1989

Novel & Short Story Writer's Market

Editor: Laurie Henry

Assistant Editor: Robin Gee

Cincinnati, Ohio

Writer's Digest Books

Distributed in Canada by Prentice-Hall of Canada Ltd., 1870 Birchmount Road, Scarborough, Ontario M1P 2J7.

Managing Editor, Market Books Department:
Constance J. Achabal

1989 Novel & Short Story Writer's Market.
Copyright © 1989
by Writer's Digest Books, an imprint of F&W Publications, 1507 Dana Ave., Cincinnati, Ohio 45207.

International Standard Serial Number
0275-2123
International Standard Book Number
0-89879-341-6

Contents

From the Editor

Welcome to the ninth edition of this book, which comes to you with a new title and a new paperback format. After being known for eight years as *Fiction Writer's Market*—and sometimes being confused with other writing titles—we've changed our name to *Novel and Short Story Writer's Market*, a title which tells you *exactly* for whom this book is written. And, unlike the majority of annually updated publications, *Novel and Short Story Writer's Market* is actually selling for a lower price this year than *Fiction Writer's Market* did last year.

This year's book contains over 1,900 listings, over 125 more than appeared in last year's book. All of the sections in this year's edition have grown; you'll find a particularly noticeable increase in the little/literary magazine and literary agent categories, and among the foreign markets. This year for the first time we're also detailing what happened to the listings in last year's book that don't appear in the 1989 edition—check the end of each section to find if last year's magazine, book or comic book/graphic novel publisher, contest or literary agent is out of business or simply overstocked with submissions.

A telephone survey of our readers last spring helped us reach a better understanding as to what readers look for in the articles on writing techniques and in the close-up interviews we publish. So we've commissioned more original pieces and looked for outstanding reprints with as much practical, nuts-and-bolts information as possible on the writing and submission process. You'll find articles on mistakes talented beginners make that can keep them from being successful with their writing ("How *Not* to Keep Yourself From Making It," by J.N. Williamson) and a judge's inside view of how fiction-writing contests work and how you can improve your chances of winning one ("You be the Judge: A Guide to Fiction Contests," by Barbara Warnecke Durkin).

We're also including articles like Gayle Feldman's "Is there a Short Story Boom?" and, as usual, the introductions to each of the major sections in the book help you keep in touch with recent publishing trends.

Our survey also showed that of all of the sections of the book, readers were most likely to overlook the Category Index, on page 636 don't make this mistake! Of course studying the category index is no substitute for reading sample copies and book catalogues, but if, say, you're looking to narrow down the 629 listings in the little/literary section for the 38 magazines that might be interested in a condensed version of your novel, or the 166 that accept translations, you'll save hours by checking the category index to see exactly which ones are at all likely to be interested in your manuscript.

Beginners can probably find homes (if not always paying homes) for their short stories, but even very experienced writers may find it more difficult today to place their novels with a major publisher. With persistence, however, chances are you will be able to find the right publisher for your book manuscript. We're here to make your search a little easier, and to provide assistance and inspiration you might need to make the writing process enjoyable as well.

Laurie Henry

Acknowledgments

The editor wishes to thank the following for their original contributions to the 1989 edition of *Novel and Short Story Writer's Market*:

Barbara Wernecke Durkin, "You Be the Judge: A Guide to Fiction Contests"
David Huddle, "The Writing Habit"
J. N. Williamson, "Learning Not to Prevent Yourself from Making It"

The editor of *Novel and Short Story Writer's Market* gratefully acknowledges the following publishers, authors and agents for granting permission to publish their articles and book excerpts:

Stephanie Kay Bendel, "Point of View," from *Making Crime Pay,* copyright © 1983. Used by permission of the publisher, Prentice-Hall Inc., Englewood Cliffs NJ.
Hal Blythe and Charlie Sweet, "Collaborwriting," from *Writers on Writing,* edited by Tom Waldrep, copyright © 1985 by Random House, Inc. Reprinted by permission.
Daryln Brewer, "The Plight of the First Novel," from *The Writing Business.* Reprinted by permission, copyright © 1985 by Poets & Writers, Inc.
Janet Burroway, "Is and Is Not," from *Writing Fiction: A Guide to Narrative Craft,* second edition, pages 308-323, copyright © 1987 by Janet Burroway. Reprinted with permission of Scott, Foresman and Company.
Richard Curtis, "Payout Schedules: On the Important Subject of Getting Paid," copyright © Richard Curtis. Reprinted with permission of the author.
David Daniel, "An Interview with Stanley Elkin," reprinted by permission of the *AWP Newsletter.*
Peter Elbow, "Thoughts on the Teacherless Writing Class," from *Writing Without Teachers.* Copyright © 1973 by Oxford University Press, Inc. Reprinted by permission.
Gayle Feldman, "Is There a Short Story Boom?" from the December 25, 1987 issue of *Publishers Weekly.* Reprinted with permission of the author.
Peter Heck, "The Man Who Built Moonshae," interview with Douglas Niles, reprinted from Vol. XXX, June-July 1988 issue of *Xignals.* Reprinted with permission of Walden Book Company, Inc., Stamford CT.
André Jute, "Breathing Life into Characters," from *Writing a Thriller,* copyright © 1986 by André Jute, St. Martin's Press Inc., New York. Reprinted with permission of the publisher.
William Manners, "How to Write Proifically in Your Spare Time," from *Wake Up and Write,* copyright © 1962, 1965, 1977 by Arco Publishing Co., Inc. Reprinted with permission of the author.
Valerie Martin, "Waiting for the Story to Start," copyright © 1988 by the New York Times Company. Reprinted by permission.
Lynne Sharon Schwartz, "Remembrance of Tense Past," from Vol. X, Number 2, Winter 1987 issue of *New England Review and Bread Loaf Quarterly,* copyright © 1987 by Middlebury College Publications, Middlebury VT. Reprinted by permission of the author.
Susan Shreve, "Writing for Children vs. Writing for Adults." Reprinted from the July 23, 1982 issue of *Publishers Weekly,* published by R.R. Bowker Company, a Xerox company. Copyright © 1982 by Xerox Corporation.
Brenda Ueland, "The Imagination Works Slowly and Quietly," from *If You Want to Write,* copyright © 1987 by the Estate of Brenda Ueland. Reprinted with permission of Graywolf Press.

Writing Techniques

Learning *Not* To Prevent Yourself From Making it

by J. N. Williamson

It's probably an old saw that a caring teacher winds up learning more from his students than the teacher teaches them. If it isn't, let's begin the bromide (not a bad TV quiz show title) now. After four year of trying to help several hundred Writer's Digest School students vault over the sawhorse into the medal-winning world of professional sales, I realized those people had instructed me generously in two areas: First, unpublished writers are inclined to make the same kinds of mistakes, to draw the same false conclusions about the business end of writing, and even *prevent themselves* from being published for strikingly similar reasons.

Second, those students I spent eighteen months with, via the mails, unknowingly reminded me that a lot of professionals who crank out several pages a day with the cozy knowledge that our words probably *will* be published somewhere never quite overcome the temptation to make the same gaffes. We simply make them on a grander scale, and have more experience in sensing the sneaky presence of such subversive boo-boos—and we know how to *conceal* them!

Regrettably, I learned for a fact, even the blunders we have allowed to infiltrate our prose are used as models of correct technique and procedure by numerous aspiring writers. Over and over, at points when I felt obliged to correct unwise sentences and paragraphs, I was answered by sharp rejoinders to the effect that such-and-such a famous pro *always* "does it that way." And the student was right.

Yet he was also wrong, for reasons that I'll discuss at greater length than I usually provide for individual students: a respected full-time writer may well have achieved success *despite* his or her rule-breaking mistakes of judgment, not because of them—unless the boo-boos in question were an irreplaceable part of the professional's style. Then, too, there is the already cited ongoing temptation to commit assorted literary sins—and something else: Exceedingly prominent authors rarely receive the same amount of sharp critical analysis newcomers get. Or, more accurately, only writers who have been published but are anxious to move on to bet-

J. N. Williamson's newest novel, The Black School, *is his 31st. His short stories include "Happy Hour," originally published in* Twilight Zone, *selected for inclusion in* The Year's Best Fantasy Stories, *and "The Book of Webster's," published in* Nightcry, *and also in a new hardcover anthology,* Urban Horrors.

ter houses and magazines get as much criticism as new comers. Editors *trust* the old pros more—especially to sell product.

None of which means that famous pro's style or his kid-glove coddling have a thing to do with an un-bought writer. They don't, and they shouldn't.

B. S. expectations

That stands for "Before Students"—and the expectations I had of them and they probably had of me, and then we'll see how it all worked out.

Frankly, when the director of the Writer's Digest School and I agreed that I'd become one of the then-forty WDS instructors, I had such respect for her and cockiness about my own skills that I believed her course and I would make an unbeatable combination. Although I know a number of writing aspirants would just not have what it takes to write professionally, I also believed there were enough talented people Out There in America to make my part-time teaching gig seem worthwhile. My idea was to treat the hopeless students decently, to honor their investments of time and money, but to focus my wondrous abilities on all those gifted men and women who merely needed a swipe or two of polish from a guy who had published twenty-some novels and edited a prize-winning, hardcover anthology. A sweet, compassionate, experienced guy who would bring well-deserved success to those diamonds in the rough by demonstrating the *right* way to craft this or that, sharing a handful of pointers he'd picked up the hard way, then winding up the course with a fiction instructor's benediction of, "Go, my son (or daughter), and sin no more."

Among the troubles with that were these:

The really talented students with a gift for language often lacked the slightest comprehension of what a plot was about or didn't have the tiniest iota of an original idea!

The people with the kind of idea I was sometimes tempted to steal because they were so dazzlingly cleaver and fresh frequently didn't know a subject from a verb, never heard of a dictionary (let alone a thesaurus), and started new paragraphs only when they got back from pouring more coffee or going to the toilet!

The gifted writers not only tended not to develop any original ideas but were disposed to scorn the obligation for pretensions of a plot; and,

The students with the great new ideas tended either to drop out, because the suggestions of a need for half-way decent sentence structure and grammar sounded to them as if I'd proposed they join the Moonies or enlist in the Afghan army *or* because they'd never actually *read* a book before and they certainly didn't propose to do so now! Generally speaking, they were intense movie buffs.

Within three weeks—maybe it was three days—after watching the first flood of literary hopes and dreams begin to pour onto my desk, I realized I'd badly underestimated this task I had taken on. Whenever a student excelled and honestly earned a B+ or an A-, I was astonished to discover that my feelings were similar to those I experienced when a story I like has just sold. Then, it seemed, the promising student got fired from his or her job, went on vacation or fell in love, told me there "just isn't enough motivation to keep going," or objected to the notion that his or her work had ever earned anything less than an A+. I hadn't felt so frustrated since, nineteen years before, I made my first major magazine sale and then was unable to use it as a steppingstone despite writing five more stories I honestly believed were better. (For the record, it was another eight years before I made the grade again at a similarly respected magazine.)

Because I was always a courteous instructor—almost always, at least—I never got any death threats as a consequence of adamantly giving students the grade I believed they had coming, but the frustrations mounted. Often it was because I agreed with Bill or Amanda that they were working incredibly hard and improving more than students who routinely drew a

B+ or A. But stories that earned a C-, even when the writer had progressed from a D-, *weren't* going to be bought, so I was constantly engaged in a war with myself. It matched the minions of False Hope on one side—a weaponless fantasy army clamoring that real effort might still win the day if sufficient sacrifices were made—and legions of invulnerable armored automatons goose stepping across the line. After I reached the point at which, with some economic justification, I could consider quitting this demanding work, I found that I was too involved. The sacrifice to be made was *me*, and I cared much more than common sense seemed to dictate—but for some good reasons:

My better and luckier students, you see, were actually beginning to *place* their work! And somehow, overnight, I was a combination of silver-haired and -tongued old Professor Williamson, Daddy, and He Who Holds the Key to upwards of five hundred strangers. Suddenly, certain students were actually *getting the hang of it*—and I found myself, as an anthologist, self-indulgently and benignly choosing some of them for my *own* books. My students were beginning to become friends—we were traveling to various places to hug and wring hands and root on—and my role was mystically metamorphosizing into a blend of the J. N. Williamson Commune for Homeless Writers and the new level of . . . of Saint Jerry!

In three anthologies I edited for publication in the years 1987 (two books) and 1989, a total of nine "slots" were filled by former WDS students of mine. The point is not to ask if all the students I helped into publication deserved it or not. Most of them definitely did. Another ex-student is now publishing a well-liked small press horror magazine. At least two of these people may well succeed in placing their first novels; in at least one instance, I shall be amazed if the author does not become a particularly outstanding writer of books.

The point is that there were a number of other students I strove to teach who *might* have become commercially acceptable but did not do so. The failure, in part, seems mine and I can't adequately express how disappointed I am in them and me. How many of them were there? The estimate is hard to make, but as many as twenty-five to thirty people. A few, in my opinion, had the imagination and talent to have moved up the literary ladder of accomplishment just about as far as they wished.

They could have done it

For such reasons I set out to categorize the kinds of students who could have enjoyed fine fiction-writing careers but probably will not do so. They are those who might have learned not to keep themselves from breaking into print—and some of their misunderstandings or mistakes might well be your own:

*1. People who really want to become writers who have **already** existed!* It took me quite awhile, as a new teacher, to recognize some of the students—for two reasons: I haven't read everything, and a few of them created such deft pastiches of the writers they admire that they might almost continue the fiction begun by their idols. Because I was primarily an instructor in horror and fantasy, the writers whose styles, interests, even characters were most emulated unquestionably were Stephen King, H.P. Lovecraft, Edgar Allan Poe, Ray Bradbury and J.R.R. Tolkien. With a generous scattering of sometimes-unconscious *homages* to Dean R. Koontz, Shirley Jackson, Robert Heinlein, Arthur C. Clarke—and the *television* people associated with Gene Roddenberry who wrote or write for the "Star Trek" series.

King is alive. So is Bradbury. Editors as well as readers are delighted with the fact, Steve did not sell his first novel ripping off anybody; Ray has always been an original, a one-of-a-kind. We don't need impersonators.

Lovecraft, Poe, Jackson, etc., are *deceased* giants. Were they beginning to write today, they would write quite differently.

Save your wonderful imitations of the titans you admire for anthologies that are sold as such. However well-crafted they are, your works are not theirs—and you have no moral or, in most cases, legal right to their voices, ideas or styles.

2. *People who have good ideas but who lack the discipline to create salable, complete* **stories** *within the framework of a contemporary professional plot.* A mastery of characterization is not by itself enough to make a salable yarn today, if it ever was, and an idea is the necessary starting point but it shouldn't be evolved the way a comedian tells a funny story. It demands a peopling and a setting, all the elements of sound fiction. It's also less likely to sell if you insist upon placing your plot in the past. Most contemporary editors prefer contemporary settings.

3. *People who are unfamiliar with what is already written in the genre they prefer* and consciously or unconsciously—are creating what seems to editors like clichés. Anyone entering business with a personal investment knows what the competition is doing, and also knows how that particular business reached the point of acceptance it possesses. A writer has the same obligation. There are certain premises in every kind of fiction writing that professionals in that field understand are virtually unmarketable because they been written over and over. Therefore, when the professional writer has an idea linked to such clichés, he tends to lie down until it passes through and no longer tries to plague him or her into wasting valuable time on it.

A new writer, ideally, should jump upon such a notion and throttle it by the neck as if it were a demon attemping to inhabit his soul.

4. *People who are basically movie-educated and actually writing screen treatments, not* **publishable prose.** This problem infects the community of would-be horror writers more, perhaps, than other genres, but none of them is immune. We all live in a world where films long ago overcame books as the principal moral means of entertainment or escape; we may not like it that way, but it's a fact. Consequently, to an editor or an author who believes motion pictures are overrated, the submission of a story or an idea that is fundamentally suited to film and not to fiction seems insulting.

Elsewhere I've written that too many people by far—for my tastes—confuse horror novels and stories with horror flicks. Some of the latter are excellent; most, I think are not. The distinctions are too complex to get into here, but if you think you want to write horror, or science fiction, yet you go to the movies and never read books or magazines, you are centering your ambitions on the wrong medium.

5. *People with general misconceptions about length who cram novel ideas into a short* **story.** Most writers starting out and some professionals have no capacity for judging the length of a fictional piece before they write it. I still have that difficulty with many of my short stories, since they are rarely outlined.

But beginning people have quite severe problems in estimating length for reasons that usually are not a challenge to pros. This became clear to me when the majority of my students foisted off on me stories that were meant, by the rules of the course, to run a specified maximum length—and they seldom were. I attempted to instruct them that printed editorial guidelines are often very clear and mean what they say. A magazine editor who goes to the trouble of filling out forms for *Writer's Digest* and other publications stating that he seeks material between 2,000 and 4,000 words does not mean between 1,500 and 4,500 words. He does not expect such variations and, unless the writer is a pro, probably will not take them.

His boss has told him how much room is permitted for short fiction and the editor wishes to keep his job. Since even teenage wordsmiths these days seem to have access to computers, there is even less reason now to give serious consideration to submissions that violate the preferred minimum and maximum lengths. Using such gadgetry, a writer can find out during the writing of a story—at any moment—just how long it is running.

I believe I have heard every possible reason or excuse for submissions being in excess of what was proscribed, ranging from the aesthetic to the apathetic and to a rare confession that they just "didn't know" the yarn would get out of hand. When a professional's tale runs to a greater length than originally planned—perhaps because he knows the editor pays by the word and would like to get a higher payment—chances are that he or she will merely submit it to a different publication.

However, an author with a few novels plus four of five stories almost always knows when an idea is suitable for "something short" and when it is actually a novel or novella concept. Among the ways this detective work is achieved are the following: A thoughtful evaluation of the story line's complexity; the number of characters to be featured and involved; the time period to be covered from start to finish; and the *kinds* of scenes constituting the particular work of fiction. Let me explain:

Most short stories do not have a subplot or subtext, cover more time than a few months (unless the flashback or flash-forward for many years is presented by no means trickier than a bit of extra spacing) or feature more than a few speaking characters. (I should note that the short story protagonist tends to be a changed or different person, because of what happens to him or to her, by the end of the plot.) Stories are *episodes*, you see, moments in a protagonist's life—not the whole life. Casts of thousands are for novels and old Cinemascope movies. So are histories of the world and multigenerational sagas. Short fiction does its thing tautly, briefly—just the way the word "short" suggests.

About the types of scenes I mentioned. Newcomers need to learn that editors unconsciously judge the real length of a story by how long it appears to be when they read it. Narratives with little dialogue consume more of the editor's time. Ordinarily, dialogue and action both can make the yarn seem shorter, especially if the latter is "told" with punchy, pungent words matching the tension of your argument, escape, battle, or whatever comprises the action. Lengthy descriptive scenes are generally better suited for the long form, not the short—for novels not stories.

I believe it goes without saying that any good reader can point to a dozen stories or novels that make such rules of thumb seem entirely wrong. They are not; the fiction you want to cite is merely a marvelous exception.

6. *People who have come up with one outstanding basic premise that isn't enough in itself to make it a real story or novel*. At least half my students had one idea I was able to like, even cheer for; most of them proceeded to develop it with so little flesh on its bones that the story ultimately would not sell. Worse, ultimately, it often was not even a story.

This is not the place to define "story" or "story line," but it is the time to point out that too many aspiring writers made it clear to me they imagined that their interesting yet frail concept was adequate. As a result, their stories tended not only to lack plot but a discernible or viable protagonist, antagonist, suspense, atmosphere, characterization, and so forth. It was as if the student conceived of a vampire whose victim had AIDS, or an army corporal who turned out to be Adolf Hitler, and believed it was necessary only to come up with a variation of "Count Alacard" (for a man with no mustache yet whose hair kept falling over one eye) and "tell" the ending as if it were a punchline.

Fundamentally, there's nothing wrong with either thought that just occurred to me. While a pro would not automatically discard either premise, he or she would be at great pains to decide whether or not to tell readers *immediately* that the count's victim might possess a new way to kill the vampire, or that the corporal's name was Hitler, but as the yarn progresses, the soldier loses his life—and he turns out to be a descendant of Adolf who possibly committed suicide to be sure he would never turn out like his ancestor. Comprehending the differences between the amateur and professional approaches to the same two ideas can enable you to make a quantum jump in that vital matter known as "plot" while simultaneously teaching you the distinctions between the "basic premise," the "frail concept" I mentioned, and how to begin plotting your fiction.

7. *People who really are teaching or preaching their ideals and writing political or religious tracts*. For four years, a steady percentage of my own WDS students presented story ideas to me that clearly were meant to become thinly disguised statements of principle, belief, mission. I was never fooled but usually allowed them to develop the idea, except for one encounter with a man who seemed eager to eradicate every minority group on the planet. With the director's approval, I told him to get lost.

But I also attempted to caution my students that if they could not figure out ways to integrate their principles and ideals with realistic characters who were then propelled through that maze of difficulties lying at the heart of most good fiction, they might wind up only with good speeches—not stories. Most of the time they claimed they understood and then proceeded to craft polemics that weren't even very good speeches.

The same thing was a basic failing of my own early writing. Discovering how to *hide* these messages I was anxious to convey and "sell" in a textured story line, one that was told in my own individual "voice," was the difference between becoming a published novelist at twenty-seven—which I wasn't—and forty-seven. It's a matter of self interest and allegiances, it's a test of how really badly you want your own dearest arguments to reach print. If you cannot imagine how to put the *story first*, not the speech, just enroll in a seminary or run for office—it's a free country.

8. *People who can't understand the obligation of working hard to place their fiction, or perceive the nature of competition among publications*. Some aspiring writers are finally successful in becoming published because it has fully dawned to them that a story or novel can be said not to exist at all until it is print. Among those talented students I hoped to help into print—that was always my *raison d'être* where those with genuine ability were concerned—were some who probably shouldn't have been crafting any kind of genre fiction. Why? Because their gifts, education or intelligence were so formidable that it's possible they will always write over the heads of their readers—and their editors!

These same exceptional, well-educated students were often the same ones who regarded themselves as being above the fray, too rarefied of talent, genes or something to send their creations out to market at all. How their stories were meant, physically, to arrive in any editor's hands, I have no idea; maybe editors were supposed to learn through the grapevines about their blessed skills and come straight to their doors, hats in hand.

Worse was the sort of extraordinary student who enrolled in WDS to achieve contacts and *knew* how wonderful he was. This sort of person believed it was possible to sell a first story to *OMNI*, a first novel—with no representation—to Alfred Knopf. All the efforts I made to explain that editors and publishers do not often work that way—to make it clear that first stories and novels are seldom accepted for any publication paying a thousand dollars for a short story or fifty-thousand dollars advance for a book—consistently fell on deaf and grandiloquent ears. The thinking on the student's part was, "I know how good I am, I begin at the top or nowhere"; the thinking on an editor's part is, "I know I can get Updike or Koontz or Welty or Michener for the next issue" and the thinking on my part was, "I know you're going nowhere."

By and large, we were all correct.

That allusion I made to commercial competition is tied to the way that major magazines, if they think of them at all, regard publications that pay less well and have a smaller readership as a farm system. They hold on to top dollar for the "name" writers who will simply sell copies. Of course, magazines don't actually *think*. Editors, more or less, do that. And since they desire to continue individually earning the *editorial* top dollar, they must produce issues that sell. Give any of them a choice between putting MAILER! or MICHENER! on the cover or a line reading, "We proudly introduce the mext Mailer (or Michener)" and see how fast they opt for the original! Much the same thing holds true for book publishers, except there is a difference: a given magazine format allows for one, maybe two, stories; a few (such as *Pulphouse* and *Twilight Zone*) plan for more. But *an* issue is *one, single* magazine for *one* month (or quarter); publishing houses produce many books during any publishing cycle. It is for that reason I told many of my windier students that their chances might literally be better writing a novel partial and then seeking an agent for it, than trying to crack *The New Yorker* or *Cosmo*. The reason amounts to sheer numbers.

So it is that the new genius who conceives a single brilliantly written story that illuminates aspects of the world's problems in such fresh terms that humanity might well be saved if *OMNI* or *Playboy* accepted it probably has less chance of success than if he had written 100 pages of a horror novel in which a "were-demon" somehow possesses Libya's Ghadafy and then forces the terrorists of the planet to devour everyone at the White House—and send it to a publisher of paperback originals. (Now that I think about it, that isn't a bad story line. Hmmm.) But again (in all probability) he will have no chance of someday collecting his wonderfully crafted artistic stories for Harper or Knopf—to include those he "let" a minor magazine print for fifty bucks or so—unless (1) he writes more than *one* great short story and (2) he circulates them all, repeatedly—while he works at producing enough short fiction that a great collection may be his in the distant future.

A final comment about competition between the 'zines and houses: Understand from the get-go that the four or five leading magazines and the four or five leading publishers are rarely impressed by appearance in publications at the entry level. Upward mobility in writing is apt to demand ever-better agents, reviews appearing in the right places by the right people, and getting to know some of the latter. In my own experience and observation, without the taint of bitterness or casual comment, I think that what I just said is the truth today.

9. ***People who mix genres in their writing, or who change the direction of their story midway through***. Such new writers do not have a realization as yet that most editors specifically seek work that fits their needs like a well-fitted glove. There may be fewer published editorial statements concerning the "slanting" of fiction now than there were a decade ago; certainly there's less than twenty-five years back. But with fewer magazines in existence than there were a quarter of a century ago—and still fewer that accept fiction at all—editors know with infinite exactitude what they want and feel free to wait until it arrives on their desks. The majority of western 'zines want no science fiction content, most sf magazines "oops" over submissions containing horror (or worse, occult themes), and horror publications have no interest in romantic encounters. Originality counts more in writing style, by far, than it does in idea content, regardless of what was said at the beginning of this article. (Observe, please—I said "counts *more*," not that originality doesn't matter at all.)

There is also a kind of new writer who hasn't thought the story line through and definitely has not outlined it, who sets the scene atmospherically, introduces a character suitable to the genre, and, on page 3, gets carried away with how funny and absurd the situation is. If you want to write humor, in spite of the fact there is little market for it, make it a humorous yarn all the way. Don't begin with a perfect locked-room mystery and have a shape-changing monster turn out to be the killer!

10. ***People who believe that a particular variety of computer will open doors magically***—or if not that, a better grade of paper; the way one's manuscript is clipped or bound; or whether or not a snapshot of the writer's crippled and aged mom is attached. A manuscript certainly must look professional. But there is far too great an impression today that acquiring a state-of-the-art computer—or *any* computer—will somehow substitute for the need to revise, check spelling, and paragraph properly. Too many beginners think their paragraphs are interchangeable while professionals have found there is a pace, a rhythm, for every segment of the work from page to page. Too many think a justified margin will improve their chances, and so on.

Good fiction sent to the right place at the right time, looking adequate, tends eventually to sell. And it can't be written in longhand.

11. ***People who think that a personally enthralling real-life experience is preferable in choosing material for a story or a novel to any imagined premise or plot***. Such people are also disposed to adhere painstakingly and with rather ridiculous fidelity to the facts of "real life" when fiction is and always shall be *make believe*. A credible *lie*. *Imaginary*. A *story*—and not in the journalistic sense of that word, either.

Most of us in writing tend to "refer back" mentally to those we have known and who have influenced us, one way or the other. The fiction writer understands that even if the character he is discussing was based on Dad, or Great-Grandma, and the plot demands that the character be devoured by gibbering great apes or left in pieces by a thermonuclear device, Dad or Granny has got to go!

12. *People who are neurotically convinced that there is a "trick" to be pried from the instructor—a secret*. But we don't have any and that holds true for teachers like me who have been repeatedly bought and published. If we're any good, we share what we have learned, generously; the way I'm presumably doing. The solitary secrets we husband are those tips about new magazines, anthologies, or eager editors which we first use for our individual advantages, then give away, gratis, to friends. To fellow professionals. Believing we have secrets says you *know* you're publishable now, and probably better than we published wordworkers are: that we're being narrow.

If, however, you think of "tricks," maybe you mean the ways with which full-time writers get by from year to year on generally less income than the clerk at your neighborhood drugstore makes. Our "magic" formulas are tedious, and you don't want to hear them. They include toiling for seventy- or eighty-hour weeks, planning one's entire life to survive on hope and shoddy payments, making mates or cronies who cheer us on and keep us producing even when New York editors change their minds a hundred times, or change jobs when you feel you're getting someplace. Throw in a need to keep up on everything happening in the genre identified for you by your talent while you locate postage money to keep your manuscripts "making the rounds" and you begin to have some notion of what it's like to continue being creative in a world that sometimes seems to be functionally bigoted against anyone who pursues a creative way of life. "Secrets" of this kind aren't particularly marketable.

But few of those mistaken views cherished by the majority of fiction newcomers had occurred to me as probable stumbling blocks before I began to teach. However, it is clear that many writing hopefuls *are* prevented from success by them in spite of the way that most such problems can be dispensed with by doing a little mental fine tuning. By, putting it plainly, adjusting to The Way Things Are.

A talented student's comments

Several weeks before I decided to stop instructing—close to being a burnt-out case as a correspondence teacher—I received a letter from a gentlemen who had been making B-level marks. After demonstrating potential for an A and beginning to place his work, he slipped under a B with his actual finished story. His comments were enlighteningly touching and I sought permission to quote from his letter directly without mentioning his name or location. The gentleman's reply: "Please feel free… . If my tale of woe can help someone else avoid some of the anguish, then I'll have been of some small service."

I will return to that follow-up missive for another remark. First, here are some of the things from his letter announcing that he would not be completing his final lessons of revision, starting with his kind assurance that his reasons had "nothing to do with you or the school":

1. "The story I submitted…was not really salvageable in its current form. It was a 3,400-4,000 word idea stuffed into a 2,500 word limit. It didn't, as you correctly and undiplomatically pointed out, have an ending. It merely stopped.

2. "I started the story too early in the course. …Frankly, I can't stand the sight of it now…a circumstance that makes it very difficult to do justice to any effort to repair the shambles.

3. "A word processing computer increases my raw writing and revision productivity and helps with spelling, formatting and the like. It *doesn't substitute* for careful proofing and thought.

4. "There is a vast difference between writing stand-alone scenes and producing a coherent story.

5. "I need a lot of work on characters, character development and characterization, with particular attention to *realistic reaction* and *consistency*.

6. "I need better work discipline. I have a streak of laziness…that will finish me in this writing game if I don't ultimately overcome it. (That) story should never have been submitted in that form.

7. "I have a thin skin which I'll have to toughen up if I'm to have any chance of coping with editors. …Your comments were, in retrospect, perfectly accurate and consistent but it was difficult for me to be objective about them at first. It's hard to stand back and accept the idea that the comments aren't aimed at me personally."

And the eighth comment by this student from his follow-up note reads as follows: "I find that I don't really do good creative work on the computer. I (now) compose my rough drafts on a manual typewriter or, more rarely, in pencil or pen on five-and-dime notework paper. (I) need the hard copy to integrate things." He adds, "I don't hesitate to use the computer for those functions for which it is uniquely suited, namely the grunt work of revision and manuscript formatting, but I still don't think well looking at a video monitor." And, "I've been a professional programmer since 1966."

A case in point to what he was saying in this letter was a mistake made in his final sentence to me: "A computers *(sic)* is a wonderful tool—but so is a crowbar, and neither is creative." Because "computers" is a word, alas, *his* spelling checker did not tell him to correct the pluralization of the word!

It is impossible for me to imagine a more honest and honorable letter, or one that more succinctly observes—from the "inside," so to speak—the innumerable difficulties which must be surmounted if a writer is to become published. Of the numbered points he made, some last-minute comments may be useful:

Final comments

1. Professional stories may sometimes seem inconclusively completed or vague, lost in subtlety. Most are not. The events of a work of fiction should be brought to a tentative conclusion, at least, when the story or novel ends; if it has "merely stopped," it gives the impression that the writer simply couldn't find a way to tie the loose ends together even in a slipknot.

2. Most professionals—were the truth known—reach a point at which they are sick of any often-revised work. *The Black School* (1989), my first Dell novel, was begun in the autumn of 1983 as a series of research notes and a basic premise. A year later, I started writing it and attempts were made to sell it as a partial during 1985. Other projects obliged me to push it aside until, in '86, I revised what I had written and "finished" some 40,000 words of it. An agent and an editor at a leading publishing house each misplaced it and, in disgust, I shelved it until I was seeking a new agent in 1987 and made a copy of the partial for her. Before she would submit it, she asked for three segments of the existing material to be changed sequentially; after a Dell editor made a firm offer on the book, she sought further changes in the book's order and cuts from two new segments I wrote. Then she quit, left Manhattan, and I was left without an editor.

Before the "completed" *Black School* went to typesetting, I was asked to slash right out of the manuscript a minimum of 20,000 words. I found ways to omit approximately 23,000 words. Then the author's galleys arrived and I discovered the copy editor had made almost 200 "requested" cuts or rewritten sentences, most of them—but not all—minor. I acceded to around 100 of these and substantially rewrote about ten scenes, with paste-ups right on the galleys. At this moment in time, while I believe it is a good novel and can't make the dramatic remark that I'm unsure what portions are still mine—since 90% of what was most worthwhile about it continues to be part of it—I certainly can say that I was unable to "stand the sight of it" a full two and a half years ahead of publication.

3. There isn't any way I can improve on this comment.

4. Not only for writing courses but also for practice, writers frequently have flashes of insight into the way certain scenes can be wonderfully written and create them. Often, they do work out, marvelously well. But when such a scene is part of nothing and laid aside—for months or years, sometimes, by pros—it is virtually impossible to recapture the mood or feeling of that magical moment, and all attempts to unify it—to integrate it into fiction—fall abysmally flat. Of late, I have tried either to see them as nothing but practice or taken the few transferrable lines to work into entirely different material with an emotion akin to pulling my own teeth. I am also trying to stop and to "listen" to what's happening during the mystical period of time when such brilliant words start to come in. Maybe I'll figure out how to sustain it if I live for another few hundred years.

5. This candid remark by a student who was obviously raw and bleeding at the time suggests something essential to any writing of a fantastic, improbable nature, regardless of the specific genre. The more difficult a scene is for a reader to "buy," the more believably and credibly, realistically and consistently must it be written—and it all begins with a complete understanding of the characters *you* have created. Do not attribute acts of venality or heroism, do not write flippant gags in the face of terrible danger, for characters based on your Uncle Bud, your mom, or your brother Willie *unless* (1) you can truly picture them performing that way under pressure and (2) you have *established* such qualities as part of your fictional characters. Just as importantly, don't allow a coward to become a hero, a villain to rescue a child from a speeding car, without having shown your readers that such characteristics are latent within them. Possible and plausible.

6. Interviewers have a way, it seems, of asking a full-time professional writer—or a full-time professional *anything*—how much time he or she invests in The Career during a given week. Expressionlessly, they make a note on their pads and it is almost never transferred to print. I think that may be because nobody *really* believes Larry Bird shows up two hours before game time and practices his free throws, that nurses work shifts in ghastly conditions that would make a horror writer sick to his stomach—or that I write, all told, upward of 750,000 words per year. After all, the interviewer can see only 250,000 words or so of mine published over the preceding twelve months. He has lost sight not only of the self-discipline required to revise one's work until it is where the writer knows it should be (even when he is cursed with the label of being prolific) but of such other things as these: Research, handwritten and then typed up. Original story or novel notes. Letters linked more to business than meet the eye. Outlines; numerous changes in outlines. And the rich diversity of work produced by most modern writers—

Because those people who are "fans" of a given writer rarely have a clue to how much he or she has written unless they become actual collectors. Just this past month, I've seen things I wrote appear as cover quotes and promos of novels, ideas tucked away in obscure small press columns, on local book pages (rewritten to the extent of two factual errors in a single column inch), and in flyers citing the merits of various writers, books and magazines. *One* new story of mine was published, visible, during the month. Yet I also proofed the galleys for one of my "Dark Corner" columns in *2AM*, wrote another from scratch—for a readership of maybe a few thousand—and answered three letters concerning a column that preceded the two in question! When a writer or his publisher send me a novel, I try to acknowledge it (even if I can't read all of them)—and none of those written words materialized by themselves. They had to be put down by no one but me.

Laziness sometimes masquerades as "getting ready," general (unspecified) research, and the put-me-in-the-mood blissful reading that beginners imagine professionals allow themselves each day. Even my pleasure reading is squeezed in after midnight. My former student described it properly. And the single way a lazy writer gets well is by forgetting about inspiration; by producing, self-critically; by sending it out to be considered, over and over again —

And (number 7) taking the knocks that often as not come from one's own agent or editors! Thin skin toughens up by being mutilated by criticism, then picking out the shards of broken glass that you can identify as useful and applicable—especially the shrapnel that's under your control (since you will never get everything about your writing done perfectly). Then you rewrite until *you're certain*—mentally, not emotionally—that what you have written is very good. Not good for *you*. Good for any writer. One reason I accept beginners into anthologies is that those people somehow came to see that more is expected of them than from the top pros! The stories they have created using everything they have may actually be superior in some way to the work they will write five years from now! Fair or not, it is harder for beginning writers to break into print at all than it is for those writers you know from their first names—Dean, Jackie, Norman, Judith, Stephen, Ray, Isaac or J.N. Crying that it's unfair takes anything from a minute to an hour that you could be using to make it.

My Writer's Digest School students taught me a lot. They made me, I think, a better writer; I know I am a better editor, and I'm indebted to them.

In the end, only an unpublished writer can learn not to prevent himself or herself from doing away with that detested word, "unpublished." These have been some of the ways to set about *not* doing it!

66 *I've always disliked words like* inspiration. *Writing is probably like a scientist thinking about some scientific problem, or an engineer about an engineering problem.* **99**

—Doris Lessing

Stanley Elkin

by David Daniel

The following interview took place in December 1987 and ran in the Associated Writing Programs (AWP) newsletter.

AWP: Is there a question which you've always wanted an interviewer to ask you? What is your answer to that question?

Stanley Elkin: Yes, whether I sleep in the nude. I sleep in pajamas. Under my pajamas I sleep in the nude. But I'm setting you up. Interviewers usually ask the "What question would you want an interviewer to ask?" question. It's rather like that pro forma question they say would-be presidential appointees always get—"Is there anything in your background which would embarrass the President if it came out?" And of course they're always too embarrassed, or too eager to be appointed, to say anything but "No." I assume, however, that you're really asking about one's personal bottom line. And the answer to that one has to be "Yes." A qualified yes, but yes nonetheless.

AWP: How did you get started as a writer? You said somewhere that you published in small places and that this gave you confidence to keep writing. Do you want to elaborate on this?

SE: That's easy. By being just clever enough to master the small stuff, the unit of thought called the imagination, as it pops up in the sentence and exists in fiction, but not quite patient enough or maybe just not quite smart enough to handle the details of an out-and-out discipline—law, say, medicine, poetry, arbitrage, science.

As to the little magazines, things haven't changed that much. Writers have to be stroked in order to continue doing what no one cares whether they continue doing or not. The literary magazines would prefer to stroke Nobel Prize winners, National Book Awardees, but they're stuck, too, and they stroke what they get, so the kids in these writing programs ought to be made to send their stuff out. Now that I think of it, maybe I'll ask to see rejection slips, won't let them continue in the program after their first year without one, a sort of literary carding, like something done in a bar.

AWP: Was (Is) there an editor who was particularly important to your success and development?

SE: I've had five editors thus far—Joe Fox at Random House, Aaron Ascher at Farrar, Straus & Giroux, Henry Robins and Jack McRay at E. P. Dutton, and Bill Whitehead at Dutton and Scribners'. Henry and Bill died, Jack moved, and Aaron is mad at me because I didn't sell enough *Franchiser's*. Joe Fox, whom I started with and worked with on five books, was, page for page and sentence for sentence, probably the hardest working of my editors, the most schoolmasterly, the one, I mean, who kept the strictest accounts, who questioned me closest and was, if not the most important to my success, then certainly the most important to my development.

AWP: What has been the most significant event of your writing life?

SE: June 6th, 1979, when my word processor was delivered. Not just any word processor, but what's known as a dedicated word processor. Not even just a dedicated word processor, finally, but a devoted one as well.

AWP: How would you place your work among what you consider to be the great work of the past?

David Daniel, *former Publications Manager for the* AWP Newsletter *is now living in Cambridge, Massachusetts and teaching at Emerson College.*

SE: Oh *please*.

AWP: What's your favorite book of yours? Why?

SE: One customarily names either the book one is working on or, if nothing's shaking, the last book published—superstitious talent's 5 year/50,000 mile condition, its you-ain't-seen-nothing-yet one. But my favorite is *George Mills*, a novel I published in 1982. I like that book because it's a kind of perpetual-motion story machine in which my imagination was whipped into a sort of full-court press. When I was writing it I had the direct impression that I owned the language.

AWP: Do you have a favorite book (or author) that has been neglected? How and why is it important to you? Why is it neglected?

SE: I'm not a very adventurous reader. I'm no literary archaeologist, no duster-off of the obscure. If my favorite authors had been neglected, I'm afraid I'd probably be one of the neglectors. Although he's hardly neglected, a writer I'm *very* fond of is William Trevor. He's so good I'd be hard pressed to say which of his books is my favorite.

AWP: Who gave you good advice? What was it?

SE: Phil Yordan, the screen writer and movie producer, once told me about a group of film folks who took turns hosting this floating poker game in Beverly Hills. They'd come up the gorgeously banked driveway of each other's mansions and wait in upholstery like the interiors of cows for their chauffeurs to open the doors of their limousines for them. They didn't instruct the drivers to go on errands that would last the length of the game, or make any of the Missy-will-be-needing-the-car-at-ten arrangements. This was back in the days before limousine pooling. If you couldn't afford to have a car the price of a small yacht stand idly by while you relaxed in a pal's kitchen playing fifteen-buck ante and a twenty-dollar limit, you hired one, or took cabs. The chauffeurs knew each other, of course, and spent their time chatting, catching up. Well, this one night it rained. A terrible storm, rarer in Los Angeles than an earthquake. Yordan saw the lightning, the drenched drivers, and sent his butler to invite them in.

"Not my driver," George Jessel said.

"But George, it's pouring."

"If he dries his pants, maybe I'll let him sit in the car."

"It's muggy, it's hot. He'll stifle in a closed car."

"I didn't tell him to go into his profession," George Jessel said.

I love that story. It's the best advice I ever heard and I try to remember it—when the bee stings, when the dog bites, when I'm feeling bad. Nobody told me to go into *my* profession either.

AWP: You've said that Randall Jarrell was probably the best teacher you've had. Would you talk about him? Has he influenced your teaching?

SE: Not my teaching, no. And not my writing either really. Maybe, in a way, my morals. Or perhaps, by nature, I'm attracted to the Jessel/Jarrell principles of assuming responsibility for your actions. Whenever a student asks me a particular question which, sooner or later, almost all serious students get around to asking, I tell this story about Mr. Jarrell:

He told us on the first day of class that he'd have nothing to say about our stories until we had our conference with him toward the end of the semester, a conference, incidentally, which we signed up for that first day. We'd turn the stories in but they were never discussed in class. Class was where we talked about Chekhov. Well, I wasn't scheduled to have my meeting with Mr. Jarrell until late in April, and when my appointment finally came up I was very nervous—and anxious—to hear what he'd say about my work. I was right on time—Tuesday 10 a.m. on the dot. But when I knocked on the door to his office no one was home. I waited 15 minutes, 20, but no Randall Jarrell. At first I was hurt because he'd forgotten, then mad, so I did what no one did in those days. I called the professor's home. It was obvious, even over the telephone, and even at that late hour, that I'd awakened him. He told me that I should go down and wait outside Lincoln Hall and that he'd be by in his red Oldsmobile convertible to pick me up. Well, when he showed up he was still in his pajamas. He was wearing carpet slippers. He told me to get in, we'd drive around, we'd do the conference in the car. The stories I'd written were on the seat between us. We drove around Urbana for two hours. He knew my stories at least as well as he knew Chekhov's. He knew them so well he could tell me the page number he wanted me to turn to. It was devasting. His observations about my stories were shrewd and cruel and withering. When he let me out that afternoon I was at once incredibly depressed and incredibly exhilarated. Depressed because what he had to say was so annihilating, exhilarated because no one had ever taken me so seriously before.

There were perhaps 25 students in that class, and when, at the end of the semester, he posted the grades, I saw that I was one of only two people to have been given an A. I was astonished. *After what he'd put me through?*

Well, I saw him one last time before he left Illinois. In the hall. I went up to him and reminded him who I was. "I was in your writing class, Professor Jarrell. My name is Stanley Elkin? You gave me an A?" "Yes?" Jarrell said. "Well," I said, "it's just that there were 25 people in that class, only two A's." "Yes?" "My name is Stanley Elkin," I said, "you gave me an A." And went on like that, reminding him who I was, saying my name over, locating myself for him in the class, telling him about my A, pointing out how he'd only given two of them. "Yes," he said, "what do you want?"

So I told him how important it was for me to become a writer. And made this speech about how I knew Rome wasn't built in a day, that it would take time, and dedication, and patience and practice, will and sacrifice, perseverance and all the harder virtues, saying my name for him again, in case it had slipped his mind in the few seconds that had gone by since the last time I'd said it, reminding him that mine was one of the two A's he'd given. "What?" he said. *"What?"*

"Well, just if I do all that, the perseverance, the practice, the sacrifice and will and dedication, do you think, if I live long enough and get better and better—I was in your class, you gave me an A, you gave only two, my name is Stanley Elkin—I'll publish just one story before I die?"

He looked at me and shrugged. He said, "I don't know."

AWP: How did you learn to write so well?

SE: Time, dedication, patience, practice, will, sacrifice and perseverance.

AWP: The story of your teaching . . . has it been a story?

SE: If it has, *I* couldn't tell it. It's like that story I just told you about Randall Jarrell. The teacher goes into class and gives what he can to his students and, often as not, ends up as an anecdote—Jarrell's slippers and p.j.'s in the red convertible. Well *most* students mythologize their teachers, give them horns, hubris, make them humpbacks from Hell. We become, if not their first or best, then certainly their most overdrawn characters, a known, shared denominator.

AWP: What responsibility do you feel toward your students? What do you expect from them?

SE: I teach writing, or try to. One responsibility I have toward my students is to be as truthful with them about their work as I can. Another is to try to point out what their strengths are, their weaknesses. But you know, teaching writing isn't all that different from teaching anything else. I sit in judgment on their imaginations but so does any teacher.

As far as what I expect from them is concerned, I really have no right to expect *anything* from them. Just that—we're in a workshop situation—they turn their work in on time and come prepared to discuss the work of their fellows.

AWP: If you were a young writer today and looking (would you be looking?) for a writing program, what would be foremost in your mind in choosing a place to study? A particular writer, mentor? The kind of program itself? The place of the program? Romance? Money?

SE: What worked for me was to learn about literature, to get my Ph.D. Of course, in the '50s, when I was a graduate student, writing programs weren't invented yet—well, Iowa, of course, and maybe Stanford, but the industry wasn't an industry yet—but if I *were* starting out and *were* looking for a program, chances are I'd go where a writer I admired was. I'd be this Old Masters type, this School of Michaelangelo, School of Rembrandt sort of fellow. I don't think geography would have anything to do with it. And love is where you find it, no? Money would probably be something of a factor, whether they'd tuit me my remission or whatever they call it.

AWP: What role has money played in your life, your work?

SE: I'm a great respecter of money, stand in struck dumb relation to people who have a great deal of it. Indeed, if they have enough of it, if they're *big* rich, I get inarticulate, I go all melt-mouth, my tongue goes all-thumbs. Yet, for all that I happen to be saddled with this particular perversion, I have no real desire to *get* money. There's not much I want I can't really afford, and nothing I *need*. As to the work, I tried to strike off a really rich man, a minor character, in *George Mills*. Oh yes, and in *The Making of Ashenden*.

AWP: Is there one animating, central spirit which characterizes your best students?

SE: Yes, that they have enough talent not to need me.

AWP: What would you be doing if you weren't teaching in a university?

SE: Well, what I'd *like* to be doing would be to work in the theater, go for a playwright.

AWP: How were you regarded by your peers when you first came to Washington University? How has that changed?

SE: By my peers? I was an instructor when I first came to Washington, a new kid on the block. The only peers I had who are still here were instructors. Instructor Donald Finkel, Instructor Naomi Lebowitz. And I like to think we regarded each other as just fine. And that hasn't changed. As a matter of fact, one of the nice things about teaching here is that I've met such nice people. Most of my friends are in the English Department. If your question, couched in terms of the old ad, is whether they laughed when I sat down at the piano, they did not. Academics are generally a very collegial crew, they like each other's company, they root—since there's not so much at stake—each other on. I, for example—and it *is* an example, there are plenty more like me—have never voted to deny a colleague tenure. There used, however, to be more parties in the old days. Well, we were young in the old days, now there's less energy to go around. It ain't the getting and spending that wears you out, it's the toll hope takes. Howard Nemerov has said that old age starts when you leave your house without the expectation of falling in love.

AWP: Who do you think of today as the preeminent men and women of letters?

SE: You ask this question of a gent who never cast a vote against a colleague's tenure? It's lists like these which break major bones in the heart. Let's keep it a no-names-please world here.

AWP: William Gass wrote what is most often quoted in reference to your work: "Nothing but genre blindness could prevent us from seeing that there is no warmer, wealthier poetry being written in our time." What do you think about this?

SE: No, what's most often said about my work, the book on my books, is that I do turns, shtick, one-liners. God, I hate that. Because I don't. I'm innocent, not guilty, I was framed. If anything, I write thirty-four liners, forty-three liners, three-thousand-nine-hundred-and-twelve liners. And, indeed, if what Bill says is so, it's that word "wealthier" which is the operative one—the, well, generous impulses alive and implicit in proximity. The poets are the ones who write the one-liners of course.

AWP: You said once that fiction occurs within a context and that poetry doesn't. Would you talk about that?

SE: I think what I said was that there ain't no people in poetry, and I was wrong. These things happen when you shoot from the hip and don't know what you're talking about.

AWP: How and to what extent do the people and places of your life enter your work?

SE: Not to a very great one. I used my multiple sclerosis as a metaphor for the energy crisis in *The Franchiser*, and set *The Rabbi of Lud* in New Jersey because my parents, and a lot of my family, are buried there, and chose Lodi—Lud in the novel—because when I went there for funerals, grief tunnelled my vision and left me with the impression that the town was all graveyard. There are, here and there, some minor characters in one or two of the novels and stories who've been inspired from life, but I'm damned if *I'll* name that tune. In any event, almost everything I've written is made up. Wars, had I attended any, would have been wasted on me. Ditto bankruptcies, breakdowns, love affairs, and all the rest of life's traumas. Fiction, because it's arranged, is stranger than life.

AWP: Is this the boom time it seems to be in American fiction?

SE: Hell no. I was in New York in November, my new book had just come out and I was having lunch with my publisher. "How's the book business?" I asked him, meaning, of course, How'm I doin'? You know what he said? "Stanley, there are more bookstores in this country than ever. Writers are getting bigger and bigger advances, record advances. No one is interested in serious fiction."

AWP: How do you understand the relation of the comic and the tragic?

SE: It's like that stuff—what do they call it, meat extender. Filler anyway, whatever they do to sausage and hamburger to bulk them up. Well, you get from the comic to the tragic . . . (And that's the only direction it travels, I think; it doesn't go the other way around; it doesn't *work* the other way around. Death is not mocked because Death is not mockable. If you don't believe me, read the chapter in Tom Wolfe's *The Bonfire of the Vanities* where the English reporter goes with that rich old man to the fashionable New York restaurant and the old guy dies. Wolfe does his damndest to turn the scene into farce, to "show up" the maitre d', the waiters and diners, everyone whose evening has been made uncomfortable by the man's death, to expose them, to, well—and it really does come down to something as childish— "tell on them," I suppose—God, I hate satire, it's so self-righteous—but the result is the reader's total disbelief in the scene. It's impossible to laugh where there's no trust.) You get from the comic to the tragic by following *all* the implications of the comic. If you agree with me that the best jokes come out of obsessive situations, you'll probably agree the best tragedy does too. What's a tragic flaw if not a blind spot? So you get from the comic to the tragic in exactly the same way you get from the tragic to the cathartic—by letting in the light, by the jolt recognition gives the system.

AWP: From Push the Bully to the Rabbi of Lud, is there a characteristic common to your protagonists? Selffulness? How do you see them differing from those of your contemporaries?

SE: Self certainly, but beyond self, *behind* self, intelligence. I try to give everyone the best lines. If, by my contemporaries, you mean the Minimalistas, I'd say that their characters are just as full of themselves and bright as any of mine, they just don't talk as much. Mine probably don't feel as much as theirs do. People get it wrong about minimalism. Those characters are anything but affectless. Every little thing sets off their feelings. This is a boom time in American feelings.

AWP: With each book there seems to be an increasing self-consciousness about language. How would you characterize the development of this language? Why has it happened?

SE: Two novels gave me courage early in my career, John Hawkes's *The Lime Twig* and *Omensetter's Luck* by Bill Gass. But a demurrer here, not a modest one. I wrote an article on Alfred Kinsey for *Esquire*'s 50th anniversary issue in which I discovered I'd gone maybe 19 or 30 interior clauses too far, so far, in fact, that when I recently re-read it I didn't always understand what I was trying to say. There was too much qualifying material set off by parentheticals and one-em dashes. It was sort of two essays for the price of one. It got to the point where I'd almost invented a new form—the counter essay. I'm going to have to watch that, shoot not so much for a plainer English sentence as a better organized one. And I think I know why it happened. I think it's the down side of my imagination, the anything-goes syndrome, the notion that if I thought it up that gives me the right to put it down, the feeling I told you about when I was writing *George Mills* that I owned the language. Because *no*body owns the language, the best deal you can hope for is to time share.

AWP: In "The State of the Art," God, explaining His creation, says, "*Goodness?* No. It was Art. It was always Art. I work by contrast and metrics, by beats and silences. It was all Art.

Because it makes a better story is why." What makes a better story?

SE: Good gossip. Bad news.

AWP: Later God annihilates everything, "Because I never found My audience." Who is His audience? Who is yours? Have you found it?

SE: Well, I think the point of God's complaint is that, since He's God, it's impossible for Him to find His audience. There aren't connoisseurs smart enough, holy enough. That's just in the nature of things. What with it being so lonely at the top.

My audience? Of course I've found my audience, every writer does. I could wish it larger, but it is what it is.

AWP: God, even if He's absent, must be one of your favorite characters, the ultimate stylist, the great shoptalker of the universal guild, and it seems several of your later protagonists play His straight man, or at least have some sort of special relationship with Him. Do you have anything to say about this?

SE: No one has a special relationship with God. He's ultimately an equal-opportunity Lord. He's no respecter of persons, that is, has no favored-nation alliances. In *The Rabbi of Lud*, my character, Jerry Goldkorn, however lousy his credentials as a rabbi, knows that much at least. That's why, knowing it can't do him any harm, he gets off on the I/Thou's—that's why *I* do—takes such pleasure in sending off his mixed signals, relishes not apostasy but how close he can come to the bone. But, without being particularly aware of it, he's set a stunning example for his daughter, Connie, who turns around, turns the tables, and gives as good, not as she's gotten, but as Goldkorn, showing off, has permitted her to overhear. And pokes her daddy with devastating I/Thou's of her own.

AWP: What is your view of the hero and the heroic? How does it compare to the "anti-hero" and "anti-herioc" of, say, Bob Slocum in Heller's *Something Happened*?

SE: I've never understood this business of the anti-hero. Probably because I've never set much store in the heroic. We are not, by and large, Take Charge people. It's all most of us can do to handle our own lives. That's plenty heroic enough for me. So when critics and reviewers natter away about the "losers" in my books, I really don't know what they're talking about. I really don't. I don't regard them as losers, or as anti-heroes either. Fiction is about whatever the world or other people do to us to move us off the dime, and whatever we do back to them to climb back onto it again. It's about, I mean, a quest for purchase and stability, the attainment of the quiescence we came in with.

As to *Something Happened*, I'd like to make a sort of public retraction here. I was on the fiction panel when it was up for the National Book Award. I didn't vote for it, and two other novels, both quite wonderful, shared the prize that year. Fifteen or so years later, however, I find I've a better memory of Heller's book than I do of either of the others.

AWP: In "The Conventional Wisdom," Ellerbee, in Hell, hopes to go mad, "but there was no madness in Hell—the terrific vocabulary of the damned, their poet's knack for rightly naming everything was the failsafe of Reason—and he could find peace nowhere." Articulation, in speech or touch or sight, is both the damnation and salvation of our human beingness, the joy of naming our pain and pleasure, of differentiating and thereby being able to search for sameness, of entertaining ourselves despite everything. Is this a question? If so, it has to do with something basically celebratory in your work that separates it from what's called "black humor."

SE: I should hope so. Let me just say something. You know, I wouldn't even tell a black humor joke, and I almost certainly wouldn't laugh if you told me one. Black humor is pointless cruelty for pointless cruelty's own sake. It's not dark, it's not even gallows humor, so much as a cry for attention, self-serving as satire. Black humor, not poetry, is without any context save the reflexive and self-referential. I don't know how it ever came to be a critical term—from the same folks who brought us "absurdity," I suppose. But it's been 25 or so years now and it doesn't go away.

AWP: Do you give the same advice to young people that Ben Flesh in *The Franchiser* gives the hitchhiker when the hitchhiker says he's not into cops: "There's where you make your mistake. A boy your age. You should be into everything."? If so, at what age does that change?

SE: It's good advice, though very hard, probably impossible, to follow. Though everyone ought to be into everything. Jean Cocteau said in an interview in *The Paris Review* that he tried never to turn down a commission, that everything presented its opportunities. And that's true, though of course your batteries run down, but, at least ideally, and certainly when you're young, you ought to be open to possibilities. I don't think I always was. Too chicken, too busy specializing, too taken with time, dedication, patience, practice, will, sacrifice and per-severance.

AWP: What's good about growing older?

SE: Oho. Losing, at least a little, one's self-consciousness. Learning to live with the levelling off of one's expectations. Not much.

AWP: How does metaphor give structure to your work? Why is it so important to it? How do you teach this?

SE: Well, third things first. I don't teach it. What I *do* teach, or try to teach, is the primacy of situation in fiction. Not character, and certainly not theme or style, so certainly not metaphor-as-structure, but just plain, bald old situation, the what-woulds and what-ifs. Jewish mothers in space. The inexorable literary logic, I mean, of the blind. What structures *my* work—and this is something which seems to work for me, I'm not recommending it as a formula for other people—is somebody in a vocation I haven't really thought about until I've thought about it—a professional wrestler, a department store-owning jailbird, a radio announcer, a bailbonds-man, a guy who has franchises, another with liquor stores, and another whose vocation is the blue collar curse he thinks he lives under, an obsessed fund raiser in *The Magic Kingdom*, a rabbi, and in *The MacGuffin*, the one I'm working on now, a sort of semi-pol who is Street Commissioner in a city of about one-and-a-half-million people. Those vocations become metaphors for whatever it is I find out I'm trying to say.

AWP: You said once that if you have a theme, it is a theme of self, of self and its diseases, and the disease as health. Would you talk about that?

SE: If I *have* a theme it's certainly the self, but that said I haven't told you anything, since ev-ery novel ever written is about its protagonist's self. That's why I can't enjoy detective fic-tion, because the detective usually has no self. All he has is his case, the problem he sets out to solve. All he has to do is bring his man in. And it's why I can't read science fiction either. All *those* fellows have to do is save the world. Sci-fi is too refractive. It's we-go-there or they-come-here. Whichever, the point is always sociological. There's little sociology in my own books, only a sort of received morality, emotion and theater, the diatonics and chromatics of the given. Logic, I mean, ordinary motive in the realm of the strange.

AWP: Is it true that you won't write anything without first having a contract? What does this have to do, if anything, with inspiration?

SE: Well it's true, but it has less to do with inspiration than with reassurance, some stroked sense that keeps me going over the long haul of a novel. Though to tell you the truth, this isn't the best—or even a good—way of doing business. And I do mean *business*, because you can probably get a larger advance for a novel you've completed than for one you've only pitched. The advance ties you down to the publisher who's made the offer; there's no running up the meter or picking up an additional fare on the way back from the airport. I guess I locked my-self into this bird-in-the-hand mentality when I was writing my first novel, *Boswell*, in 1962 in Rome. My mother had offered me my year's salary, plus carfare, to go off to see whether I was a writer or not, and the first day, the *first* day we moved into our villa—well, *villa*—I got a telegram from my agent saying Random House had made a $2,000 offer for the book on the merits—well, *merits*—of its opening two chapters—its only chapters. It was a minimum, though basically standard, offer for a first novel, and I snapped it up. That thousand bucks on signing, nine hundred after she took out her fee, was as much reinforcement as I needed, and gave me tremendous confidence, and I was able to finish the book in under a year. It also created the conditions wherein I found I was only comfortable writing something if I was certain there was a publisher waiting for it at the end of the rainbow. I'm like one of those contract players back in the days of the big studios in the Hollywood of the '30s and '40s.

AWP: How has your Ph. D. helped or hindered your writing? What do you think about Ph. D.'s with creative theses?

SE: It hasn't hindered it at all. I've published, counting limited editions (*Early Elkin, The Six-Year-Old Man* and *The Coffee Room*) and anthologies I've edited or written introductions for, about fifteen books. I've been able to write almost all of them while teaching in a university, either Washington, or as a Visiting Professor somewhere else. I don't believe I'd have written any more if I hadn't gotten my Ph. D. and gone into teaching. Indeed, I expect I'd have written less, or maybe not at all, since I know of no other job where they encourage you to write books and, as I say, I've always been this contract player, dependent on the institution—the publishing institution, the Ph. D., academic one. If this makes me a moderately gutless sort of wonder, well, we all find our comfortable ways—and wheres—of doing business, and mine keep me pretty close to the reservation. If you're not a brave man, you'd better make sure you're a cautious one.

I think I'm probably against the Ph. D. creative thesis. I mean, what the hell, why push it? We've still got to make the M.F.A. or M.A. creative thesis respectable.

AWP: What magazines, if any, do you now anticipate reading with great curiosity?

SE: Well, since I don't really subscribe to any magazines, I don't think I can answer the question, though I like *Grand Street* and *The Denver Quarterly* and *The New Yorker* when I see them, and I'll look through an *Esquire* on a plane.

AWP: What do you think AWP could be doing to better serve writers?

SE: "All that can be done is being done," as the docs say. Or, "All we can do is try to make them more comfortable." Because, as they also say, "It comes down to the *will* to live."

AWP: What's next?

SE: The Macguffin, and a long story, maybe long enough to be a novella, called "Her Sense of Timing," about a fellow my own age and with something maybe a bit more severe than my own physical deficits whose wife walks out on him.

AWP: Any regrets?

SE: What, this is it? We can't talk about *me* anymore?!

The Imagination Works Slowly and Quietly

by Brenda Ueland

Now I am going to try to tell you what the creative power is, how you can detect it in yourself and separate it out from all your nervous doubts and checks. And how you can separate it from mere memory. For memory and erudition (i.e., the superimposed lumber of all the hard facts you have learned) can smother it very easily.

When we hear the word "inspiration" we imagine something that comes like a bolt of lightning, and at once with a rapt flashing of the eyes, tossed hair and feverish excitement, a poet or artist begins furiously to paint or write. At least I used to think sadly that that was what inspiration must be, and never experienced a thing that was one bit like it.

But this isn't so. Inspiration comes very slowly and quietly. Say that you want to write. Well, not much will come to you the first day. Perhaps nothing at all. You will sit before your typewriter or paper and look out of the window and begin to brush your hair absentmindedly for an hour or two. Never mind. That is all right. That is as it should be—though you must sit before your typewriter just the same and know, in this dreamy time, that you are going to write, to tell something on paper, sooner or later. And you also must know that you are going to sit here tomorrow for a while, and the next day and so on, forever and ever.

Dare to be idle

Our idea that we must always be energetic and active is all wrong. Bernard Shaw says that it is not true that Napoleon was always snapping out decisions to a dozen secretaries and aides-de-camp, as we are told, but that he moodled around for months. Of course he did. And that is why these smart, energetic, do-it-now, pushing people so often say: "I am not creative." They are, but they should be idle, limp and alone for much of the time, as lazy as men fishing on a levee, and quietly looking and thinking, not *willing* all the time. This quiet looking and thinking is the imagination; it is letting in ideas. Willing[1] is doing something you know already, something you have been told by somebody else; there is no new imaginative understanding in it. And presently your soul gets frightfully sterile and dry because you are so quick, snappy and efficient about doing one thing after another that you have not time for your own ideas to come in and develop and gently shine. When you will, make a resolution, set your jaw, you are expressing an imaginative fear that you *won't* do the thing. If you knew you would do the thing, you would smile happily and set about it. And this fear (since the imagination is always creative) comes about presently and you slide down into the complete slump of several weeks or years—the very thing you dreaded and set your jaws against.

And why do these grim-resolution people will? Because they are full of fear which drives them to try to dominate themselves and others for the purpose of making money or getting some kind of security. If you dominate and boss your children all the time, it means you are afraid *they* will not be secure, foolishly thinking that your bossing will guarantee this, that *you*

Brenda Ueland *was a noted writer, editor and teacher of writing. In addition to her book on writing* If You Want to Write, *first published in 1938, her works include* Me *and* Mitropoulos & the North High Band.

know just how they should grow. Or by willing you try to dominate yourself so that your importance, financial or artistic or ethical or whatever, will be secure.

But the great artists like Michelangelo and Blake and Tolstoi—like Christ whom Blake called an artist because he had one of the most creative imaginations that ever was on earth—do not want security, egoistic or materialistic. Why, it never occurs to them. "Be not anxious for the morrow," and "which of you being anxious can add one cubit to his stature?"

So they dare to be idle, i.e., not to be pressed and duty-driven all the time. They dare to love people even when they are very bad, and they dare not to try and dominate others to show them what they must do for their own good. For great and creative men know what is best for every man is his own freedom so that his imagination (it can also be called the conscience or the Holy Ghost) can grow in its own way, even if that way, to you or to me, or to policemen or churchgoers, seems very bad indeed.

But since I would not be a critic for anything, i.e., tell you where you are all wrong without telling your something that might make you feel like changing, know that I will do so. I will try to show the grim-resolution people how they might become imaginative, creative ones.

Imagination needs moodling

It is these fool, will-worshipping people who live by maxims and lists of chores and the Ten Commandments—not creatively as when a fine, great maxim occurs to you and bursts a little, silent bomb of revelation in you—but mechanically.

". . . Honor thy father and thy mother" . . . the active, willing, do-it-now man thinks and makes note of this daily, sets his jaw, and thinks he *does* honor them, which he does not at all, and which of course his father and mother know and can feel, since nothing is hidden by outer behavior.

The idle creative man says:

" 'Honor thy father and mother.' . . . That is interesting . . . I don't seem to honor them very much . . . I wonder why that is?" and his imagination creatively wanders on until perhaps it leads him to some truth such as the fact that his father is a peevish and limited man, his mother unfortunately rattle-brained. This distresses him and he puzzles and thinks and hopes again and again for more light on the subject and tries everything his imagination shows to him, such as being kinder or controlling his temper; and perhaps he comes to think: "Is it *they* who are peevish and boring, or is it just that I, being a small man, think so?" And he goes on and seeks and asks for the answer with his imagination. And who knows, in time he even may come to understand what Christ did (who as I said was one of the most imaginative men who ever lived and whose life was fiercely and passionately directed against following mechanically any rules whatever): how if one is great and imaginative enough one can honor and love people with all their limitations.

So you see the imagination needs moodling—long, inefficient, happy idling, dawdling and puttering. These people who are always briskly doing something and as busy as waltzing mice, they have little, sharp, staccato ideas, such as: "I see where I can make an annual cut of $3.47 in my meat budget." But they have no slow, big ideas. And the fewer consoling, noble, shining, free, jovial, magnanimous ideas that come, the more nervously and desperately they rush and run from office to office and up and downstairs, thinking by action at last to make life have some warmth and meaning.

The great mystic philosopher Plotinus said about this:

"So there are men too feeble for contemplation." (This is his word for what I call the imagination.) "Being unable to raise themselves to contemplation from the weakness of their

---

[1]No doubt my terms would horrify a psychologist but I do not care at all.

Soul, unable to behold spiritual reality and fill themselves with it, but desiring to see it, they are driven to action that they may see that which they could not see with the spiritual eye."

Good thoughts come slowly

But I must go back to my subject—writing. If you write, good ideas must come welling up into you so that you have something to write. If good ideas do not come at once, or for a long time, do not be troubled at all. Wait for them. Put down the little ideas however insignificant they are. But do not feel, any more, guilty about idleness and solitude.

But of course I must say this:

If your idleness is a complete slump, that is, indecision, fretting, worry, or due to over-feeding and physical mugginess, that is bad, terrible and utterly sterile. Or if it is that idleness which so many people substitute for creative idleness, such as gently feeding into their minds all sorts of printed bilge like detective stories and newspapers, that is too bad and utterly un-creative.[2]

But if it is the dreamy idleness that children[3] have, an idleness when you walk alone for a long, long time, or take a long, dreamy time at dressing, or lie in bed at night and thoughts come and go, or dig in a garden, or drive a car for many hours alone, or play the piano, or sew or paint alone; or an idleness—and this is what I want you to do—where you sit with pencil and paper or before a typewriter quietly putting down what you happen to be thinking, that is creative idleness. With all my heart I tell you and reassure you: at such times you are being slowly filled and re-charged with warm imagination, with wonderful, living thoughts.

Now some people when they sit down to write and nothing special comes, no good ideas, are so frightened that they drink a lot of strong coffee to hurry them up, or smoke packages of cigarettes, or take drugs or get drunk. They do not know that good ideas come slowly, and that the more clear, tranquil and unstimulated you are, the slower the ideas come but the better they are.

It was Tolstoi who showed me this. I used to drink coffee all day and smoke two packages of cigarettes. I could thus pump myself up to write all day and much of the night, for a few days. But the sad part of it was, what I wrote was not very good. It came out easily, but it wasn't much good. It was interlarded with what was pretentious, commonplace and untrue.[4]

This is what Tolstoi said about it:

" 'If I do not smoke I cannot write. I cannot get on. I begin and I cannot endure,' is what is usually said and what I used to say. What does it really mean?

[2]I personally include much of the shouting, broken, perfunctory talk of social life, most card playing, and all reading that passes over a person without affecting him in the least. I mean reading that just passes time. But of course that affects him,—slowly rotting his soul.

[3]You will say that children are not alone for hours every day, or they do not want to be, and they are creative. But children are not willing all the time. They have lifted off them all duty, all anxiety. When a child is taken somewhere by his parents he is not thinking nervously: are they late or early? is the furnace running at home? etc., but he is at rest and looks out the window and sees and thinks. He lives in the present. That is why children enjoy looking and listening so much. Why they are such wonderful mimics of grown-ups. They have tremen-dous concentration because they have no other concern than to be interested in things. Later they are trained to force concentration and become as imaginatively muddy and uneasy as the rest of us.

[4]I tell in another chapter why things that are so, are uninteresting. Though I filled a whole British Museum with such stuff, not only would nobody care to read it, but it would do me no good to write it.

If I wrote something true and good that nobody cared to read, it would do *me* a great deal of good.

"It means either that you have nothing to write, or what you wished to write has not yet matured in your consciousness, but it is only beginning dimly to present itself to you, and the appraising critic within[5] when not stupefied with tobacco, tells you so.

"If you did not smoke, you would either abandon what you have begun, or you would wait until your thought has cleared itself dimly in your mind; you would try to penetrate into what presents itself dimly to you,"—(by, as I say, idling, by a long, solitary walk, by being alone)—"would consider the objects that offer themselves and would turn all your attention to the elucidation of the thought. But you smoke and the critic within you" (the truth-seeking creative critic) "is stupefied and the hindrance to your work is removed. What to you, when not inebriated by tobacco, seems insignificant, again seems important; what seemed obscure, no longer seems so; the objections that present themselves vanish and you continue to write and write much and rapidly."

I am not urging you not to smoke. Each must find out all things for himself. But I want to show how Tolstoi knew good thoughts come slowly. And so it is nothing for you to worry about or to be afraid of, and it is even a bad plan to hurry them artificially.

For when you do so, there may be suddenly *many* thoughts, but that does not mean that they are specially good ones or interesting. It is just as when you give a thoughtful, slightly tired person a stiff drink. Before the drink he says nothing but what seems to him interesting and important. He mentally discards the thoughts that are not important. He mentally discards the thoughts that are not important enough to make up for the fatigue of saying them. But after the drink, all his thoughts come out head over heels, whatever crosses his mind. There are suddenly *many* thoughts; but they are just like the flutter of thoughts that come out of one of those unfortunate people who cannot keep from talking all the time. This kind of talking is not creation. It is just mental evacuation.

And it is Tolstoi who showed me the importance of being idle—because thoughts come so slowly. For what we write today slipped into our souls some *other* day when we were alone and doing nothing.

Tolstoi speaks of the hero of Dostoevsky's *Crime and Punishment*.

"Raskolnikof lived his true life, not when he murdered the old woman or her sister. When murdering the old woman herself, and especially when murdering her sister, he did not live his true life, but acted like a machine doing what he could not help doing—discharging the cartridge with which he had long been loaded. Raskolnikof lived his true life . . . at the time when he was lying on the sofa in his room . . . And then—in that region quite independent of animal activities—the question whether he would or would not kill the old woman was decided. That question was decided when he was doing nothing and only thinking; when only his consciousness was active and in that consciousness tiny, tiny alterations were taking place. It is at such times that one needs the greatest clearness to decide correctly the questions that have arisen, and it is just then that one glass of beer, or one cigarette, may prevent the solution of the question, may postpone the decision, stifle the voice of conscience, prompt the decision of the question in favor of one's lower animal nature, as was the case of Raskolnikof."

I tell you this not to persuade you to give up drinking and smoking (though that might be a good thing too) but to show you that what you write today is the result of some span of idling

---

[5]By "critic" he means here what I call the true self, the imagination, or the Holy Ghost, or the Conscience. It is what is always searching in us and trying to free what we *really* think, from what we think we ought to think, from what is superimposed by bossy parents, teachers or literary critics.

This critic in us all, I love. The critic I abhor is the one (inside or out) which is always measuring, comparing, cautioning and advising prudence and warning against mistakes and quoting authorities and throwing dry, anxious doubt into everyone, by showing them just the way they must go.

No, each man must go by his own conscience, by his own creative, truth-searching critic.

yesterday, some fairly long period of protection from talking and busyness.

It was Raskolnikof lying on the couch, ill and miserable and in despair about his destitute mother and sister, and wondering what to do—it was then he created the murder that came many days later.

Your true self

In the same way what you write today you thought and created in some idle time on another day. It is on another day that your ideas and visions are slowly built up, so that when you take your pencil there is something to say[6] that is not just superficial and automatic, like children yelling at a birthday party, but it is true and has been tested inwardly and is based on something.

And why it must be true I will explain later. I do not mean it must be a statement of fact such as "Columbus discovered America in 1492," but it must come from your true self and not your theoretical self, from what you really think, love and believe, not from your hope to make an impression.

The is why I hope you can keep up this continuity and sit for some time every day (if only for a half hour, though two hours is better and five is remarkable and eight is bliss and transfiguration!) before your typewriter—if not writing then just thoughtfully pulling your hair. If you skip for a day or two, it is hard to get started again. In a queer way you are afraid of it.[7] It takes again an hour or two of vacant moodling, when nothing at all comes out on paper; and this is difficult always because it makes us busy, efficient Anglo-Saxons with our accomplishment-mania, feel uneasy and guilty.

You see I am so afraid that you will decide that you are stupid and untalented. Or that you will put off working as so many wonderfully gifted people do, until that time when your husband can retire on full pay and all your children are out of college.

---

[6]Though remember this: you may not be conscious, when you sit down, of having evolved something important to say. You will sit down as mentally blank, good natured and smiling as usual, and not frowning solemnly over the weight of your message. Just the same, when you begin to write, presently something will come out, something true and interesting.

[7]I hope to explain why you are afraid of it before this book is finished and to show you why you need not be at all.

__ *Thoughts on the Teacherless Writing Class*

by Peter Elbow

The main idea behind the teacherless writing class is that you can't trust theory, you can only trust facts. The only trouble is that you can't get away from theory. Facts are always dirty with some theory: no one can "see a fact" or "say what really happened" without using an implicit model or theory. On top of everything else, I love theories and models so much that I wouldn't leave them out if I could.

As I tried to write about the teacherless writing class, I was constantly derailed by digressions into theory-making and model-building. I finally realized I should collect it all here.

How I came to this approach

The main thing has been my experience as a teacher trying to comment on student papers. During my first years as a teacher, my head would swim and I'd become completely baffled as I tried to think of useful things to say about student papers. But after a number of years this changed. Slowly I developed a more or less firm and communicable idea of what I was looking for: clear, not-too-wordy sentences; paragraphs each organized around a clear, discrete point; a shaped or logical structure to the whole thing; and adequacy of argument and documentation. These standards could probably be called the main academic line in rhetorical taste: clean writing—writing that tries to call more attention to its message than to itself.

At last I knew what I was doing when I graded and commented on papers. No longer the nightmare of groping in the dark. I knew what a good paper was. I felt justified in using these standards because they weren't too narrow or idiosyncratic. I felt I could specify where a paper fell down and what changes the writer should make. As long as my unspoken premises held together it seemed to me I was a competent and useful commenter.

But my premises didn't hold together. After some years it began to happen that I would find myself in the middle of writing a comment and begin to wonder whether it could really be trusted, whether it was really useful. Perhaps I was telling someone about his flowery and wordy diction. His diction was indeed wordy and could be called flowery. But I began to wonder if this was *why* I was complaining about it. I sometimes found myself suspecting it was something else I couldn't put my finger on that bothered me but floweriness was more available. If I were in a different mood or the paper were in a different place in the stack, perhaps I wouldn't have made the comment I did.

Or sometimes the floweriness did seem to be the culprit but in a peculiar way: he was having such fun writing it and any reader who was in the right frame of mind could also have fun reading it. But I, in my writing, *can't* have fun with this kind of diction, and in my reading I don't seem to be able to have fun with it; and so it makes me mad.

Or perhaps I was pointing out the flaws in someone's organization or argument. But something made me realize I was really *looking* for something the matter. I could probably find other papers with similar structure I didn't complain of. I could even imagine being very sympathetic and persuaded by just such an argument—could find just such an organization

Peter Elbow, *director of the Writing Program at the State University of New York at Stony Brook, has also taught at Wesleyan University, MIT and Franconia College. Known as an advocate of innovative teaching methods, he is also author of* Writing with Power: Techniques for Mastering the Writing Process.

clear—if other circumstances had been different. These things *could* be called flaws, yet the more I thought about it, the more it seemed that these professional, objective matters of diction, paragraphing, organization and argument *weren't what determined how I responded to the paper*.

But if I tried to say *how* and *why* I actually did respond, I was immediately out of bounds: it was all mixed up with my mood and my personal quirks or taste and my temperament. It wouldn't seem fair either. I would clearly like some papers that seemed to me worse than others, and hate some that seemed really quite good.

Subjectivity worked better

My frustration grew and I finally said what the hell. If there is something fishy in my attempt to be fair and objective, how about trying to be as subjective as I can. So then I became intrigued with trying to be good at being subjective: actually trying to give a full and accurate report of what went on in me as a result of reading the words on the paper: no matter how little I understood why I was having these thoughts and feelings and even if they seemed nutty.

I found this was no easier than trying to be objective. All my habits worked against me. Sometimes I didn't know what my reactions were. And often I felt odd and vulnerable trying to tell reactions when I didn't understand why I was having them. No doubt I often missed the real truth about my reactions. But the new struggle seemed better. I felt it made the whole transaction between writer and reader much more genuine. I felt it helped the student's writing a bit more. It was much more fun. And it seemed to increase my powers of perception: simply to start writing a comment of this sort often led me to notice something about the paper that was very interesting—and helpful to the student—but something I never would have noticed if I had stuck with trying to be fair, professional and objective.

In other words, when my teaching began, I had an experience of the student's paper, but I had no idea what to tell the student. But then I gradually moved farther away from my experience of the paper: instead of noticing my reactions, I noticed where the writing fit my model of good writing and praised those parts, and noticed where it departed from my model of good writing and criticized those parts, and told the student how to make improvements. I could afford to ignore my experience and reactions because at last I had a workable model. And it was a great relief—not just because I finally felt I had something useful to say, but because it's too exhausting to experience and react to a stack of 20, 40, or 60 papers. To bring to bear the whole organism and all its reactors is too much. To bring a good model to bear is much easier, much more sanity-conserving. When I got good at it, I found I could often short-circuit the experiencing process altogether: simply notice diction, paragraphing, organization and argument, and not experience the paper at all. And still apply the model well.

I would also use the model with respect to "content"—not just form or style. When there are a lot of papers, it's hard actually to experience each person's whole argument. It's easier simply to hold it up against one's own model of what the argument should be. That's why so much essay grading and commenting is a process whereby the teacher "checks off" the "points" a student makes against a kind of inner master list. In short, there is a terrific pressure for the English teacher to minimize his experience of a set of words and maximize his construction of a model (perhaps implicit) in order to check off a piece of writing against it. And so, bit by bit, one *has* less and less experience of a set of words that one could transmit to a student.

When I finally embarked on trying to transmit my experience of his words, it didn't take me long to realize that it would be better if the student could get the experience of more than one reader. He would get a wider range of reactions to offset the onesidedness of a single reaction. And so I began to try to get the whole class to give reactions in this way.

Another experience confirmed this approach for me. During this period I participated in a couple of encounter groups and joined a therapy group conducted by a psychoanalyst. In these settings I often learned other people's reactions to something I said and suddenly realized that I had just learned more about that piece of speech than I usually was able to learn about words I had written on paper. This feedback consisted of people telling what the words had made happen in them.

Huh?

I've often had a kind of surreal, underwater vision of social reality. It usually seemed as though this was a purely private and aberrant experience. But now the teacherless class reinforces it.

Everyone walks around mostly out of communication with everyone else. Someone has turned off the sound, cut the wires. It's all fog and silence. If we really said what we were feeling in many situations, it would be, "Did you say something? I thought maybe I saw your mouth moving, but I wasn't sure. I guess you did look sort of worked up."

We don't admit this Faulknerian vision. We pretend we heard and understood words when we only saw the other person's mouth move. In fact I think that the fear of honest feedback is not so much a fear that the other person will think us wrong, childish, evil or stupid. Those are easy to take in comparison with our worst fear: that our words were not heard at all; or that they were perceived as merely random, meaningless babble; that the only honest feedback an audience could give would be to stare at us uncomprehendingly, mouth slightly open, and say, "Huh?"

It's usually only adolescents and people in emotional crisis who go around saying, "No one understands me! No one understands what I am trying to say!" For it is they who most need to send complex messages about the way they feel and the way they perceive the world, and to have these messages understood. Most of the rest of us discover that only simple, trivial messages get through and so we give up sending complicated ones. Pass the salt. What's playing at the movies? Where are you going tomorrow? We no longer try to describe important things like what life is like and how we live and what we need. That's why it is so magical when you have a friend who actually understands much of what you are trying to say. It makes you want to say things you never thought you had in you.

I see all this in the classes now. At first people try to be polite and nice. They try to think they hear and understand messages. But before long a couple of brave souls finally say it. "Huh?" Here's this long piece of language: probably carefully and painfully written. They see mouths moving and hear noises, but really they can't understand a thing.

This is frustrating for the writer, but it is also a relief. At last what he suspected all along is out on the table. Finally, there is no longer this pretence that communication is going on. Finally one can get down to business and notice the stray phrase or passage that actually *does* get through. There is no hope of separating real communication from static when people pretend that the whole thing is communication.

When noncommunication is more out in the open, good communication can begin. People eventually start to hear each other very well. This explains something about these classes that had perplexed and even perturbed me. When I set up a writing class or invited people to join one, I often put a big emphasis on pragmatic writing—committee reports, letters, writings for a job, writing essays for some other class: trying to make words do a real-live job where you can tell in a concrete way whether they have done the job you wanted. I'm not a "creative writing" person and I've always felt insecure about it. But I've found that many people who start a course with a desire to work on pragmatic kinds of writing, as I had encouraged them to do, begin after a while to ignore these goals and move toward more personal, imaginative or creative writing. Now I think I know why. When people not only begin to improve their writing ability but also find themselves in a group where their words are heard and understood better than they usually are, they discover messages they want to send which they had forgotten were on their minds. They want to say things that are complex and difficult to express which they had previously learned to ignore because it had always been impossible to get them heard.

Writing made easier: two conditions

Most people can learn to write much more easily. This does not solve all their problems. Perhaps they still write badly. But now they write. Now they get pleasure from writing. They write more and this too helps their writing. And they can direct more energy into trying to write well instead of needing it all—and then some—simply to get words down.

There are two conditions that help you produce words easily. These two conditions are usually absent when you write, but the teacherless class helps to produce them.

The first condition is to know how people are reacting to your words. Usually you know this when you are having a conversation with someone, and so you don't find it hard to speak meaningfully and fluently. Before you go on to the second thing you have to say, you get a feel for how your listener reacted to the first thing. You can tell not only from what he says but from how he says it—little physical movements and postures—whether he is understanding you, whether he agrees with you at all, or whether he is beginning to think you are crazy.

Think of peculiar speaking situations in which you don't know how a listener is reacting to your words. It is much harder to produce meaningful speech. There is a bit of this problem when you are talking to an absolute stranger. He is hard to "read." He might have very different responses from those you are used to. When you get *no* clues, speaking is especially difficult. Perhaps the person is paralyzed, or he is from such a foreign culture that you can't read him at all, or he is a social scientist conducting an experiment in withholding feedback, or perhaps he is just a psychiatrist. Sometimes you actually talk *more* during the first moments of such a situation: the silence is so embarrassing that you babble a bit. But usually words soon dry up.

In writing, however, this is the normal condition. No wonder it is agony. As you are writing you get no clues as to how readers will react. You have to write the whole thing out, keep going till the end, even though you have no idea whether the reader is lost or thinks you are crazy at the end of the first paragraph. Not only that, you don't even know *who* will read it. Once your words are on paper, they can be easily transported before the eyes of anyone—no matter how you feel about him, no matter how little he knows or understands you. (Notice how often people use metaphors of nakedness to describe what it feels like when they write.) In writing, there is only one way to be sure who will read it: rip it up and throw it in the wastebasket. No wonder that's what usually happens.

The teacherless class comes as close as possible to taking you out of the dark about how your words are experienced, and thus making it easier to produce meaningful words on paper.

There's another condition that makes it easy to produce language: *not worrying* how the audience experiences your words.

There are times when you simply have to speak out. The chips are down. Damn the torpedoes. It's the only way to maintain your very integrity or self-respect. In such situations, once you have started, you are usually surprised how fluent (and powerful) your words are.

Most people, no matter how hard it is ordinarily for them to write, have had one or two experiences of this sort when writing came easily. Perhaps it was an important personal letter in which you finally had to say how you felt no matter what the consequences. Perhaps it was a written test where desperation and not-caring added up right, so you could say, "Well, what the hell." Perhaps it was a paper that was so late you finally had to stop worrying about how it would be perceived. This is why so many people can only write something when it is overdue. Sometimes only desperation is powerful enough to make you stop worrying about how your words will be received.

The teacherless class will also help you reach this blessed state of not worrying, if you stick with it for a while. At first the class makes you depend on all this feedback you are getting: you wonder how you wrote anything before without it. But after a while you don't care about it so much. After a while you get enough reactions from enough people that finally you begin to develop a trustworthy sense of the effects of your words. You have learned the feel of real readers. For another thing, the class helps you worry less about whether people *like* what you wrote. You notice that in most cases it is impossible to please everyone. People's reactions are too different. There's no piece of writing in the world that would please everyone in the class. You eventually learn that it's not even very useful to learn someone's judgment of your words compared to learning his perceptions and experiences of them. So instead of letting the standards of the readers call the shots for you, gradually you come to make your own decisions as to what is good and bad, and use the responses of others to help you fulfill *your own goals*, not their goals. You are interested in their responses and you learn from them, but you no longer worry about them. This nonworrying frees your writing.

Writing made better: the right readers

Probably the most helpful thing about the class is that you get many readings of your words, not just one. But if these readers don't know any more about writing than you do, how do they help you? They help you by being, in one sense worse readers, but in another sense better readers, than a regular teacher.

A teacher is usually too good a reader in the following ways. He usually reads and writes better than you do and knows more about the subject you are writing about. You are probably writing the thing because he asked you to, and, if it's an essay, he may well have picked a topic that he knows a lot about. If writing is an exercise in getting things into readers and not just onto paper, then usually it is too easy to get everything into the teacher's head. *Yet at the same time too hard to get anything in.* What I mean is that though he can usually understand everything you are trying to say (perhaps even better than you understand it); nevertheless he isn't really listening to you. He usually isn't in a position where he can be genuinely affected by your words. He doesn't expect your words actually to make a dent on him. He doesn't treat your words like real reading. He has to read them as an exercise. He can't hold himself ready to be affected unless he has an extremely rare, powerful openness.

So one of the genuinely valuable aspects of the reading you get from the teacherless class is that in a sense it is inferior: it will have "mistakes," the readers will miss some meanings that a teacher would get. The most obvious example is that these readers give you better evidence of what is unclear in your writing. They're not just telling you the places where they think your writing is awkward because it doesn't comform to their idea of what good writing is. They are people telling you where you actually confused them. A diverse group of readers constitutes an ideal array of "channels" for "sending your message across." You find out where there is too much static or where the message is too weak. Sometimes someone who knows very little about the subject is most useful here.

I have often seen the following process. Someone writes something about a field he is expert in. He gets other experts to read it. They understand it fine, at least they have no questions and seem to display no problems in understanding it. But they don't like it very well, they are rather unpersuaded by it, or somehow the writing doesn't affect them as the writer thinks it should. He senses an importance in what he wrote and they just don't seem to get it. But someone who *doesn't* understand the matter at all shows the writer where the problem is: places where the idea is there, yes, and the expert readers felt they were understanding it, but really they weren't hearing it as the writer intended it, weren't seeing it as the writer was. They just read right through and said, "uh huh, yes, I see," but if they had really seen it as the writer saw it, they would have been forcibly struck.

Though the members of a teacherless class read, in a sense, worse than a teacher, they also read better. They see your writing every week. They hear you read things out loud. They hear you react to other people's writing. They can listen fully to your words—just listen and attend to their reactions—because they don't have to try to evaluate or give a grade. They get to know your language, your way of handling words, so they can hear ideas, feelings and nuances that are only partially encoded in the words. They hear the message behind the fog.

But how will it help you write better if they tell you that a message got across when "in the real world" it wouldn't have gotten across? I remember the evening when I first wrestled with this question. I was teaching an evening adult education class. I thought of my method as "hard nosed," "tough," "realistic." I was comfortable and in fact pleased with how useful it is for readers to be, as it were, *meaner* than a teacher would be to a piece of writing. But on this particular evening, three or four weeks into the course, the class was *nicer* than I would have been. There was a poem. People read it on paper. Everyone was left pretty cold. It clearly didn't work. But then someone asked the woman to read it out loud. Still nothing much. But the same reader asked her to read it once more—perhaps out of embarrassment at having nothing to say about the poem. And now people began to respond to it, hear things in it, finally be touched by it. It seemed to me these people weren't being hardnosed enough. I was sure it wasn't a very good poem, and reading it out loud didn't make it any better. They weren't supposed to like it like this. Here I thought I had a good empirical, real-world laboratory when now it looked as though perhaps I just had a too-easy, self-indulgent hot-house that will let people be too nice to each other.

I was very bothered but I still thought the class helped people, so I kept trying to figure out why. I came to a way of understanding the feedback process that I wouldn't otherwise have thought of.

Getting through

This woman had written a poem—not a very good poem as far as I could tell—but on that evening she had the main experience that makes people write more poems: her words got through to the readers. She sent words out into the darkness and heard someone shout back. This made her want to do it again, and this is probably the most powerful thing that makes people improve their writing. (It's not that the members of the class were "trying to say something nice." They were actually getting an important meaning or experience from the words. There is one sort of good teacher who always seems to have something good to say about a student's writing. If you try to emulate this teacher's "technique" and always say something nice, it sounds false and doesn't seem to work. His "technique" didn't consist of saying nice things but rather of being such a good reader that he actually heard in the words much of what the writer put in.)

You could describe the previous situation with the poem by saying that the woman's "message" was all right (surely there's no thought or feeling which wouldn't make a good poem if transmitted in the right language); but there was too much fog or static—she didn't have the right words; yet in the end this audience finally got through the static to the message itself and liked the poem.

But there's something wrong with describing the situation this way. In the last analysis there is no such thing as static. Human behavior, especially verbal behavior, is never random. We could only speak of static in a piece of writing if the writer had St. Vitus's Dance and kept hitting random keys of the typewriter, or splashed ink randomly across the page. Any other weakness or mistake must be thought of as understandable if you only get to know this person's coding behavior. Even completely mistaken uses of a word are understandable to a listener who knows the speaker very well.

I'm not trying to say that writing which looks weak is really strong. I'm simply saying that all the weak, static-like, or fog-like elements in it are really decipherable, really meaningful, really messages. Most of them consist of too many and too conflicting messages which *func-*

tion as static because they are only half-coded and not in good order.

It is the human condition that when we emit words in speaking or writing, we are sending out lots and lots of messages. The reason why our word production is so unpowerful and ineffective is that we let all those messages mush in together and get in each other's way. What is rare is simply to send a message with no other conflicting messages. This explains that strange but crucial phenomenon in writing: someone writes something that is not original or earthshaking, writes it not elegantly and in a sense even well, but somehow writes it with such directness and purity that it ends up hitting the reader with great force. He has fully managed to get rid of what *looks* like static, namely, all the half-coded, irrelevant messages, and all the undertones and overtones that get in the way of his utterance.

The idea that there's no such thing as static helps us understand how to improve a piece of writing: it does no good to say to someone, "get rid of the static here." He didn't write any static, he wrote nothing but messages. But he wasn't aware of most of those intruding or badly coded messages. Take a simple example: a letter which asks for something but doesn't succeed in making it happen. The letter was understandable but it simply didn't work. A reader who doesn't know the writer at all could point out some mistakes and places where it might be clearer, but when asked why it didn't work would have to say, "I don't know. It's just not convincing." And if the receiver of the letter doesn't know the writer, that is probably the only feedback he could give. But readers who know the writer well and his ways of using and responding to words can usually say much more. They will be able to hear messages throughout, even though they are faint: implications that the writer doesn't like the person he's writing to, or fears him, or that he doesn't really expect his request to be granted, or doesn't really believe some of his own reasons. These are not messages that the writer intended to send. He will not be aware of them till he hears about them from readers who know his coding habits well.

The important learning process here is that there is something you must *stop* doing—inhibit those intrusive messages—but you can't stop doing something you are unaware of doing. If someone is trying to stop tightening or clenching a muscle he is unconsciously keeping tight, he must first experience this tightening.*

So when a teacherless writing class gets going well, readers don't just hear the writer's intended message behind the fog. They also hear how the fog itself consists of unintended messages. The writer is persistently being told that there are implications in his words he didn't think he put there. When a writer hears often enough that readers have such and such a response, he finally has to suspect that perhaps the response is appropriate. When he begins to acknowledge and then finally to experience his sending of some message, he begins to be able to stop sending it. *Or*—and this can be a very powerful move toward better writing—he begins to be able to send it louder and clearer.

---

*The Alexander technique of kinesthetic training is based on this constructive analysis of inhibition. See *The Resurrection of the Body; Selected Writings of F. Matthias Alexander*, Edward Maisel, editor.

The Writing Habit

by David Huddle

The major difficulty a writer must face has nothing to do with language: it is finding or making the circumstances that make writing possible. The first project for a writer is that of constructing a writing life.

Achievement in writing requires many hours and many pages of concentrated effort. That work must be carried out in a sustained fashion: a writer must be able to carry what has been learned from one day's writing into the next, from one week's writing into the next, and so on. Significant accomplishment in writing depends on growth. A writer's development depends on being able to write regularly and without distraction.

The actual details of writing lives differ with the personalities of individual writers. I remember a lecture given by the novelist Don Bredes, a very down-to-earth man, in which he set forth what he thought were the requirements of a writing circumstance. Shelves, he said, were necessary, in order to set out one's manuscripts, supplies, and reference materials. A phone immediately at hand was neccasary so that one would not be ripped away from one's desk when the phone rang in another part of the house. A window with a view was necessary, but I don't remember if Don thought one's desk should face toward the window or away from it. And a plant, preferably a cactus, was necessary. I haven't remembered why Don thought one needed a plant—probably something to do with the benign influence of a low-profile living presence. At the time I was listening to him, I agreed with him about the shelves, disagreed with him about the phone, had no opinion about the window and thought the cactus was patently absurd. It's been about eight years since he gave that lecture; Don would have reason to smile to himself if he could see my study now, complete with shelves, a phone, and an aloe plant on the bookcase underneath the skylight.

In her memoir of her father, Susan Cheever describes the young John Cheever putting on a suit and tie each morning, riding the elevator down to a basement storage room of their Manhattan apartment building, taking off his trousers and hanging them up with his coat to prevent wrinkling, and in his boxer shorts sittting down to his writing desk for his day's work. The established Cheever claimed to have written each of his later books in a different room of his Ossining, New York, home.

My Lake St. Clair experience

I have had various writing circumstances, some of them refined to a state of high peculiarity. Perhaps the most productive ones were the winter of 1978 when I lived alone in a cottage beside a small lake. I rose at sun-up, did fifteen minutes of calisthenics, showered, made coffee and ate a light breakfast. Then I worked at "fresh" writing, beginning around seven or seven-thirty. I tried not to excuse myself before eleven, though if momentum was with me, it was o.k. to stay later. My desk faced a large window that overlooked a woodsy hillside where I had set out bird food. I allowed myself many minutes of bird-watching; the finches, jays, chickadees, and nuthatches seemed to go very well with my writing, offering me a healthy distraction. My output for those hours was three to six pages of fresh prose each morning. I composed on a portable electric typewriter, the humming of which always seemed to me like very good company.

David Huddle *teaches at the University of Vermont and at the Bread Loaf School of English. His new book is titled* Stopping by Home. *His other work includes* Only the Little Bone *and a short story collection,* The High Spirits.

Those months of living beside Lake St. Clair were the one period of my life when I have been a runner, or more accurately a jogger. My run was my reward for having worked through my morning hours. Just as I had to work up to my three or four hours of fresh writing a day, I had gradually to increase my running distance. The road around Lake St. Clair is a very hilly 2.3 miles long. When I began running in early February, I could trot only about a quarter of the way around it without stopping to walk. When I left Lake St. Clair in mid-May I was jogging (vigorously) around it twice without stopping.

When I returned from jogging, I did some stretching, took a shower, and fixed myself a light lunch. My discipline at Lake St. Clair included small portions of food for meals, no snacks and no desserts; I ate more reasonably than I had before or I have since those months. During lunch, for the first time in the day, I listened to the radio. I neither read nor was I tempted to read any newspapers during my lakeside tenure.

After washing my lunch and breakfast dishes, I was in my "free period." I could do whatever I wanted. Whatever I wanted was almost always to read for a while and then to take a nap. Among the books I read during those months were R. P. Warren's *Selected Poems*, John Ahsbury's *Houseboat Days* and *Portrait in a Convex Mirror*, John Casey's *An American Romance*, Tim O'Brien's *Going After Cacciato*.

A few words here about naps: I'm convinced that naps are an essential part of a writing life, that they "clean" the brain by discharging the clutter and allowing the subconscious to address some of the central issues of the morning's writing. If I know I want to do some more writing in the afternoon, I'll always try to schedule that session immediately after a nap. It's rare for me to try to accomplish fresh writing in the afternoon, but I often try to carry out revisions if I have at least an hour or more of afternoon time available to me.

When I woke from a nap at Lake St. Clair, I had the delicious sensation of having nothing pressing to do and not having to hurry with whatever I chose to do. Most often I simply lay in bed, letting my mind wander as it would. Because I had minimum distraction there, whatever I was writing was what I thought about most of the time. It wasn't long after I waked from my nap that I would turn to my manuscript; usually I'd be curious about the pages I'd written that morning and want to check them out. Of course, as I read, I reached for a pen to make corrections, changes, notes, and it wasn't uncommon for me to find myself again sitting before the typewriter, retyping the morning's pages, perhaps even proceeding into a page of "fresh writing" without consciously deciding to do so. These afternoon writing sessions usually lasted only an hour or two, but I always considered them a bonus. Because my writing days became so productive, I felt more and more virtuous while I lived at Lake St. Clair.

At the end of an afternoon work session, I rewarded myself with a walk around the lake. I made myself walk slowly and try to observe my surroundings as carefully as I could. The world itself seemed especially charged with energy; it became an intense presence in my life. I was primarily interested in birds—I'd bought a field guide and begun keeping a list of the birds I saw—but I also became a student of the landscape, the variety and quality of light in different weathers and at different times of day. I suspect that the attention I paid to the world of my 2.3 mile walks around Lake St. Clair was of benefit to me in my writing. The fiction I wrote during those months seems to me to hold more of the world's presence, to articulate more of a connection between my characters and the world around them.

As the days grew longer and more daylight became available after my dinner hour, I began taking after-dinner walks, too—at first very short ones, but it wasn't long before I was taking a whole loop around the lake just at sunset (arguably the best time of day for a walk). The deeper my involvement with my work became, the more avid was my appetite for the world; my experience in this regard runs counter to the conventional wisdom that art is an escape from "real life," or that art takes its practitioners away from the world.

In the evenings I listened to the radio. Sometimes I worked on my writing. Evening work sessions were rare and likely to come about only if I was trying to complete a finished draft of a story and what had to be done was merely typing clean copy. Mostly I read, because reading had become unusually exciting to me: I felt as I were reading on two levels, for the usual pleasure of poetry and narrative and also for my writerly education. In the works of other authors, I was able to observe technical achievement that I thought would be of eventual use in my own work.

I got sleepy early. It was rare that I didn't turn out my bedside light by ten or ten thirty. I went to sleep thinking about the writing I'd accomplished and about the work I meant to do the next morning.

When a writing life is in good order, as mine was then, everything is relevant to it; every detail of one's day has a connection to one's writing. I confess that I am presenting an idealized version of my months at Lake St. Clair. My mail, for instance, always a distraction, was less so because it didn't come directly to me, but I was not able to avoid giving it more attention than it merited. The telephone did ring now and then, and I had visitors, visitors I wanted and ones I didn't want. But what I had mostly was solitude, which instructed me: the more of it I had, the more I learned to make use of it.

I have been a resident of artists' colonies at Yaddo and the Virginia Center for the Creative Arts; on some occasions I have been able to work better at those places than at home, but in my best colony experience I've been only about fifty percent as productive as I was at Lake St. Clair. The obvious difference is that colonies have a social life that one must attend: one is guaranteed solitude during the day, but in the evenings one eats with the other colonists; one chats after dinner; one makes friends; and so on. This social life can be healthy influence in a writing life, especially if two writers begin exchanging manuscripts and criticism. Along with valuable friendship, a writer can also find inspiration and illumination from visual artists and composers. But finally a social life is a distraction. Instead of having the evening hours to compose oneself, to let one's mind wander back to the writing, one becomes involved with others. In the morning, when there should be minimum obstacles between self and work, one finds that one is reviewing last night's conversation.

Lake St. Clair was a temporary situation for me brought about by lucky circumstances. I have often wondered how different things would have been if I had had to think of it as my permanent circumstance. Would all that solitude have seemed so luxurious then, or would it have seemed a punishment, a burden, an entrapment? Would I have found my work so fulfilling if I had known that is had to take the place of my family? I know that a large measure of what made Lake St. Clair such an ideal working circumstance for me was its temporariness.

Back to the real world

When I left the lake, I had come to think of myself as a kind of aesthetic saint. I had lost weight. I was in excellent physical condition. I had stripped my life down to what was essential to me. I had accomplished a greater quantity and a higher quality of writing than I ever had before. I had established a meaningful connection between myself and the natural world. I felt this exhilarating rightness to my life. I felt certain that I would be able to transport the habits I had formed into my "regular life," which now (from my saintly viewpoint) seemed cluttered, distracting, piggish, physically and aesthetically unhealthy.

The disintegration took about a week. If I did my early morning calisthenics anywhere in the house, I made such a clatter that I woke my wife and daughter. My wife had to go to work and my daughter to daycare; their preparations necessarily disturbed my concentration on my work. Near my house there was nowhere to run or walk without encountering traffic and carbon monoxide. In the house, everywhere I looked, there were little chores that needed doing, dishes to be washed, toys to be picked up, stacks of magazines to straighten, bills to pay, a screen with a hole in it, a borrowed book that needed to be returned. The phone rang more often now that I was back in my own community. I played tennis, I met a friend for lunch, I attended a surprise birthday party. I snacked between meals. I watched TV. In short, I drifted away from my writing life. My Lake St. Clair habits were not transportable.

Before and after my tenure at Lake St. Clair, I was a sporadic writer—if I had something I was working on, I worked at it until I finished it; then I didn't write again until something else pressed me urgently enough to begin it and pursue it. For periods of as long as a year, I wrote nothing. I had a rationale worked out about being a sporadic writer: I wasn't a factory, and it was only because of a national assembly-line mentality that American writers felt obligated to churn out books. Who needed another piece of writing anyway? If I wasn't writing, it probably meant I had nothing worthwhile to say. And so on. But my Lake St. Clair experience demonstrated to me what it felt like to have a real writing life, to have something that held my attention over a period of time, to have ongoing, deeply fulfilling work. I have never been able to duplicate that experience, but because I had it that once, it gave me something to aspire to again. I've gotten better and better at constructing a writing life for myself in the midst of my "regular life." I don't have any remarkable secrets about it, but I do have what I think are a few useful concepts.

Clearing the way

To write well one must use one's "good hours" for one's writing. My good hours are the first three or four of my day. If I want to use them for my writing, that means I have to get up early and start writing before other demands are made on me. A few people I know have their good hours late at night, and that's when they should be writing. A poet I know warms up slowly; she finds her good hours to begin around mid- or late-morning.

Since I teach school for a living and since much of the work of my teaching involves reading and responding to student manuscripts, I find that I have to use my "next-best hours" (late morning or afternoons) for that work. But responding to student manuscripts is almost always in direct competition with my own writing for my good hours. I have to be clever and disciplined to manage a heavy teaching load with a productive writing schedule. On a day when I teach my first class at 9:25 and I have a dozen student stories to respond to, I'll need to get up at 4, be at the writing desk by 4:45, work on my own writing until 6, write my responses until 8:30, and get to my office by 9:15.

Along with using my good hours for my writing, I've learned more about how to use my less-good hours for clearing the way for efficient use of my writing time. I used to be convinced that I had to pay my bills before I could begin my writing. So I spent valuable morning time writing checks and putting them in envelopes. It is still the case that I need to have order in the room where I'm working. I need to have no evidence of distracting little chores that need to be done. I'm a house-husband, which means that I have cooking, laundry, cleaning, and child-care duties to attend to and like most writers I am very distractable; house-husbanding can devour my good writing hours if I let it. But nowadays my motto is that everything has to get done sometime. Taking a break from my writing, I'll wash the dishes because doing that little task is just distracting enough to give me a new "take" on whatever it is I'm working. Putting away laundry can often be a very useful fifteen-minute writing break. I can pay my bills while my printer is typing up a manuscript. What I understand better and better is how to clear the way to my good hours with my writing. Before I go to bed I try to have my little computer, with its battery charged, waiting for me, preferably with the document I'm working on ready to come up on the screen when I switch it on. I want my reading glasses right where I can find them, my coffee thermos clean, and the room straightened up. If I have bills to pay or letters that need to be answered, I want them neatly stashed where they won't catch my eye first thing when I sit down to write.

Robert Hass' poem "Measure" uses the phrase "the peace of the writing desk." These words have come to be an accurate description of the experience of writing for me. My writing time is when I set my life in order. I examine my life through the act of writing. Although I try to sell most of my writing, my first desire for it is that it be as truthful and beautiful as I can make it out of what I know and think and feel. Therefore writing is to me a kind of meditation. It isn't a purely spiritual activity, but it is one in which my spirit is nourished. Writing has become so essential to my daily life that I feel denied if I miss a day of "the peace of the writing desk."

When I tell people that I get up at 4:30 or 5 to do my writing, they often praise my discipline, but now that my writing life has been established, discipline has nothing to do with it. Getting up to do my writing requires no more discipline than sitting down to eat a meal or going to bed at night to get some sleep. It's natural and necessary.

Change

Flux has never been an easy principle for me to understand or to incorporate into my life. My make-up is conservative. My instinctive way of doing things is to try to get them just right and then to keep them that way. Some nasty lessons have taught me that I had better give flux its due. Thus it was silly of me to try to import my Lake St. Clair writing habits into the life I lived in my home with my family. Instead of becoming frustrated because I couldn't repeat my successful methods, a more intelligent course of action was to try to discover the different writing habits that would work in a different situation.

One must be ready to change with circumstance and one must understand that one's personal needs and instincts are constantly changing: Cheever needed different rooms of his house because at different times of his life, he was a different writer and was writing different books. My attic study, equipped with a computer and a printer, has given me many productive hours of writing, but it is located directly over the master bedroom of the house; increasingly it bothered me that I chanced disturbing my wife's sleep by trudging up the creaking stairway in the early morning hours. My hesitation to go upstairs became an obstacle of my writing. The solution has been a laptop computer that allows me to do my early morning writing downstairs in the living room. How long this laptop method will last I don't know. What I do know is that I have to stay alert to changes in both circumstance and personal inclination.

Self-knowledge

Learning to understand and monitor one's own writerly needs is the main project of a writer's education. Beginning writers almost always feel that they have to master a body of knowledge—they have to learn the secrets!—that somehow all successful writers have mastered. They think they need to take possession of something outside themselves. Writing teachers are often frustrated that they can't make students see that they're looking in the opposite direction of the place where the real secrets are located. The elements of a writer's making are within the individual, and they are different with each individual. Each writer makes his own habit.

What a student needs to find out is not how someone else works but how he or she is inclined to work. One must determine one's good hours, the writing tools and the writing environment that best suit one, the limitations that one can overcome and the best methods for dealing with the limitations one can't overcome.

One must also become aware of one's inclinations toward laziness, dishonesty, glibness, and other personal foibles. One must become skillful at outwitting those negative aspects of character. For instance, I know that I am inclined to send manuscripts out before they're really ready to be submitted any place—before they're finished. I haven't been able to correct this failure, but I've gotten so I can delay my sending out a manuscript by giving copies of it to certain friends of mine to read and respond to it before I make up a "final copy." The more friends who give me responses to a manuscript, the more drafts I'll run it through. I know I am going to have to keep chipping away at this negative quirk of mine for a long time before I can depend on myself to send out a "mature manuscript."

Like most writers, I'm a highly skilled procrastinator. I've had to develop the appropriate counter-skills. One of my more successful counter-procrastinating techniques is the bend-and-snap-back move: I'll tell myself yes, I really do need a nap right now, but the only way I can justify it is by contracting with myself to go back to the writing desk at exactly such-and-such a time.

These external maneuverings of self against self for the good of getting one's work done are not unlike similar moves one learns for improving the writing itself. For instance, I have come to understand that I am weak when it comes to portraying female characters as whole human beings. My natural, porcine inclination is toward second-rate versions of characters like Hemingway's Maria, Faulkner's Eula Verner Snopes, Nabokov's Lolita, and Terry Southern's Candy. My more responsible writing self must always be questioning and arguing with this lesser Huddle. The tension between these two impulses is a healthy one for my writing; in a few instances I've been able to write about female characters who have both sexual force and emotional-intellectual complexity. And I count myself lucky that I'm able to write across gender even as well as I have been able to so far.

Tension-management is an ability that must be cultivated by a writer both in and out of the work. Often one's natural inclinations are less than admirable, but rather than trying to elimiate such inclinations from one's personality, one must learn how to convert them into positive elements of one's writing: Thus one can convert one's inclination toward distraction and procrastination into habits that will clear the way toward using one's good hours for concentrated writing. Thus one can convert one's inclination toward fantasizing about wish-fulfilling female characters into the creation of appealingly whole human-beings. Such alchemy is still possible in a well-constructed writing life.

Once one understands that one's negative qualities can be put to use both inside and outside one's writing, one can begin to be kind to oneself. No longer neccessary are those lectures to the self, "You lazy such and such, you took a nap when you should have been writing; you can't write about women; you sent out that story too soon; you . . ." Instead of flailing away at yourself, you can become crafty and learn how to use your whole self in your writing.

The writing life

Hemingway had a rule that has been especially useful for my work. He thought you ought to stop writing for the day at a point where you knew what your were going to do next. I like that notion just as it stands—often at the end of my morning's writing session, I will make a few notes about what I think ought to come next. I also think a writer needs to stop work with a little bit of energy left. I feel good when I've written enough to be tired, but if I've written myself into a state of exhaustion, I don't feel so eager to get back to work the next day.

Hemingway's quitting-time axiom is one version of what seems to me a basic principle of the writing life: one must nourish the "ongoingness" of the work. Sometimes I feel that what is curcial is to finish this piece or that piece of writing, that the only thing that matters is to get this manuscript in the mail. But a real writing life is nothing so desperate as all that, is not something one does merely for a day or a month or a year. Stories, poems, essays, and books are the by-product of a writing life; they are to be cherished, but they separate themselves from their creators and they may be misused or harmed by editors, reviewers, or obtuse readers. For a writer, what's valuable is the ongoing work. It may take some getting used to, but after a while it becomes so natural as to be almost invisible. The writing habit is the real treasure, and it safely belongs only to the writer.

Write Prolifically in Your Spare Time

by William Manners

Writers—somehow—are especially conscious of time. When they're writing well, days are only minutes long. They may then get melodramatic and proclaim that they're racing Death to get their next piece of work done—even if it's nothing more than a filler on modern plastics.

A writer told me that he works best when he ignores time, by regarding it as a continuous stream—instead of the bits into which it is hacked by the clock and the calendar. He then doesn't feel its pressure—only its laving calm.

But this is not an indulgence for the individual who must work all day, and, if he is to write, must do it in his spare time. Spare time consists in such cases of time in the evening and/or night and on weekends. This is what is usually meant by spare time. But I say to you, don't overlook spare time on your job, or when you brush your teeth, or when you lie awake at night and can't sleep.

Redefining spare time

Your job, no matter what its nature, offers you spare time. Justify using it for your personal writing ends by assuring your conscience that one's employer deserves to be a patron of the arts. Some clever, shrewd, facile, ambitious editors that I have known have found enough free moments in the office to write, actually write, stories, articles, big hunks of novels. So if you're a barber, don't throw away slack afternoons by leafing lazily through the magazines that are around for the customers. Or if you're a musician in the pit of a loud musical, don't spend the quiet, non-musical interludes reading; put your instrument to one side and write. Or if you're a commuter and your train stops between stations, for some reason known only to trains, and sits and sits, as such trains so often do, write.

Because of all these on-the-job opportunities, if you're to be a prolific spare-time writer, spare time must be redefined. It is more than the conventional after-dinner and weekend hours; *it is any time that can be utilized.* This may sound terribly Spartan and arduous. But whether it does or not depends on how much you want to write, how much you really want to, how much writing means to you.

James Thurber was a full-time, professional writer—as you all know—but his use of spare time is significant for the spare-time writer.

"I never quite know when I'm not writing," Thurber once said. "Sometimes my wife comes up to me at a party and says, 'Dammit, Thurber, stop writing.' She usually catches me in the middle of a paragraph. Or my daughter will look up from the dinner table and ask, 'Is he sick?' 'No,' my wife says, 'he's writing something.' "

That you do what Thurber did is very important if you're going to be more than just a dilettante. If you're an elevator operator, for example, you can hardly set up a typewriter beside your up-and-down control. But you can do a lot of work in your head, especially when you're on the ground floor waiting for the car to fill up and for the starter to send you on your way. You can plot. You can observe the people who enter your elevator. A meticulous mustache

William Manners *is one of the founding editors of* Alfred Hitcock's Mystery Magazine. *Author of* Patience and Fortitude *and* T. R. and Will, *his diverse writing career has included articles, biographies and a popular cookbook. Manners is currently working on a novel.*

may enter jauntily. Notice clothing. Wonder if the girl with the empty expression really has something in her mind, and what it might possibly be. Listen to speech. See it as dialogue on a page. Note its rhythm; its structure.

No matter what your job, you can—to lesser or greater degree—do this kind of writing work. A cop on a stake-out, a dentist prying out a recalcitrant tooth, a strip tease promenading and removing, a politician smiling and shaking hands.

All this is very important spare-time work, for the spare-time writer. It readies him for the time when he sits down at the typewriter to write, for at that time, if he is to be prolific, he must write and do nothing else. That is not the time to wonder and figure and ponder, for if this time is used in this way nothing will be produced but discouragement and futility.

Getting started

But let us say that you've come home from a hard day at the office. Let us also assume that this is an evening that you've decided to work. Perhaps what made it a hard day at the office brought you around to that decision. Your work is routine, uncreative, unsatisfying. You therefore want to express yourself. And you also daydream; you've written a runaway best-seller; you're wealthy; you're a name worthy of being dropped.

Remember how tired you are, and remember your dream. You rush through dinner, because you only have a couple of hours before you'll have to brush your teeth and get to bed, so that you'll be bright and alert the next day for that job of yours that you hate.

You go into the bedroom where your typewriter squats stolidly under its cover. You take off the cover. It's as if you've seen that typewriter for the first time. Why, the thing's a solid lump of unfeeling metal. To spend two hours with it is suddenly abhorrent.

You start telling yourself interesting things. An artist, you remind yourself, doesn't create on order, doesn't hand ultimatums to his soul. How could you possibly have forgotten that? Besides you're tired. If you wrote, it would just be drivel. And this isn't just an excuse to get out of writing; it's just plain common sense. And after a hard day, didn't the writer deserve a little recreation? God, he didn't want his whole life to be work, work, work and nothing but work. He might drop dead next week—after all he was in the fatal forties—and look at all that he would have missed. For what? He might as well go out and watch TV. That's right, he remembers, there's a very good show on. It'd be a shame to miss it; he might get a lot of ideas from it. It was important to keep up with the good things that were being done.

Then as he marches out to the TV set which his wife is watching without any feelings of guilt—looking as if Euphoria is her middle name—he gets good and sore. Why did he have to give all those excuses to himself, just to go out and watch a simple, little TV show? He hadn't committed a crime by not sitting down there and writing. He didn't have to write. He had to go to work in the morning, but damned if he had to write when he was dead tired and besides . . .

At this point, his wife, whom he really loves, asks, without lifting her eyes from the TV set, "How'd the writing go, dear? Are you all done?"

So what else can he say, but, "Yeah, yeah, I'm all done." And by done, he means through, finished, washed-up.

To be prolific in your spare time, you must go about the whole matter in a somewhat different way.

In order to be fair, let's take the same individual; tired, disgusted with his job, determined to create. What is important is that there is a break—especially a psychological one—between his job and his session at the typewriter.

A long, hot shower goes a long way to remove the grime of the job. Make a ritual of it, a ritual of purification. Many like to include a sacramental cocktail as part of the deal. One—or maybe two—drinks are all that the liturgy allows. Remember that the bulk of the service is to be a sober wrestling with your typewriter.

This liquid break—of shower and cocktail—should give you the feeling that you're starting a new day joyously, instead of ending one miserably. And if you still have an inclination to do something other than write, like watch TV, recall that once you get started, writing is much more enjoyable than a somnolent, guilty viewing of something that is television-terrible.

Hemingway had a method of getting started at the typewriter that may be of value to you. This applies to a piece of work already begun. Whenever you finish for the day or night, stop while you're going along at a fast clip and with enthusiasm, stop in the middle of a paragraph, even before the completion of a particular sentence. It is much easier to take up from such a point, than from a solid block of writing complete in every respect.

One step at a time

So you get started. It's important now not to feel the pressure of time. Writing at top speed is fine, but you mustn't feel pursued. You mustn't start paying attention to those thoughts, flowing along under your writing thoughts, that you haven't much time, and that what you get done in the little time that you have will be negligible. Once the clock starts chasing you, all sorts of glands let go to protect you as an organism. But the final result is a harried, unhappy individual. And if you're going to be prolific as a spare-time writer, you have to pace yourself so that you're happy while working, so that you, as a consequence, can work night, after night, after night—and on week ends, too. And do it for years, even for decades.

There are sly ways of getting around this need for a feeling of accomplishment, even though the period of your work is no more than an hour or two in duration. There are writers who specialize in fairly short short stories, ones that they can do at a sitting. But if you're working on, let us say, a novel—even a very long novel—break it up for the sake of your psyche into segments or scenes that you can write in an evening. Moving your hero, for example, from the basement where he is growing mushrooms to the kitchen where he quaffs a can of beer is a good evening's work and should make you quite pleased with yourself.

When engaged on a long book, refrain from thinking, "My God, I've hardly done anything. And I've got so much more to do. The trouble is, I don't have enough time. An hour here, and an hour there, it's just no good. This spare-time writing is for the birds . . ."

Do one little chore at a time. And, if you must, tell yourself that big oaks from little acorns grow. And more important is this fact: if you're working and writing in your spare time, you don't have the economic pressure of the full-time writer. What you write doesn't have to sell. And what's more, you may write whatever you please and don't have to write the sort of thing that may actually repel you. So just remember, when you start griping to yourself and to others, that spare-time writing has its advantages, too.

Perhaps one reason that your spare time is inadequate is that you're fastidious. Just as the full-time writer often demands that the conditions of his environment be absolutely perfect, the spare-time writer—in his spare time, of course—carries on in an equally temperamental fashion.

Abraham Lincoln walking miles to school and doing his homework by firelight is still thrown up to students who have their own car and good reading lamps, but get bad grades just the same. So the spare-time writer, complaining bitterly about the conditions under which he must write, should take a look at what other writers have accomplished in far from ideal settings.

Jane Austen, history tells us, wrote in the midst of family conversations. William Faulkner wrote *Sanctuary*, a terrific popular success, in the boiler room of a power plant in which he was employed. He worked on the book between twelve midnight and four in the morning. He wrote it on a table improvised out of a turned-over wheelbarrow, while a dynamo near by made a steady, humming noise. Trollope, a notably prolific writer, worked in a post office, and so he did his writing before he went to work, and on his way to work, in trains and on horseback. His mother was no slouch either. Trollope in his autobiography had this to say of her writing prowess: "She was at her writing table at four in the morning, and had finished her work before the world had begun to be aroused . . . She continued writing up to 1856, when she was seventy-six years old, and had at that time produced one hundred and fourteen volumes, of which the first was not written till she was past fifty . . . Her career offers encouragement to those who have not begun early in life, but are still anxious to do something before they depart hence."

And let us not overlook Abraham Lincoln, in this connection; he might very well be thrown up to complaining writers—as he is to non-exemplary students. He wrote what he called his "little speech" under trying circumstances. His son Tad was gravely ill; the Civil War was being fought. He wrote a hurried first draft, using both pencil and ink, using both—no doubt—because pencil points always seem to break when you're in a rush, and pens, maniacally, run out of ink. But that "little speech" of Lincoln's, its 268 words, is known, with reverence and respect, as The Gettysburg Address.

By now the point must be fairly clear, and emphasized, that the spare-time writer—especially the spare-time writer—must not be overly fussy. He must not pamper himself. Granted, his time is limited. Why, then, limit it further by making special demands of it?

Writing at will

A writer told me how he made use of two hours traveling time every day on the New York, New Haven and Hartford Railroad.

"It was like a race," he said. "That on your mark, get set, go, business. When I got on the train in the morning, I knew in a general way what writing ground I was going to cover. And before the other passengers could unfold their newspapers, I was writing away. I didn't let up either, until we pulled into Grand Central . . ."

There was always the danger that he would sit down beside someone who talked, or who wanted to talk. He fought this sort of individual with reticence. And the dedicated, almost furious, way he went at his writing hinted to the talkative one beside him that this was something he must do.

The movement of the train and its noises, he found soothing rather than disturbing. The pattern of swaying and jerks and sounds, repeated in a kind of endless monotony, induced a dreamlike state that helped him creatively. He not only produced a lot of copy, but what he did proved to be good and required very little revision.

Early, very early morning writing—in the case of another writer—produced a similar dream-like state comparable to that condition induced by the train. The darkness surrounding his spotlighted typewriter, the utter quiet and sense of aloneness and his not being completely awake as yet contributed to the effect.

"Somehow," he said, "I had fewer inhibitions—working early in the morning. Maybe it takes being fully awake to be aware of all there is to be afraid of—imagined, and real."

When you work doesn't matter. Work, when you work most efficiently and with the greatest amount of pleasure. The important thing is that you write. And if you enjoy writing, you'll write more.

The spare-time writer must cultivate the knack of writing on order, his own order. Writing must appear on the page like a response to a stimulus.

Robert Penn Warren has this facility. He can, therefore, make full use of any quantity of free time.

As a friend of his said, with some amazement, "He simply goes to the typewriter, picks up where he left off, and pounds ahead."

Even in the matter of plotting, putting words down on paper is better, far better, than merely sitting and thinking. Write your thoughts. Call yourself names, in writing, if what you have thought is absurd. Tell yourself, in writing, what you still need to find to complete your story.

Write something like this, for example, "I need a good juicy black moment. I need something to really jar the reader, make him feel that the hero will never get out of the jam he's in. Perhaps when the hero comes to meet the girl, she doesn't show up. He thinks that perhaps he misunderstood and he is supposed to meet her at his place. So when he goes there . . . Let's see, considering the girl's character, what might he find? Maybe he witnesses something that is not in her character at all. What could it be that he sees? Perhaps . . ."

Writing away in this manner, more ideas will come to you in five minutes than you can think of in an hour. This is a method that is especially valuable to you as a spare-time writer, for you're putting words down on paper and at no time do you feel that you've run hopelessly into the dead end of a plot.

Keep a steady flow

To get started writing, use any trick or approach that will work for you. Sometimes, just sitting down with paper and pencil may seem less formidable than working at the typewriter. Then, by all means, use paper and pencil. And, when it suits your mood, switch back to the typewriter.

If yellow paper, which means a first draft, works better for you than white paper, which stands for finished copy, stick to yellow paper.

Whatever works for you—that is, a steady flow of copy coming out of your typewriter—is the right approach. Search it out, by trial and error. Use it. Don't apologize for it because it is different—even vastly different—from the working methods of others.

You may find that you need the discipline of a course in writing in order to get started and to gain the momentum that will keep you going on your own. From a writing-prolifically standpoint, study at home is better than a weekly trek to a classroom. How fast you go is then completely up to you. However, a correspondence course may simply not be for you. To be stimulated, your temperament may require direct, personal contact with a teacher—and the presence of other students who share your interests and your objectives. Many universities have journalism departments, offering adult courses, evening classes, summer programs. By making inquiries, you should find just what you want.

And once you get started writing, you—as a spare-time writer—must be especially responsive to the words that come to you out of nowhere, or the subconscious, as it has been glibly labeled. Put them down quickly, with only a slight, evaluative hesitancy. You will find that they are usually apt and can't be improved upon.

The times that you are writing especially well and fluently, you will invariably feel a certain excitement about what is going down on the paper before you, and it will carry you away from the bare outline or summary or idea from which you are working. You may find yourself expanding something in an entirely new and different direction—going on because of this feeling that you have that what you are doing is good.

The catalyst for this sort of performance is a pressure of sorts. The desire to spill your guts, or entertain, or instruct blended with the desire to get on with it. This pressure must not be burdensome; it must merely be a gentle goad.

The feeling that you will have, when excitement and pressure are in just the right proportions, will be of sailing along exhilaratedly.

Avoid distractions

Though there are relatively few things that will get you under way, the possible interruptions are without number. Then, too, there are quite a few things that will "just come up" to keep you from even getting started.

I've already mentioned the talkative man on your seat on the train. He takes many forms, none of them speechless.

Then there are the staple rationalizations, typified by, "So what if I don't work this time?" When you use this one, you are being humble. You imply, pleasurably, that keeping the spigot of your prose turned off for a time isn't going to make or break the world. There's no arguing that, either.

Another approach is to cover your not working with, "Oh, I'm just lazy that's all," and smile when you say it, implying that though you may be lazy, you are a good guy, who doesn't take himself too seriously and who has a terrific sense of humor.

Then there's that analogy of dubious validity. It skips along like this: A tennis player doesn't play tennis for awhile. You'd think that this layoff would make him stale, wouldn't you? But it doesn't. When he resumes play, he's better than when he stopped. The answer, of course, is that he's never really stopped, not in a complete sense. While he lay in the hammock, his right arm hanging limply over the gunwale, his subconscious worked furiously on his faulty backstroke. The conclusion to be drawn from all this is that it might be a nice, relaxing idea to get away from the typewriter for awhile.

And if you really want to keep from writing in your spare time, don't worry; you'll get all kinds of help. In this connection, you'll find your spouse to be just wonderful, finding things for you to do around the house that after a hard day's work you could never have thought of all by yourself.

Then there's social life, which, of course, also involves your spouse—and your friends. You can't be a stick-in-the-mud, or a hermit, or anti-social, or a world all to yourself. You have to spend quite a bit of time at the typewriter, but you also definitely must get out and have a good time with people, real, live, nonfiction people.

Social life is versatile; it can interfere with your writing in all sorts of ways and it can also help it. The spare-time writer must gauge how much of it he wants, how much his time permits, how much is actually beneficial. Such calculation may seem cold, but calculation usually is—especially, if you want to get the right answer.

Your other job

Another factor to be considered in the matter of writing prolifically in your spare time is the nature of your 9-to-5 job.

Many spare-time writers feel that if they could trade their particular job for an editorial job, they would be all set, In the main, this is a misconception.

First, I would like to point out the advantages of having an editorial job as your full-time job, while writing in your spare time. For one thing, you acquire an understanding of the whole editorial process—and this is invaluable. You see why manuscripts are accepted; why they're rejected; how they're edited. And by participating in the entire routine—issue after issue, or book after book—it becomes a part of you.

An editorial job may also give you the disdain of. confidence. A writer told me that she hadn't thought of being a writer until she had been an editor for awhile.

"I worked on manuscripts written by name writers," she said, "And some of the stuff needed heavy editing. Well, I got the feeling that I could do as well as these big-name boys did. And the thought of making their kind of money, let me tell you, was awfully appealing."

Still, going from your editorial desk to your spare-time writing desk has at least one pretty serious drawback. The work in both cases is too similar. You sit. You juggle words. But should your full time job consist of plumbing or delivering letters or driving a cab, you might more readily look forward to a stint at the typewriter. So, it can safely be said, that the greater the difference between your full-time and your spare-time job, the easier it is to switch from the one to the other.

The time has come to point out that some publishers forbid their editors to write in their spare time. Their editors may do anything else in their spare time, but they must not write. Behind this ordinance is the belief that if an editor gets too involved in writing, his heart won't be completely in his editing.

But editing, and allied jobs, tend to give an individual a special incentive and drive to write in his spare time. After awhile, editing may be viewed as menial. And working on someone else's writing, instead of one's own, may become irksome. So an editor may labor in his spare time, with the idea in the back of his mind that eventually he will give up editing altogether.

A veteran newspaper reporter told me, "It's wonderful being a newspaperman, for a short time. But if you stick with it too long, it'll ruin you as a writer. And I've seen it happen."

So, many newspaper reporters are driven to a more creative writing, which they must do in their spare time. And this is true of advertising copywriters and those who write for the movies.

Their choice is usually fiction. But nonfiction shouldn't be overlooked. Though it does present special problems; so nonfiction may not be for you. Whether it is or not, depends—in large measure—upon the amount of pleasure writing nonfiction can give you. The hedonistic yardstick must be applied to all writing—especially to spare-time writing—for if you don't derive fun from it, you're not going to continue at it for very long.

Different writing, different demands

To enjoy doing nonfiction, you must enjoy research. This is the case because research is more than half the work. Actually, as much as seventy-five per cent of your time may be taken up with research. Aside from whether you enjoy it or not, research may be difficult to fit into a spare-time schedule if a considerable amount of interviewing is involved. To cite an extreme example, the definitive biography of Sinclair Lewis by Mark Schorer required that well over a thousand persons be interviewed.

The personal-experience piece, obviously, doesn't require research. It's therefore ideal for a spare-time arrangement. But since such a piece has to be based on an uncommon experience like building a submarine in your back yard or reducing on five square meals a day, the number of such pieces that you can do is of necessity limited.

For some writers doing both fiction and nonfiction is the answer. The writer then does whichever suits his purpose best at a particular time.

No matter what you write in your spare time, if you write prolifically and sell a respectable percentage of your copy, it is inevitable that you will begin to toy with the idea of quitting your job in order to write full time.

But you should interrupt this pleasant dream, in which you are your own boss, writing when you want to and in whatever part of the world suits your fancy, to ask yourself a fairly important question.

"Can I," you should ask, "make enough money writing in my spare time to pay the rent and buy a little food once in awhile?"

You may reason, with what appears to be logic, that if you can make a certain amount of money writing ten hours a week, you should be able to turn out four times that much copy in a forty-hour week and make four times as much money. Two more questions that you certainly won't like to ask of yourself, should be asked: 1. Can I write four times as much as I'm writing in my spare time? 2. And if I am able to write four times as much, would I automatically make four times as much money?

I know one writer who turned with great elation and enthusiasm from spare-time to full-time writing. He'd figured every angle. He was sure he had it licked. Then, to his horror, he discovered that he had written more in his spare time than he did when he devoted all of his time to writing. He admitted that he missed the security of a weekly pay check. And because of this lack in his life, he found it impossible to write easily and quickly, expressing himself naturally. One thought always loomed like a dark, threatening cloud in the fore part of his head, "Will it sell?"

His first rejection, as a full-time writer, hurled him into a state of panic. What hurt him was not that his story had been rejected, but that a full week's work had been. And what if further submissions didn't sell the thing? That would mean that he had worked an entire week for nothing.

This was the spare-time writer who thought he had figured every angle—in the psychology and economics areas, too. Unfortunately, he had to give up his dream in a hurry and go back to spare-time writing.

The principal mistake this writer had made when switching from spare-time to full-time writing was in doing speculative writing. If you turn full-time, freelance writer, in order to survive you must reduce the speculative element of what you do to a minimum. Any hours or days that you work without a contract or an assignment is time for which you may never receive remuneration. So if you're doing an article, send a query and get a go-ahead before doing the article. The query itself, you will find, is a considerable investment of time.

Some magazines will say that they would like to see the piece, as described in your query, but can't promise an acceptance or payment. Others offer conditional go-aheads: the payment of a few hundred dollars, even if they don't buy the piece. This is the kind of jungle growth through which you must find your way, circling daintily around the quicksand and sprinting when a fairly smooth piece of terrain shows up.

Getting paid

The question of how individual writers write is often raised. There are those who want desperately to believe that good writers should be undernourished. They admire Stephen Crane for having died at the age of twenty-eight, felled by tuberculosis which had been enhanced by money worries. And they insist that next to a writer's not being recognized in his lifetime, poverty just can't be beat for lending a writer a romantic air.

I'm therefore sorry to say that all writers, so it seems, write faster and better if they know they're going to be paid for their output. It's just one of those quirks of human nature that one can't do much about. Of course, if you're writing in your spare time, you can afford to write for the pure love of it, but this obviously can not be done if your writing must provide you with a livelihood. So payments for articles should be guaranteed. Contracts and initial payments should be obtained, in the case of books, for a few chapters and an outline. Forget the short story—for they have been stamped speculative—unless an editor should order one from you; but this sort of thing is rare.

And you might look into the matter of being subsidized by a publisher. This sort of arrangement didn't agree with Sherwood Anderson, but it has helped others get work done.

During the depression, when John O'Hara had no money, but a lot of debts, he also had 25,000 words of *Appointment in Samarra*. He used those 25,000 words to induce a publisher to pay him fifty dollars a week for three months. And during that three-month period, he finished the novel.

Nelson Algren had an even better arrangement. He asked a publisher for fifty dollars a week for a year so that he write a novel for them. Because this publisher wanted Algren to write for them, he graciously consented to pay Algren sixty dollars a week for two years. The novel that Algren wrote for the considerate publisher was *The Man With the Golden Arm*.

There is one and only one moral to be deduced from all this: Don't quit your job too soon, but be happy writing prolifically in your spare time.

Waiting for the Story to Start

by Valerie Martin

Unlike babies, not all stories come from the same place, and not all people who create stories go about it in the same way. Every writer who has succeeded in bringing a story to life has also managed to kill a few, usually by force. Most of us have lost a few along the way too—stories that started as ideas, stories that came from arguments or from a desire to set the record straight.

Taking time

Students who want to write stories are often puzzled about how to begin. How do writers get started on a story? they ask. And, once started, how do writers keep their stories alive? Do storytellers have extraordinary lives? Do they write only what they know? It's not difficult to find examples of authors who have addressed these questions. They give their answers in journals, in letters and in essays written to turn a buck on the modern reader's peculiar fascination with writers as people. There are some surprising similarities in the responses they give.

Virginia Woolf, in her diary, described her early work on a book entitled *The Moths*. (Woolf never wrote a book with this title. The work eventually became *The Waves*.) She wrote:

> Now about this book, *The Moths*. How am I to begin it? And what is it to be? I feel no great impulse; no fever; only a great pressure of difficulty.
> . . . Every morning I write a little sketch, to amuse myself. I am not saying, I might say, that these sketches have any relevance. I am not trying to tell a story. Yet perhaps it might be done in that way. A mind thinking. They might be islands of light—islands in the stream that I am trying to convey; life itself going on. The current of the moths flying strongly this way. A lamp and a flower pot in the centre. The flower can always be changing.

Joyce Carol Oates spoke of a similar percolating condition in an interview she gave shortly after completing *Wonderland*: "At times my head seems crowded, there is a kind of pressure inside it, almost a frightening physical sense of confusion, fullness, dizziness. Strange people appear in my thoughts and define themselves slowly to me."

The pressure to begin

In his essay "The Art of Fiction," Henry James described not his own method of beginning but that of "an English novelist, a woman of genius":

> She was much commended for the impression she had managed to give in one of her tales, of the nature and way of life of the French Protestant youth. She had been asked where she learned so much about this recondite being, she had been congratulated on

Valerie Martin *is the author of the novel,* A Recent Martyr. *Her recently published collection of short stories is titled* The Consolation of Nature.

her peculiar opportunities. These opportunities consisted in her having once, in Paris, as she ascended a staircase, passed an open door where, in the household of a pasteur, some of the young Protestants were seated at table round a finished meal. The glimpse made a picture, it lasted only a moment, but that moment was experience.

Thus James lays to rest the old chestnut "write what you know." The necessary experience can be had in one moment on the right staircase. "Of course all writing is based on personal experience," Margaret Atwood observed in an essay on this subject. "But personal experience is experience—wherever it comes from—that you identify with, *imagine* if you like, so that it becomes personal to you."

The writer, James concluded, must always be "one on whom nothing is lost." Flannery O'Connor put it a slightly different way: "There's a certain grain of stupidity that the writer of fiction can hardly do without, and this is the quality of having to stare, of not getting the point at once." To begin, then, young writers must feel the pressure to begin. They must open their eyes to the world and "experience" what's out there.

What next?

William Faulkner, in an interview he gave following his last public reading, was asked about the beginning of *The Sound and the Fury*. "That began as the story of a funeral," he responded. "The first thing I thought of was the picture of the muddy seat of that little girl's drawers climbing the pear tree to look in the parlor window to see what in the world the grown people were doing that the children couldn't see."

Here are John Fowles' published "Notes" on the beginning of *The French Lieutenant's Woman*; in them he describes not only how he got started but how the story stayed alive for him, almost insisting on being written:

It started four or five months ago as a visual image. A woman stands at the end of a deserted quay and looks out to sea. That was all. This image rose in my mind one morning when I was still in bed half asleep. It responded to no actual incident in my life (or in art) that I can recall, though I have for many years collected obscure books and forgotten prints, all sorts of flotsam and jetsam from the last two or three centuries, relics of past lives—and I suppose this leaves me with a sort of dense hinterland from which such images percolate down to the coast of consciousness.

These mythopoeic 'stills' (they seem almost always static) float into my mind very often. I ignore them, since that is the best way of finding whether they really are the door into a new world.

So I ignored this image; but it recurred. Imperceptibly it stopped coming to me. I began deliberately to recall it and to try to analyze and hypothesize why it held some sort of imminent power. It was obviously mysterious. It was vaguely romantic. It also seemed, perhaps because of the latter quality, not to belong to today. The woman obstinately refused to stare out of the window of an airport lounge; it had to be this ancient quay—as I happen to live near one, so near that I can see it from the bottom of my garden, it soon became a specific ancient quay. The woman had no face, no particular degree of sexuality. But she was Victorian; and since I always saw her in the same static long shot, with her back turned, she represented a reproach on the Victorian age. An outcast. I didn't know her crime, but I wished to protect her. That is, I began to fall in love with her. Or with her stance. I didn't know which.

All of these descriptions have one thing in common: they begin with an image, coming from within or without, strangely persistent in the writer's imagination. This is important. It has to do with the basic necessity of all stories, that quality that makes literature, in my view, the most sublime of the arts: the ability of the story to engage the senses of the reader. This is more than being concrete, though concreteness is essential to create a world. It's the engagement—sudden, unexpected and complete—of our senses that moves us, in reality as well as in fiction. As writers begin, it is this sense of an intrusion of reality that sends them off into fiction in the form of an image that, as Mr. Fowles puts it, is "the door into a new world." "Reality," Gustave Flaubert wrote to his sentimental mistress, Louise Colet, "if we are to reproduce it well, must enter us until we almost scream."

The desire at the start is not to say anything, not to make meanings, but to create for the unwary reader a sudden experience of reality. No writer has put this more succinctly than Joseph Conrad, who described his purpose as always "to render the highest possible justice to the visible universe." This is a definition of purpose I think few writers would dispute. It's a laudable goal, rendering justice, and should be distinguished from passing judgment, which is not the fiction writer's province.

The notion of surprise

A second requirement of the developing story is a sense of free play. Most of us can claim to have been visited by an image like John Fowles' woman on the quay, but few of us have any idea how to make her turn her face to us so we can make out more about her. It won't work to try to force her; if you want to know someone, in life or in art, you always have to wait. In his "Notes," Mr. Fowles makes this observation about his steadfast lady, who has by this time, through his patience, revealed to him her face, her name, her situation, but not her soul:

"I was stuck this morning to find a good answer from Sarah at the climax of a scene. Characters sometimes reject all the possibilities one offers. They say, in effect: I would never say or do a thing like that. But they don't say what they would say; and one has to proceed negatively, by a very tedious coaxing kind of trial and error. After an hour over this one wretched sentence, I realized that she had in fact been telling me what to do; silence from her was better than any line she might have said."

Joyce Carol Oates has described this same obstinacy of the developing character. "My 'characters' really dictate themselves to me," she reports. "I can not force them into situations they haven't themselves willed." Perhaps Faulkner explained the writer's relationship with his character most directly in his answer to a naïve question about whether, when his characters got into some sort of trouble, he didn't feel tempted to help them out. "I don't have time," he replied. "By that time I'm running along behind them with a pencil trying to put down what they say and do."

This element of surprise is the most difficult for critics and students to understand. Their notion is that writers have set out to create something "meaningful," and that to do so they must lace the work with clues to its meaning, usually symbols that have to do with colors or nature, the location of a river or a train track. Many students want to believe that writing is a kind of craft, a superior form of cooking or tapestry weaving, in which the writer is in total control from start to finish. No amount of denial is sufficient to obviate this notion. The teacher's impassioned cry, "No surprise for the writer, no surprise for the reader," falls on deaf ears.

Margaret Atwood goes so far as to call this element of surprise the pivot upon which the question of "art" turns. "Nevertheless," she declares, "art happens. It happens when you have the craft and the vocation and are waiting for something else, something extra, or maybe not waiting; in any case it happens. It's the extra rabbit coming out of the hat, the one you didn't put there."

I think the resistance to this notion of surprise is caused by the fact that good stories just don't seem to be accidental. They look meaningful; they contain symbolic patterns; you can take them apart and find pieces that fit right back together again. They are organic, like flowers; they have an internal and external structure. In fact, like the hands that deal them out, they show their cards now and then; they appear to have a subconscious as well as a conscious level.

This analogy to our thinking may explain why stories are so important to us and why they appear meaningful. Stories think, and they do it the same way we do. They talk straight sometimes, right to the heart, but they have always a deep, symbolic understanding of reality that can dictate what happens on the conscious level. They speak to us, as dreams speak to us, in a language that is at once highly symbolic and childishly literal. They mirror our consciousness exactly because they are composed through a process both conscious and subconscious.

The mirror the contemporary story often holds up to the reader reflects a world that is so vapid, so devoid of hope or humanity that the writer may be reduced to presenting it as if it were a stack of obscene snapshots; there's just no point in trying to say much about such pictures. This "reality" looks like a nightmare from which no amount of screaming can wake us. Yet we continue to need, read and pay people to write stories. In a world where the ultimate power to destroy human life lies in the hands of people we can neither admire nor trust, and with the certain knowledge that this extraordinary power is held by people we may even despise, one must assume that the average person is making up stories all the time. Otherwise we would simply go mad from anxiety.

Teaching people to write stories requires, first of all, that for a limited period of time they will be forced to open their eyes and ears, to take off the blinders and let the images pour in—a necessary first step toward taking life seriously and even, I suspect, a good way to start taking responsibility for themselves and for the world they can finally see.

66 *There is only one trait that marks the writer. He is always watching. It's a kind of trick of mind and he is born with it.* **99**

—*Morley Callaghan*

Collaborwriting

by Hal Blythe and Charlie Sweet

Two heads are better than one might be a cliché, but in our case the old saw still cuts it. As partners in crime—well actually, writing about crime—we have found that what we call collaborwriting pays (though not enough).

Since the Longfellowian April of '75, we have turned out as a team everything from a critical piece on the motivations of Browning's Ferrara to a monthly column in *Byline* to the lead novella in *Mike Shayne Mystery Magazine*. From almost ten years we have collaborated on over 250 published works, and all of them are products of a single methodology on whose cornerstone is inscribed WRITING DEMANDS DISCIPLINE.

Under the golden arches

Perhaps the best way to illustrate why Hal and Charlie (a/k/a Hal Charles, Brett Halliday, Charlene Herrald) can write is to take you through an ordinary writing day. Since our primary profession is teaching and we both have families, we have a limited amount of time. Fortunately, writing is a full-time occupation we have learned to practice part-time.

Our teaching schedules, we make certain, are set up so as to allow us a compatible block of time during the day. Our synergy level peaking early, we arrange to be free from classes every day between 10:30 and 1:00. Perhaps this very brevity forces us to use our time efficiently. We write only on weekdays, but in our ten years of collaboration neither of us has ever missed a day because of illness or other commitments. We write forty-eight weeks a year, allowing two weeks at the end of each semester to recharge our individual batteries. This discipline has caused us at various times to write in homes, hospitals and airports.

Normally, though, we write at one specific place. When we were just getting started, we received a very useful piece of advice from a Hollywood writer who was visiting campus. Jack Sowards, who wrote *Star Trek II* among other things, told us that instead of setting aside a room at his house, he got up every morning and drove to a rented office in downtown L.A. Separated from the usual associations and demands of home life, he found the typewriter and books put him in the right frame of mind for writing—the separate office reinforced his professional commitment. For us, getting away from the constant interruptions at our office by colleagues, students and book salesmen is a similar necessity. Unfortunately, we can't afford to rent a downtown office. Our compromise? For a mere 70 cents a day we can get two cups of coffee and a booth at the local McDonald's. After all, Scott and Ernie labored in the smoke-filled haze of Paris bistros, so why not work under the glow of the Golden Arches? Furthermore, Papa couldn't get a Big Mac. After six years of sitting in the same booth five days a week amidst cheerful muzak and Happy Meals, in fact, we were honored. While he couldn't present us with the Pulitzer Prize, the owner dedicated our booth by placing over it a plaque and our portrait ("Hey, Sundance, who are those guys?").

A structured routine

Each writing session is structured. While we absorb that first jolt of caffeine, we talk over anything interesting we've run across in the media or personal experience. "Where do you

---

Hal Blythe *and* ***Charlie Sweet*** *have collaborated on a third novel featuring their creation, private investigator Aaron Holliday. They write a monthly column for* Byline *and are involved in the writing, direction and production of murder and mystery "weekends" for Murder, Ink of Lexington, Kentucky.*

guys get all your ideas?'' we're always being asked at writers' conferences. Essentially we're both sponges absorbing information, events and personalities around us. It's in this initial and informal brainstorming conversation that we hear ourselves and each other talking. Somehow this process gives us a focus on ideas that might otherwise escape our attention; thus, this interchange becomes a primary advantage of team-writing. Then, too, we subscribe to what we call the three burner theory. Besides the primary piece we're bringing to a boil on any given day, we like to have a second starting to bubble, and a third we've just put on the stove. Usually we jot down what we discuss and try to rough out vaguely what we might do with it.

Stage two is the read-through of what we wrote the previous session. Hal's reading the material aloud helps us correct any problems in form or content. Misspellings, overused sentence patterns, unnatural-sounding dialogue—all are exorcised at this point in our daily ritual. Further, this reading shifts us into the flow of the piece. It is here that we leave the booth in a Kentucky McDonald's and enter the mean streets of Miami or the wine cellar of Montresor.

Stage three is the actual writing. Charlie plays scribe because Hal writes as though he has a medical degree. Here as in everything else the collaboration is total. Our idols Manny Lee and Fred Dannay (Ellery Queen) divided up the chores so that one wrote the plot outline, the other filled in the story, and on Fridays they met to revise. We, on the other hand, write every word facing each other across the paper-filled Formica.

During this stage we usually work from a rudimentary outline constructed in an earlier session. It's a free exchange of ideas. Hal might say, "What if . . . ?" and Charlie will pick up the cue and supply some details. If we reach the point in the wood at which the roads diverge and Hal wants to travel one while Charlie the other, we talk out the situation until we both take the same path. The more we write together, the less we encounter divergencies and the more we seem to be able to finish each other's sentences. We usually work out scenes by dramatizing the parts. A scene really comes alive when Hal playing Mike Shayne interrogates Charlie the Gat. Once, in fact, we got so wrapped up in the role-playing that a McDonald's employee who overheard but didn't know us, asked almost hopefully, "Are you guys . . . detectives?" Three cheers for credibility! We try to end each writing session at an exciting juncture, making the starting point of the next day's writing easier.

Stage four is the only time we work alone. Every night Hal does any necessary research for the next day and handles our correspondence. Meanwhile, Charlie plays with our newest investment, transferring the day's material onto a floppy disk and running off a copy for the next day's proofreading. Changing over from the old Smith-Corona to the Apple IIe in the last year has improved both the quality and the quantity of our writing. We're more open to revision since the magic of word processing makes the chore easier than in the old days, when even a minor change meant a totally retyped manuscrtipt. Our word count—and yes, we do consider that part of the discipline—has more than doubled. When Charlie types, he also provides an extra reading.

The next day we repeat the cycle. When the project is ready to be taken off the burner and presented for consumption, we do a final read-through, checking for any errors in logic or mechanics. The finished product, then, has usually been through at least five readings in part or in whole.

Charlie's right brain, Hal's left

Establishing a routine and following it religiously has the same value we believe for the writer as it does for the athlete. The whole process, like a Boston Celtic guard dribbling behind his back, has become second nature for us, something we rarely consider. It's only when we get the inevitable writers'-conference question, "Why do you guys write together?" that we stop to analyze. Actually, there's more than one reason we continue our collaboration.

How many writers have complained that writing is a lonely, agonizing time? For us, it's not. It's a period when we can socialize, when we can exchange and fictionalize our views on everything from departmental gossip to nuclear terrorism. One of us is a big-city, Southern

Baptist good-ole-boy, while the other is a small-town Connecticut Yankee. Part of the fun of our cross-pollination is reconciling our two varied viewpoints on many issues.

All writers need reinforcement and support. Consider Gustave Flaubert, who wrote his first work in a vacuum. When he showed what he thought was the finished product to a circle of friends, he was devastated by their criticism. Our support is constant, and so too is our criticism. If Charlie suggests what he considers an innocent line of dialogue, Hal, seeing it in a different light, might point out its lack of logic. We've long since passed the point of individual egotism and thin-skinnedness. Even now, rereading this paragraph, we can't remember if Hal said this or Charlie said that; *we* said it all. Some of our colleagues have commented, in fact, that our greatest fictional creation is Hal Charles.

Maybe our collaborwriting isn't so much two heads but, as psychological studies are showing, an instance of being able to integrate Charlie's right brain and Hal's left brain. We're not saying that we're a pair of half-wits, but that we have complementary personalities. Let us illustrate with the genesis of a Mike Shayne story published in the August 1984 issue of *Mike Shayne Mystery Magazine.*

The bulk of our fiction originates from an isolated idea Charlie has—in this case he had three. In our brainstorming portion he threw out a trio of plot seeds that intrigued him:

1. What if Santiago and Manolin had been trolling the Gulfstream circa 1984 and had found not the big fish, but a floating bale of marijuana?

2. A newspaper article that described a teenager paying for a new Mercedes by pulling $40,000 out of his lunchbox.

3. A couple who kept their marriage from becoming stale by pretending she was a prostitute and he was a regular.

Hal, being the Mr. Spock of our enterprise, ran the ideas through his mystery filter and suggested combining all three. Logical, Charlie said, but how? For Hal, the figure in Charlie's carpet was a crime ring, a drug-smuggling Fagin who employed street kids as runners and whose operation was threatened by a blackmailing streetwalker who had stumbled into his illegal activities. Fine, said Charlie, how do we get Mike Shayne in? Oh, he needs a client. Who? Suppose the prostitute shows up dead and one of her clients retains Miami's number-one P.I. Why hire Shayne? Suppose the john cared? Why would he? And so it goes.

In essence, what we do is eventually apply the usual pattern of a hardboiled mystery to set up our episodes. By continually asking a kid's favorite question, "Why?" we evolve a rough outline of the plot that we feel free to add or subtract from as we write. And scholarship/criticism begins the same way. For instance, after teaching Browning, Hal once expressed a dissatisfaction with the traditional explanation of Ferrara's motivation. Off the top of his head, Charlie wondered if the Duke might have been impotent. "Why," Hal asked, picking upon the chance remark, "did you say that?" Charlie didn't know. A close examination of the text offered tenuous support. Hal noticed an image cluster, and then we did some research. With two of us, that takes half the time. Bits and pieces were culled from previous scholarship, an outline was constructed around the usual pattern for a critical paper, and the writing process began. The end product appeared in *Studies in Browning and His Circle.*

Another advantage to collaborating is that we rarely encounter the traditional nemeses of writers. One of the reasons we haven't missed a day of writing in so long is a sense of obligation. On a particular day Charlie may feel like anything but a trip to Ronald's Room, but he knows Hal is depending on his being there, so he shows up. Writer's block? Never! One of us always has a fresh idea or a new slant on an old one. False starts? Hardly! Because we talk out virtually everything step by step beforehand, we usually have a pretty good idea of our destination as well as a map of how to get there before we start the actual work. Burnout? Impossible! With our constant exchanges, frustrations are always brought into the open and never allowed to fester. And with the three burners operating, if we get tired of one project, we can always switch to another.

In our new math, then, $1 + 1 \rangle 2$.

Breathing Life into Characters

by André Jute

Characters are the glue that sticks the parts of your novel together, and the umbilical cord that holds your reader's attention. Characters explicate concepts in action, characters by their actions expound your plot, characters (rather than plots) provide the emotional link—"identification" in the jargon—between your reader and your theme and are consequently the main motivators of tension. Ergo, effective creation and presentation of characters are the most important of your writing skills; without effective characters, there will be no reader identification, without reader identification no tension—and without tension, no novel, never mind a thriller. More, the modern thriller writer requires greater skill in character creation than the "straight" novelist; this is because the increased respectability of the better thrillers has been won at the cost of having the highest critical standards applied to nearly all thrillers, and the difficulty is compounded by the requirement for pace, which inevitably imposes very tight space restrictions on characterization.

How high should you aim?

All that said, various classes of thrillers require different levels of skill with characterization. The classic locked room mystery can still get away, though only barely, with cardboard characters because the main thing is the puzzle, but even here it is noticeable that the characters of even the worst offenders are decidedly less stiff than, say, those in the whodunnits of pre-War authors. Equally, because pace is paramount in the adventure story, which is generally accepted as being modestly less sophisticated than the thriller, readers and most professional critics will sometimes, if the tale is otherwise exceptional, make allowances for skimpily sketched characters. However, charity does not invariably prevail, and you could find your work unfavourably compared with that of a top professional adventure writer, say Wilbur Smith, who has both excellent quickly sketched characters and riveting pace. It would therefore be self-defeating to select your place in the spectrum of thrillers according to your present skill at characterization. Far better to write what you want to write and to work at improving your characterization, not only to the required minimum but to the highest achievable level; if your characterization is richer than expected in your chosen class of thriller, so much the better for your chances of publication.

Character vs. pace. If, in the early stages of your apprenticeship, you are faced with a choice between characterization and pace, choose to round the character at the expense of pace; you can always come back later and cut or compress to enhance the pace—a much simpler matter than trying to blow the spark of life into a character who was stillborn or grew up deprived. Do not despair: the skill of quick, even instant characterization, is, like all the others, learnt rather than inherent. Perseverance will triumph.

You already know your characters

You can, but only in a matter of speaking, create a character from scratch so that he or she

---

André Jute *is the author of* Reverse Negative *and* Writing a Thriller. *He's currently working on a book about Iditarod and Alaskan dog-sled racing.*

seems to bear absolutely no relation to anyone you have ever met or read about. Some writers may sincerely believe this is what they do, but many know that the process of creating characters from a handful of dust does not stand close examination, while true faith in it (as contrasted with lip service induced by fear of the libel laws) can be an important impediment to the regular and consistent creation of varied, individual characters. The professional writer, who must create a new set of characters at least once a year, cannot depend on the lottery of inspiration. In any event, "inspiration" is merely the convenient name for doing subconsciously what we here propose to do more efficiently with our wits about us.

Concept characters A number of characters will be inherent in the concept. These may or may not be your central character(s). It was obvious from the start that my disaster novel *Sinkhole*, about a city falling into hole in the ground, would or at least could have characters from the police, fire, hospital and other emergency services; if the disaster was bad enough, the National Guard could be called out; journalists would cover the disaster. However, while people from all these organizations had substantial parts, I chose to make my hero a car salesman and part-time mountaineer because my concept was to tell the story from the spearhead of the rescue attempts rather than from the command or even national (Washington) viewpoint. Now, I can state categorically that I have never met a mountaineering car salesman. That is the truth, and nothing but the truth—but is it whole? No, it is not: I have met and read about many mountaineers; in advertising I worked with and collected tales about a great many car salesmen from corner used car lots right up to Henry Ford. Even the name I chose for my hero was suggested to me by no fewer than three men I know who were christened Quinten and hate the name. None of these facts are listed in my notes for the novel and it took me a while to dredge them out of my memory; you can be certain there are other indicators locked into my subconscious that I have not managed to unlock.

Character transmutation The character each of us knows best is our own and, by extension, it is often said that the characters in an author's novel are merely representations of the varied facets of himself. There is a kernel of truth in this—and the introspective-navel novels that so blight our literary epoch are extreme cases—but most authors instinctively command the common sense to transform what they know at first hand through the filter of observed real world experience: people in their own families, at work, in other people's fiction. The process can be either subconscious or conscious and consists of taking something from here and something from there until you have a coherent whole. Further differentiation between characters is provided in the writing by their attitudes, actions, dialogue and so on, the mechanics of which we shall come to.

Libel

You must not name real people as characters in your novels, or describe them in such a way that they may be recognized. If you do, and the actions ascribed to them are such that they may be held up to ridicule of suffer loss in their community of profession, you may be liable for damages or even be imprisoned. Even if no evil is ascribed to their characters in your novel, their mere appearance in it (can you *guarantee* some bilious critic won't call your novel a disreputable travesty?) may bring them into disrepute and therefore be actionable. Don't!

Don't, even in jest, threaten to put your friends in your novels. They may no longer be your friends when, ten years hence, your subconscious drags up some characteristic of the friend, sticks it on the baddie in your current novel, and forgets to inform your conscious mind until the writ arrives.

Don't use names from the telephone book for your characters. Use town names from a gazetteer (at the back of a geographical or road atlas) instead, then check in the voters' roll for the town your story is set in that no one of the name lives there (the telephone book is second-best if you can't get hold of the voters' roll); if you give a character a profession, you should also check that no one of that name practices the profession anywhere in the *country* where the story is set; finally, you should check *all* names (persons, companies, organizations, institutions) against all the references and directories (*Who's Who*, Kelly's etc.) your library has.

Don't quote the car license number or telephone number of any character without first ascertaining from the appropriate authorities that such numbers are nonexistent; some authorities have a reserve of numbers used only in fiction from which they will allocate you one if you ask politely. Heed the lesson of the famous story about the television writer/director who, up against a deadline, used his own license plate on the car the actor playing the child molester drove in a piece of television only a moron could mistake for anything but fiction. The week after the episode was screened, the writer and his car (with his registration plate back on it) were attacked in the High Street of his village by shoppers who did substatial damage before the police arrived and explained he wasn't wanted for child molesting. The likely libel damages if he had used someone else's number do not bear thinking about.

In most places in the world, ignorance or the absence of malicious intent is *not* a defense against libel, but proof that you checked to the very best of your ability that you were libelling no one may be taken as a mitigating circumstance. In some countries a defense against a charge of libel is possible by proving disclosures were made in the public interest, which of course implies an admission of intent to libel, and the onus of proof then falls on the libeller (the accused—you), a prospect that turns the staunchest legal stomach.

When you get your first publishing contract, you will find its most horrifying clause, and the only one which no publisher will allow you to delete or alter, gives the publisher an unconditional guarantee that you will foot the bill for damages and legal costs in any case involving obscenity, defamation or libel. If publishers are scared sick, it behooves mere authors to tread carefully.

Now let us denigrate great men and famous In theory at least, you can say what you like about dead men; in practice there are ways in which the surviving relatives of the late traduced, especially if they are rich and well connected, can act against you.

It is also modern practice to include the living great in modern novels, not just as representative of the great office they hold, but often by their given names and described by their peculiarities either lovable or disgraceful, according to the author's inclination. As a rule, it is beneath the dignity of such men (and Mrs. Thatcher) to sue mere novelists but there is no legal bar to them doing so. A lawyer I met socially gleefully volunteered the frightening information that Yuri Andropov, then Chairman of the KGB, should he desire to retire a multi-millionaire in the West, need only sue me and a dozen other thriller writers *and our rich publishers* (if even lawyers know writers have no money, the KGB knows too) for libelling him in our novels.

Plot flows from character

The greatest care is required in choosing and delineating your characters, because so much follows. In particular, the twists and turns of the detailed plot will owe a great deal to the friction between the characters and to their opposing goals. Take *Sinkhole*; it is wisdom after the event, with the book written, to say that the chief character could have succeeded only through unflagging drive and an obstinate unwillingness to be beaten back by petty bureaucrats and nature alike. But, when I created the character, I did not make him a mountaineer because I knew he would need an indomitable will in bureaucratic battles—it was the other way round: I first gave him an indomitable will and then made him a mountaineer (as second choice to a pot-holer or spelunker because Trevanian's *Shibumi* had just appeared) because I already knew something about the techniques of mountaineering and could present it convincingly. From there the next step was that such a man (especially if he was self-made, hence his profession as a car distributor) would not let petty bureaucrats deter him long and, since the concept itself suggested there would be some bureaucrats, one major strand of human conflict thus developed from the single word I wrote down as my player's leading characteristic: "iron-willed." This is of course an ultra-simplified version of what happened: in reality I had many choices—my strong-willed hero could be in conflict with bureaucracy (two kinds in the novel as published), another strong-willed rescuer with different priorities, his own conscience (by rescuing some from certain death, he risks others), one or more of the victims, members of his own team challenging for the leadership. What all these possible strands of conflict have in common is that they involve other people and their characteristics.

Naming your characters Many professional novelists agonize over the choice of names for their characters and with good cause. Suppose Ian Fleming had called 007 Isadore Wimp, do you suppose his books would have sold? George Smiley sounds like a regular guy, Bill Hayden rolls off the tongue as being slightly suspicious and not quite British before one finds out anything else about him, Toby Esterhase is obviously an untrustworthy creepy-crawly, and Karla implies something sly and vicious and treacherous—exactly what I would call an Alsatian dog! Joe Lampton could only be a coal miner or a Yorkshireman on the make; if he were a pattern-maker or a precision molder, he would be called Albert, not Al or Bert, and you'd have to drop the Lampton because Albert Lampton doesn't ring euphoniously, whereas Joe Lampton has an admirable inevitability. An important editor says a felicitous selection of character names is one of the handful of criteria he considers in those ten or fewer pages he reads of unsolicited novels that wash in over the transom (his brutal metaphor, not mine); if the names are wrong, he won't read on, if they're right and nothing else is obviously incompetent, he might read on.

Writing down characters Just as you wrote down your concept, so you should write down your characters. John Braine suggests a minimum: age, physical appearance, profession, ages of children etc.—and to keep it as brief as possible. I read Braine's book *Writing a Novel* only after I finished the first draft of this book, but I wish I had had that advice when I started out as a novelist. Then I wrote reams of character descriptions extraneous to the thriller itself. An utter waste. What you want is one side of a sheet of paper per character to keep beside you to refer to during the detailed plotting and perhaps while you write the novel. Don't try to fill the sheet: just write down what you consider essential.

Stop that character

The reason long character descriptions are such a waste is that character, for the narrative novelist in general but in particular for the thriller writer who has less space for character development, is created most satisfactorily not in description but *in action*. Even at its most basic, defining a man by his possessions, it is dull to write "He had a Bentley Mulsanne Turbo" and hardly more inspired to show him driving routinely to his office in it, but riveting to show him racing across Germany in it to save the girl while being chased by baddies in equally fast cars. There are two points here: *relevance to character* and *relevance to action*. In the first two examples, the car may be relevant to the character to show either wealth or snobbery (and then should be better handled in the second sense of relevance); in the chase example the car is relevant to the action and tells us as much about the character as in the other two while additionally furthering the plot and creating a thrill for the reader.

It is a trap to conclude from this that only those characteristics that may be described in action should find a place in your novel, but you should, in the interest of pace, search very hard for ways to build a fully rounded character as largely as possible in action and in friction with other characters rather than lying on his bed examining his own navel. The only time to back off (should you be so fortunate as to arrive at this point) is where the character and the reader are seeing too much action without pause for breath or thought. What you do then depends on the cause: too much plot, the most common cause, you fix by cutting and saving the surplus events for your next novel. In that rare case where your character is so complex that he won't fit the confines of whatever length you are writing to (60,000-100,000 words are your best bet), you must then simply go to greater length or contrive to squeeze more character development into each activity.

"Right" and "wrong" characters "Wrong" characters are wallflowers at the party: they relate to no one else, they don't spark off anybody, nobody wants to know their secrets (now that *defines* dull), and they suggest nothing interesting they can do either with or in opposition to the leading characters. If they are your leading characters, you're in trouble and must start again because you've gone wrong somewhere, but this is fortunately a rare occurrence; far more commonly they are subsidiary characters and by their very uselessness declare their irrelevance to the story you're telling. Write them out.

"Right" characters are different, they sparkle with contradictions, they spark off all the other characters but especially the main characters, whom they also complement like spoons in a drawer; they have secrets and hidden dreams that others would pay to discover; in a word, they are interesting, not dull, perhaps even fascinating. An elevated, even exalting, state of "rightness" arises when a character self-generates so much plot that you can barely keep him under control, a process known derogatively as "the character running away with the author" (you'd be a very poor specimen if you couldn't control a character you had yourself created on paper rather than in a laboratory); such characters are a joy and a pleasure and almost write the books they appear in. You collect such characters every moment that you can find, worrying at them like a dog at a bone for that last little scrap of interaction with the other characters and the reasons behind it. But beware, many "overwritten" novels (a fatal description in editorial offices) result from the author's fascination with and pleasure in just such appealing characters; by all means write it all down but be prepared to murder your darlings ruthlessly if they hold up the forward momentum of the action.

Now for the bad news: you can't find out about the right and the wrong characters without actually writing the story. It is impossible to find those characters you can or should do without except by creating them on paper at some considerable length. And, since they won't reveal themselves except in relevant action, you cannot do this in some dry description apart from the story you want to tell, you must do it in your novel. This is one advantage of the "John Braine method" of writing a complete first draft at high speed before coming back to refine character descriptions and plot outline prior to writing a completely new draft: all the dud characters can be eliminated in a draft you are already resigned to scrapping.

Dull characters There is another class of characters. They would, in real life, be worthy people, they may even in your novel be worthwhile characters, but they suffer from a terminal illness: they bore *you* stiff. As examples, I would not in a novel of mine have, except as a very minor character, a social worker or miner or missionary, simply because they bore me to tears; an author who has no feeling either sympathetic or antipathetic to a character does not present a neutral depiction—there is no such thing—but a boring one. If you find a character bores you, don't try to jazz it up because your readers won't be fooled; get rid of it.

Contrasts and foils You should, however, differentiate intrinsically boring characters from those which serve, usually in minor parts, as contrasts or foils to your leading characters; for instance, in *Sinkhole* I deliberately created a neurotic housewife (whose stupid hopelessness depressed me terribly) as a mirror to the cheerful self-reliance of her friend who is one of the victims waiting to be rescued. The negative effect of such necessary characters can be minimized by showing them always in action and as briefly as will convey the point. Don't misunderstand me; there is no need to become the Norman Vincent Peale of the thriller world—if you want to present negative characters who are relevant to the story and for whom you feel sympathy (or antipathy), fine, but not characters who bore you-the-writer.

Good guys and bad guys

It is coarsely held to be axiomatic that the writer is in perfect empathy with the hero and to lesser degrees with the other good guys; the writer is also taken to be 'agin' the bad guys. Axiomatic, that is, in the crudest kind of Western. The modern thriller offers this dichotomy only at its very lowest levels. Loyalty and guilt, courage and patriotism, faith and cynicism, friendship and love, are more subtly layered the higher one ascends the ladder until, at the top, it is often very difficult indeed to decipher whose side the author is on, if he is indeed on anyone's—and sometimes even if there are sides! I don't for a moment suppose authors choose their own position on this scale. Instead, it seems to me that their skill at creating and presenting ever more complex characters at the same time increases the subtlety of their narrative. If you read in chronological order the books of serious author (McCarry, rather than Ludlum) you like and admire, the development becomes clear. With others, you will find a high point and then a decline which often coincides with bestsellerdom and uncritical acceptance. ("Oh, that's because he believes his own publicity," a Grand Old Man told me when I complained that the latest from his friend the Famous Author was poor stuff.)

This subtlety is of course worthless if practiced for its own sake and, clumsily done, is mere obscurantism soon recognized and damned by readers for its pompous pretense. But, if it flows from a genuine understanding of all characters, good, bad or indifferent (but not boring!), that is, as a result rather than a mere mechanical cause, it is a Good Thing. Unfortunately, study of the leading texts reveals amazingly little to the novice (except how easily Len Deighton or Victor Canning gets away with breaking most of the rules in every book on the subject—the prerogative of the master craftsman) exactly because subtlety is not a technique in itself but an effect. How then to know and present your characters so that their actions and the frictions between them accurately reflect your own growing perception of the issues underlying the visible plot—and in the process exalt your writing step by step until one day it bears comparison with the masters?

Viewpoints

The point from which the writer, and perforce his reader, views the tale to be told reflects his attitude to each of his characters. There is no such thing as an author who is truly neutral to his characters, but there are ways of pretending more or less successfully, if that should be necessary and desirable for your tale, that you are giving every character equal time at the bat. Equally, there are ways in which your commitment to a certain character or small group of characters may be signalled to your reader.

The author's viewpoint owes its primacy in classroom and other structured literary discussion to its obvious utility as an analytical device. But the practicing author, and especially the novice, does not normally use it as a constructional tool, simply because the point of view normally comes to him as part of the concept. As with the tone of voice, decision about point of view is usually thrust upon the writer only when things go awry in the writing. If you realize late in the novel that you are telling the story from the wrong character's point of view, this often also means you're telling the wrong story (because a different "hero" will lead the story in different directions) and you will probably have to start afresh. The other, and fortunately most common, point at which you will have to face the choice arises which you wish to include something invisible from the existing viewpoint; at this stage you will suddenly become aware that it is possible to change viewpoints even in mid-narrative and can select one or more of those listed below. As for the advice sometimes offered that the novelist should decide his point of view as a planning procedure, I doubt the efficacy of this counsel for any but the most professional novelists and then only for their simplest and most straightforward books. By all means consider the possibilities but don't torture yourself with them; in your original draft, follow your first inclination and tell it the way it seems natural—you'll find out soon enough if you go wrong.

First-person The first-person narrative most definitely provides instant identification with the hero for both author and reader. Even when the "I" of the tale is less than savory, the implication is that his circumstances allow of no better behavior, or that only the hardhearted would condemn a man so charming for a few small peccadillos (think of an Eric Ambler hero). This approach at first seems to hold many attractions for the new novelist: after all, the narrative form we most practice is "And then I did so and so"; many plotting problems melt away for the first person narrator; the requirements of several differentiated and rounded characters and of character contrasts become less acute; and the changes of outlook inherent in many other narrative techniques, which are in themselves stumbling blocks for the novice struggling to control a single viewpoint, are eliminated. Unfortunately, the first person narrative has very great disadvantages too: plotting can become very difficult when there seems no way to introduce certain information to the narrator without ludicrous contortions either by him or another character; the requirement that a first person narrator feels so much more deeply and experiences the events of the story so much more acutely than characters with whom the reader identifies less closely can trip up even experienced authors; characterization, unless controlled with a very firm hand, can more easily than in other formats encroach on space better reserved for action. It is true that in one of my earliest novels, *Reverse Negative*, I knew no better than to use a first-person narrator but, to keep the story under control, I was soon driven to include computer-generated probability studies* of what the other characters were doing. There is no doubt that most of my problems with that novel stemmed from the use of first-person narrative; conversely, when a dozen novels later, I tackled a sequel, *Friday's Spy*, my greater experience helped me keep the computer syntheses down to less than one tenth of the narrative as compared with nearly half in the earlier book.

Single-person A compromise that offers most of the benefits and avoids almost all the pitfalls of first-person narrative is the single-person viewpoint where everything is seen through the eyes of the leading character. A good example is Andrew Garve's *A Hero for Leanda*, where we are given absolutely nothing the hero doesn't experience first-hand or isn't told within the reader's hearing.

God's-eye view The most common narrative form is the god's-eye view (third person impersonal in the jargon) where the author shows each character when his actions are relevant to the story and fills gaps in the essential fabric of knowledge for the reader. In practice, this viewpoint follows, and identifies with, one or a very small number of characters who enjoy the author's implicit approval. It is such a common form because it offers the best of all worlds to both author and reader but, please, don't choose it automatically without considering whether one of the admittedly more difficult viewpoints would not be more apt to the story you are about to tell.

Equal time A far more difficult—and very unusual—version of the god's eye view is that in which the author bends over backwards to be fair to all his characters; here each gets not only equal time but an equal entitlement to the balance of doubt for his argument. This approach is most suited to the higher reaches of the thriller, where moral questions are canvassed. It is ferociously difficult to be fair to all characters because the author, however hard he tries, is never truly neutral. However, I suggest that you try and write at least one draft of your novel from this viewpoint, because it will exercise your growing skill in another direction, that of giving the baddies a credible voice of their own.

---

*If you know how a certain individual behaved under known historical circumstances, you can feed this information to a computer together with information on how people in general or others in his profession react to various stimuli and you can then have the computer tell you how the chosen individual will behave in different-but-related hypothetical circumstances or probably did behave in known-but-unobserved circumstances. The computer's answers are normally, in the versions used by commercial and national security organizations, in the form of a number of possible responses graded by their statistical probability. Tables and graphs qualified by confidence levels are of course not the stuff of tension (quite apart from readers' inability to interpret them) so I cheated by presenting these probability studies as narratives "written" by the computer.

Cheating readers Red herrings are admirable, cheating readers deplorable. A red herring is set up by a thoroughly motivated action that is *in character* with the character performing it and which directs the reader's eye away from the real culprit. Cheating occurs when the author breaks faith with the reader. If you do not take your reader inside a character's thoughts, fine, the readers know what to expect. But, once you've invited your reader into a character's head, you have made a commitment to tell the reader everything relevant to the story going on in that character's mind, unless you've somehow made it clear that the visit won't be repeated. For instance, Noel Hynd's otherwise excellent *False Flags* is spoiled because he repeatedly takes us inside the head of one character and shows us everything she thinks except the most important part of her thoughts; ditto for her actions. Then, right at the end of his book we find out she's the guilty party. This is as much a cheat as *deus ex machina* and both author and editor are culpable for not cutting the offending sections which add nothing to the book.

Credible black hats

Of the many reasons why so many fictional baddies are cardboard cutouts, two are more culpable than the others: authors naturally identify with the good guys rather than the bad; and, in most of the thriller classes accessible to the novice, the amount of space available for developing characters other than the leading one is extremely limited. At the lowest level of thrillers, cardboard baddies may well be accepted, even expected, by readers; this is the solace of the familiar, and the professional author who scoffs at it is a snob. However, the market moves up all the time, and this segment of it is in serious decline; aside from this commerical consideration, most aspirants will *want* to do better if they can.

The devil within? It is important to understand that there is no such thing as a will to evil. Children up to five may tell you they will "do bad things" but adults commit outrages against society or their fellow men from madness (psychopaths) or greed or need (common crime) or fear (violence) or ideological or chauvinist conviction (political crimes). Most might make a case, however cynical and shaky, that the means justify the end; even the vandal is inspired not by an urge to evil but by boredom or envy. I'm not constructing a Marxist argument that crime is society's fault, which is a matter of definition, but that the perceptive author will see, not a crowd of hooligans destroying property for the sake of destruction, but a number of individuals with multiple individual motivations.

Don't particularize your baddies by physical disabilities or peculiarities or by race alone. Sapper could count on kneejerk reflexes to huns, krauts, jerries and Jewish financiers with nasal drips; exactly the same characterizations will ensure that you remain unpublished.

Ways and means In *Reverse Negative*, where my emotional commitment to the narrator was great—what else could it be when I was telling his story through his diary?—I finally overcame the disadvantage the black hats suffered because of this by writing the computer sytheses in which they appeared as a separate book seen from their viewpoint with the lot of them, traitors and innocent dupes, behaving absolutely righteously and in good faith as if they were the good guys and my diarist wore the black hat. Part of the strength of the book lies in this meeting of immovable object with irresistible force, so that the reader is torn between conflicting loyalties almost to the end of the tale. However, this presupposes a narrative structure which can conveniently be split into two (or more) self-contained parts in its creation, to be merged later, and is therefore of limited application.

Another solution is to make your baddie rather likeable, except for the single very serious character flaw which causes him to threaten to destroy the world or whatever. This is most easily done by demonstrating that he has the right instincts—through having the hero sympathize with some of his reasons for committing an outrage, for instance—but his means are despicable or out of proportion to the injustice he seeks to right. Karla, the Soviet spymaster in the Le Carré stories, becomes a sympathetic character even while he opposes the character we identify with, George Smiley, because the author chooses to tell us that Karla suffered for his commitment to his ideology by being imprisoned under Stalin and yet did not waver in his faith. Of course, Le Carré has created an admirable opponent rather than a likeable one, but that merely requires greater skill; the principle is the same.

Character development

A generation ago, Ian Fleming's character James Bond was accepted without comment as a cad and a thug—already everyone knew which class of person became successful secret policemen and that the pre-War beau ideal was no longer tenable even in escapist fiction—but critics found Fleming's plots more than a little ludicrous. At the time, it was not thought worth much comment that Bond did not develop as a character through the book or even much over a series of books but it is doubtful if Bond would be such a huge success today. (The latter-day continuation of the Bond saga by the excellent John Gardner conforms to modern practice by having Bond's character develop or, where that is impossible, by sending him up, and cannot be fairly compared to the originals, not least because Fleming altogether lacked Gardner's infectious sense of humour). Plots that Fleming himself might have thought over the top are now breakfast commonplaces, taken from the media with our wheaties. There has also been a tenfold rise in the availability of the ersatz medium, television, which offers instant characterization (you like the actor's face or you don't) much more intimately in your living room than the big screen ever could, and then fills the rest of the time with instant action. Partly in self-defense against exterior attack, and partly as an inevitable historical process of growth, the thriller has pulled itself up by its bootstraps in the eyes of both critics and readers. Improved character delineation was both a cause and an effect in this process. But that is not the way it is expressed: nobody says, "You must offer better delineated characters"; instead, we hear much about "character development."

Now, most of us have our characters set in concrete before we are thirty and many of us are likely to laugh at those lost souls who, at forty, are still "searching for the real me." We *know* character does not develop much after one's teens, barring only major crises, and that even catastrophes are more likely to induce minor changes in personality (a mellowing, say) rather than a 180° conversion of the kind found in inspirational literature. Character development in the literary sense therefore implies something different from the common everyday meaning of the word (except when we are dealing with children and teenagers). What is this particular meaning, and how can the new author best portray developing characters? By measuring each character, however minor, against each of these criteria—major characters must satisfy most or all.

Developing characters develop This tautology means only that a character (unless a mere walk-on) who can be instantly presented, like Athena from the helmet of Zeus, is quite likely to fall as flat as a board and be as interesting. In real life, who is more boring than the person you meet at a party who spends ten minutes telling you all about himself and then has nothing interesting left to say? So, reveal your fictional character slowly, and preferably in relevant action rather than holding up action merely to describe the character. If you can still be peeling the onion of personality in the very last line, so much the better. Character in this sense is a fine tension-building device.

Developing characters are complete John Braine (p. 132 of *Writing a Novel*) defines the well-made novel as one which leaves no question unanswered in the reader's mind; the same is true of characters. There is no paradox in developing characters also being complete—we are not discussing a fixed point in time but the shifting perception of the character by the reader at any sequential point in the narrative, a compound of the reader having been told everything he could reasonably expect to be told about the character, and the resulting rational expectation that anything relevant *will* in due course be imparted by the author.

Developing characters are internally consistent All the parts of the whole must gel. This is not a difficult requirement to meet; the danger lies in exceeding it and creating a stereotype or caricature. A Colonel Blimp is a lot easier to paint on the page than a 'neutral' retired Army officer. Fortunately, another facet of the developing character almost always saves the thoughtful novice writer.

Developing characters have quirks This is unpredictability rather than inconsistency. If a character astounds by doing something unmotivated, you will lose your reader's faith in your ability to present a complete, consistent character. If your character surprises and delights the reader with an unpredicted trait, you have fixed your character on the reader's mind as if with photographic chemicals. An example: in *Reverse Negative* the first person narrator is an elderly bachelor, neat to the point of fussiness (he knows his house was searched because the blankets on his bed are now tucked in at the sides before the bottom), pedantic, patriotic, finicky (he has spent his whole life on twentieth-century British history), sarcastic to anyone who speaks imprecisely, and so on. Yet, while assassins shoot at him, this sedentary scholar tarries to rescue his cat. The cat made the book for many people; I know this from letters I received from readers and from the fact that some critics, who were otherwise repelled by the deliberately cold tone of the book (as I've described, half of it was supposed to be written by a computer), mentioned the cat; virtually all the favorable reviewers also seemed keen on the cat. Frankly, I'm no T. S. Eliot or Derek Tangye (I freely admit a preference for dogs), so it is safe to assume that my cat is no better, nor any worse, than your cat or anyone else's cat; what made this cat notable was not the cat itself, but that this almost-stereotype dried-up don cherished it. And, because of his love for his cat, he stood out from the crowd of everyone else's dried-up dons and became memorable. Note that there is nothing caricatured or eccentric here: the English are known to be animal-lovers: if he had been a dried-up French don, I would not have given him a cat.

The developing character reverberates This refers to the character's relationship to the world and people beyond the narrow slice of his life-at-crisis-point you are presenting to the reader. I found out about this by a combination of circumstances: I wanted to write a big novel about the arts in Australia and had a first draft of about 250,000 words. However, my American publishers hated the idea of a novel about the arts and, worse, set in Australia; my London publishers bribed me by commissioning two other novels for about six times what they said they would pay for the arts novel; my Australian publishers offered me as much as they could afford, which would not have paid household expenses while I wrote the book; the Australian Literature Board declined to give me a grant to make up the difference. Then my London paperback publishers built a big warehouse in Australia and, to have something to distribute through it (this is all true), offered to finance the novel if I could deliver quickly and would confine the plot to the thriller sub-plot I had mentioned over lunch (they didn't have time to read the big draft). Reducing 250,000 words to 80,000 produced a novel in which the various characters almost seem to glow with undercurrents of past history and associations, sparking off each other like a telephone exchange. (I'm indebted to the freelance editor Shirley Young for the phrase "reverberation" and for pointing out the cause of the phenomenon.) But not every novel suffers such a chain of fortuitous misfortune and it would be malicious to suggest you overwrite and then cut because mere overwriting, to fill the space, is not the same as writing a long novel with all the events motivated and then coralling a sub-plot for publication. But, ever since I found out about reverberation and had its benefit confirmed when I cut another novel from 125,000 to 70,000 words, I have been consciously providing my characters with a life beyond what I write down, with a past, with friends the reader need never hear about, whatever would fill the character out in real life, away from the present consuming crisis; I do not write down these perspectives-exterior-to-the-novel (not only a waste of time but too rigid) but let them illuminate each action in my mind as I work out the character's story on paper.

Developing characters enjoy life after death At the end of the novel, the characters will disappear back onto the library shelf. It is a small, literary death. And that is exactly what you want your readers to feel, that they have suffered the loss of old friends. This cannot be done if readers feel they have exhausted the potential of the characters (has-beens are a bore). Thus the reader must feel there is an unexplored corner of the character he wants to know more about; this is not the same as an unanswered question, more a vague feeling that it would be good to have the characters around a while longer. Of course, the characters' other-life reverberations contribute to this, and so does the strength of character of the leading actors, but a little sleight of plot can also help.

Developing characters change No matter that it doesn't happen often in real life, this is one of the conventions of literature and the thriller can claim no exemption; novels are in any event records of the exceptional. The change need not be large, but it must be consistent with character and also the magnitude of events—film jargon would have it that the reaction must be "established" by prior events arranged in a chain of motivation. In the superior thriller reactions are likely to be both subtle and subtly presented by the author. As an example subtle enough to make the point but not so delicate as to be elusive, take the culmination of Smiley's *Quest for Karla*, where Smiley takes delivery of Karla at the Berlin Wall. We know Karla has been forced to defect through love of his daughter and may feel sorry for him. But eyes on Smiley: Karla drops the lighter which he stole from Smiley thirty years ago. The lighter had been a gift to Smiley from his unfaithful wife and is a symbol of the manipulations and humiliations he has suffered from Karla through his puppets, the traitors. The gesture is both Karla's admission of defeat and his statement of defiance. *But Smiley does not pick up the lighter.* This is his acceptance of a pyrrhic victory, his rejection (at last! we've been suffering the bloody woman for over a thousand pages) of his faithless wife, and—in the very closing lines of the novel series—it is Smiley's valedictory. It leaves us indescribably sad because we know there is nothing left for him to do except die. Here, at nearly seventy, Smiley takes, in a few paragraphs, new directions; this culmination is the reader's reward for staying with the character.

Emotional catharsis is of course not the only reward the reader may be offered: you may choose to confirm his prejudices, relieve his anxieties, strengthen his faith in the status quo, induce him to examine the bases of his ratiocination, whatever—but change is expected and must be provided. The only exception is when the very point of the novel is that *nothing has changed* and this is very tricky to put over convincingly even if you can find a valid example (which would not include the hero failing tragically to achieve his aims, for this is a point of another kind).

Dialogue, action and description

Nabokov said *ad nauseam* that he considered writers who use more than a page of dialogue at a time to be lazy sods and would therefore not read their novels. This kind of snobbery is a trap into which many new writers and some of the slower critics regularly fall. There is no workable prescriptive theory apportioning the space you should allocate to static description, dialogue and action. Dianne Doubtfire in *Teach Yourself Creative Writing* advocates a third each for dialogue, action and introspection (!); I find this and other similar advice a faintly ludicrous attempt to mechanize art and suggest that instead, without thinking about it too much, you let the story tell itself in the manner that will put it over most effectively.

Defining our terms Static description is the author telling the reader what a place or object or person looks like; static description is also the author *telling* the reader the salient characteristics of the character. The trouble with such description is proving that it is irrelevant, especially if it is well written, which accounts for so much of the flatulent description which obscures the true thread even in many good novels. Dialogue is what the characters say to each other and to themselves (strictly speaking, interior monologue) and reveals character and furthers the action; empty talk is easy to spot and cut. Action is a mixture of dialogue and description distinguished by the forward momentum of the event being played out. We have already decided that characters are best developed in action rather than through static description.

It would be self-defeating to write "Joey was apolitical" when you could instead have him say "I make bombs for fun, man," which tells you much more about Joey than merely his lack of interest in politics, builds his character in the reader's mind by the chosen vocabulary, still takes up only the same single line of text (publishers' word counts reckon a broken line of text at as many words as a full line) and, not least of all, is both more interesting and more convincing for the reader than your blunt say-so.

There are dissenting schools of thought but it seems to me that the modern novel, and in particular the thriller, is less bogged down with static description than previously. By now it should be no secret that I consider this new, leaner aspect of the thriller a good thing. If you want to buck the trend, be sure you have a reason good enough to persuade a publisher.

Dialogue The primary test for good dialogue is that it must lend itself to reading aloud, and a great many novelists speak their dialogue as they write it. This does not mean that you can tape-record and transcribe everyday conversations: they contain too many pauses, repetitions, irrelevancies and incomplete sentences. You learn to write good dialogue not by listening to people talk but by reading persuasive authors and practicing at your typewriter. The next test you apply, if the dialogue "scans," is whether you can distinguish the "voices" of your characters: does each character have his own vocabulary and rhythm of speech? (One way I differentiate my characters is by asking about each one, "What does this character fear most of all?" Somehow, if I know what he fears, I know how he speaks. I can't guarantee the method but it may work for you as well.) One easy way to differentiate characters' dialogue is to have one person who always speaks precisely and to the point, another who uses circumlocutions and yet another who waffles, but only if it suits the characters you have already developed. If a character stammers, say so, show his handicap once in action, then write his dialogue as if he has no handicap. Similarly, don't let a garrulous character bore the reader; show him in full flow once, then summarize what he said (" . . . but Bill no longer listened to the tale of all John's conquests.") except where you can use his failing to prolong the tension. Don't try to render a foreigner's speech phonetically: his vocabulary, sentence construction, speech rhythm and the odd outright error (don't overdo it) will set him apart far more efficiently. In action, dialogue should have a shorter beat than in the more restful scenes. Use the description "he said" and "she said" or "Jack said" rather than tiresomely trying to differentiate each speech; when you do then have cause to write "Jack shouted angrily," the reader will also have cause to notice.

Dialect writing Don't. Many registered library-card holders refuse even to attempt dialect books, several paperback publishers have a definite veto on them, and, if these commercial considerations aren't enough, dialect destroys the pace of a thriller while the reader tries to decipher your character's message. Read Leo Rosten's introduction to the collected *Kaplan* stories for an expert's view on dialect. If you want to see how dialect can be suggested by vocabulary and rhythm, turn to the master and refresh your memory about James Joyce's Irish in *Ulysses*. Or read Jon Cleary's *A Very Private War*, where he never lets the reader forget that the indigenes speak pidgin yet offers only three actual examples.

Is and Is Not: Comparison

by Janet Burroway

As the concept of distance implies, every reader is a self-deceiver. We simultaneously "believe" a story and know that it is a fiction, a fabrication. Our belief in the reality of the story may be so strong that it produces physical reactions—tears, trembling, sighs, gasps, a headache. At the same time, as long as the fiction is working for us, we know that our submission is voluntary; that we have, as Samuel Taylor Coleridge pointed out, suspended disbelief. "It's just a *movie*," says the exasperated father as he takes his shrieking six-year-old out to the lobby. For the father the fiction is working; for the child it is not.

The necessity of disbelief was demonstrated for me some years ago with the performance of a play that ended with too "good" a hanging. The harness was too well hidden, the actor too adept at purpling and bloating his face when the trap fell. Consternation rippled through the audience: my God, they've hanged the *actor*. Because the illusion was too like reality the illusion was destroyed, and the audience was jolted from its belief in the story back into the real world of the performance.

Simultaneous belief and awareness of illusion are present in both the content and the craft of literature, and what is properly called artistic pleasure derives from the tension of this *is and is not*.

The content of a plot tells us that something happens that does not happen, that people who do not exist behave in such a way, and that the events of life—which we know to be random, unrelated, and unfinished—are necessary, patterned, and come to closure. When someone declares interest or pleasure in a story "because it really happened," he or she is expressing an unartistic and antiartistic preference, subscribing to the lie that events can be accurately translated into the medium of words. Pleasure in artistry comes precisely when the illusion rings true without, however, destroying the knowledge that it is an illusion.

In the same way, the techniques of every art offer us the tension of things that are and are not alike. This is true of poetry, in which rhyme is interesting because *tend* sounds like *mend* but not exactly like; it is true of music, whose interest lies in variations on a theme, of composition, where shapes and colors are balanced in asymmetry. And it is the fundamental nature of metaphor, from which literature derives.

Just as the content of a work must not be too like life to destroy the knowledge that it is an illusion, so the likeness in the formal elements of art must not be too much alike. Rich rhyme, in which *tend* rhymes with *contend* and *pretend*, is boring and restrictive, and virtually no poet chooses to write a whole poem in it. Repetitive tunes jingle; symmetrical composition tends toward decor.

Metaphor is the literary device by which we are told that something is, or is like, something that it clearly is not, or is not exactly like. What a good metaphor does is surprise us with the unlikeness of the two things compared, while at the same time convincing us of the aptness or truth of the likeness. A bad metaphor fails to surprise or to convince or both.

Janet Burroway *is a Foundation Professor of English Literature and Writing at Florida State University. She is author of novels including* Opening Nights, Raw Silk *and* The Buzzards. *Her short stories, poetry and articles have appeared in* Mademoiselle, Ms. *and* The New Statesman. *She is completing her seventh novel,* Cutting Stone, *set in Arizona in 1914.*

Types of metaphor and simile

The simplest distinction between types of comparison, and usually the first one grasped by beginning students of literature, is between *metaphor* and *simile*. A simile makes a comparison with the use of *like* or *as*, a metaphor without. Though this distinction is technical, it is not entirely trivial, for a metaphor demands a more literal acceptance. If you say, "a woman is a rose," you ask for an extreme suspension of disbelief, whereas "a woman is like a rose" is a more sophisticated form, acknowledging the artifice in the statement.

Historically, metaphor preceded simile, originating in a purely sensuous comparison. When we speak of "the eyes of a potato," or "the eye of a needle," we mean simply that the leafbud and the thread hole look like eyes. We don't mean to suggest that the potato or the needle can see. The comparisons do not suggest any essential or abstract quality to do with sight.

Both metaphor and simile have developed, however, so that the resonance of comparison is precisely in the essential or abstract quality that the two objects share. When a writer speaks of "the eyes of the houses" or "the windows of the soul," the comparison of eyes to windows does contain the idea of transmitting vision between the inner and the outer. When we speak of "the king of beasts," we don't mean that a lion wears a crown or sits on a throne (though it is relevant that in children's stories the lion often does precisely that, in order to suggest a primitive physical likeness); we mean that king and lion share abstract qualities of power, position, pride and bearing.

In both metaphor and simile a physical similarity can yield up a characterizing abstraction. So "a woman" may be either "a rose" or "like a rose." The significance of either lies not in the physical similarity but in the essential qualities that such similarity implies: slenderness, suppleness, fragrance, beauty, color—and perhaps the hidden threat of thorns.

Every metaphor and simile I have used so far is either a cliché or a dead metaphor (both of which will be discussed later): each of them may at one time have surprised by their aptness, but by now each has been used so often that the surprise is gone. I wished to use familiar examples in order to clarify that the resonance of comparison depends on the abstractions conveyed in the likeness of the things compared. A good metaphor reverberates with the essential; this is the writer's principle of choice.

So Flannery O'Connor, in "A Good Man Is Hard to Find," describes the mother as having "a face as round and innocent as a cabbage." A soccer ball is also round and innocent; so is a schoolroom globe; so is a streetlamp. But if the mother's face had been as round and innocent as any of these things, she would be a different woman altogether. A cabbage is also rural, heavy, dense and cheap, and so it conveys a whole complex of abstractions about the woman's class and mentality. There is, on the other hand, no innocence in the face of Shrike, in Nathanael West's *Miss Lonelyhearts*, who "buried his triangular face like a hatchet in her neck."

Sometimes the aptness of a comparison is achieved by taking it from an area of reference relevant to the thing compared. In *Dombey and Son*, Charles Dickens describes the ships' instrument maker Solomon Gills as having "eyes as red as if they had been small suns looking at you through a fog." The simile suggests a seascape, whereas in *One Flew Over the Cuckoo's Nest*, Ken Kesey's Ruckly, rendered inert by shock therapy, has eyes "all smoked up and gray and deserted inside like blown fuses." But the metaphor may range further from its original, in which case the abstraction conveyed must strike us as strongly and essentially appropriate. William Faulkner's Emily Grierson in "A Rose for Emily" has "haughty black eyes in a face the flesh of which was strained across the temple and about the eyesockets as you imagine a lighthouse-keeper's face ought to look." Miss Emily has no connection with the sea, but the metaphor reminds us not only of her sternness and self-sufficiency, but also that she has isolated herself in a locked house. The same character as an old woman has eyes that "looked like two pieces of coal pressed into a lump of dough," and the image domesticates her, robs her of her light.

Both metaphors and similes can be *extended*, meaning that the writer continues to present aspects of likeness in the things compared.

> There was a white fog . . . standing all around you like something solid. At eight or nine, perhaps, it lifted as a shutter lifts. We had a glimpse of the towering multitude of trees, of the immense matted jungle, with the blazing little ball of the sun hanging over it—all perfectly still—and then the shutter came down again, smoothly, as if sliding in greased grooves.

> —Joseph Conrad, *Heart of Darkness*

Notice that Conrad moves from a generalized image of "something solid" to the specific simile "as a shutter lifts"; reasserts the simile as a metaphor, "then the shutter came down again"; and becomes still more specific in the extension "as if sliding in greased grooves." Also note that Conrad emphasizes the dumb solidity of the fog by comparing the larger natural image with the smaller domestic one. Metaphor may equally work when the smaller or more ordinary image is compared with one larger or more intense, as in this example from Katherine Anne Porter's "Flowering Judas."

> Sometimes she wishes to run away, but she stays. Now she longs to fly out of this room, down the narrow stairs, and into the street where the houses lean together like conspirators under a single mottled lamp.

A *conceit*, which can be either metaphor or simile, is a comparison of two things radically and startlingly unlike—in Samuel Johnson's words, "yoked by violence together." A conceit is as far removed as possible from the purely sensuous comparison of "the eyes of the potato." It compares two things that have very little or no immediately apprehensible similarity; and so it is the nature of the conceit to be long. The author must explain to us, sometimes at great length, why these things can be said to be alike. When John Donne compares a flea to the Holy Trinity, the two images have no areas of reference in common, and we don't understand. He must explain to us that the flea, having bitten both the poet and lover, now has the blood of three souls in its body.

The conceit is more common to poetry than to prose because of the density of its imagery, but it can be used to good effect in fiction. In *The Day of the Locust*, Nathanael West used a conceit in an insistent devaluation of love. The screenwriter Claude Estee says:

> Love is like a vending machine, eh? Not bad. You insert a coin and press home the lever. There's some mechanical activity inside the bowels of the device. You receive a small sweet, frown at yourself in the dirty mirror, adjust your hat, take a firm grip on your umbrella and walk away, trying to look as though nothing had happened.

"Love is like a vending machine" is a conceit; if the writer didn't explain to us in what way love is like a vending machine, we'd founder trying to figure it out. So he goes on to develop the vending machine in images that suggest not "love," but seamy sex. The last image—"trying to look as though nothing had happened"—has nothing to do with the vending machine; we accept it because by this time we've fused the two ideas in our minds.

Tom Robbins employs conceit in *Even Cowgirls Get the Blues*, in a playfully self-conscious, mock-scientific comparison of Sissy Hankshaw's thumbs to a pearl.

> As for the oyster, its rectal temperature has never been estimated, although we must suspect that the tissue heat of the sedentary bivalve is as far below good old 98.6 as that of the busy bee is above. Nonetheless, the oyster, could it fancy, should fancy its excremental equipment a hot item, for what other among Creation's crapping creatures can convert its bodily wastes to treasure?

> There is a metaphor here, however strained. The author is attempting to draw a shaky parallel between the manner in which the oyster, when beset by impurities or dis-

ease, coats the offending matter with its secretions—and the manner in which Sissy Hankshaw, adorned with thumbs that many might consider morbid, coated the offending digits with glory.

The vignette of the oyster is a frivolous digression, relevant only in the making of the pearl. The comparison of pearl and thumbs is a conceit because sensuous similarity is not the point. Sissy's thumbs are not necessarily pale or shiny. The similarity is in the abstract idea of converting "impurities" to "glory."

A *dead metaphor* is one so familiar that it has in effect ceased to be a metaphor; has lost the force of the original comparison and acquired a new definition. Fowler's *Modern English Usage* uses the word *sift* to demonstrate the dead metaphor, one that has "been used so often that speaker and hearer have ceased to be aware that the words used are not literal."

> Thus, in *The men were sifting the meal* we have a literal use of *sift*; in *Satan hath desired to have you, that he may sift you as wheat*, *sift* is a live metaphor; in *the sifting of evidence*, the metaphor is so familiar that it is about equal chances whether *sifting* or *examination* will be used, and that a sieve is not present to the thought.

English abounds in dead metaphors. *Abounds* is one, where the overflowing of liquid is not present to the thought. When a man *runs* for office, his legs are not present to the thought, nor is an arrow when we speak of his *aim*, hot stones when we go through an *ordeal*, headgear when someone *caps* a joke. Unlike clichés, dead metaphors enrich the language. There is a residual resonance from the original metaphor but no pointless effort on the part of the mind to resolve the tension of like and unlike. English is fertile with metaphors (including those eyes of the potato and the needle) that have died and been resurrected as *idiom*, "a manner of speaking."

Metaphoric faults to avoid

Comparison is not a frivolity. It is, on the contrary, the primary business of the brain. Some eighteenth-century philosophers spoke of the human mind as a *tabula rasa*, a blank sheet on which sense impressions were recorded, compared and grouped. Now we're more likely to speak of the mind as a "computer" (notice that both images are metaphors), "storing" and "sorting" "data." What both acknowledge is that comparison is the basis of all learning and all reasoning. When a child burns his hand on the stove and his mother says, "It's hot," and then goes toward the radiator and the mother says, "It's hot," the child learns not to burn his fingers. But the goal of reasoning is fact, toward a mode of behavior. When we speak of "the flames of torment," our impulse is comprehension and compassion. The goal of literary comparison is not fact but perception, toward scope of understanding.

Nevertheless, *metaphor* is a dirty word in some critical circles, because of the strain of the pursuit. Clichés, mixed metaphors, similes that are inept, unapt, obscure, or done to death mar good prose and tax the patience of the most willing reader. After eyes have been red suns, burnt-out fuses, lighthouse keepers, and lumps of coal, what else can they be?

The answer is: always something. But because by definition metaphor introduces an alien image into the flow of the story, metaphor is to some degree always self-conscious. Badly handled, it calls attention to the writer rather than the meaning and produces a sort of hiccup in the reader's involvement. A good metaphor fits so neatly that it fuses to and illuminates the meaning; or, like the Robbins passage quoted above, it acknowledges its self-consciousness so as to take the reader into the game. Generally speaking, where metaphors are concerned, less is more and, if in doubt, don't.

(Now I want to analyze the preceding paragraph. It contains at least seven dead metaphors: *alien, flow, handled, calls, fits, fuses* and *illuminates*. A metaphor is not a foreigner; a story is not water; we do not take comparisons in our fingers; they have no vocal cords; they are not puzzle pieces; they do not congeal; and they give off no light rays. But each of these words has acquired a new definition and so settles into its context without strain. At the same time, the metaphoric echoes of these words make them more interesting than their abstract synonyms: *introduces an image from a different context into the meaning of the story . . . badly written, it makes us aware of the writer . . . a good metaphor is so directly relevant that it makes the meaning more understandable*—these abstract synonyms contain no imagery, and so they make for flatter writing. I have probably used what Fowler speaks of as a "moribund or dormant, but not stone-dead" metaphor when I speak of Robbins "taking the reader into the game." If I were Robbins, I'd probably have said, "inviting the reader to sit down at the literary pinochle table," which is a way of acknowledging that "taking the reader into the game" is a familiar metaphor; that is, it's a way of taking us into the game. I have used one live metaphor—"produces a sort of hiccup in the reader's involvement"—and I think I will leave it there to defend itself.

There are more *don'ts* than *do's* to record for the writing of metaphor and simile, because every good comparison is its own justification by virtue of being apt and original.

To study good metaphor, read. In the meantime, avoid the following:

Cliché metaphors are metaphors on their way to being dead. They are inevitably apt comparisons; if they were not, they wouldn't have been repeated often enough to become clichés. But they have not acquired new definitions, and so the reader's mind must make the imaginative leap to an image. The image fails to surprise, and we blame the writer for this expenditure of energy without a payoff. The metaphor is not original.

It's a sad fact that because you have been born into the twentieth century you may not say that eyes are like pools or stars, and you should be very wary of saying that they flood with tears. These have been so often repeated that they've become shorthand for emotions (attractions in the first and second instances, grief in the third) without the felt force of those emotions. Anytime you as a writer record an emotion without convincing us to feel that emotion, you introduce a fatal distance between author and reader. Therefore, neither may your characters be hawk-eyed nor eagle-eyed; nor may they have ruby lips or pearly teeth or peaches-and-cream complexions or necks like swans or thighs like hams. I once gave a character spatulate fingers—and have been worrying about it ever since. If you sense—and you may—that the moment calls for the special intensity of metaphor, you may have to sift through a whole stock of clichés that come readily to mind before you find the fresh comparison that is both apt and startling.

Nevertheless, *pools* and *stars* have become clichés for *eyes* because they capture and manifest something essential about the nature of eyes. As long as eyes continue to contain liquid and light, there will be a new way of saying so. And a metaphor freshly pursued can even take advantage of the shared writer-reader consciousness of familiar images. Here William Golding, in *The Inheritors*, describes his Neanderthal protagonist's first tears, which mark his evolution into a human being.

> There was a light now in each cavern, lights faint as the starlight reflected in the crystals of a granite cliff. The lights increased, acquired definition, brightened, lay each sparkling at the lower edge of a cavern. Suddenly, noiselessly, the lights became thin crescents, went out, and streaks glistened on each cheek. The lights appeared again, caught among the silvered curls of the beard. They hung, elongated, dropped from curl to curl and gathered at the lowest tip. The streaks on the cheeks pulsed as the drops swam down them, a great drop swelled at the end of a hair of the beard, shivering and bright. It detached itself and fell in a silver flash.

In this sharply focused and fully extended metaphor of eyes as caverns, Golding asks us to draw on a range of familiar light imagery: starlight, crystal, the crescent moon, silver. The light imagery usually associated with eyes attaches to the water imagery of tears, though neither eyes nor tears are named. There is a submerged acknowledgment of cliché, but there is no cliché; Golding has reinvested the familiar with their comparative and emotional force.

Mixed metaphors and metaphors too close together may be used for comic or characterizing effect. *The New Yorker* has been amusing its readers for decades with a filler item called "Block That Metaphor." But the laugh is always on the writer/speaker, and put-down humor, like a bad pun, is more likely to produce a snicker than an insight. Just as writers are sometimes tempted to put a cliché in quotation marks, they are sometimes tempted to mix metaphors and then apologize for it, in some such phrase as "to mix the metaphor," or, "If I may be permitted a mixed metaphor." It doesn't work. Don't apologize and don't mix.

Obscure and *overdone metaphors* falter because the author has misjudged the difficulty of the comparison. The result is either confusion or an insult to the reader's intelligence. In the case of obscurity, a similarity in the author's mind isn't getting onto the page. One student described the spines on a prickly pear cactus as being "slender as a fat man's fingers." I was completely confused by this. Was it ironic, that the spines weren't slender at all? Ah no, he said, hadn't I noticed how startling it was when someone with a fleshy body had bony fingers and toes? The trouble here was that the author knew what he meant but had left out the essential abstraction in the comparison, the startling quality of the contrast: "the spines of the fleshy prickly pear, like slender fingers on a fat man."

In this case, the simile was underexplained. It's probably a more common impulse—we're so anxious to make sure the reader gets it—to explain the obvious. In the novel *Raw Silk*, I had the narrator describe quarrels with her husband, "which I used to face with my dukes up in high confidence that we'd soon clear the air. The air can't be cleared now. We live in marital Los Angeles. This is the air—polluted, poisoned." A critic friend pointed out to me that anybody who didn't know about LA smog wouldn't get it anyway, and that all the last two words did was ram the comparison down his throat. He was right. "The air can't be cleared now. We live in marital Los Angeles. This is the air." The rewrite is much stronger because it neither explains nor exaggerates; and the reader enjoys supplying the metaphoric link.

66 Why shouldn't *truth* be *stranger* than fiction? Fiction, after all, has to make sense. **99**

—Mark Twain

Remembrance of Tense Past

by Lynne Sharon Schwartz

I became aware, some years ago, of the spreading use of the present tense in fiction the way one becomes aware of an epidemic of flu. So many people you meet are afflicted by it, until not to be hints at some dubious immunity, almost a standoffishness, an unwillingness to partake of the *Zeitgeist*. But while influenza does its worst to old people, the present tense for the most part strikes at the young. In that regard it might be better likened to the miniskirt in one of its brief flowerings two decades ago (a time, incidentally, when magazine editors were known to reject present-tense stories for impropriety). Likewise, the present tense has gone beyond stylish to positively *de rigueur*, so that a writer of my age will try it on in the privacy of her boudoir, wistfully regarding her image and thinking: Can I? Should I? Will I pass or simply look ridiculous?

Just when women were refusing to be regarded solely as objects of sexual desire, they began showing more sexy parts. A double and contradictory message? Or maybe an even more difficult challenge, namely: by showing our desirability more than ever, we're making it tougher for you to meet our demands. This ambiguity and quasi-perverseness should be kept in mind while examining the meanings and ramifications of the present tense—not with a view to extirpating it like the flu, but to understanding what it implies about fiction and those who write it.

Having grown up on fiction written in the past tense, I would at once notice the present tense, especially in the work of students, as a deviation. I was aware of the writer's immanence, not as narrative voice, which I would have applauded, few things being so appealing as the sound of a human voice, but as technician. It was the auditory jolt that bothered me, not the break with convention, good writing by its nature being a break with convention. Granted that I may be an aesthetic Luddite, yet I was concerned with whether this particular technology was adopted for a conscious reason or was a mindless succumbing to fad. When breaking with convention it is wise to know exactly why you are doing so, and what you may gain and lose, and whether you are simply substituting another convention with new and more disguised disadvantages.

Writing in the immediate

I began asking my students why they wrote—and read—in the present tense. They chorused a short-answer reply: it gave a greater feeling of immediacy. When pressed to define what they meant by "immediacy," they said: that it's happening now, as you read.

What is the notion that the action is happening as one reads? John goes to the window, he parts the curtains and looks out; he sees a neighbor starting his car; his wife enters the room and says she is going to the store, and so on. Barely worth a yawn. However, it is happening as you read, or so we agree to believe, in the tacit contract between reader and writer. This contract asks for a considerable suspension of disbelief: the reader agrees to assume also that what appears on the page has objective truth and merits his time and attention. We all know,

Lynne Sharon Schwartz *is a novel and short story writer. She has published six novels—her most recent,* Leaving Brooklyn, *in 1989.*

of course, that the writer has made it up. She has thought it over and manipulated it, revised it in a calculated fashion, after which it has been set in type, printed, corrected, bound in hard covers, and distributed on trucks or through the mail. But we put aside such knowledge when reading fiction. So in actuality, the use of the present tense requires a further suspension of disbelief: despite all of the above, we are asked besides to believe the story is happening as we read.

Moreover, if a reader is presented with a series of incomplete actions, "happenings-as-he-reads," reflection and evaluation (comprehension) may be suspended indefinitely. In the guise of a spurious immediacy, the action is thrust so close that the reader is overwhelmed, or supposed to be overwhelmed, anyway, and must rely on the most superficial and quickest of responses, which are not always the best or truest. His participation in the work becomes less an imaginative, reflective act than a passive, reflexive one, like a leg jerking when a doctor taps the knee.

"Immediate" means without mediation, without any barriers between subject and object, statement and response, action and reader. If the present tense, for my students, produces immediacy, then the past tense presumably acts as an intermediary. That is, no matter how intense an event or episode may have been, by virtue of being past it is less crucial and cannot have as forceful an impact. In short, the choice of the present tense implies a specific and curious value judgment that raises questions of what fiction is all about.

A belief in living in the moment, without the native hue of resolution sicklied o'er with the pale cast of thought, is more salutary for real life than for fiction. Because life is chaotic, constantly recreating and rearranging itself, the past can be a constraint: we need to be free, available and spontaneous enough to seize what comes our way. Fiction, on the contrary, presents made-up people whose stories are told precisely because they have more than ephemeral import. Fiction is an artifice giving coherence and boundaries to arbitrary swatches of life. To understand a character we need to see the trajectory of his or her experience: fiction *is* the trajectory—the shape of the fiction is. The present tense can be a way of evading scrutiny of that trajectory, evading the obligation of applying sensibility and evaluation. Thus after reading some present-tense fiction we may be left with no more sense of what the characters' lives have been about, or mean, than we have of the lives of strangers glimpsed on the street. The implication is that all we can ever understand is what can be understood from a glimpse.

It might be argued that if art imitates life, what better way to do so than to seize this very means—the fleeting glimpse? Surely that is a bit facile. If art imitates life, perhaps photography, of all the arts, can be made to give the most accurate picture. But photographs have a frame; most photographers arrange their subjects and do not snap at random. And even so, the result is a photograph and not a painting. (Those who study the subtle aesthetics of photography might urge that it is as "invented" as painting, but we will leave them aside for the moment.) The difference between the fiction in question and the more durable kind is like the difference between a photograph and a painting, one a copy of life and the other a copy of a vision of life, which is why some fiction is reminiscent of photo-realism. As far as art imitating life: while its subject matter resembles that of life, its procedures are quite the opposite.

Fashion and the future

The fashionableness of the present tense is linked to several adverse and well-known cultural developments. Naturally if we feel we have no long-range future to speak of, we may come to feel we have had no past, or that we might as well behave as though we hadn't. The decline of a sense of history is exacerbated by a narrowing of the scope of education; what is taught appears increasingly to be determined by what students are willing to learn, and the sense of history is not, regrettably, an innate craving. But since the past is undeniably there, regardless of nuclear or ecological threats, the young as well as the old would do well to be aware of what it consists of, to acknowledge continuity. The present tense, in fiction, seems to come out of nowhere; the experiences of reader and writer are not connected by a common past nor by a past elucidated and made common in the work, but by the use of brand names known to all. Thus consumerism rather than the continuity of the human spirit informs our fiction. Thus we have stories where we know what brand of shaving cream or cereal a character uses but not if he ever had a mother or father or what part of the world he grew up in. The shaving cream is taken to be more indicative than the father or mother.

The use of the present tense derives equally from another notoriously anti-historical phenomenon. For a long time, much new fiction reminded me of something familiar, so familiar that I could not place it right away. John goes to the window; he parts the curtains and looks out. He sees his neighbor, etc. What does this sound like? Exactly what you might get when a person describes to someone in the next room what is happening on a screen. A television screen. Instead of being more immediate, the experience is twice removed.

Through the ubiquity of television, the present tense is linked to the way current history is made—similarly removed, carefully selected, and displayed to us on a screen. Consider an event that can easily be made to sound like the fiction in fashion: The President is standing in the open car waving to the onlookers. His wife is beside him, smiling, wearing a pink suit. The President is falling. It appears he has been shot. Blood streams, etc. A blank space on the page denotes the passage of time and a new scene. Lee Harvey Oswald is walking down a corridor with a guard on either side. A man appears at the end of the corridor, holding a gun . . . .

The space shuttle disaster of 1986, as transmitted on television, sounded very much like that. Inevitably—it was taking place live. The television newsman cannot interpret; he has neither the time nor the responsibility and must simply report what he sees. The artist has the time and the privilege of reflection and moreover is in control of the material. One has to wonder why he or she declines to use it and assumes instead the persona of a TV newscaster.

One reason may be that in a visually oriented age, visible action is accorded high value. Fiction is rooted not in action but in character and destiny. Its major events are often spiritual or emotional journeys impossible to illustrate by physical gestures—which may be why novels like *Mrs. Dalloway* or *Middlemarch* do not find their way to the big screen. The present tense has the questionable facility of suggesting action when nothing visibly significant is taking place, witness the example of John's looking out the window and seeing his neighbor's car, then hearing his wife announce her intention to go to the store. While the action described is devoid of interest, the real action may be taking place inside the character—if, for instance, John, a suspicious person, is shaken by the coincidence (?) of his wife and the neighbor going out at the same moment. The writer has offered the visible, however boring, and left us to infer the rest, like a host who serves his guests tuna fish and lets them smell the hidden caviar.

In sum, if the present tense makes things immediate, the critical issue remains: what aspect of the character's experience is being made immediate?

How much involvement?

The use of the present tense to give the illusion of significance might be tested by transforming a passage into the past tense and seeing how viable it is. The following—with the tense changed for illustration—is from "Three Thousand Dollars," by David Lipsky, in the November 11, 1985, issue of *The New Yorker*. The narrator is a young man of nineteen on the subject of his mother.

> She taught art at a grammar school a few blocks up from our house, and the walls of our apartment were covered with her drawings. That's the way she taught. She stood over these kids while she had them drawing a still-life or a portrait or something, and if they were having trouble she sat down next to them to show them what to do, and usually she ended up liking her own work so much that she brought it home with her. We had all these candlesticks and clay flowerpots that she made during class.

The half-affectionate, half-contemptuous attitude towards the mother, making her into a "cute" character, substitutes for the adolescent's complex feelings: in the course of the story he lies to her about money, driving her into misery and confusion. A little further on, the narrator makes a crucial mistake, "forgetting" that through his own perverseness he hasn't the money to return to college after the summer.

> I got a job working at a B. Dalton bookstore. The manager had to fill out some forms, and when he asked me how long I would be working—for the whole year or just for the summer—I said, "Just for the summer," without thinking, and by the time I realized, he had already written it down and it didn't seem worth the trouble of making him go back and change it. Still, I went through the rest of the day with the feeling that I'd done something wrong.

So much for the crucial issue. In effect the reader is expected automatically to supply the requisite emotion.

> I was sent to the main floor, to the middle register, where old women came in pairs and shuffled through the Romance section. I ate lunch in a little park a block from the store, where a man-made waterfall kept tumbling down and secretaries drank diet soda. There was a cold breeze because of the water.

Admittedly, these sentences sounded more alive in the present tense. They sounded as though something, however amorphous, was being conveyed; thus we can agree that the writer made a wise choice of tense. Specifically, the novelty or "immediacy," if you will, of the present tense masked the poverty of diction and sensibility. But when we change the tense, what is left? Rather than substance, an intelligent technical choice, and avoidance of the task at hand.

Another example: the conclusion of "Pupil," a story by Frederick Barthelme in the August 5, 1985, *New Yorker*, written in the present tense, here transposed to the past. The narrator, a teacher, has invited an eighteen-year-old student over for dinner and, finding her unexpectedly baffling and sly, is ambivalent about whether to sleep with her.

> I took the bowl and dumped the chicken into the paper bag under the kitchen sink. Then I got a plastic trash bag from the closet and put the paper bag in the plastic bag. I scraped the rest of the plates into the paper bag, and put the dishes in the sink, then turned on the tap full blast and used the built-in spray nozzle to rinse the plates and glasses and the silverware. Tracy was watching me do all this. I got some paper towels and wetted them, wiping the countertops and the top of the stove, then the dining table. I shook the placemats over the sink, rinsed everything again, then led her out of the kitchen, hitting the light switch as we went.
>
> "So now we start stuff, right?" she said. She grinned after she said it, reaching for one of the buttons on her shirt.
>
> She was so beautiful. Her braces were shining. On one of her front teeth there was a tiny reflection of me and of the living room behind me. I thought about touching the white down on her face. I moved her hand away from the button.

The reflection in the braces is a delicate touch, a little epiphany, unfortunately too small and too late to redeem the pages of preparatory banality. The domestic details are used to create a feeling of tension, of waiting for the sexual part, or the renunciation of sex, as it appears. But in the past tense, is there really emotional, psychological and sexual tension, or is there a lesson in cleaning up?

The reason why contemporary writers abstain from reflection (and expression) is hardly a deep mystery. Received modernist wisdom has it that after the intellectual upheavals of Freud, Marx and Darwin, after the theories of relativity and probability, the writer no longer feels she has a privileged position regarding the meaning or value of anything, not even, alas, her own fantasies. To be judgmental has become the sin of the artist, just as to be immortal or subversive was his sin in former ages. Values still exist, to be sure, but, no longer held in common, they jostle under siege. Somehow the result is not a free, sophisticated, happy state of moral relativism, but one of timidity, with writers prudently staking no claims. The credo seems to be the less said on such matters, the better, or safer. The present tense serves this timidity admirably, as the writer can pretend to be simply reporting observations—the Sorry Madam I only work here posture.

The predicament is not the same as an honestly amoral stance on the fiction writer's part, which would be: You can think whatever you like about what I am about to show you, I do not presume to tell you what to think. Such utter objectivity would be almost impossible in any event. The stance of the present tense is rather: You can think whatever you like about what I show you, I am not going to tell you what I think, though you can bet your life I think something. In other words, we are not dealing with freedom of thought but with hedging.

Yet here, too, the present tense is paradoxical. Indirectly, the writer must be telling what she thinks because the material is not there by chance, as in an amateur snapshot. Its choice is every bit as meticulous as in older-fashioned fiction. As with the mini-skirt, a sort of double message or challenge is operating. While the writer pretends to take no discernible stance, the reader is more constrained than usual, misled about the degree of manipulation exercised. Compare this to the tactics of, say, Dickens, who makes it abundantly clear what a reader is to think and feel. Anyone diverging from Dicken's viewpoint, in the more sentimental passages, for instance, is free to laugh and say, Come on, I don't feel that way at all. Thus Oscar Wilde could quip that anyone not laughing at the death of Little Nell could not have a heart. The reader does not have the same freedom of rejection with most fiction in the present tense, for the writer's attitude cannot be accurately located. The reader is less free under the guise of bind more free—an Orwellian situation.

Is complexity lost?

It seems to me, though I have not made a scientific study, which some Ph.D. candidate might eventually undertake, that stories written in the present tense tend to sound more like each other, that is, to speak in the same voice, than stories in the past tense. I suspect it has to do with syntax and sentence structure. The present tense (with notable exceptions) has a colloquial tone and does not lend itself easily to complex structures, which make it sound inflated and self-conscious. Also, the reflexive response sought can be more readily attained by simple prefabricated language of the kind cited earlier (catering, incidently, to the limitations of today's readers).

The sentences of Proust, James, Faulkner or Woolf are complex because the shapes of their visions are complex—circular, convoluted, labyrinthine—as the world is complex; they use subordination, relative clauses, and other grammatical baggage to portray the emotional, psychological or intellectual contours of what is being offered. The present tense is commonly employed in a linear way, suggesting that nothing in the work at hand is terribly complex and that understanding, such as it is, can be reached by naming objects or accumulating data. But in truth very little in fiction's realm is simple or linear; all events are interwoven and interdependent.

Some exceptions might reinforce the case. The following, from Russell Banks' story, "Firewood," in *Success Stories*, demonstrates that the present tense need not always be used in the service of a reductive world-view. The character described, Nelson Painter, is an alcoholic who has spent the morning, as well as his whole life, becoming progressively more drunk.

> It's [the snow's] deeper than he expected, eight or ten inches already, and drifting, a heavy, wet snow driven by a hard northeast wind and sticking to every surface that faces it, trees, houses, barns, chimneys and now Nelson Painter, working his way down his driveway from the huge open door of the barn, a man turning quickly white,

so that by the time he reaches the woodpile he's completely white, even his face, though he's pulled his head down into his coat as far as he can and can barely see through the waves of wind-driven snow before him.

And at the close, trying to return to the barn:

It seems so far away, that dark opening in the white world, miles and years away from him, that he wonders if he will even get there, if he will spend years, an entire lifetime, out here in the snow slogging his way toward the silent, dark, ice-cold barn where he can set his three pieces of firewood down, lay one piece of wood on the floor snugly against the other, the start of a new row.

How often do we find the present tense so exhaustively exploited to render, verbally and rhythmically, the feel of a character's being-in-the-world? What Banks has done, and most present tense writers are loath to do, is absorb his character's experience and let it permeate his own voice.

Another exception is Alice Adams, who frequently writes in the present tense, yet whose voice is among the few today one immediately recognizes. Here is the opening of "New Best Friends," from *Return Trips*.

"The McElroys really don't care about seeing us anymore—aren't you aware of that?" Jonathan Ferris rhetorically and somewhat drunkenly demands of his wife, Sarah Stein.

Evenly she answers him, "Yes, I can see that."

But he stumbles on, insisting, "We're low, *very low*, on their priority list."

"I *know*."

Jonathan and Sarah are finishing dinner, and too much wine, on one of the hottest nights of August—in Hilton, a mid-Southern town, to which they moved (were relocated) six months ago; Jonathan works for a computer corporation. They bought this new fake-Colonial house, out in some scrubby pinewoods, where now, in the sultry, sulfurous paralyzing twilight no needle stirs, and only mosquitoes give evidence of life, buzz-diving against the window screens.

Adams is not reluctant to let her voice be heard, nor to use modifiers that convey an attitude towards the proceedings. Her story, "Sintra," opens:

In Lisbon, Portugal, on a brilliant October Sunday morning, an American woman, a tourist, experiences a sudden rush of happiness, as clear and pure as the sunshine that warms the small flowers near her feet. She is standing in the garden of the Castelo de Sao Jorge, and the view before her includes a great spread of the city: the river and its estuary, the shining new bridge; she can see for miles!

The voice is distinguishable by its intelligence and sensibility; it is keenly aware of location in time and space and on a spectrum of emotions. The sentences seem to have been born in the present tense, rather than cast there for fashion or convenience.

On the other hand it is doubtful whether the past masters of elaborate structure could have worked their complex spells in the present tense. We might experiment, begging their indulgence. Listen to Proust, in a passage from *The Captive*, transposed to the present tense:

As in the old days at Combray when my mother left me without soothing me with her kiss, I want to rush after Albertine, I feel that there will be no peace for me until I have seen her again, that this renewed encounter will turn into something tremendous which it has not been before . . . . I spring out of bed when she is already in the room, I pace up and down the corridor, hoping that she will come out of her room and call me; I stand stock still outside her door for fear of failing to hear some faint summons, I return for a moment to my own room to see whether she many not by some lucky chance have forgotten her handkerchief, her bag, something which I may appear to be afraid of her needing during the night, and which will give me an excuse for going to her room. No, there is nothing. I return to my station outside her door, but the crack beneath it no long-er shows any light. Albertine has put out the light, she is in bed; I remain there motion-less, hoping for some lucky accident which does not occur; and long afterwards, fro-zen, I return to bestow myself between my own sheets and cry for the rest of the night.

What happens, paradoxically, is that all immediacy is lost; the passage is cheapened and made melodramatic. It depends for its great effect—in the original past tense—on the narra-tor's relating a completed episode and reflecting upon its meaning as a station in the course of his developing obsession with Albertine. So that along with the charged emotional content, there is a philosophical and intellectual content as well. The past tense delivers both; the present, only the emotional part.

Here is an example from Henry James, the famous passage somewhat past the middle of *The Portrait of a Lady*, where Isabel Archer reflects on how awful her marriage to Gilbert Os-mond has turned out to be. As before, I have changed the original past tense to the present.

. . . her soul is haunted with terrors which crowd to the foreground of thought as quick-ly as a place is made for them. . . . Her short interview with Osmond half an hour ago is a striking example of his faculty for making everything wither that he touches, spoiling everything for her that he looks at. . . . It is as if he has the evil eye; as if his presence is a blight and his favour a misfortune . . . ; a gulf has opened between them over which they look at each other with eyes that are on either side a declaration of the deception suffered. . . . It is not her fault—she has practised no deception; she has only admired and believed. She has taken all the first steps in the purest confidence, and then she has suddenly found the infinite vista of a multiplied life to be a dark, narrow alley with a dead wall at the end. Instead of leading to the high places of happiness, from which the world seems to lie below one, so that one can look down with a sense of exaltation and advantage, and judge and choose and pity, it leads rather downward and earthward, in-to realms of restriction and depression, where the sound of other lives, easier and freer, is heard as from above, and where it serves to deepen the feeling of failure. It is her deep distrust of her husband—this is what darkens the world.

Identity and voice

Oddly enough, it is not as bad as one might expect; apart from the awkwardnesses of tran-position, the meaning and images are clear. But something is missing—the weight of James, the specific gravity. Above all, the sense of progression, the narrative's moving force, is lost in the present tense. The passsage feels lightened and less consequential, while in the original it is heavy with foreboding: a life being assessed, on its path to tragic and universal conclu-sions. This is only possible when something is looked at from a distance, as Isabel looks at her life. In the present tense everything looms too close to focus clearly.

When syntax and sentence structure are limited, the opportunities for diversity in voice are reduced, so that works in the present tense will naturally resemble each other to some degree. And possibly that is what beginning writers want. Given the pressures of the marketplace and the difficulty of getting unconventional work published, they may feel they have a greater chance of success as talented young people see their contemporaries winning acclaim at em-bryonic stages of their careers. So their voices tend to merge the way voices on a telephone are less distinct and more alike than they are in real life, and reading work in the present tense, one has the sense of hearing a telephone voice—in the worst of cases, the computer voice that gives the number when you call Information, which has all the hallmarks of a real voice ex-cept the breath and inflections of life.

This is a sharp contrast to the situation of, say, fifty years ago, when writers prided themselves on distinctiveness of voice rather than uniformity. Frank O'Connor, I am told, said that what is absent from contemporary fiction is the sound of a human voice. Just as a speaker's voice shows her degree of attachments to the words, and a monotone empty of affect can deaden a listener, so the writer's voice shows whether his connection to the story is authentic and live, or dead and inconsequential. The widespread use of the present tense suggests that, in addition to following trends, writers are resisting, and perhaps even afraid of the sound of their own voices (the same point is raised in an essay by Rosellen Brown in *The Boston Review*). To understand the reasons for this resistance to the human voice, we need to look beyond the deplorable state of publishing to the inner pressures assailing individuality.

Despite the recent wave of censorship, we in the West still possess the freedom to say safely in fiction almost anything about ourselves or our society: safely, meaning we will not be thrown in jail or be shunned by our neighbors, though we may be shunned by publishers and certain schools and libraries. We can speculate about the universe unhindered as well as write of the intimacies of private lives as we please. This should yield a gorgeous array of possibilities. How are writers using their freedom? Besides doing sexually explicit things on the page, contemporary characters tend towards a vague nihilism and lead passive, meaningless or unexamined and unexamining lives. But this is hardly original. Bungled or wasted lives are among traditional fiction's most fertile and hallowed themes. Nor are they being handled with startling originality. The best novel about idleness and passivity remains Goncharov's *Oblomov*, written in the far more repressive society of nineteenth-century Russia, in the past tense; having read *Oblomov* one cannot be too unsettled or aroused by the work of Frederick Barthelme or Deborah Eisenberg.

More important, these passive characters' lives, these sexually explicit scenes, are presented over the telephone, as it were, and not face to face. Writers today may feel comfortable physically exposed, as the promotion of some books indicates, yet they seem diffident about their fantasies, about the contents of their minds. Rather than saying, the character I have invented *did* such and such, which means an accomplished act, they say, my character *does* such and such, a more tentative act always in the making, for which one need not take full responsibility, yet. Can it be that they wish to separate themselves from what they are writing, mumble or murmur or mask their voices, as we do when we are uncomfortable about our words and prefer not to be held accountable for them? Very likely, since there is nothing more revealing than the naked imagination and the naked sound of the intimate voice. In this aspect, earlier writers, even Victorians, even those living under repressive political systems, were more daring and courageous about showing themselves than we are.

Not the human body but the individual sensibility is the essence of identity: not our thoughts but how we think, not what we see but how we look at things, not what has happened to us but what our intimate responses have been, and what our assessments are. The sensibilities, made audible in the voice, is what is inhibited in beginning writers today. And the inhibition is encouraged by the impersonal, generalized present tense.

As distinct from most present-tense fiction, the sensibility of the writer can be heard in the following examples.

> Standing before the kitchen sink and regarding the bright brass faucets that gleamed so far away, each with a bead of water at its nose, slowly swelling, falling. David again became aware that this world had been created without thought of him. He was thirsty, but the iron hip of the sink rested on legs tall almost as his own body, and by no stretch of arm, no leap, could he ever reach the distant tap. Where did the water come from that lurked so secretly in the curve of the brass? Where did it go, gurgling in the drain? What a strange world must be hidden behind the walls of a house! But he was thirsty.

That is the opening of Book I of *Call It Sleep,* by Henry Roth. The viewpoint is a six-year-old's, the language an adult's. From so homely an object as a dripping faucet the mystery of the world is evoked. From the directness of tone, sensual detail, and precision of diction, a reader is convinced that Roth has inhabited his character, breathed spirit into him, and, in the writing, shared his place and identity.

The German author Heinrich von Kleist wrote the novella, *Michael Kohlhaas*, in 1808; this is the opening:

> Towards the middle of the sixteenth century, there lived on the banks of the Havel a horse dealer by the name of Michael Kohlhaas, the son of a schoolmaster, one of the most upright and at the same time one of the most terrible men of his day. Until his thirtieth year this extraordinary man would have been thought the very model of a good citizen. In a village that still bears his name, he owned a farm on which he quietly earned a living by his trade; the children with whom his wife presented him were brought up in the fear of God to be industrious and honest; there was not one of his neighbors who had not benefited from his benevolence or his fair-mindedness—the world, in short, would have had every reason to bless his memory, if he had not carried one virtue to excess. But his sense of justice turned him into a brigand and a murderer.

Kleist's voice does not shrink from stating the subject in authoritative terms. The rhythm is temperate and measured; not so what follows. The story becomes an obsessive, furious and violent quest for retribution. Totally absorbing, it makes the reader, in imagination, into a brigand and murderer as well—*there* is real immediacy. While events move at a galvanized pace, the writing keeps the controlled quality till it sounds like a madman trying with all his might to appear sane, in the same way that a drunkard walks with exaggerated precision. Besides being tremendously exciting, the prose is an accurate picture of the mind of Kleist, in whom passion and a constraining, compulsive logic were at war. The voice is the writer revealed.

Finally, the voice of Cynthia Ozick, in the story called "Puttermesser and Xanthippe," from *Levitations*. The heroine has attained a high place in New York City's municipal bureaucracy.

> The truth was that Puttermesser was now a fathomer; she had come to understand the recondite, dim, and secret journey of the city's money, the tunnels it rolled through, the transmutations, investments, multiplications, squeezings, fattenings and battenings it underwent. . . . . Every day, inside the wide bleak corridors of the Municipal Building, Puttermesser dreamed an ideal Civil Service: devotion to polity, the citizen's sweet love of the citizenry, the light rule of reason and common sense, the City as a miniature country crowded with patriots—not fools and jingoists, but patriots true and serene; humorous affection for the idiosyncrasies of one's distinctive little homeland, each borough itself another little homeland, joy in the Bronx, elation in Queens, O happy Richmond! Children on rollerskates, and over the Brooklyn Bridge the long patchwork-colored line of joggers, breathing hard above the homeland-hugging green waters.

Ozick is one of our scarce visionaries, albeit here with tongue-in-cheek. Few attempt such flights nowadays, maybe because exuberance is often mistaken for naiveté. What is most winning, I think, is that she shows no diffidence about being a *writer*, having a vocabulary and an ear—the primitive writerly goods, after all—and using them.

However diverse, these three writers share an equanimity, even abandon, in revealing the paths and by-ways of their imaginations. Such revelation should not be confused with self-expression, which is merely the other face of self-concealment, neither producing memorable writing. Roth, Kleist and Ozick labor instead to construct, to translate a vision of the world, using their sensibilities as instruments—without coyness, without arrogance.

The question of tense led to voice, and voice leads to the center of where fiction comes from. What is real immediacy? To begin with, it has little to do with whether a story purposes to be happening in the past or the present and a great deal to do with the truthfulness of the emotion informing the work. If a writer does not appear to be invested in the fates of his characters, clearly no one else can be. I am not alluding to superficial "warmth" or "caring" of the kind one desires from a friend or relative. Successful writing can be "cold" and unsentimental—witness *Madame Bovary* or the works of Nabokov or Céline. But the characters' destinies must matter, must have a place in a scale of values—the writer's scale of values—where there is such a thing as better or worse, joy or misery, where the end may be ineluctable, like Oedipus's or Othello's, yet is not depreciated with a shrug.

I can anticipate austere postmodernists objecting that the writer's allowing her scale of values to be known—perhaps even having one—is somehow "interfering" with the reader's response. Since when is showing how you feel and where you stand interfering? Interfering, manipulating, is the opposite, concealing how you feel but prying a response out of others.

Suited to intimacy

A writer needs to love his characters not with personal fondness but with the kind of love that is thorough comprehension. It is no wonder that sexual love is called carnal knowledge; it does not necessarily follow that the people love each other warmly or even care to meet for lunch. The writer's kind of love is spiritual knowledge, the non-physical equivalent. Ideally, after carnal knowledge (excluding rapists and sadists with mad agendas), whatever one feels for the other person, one acknowledges her particular way of being in the world, the unique style in which his spirit moves the flesh and occupies space. The writer needs to feel the same. He may (unlike a lover, one hopes) loathe his characters, scorn them, even ultimately kill them, but he loves them in an existential way, granting their position in the scheme of things. This is something a reader can tell instinctively; aside from the formal merits of a work, it is what binds a reader to a book.

Well, how does a writer get to this comprehensive love? What is behind it, what makes it possible? She reaches it, with difficulty, by thoroughly knowing why she has chosen the story she has, where exactly it comes from, what it is really *about*. Not necessarily at the start of a work, but eventually, and then there arrives a great feeling of transcendence. "The reward of art is not fame or success but intoxication," Cyril Connolly wrote in *Palinurus*. When intoxicated, you feel like yourself enlarged, a better, more buoyant self, an enhanced, and, for the moment, fully realized self.

How to reach this secret, crucial knowledge? Joyce Carol Oates once said the prime trait a writer must possess is patience. Another well-known writer said perseverance. To these I would add nerve. Many writers have courage, many are intrepid; nerve is a bit different. There is a dashing, swift quality to it, to the word itself, a sense of peeking or lurching into something dangerous but thrilling, a cavalier, more than noble, quality. Nervy people are not so much brave as a little outrageous. A writer's nerve consists in serving as his own specimen of human nature and looking at the very things he would most like to overlook—not only the standard character flaws, but the secret wickednesses, the perversities of every kind, the meannesses and stupidities, the fears, obsessive mistakes, blindness and deafness, grossness, and the whole residue of infantile cravings. Not looking at them with a view to correct or ameliorate, as one might do for therapeutic or practical purposes, but with a view to comprehend. And comprehending, to bring to light. These qualities need never explicitly appear as the writer's own nor attached to any invented character (that is, need not produce confessional writing—a term, by the way, usually applied to women's subjective fiction and rarely to men's). Simply the awareness of them, the appropriate ones for the story, must radiate from the words like an aura. The aura of knowledge and acceptance is what gives great works their magic and lucidity. The integrity of the work comes to reflect the integrity of the writer.

(Certainly the writer's awareness of human virtues may play a part as well. They need not be stressed since as a rule we tend not to overlook them as effectively as we do our flaws. As a matter of fact one sees the virtues of student writers poignantly and blatantly displayed—

"look what a decent person I am"—to the detriment of objective truth as well as fiction.)

The present tense is ideally suited for writing from the core of this intimate comprehension of the work. Because of the requirements of narrative, few works can take place there all the time. But when one has gotten as close to the bone as one is going to get, the present tense does indeed give immediacy. A good contemporary example is Graham Swift's novel, *Waterland*, where the present and past tenses' interweaving is beautifully appropriate to display the simultaneity of past, present and future in human destiny. The stories of Alice Munro too are firmly grounded in history: their protagonists have fully documented pasts, yet commit anomalous acts springing from obscure sources. For this kind of mystery, the juxtaposition of present and past tense serves well. J. M. Coetzee's superb novel, *Waiting for the Barbarians*, is written almost entirely in the present tense, and almost all of it takes place in the marrow of the spirit.

A final example from Proust—undoctored this time—demonstrates a potent, and once obvious, use of the present tense. Again, from the narrator's musings and frettings about Albertine:

> As soon as Albertine had gone out, I felt how exhausting was her perpetual presence, insatiable in its restless animation, which disturbed my sleep with its movements, made me live in a perpetual chill by her habit of leaving doors open, and forced me—in order to find excuses that would justify my not accompanying her, without, however, appearing too unwell, and at the same time seeing that she was not unaccompanied—to display every day greater ingenuity than Sheherezade. Unfortunately, if by a similar ingenuity the Persian storyteller postponed her own death, I was hastening mine. There are thus in life certain situations . . . in which . . . the problem of whether to continue a shared life or to return to the separate existence of the past poses itself almost in medical terms: to which of the two sorts of repose ought we to sacrifice ourselves (by continuing the daily strain, or by returning to the agonies of separation)—to that of the head or that of the heart?

About halfway through the passage Proust makes a switch, from the past tense in discussing a specific instance, to the present for a general comment about such quandaries. This was at one time a natural use of the present tense—for stating truths we all participate in, brought into high relief by the fictional situation. It is no longer fashionable to state such truths; there is implied doubt that they exist at all, and if they do, the reader is supposed to deduce them on her own. But given the force and reverberation—and wit—of Proust's paragraph, perhaps we might reconsider how the two tenses could work together to reaffirm the commonality of human experience and to link not only past and present, but specific and general, action and effect, character and reader: the world of the story and the world outside.

Making Crime Pay: Point of View

by Stephanie Kay Bendel

Selecting the proper point of view from which to tell your story is a critical decision. You are, in effect, deciding what information your readers will and will not have, what emotions they will experience, with which characters they will sympathize, and what feelings they will have at the end of the story.

Consider the following plot idea: Arthur murders his wife, Millicent, and makes it look like an accident. Sarah, Arthur's stepdaughter, suspects the truth. Dan, an insurance investigator, is trying to establish what actually happened.

Because readers tend to identify with that person from whose point of view the story is told, the selection of the point of view is also a decision about the kind of story we are going to tell.

Suppose we decide to tell this story from Dan's point of view. The readers will step into his shoes. They'll know nothing about the relationships among Arthur, Sarah and Millicent except what Dan is able to learn in the course of his investigation.

His goal—to determine exactly how Millicent died—is now theirs. Their energies will be directed toward trying to figure out what happened, who did it, and how to prove it. They will feel satisfaction when Dan captures Arthur.

We could also tell the story from Sarah's point of view. Now the readers will step into the shoes of a young woman whose mother has died suddenly under questionable circumstances. Because the readers are in Sarah's mind, they know how Sarah got along with her mother and stepfather. They also know as much as Sarah knows about the relationship between Arthur and Millicent.

Sarah's life may be in danger if Arthur realizes that she suspects him. And now along comes Dan, a young insurance investigator who is ready to write off Millicent's death as accidental. Can Sarah convince him otherwise? Can he help her prove that her stepfather is a murderer? How will Sarah protect herself?

Sarah's goals are a little different from Dan's. Now the readers are not so much concerned with who did it or why but with how it was done and how to prove it. And how to maintain Sarah's safety in the meanwhile. They'll feel satisfaction when Arthur is caught. They'll also feel relief that Sarah is out of danger.

We could even tell the story from Arthur's point of view. We might see that Millicent was a horrible tyrant who took sadistic pleasure in making poor Arthur miserable. She manipulated him and bullied him until he felt he had no choice but to kill her. Although the murder was committed on impulse, the terrified Arthur tried to make it look like an accident. He's almost gotten away with it, except for his nosy stepdaughter who is terrifyingly like her mother. That nice insurance investigator seemed to be satisfied until Sarah got hold of him. Now she's raising suspicions. What can Arthur do?

In this case the readers will be certain of the details of Millicent's death from the beginning. Because they understand things from Arthur's point of view, they will be rooting for him to find some way out of this mess. They won't care for Sarah and will be hoping that Dan isn't

Stephanie Kay Bendel, *a former regional vice president of the Mystery Writers of America, is the author (under the pseudonym Andrea Harris) of a suspense thriller, A Scream Away and a collection of mystery short stories under the pen name Hilary Stevens.*

clever enough to figure out what really happened.

Who should your viewpoint character be? It depends upon which story you want to tell. And once you've made that decision, you still have several more to consider: Should you tell your story objectively or subjectively? And what about using mixed or omniscient viewpoints?

To a certain extent, your choices may be limited by the nature of the story. Some material can only be effectively presented in one particular viewpoint. There are times, however, when you do have a choice. In such instances it is best to write in the viewpoint that feels most comfortable.

Let's take a look at some of the methods of handling the point of view and analyze their strengths and weaknesses.

First-person viewpoint

Nearly all fiction is written in either the first or the third person. Stories written in the first person sound as though they are being told directly by the one who lived through the events in the story. This narrator may be either the protagonist or an observer who describes what happens to the protagonist.

The narrator/protagonist

I stopped the car at the entrance to the grounds. The driveway was full of chuckholes big enough to drown a horse. I looked over at Melanie. The poor kid was still blinking back tears. I realized I'd been pretty hard on her.

"Come on, Mel," I said. "We have to walk the rest of the way."

Her legs weren't too steady, so I gripped her arm as we walked to the main entrance of the house. While I was fumbling in my pocket for the key Reynard had given me, I noticed a bloody fingerprint on the doorknob. The blood was still fresh.

What in hell were we getting into?

I glanced at Melanie, who was dabbing at her eyes with her handkerchief. She was so young. So vulnerable. And she trusted me.

I had to get her out of there.

"Damn!" I muttered. "Would you believe I lost the key? We'll have to go back to town."

This story is being told by the unnamed protagonist. The readers know everything the narrator sees and does *as well as what he knows, thinks and feels*. Everything is seen subjectively. It is as if the readers were stepping into this person's mind.

There is one great advantage in writing a story this way. Because the readers feel as though they were in the protagonist's mind, the level of reader identification is very high.

On the other hand, you are faced with all those first person pronouns: *I, me,* and *my.* Somehow, the pronouns *he* and *she* never seem to jump off the page the way *I* does. It takes a bit of skill to construct your sentences so that every other one doesn't begin with a first-person pronoun.

Then, too, the entire text must be written in the speech patterns that that character would use. In the foregoing example, the protagonist speaks of "chuckholes big enough to drown a horse." If another character were telling this story, the holes in the driveway might be described differently. For example, Melanie might say, "The driveway was sadly neglected. It was peppered with deep holes."

Keeping the speech patterns consistent with the narrator's character throughout the story helps a great deal in making the reader feel that they are truly inside of someone else's mind, but it takes a lot of concentrated effort. Every sentence must be weighed, not only to see whether or not it says what we want it to say and whether or not it is constructed as well as possible but also to see whether or not it sounds like the narrator speaking.

There is one other subtle drawback to the use of the narrator/protagonist viewpoint, and that is a slight lowering of tension. It comes about because the readers are certain from the outset that the protagonist survived whatever ordeals are being described; otherwise he or she wouldn't be around to tell this story!

The narrator/observer

Another method of writing in the first person is that in which the narrator is not the protagonist. The readers are still in the mind of the narrator. They know what he sees and does, thinks, knows and feels, but the narrator is no longer the chief character in the story. The readers are outside of the protagonist and can only observe him or her.

If this sounds confusing, remember that Sir Arthur Conan Doyle used this viewpoint in his Sherlock Holmes stories. While Holmes is the protagonist, the story is told through the eyes of Dr. Watson and in Dr. Watson's voice.

Reader identification is affected by this technique. The tendency to identify with the narrator is diluted by the fact that the protagonist is a far more interesting character who also invites reader identification.

We have some other limitations as well. Let's return to the previous example and rewrite it in the viewpoint of the narrator/observer. Now the story is being told by a fellow named Rusty who is sitting in the backseat of the car:

> Lucas pulled the car up at the entrance to the grounds. I leaned forward from the backseat and saw why he'd stopped. The driveway was chock full of holes.
>
> In the passenger seat Melanie was still blinking back tears. Lucas looked at her and the lines around his mouth softened. He knew he'd been too hard on her.
>
> "Come on, Mel," he said. "We have to walk the rest of the way." He looked back at me. "You coming, too, Rusty?"
>
> Melanie stumbled and Lucas gripped her arm as we walked to the main entrance of the house. As he fumbled in his pocket for the key Reynard had given him, I saw Lucas stiffen suddenly. I followed his gaze to the doorknob. There was a fresh bloody fingerprint on it.
>
> Lucas frowned and glanced at Melanie, who was dabbing her eyes with her handkerchief again. Then his face relaxed.
>
> "Damn!" he muttered. "Would you believe I lost the key? We'll have to go back to town."

Let's take a look at the necessary differences in writing this scene from the viewpoint of a narrator who is not the protagonist.

The story is still about Lucas. He is the active person and we are interested in what he says and does. But now we are outside of Lucas, looking at events through Rusty's eyes. We can only see what Rusty sees. We even have to lean forward from the backseat to find out why the car has stopped. The driveway is now described in Rusty's words, "chock full of holes."

When Lucas looks at Melanie, we can't know what he's thinking. We can, however, see the lines around his mouth soften and surmise his thoughts. This is what Rusty does: "He knew he'd been too hard on her." In this instance Rusty is correct, but he could as easily be mistaken when he tries to guess what Lucas is thinking. This sometimes offers a nice opportunity to let our readers mislead themselves.

Notice that we cannot say, "Lucas saw the bloody fingerprint." We are limited to what Rusty can see and infer. In this case Rusty sees Lucas stiffen, sees him looking in the direction of the doorknob, and *concludes* that Lucas is reacting to the bloody fingerprint. Such details may seem unnecessarily picky, but remember that our readers are feeling a certain inclination to identify with Lucas as well as Rusty. If we accidentally slip into Lucas's point of view from time to time, the readers will feel manipulated, particularly when Lucas obviously has information that the narrator doesn't have.

As you can see, there is a certain artificiality about this viewpoint and it is best to use it only when necessary. The best reason for using it is that at a given point in the story, the protagonist must know more than the reader can be allowed to know.

Third-person viewpoint

This point of view is probably the most popular with both writers and readers. The narrative is told in the third person, describing the protagonist as *he* or *she*. The reader may be either in the protagonist's mind (a subjective view of events) or looking over the protagonist's shoulder (an objective view).

Let's go back to our example and see what happens when it is done in the third person.

Third person—subjective view

Lucas stopped the car at the entrance to the grounds. The driveway was full of chuckholes big enough to drown a horse.

He looked at Melanie. The poor kid was still blinking back tears. Maybe he shouldn't have been so hard on her.

"Come on, Mel. We have to walk the rest of the way." She was still unsteady, and he gripped her arm as they walked up to the main entrance of the house.

As he fumbled in his pocket for the key Reynard had given him, Lucas saw a bloody fingerprint on the doorknob. The blood was still fresh.

What in hell were they getting into?

He glanced at Melanie who was dabbing her eyes with her handkerchief again. She was so young. So vulnerable. And she trusted him.

He had to get her out of there.

"Damn!" he muttered. "Would you believe I lost the key? We'll have to walk back to town."

If you compare this with the example done in the first person with a narrator/protagonist, you can see that there is not a great deal of difference in the material except for the use of third-person pronouns instead of first. Besides knowing what Lucas says and does, we know what he knows, thinks and feels. Because we are in the protagonist's mind, we have a high level of reader identification.

On the other hand, one of the drawbacks of telling a story from a subjective point of view (in the character's mind) is that the character can't see himself (unless, of course, he's looking in a mirror), and we can't describe the character as if the readers were seeing him.

The logic of this seems more obvious in the first person. Few beginning writers would say:

I ran my fingers through my sandy hair and shrugged my broad shoulders. There seemed to be no way out.

Yet it is common to find the same illogic in a beginner's third-person manuscript:

Lucas ran his fingers through his sandy hair and shrugged his broad shoulders. There seemed to be no way out.

In one sentence the readers are outside of Lucas, looking at his hair and shoulders. In the next sentence they are inside his head. Such a change of viewpoint is unsettling, and readers will have trouble identifying with Lucas. They may not consciously realize that the viewpoint is changing back and forth, but they will be very aware that something is not quite right.

By the same logic, when we are writing from a subjective viewpoint, we cannot say:

> There was a small grease spot on the back of Lucas's collar.

Unless, of course, Lucas is doing contortions in front of a mirror or he has taken the shirt off and is looking at it. If we need to have the readers know that the spot is there, we might have Melanie notice it and comment upon it.

Nor can we write such sentences as:

> When Lucas left the house that morning, he forgot to take his gun.

Why not? Because when he left the house, he obviously wasn't aware that he'd forgotten the gun. In the subjective viewpoint we are limited to know only what he knows, so we can't be aware that he's forgotten the gun, either.

Similarly, it is unacceptable to write:

> Lucas didn't realize that the elevator had stopped.

or:

> Unconsciously, he reached for the telephone.

It takes a little thought to avoid such sentences as these, but after all the work we've gone through to get our readers into the character's mind, it's worth expending a little effort to keep them there.

Whether we are writing in the first person or the third person, one crucial limitation in writing with a subjective point of view is that we cannot fairly withhold any information from the readers if the protagonist has it. Consider the following passage:

> Lucas wondered what he was going to do. There wasn't much time.
> The phone rang. Inspector Holloway was on the line. Lucas listened grimly. When he replaced the receiver, he turned to Melanie.
> "I've got to leave for a while. Lock the place up tight and don't let anyone in!"

Until now, our readers have been in Lucas's mind, sharing his thoughts and feelings. But as soon as we say *Lucas listened grimly* without saying what he heard, we have cheated. In effect, we are saying to the readers, "Now Lucas is getting a piece of information that I'll tell you about later." Our readers are suddenly aware that they are not in Lucas's mind after all. The fantasy has been shattered. The result is disappointment.

Occasionally, under certain conditions, an author can get away with withholding information. However, in general, when you find that your protagonist must logically have information that cannot be shared with the readers immediately, you should consider changing your viewpoint so that your protagonist is seen objectively.

Third person—objective view

In this viewpoint the story is told as if the readers were watching the main character in much the same way that they might watch a character in the movies or on television. They know what the protagonist does and says and what happens to him, but they cannot enter his mind.

The passage describing Lucas and Melanie arriving at the house might now go like this:

> Lucas stopped the car at the entrance to the grounds. The driveway was full of potholes.
> He looked at Melanie. She was still blinking back tears. He reached over and squeezed her hand. "Come on, Mel. We've got to walk the rest of the way."
> She stumbled and he gripped her arm as they walked up to the main entrance of the house. As he fumbled in his pocket for the key Reynard had given him, Lucas's gaze fell upon the doorknob. There was a bloody fingerprint on it, and the blood was still

fresh.

He glanced at Melanie, who was dabbing her eyes with her handkerchief again. "Damn!" he muttered. "Would you believe I lost the key? We'll have to go back to town."

Notice that the description of the driveway is not strictly objective. Rather than describing it in the way that Lucas would, we are simply conveying the facts to the readers.

We show that Lucas feels sympathy for Melanie by having him reach over and squeeze her hand. We cannot show that he regrets any earlier actions unless he *says* so. The readers have to interpret Lucas's motives from his speech and actions. Thus, we have to be certain that his speech and actions clearly reveal everything we want our readers to know.

Because we are not inside the protagonist's mind, reader identification is lowered, and it is best to compensate for this by having plenty of action and drama.

From a practical stance, the third-person objective viewpoint often serves nicely for a short piece, but it is difficult to write an entire book from that viewpoint because of the stringent limitations on the author. It can be done, however; Gregory McDonald does it very effectively in his Fletch novels.

Mixed viewpoint

Some stories are best told from the viewpoint of more than one character. To insure that the readers feel neither confused nor manipulated, it is a good idea to compartmentalize the book. For example, we might change viewpoints with each chapter. Or we might divide the book or the chapters into sections, each in a particular viewpoint. Within a chapter or a section, however, the viewpoint should be consistent.

We are still bound by the same rules as before: when we are in Lucas's mind, we are limited to what he knows and we may not withhold any information he has. When we switch to Melanie's mind, we know what is going on in her mind but not in his.

If you are writing a whodunit using several viewpoints, you may unwittingly be eliminating a number of possible suspects because once the murder has been committed, we cannot enter the mind of the murderer without knowing it.

When Agatha Christie wrote *The Murder of Roger Ackroyd,* some critics argued that she had violated this principle. A thoughtful reading, however, will show that she did not.

On the other hand, a superb unconventional mystery that uses mixed viewpoint, one of which *is* that of the murderer, is Ira Levin's *A Kiss Before Dying*. It is worth studying to see the skillful use of mixed viewpoint.

As a rule, reader identification is quite low with a mixed viewpoint, and it helps if you have one viewpoint that is more prominent than the others.

It also helps if the connections between the various viewpoint characters are made clear before the story is too far underway. The readers shouldn't have to wonder whether they are still reading the same story.

Omniscient viewpoint

In this viewpoint the author is free to put the readers inside anyone's mind at will. Furthermore, the author can state facts that none of the characters are aware of.

Laura Anderson poured another cup of coffee for Harold. If only it hadn't rained again! She had wanted to go shopping so badly.

Harold folded his paper and sniffed in self-pity. Damn cold! It was the worst time of year to have a cold, too.

Half a mile to the rear of the Anderson house, the crack in the dam to the Hammond Reservoir grew wider.

In the truly omniscient viewpoint, reader identification is quite low. Also, any information that is withheld from the readers is withheld arbitrarily by the author. Thus, there is the danger that the readers may feel cheated. In general, it takes an intricately plotted story to compensate for these potential problems, and conventional mysteries are not often written in the omniscient viewpoint.

However, long, complex suspense novels often lend themselves to this treatment. In such stories there are usually a number of characters plotting at cross purposes, and suspense is derived from the fact that the readers know more than any one of them and can foresee possible consequences. Suspense is also kept high because there are several problems being dealt with and at any given time somebody is in deep trouble. Ken Follett's *The Eye of the Needle* and Frederick Forsyth's *The Odessa File* are good examples of writing in the omniscient viewpoint.

Other uses of viewpoint

Careful use of viewpoint can be effective for directing readers' suspicions in the mystery. To illustrate, let's look at a passage in the third-person subjective view:

> Simon found Iris in the gallery. The poor child was crying. "Here." He offered her his handkerchief. "Let's sit by the fire for a while, shall we?"

Iris is being seen through Simon's eyes. He feels sorry for her, and the readers are invited to feel sorry for her, too. This can be useful if we don't want the readers to consider Iris a likely suspect at this point.

In the same way we can use Simon's emotions to sway the readers against a character.

> Ruby came down the stairs, her eyes still swollen from crying. Simon wondered whether she always used tears to get her way. She'd been doing enough of that this weekend!
> "I suppose you think I'm wrong," she said softly.
> "I think," Simon said, looking her in the eye, "that you should grow up."

Our readers are not likely to care very much for Ruby because Simon—through whose eyes they are seeing things—doesn't like her.

Misinterpretation

If our readers are seeing events through a character's eyes, it is not unfairly misleading the readers if that character misinterprets what he sees.

> As Simon approached the main house, he saw Alex struggling with the key to the front door. "I'm glad you've come home," Simon said as he mounted the steps. "I have to ask your mother some questions. I'd prefer you to be there."
> "Of course." Alex held the door for him. "Mother! I'm home!" His voice rang hollowly in the large hall. There was no reply.
> "Perhaps she's napping." Simon said.
> "She doesn't usually." Alex pushed open the door to the library and froze. "Oh, my God!"
> Mrs. Renfield lay in a pool of blood by the hearth.

At this point, Simon won't suspect Alex because it appears that Alex only just arrived. But that is really an assumption on Simon's part. If, later in the book Simon realizes that Alex could just as well have been *locking* the door on his way *out* of the house, our readers will wonder why they didn't realize that themselves.

We have not misled them. We showed them what Simon saw and told them how Simon interpreted it. It is up to the readers to realize that Simon's interpretation is not necessarily the correct one.

Pointing out a significant thought

The first-person viewpoint is sometimes used to distinguish thoughts from speech in a narrative that is otherwise third-person. When combined with the use of italics, it is particularly useful to make sure the readers realize the significance of the thought. This technique is most often used in the following situations:

1. *When a character is remembering a statement to which you want to call the readers' attention.* This is a handy way to remind the readers of something that may have been said several chapters earlier or that may have been passed over lightly at the time and has now taken on a new significance.

> As Lucas helped Melanie into the car, his mind was on that bloody fingerprint. They said Waldo had been wounded in the prison break.
> *I'm going to get those Harringtons for what they did to me. Every last one of them!*
> Lucas slid behind the wheel and gripped it tightly. Melanie *was* the last Harrington.

Here we are reminding the readers that Waldo threatened Melanie's entire family. These are words the readers have seen before. Because they are quoted exactly, in the first person, and italicized, great importance will now be attached to them.

Compare the lesser impact of reminding the readers of the same threat by simply giving them the necessary information:

> Lucas remembered that Waldo had threatened the entire Harrington family at the time of his conviction.

The same technique is useful in another situation:

2. *When the character is making an important unspoken promise to himself or to someone else.* In this case, we want to point out the character's motives to make sure that the readers understand we are dealing with a matter of importance.

> Lucas released the brake and backed the car onto the road.
> *Don't worry, Mel. I'm going to get you out of this if it's the last thing I do. I promised your father I'd take care of you.*
> He smiled at her. "Are you all right?"
> She nodded.

The use of first person and italics makes Lucas's resolve appear far stronger and more dramatic than if it were simply stated directly:

> Lucas released the brake and backed the car onto the road. He had to get Melanie out of this, if it was the last thing he ever did. He'd promised her father.
> He smiled at her. "Are you all right?"
> She nodded.

Summary

The skillful use of viewpoint can aid reader identification with the protagonist, explain the protagonist's motives, maintain a logical sequence of information that is to be given to the readers, lend emotional coloring to the events in your story, and help the reader appreciate the significance of certain thoughts.

Obviously, the selection of a viewpoint from which to tell a story is not one that should be made lightly. And until you have mastered the art of handling viewpoints, it is a good idea to check your manuscript sentence by sentence to be sure that you are being consistent and that you are viewing events from the best possible perspective.

Writing for Children vs. Writing for Adults

by Susan Shreve

Recently, I found a picture of a fairy I had drawn the Halloween I was in first grade. The fairy had blond curly hair (which I don't have), large blue eyes (which I don't have) and a huge white tulle dress that my mother made for me to wear that Halloween. Underneath the picture I have written: "This is me as a fairy. Only I will be much better still."

It occurred to me that the sweet blond fairy I drew years ago suggests the dilemma for a realistic writer of fiction for adults and children. The impetus to draw the fairy must have come of wanting her to look like my finest imaginings of myself. Imagining fairies, I have the same concerns and seriousness whether I am writing for adults or children.

My third child, a son who was ten at the time, asked me at dinner one day if I would please write a book about him—"just a book about a regular boy named Caleb Shreve who looks like me and acts like me, only he is even more amazing. Make it a very good book," he added, as though he worried that I might put this amazing boy in a bad one. Certainly what I am after in writing fiction for adults and children is a kind of order that distinguishes stories from the randomness of our ordinary lives. Most of my books have owed their beginnings to real situations and my attempt to make sense of them.

In the beginning, I wrote for adults because I was one and knew in a personal sense what I was talking about. I worte my first book about a woman my age, a widow with a young son. It was not exactly autobiographical, but—like a lot of first novelists—I started with my own life, which did not include being a widow. The publisher, however, was certain that I had fictionalized my true story. My agent, whom I met for the first time when I was several months pregnant, was surprised to learn, he said, that I had remarried with such speed. There is truth in these stories that has to do with the nature of realistic fiction as a process of discovery and self-discovery. When I wrote my first novel, I wasn't ready to write for children because I hadn't rediscovered the child in myself. My own children helped me do that.

The same concerns

My first children's book grew out of a suggestion by my brother, also a writer. I should try to make a financial killing, he advised, so I could stop teaching school. The book is called *The Nightmares of Geranium Street* and is an adventure story about a benevolent gang of children in northwest Philadelphia. It was to take me three months to write—the "killing" was to be the result of a series of ten books about the same gang. As it turned out, the book took a year to write. Although it received respectable reviews and a paperback sale, there has been no sequel and neither Knopf nor I have made a "killing."

After several rewrites of *The Nightmares* I did, however, learn a number of important lessons as an adult writing for children. I tend to build a complicated structure, particularly for the time scheme, writing in short takes as opposed to long narrative passages. Often I have a Hollywood cast of thousands with characters making brief appearances. My style is both spare and elliptical; it requires something of the reader. In the development of character, I am

Susan Shreve *is a professor at George Mason University and regular essayist on the MacNeil-Lehrer Newshour. She is working on a novel,* A Country of Strangers, *to be published this year.*

suggestive rather than explicit.

None of this is particularly important in writing for children, who need to feel immediately secure in a book. With *The Nightmares*, I became more direct in terms of characters and more linear in terms of time scheme, and I learned to *plot*, since children expect something to happen. To write a page turner that matters beyond the simple story told is certainly the ultimate goal of realistic writers for children and adults. And children have little patience with digression from the matters at hand. I have learned a lot about structure from the high expectations of an audience of children.

A number of years ago, when Flannery O'Connor was teaching writing at the Iowa Writers' Workshop, a student came in to see her with the usual terrible crisis for writers in graduate school.

"I have nothing to write about," she said.

To which Miss O'Connor replied. "All you need is a childhood."

When I began in earnest to write books for children, they came out of my own childhood, not so much specific experiences as a state of mind. I wanted to write stories about children in real and serious situations that told about their lives with a dimension of nobility—which they in fact have.

I was 21 when I started to teach school. I taught grammar school, drawn to that age child as a result of the perfectly terrible teachers I had had (save Miss Hardell in grade four), whose interests in the profession must have come from a fundamental dislike for children. (Maurice Sendak would draw brilliantly my nightmare memories of teachers.) So I spent my childhood in and out of trouble all the time. All of my protagonists are in one way or another peripheral characters, rebels, self-examiners and examiners of the world in which they live. One of my motives in writing for children was to examine that little girl who spent her childhood in the principal's office. How come, and was she really a bad seed?

Another reason for writing the kind of books I write for children is similar to my decision to be a teacher when I was young. There were a lot of books around in the 1940s and 1950s about sweet girls leading sweet lives unacquainted with grief or the details of the principal's office.

I have the same concerns in writing for children that I have in writing for adults, the same affections, and worries for my characters and how they make out in the world they have inherited. I approach both kinds of books not with the same requirements, but with the same seriousness. It is not a seriousness shared by publishing houses or critics. When I started teaching school, kindergarten through sixth grade, I was quickly aware of being a second-class citizen. Obviously I wasn't so smart if I taught little children, or as serious or professional as if I were teaching in high school or college. I wasn't paid as much. The institutional attitude was that teachers are delivered to schools *en masse* and placed according to their intelligence and ability, so the worst are on the bottom.

Sadly, the same attitude I found in schools prevails in the approach to children's books. One adult publisher suggested I publish children's books under a different name, so as not to diminish my reputation as a novelist. It was suggested once that I leave the names of my children's books off the list of books in a new novel I had written. Book editors arbitrarily will give books for children to reviewers who may or may not have any sympathy or understanding for the book, whereas they use great care in selecting reviewers for adult fiction. I know a couple of children's book authors who are writing their first adult novels with an attitude inherited from the industry: They are finished with their apprenticeship and ready for the big time. The message is clear and absolutely false—you've got to be smarter, wiser, better, to write for adults—and the same goes for teaching in high school or college.

Different point of view

There is no fundamental difference in writing for children and adults. I have learned, however, that there is a difference in point of view. All of my books have children in them, even my adult books, because I like to write about them. They are funny and wise and irreverent. But when I write about children for adults, I am thinking about them from the perspective of an adult who has come to understand some of her childhood. I wrote a book for adults called *Children of Power*, which is about the sins of the fathers visited on their children. The main characters are children, but the point of view is essentially adult because only the fathers can understand the nature of such sins. In another adult book, *Miracle Play*, the children provide, as children often do in life, the balance and comedy that keep our lives on course.

When I write a children's book or a young adult novel, I think in terms of the vision of the hero—that the story not move into territories beyond that vision. In *The Revolution of Mary Leary*, a young adult novel, I have written a first-person, present-tense story about the revolt of a young girl against her strong Catholic mother. Mary Leary is an unreliable narrator, and until she sees the world she lives in for what it is, we have to accept—even if we doubt—her point of view. So her discovery is our discovery.

Whatever book one writes, one must think of the possible scope of that book and honor it. I am conscious of certain unwritten rules when I write for children. I think of a single story, not several as I tend to with adult books, a story whose events affect primarily the hero, just one hero. As a result of these events the hero changes. Grows up, really. This is not substantially different from the considerations I have in writing an adult book. I simply think of a book for children in terms of a single point of view and issue and resolution.

Another important problem in writing books for children arose for me some time ago when I was on a panel with a respected writer of fiction for very young children.

"Why," she asked me, "is there such a category as young adults? At that age, children should be reading Dickens."

I didn't have an answer right away. I panicked and thought, "Jeez, she's right," and went home to tell two of my older children to read Dickens right away. Which they didn't do. I would have an answer now. To the extent that literature is a history of our time, children have a new role in the 20th century that requires a voice. They are no longer just like adults, only smaller, as they were once considered, but a society unto themselves with special problems and histories and adjustments that have been approached lately with zealous enthusiasm. Of course they should want their own stories that tell about their lives in familiar ways and give dignity to them. Which is not to dismiss Dickens any more than we'd dismiss him for ourselves.

I believe that a book for children should not be without hope. When I was small, an aunt of mine gave me a series of opera books for children that I cherished, read again and again, and rewrote. My children have the books now and they have pointed out to me what I had forgotten. At the end of each opera, when the hero is dying and the world is tumbling down, I had crossed out the final paragraphs and in my child's script had substituted, "And they all lived happily ever after."

Shortly after my first adult book came out, a journalist friend whom I admire said to me, "The book's all right but I didn't like the ending. You know better than that. There are no happy endings." Nevertheless, I must be fundamentally committed to a sense of a future, whatever the prospects for our lives in these dark and complicated times, convinced that for children and adults there must be the possibility of fairies who will be in real life much better still.

Douglas Niles

by Peter Heck

Doug Niles is a new name to fantasy readers; his first novel, *Darkwalker on Moonshae*, is barely a year old. But to fans of role-playing games, Niles is already a familiar name. As a game designer at TSR, he has been responsible for several of the best-received games in their recent history, notably the 1985 H.G. Wells Award winner, *AD&D Battlesystem*.

Niles's "Moonshae" trilogy (the second volume, *Black Wizards*, appeared in June, 1988) is part of TSR's newest campaign setting: the Forgotten Realms. In addition to the two novels, Niles has written the *Moonshae* game accessory volume, full of fascinating background on the setting of his books, as well as a challenging setting for a party of gamers.

We spoke to Niles by phone from his office at TSR. Given the number of fans interested in the "Dungeons and Dragons" universe, we also took the opportunity to get his insider's view of the gaming world. Meet Doug Niles: the man who built the Moonshaes.

XI: How did the Moonshae Islands and your trilogy of novels come about? Had you been working on them for a long time?

DN: Darkwalker had kind of a long evolution, starting when I was a high school teacher, before I came to work for TSR. I started working on a novel, without any real plans ever to get it published, but just for fun. This would have been back in 1981. It was a short novel, about a prince and about the king's ward, who becomes his lady later on in life. I was aiming it toward a teenage reading level, I guess, and at the time I was also playing a lot of D&D. One of my students in high school had been Heidi Gygax, and that's how I happened to hear about the game. One day she had asked me to sign a permission slip to miss the next day's class, because she was going to an interview with *People* magazine. I thought that was kind of interesting and asked her why and she asked if I'd ever heard of the game *Dungeons and Dragons*. When I said yes, she told me her father had designed it. I told her how I was interested in the game, and she have me a copy of it, which is how I started playing.

XI: You were living in Lake Geneva at the time?

DN: In Delavan, which is about ten miles down the road from TSR. So when I heard, about a year later, that they were hiring editors, I thought I would try to convince them to hire me. I was an English and Speech teacher, and I had this novel I had written, so I applied for the editing job. I did just horribly on the editing test they gave—I guess I'm not cut out for that job—but I found out they were also hiring game designers, and actually that sounded like a more interesting position to me. So I did a sample game design for them, went for four or five interviews, and showed them the novel (which I'd completed shortly before), as part of my job application, if only to prove I knew how to put words together. They eventually hired me, in January of 1982, and then the novel just sat for about five years. I didn't look at it; I was busy doing game modules and board games and all kinds of stuff.

XI: What made you take another look at it?

DN: Well, I recalled the urge I'd had to write a novel and I dragged it out and looked at it—it was pretty bad. [Laughs] It was really the first writing I'd done since college, and I wasn't too impressed with it. I did like some of the basic plot ideas, and kept them for *Darkwalker on*

Peter Heck, *a long-time science fiction reviewer for* Newsday, *is the editor of two newsletters published by the Walden Book Company—*Xignals *(science fiction) and* Crime Time *(mystery). This interview ran in* Xignals.

Moonshae. Then, in 1986, several of the British TSR game designers came over to discuss a game project for a Celtic land, and we were hoping to do a novel project for that. So that got me started thinking of converting my plot idea to their islands, which were based roughly on the United Kingdom. As things turned out, that project never made it onto the schedule, but at around the same time we came up with the "Forgotten Realms."

XI: Did that project include original fantasy novels from the beginning?

DN: Oh, yes, it was going to use an entire world as a campaign setting, more extensive than anything we'd ever done before. And we knew from the start the line was going to include novels as well as game materials. So again, I started to think maybe this was finally the niche for my story. But the Moonshae Islands in the early version of the "Forgotten Realms" setting were going to be quite a different sort of territory, a bunch of small islands grouped together without any particular historical background. So as we were starting to work on it, I asked if these could be converted to a Celtic kind of culture, which was still pretty easy to do at that stage of the game. We kept the name Moonshae, which was Ed Greenwood's idea, and details from some of the original story I'd written. Other characters, the monster Kazgaroth for example, came from the British game designers. So all these elements finally came together at the same time and gave me the chance to do a novel based on the Moonshae Islands in the "Forgotten Realms," and I spent the last half of 1986 writing the novel.

XI: How much of your first version did you end up using?

DN: I ended up using some ideas from the original story: Tristan and Robyn were my old characters, but with names to fit the Celtic atmosphere, and the magic sword was there in my first version. But basically, it was written from scratch. It was certainly the most exciting project I'd ever worked on, and at that point I'd written quite a few role-playing modules and several "Endless Quest" books. But writing the novel was just an exhilarating experience, beyond any other writing I had done.

XI: How much of what you'd learned in those other kinds of writing turned out ot be useful in fiction?

DN: Description is an important part of module and game writing; you're always describing things. That was something I had a lot of practice in. On the other hand, I got almost no practice in writing characters while doing role-playing adventures. The players become the characters, and what you're trying to do is give them a rich setting; in a novel, you have to do both. Luckily, we have some good editors here, who are very conscientious about helping writers develop their skills, and I've enjoyed working with them tremendously, on both books. Another thing that came out of the games was a feeling for magic, for unusual creatures, and for battles. One of my favorites, among the games I've created, is the *Battlesystem*, which lets you fight mass battles within the "Dungeons and Dragons" rules—so that instead of one human against one monster, you can have whole armies of humans and monsters. I've always been a military history buff, and my favorite fantasy novels are those that put their fantasy against the background of an all-encompassing war: Tolkien's books, or Lloyd Alexander's. In fact, I ended up cutting out a lot of battle description in *Darkwalker* because my editor felt I was going a bit overboard in explaining how the left flank advanced, and things like that. But since that was one of the areas I had strong experience in, from game designing, it was what I focussed on.

XI: How deep does the background of Moonshae go? Are there large areas of geography and history that aren't in print yet?

DN: Well, of course, the *Moonshae* gaming sourcebook takes the setting quite a bit deeper than either of the novels do. Because it was designed for players who might want to take their characters anywhere on the Moonshae Islands, it had to have a lot more detail. In fact, that turned out to be a really useful aid when I started writing the novels. It forced me to decide what Moray was like, and what Snowdown was like. Making those decisions gave me a lot more background to draw on, especially when I began *Black Wizards*. For *Darkwalker*, I had basically worked out the kingdoms of the Ffolk, and how their culture worked, and their conflict with the Northmen, who controlled the other half of the Moonshae Islands. But I didn't really establish, even for myself, an awful lot of detail beyond what was needed for that novel. Now I have a complete background for the Moonshaes, even beyond the sourcebook. It's not a bottomless pit, but there is material I have not been able to use yet.

XI: "Game Designer" is one of those job titles like "Wine Taster" or "Professional Fanzine Editor," in that a lot of people are probably jumping up and down saying, "I want to do that!" What does a game designer really do? Obviously, it isn't throwing dice all day.

DN: No, just on Thursday afternoons. [Laughs.] I would say 50% of the job is writing. At TSR, it's at least a forty-hour-a-week job, and a light week when you're done after forty hours. Because of the nature of the work, you can do a lot of it at home; some nights, I'll stay up to one or two o'clock, just because I'm on a roll. Other days are a lot slower. Some projects are assigned: I'll be told, " We need a Sourcebook on the land of Calimshan; it's got to be 64 pages long, with a map, and it's due on such and such a date." That's fairly standard, especially when somebody's just starting out. For my first several years here, most of my projects were assignments like that. In a "Forgotten Realms" Sourcebook, eighty to ninety percent of your design is writing. The designer for a book like that also has to tell the art department, as much in advance as possible, how many illustrations and of what size, plus specific suggestions for subjects, i.e, "Let's have a cleric and a fighter, the fighter has a two-handed sword and the cleric has a staff, and they've just discovered a giant in his lair"—something like that. The designer generally will do a rough copy of any of the maps we're going to use, and we send those over to our cartographers. In a couple of cases—I'm thinking of a famous module by Tracy Hickman, called *Ravensloft*, and one that Michael Dobson and I have just written, *The Bloodstone Throne*—the mapmaker is involved from an early stage. In both those cases, it was Dave Sutherland, who for my money is the most talented cartographer in the industry, and we're lucky enough to have him working here. For *The Bloodstone Throne*, we wanted a map of the lair of Orcus—one of the highpowered monsters in the AD&D game. And this was very other-worldly kind of place, and I didn't feel that my own graphics talent was up to creating a map of it. So I talked to Dave about it, and he put together a 3-dimensional cutaway-view map of Orcus's castle. It's a nightmarish place, which is just what we wanted—the kind of place that we hope very high-level characters will enter and then drop their teeth from sheer fright! The map is an integral part of that, and I found it an ideal way to work on the project. Then we write it up, on a word processor, and the files go to the editor, who takes over the project and coordinates it through the rest of the process. That's for a role-playing module: a board game, which is another thing I love to do, involves a lot more play testing and a lot more sitting down and thinking. For *The Hunt for Red October*, at least half the work was done before I ever wrote a line. I had a prototype map made up, with prototype pieces, and started playing the game. It blew up horribly, so we had to go back and make new pieces and new rules, and it blew up again. I do that kind of work with pencil and paper, cross out and start again; this is pretty standard procedure. Finally we had something that didn't blow up, and then I sat down and started writing the game. So there are two entirely different procedures.

XI: One of the subjects you taught in school, I understand, was drama. What do you see as the connections between role-playing and drama in the more conventional sense?

DN: Acting and role-playing are practically the same thing. An actor is obviously a lot more physical about it, with costume and make-up to really look the part and get into the performance of it. In a game, you don't go so heavily into the physical components of it, but in the sense that you don't know what's going to happen next, it's a lot *purer* kind of role-playing. A role-playing game is very much like an improvisational theatre performance. When I was teaching drama in high school, my main responsibility was directing plays, and I found that being a Dungeon Master was very similar to being a director. As a DM, you may have less control over the players, but you have complete control over the setting. I like to think that people who are good actors would, generally, be good DMs, good role-players. They can understand what it means to get into a character, and they have the skills to present that character in an amusing and entertaining fashion. Part of a good role-playing game is watching your friends play *their* characters. If you have a good group of players, who are really enjoying themselves in a communicative fashion, watching somebody play a character well is as much fun as going to a play.

XI: What kind of things did you read as a kid? Were you a fantasy fan?

DN: I loved Tarzan when I was a kid. I think I've read each of the books at least three times, many of them more than that. I was also very much into the Hardy Boys, and had an extensive collection of them, back when I was 10 or 11. And military history—my father was very much into W.W.I. aviation, and so at an early age I could tell a Spad from a Sopwith Camel and Fokker Triplane from an Albatross. But W.W.II became my particular area of historical interest, and I spent most of my high school years reading every book I could get my hands on about W.W.II, particularly the aviation. Oh, and Alistair MacLean, everything I could get, and Fritz Leiber's "Faffhrd and the Grey Mouser" stories.

XI: What have you enjoyed reading recently?

DN: My favorite writer, right now, has got to be Tom Clancy. I'd put *Red Storm Rising* right at the top of my list of favorite novels. I've read it twice and probably will be going back to it again. Robert Ludlum is another of my favorites. And I still very much enjoy historical fiction, especially set in the W.W.II period. In fact, that's a period in which I hope, eventually, to be able to write some novels of my own.

XI: What else have you got on the drawing board?

DN: I'm working on the outline for the third book of the "Moonshae" trilogy. I've been working on the board game for *Red Storm Rising*, which is going to link to the *Hunt for Red October* board game. And I had a chance to design a role-playing game for TSR, the *Top Secret SI* game. I'm hoping to write a series of modules to follow up on that. I look forward to that, because I really enjoy playing *Top Secret*, and writing modules is a great excuse to get my friends over and play the game!

❝ *A good science fiction story is a story with a human problem, and a human solution, which would not have happened without its science content.* **❞**

—Theodore Sturgeon

Is There a Short Story Boom?

by Gayle Feldman

Once upon a time there was the short story. It was written by Poe and Melville and Hawthorne and James and was quintessentially American, best suited of all our literary forms to express whatever American writers wanted to say. It went on to find its golden age in the '20s and '30s of this century, when Fitzgerald and Hemingway told their tales, and then, alas!, war came, followed by the apocalypse—also known as TV—and decline set in until, miraculously, the story was rediscovered in the 1970s and all was happy ever after. But the short story was also wonderfully French. It was written by people called Stendhal and de Maupassant and Camus and Sarraute. And it was marvelously Russian, with authors whose names were Turgenev and Chekhov. And it was specially Irish, being spun by the likes of a Joyce or a Trevor, and English and Argentinian, and . . .

And if that were not perplexing enough, how is it that when American stories were deemed to be dead—in the quiet between the setting down of Fitzgerald's pen and the taking up of Raymond Carver's—there happened to be an O'Hara and an O'Connor and a Cheever and a Roth? And a magazine called the *New Yorker* that managed to print, year in and year out, short story after short story? And what of today's literary phoenix risen from the ashes? Do we only have, as we are so often told, sparsely plumed, minimalist birds? Can it be possible for all manner of creatures still to take flight?

The short story is a complicated form, through its very compactness, its elliptical quality and compression in time; and it is a complicated thing to write about, since editors, teachers and writers speak feelingly about it and passion does not often make for a smooth convergence of views. Are we indeed seeing a resurgence today, and if so, how and why? Are there more writers, more stories, more magazines, more books and, not least, more money for all those involved along the way? Is there something very different about the stories or the writers that are with us now? Where does the short story fit into the American publishing scheme of things?

The seven sources

Stories come to us primarily in seven different packages. We read them in the pages of mass-audience magazines like the *Atlantic,* the *New Yorker, Esquire, Playboy, Mademoiselle*; in literary magazines like *Paris Review, Antaeus*, the *Quarterly, Georgia Review, Grand Street* and many lesser-known periodicals; in book form published by small presses like Ecco and Algonquin; in the *O. Henry, Best American Short Stories* and *Pushcart Prize* annual collections; in ad hoc anthologies often brought out by publishing houses that commonly anthologize all manner of things, like Norton and Oxford; in university press collections, usually single-author volumes; and in books by individual writers published by mainstream commercial houses.

Most people agree that if the days of Hemingway and Fitzgerald are to be construed as special for the short story, a great deal of that golden aura is attributable to the numbers of popu-

Gayle Feldman *is both Professional Publishing Editor and a contributing editor for* Publishers Weekly. *Her articles appear in a number of other publications including the* Los Angeles Times, New Woman *and* The Bookseller *(U.K.).*

lar, mass-audience magazines around at the time that featured and paid very handsomely for short fiction. In the '20s and '30s, writers could live rather well off their stories in a way that today's practitioners cannot. Short stories combined art, entertainment and, as the *New Yorker's* Charles McGrath says, served "a kind of journalistic function—bringing news of how people lived in other parts of the country and other parts of the world." They were an essential component of magazines, a component that appealed to publishers and advertisers and subscribers alike. And magazines, along with radio and movies, were the popular entertainment trinity, as yet unchallenged by television.

After World War II, when that challenge came, the economics of short story publishing changed dramatically. There is no longer a *Saturday Evening Post* or a *Colliers* or a *Saturday Review*, and one of the few things that all of the writers interviewed for this article agreed on was that mass-market magazine, with a few exceptions, are finding less room for short fiction and are taking a different attitude to publishing it. Even writers who are regarded as commercially successful feel this way. Ann Beatie says, "If I tried to support myself solely by writing short stories, I'd have an annual income of under $10,000 a year, but it's always assumed I'm doing fine. If you're a really talented writer with a new voice, you'll be found and make your way into print—but you probably will not be able to live off it."

Mary Evans, an agent at Virginia Barber who counts many short fiction writers—like Alice Munro—among her clients, feels that "at a lot of mass market magazines, short fiction doesn't get much esteem from editors, since it's hard to explain its value (as opposed to extracts from a blockbuster novel) to advertisers."

The magazines that count

On the other hand, the *Atlantic*, and particularly the *New Yorker*, have continued to print, nurture and pay for short fiction, whatever was happening elsewhere. Even as some other mass audience magazines faded from the scene, and as commercial book publishers responded quixotically to bringing out single-author collections of stories, short fiction flourished within the pages of the *New Yorker*. Charles McGrath says, "We very much want to resist the idea that the *New Yorker* is the museum of literature, although we are so often perceived as such. But part of this perception comes from the fact that we are one of the few magazines left that pays reasonable money for fiction." Ben Sonnenberg. whose *Grand Street* is applauded by writers and agents alike for its unusual largesse, reflects that "the *New Yorker* must be the most fruitful and generous institution of short fiction there is in the United States."

Certainly, the importance of the *New Yorker* to the book publishing side of the short fiction equation should not be underestimated. One obvious example of this is the fact that so many stories that find their way into anthologies start their printed lives within the pages of the *New Yorker*. Of the 20 stories in the 1988 *O. Henry* volume, four came from the magazine; ditto four of the 23 tales in *The Breadloaf Anthology*; ditto five of the 20 from the 1987 *Best American Short Stories* collection. Another indicator comes from Mary Evans: "From the agent's perspective, it is hard selling a collection of short fiction by a new writer unless that writer has been represented in the *New Yorker* and the *Atlantic*." Harper & Row's Ted Solotaroff, who edited the *New American Review*—in its day one of the most important ventures for short fiction—is not particularly sanguine about the scene today. Solotaroff feels that "the short story is now the sun-dried tomato of the literary world," but he, too, thinks that for a short fiction writer to attract the attention of a book publisher, "you could cynically say that the optimal combination is to have published six stories in the *New Yorker*, two in a woman's magazine and one in something like *Vanity Fair*."

However, for many voices involved in the debate over the state of health of the American short story, the question of whether there is a resurgence centers not on the doings of an "institution" like the *New Yorker*, but much more on the world of the smaller-scale presses and literary magazines. When talking about the short story, statistics are not very precise. *Publishers Weekly* estimates roughly—very roughly—that 40 volumes have been brought out by mainstream book publishers in each of the past two years. However, the statistics for smaller-scale operations are rather more interesting. *The International Directory of Little Magazines and Small Presses*, published annually by Len Fulton's Dustbooks, now contains about 4,400 entries, and 19 percent of the presses (666) and 43 percent of the magazines (802) publish fiction. Surprisingly, says Fulton, the growth rate in the number of small presses has overtaken magazines since 1979. He feels that "a lot of magazines have transmogrified into book publishers in the past 10 years in part because of the grant situation. There is a lot more competition for the magazine grant dollar than there is for the book equivalent. Also, the technology of book printing has something to do with it, since it is much easier these days to do a backyard operation."

The small press renaissance

For Bill Henderson, publisher of *The Pushcart Prize*—which with Houghton Mifflin's *Great American Short Stories* collection and Doubleday's *O. Henry Prize* volume comprises the trilogy of annual anthologies of record—"There has been a renaissance in short fiction publishing, but not through the sales of books published by Knopf or Viking. It's through the resilience and increase in small magazine and press publishing." Although *The Pushcart Prize* is the only yearly anthology dedicated solely to this area, William Abrahams, who has shepherded the *O. Henry* annual for the past 22 years, is finding that more little magazines are contributing to the stock of stories from which he makes his yearly cull. Shannon Ravenel, senior editor for Algonquin Books, who since 1978 has provided the support framework for the guest editors of the Houghton series, also has remarked an increase in small journals coming through her letterbox. When Houghton Mifflin changed the format of the *Best American* collection and engaged Ravenel to do the preliminary sifting for its visiting editors, she was surveying about 900 stories a year. She now reads 2,000.

One periodical that has attracted a lot of attention since starting life earlier this year, and that has often been cited as evidence for the burgeoning of literary magazines, is the *Quarterly*. Since it is being underwritten by Random House, it cannot exactly be termed a little magazine. Edited by Knopf's Gordon Lish, who in a previous life as fiction editor at *Esquire* did a great deal to promote the careers of writers like Raymond Carver, Mary Robison and Barry Hannah, the magazine has provoked not a little controversy. Lish says he started it "because the short story is my passion, and having lost the opportunity I had at *Esquire* to have on a regular basis the pleasure of putting good stories before a serious readership, I had to find another way to do it. The magazine aggressively seeks the new, young writers, people like Yannick Murphy and Amy Hempel. They are far more interesting than many people who have been publishing stories for years and may have achieved great things in the past but haven't kept themselves as energetically in touch with English sentences as they once did." Some others in the literary world tend to view the *Quarterly* rather more critically. They comment that many of the writers whose works are published within its pages have been tied to the writing workshops that Lish conducts, and that the voices of the magazine are, as a result, rather unvarying.

The writing school boom

But certainly the *Quarterly* is indicative of one very important factor in the state of the American short story today. Given that there are more magazines and small presses publishing short fiction, and more stories coming over the transom for consideration, the increase in volume has much to do with the mushrooming of writing programs throughout the country. According to William Abrahams, "Since the end of World War II, we've seen a tremendous rise in writing programs in American universities. It began with the Iowa Writers Workshop, but at present I believe there are over 300 programs nationwide. And that's only the beginning. There are summer meetings, conferences, adult education centers, all trying to teach people how to write fiction. This is a new phenomenon in the history of the short story."

Why so many writing programs? Shannon Ravenel comments, "It's said by some people that M.F.A. writing courses are financially useful, and that they can create publicity for English departments, among other things. A well-known writer supposedly brings glamour to academe. I'd speculate that more than half of our 'known' writers support themselves by taking jobs in writing programs or conferences." And it should be remembered that people from these courses themselves often start up little magazines and buy collections of stories, thus completing the circle.

But controversy about whether this proliferation is a good or bad thing is almost constant. Gordon Lish says, "I believe that each of us has that within ourselves from which great literature can be made. Talent is really an uninteresting and an entirely irrelevant question—energy and will and a great wanting are what are relevant. My activities as a teacher are aimed at facilitating the progress of a student's will and character to behavior on the page." Others view the role of the writing teacher and the programs somewhat differently. Bill Henderson, who teaches in Princeton's undergraduate program, says, "Classes can be fun. But I tell my students, if you want to be a real writer you should be looking for the exit from this classroom, to find your own voice in the world of experience outside." Others think that some programs have developed along unhelpful lines. Walton Litz, who edited Oxford's *Major American Short Stories* anthology and has been a professor of English at Princeton for many years, feels "some programs have conventionalized things in a kind of hermetic world, where writing and talking about short fiction are akin to group therapy. Such workshops have produced a narrative that is limited in scope and all too often is written for a market in imitation of certain stories that have been commercially successful." Stanley Lindberg, editor of the *Georgia Review*—mentioned by many in the field as one of the best literary magazines around—feels that some writing schools have had a particularly negative effect. "The best fiction I see comes from people who have a fresh angle on life, who aren't interested in what the current fashion is in New York. A lot of America speaks with voices from the provinces and not from the cities. I don't find the current school of charismatic writers who live in the present tense and project their angst on the page a creative phenomenon."

Front page attention

Having looked at the mass and not-so-mass magazine side of things, having delved into the world of the small press and of the writing program, what is the short story doing in the world of the commercial publisher? Isn't that where this renaissance is supposed to have taken place during the past few years? Raymond Carver says, "I've never seen a time like this, where books of short stories whose authors have never published a novel are being reviewed on the front page of the *New York Times Book Review*, and where short story writers are able to command advances." Shannon Ravenel feels "many more publishers are actually willing to consider single-author collections in the hope that they will catch fire. In the '60s, the conventional wisdom was that you should persuade the author to publish a novel first." Viking Penguin's Kathryn Court thinks that "there is not much difference between what we can sell of a very good short story collection by an unknown writer and a first novel by an unknown. The numbers for new fiction are very small anyway—we'd print 4,000-6,000 copies for a story collection, and 5,000—7,500 copies for a novel. Our view is that when we take on an author, we take on an author, rather than one novel or one collection of tales."

Despite such encouraging statements, many publishing voices are more cautious about the ease with a short story collection by a single author can get published. Mary Evans reflects, "As an agent representing someone who comes along with a story collection, it still is difficult to sell without a novel in tow. I don't think I've ever sent something out without the editor coming back and asking if the author is writing a novel. It is very hard for an agent to take on someone who just writes short stories. It is an arduous process to establish a new writer, and there are so few places that pay any real money for short stories. The potential for the author's livelihood is much more limited—it is rare to be able to sell movie and other rights to a story." Charles McGrath says, "I don't really see a renaissance in the short story situation in terms of commercial publishers. The novel is less of a risk to them, and the financial situation is never very good, which is not lost on agents. One could say that some agents really lean on their writers to produce novels."

More often than not, if a short story writer is taken on by a commercial publishing house, he or she is given a two-book contract. Ted Solotaroff, looking at the situation as one who has been around both magazine and book publishers a very long time, comments, "Young writers are currently in vogue, and high prices are going for these writers when they hit it big. Many publishers think: If I can get this writer to agree to a two-book contract now, taking the stories but also signing for a novel, I may be saving myself a lot of money in the long run." Raymond Carver: "Ten years ago, there would have been no such talk as a two-book contract for a young writer. Most publishers would only have offered a contract for a novel."

The significance of hype

Many people feel that there is no special resurgence of short fiction publishing by commercial houses; but rather that the printed life of the story has always been cyclical, and that currently writers of short stories, like writers of novels, are affected by a situation where, for better or for worse, books are being hyped. Ann Beattie reflects that "when John Cheever was writing, it was a different time socially. The media didn't want to hype him. To my intense surprise, writers are now considered to be inherently interesting, because the media are making stars of writers." Further evidence of this "star quality" is seen in the Perfect Presence series from Minneapolis's Redpath Press. These are illustrated individual short stories by writers as diverse as Woody Allen, Roald Dahl and Mark Twain, which are packaged as upscale greeting cards under the rubric "Good Stories Make Great Gifts."

Media interest in the short story also has to do with the cycle whereby one or two writers "break through." Many would say that Beattie herself, and certainly Raymond Carver, were taken up by the media and that a lot of other writers jumped onto their coattails. The writing schools also enter into the equation. Solotaroff reflects that "the renaissance of the short story is a marketing thing plugged directly into a reachable market. The kids in the writing programs buy the books, feeling they must read the new, young, published writer that any potential writer should read." Shannon Ravenel agrees that "educated young people who may have had a few years in a writing program are the new market for these stories. They are very susceptible to hype. But as a publisher I feel the market for individual collections still remains rather limited. Many people don't want to read a whole series of stories by one person . . . that can be more difficult than reading a novel. A lot of people therefore turn to anthologies, wanting a variety of voices and someone to have picked them out."

Certainly, anthologies are doing rather well these days. Algonquin's *New Stories from the South*, a brand-new anthology of unknowns from a small press, came out in 1986 and sold 6,000 copies. When Shannon Ravenel first started working on the Best American Short Story series, it was available only in hardcover and sold about 7,000 copies a year. In 1984, Houghton Mifflin instituted a joint hard/soft publication and combined sales jumped to around 25,000, where they have stayed roughly ever since. The *O. Henry* collection has a similar tale to tell. When it was only in hardcover, the volume sold about 10,000 copies a year. About five years ago a trade paperback edition was added, and the book started to sell an additional 12,000 copies per year. And a sprinkling of other anthologies—Dan Halpern's volume for Penguin, the *Breadloaf Anthology,*, and *The New Generation: Fiction of Our Time from America's Writing Programs* (coming soon from Doubleday)—prove that anthologies, which are eminently useful for writing and English courses of all sorts, are flourishing.

University press activity

Libraries are great supporters of anthologies and also make it possible for university presses to do some of the more interesting short fiction publishing around. For a university press, involvement in fiction publishing can be arduous, but it is also an exciting change from scholarly monographs. Library sales make all the difference. The university press is not subject to fads or hype in quite the way a commercial publisher is, and in the mid-'70s, partly in response to the swelling of story writers' ranks courtesy of the writing programs, several presses—like Louisiana State—started to publish occasional volumes of stories. In 1975, the University of Illinois began the Illinois Short Fiction series, publishing four titles a year. Since then, Georgia has instituted the Flannery O'Connor series, Pittsburgh started the Drue Heinz prize, Johns Hopkins and others have got going on the fiction scene. Ann Lowry Weir, who has been responsible for the books in the Illinois series since 1979, says that her press normally prints 1,500 copies of each and that about one in four are reprinted. All of this year's crop were reviewed in the *New York Times*, and the *Chicago Tribune*, which has made a great difference to sales—two of them are already being reprinted, less than six months after publication. Weir looks at the short story scene from an interesting perspective: "Perhaps only a few of our 50 authors so far have been under 30. We get about 200 fiction manuscripts each year, many of which are autobiographical, written by people in their 20s. But we are looking for variety, and people who are 25 or so, unless truly exceptional, just don't come up with that kind of variety. It is difficult for them to write with distance, and to use voices of different generations."

Joyce Carol Oates, who has written a story or two in her time and is currently teaching at Princeton, comments, "One can't judge one's contemporaries very objectively. To expect a great story from somebody who is 25 might be unjustified. When I was writing in the 1960s, I was technically more experimental than I am now, when I am more interested in stories that have the density of a small novel. I have taught writing to graduate students from their 20s to their 50s, and you can't have any substitute for life experience. Writing deepens as you get older."

Although there may be a proliferation of little magazines and presses, a bigger hype of writers, including those who engage in short fiction, and more review space devoted to the short story these days, does that mean that there is also some considerable increase in the number of great writers of the genre? Gordon Lish feels that "we are seeing as many great stories now as in the '20s or '30s, but the numbers are no greater than before." William Abrahams feels that "the writing programs have caused there to be fewer really appalling stories, but then there is the talent factor. There may be more people writing, but that doesn't make a difference to the number of truly transcendent voices around."

What's in it for writers?

Why do writers turn to the short story, and is there a dominating characteristic among the stories of the moment? For Ann Beattie, short fiction is attractive because "you operate more intensely than in a novel. You are always aware of the fact that you are dealing in compressed time. In stories, people write about things that to some extent disturb them—wonderful stories have the ability to surprise, and to articulate something that is mysterious to the author." For Richard Ford, stories give "the opportunity to write something I could finish. When you're working on a long novel, you feel it won't ever stop, that you'll be muddling around forever. So I wanted to do something compact, something that I could finish. I'm always driving for stories in which I've discovered some piece of human intelligence—how we understand moments in our lives, what we say under duress."

People these days talk about minimalism—about a sparseness, a holding back, a less-is-more approach—and link the term to names like Beattie and Carver, and to the young who write in imitation of those authors. But such terminology is not particularly helpful and denies the variety that is present in the best stories of an exceptional writer's work. What does seem to be true is that people like Carver, Ford, Frederick Barthelme and Joyce Oates often write about people who were rarely the subject of short fiction before; blue-collar workers, people on the margin, people who might, in another time, have appeared in a painting by Edward Hopper.

William Abrahams, looking over the years that he's edited the *O. Henry Prizes*, comments, "I don't see any big differences—some changes in apparent subject matter, but in the very first collection there were stories by Oates and Updike, and they will be appearing in next year's collection as well. If anything does characterize today's stories, it is that we are living in a time of people writing privately; political concerns, and those of the outside world, are only rarely treated."

Joyce Oates says that the rise in feminism has caused more female voices to break through in the '70s and '80s; Gordon Lish claims that young writers are being influenced by Garcia Márquez and by the French; and Dan Halpern claims that nobody is doing anything today that Borges didn't already do 50 years ago. Looking at the list of writers whose names came up over and over again in the course of conversations for this article—Ozick, Mason, Hood, Hempel, Erdrich, Irving, Boyle, Munro, Welty, Minot, Paley, Gilchrist, Gallant, Banks, Brodkey, Bell, Robison—the art of the tale is certainly not dead. As Raymond Carver and William Abrahams both remarked, Chekhov, in writing about himself, once said he "lacked a political, religious and philosophical world view. I change it every month, so I'll have to limit myself to the descriptions of how my heroes love, marry, give birth, die and how they speak."

A resurgence in the American short story? Perhaps that is not a particularly relevant question to address. The tale carries on whether there is hype or no hype, writing programs or no writing programs, and the few transcendent writers in every generation always manage to rise above the rest.

❝ *Nice writing isn't enough. It isn't enough to have smooth and pretty language. You have to surprise the reader frequently; you can't just be nice all the time. Provoke the reader. Astonish the reader. Writing that has no surprises is as bland as oatmeal. Surprise the reader with the unexpected verb or adjective. Use one startling adjective per page.* **❞**

—Anne Bernays

The Plight of the First Novel

by Daryln Brewer

When Marilynne Robinson finished her first novel, *Housekeeping*, she showed it to a friend, also a novelist, who said, "This is a lovely book, but you'll never get it published." He sent it to his agent, Ellen Levine, anyway, who said, "This is lovely, but it may be difficult to get it published." Nevertheless, Levine agreed to represent Robinson, and sent the book to Pat Strachan at Farrar, Straus & Giroux. Strachan said, "It's a lovely book, but we can't predict it will sell well." Regardless, Strachan signed up the book and Farrar, Straus & Giroux published it.

The hardcover edition of *Housekeeping* had multiple printings, was nominated for the PEN/Faulkner Award, and won the $7,500 Hemingway prize. Robinson also won the $3,000 Richard and Hilda Rosenthal Award from the American Academy and Institute of Arts and Letters. The book sold to England, Norway, France, Germany, Israel, Holland, Italy, Spain, Denmark and Sweden. Bantam published a paperback edition in this country and Penguin published one in England. *Housekeeping* spent several weeks on the *Washington Post* best-seller list.

An avid readership

"It would be churlish of me to be cynical about publishing and the first novel," says Marilynne Robinson. "I had an amazing experience and people went out of their way for a book they considered a bad commercial risk." Robinson believes an avid and charitable readership awaits good fiction. "I've received many fan letters, some very emotional. It's odd how many say *Housekeeping* reads like poetry—as if that is the ultimate compliment—and yet publishers feel that poetic fiction won't sell. I think a market does exist for poetic fiction, in spite of the cynicism about public taste. Readers do exist who don't like being condescended to, catered to or exploited," she says.

"We publish the fiction we want at Farrar, Straus & Giroux and we've been very successful," says Pat Strachan. "Editors at some houses may have problems signing up serious first novels, but we don't consciously limit ourselves to a certain number. We just try to find special ones, since exceptionally fine writing is rarely lost on reviewers or readers. Early praise from Doris Lessing, Walker Percy and John Hawkes certainly didn't hurt, but the overwhelming reaction to *Housekeeping* is attributable to the text," she says.

"It was very important that my book was published by Farrar, Straus & Giroux," says Robinson. "The title, for instance, turned out to be a curse on the book. Some men wouldn't have looked at it if it hadn't been published by such a fine house." Her one complaint was that "Farrar, Straus & Giroux didn't advertise the book very much. It never got into the Cleveland stores. I have the best spies there—my relatives," she says.

Robinson advises a first novelist to "write for yourself—stay close to what you feel is your compulsion for writing. Don't try to calculate—if you do, your writing will be false and tired. Getting published is a long shot, but it's easier if you speak with your own authentic voice."

Daryln Brewer, *editor of* Poets & Writers, *lives and writes in New York City.*

Like sending a child off

Lee Goerner, an editor at Alfred A. Knopf, has been the editor of many first novels. For him, the most exciting part of publishing is "to get in on the beginning of a career. I like to make noise and get attention for a writer. I hope their career builds and builds, and that they grow as writers. The first book is just a step in a career—and though that first book may not represent a writer's best work, it has something especially exciting for a publisher. It's like sending a child off.

"Of course you don't send it off alone and unprotected," says Goerner. "This means you write personal notes to people in the industry, you present it enthusiastically to the salespeople, and even give copies to strangers in the street. In general, you become a pest. I want to be obsessive about a book," he says. "If you can't be, maybe it's better for everyone involved not to publish it."

Sometimes it's tough for publishers to convince a salesperson to push a first novel, but not at Knopf. "Our salespeople are extremely helpful and have a tremendous respect for first novels," says Goerner.

"I'm optimistic about the writing of first novels and about publishing them," he says. "In fact, I'd like to accept more first novels than I do—the problem is, I just don't get as many good ones as I'd like."

.001% of the population

Elisabeth Sifton, Editor-in-Chief of the Viking Press, agrees. Writing in the *Nation*, she said, "The unpalatable truth is that most of the novels sent to us are not good . . . most are mad, bad, banal, derivative or imitative—and apparently purposeless." If there is a crisis in the publishing of first fiction, Sifton blames it on the reader. "The American people are not reading serious books the way they used to and especially they are not reading novels. The average first novel sells only about 2,000 to 4,000 copies. This readership represents about .001 or .002 percent of the population." Publishers, she said, were not to blame. "If the books are not selling, the publishers will not have money to offer authors, much less to advance for a book not yet completed."

Gangland—four years in the rewriting

Although a first novel may indeed be completed when signed up by an editor, that doesn't necessarily mean it's ready for publication. Lee Goerner signed a contract with David Winn for his first novel, *Gangland*, and worked with Winn on three versions of the novel before it was finally published. "Publishing is also about setting up a relationship," says Goerner. "Taking on a first novelist depends on the rapport between the author and editor."

Gangland began as a series of short stories which were published in tiny, not just little, magazines such as *Synapse*, *Big Breakfast* and *Thrilling Janitor*. The stories were written while Winn was at the University of California at Irvine as a graduate student, at the University of Colorado as a writing fellow, and finally in 1977 at the Squaw Valley Writers Conference. In Squaw Valley, he met novelist and critic Francine du Plessix Gray, who liked his work, and subsequently mentioned him in a *New York Times Book Review* article on writers' conferences. Soon Winn began to receive mail from publishers and agents. For that reason, he advises a first novelist to make connections. "I know conferences often get laughed at," he says, "but many are very good and you do meet agents and editors who can help you." After reading the article in the *Book Review*, Maureen Howard, whom Winn had previously met at the Colorado Writers Conference, called to congratulate him. She recommended Gloria Loomis, a literary agent who has her own agency in New York. "Good thing she called, because I was very impressed by the Little, Brown and Harper & Row stationery," says Winn. He might have succumbed and gone directly to a publisher without an agent—but he thinks writers need agents. "Publishing is a commercial business and a writer isn't able to look after his own interests."

A persistent agent and lots of luck

Loomis sold *Gangland* within three months. "You must have a persistent agent and a certain amount of luck," says Winn. Although he always felt that he would somehow get published, Winn cites a book by a friend, which he says is "somewhat better than mine," and still hasn't found a publisher after eighteen months.

"Lee Goerner was an extremely fortunate choice as an editor," says Winn. "His sympathetic wit and bedrock realism couldn't be found in all editors. What separates Knopf from other houses is that editors are encouraged to find first novelists."

Bob Gottlieb (Knopf's former Editor-in-Chief) presented Winn's book at sales conferences, which helped to launch it. "Of course I'm concerned about sales," says Winn, "but there's little rhyme or reason to it—it's a hapless attitude to think you can affect sales.

"People are receptive to fiction," says Winn. "Go back to the *Library Journal* articles on first novelists and count how many there are. There has to be an audience and a commitment from publishers if that many first novelists are being given an opportunity to publish. I'm at odds with the shop talk that says there's no market for new fiction. The novel isn't dead. It's changing, vital and alive."

Winn hasn't made a living from writing fiction, though. To supplement his income, he teaches at Hunter College in New York City. "There is a generation and a half of illiterate Americans," he says. "I feel an obligation to teach people to read and write."

The Times: searching out first novels

Gangland was reviewed at the *New York Times* by book review editor Le Anne Schreiber [who has since left the *New York Times Book Review*]. "The single most gratifying thing for me is finding a first novel and taking it on its way to a reviewer or reviewing it myself," says Schreiber. "I get more feedback from reviews I write of first novels than from anything else," she says. "People tell me they buy first novels because they've read my reviews. I don't know how large the market for first novels is, but these readers are certainly engaged and interested in new talent.

"The *Times Book Review* is very interested in reviewing first novels, but time is needed to ferret out a special one—so many are touted by the publishers." says Schreiber. "Sometimes you have to go through five first novels to find one you want to review."

Schreiber thinks fiction is taking a fascinating turn. "In the last ten to fifteen years, fiction has been dominated by sociological concerns. Changes wrought by the women's movement were the subject of the novel. People have been reading for therapy as well as literary pleasures. Maybe this is coming to an end—now there is more possibility for the publication of novels which are less socially narcissistic, more about the creation of imaginative reality or the metaphysical, such as *Housekeeping* and *Gangland*."

Thirty editors who care

"The part of my job that gives me the most pleasure is opening the manuscript box, not knowing what's inside and finding a first novel like *Housekeeping*," says New York literary agent, Ellen Levine. In addition to selling *Housekeeping*, Levine has sold many other first novels. "But fewer publishers are willing to take a risk today—it used to be easier," she says. "You must make the distinction between commercial and literary fiction, though. A first novel that's a horror story, mystery or a family saga, particularly one suitable for paperback publication, may not be as much of a problem to get published. Serious fiction is much harder.

"I have encountered situations in which a sponsoring editor wanted to acquire a first novel—one with an estimated sale of 2,000-5,000 copies—and had to struggle against editorial boards." Levine estimates New York has thirty editors who are really interested in serious first novels. But that doesn't tell the whole story: an editor may care about first fiction but be working for a house that doesn't. Levine believes that "a novel which is appealing, shows talent and promise in a writer, but is not necessarily a masterpiece or a little jewel, might in better times have been published just to introduce a writer to the reading public."

Levine agrees there is an audience for fiction, but is unhappy about the cost of hardcover fiction. "Good reviews attract a reader, but that reader might be a college student or someone who can't afford $13.95 or $14.95 for a first novel. We must re-think the format—perhaps first novels should be published in trade paperback, making these books available at $5.95 or $7.95. When paperbacks are reviewed regularly, perhaps mass-market paperback houses will think about consistently publishing original serious fiction. In fact, several houses such as Bantam and Avon have already begun to do so.

"Although there are more agents than ever, it's more difficult to find an agent for first novels because it's so hard to place first novels," says Levine. "Agents are more likely to take on nonfiction writers."

For first novelists having a difficult time, Levine recommends the small press. "The small press is a growing phenomenon fulfilling a need," she says. "The advances are more modest, the printings smaller, and distribution isn't the same, but it's worth a try. After twenty commerical publishing houses have turned down a book, I try the small press. When you love a book, you can't give up. If a writer gets a first book published by the small press, perhaps the bigger publishers will pay attention to the second novel." Levine cited small presses such as North Point, Creative Arts, Capra, Ecco and Persea, and university presses such as Pittsburgh, Louisiana State and Illinois.

"I always tell a first novelist what I think his or her chances are at the beginning," says Levine. Still, she advises, "Don't be discouraged. The main thing is not to give up. More than a few houses will stay committed to first fiction. As long as people like us are around, first fiction will get published."

66 *To me a novel is something that's built around the character of time, the nature of time, and the effects that time has on events and characters. When I see a novel that's supposed to take place in twenty-four hours, I just wonder why the man padded out the short story.* **99**
—*Frank O'Connor*

—— *Cover Letters and Queries: When and Why?*

by Laurie Henry

Cover Letters

The letter below combines aspects of the worst of all the cover letters described by the 315 little/literary magazine editors and 89 commercial periodical editors who responded to a recent *Novel and Short Story Writer's Market* survey on the subject. Needless to say, a note like this one is unlikely to encourage any editor to give a story a second look.

> To Whom it May Concern:
>
> I've never seen your magazine but here is an unpublished story I had in my files. It has been rejected by many other publications, and you are my last chance. I am also sending it to 6 other magazines. It is not my best story (which I sent to The New Yorker because it is a better magazine).
>
> The story is about an adventure my cats had, but symbolicly it is really about life itself. Do'nt worry—the dog is caught in the end (page 65). I have 2 cats, named Shakspear and Hemminway, only I just found out, Shakspear is really a girl!!!!! My freinds say I am as good as Falkner, and I know this is true. You are lucky I sent you this. I know you will buy it, so I am not including a SASE, because you or your staff might just tare off the stamp and use it. I'll slit my writsts if you don't buy first North American serial rights for $1,000, even though you 'claim' you only pay in copies.
>
> Your freind,
> A. Writer

Still, most editors really do prefer to receive some kind of letter along with the story submitted to them. In fact, two hundred and twenty of the literary magazine editors (70%) and 54 of the commercial magazine editors (60%) said they appreciated receiving cover letters. As Margaret Ann Roth, editor of *The Boston Review* says, "The cover letter is really to the writer's advantage; it sometimes brings the entire submission to the top of the pile." Only 10 editors said they actively dislike cover letters—others said it didn't make a difference to them one way or another.

Most of the listings in *Novel and Short Story Writer's Market* do say whether an editor prefers a cover letter, and, if so, what the editor looks for—not surprisingly, the type of preferred letter varies a great deal from editor to editor. Still, most agree on a few basic points.

Brevity

The word "brief" appeared in 68 magazine editors' suggestions for good cover letters. In no case should a cover letter be longer than a page; in most cases, you'll want to be much briefer than that. Tess Gallagher, whose published work includes *Amplitude: New & Selected*

Laurie Henry *is the editor of* Novel and Short Story Writer's Market. *Her fiction and poetry have appeared in* Silverfish Review, Missouri Review, Antioch Review, Poetry, Poetry Northwest *and* American Poetry Review.

Poems (Graywolf Press, 1987), *The Lover of Horses* (Harper & Row, 1986) and *Willingly* (Graywolf Press, 1984), says, "Since the work is the main convincing element, the letter should be short. No more than five lines, I should think." And Scott Russell Sanders, author of *The Paradise of Bombs* (University of Georgia Press, 1987), *Stone Country* (Indiana University Press, 1985) and *Fetching the Dead* (University of Illinois Press, 1984), says, "In general, for writers of fiction, I think the less you say in a cover letter, the better. If the fiction draws upon some body of knowledge or experience to which you have special access, you might mention that. Be as brief, precise, and unpretentious as you can."

Previous publications

Tess Gallagher says, "I mention whether the story is part of a book about to be published. I may also give an idea of where I've published previously if the editor is unfamiliar with my work." Indeed, most editors like to hear about the writer's previous publications, although some hasten to add, like Richard Behm, managing editor of *The Northern Review*, that this information is only requested in order to "save time in requesting a contributor's note should we take the story"—and does not affect the acceptance or rejection process. In theory anyway, a lack of previous publications won't work against a good story, and most editors agree with Bruce W. Hozeski, editor in chief of *Ball State University Forum*, that "previous publications are not necessary, but mention of previous publications helps." Listing any previous fiction publications probably will get you a closer reading at most magazines than you might have had otherwise; editors are human and most will be reassured to know that other editors have also been impressed by your work.

A few editors say they are completely indifferent to whether a writer has published fiction previously—as Deborah Pursifull, managing editor of *The Pennsylvania Review*, says, "I'm interested in the work that is sent, and not in knowing where the writer has published previously." And mentioning *some* previous publications might actually hurt. Meg Mac Donald, editor of *Pandora* says, for example, that the "inclusion of irrelevant publication credits, i.e. nonfiction, vanity press, etc." is a mistake she often sees in cover letters. In general, mention nonfiction publications only if you are writing for a specialized market—such as children's magazines. Editor Elizabeth A. Rinck, of *Children's Digest*, for example, suggests the inclusion of "any special knowledge the writer might have of his or her subject matter."

Most editors see no advantage in a writer's listing more than four previous publications. C. Michael Curtis, senior editor of *The Atlantic Monthly*, for example, remarks that too lengthy a list of prior publications is a common mistake he sees.

If you have more than four previous publications, choose either the most prestigious magazines in which your fiction has appeared, or else those most relevant to the type of publication to which you're now sending work—science fiction publications, if you're now submitting to a science fiction magazine, for example. Unless you're currently a high school student, don't mention high school literary magazines, and avoid mentioning any publications to which only a few people (members of your writer's group, or people who live in a certain city) are eligible to submit.

What about beginners?

Not all writers face the problem of choosing which previous publications to list in a cover letter. Editors are divided as to whether beginners should admit that they have never published anything at all, but most really do want to encourage new writers and are excited—at least initially—to hear from any new *talented* fiction writer. Askold Melnyczuk, editor of the *Agni Review,* suggests, for example, "if the writer is really a beginner, or a student, mentioning that might be helpful," and Eleanor Sullivan, editor of *Ellery Queen's Mystery Magazine*, says, "We especially like to know if the story would represent the author's first professional published fiction should we buy it."

On the other hand, Steven Brady, editor of *Cache Review*, says that a common mistake is "beginners admitting they're beginners," and Jeannette M. Hopper, editor of *Gas*, says, "beginning writers should not tell an editor that they've never been published."

There's no shame in being unpublished—everyone was a beginner once. Some editors do look askance, though, at a writer who mentions having been submitting work for 20 years without an acceptance. If you have been sending out stories for several years but have not yet had anything published, it is best not to mention that fact. If you've just begun to send out your fiction and want an editor to know this, on the other hand, try putting it in a positive light—for example, "I've just begun to send out my work and hope you find it of interest."

Personal Information

Next to information about publishing credits, editors most often ask for personal information about the writer. Specialized magazines do this most frequently, and unless a listing states otherwise, it's a good idea to say something about your ties to the subject or region of a magazine to editors of periodicals ranked *IV* in this book. Anne Dinnan, editor of *Christian Living for Senior Highs*, says, "Writers should include a word about their Christian commitment and their experience with senior highs." Valerie Eads, editor of *Fighting Woman News*, says, "It's always nice to have a bit of info on the writer's background in the martial arts. Makes it easier to focus any suggestions."

C. Michael Curtis of *The Atlantic Monthly*, says "cover letters are sometimes helpful, particularly if they cite prior publications or involvement in writing programs." If you are or have been a student in a graduate-level writing program, it's a good idea to say so: many editors are particularly open to writers who have attended these programs. If you have taken a single night school course, or are a member of a writer's group to which there are no particular admissions standards, however, don't bother mentioning that in a cover letter—unless, say, it's a mystery-writing group, and you're submitting a mystery to a very small magazine.

Reta Finger, editor of *Daughters of Sarah*, says she "Generally prefers the human touch," and this is a concept that recurs again and again, especially with editors of smaller magazines. Frederick A. Raborg, Jr., editor of *Amelia* goes on to say, "An honest display of personality is helpful, because it often helps to define the approach to a story." And Pat Schneider, of *Peregrine*, says cover letters "should sound like a real human being talking to another real human being. Putting out a small literary journal is hard, sacrificial volunteer work. We're human, and appreciate letters which seem to reflect a real person." Editors who are also the publishers/typesetters/proofreaders/designers of their magazines tend to be especially interested in personal—even chatty—cover letters. This may seem odd, since it's these editors who probably have the least amount of time to spend reading cover letters—but really it's the editors of one-person publications who are often most interested in knowing that someone appreciates their work.

Not all editors of small publications want to know everything about their authors, at least not right away. As Molly Giles, whose *Rough Translations* won the 1985 Flannery O'Connor Award for Short Fiction from the University of Georgia Press, remarks, "I have only one basic rule for my students at San Francisco State: 'Don't tell the names of your cats.' Don't get too personal, too cute, or—it happens so easily with beginning writers—too pathetic."

It's a good idea to try to let the personal information you provide in a letter relate at least tangentially to your writing background or to your story. Karen Campbell, editor of *Writers' Rendezvous*, for example, discourages "extraneous comments (e.g. 'I am the father of one and a second due next week')," but welcomes personal details that relate to the story, "(e.g., 'I am a legal secretary who has been around law offices for 10 years,' for a manuscript dealing with law or lawyers)."

Kelly Cherry, author of *Natural Theology* (Louisiana State University Press, 1987), *Conversion* (McPherson & Co., 1979) and *Relativity: A Point of View* (Louisiana State University

Press, 1977), sums up of the advice of many editors: "Don't be weirdly casual; be brief and professional; but don't be stiffly formal either. Again, it was time that taught me this. Unless you're from a privileged—say, Ivy League—background, you're apt, like me, to begin by thinking of editors as powerful, all-wise authority figures to be pleased and placated. Eventually, though, you grow older and they grow younger—sometimes, like doctors and lawyers, astonishingly young—and from this changed perspective, you perceive them at last as just people. Best to write to them as such."

Why this magazine?

Tess Gallagher says, "It is good to let the editor know you have *chosen* the story for *that particular* magazine and this means *reading* the magazines before sending!" and most editors agree. If you're sending to *The New Yorker* or any other large-circulation periodical, of course, it would sound strange if you mentioned how you heard about the magazine or why you're sending your work there: your reasons are pretty obvious. If you're sending to a little magazine you *never* heard of before seeing a listing in *Novel and Short Story Writer's Market*, though, you'll find most editors interested in knowing just how you decided to submit to them. Noemie Maxwell, co-editor of *Sub Rosa*, says, "We like cover letters because we are curious about the people who send us work, and because we like to feel that the author has chosen *Sub Rosa* as a possible place to publish for rational or even whimsical reasons rather than as part of a statistical ploy to send to as many (unknown) magazines as possible." And Betsey McDougall, managing editor of *Southwest Review*, comments, "A cover letter is some reassurance that the author has taken the time to check a current directory for the editor's name. Where there isn't a cover letter we wonder whether the same story is on 20 other desks around the country."

Editors of very small magazines are sensitive to the fact that there are more people who want to write for them than who want to read them—but don't presume that editors of commercial periodicals aren't also interested in your knowledge of the magazine. As Marc Silver, editor of *B'nai B'rith Jewish Monthly*, says, "A writer who submits a manuscript without a cover letter doesn't seem to have an awareness of/interest in our publication."

If you really are a regular—or occasional—reader of a very small magazine, mention that in your cover letter, rather than simply that you heard about the magazine in *Novel and Short Story Writer's Market*. If you've never even seen a sample copy, it's best to avoid the issue entirely.

About the story

Most editors don't want to read *about* the story in a cover letter before they read the story itself—they want to be free to make up their own minds. As Clint McCown, editor of the *Beloit Fiction Journal*, says, "Cover letters can be helpful, but not when they attempt to give a plot synopsis or psychological analysis of the story. Ultimately no cover letter will help a weak story or hurt a good one." Editors also agree with Nancy Peavler, editor of *Capper's*, who says, "Cover letters shouldn't try to convince us to buy the story; only the story itself can do that."

Mechanics

James Gunn, author of *Crisis* (Tor, 1986), *The Listeners* (Ballantine, 1985), and *Tiger! Tiger!*, (Chris Drumm Books, 1984), says, "I've never found cover letters useful unless the circumstances of the story are not self-explanatory: it is part of a series, say, or timeliness is important—it will be published as part of a novel soon, or it is a multiple submission because the subject may vanish from the news." Occasionally, you too might need to include a cover letter with a submission even to an editor who might not really want one, because it's important that the editor know something in particular about you or your work. Helen DelMonte, fiction editor of *McCall's*, says, for example, "If some other editor has recommended *McCalls*, tell us that." Don't mention this kind of information in a letter, of course, unless the editor who suggested the other market is someone this editor is likely to respect. And Lou Thomas, editor of *FirstHand Magazine*, says cover letters are "a must" because so many *FirstHand* writers use pseudonyms, and it's important to be absolutely sure that the payment check is made out to the right person.

Patricia Pingry, vice president and publisher of *Ideals*, wants to know about any restriction on rights offered. If you are submitting a story that has already been published elsewhere, it's vital to include this information. Note, however, that any other information about rights offered is not usually appropriate in a cover letter sent with a submission to a literary magazine—as Robert R. Ward, editor of *Bellowing Ark* states, "I always just cringe when I see a letter stating the 'rights' offered!" Most literary magazine editors take it for granted that your story has never been published elsewhere, and that you would ask the original publisher for permission before submitting it to another magazine.

If you're submitting a manuscript to a contest offered by a magazine, mention that, or risk the problem Ben Johnston, editor of *The Associate Reformed Presbyterian*, describes: "In a couple of instances this year we returned stories which were intended for our contest, simply because the would-be contestants were not aware of the contest rules."

Stanley Schmidt, editor of *Analog Science Fiction/Science Fact* wants to be reminded if a story "is a rewrite I suggested, or if the piece is already scheduled for book publication," and Martha Roth, co-executive editor of *Hurricane Alice*, says, "writers should be sure to tell us if a piece was commissioned by one of the editors."

Bad typing

Sloppiness of any kind will lessen the chances of your manuscript being read—editors seeing a badly spelled, punctuated and typed cover letter are usually justified in expecting a poorly spelled, punctuated and typed manuscript as well—and bad spelling, punctuation and typing—rightly or wrongly—are often used to judge the abilities of a writer. Stan Goredon, editor of *Tyro*, complains that "cover letters are often handwritten notes rather than proper business letters." And Lisa Roose Church, editor of *Poetry Magic* says she sees "too many typing errors and spelling errors."

Editors sometimes ask to be told in cover letters whether the story is a simultaneous submission—and if you know that a magazine accepts simultaneous submissions, it's only polite to provide this information. Obviously, if you are simultaneously submitting a manuscript to a publication that does *not* accept simultaneous submissions, you are not helping yourself by mentioning that fact. If you submit a multiple submission to a magazine that does not accept them, you are, of course, risking great irritation by the editor if you are found out. If you are *not* simultaneously submitting a story to a magazine that does not accept simultaneous submissions, you might want to reassure the editor of that fact in your letter.

Critiques

Unless you have reason to believe that the editor enjoys critiquing manuscripts—like Liz Shaw, editor of *Adara*, who says, "If you ask for a critique, I'll be glad to give you one," don't ask for criticism of your story. Barbara Cunningham, editor of *Catholic Forester*, explains that "many writers ask for comments on their stories and want to be told why the stories were rejected. We understand how they feel and are sympathetic, but to explain all the things wrong with a story, or why we can't use it, or how they could improve it is much too time consuming. In many cases we would just be acting as a teacher, and editors really don't have time to also be teachers." Scott Sanders agrees, saying, "Don't ask for critical advice. Editors are in the business of evaluating manuscripts, and they don't like having their elbows nudged. And if they have the time and interest to offer critical advice, they will do so without being asked. *All* editors have too much to read. Let your fiction speak for itself."

Responding to personalized rejections

If an editor rejects your story but offers encouraging words and asks you to submit again, by all means do so. No editor makes this kind of request insincerely. Once you have received a personalized rejection from an editor, it is definitely to your advantage to make the relationship between you and the editor a little more personal. A remark like "thank you for your comments on *What the Butcher Saw*; here's a new story, *Killer in Kentucky*" can remind the editor of your previous work and bring your story to the top of a pile. As Michael Martone, author of *Alive & Dead in Indiana* (Knopf, 1984), says, "An important letter is the one that begins an exchange between writer and editor after the manuscript has been returned. If an editor has taken the time to dash a note while rejecting, the writer should respond directly, even without a new manuscript. It is a lonely business being a writer. And it is lonely being an editor. Correspondences outside the business exchange are things of value, something to be desired."

Some editors might even think you impolite if you *don't* respond to a personal note, as Kelly Cherry states: "Eventually, I arrived at a point where editors knew my name, and I knew their names, and at that point, the question of whether or not to enclose a cover letter answered itself: it seemed rude to address a manuscript to somebody in particular without acknowledging his or her existence by a cover letter."

Serious mistakes

Here's a roundup of some of the worst mistakes editors have seen in cover letters recently:
- Nathasha Brooks, editor, *Jive/Intimacy*: "Writers try to be cute in their letters or tell me they're not black." [8 editors mentioned the word "cute" as a negative factor in the cover letters they see.]
- Mark Williamson, fiction editor, *Easyriders*: "Don't tell us friends really liked it."
- Edie Clark, fiction editor, *Yankee Magazine*: "If the writer has no publishing history, it is pointless (yet some do) to go on for 3 paragraphs about how you don't but wish you did."
- Sheila Williams, managing editor, *Isaac Asimov's Science Fiction Magazine*: "Don't tell us if the story's been rejected elsewhere."
- A.E. Burke, editor, *The Prairie Journal of Canadian Literature*: "People tell me they sent their best work elsewhere, so I wonder why they are sending me their worst."
- Ruth Berman, assistant editor, *Sing Heavenly Muse*: Being too "hard sell—saying 'you will love this.' " ["Hard sell" methods are always inappropriate. Molly Giles mentions an unsuccessful cover letter she once wrote: "Here it is! At last! The story you've been waiting for!"—describing it as an attempt that "failed on contact."]
- Andy Solomon, fiction editor, *Tampa Review*: "Unnecessary length and extremes of tone, arrogant or overly humble."
- Jason Sherman, editor, *What*: "Never write: 'Publish this or I'll blow my brains out' or 'This is my last chance.' "
- Christopher B. Hughes, editor, *The Magazine for Christian Youth*: "Don't disclose that you want to be a writer. That is obvious."
- Ellen Datlow, fiction editor, *Omni Magazine*: "Never address an editor by the first name unless you have met him/her and are on a first-name basis because of that meeting."
- Valerie Eads, editor, *Fighting Woman News*: "Stating outright 'I've never seen your magazine,' is a very common mistake, as is 'here are some unpublished pieces I had in my files.' "

Query letters

If you have not yet finished a novel or a story collection, you may not yet be concerned with query letters. But most publishers of books do look for query letters before a complete manuscript is sent. Rosalyn Drexler, whose books include *Transients Welcome* (Broadway Play

Publishing, 1984) and *Bad Guy* (E.P. Dutton, 1982), suggests, "I think a letter asking permission to send an outline and 40 pages might work." Barbara Grier, vice president and general manager, of Naiad Press, says, "No one has time to look at piles of manuscripts to the ceiling, and we are fast approaching that stage." And David M. Harris, executive editor of Omeiga, points out, "A novel that comes complete and unannounced will wait until someone has time to look at it—possibly months." The most common—though not universal—exception to the rule of sending query letters before entire manuscripts is with editors of children's books; a number of children's book editors do prefer to see the complete manuscript right away.

You should send your letter to a specific editor, if possible; if no name is listed in *Novel and Short Story Writer's Market*, call the publisher and ask for the name of the acquisitions editor. If it's impossible for some reason to learn the name of the acquisitions editor, send your query to "Fiction Editor"—and then, if you receive a go-ahead to submit the complete manuscript, address it to the person who answers your letter.

Brevity is not always the key with a query letter, as Toni Simmons, editor of Ballantine/Epiphany Books says: "A common mistake is to try to describe a lengthy novel in a brief query letter without including a synopsis! It's impossible to assess a novel from a writer's brief description." Many other editors also prefer a synopsis or outline sent along with a query letter—and the amount of material desired varies with each editor. Here are some book editors' preferences as to what they like to see from an author who is contacting the company for the first time:

• John Ruemmler, editor, Iron Crown Enterprises: "A good query is 1-2 pages and outlines the plot, characters and 'hook' of the book."
• Susann Brailey, administrative editor, Loveswept/Bantam Books: "Query letters should be no more than 2 to 3 pages. Content should be a brief description of the plot and the two main characters. Writers should be familiar with the Loveswept line before submitting." [Note that most romance book publishers print up "tip sheets" for potential authors; these are available for a SASE.]
• Nachama H. Loeshelle, associate editor, Margaret K. McElderry Books: "In the case of a novel, we feel it is also helpful for us to receive a sample chapter along with the query letter."
• Irene Zahava, editor, WomanSleuth series, Crossing Books: "I don't want to receive a completed manuscript if it is unsolicited. Prefer chapter outline or synopsis and 3-4 sample chapters."
• John Oakes, co-publisher, Four Walls Eight Windows: "Query letter accompanied by sample chapter and SASE is best."
• Laurie Schneider, publisher, Score Publications: "Writers should send a short 1-2 page sample from manuscript. Since we publish only nontraditional forms, writers *must* query."
• June Cussen, executive editor, Pineapple Press: "1-page synopsis and sample chapters, including the first chapter."
• Leora Zeitlin/Ed Hogan, editors, Zephyr Press: "We prefer a sample chapter with a query letter to give us a sense of the writer's style and writing ability, as well as the plot."
• Roberta Kalechofsky, general editor, Micah Publications: "Send 30 pages of writing and outline."
• Lee Anne Martin, associate editor, Farrar, Straus and Giroux: "Query letter plus 3 sample chapters."
• Betsy Uhrig, editor, Faber and Faber: "Prefer query and 1 or 2 sample chapters. Require synopsis/description—cannot consider manuscripts without this. Many beginning writers make the mistake of submitting entire manuscript without even a cover letter."
• Janna E. Silverstein, assistant editor, Bantam Spectra/Doubleday Foundation: "We prefer to see query letters first including a couple of paragraphs summarizing the story."
• Ted Griffin, managing editor, Crossway Books: "Queries first. Include synopsis and 2 sample chapters."

If you do send sample chapters, remember that almost all editors want *consecutive* sample chapters—it's hard to follow the plot of a novel if only the first, middle and last chapter are included.

Take time to write it

As James Gunn points out: "Books are a big investment of time, and queries about books are a reasonable way to budget time." Don't write your query letter without giving it as much time as it deserves—it's important to take the time to make it look as professional as possible. Karen Palmer, packager/editor of Bogie's Mystery Books, notes that "beginning authors often send poorly written letters, which are taken as an example of their writing ability." And Charles W. Oddo, vice president of Oddo Publishing, says, "Beginning writers tend not to send manuscripts prepared in a neat and organized manner." Alice Harron Orr, fiction editor at Walker and Company, notes that common mistakes are "sounding unprofessional (i.e. too chatty, too braggardly)."

Your letter should be a formal business letter, without typographical or spelling errors, or unnecessary digressions. A helpful book is Lisa Collier Cool's *How to Write Irresistible Query Letters*, published by Writer's Digest Books. Note that most editors prefer *not* to be phoned by writers with whom they haven't worked previously.

Mechanics

Feroze Mohammed, senior editor at Worldwide Library, says that authors "should try as best they can to establish the category or genre in which their novel fits." This will ensure that your book is sent along to the right editor and is an important step if you are sending a genre manuscript to a house that publishes many different types of genres.

Remember too that some publishers print up specific guidelines for writers. Lyn Miller-Lachman, of Square One Publishers, says, "Read our guidelines to make sure your manuscript is going to the right place."

Jerry Gold, editor of Black Heron Books, says, "A query letter should tell me: 1) number of words 2) number of pages 3) is manuscript available on floppy disk 4) have parts of novel been published? 5) where?" For a book, your estimated word count does not have to be too exact—if you can get it to the nearest thousand words, that's fine. Check the Manuscript Mechanics chapter (page 131) for a description of how to estimate your manuscript's word count.

Writer's qualifications

It's important to establish your credibility as a writer as quickly as possible in your query letter—and this means both mentioning your writing experience and avoiding making statements that will make the editor question your competence. If you've had anything published, you'll want to mention it—even publications not related to your current project, if you've published no fiction in the past. As Jean Campbell, Starblaze editor, says, "Writers need to list their writing experience in a cover letter."

James R. Hepworth, publisher of Confluence Press, says, "We especially welcome reviews of writers' previous books, publication histories and résumés." And Lee Smith, assistant editor at Ecco Press, looks for "prior publications, education."

Michael R. Hutcheson, publisher of Green Street Press, advises, "The cover letter should be straightforward, honest and avoid displays of hubris." Remember—you're writing to a human being! And Toni Simmons of Ballantine/Epiphany Books, says, "It looks amateurish when a writer states that his/her work is copywritten and when he/she states an expected advance." Don't mention which other publishers have already rejected your manuscript—unless another editor has particularly recommended you send it to another house.

Relevance to list

Your letter should also reflect that fact that you have a good knowledge of what kind of books the company publishes. As John Ruemmler of Iron Crown Enterprises points out, "Most beginning writers do not study our specialized market—interactive fiction, or quest-books, which are as much games as they are fiction." And Gregg Fedshak, publisher of Night Tree Press, asks that authors reflect how their manuscripts "relate to the far north country of New York State." Mistakes he sees in query letters include "incredibly inept marketing; pornography, craft books proposals; novels set in Albania—we're a *regional* press, damn it!" It's a good idea to look at a publisher's catalog before sending a query letter—publishers that seem at a casual glance to be good bets for your manuscript might not turn out to be after all. Jenny Wrenn, publisher of Clothespin Fever Press, says, for example, "Most writers assume that since we are a lesbian publisher that we publish work on AIDS. Our audience is not gay male and therefore we are not interested in the topic of AIDS."

Marketing

Edward Field, poet and author of the novel *Village* under the pseudonym Bruce Elliot, says, "In writing the cover letter for a novel proposal (along with a synopsis and/or outline, plus sample chapter), I think one ought to include a brief summary of the book in a sentence or two. It might also be helpful to make clear what audience the book would appeal to, for not many books are published these days that do not have a sales potential." Editors at commercial publishers do welcome some indication that authors know their books are supposed to make a profit both for themselves and the publishing company.

Mark Plunkett, director of Standard Publishing, suggests that query letters "should include synopsis and general description of perceived market," a good idea for writers submitting to most publishing houses. Michael Hutcheson of Green Street Press (which does not require an advance query), says, "One common error in the query letters we do receive is that they are too general. The information most often omitted is: for what audience is the work written? (There is a world of difference between Beverly Cleary's account of what it is like to be 17 and J.D. Salinger's); and, what is the tone of the work?"

Note, however, that it's possible to go too far with your marketing ideas: Regina Griffin, senior editor of Apple, Point and Scholastic Books, says, "Query letters should describe the genre of the book (mystery, sci-fi, etc.) and give a brief plot description. One common mistake I see is that I get letters that go on and on about marketing possibilities, but neglect to describe the book at all. This makes me feel I'm dealing with someone who wants to be a 'writer' but doesn't really take writing seriously enough."

Someday you can stop

Asked about the query letters he's written, Isaac Asimov states, "I'm afraid I can't be very useful to you. I have never written a query letter in my life. Publishers have written query letters *to me*, but that's their problem. As for covering letters, I just write: 'Here is the manuscript I promised you. Please send check as soon as you can.' That's not very useful either, is it?" Not exactly useful—but encouraging, in a way. Someday you might not have to bother about cover letters and queries either. In the meantime, while taking a little care in your correspondence may not mean the difference between an acceptance and a rejection (although it just might), certainly your letters *can* help bring about a faster editorial response time and could result in a closer relationship between you and an editor. Ultimately, however, your work has to speak for itself, as Greg Ruggiero, editor of *Open Magazine* reminds us: "Whether a cover letter is brilliant, funny, memorable or dumb, in the end it is a writer's work that gets scrutinized and discussed. Following the guidelines espoused by the latest 'how to' article makes for efficient but ultimately unmemorable letters. To thine own self be true."

Payout Schedules: Getting paid

by Richard Curtis

While the size of the advance is the criterion by which most authors measure the commercial value of their books, the size and timing of the installments in which the advance is paid are just as significant, and sometimes more so. Because the "payout schedule" directly affects the cash flow of publishers and authors, it is often a bone of bitter contention in negotiations, and many a player has walked away from an otherwise good deal because the payout schedule nullified advantages gained in the negotiation.

With few exceptions, advances are paid in installments. Part of the total money is payable upon signing the contract, the balance payable on acceptance of partial, complete or revised manuscript; on certain calendar dates; on publication; and even after publication. Although the payout formula may be fairly simple when the advance is small, publishers and agents devote a great deal of attention to it when the stakes get high. The reason, of course, is the cost of money.

Until recently, when the inflation rate ground to a comfortably low single-digit crawl, it could be projected that the value of one thousand dollars deferred for one year was nine hundred dollars. At the same time, double-digit interest rates until late 1985 appreciated the value of that thousand dollars to something like twelve hundred in a year. Thus, between inflation and interest, a year's postponement of payout to an author meant a swing of some thirty percent in the value of that money.

Both interest rates and inflation have, at this writing at any rate, returned to manageable levels, but for both publishers and authors, even ten percent per annum is worth fighting over and may indeed make a significant difference to their balance sheets.

Payment before publication

Let's take a closer look at payout schedules installment by installment and sketch some ways authors may improve their position when the haggling begins.

Payment due on signing of the contract. All contracts large and small require a consideration to be paid on signing, even if it be no more than one dollar, in order to bind the agreement. If the total advance is small enough, it may be payable in full upon signing. Most publishers today, however, have policies prohibiting payment in full on signing, and editors are ordered to defer some part of the advance in negotiation. Even if your book is a flawless gem requiring not a jot of revision, an editor may contrive to pay a second installment of your advance "upon acceptance of revisions" in order to satisfy company policy. Then, a week or two after vouchering the signature installment, the editor will put through the acceptance installment as well.

If the book is a commissioned work, the advance will be divided at least into an on-signing payment and an acceptance one to create an incentive for the author to deliver the book. The publisher may try to divide the advance even further, into installments payable on delivery of a partial manuscript or first draft.

Richard Curtis *is a New York agent. The above article is excerpted from his forthcoming book,* Beyond the Bestseller: A Literary Agent Takes You Inside Publishing.

You will have to do some solid reckoning before accepting too small an installment on signing; otherwise, you'll run out of money before you turn in material qualifying you for the next installment. First you must subtract your agent's commission if any, then calculate the amount of time that will pass until you are entitled to the next payment. You then have to figure whether your living costs (including anticipated lump sum payments like school tuition, income taxes, or insurance premiums) during that period will be covered by what you collect when you sign your contract. A $50,000 advance may seem attractive to you, but if your publisher wants to pay you $10,000 on signing and it takes you six months to write the book, and your monthly net is $3,000, you're gong to be up the creek halfway through the writing of the book. So you must bargain hard for a down-payment that will sustain you until you've turned your manuscript in.

Payment due upon delivery of partial manuscripts or first draft. These installments are generally known in the book trade as "satisfactory progress" payments. To help bridge the gap between the on-signing and the acceptance checks, and to encourage or compel progress, publishers frequently negotiate installments payable when the author turns in part of the book. A typical deal might be structured: One third on signing the contract, one third on delivery of half the manuscript, and one third on delivery and acceptance of the complete manuscript.

Of the many ploys cooked up by publishers to stretch out their money, Satisfactory Progress is the shabbiest, and if it weren't so dangerous it would be just plain silly. At the very least, Satisfactory Progress is satisfactory neither to authors nor publishers, and the only thing it does for progress is halt it.

In a Satisfactory Progress situation, an author faces a number of choices, all of them terrible. *Regardez*: he can turn in a rough draft, which is usually an embarrassing mess that will send most editors into respiratory arrest, or at least provoke them to request revisions that the author would ordinarily make on his own when tackling the final draft. Or he can stop work in the middle of the book, polish and retype what he's done so far, and turn a partial manuscript in. Either way, he will have to suspend work on his book until he has received some feedback from his editor. Even if his editor offers no feedback whatever, it may take weeks or longer to get that editorial reaction, and such delays are inevitably harmful to creativity and cash flow. If the editor does have criticisms, the author may be required to rework what he's turned in in order to get his hands on that money. To avoid all that hassle, therefore, an author may choose to forego his Satisfactory Progress payment and forge ahead with the rest of the book, which defeats the purpose of such interim payments. Most authors do not polish chapters after drafting them, but prefer to finish a rough draft and polish it in the final draft. Thus the time between the completion of a first draft and final draft, or delivery of half the manuscript and all of it, may be of such brief duration that the machinery for putting through the Satisfactory Progress installment will scarcely have begun turning when it will be time to put through the final acceptance payment. Furthermore, many editors feel it's silly to read a partial manuscript or first draft when the final product will be turned in a few weeks or a month later.

In short, Satisfactory Progress payments reflect little understanding of how authors work, and pose a genuine threat to both the quality of a book and the timeliness of its delivery. Ultimately, this ends up hurting the publisher as badly as it hurts the author.

If there is no way that you can avoid this onerous arrangement, at least negotiate for a time limit on editorial approval of your partial manuscript. If you've had no word in, say, two weeks then the material you've turned in should be deemed satisfactory and the check due at that time must be vouchered.

Payment due on acceptance of the manuscript. Whenever possible, the balance of the advance on a commissioned book should be payable no later than upon acceptance. A number of contracts stipulate that a manuscript is deemed acceptable unless the publisher notifies the author to the contrary within a period of time, 30 days, 60 days, or thereabouts. This is a very desirable feature and one worth fighting for if it does not appear in the boiler plate of your contract.

In most contracts the definition of acceptability embraces revisions. If serious revisions are required by a publisher, the acceptance segment of the advance may be delayed until satisfactory revisions are turned in. If the revisions are minor, however, the publisher can often be prevailed upon to put through the acceptance money and take it on faith that the author will turn in acceptable revisions. There is an in-between state where revisions are necessary but the author cannot afford to do them with some sort of financial relief. In such cases the publisher may be persuaded to release some of the acceptance money to carry the author during the revision period.

I've expressed myself in a previous column about the prevailing requirement in publishing contracts that an author must repay the on-signing installment of his advance if his manuscript is rejected. In case you've forgotten—I think it stinks. The on-signing advance should be regarded as a forfeitable investment, not a refundable loan.

Payment after publication

Payments due on publication. The purpose of publication installments is to enable publishers to start recouping what they've paid the author as soon as possible after disbursing his advance. Publication payments used to be the norm in American publishing. Then the rise of strong agents in the 1960s drove publication payments out of favor. But when money started to get expensive again in the 1970s publishers pushed the agents back, and it is now common for publication installments to be paid. In some foreign countries such as England, the publication installment is an article of faith.

The most common mistake authors make when agreeing to publication payments in a negotiation is failing to fix a time limit on them. Unacceptable language is, "$5,000 payable upon publication of the Work." Acceptable: "$5,000 payable upon publication of the Work or twelve months after acceptance, whichever date is sooner." The reason should become obvious if you think it through. Few contracts require publication of a book in fewer than twelve months after its acceptance, and many allow for publication in eighteen or even twenty-four months. Tacked on to these times are grace periods giving publishers an additional six months or more beyond the deadline to publish the work upon notification by the author that the deadline has passed. A publication payment may therefore not be due for as much as three years after a book has been accepted.

What is worse, publication of a book may be cancelled entirely for any of a number of reasons: staff changes, new policies, or events or trends that date the book. That means that the publication portion of the advance will not be payable at all, at least not according to the publisher's interpretation of the contract. I don't know if the point has been tested in court, but it can certainly be argued that if you sell a book to a publisher for $25,000 and the publisher cancels publication—well, you *still* sold the book for $25,000 even if some of that sum was to have been paid, for the publisher's convenience, on publication. Therefore, whenever you negotiate a publication advance, you should always stipulate that the installment will be due on publication *or X months after acceptance, whichever date comes first.* The X is negotiable, but should be no longer than the outside date by which the publisher is required to publish your book.

Post-publication payments. Publishers have devised a fascinating array of gimmicks to postpone the day of reckoning to authors. Among these is the post-publication advance. Such installments may be payable on a specific date—X months after publication, say—or, in the case of a hardcover-softcover deal, one installment may be payable when the hardcover edition is published, another when the paperback edition is brought out. There are other creative variations on this theme, but because a book begins earning royalties from the date it's shipped, all post-publication advances amount to the same thing: paying authors with their own money.

Authors may want to try to negotiate payout schedules advantageous to their income tax statuses. An author who had already made a lot of money in a year may not want to receive a large on-signing payment that same year. A deal can be structured, therefore, so that only a token amount is paid on signing and the balance of the on-signing advance paid on January 2nd of the following year. Not surprisingly, publishers like such setups since they enable them to keep authors' money for several months. Literary agents, however, are not always thrilled to have their commissions deferred just because a client is enjoying a good year, so I don't feel your agent is out of line to request his commission on the full on-signing advance now, and to take no commission when your money comes in January. If your agent wants his commission now, he could negotiate $1,000 on signing of the contract to be retained entirely by him as commission (assuming a ten percent commission, then $9,000 payable in January on which he would take no commission at all.

If you do want to structure installments in a way that you feel is advantageous to you tax-wise, and your publisher is agreeable to the arrangement, the time to do it is when your contract is negotiated. If a contract is already in force and you ask your publisher to defer until next January a payment that is due this October because you don't want more money this year, the Internal Revenue Service may disallow it if you are audited and your publishing contract examined. The same holds true of requests to agents to hold money until the following January. The law makes it quite clear that money received by a fiduciary—a literary agent, for example—is construed to have been received by the author. This is not to say that publishers and agents do not hold money for authors in such circumstances, but getting away with it doesn't alter the statutes concerning "constructive receipt," and you may be liable for an adjustment in tax for that year plus interest and penalties.

Not long ago a publisher approached me with an intriguing idea for payout of the advance on a deal with a superstar client. He suggested structuring the terms in the same way that they are structured for superstar ball players to help prevent them from paying too much in taxes in any given year. A million dollar advance, for example, might be payable over twenty years to hold the tax bite down. However well or poorly the book did, the publisher reasoned, and whether the author was working or retired over the next twenty years, he could look forward to a check for $100,000 every year.

I said, "Thanks but no thanks." For one thing, between inflation, interest and revenue earned on the book, the million dollar advance would actually cost the publisher close to nothing. Second, most authors who have achieved superstar status will probably have incorporated themselves, and deferred compensation for corporations is not as desirable as it is for mere mortals. Even if you are nothing more than a working-stiff type writer, it's still a good idea to get as much money up front as you can. A smart agent and a smart accountant will help you to structure your cash flow so that your hide is relatively intact every April 15th. Don't let publishers earn interest on your money. Remember, the sooner you get your hands on it, the sooner you can start blowing it on stupid investments.

You Be the Judge: A Guide to Fiction Contests

by Barbara Wernecke Durkin

I'd always known I loved fiction, especially the short story. I'd built my modest career on it, and therefore felt flattered and delighted when a local literary agent asked me if I'd like to judge her short story contest.

"I _love_ fiction!" I bubbled, falling all over myself to thank her for asking me. "I can't _wait_ to see the manuscripts." As a teacher of writing, I felt doubly qualified to read and evaluate these little 10-page gems. "This is going to be _fun!_" I cried.

The first bundle of manuscripts arrived, and I dove into them face first. The agent's rules before me, I sat down at once to feast upon these treasures.

But wait. The first one was at least five pages over the limit stated clearly in those rules. What should I do? Read it anyway? Disqualify it? I set it aside.

The second one had some interesting characters, but when I got to the end, I found that absolutely nothing had happened. Nothing at all. It was a character study, and not a short story at all. Hmm. I thought I'd better set it aside.

The third story was sweet, a story about a good dog, told from the dog's viewpoint. Not badly written at all, but golly Ned, was it salable in today's market? Gee. Better set it aside and see if my agent friend was interested in stories she could _sell_, or stories she could simply _admire_.

Next came a little slice of life that was interesting, but that went no place. After that, a little slice of out-and-out porn. Gulp. I set those two aside.

There were four more to consider from the first group of submissions. They stared at me from their bland manila folders. I stared back, then averted my eyes in confusion.

Somebody was just going to have to come up with a set of standards for my judging. I couldn't be awarding points willy-nilly on the basis of my personal whims and caprices, depending on the freshness of my eyes, the lateness of the hour, my own prejudices and viewpoints, politics, or level of crabbiness and generosity. This was one job that would have to be done, at least partially, by the numbers.

That same night I set up my personal criteria for judging the short stories for the contest. As I labored over this task, it occurred to me that many of the would-be winners of all the fiction contests in the world would do well to know beforehand what a judge like me might be looking for. I then thought that my own requirements might act as a handy yardstick for all beginning writers of short fiction, since what is an editor if not a "judge"? The writer who has the essentials in mind as she writes should surely stand a better chance of hitting the mark than the totally uninformed.

Here goes, then:

General rules

Has this manuscript come in on time, according to the contest rules? Is it in proper form? Typed, double-spaced, on standard-size paper? Has the contestant followed proper procedure

Barbara Wernecke Durkin _is an instructor for the Institute of Children's Literature and recently served as judge for a fiction contest sponsored by agent Elaine Davie. She is currently working on a novel and a book on the effect of cults on youth._

and format? Enclosed all fees? Sent SASE if requested?

Be assured that contest people make the rules they make for good reasons. They've devised systems for submission they must adhere to in order to give everyone a fair chance and to keep order. Do not deviate from their requirements or ask for extensions, waivers, etc. Do what is asked, or bow out.

And be sure to check out the contest to see if it has a particular slant or emphasis. Some are strictly for juvenile fiction, some specify themes, etc. Be alert to all that fine print, and don't waste everyone's time by submitting unsuitable material.

Appearance of manuscript

Is this manuscript free of smudges, strikeovers, typos, coffee stains? Is it properly fastened according to our directions? Are the pages properly numbered and named, and are there large margins?

Don't kid yourself. The appearance and presentation of your material *is* important, and can make a difference in the judge's perception of your work. A sloppy, nasty-looking, unprofessionally prepared manuscript is more likely to be shoved aside. After all, if you don't care, why should we? If it isn't "special" to you, why should we even take a second glance at it?

Mechanics

Is the manuscript relatively error-free? Does the writer have a command of the language? Are spelling, grammar, usage, etc., competent? Are there run-on fragments, too many commas, incorrect capitalization? Is dialogue properly punctuated? If you're in doubt of any of this, don't think that judges just smile indulgently and wave it all away in order to concentrate on "art." Such an approach is unprofessional and tacky. Trust me on this and consult your handy "English Fixit" book before you submit that manuscript.

Plot

Does this story have a beginning, a middle and an end? Does the writer get to the conflict/tension within the first few paragraphs? Is there a definite climax? Does the writer know when to stop? Is the plot original? Gripping? Special in some way?

Sometimes new writers read a lot of very "literary" stories and believe they've hit upon the easiest way on earth to make a living: just give 'em a slice of life and let it go. Readers don't want a little slice of life; they want the whole cake, the whole loaf, the whole shmear. You don't have to give them a 100-year saga to satisfy them, but they need to know who did what to whom and where and when and why, or they feel cheated. I do, and I'm just as fond of "literary" stories as the next guy. But the deft and skillful writer can weave elements of exposition, background and motivation into the current action without impeding the progress of the story, and when this happens, the reader gains so much insight into what's happening. All this plot enhances character and theme, and is valuable.

Character and dialogue

Are all characters necessary to the story? Does each have a specific function in the story? Is the main character the viewpoint character consistently throughout? Does the writer waffle on viewpoint? Does the main character undergo change? Are characters identifiable? Real? Is their dialogue realistic? Revealing? Do we have reason to *care* about the character(s)?

Mood and setting

Do we have a sense of time and place for this story? Is the setting an integral part of the plot, significant to the story? Can the reader see and feel the places, the rooms, the weather? Can she imagine the setting as if she were seeing movie scene? Do the scenes linger and haunt or dance in the mind even after the story is over?

Language and technique

Does the writer make use of evocative language, metaphors, similes, images, symbolism? Does she use a special diction to enhance mood, tone and character? Does she *show* and not simply *tell*? Does the overall tone fit the plot and theme? Is there a rhythm and movement to the narrative, as well as evidence of the careful choice of words? Is there an absence of clichés, a freshness and economy of expression?

Theme

What's the essential message here? Is the story worth my time? Is the writer dealing with a matter of some genuine significance, or is he wasting my time with hackneyed situations and trivial revelations? Does this work show insight, vision and maturity? Some grasp of man's position in the universe? The dilemma of the human condition? Is the story enriching, life-enhancing, even didactic? Does it leave us with something to ponder, to care about, to hang on to?

General impression

Is the story entertaining? Did it keep my attention? Did it come leaping off the page at me with its sparkle and pizzazz? Did it sing to me, make me chuckle, bristle, growl, shiver, look over my shoulder in terror? Did it *move*? Did it *touch* me? Will it *stay* with me? Did I find myself inside it? How far would I go to defend it as my "winner"?

Nobody earned a perfect score in all these categories, of course. And in the end, this business of judging other people's writing is so subjective that no two judges are ever in total agreement. Such was the case with the other fiction judge in this contest and me. But that was good, I think. Our disagreements forced us to ask ourselves how we could defend our final choices against the other's criticisms, and we eventually realized that there was that one special story that did fulfill the other judge's art-and-conscience approach, my entertainment-salability viewpoint, and the agent's beauty-and-truth requirements. All in all, it was a good story, a great story, in fact. We all agreed on that, and were proud to award the first prize in fiction to a slightly older-than-middle-aged lady with a wealth of life experiences and sensitivity to bring to her well-crafted story.

To this day, that story wanders in and out of my heart and mind like a restless friend who comes by occasionally to stroll and chat.

I love the writer for that. It's a gift she's given me, that story of hers.

When you write for your favorite fiction contest, try offering your story as a gift to the judge. See it that way as you write; feel it that way in your heart and spirit as you write. Give that judge something she *wants*.

The judges will thank you

Maybe even with a prize.

Important Listing Information

- *Listings are not paid advertisements. Although the information herein is as accurate as possible, the listings are not endorsed or guaranteed by the editor of* Novel & Short Story Writer's Market.
- Novel & Short Story Writer's Market *reserves the right to exclude any listing that does not meet its requirements.*

Market conditions are constantly changing! If you're still using this book and it is 1990 or later, buy the newest edition of Novel & Short Story Writer's Market at your favorite bookstore or order directly from Writer's Digest Books.

The Markets

Finding Your Market

If there is a certain publisher or publication to which you want to submit your work, turn to the general alphabetical index starting on page 653 to find it in the book. If you have a story or novel manuscript ready to submit but are not sure where to send it, refer first to the category index immediately preceding the general index on page 636. The category index is divided into five sections: little/literary magazines, commercial periodicals, small presses, commercial publishers and agents. The listings within these sections are indexed by category or genre (e.g. children's, history, humor), and each category includes all those magazines, book publishers and agents in the book that look for stories or novels of that type. You'll still want to browse through *Novel and Short Story Writer's Market* to find publishers who publish fiction that doesn't really fit into any of our categories.

After finding a market to pursue, read the entire listing *carefully* before submitting your manuscript—editors sometimes ask not to be listed in *Novel and Short Story Writer's Market* because their listings have attracted too many manuscripts totally incompatible with their needs. If you are looking for a publisher for your novel, for example, check carefully to see if the editors would prefer to read a query letter before seeing your entire manuscript. Submitting a novel manuscript is expensive; don't waste your time by sending a complete manuscript to an editor likely to return it unread.

Magazine and book publishers outside the U.S. and Canada are listed at the end of each section in the book. Remember that when sending manuscripts or query letters to another country (including Canada for U.S. writers), you must include the correct number of International Reply Coupons (IRCs) with your manuscript for your work's return if it is not accepted. IRCs are available at most post offices for 95¢. If you live outside the U.S. and are submitting to a U.S. publisher, you must also use IRCs if you want your submission to be returned.

A dagger (‡) before a listing means that listing is new to the '89 edition of *Novel and Short Story Writer's Market*. We have also ranked the magazine and book publishers in the book with the following codes, to help you select the markets most appropriate for your work.

I   Open to beginners. Especially encourages new writers to submit fiction;
II   Accepts work both from beginning and established writers, depending on quality;
III   Prestige market, generally hard to break into, usually accepting work only by established or agented writers, and a very few outstanding new writers;
IV   Specialized publication or press, limited to contributors from certain regions or within a specific age group, or to those writing on specialized subjects or themes.

Unlisted addresses

Occasionally we receive letters asking why a certain magazine, book publisher, award or agent is not listed in *Novel and Short Story Writer's Market*. Chances are, we have already contacted the party in question, but the editor or agent has elected not to list with us for one of several reasons:

● The magazine or publisher may use very little fiction, or it may be overstocked with manuscripts, consider only solicited material, or work by a select group of writers.

● The magazine or press may be in financial difficulty, or its policies may be in a state of flux at our press time.

● A listing in *Novel and Short Story Writer's Market* means additional manuscripts. While many editors are grateful for an expanded choice of material and exposure to new talent, other publishers may not have the time or staff to respond to the additional submissions a listing in the book will bring. For this reason, some publishers ask not to be listed in the book.

● The decision to list a market may also be ours—to protect you, the writer. We investigate complaints about misrepresentations by editors or agents in the information they provide us, or about any unethical or unprofessional activities in their dealings wtih writers. If we find these reports to be true, after thorough investigation, we will delete the listing.

At the end of each section, you'll find a list of the markets that appeared in the 1988 edition of *Fiction Writer's Market* which do not appear in the 1989 edition of *Novel and Short Story Writer's Market*—along with a brief explanation as to why they do not appear in this year's book.

Let us know

The listings in *Novel and Short Story Writer's Market* are based on correspondence, questionnaires and phone conversations with editors, publishers, awards coordinators and agents. The information is updated annually and is as current as we can make it. The publishing industry is volatile, however, and changes in addresses, policies, editorial staffs, needs and submission requirements occur frequently.

To keep abreast of these changes, we suggest you check the monthly Markets column in *Writer's Digest* for updated information throughout the year. We also ask your help. If you become aware of changes or problems with a particular market, or if you know of a new magazine or press publishing fiction—or if you have suggestions on how we can publish a better book—we encourage you to write us.

Manuscript Mechanics

You've written a 300-word story or a 1,000-page novel that you are proud of, and you're ready to send it to an editor or agent. Before you run your paper through the typewriter or printer one last time, remember to review the sometimes irksome, but always necessary, business of properly preparing your work for submission.

Unfortunately, a well typed and efficiently submitted manuscript still won't guarantee your work's quick acceptance. If it did, our most famous writers might be professional typists and postal workers. But the truth is, a sloppily presented manuscript will start its life with unnecessary strikes against it, which might keep it from ever being read at all.

Here are some points you should check before sending out your work.

Type of paper. The paper on which you type your work _must_ be white and measure 8½x11. You might be able to find 100 sheets of paper for under a dollar at a grocery store, and this type of paper is fine—for rough drafts. A hundred pages of 25% cotton-fiber content paper at an office-supply store, on the other hand, can cost as much as $5. Not surprisingly, editors strongly prefer this more expensive, heavy-weight (16-lb—or better still—20-lb) paper, which feels good to the touch, shows type neatly, and holds up under occasional white-outs or erasures. It's cheaper to buy a ream of 500, and you can use the box later for sending out long manuscripts.

Editors almost unanimously discourage the use of erasable bond paper for manuscripts, as it tends to smear when handled and is hard to write on with a pen or pencil. And never use onionskin, or paper with notebook holes or a red line down the left margin.

Your typewriter or printer. Both pica (10 characters per inch) and elite (12 characters per inch) are acceptable to editors, although many find pica easier to read. Editors _do_ object to hard-to-read or unusual typefaces such as script, Old English, italics or all-capital letters.

If you have a dot-matrix printer that prints so few dots per letter that you can actually _see_ the dots, you may find that many editors object. If a cheap dot-matrix printer is your only source of type, you may want to consider hiring a typist or, if you do a lot of typing, buying another printer.

Always use a good black ribbon; the one-time, non-reuseable kind, although more expensive, makes a crisper impression than a multi-use ribbon and is preferred by editors.

If the characters in the letters a, b, e, o, etc. get inked in, it's time to clean your keys. Inexpensive kits are available at office-supply stores. Occasional retyping over erasures or use of white-out is acceptable, but strikeovers give a manuscript a sloppy, careless appearance. Sloppy typing is viewed by many editors, rightly or wrongly, as indicative of sloppy work habits—and of careless writing and thinking habits as well. Strive for a clean, professional-looking manuscript that reflects your justifiable pride in your work.

File copies. Always make a carbon or photocopy of your manuscript before you send it out. You might want to make several photocopies while the original manuscript is still fresh and crisp looking—especially if you've decided to submit the manuscript to different editors at the same time. Many writers keep their original story or novel as the file copy and submit a good-quality photocopy to an editor. If your original manuscript contains a lot of corrections, it's an especially good idea to send a photocopy instead of the original, unless of course the editor says in _Novel and Short Story Writer's Market_ that photocopied submissions will not be accepted.

If you have unlimited access to a photocopier, you might tell the editor simply to discard the manuscript if it is not accepted, and to notify you with a stamped, business-sized envelope (which you have enclosed). This saves on postage and is a particularly good idea if you are submitting work to foreign markets.

Page format. In the upper left corner of the first page, type your name, address and phone number on four single-spaced lines. What you put in the upper right hand corner depends on where you're sending your manuscript. For a commercial periodical, indicate on three single-spaced lines the approximate word count of the manuscript, the rights you are offering for sale and your copyright notice. Note that it is not customary to include the word count, rights offered or copyright notice when sending work to most literary magazines. Most little magazines are copyrighted and that copyright will safeguard your story. Permission to reprint stories that have appeared in magazines and anthologies is routinely granted by little-magazine editors. You don't need to bother stating rights offered or including a copyright notice with a book manuscript—but most editors do prefer a word count.

Now center the title of your story or novel in capital letters about a third of the way down the page. To center, tab until you reach the exact horizontal center of the page, then slowly begin to spell the title of your story, either mentally or aloud, and press the backspace key once for every two characters of your title. Don't ignore spaces or marks of punctuation, which must be counted as well as the letters. When you're done spelling, simply type the title, and you'll see that it is correctly centered on the page.

Now center your name a triple-space below the title. If you are writing under a pen name, this is the place to put it. It will let the editor know that you want to publish your story or novel under a pen name, while making sure your legal name is clearly visible on the first page for mailing and payment purposes. If you are not using a pseudonym, you don't need to type your name again below the title. If you are typing a novel, center the words "Chapter One," or the title of the chapter, a triple-space below the title. Then triple-space again, indent, and start typing. Remember to leave a 1¼" margin on all sides of your pages.

On every page after the first, type your last name, a dash or a slash, and the page number, in the upper right-hand corner. Number your pages consecutively: If the last page of the first chapter is 26, the first page of the second chapter will be 27. Each new chapter should begin on a new page, even if the last page of the previous chapter contains only a few lines.

Estimating word count. A quick and accurate way to estimate the word count of your story or novel is to count the exact number of words on three full pages of your manuscript, divide the total by three, and multiply the result by the number of pages. For example, if you have a 12-page story with three page-number totals of 265, 316 and 289 words, divide your total of 870 by three to get 290. Now multiply 290 by 12 pages to get 3,480. On manuscripts over 25 pages, count five pages instead of three, then follow the same process but divide by five to get the average number of words per page. Remember that your first and last pages are likely to be less than full, and adjust your count accordingly. And round your number to the nearest 10, since it is, after all, only an estimate.

Cover letters. In most cases, a brief (less than one page) cover letter is helpful in personalizing your submission. Nothing you say about your story or novel will ensure its acceptance, but the editor will probably be interested in hearing what you have to say about yourself, your publishing history, and any particular qualifications you have for writing the manuscript you are submitting. If you have written to the editor earlier, a brief reminder—"Here is the story we discussed earlier. I look forward to hearing from you at your earliest convenience"—is enough.

If you are writing to a particular magazine or publishing house for the first time, make sure you are using the editor's correct name and title. Your chances for acceptance decrease when you send a cover letter merely to "Fiction Editors." This kind of impersonal submission will probably result in your manuscript being read by an underpaid (or unpaid) reader with no real authority to accept a manuscript—but complete authority to reject it.

Mailing your manuscript. Except when working on a specific assignment from a magazine, or when under contract to write a novel for a publisher, *always* enclose a self-addressed, stamped envelope (SASE) when you send out your manuscript. Manuscript pages should never be stapled together—and using a rusty paperclip is unwise, since an editor is likely to

Jones (Pseudonym)—2

Begin the second page, and all following pages, in this manner—with a page-number line (as above) that includes your name, in case loose manuscript pages are accidentally shuffled. You may include the title of your manuscript or a shortened version of the title to identify the Jones to whose manuscript this page 2 belongs.

Chris Jones
1234 Any Street
City, ST 12345
(123)456-7890

About 3,000 words
First Serial Rights

YOUR STORY OR NOVEL TITLE HERE

CHAPTER ONE

By Sue Pseudonym

The manuscript begins here—about halfway down the first page. It should be cleanly typed, double-spaced, using either pica or elite type. Use one side of the paper only, and leave a margin of about 1¼ inches on all four sides.

To begin a new paragraph, drop down one double-space and indent. Don't leave extra white space between paragraphs.

NEATNESS COUNTS. *Here are sample pages of a manuscript ready for submission. If the author uses a pseudonym, it should be placed on the title page only in the byline position; the author's real name must always appear in the top left corner of the title page for mailing and payment purposes. On subsequent pages, list the real name, then the pen name in parentheses, followed by a slash or a dash and the page number.*

remove it to read the story and then leave a second indented mark by putting it back in a new place. Do not use a binder when submitting a story or novel unless a publisher requests it.

To submit work to foreign publications and publishers, including Canadian markets, enclose an International Reply Coupon (IRC), available for 95¢ at larger post offices. You will have to buy more than one if your manuscript is very heavy. Editors in Canada and other countries generally accept IRCs, but they will not accept U.S. checks or money orders. It's a good idea to send a manuscript to Europe, South America or Asia via airmail; a manuscript sent by seamail could take months even to reach the country to which you have sent it.

Most editors won't object if story manuscripts under five pages are folded in thirds and mailed in a letter-sized envelope. However, there is a preference for flat mailing in 9x12 or 10x13 envelopes for manuscripts over four pages. Your manuscript will look best if you mail it out in the smallest envelope into which it will fit—so it doesn't move around inside the envelope while in transit. Fold the return envelope in half, address it to yourself, stamp it, and put it into the outgoing package.

Mark both of your envelopes FIRST CLASS MAIL or SPECIAL FOURTH CLASS MANUSCRIPT RATE, as desired. First Class mail costs more but assures better handling and faster delivery. Special Fourth Class is handled the same as Parcel Post (Third Class), but is less expensive than both First and Third Class. You can only use Special Fourth Class rate for manuscripts mailed in and to the U.S., and for manuscripts weighing over one pound. If your manuscript weighs less than a pound, it's best to send it First Class. If you plan to send out a lot of work, invest in a postal scale and stock up on stamps, to save trips to the post office.

Note that if you use an office or personal postage meter, it's important not to indicate a date on the return envelope; this can cause trouble with the postal authorities.

First Class mail is forwarded or returned automatically, but Third Class and Special Fourth Class mail are not. To make sure you get your Special Fourth Class submission back if it proves undeliverable, print "Return Postage Guaranteed" below your return address.

You may enclose a cover letter with your manuscript sent at the Special Fourth Class rate, but legally you must also add enough first class postage to cover the letter and write FIRST CLASS LETTER ENCLOSED on the outside of your package.

Many writers have described postal workers who insist that Special Fourth Class rate applies only to published books; this is not true, and you should insist on your rights in this matter if challenged.

Postal insurance is payable only on the tangible value of what is in the package (i.e. typing paper), so your best insurance is to keep a copy of what you send at home. Publishers do not appreciate receiving unsolicited manuscripts marked Certified, Registered or Insured, especially if they have to make a special trip to the post office to get them.

The United Parcel Service can be less expensive than First Class mail for mailing book manuscripts when you drop the package off at UPS yourself. Check with UPS in your area to see if it has benefits for you. The cost depends on the weight of your manuscript and the delivery distance.

Mailing book manuscripts. Book manuscript pages should be mailed in a box (a ream-size typing paper box is perfect) without binding. It's a good idea to tape the box closed, and reinforce the corners of the box with tape as well. The flimsier cardboard boxes provided by copy centers often do not hold up well in the mail. To ensure your manuscript's safe return, enclose a folded self-addressed and stamped insulated bag mailer. Many publishing house readers discard the mailer a manuscript arrives in, then read and circulate the manuscript as necessary for editorial consideration, and, if the manuscript is rejected, finally route it through the mail room back to you with a letter or rejection slip. This kind of handling makes it likely that a freshly typed manuscript will be in rough shape after one or two submissions. Thus, it is wise to have several photocopies made of a long manuscript while it is still fresh.

Electronic submissions. It's important to query before sending a story via disk or modem, even if an editor has indicated a willingness in *Novel and Short Story Writer's Market* to receive such material. In any case, be sure to follow the editor's directions regarding electronic submissions very carefully. Some editors want material they have already accepted re-sent electronically but will not look at unsolicited submissions on the computer.

The waiting game. The writer who sends off a story or book manuscript to an editor should turn immediately to other ideas and try not to think too much about the submission. Unless you are under contract to do a story or book—in which case a phone call to your editor saying the manuscript is in the mail is quite appropriate—it's best to use your time on other writing projects and let the submission take care of itself. But if an editor has been holding onto a manuscript for more than a month longer than the listing in *Novel and Short Story Writer's Market* leads you to believe it should be kept, it's time to inquire further. Don't feel timid about doing this; an editor would probably think it odd if you *didn't* worry about the status of a manuscript that had been held for an unusual length of time.

Write a brief letter to the editor asking if your manuscript (give the title, a brief description and the date you mailed it) has in fact reached the publisher's offices, and if so, if it is still under consideration. Don't give the impression of being impatient with the editor, who may be swamped with work or short-handed or about to give your manuscript another reading. An impatient or angry attitude from you could alienate the editor against you for a long time. Be polite and professional. Enclose another SASE to expedite a response. This is usually enough to stir a decision if matters are lagging in an editorial office.

If you hear nothing from a publisher one month after your follow-up letter, send the editor a short note asking if your previous follow-up was received. If after another month you have still heard nothing, send a polite letter saying that you are withdrawing the manuscript from consideration (include the title, date of submission, and dates of follow-up correspondence), and ask that the manuscript be returned immediately in the SASE you sent with it. You are now free to market the manuscript elsewhere.

Even if matters do not work out with a publisher, and you have lost months of marketing time, be cool and professional as you set about the business of finding another publisher for your work. Move on to the next name on your list, submitting your manuscript with a personal cover letter and the same methods outlined above. In the meantime, continue working on your new writing projects, remembering that the creation of good fiction is in itself an worthy and admirable goal.

Little/Literary Magazines

If you've been submitting your work to literary magazines for some time, you probably already have a list of fifteen or twenty favorites to which you send your best stories—and maybe a longer, but less promising list to which you turn if a story isn't taken by one of your top choices.

If you're a new writer, though, or have just started sending work to literary magazines, the idea of reading through the 630 US and Canadian literary magazines listed here to find the right markets for your work might seem a little daunting. You'll soon find it's well worth the trouble though—and that sending out stories more or less at random is really a waste of time. A number of editors agree with David Nalle, editor of *Abyss Magazine*, who complains, "More than half of what we get is completely inappropriate." Check the category index on page 636 for help, too. Remember, though, that not all of the magazines listed in the section are to be found in the category index—editors who don't specify a particular category but say "we consider all types of fiction," for example, aren't in the category index.

Ordering and reading sample copies before you submit will save you time and postage in the long run, helping you choose the magazines whose editors are most likely to appreciate your work. Try to visit the periodical room at a college or university library; this kind of library is usually the best place for writers to learn about a lot of different literary magazines at once. If you're a new writer of genre fiction—science fiction, horror or fantasy in particular—you'll probably find the little magazines in those fields hard to locate even in the largest cities, however.

A few generalizations can be made just by looking at the names of the magazines in this section:

• Most journals affiliated with colleges and universities, or with states in their names (like the *Missouri Review*), are most interested in literary fiction, often including prose poems, and will not consider horror, romance or work for children.

• Writers at the *very* beginning of their careers might want to turn to magazines with the word "Writer" or "Writing" in their names (although not *Writers' Forum*, a university-published literary magazine), for easy and quick publication.

• Magazines with offbeat names, like *Baby Sue* and *Blonde on Blonde*, are most likely to be interested in more experimental, avant-garde fiction.

Note that listings in this section also include a grab bag of magazines like *Day Care and Early Education* that are more similar to commercial periodicals than to little magazines except for one thing: They do not pay.

Whatever you do, don't go through the little/literary magazine category alphabetically, beginning with *Abbey* and sending a story out until it gets taken—maybe by a magazine in the "As" and maybe not even by *Zyzzyva*, the last listing in the section. Experience shows so many writers submit alphabetically that magazines early in the book are flooded with submissions, while many of those that come later are not.

After advice like "the writer should familiarize himself/herself with the type of fiction published in literary magazines as opposed to family magazines, religious magazines, etc.," (Betty Rossi, editor, *Loonfeather*), and the even more pointed "Know your market!" (Meg Mac Donald, editor, *Pandora*), the most common advice to new writers is that given by Jim Barnes of *The Chariton Review*: "Know the simple mechanics of submission—SASE, no paper clips, no odd-sized SASE." As Frederick Raborg, Jr., of *Amelia*, urges, "Study manuscript mechanics and submission procedures. Neatness does count."

Low pay, high prestige

Many of the magazines listed here, including some quite prestigious ones, like *Cimarron Review*, *Gargoyle*, *Kansas Quarterly*, *New Virginia Review* and *The North American Review* pay little or nothing. These publications, though, offer advantages that might prove more valuable than cash. Literary agents, for example, peruse the best literary magazines (especially those ranked III) avidly to find promising new writers. Being published in literary magazines will definitely help if you hope to be asked to give readings of your fiction, or if you're looking to get a collection of your stories published—with or without an agent.

In smaller, more specialized or regional magazines (like *The Icelandic Canadian*), you can count on the stories being read by exactly the audience who will most appreciate your work, a gratifying experience. And publication in even the very smallest magazines will improve your list of credits and help you develop a real audience. Note too that some magazines, such as *The American Voice* and *The Paris Review*, really do pay very well. If cash is important to you, be sure to check the contest section for awards offered by magazines like *Japanophile* and *Quarterly West*, which normally pay little—except to contest winners.

Not all little/literary magazines belong to the elite, prestigious category. There are many, most of them ranked I, published from the editor's basement or from a local copy center. If the appearance of the magazine publishing your work is important to you, make doubly sure you've seen a copy of a magazine before submitting your stories, or at least check the listing for a description of the magazine itself—remember that 20 lb paper is the weight of normal typing paper, and "20 lb cover stock" is often your main clue in a listing that the magazine in question is very modest in appearance.

Problems

Unfortunately, little/literary magazines go out of business more often than any other category of listing in the book. The most common problems arise when editors starting out don't foresee just how much running a magazine will cost. Of the 166 new listings that appeared in the little/literary magazine section in the 1988 edition of *Fiction Writer's Market*, for example, 51 are not in the 1989 *Novel and Short Story Writer's Market*. So when you're dealing with a magazine founded in 1988, be sure to see a sample copy before submitting, to make certain the publication has survived that important first year.

Another common problem writers have with literary magazine editors deals with very slow response times. As long as you are sure the publication is still in business, patience is usually the key here. An editor may fully intend to report on a story in a week or two, but this goal often proves unrealistic. An editor whose magazine comes out only once a year might let the stories collect for nearly that long before making a choice. Note too that many of the magazines sponsored by colleges and universities do not read manuscripts during the summer. It's best to wait three months or so, no matter what a listing in *Novel and Short Story Writer's Market* says, before querying about your piece.

A promising development for writers is the recent agreement by the highly thought-of magazine *Ploughshares* and the National Writers Union. The contract agrees that the magazine will shorten response time to a maximum of five months, will allow multiple submissions, and defines specific publishing conditions as well as copyright and payment terms. "As it is now, many writers believe magazines take so long to respond out of negligence," says *Ploughshares* managing editor Jennifer Rose. "In fact, most editors are writers themselves and know what it's like to be at the other end. But with volunteer staff and thousands of manuscripts coming in, it's impossible to consider them all quickly." We can hope that other magazines will follow *Ploughshares'* lead and standardize their policies in the future.

More listings

If you're drawn to fanzines, those eccentric—even bizarre—publications that often combine graphics and stories, you'll want to read the quarterly magazine *Factsheet Five* (6 Arizona Ave., Rensselaer, NY 12144-4502), which describes hundreds of fascinating, unusual amateur publications. If you also write poetry or nonfiction and want a list of little/literary magazines that includes those subjects, see *Poet's Market* (Writer's Digest Books) or *The International Directory of Little Magazines and Small Presses* (Box 100, Paradise CA 95967).

Here's the ranking system we've used to categorize the listings in this section.

> I *Publication encourages beginning or unpublished writers to submit work for consideration and publishes new writers frequently;*
>
> II *Publication accepts work by established writers and by new writers of exceptional talent;*
>
> III *Publication does not encourage beginning writers; prints mostly writers with previous publication credits and a* very *few new writers;*
>
> IV *Special-interest or regional publication, open only to writers in certain genres or on certain subjects, or from certain geographical areas.*

ABBEY (II), White Urp Press, 5360 Fallriver Row Court, Columbia MD 20144. Editor: David Greisman. Magazine: 8½x11; 18-26 pages; Xerox paper; illustrations. "Unassumed intelligence in a publication of finite production for the type of person who knows the pure poetry of Molson Ale." Quarterly. Estab. 1970. Circ. 200.
Needs: Literary, contemporary, prose poem, science fiction and regional (appreciation of Maryland). "Nothing political! Nothing pornographic." Accepts 3-6 mss/year. Receives approximately 5 unsolicited fiction mss each month. Does not read mss in summer. Length: 1,000-2,000 words. Sometimes recommends other markets.
How to Contact: Query with SASE. Accepts computer printout submissions. Reports in 1 month. Publishes ms 3-9 months after acceptance. Sample copy 50¢.
Payment: 1-2 free author's copies.
Terms: Acquires one-time rights.
Advice: "Plug in the typewriter. Buy stamps. Don't imitate Thomas Hardy. Drink less than Behan or Thomas. Tell stories like Frederic Raphael." Most mss are rejected because "the stories themselves aren't interesting. Also, too many writers tend to lose their narrative strengths by introducing gimmicks and tricks where they are least needed. I'll accept nothing more than 6-7 pages. Know the mag you submit to. A good 'fit' does the writer and the magazine proud."

ABYSS MAGAZINE (II, IV), "Games and the Imagination," Ragnarok Enterprises, 3716 Robinson, Austin TX 78722. (512)472-6534. Editor: David F. Nalle. Fiction Editor: Patricia Fitch. Magazine: 8½x11; 28 pages; bond paper; glossy cover; illustrations; photos. "Heroic fantasy fiction: some fantasy, horror, SF and adventure fiction, for college-age game players." Bimonthly. Plans special fiction issue. Estab. 1979. Circ. 1,500.
Needs: Adventure, fantasy, horror, psychic/supernatural/occult, cyberpunk, science fiction, heroic fantasy, sword and sorcery. "Game-based stories are not specifically desired." Receives 20-30 unsolicited mss/month. Buys 1 ms/issue; 7 mss/year. Publishes ms 1-12 months after acceptance. Recently published work by Antoine Sadel, Ardath Mayhar, Lewis Bryson; published new writers within the last year. Length: 2,000 words average; 1,000 words minimum; 4,000 words maximum. Publishes short shorts occasionally. Sometimes critiques rejected mss or recommends other markets.
How to Contact: Send for sample copy first. Reports in 1 month on queries; 2 months on mss. "Do send a cover letter, preferably entertaining. Include some biographical info and a precis of lengthy stories." SASE. Photocopied submissions OK. Accepts computer printout submissions, including dot-matrix. "Call IIBBS at (512)472-6905 for modem ASCII info." Sample copy and fiction guidelines $2.
Payment: Pays 1-3¢/word or by arrangement, plus contributor's copies.
Terms: Pays on publication for first North American serial rights. Publication copyrighted.
Advice: "We are particularly interested in new writers with mature and original style. Don't send us fiction which everyone else has sent back to you unless you think it has qualities which make it too strange for everyone else but which don't ruin the significance of the story. Make sure what you submit is appropriate to the magazine you send it to. More than half of what we get is completely inappropriate. We plan to include more and longer stories."

ACM, (ANOTHER CHICAGO MAGAZINE) (II), Another Chicago Press, Box 11223, Chicago IL 60611. (312)524-1289. Editors: Lee Webster and Barry Silesky. Fiction Editor: Sharon Solwitz. Magazine: 5½x8½; 150-200 pages; "art folio each issue." Estab. 1977.
Needs: Contemporary, literary, experimental, feminist, gay/lesbian, ethnic, humor/satire, prose poem, translations and political/socio-historical. Receives 75-100 unsolicited fiction mss each month. Recently published work by Fred Nadis, Curtis White, Gary Soto; published new writers in the last year. Sometimes recommends other markets.
How to Contact: Unsolicited mss acceptable with SASE. Accepts computer printout submissions. Publishes ms 6-12 months after acceptance. Sample copies are available for $3.50 ppd. Reports in 8 weeks.
Payment: Small honorarium plus contributor's copy.
Terms: Acquires first North American serial rights. Publication copyrighted.
Advice: "Get used to rejection slips, and don't get discouraged. Keep query and introductory letters short. Make sure ms has name and address on every page, and that it is clean, neat and proofread. We are looking for stories with freshness and originality in subject angle and style."

‡ACTA VICTORIANA (I, II), 150 Charles St. West, Toronto Ontario M5S 1K9 Canada. Editor: Elias Polizoes. Magazine: 8½x11; 32 pages; glossy paper; cornwall cover; illustrations and photos. "We publish the poetry, prose, drawings and photographs of university students as well as of other writers. The magazine reaches the University of Toronto community as well as students of other universities. Semiannually. Estab. 1987. Circ. 1,200 + .
Needs: Contemporary, ethnic, experimental, humor/satire, literary, mainstream, prose poem. Accepts 4-5 mss/issue; 8-10 mss/year. Publishes ms 2 months after acceptance. Recently published work by Craig Stephenson, Peter McCallum and Douglas Brown; published new writers within the last year. Length: 1,500 words maximum.
How to Contact: Send complete manuscript with cover letter, which should include information about the writer's previous publishing credits. Reports in 2 months on mss. SASE. Simultaneous and photocopied submissions OK. Accepts computer printout submissions, including dot-matrix. Sample copy and fiction guidelines for $3 and 8½x11 SAE.
Payment: Pays contributor's copies.
Terms: Publication copyrighted.
Advice: "University publications such as ours offer beginning fiction writers good opportunities to get published. If your piece is innovative and exciting, yet at the same time well-crafted, you will have a good chance of getting published. Editors change yearly in this student journal, yet our editorial policy remains roughly the same."

‡ACTION TIME (IV), 15854 Montview Dr., Dumfries VA 22026. (703)680-5803. Editor: Erik Grotz. Magazine: 8½x11; 20 pages and up; 60 lb paper and cover stock; Xeroxed illustrations; halftone photos. "Mostly for exposure of varied underground music; interviews bands; reviews records and magazines; also likes to print fiction, but it is not my 'main theme.' Audience is mostly 14-30, into 'alternative/underground music.' " Quarterly. Estab. 1985. Circ. 300.
Needs: Experimental, horror, humor/satire, prose poem, science fiction, music. "An odd perspective or views on these topics may help." No length limits. Publishes short shorts. Sometimes recommends other markets.
How to Contact: Query first. "Call or write." Reports in less than 1 week. Simultaneous, photocopied and reprint submissions OK. Accepts computer printouts, including dot-matrix. Accepts electronic submissions via Apple IIe disk. Sample copy $1. Fiction guidelines free.
Payment: Pays in contributor's copies.
Terms: Acquires one-time rights. Publication "will be copyrighted."
Advice: "I like a varied perspective and outlook—I also publish comic strips, artwork, etc. I'll accept anything interesting, weird, demented or other that I find to my (low) standards. Send it! I may like it!"

ADARA (IV), 305 Summerwood Dr., Clarkston GA 30021. (404)296-8463. Editor: Elizabeth Shaw. Magazine: 8½x11; 100 pages; 60 lb cover stock; illustrations; photos. *All materials must be related to Doctor Who.* Semiannually. Estab. 1986. Circ. 100.
Needs: Adventure, fantasy, feminist, gay, historical, humor/satire, prose poem, science fiction, serial-

✚ *The double dagger before a listing indicates that the listing is new in this edition. New markets are often the most receptive to freelance contributions.*

ized/excerpted novel and Doctor Who. No "Mary Sue" (authoress gets Doctor) stories; nothing sexual, obscene, or explicitly gory. Buys 5 mss/issue; 10-12 mss/year. Manuscripts usually published in next issue after acceptance. Recently published work by Janet Reedman, Ed Oram and Autumn Lee. Published new writers within the last year. Length: 7,500 words preferred. Publishes short shorts. Length: 2 pages. Sometimes critiques rejected mss and recommends other markets.

How to Contact: Send complete ms with cover letter, which should state "where else author has been published, if story is simultaneous submission, whether it has been published elsewhere." Reports in 2 weeks on queries; 1 month on mss. SASE for ms, not needed for query. Photocopied submissions OK. Accepts computer printout submissions, including dot-matrix. Accepts electronic submissions via IBM compatible computer, 5¼ disk, in RFT/DCA on Displaywriter 3. Sample copy $8. Fiction guidelines free.

Payment: Pays in contributor's copies.

Terms: Acquires one-time rights. Sends galleys to author. Publication copyrighted.

Advice: "Grammar and spelling are very important. I do reject incoherent stories, which I don't consider 'modern' or 'experimental'—just incoherent. My readers are international (Canada, Great Britain and Australia as well as the USA), so few local-interest-only references should be used. No one is ever turned down for too *high* an intellectual content. Stories emphasizing character over action are preferred, especially those demonstrating that we are all, and have all felt, alien *somewhere*, and we can, nevertheless, get along."

ADRIFT (II), Writing: Irish, Irish American and . . ., #4D, 239 E. 5th St., New York NY 10003. Editor: Thomas McGonigle. Magazine: 8x11; 32 pages; 60 lb paper stock; 65 lb cover stock; illustrations; photos. "Irish-Irish American as a basis—though we are interested in advanced writing from anywhere." Semiannually. Estab. 1983. Circ. 1,000+.

Needs: Contemporary, erotica, ethnic, experimental, feminist, gay, lesbian, literary, translations. Receives 40 unsolicited mss/month. Buys 3 mss/issue. Recent issues have included work by Francis Stuart. Published new writers within the last year. Length: open. Sometimes critiques rejected mss and recommends other markets.

How to Contact: Send complete ms. Reports as soon as possible. SASE for ms. Photocopied submissions OK. Accepts computer printout submissions. Sample copy $5.

Payment: Pays $7.50-$300.

Terms: Pays on publication for first rights. Publication copyrighted.

Advice: "The writing should argue with, among others, James Joyce, Flann O'Brien, Juan Goytisolo, Ingeborg Bachmann, E.M. Cioran, Max Stirner, Patrick Kavanagh."

THE ADROIT EXPRESSION (I), Box 73, Courtney PA 15029. (412)379-8019. Editor: Xavier F. Aguilar. Newspaper: 8½x11; 3-5 pages; 20 lb paper and cover stock; some illustrations. For the aspiring writer, poet and artist. Triannually. Estab. 1986. Circ. 75.

Needs: Adventure, contemporary, experimental, fantasy, literary, mainstream, prose poem, romance (contemporary). No erotica. Receives 5 unsolicited mss/month. Accepts 1-2 mss/issue; 3-6 mss/year. Does not read mss July 15-Dec. 31. Recently published work by Becky Knight, Marsha Powers and Deborah T. Johnson. Published work by previously unpublished writers in the last year. Length: 500 words minimum; 2,000 words maximum. Publishes short shorts.

How to Contact: Send complete ms. Reports 2 weeks on queries; 1 month on mss. "Please keep copies of works submitted as none can be returned." SASE. Photocopied submissions and reprint submissions OK. Sample copy $4 and 1 first class stamp.

Payment: "A byline is disbursement for contributions and all rights remain with authors."

‡AEGEAN REVIEW (IV), Suite 2A, 220 West 29th St., New York NY 10011. (212)995-9835. Editor: Dinos Sitotis. Fiction Editor: Barbara Fields. Magazine: 7x10; 80 pages; 60 lb paper; laminated cover; illustrations and photos. "*Aegean Review* is devoted to subjects Greek, fiction, essays, poetry and art. Authors are American Greeks in translation and Greek-Americans. Our subscribers are Greek-American predominantly, but we have many readers who are simply interested in literature or in Greece." Semiannually. Estab. 1986. Circ. 2,000.

Needs: Greek subjects. "Fiction must be well-written and have a tie to Greece, however tenuous." Receives 5 unsolicited mss/month. Buys 2 mss/issue; 4 mss/year. Publishes ms within one year of accept-

Market categories: (I) Beginning; (II) General;
(III) Prestige; (IV) Specialized.

ance. Recently published work by Jorge Luis Borges, Menis Koumandareas and Truman Capote. Length: 4,000 words average. Publishes short shorts. Length: 600 words.

How to Contact: Send manuscript and cover letter. Cover letter should include basic information about writer and manuscript. Reports in 1 month. SASE for ms. Simultaneous, photocopied and reprint submissions OK. Accepts computer printout submissions, including dot-matrix. Sample copy for $5 and SAE "to fit."

Payment: Pays $25-$100, "but if we found something we liked very much and it was more, we would pay for it."

Terms: Pays on publication for first rights or first North American serial rights. Sends galleys to author. Publication copyrighted.

Advice: "Choosing fiction is largely a subjective and personal matter for us. We try to emphasize excellence in writing. We find that we receive quite a few amateurish manuscripts, almost unreadable. We solicit manuscripts from writers who we know have had either professional or personal experiences with Greece or Greek literature."

‡AERIAL (II), Box 25642, Washington DC 20007. (202)333-1544. Editor: Rod Smith. Magazine: 6x9; 64 pages; 75 lb paper; 10 pt. CIS cover stock; photos on cover only. Semiannually. Estab. 1984. Circ. 750.

Needs: Experimental, literary, translations. Receives 10 mss/month. Accepts 1-2 mss/issue; 3-4 mss/year. Publishes ms within 3-12 months of acceptance (average). Length: ½ page-10 pages. Sometimes critiques rejected mss.

How to Contact: Send ms—short fiction or excerpts—with or without cover letter. Reports in 1 week to 1 month. SASE. Photocopied and reprint submissions OK. Accepts computer printout submissions, including dot-matrix. Sample copy for $6.

Payment: Pays in contributor's copies.

Terms: Acquires one-time rights. Publication copyrighted.

AETHLON (I,II,IV), (formerly *Arete*), San Diego University Press, San Diego State University, San Diego CA 92182. (619)265-6220 (Press), (619)265-5184 (Editor). Editor: Alfred F. Boe. Magazine: 6x9; 180-240 pages; illustrations and photographs. "Theme: Literary treatment of sport. We publish articles on that theme, critical studies of author's treatment of sport and original fiction and poetry with sport themes. Most of our audience are academics." Semiannually. Plans "possible" special fiction issue. Estab. 1983. Circ. 800.

Needs: Sport. "Stories must have a sport-related theme and subject; otherwise, we're wide open." No personal experience memoirs. Receives 10-15 fiction mss/month. Accepts 4-8 fiction mss/issue; 10-15 fiction mss/year. Publishes ms "about 6 months" after acceptance. Length: 2,500-5,000 words average; 500 words minumum; 7,500 words maximum. Publishes short shorts of 500 + words. Sometimes critiques rejected mss.

How to Contact: Send complete ms with cover letter. Reports in 6 months. SASE. Simultaneous, photocopied and reprint submissions OK. Accepts computer printout submissions, including dot-matrix. Sample copy $12.50.

Payment: One contributor's copy and 10 offprints.

Terms: Sends pre-publication galleys to author. Publication copyrighted.

Advice: "Too many people with no talent are writing. Too many people think a clever idea or an unusual experience is all it takes to make a story. We are looking for well-written, insightful stories. Don't be afraid to be experimental."

THE AGNI REVIEW (II), Creative Writing Program, Boston University, 236 BayState Rd., Boston MA 02215. (617)354-8522. Editor-in-Chief: Askold Melnyczuk. Magazine: 5½x8½; 212-300 pages; 55 lb booktext paper; glossy cover stock; occasional illustrations and photos. "Eclectic literary magazine publishing first-rate poems and stories." Semiannually. Estab. 1972.

Needs: Stories, excerpted novels, prose poems and translations. Receives 150 unsolicited fiction mss/month. Accepts 4-7 mss/issue, 8-12 mss/year. Recently published work by Stephen Minot, Suzanne Gardinier, and Marco Papa. Rarely critiques rejected mss or recommends other markets.

How to Contact: Send complete ms with SASE and cover letter listing previous publications. Simultaneous and photocopied submissions OK. Accepts computer printout submissions. Reports in 4 weeks. Sample copy $5.

Read the Manuscript Mechanics section to learn the correct way to prepare and submit a manuscript.

Payment: Pays $8/page; 3 contributor's copies; extra copies 60% of retail price.
Terms: Pays on publication for first North American serial rights. Sends galleys to author. Publication copyrighted.
Advice: "Read *Agni* carefully to understand the kinds of stories we publish. Read—everything, classics, literary journals, bestsellers."

ALABAMA LITERARY REVIEW (II), Smith 264, Troy State University, Troy AL 36082. (205)566-3000, ext. 306. Editor: Theron Montgomery. Fiction Editor: Jim Davis. Magazine: 11½x6; 100+ pages; top paper quality; some illustrations; photos. "National magazine for a broad range of the best contemporary fiction, poetry and essays and drama that we can find." Semiannually. Estab. 1987.
Needs: Condensed novel, contemporary, erotica, ethnic, experimental, fantasy, feminist, gay, historical (general), humor/satire, lesbian, literary, prose poem, regional, science fiction, serialized/excerpted novel, suspense/mystery, translations. "Serious writing." Receives 50 unsolicited fiction mss/month. Buys 2 fiction mss/issue. Publishes ms 5-6 months after acceptance. Recently published work by Joseph Lane, Thomas Wooten, and Mary Jane Mayo; published new writers within the last year. Length: 1,500-2,000 words average. Publishes short shorts of 500 words. Sometimes comments on rejected mss and recommends other markets.
How to Contact: Send complete ms with cover letter or submit through agent. Reports on queries in 2 weeks; on mss in 2-4 weeks. SASE. Simultaneous submissions OK. Accepts computer printouts, no dot-matrix "unless Xeroxed." Sample copy $4 plus 50¢ postage.
Payment: Pays in contributor's copies.
Terms: Publication copyrighted. First rights returned to author.
Advice: "There is too much influence from the northeastern seaboard, the most negative qualities pertaining to gimmickry and a self-centered point of view. We are interested in any kind of story if it is *serious* and *honest* in the sense of 'the human heart in conflict with itself.' "

ALASKA QUARTERLY REVIEW (II), University of Alaska, 3211 Providence Dr., Anchorage AK 99508. (907)786-1327. Fiction Editor: Ronald Spatz. Magazine: 6x9; 146 pages; 60 lb Glatfelter paper; 10 pt. C15 black ink varnish cover stock; photos on cover only. Magazine of "contemporary literary art and criticism for a general literary audience." Semiannually. Estab. 1982.
Needs: Contemporary, experimental, literary, prose poem and translations. Receives 50 unsolicited fiction mss/month. Accepts 5-8 mss/issue,15 mss/year. Does not read mss May 15-August 15. Published new writers within the last year. Publishes short shorts. Occasionally critiques rejected mss.
How to Contact: Send complete ms with SASE. Photocopied submissions OK. Reports in 2 months. Publishes ms 6-12 months after acceptance. Sample copy $4.
Payment: 1 free contributor's copy.
Terms: Acquires first rights. Publication copyrighted.
Advice: "We have made a significant investment in fiction. The reason is quality; serious fiction *needs* a market. Try to have everything build to a singleness of effect."

‡THE ALBANY REVIEW (II), 4 Central Ave., Albany New York 12210. (518)436-5787. Editor: Theodore Bouloukos II. Fiction Editor: Thomas H. Littlefield. Magazine: 11x14; 56-68 pages; premium 50 lb white paper; 91 lb media print satin cover stock; illustrations and photographs. "We consider ourselves a monthly feast for upscale, 28-56, literate, lively and interested readers." Monthly. Estab. 1987. Circ. 15,000.
Needs: Contemporary, experimental, humor/satire, literary, mainstream, prose poem, translations. "Second-person narration, coupled with minimalist prose, is a yawn for us. As well, we like generic romance only in our private lives." Receives 90-150 unsolicited mss/month. Accepts 5 mss/month; 3 mss/issue. Publishes ms 2-3 months after acceptance. Length: 3,000-4,000 words average; 750 words minimum; 3,500 words maximum.
How to Contact: Send complete ms with cover letter. Cover letter should include "brief biography with published credits." Reports in 2 weeks on queries; 3-4 weeks on mss. SASE. Reprint submissions OK. Computer printout submissions OK. Electronic submissions via Macintosh only. Sample copy $1.50. Fiction guidelines free for #10 SASE.
Payment: Pays in contributor's copies; charges for extras.
Terms: Acquires first rights. Publication copyrighted.
Advice: Looks for "good solid, exact writing, whose flow of imagery conveys more than a spiritual strength but rather a resonance in the mind and soul. Strong, powerful writing is measured by form, function and tight composition. Obviously, well-developed characters and settings that take you there are rudimentary to all finished work—so we often look for surprises. As well, what Robert Frost said about the image a poem makes is true of good fiction: 'It all begins in delight and ends in wisdom.' "

‡ALDEBARAN (II), Roger Williams College, Ferry Rd., Bristol RI 02809. Editor: Jodi L. Kehn. Magazine: 5½x8½; 60-80 pages; illustrations; photos. Literary publication of prose and poetry for a general audience. Published annually or twice a year. Estab. 1970.
Needs: Will consider all fiction. Receives approximately 10 unsolicited fiction mss each month. Does not read mss in summer. Preferred length: 10-15 pages or shorter. Critiques rejected mss when there is time.
How to Contact: Send complete ms with SASE and cover letter, which should include "information for possible contributor's notes—but cover letters will not influence decision on publication." Accepts computer printout submissions. Reports in 1 month. Sample copy $1 with SASE.
Payment: 2 free author's copies.
Terms: Publication copyrighted. Copyright reverts to author on publication.
Advice: Mss are rejected because of "incomplete stories, no live character, basic grammatical errors; usually returned with suggestions for revision and character change."

ALLEGHENY REVIEW (IV), A National Journal of Undergraduate Literature, Box 32, Allegheny College, Meadville PA 16335. (814)724-6553. Editors: Tony Monta, Megan Schneider. Magazine: 6x9; 100 pages; 60 lb White Wove paper; illustrations; photos. "The *Allegheny Review* is an annual journal composed *entirely* of undergraduate contributions selected from submissions from colleges across the nation. Short fiction topics are open, the only restriction being status as an undergraduate student. Volume is aimed at the undergraduate student with an aim towards providing the missing communications link between undergraduate writers in this nation." Annually. Estab. 1983. Circ. 1,000.
Needs: Confession, contemporary, experimental, humor/satire, literary with any topic, mainstream. "All mss must possess adequate literary merit to be regarded as serious literature. Topics are open. The *Review* is intended primarily as a creative outlet for the undergraduate writer, and is suitable as a creative writing text. In the past three issues we have found the content to be extremely interesting to all levels of readers." Accepts 10-15 fiction mss per volume/year. Published new writers within the last year. Length: 5,000 words average. "Length necessary to tell the tale." Also publishes short shorts. Sometimes recommends other markets.
How to Contact: Query first or send complete manuscript with cover letter (name of school author currently attending; some background on the evolution/creation of the piece). Reports in 2 weeks on queries; 2 months on mss following Jaunary 31 deadline. No response in summer. SASE for query and ms. Photocopied submissions OK. Accepts computer printouts including dot-matrix. Sample copy for 8x11 SAE and 3 first class stamps.
Payment: Free subscription to magazine, contributor's copies, charge for extras.
Terms: Acquires first rights. Publication copyrighted.
Advice: "Selected story judged most outstanding by editors receives $50 award. Although we are entirely student run, we expect submissions with a high level of quality. Be professional and serious—*we are*. The *Review* is ideal for the developing writer to see how and what others in peer group are creating."

ALPHA ADVENTURES SF&F (II), Suite 348, 12322 Poway Rd., Poway CA 92064-4219. Editor: Scott C. Virtes. Magazine: 5½x8½; 48 pages; bond paper; heavy cover stock; illustrations. "We use science fiction and fantasy fiction and poetry" for SF/F readers. Published 4 times/year. Estab. 1981.
Needs: Fantasy, horror, humor/satire, psychic/supernatural/occult and science fiction. No media-based fiction. Receives 150 unsolicited mss/month. Buys 5-10 mss/issue; 4 mss/year. Recently published Doug Beason, Kevin J. Anderson and Uncle River; published new writers within the last year. Length: 4,000 words average; 1,000 words minimum; 11,000 words maximum. Usually comments on rejected mss.
How to Contact: Send complete ms and cover letter. "I like to hear about people and their sales. I usually can't respond on matters not associated with writing, but I do enjoy reading about people and hearing about their successes in the field." Reports in 2-6 weeks. SASE. Photocopied submissions OK. Accepts computer printout submissions. Prefers letter-quality. Sample copy $2. Fiction guidelines for #10 SAE and 1 first class stamp.
Payment: ½¢/word plus contributor's copy; extra copies at wholesale rates.
Terms: Pays on publication for first North American serial rights.
Advice: "Fantasy seems to be dominating science fiction these days; as such, we have a hard time getting enough SF to balance the fantasy we use. We're most eager to get mid-length stories from 2,000 to 8,000 words. Study the markets before sending anything, and try to meet with other writers (famous or nonfamous) where possible."

ALPHA BEAT SOUP (IV), 5110 Adam St., Montréal Québec H1V 1W8 Canada. (514)255-3159. Editor: Dave Christy. Magazine: 7½x9; 95-125 pages; illustrations. "Beat and modern literature—prose, reviews and poetry." Semiannually. Plans special fiction issue. Estab. 1987. Circ. 150.

Needs: Erotica, experimental, literary and prose poem. Recently published work by Carles Bukowski, Joy Walsh and Arthur Knight; published new writers within the last year. Length: 600 words minimum; 1,000 words maximum. Sometimes recommends other markets.
How to Contact: Query first. Reports on queries ASAP. SASE. Simultaneous, photocopied and reprint submissions OK. Sample copy for $2.
Payment: Pays in contributor's copies.
Terms: Rights remain with author. Publication not copyrighted.
Advice: "We've grown! Have published 2 poetry chapbooks; much more planned. *ABS* is the finest journal of its kind available today, having, with 3 issues, published 45 different writers—both published and unpublished."

‡**ALPHA LITERARY MAGAZINE (I)**, Either/Or Publications, Box 1269, Wolfville, Nova Scotia B0P 1X0 Canada. Editor: Siân Morris Ross. "*Alpha* is a literary magazine interested in developing new authors. We publish mostly short fiction and poetry." Semiannually. Estab. 1970. Circ. 560.
Needs: Literary, prose poem. "No concrete or experimental fiction." Receives 8-10 unsolicited mss/month. Accepts 4 mss/issue; 8 mss/year. Length: 2,500 words average; 2 words minimum; 6,000 words maximum. Sometimes critiques rejected mss.
How to Contact: Send complete ms. Reports in 3 weeks on queries; 2 months on mss. SAE, IRC for mss. Simultaneous submissions OK. Sample copy for $2 and large manila envelope.
Payment: Pays 2-3 contributor's copies.
Terms: All rights retained by author. Publication copyrighted.
Advice: "Unfortunately, writers seem to hide in obscure prose; the trend now seems to be to move away from clear fiction, as it is difficult to master. Clean, readable copy is necessary; lucid style is appreciated."

Amelia is a perfect bound 5½x8½ magazine published quarterly which uses four-color covers, original illustrations or b&w photos for covers. It publishes "fine fiction, poetry, criticism, belles lettres, one-act plays, . . . book reviews and translations of both fiction and poetry for general readers with catholic tastes for quality writing." Cover illustration by Adam Niklewicz.

MERRILL JOAN GERBER
EUGENE DUBNOV
ADAM NIKLEWICZ
LEV RAPHAEL

AMELIA (II), 329 E St., Bakersfield CA 93304. (805)323-4064. Editor-in-chief: Frederick A. Raborg Jr. Magazine: 5½x8½; 124-136 pages; perfect bound; 60 lb high quality moistrite matte paper; kromekote cover; four-color covers; original illustrations; b&w photos. "A general review using fine fiction, poetry, criticism, belles lettres, one-act plays, fine pen-and-ink sketches and line drawings, sophisticated cartoons, book reviews and translations of both fiction and poetry for general readers with catholic tastes for quality writing." Quarterly. Plans special fiction issue each July. Estab. 1984. Circ. 1,250.
Needs: Adventure, contemporary, erotica, ethnic, experimental, fantasy, feminist, gay, historical (general), humor/satire, lesbian, literary, mainstream, prose poem, regional, science fiction, senior citizen/retirement, sports, suspense/mystery, translations, western. Nothing "obviously pornographic or

patently religious." Receives 160-180 unsolicited mss/month. Buys up to 9 mss/issue; 25-36 mss/year. Published 4 new writers within the last year. Recently published Judson Jerome, Jack Curtis, Eugene Dubnov and Merrill Joan Gerber. Length: 3,000 words average; 1,000 words minimum; 5,000 words maximum. Usually critiques rejected ms. Sometimes recommends other markets.

How to Contact: Send complete manuscript. Cover letter with previous credits if applicable to *Amelia* and perhaps a brief personal comment to show personality and experience. Reports in 1 week on queries; 2 weeks-3 months on mss. SASE. Photocopied submissions OK. Accepts computer printout submissions; prefers letter-quality. Sample copy for $6.50. Fiction guidelines free for #10 SAE and 1 first class stamp.

Payment: Pays $35-$50 plus 2 contributor's copies; extras with 20% discount.

Terms: Pays on acceptance. Buys first North American serial rights. Sends galleys to author "when deadline permits." Publication copyrighted.

Advice: "Write carefully and well, but have a strong story to relate. I look for depth of plot and uniqueness, and strong characterization. Study manuscript mechanics and submission procedures. Neatness does count. There is a sameness—a cloning process—among most magazines today that tends to dull the senses. Magazines like *Amelia* will awaken those senses while offering stories and poems of lasting value."

AMERICAN ATHEIST (II, IV), A Journal of Atheist News and Thought, American Atheist Press, Box 140195, Austin TX 78714-0195. (512)458-1244. Editor: R. Murray-O'Hair. Magazine: 8½x11; 44 pages; 60 lb offset paper; 80 lb glossy cover; illustrations and photographs. "The *American Atheist* is devoted to the history and lifestyle of atheism, as well as critiques of religion. It attempts to promote an understanding of atheism, while staying aware of religious intrusions into modern life. Most of its articles are aimed at a general—but atheistic—readership. Most readers are college or self-educated." Monthly. Estab. 1958. Circ. 30,000.

Needs: Contemporary, feminist, historical (general), humor/satire, atheist, anti-religious. "All material should have something of particular interest to atheists." No religious fiction. Receives 0-6 mss/month. "We would like to publish 1 story per issue; we do *not* receive enough quality mss to do so." Publishes ms "1-3 months" after acceptance. Length: 2,000-3,000 words preferred; 800 words minumum; 5,000 words maximum. Sometimes critiques rejected mss.

How to Contact: Send complete ms with cover letter and biographical material. Reports in 8 weeks. SASE. Photocopied submissions OK. Accepts computer printout submissions, including dot-matrix. Accepts electronic submissions, "Word Perfect compatible or in ASCII. Should be accompanied by printout." Sample copy 9x12 SAE or label. Fiction guidelines for #10 SASE.

Payment: $15/thousand words, free subscription to the magazine and contributor's copies.

Terms: Pays on acceptance for one-time rights. Publication copyrighted.

Advice: "Our magazine has a preponderance of serious 'heavy' reading matter. Sometimes our readers need a break from it. There's so little atheist fiction, we would like to encourage it."

AMERICAN FICTION '89 (II) Wesley Press, Suite C-201, 309 Farmington Ave., Farmington CT 06032. Editor: Michael C. White. Magazine: 5¾x8¼; 200-300 pages; illustrations. Annually. For "serious readers of fiction." Circ. 1,500 paper; 150 hardcover.

Needs: Contemporary, experimental, literary. Receives 500-600 mss/year. Buys or accepts 15-20 mss/year. Does not read mss January-October. "Send *only* after our *AWP* and *Poets & Writers* ads appear." Publishes ms within 3-4 months of acceptance. Charges $7.50 reading fee. Recently published work by Ursula Hegi, Burton Raffel, Leslee Becker. Length: 5,000 words average 10,000 words maximum. Publishes short shorts. Sometimes critiques rejected mss.

How to Contact: "Send ms, cover/bio, after reading our ads in *AWP* and *Poets & Writers*." SASE for query. "We don't return mss." Simultaneous and photocopied submissions OK. Accepts computer printout submissions, including dot-matrix. Sample copy for $6 and $1 postage. Fiction guidelines for #10 SAE and 1 first class stamp.

Payment: Pays $50 maximum and contributor's copies. "$500, $200, $100 awards to top 3 stories based on guest judge's decision."

Terms: Pays on publication for first North American serial rights. "The *American Fiction* series is a contest. Top 15-20 stories published, with awards given to judge's top 3 stories. 1988 judge was Raymond Carver."

Advice: Looks for "moving, interesting, engaging characters, action, language."

‡AMERICAN SCREAMER (IV), Box 2158, Joliet IL 60434. Editor: Stephen D. Black III. Magazine: 5½x8½; 56 pages; 10M-S20 paper; camera-ready illustrations. "*American Screamer* is a literary (prose, poetry, artwork) magazine with a satirical, parodying, aggressively humorous bend. Some 'serious' works published if the editor likes them." Quarterly. Estab. 1987. Circ. 300.

Needs: Humor/satire, "Any or all if written 'tongue-in-cheek.' " Receives 12 mss/month. Accepts no more than 6 mss/year. Publishes ms within 3 month period unless otherwise specified. Recently published work by Tom Lane, Karen I. Frank, Steve Siedler. Length: 2,000 words average. Publishes short shorts. Length: 300 to 500 words. Sometimes critiques rejected mss and recommends other markets.

How to Contact: Query first. Reports "usually within three-month period, though no responsibility taken for unsolicited manuscripts." SASE. Simultaneous, photocopied and reprint submissions OK. Accepts computer printout submissions, including dot-matrix. Sample copy $3 (four-issue subscription is $10). Fiction guidelines for #10 SAE and 1 first class stamp.

Payment: Pays in contributor's copies.

Terms: Acquires one-time rights. Publication copyrighted.

Advice: "Best idea is to purchase a sample subscription or copy and ascertain what type of writing is considered by *American Screamer* to be satirical, funny, etc. Don't inhibit yourself. Send it in as is; if I like it, I will use it as close to verbatim as possible; if I don't like it, try somewhere else. It might fit better in a different publication. Just because it doesn't fit in *American Screamer* doesn't mean it is bad; keep trying; somebody, somewhere, will probably want to use it."

THE AMERICAN VOICE (II), Ste 1215, Heyburn Bldg, Broadway at 4th Avenue, Louisville KY 40202. (502)562-0045. Editors: Sallie Bingham and Frederick Smock. Magazine: 6x9; 110 pages; acid-free paper; 80 lb cover; photos occasionally. "An eclectic reader, publishing work by new and established writers in the U.S., Canada and South America, for a usually—but not necessarily—college educated audience." Quarterly. Estab. 1985. Circ. 1,500.

Needs: Experimental, feminist, gay, humor/satire, lesbian, literary, serialized/excerpted novel, translations. "Nothing that is racist, sexist, homophobic or classist." Receives 400 unsolicited mss/month. Buys 5 mss/issue; 20 mss/year. Publishes ms approximately 5 months after acceptance. Agented fiction 5%. No preferred word length. Publishes short shorts. Occasionally critiques rejected mss and recommends other markets.

How to Contact: Send complete ms with cover letter, which should include the writer's publishing history. Reports in 6 weeks on mss. SASE. Simultaneous and photocopied submissions OK. Accepts computer printout submissions, including dot-matrix. Sample copy for $5.

Payment: Pays $400—prose; $150—translator of prose, and free subscription to magazine.

Terms: Pays on publication for first North American serial rights. Sometimes sends galleys to author. Publication copyrighted.

THE ANGLICAN MAGAZINE (II), The Anglican Church of Canada, 600 Jarvis St., Toronto Ontario M4Y 2J6 Canada. (416)924-9192. Editor: John Bird. Magazine: half tabloid; 48 pages; upgraded newsprint paper; glossy cover stock; b&w illustrations; b&w inside photographs; color cover. "*The Anglican Magazine* calls forth from its readers a Christian response to family and social concerns. Encourages and aids the ministry of clergy and lay people. Especially interested in human rights and justice issues. Our readers are committed Christians, especially of the Anglican Church (Episcopal). Readers want to know about Anglican and other Christian life in all areas of the world. They want to know how they can minister with people in local communities." Published seven times a year. Estab. 1889. Circ. 10,000.

Needs: Literary, contemporary and humor. "We do not require religious/inspirational stories. No sentimental writing; no moralizing please!" Buys up to 1 ms/issue. Receives approximately 10 unsolicited fiction mss/month. "We publish work by little known authors. We definitely favour Canadian writers." Length: 1,000-1,500 words.

How to Contact: Send complete ms with SAE and IRC (*not US stamps*). Reports in 1 month on ms. Publishes ms 3-6 months after acceptance. Free sample copy.

Payment: Pays in author's copies.

Terms: Publication copyrighted.

Advice: "Don't write long letters to the editor. Make sure you study the market; read the whole magazine, not just the fiction. We receive very few good stories. If you can write simply, with insight and sensitivity, let us see your work. If it's done well, fiction can be highly effective in informing and helping the reader to understand and respond to an issue—to know what it feels like to be a certain person in a certain situation. Stories do not have to be overly 'religious' to reflect the truth about God's children." Mss are rejected because they are "too long or there is too much moralizing. We sometimes 'discover' a beginning writer who has potential."

‡ANOTHER POINT OF VIEW (I), 906 N. Evergreen Ave., Arlington Heights IL 60004. (312)253-5226. Editor: Todd Brown. Magazine: 8½x11; number of pages varies; copying paper and cover stock; illustrations. "*APoV* is open to anyone interested; so far, writers, artists, thespians, poets, political activists, other 'zine editors, and people who can read have seen it (oh, and a high school teacher)." Bimonthly. Plans special fiction issue in the future. Estab. 1988. Circ. 200.

Needs: Adventure, confession, contemporary, erotica, experimental, fantasy, feminist, historical (general), horror, humor/satire, literary, regional, science fiction, serialized/excerpted novel, suspense/mystery, translations, western.

How to Contact: Query first with clips of published work or send complete ms with cover letter, which should include "any info the author wishes to include (intended message, theme, inspiration, etc.), name and possible other works. If it fits comfortably into my mag, I'll be more than happy to print it there. If it's too long, I can work in conjunction with another editor to print an actual micro-novella." Reports in 1-3 weeks. Simultaneous, photocopied and reprint submissions OK. Computer printout submissions OK. Sample copy and fiction guidelines free.

Payment: Free subscription to magazine.

Terms: "If someone sends me a piece with some sort of ownership statement, I assume they have the rights to it. Otherwise it can be republished with or without consent." Sends pre-publication galleys to author.

Advice: "Underground works like *APoV* are more lenient (but not that much!) in what sorts of pieces they choose. The underground is an excellent vehicle for one's creative efforts because communication between editor and contributor is much more personal than with professional publications, and criticism is both easier to give and more accurate yet supporting in such a situation. If a writer is going to send me a work, I want that writer to feel that it deserves publication. I don't want to see second-rate works that a writer had nothing better to do with than send it to some small-time publisher of avant material in hopes of a little recognition."

ANTAEUS (III), The Ecco Press, 18 W. 30th St., New York NY 10001. (212)685-8240. Editor-in-Chief: Daniel Halpern. Managing and Associate Editor: Lee Ann Chearneyi. Magazine: 6½x9; 275 pages; Warren old style paper; illustrations and photographs sometimes. "Literary magazine of fiction and poetry, literary documents, and occasional essays for those seriously interested in contemporary writing." Quarterly. Estab. 1970. Circ. 5,000.

Needs: Contemporary, literary, prose poem, excerpted novel, and translations. No romance, science fiction. Receives 600 unsolicited fiction mss/month. Recently published fiction by Richard Ford, Donald Hall, Joyce Carol Oates; published new writers within the last year. Rarely critiques rejected mss.

How to Contact: Send complete ms with SASE. Photocopied submissions OK; no multiple submissions. Accepts computer printout submissions; prefers letter-quality. Reports in 6-8 weeks. Sample copy $5. Fiction guidelines free with SASE.

Payment: Pays $10/page and 2 free contributor's copies. 40% discount for extras.

Terms: Pays on publication for first North American serial rights and right to reprint in any anthology consisting of 75% or more material from *Antaeus*. Publication copyrighted.

Advice: "Read the magazine before submitting. Most mss are solicited, but we do actively search the unsolicited mss for suitable material. Unless stories are extremely short (2-3 pages), send only one. Do not be angry if you get only a printed rejection note; we *have* read the manuscript. Always include an SASE. Keep cover letters short, cordial and to the point."

ANTIETAM REVIEW (II,IV), Washington County Arts Council, 82 W. Washington St., Hagerstown MD 21740. (301)791-3132. Editor: Ann B. Knox. Magazine: 8½x11; 42 pages; photos. A literary journal of short fiction, poetry and black-and-white photographs. Annually. Estab. 1982. Circ. 1,000.

Needs: Contemporary, ethnic, experimental, feminist, literary and prose poem. "We read manuscripts from our region—Maryland, Pennsylvania, Virginia, West Virginia and Washington D.C. only. We read from October 1 to March 1." Receives about 100 unsolicited mss/month; accepts 7-9 stories/year. Recently published work by Rachel Simon, Elisavietta Ritchie, Philip Bufithis; published new writers within the last year. Length: 3,000 words average.

How to Contact: "Send ms and SASE with a cover letter. Let us know if you have published before and where." Photocopies OK. Accepts computer printouts; prefers letter-quality. Reports in 4 to 8 weeks. "If we hold a story, we let the writer know. Occasionally we critique returned ms or ask for rewrites." Sample copy $4.50.

Payment: "We believe it is a matter of dignity that writers and poets be paid. We have been able to give $100 a story and $25 a poem, but this depends on funding. Also 2 copies." Prizes: "We offer a $100 annual literary award in addition to the $100, for the best story."

Terms: Acquires first North American serial rights. Publication copyrighted. Sends pre-publication galleys to author if requested.

Advice: "We look for well crafted work that shows attention to clarity and precision of language. We like relevant detail but want to see significant emotional movement within the course of the story—something happening to the central character. This journal was started in response to the absence of fiction markets for emerging writers. Its purpose is to give exposure to fiction writers, poets and photographers of high artistic quality who might otherwise have difficulty placing their work."

THE ANTIGONISH REVIEW, St. Francis Xavier University, Antigonish, Nova Scotia B2G 1C0 Canada. (902)867-3962. Editor: George Sanderson. Literary magazine for educated and creative readers. Quarterly. Estab. 1970. Circ. 800.
Needs: Literary, contemporary, prose poem and translations. No erotic or political material. Accepts 6 mss/issue. Receives 25 unsolicited fiction mss each month. Recently published work by Arnold Bloch, Richard Butts and Helen Barolini; published new writers within the last year. Length: 3,000-5,000 words. Sometimes comments briefly on rejected mss.
How to Contact: Send complete ms with cover letter. SASE or IRC. Accepts disk submissions compatible with Apple and Macintosh. Prefers hard copy with disk submission. Reports in 12 weeks. Publishes ms 3-12 months after acceptance.
Payment: 2 free author's copies.
Terms: Acquires first rights. Publication copyrighted.
Advice: "Learn the fundamentals and do not deluge an editor." Rejects mss because of "poor style—usually foggy, dull or unclear."

ANTIOCH REVIEW (II), Box 148, Yellow Springs OH 45387. (513)767-7386. Editor: Robert S. Fogarty. Associate Editor: Nolan Miller. Magazine: 6x9; 128 pages; 60 lb book offset paper; coated cover stock; illustrations "seldom." "Literary and cultural review of contemporary issues in politics, American and international studies, and literature for general readership." Quarterly. Published special fiction issue last year; plans another. Estab. 1941. Circ. 4,000.
Needs: Literary, contemporary, translations and experimental. No children's, science fiction or popular market. Buys 3-4 mss/issue, 10-12 mss/year. Receives approximately 175 unsolicited fiction mss each month. Approximately 1-2% of fiction agented. Published new writers within the last year: Miriam Kugnets, Hiram Moody and Doug O'Hara. Length: any length the story justifies.
How to Contact: Send complete ms with SASE, preferably mailed flat. Accepts computer printout submissions, prefers letter-quality. Reports in 2 months. Publishes ms 6-9 months after acceptance. Sample copy $5; free guidelines with SASE.
Payment: $10/page; 2 free author's copies. $2.70 for extras.
Terms: Pays on publication for first and one-time rights (rights returned to author on request). Publication copyrighted.
Advice: "Our best advice, always, is to *read* the Antioch Review to see what type of material we publish. Quality fiction requires an engagement of the reader's intellectual interest supported by mature emotional relevance, written in a style that is rich and rewarding without being freaky. The great number of stories submitted to us indicates that fiction apparently still has great appeal. We assume that if so many are writing fiction, many must be reading it."

L'APACHE (II), An International Journal of Literature and Art, Kathryn Vilips Studios, Inc., P.O. Drawer G, Wofford Heights CA 93285. (619)376-3634. Editor: Kathryn Vilips. Fiction Editor: Bill Jackson. Journal: 6x9; 144 pages and up; 70 lb stock; varnished 4-color cover; illustrations and photos. "Heavy stock; excellent quality; perfect bound. Literature and writing on art, history, anthropology, archaeology and Indians for a university-level audience." Semiannually. Estab. 1986.
Needs: Ethnic, historical (general), literary, prose poem, translations, art history, Indians, foreign. No violence, erotica, science fiction or witchcraft. Buys 2 mss/issue; 8 mss/year. Publishes ms 3-6 months (sometimes less) after acceptance. Length: 3,000 words average. "We will not reject a good story that is under or over the word length." Publishes short shorts. Occasionally critiques rejected mss or recommends other markets.
How to Contact: Send complete ms and "a short bio, and, in the case of a contest, a 5x7 (or smaller) black and white glossy, if desired. Do *not* send originals." Reports in 3 months or less. SASE. Photocopied submissions OK. Accepts computer printout submissions, including dot-matrix. Sample copy for $5, 8x11 SAE and $1 postage. Fiction guidelines for #SAE and 1 first class stamp.
Payment: Pays $25-$50 "except for contests." Pays double for translations when both English and foreign language versions are sent.
Terms: Pays on publication for first and foreign rights. Publication copyrighted.
Advice: "Bring the story full circle. Tie up the ending with the beginning. I like stories that sometimes begin in the middle. Love is fine, but no descriptive sex scenes. Indian stories, legends, fiction based on reality, archaeology or history get a good chance of being published. I especially seek submissions from Indian writers, black writers and readers from foreign universities and libraries. Despite writer's guidelines *L'Apache* still receives 7 to 8 mss a week that are written in bad taste. They are rejected immediately. My best stories have come from unpublished writers, apparently because they haven't fallen into the trap of sex, violence or drugs in their stories."

APAEROS (I), 960 S.W. Jefferson Ave., Corvallis, OR 97333. Clerks: Kathe and John Burt. Newsletter: 8½x11; 24-32 pages; photos if photocopyable. "Sex, erotica, relationships (het, lesbian, gay), turn-ons, nudism, VD and rape prevention, etc. For sharing feelings, knowledge, questions, problems, stories, drawings and fantasies. Ready-to-photocopy pages published unedited." Bimonthly. Estab. 1985. Circ. 60.
Needs: Confession, erotica, feminist, gay, lesbian, romance (contemporary, historical, young adult), prose poem, science fiction, serialized/excerpted novel, spiritual. Published new writers within the last year. Publishes short shorts. Sometimes comments on rejected mss or recommends other markets.
How to Contact: Send $2 and SASE for sample and guidelines. SASE for mss. Simultaneous, photocopied and reprint submissions OK. Accepts computer printouts, including dot-matrix. Sample copy and guidelines for 9½x4 envelope and 1 first class stamp. "State that you are over 18."
Payment: "Increased pages; maybe free subscription extensions."
Terms: Publication copyrighted via "common law."
Advice: "*Apaeros* is *un*edited, reader-written. The amateur press is good for learning the trade."

APALACHEE QUARTERLY (II), Apalachee Press, Inc., Box 20106, Tallahassee FL 32316. (904)878-1591. Editors: Barbara Hamby, Bruce Boehrer, Paul McCall, Pam Ball and Claudia Johnson. Magazine: 50-100 pages; heavy paper; illustrations; photos. Contemporary journal of fiction, poetry and drama. Quarterly. Published special fiction issue last year; plans another. Estab. 1972. Circ. over 500.
Needs: Literary and contemporary. "We want high quality, modern fiction and poetry." Buys 30 mss/issue, 120 mss/year. Receives 200 unsolicited fiction mss month. Published 10 unpublished writers within the last year. Length: 700-6,000 words. Also publishes short shorts. Critiques rejected mss when there is time. Does not read mss in summer. Sometimes recommends other markets.
How to Contact: Send complete ms with SASE. Accepts computer printout submissions. Prefers letter-quality. Reports in 3 months. Sample copy $3.50.
Payment: 2 free author's copies. Payment when funds are available.
Terms: Acquires first rights. Publication copyrighted.
Advice: "We sometimes sponsor regional or statewide contests, depending on grant money. Don't send early drafts. Polish your work. Read modern fiction and poetry. And work on finding your own voice."

APPALACHIAN HERITAGE (I, II), Berea College, Hutchins Library, Berea KY 40404. (606)986-9341. Editor: Sidney Farr. Magazine: 9½x7; 80 pages; 60 lb stock; 10 pt Warrenflo cover; drawings and clip art; b&w photos. "*Appalachian Heritage* is a southern Appalachian literary magazine. We try to keep a balance of fiction, poetry, essays, scholarly works, etc., for a general audience and/or those interested in the Appalachian mountains." Quarterly. Estab. 1973. Circ. 1,100.
Needs: Regional, literary, historical. Receives 20-25 unsolicited mss/month. Accepts 2 or 3 mss/issue; 10 or more mss/year. Recently published work by Robert Morgan, Richard Hague and James Still; published new writers within the last year. No reading fee, but "would prefer a subscription first." Length: 2,000-2,500 word average; 3,000 words maximum. Publishes short shorts. Length: 500 words. Occasionally critiques rejected mss and recommends other markets.
How to Contact: Send complete ms with cover letter. Reports in 1-2 weeks on queries; 3-4 weeks on mss. SASE for ms. Simultaneous, photocopied submissions OK "if clear and readable." Accepts computer printout submissions, no dot-matrix. Sample copy for $4.
Payment: 3 free contributor's copies; $4 charge for extras.
Terms: Acquires one-time rights. Publication copyrighted.
Advice: "Trends in fiction change frequently. Right now the trend is toward slick, modern pieces with very little regional or ethnic material appearing in print. The pendulum will swing the other way again, and there will be a space for that kind of fiction. It seems to me there is always a chance to have really good writing published, somewhere. Keep writing and keep trying the markets. Diligent writing and rewriting can perfect your art. Be sure to study the market. Do not send me a slick piece of writing set in New York City, for example, with no idea on your part of the kinds of things I am interested in seeing. It is a waste of your time and money. Get a sample copy, or subscribe to the publication, study it carefully, then send your material."

THE APPLE BLOSSOM CONNECTION (II), Peak Output Unlimited, 122 S. Broad St., Box 325, Stacyville IA 50476. (515)737-2269. Editor: Mary M. Blake. Fiction Editor: Jacquelyn D. Scheneman. Digest: 5½x8½; 32-36 pages; 60 lb offset paper; colored text cover; occasional illustrations and photographs. "*ABC* is for writers of all experience levels. Material is for both writers and the general audience." Monthly. Plans special fiction issue. Estab. 1987. Circ. approaching 3,000.
Needs: Adventure, contemporary, ethnic, historical (general), horror, humor/satire, juvenile (5-9 years), literary, mainstream, prose poem, regional, religious/inspirational, romance (contemporary, historical, young adult), science fiction, senior citizen/retirement, suspense/mystery, western, young adult/teen (10-18 years). "Nothing off color, lewd, insensitive." Receives 100-150 unsolicited mss/

month. Accepts 1-3 mss/issue; 12-36 mss/year. Publishes ms 2-6 months after acceptance. Recently published work by Bobby G. Warner, Michael C. McPherson and Dee Stuart; published new writers within the last year. Length: 1,000 words average; 500 words minimum; 1,800 words maximum. Publishes short shorts. Length: 300-500 words. Sometimes critiques rejected mss and recommends other markets. "Considers every submission for possible publication in all of Peak Output's current publishing projects."

How to Contact: Send complete ms with cover letter. "We like to know a little something about the writer. A 50-100 word autobiographical sketch, sometimes condensed, is usually shared with our readers." Reports in 1-8 weeks. SASE vital. Simultaneous, photocopied and reprint submissions OK. Accepts computer printout submissions, including dot-matrix. Sample copy for $5; fiction guidelines for SASE.

Payment: Pays $1-$85 plus contributor's copy.

Terms: Pays on publication for First North American serial rights and/or one-time rights. Publication copyrighted. Offers The Big Apple Award 3 times/year with a $50 prize. Send SASE for details.

Advice: "Our small press publication is a good place for a beginning writer to get his/her foot in the door. Use a standard format when submitting your manuscript. Create believable characters. Don't waste words. We send a permission release form requiring author's signature with every acceptance; your SASE is *vital*. SASPs (postcards) can only be used to acknowledge *receipt* of your manuscript, *not* acceptance."

‡ARBA SICULA (II, IV), Box D, c/o Saint Finbar's Parish, 138 Bay 20th St. Brooklyn NY 11214. Editor: Gaetano Cipolla. Magazine: 6x9; 85 pages; top-grade paper; good quality cover stock; illustrations; photos. Bilingual ethnic literary review (Sicilian-English) dedicated to the dissemination of Sicilian culture. Published 2-4 times a year. Plans special fiction issue. Estab. 1979. Circ. 1,500.

Needs: Accepts ethnic literary material consisting of various forms of folklore, stories both contemporary and classical, regional, romance (contemporary, historical, young adult) and senior citizen. Material submitted must be in the Sicilian language, with English translation desirable. Published new writers within the last year. Critiques rejected mss when there is time. Sometimes recommends other markets.

How to Contact: Send complete ms with SASE and bio. Reports in 2 months. Publishes ms 1-3 years after acceptance. Simultaneous submissions and reprints OK. Sample copy $8 with 8½x11 SASE and 90¢ postage.

Payment: 5 free author's copies. $4 for extra copies.

Terms: Acquires all rights. Publication copyrighted.

Advice: "This review is a must for those who nurture a love of the Sicilian language." Mss are rejected because of "poor Sicilian language. Provide both Sicilian and English. If you have good clean stuff for a literate market, we're interested."

ARGONAUT (II), Box 4201, Austin TX 78765-4201. Editor: Michael Ambrose. Magazine: 8¼x5¼; 48 pages; 60 lb paper; varied cover stock; illustrations; photos. "*Argonaut* is a weird fantasy/science fiction magazine. The word 'fantasy' carries few restrictions here. *Argonaut* readers want original, literate, unusual stories." Annually. Estab. 1972. Circ. 500.

Needs: Science fiction, fantasy, horror and prose poem. Buys 5-8 mss/issue. Receives 40-50 unsolicited fiction mss each month. Reading period is October 1-March 31. Recently published work by Kiel Stuart, James W. Holzer and Elizabeth Massie. Length: 2,500-10,000 words. Sometimes recommends other markets.

How to Contact: Send complete ms with SASE. "It is nice to know a little something about the author." Reports in 1-2 months. Sample copy $3.

Payment: 2 or more copies. $3 charge for extras or 5 copies or more at 40% discount.

Terms: Acquires first North American serial rights. Publication copyrighted.

Advice: "Read *Argonaut* and other small press magazines before submitting anything. Don't submit more than one story at a time, and keep trying when rejected. *Argonaut's* infrequent publishing schedule compels me to be very selective of the stories I receive. It takes more than a polished style with no originality of idea, or all idea with no style on the other hand, to get me interested. Be willing to work with an editor to improve material."

ARNAZELLA (II), Arnazella's Reading List, English Department, Bellevue Community College, Bellevue WA 98009. (206)641-2341. Advisor: Roger George. Magazine: 6x5; 104 pages, 70 lb paper; heavy coated cover; illustrations and photos. "For those interested in quality fiction." Annually. Estab. 1976. Circ. 500.

Needs: Adventure, contemporary, erotica, ethnic, experimental, fantasy, feminist, gay, historical, humor/satire, lesbian, literary, mainstream, prose poem, regional, religious/inspirational, science fiction, suspense/mystery, translations. Receives 7 unsolicited mss/month. Submit in Fall and Winter for issue to be published in Spring. Published new writers within the last year. Publishes short shorts. Sometimes critiques rejected mss.

How to Contact: Send complete ms with cover letter. Reports on mss in 2 months. SASE. Photo-copied submissions OK. Accepts computer printout submissions, including dot-matrix. Sample copy for $5. Fiction guidelines for #10 SAE and 1 first class stamp.

Payment: Pays in contributor's copies.

Terms: Acquires first rights. "Best student story earns $25."

Advice: "Read this and similar magazines, reading critically and analytically."

‡THE ARRASTRA (I,II,IV), Chaffee County's Literary Magazine, 15985 Transmission Rd., Buena Vista CO 81211. (719)395-8765. Editor: Mike Dolan. Magazine: 8½X5½; 44 pages; 20 lb dupli-cator paper; bristol cover stock; illustrations. "Fiction with a Chaffee County background is preferred, but not required. Each issue has a different topic or theme. A 6-issue schedule is available. For local readers and former Chaffee County residents living nationwide." Quarterly. Plans special fiction issue. Estab. 1981. Circ. 100.

Needs: Adventure, experimental, fantasy, horror, humor/satire, juvenile (5-9 years), literary, main-stream, psychic/supernatural/occult, regional, contemporary/young-adult romance, science fiction, sports, suspense/mystery, western, young adult/teen (10-18 years). "Should relate to Chaffee County and the high river valleys of the central Colorado rockies, because this is where our readers live, or used to. However, I've also used stories set in Utah's mesa country, rural California, and eastern or midwest-ern cities in the nostalgic past. And SF and fantasy can take place anywhere!" No 'urban' fiction. No 'mean streets.' Writers *must* know their genre! Be honest. No language or topic taboos, but stories must not be unnecessarily offensive." Receives less than 12 mss/month. Accepts 6-12 mss/issue; 24-48 mss/year. Publishes ms within 3-6 months of acceptance. Recently published work by Linda Lehmann, Arlene Shovald and Jack Michaels. Length: 1,500 words preferred; 600 words minimum; 3,000 words maximum. Publishes short shorts. Length: 400 words. Sometimes critiques rejected mss; recommends other markets if possible.

How to Contact: Query first or send complete manuscript with cover letter. "Visit Chaffee Country and let it inspire you. Then send us the result." Cover letter should include "real name, age, brief per-sonal background." Reports in 2 weeks. SASE. Accepts computer printout submissions, including dot-matrix. Sample copy $2.50, #10 SAE and 1 first class stamp.

Payment: Pays contributor's copies, charge for extras.

Terms: Acquires one-time rights. Sends galleys of stories to author.

Advice: "The best new fiction is being written and published *outside* the mainstream!" Looks for "quality and originality; a complete plot that makes sense; and ending that leaves you feeling good, and feeling that you know more about life, and people, than you did when you started reading; a quick begin-ning and a fast pace; inspiration, not a mechanical knocked-together job; something new and fun."

‡ART BRIGADE (IV), 1603 Bonham, Amarillo TX 79102. (806)372-8466. Editor: Ben Davis. Fiction Editors: Ben Davis and Mark Capps. Tabloid: 11x14; 24-32 pages; newsprint paper; book stock cover; illustrations and photographs. "*Art Brigade* exists for the purpose of publishing bold new fiction and poetry, covering personalities in the arts, and helping people link up with other alternative media outlets. For other writers, musicians, independent publishers and artists. Also distributed to college students and others in Texas." Bimonthly. Plans special fiction issue. Bimonthly. Estab. 1987. Circ. 5,000.

Needs: Contemporary, erotica, experimental, fantasy, feminist, gay, horror, humor/satire, lesbian, lit-erary, science fiction, serialized/excerpted novel, translations, political. "No pointless pornographic nonsense, insipid or two-dimensional genre fiction, hate literature, pieces with a specialized perspec-tive, aimless or amateurish ranting, anything incoherent, new age/pseudoscientific gobbledygook." Receives 25 unsolicited fiction mss/month. Accepts approx. 10 mss/issue; 40-50 mss/year. Publishes fiction an average of 1 month after acceptance. Length: 3,500 words averge; 4,500-5,000 words maxi-mum. Publishes short shorts. Sometimes comments on rejected mss and recommends other markets.

How to Contact: Send complete manuscript with cover leter. Reports in 1 week on queries; 2 weeks on mss. Simultaneous, photocopied and reprint submissions OK, including dot-matrix. Computer printout submissions OK. Sample copy $1; fiction guidelines free.

Payment: Pays in contributors copies.

Terms: Acquires one-time rights. Sends pre-publication galleys to author. Publication copyrighted.

Advice: "Genre fiction and specialized kinds of stuff seem to be flourishing, while general-interest or literary fiction is suffering from a slowly declining readership. The alternative small press does provide an outlet for most kinds of fiction, however, and this is a healthy trend. Be confident and be sure what you are doing is good and worthwhile, and be persistent and aggressive. Any good writer can find an en-thusiastic readership if he tries hard enough, and works on his craft. Be original, innovative, and don't rely on the obvious, but seek to teach and reveal as well as teach or shock. Whatever else, be true to your own personal literary instincts, and persevere."

‡**ART:MAG (II)**, 5055 E. Charleston, F110, Las Vegas NV 89104. (702)459-8475 or (702)383-8624. Editor: Peter Magliocco. Magazine: 5½x8½; 60 pages; 20 lb bond paper; b&w pen and ink illustrations and photographs. Publishes "irreverent, literary-minded work by committed writers," for "small press, quasi-'art-oriented' " audience. Estab. 1984. Circ. under 100.

Needs: Condensed/excerpted novel, confession, contemporary, erotica, ethnic, experimental, fantasy, feminist, gay, historical (general), horror, humor/satire, lesbian, literary, mainstream, prose poem, psychic/supernatural/occult, regional, science fiction, suspense/mystery, translations and arts. No "slick-oriented stuff published by major magazines." Receives 1 plus ms/month. Accepts 1-2 mss/issue; 4-5 mss/year. Publishes ms within 3-6 months of acceptance. Recently published work by Wayne Allen Sallee and Warren C. Miller. Length: 5,000 words preferred; 250 words minimum; 10,000 words maximum. Sometimes critiques rejected mss and recommends other markets.

How to Contact: Send complete ms with cover letter. Reports in 3 months. SASE for ms. Simultaneous and photocopied submissions OK. Sample copy $2.50, 6x9 SAE and 79¢ postage. Fiction guidelines for #10 SAE and first class stamp.

Payment: Pays contributor's copies.

Terms: Acquires one-time rights. Publication copyrighted.

Advice: "Seeking more novel and quality-oriented work, usually from solicited authors. Magazine fiction today needs to be concerned with the issues of fiction-writing itself—not just with a desire to publish or please the largest audience. Think about things in the fine art world as well as the literary one and keep the hard core of life as an in between, guiding ballast for good measure."

ARTEMIS (IV), Artists and Writers from The Blue Ridge Mountains, Box 8147, Roanoke VA 24014. (703)774-8440. Contact: Fiction Editors. Magazine: 6x6; 85 pages; heavy/slick paper; colored cover stock; illustrations; photos. "We publish poetry, art and fiction of the highest quality and will consider any artist/writer who lives or has lived in the Blue Ridge. General adult audience with literary interest." Annually. Estab. 1976. Circ. 2,000 in '89.

Needs: Literary. Wants to see "the best contemporary style." Receives 35 unsolicited fiction mss/year. Accepts 3-4 mss/issue. Does not read mss Jan.-Aug. Publishes ms 4-5 months after acceptance. Recently published works by Rosanne Coggeshall, Jeanne Larsen, Kurt Rheinheimer; published work by new writers within the last year. Length: 1,500 words average; 2,000 words maximum. Sometimes critiques rejected mss.

How to Contact: Submit unpublished ms between Sept. 15-Nov. 15, name on each page, short bio. Reports in 2 months. SASE for ms. Photocopied submissions OK. No multiple submissions. Accepts computer printout. No dot-matrix unless high quality. Sample copy $7.

Payment: 1 complimentary copy. Discount for extra copies.

Terms: Acquires first rights.

Advice: "We went from two to four fiction works in the last issue. We look for polished quality work that holds interest, has imagination, energy, voice."

ARTFUL DODGE (II), Department of English, College of Wooster, Wooster, OH 44691. Editor-in-Chief: Daniel Bourne. Magazine: 100-130 pages; illustrations; photos. "There is no theme in this magazine, except literary power. We also have an ongoing interest in translations from Eastern Europe and elswhere." Semiannually. Estab. 1979. Circ. 750.

Needs: Experimental, literary, prose poem, translations. "We judge by literary quality, not by genre. We are especially interested in fine English translations of significant contemporary prose writers." Receives 30 unsolicited fiction mss/month. Accepts 2-3 mss/issue, 5 mss/year. Recently published work by Elizebeth Bartlett and Tom Hozuka; published 1 new writer within the last year. Length: 10,000 words maximum; 2,500 words average. Occasionally critiques rejected mss.

How to Contact: Send complete ms with SASE. Do not send more than 30 pages at a time. Photocopied submissions OK. Reports in 2-3 months. Sample copies of older, single issues are $2.75 or five issues for $5; recent issues are double issues, available for $5.75. Free fiction guidelines for #10 SAE and 1 first class stamp.

Payment: 1 free contributor's copy (subject to change for the better).

Terms: Acquires first North American serial rights. Publication copyrighted.

Advice: "If we take time to offer criticism, do not subsequently flood us with other stories no better than the first. If starting out, get as many readers, good ones, as possible. Above all, read contemporary fiction and the magazine you are trying to publish in."

THE ASYMPTOTICAL WORLD (II), Box 1372, Williamsport PA 17703. Editor: Michael H. Gerardi. Magazine: 8½x11; 54 pages; glossy paper; illustrated cover; b&w illustrations. "*The Asymptotical World* is a *unique* collection of psychodramas, phantasies, poems and illustrations which elucidates the moods and sensations of the world created in the mind of men, for 18 year olds and older; those who enjoy work completed in style and mood similar to Poe." Annually. Estab. 1984. Circ. 1,300.

Needs: Experimental, fantasy, horror, psychic/supernatural/occult. Receives 30 unsolicited fiction mss/month; accepts 10 fiction mss/issue. Publishes ms 6-12 months after acceptance. Length: 1,000 words minimum; 2,000 words maximum.
How to Contact: Query first. SASE. Reports in 1-2 months on queries; 1-2 months on mss. Simultaneous and photocopied submissions OK. Accepts computer printouts including dot-matrix. Sample copy $6.95 with SAE and 8 first class stamps. Fiction guidelines for 4x9 SAE and 1 first class stamp.
Payment: Pays $20-$50.
Terms: Pays on publication. Acquires first rights. Publication copyrighted.
Advice: "*The Asymptotical World* is definitely unique. It is strongly suggested that a writer review a copy of the magazine to study the format of a psychodrama and the manner in which the plot is left 'open-ended.' The writer will need to study the atmosphere, mood and plot of published psychodramas before preparing a feature work."

‡ATALANTIK (II, IV), 7630 Deer Creek Drive, Worthington OH 43085. (614)885-0550. Editor: Prabhat K. Dutta. Magazine: 8½x11; approx. 80 pages; paper quality and cover stock vary; illustrations and photos. "The publication is bilingual: Indian (Bengali) and English language. This was started to keep the Indian language alive to the Indian immigrants. This contains short stories, poems, essays, sketches, book reviews, cultural news, children's pages, etc." Quarterly. Plans special fiction issue. Estab. 1980. Circ. 400.
Needs: Adventure, condensed novel, contemporary, ethnic, experimental, historical (general), humor/satire, juvenile (5-9 years), literary, mainstream, psychic/supernatural/occult, romance, science fiction, suspense/mystery, translations, travelogue, specially to India. No politics and religion. Receives 10 unsolicited fiction mss/month. Publishes about 2-4 fiction mss/issue; about 30 mss/year. Publishes ms an average of at least 6 months after acceptance. Length: 5,000 words average. Publishes short shorts. Length: 1-2 pages. Sometimes comments on rejected mss and recommends other markets.
How to Contact: Query with clips of published work or send complete ms with cover letter; "author's bio-data and a synopsis of the literary piece(s)." Reports on queries in 1 month; on mss in 4 months. SASE. Photocopied submissions OK, including dot-matrix Computer printout submissions OK. Sample copy $6; fiction guidelines for #10 SASE.
Payment: Pays in contributor's copies; charge for extras.
Terms: Acquires all rights. Publication copyrighted. Sponsors contests for fiction writers.
Advice: "A short story has to be short and should have a story too. A completely imaginative short story without any real life linkage is almost impossible. The language should be lucid and characters kept to a small number. A short story is not simply the description of an incident. It goes far beyond, far deep. It should present the crisis of a single problem. Usually a successful short story contains a singular idea which is developed to its most probable conclusion in a uniquely charted path."

ATHENA INCOGNITO MAGAZINE (II), 1442 Judah St., San Francisco CA 94122. (415)665-0219. Editors: Ronn Rosen and Kurt Cline. Magazine: 8½x11; approximately 30-40 pages; illustrations; Xeroxed photos. "Open-format magazine with emphasis on experimental and/or any type of quality writing. Emphasis on poetry especially." Quarterly. Estab. 1980. Circ. 100.
Needs: Any subjects OK. Receives 15 unsolicited mss/month. Publishes mss usually 2-3 months after acceptance. Requires magazine subscription "to cover postage and expense of publication" of $3 (for 1 issue) before reading ms. Published new writers within the last year. Publishes short shorts. No long pieces over 2 pages. Sometimes critiques rejected mss.
How to Contact: Send complete ms with cover letter. Reports in 2 weeks to 1 month. SASE. Simultaneous, photocopied and reprint submissions OK. Accepts computer printout submissions, including dot-matrix. Sample copy for $3; fiction guidelines for SAE and 1 first class stamp.
Payment: Pays in contributor's copies.
Terms: Acquires all rights. Publication not copyrighted.
Advice: "Experiment and practice eclecticism of all kinds! Discover! Pioneer! Dada lives!"

‡ATLANTIS (I), Speculative Fiction Quarterly, Xyder Press, Box 5609-Station B, Victoria, British Columbia V8R 6S4 Canada. (604)477-0951. Editor: David Gordon-MacDonald. Magazine: 8½x11; 64 pages; 20 lb letter bond paper; card cover; b&w illustrations; b&w photographs. "Science fiction, fantasy, horror, some detective and suspense. Explores speculative or fantastic themes." Quarterly. Plans special fiction issue. Estab. 1984. Circ. 1,500.
Needs: Adventure, fantasy, historical (general), horror, humor/satire, science fiction, suspense/mystery. "No manuscripts promoting racial, ethnic, religious or sexual bias." Receives 50 unsolicited mss/month. Accepts 10 mss/issue; 40-50 mss/year. Publishes ms 4-8 months after acceptance. Recently published work by A. David Moncrieff; Jeffrey D. S. Taylor; Carla Luna; published new writers within the last year. Length: 7,000 words average; 500 words minimum; 15,000 words maximum. Sometimes critiques rejected mss and recommends other markets.

How to Contact: Send complete manuscript with cover letter, which should include "short bio; history of past publications (if any); story synopsis." Reports in 4 weeks. SASE. Simultaneous, photocopied and reprint submissions OK. Accepts dot-matrix computer printouts. Sample copy for $2. Fiction guidelines for #10 SAE and 2 first class stamps.
Payment: Free subscription to magazine and contributor's copies.
Terms: Acquires one-time rights. Publication copyrighted.
Advice: Looks for "originality; clear, correct diction; a strong narrative voice; engrossing plots. Don't submit D & D or other role-playing scenarios. Don't submit slightly re-written Stephen King."

ATROCITY (I), Publication of the Absurd Sig of Mensa, 2419 Greensburg Pike, Pittsburgh PA 15221. Editor: Henry Roll. Newsletter: 8½x11; 8 pages; offset 20 lb paper and cover; illustrations; photographs occasionally. Humor and satire for "high IQ-Mensa" members. Monthly. Estab. 1976. Circ. 250.
Needs: Humor/satire. "Liar's Club submissions for those unfamiliar with our contents." Receives 20 unsolicited mss/month. Accepts 5 mss/issue. Publishes ms 3-6 months after acceptance. Recently published work by Bruce Filbeck, Dorothy Heaton and Ted Kelly; published new writers within the last year. Length: 150 words preferred; 650 words maximum. Sometimes recommends other markets.
How to Contact: Send complete ms. "No cover letter necessary if ms states what rights (e.g. first North American serial/reprint, etc.) are offered."Reports in 1 month. SASE. Simultaneous, photocopied and reprint submissions OK. Accepts computer printout submissions; no dot-matrix. Sample copy for 50¢, #10 SAE and 1 first class stamp.
Payment: Pays with free subscription to magazine and contributor's copies.
Terms: Acquires one-time rights. Publication copyrighted.
Advice: "Be funny."

AURA Literary/Arts Review (II), University of Alabama in Birmingham, Box 76, University Station, Birmingham AL 35294. (205)934-3216. Editor: Wendy Freeman Miles. Magazine: 6x9; 150 pages; illustrations and photos. "We publish various types of fiction with an emphasis on short stories. Our audience is college students, the university community and literary-minded adults, the arts community." Semiannually. Estab. 1974. Circ. 1,000.
Needs: Literary, contemporary, science fiction, regional, romance, men's, women's, feminist and ethnic. No mss longer than 7,000-8,000 words. Accepts 3-4 mss/issue. Receives 15-20 unsolicited fiction mss each month. Recently published works by Nickell Romjue, Josephine Marshall, Rodolfo Tomes; published new writers within the last year. Length: 2,000-8,000 words. Publishes short shorts; length according to editor's decision. Critiques rejected mss when there is time.
How to Contact: Send complete ms with SASE. No simultaneous submissions; please include biographical information. Reports in 2 months. Publishes ms 1-2½ months after acceptance. Sample copy $2.50
Payment: 2 free author's copies.
Terms: Acquires first North American serial rights.
Advice: "If it's fiction, we will consider it."

AXE FACTORY REVIEW (III), The Axe Factory, Box 11186, Philadelphia PA 19136. (215)331-7389. Editor: Louis McKee. Fiction Editor: Joseph Farley. Magazine: 8x10; 56 pages. Published irregularly. Estab. 1986. Circ. 500.
Needs: Contemporary, erotica, humor/satire, literary. Receives 2-4 unsolicited mss each month. Does not read during the summer. Publishes short shorts. Sometimes critiques rejected mss.
How to Contact: Send complete ms with cover letter. Reports in 2 weeks on queries; 2-6 weeks on mss. SASE. Simultaneous submissions OK. Accepts computer printout submissions; no dot-matrix. Sample copy for $5.
Payment: Pays 2 contributor's copies.
Terms: Acquires first rights. Publication copyrighted.

THE AZOREAN EXPRESS (I, IV), Seven Buffaloes Press, Box 249, Big Timber MT 59011. Editor: Art Cuelho. Magazine: 6¾x8¼; 32 pages; 60 lb book paper; 3-6 illustrations/issue; photos rarely. "My overall theme is rural; I also focus on working people (the sweating professions); the American Indian and Hobo; the Dustbowl era; and I am also trying to expand with non-rural material. For rural and library and professor/student, blue collar workers, etc." Semiannually. Estab. 1985. Circ. 600.
Needs: Contemporary, ethnic, experimental, humor/satire, literary, regional, western, rural, working people. Receives 10-20 unsolicited mss/month. Accepts 2-3 mss/issue; 4-6 mss/year. Publishes ms 1-6 months after acceptance. Length: 1,000-3,000 words. Also publishes short shorts 500-1,000 words. "I take what I like; length sometimes does not matter, even when longer than usual. I'm flexible." Sometimes recommends other markets.

How to Contact: "Send cover letter with ms; general information, but it can be personal, more in line with the submitted story. Not long rambling letters." Reports in 1-4 weeks on queries; 1-4 weeks on mss. SASE. Photocopied submissions OK. Accepts computer printouts including dot-matrix. Sample copy $3. Fiction guidelines for SASE.
Payment: Contributor's copies. "Depends on the amount of support author gives my press."
Terms: Acquires first North American serial rights. "If I decide to use material in anthology form later, I have that right." Sends pre-publication galleys to the author upon request. Publication copyrighted.
Advice: "There would not be magazines like mine if I was not optimistic. But literary optimism is a two-way street. Without young fiction writers supporting fiction magazines the future is bleak, because the commercial magazines allow only formula or name writers within their pages. My own publications receive no grants. Sole support is from writers, libraries and individuals."

‡BABY SUE (I), Box 1111, Decatur GA 30031. (404)288-2073. Editor: Don W. Seven. Magazine: 8½x11; 20 pages; illustrations and photos. "*Baby Sue* is a collection of music reviews, poetry, short fiction and cartoons," for "anyone who can think and is not easily offended." Quarterly. Plans special fiction issue. Estab. 1983. Circ. 1,500.
Needs: Erotica, experimental and humor/satire. Receives 5-10 mss/month. Accepts 3-4 mss/year. Publishes ms within 1 month of acceptance. Publishes short shorts. Length: 1-2 single-spaced pages.
How to Contact: Query with clips of published work. Reports in 4 weeks. SASE. Accepts computer printout submissions, including dot-matrix. Sample copy for #10 SAE and first class stamp.
Payment: Pays 1 contributor's copy.
Terms: Publication copyrighted.
Advice: "There's more places to get work printed than ever before. The underground press circuit is *great*! If no one will print your work, start your own publication!"

BACKBONE MAGAZINE (I,II,IV), A Journal of Women's Literature, Box 95315, Seattle WA 98145. (206)547-7173. Editor: Lauren Fortune. Magazine: 5½x8½; 80 pages; 80 lb paper; 100 lb cover stock. "Feminist publication—we encourage women who have never been published to submit work that inspires poetic, feminist, spiritual and political dialogue." Semiannually. Estab. 1984. Circ. 1,000.
Needs: Contemporary, ethnic, experimental, feminist, lesbian, literary, regional, translations. "We're looking for new models for women. No violence or degradation." Receives 12 or more unsolicited mss/month. Accepts 15 or more mss/issue; 30 or more mss/year. Published work by new writers within the last year. Length: 2,000-4,000 words. Publishes essays, poems and short shorts. Occasionally comments on rejected mss.
How to Contact: Send complete ms with cover letter and SASE. Reports in 4 weeks on queries; 1 month before publication on mss. SASE. Simultaneous submissions and photocopied submissions OK. Accepts computer printouts. Sample copy $4.50; writer's guidelines free.
Payment: 1 contributor's copy. "If there is cash payment it varies, depending on funding source."
Terms: Pays on publication. Publication copyrighted.
Advice: "Well-crafted stories are accepted. Good spelling is a must."

BAD HAIRCUT QUARTERLY (II), 12922 Harbor Blvd. #942, Garden Grove CA 92640. Editors: Ray GoForth, Kim Richards. Magazine: 8½x11; 100 pages; illustrations. Quarterly. Estab. 1987. Circ. 200.
Needs: Contemporary, experimental, historical (general), horror, humor/satire, mainstream, prose poem, psychic/supernatural/occult, science fiction, translations, political, world-conscious. No pornography, Receives 1 fiction ms/month. Accepts 1-3 mss/issue; 4-12 mss/year. Publishes short shorts. Sometimes critiques rejected mss and recommends other markets.
How to Contact: Query with or without clips of published work; send complete ms with cover letter; or "send by special messenger." Reports in 1 week on queries; 2 months on mss. SASE. Simultaneous, photocopied and reprint submissions OK. Accepts computer printout submissions, including dot-matrix. Sample copy $4. Fiction guidelines for #10 SAE and 1 first class stamp.
Payment: $0-$75; free subscription to magazine; contributor's copies; charge for extras. Payment "depends on our mood."
Terms: Pays on publication for first North American serial rights. Publication copyrighted.
Advice: "Keep on trying. You reap what you sow. Love is love. Enjoy your life."

BAD NEWZ (IV), Artists & Writers Underground, c/o Sarris Bookmarketing, 125 E. 23d St., #300, New York NY 10010. (718)636-3845. Editor: Bob Z. Magazine: 8½x11; 36-40 pages; 20 lb paper; 70 lb glossy cover; illustrations throughout. "Accepts writing only from punks or those living on the fringes of society." For an audience of "anyone who can take it." Quarterly. Estab. 1986. Circ. 1,000.
Needs: Erotica, experimental, horror, humor/satire, psychic/supernatural/occult, music. "All literature must be written from the point of view of someone *outside* the mainstream." Receives 15-20 unsolicited fiction mss/month. Accepts 2-3 mss/issue; 8-12 mss/year. Publishes ms 2-3 months after accept-

ance. Length: 300-500 words preferred; 1 word minimum; 1,000 words maximum. Sometimes comments on rejected mss and recommends other markets.
How to Contact: "Since we only print very short pieces, just send the piece(s). We don't reply to queries—only to mss." SASE. Simultaneous, photocopied and reprint submissions OK. Accepts computer printouts, including dot-matrix. Sample copy $2. Fiction guidelines for #10 SAE and 1 first class stamp.
Payment: Pays in contributor's copies.
Terms: Acquires first North American serial rights. Publication not copyrighted.
Advice: "The market is terrible. It's no better now than it was when Franz Kafka was being ignored, and the chances that another Kafka is being ignored right now are very good. That's why we welcome the strange and offbeat as much as possible, even encourage it—we accept things that other editors won't even read."

BALL STATE UNIVERSITY FORUM (II), Ball State University, Muncie IN 47306. (317)285-8456. Editor: Frances M. Rippy; Editor-in-Chief: Bruce W. Hozeski. Magazine: 6½x9½; 80 pages; excellent paper quality; heavy paper cover. Magazine for "educated non-specialists." One issue a year devoted to fiction of all types. Quarterly. Estab. 1960. Circ. 1,000.
Needs: Adventure, condensed or excerpted novel (30 pages or less), contemporary, ethnic, experimental, fantasy, feminist, gothic/historical romance, historical (general), humor/satire, literary, mainstream, prose poem, psychic/supernatural, religious/inspirational, science fiction, suspense/mystery, translations and western. No "box-office and sex and violence." Receives 30 unsolicited fiction mss/month. Accepts 15 mss/year. Publishes ms "usually 18 months maximum" after acceptance. Recently published work by Thomas A. Long, Paul Grussendorf and Barbara Rodman. Published new writers in the last year. Length: 200 words minimum, 6,000 words maximum, 4,000 words average. "Only occasionally" critiques rejected mss.
How to Contact: Send complete ms with SASE. Photocopied submissions OK. Accepts computer printout submissions, including dot-matrix. Discourages multiple submissions. Reports in 3-4 months. Sample copy $6.
Payment: 1 free contributor's copy.
Terms: Acquires all rights. Publication copyrighted.
Advice: "Send an original, polished story in a clean copy. If it is rejected, we tell you if the vote was close and suggest sending another. Read broadly, write carefully, revise painstakingly, submit mss persistently. Short stories from the *Forum* have been listed in the Houghton Mifflin edition of *Best American Short Stories*; one was reprinted in *Prize Stories O. Henry Awards*."

‡LA BELLA FIGURA (I,II,IV), Box 411223, San Francisco CA 94141-1223. Editor: Rose Romano. Magazine: 5½x8½; 36 pages. Publishes "work by Italian-American women, mostly about us." Quarterly. Estab. 1988. Circ. 150.
Needs: Ethnic, feminist, lesbian, literary, prose poem, translations and Italian-American culture and heritage. "It is the purpose of *LBF* to provide a space for a much-neglected group of people. It is our space to share ourselves with each other and to help others understand us." Receives 10-15 mss/month. Accepts 1-2 mss/issue; 4-8 mss/year. Publishes ms within 2-3 months of acceptance. Recently published work by Rachel DeVries, Maria Gillan and Rina Ferrarelli. Length: about 10 double-spaced pages preferred. Publishes short shorts. Sometimes critiques rejected mss and recommends other markets.
How to Contact: Send complete manuscript with cover letter, which should include previous publications and any other credits. Reports within 1 month after appropriate theme deadline. SASE. Photocopied and reprint submissions OK. Accepts computer printout submissions, including dot-matrix. Sample copy $3. Fiction guidelines for #10 SAE and first class stamp.
Payment: Pays 2 contributor's copies; charge for extras.
Terms: Acquires one-time rights. Publication copyrighted.
Advice: "There's not enough work by and about Italian-American women (especially lesbians) published yet. The writer must find that space between stereotyped and assimilated."
awards for fiction writers. "Entry is automatic upon publication. Prize at least $200."
Advice: "Prefer unusual stories. I would rather not have to edit. I am interested in beginning writers; don't worry about making impressions."

‡THE BELLADONNA (I), Box 935, Simpsonville SC 29681. Editor: Kelly E. Finnell. Magazine: 10x8; 16-20 pages; gloss paper; gloss/color cover; illustrations and photos on cover. Publishes poetry, short stories, articles, song poems/lyrics and artwork on new age topics. Semiannually. Estab. 1988.
Needs: Adventure, contemporary, erotica, experimental, fantasy, feminist, horror, lesbian, literary, prose poem, psychic/supernatural/occult, romance (contemporary), science fiction, suspense/mystery. No children's, western, religious, humor. Accepts 2-3 mss/issue; 12+ for 1989. Publishes short shorts. Sometimes critiques rejected mss and recommends other markets.

How to Contact: Query or send complete manuscript with cover letter. Reports in 1-2 weeks on queries; 1 week to 2 months on mss. Photocopied and reprint submissions OK. Accepts computer print-out submissions, including dot-matrix. Sample copy for $5. Fiction guidelines for #10 SAE and 1 first class stamp.
Payment: 1 contributor's copy to nonmembers; 2 copies to members "if 3 single-space pages or more."
Terms: Acquires one-time rights. Publication copyrighted. Sponsors awards for fiction writers. "Entry is automatic upon publication. Prize at least $200."
Advice: "Prefer unusual stories. I would rather not have to edit. I am interested in beginning writers; don't worry about making impressions."

THE BELLINGHAM REVIEW (II), Box 4065, Bellingham WA 98227. Editor: Shelley Rozen. Magazine: 8x5½; 64 pages; 60 lb white paper; varied cover stock; photos. "A literary magazine featuring original short stories, novel excerpts, short plays and poetry of palpable quality." Semiannually. Estab. 1977. Circ. 700.
Needs: All genres/subjects considered. Acquires 1-2 mss/issue. Publishes short shorts. Submission period: September 15 to May 1. Published new writers within the last year. Length: 5,000 words or less. Critiques rejected mss when there is time.
How to Contact: Send complete ms. Reports in 2 weeks to 2 months. Publishes ms an average of 1 year after acceptance. Sample copy $2.
Payment: 2 1 free author's copy plus 2-issue subscription. $1.50 for extras.
Terms: Acquires first North American serial and one-time rights. Publication copyrighted.
Advice: Mss are rejected for various reasons, "but the most common problem is too much *telling* and not enough *showing* of crucial details and situations. We also look for something that is different or looks at life in a different way."

BELLOWING ARK (II), A Literary Tabloid, Box 45637, Seattle WA 98145. (206)545-8302. Editor: R.R. Ward. Tabloid: 11½x16; 20 pages; electro-brite paper and cover stock; illustrations; photos. "We publish material which we feel addresses the human situation in an affirmative way. We do not publish academic fiction." Bimonthly. Plans special fiction issue. Estab. 1984. Circ. 500.
Needs: Contemporary, literary, mainstream, serialized/excerpted novel. "Anything we publish will be true." Receives 100-150 unsolicited fiction mss/year. Accepts 1-2 mss/issue; 7-12 mss/year. Time varies, but publishes ms not longer than 6 months after acceptance. Recently publshed work by Kim Silvera Wulterbeek, Patrick Barry Smid and Catherine Marley; published new writers within the last year. Length: 3,000-5,000 words average. Publishes short shorts. Sometimes critiques rejected mss and recommends other markets.
How to Contact: Send complete ms with cover letter and short bio. "I always cringe when I see letters listing 'credits' and stating the 'rights' offered! Such delights indicate the impossible amateur. Many beginners address me by first name—few of my close friends do." Reports in 2 weeks on queries; 6 weeks on mss. SASE for ms. Sample copy for $2, 9x12 SAE and 85¢ postage.
Payment: Pays in contributor's copies.
Terms: Acquires first rights. Publication copyrighted.
Advice: "Learn how to tell a story before submitting. Avoid 'trick' endings—they have all been done before and better."

BELOIT FICTION JOURNAL (II), Box 11, Beloit College WI 53511. (608)365-3391. Editor: Clint Mc-Cown. Magazine: 6x9; 112 pages; 60 lb paper; 10 pt. CIS cover stock; illustrations and photos on cover. "We are interested in publishing the best contemporary fiction and are open to all themes except those involving pornographic, religiously dogmatic or politically propagandistic representations. Our magazine is for general readership, though most of our readers will probably have a specific interest in literary magazines." Semiannually. Estab. 1985.
Needs: Contemporary, literary, mainstream, prose poem, spiritual and sports. No pornography, religious dogma, political propaganda. Receives 75 unsolicited fiction mss/month. Accepts 8-10 mss/issue; 16-20 mss/year. Replies take longer in summer. Publishes ms within 9 months after acceptance. Recent issues have included work by Alvin Greenberg, Erin McGraw and Tony Ardizzone; new writers published within the last year. Length: 5,000 words average; 250 words minimum; 10,000 words maximum. Sometimes critiques rejected mss and recommends other markets.
How to Contact: Send complete ms with cover letter. Reports in 1 week on queries; 1-6 weeks on mss. SASE for ms. Simultaneous and photocopied submissions OK, if identified as such. Accepts computer printouts including dot-matrix. Sample copy $5. Fiction guidelines free for #10 envelope and 1 first class stamp.
Advice: "Many of our contributors are writers whose work we have previously rejected. Don't let one rejection slip turn you away from our—or any—magazine."

BERKELEY FICTION REVIEW (II), 700 Eshelman Hall, University of California, Berkeley CA 94720. (415)843-0196. Editor: Mark Landsman. Magazine: journal size; 200 pages; some illustrations and photographs. "We publish fresh, inventive fiction and poetry." Published irregularly. Estab. 1981. Circ. 500.
Needs: No "self-consciously trendy or fashionable fiction." Receives up to 50 unsolicited mss/month. Accepts 8-20 mss/issue. Published work by new writers in the last year. Occasionally critiques rejected mss.
How to Contact: Query first (with clips if possible), send complete ms, or submit through agent. SASE. Photocopied submissions OK. Sample copy $4.50.
Payment: 3 free contributor's copies.
Terms: Publication copyrighted.

BEYOND . . . SCIENCE FICTION & FANTASY (I,II,IV), Other Worlds Books, Box 1124, Fair Lawn NJ 07410. (201)791-6721. Editor: Shirley Winston; Fiction Editor: Roberta Rogow. Magazine: 8½x11; 48 pages; illustrations. Science fiction and fantasy fiction, art and poetry. Audience is "mostly adults, some younger." Quarterly. Estab. 1985. Circ. 300.
Needs: Fantasy and science fiction. No pornography. Receives 100 unsolicited mss/month. Accepts 10 mss/issue; 40 mss/year. Publishes ms "up to 2 years after acceptance." Length: 5,000 words average; 500 words minimum; 12,000 words maximum. Publishes short shorts. Sometimes critiques rejected mss and recommends other markets.
How to Contact: Send complete ms with cover letter. Reports in 2 months. SASE. Photocopied submissions OK. Accepts computer printout submissions including dot-matrix. Sample copy $4.50; fiction guidelines free for SASE.
Payment: ¼¢ per word and contributor's copies.
Terms: Pays on publication for first North American serial rights. Publication copyrighted.

BIG TWO-HEARTED (II,IV), Mid-Peninsula Library Cooperative, 424 Stephenson Ave., Iron Mountain MI 49801. (906)774-3005. Editor: Gary Silver. Magazine: 8¼x5½; 60 pages; 20 lb bond; 60 lb stock. "Creative, wholesome and understandable stories and poems about nature and the independent human spirit." Published every 4 months. Estab. 1985. Circ. 110.
Needs: Humor/satire, literary, prose poem and regional. No profanity, morbidity or erotica. Receives 3 mss/month. Accepts 3 mss/issue. Publishes ms within 3-6 months of acceptance. Recently published work by John O'Connor and Gene Washington; published new writers within the last year. Length: 2,000 words preferred; 500 words minimum; 3,000 words maximum. Sometimes critiques rejected mss.
How to Contact: Send complete ms with cover letter, which should include a short bio. Reports in 3 months. SASE. Photocopied submissions OK. Accepts computer printout submissions, including dot-matrix. Sample copy for $1 and 6x9 SAE.
Payment: Pays in contributor's copies.
Terms: Acquires all rights (returned to author). Publication copyrighted.
Advice: "Tell a good story. Send us a clean manuscript with double-checked spelling and punctuation. Use of the traditional taboo words is an automatic rejection. Our readers like upbeat stories set in the out-of-doors."

BILINGUAL REVIEW (II, IV), Hispanic Research Center, Arizona State University, Tempe AZ 85287. (602)965-3867. Editor-in-Chief: Gary D. Keller. Scholarly/literary journal of US Hispanic life: poetry, short stories, other prose and theater. Magazine: 7x10; 96 pages; 55 lb acid-free paper; coated cover stock. Published 3 times/year. Estab. 1974. Circ. 2,000.
Needs: US Hispanic creative literature. "We accept material in English or Spanish. We publish original work only—no translations." US/Hispanic themes only. Receives 50 unsolicited fiction mss/month. Accepts 3 mss/issue, 9 mss/year. Often critiques rejected mss. Recently published work by Nash Candelaria, Ana Castillo, Ron Arias, Rolando Hinojosa. Published work of new writers within the last year.
How to Contact: Send 2 copies of complete ms with SAE and loose stamps. Simultaneous and high-quality photocopied submissions OK. Reports in 4 weeks on mss. Publishes ms an average of 1 year after acceptance. Sample copy $7.
Payment: 2 contributor's copies. 30% discount for extras.
Terms: Acquires all rights (50% of reprint permission fee given to author as matter of policy). Publication copyrighted.
Advice: "We do not publish literature about tourists in Latin America and their perceptions of the 'native culture.'"

‡BLACK DOG (I), Real Good Stuff, S&M Productions, 1111 W. 7th, #A, Austin TX 78703. (512)499-8209. Editor: Sam DeSanto. Tabloid: 10x13; 16 pages; newsprint paper and cover; illustrations and photos. "We provide an open forum for artists, poets and writers." Semiannually. Estab. 1987. Circ. 10,000.

Needs: Contemporary, erotica, ethnic, experimental, feminist, gay, lesbian, literary, prose poem, translations. No New Age, fantasy, sci-fi. Receives 3-4 unsolicited fiction mss/month; accepts 1-2 mss/issue; 4 mss/year. Publishes mss 3 months after acceptance. S. DeSanto, Jeff Coats and Brian Cuteau; published new writers within the last year. Length: open. Publishes short shorts. Sometimes critiques rejected mss and recommends other markets.

How to Contact: Send complete ms with cover letter or "come by with a six pack of beer." Reports on queries in 2 weeks; on mss in 3 weeks. SASE. Simultaneous, photocopied and reprint submissions OK. Accepts computer printouts, including dot-matrix. Sample copy $1. Fiction guidelines free.

Payment: Pays free subscription to magazine and contributor's copies.

Terms: Acquires one-time rights. Publication copyrighted.

Advice: "It is hard for even a good writer to be published today. But there is hope in the fact that a vast audience is out there eager to devour any material that is made readily available."

BLACK JACK (I), Seven Buffaloes Press, Box 249, Big Timber MT 59011. Editor: Art Cuelho. "Main theme: Rural. Publishes material on the American Indian, farm and ranch, American hobo, the common working man, folklore, the Southwest, Okies, Montana, humor, Central California, etc. for people who make their living off the land. The writers write about their roots, experiences and values they receive from the American soil." Annually. Estab. 1973. Circ. 750.

Needs: Literary, contemporary, western, adventure, humor, American Indian, American hobo, and parts of novels and long short stories. "Anything that strikes me as being amateurish, without depth, without craft, I refuse. Actually I'm not opposed to any kind of writing if the author is genuine and has spent his lifetime dedicated to the written word." Buys 5-10 mss/year. Receives approximately 10-15 unsolicited fiction mss/month. Length: 3,500-5,000 words (there can be exceptions).

How to Contact: Query for current theme with SASE. Reports in 1 week on queries, 2 weeks on mss. Sample copy $4.75.

Payment: Pays 1-2 author's copies.

Terms: Acquires first North American serial rights and reserves the right to reprint material in an anthology or future *Black Jack* publications. Publication copyrighted. Rights revert to author after publication.

Advice: "Enthusiasm should be matched with skill as a craftsman. That's not saying that we don't continue to learn, but every writer must have enough command of the language to compete with other proven writers. Save postage by writing first to the editor to find out his needs. A small press magazine always has specific needs at any given time. I sometimes accept material from country writers that aren't all that good at punctuation and grammar but make up for it with life's experience. This is not a highbrow publication; it belongs to the salt-of-the-earth people."

‡BLACK RIVER REVIEW (II), 855 Mildred Ave., Lorain OH 44052. Editor: Kaye Coller. Fiction Editor: Jack Smith. Magazine: 8½x11; 60 pages, "quality stock" paper; mat card cover stock; b&w drawings. "Contemporary writing and contemporary American culture; poetry, book reviews, essays on contemporary literature, short stories." Annually. Estab. 1985. Circ. 300.

Needs: Contemporary, experimental, humor/satire and literary. No "erotica for its own sake, stories directed toward a juvenile audience." Receives 12-20 contest entries/year. Accepts 1 ms/year. Does not read mss May 1-Dec. 31. Publishes ms no later than June of current year. Charges $2 entry fee (each story) for annual contest. Recently published work by Tim Coats and Dan Gallik. Length: up to 3,000 words maximum. Publishes short shorts. Sometimes critiques rejected mss and recommends other markets.

How to Contact: Send SASE for current year writing competition guidelines. Reports on mss about 1 month after contest deadline (May 1 to June 1). SASE. Photocopied submissions OK. Sample copy $3 back issue; $3.50 current. Fiction guidelines for #10 SAE and 1 first class stamp.

Payment: Pays $50 (1st place); $30 (2d place); $15 (3rd place); contributor's copies; charge for extras. Prize winners receive their prizes when notified. Acquires one-time rights. Publication copyrighted. We will consider publishing one additional story outside the contest (from submissions) if quality of mss and space warrant."

Advice: "Since it is so difficult to break in, much of the new writer's creative effort is spent trying to match trends in popular fiction, in the case of the slicks, or adapting to narrow themes ('Gay and Lesbian,' 'Vietnam War,' 'Women's Issues,' etc.) of little and literary journals. An unfortunate result, from the reader's standpoint, is that each story within a given category comes out sounding like all the rest. Among positive developments of the proliferation of small presses is the opportunity for writers to decide what to write and how to write it. My advice is support a little magazine that is both open to new writers and prints fiction you like. 'Support' doesn't necessarily mean 'buy all the back issues,' but, rather, direct involvement between contributor, magazine and reader needed to rebuild the sort of audience that was there for writers like Fitzgerald and Hemingway."

BLACK WARRIOR REVIEW (II), Box 2936, Tuscaloosa AL 35487. (205)348-4518. Editor-in-Chief: Jeff Mock. Fiction Editor: Thomas Alan Holmes. Magazine: 6x9; approx. 144 pages; good paper; illustrations and photos sometimes. "We publish contemporary fiction, poetry, reviews, essays and interviews for a literary audience." Semiannually. Estab. 1974. Circ. 1,300-2,000.
Needs: Contemporary, literary, mainstream and prose poem. No types that are clearly "types." Receives 100 unsolicited fiction mss/month. Accepts 5 mss/issue, 10 mss/year. Approximately 25% of fiction is agented. Recently published work by Scott Gould, Max Phillips and Lynda Sexson. Published new writers within the last year. Length: 7,500 words maximum; 3,000-5,000 words average. Occasionally critiques rejected mss.
How to Contact: Send complete ms with SASE. Photocopied submissions OK. Reports in 2 months. Publishes ms 2-3 months after acceptance. Sample copy $3.50. Free fiction guidelines for SAE and 1 first class stamp.
Payment: $5-$10/page and 2 contributor's copies.
Terms: Pays on publication. Publication copyrighted.
Advice: "Become familiar with the magazine(s) being submitted to; learn the editorial biases; accept rejection slips as part of the business; keep trying. We are not a good bet for 'commercial' fiction. Each year the *Black Warrior Review* will award $500 to a fiction writer whose work has been published in either the fall or spring issue, to be announced in the fall issue. Regular submission deadlines are August 1 for fall issue, January 1 for spring issue."

BLACK WRITER MAGAZINE (II), Terrell Associates, Box 1030, Chicago IL 60690. (312)995-5195. Editor: Mable Terrell. Fiction Editor: Herman Gilbert. Magazine: 8½x11; 40 pages; glossy paper; glossy cover; illustrations. "To assist writers in publishing their work," for "all audiences, with a special emphasis on black writers." Quarterly. Estab. 1972.
Needs: Ethnic, historical, literary, religious/inspirational, prose poem. Receives 20 unsolicited mss/month. Accepts 15 mss/issue. Publishes ms an average of 6 months after acceptance. Recently published work by Margaree Renas and Maria Macon; published new writers within the last year. Length: 3,000 words preferred; 2,500 words average; 1,500 words minimum. Sometimes critiques rejected mss and recommends other markets.
How to Contact: Send complete ms with cover letter, which should include "Writer's opinion of the work, and rights offered." Reports in 3 weeks. SASE. Simultaneous submissions OK. Does not accept dot-matrix computer submissions. Sample copy for 8½x11 SAE and 70¢ postage. Fiction guidelines for SASE.
Payment: Free subscription to magazine.
Terms: Acquires one-time rights. Publication copyrighted. Sponsors awards for fiction writers. Contest deadline May 30.
Advice: "Write the organization and ask for assistance."

‡THE BLIZZARD RAMBLER (I), World's Most Unique Magazine, Box 6296, Ventura CA 93006. (805)649-1507. Editor: Ron Blizzard. Fiction Editor: Dale Blizzard. Magazine: 7x8½; 40-80 pages; 20 lb paper; 60 lb cover; line drawings. Publishes "humor/satire and adventure (SF, fantasy, western), for those who don't take themselves too seriously." Quarterly. Plans special fiction issue. Estab. 1983. Circ. 200.
Needs: Adventure, fantasy, horror, humor/satire, prose poem, suspense/mystery, western. "We also like fictional 'news' stories." No erotica. Receives 5-10 unsolicited mss/month. Buys 6-10 mss/issue; 30-40 mss/year. Publishes ms 2-6 months after publication. Recently published work by Tony Blizzard, Al Hamon, Frank Donato. Length: 3,000 words preferred; 2,500 words average; 50 words minimum; 8,000 words maximum. Sometimes critiques rejected mss and recommends other markets.
How to Contact: Send complete ms with cover letter. "Cover letter optional." Reports in 1-3 weeks on queries; 2-4 weeks on mss. Photocopied submissions OK. Accepts computer printout submissions, including dot-matrix. Sample copy for $2 with writer's guidelines. Fiction guidelines for #10 SAE and 1 first class stamp.
Payment: Pays ¼¢/word. Free contributor's copies.
Terms: Pays on acceptance. Acquires first rights. Sends galleys to author if requested. Publication copyrighted.
Advice: "Is it entertaining? Is it a story, or just part of one? Is it clear what's happening? We would like to see old style westerns submitted. Send for a sample copy or writer's guidelines. Aim to entertain and send in the stories."

‡**BLONDE ON BLONDE MAGAZINE (I)**, 3400 Montrose Blvd. #920, Houston TX 77006. (713)526-1262. Editor: Jeff Troiano. Fiction Editor: Mike Troiano. Magazine: 11x16; 28-36 pages; 45 lb paper and cover; illustrations and photographs. "Progressive general interest magazine. Art-oriented." Monthly. Plans special fiction issue. Estab. 1987.
Needs: Condensed/excerpted novel, contemporary, experimental, fantasy, humor/satire, literary, prose poem, psychic/supernatural/occult, regional and science fiction. Receives 25-30 unsolicited mss/month. Buys 3-5 mss/issue; 36-60 mss/year. Length: 1,000-1,250 words preferred. Sometimes critiques rejected mss and recommends other markets.
How to Contact: Send complete ms with cover letter. Reports in 6 weeks. SASE. Simultaneous, photocopied and reprint submissions OK. Accepts computer printout submissions, including dot-matrix. Sample copy for $1. Fiction guidelines for SAE.
Payment: Pays in contributor's copies.
Terms: Acquires first rights. Publication copyrighted. Sponsors awards for fiction writers. "Contests are advertised in pages of magazine."
Advice: "Most publications do not publish enough fiction. I believe that fiction is making a comeback in major American magazines. Fiction must fit progressive format. Lengthy cover letters do not influence editors."

THE BLOOMSBURY REVIEW (II), Owaissa Communications, Inc., Box 8928, Denver CO 80201. (303)892-0620. Editor-in-Chief: Tom Auer. Fiction Editor: John Roberts. "*The Bloomsbury Review* is a book magazine. We publish book reviews, essays, poetry and interviews with book-related persons." Bimonthly. Estab. 1980. Circ. 10,000.
Needs: Contemporary, literary and mainstream.
How to Contact: Send complete ms with SASE. Simultaneous and photocopied submissions OK. Reports in 2 months on queries and mss. Sample copy $3.50 with 8x10 SAE and 70¢ postage. Guidelines for #10 SAE and 1 first class stamp.
Payment: $5-$25; $14/year subscription to magazine and 10 free contributor's copies.
Terms: Pays on publication for first rights. Rights revert to writer. Publication copyrighted.
Advice: "Can be experimental or traditional. The bottom line is good quality writing."

BLUE SKY JOURNAL (II), 1710 Decker Rd., Malibu CA 90265. (213)457-4613. Editor: Laura Gillberg. Newsletter: 8½x11; 15-25 pages; bond paper cover. "Publication dealing with creativity as it relates to wholeness and living well. Our audience especially includes people who are creative and have not yet tapped that part of themselves. The journal encourages and inspires creative expression for the purpose of healing oneself and others." Semiannually. Estab. 1982. Circ. 200-250.
Needs: Fantasy, humor/satire, literary, mainstream. Receives 5-10 unsolicited mss/month. Length: "Not longer than 3 pages single spaced." Publishes short shorts. Recently published work by Sue Roben and Beverly Clark; published new writers within the last year.
How to Contact: Send complete ms with cover letter, which should include "personal info, writing history or non-writing history." Reports mss in 2 months. SASE for ms. Sample copy for $3.
Terms: Publication copyrighted.
Advice: "Be concise."

BOGG (II), A Magazine of British & North American Writing, Bogg Publications, 422 N. Cleveland St., Arlington VA 22201. (703)243-6019. U.S. Editor: John Elsberg. Magazine: 8½x11; 60-64 pages; 50 lb white paper; 50 lb cover stock; line illustrations. "American and British poetry, prose poems and other experimental short "fictions," reviews, and essays on small press." Published 3 times a year. Estab. 1968. Circ. 650.
Needs: Very short experimental and prose poem. Nothing over 1 typewritten page. Receives 25 unsolicited fiction mss/month. Accepts 2-3 mss/issue; 6-8 mss/year. Published 50% new writers within the last year. Occasionally critiques rejected mss.
How to Contact: Query first or send ms (2-6 pieces) with SASE. Photocopied submissions OK. Accepts computer printout submissions. Prefers letter-quality. Reports in 1 week on queries; 2 weeks on mss. Publishes ms 6-12 months after acceptance. Sample copy $3.50.
Payment: 2 contributor's copies. Reduced charge for extras.
Terms: Acquires one-time rights. Publication copyrighted.
Advice: "Read magazine first. We are most interested in work of experimental or wry nature to supplement poetry. No longer (with issue #60) accepts traditional narrative short stories."

‡**THE BOOK OF CONTEMPORARY MYTH (II)**, The Caitlin Press, Box 2385, Pittsfield MA 01202. Editor: D.C. Bradburd. Book: 5½x8½; 64 pages; 60 lb paper; 60 lb textured cover; illustrations. "Myth is luminous, a metaphor for life that speaks true and straight, illuminating our inner journeys and our outer signposts, our growth, our relationships, our spirit and purpose, hurt and joy. Any work that brings

to life the archetypes and metaphors of our existence will be considered, particularly those that do so through themes that make clear the essentially mythic in the contemporary world or in the timeless world of the soul." Annually. Estab. 1987.

Needs: Contemporary, experimental, literary, prose poem, psychic/supernatural/occult, mythical. Accepts 1-4 story mss/issue. Publishes short shorts.

How to Contact: Send complete ms with cover letter after obtaining and reading writer's guidelines. Cover letter should include background of publication history. Reports on mss in 6-8 weeks. SASE. Photocopied and reprints submissions OK. Accepts computer printout submissions, including dot-matrix. Sample copy for $5.50. Fiction guidelines for #10 SAE and 1 first class stamp.

Payment: Pays in contributor's copies; charge for extras "at discount."

Terms: Acquires rights for all editions of book. Publication copyrighted.

Advice: "Read the guidelines; write from the heart."

BOULEVARD (III), Journal of Contemporary Writing, Opojaz Inc., 2400 Chestnut St., Philadelphia PA 19103. (215)561-1723. Editor: Richard Burgin. Magazine: 8½x5½; 150-220 pages; excellent paper; high-quality cover stock; illustrations; photos. "*Boulevard* aspires to publish the best contemporary fiction, poetry and essays we can print." Published 3 times/year. Estab. 1986. Circ. about 2,500.

Needs: Contemporary, experimental, literary, prose poem. Does not want to see "anything whose first purpose is not literary." Receives over 100 mss/month. Buys about 6 mss/issue. Publishes less than a year after acceptance. Agented fiction ⅓-¼. Length: 5,000 words average; 10,000 words maximum. Publishes short shorts. Recently published work by Madison Smartt Bell, Francine Prose, Alice Adams. Sometimes critiques rejected mss and recommends other markets.

How to Contact: Send complete ms with cover letter. Reports in 2 weeks on queries; 2 months or less on mss. SASE. Simultaneous and photocopied submissions OK. Accepts computer printout submissions, including dot-matrix. Accepts electronic submissions. Sample copy for $5 and SAE with 5 first class stamps.

Payment: Pays $50-$150; contributor's copies; charges for extras. $1,000 annual prize for best story published in *Boulevard* during the year.

Terms: Pays on publication for first North American serial rights. Does not send galleys to author unless requested. Publication copyrighted.

Advice: "We are substantially increasing the amount of fiction we publish. Master your own piece of emotional real estate. Be patient and persistent."

BREAKFAST WITHOUT MEAT (IV), 1827 Haight St., Room 188, San Francisco CA 94117. Editors: Lizzy Gray and Gregg Turkington. Magazine: 8½x11; 20 pages; 60 lb cover stock; illustrations; photos. "Humor, satire, Richard Harris fanaticism." 3 issues/year. Estab. 1983. Circ. 800.

Needs: Adventure, condensed novel, confession, ethnic, experimental, feminist, humor/satire, juvenile (5-9 years), preschool (0-4 years), psychic/supernatural/occult, religious/insipirational, senior citizen/retirement, suspense/mystery, Frank Sinatra Jr., lunacy. Receives 15 unsolicited mss/month. Accepts 2 mss/issue; 6 mss/year. Publishes ms 3 weeks to 6 months after acceptance. Length: 200 words average; 2 words minimum; 501 words maximum. Sometimes critiques rejected mss and recommends other markets.

How to Contact: Writers should contact "telepathically." Cover letter should include "money and candy." Reports in 5 weeks. SASE. Simultaneous and photocopied submissions OK. Accepts computer printout submissions, no dot-matrix. Sample copy for $1.25. Fiction guidelines for 25¢ or # SAE with 1 first class stamp.

Payment: Pays in contributor's copies.

Terms: Buys all rights. Publication copyrighted.

BRILLIANT STAR (II), National Spiritual Assembly of the Baha'is of the U.S., 2512 Allegheny Dr., Chattanooga TN 37421. Magazine: 8½x11; 33 pages; matte paper; glossy cover; illustrations; photos. "Central objective and theme is to develop children's conscious awareness of the oneness of humanity and appreciation of diversity." For children approx. 5-12 years old. Bimonthly. Plans special fiction issue. Estab. 1969. Circ. 2,300.

Needs: Adventure, ethnic, fantasy, historical (general), humor/satire, juvenile (5-9 years), preschool (1-4 years), science fiction, spiritual, suspense/mystery, young adult/teen (10-18 years). "Accepts inspirational fiction if not overtly preachy or moralistic and if not directly Christian and related directly to Christian holidays." Receives 30 unsolicited mss/month. Accepts 3-4 mss/issue; 18-24 mss/year. Publishes ms no sooner than 6 months after acceptance. Recently published work by Dottie Smith and Susan Allen; published new writers within the last year. Length: 1,000 words preferred; 500 words minimum; 1,300 words maximum. Publishes short shorts. Always critiques rejected mss and may recommend other markets.

How to Contact: No queries. Send complete ms. Cover letter not essential. Reports in 6-8 weeks on mss. SASE. Simultaneous and photocopied submissions OK "but please make a notation that it is a simultaneous sub." Accepts computer submissions, including dot-matrix. Sample copy for 9x12 SAE and 5 oz. postage. Fiction guidelines for #10 SAE with 1 first class stamp.

Payment: Pays in contributor's copies (single complimentary issue only); charges for extras.

Terms: "Writer can retain own copyright or grant to the National Spiritual Assembly of the Baha'is of the U.S." Publication copyrighted.

Advice: "We enjoy working with beginning writers and try to develop a constructive collaborative relationship with those who show promise and sensitivity to our aims and focus. We feel that the children's market is open to a wide variety of writers: fiction, nonfiction, science, photo-essays. Our needs for appealing fiction especially for pre-schoolers and young readers make us a good market for new writers. *Please*, have a story to tell! The single main reason for rejection of manuscripts we review is lack of plot to infuse the story with energy and make the reader want to come along. Seeking writers from Afro-American, Hispanic, Asian and Native American backgrounds to increase multi-ethnic focus of our magazine."

BRONTË STREET (II), A Contemporary Journal of Short Stories & Poems, 542 E. Ingram, Mesa AZ 85203. Editor: Linda S. Valentine. Magazine: 5½x8½; 60+ pages; 60 lb offset paper; glossy cover. "We are striving to provide an attractive forum for talented writers and are receptive to all kinds of short stories and poems." Semiannually. Estab 1987. Circ. 500.

Needs: Contemporary, ethnic, experimental, fantasy, feminist, historical, humor/satire, literary, mainstream, prose poem, science fiction, spiritual, suspense/mystery. No pornographic or racist material. Receives 150 unsolicited fiction mss/month; accepts 10-20 mss/issue; 20-40 mss/year. Publishes ms 5-10 months (or less) after acceptance. Recently published work by Dave Turnburke, Jeanne M. Pinneo, Sheryl L. Nelms; published new writers within the last year. Length: 2,000-4,000 words preferred; 6,000 words maximum. Publishes short vignettes under 800 words. Sometimes critiques rejected mss.

How to Contact: Send complete ms with or without cover letter. Reports on queries in 2 weeks; on mss in 6 weeks. SASE. Simultaneous ("if informed"), photocopied and reprint submissions OK. Accepts computer printouts. Sample copy for $4. Fiction guidelines for #10 SAE and 1 first class stamp.

Payment: $20 minimum; 1 contributor's copy. Buys first rights. Publication copyrighted.

Terms: Pays "usually several weeks prior to publication" for first rights or one-time rights. Publication copyrighted. Sponsors contests for fiction writers; send #10 SASE for guidelines.

Advice: "Subscribe to *Brontë Street*, as well as to other literary magazines. Concentrate on characterization. Write clearly. Keep trying. Perfect your craft and be determined!"

BROOMSTICK (II, IV), A National, Feminist Periodical by, for, and About Women Over Forty, 3543 18th St. #3, San Francisco CA 94110. (415)552-7460. Editors: Mickey Spencer and Polly Taylor. Magazine: 8½x11; 40 pages; line drawings. "Our first priority in selecting and editing material is that it convey clear images of women over 40 that are positive, that it take a stand against the denigration of midlife and long-living women which pervades our culture, and that it offer us alternatives which will make our lives better." For "women over 40 interested in being part of a network which will help us all develop understanding of our life situations and acquire the skills to improve them." Bimonthly. Estab. 1978. Circ. 3,000.

Needs: Feminist experience in political context, old women, age, and ageism, humor, ethnic. No mss of "romantic love, nostalgic, saccharine acceptance, by or about men or young women." Receives 10 unsolicited fiction mss/month. Accepts 2-3 mss/issue; 20 mss/year. Recently published work by Ruth Harriet Jacobs, Ursula LeGuin, Astra Margaret Randall; published new writers within the last year. Recommends magazine subscription before sending ms. Critiques rejected mss.

How to Contact: Send complete mss with 2 SASEs. Simultaneous, photocopied and previously published submissions OK. Accepts computer printout submissions. Prefers letter-quality. Reports in 3 months on queries and mss. Sample copy for $3.50. Writer's guidelines for $2.50.

Payment: 2 free contributor's copies; $3.50 charge for extras.

Advice: "Don't use stereotypes to establish character. Give protagonists names, not just roles (e.g. 'mother'). Avoid using "you," which sounds preachy. Read our writer's packet."

BUGLE (II), The Quarterly Journal of the Rocky Mountain Elk Foundation, Rocky Mountain Elk Foundation, Box 8249, Missoula MT 59807. Editor: Lance Schelvan. Magazine: 8½x11; 84-132 pages; 70 lb gloss paper; 80 lb gloss cover; illustrations; 4-color photos. Publishes material on "elk and the future of elk across the North American continent, for elk hunters, hunters in general and conservationists." Quarterly. Estab. 1984. Circ. 120,000.

Needs: Adventure, condensed novel, experimental, historical, humor/satire, western. Receives 40-50 unsolicited fiction mss/month. Publishes ms 3-6 months after acceptance. Recently published work by John Hairland, M. Andrew Taylor; published new writers within the last year. Length: 2,000 words av-

erage; 1,500 words minimum; 3,000 words maximum. Publishes short shorts. Sometimes recommends other markets.
How to Contact: Send complete ms with cover letter, which should include short biographical sketch of author. Reports in 2-3 weeks. Simultaneous, photocopied and reprint submissions OK. Accepts computer printouts, including dot-matrix. Sample copy for $4; fiction guidelines free.
Payment: Free subscription to magazine and contributor's copies.
Terms: Publication copyrighted.
Advice: "Stay away from 'formula' outdoor writing."

‡**BURNING TODDLERS (I)**, FRANK Publications, Box 56942, Phoenix AZ 85079. Editor: P. Petrisko, Jr. Magazine: 5½x8½; 40 pages; illustrations; occasionally photographs. Publishes "fiction and non, both humorous and serious, topics of which include religion, politics, social issues, personal experiences and the mass media. A magazine by and for those attempting to survive the mass-media (r)age." 3 issues/year. Estab. 1987. Circ. 400.
Needs: Confession, experimental, humor/satire, literary, serialized/excerpted novel. "The humor published runs the gamut, from satire to black humor to gallows humor." No erotica, mainstream. Publishes ms 2-6 months (at most) after acceptance. Length: 550-600 words preferred; 1,650 maximum. Occasionally critiques rejected mss and recommends other markets.
How to Contact: Send complete ms with cover letter. "Contact information, publishing history (if applicable), any personal information the writer wants to share." Reports on mss in 4-6 weeks. SASE for ms. Simultaneous ("if noted") and photocopied submissions OK. Accepts computer printout submissions, including dot-matrix. Sample copy for $2.
Payment: 1 contributor's copy.
Terms: Acquires one-time rights. Publication copyrighted.
Advice: Publishes fiction "to preserve this medium and re-introduce the written word to those who have grown accustomed to the 'quick fix' provided by the television medium. Your writing should be entertaining, thought-provoking, or both."

‡**BVI-PACIFICA NEWSLETTER (I)**, Tahuti/Quetzlcoatl Press, Box 45792, Seattle WA 98145-0792. (206)547-2364 or 547-2202. Editor: Yael Dragwyla. Magazine: 5½x8½; 32-36 pages; 20 lb paper; 60 lb cover; illustrations; some photographs. "Theme: Breaking new trails in the Inner Planes (world of the mind)." Quarterly. Plans special fiction issue. Estab. 1985. Circ. 200 + .
Needs: Erotica, experimental, fantasy, horror, humor/satire, psychic/supernatural/occult, science fiction, serialized/excerpted novel, suspense/mystery, SubGenius. "We want fiction, humor, poetry or graphics that make the mind turn unusual or new corners—like juxtaposition of dissonant material such that it almost makes sense—like good satire, with Punken, SubGenius or end-of-the-world overtones. No romance, children's, New Ager or Norman Vincent Peale-type inspirational, anything saccharine." Receives 1-2 unsolicited mss/month. Accepts 6-12 mss/issue; 6-24 mss/year. Publishes ms 3 months-1 year after acceptance. Length: 450 words preferred; 100 words minimum; 1,000 words maximum. Sometimes critiques rejected mss and recommends other markets.
How to Contact: Send complete ms with cover letter. Reports in 1-4 weeks. SASE. Simultaneous, photocopied and reprint submissions OK. Accepts computer printout submissions, including dot-matrix. Sample copy for $2.50.
Payment: Pays in contributor's copies.
Terms: Acquires first North American serial rights. Publication copyrighted.
Advice: "Write with your heart as well as your head. As the state of the world today is both horrifying and disgusting in many places and respects, often the most honest and gripping fiction and the best humor deals with the terror and anger this provokes, head-on. We want fiction, humor, poetry and graphics that free up and change the mind, so that the actions underlaid by mind will change, and in the changing, maybe open up new cracks in the Cosmic Egg."

BYLINE (II), Box 130596, Edmond OK 73013. (405)348-3325. Editor-in-Chief: Marcia Preston. Managing Editor: Kathryn Fanning. Monthly magazine "aimed at encouraging and motivating all writers toward success, with special information to help new writers." Estab. 1981.
Needs: Literary, suspense/mystery and general fiction. Especially like stories with a literary or writing twist. Receives 50-75 unsolicited fiction mss/month. Accepts 1 ms/issue, 12 mss/year. Recently published work by Ann Collette and Nell Abbott. Published many new writers within the last year. Length: 3,000 words maximum; 1,000 words minimum.
How to Contact: Send complete ms with SASE. Photocopied submissions OK. "For us, no cover letter is needed." Reports in 2-6 weeks. Publishes ms an average of 3 months after acceptance. Sample copy, guidelines and contest list for $3.
Payment: $50 and 1 free contributor's copy.
Terms: Pays on acceptance for first North American rights. Publication copyrighted.

Advice: "We're very open to new writers. Submit a well-written, professionally prepared ms with SASE. No erotica or rape-and-revenge; otherwise, we'll consider most any theme. Writing connection is a plus. We also sponsor short story and poetry contests."

CACHE REVIEW (II), Cache Press, Box 19794, Seattle WA 98109-6794. (602)748-0600. Editor: Steven Brady. Magazine: 8½x11; 50 pages; 20 lb bond paper; classic laid cover; cover photos and illustrations. Magazine which publishes "quality writing in all styles." Semiannually. Estab. 1982. Circ. 200-500.

Needs: Experimental, fantasy, historical (general), horror, humor/satire, mainstream, prose poem, regional, science fiction, serialized/excerpted novel, sports, suspense/mystery and translations. Receives 10-20 unsolicited fiction mss/month. Accepts 3-6 mss/issue, 6-12 mss/year. Does not read June-August. Recently published work by Joe Lane, John Bradley, Susan Polkicoff. Length: 10,000 words maximum. Publishes short shorts.

How to Contact: Send complete ms with SASE. Photocopied submissions OK, "but we prefer the original." Accepts computer printout submissions. Prefers letter-quality. Reports in 1 month on mss. Publishes ms 6-12 months after acceptance. Sample copy $3. Fiction guidelines free with # 10 SAE and 1 first class stamp.

Payment: 2 free contributor's copies; $1.50 charge for extras.

Terms: All rights revert to the author. Publication copyrighted. "Cash awards may be presented for the best pieces of fiction and/or poetry in each issue."

Advice: "Send your best. Don't be afraid to experiment, but remember that editors have seen all the tricks."

CAESURA (I), English Dept., Auburn University, Auburn AL 36849. (205)826-4620. Editor: R.T. Smith. Magazine: 6x9; 60-80 pages. Literary journal of fiction and poetry, for a college-educated audience. Quarterly. Estab. 1984. Circ. 600.

Needs: Contemporary, literary, mainstream. Does not want to see work by any whose goal is to fit a genre formula. Receives 10 unsolicited mss/month. Accepts 3-6 mss/issue; 12-15/year. Doen not read mss in summer. Publishes ms 3-9 months after acceptance. Requires magazine subscription of $3 before reading ms. Length: 3,000 words average; 2,000 words minimum; 5,000 words maximum. Publishes short shorts. Occasionally critiqes rejected ms.

How to Contact: Query first. Reports in 1 month on queries; 3 months on mss. SASE. Accepts computer printout submissions, no dot-matrix. Sample copy $3.

Payment: Free subscription to magazine and contributor's copies.

Terms: Acquires one-time rights. Publication copyrighted. Holds annual contest for short stories.

Advice: "For whatever reason, the short story seems to be enjoying great popularity with yuppie types and surviving rebels as well. Avoid the most obviously fashionable (Ray Carver) style, as well as stilted language and dialogue-less stories. If the the story is about a meeting with a bear, don't preface it with information about the character's wardrobe and love life; *bring on the bear.*"

IL CAFFÈ (II, IV), The Italian Experience, Suite 2065, 1582 Response Rd., Sacramento CA 95815. (916)927-6368. Editor: R.T. LoVerso. Fiction Editor: Lloyd Bruno. Magazine: 8x12; 36 pages; illustrations and photos. Publishing serialized novels, short stories, interviews, politics, economy and art for American and Italian-American professional people. Bimonthly. Estab. 1981. Circ. 20,000.

Needs: Adventure, comics, condensed novel, confession, contemporary, ethnic, humor/satire, literary, mainstream, prose poem, romance (contemporary, historical, young adult), serialized/excerpted novel and translations. Receives 5 unsolicited mss/month. Accepts 1-2 mss/issue; 6-12 mss/year. Recently published work by Masini; published new writers within the last year. Length: 3,000 words average. Also publishes short shorts. Occasionally critiques rejected mss.

How to Contact: Send complete ms with SASE. Reports in 1 month. Publishes ms 2-6 months after acceptance. Simultaneous, photocopied and previously published submissions OK. Accepts computer printout submissions. Prefers letter-quality. Sample copy $2.25.

Payment: Pays in contributor's copies; $1.25 charge for extras.

Terms: Acquires first rights. Buys reprints. Publication copyrighted.

Advice: Fiction should reflect "international views."

‡CALAPOOYA COLLAGE (II), Box 309, Monmouth OR 97361. Editor: Tom Ferté. Tabloid: 12x16; 40 pages; b&w photographs. Annually. Estab. 1975. Circ. 1,500.

Needs: Mainstream, native american. Receives 2-4 unsolicited mss/month. Accepts 1 or 2 mss/issue. Does not read mss in summer. Length: 1,600 words preferred; 1,200 words minimum; 2,000 maximum. Publishes short shorts. Sometimes recommends other markets.

How to Contact: Send complete ms with cover letter. Reports in 2 months on mss. SASE. Does not accept dot-matrix computer printouts. Sample copy for $4.

Payment: Pays in contributor's copies.
Terms: Publication copyrighted.

‡CALIFORNIA QUARTERLY (I), 100 Sproul Hall, U.C. Davis, Davis CA 95616. Editor: Elliot L. Gilbert. Fiction Editor: Robert Clark Young. Magazine: 6x10; 80 pages; "book quality" paper; glossy cover; drawings and glossy photos. Magazine for fiction, poetry and graphics. Estab. 1969.
Needs: Contemporary, experimental and literary. Receives approximately 300 mss/month. Does not read mss from mid-June to the end of September. Recently published work by Chris Mazza and David Jauss; published new writers within the last year. Length: 8,000 words average.
How to Contact: Send complete manuscript. Reports in 4-6 weeks on mss. SASE. Simultaneous and photocopied submissions OK. Accepts computer printout submissions; prefers letter-quality. Sample copy for $2.50 and 50¢ postage.
Payment: $3/page and 2 contributor's copies.
Terms: Pays on publication for first North American serial rights. Publication copyrighted.
Advice: "Read publication thoroughly before submitting a manuscript. We are not interested in adolescent romances, pet stories, implausible fantasy or science fiction material, sexist stories (including the currently popular all-men-are-bastards genre), actionless 'mood pieces,' miniatures, autobiography which is self-pitying and/or not yet concealed into a fictive matrix, contrived plots, unleavened characters or trite language. When we see any of this, we do not read beyond the first or second page. Our advice: Take your best story, rewrite it two more times, and submit a professional copy—that means no onionskin, no folding, and no 20-year-old ribbons. SASE. If it's been rejected by every major magazine in the East, don't assume our standards are any lower simply because we're 'small.' Read Mailer for texture, Pynchon for ideas, Kerouac for heart, and Flannery O'Connor for structure.'"

CALLALOO (II, IV), A Journal of Afro-American and African Arts and Letters, Dept. of English, University of Virginia, Charlottesville VA 22903. (804)924-6637. Editor: Charles H. Rowell. Magazine: 7x10; 200 pages. Scholarly magazine. Quarterly. Plans special fiction issue in future. Estab. 1976. Circ. 1,000.
Needs: Contemporary, ethnic (black culture), feminist, historical (general), humor/satire, literary, prose poem, regional, science fiction, serialized/excerpted novel, translations. Accepts 3-5 mss/issue; 10-20 mss/year. Length: 2,500 words average.
How to Contact: Submit complete ms and cover letter with name and address. Reports on queries in 2 weeks; 2-3 months on mss. Simultaneous, photocopied and previously published work "occasionally" OK. Accepts computer printout submissions. Sample copy $5.
Payment: Contributor's copies.
Terms: Acquires all rights. Sends galleys to author. Publication copyrighted.
Advice: "Submit clean copy—finished work with serious literary intent."

CALLIOPE (II, IV), Creative Writing Program, Roger Williams College, Bristol RI 02809. (401)253-1040, ext 2217. Advisory Editor: Martha Christina. Magazine: 5½x8½; 40-56 pages; 50 lb offset paper; vellum or 60 lb cover stock; occasional illustrations and photos. "We are an eclectic little magazine publishing contemporary poetry, fiction and occasionally interviews." Semiannually. Estab. 1977. Circ. 300.
Needs: Literary, contemporary, experimental/innovative. "We try to include 2 pieces of fiction in each issue." Receives approximately 10-20 unsolicited fiction mss each month. Does not read mss mid-March to mid-August. Published new writers within the last year. Length: 3,750 words. Publishes short shorts under 15 pages. Critiques rejected mss when there is time.
How to Contact: Send complete ms with SASE. Reports immediately to 3 months on mss. Sample copy $1.
Payment: 2 free author's copies and year's subscription beginning with following issue.
Terms: Rights revert to author on publication. Publication copyrighted.
Advice: "We are not interested in reading anyone's very first story. If the piece is good, it will be given careful consideration. Reading a sample copy of *Calliope* is recommended. Let the characters of the story tell their own story; we're very often (painfully) aware of the writer's presence. Episodic is fine; story need not (for our publication) have traditional beginning, middle and end."

CALLI'S TALES (I, II), Box 1224, Palmetto FL 34220. (813)722-2202. Editor: Annice E. Hunt. Magazine: 8½x11; 18-20 pages; 20 lb bond paper and cover; b&w clip art. Quarterly for "animal lovers of all ages; those who care about pets, wildlife and the environment." Estab. 1981.
Needs: Adventure, fantasy (wildlife), historical (general), juvenile (5-9 years), preschool and young adult/teen. "Stories must relate to animals. No gory details about dying animals; no profanity." Accepts 8-10 unsolicited mss/year. Next reading period January 1 to May 31, 1989. Published new writers within the last year. Length: 600 words average; 450 words minimum; 800 words maximum. Publishes short

shorts, 250 words or less. Occasionally critiques rejected mss. Sometimes recommends other markets.
How to Contact: Query first or send complete ms. Reports in 5 weeks on queries; 8 weeks on mss. SASE. Simultaneous, photocopied and previously published submissions OK. Publishes ms an average of 9 months after acceptance. Sample copy $2. Fiction guidelines for SASE.
Payment: 1 free contributor's copy; $2 each for extras.
Terms: Acquires one-time rights only. Publication copyrighted.
Advice: "A writer can make an editor's job easier by deleting unnecessary words and typing neatly. Keep revising and rewriting. We have a big backlog at the present time."

CALYX (II), A Journal of Art & Literature by Women, Calyx, Inc., Box B, Corvallis OR 97339. (503)753-9384. Co-Managing Editors: Margarita Donnelly and Lisa Domitrovich. Associate Editors: Rebecca Gordon, Cheryl McLean, Catherine Holdorf, Linda Varsell Smith, Susan Lisser, Carol Pennock and Eleanor Wilner. Magazine: 7x8; 120 pages per single issue, 250 per double; 60 lb coated matte stock paper; 12 point chrome coat cover; original art. Publishes prose, poetry, art, essays, interviews and critical and review articles. "*Calyx* editors are seeking innovative and literary works of exceptional quality." Triannually. Estab. 1976. Circ. 3,000.
Needs: Accepts 3-5 fiction mss/issue, 9-15 mss/year. Receives approximately 300 unsolicited fiction mss each month. Recently published works by Ruthann Robson, Shirley Sikes, S.C. Wisenberg. Published new writers within the last year. Length: 5,000 words maximum.
How to Contact: Send ms with SASE and biographical notes. Reports in up to 6 months on mss. Publishes ms an average of 2 months after acceptance. Sample copy $6.50 plus 75¢ postage.
Payment: Pays in copies.
Terms: Publication copyrighted.
Advice: Most mss are rejected because "the writers are not familiar with *Calyx*—writers should read *Calyx* and be familiar with the publication."

CANADIAN AUTHOR & BOOKMAN (II), Canadian Authors Association, Suite 104, 121 Avenue Rd., Toronto, Ontario M5R 2G3 Canada. (416)926-8084. Editor: Diane Kerner. Magazine: 8½x11; 32 pages; illustrations; photos. "Craft magazine for Canadian writers, publishing articles that tell how to write and where to sell. We publish a dozen poems and one short story per issue as well as the craft articles. We aim at the beginning or newly emerging writer." Quarterly. Estab. 1921. Circ. 3,000.
Needs: Contemporary, humor/satire, literary. "Will not accept writing for children or 'young' adult market." Receives 50-100 unsolicited mss/year. Buys 8-10 mss/issue, 30-40 mss/year. Publishes ms 3-6 months after acceptance. Published new writers within the last year. Length: 2,500 words average; 2,000 words minimum; 3,000 words maximum. Occasionally recommends other markets.
How to Contact: Send complete ms with cover letter, which should include introduction and brief bio. Reports in 1-2 months on mss. SASE. Photocopied submissions OK. Accepts computer printout submissions, including dot-matrix. Sample copy $4.50, 9x12 SAE and IRC. Fiction guidelines #10 SAE and IRC.
Payment: "Our magazine publishes one short-fiction piece per issue, which receives the Okanagan Short Fiction Award of $125 Canadian funds." Contributor's copy to the author.
Terms: Pays on publication for first North American serial rights. Publication copyrighted.
Advice: "We are looking for originality, flair and imaginative work. The writer's strategy is examined from the overall structure, to the rise and fall of the sentences to the placement of the punctuation. For more specific information, send $2.50 Canadian funds to the Canadian Authors Association with your request for a reprint of *The Green Glad Bag Review*, by Geoff Hancock."

CANADIAN FICTION MAGAZINE (II,IV), Box 946, Station F, Toronto, Ontario M4Y 2N9 Canada. Editor: Geoffrey Hancock. Magazine: 6x9; 148-300 pages; book paper; overweight cover stock; 16-32 page portfolio. "This magazine is a quarterly anthology devoted exclusively to the contemporary creative writing of writers and artists in Canada and Canadians living abroad. Fiction only, no poetry. The ideal reader of *CFM* is a writer or somebody interested in all the modes, manners, voices, and conventions of contemporary fiction." Quarterly. Estab. 1971. Circ. 1,800.
Needs: Literary. "Theme, style, length and subject matter are at the discretion of the author. The only requirement is that the work be of the highest possible literary standard." Buys 10 mss/issue, 35 mss/year. Publishes short shorts. Published new writers within the last year.
How to Contact: Send complete ms with SASE or IRC. Reports in 6 weeks on mss. Publishes ms up to 18 months after acceptance. "It is absolutely crucial that three or four issues be read. We sell back issues up to 1976 for $3; current issue $6.50 (postage included). Some double issues are $12."
Payment: $10/page plus one-year subscription.
Terms: Pays on publication for first North American serial rights. Sends galleys to author.
Advice: "*CFM* publishes Canada's leading writers as well as those in early stages of their careers. A wide knowledge of contemporary literature (in English and in translation) plus expertise in creative writ-

ing, modern fiction theories, current Canadian literature, and the innovative short story would be of great help to a potential contributor. *CFM* is an independent journal not associated with any academic institution. Each issue includes French-Canadian fiction in translation, interviews with well-known Canadian writers on the techniques of their fiction, forums and manifestoes on the future of fiction, as well as art work and reviews. $500 annual prize for the best story submitted in either French or English. Previous winners include John Metcalf, Mavis Gallant, Leon Rooke, W.P. Kinsella, Anne Copeland, Keath Fraser, Guy Vanderhaege, Matt Cohen, Patrick Roscoe, Douglas Glover, Robinton Mistry, Frances Irani, Sharon Butalu."

THE CAPILANO REVIEW (II), 2055 Purcell Way, North Vancouver, British Columbia V7J 3H5 Canada. (604)986-1911. Editor: Dorothy Jantzen. Fiction Editor: Crystal Hurdle. Magazine: 5 3/8x8 1/8 cm; 80-100 pages; glossy paper; photos. Magazine of "fresh, innovative art and literature for literary/artistic audience." Quarterly. Estab. 1973. Circ. 850.
Needs: Contemporary, experimental, literary and prose poem. Receives 20 unsolicited mss/month. Accepts 1-2 mss/issue; 4 mss/year. Recently published works by K. D. Miller, Dorothy Speak and Gladys Hindmarch. Published "lots" of new writers within the last year. Length: 2,000-6,000 words. Publishes short shorts. Occasionally recommends other markets.
How to Contact: Send complete ms with cover letter. Simultaneous and photocopied submissions OK. Sample copy $5.
Payment: Pays $48 maximum and 2 contributor's copies.
Terms: Pays on publication. Publication copyrighted.

THE CARIBBEAN WRITER (IV), The Caribbean Research Institute, RR 02, Box 10,000—Kingshill, St. Croix, Virgin Islands 00850. (809)778-0246. Magazine: 7x10; 110 pages; 60 lb paper; glossy cover stock; illustrations and photos. *"The Caribbean Writer* is an international magazine with a Caribbean focus. The Caribbean should be central to the work, or the work should reflect a Caribbean heritage, experience or perspective." Annually. Estab. 1987. Circ. 1,000.
Needs: Contemporary, experimental, historical (general), humor/satire, literary, mainstream and prose poem. Receives 50 unsolicited ms/year. Accepts 6 mss/issue. Length: 300 words minimum; 3,750 words maximum.
How to Contact: Send complete ms with cover letter. "Blind submissions only. Send name, address and title of ms on separate sheet. Title only on ms. Mss will not be considered unless this procedure is followed." Reports "once a year." SASE. Simultaneous and photocopied submissions OK. Accepts computer printout submissions including dot-matrix. Sample copy for $7 and $2 postage. Fiction guidlelines for SASE.
Payment: 1 contributor's copy.
Terms: Acquires one-time rights. Publication copyrighted.

A CAROLINA LITERARY COMPANION (II), Community Council for the Arts, Box 3554, Kinston NC 28501. (919)527-2517. Editors: Nellvena Duncan Eutsler, Mike Parker. Magazine: 5 1/2x8 1/2; 65-75 pages; 80 lb matte paper; 80 lb card matte cover. "The original focus of the magazine was on providing a forum for NC writers, but that emphasis has been expanded to include both established and emerging writers from any geographic area. Accordingly, priority is given to manuscripts submitted by writers living in or natives of the following states: Alabama, Florida, Georgia, Kentucky, Maryland, North Carolina, South Carolina, Tennessee, Virginia, West Virginia. Subscriptions are held by individuals, academic and public libraries." Annually. Estab. 1985. Circ. 500.
Needs: Adventure, contemporary, ethnic, historical, humor/satire, literary, mainstream, regional, senior citizen/retirement, suspense/mystery. No horror stories, religious material, children's/teenager's stories, erotic or specifically sexually oriented fiction. Receives 6-10 unsolicited mss/month. Accepts 5-6 mss/issue; 10-12 mss/year. "Recently published work by Ron Rash, who won a General Electric Foundation 1987 Award for Younger Writers, sponsored by The Coordinating Council of Literary Magazines." Published new writers within the last year. Publishes short shorts.
How to Contact: Send complete ms with cover letter. Reports in 1-2 weeks on queries; 2-4 months on mss. Photocopied submissions OK. Accepts computer printout submissions, including dot-matrix. Sample copy for $4.25, 6x9 SAE and 3 first class stamps.
Payment: Publication in contributor's copies.
Terms: Publication copyrighted.
Advice: "Submit! Just be sure your manuscript is legible, correctly spelled and correctly punctuated (the number of illegible and/or misspelled/mispunctuated submissions we receive is appalling). Fiction published in *A Carolina Literary Companion* is limited by space requirements to short and short-short stories."

CAROLINA QUARTERLY (II), Greenlaw Hall 066A, University of North Carolina, Chapel Hill NC 27514. (919)962-0244. Editor-in-Chief: Robert Rubin. Fiction Editor: Paul Lyons. Literary journal: 90-100 pages; illustrations; photos. "Fiction, poetry, graphics and some reviews, for that audience—whether academic or not—with an interest in the best in poetry and short fiction." Triquarterly. Estab. 1948. Circ. 1,000.
Needs: No pornography. Receives 150-200 unsolicited fiction mss/month. Buys 5-7 mss/issue, 15-20 mss/year. Publishes ms an average of 10 weeks after acceptance. Recently published work by Ian Mac-Millan, Jessica Weber, Ron Carlson. Published new writers within the last year. Length: 7,000 words maximum; no minimum; no preferred length. Also publishes short shorts. Occasionally critiques rejected mss.
How to Contact: Send complete ms with cover letter (no synopsis of story) and SASE to fiction editor. Photocopied submissions OK. Reports in 2-4 months. Sample copy $4; writer's guidelines for SAE and $1 postage.
Payment: $3/printed page; 2 free contributor's copies. Regular copy price for extras.
Terms: Pays on publication for first North American serial rights. Publication copyrighted.
Advice: "We publish a good many unsolicited stories and yes, I love publishing a new writer for the first time; *CQ* is a market for newcomer and professional alike. Write 'Fiction Editor' on envelope of submitted manuscript. Keep story to decent length—it's hard to publish very short and very long stories. Also—read what gets published in the journal/magazine you're interested in. Write the kind of story you would like to read. Make your packet look professional yet modest."

‡THE CASTLE (I,IV), FanTek—a SciFi & Fantasy & Gaming Club, Box 128, Aberdeen MD 21001. (703)360-2292. Editor: Bruce Eury. Fiction Editor: Cheryl Abrams. Magazine: 8½x5½; 16-20 pages; 60 lb offset paper; 60-69 lb color cover; illustrations and "very fine" photographs. "SF and fantasy, gaming, humorous fiction—main emphasis on club activities. Sent only to club members." Quarterly. Estab. 1983. Circ. 2,000.
Needs: Fantasy, humor/satire, science fiction. Does not want "anything serious." Receives very few unsolicited mss/month. Accepts 1-2 mss/issue; 5-10 mss/year. Publishes ms in next issue after acceptance. Recently published work by David Robeson, D. Allen Murphy and Greg Lanson. Length: 400 words average; 2 words minimum; 600 words maximum. Sometimes critiques rejected mss or recommends other markets.
How to Contact: Send complete ms with cover letter or "join our club ($5 dues per year) or come to conventions." Reports in 3 weeks. SASE. Photocopied submissions OK. Accepts computer printout submissions, including dot-matrix. Sample copy for 6x9 SAE and 2 first class stamps. Fiction guidelines for #10 SAE and 1 first class stamp.
Payment: Free subscription to magazine.
Terms: Acquires one-time rights. Publication copyrighted. "We do have a 'Writers' Group,' which holds workshops at our SF conventions. Future plans include awards."
Advice: "In our genres, it is almost impossible for a new author to get started in the very small handful of magazines still in 'professional' publication. We prefer things that touch on some aspect of our club's interests and activities. There are more nonfiction than fiction pages available, but poetry and fiction are fine. We are a family-type group and do not print foul language or erotic stuff. We like humor."

‡CATHEDRAL OF INSANITY (II), 1216 W. Ivesbrook, Lancaster CA 93534. Editor: Julie. Magazine: 8½x5½; 120 pages; illustrations. "The theme is mainly humor with a bit of seriousness. Publishes short stories and poetry for underground intellectuals." Bimonthly. Estab. 1988. Circ. 50.
Needs: Contemporary, experimental, humor/satire, psychic/supernatural/occult, serialized/excerpted novel and strange personal experiences. "I would like something with an underground or avant-garde feel. Nothing mainstream." Accepts 1 mss/issue; 2 mss/year. Publishes ms within 1-2 months of acceptance. Publishes short shorts. Sometimes critiques rejected mss.
How to Contact: Query with clips of published work. Reports in 2 weeks. Simultaneous and reprint submissions OK. Accepts computer printout submissions, including dot-matrix. Sample copy for $1. Fiction guidelines free.
Payment: Pays in contributor's copies.
Terms: Publication copyrighted.
Advice: "Send some work. My magazine is eager for material. I want a story that can be broken into about 3 segments (or 4 depending on length) to be used in 3 issues. Something humorous/satirical (I am fond of word play) or unnatural (drug experiences) is a good thing to send."

CEILIDH (II), An Informal Gathering for Story & Song, Box 6367, San Mateo CA 94403. (415)591-9902. Editors: Patrick S. Sullivan and Perry Oei. Associate Editor: Denise E. Sullivan. Magazine: 8½x5½; 32-64 pages; illustrations. "We are a growing literary magazine looking for literary fiction, drama and poetry." Quarterly. Two issues annually devoted to fiction. Estab. 1981. Circ. 500.

Needs: Experimental, literary, prose poem, science fiction, serialized/excerpted novel and translations. No romance, juvenile, erotica, preschool or young adult. Receives 25 unsolicited mss/month. Accepts 5 mss/issue; 10-12 mss/year. Recently published work by Karlton Kelm and Anne Brashler. Published new writers within the last year. Length: 3,000 words average; 6,000 words maximum. Also publishes short shorts. Sometimes recommends other markets.
How to Contact: Send complete ms with SASE. Reports in 6-8 weeks. Photocopied submissions OK. Accepts computer printout submissions. Publishes 2-3 months after acceptance. Sample copy $3.50. Fiction guidelines for #10 SAE and 1 first class stamp.
Payment: 2 contributor's copies; $3 charge for extras.
Terms: "At this point we cannot pay for every piece, but we occasionally sponsor a contest." Acquires one-time rights. Publication copyrighted.
Advice: "We lean toward experimental, more serious fiction, with a strong sense of voice. Send a neat manuscript with a descriptive cover letter, SASE. Fiction is a good voice for our times. Poetry is also, but people seem to enjoy a short story over a long poem."

THE CELIBATE WOMAN (IV), A Journal for Women Who Are Celibate or Considering This Liberating Way of Relating to Others, 3306 Ross Place NW, Washington DC 20008. (203)966-7783. Editor: Martha Allen. Journal for women interested in the issue of celibacy. Published irregularly. Estab. 1982.
Needs: Celibacy. Receives 10-15 unsolicited mss/issue.
How to Contact: Send complete ms with SASE. Reports in weeks on queries and mss. Simultaneous, photocopied and previously published submissions OK. Accepts computer printout submissions. Sample copy $4.

CENTRAL PARK (II), A Journal of the Arts and Social Theory, Neword Productions, Inc. Box 1446, New York NY 10023. (212)362-9151. Editor: Stephen-Paul Martin. Magazine: 7 1/2x10, 100 pages; glossy cover stock; illustrations; photos. Magazine of theoretical essays, poetry, fiction, photos and graphics for intellectual audience. Semiannually. Estab. 1981. Circ. 1,000.
Needs: Contemporary, erotica, ethnic, experimental, feminist, gay, historical (general), lesbian, literary, prose poem, serialized/excerpted novel and translations. Approximately 10% of fiction is agented. Receives 50 unsolicited mss/month. Publishes short shorts of 5-10 pages. Accepts 5 mss/issue; 10 mss/year. Recently published works by Ron Sukenick, Clarence Major, Dick Higgins. Published new writers within the last year. Usually critiques rejected mss. Sometimes recommends other markets.
How to Contact: Send complete ms and cover letter with "publication credits, relevant personal data, reasons for sending to us. We prefer submissions from people who are familiar with the magazine. We suggest that prospective contributors order a sample copy before submitting." Reports in 2 months. SASE. Simultaneous and photocopied submissions OK. Accepts computer printout submissions. Publishes ms an average of 3 months after acceptance. Sample copy $5.
Payment: 2 contributor's copies; $5 for extras.
Terms: Acquires first rights. Publication copyrighted.
Advice: "We would like to publish more short fiction, especially if it is experimental, aggressively sexual and political in nature. Write what seems to be an authentic representation of how *your* feelings interact with the social world. Let your imagination have free reign in evolving the form your work takes. Be aware of, *but not harnessed by*, conventions. We like to know who our writers are: what they do, their literary background and activities. Writers should include a cover letter and expect a personal letter in response."

THE CHARITON REVIEW (II), Northeast Missouri State University, Kirksville MO 63501. (816)785-4499. Editor: Jim Barnes. Magazine: 6x9; 100 + pages; 60 lb paper; 65 lb cover stock; photographs on cover. "We demand only excellence in fiction and fiction translation for a general and college readership." Semiannually. Estab. 1975. Circ. 700 + .
Needs: Literary, contemporary and translations. Buys 3-5 mss/issue, 6-10 mss/year. Recently published work by Steve Heller, John Deming, Judy Ray. Published new writers within the last year. Length: 3,000-6,000 words. Critiques rejected mss when there is time. Sometimes recommends other markets.
How to Contact: Send complete ms with SASE. Reports in less than 1 month on mss. Publishes ms an average of 6 months after acceptance. Sample copy $3 with SASE.
Payment: $5/page up to $50 maximum. Free author's copy. $2.50 for extras.
Terms: Pays on publication for first North American serial rights; rights returned on request. Publication copyrighted.
Advice: "Write well and study the publication you are submitting to. We are interested only in the very best fiction and fiction translation. We are not interested in slick material. We do not read photocopies or

carbon copies. Know the simple mechanics of submission—SASE, no paper clips, no odd-sized SASE, etc. Know the genre (short story, novella, etc.). Know the unwritten laws."

THE CHATTAHOOCHEE REVIEW (II), DeKalb College, 2101 Womack Rd., Dunwoody GA 30338. (404)390-3166. Editor: Lamar York. Magazine: 6x9; 150 pages; 70 lb paper; 80 lb cover stock; illustrations; photographs. Quarterly. Estab. 1980. Circ. 1,250.
Needs: Contemporary, erotica, experimental, feminist, gay, humor/satire, literary, mainstream, regional and translation. No juvenile, romance, sci-fi. Receives 100 unsolicited mss/month. Accepts 5 mss/issue. Recently published work by Leon Rooke, R.T. Smith; published new writers within the last year. Length: 2,500 words average. Sometimes critiques rejected mss and recommends other markets.
How to Contact: Send complete ms with cover letter, which should inlcude sufficient bio for notes on contributors' page. Reports in 4 months. SASE. Photocopied submissions OK. Accepts computer printout submissions, including dot-matrix. Sample copy $3.50. Fiction guidelines printed in magazine.
Payment: Pays in contributor's copies.
Terms: Acquires first rights. Publication copyrighted. "We sponsor a prize awarded to the best story printed in *The Review* throughout the year. Judged by professional writer, not the editor."
Advice: "Arrange to read magazine before you submit to it."

‡CHELSEA (II), Chelsea Associates, Inc. Box 5880, Grand Central Station, New York NY 10163. Editor: Sonia Raiziss. Magazine: 6x9; 185-235 pages; 60 lb white paper; glossy cover stock; artwork; occasional photos. "We have no consistent theme except for single special issues. Otherwise, we use general material of an eclectic nature: poetry, prose, artwork, etc., for a sophisticated, literate audience interested in avant-garde literature and current writing, both national and international." Annually. Estab. 1958. Circ. 1,100 +.
Needs: Literary, contemporary , prose poem and translations. No humorous, scatological, purely confessional or child/young-adult experiences. Receives approximately 25 unsolicited fiction mss each month. Approximately 1% of fiction is agented. Recently published work by Ronald Tobias, Paul Rovina and Harold Jaffe. Length: not over 25 printed pages. Publishes short shorts of 4-6 pages. Critiques rejected mss when there is time.
How to Contact: Query with SASE and succint cover letter with previous credits. Accepts computer printout submissions. Prefers letter-quality. Reports in 3 weeks on queries, 2 months on mss. Publishes ms within a year after acceptance. Sample copy $5 plus postage.
Payment: Author's copies, plus $5 per printed page.
Terms: Acquires first North American serial rights plus one-time non-exclusive reprint rights. Publication copyrighted.
Advice: "Familiarize yourself with issues of the magazine for character of contributions. Manuscripts should be legible, clearly typed, with minimal number of typographical errors and cross-outs, sufficient return postage. Most mss are rejected because they are conventional in theme and/or style, uninspired, contrived, etc."

CHESS LIFE (IV), U.S. Chess Federation, 186 Route 9W, New Windsor NY 12550. (914)562-8350. Editor: Don Maddox. Magazine: 8¼x10¾; 68 pages; slick paper; illustrations and photos. "Chess: news, theory, human interest, for chess players (mostly male)." Monthly. Circ. 58,000.
Needs: "Chess must be central to story." Receives 3 unsolicited mss/month. Accepts 2 mss/year. Publishes short shorts. Occasionally critiques rejected mss.
How to Contact: Query first. Sample copy and fiction guidelines free.
Terms: Publication copyrighted.

CHICAGO REVIEW, Faculty Exchange, Box C, University of Chicago, Chicago IL 60637. (312)702-0887. Fiction Editor: Emily McKnight. Magazine for a highly literate general audience: 6½x9; 96 pages; offset white 60 lb paper; illustrations; photos. Quarterly. Estab. 1946. Circ. 2,000.
Needs: Literary, contemporary, and especially experimental. Accepts up to 5 mss/issue, 20 mss/year. Receives 80-100 unsolicited fiction mss each month. No preferred length, except will not accept book-length mss. Critiques rejected mss "upon request." Sometimes recommends other markets.
How to Contact: Send complete ms with cover letter. SASE. Simultaneous submissions OK. Accepts

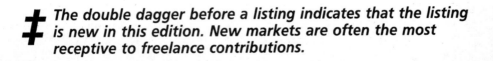

The double dagger before a listing indicates that the listing is new in this edition. New markets are often the most receptive to freelance contributions.

computer printout submissions if of good quality. Reports in 4-5 months on mss. Sample copy $4.50. Free guidelines with SASE.

Payment: 3 free author's copies and subscription.

Terms: Publication copyrighted.

Advice: "We look with interest at fiction that addresses subjects inventively, work that steers clear of clichéd treatments of themes. We're always eager to read writing that experiments with language, whether it be with characters' viewpoints, tone or style."

CHIPS OFF THE WRITER'S BLOCK (I), Box 83371, Los Angeles CA 90083. Editor: Wanda Windham. Newsletter. "Freelancer's forum, the beginner's chance to be published." Bimonthly.

Needs: "We will consider all categories of fiction, as our publication gives writers a chance to be 'critiqued' by fellow writers." No pornographic or offensive material. Published new writers with the last year. "Always" critiques rejected mss.

How to Contact: Submit complete ms. "Cover letters are not necessary. Please note the word count on the first page of the story." Reports in 3 weeks on queries; 1 month on mss. SASE. Considers simultaneous submissions; "prefers" photocopies. Accepts computer printout submissions, no dot-matrix. Sample copy $1. Fiction guidelines for #10 SAE and 1 first class stamp.

Payment: Payment is in copies.

Advice: "The editor works directly with the author if editing is necessary or if the story needs to be reworked. The writer's peer group also sends in comments, suggestions, etc., once the story is in print. The comments are discussed in later issues."

‡CHIRICÚ (IV), Ballantine Hall 849, Indiana University, Bloomington IN 47405. Editor: John Lashmett. "We publish essays, translations, poetry, fiction, reviews, interviews and artwork (illustrations and photos) that are either by or about Hispanics. We have no barriers on style, content or ideology, but would like to see well-written material." Annually. Estab. 1976. Circ. 500.

Needs: Contemporary, erotica, ethnic, experimental, fantasy, feminist/lesbian, gay, humor/satire, literary, mainstream, prose poem, science fiction, serialized/excerpted novel, translations. No fiction that has nothing to do with Hispanics (when not written by one). Recently published work by Sam Dean Dunning, Margarita Mondrus Engle, William Reyes; published new writers within the last year. Length: 7,000 words maximum; 4,000 words average. Occasionally critiques rejected mss. Sometimes recommends other markets.

How to Contact: Send complete ms with cover letter. "Include some personal information along with information about your story. "SASE. Photocopied submissions OK. Reports in 5 weeks. Publishes ms 6-12 months after acceptance. Sample copy $4.50.

Terms: Publication copyrighted.

Advice: "Realize that we are an Hispanic literary review so that if you are not Hispanic, then your work must reflect an interest in Hispanic issues or have an Hispanic bent to it in literature." Mss rejected "quite simply because beginning writers force their language instead of writing from genuine sentiment and natural language."

‡CHOPLOGIC (I,II), 151 First Ave., Studio D, New York NY. 10003. (212)713-5754. Editor: Eric Gunnar Rochow. Magazine: 7x8½; 24 pages; 20 lb bond paper; self cover; illustrations and photographs. "We feel the title describes our content. Good writing, thought-provoking visuals, intelligence." Magazine is "distributed internationally (Europe mainly), predominantly 'East Village' in NYC, but read by variety of people, even my mother." Quarterly. Plans special fiction issue. Estab. 1988. Circ. 1,500.

Needs: Adventure, condensed novel, contemporary, experimental, humor/satire, mainstream. "I like writing that moves, is concise and doesn't drag along like some piece of wordy noise. No heavy romance/erotica." Receives 15-20 unsolicited mss/month. Accepts 3-5 mss/issue. Publishes ms 2-3 months after acceptance. Length: 250-500 words preferred.

How to Contact: Send complete ms with cover letter. Cover letter should include "short letter of introduction, orientation to the moon at time of writing." Reports in 2-3 weeks. SASE. Sample copy for $1, 7x10 SAE and 2 first class stamps.

Payment: Pays in contributor's copies.

Terms: Acquires one-time rights. Publication copyrighted.

Advice: "I can be optimistic to those that write from the heart and not in a dictated style of some academic standard. Though William Safire is not a fiction writer, he is good with words. Write what you want rather than what you think will sell. If you want to prostitute yourself, join the Writer's Guild. Just be cool, be yourself, let us get to know you through your work and enjoy it rather than having to labor through the piece and shelve it."

CHRONOSCOPE, Aegis Unicorne, Box 1972, Davis CA 95617-1972. (916)753-9510. Editor: Tristan A. MacAvery. Fiction and Art Editor: Patrick J. Williams. Magazine: 5½x8½; 48+ pages; 20 lb paper; 110 lb cover; illustrations. "Features both finished works and works-in-progress from new and established authors. We encourage direct communication between artists and audience by publishing (with permission) artists' addresses in each issue, creating a forum for sharing." Bimonthly. Plans special fiction issue. Estab. 1986. Circ. 250+.
Needs: Contemporary, ethnic, experimental, fantasy, gay, historical (general), horror, humor/satire, lesbian, literary, mainstream, prose poem, psychic/supernatural/occult, romance (contemporary, historical), science fiction, serialized/excerpted novel, suspense/mystery, translations, western, young adult/teen. "No porn for its own sake; no experimentation just to be different; and absolutely no pretentiousness! Fake people or writing is rejected without a second glance." Receives approximately 30 fiction mss/month. Accepts 3-5 mss/issue; 40-60 mss/year. Recently published work by Wayne Allen Sallee, Michael Pagion, Catherine Buckaway; published new writers within the last year. Length: 2,500 words average; serialization possible. Publishes short shorts. Length: 500 words. Sometimes critiques rejected mss and recommends other markets.
How to Contact: Send complete ms with cover letter. "Tell us something about the work, about yourself. Don't be afraid to be personal, friendly, fun. We like people, not androids churning out a manuscript to the next name on the list. Art and artists are not easily separated, and we like that! We acknowledge all received manuscripts with a postcard; if the author does not hear back within 3 months, he may return the postcard for priority consideration and a free 3-issue (6 month) subscription to the magazine." SASE. Simultaneous, photocopied and reprint submissions OK. Accepts computer printout submissions, including dot-matrix. Sample copy $3. Fiction guidelines for #10 SAE and 1 first class stamp.
Payment: Pays in contributor's copies; charge for extras (2-for-1).
Terms: "For the sake of easy copyrighting of the magazine, we purchase all rights as a 'work for hire,' then reassign all rights, in writing, to author after publication." Sponsors contests for writers. "*Chronoscope* sponsors a semiannual fiction and poetry contest. Rules and entry form available for SASE."
Advice: "Don't be afraid to be personal, open, and give us your best shot. We try to make a comment on every manuscript that goes through here, and we make a policy of being constructive. Everyone working here has garnered enough rejection slips to cover any wall you care to name; we've been there, we understand! Most 'little' magazines are the same way, and 'The Big Boys' aren't out to bite your head off, either. Just remember: No one else in this world could write *your* story *your* way; both you and your work are one-of-a-kind material. That alone makes you special enough to merit a moment of an editor's time. Use that moment to make a good, personal impression, and you'll earn still more time—and that gets your story read carefully. From there, it's time for publication!"

CIMARRON REVIEW (II), Oklahoma State University, 205 Morrill, Stillwater OK 74078-0135. (405)744-9476. Editor: John K. Crane. Managing Editor: Deborah Bransford. Magazine: 6x9; 100 pages; illustrations on cover. "Poetry and fiction on contemporary themes; personal essay on contemporary issues that cope with life in the 20th century, for educated literary readers. We work hard to reflect quality." Quarterly. Estab. 1967. Circ. 500.
Needs: Literary and contemporary. No collegiate reminiscences or juvenilia. Accepts 6-7 mss/issue; 24-28 mss/year. Recently published works by Peter Makuck, Mary Lee Settle, John Timmerman; published new writers within the last year. Sometimes recommends other markets.
How to Contact: Send complete ms with SASE. "Short cover letters are appropriate but not essential, except for providing *CR* with the most recent mailing address available." Accepts computer printout submissions, prefers letter-quality. Reports in 1 month on mss. Publishes ms 6-9 months after acceptance. Free sample copy with SASE.
Payment: 5 free author's copies.
Terms: Acquires all rights on publication.
Advice: "Short fiction is a genre uniquely suited to the modern world. *CR* seeks an individual, innovative style that focuses on contemporary themes such as modern man's triumph over technology. Fiction especially focuses on humanism. Avoids childhood recollections and self-indulgent themes."

CLIFTON MAGAZINE (II), University of Cincinnati Communications Board, 204 Tangeman University Center, Cincinnati OH 45221. Editor: Lewis M. Wallace. Fiction Editors: Joanne Centa and Otis Pippins. Magazine: 8x11; 48 pages; 70 lb enamel coated paper; illustrations; photos. "*Clifton* is the magazine of the University of Cincinnati, presenting fiction, poetry and feature articles of interest to the University community. It is read by a highly literate audience of students, academics and professionals looking for original and exciting ideas presented in our award-winning format." Quarterly. Estab. 1972. Circ. 13,000.
Needs: Literary, contemporary, science fiction, fantasy, feminist, erotica, humor, prose poem, spiritual, regional and ethnic. "Will consider anything we haven't read a thousand times before. We try to have

no preconceptions when approaching fiction." Accepts 1-2 mss/issue, 5 mss/year. Recently published work by Karen Heuler, Evelyn Livingston and Adrienne Gosselin. Length: 6,000 words maximum. Publishes short shorts. Receives approximately 25 unsolicited fiction mss each month.

How to Contact: Send complete ms with SASE. Reports in 1 month on mss. Sample copy $1.75. Free guidelines with #10 SASE.

Payment: 5 free author's copies.

Terms: Acquires first rights. Publication copyrighted.

Advice: "*Clifton* often publishes work by unpublished authors and is quite open to any fiction. We look forward to continuing the publication with both young and established writers. *Clifton* tries to find mechanically sound, intricate, original work for publication. The unusual is popular. Be unique. Don't give up. Send at least one follow-up letter."

CLOCKWATCH REVIEW (II), A Journal of the Arts, Driftwood Publications, 737 Penbrook Way, Hartland WI 53029. (414)367-8315. Editor: James Plath. Magazine: 5½x8½; 64 pages; coated stock paper; glossy cover stock; illustrations; photos. "We publish stories which are *literary* as well as alive, colorful, enjoyable—stories which linger like shadows," for a general audience. Semiannually. Estab. 1983. Circ. 1,500.

Needs: Contemporary, experimental, humor/satire, literary, mainstream, prose poem and regional. Receives 50-60 unsolicited mss/month. Accepts 2 mss/issue; 4 mss/year. Recently published work by Ellen Hunnicutt, V.K. Gibson, J.W. Major; published new writers within the last year. Length: 2,500 words average; 1,200 words minimum; 4,000 words maximum. Occasionally critiques rejected mss if requested.

How to Contact: Send complete ms. Reports in 2 months. SASE. Photocopied submissions OK. Accepts computer printout submissions. Prefers letter-quality. Publishes ms 3-12 months after acceptance. Sample copy $3.

Payment: 2 contributor's copies and hand-crafted cut-out coin jewelry. "We also offer a cash prize for the best short story published in *CR* each year."

Terms: Acquires first serial rights. Publication copyrighted.

Advice: "Give us characters with meat on their bones, colorful but not clichéd; give us natural plots, not contrived or melodramatic. Above all, give us your *best* work."

‡COCHRAN'S CORNER (I), Box 2036, Waldorf, MD 20601. (301)843-0485. Editor: Debra G. Tompkins. Magazine: 5½x8; 52 pages; "good" paper. "We publish both fiction and nonfiction and poetry. Our only requirement is no strong language." For a "family" audience. Plans a special fiction issue. Quarterly. Estab. 1986. Circ. 500.

Needs: Adventure, historical (general), horror, humor/satire, juvenile (5-9 years), preschool (1-4 years), prose poem, religious/inspirational, romance, science fiction, suspense/mystery and young adult/teen (10-18 years). "Mss must be free from language you wouldn't want your/our children to read." Receives 50 mss/month. Accepts 4 mss/issue; 8 mss/year. Publishes ms by the next issue after acceptance. Recently published work by Juni Dunkin, Ruth Cox Anderson, Becky Knight. Length: 500 words preferred; 300 words minimum; 1,000 words maximum. Sometimes critiques unsolicited mss and recommends other markets.

How to Contact: Send complete ms with cover letter. Reports in 3 weeks on queries; 3 months on mss. SASE for manuscript. Simultaneous, photocopied and reprint submissions OK. Accepts computer printout submissions, including dot-matrix. Sample copy for $3, 5x9 SAE and 90¢ postage. Fiction guidelines for #10 SAE and 1 first class stamp.

Payment: Pays in contributor's copies.

Terms: Acquires one-time rights. Publication copyrighted.

Advice: "I feel the quality of fiction is getting better. The public is demanding a good read, instead of having sex or violence carry the story. I predict that fiction has a good future. We like to print the story as the writer submits it if possible. This way the writer can compare their work with their peers and take the necessary steps to improve and go on to sell to bigger magazines. Send for a sample copy, then send us your best work. If we can't use it, we'll tell you why."

‡THE COE REVIEW (II), Student Senate of Coe College, 1220 1st St., Cedar Rapids IA 52402. Contact: Becky L. Rieniets. Magazine: 8½x5½; 100-150 pages; illustrations; photos. Annual anthology of "quality experimental writing in both poetry and fiction. Especially directed to an academic or experimental literary audience that is concerned with current literature." Annually. Estab. 1972. Circ. 500.

Needs: Literary, contemporary, psychic/supernatural, science fiction, fantasy, feminist, gay/lesbian, erotica, quality ethnic, regional, serialized and condensed novels, translations. "We publish students, unsolicited professional and solicited professional mss. *The Coe Review* is growing and it is our goal to become nationally acknowledged in literary circles as a forerunner in the publication of experimental writing. We support writing workshops and invite both writing professors and student writers to sub-

mit." No "religious propaganda, gothic, romance, western, mystery or adventure. We avoid 'sap' and predictability." Length: 500-4,000 words.
How to Contact: Send complete ms with SASE. "Mss sent in summer will possibly not be returned until fall depending on availability of a fiction editor in summer." Accepts computer printout submissions. Sample copy $4.
Payment: $25-$100 for solicitations. 1 free author's copy. $4 charge for extras.
Terms: Pays on publication for all rights "but possibly sooner with solicited mss. Upon request we will reassign rights to the author."
Advice: "We desire material that seeks to explore the vast imaginative landscape and expand the boundaries thereof. Study experimental writers such as Borges, Vonnegut, Brautigan, J. Baumbach and Manual Puig. Avoid sentimentalism. Do not be afraid to experiment or to write intelligent fiction."

COLD-DRILL MAGAZINE (IV), English Dept., Boise State Univ., 1910 University Dr., Boise ID 83725. (208)385-1999. Editor: Tom Trusky. Magazine: 6x9; 150 pages; Beckett text paper; illustrations; photos. Material submitted must be by Idaho authors *or* deal with Idaho. For adult audiences. Annually. Estab. 1970. Circ. 500.
Needs: Adventure, contemporary, erotica, ethnic, experimental, fantasy, feminist, gay, horror, humor/satire, lesbian, literary, mainstream, science fiction, serialized/excerpted novel, suspense/mystery, translations, western, Idaho topics. "Manuscripts are selected in December for the annual issue in March. Authors may submit any time, but they will not be notified unless they are selected; if they are, notification will be in late December, early January." No children's literature, romance, gothic, true confession, psychic, religious or inspirational. Receives 10 fiction mss/month. Accepts 5-7 mss/issue; 5-7 mss/year. Publishes short shorts.
How to Contact: Query first. Reports in 2 weeks. SASE. Simultaneous and photocopied submissions OK. Accepts computer printouts including dot-matrix. Sample copy $5. Fiction guidelines for #10 SAE and first class stamp.
Payment: Contributor's copies.
Terms: Acquires first rights. Publication copyrighted.
Advice: "We publish the best in Idaho literature, regardless of the genre. Know the publication."

COLLAGES AND BRICOLAGES (II), The Journal of International Writing, Office of International Programs, 212 Founders Hall, Clarion University of Pennsylvania, Clarion PA 16214. (814)226-2340. Editor-in-Chief: Marie-José Fortis. Fiction Editor: Trudy Call. Consultant: Terry Caesar. Magazine: 8x11; 65-100 pages; illustrations and photographs. "The theme, if there is any, is international post-modern/avant-gardist culture. The magazine may include essays, short stories, short plays, poems that show innovative promise." Annually. Estab. 1987. Plans special fiction issue.
Needs: Contemporary, ethnic, experimental, feminist, humor/satire, literary, mainstream, philosophical, prose poem and science fiction. "Also post-modern, surrealist designs/illustrations are welcome." Receives 3-4 unsolicited fiction mss/month. Publishes ms 3-4 months after acceptance. Recently published work by Joe McCullough, Wayne Miller, Roland Perez; published new writers within the last year. Publishes short shorts. Sometimes critiques rejected ms; recommends other markets when there is time.
How to Contact: Send complete ms with cover letter. Reports in 4 weeks. SASE. Simultaneous submissions OK. Accepts computer printout submissions including dot-matrix. Sample copy $3.
Payment: Free subscription to magazine.
Terms: Acquires first rights.
Advice: "As far as fiction is concerned, it seems that everything has been said before. Hence, the writer's despair. This literary despair should be an asset to today's young writer. It should be his motif. The only innovation that can still be done is language innovation, playfulness, humor (with a sense of doom). We are now living in a neo-dada age, in a 'post-modern aura.' Hence, the writer's input should concentrate on these premises. Writing about the decadence of inspiration can bring us to a new age in literature. (The Dadaist despair was, after all, answered with surrealism.)"

COLORADO-NORTH REVIEW (I, II), University of Northern Colorado, Greeley CO 80639. Magazine: 8½x5½; 64 pages; 70 lb paper; 80 lb cover stock; illustrations; photos. Magazine of poetry, short fiction, translations, photography, interviews and graphic arts for writers or those interested in contemporary creativity. Published in winter and spring. Estab. 1968. Circ. 2,500.
Needs: Contemporary, literary and prose poem. Receives 100 unsolicited fiction mss/month. Accepts 70 mss/issue (including poetry), 140 mss/year. Recently published work by James Lentestey and Dennis Vannatta. Published new writers within the last year. Length: 1,000 words maximum. Critiques rejected mss by request.
How to Contact: Send complete ms with SASE and brief biographical info for contributor's section. Photocopied submissions OK. Reports in 3 months. Publishes ms 2-3 months after acceptance. Sample

copy $3.50; free guidelines with SASE.
Terms: Pays in contributor's copies. Publication copyrighted.
Advice: "We print primarily poetry; however, the short fiction is well received and very competitive. Simultaneous submissions are frowned upon. We strive for variety and short stories of different themes. Too often the best two or three stories are of the same theme and so we pick only one. Too many writers are confined to the novella, or bare character studies. We appreciate your best. Recent fiction inclusions have been extremely unconventional, often what has been called 'anti-fiction.' Abstract, bizarre and apparently 'new' fiction read eagerly."

‡COLORADO REVIEW (II), English Department, Colorado State University, Fort Collins CO 80523. (303)491-6428. Managing Editor: Bill Tremblay. Fiction Editor: David Milofsky. Translation Editor: Mary Crow. Literary magazine: 80-100 pages; 70 lb book weight paper; gloss cover stock. Semiannually. Estab. 1977. Circ. 1,000.
Needs: Contemporary, ethnic, experimental, literary, mainstream, translations. Receives 100 unsolicited fiction mss/month. Accepts 8-10 mss/issue. Recently published work by Rita Ciresi, Stephen Minot and Michael Fontana. Published new writers within the last year. Length: under 6,000 words. Does not read mss May-August. Occasionally critiques rejected mss and recommends other markets.
How to Contact: Send complete ms with SASE and brief bio and previous publications. Accepts computer printout submissions; prefers letter-quality. Reports in 3 months. Publishes ms 3-6 months after acceptance. Sample copy $5.
Payment: $10/printed page; 1 subscription to magazine; 2 free contributor's copies; $5 charge for extras.
Terms: Pays on publication for first North American serial rights. "We assign copyright to author on request." Sends galleys to author "when time permits." Publication copyrighted.
Advice: "We are interested in manuscripts which show craft, imagination and a convincing voice. Character development, strong story lines and thematic insight are always desired. If a story has reached a level of technical competence, we are receptive to the fiction working on its own terms. The oldest advice is still the best: persistence. Approach every aspect of the writing process with pride, conscientiousness—from word choice to manuscript appearance."

COLUMBIA: A MAGAZINE OF POETRY & PROSE (II), 404 Dodge Hall, Columbia University, New York NY 10027. (212)280-4391. Editors: Rotating. Magazine: 5¼x8¼; 180 pages approximately; coated cover stock; illustrations, photos. "We accept quality short stories, novel excerpts, translations, interviews, nonfiction and poetry." Annually.
Needs: Literary, prose poem and translations. Accepts 3-10 mss/issue. Receives approximately 125 unsolicited fiction mss each month. Does not read mss April 1 to August 31. Recently published work by Philip Lopate, Amy Hempel, Madison Smartt Bell; published 5-8 unpublished writers within the year. Length: 25 pages maximum. Publishes short shorts.
How to Contact: Send complete ms with SASE. Accepts computer printout submissions. Reports in 1-2 months. Sample copy $5.
Payment: Pays in author's copies. $3 charge for extras. Offers annual fiction awards.
Terms: Publication copyrighted.
Advice: "Don't overwhelm editors. Send work that's not longer than 20 pages."

COLUMBUS SINGLE SCENE (II, IV), Box 30856, Gahanna OH 43230. (614)476-8802. Editor: Jeanne Marlowe. Magazine: 8x11; 24 pages; illustrations; photos. Single living, male-female relationship topics covered for single adults. Monthly. Estab. 1985. Circ. 4,000.
Needs: Confession, contemporary, experimental, fantasy, humor/satire, mainstream, suspense/mystery. Buys 12 mss/year. Publication time varies "now that I have a backlog." Recently published work by C. Heath Johnson, Jan Maxwell, Jonathon Lowe; published new writers within the last year. Length: 5,000 words maximum; "shorter ms more likely to be accepted." Publishes short shorts. Occasionally critiques rejected mss.
How to Contact: Send complete ms with cover letter, which should include a statement granting one time rights in exchange for copies. Reports in 1 week on queries; 2-4 weeks on mss. SASE for ms, "unless you don't want ms returned." Simultaneous, photocopied and reprint submissions OK, "if not from local publications." Accepts computer printout submissions, including dot-matrix. Sample copy $1.
Payment: Contributors copies and advertising trade for most; $25 plus advertising trade maximum.
Terms: Pays on acceptance for one-time rights. Publication copyrighted.
Advice: "Good story telling will always be needed. Fiction may take a year to be published after acceptance. For my publication the work should concern meeting people, dating/relating to the other sex."

COMMON LIVES/LESBIAN LIVES (IV), A Lesbian Quarterly, Box 1553, Iowa City IA 52244. Contact: Tess Catalano and Tracy Moore. "*CL/LL* seeks to document the experiences and thoughts of lesbians for lesbian audience." Magazine: 8½x5; 112-128 pages; illustrations; photos. Quarterly.
Needs: Adventure, comics, contemporary, erotica, ethnic, experimental, fantasy, feminist, historical (general), humor/satire, juvenile, lesbian, prose poem, psychic/supernatural/occult, regional, romance, science fiction, senior citizen/retirement, suspense/mystery, western and young adult/teen. "All pertaining to lesbian culture." Length: 4-10 pages. Occasionally critiques rejected mss.
How to Contact: Send complete ms with cover letter; a short bio sketch is required. Reports in 4 months. SASE. Photocopied submissions OK. Accepts computer printout submissions. Publishes ms up to 4 months after acceptance. Published "many" new writers within the last year. Sample copy $4.
Payment: 2 contributor's copies. Publication copyrighted.
Advice: "Readers relate stories to their lives; fiction is an interesting and accessible way for lesbians to document their experience and express their opinions."

A COMPANION IN ZEOR (I,II,IV), 17 Ashland Ave., RR 5, R Box 82, Cardiff NJ 08232. Editor: Karen Litman. Fanzine: 8½x11; 60 pages; "letter" paper; heavy blue cover; b&w line illustrations; occasional b&w photographs. Publishes science fiction based on the various Universe creations of Jacqueline Lichtenberg. Occasional features on Star Trek, and other interests, convention reports, reviews of movies and books, recordings, etc. Irregular. Estab. 1978. Circ. 300.
Needs: Fantasy, humor/satire, prose poem, science fiction. "No vicious satire. Nothing X rated. Homosexuality prohibited unless *essential* in story. We run a clean publication that anyone should be able to read without fear." Occasionally receives one manuscript a month. Accepts "as much as can afford to print." Publication of an accepted ms "can take years, due to limit of finances available for publication." Occasionally critiques rejected mss and recommends other markets.
How to Contact: Query first or send complete ms with cover letter. "Perfer cover letters about any writing experience prior, or related interests toward writing aims." Reports in 1 month. SASE. Simultaneous and photocopied submissions OK. Accepts computer printout submissions, including dot-matrix. Sample copy price depends on individual circumstances. Fiction guidelines for #10 SAE and 1 first class stamp. "I write individual letters to all queries. No form letter at present." SASE preferred for guidelines, but not required at present (our present contact with writers is small). If volume of inquiries becomes larger, a SASE will be required.
Payment: Pays in contributor's copies.
Terms: Acquires first rights. Publication copyrighted.
Advice: "We take fiction based on any and all of Jacqueline Lichtenberg's published novels. The contributor should be familiar with these works before contributing material to my fanzine. Also accepts manuscripts on cassette from visually handicapped if submitted. 'Zines also on tape for those individuals."

COMPASSION MAGAZINE (IV), Pittenbruach Press, Box 553, Northampton MA 01061. Editor: Teddy Milne. Magazine: 11x7; 24-48 pages; b&w line illustrations. "Socially responsible fiction—send SASE for guidelines." Quarterly. Estab. 1988.
Needs: Accepts 8-12 mss/issue. Recently published work by Dominique Mazeaud, Rodolfo Torres, Virginia Royce Clark; published new writers within the last year. Publishes short shorts.
How to Contact: Send SASE for guidelines. Photocopied and reprint submissions OK. Accepts computer printout submissions, including dot-matrix. Sample copy $4.95.
Payment: Pays in contributor's copies; half price for extras.
Terms: Acquires one-time rights.
Advice: "You decide on the plots, but try to keep in mind that we want to emphasize social responsibility, sense of community, appreciation of nature, attunement with the universe and with each other, friendship (perhaps particularly friendships between men and women which don't assume that sex is the first step or the end goal—whether or not that happens); and hopefully, a kind of vision of the world as it

❝ *The main suggestion from me is read. It is impossible for a writer to be able to write honestly and eloquently without having at one time or another acquainted himself with such writers as Sir Thomas Browne.* **❞**

—*William Styron*

could be if we emphasized the good instead of the bad. Write good stories about interesting, but normal, people. We're sick of psychos."

‡COMPOST NEWSLETTER (IV), Compost Coven, 729 Fifth Ave., San Francisco CA 94118. (415)751-9466. Editor: Valerie Walker. Newsletter: 8½x11; 20 pages; bond paper and cover; illustrations and scanned photographs. Publishes "humor/satire from a pagan/punk perspective." Published 8 times/year. Estab. 1981. Circ. under 100.
Needs: Experimental, fantasy, feminist, gay, humor/satire, lesbian, psychic/supernatural/occult, science fiction, serialized novel, pagan. No Christian. Publishes ms within 1 or 2 issues after acceptance. Length: 500 words minimum; 2,000 words maximum.
How to Contact: Query with clips of published work. Reports in 2 months. SASE. Simultaneous, photocopied and reprint submissions OK. Accepts dot-matrix computer printouts; accepts electronic submissions via Macintosh disk. Sample copy $1.
Payment: Pays in contributor's copies.
Terms: Acquires one-time rights. Publication not copyrighted.
Advice: "If you don't like the magazine market, go out and make one of your own. Type single space on white paper, or send a Macintosh disk in MacWrite or Microsoft Word. Don't bother to format unless it's essential for the feel of the piece. Entertain us, even if you're serious. Get strange." Publishes ms "if it is funny, bizarre, or we agree with its politics."

CONDITIONS: A Feminist Magazine With an Emphasis on Writings by Lesbians (II), Box 159046, Van Brunt Station, Brooklyn NY 11215-9046. Collective of editors. Magazine: 8½x11; 200 pages; good paper; color cover stock; illustrations and photographs. A magazine of work "by published and unpublished writers of many different backgrounds for women of all ages and backgrounds who feel that a commitment to other women is an integral part of their lives." Annually. Estab. 1976.
Needs: Ethnic, feminist, lesbian, literary, prose poem, translations. Wants to see mss "which reflect the experiences and viewpoints of Third World, working-class and older women." Receives 10 unsolicited fiction mss/month. Accepts 12 mss/issue. Recently published work by Shay Youngblood, Mariana Romo-Carmona, Leslea Newman; published new writers in the last year. Length: 500 words minimum, 10,000 words maximum, 5,000 words average. Occasionally critiques rejected mss.
How to Contact: Send complete ms with SASE. Photocopied submissions OK. Reports in 2 months. Sample copy $8.95.
Payment: 2 free contributor's copies.
Terms: Publication copyrighted.
Advice: "Buy a copy first to understand purpose of magazine. Revise, revise, revise, and keep trying."

CONFRONTATION (II), English Dept., C.W. Post of Long Island University, Greenvale NY 11548. (516)299-2391. Editor: Martin Tucker. Fiction Editor: William Fahey. Magazine: 6x9; 190-250 pages; 70 lb paper; 80 lb cover; illustrations; photos. "We like to have a 'range' of subjects, form and style in each issue and are open to all forms. Quality is our major concern. Our audience is literate, thinking college students; educated and self-educated lay persons." Semiannually. Published special fiction issue last year; plans another. Estab. 1968. Circ. 2,000.
Needs: Literary, contemporary, prose poem, regional and translations. No "proseletyzing" literature. Buys 30 mss/issue, 60 mss/year. Receives 400 unsolicited fiction mss each month. Does not read June-September. Approximately 10-15% of fiction is agented. Recently published work by Jerzy Kosinski, Irvin Faust, Mae Briskin. Published new writers within the last year. Length: 500-4,000 words. Publishes short shorts. Critiques rejected mss when there is time. Sometimes recommends other markets.
How to Contact: Send complete ms with SASE. "Cover letters acceptable, not necessary. We accept simultaneous submissions but do not like it." Accepts computer printout submissions, letter-quality only. Reports in 6 weeks on mss. Publishes ms 6-12 months after acceptance. Sample copy $3.
Payment: $10-$100. 1 free author's copy. Half price for extras.
Terms: Pays on publication for all rights "with transfer on request to author." Publication copyrighted.
Advice: "Keep trying."

CONJUNCTIONS (II), 33 W. 9th St., New York NY 10011. Editor: Bradford Morrow. Magazine: 6x9; 294 pages; 55 lb woven paper; heavy cream laid paper cover stock; illustrations; photos. "*Conjunctions*: a conjoining of texts by many diverse writers: a forum of work-in-progress by both well-known and new writers. We represent no clique but are concerned solely with publishing works of high artistic and technical calibre." Semiannually. Estab. 1981. Circ. 5,500.
Needs: Experimental, literary and translations. Receives 100 unsolicited fiction mss/month. Accepts 65 mss/year. "Recent issues have included new work by John Hawkes, William T. Vollman and Mary

Caponegro."Published new writers within the last year. No preferred length.
How to Contact: Send complete ms with SASE. Reports in 8-12 weeks on mss.
Payment: 3 free contributor's copies; extra copies available at 40% discount to contributors.
Terms: Acquires one-time rights. Sends galleys to author. Publication copyrighted.
Advice: "Gain a far wider personal experience than that which is possible in writing schools. A broader reading base than is evident in most of the unsolicited work we receive would be useful. So much has already been accomplished, and it seems to us the literacy rate among writers is only barely higher than any other community or profession."

THE CONNECTICUT WRITER (I), Box 10536, West Hartford CT 06110. Editor: R. Lucas. Fiction Editor: Sara Maxson Medvitz. Magazine: 5⁷/₁₆x8³/₈; 78 pages; excellent paper; heavy, glossy stock. "We publish short poetry and fiction." Annually. Estab. 1982. Circ. 500.
Needs: Condensed/excerpted novel, contemporary, historical (general) humor/satire, literary and mainstream. Charges $3/entry reading fee. Recently published work by Martha Clark Cummings, Holly Keith and Immy Wallenfels. Length: 1,500 words preferred; 3,000 words maximum. "We haven't published stories under 500 words, but I see no reason why we wouldn't if we like something that short."
How to Contact: "We read only contest entries now. Send SASE for guidelines." Accepts computer printout submissions, including dot-matrix. Sample copy $6. Fiction and poetry guidelines for #10 SAE and 1 first class stamp.
Advice: "We usually don't like things that are wordy, pretentious, not carefully thought out. Beginners should read good short stories, see what makes them good and be guided by them in their writing."

COSMIC LANDSCAPES (I), An Alternative Science Fiction Magazine, % Dan Petitpas, 6 Edson St., Hyde Park MA 02136. (617)361-0622. Editor: Dan Petitpas. Magazine: 7x8½; 32-56 pages; white bond paper and cover stock; illustrations; photos occasionally. "A magazine which publishes science fiction for science-fiction fans; also articles and news of interest to writers and SF fans. Occasionally prints works of horror and fantasy." Annually. Estab. 1983. Circ. 100.
Needs: Science fiction. Receives 10-15 unsolicited mss/month. Accepts 8 mss/issue. Recently published work by Susan Linville, Alan McElroy, Michael Ashley; published new writers in the last year. Length: 2,500 words average; 25 words minimum. Will consider serials. "Every manuscript receives a personal evaluation by the editor." Sometimes recommends other markets.
How to Contact: Send complete ms with info about the author. Reports usually in 1 week-3 months. SASE. Photocopied submissions preferred. Accepts readable computer printout submissions. Sample copy $3. Fiction guidelines free with SASE.
Payment: 2 contributor's copies; charge for extras: $1.50.
Terms: Acquires one-time rights. Publication copyrighted.
Advice: "Writers don't know letter formats for business-style letters. Or they don't include a return address. I like to know a little about them. Some background, and how the story pertains to their experience. Learn manuscript formats. Get E. B. White's *Elements of Style*. Don't get all your ideas from TV shows or movies. Try to get the basics. It would have helped if you paid attention in English classes."

COTTON BOLL/ATLANTA REVIEW (II), Sandy Springs, Box 76757, Atlanta GA 30358-0703. Editor: Mary Hollingsworth. Magazine: 5½x8½; 100-125 pages; 60 lb bond paper; cardboard cover; illustrations and photographs. Quarterly. Estab. 1985. Circ. 750.
Needs: Contemporary, experimental, humor/satire, literary, prose poem. Preference is for reflection of the contemporary South or general applicability." No pornography, religion, lovelorn or racism; or genre such as sci-fi or romance. Receives 12-15 fiction mss/month. Accepts about 3 mss/issue; 12-15 mss/year. Publishes ms 3 months to 1 year after acceptance. Recently published work by Joseph C. Thackery, Ellyn Bache, and Gloria Durham; published new writers within the last year. Preferred length: 3,500 words.
How to Contact: Send complete ms with cover letter. Reports on queries in 2 weeks; on mss in 12 weeks. SASE. Computer printout submissions OK, including dot-matrix. Sample copy $5.50. Fiction guidelines for #10 SAE with 1 first class stamp.
Payment: Pays in contributor's copies; reduced charge for extras.
Terms: Acquires one-time rights. Publication copyrighted. Sponsors contests and awards for fiction writers.
Advice: "Study the magazine; read the guidelines. Don't be in too great a hurry for publication. Be sure your material is the best you can do."

‡**THE COUCH POTATO JOURNAL (I, II, IV), A Quarterly Fanzine of Fiction, Poetry, Art and Essays**, 6861 Catlett Rd., St. Augustine FL 32084. (904)824-6581. Editor: T. M. Spell. Magazine: 5½x8½; 72 pages; 20 lb bond paper and cover; b&w illustrations. "Publication to entertain readers with

fiction, poetry, art and essays based on science fiction and fantasy television shows. It is also our desire to provide an outlet for creative expression among fan artists and writers who have not yet achieved professional publication, but who have goals in that direction." Quarterly. Plans special fiction issue. Estab. 1988. Circ. approx. 200.

Needs: Adventure, fantasy, prose poem, romance, science fiction and suspense/mystery. Special interests: high fantasy, dark fantasy, sword and sorcery, space opera, cyberpunk, science gone mad, all related to sf/f television shows. "The shows we give the most attention to are *Beauty and the Beast*, *Friday the 13th: The Series*, *Max Headroom*, *Probe*, *Shadow Chasers*, *Werewolf* and *The Wizard*, but we will consider work based on any sf/f television show. No pornography: nothing degrading or sadistic; stories written for their gore, shock or disgust value alone, that have no independent plot; "Mary Sue" stories (author's character 'gets' series character) without an independent plot line of some sort." Receives 10-25 unsolicited mss/month. Buys 5-10 mss/issue; 20-40 mss/year. Publishes ms 3-6 months after acceptance. Length: 250 words minimum; 25,000 words maximum. Sometimes critiques rejected mss and recommends other markets.

How to Contact: Send complete ms with cover letter. "Tell me a little about what you're submitting (is it a story, poem(s), or essay?) and what series your work is based on." Reports in 1-3 weeks on queries; 2-8 weeks on mss. SASE. Photocopied submissions OK. Accepts computer printout submissions, including dot-matrix. Sample copy for $3. Fiction guidelines for #10 SAE and 1 first class stamp.

Payment: Pays free subscription and contributor's copies.

Terms: Acquires one-time rights.

Advice: "Know and love sf/fantasy—not just the shows and movies, but the books and magazines as well. It helps to know what's been done to death and what territory is wide open for exploration. Still, don't be afraid to tackle an idea that's been used often (alien invasion, for instance); write about it from your point of view and the chances are the resulting story will be fresh and moving. It helps to love the show you write about to the point of maniacal obsession (most fans, myself included, do). Fandom is a way of life and that devotion will rub off on your fiction, often overcoming all but the worst stylistic flaws. Something to keep in mind: most of the bestselling *Star Trek* novels were written by *Star Trek* fans, and a great many fan writers go on to be *selling*, professional writers."

COYDOG REVIEW (II, III), A Journal of Poetry, Short Fiction, Essays and Graphics, Box 2608, Aptos CA 95001. (408)761-1824. Editor: Candida Lawrence. Magazine: 7x9½; 125 pages; Xerox paper; fine press cover; b&w art and photos. "*Coydog Review* seeks honest, original work on any subject, in any style, for a literate audience that enjoys reading about everyday experiences." Annually. Estab. 1984. Circ. 200-500.

Needs: Erotic, ethnic, experimental, feminist, gay, humor/satire, lesbian, literary, mainstream, prose poem, regional, science fiction, excerpted novel and autobiographical. No obvious porn. Receives 60 unsolicited mss/month. Accepts 20 mss/issue. Recently published works by Michelle Dionetti, Robert Bly, Paul Milenski; published new writers within the last year. Length: under 10,000 words average. Also publishes short shorts. Occasionally critiques rejected mss and recommends other markets.

How to Contact: Send complete ms with SASE. Reports in 1 month on mss. Simultaneous and photocopied submissions OK. Accepts computer printout submissions. Sample copy $5.95.

Payment: 2 contributor's copies. Sometimes offers prize money for special themes.

Terms: Acquires one-time rights. Publication copyrighted.

Advice: "Write about what you know, not what you think you ought to know or feel, and do not imitate a sophistication which is false. Risk reading your work out loud to yourself before sending. The editor is especially interested in work which tips toward autobiography but avoids self-indulgence. Getting published *anywhere* is a thrill for a beginning or continuing writer. The thrill translates into more devotion to craft. Avoid over-explanation of motive or character. Dramatic flashbacks are becoming *very* trite and ho-hum."

CRAB CREEK REVIEW (II), 4462 Whitman Ave. N., Seattle WA 98103. (206)633-1090. Editor: Linda Clifton. Fiction Editor: Carol Orlock. Magazine: 6x10 minitab; 32 pages; ultrabright newsprint paper; self cover; line drawings. Magazine publishing poetry, short stories, art and essays for adult, college-educated audience interested in literary, visual and dramatic arts and in politics. Triquarterly. Estab. 1983. Circ. 350.

Needs: Contemporary, humor/satire, literary and translations. No confession, erotica, horror, juvenile, preschool, religious/inspirational, romance or young adult. Receives 20 unsolicited mss/month. Accepts 2 mss/issue; 6 mss/year. Recently published work by Carol Orlock, Rebecca Wells, Robert Neuman; published new writers within the last year. Length: 3,000 words average; 1,200 words minimum; 4,000 words maximum. Publishes short shorts. Occasionally critiques rejected mss.

How to Contact: Send complete ms with short list of credits. Reports in 2 months. SASE. Photocopied submissions OK "but no simultaneous submissions." Accepts computer printout submissions; prefers letter-quality. Sample copy $3.

Payment: 2 free contributor's copies; $2 charge for extras.
Terms: Acquires first rights. Rarely buys reprints. Publication copyrighted.
Advice: "We appreciate 'sudden fictions.' Type name and address on each piece. Enclose SASE. Send no more than one story in a packet (except for short shorts—no more than 3, 10 pages total)."

CRAZYHORSE (III), Dept. of English, Univ. of Arkansas at Little Rock, AR 72204. (501)569-3160. Managing Editor: Zabelle Derounian. Fiction Editor: David Jauss. Magazine: 6x9; 128 pages; cover and front page illustrations only. Publishes original, quality literary fiction. Past contributors include Lee K. Abbott, Frederick Busch, Andre Dubus, Pam Durban, H.E. Francis, James Hannah, Gordon Lish, Bobbie Ann Mason and Maura Stanton. Biannually. Plans special fiction issue. Estab. 1960. Circ. 750.
Needs: Literary. No formula (science-fiction, gothic, detective, etc.) fiction. Receives 100-150 unsolicited mss/month. Buys 4-5 mss/issue; 8-10 mss/year. Does not read mss in summer. Publishes short shorts. Published new writers within the last year. "Rarely" critiques rejected mss.
How to Contact: Send complete ms with cover letter. Reports in 1 week on queries; 1-4 weeks on mss. SASE. Photocopied submissions OK. Accepts computer printout submissions. Sample copy $3.
Payment: Pays $5/page and contributor's copies.
Terms: Pays on publicaton for first North American serial rights. Publication copyrighted. *Crazyhorse* awards $250 to the author of the best work of fiction published in a given year.
Advice: "Read a sample issue and submit work that you believe is as good as or better than the fiction we've published."

CRAZYQUILT (II), 3341 Adams Ave., San Diego CA 92116. (619)576-0104. Editor: Marsh Cassady. Magazine: 5½x8½; 80 pages; illustrations and photos. "We publish short fiction, poems, nonfiction about writing and writers, one-act plays and b&w illustrations and photos. Quarterly. Estab. 1986. Circ. 175.
Needs: Contemporary, ethnic, fantasy, historical, humor/satire, literary, mainstream, science fiction, excerpted novel, suspense/mystery. "Shorter pieces are preferred." Receives 85-100 unsolicited mss/quarter. Accepts 1-3 mss/issue; 4-12 mss/year. Publishes 6-12 months after acceptance. Recently published work by Frederick A. Raborg, Jr., Peter Telep, Robert W. McCray; published new writers within the last year. Length: 1,500 words minimum; 5,000 words maximum. Publishes short shorts. Occasionally critiques rejected mss.
How to Contact: Send complete ms with cover letter. Reports in 3 months on mss. Simultaneous and photocopied submissions OK. Accepts computer printout submissions, including dot-matrix. Sample copy $4 ($2 for back issue). Fiction guidelines for SAE and 1 first class stamp.
Payment: 2 free contributor's copies.
Terms: Acquires first North American serial rights or one-time rights. Publication copyrighted. Holds annual poetry and fiction contest ($100, $50 and $25 prizes) and annual chapbook contest.
Advice: "Write a story that is well constructed, develops characters and maintains interest."

THE CREAM CITY REVIEW (II), University of Wisconsin-Milwaukee, Box 413, Milwaukee WI 53201. (414)229-5041.Editor: Ron Tanner. Fiction Editor: Ellen Barclay. Magazine: 8½x5½; 120-200 pages; 70 lb offset/perfect bound paper; 80 lb cover stock; illustrations; photos. "General literary publication—an electric selection of the best we receive." Semiannually. Plans to publish special fiction issue Semiannually. Estab. 1975. Circ. 1,000-1,500.
Needs: Ethnic, experimental, humor/satire, literary, prose poem, regional and translations. Receives approximately 100-200 unsolicited fiction mss each month. Accepts 6-10 mss/issue. Recently published works by Eve Shelnutt, Ellen Hunnicut and F.D. Reeve; published new writers within the last year. Length: 1,000-10,000 words. Publishes short shorts. Critiques rejected mss when there is time. Recommends other markets "when we have time."
How to Contact: Send complete ms with SASE. Photocopied submissions OK. Reports in 2 months. Sample copy $4.50.
Payment: 2 free author's copies.
Terms: Acquires first rights. Sends galleys to author. Publication copyrighted. Rights revert to author after publication.
Advice: "Read as much as you write so that you can examine your own work in relation to where fiction has been and where fiction is going."

CREATIVE KIDS (I, IV), GCT, Inc., Box 6448, Mobile AL 36660. (205)478-4700. Editor: Fay L. Gold. Magazine: 8½x11; 32 pages; illustrations; photos. Material by children for children. Published 8 times/year. Estab. 1980. Circ: 10,000.
Needs: "We publish work by children ages 5-18." Juvenile (5-9 years); young adult/teen (10-18 years). No sexist, racist or violent fiction. Accepts 8-10 mss/issue; 60-80 mss/year. Publishes ms up to one year after acceptance. Published new writers within the last year. Publishes short shorts.

How to Contact: Send complete ms with cover letter, which should include name, age, home address, school name and address. Reports in 2 weeks on queries; 4 weeks on mss. SASE. Accepts computer printout submissions, no dot-matrix. Sample copy $2.50.
Payment: Pays contributor's copy only.
Terms: Acquires all rights. Publication copyrighted.
Advice: "Ours is a magazine to encourage young creative writers to use their imaginations, talent and writing skills. Type the manuscript—double space. Include all vital information about author. Send to one magazine at a time."

THE CREATIVE SPIRIT (I), Creative Press, Manchester Mall, 811 Main St., Box 10, Manchester CT 06040. Editor: Bea Sheftel. Magazine: 8½x11; 20-40 pages; bond paper; paper cover; illustrations. "General interest fiction. Strong characters—especially like women as heroine." Published 3 times/year. Press established in 1982. Circ. 1,200.
Needs: Confession, contemporary, fantasy, feminist, historical (general), horror, humor, mainstream, prose poem, regional, religious/inspirational, romance (contemporary, historical), science fiction, suspense/mystery. Looks for "romance between mature adults, science fiction with more characters than machines. We like great fantasy with romance." Receives 6 fiction mss/month. Tries to accept 10-15 fiction mss/issue. Published new writers within the last year. Length: 750 words average; 500 words minimum; 1,500 words absolute maximum. Publishes short shorts. Length: 300-450 words. Anything longer than 5 pages returned unread!
How to Contact: Send complete ms with cover letter. Reports in 2 months. SASE. Photocopied and simultaneous submissions OK. Accepts computer printout submissions, including dot-matrix. Sample copy $4. Fiction guidelines for #10 SAE and 2 first class stamps.
Payment: One copy. "Chance at prizes for best of issue, reader selected."
Terms: Acquires one-time rights. Publication copyrighted. Offers prizes for best stories published.
Advice: "Have some plot and characterization even in a short piece. Don't send me suicides, AIDS or other depressing stories. Romantic humor is my favorite."

THE CREATIVE WOMAN (I,IV), Governors State University, University Park IL 60466. (312)534-5000, ext. 2524. Editor: Dr. Helen Hughes. Magazine: 8½x11; 48 pages; illustrations; photos. "Focus on a special topic each issue, presented from a feminist viewpoint." Estab. 1977. Circ. 800.
Needs: Feminist, humor/satire, prose poem, spiritual and sports. Receives 5 unsolicited fiction mss/month. Accepts 1 ms/issue; 3 mss/year. Publishes ms 3-12 months after acceptance. Recently published work by Susan Griffin. Also publishes short shorts. Occasionally critiques rejected mss and recommends other markets.
How to Contact: Send complete ms with cover letter. Report time varies. SASE for ms. Photocopied submissions and reprints OK. Accepts computer printouts. Sample copy $3.
Payment: Pays in contributor's copies.
Terms: Publication copyrighted.
Advice: "Read our magazine before submitting. Don't give up."

CROSS TIMBERS REVIEW (II), Cisco Junior College, Cisco TX 76437. (817)442-2567. Editor: Monte Lewis. Fiction Editor: Ken Hammes. Magazine: 9½x6; 72 pages average; 65 lb paper; 80 lb cover stock; pen and ink illustrations. "To serve as a medium through which regional ideas and works may be presented to a broader readership, while at the same time not excluding the works of international writers, for academic and general audience." Semiannually. Estab. 1983. Circ. 250.
Needs: Adventure, ethnic, historical (general), humor/satire, literary, regional, western, southwestern material. Receives 5-10 unsolicited fiction mss/month. Accepts 2-3 mss/issue; 4-6 mss/year. Does not read mss June/July. Publishes ms 3-6 months after acceptance. Length: 3,000-4,000 words average; 1,000 words minimum; 4,000 words maximum. Sometimes critiques rejected mss.
How to Contact: Send complete ms with cover letter with name, address. Reports in 6 weeks on queries; 6 months on mss. SASE for ms. Photocopied submissions OK. Accepts computer printouts including dot-matrix. Sample copy $3.
Payment: Pays in 3 contributor's copies, $3 charge for extras.
Terms: Acquires one-time rights. Sends galleys to author. Publication copyrighted.
Advice: "We like stories with *impact*. The story must say something with preciseness and punch. The Southwest has a rich tradition of fiction; we want to encourage writers to keep the tradition alive. We attempt to showcase Texas writers."

CROSS-CANADA WRITERS' MAGAZINE (II), Box 277, Station F, Toronto, Ontario M4Y 2L7 Canada. Editor-in-Chief: Ted Plantos. Magazine: 8½x11; 32 pages; 70 lb paper; card-coated cover stock; illustrations; photos. "The Canadian literary writer's magazine." Published 3 times/year. Estab. 1978. Circ. 2,000.

Needs: Literary, prose poem and regional. "We welcome submissions of fiction from American authors. We offer American as well as Canadian writers the most comprehensive, current literary market listings published in Canada. We keep our readers in touch with the Canadian literary scene and available markets for their work." Receives 15-20 unsolicited fiction mss/month. Accepts 1-2 mss/issue, 3-6 mss/year. Recently published work by Don Bailey, Patricia Stone and Renato Trujillo. Published new writers within the last year. Length: 3,000 words maximum. Publishes short shorts. Occasionally critiques rejected mss.
How to Contact: Send complete ms with SASE with bio. Photocopied submissions OK. Accepts computer printout submissions; prefers letter-quality. Reports in 2 weeks on queries; 5 weeks on mss. Publishes ms "up to one year" after acceptance. Sample copy $3.95.
Payment: Honorarium.
Terms: Acquires first rights and one-time rights. Publication copyrighted.
Advice: Recommends studying an issue before submitting. Subscriptions: $14 (individuals Canadian); $16 (individuals abroad); $18 (institutions Canadian); $21 (institutions abroad)."Before submitting, a writer should read the story as though he/she is a magazine subscriber encountering it in print cold: i.e., put self in the reader's shoes. Does the story entertain, hold interest?"

CROSSCURRENTS (III), 2200 Glastonbury Rd., Westlake Village CA 91361. Editor: Linda Brown Michelson. Magazine: 6x9; 176 pages; 70 lb paper stock; laminated cover; line drawings and halftone photos. "*Crosscurrents* is a literary magazine offering another corner for today's artistry. We publish short fiction, poetry, graphic arts and nonfiction. We direct our publication toward an educated audience who appreciate good writing and good art and who enjoy a periodic sampling of current trends in these fields." Quarterly. Estab. 1980. Circ. 3,000.
Needs: Most categories except heavy erotica, juvenile and young adult. "Good writing is what we look for and consider first. We want high quality literary fiction." Buys 7-12 mss/issue, 45 mss/year. Approximately 10% of fiction is agented. Recently published fiction by Alvin Greenberg, Joyce Carol Oates and Alice Adams; published new writers in the last year. Length: 6,000 words maximum. Critiques rejected mss when there is time.
How to Contact: Send complete ms with SASE. Reviews material June 1-Nov 30 each year. No simultaneous submissions. Accepts computer printout submissions. Prefers letter-quality. Reports in 6 weeks on mss. Publishes ms 4-6 months after acceptance. Sample copy $5.
Payment: $35 minimum. Offers 50% kill fee for assigned ms not published.
Terms: Pays on publication for first North American serial rights. Publication copyrighted.
Advice: "Look at a sample issue to see what we publish. Include a short letter with your manuscript to let us know who you are. If given encouragement, submit three or four times each year, not every week. Study the awards collections and make sure your work measures up. Even small publications receive submissions from Nobel winners, and so self-monitoring will, in the long run, save postage."

CRYSTAL RAINBOW (I), 340 Granada Drive, Winter Park FL 32789. Editor: Louise M. Turmenne. Newsletter: 7x8½; 12 pages; 20 lb bond paper and cover; illustrations. *Crystal Rainbow* publishes "To uplift, inspire, encourage creativity and praise. Publishes seasonal/inspirational material." Quarterly. Estab. 1987. Circ. 120.
Needs: Adventure, prose poem, religious/inspirational and suspense/mystery. "Mostly seasonal material and regular column needs and devotionals. I'll look for attitude in the writing as well as quality. Neatness also counts. No sex, violence, erotica, gay or gore." Accepts 1-2 mss/issue; 4-8 mss/year. Publishes ms 9 months or more after acceptance. Length: 300 words average. Usually comments on rejected ms and "if possible" recommends other markets.
How to Contact: Query first with or without clips of published work or send complete ms with cover letter, which should include a brief bio. Reports in 2 weeks-1½ months. SASE. Simultaneous, photocopied and reprint submissions OK. Accepts computer printout submissions, including dot-matrix, and electronic submissions. Sample copy $1.75, #10 SASE and 45¢ postage. Fiction guidelines for #10 SAE and 1 first class stamp.
Payment: Pays in contributor's copies; extras for 75¢.
Terms: Acquires first rights, first North American serial rights, one-time rights or simultaneous rights. Sends galleys to author "if requested." Send for contest rules and requirements.
Advice: "Don't write 'above the heads' of readers. Intellectual displays of writing powers aren't necessary if they only lead to confusion for the reader. Write the way you talk. Watch spelling and neatness. They say so much about you and often precludes a good mark for writing. You may be forfeiting acceptance and publication if you don't care."

‡CUBE LITERARY MAGAZINE (II), An Eclectic Collection, Box 2637, Newport News VA 23602. (804)874-7766/(804)838-9735. Editor: Eric Mathews. Fiction Editor: Michele Maroney. Newspaper: 8½x11; 56-60 pages; 70 lb offset paper; 63 lb cover; b&w illustrations. "A serious literary magazine, seeking the unique and innovative voices of short fiction and poetry." Quarterly. Plans special fiction issue. Estab. 1988. Circ. 500.

Needs: Adventure, condensed/excerpted novel, confession, contemporary, ethnic, experimental, fantasy, horror, humor/satire, literary, mainstream, prose poem, psychic/supernatural/occult, science fiction, suspense/mystery, translations. "No romance or religious and/or inspirational." Receives 20 unsolicited mss/month. Buys 4-7 mss/issue; 20-28 mss/year. Publishes ms 2 months maximum after acceptance. Recently published work by Isak Romun, Lewis Owens, Doris Gwaltney. Length: 3,000 words preferred; 100 words minimum; 5,000 words maximum. Always critiques rejected mss and recommends other markets.

How to Contact: Send complete ms with cover letter. Cover letter should include "author's writing experience (what and where published); where and when writer heard of *CUBE Literary Magazine*." Reports in 1 week on queries; 1 month on mss. SASE. Photocopied and reprint submissions OK. Accepts computer printout submissions, including dot-matrix. Sample copy for $3. Fiction guidelines for #10 SAE and 1 first class stamp.

Payment: Pays in contributor's copies; charge for extras.

Terms: Acquires first North American serial rights. Publication copyrighted.

Advice: "What seems most prevelent in today's magazine fiction is the 'when I was young' story. Aren't most of us bored with these when coming from our (grand)parents, let alone from strangers? We are tired of seeing potentially talented writers wasting their time trying to imitate Stephen King. We enjoy seeing experimental fiction, no matter where it crops up. Of course, this is with the understanding that 'experimental' does not connote 'indecipherable.' The biggest problems we encounter with new or unpublished writers are weak or contrived endings. Some new writers also seem to be under the impression that vague and/or confusing stories leave readers 'options' for interpretation. Balogna. All such stories are is unpublishable. Don't copy stories we've already published, do exactly the opposite. Remember there are no real restrictions at *CUBE*. Don't, however, send us sleazy material, only quality fiction that touches the bounds of what hasn't been done before. Please, prepare your manuscripts properly. Type your name and address on all title pages, not just on your cover letters (most of which find their way to the trash, quickly). Make sure all pages are numbered and unstapled. Never, ever, forget your SASE."

CUTBANK (II), English Department, University of Montana, Missoula MT 59812. (406)243-5231. Fiction Editor: Tom Stone. Magazine: 5½x8½; 115-130 pages. "Publishes highest quality fiction, poetry, artwork, for a general, literary audience." One double issue/year. Estab. 1972. Circ. 450.

Needs: "No overt stylistic limitations. Only work of high qualtity will be considered. Receives 200 unsolicited mss/month. Accepts 6-12 mss/year. Does not read mss from February 2-August 15. Publishes ms 2-4 months after acceptance. Published new writers within the last year. Length: 3,750 words average; 1,000 words minimum; 12,500 words maximum. Occasionally critiques rejected mss and recommends other markets.

How to Contact: Send complete ms with cover letter, which should include "name, address, publications." Reports in 1 month on queries; 1-6 months on mss. SASE. Accepts computer printout submissions, no dot-matrix. Sample copy $3 (current issue $9.00) and 6½x9 SAE. Fiction guidelines 50¢, #10 SAE and 1 first class stamp.

Payment: Free contributor's copies, charges for extras, 10% discount for over 15 copies.

Terms: Acquires all rights. Publication copyrighted. Rights returned upon writtern request.

Advice: "Tight market, improving. Every submission is read several times, by several editors. We have published both numerous new and established fiction writers, including William Pitt Root, Ralph Beer, Neil McMahon, Gordon Lish, Madeline Defrees, Julie Brown, Fred Haefele, William Yellow Robe, Leonard William Robinson, etc. Read latest issue. Send only your best work."

THE DALHOUSIE REVIEW (II), Room 314, Dunn Building, Dalhousie University, Halifax, Nova Scotia B3H 3J5 Canada. Editor: Dr. Alan Andrews. Magazine: 14cmx23cm; approximately 165 pages; photographs sometimes. Publishes articles, short stories and poetry. Quarterly. Circ. 1,000.

Needs: Literary. Length: 5,000 words maximum.

How to Contact: Send complete ms with cover letter. SASE (Canadian stamps). Sample copy $5 (Canadian dollars) plus postage.

DAN RIVER ANTHOLOGY (I), Box 123, South Thomaston ME 04858. (207)354-6550. Editor: R. S. Danbury III. Book: 5½x8½; 156 pages; 60 lb paper; gloss 65 lb full-color cover; b&w illustrations. For general/adult audience. Annually. Estab. 1984. Circ. 1,200.

Needs: Adventure, contemporary, ethnic, experimental, fantasy, historical (general), horror, humor/satire, literary, mainstream, prose poem, psychic/supernatural/occult, regional, romance (contemporary and historical), science fiction, senior citizen/retirement, suspense/mystery and western. No "evangelical Christian, pornography or sentimentality." Receives 20-30 unsolicited mss/month. Accepts about 8-10 mss/year. Reads "mostly in March." Recently published work by Geoffrey Clark. Published new writers the last year. Length: 2,000-2,400 words average; 800 words minumum; 4,000 words maximum.

How to Contact: Send complete ms with SASE and $1 (cash) reading fee. Reports in April each year. Previously published work not accepted. Accepts computer printout submissions, prefers letter-quality. Sample copy $9.95 paperback, $19.95 cloth, plus $1.50 shipping. Fiction guidelines for #10 SAE.

Payment: 10% of all sales attributable to writer's influence: readings, mailings, autograph parties, etc., plus up to 50% discount on copies, plus other discounts to make total as high as 73%.

Terms: Acquires first rights. Publication copyrighted.

DARK STARR (I,IV), M. Talarico & Daughter, Publishers, Drawer 417, Oceanside CA 92054. (619)722-8829. Editor: Marjorie Talarico. Magazine: 8½x14; 95-105 pages; illustrations. "We publish short shorts, short stories, some poetry, for mature readers of all ages." Quarterly. Plans special fiction issue. Estab. 1986. Circ. 200.

Needs: Fantasy, horror, science fiction, suspense/mystery. "Experimental, if in horror, fantasy, genre. Can be erotic but not outright pornographic; graphic, but not gross." No fiction on "life-threatening diseases, e.g. AIDS. No pornography, no 'The butler did it,' and no murderous household appliances." Receives 50-70 unsolicited fiction mss/month; accepts 20-25 mss/issue. Publishes ms 6-8 months after acceptance. "No fees charged unless contest entry fee." Critique service available for nominal fee. Rates available for SASE. Ask about our new Chapbook Service." Recently published work by David A. Lindschmidt, D.M. Rectenwalt, Bentley Nittle. Published new writers within the last year. Length: 2,500 words average; 600 words minimum; 5,000 words maximum. Publishes short shorts 175-400 words. Sometimes recommends other markets.

How to Contact: Submit complete ms. Query only on serialized/condensed novels. Reports on queries in 6-8 weeks; on mss in 8-12 weeks. SASE. Accepts computer printout submissions, including dot-matrix. Sample copy $4, #10 SAE and 90¢ (third class) or $2.40 (first class) postage. Fiction guidelines for #10 SAE.

Payment: Pays in contributor's copies; charge for extras.

Terms: Acquires first North American serial rights. Publication copyrighted. List of contests and awards available in October of each year for SASE.

Advice: "Give me some good horror with strong characters—we welcome vampires, ghouls, etc. I like to give beginning writers a break, so if they have a good sci-fi plot, a mystery with a twist or fantastic fantasy, chances are I'll have a spot for them."

‡DARK VISIONS (I,II), #422 Risley Hall, Cornell University, Ithaca NY 14853. (607)253-2696. Editor: Ted Quester. "A magazine of short horror fiction, for those who like to be scared." Quarterly. Estab. 1988. Circ. 500.

Needs: Fantasy, horror, psychic/supernatural/occult. No "pornographic fiction and fiction which is disgusting but not scary." Receives 50-100 unsolicited fiction mss/month; buys 8-10 mss/issue; 30-40 mss/year. Recently published work by John B. Rosenman. Length: 4,000 words maximum. Publishes short shorts. Sometimes critiques rejected mss or recommends other markets.

How to Contact: Send complete ms with cover letter. Reports in 2 weeks. SASE. Simultaneous, photocopied and reprint submissions OK. Accepts computer printout submissions, including dot-matrix. Fiction guidelines free.

Payment: ¼¢-2¢/word.

Terms: Pays on acceptance for first North-American serial rights. Sends pre-publication galleys to author. Publication copyrighted.

Advice: "There are very few professional markets for short horror fiction. Small press fills the gap. Strive for originality. Write about what scares *you*, not about what you think will scare others."

DAY CARE AND EARLY EDUCATION (II, IV), Human Sciences Press, 72 Fifth Ave., New York NY 10011. (212)243-6000. Editor: Randa Roen Nachbar. Magazine: 8½x11; 48 pages; illustrations and photographs. "Articles for classroom practice with child 0-6, for teachers and administrators in early education." Quarterly. Estab. 1973. Circ. 5,000.

Needs: Juvenile, preschool (0-4 years). No "didactic" fiction. Receives 2 fiction mss/month. Accepts 0-1 ms/issue; 2-3 mss/year. Publishes ms 6 to 9 months after acceptance. Published new writers within the last year. Length: 1,000-2,000 words average. Publishes short shorts. Sometimes critiques rejected ms.

How to Contact: Send complete ms with cover letter. Reports on queries in 3 weeks; on mss in 3 months. SASE. Photocopied submissions OK. Accepts computer printout submissions, including dot-matrix. Sample copy and fiction guidelines for 8½x11 SAE.

Payment: Pays 2 contributor's copies; charge for extras ($2.40 each). Sends prepublication galleys to the author. Publication copyrighted.

‡**DEATHREALM (II)**, 3223-F Regents Park, Greensboro NC 27405. (919)288-9138. Editor: Mark Rainey. Magazine: 5½x8½; 50-60 pages; 20 lb bond paper; 8 pt glossy coated cover stock; pen & ink, screened illustrations; b&w photos. Publishes "fantasy/horror," for a "mature" audience. Quarterly. Plans special fiction issue. Estab. 1987. Circ. 1,000.
Needs: Experimental, fantasy, horror, psychic/supernatural/occult and science fiction. "Sci-fi tales should have a horror slant. *Do not* send tales that are not in the realm of dark fantasy. *Strongly* recommend contributor buy a sample copy of *Deathrealm* before submitting." Receives 200 mss/month. Buys 6-8 mss/issue; 30 mss/year. Publishes ms within 1 year of acceptance. Recently published work by Wayne Allen Sallee, William C. Rasmussen and Jessica Amanda Salmonson. Length: 5,000 words average; 10,000 words maximum. Publishes short shorts. Sometimes critiques rejected mss and recommends other markets.
How to Contact: Send complete manuscript with cover letter, which should include "publishing credits, some bio info, where they heard about *Deathrealm*. Never reveal plot in cover letter." Reports in 1 week on queries; 2-6 weeks on ms. SASE. Photocopied submissions OK. Accepts computer printout submissions, including high-quality dot-matrix. Sample copy for $3.50 and 65¢ postage. Fiction guidelines for #10 SAE and 1 first class stamp.
Payment: Pays $5 minimum; $8 maximum; contributor's copies.
Advice: "Concentrate on characterization; development of ideas; strong atmosphere, with an important setting. I frown on gratuitous sex and violence unless it is a mere side effect of a more sophisticated story line. Stay away from overdone themes—foreboding dreams come true; being a frustrated writer; using lots of profanity and having a main character so detestable you don't care what happens to him."

THE DEKALB LITERARY ARTS JOURNAL (II), DeKalb Community College, 555 N. Indian Creek Dr., Clarkston GA 30021. (404)299-4119. Editor: Frances Ellis. Magazine: 6x9; 85 pages; 80 lb sunray crystal vellum paper; 10 pt cl5 cover stock. Magazine of original/creative writing: short stories, drama, poetry, b&w visual art and music, for general audience. Estab. 1966. Publishes 2 or 3 issues annually.
Needs: Humor/satire and literary. No prose over 25 pages. Receives 50 mss/month. Publishes short shorts of 3-10 pages. Accepts 50+ mss/year. Published new writers within the last year.
How to Contact: Send complete ms with SASE and brief bio. Reports in 6 months on mss. Sample copy for $4. Fiction guidelines free with SASE.
Payment: Pays 1 contributor's copy; charge for extras: $4 each.
Terms: Accepts one-time rights.
Advice: "Please be willing to revise. Take a course or read a book on creative writing. Readers still enjoy a good story: characters, motives, action, language."

‡**DEMENTIA (II,IV)**, 9412 Huron Ave., Richmond VA 23229. (804)270-9187. Editor: Roger W. Reus. Magazine: 8½x11; number of pages varies; paper varies; card stock cover. "*Dementia* is very much a horror fiction magazine, specializing in that genre as well as in dark fantasy. Also, nonfiction essays, articles and interviews are considered on the fields. For an audience of horror fans who have grown jaded of the 'gross out' short story. *Dementia* readers expect a more original and subtle telling which ultimately leads to a more powerful effect." Published irregularly. Estab. 1986. Circ. varies (1,000 of #1 printed).
Needs: Dark fantasy and horror. "*No* science fiction. No stories that rely on a 'shock ending' which is usually obvious early on in the story. If used effectively, gore could be acceptable, but don't use it unwisely." Receives over 50 mss/month. Accepts 10-18 mss/issue. Publishes ms within 4-8 months of acceptance. Recently published work by J.N. Williamson, Janet Fox and John Maclay. Length: "wide open;" 10,000 words maximum. Publishes short shorts. Sometimes critiques rejected mss and occasionally recommends other markets.
How to Contact: Query first with "basic info—publishing credits, bit of info on self." Reports in 4 weeks. SASE. Simultaneous and photocopied submissions OK. Accepts computer printout submissions, including dot-matrix. Sample copy $1.
Payment: Pays in contributor's copies.
Terms: Acquires one-time rights. Sends galleys to author. Publication copyrighted. Sponsors awards for fiction writers. "Beginning with #2, each issue shall have a contest in which the readers judge the three best authors in each issue, with the top three receiving cash prizes."
Advice: "In the field upon which I'm most associated, the horror small press 'scene,' there seems to be an explosion of quality mags appearing. I've never seen this field as strong as it is now and some are calling it the 'golden age' of modern horror. Respected horror authors are now appearing occasionally in these more-or-less amateur mags. It has never been so good for us. I'm open to any horror and dark fantasy short stories. Many mss which I reject are simply rehashes on themes I've encountered far too often in the field: vampires, haunted houses, werewolves, etc. Try something original and build up a bit of suspense (as well as a bit of characterization) and do not rely on a cheap, shock ending."

DENVER QUARTERLY (II, III), University of Denver, Denver CO 80208. (303)871-2892. Editor: Donald Revell. Magazine: 6x9; 144-160 pages; occasional illustrations. "We publish fiction, articles and poetry for a generally well educated audience, primarily interested in literature and the literary experience. They read *DQ* to find something a little different from a strictly academic quarterly or a creative writing outlet." Quarterly. Estab. 1966. Circ. 1,200.
Needs: "We are now interested in experimental fiction (minimalism, magic realism, etc.) as well as in realistic fiction."
How to Contact: Send complete ms with SASE. Does not read mss May-September 15. Do not query. Reports in 1-2 months on mss. Publishes ms within a year after acceptance. Recently published work by Joyce Carol Oates, Jay Clayton, Charles Baxter. Published new writers within the last year. No simultaneous submissions. Sample copy $5 with SASE.
Payment: Pays $5/page for fiction and poetry. 2 free author's copies plus 3 tear sheets.
Terms: Acquires first North American serial rights.
Advice: "We'll be looking for serious, realistic and experimental fiction. Nothing so quickly disqualifies a manuscript as sloppy proofreading and mechanics. Read the magazine before submitting to it. Send clean copy and a *brief* cover letter. We try to remain eclectic and I think we do, but the odds for beginners are bound to be long considering the fact that we receive nearly 8,000 mss per year and publish only about 16 short stories."

DESCANT (II), Department of English, Texas Christian University, Fort Worth TX 76129. (817)921-7240. Editors: Betsy Colquitt, Stanley Trachtenberg. "*Descant* uses fiction, poetry and essays. No restriction on style, content or theme. It is a little literary magazine, and its readers are those who have interest in such publications." Semiannually. Estab. 1955. Circ. 500.
Needs: Literary, contemporary and regional. No genre or category fiction. Receives approximately 50 unsolicited fiction mss each month. Does not read mss in summer. Published new writers within the last year. Length: 1,500-5,000 words. Publishes short shorts. Sometimes recommends other markets.
How to Contact: Send complete ms with SASE. Accepts computer printout submissions. Prefers letter-quality. Reports usually within 6 weeks on ms. Sample copy $4.50 (old copy).
Payment: 4 free author's copies. $4.50 charge/extra copy.
Terms: Acquires first North American serial rights. Publication copyrighted.
Advice: "Submit good material. Even though a small publication, *Descant* receives many submissions, and acceptances are few compared to the total number of mss received." Mss are rejected because they "are badly written, careless in style and development, shallow in characterization, trite in handling and in conception." We offer a $300 annual prize for fiction—the Frank O'Connor Prize. Award is made to the story considered (by a judge not connected to the magazine) to be the best published in a given volume of the journal."

DESCANT (II), Box 314, Station P, Toronto, Ontario M5S 2S8 Canada. (416)927-7059. Editor: Karen Mulhallen. Magazine: 5¾x8¾; 100-300 pages; heavy paper; good cover stock; illustrations and photos. High quality poetry and prose for an intelligent audience who wants to see a broad range of literature. Published 4 times/year. Published special fiction issue last year; plans another. Estab. 1970. Circ. 1,000.
Needs: Literary, contemporary, translations. "Although most themes are acceptable, all works must have literary merit." Receives 100-200 unsolicited mss/month. Recently published work by David Carpenter, Katherine Govier, Rohinton Mistry. Publishes short shorts. Critiques rejected mss when there is time.
How to Contact: Send complete ms with cover letter. SAE, IRC. Reports in 4 months on mss. Sample copy $7.50 plus $2 for postage to U.S.
Payment: Pays a modest honorarium and 1 year subscription. Extra author's copies at discount.
Terms: Varies.
Advice: "*Descant* has plans for several special issues in the next two years. Unsolicited work is less likely to be accepted in the coming months, and will be kept on file for longer before it appears."

DESERT SUN, 1235-D Ortiz SE, Albuquerque NM 87108. (505)256-7694. Editor: Craig W. Chrissinger. Magazine: 7x8½; 24-40 pages; 20 lb bond paper and cover; illustrations and photographs. Theme: science fiction, fantasy and horror. Publishes fiction, articles, essays, book reviews, movie reviews, interviews. Semiannually. Estab. 1986. Circ. 120.
Needs: Science fiction, fantasy, horror, humor/satire, erotica. "Almost any element is allowed as long as it ties in with science fiction, fantasy or horror." Receives 10-15 fiction mss/month. Accepts 10-20 mss/issue. Does not read mss March-May or August-December. Publishes ms 2-4 months after acceptance. Recently published work by William Rasmussen, D.M. Vosk, Anke Kriske; published new writers within the last year. Length: 1,000-2,000 words average; 3,800 words maximum. Sometimes critiques rejected ms and recommends other markets.

How to Contact: Send complete ms with cover letter and name, source of information about magazine. Reports on queries in 1 month; 2 months on mss. SASE. Photocopied submissions OK. Accepts computer printout submissions, including dot-matrix. Sample copy $2. Make all payments to Craig Chrissinger. Fiction guidelines for #10 SAE.
Payment: Pays in contributor's copies; charge for extras.
Terms: Acquires one-time rights. Publication copyrighted.
Advice: "Watch out for typographical errors and misuse of punctuation marks. Write every day. Know about the magazine's genre(s) and send only appropriate material."

‡**DETECTIVE STORY MAGAZINE (I,II)**, Gryphon Publications, Box 209, Brooklyn NY 11228. Editor: Gary Lovisi. Magazine: digest size; over 50 pages; offset paper; card stock cover; illustrations. Publishes "stories 2,000-4,000 words where detective (in whatever guise) is central character—stories should be *fun* and enjoyable to read." Quarterly. Estab. 1988.
Needs: Some mystery, but mostly detective. No "blood for blood's sake." Receives 20 mss/month. Accepts 9-12 mss/year. Publishes ms within 3 months to a year of acceptance. Recently published work by Will Murray, Robert Sampson and C.J. Henderson; published new writers within the last year. Length: 2,000 words minimum; 4,000 words maximum. Sometimes critiques rejected mss and recommends other markets.
How to Contact: Query first or send complete ms with cover letter. Reports in 2 weeks on queries; 4 weeks on mss. SASE. Photocopied and some reprint submissions OK. Accepts computer printout submissions, including dot-matrix. Sample copy $4.
Payment: Pays in contributor's copies.
Terms: Acquires first North American serial rights. Publication copyrighted.

DEVIANCE, Opus II Writing Services, Box 1774, Pawtucket RI 02862. (401)722-8187 (evenings, weekends only). Editor: Lin Collette. Magazine. 8½x11; 36-48 pages; 20 lb bond paper; heavier bond cover; b&w drawings; b&w photographs on occasion. "*Deviance* is a magazine dedicated to publishing work by persons espousing views that may not be in favor of the 'majority.' This includes feminists, lesbian/gay, non-religious or religious (i.e. discussions of religious issues that are not Judeo-Christian or which may be an unorthodox view of Christianity or Judaism), political (non-republican or democrat) and so on. Published three times yearly. Plans special fiction issue. Estab. 1987. Circ. 500.
Needs: Condensed novel, contemporary, erotica, ethnic, experimental, fantasy, feminist, gay, historical (general), horror, humor/satire, lesbian, literary, prose poems, psychic/supernatural/occult, science fiction, senior citizen/retirement, serialized/excerpted novel, spiritual, suspense/mystery, translations. Nothing homophobic, racist, sexist, violent for violence's sake. Receives 5 fiction mss/month. Accepts 1-2 mss/issue. May publish ms up to 2 years after acceptance. Recently published work by Krussick; published new writers within the last year. Length: 2,500 words average; 25 words minimum; 2,500 words maximum. Sometimes critiques rejected ms and recommends other markets.
How to Contact: Send complete ms with cover letter, a biography including other places published, a whimsical description of author, no longer than 10 lines. Reports on queries in 2 weeks; 1 month on ms. SASE. Simultaneous, photocopied and reprint submissions OK. Accepts computer printout submissions, inlcuding dot matrix. Sample copy $3.50, SAE with 69¢ postage. Fiction guidelines for #10 SAE with 1 first class stamp. Checks make out to Lin Collette please!
Payment: Pays in contributor's copies; $3.50 charge for extras.
Terms: Acquires first rights. Publication copyrighted.
Advice: "Read the magazine! We have people sending in material that is so 'mainstream' (as in inspirational, children's, Harlequin-type love stories) that we know nobody's bothering to check us out. If you can't afford a back issue, at least send for guidelines. We are looking for offbeat ways of looking at the world—we publish gay, lesbian, feminist, horror, slice-of-life, *New Yorker*-style pieces, so if you've been rejected by *The New Yorker*, give us a try."

‡**DOOR COUNTY ALMANAK (IV)**, The Dragonsbreath Press, 10905 Bay Shore Dr., Sister Bay WI 54234. (414)854-2742. Editor: Fred Johnson. Magazine: 6x9; 200-300 pages; good uncoated paper; antique vellum cover stock; illustrations; photos. "The major focus is Door County WI and its surrounding areas. Covering the history, recent and distant, of the area and its people, including contemporary profiles of people and businesses. Each issue has a major theme. Also uses poetry and fiction for general audience, mainly aimed at people familiar with the area." Annually. Estab. 1982.
Needs: Adventure, contemporary, fantasy, historical (general), humor/satire, literary, regional, suspense/mystery. "Prefer to have the fiction in some way related to the area, at least to the issue's theme." No romance. Receives 10-20 unsolicited fiction mss/month. Buys 1-2 mss/issue. Does not read mss April-September. Published new writers within the last year. Length: 4,000 words average; 500 words minimum; 6,000 words maximum.
How to Contact: Query first. Reports in 3-4 weeks on queries; 2-3 months on mss. SASE for query

and ms. Simultaneous, photocopied submissions and reprints OK. Accepts computer printouts including dot-matrix. Sample copy: $5.95 for issue #2; $7.95 for issue #3 and 7x10 SAE and $1 postage. Fiction guidelines free for #10 SAE and 1 first class stamp.

Payment: Pays $10-$35 plus contributor's copies.

Terms: Pays on publication for first North American serial rights and other rights. Publication copyrighted.

Advice: "Query first to find out what coming issue's theme is and what the needs are. We're always looking for nonfiction articles also. Keep in mind this is definitely a regional magazine."

DREAM INTERNATIONAL/QUARTERLY (II, IV), U.S. Address: Charles I. Jones, 121 N. Ramona St. ‰25, Ramona CA 92065. Japanese address: Les Jones, 1-17-7 Ushita Waseda, Higashi-ku, Hiroshima 732 Japan. Editors: Les and Chuck Jones. Magazine: 7x5; 60-80 pages; Xerox paper; parchment cover stock; some illustrations and photos. Publishes fiction and nonfiction that is dream-related or clearly inspired by a dream. Quarterly. Estab. 1981. Circ. 200.

Needs: Adventure, confession, contemporary, erotica, ethnic, experimental, fantasy, historical (general), horror, humor/satire, juvenile (5-9 years), literary, mainstream, prose poem, psychic/supernatural/occult, romance, science fiction, senior citizen/retirement, serialized/excerpted novel, spiritual, suspense/mystery, translations, western, young adult/teen (10-18). Receives 20-40 unsolicited mss/month. Ms published 6-8 months after acceptance. Length: 1,500 words minimum; 2,000 words maximum. Publishes short shorts. Published new writers within the last year. Length: 1,000 words. Occasionally critiques rejected mss. Sometimes recommends other markets. "Accepted mss not returned unless requested at time of submission."

How to Contact: Reports in 6 weeks on queries; 3 months on mss. SASE. Photocopied and reprint submissions OK. Accepts computer printout submissions, including dot-matrix "if legible." Sample copy for $4, SAE and 2 first class stamps. Guidelines for $1, SAE and 1 first class stamp. "Accepted mss will not be returned unless requested at time of submission."

Payment: Pays in contributor's copies; sometimes offers free magazine subscription.

Terms: Acquires one-time rights. Publication copyrighted.

Advice: "Use your nightly dreams to inspire you to literary flights. Avoid stereotypes and clichés. Avoid Twilight Zone type stories. When contacting editor, make all checks, money orders, and overseas drafts payable to *Charles Jones*."

DREAMSHORE (IV), A Psychedelic Journal, Box 1387, Bloomington IN 47402-1387. (812)336-9943. Editor: Jan Byron. Magazine: 5½x8½; 25-35 pages; 16 lb paper and cover; illustrations; photos "if they can be 'screened' for printing." Magazine concerned with "dreams, fantasy, imagination—the importance of subjective reality—the importance of childhood perceptions-psychic phenomena-UFOs-folklore-mythic symbols, themes and archetypes," for "adults (or children) who enjoy the above subjects and have a sense of wonder." Semiannually. Estab. 1982. Circ. 125.

Needs: Experimental, fantasy, juvenile (5-9 years), preschool (1-4 years), psychic/occult, prose poem, young adult/teen (10-18 years), psychedelic "60's" style. "Stress is on the idea that magic is real, and that mystery and wonder are to be affirmed and celebrated." No "New Age." No horror, violence for its own sake, mainstream, Judaeo-Christian inspirational, Dungeons & Dragons, macabre. Receives 3-5 unsolicited fiction mss/month. Accepts 8-10 mss/issue; about 15-20 mss/year. Recently published work by Larry Sams, Lauren Stevens and David Bota. Length: 800 words maximum. Submissions to *Dreamshore* should be typed *single spaced* in 35-character columns. Occasionally critiques rejected mss and recommends other markets.

How to Contact: Query first or send complete ms with cover letter, which should include "information about where they heard of *Dreamshore* and how the story came to be written. If query is sent, I send a *Dreamshore* writer's guide." Reports immediately on queries; 2-4 weeks on mss. SASE. Simultaneous, photocopied and reprint submissions OK. Accepts computer printout submissions; no dot-matrix. Sample copy for $1. Fiction guidelines for #10 SAE and 1 first class stamp.

Payment: Pays in contributor's copies.

Terms: Acquires first North American serial rights. Sends galleys to author if requested. Publication copyrighted.

Advice: "We aim to encourage positive, creative fantasy as 'far out' and 'wild' as possible. Also, actual subjective experiences (such as seeing a UFO, having a vision of supernatural beings, etc.) are well expressed in the Western world through telling them as stories. The feeling of *Dreamshore* is often expressed in the imagery of Stevie Nicks-type rock videos. Seeking illustrators/artists."

‡DV-8 (II), 437 W. 13th St., Box 30911, New York NY 10011. (212)586-5667. Editor: Laurie Litchford. Magazine: 8½x11; 48 pages; 60 lb semi-coated paper; 100 lb coated cover; charcoal, ink, painted illustrations; b&w photographs. Publishes material on "new music, art and fashion. Alternative, thoughtful publication. Most readers are 18-34." Bimonthly. Plans special fiction issue. Estab. 1988.

Circ. 10,000.

Needs: Excerpted novel, contemporary, ethnic, experimental, humor/satire, literary. No "stream of consciousness leading nowhere." Receives 10 unsolicited mss/month. Buys 1 ms/issue; 6 mss/year. Publishes ms 1 month after acceptance. Recently published work by Emily Carter, Michael Greenberg. Length: 2,000 words preferred; 250 words minimum; 3,000 words maximum. Sometimes critiques rejected mss and recommends other markets.

How to Contact: Send complete ms with cover letter. Cover letter should include "name, pseudonym,(if desired), address, telephone number, other publications in which writing appears." Reports in 4 weeks on queries; 6 weeks on mss. SASE. Simultaneous, photocopied and reprint submissions OK. Accepts computer printout submissions, including dot-matrix. Sample copy for $2, 9x12 SAE and $1.41 postage. Fiction guidelines for #10 SAE and 1 first class stamp.

Payment: Pays $20 maximum. Free contributor's copies.

Terms: Pays on publication for first North American serial rights. Sends galleys to author. Publication copyrighted. Sponsors awards for fiction writers.

Advice: "Conventional literary fiction is, for me as a reader, the primary model upon which a good story is considered. After certain prerequisites have been met (i.e., dramatic tension, resolution, character development, verity of emotion, original vision), then experimentation is certainly also encouraged. Submit clean drafts. Include other clips—always enjoyable to read other pieces of writing by the author."

EARTH'S DAUGHTERS (II), A Feminist Arts Periodical, Box 41, Central Park Station, Buffalo NY 14215. (716)837-7778. Collective editorship. Business Manager: Bonnie Johnson. Magazine: usually 5½x8½; 50 pages; 60 lb paper; coated cover; 2-4 illustrations; 2-4 photos. "We publish poetry and short fiction; also graphics, art work and photos; our focus is the experience and creative expression of women." For a general/women/feminist audience. Quarterly. Published special topical issues last year; plans more this year. Estab. 1971. Circ. 1,000.

Needs: Contemporary, erotica, ethnic, experimental, fantasy, feminist, humor/satire, literary, prose poem. "Keep the fiction short." Receives 25-50 unsolicited fiction mss/month. Accepts 2-4 mss/issue; 8-12 mss/year. Recently published work by Gabrielle Burton, Mary Jane Markell, Meredith Sue Willis and Julia Alvarez. Published several new writers within the last year. Length: 400 words minimum; 1,000 words maximum; 800 words average. Occasionally critiques rejected mss and recommends other markets.

How to Contact: Send complete ms. SASE. Simultaneous and photocopied submissions OK. Accepts computer printout submissions, "must be clearly legible." Reports in 3 weeks on queries; 3 weeks to 3 months on mss. Publishes ms an average of 1 year after acceptance. Sample copy for $4.

Payment: 2 free contributor's copies, additional copies half price.

Terms: Acquires first rights. Copyright reverts to author upon publication.

Advice: "We require work of technical skill and artistic intensity; we welcome submissions from unknown writers. Send SASE in April of each year for themes of upcoming issues. Please do not inquire as to the status of your work too soon or too often—the US Mail is dependable, and we have yet to lose a manuscript."

‡EDGES (II), the new literary magazine, Weinlos Bldg, 3rd flr, 10022 103d St., Edmonton Alberta T5J 0X2 Canada. Editor: Andrew Thompson. Magazine: 7½x8½; 48 pages; 20 lb bond paper; card stock cover; b&w illustrations. "*edges* is dedicated to publishing all styles of writing in the fields of short fiction and poetry." Quarterly. Estab. 1986. Circ. 150.

Needs: Adventure, contemporary, erotica, ethnic, experimental, fantasy, feminist, gay, horror, humor/satire, lesbian, literary, mainstream, prose poem, psychic/supernatural/occult, regional, science fiction, senior citizen/retirement, sports, suspense/mystery. "All well-written fiction may be considered." Receives 15-18 unsolicited mss/month. Accepts 2-5 mss/issue; 12 mss/year. Publishes ms 3-6 months after acceptance. Recently published work by Nancy Holmes, Gerald Osborn, Anya Wassenberg-Bruce; published several new writers within the last year. Length: 3,500 words maximum. Publishes short shorts. Sometimes critiques rejected mss.

How to Contact: Send complete ms with cover letter. Cover letter should include "brief biography and previous credits, if any." Reports in 1 month on queries; 2-3 months on mss. SASE. Photocopied submissions OK. Accepts dot-matrix computer printout submissions. Sample copy for $3. Fiction guidelines for #10 SAE and 38¢ Canadian postage. "Remember, this is a Canadian magazine."

Payment: Pays $10 (Canadian) or free subscription to magazine; free contributor's copies; charge for extras.

Terms: Pays on publication for first North American serial rights. Publication copyrighted.

Advice: "Basically, fiction should be well-written, regardless of its subject matter and should show a clear image or convey an idea that readers today will be interested in reading. In short, the criterion we rely upon is quality both in expression and execution."

EIDOS: (IV), Erotic Entertainment for Women, Men & Couples, Box 96, Boston MA 02137. (617)262-0096. Editor: Brenda L. Tatelbaum. Tabloid: 10x14; 48 pages; web offset printing; illustrations; photos. Magazine of erotica for women, men and couples of all sexual orientations, preferences and lifestyles. "Explicit material regarding language and behavior formed in relationships, intimacy, moment of satisfaction—sensual, sexy, honest. For an energetic, well informed, international erotica readership." Quarterly. Estab. 1984. Circ. 7,000.

Needs: Erotica. Humorous or tongue-in-cheek erotic fiction is especially wanted. Publishes at least 4 pieces of fiction/year. Published new writers within the last year. Length: 2,000 words average; 500 words minimum; 3,500 words maximum. Occasionally critiques rejected mss and recommends other markets.

How to Contact: Send complete ms with SASE. "Cover letter with history of publication or short bio is welcome." Reports in 2 months on queries; 3 months on mss. Simultaneous and photocopied submissions OK. Accepts computer printout submissions. Sample copy $5. Fiction guidelines free for #10 envelope with 1 first class stamp.

Payment: Contributor's copies.

Terms: Acquires first North American serial rights on publication.

Advice: "We receive more erotic fiction manuscripts now than in the past. Most likely because both men and women are more comfortable with the notion of submitting these manuscripts for publication as well as the desire to see alternative sexually explicit fiction in print. Therefore we can publish more erotic fiction because we have more material to choose from. There is still a lot of debate as to what erotic fiction consists of. This is a tough market to break into. Manuscripts must fit our editorial needs and it is best to order a sample issue prior to writing or submitting material. Honest, explicitly pro-sex, mutually consensual erotica is void of power, control and degradation—no rape or coercion of any kind."

ELDRITCH TALES (II, IV), Yith Press, 1051 Wellington Rd., Lawrence KS 66044. (913)843-4341. Editor-in-Chief: Crispin Burnham. Magazine: 5½x8; 120 pages (average); glossy cover; illustrations; "very few" photos. "The magazine concerns horror fiction in the tradition of the old *Weird Tales* magazine. We publish fiction in the tradition of H.P. Lovecraft, Robert Bloch and Stephen King, among others, for fans of this particular genre." Semiannually. Estab. 1975. Circ. 1,000.

Needs: Horror and psychic/supernatural/occult. "No mad slasher stories or similar nonsupernatural horror stories." Receives about 8 unsolicited fiction mss/month. Accepts 12 mss/issue, 24 mss/year. Recently published work by J.N. Williamson, William F. Wu and Charles Grant. Published new writers within the last year. Length: 50-100 words minimum; 20,000 words maximum; 10,000 words average. Occasionally critiques rejected mss. Sometimes recommends other markets.

How to Contact: Send complete ms with SASE and cover letter stating past sales. Photocopied and previously published submissions OK. Accepts computer printout submissions, prefers letter-quality. Reports in 4 months. Publication could take up to 5 years after acceptance. Sample copy $6.

Payment: ¼¢/word; 1 contributor's copy. $1 minimum payment.

Terms: Pays in royalties on publication for first rights. Publication copyrighted.

Advice: "Buy a sample copy and read it thoroughly. Most rejects with my magazine are because people have not checked out what an issue is like or what type of stories I accept. Most rejected stories fall into one of two categories: non-horror fantasy (sword & sorcery, high fantasy) or non-supernatural horror (mad slasher stories, 'Halloween Clones,' I call them). When I say that they should read my publication, I'm not whistling Dixie. We hope to up the magazine's frequency to a quarterly. We also plan to be putting out one or two books a year, mostly novels, but short story collections will be considered as well."

‡THE ELEPHANT-EAR (II, IV), Irvine Valley College, 550 Irvine Center Dr., Irvine CA 92720. (714)559-3327. Editor: Elaine Rubenstein. Magazine: 6x9; over 150 pages; matte paper and cover stock; illustrations and photos. "The journal prints the work of Orange County writers only." Annually. Estab. 1983. Circ. 2,000.

Needs: Contemporary, ethnic, experimental, feminist, humor/satire, literary, regional, science fiction, suspense/mystery, western. "We cannot print pornographic fiction." Receives 50 mss/month. Accepts 5 mss/issue. "Reads only between Feb. 14 and March 1; reports thereafter." Publishes ms within 3 months of acceptance. Length: 25 pages maximum. Publishes short shorts. Sometimes critiques rejected mss.

How to Contact: Send 2 copies of completed ms with cover letter, which should include "the name, address and phone number of author, the title(s) of work submitted. Author's name must not appear on manuscript." SASE. Photocopied submissions OK. Accepts computer printout submissions, including dot-matrix. Sample copy for 6x9 SAE. Free fiction guidelines.

Payment: Pays in contributor's copies.

Terms: Acquires one-time rights. Publication copyrighted.

Artist Susan Linder created this whimsical cat illustration for The elephant-ear, a journal which publishes the work of Orange County, California writers. By co-incidence, the issue on which this illustration ran contained two cat stories; one that was written by the artist's husband, Richard Linder.

‡ELLIPSIS. . .(II), 105A N. Santa Cruz Ave., Los Gatos CA 95030. Editor: Jonathan Ther. Associate Editors: Ruth McCue and Joy Oestreicher. Journal: 80-96 pages; illustrations. "*Ellipsis*. . . represents those writings which have been mistakenly omitted from academic literature. We publish unique literary poetry and short fiction and essays of social or epistemological comment." Quarterly. Estab. 1988.
Needs: Literary, humor/satire, prose poem, experimental. "We're interested in serious fiction and poetry which has a humorous twist and vice versa. In particular, we are looking for work which contains a strong, philosophical, psychological or social theme." Receives 50 mss/month. Accepts 15-20 mss/issue. Publishes ms within 1-6 months of acceptance. Length: 2,500 words preferred; 5,000 words maximum. Publishes short shorts. Sometimes critiques rejected mss and recommends other markets.
How to Contact: Does not accept work without prior contact. Reports on mss in 1-6 months. SASE. Simultaneous and photocopied submissions OK. Accepts computer printout submissions, including dot-matrix (please use a dark ribbon). Accepts electronic submissions (Macintosh). Writer's guidelines included with sample copy, $6.
Advice: "In order to be published in *Ellipsis* . . ., a poem or short story must feature strong, creative use of the language. We see too many stories that don't have a strong sense of direction or that simply meander for 10 pages, and then stop. We are looking for writing which shows the passionate writer's command of language, either through a unique use of the written word, and/or through the subtle and creative use of literary imagery and metaphor. It is intended that every issue be enjoyed more than once by the reader. As such, we seek writing which has within it such seeds of social or philosophic comment that the reader is left with a sense that something important and wonderful has been said. (Not to make the whole thing sound too forbidding, we also happen to like puns, and are not above including odd or cute stories that just happen to strike our fancy.)"

‡emPo MAGAZINE (II), emPo Publications, 1002 E. Denny Way, #202, Seattle WA 98122. Editor: Trudy Mercer. Magazine: size varies; 24-70 pages; 20-24 lb paper; 24-70 lb cover; illustrations and photographs possible. Publishes "experimental/avant garde visual poetry/experimental writing in many forms." "Spontaneous." Estab. 1988. Circ. 250-300.
Needs: Experimental, prose poem. Receives 12 unsolicited mss/month. Accepts 1-2 mss/issue. Does not read mss July-August. Recently published work by Charlie Burks and Kathleen K. Length: 1,000 words maximum. Publishes short shorts (preferred). Sometimes critiques rejected mss.
How to Contact: Send complete ms with cover letter. Cover letter should include "acknowledgements, if I can publish only part (excerpt), other places it is submitted." Reports in 1 month on queries; 2-3 months on mss. SASE. Photocopied submissions OK. Accepts dot-matrix computer printout submissions. Sample copy for $2, #10 and 4 first class stamps. Fiction guidelines for #10 SAE and 1 first class stamp.

Payment: Pays in contributor's copies.
Terms: Acquires one-time rights. Publication copyrighted.
Advice: "Emphasis on visual poetry and experimental writing."

EMRYS JOURNAL (II), The Emrys Foundation, Box 8813, Greenville SC 29604. (803)288-5154. Editor: Linda Julian. Magazine: 6x9; 96 pages; 60 lb paper and cover stock; calligraphy illustrations. "We publish short fiction poetry, essays and book reviews. We are particularly interested in hearing from women and other minorities. We are mindful of the southeast but not limited to it." Annually. Estab. 1984. Circ. 300.
Needs: Contemporary, feminist, literary, mainstream and regional. "We read only during December 15-February 15. During reading periods we receive around 500 manuscripts." Accepts 3-7 stories per issue. Publishes ms 2 months after acceptance. Length: 3,500 words average; 2,500 word minimum; 6,000 word maximum. Publishes short shorts. Length 1,600 words. Sometimes recommends other markets.
How To Contact: Send complete ms with cover letter. Put no identification on manuscript; include separate sheet with title, name, address and phone. "No queries." Reports in 2 months. SASE. Photocopied submissions OK. Accepts computer printout submissions, including dot-matrix, if legible. Sample copy $4 and 7x10 SAE with 4 first class stamps. Fiction guidelines for #10 SAE and 1 first class stamp.
Payment: Pays in contributor's copies.
Terms: Acquires first rights. Publication copyrighted. Sponsors contests and awards for fiction writers. "Send to managing editor for guidelines."

ENFANTAISIE (II, IV), 2603 S.E. 32nd Ave., Portland OR 97202. (503)235-5304. Editor: Viviane Gould. Fiction Editor: Michael Gould. Magazine: 8½x11; 32 pages; 20 lb bond paper; 70 lb glossy cover; illustrations; photos. "We are an educational French-language publication, designed to be a supplementary material in the classroom to teach the language. We are an activity reader, containing games, puzzles, short stories and cultural articles for children studying French, from elementary through high school." Bimonthly. Estab. 1983. Circ. 2,000.
Needs: Young Adult/Teen (12-18 years). No religious/inspirational or psychic mss. Receives 30-40 unsolicited mss/month. Buys 1 ms/issue; 4 mss/year. Publishes ms 6 months after acceptance. Recently published work by A.J. Schut, Frank Ananicz and Michael Gould. Length: 1,000 words average. Publishes short shorts. Occasionally critiques rejected mss.
How to Contact: Send complete ms. "Prefer *no* cover letter." Reports in 3 weeks on queries; 3-6 weeks on mss. Simultaneous, photocopied and reprint submissions OK. Accepts computer printout submissions, including dot-matrix. Accepts electronic submissions via Macintosh. Sample copy for $3 and 9x12 SAE and 4 first class stamps.
Payment: Pays $20 per published full-length feature and 3 contributor's copies; charge for extras: $2 copy, 10 copies maximum.
Terms: Acquires one-time rights. Publication copyrighted.
Advice: "As an educational magazine for classroom use, we find that short stories provide an excellent tool for learning French. Avoid being 'cute' and overly moralistic. Treat realistic themes involving real people in everyday situations, but avoid violence and depressing topics. Simple style preferred; do not strive for richness of vocabulary, since we have to simplify when we translate into French. Dialogue should be a strong component. Humor, irony are welcome. Aim for higher age group. Most of our mss are rejected because they are geared to very small children."

EOTU (I, II), Fiction from the Edge, 1810 W. State, #115, Boise ID 83702. Editor: Larry D. Dennis. Magazine: 5½x8½; 70-80 pages; 20 lb paper; 70 lb cover; illustrations. "We publish short stories that try to say or do something new in literature, in prose. New style, new story structures, new voice, whatever." Bimonthly. Estab. Feb., 1988. Circ. 500.
Needs: Experimental, prose poem. No stories whose express purpose is to advance a religious or political belief. No pornography. Receives 150-200 unsolicited fiction mss/month; accepts 10-12 mss/issue; 60-70 mss/year. Publishes ms 4-6 months after acceptance. Recently published work by Don Webb, Bruce Boston, Conger V. Beasley; published new writers within the last year. Length: 2,500 words average; 2 words minimum; 7,000 words maximum. Sometimes comments on rejected mss or recommends other markets.
How to Contact: Send complete ms. "Cover letter isn't really necessary, but it's nice to know where they heard of us." Reports on queries in 1 week; on mss in 6-8 weeks. SASE. Photocopied submissions OK. Accepts computer printouts, including dot-matrix. Sample copy for $4; fiction guidelines for #10 SAE and 1 first class stamp.
Payment: Pays $5 minimum; $25 maximum, and contributor's copies.
Terms: Pays on acceptance for first North American serial rights. Sends pre-publication galleys to au-

thor "only when a story has been edited and a writer's approval of the changes is needed." Publication copyrighted.

Advice: "I've got this time and money and want to invest it in something. So, do I buy a Jiffy Lube or start a new Wendy Burger place? Or do I choose to create a business that caters to my strengths, my loves and desires? Well, that's what I'm doing. I always wanted to publish a magazine, and I've always loved short stories. I urge beginning writers to keep sending stories out. You'll never sell the one in your drawer. If a story comes back with a handwritten note, if it looks like someone really read it, send that editor another. When an editor takes time to critique, it means he's interested and he's trying to help."

EPOCH MAGAZINE (II), 251 Goldwin Smith Hall, Cornell University, Ithaca NY 14853. (607)256-3385. Editor: C.S. Giscombe. Magazine: 6x9; 80-100 pages; good quality paper; good cover stock. "Top level fiction and poetry for people who are interested in and capable of being entertained by good literature." Published 3 times a year. Estab. 1947. Circ. 1,000.

Needs: Literary, contemporary and ethnic. Buys 4-5 mss/issue. Receives approximately 100 unsolicited fiction mss each month. Does not read in summer. Recently published work by Dallas Wiebe, Sherley Anne Williams, Lee K. Abbott; published new writers in the last year. Length: 10-30 typed, double-spaced pages. Critiques rejected mss when there is time. Sometimes recommends other markets.

How to Contact: Send complete ms with SASE. Accepts computer printout submissions. "No dot-matrix please." Reports in 2-8 weeks on mss. Publishes ms an average of 3 months after acceptance. Sample copy $3.50.

Terms: Pays on publication for first North American serial rights. Publication copyrighted.

Advice: "Read and be interested in the journals you're sending work to."

ERGO! (II), The Bumbershoot Literary Magazine, Bumbershoot, Box 9750, Seattle WA 98109-0750. (206)622-5123. Editor: Judith Roche. Magazine; 6x9; 100 pages; 60 lb offset stock; 4-color gloss cover; illustrations; photos. "Magazine publishes articles of interest to the literary community, book reviews, and poems and prose by competition winners and invited writers who read at the Bumbershoot Festival." Annually. Circ. 1,500.

Needs: Literary. Accepts approximately 4 mss/issue. Agented fiction 5%. Publishes short shorts.

How to Contact: Query first. Reports in 2 weeks on queries; 2 months on mss. SASE for ms. Simultaneous, photocopied and reprint submissions OK. Accepts computer printout submissions, including dot-matrix. Sample copy for $5 and 9x12 SAE.

Payment: $25-$75 for articles and reviews. $150 award honoraria for Bumbershoot writers; contributor's copies.

Terms: Pays on acceptance for one-time rights. Publication copyrighted.

Advice: Request application for annual contest.

EROTIC FICTION QUARTERLY (I, II, IV), EFQ Publications, Box 4958, San Francisco CA 94101. Editor: Richard Hiller. Magazine: 5x8, 186 pages; 50 lb offset paper; 65 lb cover stock. "Small literary magazine for thoughtful people interested in a variety of highly original and creative short fiction with sexual themes."

Needs: Any style or genre heartfelt, intelligent erotica. (Ethnic, feminist, science fiction, etc.). Also, stories not necessarily erotic whose subject is some aspect of authentic sexual experience. No standard pornography; no "men's" stories; no contrived plots or gimmicks; no broad satire, parody or obscure "literary" writing; no poetry. Published new writers within the last year. Length: 500 words minimum; 5,000 words maximum; 1,500 words average. Occasionally critiques rejected ms. "Willing to work with beginners on exceptional mss." Sometimes recommends other markets.

How to Contact: Send complete ms only with SASE. Photocopied submissions OK; non-returnable copy also OK with SASE for reply. Fiction guidelines free with SASE.

Payment: Pays $35 minimum.

Terms: Pay on acceptance for first rights. Publication copyrighted.

Advice: "I specifically encourage beginners who have something to say regarding sexual attitudes, emotions, roles, etc. Story ideas should come from real life, not media; characters should be real people. There are essentially no restrictions regarding content, style, explicitness, etc.; *originality*, *clarity* and *integrity* are most important."

THE EVERGREEN CHRONICLES (II), A Quarterly Journal of Gay & Lesbian Writers, Box 8939, Minnehaha Station, Minneapolis MN 55408. (612)824-2289. Editors: Lisa Albrecht, Douglas Federhart. Magazine: 5½x8½; 36 pages; linen bond paper; b&w line drawings and photos. "No one theme, other than works must have a lesbian or gay appeal. Works sensual and erotic are considered, but must be handled well and have a purpose beyond just sexuality. We look for poetry and prose, but are open to well-crafted pieces of nearly any genre." Quarterly. Estab. 1985. Circ. 300.

Needs: Adventure, confession, contemporary, ethnic, experimental, fantasy, feminist, gay, humor/satire, lesbian, literary, romance (contemporary), science fiction, serialized/excerpted novel, suspense/

mystery. "We are interested in works by gay/lesbian artists in a wide variety of genres. The subject matter need not be specifically lesbian or gay-themed, but we do look for a deep sensitivity to that experience. No hardcore sex or porno; no unnecessary violence; nothing homophobic." Accepts 3-4 mss/issue; 12-15 mss/year. Publishes ms approx. 6 weeks after acceptance. Recently published work by Terri Jewel, Lev Raphael and Ruthann Robson. Published new writers in the last year. Length: 3,500-4,500 words average; no minimum; 5,200 words maximum. 25 pages double-spaced maximum on prose. Publishes short shorts. Sometimes comments on rejected mss.
How to Contact: Send r copies of complete ms with cover letter. "It helps to have some biographical info included." Reports on queries in 3 weeks; on mss in 3-4 months. SASE. Photocopied and reprint submissions OK. Accepts computer printouts, no dot-matrix. Sample copy for $3.50, 6x9 SAE and 65¢ postage. Fiction guidelines for #10 SAE and 1 first class stamp.
Payment: Pays in contributor's copies.
Terms: Acquires one-time rights. Publication copyrighted.
Advice: "Perseverance is on a par with skill at the craft."

EXIT, A Journal of the Arts, Rochester Routes/Creative Arts Projects, 193 Inglewood Dr., Rochester NY 14619-1403. (716)328-8818. Editor/Publisher: Frank Judge. "Our magazine has no theme and no particular bias but *quality*. We assume our readership is the 'little magazine' audience; we've had nothing to disprove this assumption so far." Published irregularly. Estab. 1976. Circ. 1,000.
Needs: Literary, contemporary, science fiction, fantasy, mystery and translations. "Science fiction, fantasy and mystery submissions should have a 'literary' slant giving a broader appeal than that of the respective forms; query preferred for these categories." No religious/inspirational, psychic/supernatural, feminist, gay/lesbian, confession, gothic, romance, western, adventure, juvenile, young adult, ethnic, or serialized or condensed novels. Accepts 1-2 mss/issue. Receives 20-30 unsolicited fiction mss each month. Length: 2,000 words maximum. Critiques rejected mss when there is time.
How to Contact: Send query or complete ms with SASE. Accepts computer printout submissions. Accepts disk submissions compatible with PC XT/AT, Mac, Apple II +, IIc, IIe. Reports in 3 weeks on queries, 3-6 months on mss. Publishes ms 6-12 months after acceptance. Sample copy $5.
Payment: 3 free author's copies; $5 charge for extras.
Terms: Pays on publication for first North American serial rights and second serial rights. Publication copyrighted.
Advice: Mss are rejected because they are "loaded with adolescent clichés and trite concepts, revel in 'experimental' obscurantising, and/or have no sense of plot, liveliness."

EXPLORER MAGAZINE (I), Flory Publishing Co., Box 210, Notre Dame IN 46556. (219)277-3465. Editor: Ray Flory. Magazine: 8½x5½; 20-32 pages; 20 lb paper; 60 lb or stock cover; illustrations. Magazine with "basically an inspirational theme including love stories in good taste." Christian writing audience. Semiannually. Estab. 1960. Circ. 200.
Needs: Literary, mainstream, prose poem, religious/inspirational, romance (contemporary, historical, young adult) and science fiction. No pornography. Buys 2-3 mss/issue; 5 mss/year. Length: 600 words average; 300 words minimum; 900 words maximum. Occasionally critiques rejected mss.
How to Contact: Send complete ms with SASE. Reports in 1 week. Publishes ms up to 2 years after acceptance. Photocopied submissions OK. Sample copy $3. Fiction guidelines for SAE and 1 first class stamp.
Payment: Up to $25 and 1 free contributor's copy; $3 charge for extras.
Terms: Cash prizes of $25, $20, $15 and $10 based on subscribers' votes. A plaque is also awarded to first place winner.
Advice: "See a copy of magazine first; have a good story to tell—in *good* taste! Most fiction sent in is too *long*! Be yourself! Be honest and sincere in your style. Write what you know about."

EXQUISITE CORPSE (III), A Monthly of Books & Ideas, Culture Shock Foundation, English Dept., L.S.U., Baton Rouge LA 70803. Editor: Andrei Codrescu. Tabloid: 16x16; 24 pages; 60 lb offset paper; illustrations; photos. Tabloid of essays, reviews, polemics, poetry, fiction for literate audience. Monthly. Estab. 1983. Circ. 3,000.
Needs: Experimental. Receives 150 unsolicited mss/month. Accepts 1-2 mss/issue; 15 mss/year. Requires magazine subscription of $15 (12 issues) before reading ms. Published new writers within the last year. Length: 1,000 words average; 250 words minimum; 1,000 words maximum.
How to Contact: Query first. Reports in 2 weeks on queries and mss. SASE. Simultaneous submissions OK. Accepts computer printout submissions; letter-quality only. Accepts disk submissions compatible with Mergenthal system. Prefers hard copy with disk submission. Sample copy $2.50.
Payment: 5 contributor's copies.
Terms: Acquires one-time rights. Publication copyrighted.
Advice: "Break the rules. We don't much believe in genre—we like experimental work."

‡FANTASY & TERROR, New Series, Richard Fawcett, Publisher, 61 Teecomwas Dr., Uncasville CT 06382. Editor: Jessica Amanda Salmonson, Box 20610, Seattle WA 98102. Magazine: digest sized; 36 pages; 20 lb paper; 70 lb cover stock; illustrations. Magazine of "macabre-surrealist prose poems à la Baudelaire; traditional ghost stories; fables, parables, idiosyncratic non-commerical fantastic narrative artforms; romanticism for "jaded fantasy readers; aesthetic cynics; dark romantics." Published occasionally. Estab. 1973. Circ. 500.
Needs: "Still use predominantly macabre poems-in-prose." Recently published work by Marvin Kaye, Michael Bishop, Jane Yolen; published new writers within the last year. Length: short-short stories.
How to Contact: Send complete ms with cover letter. "Would like to know previous publication record, if any." Reports in 2 weeks on queries; in 4 weeks on mss. Photocopied submissions OK. Prefers letter-quality computer printouts. Sample copy $3, from publisher's address only. Sometimes recommends other markets.
Payment: Contributor's copy; 40% discount to contributors only.
Terms: Acquires one-time rights on publication. Publication copyrighted.
Advice: "*Fantasy and Terror* has nothing to do with popular trends. Be familiar with *fin-de-siècle* authors and the symbolists."

THE FARMER'S MARKET (II), Midwestern Farmer's Market, Inc., Box 1272, Galesburg IL 61402. Fiction Editor: John Hughes. Magazine. 5½x8½; 80-100 pages; 60 lb offset paper; 65 lb cover; b&w illustrations and photos. Magazine publishing "quality fiction, poetry, nonfiction, plays, etc., with a Midwestern theme and/or sensibility for an adult, literate audience." Semiannually. Estab. 1982. Circ. 500.
Needs: Contemporary, feminist, humor/satire, literary, regional and excerpted novel. "We prefer material of clarity, depth and strength; strong plots, good character development." No "romance, avant-garde, juvenile, teen." Accepts 6-12 mss/year. Recently published work by Donn Irving, Elsavietta Ritchie, David Williams. Published new writers within the last year. Occasionally critiques rejected mss or recommends other markets.
How to Contact: Send complete ms with SASE. Reports in 1-2 months. Photocopied submissions OK. Accepts computer printout submissions; prefers letter-quality. Publishes ms 4-8 months after acceptance. Sample copy for $3.50 and 80¢ postage and handling.
Payment: 1 free contributor's copy.
Terms: Authors retain rights.
Advice: "We're always interested in regional fiction. We are trying to publish more fiction and we are looking for exceptional manuscripts. Read the magazines before submitting. If you don't want to buy it, ask your library. We receive numerous mss that are clearly unsuitable."

FAT TUESDAY (II), 141 E. Glaucus #D, Encinitas CA 92024. Editor-in-Chief: F.M. Cotolo. Editors: B. Lyle Tabor and Thom Savion. Associate Editors: Lionel Stevroid and Kristen Vonoehrke. Journal: 8½x11 or 5x8; 27-36 pages; good to excellent paper; heavy cover stock; b&w illustrations; photos. "Generally, we are an eclectic journal of fiction, poetry and visual treats. Our issues to date have featured artists like B. Lyle Tabor, Dom Cimei, Mary Lee Gowland, Patrick Kelly, Cheryl Townsend, Joi Cook, Chuck Taylor and many more who have focused on an individualistic nature with fiery elements. We are a literary mardi gras—as the title indicates—and irreverancy is as acceptable to us as profundity as long as there is fire! Our audience is anyone who can praise literature and condemn it at the same time. Anyone too serious about it on either level will not like *Fat Tuesday*." Annually. Estab. 1981. Circ. 700.
Needs: Comics, erotica, experimental, humor/satire, literary, prose poem, psychic/supernatural/occult, serialized/excerpted novel and dada. "Although we list categories, we are open to feeling out various fields if they are delivered with the mark of an individual and not just in the format of the particular field." Receives 10 unsolicited fiction mss/month. Accepts 4-5 mss/issue. Published new writers within the last year. Length: 1,000 words maximum. Publishes short shorts. Occasionally critiques rejected mss.
How to Contact: Send complete ms with SASE. Photocopied submissions OK. Accepts computer printout submissions. Reports in 1 month. Publishes ms 3-10 months after acceptance. Sample copy $5.
Payment: 1 free contributor's copy.
Terms: Pays on publication for one-time rights. Publication copyrighted.
Advice: "Retain your enthusiasm. Never write and submit anything without it. Buy an issue and eat it up, page by page. Then, go into your guts and write something. If you're not on fire, we'll tell you so and encourage you to try again. Don't be self-critical when you have something to say that reflects how you feel. Most of all, be aware of life outside of literature, and then let life influence your writing. It is essential that a potential submitter buy a sample issue and experience the 'zine to understand what would work and get a better idea of what we're talking about and help support the continuation of this free form of expression that *FT* calls 'littéraire verité.'"

‡**FELICITY (I)**, Weems Concepts, Star Route, Box 21AA, Artemas PA 17211. (814)458-3102. Editor: Kay Weems-Winter. Newsletter: 8½x11; 20 lb bond paper; illustrations. "Publish articles, poetry and short stories. Poetry has different theme each month. No theme for stories." Monthly. Plans special fiction issue. Estab. 1988. Circ. 50.

Needs: Adventure, confession, ethnic, fantasy, historical (general), horror, humor/satire, juvenile (5-9 years), prose poem, psychic/supernatural/occult, religious/inspirational, romance (contemporary, historical, young adult), science fiction, senior citizen/retirement, suspense/mystery, western and young adult/teen (10-18 years). No erotica, translations. Receives 6-10 unsolicited mss/month. Buys 1 ms/issue (for *Felicity* contest); 12 mss/year (for *Felicity* contest—sometimes more for publication). Publishes ms 3-4 weeks after acceptance. $5 reading fee for contest entries. Length: 2,000 words preferred; 800 words minimum; 2,500 words maximum. Sometimes critiques rejected mss and recommends other markets.

How to Contact: Send complete ms with cover letter or enter our monthly contests. "Send SASE for return of ms or tell me to destroy it if not accepted." Reports in 1-4 weeks. SASE. Simultaneous, photocopied and reprint submissions OK as long as author still retains rights. Accepts computer printout submissions, including dot-matrix. Prefers letter quality. Sample copy for $1.50, #10 SAE and 65¢ postage. Fiction guidelines for #10 SAE and 1 first class stamp.

Payment: Pays in contributor's copies.

Terms: Acquires one-time rights. "We will be" copyrighted. "We sponsor monthly contests. Winner receives half of entry fees collected for the short story contest. Submit ms along with reading fee and you will be entered in the contest. Deadline is the 30th of each month. Read both of our publications—*Felicity* and *The Bottom Line Publications*. Our contests are listed there."

Advice: Looks for "good opening sentence, realistic characters, nice descriptions, strong plot with believable ending. Use natural conversations. Let me *feel* your story. Keep me interested until the end. Keep trying. A lot of mss I read are from new writers. Personally I enjoy stories and articles which will create a particular emotion, build suspense, or offer excitement or entertainment. Don't spell out everything in detail—keep me guessing."

FEMINIST STUDIES (II), % Women's Studies Program, University of Maryland, College Park MD 20742. (301)454-2363. Editor: Claire G. Moses. Fiction Editor: Rachel Blau DuPlessis. Business Manager: Marianna Murota. Magazine. 6x9; 250 pages; 60 lb white offset paper, 10 pt c15 cover stock; photos. Journal of feminist issues. A forum for analysis, debate and exchange. Audience consists of women's studies faculty, students, anyone interested in feminist issues and research. Publishes 3 times/year. Estab. 1972. Circ. 7,000.

Needs: Feminist, gay/lesbian and Third World women's writing. Publishes stories of 10-18 ms pages.

How to Contact: Send 3 copies of ms and abstract. Reports in 1-3 months on mss. Publishes ms 1-10 months after acceptance. Sample copy $8 for individuals, $16 for institutions. Free guidelines.

Terms: Sends galleys to author. Publication copyrighted.

FENNEL STALK (I, II), Divergent Freeway Arts Underwriters Inc., 2448 W. Freeway Lane, Phoenix AZ 85021. (602)995-5338. Editors: Peter Bailey, Karen Bowden, Ron Dickson. Magazine: 5½x8½; 64-78 pages; 20 lb copy paper; illustrations; photos. Semiannually. Estab. 1986. Circ. 250-300.

Needs: "We are primarily a poetry magazine. But we do publish 1-3 fiction pieces each issue—just depends on what we get. Looking for good writing. Don't want to discount any on basis of subject matter." No *very* long stories. Receives 6-8 unsolicited mss/year. Buys 1-3 mss/issue; 2-6 mss/year. Length: "over 10 double spaced pages is pushing it—but if we *really* liked it, we'd publish it." Sometimes critiques rejected mss (if asked to) and recommends other markets.

How to Contact: Send complete ms with cover letter. Reports in 2-3 months on mss. SASE. Photocopied submissions OK. Accepts computer printout submissions, including dot-matrix if legible. Accepts electronic submissions via IBM/PC, Word Perfect, Wordstar, Multimeate disks. Sample copy for $3.

Payment: Pays in 1 contributor's copy, charges for extras.

Terms: "All rights belong to the writer." Publication copyrighted.

Advice: "You have to begin by sending us a manuscript. Let us know if you want comment—we'll give it if we can."

FESTIVALS, Resource Publications, Inc., 160 E. Virginia St., #290, San Jose CA 95112. (408)286-8505. Editor: Ken Guentert. Magazine. 8½x11; 32 pages; 60 lb glossy paper and cover; illustrations and photographs. "We're focused on the transformation through ritual and celebration. We publish legends, fairy tales and short fiction with mythic or archetypal overtones. Readers are people who lead rituals and celebrations and festivals." Bimonthly. Estab. 1981. Circ. 8,000.

Needs: Ethnic, fantasy, feminist, humor/satire, spiritual. "Stories should put reader in touch with the 'holy' especially as it is found in the ordinary, and within the most deeply masculine, feminine, human

part of oneself. We don't want evangelical Christian stories or any other stories pushing a particular religion. But stories arising from religious traditions are okay." Receives 10 unsolicited fiction mss/month. Accepts 1 mss/issue; 6 mss/year. Publishes ms 1 year after acceptance. Length: 1,500 words average; 600 words minimum; 2,500 words maximum. Publishes short shorts.
How to Contact: Send complete ms with cover letter. Reports in 6 weeks. SASE. Photocopied submissions OK. Accepts computer printout submissions, including dot-matrix. Sample copy $3 and 9x12 SAE with 3 first class stamps. Fiction guidelines for #10 SAE and 1 first class stamp.
Payment: Free subscription to magazine and 5 contributor's copies; charge for extras.
Terms: Acquires first rights plus right to grant reprint permission for non-commercial purposes to customers. Publication copyrighted.
Advice: "We don't publish 'short stories' *per se*. But lots of fiction material—legends, fairy tales, storytelling—fits our seasonal and celebrational orientation."

FICTION INTERNATIONAL (II), English Dept., San Diego State University, San Diego CA 92182. (619)594-6220. Editors: Harold Jaffe and Larry McCaffery. Serious literary magazine of fiction, extended reviews, essays. 200 pages; illustrations; photos. "Our twin biases are progressive politics and post-modernism." Biannually. Estab. 1973. Circ. 2,500.
Needs: Literary, political and innovative forms. Receives approximately 300 unsolicited fiction mss each month. Published new writers within the last year. No length limitations but rarely uses manuscripts over 25 pages. Portions of novels acceptable if self-contained enough for independent publication. Unsolicited mss will be considered only from September 1 through December 15 of each year.
How to Contact: Send complete ms with SASE. Reports in 1-3 months on mss. Sample copy for $9: query Ed Gordon, managing editor.
Payment: Varies.
Terms: Pays on publication for first rights and first North American serial rights. Publication copyrighted.
Advice: "Study the magazine. We're highly selective. A difficult market for unsophisticated writers."

FICTION NETWORK MAGAZINE (II), Box 5651, San Francisco CA 94101. (415)391-6610. Editor: Jay Schaefer. Magazine: 8½x11; 48 pages; newsprint paper; 70 lb coated cover stock; illustrations. "Fiction Network distributes short stories to newspapers and publishes *Fiction Network Magazine*, which circulates to agents, editors, writers and others in publishing and film." Biannually. Estab. 1983. Circ. 6,000.
Needs: "All types of stories and subjects are acceptable; novel excerpts will be considered only if they stand alone as stories." No children's or young adult. Receives 500 unsolicited mss/month. Accepts 75 mss/year. Approximately 35% of fiction is agented. Recently published work by Monica Wood, Joyce Carol Oates, Bharati Mukherjee. Published new writers within the last year. Length: 2,500 words average.
How to Contact: Send complete ms or submit through agent. Reports in 16 weeks. Publishes ms 6-9 months after acceptance. SASE. "Do not ask us to return submissions from outside U.S. Do not send a second manuscript until you receive a response to the first. Please send manuscripts unfolded." Simultaneous and photocopied submissions OK. Accepts computer printout submissions. Prefers letter-quality. Sample copy $4 US and Canada; $6.50 elsewhere. Fiction guidelines for SASE.
Payment: $25-$500 and up.
Terms: Pays on publication. "*Fiction Network* buys newspaper and magazine rights for two years. Each story accepted may be sold to several periodicals, in addition to appearing in *Fiction Network Magazine*. Payments from publications that carry the story are divided 50/50 with the author."
Advice: "We're looking for quality short fiction that appeals to a wide audience. Contributors include Alice Adams, Max Apple, Ann Beattie, Ken Chowder, Andre Dubus, Bobbie Ann Mason, Lorrie Moore, Lynne Sharon Schwartz and many previously unpublished writers. Read an issue of a magazine before submitting your writing. Don't get discouraged."

THE FICTION REVIEW, Brick Lung Press, Box 12268, Seattle WA 98102. Editor: S.P. Stressman. Magazine: 8½x7; 52 pages; 70 lb paper; 80 lb cover stock; illustrations. Short fiction, essays on contemporary fiction, occasional interviews. Quarterly. Plans special fiction issue. Estab. 1987. Circ. 500.
Needs: Contemporary, experimental, literary, mainstream, prose poem. Receives approximately 200 unsolicited fiction mss/month. Accepts 5-6 mss/issue; 20-30 mss/year. Publishes ms usually 1-3 month after acceptance. 5% of fiction is agented. Recently published work by Richard Kostelanetz, Ron Carlson, Roberta Allen; published new writers within the last year. Length: 2,000-2,500 words average; 500 words minimum; 4,000 words maximum. Publishes short shorts. Sometimes critiques rejected mss and recommends other markets.
How to Contact: Send complete ms with cover letter, name and address. Reports on queries in 1 month; on ms in 1-2 months. SASE. Simultaneous and photocopied submissions OK. Accepts computer

printout submissions, including dot-matrix. Sample copy $4. Fiction guidelines for #10 SAE and 1 first class stamp.
Payment: Pays 1 contributor's copy.
Terms: Acquires first North American serial rights. Publication copyrighted.
Advice: "1. Write a cover letter, however brief, listing credits, or just presenting the story. 2. Do not send more than one story at a time. 3. We are most attracted to distinctive, vivid short stories. A story of 8-10 pages is the ideal for our publication. 4. Do not include photos, reviews from journals or other personal material to 'sell' your story. It will sell itself, if it is excellent. 5. Include SASE for return of manuscript or reply. 6. If you receive any handwritten note saying we want to see more of your work, do send more. Since we read about 200 manuscripts a month, we do not encourage people to try again unless we like their style. We plan to publish more book reviews in support of small press publications."

FIGHTING WOMAN NEWS (IV), Box 1459, Grand Central Station, New York NY 10163. Editor: Valerie Eads. Fiction Editor: Kristen Noakes-Fry. Magazine: 8 1/2x11; 16-32 pages; 60 lb offset bond paper; illustrations; photos. "Women's martial arts, self defense, combative sports. Articles, reviews, etc., related to these subjects. Well-educated adult women who are actually involved with martial arts read us because we're there and we're good." Quarterly. Estab. 1975. circ. 4,500.
Needs: Science fiction, fantasy, feminist, adventure and translations. "No material that shows women as victims, incompetents, stereotypes; no 'fight scenes' written by people who don't know anything about fighting skills." Receives very few unsolicited fiction mss. Recently published work by Robert W. Dillon, Lauren Wright Douglas and William C. White. Length: 2,500 words.
How to Contact: Query with clips of published work with SASE. Enclose cover letter with ms. Accepts computer printout submissions. "We must know if it is a simultaneous submission." Reports as soon as possible on queries and mss. Sample copy $3.50. Specify "fiction" when asking for samples. Free guidelines with #10 SASE.
Payment: Pays author's copies or subscription or $10 honorarium.
Terms: Pays on publication for one-time rights. Publication copyrighted; will print author's copyright if desired.
Advice: "We are now getting unsolicited mss from published writers who have what we want; i.e., a good, competent story that's just a bit too martial-arts oriented for their regular markets. Our readers have expressed a strong preference for more technique and theory with a few specific complaints about too much fiction or poetry. So even with a more regular publication schedule and corredsponding increase in total pages, we are not likely to use more fiction. Read the magazine before submitting. I also think the theme of death in combat can do with a rest."

‡FIRST STORIES and STORYETTE (I,II), Box 710, Santa Monica CA 90406. (213)397-4217. Editor: Davis Lott. Magazine: 10x13 print size; 32 pages; Electrobrite paper and cover; b&w illustrations and photographs. *First Stories* is for short stories by unpublished writers; *Storyette* publishes stories by published writers. Quarterly. Plans special fiction issue. Estab. 1988. Circ. 10,000.
Needs: Adventure, confession, contemporary, fantasy, historical, humor/satire, juvenile (5-9 years), literary, mainstream, romance (contemporary, historical, young adult), science fiction, senior citizen/retirement, sports, suspense/mystery, western. "All stories limited to 1,000-1,200 words." Receives 2-10 unsolicited fiction mss/month; accepts 10-14 mss/issue; 40-56 mss/year. Time between acceptance and publication varies. Requires magazine subscription before reading ms. Length: 1,000-1,200 words. Sometimes comments on rejected mss and recommends other markets.
How to Contact: Query first. Reports in 2 weeks. SASE. Simultaneous and photocopied submissions OK. Accepts computer printout submissions, including dot-matrix. Sample copy and fiction guidelines for $2 plus $1 postage.
How to Contact: Pays 2¢-5¢/word for *Storyette*.
Terms: Pays on publication. Sends galleys to author "for a $5 charge." Publication not copyrighted.
Advice: "When a story is published in either magazine, we send 100 copies to agents or markets and act as the writer's agent on a 20% fee. If he or she *has* an agent, they get 10% and we get 10%. Our magazines are designed to act as showcases for unpublished writers (*First Stories*) or lesser-known published writers (*Storyette*)."

FIVE FINGERS REVIEW (II), 553 25th Ave., San Francisco CA 94121. (415)386-2151. Editor: "rotating." Magazine: 5x8; 125-150 pages; photographs on cover. "*Five Fingers* is dedicated to publishing well wrought poetry and prose from various aesthetic viewpoints. The magazine proveds a forum from which talented writers (new and known, traditional and experimental) act as conscientious objectors, as creative witnesses to the passions and possibilities of our time." Semiannually. Estab. 1984. Circ. 1,000.
Needs: Ethnic, experimental, feminist, gay, humor/satire, lesbian, literary, regional, prose poems, prose vignettes and works that move between the genres. Receives 15-20 unsolicited mss/month. Ac-

cepts 2-5 mss/issue. Recently published work by Molly Giles, W.A. Smith and Peter Johnson; published new writers in the last year. Publishes short shorts.
How to Contact: Query with clips of published work. SASE. Simultaneous, photocopied and reprint submissions OK. Sample copy for $6.
Payment: Pays in contributor's copies.
Advice: "We are particularly looking for short-short stories, prose poems, prose vignettes and works of translation."

FLIPSIDE (II), Professional Writing Program, Dixon 104, California University, California PA 15419. (412)938-5946. Fiction Editor: Kathleen Vail. Tabloid: 11½x17; 45-60 pages; illustrations; photos. "Emphasis on 'new journalism.' Fiction, nonfiction, poetry, humor." Semiannually. Estab. 1987. Circ. 2,000.
Needs: Contemporary, experimental, literary. No genre fiction. Receives 5-6 unsolicited mss/month. Accepts 2-3 mss/issue; 6-8 mss/year. Does not read June-August. Publishes ms 1-6 months after acceptance. Length: 1,000-5,000 words average; 10,000 words maximum.
How to Contact: Send complete manuscript with or without cover letter. Reports in 2-4 weeks on queries; 1-2 months on mss. SASE. Simultaneous and photocopied submissions OK. Accepts computer printouts, including dot-matrix. Sample copy and fiction guidelines for 9x12 SAE and $1.24 postage.
Payment: 3 contributor's copies.
Terms: Acquires first North American serial rights.
Advice: "Read as much contemporary fiction as possible. It's important to read the classics, especially our American 'classic' authors (Dreiser, Lewis, Hemingway, not to mention Melville, Hawthorne, etc.)—but an aspiring writer must know what other writers are doing."

"We publish fiction of high 'literary' quality—stories that delight, instruct, and aren't afraid to take risks," says Pat Rushin, editor of The Florida Review.

Cover photo by Richard Spencer.

‡THE FLORIDA REVIEW (II), Dept. of English, University of Central Florida, Orlando FL 32816. (407)275-2038. Editor: Pat Rushin. Magazine: 5½x8½; 128 pages. Semiannually. Plans special fiction issue. Estab. 1972. Circ. 1,000.
Needs: Contemporary, experimental and literary. "We welcome experimental fiction, so long as it doesn't make us feel lost or stupid. We aren't especially interested in genre fiction (science fiction, romance, adventure, etc.), though a good story can transcend any genre." Receives 80 mss/month. Buys 8-10 mss/issue; 16-20 mss/year. Publishes ms within 3-6 months of acceptance. Recently published work by Stephen Dixon, Richard Grayson and Liz Rosenberg. Publishes short shorts.
How to Contact: Send complete ms with cover letter. Reports in 2-4 months. SASE. Simultaneous and photocopied submissions OK. Accepts computer printout submissions, including dot-matrix. Sample copy $4.50; free fiction guidelines.

Payment: Pays $5/printed page and contributor's copies. Charges for extra copies.
Terms: Pays on publication. "Copyright held by U.C.F.; reverts to author after publication. (In cases of reprints, we ask that a credit line indicate that the work first appeared in the *F.R.*)" Publication copyrighted.
Advice: "We publish fiction of high 'literary' quality—stories that delight, instruct, and aren't afraid to take risks."

‡F.O.C. REVIEW (I,II), Box 101, Worth IL 60482. Editor: Michael Ogorzaly. Managing Editor: William L. Roach. Magazine: 5¹/₂x8¹/₂; over 60 pages. "We publish original stories, poems, essays and one-act plays. In addition, we seek book and film reviews." Quarterly. Plans special fiction issue. Estab. 1988. Circ. 500.
Needs: Adventure, condensed/excerpted novel, contemporary, experimental, fantasy, feminist, humor/satire, literary, prose poem, science fiction, serialized novel, sports and suspense/mystery. No romance, erotica. Receives over 30 mss/month. Accepts 10-12 mss/issue; 36 mss/year. Publishes ms in next or following issue after acceptance. Recently published work by James Linn, Rama Rao, John Nerone; published new writers within the last year. Length: 4,000 words maximum. Publishes short shorts. Sometimes critiques rejected mss.
How to Contact: Send 2 copies of complete ms with cover letter, which should include "bio note." Reports on mss in 2 months. SASE. Simultaneous, photocopied and reprint submissions OK. Accepts computer printout submissions, including dot-matrix. Sample copy $5. Fiction guidelines for #10 SAE and 1 first class stamp.
Payment: Pays in contributor's copies.
Terms: Acquires one-time rights.

FOLIO: A LITERARY JOURNAL (II), Literature Department, American University, Washington DC 20016. (202)885-2971. Editor changes yearly. Magazine: 6x9; 64 pages. "Fiction is published if it is well written. We look specifically for language control and skilled plot and character development." For a scholarly audience. Semiannually. Estab. 1984. Circ. 300.
Needs: Contemporary, literary, mainstream, prose poem, sports, suspense/mystery, translations. No pornography. Receives 40 unsolicited mss/month. Accepts 4 mss/issue; 8 mss/year. Does not read mss during May-August or December-January. Recently published work by Paul McComas, Anne Louise Kerr, David K. Choo; published new writers within the last year. Length: 2,500 words average; 3,000 words maximum. Publishes short shorts. Length: 3 pages. Occasionally critiques rejected mss.
How to Contact: Send complete ms with cover letter, which should include a brief biography. Reports in 1-2 weeks on queries; 1-2 months on mss. SASE. Simultaneous, photocopied and reprint submissions OK. Accepts computer printout submissions, including dot-matrix. Sample copy for $4.50. Fiction guidelines for #10 SAE and 1 first class stamp.
Payment: Pays in contributor's copies.
Terms: Acquires all rights. Publication copyrighted. "$50 award for best piece of fiction. Query for guidelines."
Advice: "Don't give up, but don't forget to revise."

FOOTWORK (I,II), A Literary Collection of Contemporary Poetry, Short Fiction and Art, Passaic County Community College, College Blvd., Paterson NJ 07509. (201)684-6555. Editor: Maria Gillan. Fiction Editor: James T. McCartin. Magazine: 8x11; 88 pages; 60 lb paper; 70 lb cover; illustrations; Photos. Plans fiction issue in future.
Needs: Contemporary, ethnic, experimental, translations. "We are interested in quality short stories, with no taboos on subject matter." Receives about 30 unsolicited mss/month. Accepts 1 ms/issue. Publishes ms about 6 months to a year after acceptance. Published new writers within the last year. Length: 2,500-3,000 words.
How to Contact: Reports in 3 months on mss. SASE for query and ms; no simultaneous submissions or reprints. Accepts computer printouts. No dot-matrix. Sample copy $3.
Payment: Pays in contributor's copies. Acquires first North American rights. Publication copyrighted.
Advice: "We look for original, vital, powerful work. The short story is—when successful—a major achievement. Because we publish relatively little work, we cannot consider stories which are slight, however charming."

Market categories: (I) Beginning; (II) General;
(III) Prestige; (IV) Specialized.

FOUR QUARTERS (III), LaSalle University, 20th and Olney Ave., Philadelphia PA 19141-1199. (215)951-1171. Editor: John C. Kleis. Magazine: 7x9; 64 pages; 70 lb paper; 65 lb cover. Magazine of poetry, fiction and nonfiction for mainly academic audience. Quarterly. Estab. 1951. Circ. 750.
Needs: Literary and contemporary. "Established writers preferred." Buys 5 mss/issue, 20 mss/year. Receives approximately 40 unsolicited fiction mss each month. Recently published work by William Van Wert, T. Alan Broughton, Allen Shepherd. Length: 2,000-5,000 words. Critiques rejected mss when there is time.
How to Contact: Send complete ms with SASE. Reports in 4-6 weeks on mss. Publishes ms 4-10 months after acceptance. Sample copy $4. Free guidelines with SASE.
Payment: Pays $25 and 3 free author's copies. $1 charge for extras.
Terms: Pays on publication for all rights. Publication copyrighted.
Advice: "Technical mastery gets our attention and respect immediately. We admire writers who use the language with precision, economy and imagination. But fine writing for its own sake is unsatisfying unless it can lead the reader to some insight into the complexity of the human condition without falling into heavy-handed didacticism. We reject most of the manuscripts we receive, mostly because their ideas and expression are clichés. Learn to punctuate and be more sparing with metaphors and rhetorical flourishes."

‡THE FREELANCER'S REPORT (I, IV), Literary Publications Co., Box 93, Poquonock CT 06064. (203)688-5496. Editor: Pat McDonald. Magazine: 8½x11; 20-28 pages; bond/colored paper and cover stock; illustrations and photos. "Fiction must feature main character involved in writing (editor, agent etc., okay), photography or any form of illustration used in literature" Audience is "freelancing writers, photographers, illustrators." Bimonthly. Plans special fiction issue. Estab. 1986. Circ. 250.
Needs: Contemporary, humor/satire and romance (contemporary). Fiction "must be on theme—otherwise pretty open." No "porn—anything without a message—only tight writing accepted." Receives 30 mss/month. Accepts 1 ms/issue; 6-12 mss/year. Publishes ms within 90 days of acceptance. Length: 1,000 words minimum; 1,500 words maximum. Always critiques rejected mss; sometimes recommends other markets.
How to Contact: Send complete mss with cover letter. "Bio notes recommended. Also note that payment in copies is understood. Prefers no queries." SASE. Simultaneous, photocopied and reprint submissions OK. Accepts computer printout submissions, including "highly legible" dot-matrix. Sample copy $3.50. Fiction guidelines for #10 SAE and 2 first class stamps.
Payment: Pays in contributor's copies.
Terms: Acquires first North American serial rights and reprint rights (if applicable). Sends edited copy of ms to author "whether we accept or not."
Advice: "Fiction writers, to succeed, *must* have original, well crafted stories and a good understanding of literary craft, style, English language *and* be excellent researchers for market sources. Most of our rejected ms were not well researched—the remainder were not well-written."

FREEWAY (II), Box 632, Glen Ellyn IL 60138. (312)668-6000 (ext. 216). Editor: Billie Sue Thompson. Magazine: 8½x11; 4 pages; newsprint paper; illustrations; photos. Weekly Sunday school paper "specializing in first-person true stories about how God has worked in teens' lives," for Christian teens ages 15-21. Circ. 50,000.
Needs: Comics, humor/satire, spiritual, allegories and parables. Receives 100 unsolicited mss/month. Recently published work by Doug Peterson, Michelle Starr; published new writers within the last year. Published new writers within the last year. Length: 1,000 words average. Occasionally critiques rejected mss.
How to Contact: Send complete ms with SASE. Reports in 1 month. Simultaneous and photocopied submissions OK. Accepts computer printout submissions. Prefers letter-quality. Sample copy or writing guidelines available with SASE. Fiction guidelines free for SASE with 1 first class stamp.
Terms: Pays on acceptance for first rights. Publication copyrighted.
Advice: "Send us humorous fiction (parables, allegories, etc.) with a clever twist and new insight on Christian principles. Do *not* send us typical teenage short stories."

‡FRIGHT DEPOT (I,II,IV), 15519 Domart Ave., Norwalk CA 90650. Editor: Ronald C. Morgan II. Magazine: size varies; 68-80 pages; 20 lb paper; 60 lb cover stock; b&w illustrations. Publishes "supernatural horror and sword and sorcery." Published 3-4 times/year. Plans special fiction issue "for contest winners." Estab. 1988. Circ. 150.
Needs: Adventure, fantasy, horror, humor/satire, prose poem, psychic/supernatural/occult, romance (young adult), science fiction, serialized/excerpted novel, suspense/mystery, western and young adult/teen (10-18 years). "All subjects must have some degree of fantasy or the supernatural in them. No sex or gore, really bad language, stories with no fantasy element." Receives 10-20 mss/month. Accepts 9-13 mss/issue; 40-50 mss/year. Publishes ms within 2 months to 1 year of acceptance. Recently published

work by Dan Crawford, Bobby Warner, William Rasmussen. Length: 2,000-3,000 words preferred; 100 words minimum; 5,000 words maximum. Publishes short shorts. Sometimes critiques rejected mss and recommends other markets.
How to Contact: Send complete mss with cover letter or "query if over 5,000 words for serialization." Reports in 1-3 weeks on queries; 2-4 weeks on mss. SASE. Simultaneous, photocopied and reprint submissions OK. Accepts computer printout submissions, including dot-matrix. Sample copies: $3 for #1; $4 for #2 on. Enclose 6x9 SAE for #1; 9x12 for #2 on; 4 first class stamps for #1; 5 for #2 on.
Payment: Pays $1-$5 (more for serials), 1 contributor's copy.
Terms: Pays on publication for one-time rights. Publication copyrighted. Sponsors awards for fiction writers. "Those interested should send 10¢ and a #10 SASE for *Third Millennium Newsletter*, which explains all contests."
Advice: "I think fiction is starting to come back. Even newspapers are beginning to use some. I take supernatural or sword-and-sorcery stories, with other genres (SF, adventure, etc.) sometimes considered if combined with fantasy, and some humorous tales of the same type. Each three issues (#4, 7, 10, 13, etc.) are special subject issues, #4 being on the Cthulhu Mythos, #7 sword and sorcery, #10 cross genres only, etc. Writers must be aware of length limitations and remember that sex, gore and most bad language will require a rewrite before the story will be accepted."

FRONTIERS (II), A Journal of Women Studies, Women Studies Program, University of Colorado, Boulder CO 80300. (303)492-3205. Editor: Charlotta C. Hensley. Magazine: 8½x11; 92 pages; photos. "Women studies; personal essays; academic articles in all disciplines; criticism, book and film reviews; exceptional creative work (art, short fiction, photography, poetry)."
Needs: Feminist, lesbian. Receives 15 unsolicited mss/month. Accepts 1 ms/issue. Publishes ms 6 months after acceptance. Publishes short shorts. Sometimes critiques rejected mss and recommends other markets.
How to Contact: Send complete ms with cover letter. Reports in 1 week on queries; 3 months on mss. SASE. Accepts computer printout submissions, including dot-matrix. Sample copy for $8.
Payment: Pays 2 contributor's copies.
Terms: Buys first North American serial rights. Publication copyrighted.
Advice: "It is our stated purpose to publish exceptional creative work by women; we are a *feminist* journal."

GALACTIC DISCOURSE (II), Satori Press, 1111 Dartmouth, #214, Claremont CA 91711. (714)621-3112. Editor-in-Chief: Laurie Huff. Magazine: 8½x11; 200+ pages; 60 lb non-gloss paper; 80 lb non-gloss cover stock; illustrations; astronomical photos. Magazine of "*Star Trek* fiction (characterization and character interaction are emphasized), poetry, artwork; some visionary/science fiction poetry and art for *Star Trek* fans," *Note:* "This a 'when there's time' venture!" Published irregularly—every two years or so. Estab. 1977. Circ. 2,000.
Needs: Adventure, fantasy, feminist/lesbian, gay, humor, prose poem, psychic/supernatural/occult, science fiction, suspense/mystery. No pure adventure, x-rated (explicit erotica), or "Mary-Sue." Receives less than 5 unsolicited fiction mss/month. Accepts 8-12 ms/issue. Publishes short shorts under 100 double-spaced pages. Recently published work by Leslie Fish, Ginna La Croix, Harriett Stallings. Length: 12,000 words maximum; 5,000 words average. "We would consider publishing novellas/novels as a special issue apart from other work." Occasionally critiques rejected mss and recommends other markets.
How to Contact: Query first with SASE and cover letter with description of manuscript(s), including length. Photocopied submissions OK. Accepts computer printout submissions. Accepts disk submissions compatible with Apple II, Franklin or IBM PC. Prefers hard copy with disk submission. Reports in 6 weeks on queries; 2 months on mss. Publishes ms 6 months-2 years after acceptance. Sample copy "not offered, sorry; send SASE for purchasing info." Fiction guidelines and sample of published material for #10 SAE and 2 first class stamps.
Payment: 1 free contributor's copy; issue price charge for extras.
Terms: Acquires second serial rights. Sends galleys to author upon request. Publication copyrighted.
Advice: "We are looking for more controversial topics, psychological studies and humor." Mss are rejected because "they are poorly written, have inappropriate content and lack personal appeal. The new, lower-cost print technologies seem to be spawning more small presses. And many small presses are willing to work with beginning fiction writers. Write the story you'd like to read."

THE GAMUT (II), A Journal of Ideas and Information, Cleveland State University, 1216 Rhodes Tower, Cleveland OH 44115. (216)687-4679. Editor: Louis T. Milic. Managing Editor: Mary Grimm. Magazine: 7x10; 96 pages; 70 lb Patina Matte paper; Patina Matte cover stock; illustrations; photos. "*The Gamut* is a general-interest magazine that mainly publishes well-researched, interesting articles;

however, we like to publish one or two pieces of fiction per issue, if we find something suitable." For the college-educated audience. Triannually. Estab. 1980. Circ. 1,200.

Needs: Contemporary, experimental, feminist, humor/satire, literary, mainstream, prose poem, regional, translations, "Our only requirement is high quality fiction." No genre fiction, no fiction for specific age groups. Receives 50 unsolicited mss/month. Accepts 1-2 mss/issue; 4-6 mss/year. Publishes mss usually 3 months, certainly 1 year after acceptance. Reading fee "only when we have contest, then $5." Recently published work by Margot Livesey, Nancy Potter, John Gerlach; published new writers within the last year. Length: 3,000 words average; 1,000 words minimum; 6,000 words maximum. Often critiques rejected mss and recommends other markets.

How to Contact: Send complete ms with cover letter. Reports in 1 month on queries; 3 months on mss. SASE for ms. Simultaneous and photocopied submissions OK. Accepts computer printouts. Sample copy $2.50. Fiction guidelines for #10 SAE and 1 first class stamp.

Payment: Pays $25-$150, depending on length; contributor's copies; charges reduced rate for extras.

Terms: Pays on publication. Acquires first North American serial rights. publication copyrighted.

Advice: "We've been a little more actively looking for fiction. The best advice we have for writers who wish to be published in our magazine is that they should care about the quality of their writing. Further, we are interested in neither stale approaches to fictional situations nor avant-garde experiments that have lost touch with the purpose of literature."

GARGOYLE MAGAZINE (II), Paycock Press, Box 30906, Bethesda MD 20814. (301)656-5146. Co-Editors: Richard Peabody and Peggy Pfeiffer; London Editor: M. Maja Prausnitz % 72 Beaconsfield Rd., Seven Sisters, London N15 45J England. Magazine: 5½x8½; 480 pages; standard bulk paper; slick card cover stock; illustrations; photos. Estab. 1976. Publishes 2 times/year.

Needs: Contemporary, literary, experimental, humor/satire, prose poem, sports and translations. Recently published work by Joyce Renwick, Laurence Gonzales, Mary Kay Zuravleff; published new writers within the last year. "We like fiction in the 2-10 typed page range, but often publish much longer works. We generally print 3-6 stories per issue." Approximately 10% of fiction is agented. "We print 1 out of every 250 stories we read these days." Does not read in August. Critiques rejected ms when there is time. Sometimes recommends other markets.

How to Contact: Submit complete ms with SASE. Photocopied submissions OK. Accepts computer printout submissions. Prefers letter-quality. Reports in 1-2 months on mss. Publishes ms 6-12 months after acceptance. Sample copy for $7.95.

Payment: Free author's copy. Half the cover price for extras.

Terms: Publication copyrighted.

Advice: "Small magazines are deluged with mss. Writers should keep in mind that rejection doesn't mean that the story is bad, only that the magazine editor doesn't want to, or can't, use it. Writers have to learn to endure. Writers should always be familiar with the market. This means reading all the short stories/fiction you can get your hands on. It is also important to keep up with movements in the contemporary fiction. We're interested in printing excerpts from unpublished novels. We're consciously seeking out the new young writers (20-30 years old and younger)."

THE GARLAND, Loyola College, 4501 N. Charles St., Baltimore MD 21210. (301)323-1010. Editor: Sandy Moser. Magazine of poetry, short fiction, photography and drawing for the college community. Quarterly. Estab. 1972. Circ. 1,500.

Needs: Contemporary, fantasy, humor/satire. Receives 50 unsolicited fiction mss/month. Accepts 4 mss/issue, 10 mss/year. Approximately 20% of fiction is agented. Length: 900 words minimum; 3,000 words maximum; 2,100 words average.

How to Contact: Send complete ms with SASE. Simultaneous submissions OK. Reports in 1 month on ms. Publishes ms an average of 1-3 months after acceptance. Sample copy $1 and SAE.

Payment: 1 free contributor's copy.

Terms: Acquires all rights.

Advice: "The organization has undergone drastic format changes. We are now commercial; that is, we sell space for commercial advertising. Eventually, we would like to pay a fee for all contributions, even if the fee is nominal."

‡GARM LU (II, IV), A Canadian Celtic Arts Journal, St. Michael's College, University of Toronto, 81 St. Mary St., Toronto Ontario M5S 1J4 Canada. (416)926-1300 (Celtic Studies Dept.). Editor: Linda Revie. Fiction Editors: Linda Revie and Mary MacDonald. Magazine: 140mmx215mm; 60 pages; bond paper; almost cardboard cover; illustrations. "A register of the concerns and interests of those involved in Celtic studies." Semiannually. Estab. 1986. Circ. 400.

Needs: Adventure, condensed novel, confession, contemporary, erotica, ethnic, feminist, gay, historical, humor/satire, lesbian, literary, regional, religious/inspirational, serialized/excerpted novel, translations, Celtic. Receives 4 unsolicited mss/month. Buys 1 or 2 mss/issue; 3 or 4 mss/year. Length: 1,000

words preferred; 250 words minimum; 2,500 words maximum. Sometimes critiques rejected mss.
How to Contact: Query with clips of published work or send complete ms with cover letter. Reports in 2 weeks on queries; 3 weeks on mss. SASE. Simultaneous, photocopied and reprint submissions OK. Accepts computer printouts, including dot-matrix. Sample copy for $3 (American).
Payment: Free contributor's copy; charge for extras.
Terms: Acquires all rights. Publication copyrighted. "In future, we will be having contests that will be worth about $20 (Canadian)."
Advice: "Read it over 100 times and edit it 100 times."

GAS (I, II, IV), The Newsletter That's Not A Newsletter, For The Nonexistent Gross Americans' Society, Box 397, Marina CA 93933. (408)384-2768. Editor: Jeannette M. Hopper. Magazine: digest size; 20-50 pages; 20 lb paper; non-gloss heavy cover; pen-and-ink illustrations; photos if screened. "*Gas* is dedicated to the fine art of the gross-out; accepts humorous horror, horrible humor and blends of those genres, with an emphasis on short-short horror fiction." For "people mature enough to see that this is all strictly for fun and entertainment, and not an attempt to make any real social statement." Quarterly. Estab. 1986. Circ. 250.
Needs: Adventure, confession, contemporary, erotica, experimental, fantasy, horror, humor/satire, mainstream, prose poem, psychic/supernatural/occult, science fiction, suspense/mystery, gross humor/horror. "All fiction must have some aspect of grossness, but story is of utmost importance. Characters must be someone the reader can identify with (no utterly detestable creeps as protagonists). No scatalogical or cannibal-related stories. No hard pornography. No children placed in sexual situations. No politics, racism, religion or heavy dogma." Receives 50 unsolicited mss/month. Buys 5-10 mss/issue; 40 mss/year at most. Publishes ms 1-6 months after acceptance. Recently published work by J.N. Williamson, Bruce Boston, Cheryl Sayre; published new writers within the last year. Length: 1,500 words maximum. Publishes short shorts; 100-1,000 words. Sometimes critiques rejected mss and recommends other markets.
How to Contact: Send complete ms with cover letter, which should include brief introduction of author; previous publications. Reports in 1 week on queries; 1-2 weeks on mss. SASE. Simultaneous, photocopied and reprint (5 years after publication) submissions OK. Accepts computer printout submissions, including dot-matrix. Sample copy for $3.50. Fiction guidelines for #10 SAE and 1 first class stamp.
Payment: Pays 1/4¢/word with a $2 minimum, contributor's copies, charge for extras.
Terms: Pays on publication for one-time rights. Publication copyrighted. Occasional contests announced in magazine.
Advice: "Now concentrating more on humorous *horror*, whereas we were open to almost anything sick and funny in the past. Now the emphasis will be upon the frightening and bizarre, rather than just 'funny stuff.' I receive too many submissions from people who never should have passed English proficiency exams; spelling is terrible, punctuation is a mystery, grammar is pathetic. Master your basic tools, and that means master English. Also, read, read, read to get the feel of how the pros do it."

‡GATEWAYS (I), Rt. 10, Box 52, McKinney TX 75069. (214)548-8307. Editor: Daniel Meyer. Magazine: 8½x11; 40-80 pages; newsprint paper; 40 lb mill cover; many illustrations; some photos. "We publish anything related to science fiction or fantasy, primarily artwork and stories, for an 18-up audience." Plans special fiction issue. Estab. 1988. Circ. 500.
Needs: Adventure, erotica, experimental, fantasy, horror, science fiction, serialized novel. No westerns, straight romance, drug related. Receives 1-4 unsolicited fiction mss/month; accepts 4-15 mss/issue. Publishes ms approx. 6 months after acceptance. Recently published work by Vance Garrett, Kelli Wakefield and Jan Owens. Length: 100 words minimum; 10,000 words maximum. Sometimes comments on rejected mss and recommends other markets.
How to Contact: Send complete ms with cover letter, which should include "name, address, previous published work. Cover letter not necessary." Reports on queries in 2 months; on mss in 1 month. SASE for queries; not needed for mss. Simultaneous and photocopied submissions OK. Accepts dot-matrix computer printouts and electronic submissions, "Wordstar data only." Sample copy $3. Fiction guidelines for #10 SAE and 1 first class stamp.
Payment: Pays in contributor's copies.
Terms: Acquires one-time rights. Publication copyrighted.
Advice: "A lot of fiction I have seen lately has had excellent ideas or plots, but the author has not proofread his/her work. Please check spelling and punctuation. Do not be put off by the delays sometimes associated with small magazines; many times the editors are working with very tight budgets."

EL GATO TUERTO (II, IV), Box 210277, San Francisco CA 94121. (415)752-0473. Editor: Carlota Caulfield. Tabloid: 11x17; 16 pages; illustrations; photos. "We welcome works dealing with Spanish, Latin American and Caribbean literatures, but we are open to any kind of fiction, poetry or literary es-

says as well. We publish in Spanish and English." Quarterly. Estab. 1984. Circ. 3,000.
Needs: Adventure, confession, contemporary, ethnic, fantasy, feminist, prose poem, science fiction, suspense/mystery, translations. "Spanish, Latin American and Caribbean fiction." No horror. Receives 3-7 unsolicited mss/month. Accepts 2-3 mss/issue; 10 mss/year. Does not read mss December-January. Publishes ms 2-6 months after acceptance. Recently published work by Calvert Casey, Enrique Labrador Ruiz, Rima de Vallbona; published new writers within the last year. Length: 5-7 pages. Publishes short shorts. Length: 2 pages.
How to Contact: Query first. Reports in 3 weeks on queries; 5-7 weeks on mss. SASE. Photocopied submissions OK. Accepts computer printout submissions. Sample copy for $2 and 13x10 SAE with 56¢ postage.
Payment: Pays in contributor's copies.
Terms: Pays on publication. Publication not copyrighted.
Advice: "Inquire first about the magazine to see if your work is appropriate for the publication's format."

GAY CHICAGO MAGAZINE (II), Ultra Ink, Inc. 3121 N. Broadway, Chicago IL 60657-4522. (312)327-7271. Editor: Dan Dileo. Magazine: 8½x11; 80-144 pages; newsprint paper and cover stock; illustrations; photos. Entertainment guide, information for the gay community.
Needs: Erotica (but no explicit hard core), lesbian, gay and romance. Receives "a few" unsolicited mss/month. Accepts 10-15 ms/year. Published new writers within the last year. Length: 1,000-3,000 words maximum.
How to Contact: Send complete ms with SASE. Photocopied submissions OK. Accepts computer printout submissions. Accepts disk submissions compatible with Merganthaler Crtronic 200. Must have hard copy with disk submissions. Reports in 4-6 weeks on mss. Free sample copy for 9x12 SAE and $1.45 postage.
Payment: Minimal. 5-10 free contributor's copies; no charge for extras "if within reason."
Terms: Acquires one-time rights.
Advice: "I use fiction on a space-available basis, but plan to use more during the coming year because we have doubled our format size to 8½x11."

GENERATION (I,II), The Student Magazine, Sub-board I, Inc., SUNY at Buffalo, Harriman Hall, Box G, Buffalo NY 14214. (716)831-2249. Editor: Sean O'Sullivan. Magazine: 8½x11; 40 pages; 32 lb newsprint; glossy 50 lb cover; illustrations; photographs. "Weekly feature magazine published by students of the University of New York at Buffalo. All types of feature writing pertaining to campus issues, regional and national news, entertainment, investigative stories and humor. Weekly fiction and/or poetry pages." Readers include students, faculty and staff of SUNYAB and the surounding community. Plans special fiction issue. Estab. 1984. Circ. 12,000.
Needs: Adventure, contemporary, experimental, fantasy, feminist, historical (general), horror, humor/satire, literary, mainstream, psychic/supernatural/occult, science fiction, suspense/mystery, western. Receives 12 unsolicited fiction mss/month. Accepts 1 ms/issue; 24-48 mss/year. "We do not publish during the summer or over winter break." Length: 1,200-1,500 words average; 500 words minimum; 2,000 words maximum. Publishes short shorts. Occasionally critiques rejected mss.
How to Contact: Send complete ms with cover letter, which should include the story length and name of college attended by writer. Reports in 4-5 weeks. SASE. Accepts computer printout submissions, including dot-matrix. Sample copy for 10x13 SAE and 79¢ postage.
Payment: Pays in contributor's copies.
Terms: Publication copyrighted.
Advice: "Write about issues that affect college-aged people. We try to give the students of UB a little of everything—humor, fiction, investigative journalism, entertainment, etc."

THE GEORGIA REVIEW (II,III), The University of Georgia, Athens GA 30602. (404)542-3481. Editor-in-Chief: Stanley W. Lindberg. Associate Editor: Stephen Corey. Journal: 7x10; 216 pages (average); 50 lb woven old style paper; 80 lb cover stock; illustrations; photos. "*The Georgia Review*, winner of the 1986 National Magazine Award in Fiction, is a journal of arts and letters, featuring a blend of the best in contemporary thought and literature—essays, fiction, poetry, graphics and book reviews—for the intelligent nonspecialist as well as the specialist reader. We seek material that appeals across disciplinary lines by drawing from a wide range of interests." Quarterly. Estab. 1947. Circ. 5,300.
Needs: Experimental and literary. "We're looking for the highest quality fiction—work that is capable of sustaining subsequent readings, not throw-away pulp magazine entertainment. Nothing that fits too easily into a 'category,' e.g. adventure, erotica, ethnic, lesbian, gay, horror, psychic, religious, romance, etc." Receives about 300 unsoliicted fiction mss/month. Buys 3-4 mss/issue; 12-15 mss/year. Does not read ms in June, July or August. Recently published work by Lee K. Abbott, Jack Driscoll,

Diana Reed; published new writers within the last year. Length: open. Occasionally critiques rejected mss.

How to Contact: Send complete ms with SASE. Photocopied submissions OK; no multiple submissions. Accepts computer printout submissions. Prefers letter-quality. Reports in 2 months. Sample copy $4; free guidelines for #10 SAE with 1 first class stamp.

Payment: Minimum: $25/printed page; 1 year complimentary subscription; 1 contributor's copy, reduced charge for extra.

Terms: Pays on publication for first North American serial rights. Sends galleys to author. Publication copyrighted.

Advice: "Obviously the best way to become acquainted with any journal is to look at its recent issues."

‡THE GETTYSBURG REVIEW (II), Gettysburg College, Gettysburg PA 17325. (717)337-6770. Editor: Peter Stitt. Assistant Editor: Frank Graziano. Magazine: 6¾x10; approx. 200 pages; acid free paper; full color illustrations and photos. "Quality of writing is our only criterion; we publish fiction, poetry and essays." Quarterly. Estab. 1988. Circ. 1,500.

Needs: Contemporary, experimental, historical(general), humor/satire, literary, mainstream, regional and serialized novel. "We require that fiction be intelligent, and intelligently and aesthetically written." Receives approx. 25 mss/month. Buys approx. 4-6 mss/issue; 16-24 mss/year. Publishes ms within 3-6 months of acceptance. Recently published work by Frederick Busch, Ed Minus and Gloria Whelan. Length: 3,000 words average; 1,000 words minimum; 20,000 words maximum. Publishes short shorts. Sometimes critiques rejected mss.

How to Contact: Send complete mss with cover letter, which should include "education, credits." Reports in 3 months. SASE. Photocopied submissions OK. Accepts computer printout submissions, including dot-matrix.

Payment: Pays $20/printed page plus free subscription to magazine, contributor's copy. Charge for extra copies.

Terms: Pays on publication for first North American serial rights. Publication copyrighted.

Advice: "Be a good writer; send a carefully prepared manuscript. Always enclose a SASE. Be patient. Reporting time can take three months. It is helpful to look at a sample copy of *The Gettysburg Review* to see what kinds of fiction we publish before submitting."

THE GINGERBREAD DIARY (I, IV), Alternative Lifestyles in Interracial Love, Box 3333, New York NY 10185. (212)904-0512. Editor: Gary David. Fiction Editors: Gary David, Julie David. Magazine: 8½x11; 40-50 pages; bond paper; color Xerox paper cover; illustrations; photos. "We feature essays, stories, poems on the theme of interracial love and relating, as well as material embracing other 'human interest' topics, basically for those who are involved in, or who have thought about, interracial relationships; also those who are the products of interracial unions." Published 5 times/year. Plans special fiction issue. Estab. 1986. Circ. 50.

Needs: Erotica, ethnic, experimental, fantasy, gay, historical (general), humor/satire, lesbian, literary, mainstream, prose poem, spiritual, regional, romance (contemporary, historical, young adult). "As noted above, we accept for consideration material dealing with a broad range of subjects; bear in mind that we do not restrict ourselves to black/white issues, but include all other 'races' as well, the object being, of course, to illuminate the emotional and intellectual interplay between people of different racial and cultural backgrounds within the context of their relationship." Accepts 1-2 mss/issue; 8-9 mss/year. Publishes ms "2 issues hence" after acceptance. Length: 4,000 words average; 550 words minimum; 5,000 words maximum. Publishes short shorts. Sometimes critiques rejected mss and recommends other markets.

How to Contact: Send complete ms with cover letter, which should include "some personal information about the author, a brief genesis of his/her work and why the author chose us." Reports in 3-4 weeks on queries; 1-2 months on mss. SASE for ms, not needed for query. Simultaneous and photocopied submissions OK. Accepts computer printout submissions, no dot-matrix. Sample copy for $1.50. Fiction guidelines for #10 SAE and 1 first class stamp.

Payment: Pays in contributor's copies, charges for extras.

Terms: Acquires all rights. Publication copyrighted.

Advice: "Anyone interested in being published in the *Diary* would have to keep in mind that we are a new enterprise and, as such, are testing the waters of 'special-interest' literature in the hopes of building a readership of open-minded and intelligent people. Translation: You won't get rich and famous with us, if that is your aim. But . . . if you have a good imagination and are willing to tackle subject matter 'beyond your ken' (as interracial loving will most likely be) then we will be more than happy to consider your work. We like to think of ourselves as one of the few publications willing to take a chance on raw, undiscovered talent."

THE GLENS FALLS REVIEW (II), Loft Press, 42 Sherman Ave., Glens Falls NY 12801. (518)798-8110. Editor: Jean Rikhoff. Magazine: 8½x11; 48 pages; 30 lb paper; 60 lb cover; photos. Estab. 1981. Annually.
Needs: Contemporary fiction, prose poem, poetry, literary articles, some regional materials. Recently published work by William Kennedy, William Brock; published new writers within the last year.
How to Contact: Send complete ms with cover letter. SASE for ms. Reads from January 1 through April 15. Accepts computer printout submissions, including dot-matrix. Sample copy for $5.
Advice: "Interested in *any* type of good writing."

GOLDEN ISIS MAGAZINE (I, IV), Box 726, Salem MA 01970. Editor: Gerina Dunwich. Magazine: digest size; approx. 30-40 pages; 20 lb stock; paper cover; illustrations. "*Golden Isis* is a mystical neo-pagan literary magazine of occult fiction, Goddess-inspired poetry, artwork, Wiccan news, letters, occasional book reviews and classified ads." Quarterly. Estab. 1980. Circ. 4,000.
Needs: Psychic/supernatural/occult, bizarre fantasy and mystical Egyptian themes. "Please do not send us pornographic, religious, racist or sexist material. We will not consider stories written in present tense." Receives 40+ mss/month. Buys 2 mss/issue; 8 mss/year. Recently published fiction by Rod R. Vick, Cary G. Osborne and Gypsy Electra. Published many new writers within the last year. Length: 2,000 words maximum. Publishes short shorts. Occasionally critiques rejected mss and often recommends other markets.
How to Contact: Send complete ms with cover letter. Reports in 2 weeks. SASE. Simultaneous, photocopied and reprint submissions OK. Accepts computer printout submissions, including dot-matrix. Sample copy for $2.95. Fiction guidelines for #10 SAE and 1 first class stamp.
Payment: Payment varies from 1 free contributor's copy to $5.
Terms: Pays on publication for first North American serial rights. Publication copyrighted.
Advice: "Submit short fiction that is well-written, atmospheric and equipped with a good surprise ending. Originality is important. Quality writing is a must. Avoid clichés, poor grammar, predictable endings, unnecessary obscenity and run-on sentences, for these things will only bring you a fast rejection slip."

THE GOOFUS OFFICE GAZETTE (I), Box 259, Pearl River NY 10965. Editor: Samuel T. Godfrey. Newsletter: 8½x11; 8-12 pages; Xerographic paper and cover; illustrations; photos. "We print mostly humorous short stories, articles concerning music and the arts, silly poetry, tongue twisters, games, trivia and fictitious news (or humorous reality). Specifically we cater to those with the ability to read printed matter. All others are welcome to just come and watch or provide input." Plans special fiction issue. Estab. 1983. Circ. 300.
Needs: Humor/satire, anti-television, prose poem. "We prefer short, clever, light-hearted humor in reasonably good taste. Shaggy dog stories and folklore are needed. The feeling is always happy and foolish, good clean fun, balderdash, etc." No violence. No profanity for profanity's sake. No hurtful or distasteful remarks. No heavy, pointed satire. Receives 2 fiction mss/month; accepts at least 2 or 3 unsolicited mss/issue. Accepts "countless" fiction mss/year. Publishes ms "next issue unless special interest." Charges reading fee of $1 per 10,000 words. Recently published work by Rex Kusler, Darren O. Godfrey, Janet McCann; published new writers within the last year. Length: 500 words average; 3 words minimum; 1,000 words maximum. Comments on rejected mss. Recommends other markets.
How to Contact: Send complete ms with cover letter and return address, minor biography. "A knowledge of writer's goal is helpful to determine a common relationship between writer/publisher/reader." Reports in 2 weeks on queries; 1 month on mss. Simultaneous, photocopied and reprint submissions OK. Accepts computer printouts including dot-matrix. Sample copy $1 and #10 SAE with 39¢ postage. Fiction guidelines $1 and #10 SAE with 39¢ postage.
Payment: Free subscription to magazine; contributor's copies.
Advice: "Due to economical troubles, it becomes difficult to get a pressworthy publication in the reader's hands. Competition invades the office. Strive for a more comfortable, secure and prosperous full-time job than I have to secure a more solid position in your endeavors."

GRAIN (I, II), Saskatchewan Writers' Guild, Box 1154, Regina, Saskatchewan S4P 3B4 Canada. Editor: Mick Burrs. Fiction Editor: Byrna Barclay. Literary magazine: 8½x5½; 80 pages; Chinook offset printing; chrome-coated stock; illustrations; photos sometimes. "Fiction and poetry for people who enjoy high quality writing." Quarterly. Estab. 1973. Circ. 600-800.
Needs: Contemporary, experimental, literary, mainstream and prose poem. "No propaganda—only artistic/literary writing." No mss "that stay *within* the limits of conventions such as women's magazine type stories, science fiction; none that push a message." Receives 40-60 unsolicited fiction mss/month. Buys 4-7 mss/issue; 16-28 mss/year. Approximately 1% of fiction agented. Recently published work by Dianne Warren, Fred Stenson, Leon Rooke. Published new writers within the last year. Length: "no more than 20 pages." Occasionally critiques rejected mss.

How to Contact: Send complete ms with SAE, IRC and brief of one-two sentences. "Let us know if you're just beginning to send out." Reports in 3-6 months on mss. Publishes ms an average of 4 months after acceptance. Sample copy $4.

Payment: $35-$100; 2 free contributor's copies.

Terms: Pays on publication for one-time rights. "We expect acknowledgment if the piece is re-published elsewhere."

Advice: "Submit a story to us that will deepen the imaginative experience of our readers. *Grain* has established itself as a first-class magazine of serious fiction. We receive submissions from around the world. Canada is a foreign country, so we ask that you *do not* enclose US postage stamps on your return envelope. If you live outside Canada and neglect the International Reply Coupons, we *will not* read nor reply to your submission."

GREEN MOUNTAINS REVIEW (II), Johnson State College, Box A-58, Johnson VT 05656. (802)635-2356, ext. 339. Editor: Neil Shepard. Editor: Tony Whedon. Magazine: digest size; 90-100 pages. "*GMR*'s emphasis is on quality writing. Each issue features an essay, works of fiction or suite of poems that explores an aspect of New England life." Semiannually. Estab. 1987. Circ. 1,000.

Needs: Adventure, contemporary, experimental, humor/satire, literary, mainstream, regional (New England), serialized/excerpted novel, translations. Receives 20 unsolicited mss/month. Accepts 5 mss/issue; 10 mss/year. Publishes ms 1-2 months after acceptance. Length: 25 pages maximum. Publishes short shorts. Sometimes critiques rejected mss.

How to Contact: Send complete ms with cover letter. Reports in 1 month on queries; 2 months on mss. SASE. Simultaneous and photocopied submissions OK. Accepts computer printout submissions; no dot-matrix. Sample copy for $3.

Payment: Pays in contributor's copies.

Terms: Acquires first North American serial rights. Sends galleys to author upon request. Publication copyrighted.

GREEN'S MAGAZINE (II), Fiction for the Family, Green's Educational Publications, Box 3236, Regina, Saskatchewan S4P 3H1 Canada. Editor: David Green. Magazine: 5¼x8; 100 pages; 20 lb bond paper; matte cover stock; line illustrations. Publishes "solid short fiction suitable for family reading." Quarterly. Plans special fiction issue. Estab. 1972.

Needs: Adventure, fantasy, humor/satire, literary, mainstream, science fiction and suspense/mystery. No erotic or sexually explicit fiction. Receives 15-20 mss/month. Buys 10-12 mss/issue; 40-50 mss/year. Publishes ms within 3-6 months of acceptance. Agented fiction 2%. Recently published work by Solomon Pogarsky, Marion McGuire, Marsh Cassady. Length: 2,500 words preferred; 2,500 words minimum; 4,000 words maximum. Sometimes critiques rejected mss and recommends other markets.

How to Contact: Send complete ms. "Cover letters welcome but not necessary." Reports on mss in 8 weeks. SASE. "Must include international reply coupons." Photocopied submissions OK. Accepts computer printout submissions, including dot-matrix. Sample copy $4. Fiction guidelines free for #10 SAE and international reply coupon.

Payment: Pays in contributor's copies.

Terms: Acquires first North American serial rights. Publication copyrighted.

Advice: "Write, experiment, polish, have confidence."

GREENSBORO REVIEW (II), University of North Carolina at Greensboro, Dept. of English, Greensboro NC 27412. (919)379-5459. Editor: Jim Clark. Fiction Editor: Tom McGohey. Magazine: 6x9; approximately 120 pages; 60 lb paper; 65 lb cover. Literary magazine featuring fiction and poetry for readers interested in contemporary literature. Semiannually. Circ. 500.

Needs: Contemporary and experimental. Accepts 4-8 mss/issue, 8-16 mss/year. Recently published work by Julia Alvarez, Larry Brown and Suzanne Brown; published new writers within the last year. Length: 7,500 words maximum.

How to Contact: Send complete ms with SASE. Unsolicited manuscripts must arrive by September 15 to be considered for the winter issue and by February 15 to be considered for the summer issue. Manuscripts arriving after those dates may be held for the next consideration. Photocopied submissions OK. Sample copy for $2.50.

Payment: Pays in contributor's copies.

Terms: Acquires first North American serial rights. Publication copyrighted.

Advice: "We want to see the best being written regardless of theme, subject or style."

GROUNDSWELL, A Literary Review (II), The Guild Press/Hudson Valley Writers Guild, 19 Clinton Ave., Albany NY 12207. (518)449-8069. Editor: Kristen Murray. Fiction Editor: F.R. Lewis. Magazine: 5½x8½; 100 pages; 70 lb paper; occasional line drawings/graphics. "Variable themes; fiction, poetry reviews of small press publications, critical essays, focus on prominent writer with work (new) by focused-on writer. Semiannually. Estab. 1984.

Needs: Contemporary, ethnic, experimental, fantasy, feminist, gay, humor/satire, lesbian, literary, mainstream, regional, excerpted novel, suspense/mystery, translations. "We are open to any high quality, significant, honest fictions." No formula stories; stories that are racist, sexist; stories that ignore craft and clarity. Accepts up to 5 mss/issue; 4-10 mss/year. Recently published work by Elizabeth Adams, Ruth Tarsen; published new writers within the last year. Length: 10,000 words maximum. Publishes short shorts. Length 1-6 pages. Sometimes critiques rejected ms.

How to Contact: Send complete ms with brief bio note. "We want something that can be used as a contributor's note if the story is accepted." Reports in 3 months (varies). SASE. Photocopied submissions OK. Accepts computer printout submissions, no dot-matrix. Sample copy $6 and 6x9 SAE with 6 first class stamps.

Payment: 2 contributor's copies; other payment depends on funding.

Terms: Pays on publication for first North American serial rights. Publication in process of being copyrighted.

Advice: "Read the magazine in which you want to publish. Polish your work. Please, please—no onion skin, no dot matrix. Send work that looks like you are proud to be sending it. Before being concerned about *where* you're going to publish it, pay attention to writing well and courageously."

GRUE MAGAZINE (II, IV), Hell's Kitchen Productions, Box 370, New York NY 10108. Editor: Peggy Nadramia. Magazine: 5½x8½; 88 pages; 60 lb paper; 10 pt. CIS film laminate cover; illustrations; photos. "Quality short fiction centered on horror and dark fantasy—new traditions in the realms of the gothic and the macabre for horror fans well read in the genre, looking for something new and different, as well as horror novices looking for a good scare." Published 3 times/year. Estab. 1985.

Needs: Horror, psychic/supernatural/occult. Receives 150 unsolicited fiction mss/month. Accepts 8 mss/issue; 25-30 mss/year. Publishes ms 1 year after acceptance. Recently published work by Thomas Ligotti, Joe R. Lansdale, Don Webb; published new writers within the last year. Length: 2,500 words average; 6,500 words maximum. Publishes short shorts of 400 words (1 printed page). Sometimes critiques rejected ms and recommends other markets.

How to Contact: Send complete ms with cover letter. "I like to hear where the writer heard about *Grue*, his most recent or prestigious sales, and maybe a word or two about himself." Reports in 3 weeks on queries; 2 months on mss. SASE for ms. Photocopied submissions OK. Accepts computer printouts including dot-matrix. Accepts electronic submissions via disk. "I can read a document formatted for the Commodore 64-Paperclip word processing program." Sample copy $4. Fiction guidelines for #10 SAE and 1 first class stamp.

Payment: Pays in 2 contributor's copies plus ½¢ cent per word.

Terms: Pays on publication. Acquires first North American serial rights. Publication copyrighted.

Advice: "Editors actually vie for the work of the better writers, and if your work is good, you will sell it—you just have to keep sending it out. But out of the 150 mss I read in September, maybe three of them will be by writers who cared enough to make their plots as interesting as possible, their characterizations believable, their settings unique, and who took the time to do the rewrites and polish their prose. Remember that readers of *Grue* are mainly seasoned horror fans, and *not* interested or excited by a straight vampire, werewolf or ghost story—they'll see all the signs, and guess where you're going long before you get there. Throw a new angle on what you're doing; put it in a new light. How? Well, what scares *you*? What's *your* personal phobia or anxiety? When the writer is genuinely, emotionally involved with his subject matter, and is totally honest with himself and his reader, then we can't help being involved, too, and that's where good writing begins and ends."

‡HARVEST MAGAZINE (I,II,IV), The Reader's Hearth, 2322 Latona Dr. NE, Salem OR 97303. Managing Editors: William Michaelian and Jan Thomas Collins. Magazine: 8½x11; 24-32 pages; 60 lb sonoma gloss paper; self-cover stock; illustrations; photos. Publishes "work by people 50 and over that is illustrative of their discoveries in life." Bimonthly. Estab. 1988. Circ. 3,000.

Needs: Adventure, condensed/excerpted novel, ethnic, historical (general), humor/satire, literary, prose poem and senior citizen/retirement. Writers should be age 50 or older. Receives 20 mss/month. Accepts 6-8 mss/issue. Publishes accepted mss within 2-4 months of acceptance. Length: 2,000 words average; 200 words minimum; 7,000 words maximum. Sometimes critiques rejected mss and recommends other markets.

How to Contact: Send complete mss with cover letter. Reports on queries in 3-5 weeks; on mss in 4-6 weeks. SASE. Photocopied and reprint submissions OK. Accepts computer printout submissions, including dot-matrix. Sample copy for $2.

Payment: Pays in contributor's copies.

Terms: Acquires one-time rights. Sometimes sends galleys to author. Publication copyrighted.

Advice: "Say what you have to say in an authentic voice, both with high expectations of your reader and the result you will achieve on the page. We want to hear from you, not from an imitation of someone else."

HAUNTS (II), Tales of Unexpected Horror and the Supernatural, Nightshade Publications, Box 3342, Providence RI 02906. (401)781-9438. Editor: Joseph K. Cherkes. Magazine: 5½x8½; 80-100 pages; 50 lb offset paper; krome-kote cover stock; pen and ink illustrations. "We are committed to publishing only the finest fiction in the genres of horror, fantasy and the supernatural from both semi-pro and established writers. We are targeted towards the 18-35 age bracket interested in tales of horror and the unknown." Quarterly. Plans special fiction issue. Estab. 1984. Circ. 1,000.
Needs: Fantasy, horror, psychic/supernatural/occult. No pure adventure, explicit sex, or blow-by-blow dismemberment. Receives 100-150 unsolicited fiction mss/month. Accepts 10-12 mss/issue; 50-75 mss/year. Publishes ms 6-9 months after acceptance. Recently published work by Mike Hurley, Kevin J. Anderson, Sharon Brondos. Published new writers within the last year. Length: 3,500 words average; 1,000 words minimum; 10,000 words maximum. Publishes short shorts of not less than 500 words. Critiques rejected mss. Recommends other markets. Market open June 1 to December 1, inclusive.
How to Contact: Query first. "cover letters are a nice way to introduce oneself to a new editor." Reports in 2-3 weeks on queries; 2-3 months on mss. SASE for query. Photocopied submissions OK. Accepts computer printouts including dot-matrix, NLQ mode only. Sample copy $3.25 postpaid. Fiction guidelines for #10 SASE.
Payment: Pays $5-$50 (subject to change). Contributor's copies, charge for extras.
Terms: Pays on publication. Acquires first North American serial rights. Publication copyrighted.
Advice: "Follow writers' guidelines closely. They are a good outline of what your publisher looks for in fiction. If you think you've got the 'perfect' manuscript, go over it again—carefully. Check to make sure you've left no loose ends before sending it out. Keep your writing concise. If your story is rejected, don't give up. Try to see where the story failed. This way you can learn from your mistakes. Remember, success comes to those who persist. We plan to open to advertising on a limited basis, also plan a media campaign to increase subscriptions and distributed sales."

HAWAII PACIFIC REVIEW (II), Hawaii Pacific College, 1060 Bishop St., Honolulu HI 96813. (808)544-0259. Editor: Frederick Hohing. Magazine: 6x9; 100-150 pages; quality paper; glossy cover; illustrations and photos. "As a literary magazine located in Hawaii, we are interested in material that concerns or is set in the Pacific Rim and Asia. Categories: fiction, poetry, essays and scholarly writing." Annually. Estab. "nationwide in 1988."
Needs: Adventure, contemporary, ethnic, experimental, fantasy, humor/satire, literary, mainstream, regional, science fiction, suspense/mystery, translations. No romance, confessions, religious or juvenile. Receives approx. 25 unsolicited fiction mss/month. Accepts 4-8 mss/issue. Deadline for the Spring annual issue is January 1. Does not read in summer. Publishes ms 3-12 months after acceptance. Recently published work by Ruth Shigezawa, Marilyn Shoemaker, Susan B. Weston; published new writers within the last year. Length: 500 words minimum; 4,000 words maximum. Publishes short shorts. Sometimes critiques rejected mss or recommends other markets.
How to Contact: Send complete manuscript with cover letter, which should include a brief bio. Reports in 3 months. SASE. Simultaneous and photocopied submissions OK. Accepts computer printouts, no dot-matrix. Fiction guidelines for #10 SAE and 1 first class stamp.
Payment: Pays in contributor's copies.
Terms: Acquires first North American serial rights. Publication copyrighted. "A fiction contest is in the planning stages."
Advice: "A beginning writer should take pride in his work. Professional appearance of the manuscript, therefore, is a must."

HAWAII REVIEW (II), University of Hawaii Board of Publications, 1733 Donaghho Rd., Co-English Dept., Honolulu HI 96822. (808)948-8548. Editor: Jeannie Thompson. Fiction Editor: Barbara Gearen. Magazine: 6½x9½; 100-150 pages; illustrations; photos. "We publish short stories as well as poetry and reviews by new and experienced writers. Although the *Review* reflects the concerns of writers and artists of Hawaii and the Pacific, its interests are by no means exclusively regional." For residents of Hawaii and non-residents from the continental US and abroad. Semiannually. Plans special fiction issue. Estab. 1972. Circ. 2,000.
Needs: Contemporary, ethnic, experimental, horror, humor/satire, literary, prose poem, regional and translations. Receives 5-15 mss/month. Accepts no more than 5 mss/issue; 9 mss/year. Recently published work by William Pitt Root and Ian Macmillan; published new writers within the last year. Length: 4,000 words average; 1,000 words minimum; 8,000 words maximum. Occasionally critiques mss. Recommends other markets.
How to Contact: Send complete manuscript with SASE. Reports in 1-3 months on mss. Photocopied submissions OK. Accepts computer printout submissions, no dot-matrix. Sample copy for $3. Fiction guidelines free.
Payment: "Varies depending upon funds budgeted. Last year, we paid $35-$70 per story." 2 contributor's copies.

Terms: Pays on publication for all rights. Sends galleys to author upon request. Publication copyrighted. After publication, copyright reverts to author upon request.

Advice: "Good fiction is a *pleasure* to read. Many of our readers and subscribers turn to a story *first*."

‡HEARTLAND JOURNAL (II,IV), by Older Writers for Readers of All Ages, 3100 Lake Mendota Dr., Madison WI 53705. (608)238-4781. Editor: Lenore M. Coberly. Magazine: 8½x11; 48 pages; four-color slick paper stock; drawings and b&w photographs. "Writers must be over 60 years old." Triannually. Estab. 1983. Circ. 3,000.

Needs: Adventure, contemporary, experimental, historical, humor/satire, juvenile (5-9 years), literary, mainstream, preschool (1-4 years), regional, senior citizen/retirement, suspense/mystery, translations. No religious, fantasy, sentimental. Receives 10-15 unsolicited fiction mss/month; accepts 3-4 mss/issue. Publishes ms up to 6 months after acceptance. Recently published work by Russell Feirall, Walter Chainski and Viola Breiby. Length: 100 words minimum; 4,000 words maximum. Sometimes critiques rejected mss and recommends other markets.

How to Contact: Send complete ms. Reports in 6 months. SASE. Accepts dot-matrix computer printouts "reluctantly." Sample copy for $5.

Payment: Pays in contributor's copies.

Terms: Acquires first rights. Publication copyrighted. "Annual prize; all published authors are included automatically when published."

Advice: "Looks for "interesting story, believable characters, engaging voice, easy flow."

HEAVEN BONE (IV), New Age Literary Arts, Heaven Bone Press, Box 486, Chester NY 10918. (914)469-9018. Editors: Steven Hirsch, Kirpal Gordon. Magazine: 8½x11; 49-78 pages; 20 lb standard paper; 70 lb card cover; computer clip art, graphics, photos scanned in tiff format. "New age, new consciousness, earth and nature, spiritual path. We use current reviews, essays on new age topics, creative stories and fantasy." Readers are "spiritual seekers, healers, those familiar with channeling, your average anguished person on a city street." Semiannually. Estab. 1987. Circ. 375-500.

Needs: Experimental, fantasy, psychic/supernatural/occult, regional, religious/inspirational, spiritual, new age. "No violent, thoughtless or exploitive fiction." Receives 100-200 unsolicited mss/month. Accepts 20-30 mss/issue; 60-120 mss/year. Publishes ms 2 weeks to 6 months after acceptance. Recently published work by Richard paul Schmonsees, Jonathan London, Lynn Cochran; published new writers within the last year. Length: 3,500 words average; 1,800 words minimum; 7,000 words maximum. Publishes short shorts. Sometimes critiques rejected mss and may recommend other markets.

How to Contact: Send complete ms with cover letter, which should include short bio of recent activities. Reports in 2 weeks on queries; 2 weeks-6 months on mss. SASE. Reprint submissions OK. Accepts computer printout submissions, including high quality dot-matrix. Accepts electronic submissions via "Apple Mac plus versions in Macwrite, Microsoft Word 1.50 or Writenow." Sample copy $4.50. Fiction guidelines for SASE.

Payment: Pays in contributor's copies; charges for extras.

Terms: Buys first North American serial rights. Sends galleys to author. Publication copyrighted.

Advice: "Not only am I encouraged, but I have been generally pleased with the quality of new age fiction as it comes directly from the heart of an expanding consciousness. More attention needs to be paid, however, to the science and art of language. Spontaneity can only follow form and discipline—not precede it. Be absolutely sure you can understand your own work from an objective point of view. Being impressively specific and economical in your choice of words takes time and study and practice. Be confident that when you have something valuable to say it will be said correctly (assuming you've done your homework), and all those with ears will not be able to help but listen. Always include SASE."

HELICON NINE (II), The Journal of Women's Arts & Letters, Box 22412, Kansas City MO 64113. (913)345-0802. Editor-in-Chief: Gloria Vando Hickok. Editor: Ann Slegman. Fiction Editor: Pinky Kase. Magazine: 7x10; 96 pages; illustrations; photos. "A celebration of women in the arts, past, present and future." Semiannually. Estab. 1979. Circ. 3,500.

Needs: Condensed novel, contemporary, ethnic, experimental, fantasy, historical (general), humor/satire, literary, prose poem, translations and adult. No "militant feminist tracts." Receives 50-100 unsolicited fiction mss/month. "No set limit" on number of mss published each year. Recently published work by James Dickey, Elizabeth Kray, Colette Inez; published new writers within in the last year. Sometimes recommends other markets.

How to Contact: Send complete ms with SASE. Simultaneous and photocopied submissions OK. Reports in 3 months on mss. Publishes ms an average of 6 months after acceptance. Sample copy $8.

Payment: 2 free contributor's copies and 1 year's subscription.

Terms: Acquires one-time rights. Publication copyrighted.

Advice: "We are somewhat overstocked. Might make inquiries before submitting."

HERESIES (IV), A Feminist Publication on Art & Politics, Box 1306, Canal St. Station, New York NY 10013. (212)227-2108. Magazine: 8½x11; 96 pages; non-coated paper; b&w illustrations and photos. "We are a feminist collective. Each issue is put together by a separate group of women which forms the editorial collective." Nationwide readership gathered from alternative bookshops and women's spaces. 3 times a year. Estab. 1977. Circ. 8,000.
Needs: Feminist and lesbian. Published new writers within the last year. Publishes stories up to 10 typed pages maximum.
How to Contact: Query. Reports in 1 month on queries. Free guidelines with SASE.
Payment: Small payment post publication and free author's copies.
Terms: Publication copyrighted.
Advice: "Check back issues for special themes and content. Since each issue has its own guidelines, be specific. We only accept manuscripts directed to special issues, which are noted in the back of each publication."

HIBISCUS MAGAZINE (II), Short Stories, Poetry and Art, Hibiscus Press, Box 22248, Sacramento CA 95822. Editor: Margaret Wensrich. Magazine: 8½x11; 24-28 pages; 50 lb paper; 1 ply vellum cover stock; pen-and-ink illustrations. Magazine of short stories, poetry and drawings. Estab. 1985. Published 3 times/year. Circ. 1,000-2,000.
Needs: Adventure, contemporary, fantasy, humor/satire, literary, mainstream, science fiction, suspense/mystery and western. Receives 500 unsolicited mss/month. Buys 3 mss/issue; 9 mss/year. Does not read mss in August or December. Published new writers within the last year. Length: 1,500-2,500 words average; 1,500 words minimum; 3,000 words maximum.
How to Contact: Send complete ms with SASE. Reports in 6-8 weeks on mss. Photocopied submissions OK. Accepts computer printout submissions; prefers letter-quality. Sample copy $3.50. Fiction guidelines with #10 SAE and 1 first class stamp.
Payment: $5-$25; 2 free copies.
Terms: Pays on acceptance for first rights. Publication copyrighted.
Advice: "We do not return many manuscripts because writers and poets are *not* including enough postage on SASE. We do not attempt to return mail without enough postage. International mail, especially from Canada, does not have sufficient postage for return of ms. Writers and poets need to go to the post office and have mail weighed and then put on correct postage."

HIGH PLAINS LITERARY REVIEW (II), 180 Adams Street, Suite 250, Denver CO 80206. (303)320-6828. Editor-in-Chief: Robert O. Greer, Jr. Fiction Editor: Clarence Major. Magazine: 6x9; 135 pages; 70 lb paper; heavy cover stock. "The *High Plains Literary Review* publishes high quality poetry, fiction, essays, book reviews and interviews. The publication is designed to bridge the gap between high-caliber academic quarterlies and successful commercial reviews." Triannually. Estab. 1986. Circ. 650.
Needs: Most pressing need: outstanding essays. Serious fiction, contemporary, humor/satire, literary, mainstream, regional. No true confessions, romance, pornographic, excessive violence. Receives approximately 80 unsolicited mss/month. Buys 4-6 mss/issue; 12-18 mss/year. Publishes ms usually 6 months after acceptance. Recently published work by Richard Currey, Joyce Carol Oates and Rita Dove; published new writers within the last year. Length: 4,200 words average; 1,500 words minimum; 8,000 words maximum; prefers 3,000-6,000 words. Occasionally critiques rejected mss. Sometimes recommends other markets.
How to Contact: Send complete ms with cover letter, which should include brief publishing history. Reports in 6 weeks. SASE. Simultaneous and photocopied submissions OK. Accepts computer printout submissions, including dot-matrix. Sample copy for $4.
Payment: Pays $5/page for prose and 2 contributor's copies.
Terms: Pays on publication for first North American serial rights. Publication copyrighted. "Copyright reverts to author upon publication." Sends copy-edited proofs to the author.
Advice: *"HPLR* publishes *quality* writing. Send us your very best material. We will read it carefully and either accept it promptly, recommend changes or return it promptly. Do not send fragmented work. It *may* help to read a sample copy before submitting. Don't be a workshop writer."

HILL AND HOLLER: Southern Appalachian Mountains, Seven Buffaloes Press, Box 249, Big Timber MT 59011. Editor: Art Cuelho. Magazine: 5½x8½; 80 pages; 70 lb offset paper; 80 lb cover stock; illustrations; photos rarely. "I use mostly rural Appalachian material: poems and stories. Some folklore and humor. I am interested in heritage, especially in connection with the farm." Annually. Published special fiction issue. Estab. 1983. Circ. 750.
Needs: Contemporary, ethnic, humor/satire, literary, regional, rural America farm. "I don't have any prejudices in style, but I don't like sentimental slant. Deep feelings in literature are fine, but they should be portrayed with tact and skill." Receives 10 unsolicited mss/month. Accepts 4-6 mss/issue. Publishes ms 6 months to a year after acceptance. Length: 2,000-3,000 words average. Also publishes short shorts

of 500-1,000 words.

How to Contact: Query first. Reports in 2 weeks on queries. SASE for query and ms. Accepts computer printouts including dot-matrix. Sample copy $4.75.

Payment: Pays in contributor's copies; charge for extras.

Terms: Acquires first North American serial rights "and permission to reprint if my press publishes a special anthology." Sends galleys to author sometimes. Publication copyrighted.

Advice: "In this Southern Appalachian rural series I can be optimistic about fiction. Appalachians are very responsive to their region's literature. I have taken work by beginners that had not been previously published. Be sure to send a double-spaced clean manuscript and SASE. I have the only rural press in North America; maybe even in the world. So perhaps we have a bond in common if your roots are rural."

HOB-NOB (I), 994 Nissley Rd., Lancaster PA 17601. Editor/Publisher: Mildred K. Henderson. Magazine: 8½x11; 64+ pages; 20 lb bond paper; 20 lb (or heavier) cover stock; b&w illustrations; few photos. "*Hob-Nob* is a small (one-person), amateur publication currently with a literary emphasis on original prose and poetry. This publication is directed toward amateur writers and poets, but many of them would like to be professional. For some, appearance in *Hob-Nob* is simply an opportunity to be published somewhere, while others possibly see it as a springboard to bigger and better things." Semi-annually. Estab. 1969. Circ. 300+.

Needs: Literary, adventure, contemporary, humor, fantasy, psychic/supernatural/occult, prose poem, regional, romance, religious/inspirational, science fiction, spiritual, sports, mystery, young adult, senior citizen/retirement, very brief condensed novels, excerpts from novels. "Upbeat" subjects are preferred. "No erotica, works with excessive swearing or blatantly sexual words, gross violence, suicide, etc." Accepts 25-35 mss/issue. Does not read new contributor's submissions March 1-December 31, to prevent a backlog; any received before January will be returned. Receives 8-10 unsolicited fiction mss each month. Recently published work by Stanley Denzer, Steven A. Hess, Janet A. Novak; published many new writers within the last year. Length: preferably 500-2,000 words. Critiques rejected mss when there is time. Sometimes recommends other markets.

How to Contact: Send complete ms with SASE. Accepts computer printout submissions. Rejections in 2 weeks. Publishes ms at least 1½-2 years after acceptance. Sample copy for $3 or $2.50 for a back issue.

Payment: 1 free author's copy for first appearance only. $3 charge for extras. Readers' choice contest every issue—votes taken on favorite stories and poems. Small prizes.

Terms: Acquires first rights. Publication copyrighted.

Advice: "Include name and address on at least the first page, and name on others. State 'original and unpublished.' I especially appreciate the 'light' touch in both fiction and nonfiction—humor, whimsy, fantasy, etc. Beginning writers: Read your work out loud! Get someone else to listen to help you spot inconsistencies, unclear passages, inappropriate word choices. Bad grammar I can correct myself, but it's best to avoid, unless it is specifically meant to be dialectical. My biggest reasons for outright rejection are: lack of space, offensive subject matter or language, excessive length, and generally poor writing. I do sometimes send a story back for a rewrite when it has possibilities but 'problems.' Currently holding for 1990."

HOBO STEW REVIEW (I, II), 236 Kelton St., #14, Allston MA 02134. (617)738-6428. Editor: Hobo Stew. Magazine: 8½x11; photocopy paper; 65 lb card stock cover; illustrations (use black ink on white 8½x11 paper). "*H.S.R.* is a mixture of things: fiction, essays, letters to editor, poetry and journalism. *H.S.R.* hopes to be a medium for artists/writers to get their material viewed and critiqued." Quarterly. Estab. 1984. Circ. 40.

Needs: Contemporary, experimental, feminist, humor/satire, juvenile (5-9 years), literary, science fiction, senior citizen/retirement, translations, young adult/teen (10-18). No ageist or sexist fiction, or "slices of life that are 2 dimensional. Poorly done vignettes are extremely unfulfilling." Receives 5-10 unsolicited mss/month. Accepts 3-4 mss/issue; 8-12 mss/year. Publishes short shorts. Sometimes critiques rejected mss and recommends other markets.

How to Contact: Send complete ms with cover letter. Reports in 3-4 weeks. SASE. Photocopied submissions OK. Sample copy $2. Fiction guidelines for #10 SAE with 1 first class stamp. Subscription costs $5/year.

Payment: 1 contributor's copy.

Terms: Publication not copyrighted.

Advice: "As Hobo moves about the U.S.A. (home base for *H.S.R.* has been Eugene OR; Albuquerque NM; and currently Allston MA) the publication dates differ—as do the seasons' arrival. *H.S.R.* arrives quarterly *with* the seasons. *H.S.R.* has reduced the number of short stories, replacing them with poetry. *H.S.R.* now encourages short shorts. Send a clean copy, remember to provide return postage, if hand written make it legible—all the things taken for granted are the ones most often overlooked. Keep at it only if you can be honest."

HOOFSTRIKES NEWSLETTER (II, IV), Gweetna Press, Box 106, Mt. Pleasant MI 48858. (517)772-0139. Editor: Cathy Ford. Newsletter: 8½x11; 20 pages; offset stock; illustrations. Publishes fiction, nonfiction, poetry, art, puzzles, games. etc. "All equines are fair game including zebras, centaurs, etc. We publish only horse-related material." Quarterly. Estab. 1983. Circ. 400.
Needs: Adventure, contemporary, ethnic, experimental, fantasy, historical (general), horror, humor/satire, juvenile (5-9 years), literary, mainstream, psychic/supernatural/occult, regional, religious/inspirational, romance, science fiction, suspense/mystery, western, young adult/teen (10-18 years). "Must be horse-related material, but can use any of above themes." Receives 10-12 unsolicited mss/month. Accepts 5-7 mss/issue; 20-25 mss/year. Length: 2,000 words maximum. Publishes short shorts. Length: 1,500-2,000 words. Occasionally critiques rejected mss.
How to Contact: Send complete ms with cover letter, which should list "previously published material." Reports in 6-10 weeks. SASE. Photocopied submissions OK. Accepts computer printout submissions, including dot-matrix. Sample copy $2. Fiction guidelines for #10 SAE and 1 first class stamp.
Payment: Pays in 1-5 copies "per editor's discretion."
Terms: Acquires one-time rights. Publication copyrighted. Old Shoe Fiction award offers a plaque and cash award to a writer published in *Hoofstrikes Newsletter*.

THE HORROR SHOW (I), Phantasm Press, 14848 Misty Spring Lane, Oak Run CA 96069. (916)472-3540. Editor: David B. Silva. Magazine: 8½x11; 72-80 pages; illustrations; photos. Magazine for "all ages, young and old, who have a spark of dementia that must be satisfied." Quarterly. Estab. 1982. Circ. 54,000.
Needs: Horror. No heavy sex or violence. Receives 250 unsolicited mss/month. Buys 20 mss/issue; 80 mss/year. Recently published work by Robert R. McCammon, William F. Nolan, Skipp and Spector; published new writers within the last year. Length: 2,000 words average; 4,000 words maximum. Critiques rejected mss briefly.
How to Contact: Send complete ms with SASE. Reports in 3 weeks. Publishes ms 3-6 months after acceptance. Photocopied submissions OK. Accepts computer printout submissions. Sample copy $4.95. Fiction guidelines for SASE with 1 first class stamp.
Payment: ½-1½¢/word and 1 free contributor's copy; $3.95 charge for extras.
Terms: Pays on acceptance for first North American serial rights, one-time rights. Sometimes sends galleys to author. Publication copyrighted.
Advice: "Please take the time to read an issue of *The Horror Show*. Read as much in the horror field as possible. After that, come up with an idea which is fresh and chilling, wrap it in a unique and fascinating style, and send it my way. Hook me in the first sentence. Don't sink me in background that is not relevant. After finishing a story, put it aside for a week—then rewrite. I'm always looking for new writers with fresh ideas. We publish fiction because there aren't enough markets out there, while the hunger for good short stories is growing in the reading public."

HOR-TASY (II, IV), Ansuda Publications, Box 158-J, Harris IA 51345. Editor/Publisher: Daniel R. Betz. Magazine: 5½x8½; 72 pages; mimeo paper; index stock cover; illustrations on cover. "*Hor-Tasy* is bringing back actual *horror* to horror lovers tired of seeing so much science fiction and SF passed off as horror. We're also very much interested in true, poetic, pure fantasy."
Needs: Fantasy and horror. "Pure fantasy: Examples are trolls, fairies and mythology. The horror we're looking for comes from the human mind—the ultimate form of horror. It must sound real—so real that in fact it could very possibly happen at any time and place. We must be able to feel the diseased mind behind the personality. No science fiction in any way, shape or form. We don't want stories in which the main character spends half his time talking to a shrink. We don't want stories that start out with: 'You're crazy,' said so and so." Accepts 6 mss/issue. Receives 15-20 unsolicited fiction mss each month. Recently published work by Charmaine Parsons, M. C. Salemme, Jude Howell; published new writers within the last year. Critiques rejected mss "unless it's way off from what we're looking for." Sometimes recommends other markets.
How to Contact: Query or send complete ms with SASE. Accepts computer printout submissions; prefers letter-quality. Reports in 1 day on queries. "If not interested (in ms), we return immediately. If interested, we may keep it as long as 6 months." Publishes ms an average of 1 year after acceptance. Sample copy $2.95. Guidelines for #10 SASE.
Payment: 2 free author's copies. Charge for extras: Cover price less special discount rates.
Terms: Acquires first North American serial rights. Publication copyrighted.
Advice: "Most stories rejected are about spooks, monsters, haunted houses, spacemen, etc. Because *Hor-Tasy* is a unique publication, I suggest the potential writer get a sample copy. Only unpublished work will be considered."

‡HOUSEWIFE-WRITER'S FORUM (I), Drawer 1518, Lafayette CA 94549. (415)932-1143. Editor: Deborah Haeseler. Magazine: 7x8½; 20-24 pages and 20 lb bond paper and cover stock; illustrations. "Support for the woman who juggles writing with family life. We publish short fiction, poetry, essays, nonfiction, line drawings, humor and hints. For women of all ages; house husbands who write." Bimonthly. Plans special fiction issue. Estab. 1988. Circ. over 300.

Needs: Condensed/excerpted novel, confession, contemporary, experimental, fantasy, historical (general), horror, humor/satire, juvenile (5-9 years), literary, mainstream, preschool (1-4 years), prose poem, psychic/supernatural/occult, romance (contemporary, historical and young adult), science fiction, serialized novel, suspense/mystery and young adult/teen (10-18 years). No pornographic material. Receives 2-10 mss/month. Buys 1-2 mss/issue; 6-10 mss/year. Publishes ms within 6 months to 1 year after acceptance. Recently published work by Elaine McCormick, Carol Shenold and Sherry Zanzinger. Length: 1,500 words preferred; 500 words minimum; 5,000 words maximum. Publishes short shorts. Sometimes critiques rejected mss and if possible recommends other markets.

How to Contact: Send complete ms with cover letter. Cover letter should include "the basics." Reports in 2 week on queries; 1 month on mss. SASE. Simultaneous, photocopied and reprint submissions OK. Accepts computer printout submissions, including dot-matrix. "I'll even consider handwritten material." Sample copy for $3. Fiction guidelines for #10 SAE and 1 first class stamp.

Payment: Pays $1-$10, plus 2 contributor's copies. Charges for extra copies.

Terms: Pays on publication for one-time rights. Publication copyrighted. Sponsors awards for fiction writers. "We sponsor 15 contests geared to the interests of housewife-writers. First place and grand prize winners are published in an annual edition, *The Best of Housewife-Writer's Forum: the Contested Wills to Write*. Entry fees: $3 for subscribers, $4 for nonsubscribers. Prizes are based on the number of entries per category. Send #10 SAE with 1 first class stamp for guidelines and further information.

Advice: "Just write it the best you can and submit it. I'll share whatever thoughts come to mind as I read it. Play with your basic idea, try to imagine the plot unfolding in different ways. And this is something few other editors will say, but share with me any worries you have about your story as presently submitted. I read every submission as a friend would. I look for the good parts and encourage you to develop your strengths. At the same time, I try to help minimize your weaknesses (we all have them!). I think two heads are better than one, and as long as you realize that my opinion isn't perfect, we can learn from each other; and we'll both be better writers as a result."

‡HURRICANE ALICE (II), A Feminist Quarterly, Hurricane Alice Fn., Inc., 207 Church St. SE, Minneapolis MN 55455. Executive Editors: Martha Roth, Janet Tripp. Fiction is collectively edited. Tabloid: 11x17; 12-16 pages; newsprint stock; illustrations and photos. "We look for feminist fictions with a certain analytic snap, for serious readers, seriously interested in emerging forms of feminist art/artists." Quarterly. Estab. 1983. Circ. 600-700.

Needs: Erotica, experimental, feminist, gay, humor/satire, lesbian, science fiction, translations. No coming-out stories, defloration stories, abortion stories. Receives 20 unsolicited mss/month. Buys 1-2 mss/issue. Publishes 4-6 stories annually. Publishes ms up to 1 year after acceptance. Recently published work by Jodi Stutz, Martha Clark Cummings, Pearl Cleage; published new writers within the last year. Length: up to 3,000 words maximum. Publishes short shorts. Occasionally critiques rejected mss.

How to Contact: Send complete ms with cover letter. "A brief biographical statement is never amiss. Writers should be sure to tell us if a piece was commissioned by one of the editors." Reports in 3 months. SASE for ms. Simultaneous and photocopied submissions OK. Accepts computer printout submissions, no dot-matrix. Sample copy for $2, 11x14 SAE and 2 first class stamps.

Payment: Free subscription to magazine and 5-10 contributor's copies.

Terms: Pays on publication for one-time rights. Publication copyrighted.

Advice: "Fiction is a craft. Just becuase something happened, it isn't a story; it becomes a story when you transform it through your art, your craft."

ICE RIVER (IV), A Journal of Speculative Writing and a Quarterly Review and Marketing Tabloid, 953 N. Gale, Union OR 97883. Magazine and tabloid: 5½x8½ (magazine); 11x17 (tabloid); 60 pages (magazine); 8 pages (tabloid). "Fiction with an element of the fantastic (i.e. speculative fiction, SF, magical realism, modern fantasy and surrealism), mainly for a crossover audience between mainstream and literary SF." Quarterly (tabloid) and semiannually (magazine). Estab. 1987. Circ. 300-500 for magazine; 1,000 for tabloid.

Needs: Experimental, modern fantasy, literary, psychic/supernatural/occult, speculative prose poem, science fiction, surrealist. "We are not looking for sword-and-sorcery fantasy, Star Wars SF or stereotypical stories. This is a market for the literature of the fantastic—stories that are literary." Receives about 20 unsolicited mss/month. Accepts 4-5 mss/month for magazine; occasional fiction for newsletter; 8-10 mss/year for magazine; 3-4 mss/year for newsletter. Publishes ms an average of 6 months after acceptance. Recently published work by Mary Ann Cain, Mark Laidlaw, Don Webb. Length: 2,000-3,000

words average; 500 words minimum; 5,000 words maximum. Publishes short shorts. Sometimes critiques rejected mss and may recommend other markets.
How to Contact: Send complete ms with cover letter, which should include a brief bio and list of some previous publications. Reports in 2-3 months on mss. SASE. Simultaneous (if notified immediately) and photocopied submissions OK. Accepts computer printout submissions, if legible, letter quality or near letter quality. Subscriptions: $10 for two numbers of journal and four issues of tabloid. $13 for overseas subscriptions. Sample copy for $2.50. Fiction guidelines for #10 SAE and 1 first class stamp. Overseas orders should add $1 for postage.
Payment: Pays in 2 contributor's copies.
Terms: Pays on publication for first North American serial rights. Publication copyrighted.
Advice: "*Ice River 4* will be guest edited by Robert Frazier. He will not be reading unsolicited manuscripts. *IR* will not be reading again until April or May of 1989 for the magazine. We will be reading short-short fiction, up to 1,500 words, for the quarterly tabloid, but can only publish one story in each issue."

THE ICELANDIC CANADIAN (II), The Icelandic Canadian Club, 107-1061 Sargent Ave., Winnipeg, Manitoba R3E 0E5 Canada. Editor-in-Chief: Axel Vopnfjord. Editor: Paul A. Sigurdson. Magazine: 7x10; 64 pages; bond paper; illustrations; photos. Literary magazine promoting knowledge of Icelandic culture, activities and accomplishments of American and Canadian people of Icelandic lineage. For people interested in Iceland and Icelandic culture. Quarterly. Estab. 1944. Circ. 1,300.
Needs: Literary, contemporary, adventure, humor, ethnic (Icelandic), regional, romance, senior citizen/retirement and translations. No erotic or avant-garde. Accepts 1 ms/issue, 4-6 mss/year. Published new writers within the last year. Length: 1,000-2,000 words.
How to Contact: Send complete ms with SAE, IRC. Accepts computer printout submissions. Reports in 2 months on mss. Sample copy $4.50 with 7x10 SAE, IRC.
Payment: Free author's copy with $2 (Canadian) charge for extras.
Terms: Acquires one-time rights.
Advice: "Write an authentic story about Icelandic people or a story on your impressions of your trip to Iceland."

IMPULSE MAGAZINE (II), 16 Skey Lane, Toronto, Ontario M6J 3S4 Canada. (416)537-9551. Editors: Eldon Garnet, Judith Doyle, Carolyn White and Brian Boigon. Magazine: 8¼x10¾; 60 pages; 4-color glossy cover; illustrations and photos. "Theme is art and culture with an emphasis on experimental/innovative fiction, interviews, political and cultural analysis and artwork." Quarterly. Estab. 1971. Circ. 5,000.
Needs: "Experimental, innovative writing. We are also a visual publication and would appreciate any accompanying images, illustrations, etc." Accepts 4-5 mss/issue, 15-20 mss/year. Receives approximately 30 unsolicited fiction mss/month. Published new writers within the last year. Length: 250-2,000 words. Critiques rejected mss when there is time.
How to Contact: Send complete ms with SAE and IRCs. Accepts computer printout submissions. Reports in 4-6 months on mss. Sample copy $5.
Terms: Acquires first rights. Publication copyrighted. We have a greater commitment than previously to paying all contributors."
Advice: "Keep trying. Avoid too lengthy a manuscript. Most manuscripts are either poorly conceived or simply too conventional in style and content and do not exhibit suitable awareness of the idiosyncracies of *Impulse*. We are interested in more experimental pieces of fiction."

‡IN TRANSIT (II), Everywhichway Press, 12256 Turkey Wing Ct., Reston VA 22091. (203)476-0024. Editor: Kendra Usack. Newsletter: 8½x11; 4 pages; Xerox paper; illustrations. Publishes "Mostly sf/f, fantasy, horror, speculative, but also interested in more mainstream poetry." Monthly. Estab. 1988.
Needs: Adventure, erotica (maybe), experimental, fantasy, feminist, horror, humor/satire, mainstream, new age, prose poem, psychic/supernatural/occult, science fiction, senior citizen and suspense/mystery. Receives 1 ms/month. Accepts 1-3 mss/year. Recently published work by Al Manachino. Length: 500-1,000 words preferred; 300 words minimum; 16,000 words maximum. "2 years overstocked on long fiction." Sometimes critiques rejected mss and recommends other markets.
How to Contact: Send complete manuscript with cover letter. Reports on mss in 2 weeks-3 months. SASE. Photocopied and reprint submissions OK. Accepts computer printout submissions including dot-matrix, "depends on quality." Accepts electronic submissions via IBM-compatible disk. "I have Tandy Radio Shack 1000." Sample copy for $1. Guidelines for #10 SAE and 1 first class stamp.
Payment: Pays in free subscription to magazine or copies. Payment also arranged with more prolific contributors and for special issues.
Terms: Acquires one-time rights. Publication copyrighted. Rights revert to author.
Advice: "Fanzines are where it's at for SF/F/horror and mystery stories. Mainstream mags are pretty

much dead in the water as far as I am concerned—most stories don't have enough meat, enough to care about. Stories should be *short*. I don't have much space for fiction. Read an issue. And read as much as you can in the genre.''

IN-BETWEEN (I), Art & Entertainment Between the Lakes, Six Lakes Arts Communication, Inc., 43 Chapel St., Seneca Falls NY 13148. (315)568-4265. Editor: Stephen Beals. Magazine: 8½x11; 32 pages minimum; 60 lb offset paper; glossy cover; illustrations; photos. "Art and entertainment. Music, theatre, short stories, poetry. Exclusive to Finger Lakes region of New York State, for upscale arts enthusiasts." Bimonthly. Estab. 1987. 1,500 copies distributed to members, arts groups and media.
Needs: Historical (general), humor/satire, juvenile (5-9 years), prose poem, senior citizen/retirement, suspense/mystery, music, theatre. "We are a new magazine for the Finger Lakes. We are interested in art and entertainment with a very broad view of what constitutes art. We have a rural flavor and a 'family' audience. Work must be reflective of Finger Lakes region." No erotica, sci fi, psychic, religious, romance, gay/lesbian. Accepts 1-2 mss/issue. Publishes ms 1-3 months after acceptance. Recently published work by Richard Cicarelli, Barbara Mater and David Downey. Length: 800 words average; 500 words minimum; 3,500 words maximum. Will consider longer pieces in serial form. Publishes short shorts.
How to Contact: Send complete ms with cover letter. Reports in 2-4 weeks on queries; 4-6 weeks on mss. SASE. Simultaneous, photocopied and reprint submissions OK. Accepts computer printout submissions, including dot-matrix. Accepts electronic submissions via Apple Macintosh. Sample copy and fiction guidelines free.
Payment: Pays in contributor's copies. "Some payment for special projects; query."
Terms: Publication will be copyrighted.
Advice: "Most of our writers are first-timers. Keep in mind our audience is rural by choice and shouldn't be talked down to. Consideration is being given to publishing short stories in book form."

THE INDEPENDENT REVIEW (I), Box 2119, Independence MO 64055. Editors: M. H. Alft and Shirley Janner. Magazine: 6½x8½; approx. 60 pages; chromecoat cover; cover photos. Quarterly. Estab. 1987.
Needs: Adventure, contemporary, experimental, fantasy, feminist, horror, humor/satire, mainstream, prose poem, science fiction. No porn, family tales. Receives 10-20 unsolicited mss/month. Accepts 1-4 mss/issue. Publishes ms 1-5 months after acceptance. Published new writers within the last year. Length: 1,600 words maximum. Publishes short shorts. Sometimes comments on rejected mss and recommends other markets.
How to Contact: Send complete ms with cover letter. Reports in 3 months on mss. SASE. Simultaneous and photocopied submissions OK. Accepts computer printout submissions. Sample copy for $3.75. Fiction guidelines free for #10 SAE.
Payment: Contributor's copies.
Terms: Acquires one-time rights. Publication copyrighted.
Advice: "Much fiction is lacking one or more elements of a story (beginning, middle, end!). We especially want to see beginners! Be neat and concise. SASE a must. No erasable paper. Humor gets special attention."

INDIANA REVIEW (II), 316 N. Jordan Ave., Bloomington IN 47405. (812)335-3439. Editor: Kim McKinney. Associate Editor: Jon Tribble. Magazine: 6x9; 128 pages; 60 lb paper; Glatfelter cover stock. "Magazine of contemporary fiction and poetry in which there is a zest for language, some relationship between form and content, and some awareness of the world. For fiction writers/readers, followers of lively contemporary poetry." Triannually. Estab. 1976. Circ. 500.
Needs: Literary, contemporary, experimental, mainstream. "We are interested in innovation, logic, unity, a social context, a sense of humanity. All genres that meet some of these criteria are welcome." Accepts 6-8 mss/issue. Recently published work by Melissa Pritchard, Ron Tanner, Sharon Dilworth; published new writers within the last year. Length: 1-35 magazine pages.
How to Contact: Send complete ms with cover letter. "Don't describe or summarize the story." SASE. Accepts computer printout submissions, prefers letter-quality. Reports in 3 weeks-3 months. Publishes ms an average of 2-10 months after acceptance. Sample copy $4.
Payment: $25/story.
Terms: Acquires North American serial rights. Publication copyrighted.
Advice: "Be daring, love the language. Don't imitate anyone. Refrain from the chatty cover letter. Send one story at a time (unless they're really short), and no simultaneous submissions."

INLET (II), Virginia Wesleyan College, Norfolk VA 23502. Editor: Joseph Harkey. Magazine: 7x8½; 32-38 pages. "Poetry and short fiction for people of all ages." Annually. Estab. 1970. Circ. 700.
Needs: Literary, contemporary, mainstream, fantasy and humor. "Our main interest is well written fic-

tion." Accepts 2-5 mss/issue. Receives 10-20 unsolicited fiction mss each month. Does not read in summer. Recently published work by Myron Taube. Length: 500-1,500 words but "will consider up to 3,000." Sometimes recommends other markets.

How to Contact: "Manuscripts are read September through March only." Send complete ms to fiction editor with SASE. Reports in 2 months. Sample copy for 75¢ postage.

Payment: 2 free author's copies. Negotiates charge for extras.

Terms: Publication copyrighted.

Advice: "Write carefully and present a neatly typed manuscript with SASE. Send an example of your best work; short shorts preferred. Some rejected manuscripts are poorly written. Some are polished and professional but lack imaginative treatments of the problems they raise."

‡INNISFREE (I,II), Appleseed, Box 277, Manhattan Beach CA 90266. (213)545-2607. Editor: Rex Winn. Magazine: 8½x11; 44 pages; 90 lb cover stock; illustrations and photos. Publishes "fiction, poetry, essays—open forum." Bimonthly. Estab. 1981. Circ. 200.

Needs: Adventure, contemporary, ethnic, fantasy, literary, mainstream, regional, science fiction and suspense/mystery. No political or religious sensationalism. Accepts 8-10 mss/issue; approx. 80 mss/ year. Publishes ms within 6 months of acceptance. Recently published work by Ron Fleshman, Peter McGinn, Clem Portman and Anne Swann. Length: 3,500 words average. Publishes short shorts. Sometimes critiques rejected mss.

How to Contact: Send complete mss with cover letter. Reports in 4 weeks. SASE. Simultaneous, photocopied and reprint submissions OK. Accepts electronic submissions via IBM disk. Sample copy for $1. Free fiction guidelines.

Payment: No payment. Prizes offered.

Terms: Acquires one-time rights. Publication copyrighted. Sponsors awards for fiction writers. "$50 for best short story, $20 for best poem."

Advice: "Fiction market is on the decline. This is an attempt to publish new writers who take pride in their work and have some talent."

INSIDE JOKE (I, II), A Newsletter of Comedy and Creativity, Box 1609, Madison Square Station, New York NY 10159. Editor: Elayne Wechsler. Newsletter: 8½x11; 32 pages; 16 or 20 lb cover/stock; illustrations. "We have no theme per se—we're more defined by what we don't publish then by what we do." Readers consist of "alternative media (non-mainstream) and mutants." Bimonthly. Estab. 1980. Circ. 250.

Needs: Experimental, fantasy, humor/satire, psychic/supernatural/occult, science fiction, serialized/ excerpted story. No erotica, confessional, mainstream. Publishes ms no longer than 2 months after acceptance. Length: 500-600 words average; 1,900 words maximum. Occasionally critiques rejected mss. Sometimes recommends other markets.

How to Contact: Send for sample copy and/or writer's guidelines. SASE. Photocopied submissions OK. Accepts computer printout submissions, including dot-matrix. "I don't care if it's scrawled in blood." Sample copy $1.50. Checks *must* be made payable to "Elayne Wechsler." Fiction guidelines for #10 SAE and 1 first class stamp.

Payment: "Only staff writers receive free copies; other contributors get a discount (65¢ stamp instead of $1.50 subscription price)."

Terms: Publication copyrighted.

Advice: "To presume that a person who writes for pleasure without receiving payment is not a professional writer makes me sick. I sincerely hope mainstream presses someday come around to the realization that small independent publications have as much validity (if not more) as anything else listed in these pages."

‡INTERIM (II), Dept. of English, University of Nevada, Las Vegas NV 89154. (702)739-3471. Editor: A. Wilber Stevens. Associate Editors: James Hazen, Arlen Collier, Joe McCullough. Magazine: 6x9; 48 pages; heavy paper; glossy cover; cover illustrations. Publishes "poetry and short fiction for a serious, sophisticated, educated audience." Semiannually. Estab. 1944. Circ. 700.

Needs: Contemporary and literary. Accepts 1-2 mss/issue. Publishes ms within 6 months to 1 year of acceptance. Recently published work by Gladys Swan. Length: 4,000 words preferred; 1,000 words minimum; 8,000 words maximum. "Might" publish short shorts.

How to Contact: Send complete ms with cover letter. Reports on mss in 6 weeks. SASE. Photocopied submissions OK. Accepts computer printout submissions, including dot-matrix. Sample copy for $3.

Payment: Pays in contributor's copies and free subscription to magazine.

Terms: Acquires one-time rights. Publication copyrighted.

Advice: Looks for "quality, but would not be likely to accept anything over 20 printed pages. Primary emphasis traditionally has been on poetry."

THE IOWA REVIEW (II), University of Iowa, 308 EPB, Iowa City IA 52242. (319)335-0462. Editor: David Hamilton. Magazine: 6x9; 200 pages; first grade offset paper; Carolina CIS-10 pt. cover stock. "Stories, essays, poems for a general readership interested in contemporary literature." Published triannually. Estab. 1970. Circ. 1,200.
Needs: Receives 150-200 unsolicited fiction mss/month. Less than 10% of fiction is agented. Buys 4-5 mss/issue, 12-16 mss/year. Does not read mss May-August. Recently published work by Robert Wexelblatt, Robert Boswell, Jill Birdsall; published new writers within the last year.
How to Contact: Send complete ms with SASE. "Don't bother with queries." Simultaneous and photocopied submissions OK. Accepts computer printout submissions. Reports in 4 months on mss. Publishes ms an average of 4-12 months after acceptance. Sample copy $5.
Payment: $10/page; 2 free contributor's copies; charge for extras: 30% off cover price.
Terms: Pays on publication for first North American serial rights. Hardly ever buys reprints. Publication copyrighted.
Advice: In cover letters, "be moderate. Be decent. Be brief."

‡THE IRISH & AMERICAN REVIEW (IV), The Community Newspaper of the International Irish Community, Interstate News Services, Inc., 500 Airport Rd., #250, St. Louis MO 63135. (314)522-1300. Newspaper: tabloid size; 8-24 pages; newsprint paper and cover; photos and cartoons. "Magazine-format newspaper of Irish and Irish-American subjects for Irish readers and persons if Irish descent." Quarterly. Estab. 1985. Circ. 20,000.
Needs: Ethnic, historical (ethnic), regional, young adult, Irish. Receives 6 unsolicited mss/month; 1-3 mss/year. Publishes ms up to 6 months after acceptance. Recently published work by Jane Cosby. Length: 2,000 words maximum. Sometimes recommends other markets.
How to Contact: Send complete ms with cover letter. Reports in 6 months. SASE. Accepts dot-matrix computer submissions. Accepts electronic submissions via disk or modem. Sample copy for 5x7 SAE and 3 first class stamp; fiction guidelines for #10 SAE.
Payment: Payment negotiable.
Terms: Pays on publication for all rights. Negotiable kill fee. Publication copyrighted.

‡JABBERWOCKY (I, II), The Magazine of Speculative Fiction, Chimera Connections, Inc., 7701 SW 7th Pl., Gainesville FL 32607. (904)332-6586. Editors: Duane Bray, Jeff Vander Meer and Penelope Miller. Magazine: 8½x11; 40-70 pages; coated matte paper; gloss cover; 5-10 illustrations; 2-5 photographs; "An eclectic mix of styles within the bounds of fantasy, horror and science fiction (experimental, commercial, literary)." Semiannually. Estab. 1989. Circ. 1,000.
Needs: Experimental, fantasy, horror, humor/satire, literary, psychic/supernatural/occult, science fiction, serialized novel, translations. "No overtly religious. No Tolkien rehashes. (We will accept even extremely offensive work if scene(s) are essential to story.)" Receives 375 unsolicited mss/month. Buys 4-10 mss/issue; 8-20 mss/year. Publishes ms no more than 6 months after acceptance. "Will soon publish 1982 International Fantasy Award-winner Meredith Ann Pierce. (An original, previously unpublished story)." Published new writers in the last year. Length: 3,000 words preferred; 5,500 words maximum. Publishes short shorts. Sometimes critiques rejected mss, "always comments (if guidelines have been observed)." Sometimes recommends other markets.
How to Contact: Send complete manuscript with cover letter, which should include "where writer saw *Jabberwocky* listed. Publication credits (for bio listing if work is accepted). Something entertaining about the writer. Boring cover letter writers can expect a big man named Vinny to greet them at their doorstep shortly after our response." Reports in 1-3 weeks on queries; 3 weeks on mss. SASE. "Foreign submitters should send equivalent stamps from their own country loose along with an appropriate envelope. IRCs are a real pain; the *J* staff—all writers—can use the postage." Accepts computer printout submissions, including dot-matrix. Sample copy for $4.50. Fiction guidelines for #10 SAE and 1 first class stamp.
Payment: Pays $25 minimum; $50 maximum (for 2-part serialization). Free contributor's copy.
Terms: Pays on acceptance for First North American serial rights. Sends galleys to author. Publication copyrighted.
Advice: "Style is paramount, especially for fantasy. Obviously, characterization and setting must be fully fleshed-out (though characterization may not be essential for certain stories). We are extremely open—even mainstream material with a style or setting described in almost-fantasy terms would be considered. Writers who are unsure whether their work qualifies as speculative fiction should simply send it. Our own inluences are as diverse as Harlan Ellison, Peter Beagle, Robert Heinlein, and Clive Barker (also Ursula LeGuin and, of course, Lewis Carroll). A problem some beginners face once they've made 2 or 3 sales is focusing on the writing rather than the market. Don't get too hung up with trying to be published—especially if you're young (you've got time)."

‡JACARANDA REVIEW (II), Dept. of English, UCLA, Los Angeles CA 90024. (213) 825-4173. Editor: Cornel Bonca. Fiction Editor: Robert Metzger. Magazine: 5½x8; 124 pages; high quality paper; Archer cover stock; cover illustrations. "We publish anything that we think is high quality, for serious readers of fiction and poetry." Semiannually. Estab. 1984. Circ. 1,000.
Needs: Condensed/excerpted novel, contemporary, experimental, literary, mainstream, prose poem and translations. "We're not particularly interested in what people call 'genre' fiction. We're interested in fiction that reflects contemporary sensibilities about contemporary life." Receives 10 mss/month. Accepts 3 mss/issue; 6 mss/year. Publishes ms within 1-2 months of acceptance. Recently published work by Jorge Luis Borges, Ed Minus and Joscha Kessler; published new writers within the last year. Length: 2,500-4,000 words preferred; 500 words minimum; 7,500 words maximum. Sometimes critiques rejected mss and recommends other markets.
How to Contact: Send complete mss with cover letter. Cover letter should include "contributor's note." Reports on queries in 2 weeks; on mss in 8 weeks. SASE. Simultaneous and photocopied submissions OK. Accepts computer printout submissions, including dot-matrix. Sample copy for $3.50, 6x9 SAE and 3 first class stamps.
Payment: Pays in contributor's copies. Discount for extra copies.
Terms: Acquires one-time rights. Publication copyrighted. Sponsors awards for fiction writers. "We offer an annual prize of $100 to the best story we publish during that year."
Advice: Sees "too much *unexamined* minimalist fiction; that is, fiction that dwells in passivity and is almost ashamed of passion. Not enough fiction inspired by Garcià Marquez or Kundera. Lately we tend to like fiction that avoids minimalist mannerisms (though we do publish work in the Robison-F. Barthelme mode), that has an energetic sense of humor, and which aspires to be psychologically fearless. We're interested in good experimental fiction, too, if we can find some, and fiction about and by women. A lot of the fiction we receive seems inspired in conception but underdeveloped and unrealized in execution. Care—deeply—about the reader, and care deeply about your work."

JAM TO-DAY (II), 372 Dunstable Rd., Tyngsboro MA 01879. Fiction Editor: Judith Stanford. Co-editor: Don Stanford. Magazine: 5½x8½; 80 pages; illustrations; occasional photos. Forum for serious nonacademic poetry and fiction by unknown and little-known contemporary writers. Annually. Published special fiction issue. Estab. 1973. Circ. 400.
Needs: Literary, contemporary, science fiction and feminist. No light fiction, word-play fiction, highly allusive or allegorical fiction. Buys 3-5 mss/year. Receives approximately 35 unsolicited fiction mss each month. Published new writers within the last year. Length: 1,500-7,500. Publishes "good quality short shorts of 300-750 words." Critiques rejected mss when there is time. Sometimes recommends other markets.
How to Contact: Send complete ms with SASE. Accepts computer printout submissions. Prefers letter quality. Reports in 6 weeks on mss. Publishes ms up to 1 year after acceptance. Sample copy $4.
Payment: $5/printed page.
Terms: Pays on publication for first rights. Publication copyrighted.
Advice: "We are publishing more short stories now." Reasons for rejections: "(1) Poorly conceived: trite, uninteresting, poorly written, too academic; and (2) better suited to another market: well written and holds interest but better suited to mass-market magazine, or extraordinarily obscure but not obviously foolish and ought to go to experimental literary magazine."

JAPANOPHILE (II, IV), Box 223, Okemos MI 48864. (517)349-1795. Editor-in-Chief: Earl Snodgrass. Magazine: 8½x5¼; 50 pages; illustrations; photos. Magazine of "articles, photos, poetry, humor, short stories about Japanese culture, not necessarily set in Japan, for an adult audience, most with college background; travelers." Quarterly. Published special fiction issue last year; plans another. Estab. 1974. Circ. 600.
Needs: Adventure, historical (general), humor/satire, literary, mainstream, and suspense/mystery. Receives 40-100 unsolicited fiction mss/month. Buys 1 ms/issue, 4-10 mss/year. Recently published work by Gerald Dorset, Bobbi Crudup, Joan Van De Moortel; published new writers within the last year. Length: 2,000 words minimum; 9,000 words maximum; 4,000 words average. Sometimes recommends other markets.
How to Contact: Send complete ms with SASE and cover letter with author bio and information about story. Photocopied and previously published submissions OK. Accepts computer printout submissions. Reports in 2 months on mss. Sample copy $4; guidelines for #10 SAE and 1 first class stamp.
Payment: Pays $20 on publication. "Annual contest pays $100 plus publication for the best short story." Deadline December 31. Entry fee is $5.
Terms: Pays on publication for all rights, first North American serial rights or one-time rights (depends on situation). Publication copyrighted.
Advice: "Short stories usually involve Japanese and 'foreign' (non-Japanese) characters in a way that contributes to understanding of Japanese culture and the Japanese people. However, a *good* story deal-

ing with Japan or Japanese cultural aspects anywhere in the world will be considered, even if it does not involve this encounter or meeting of Japanese and foreign characters. Some stories may also be published in an anthology."

THE JEFFERSON REVIEW (II), 109 E. Broadway, Louisville KY 40202. (502)584-0181, ext. 242. Editor: Wanda Thomason Speckter. Fiction Editors: Norma Gaskey, Larry Perkins. Magazine: 6x9; 76 pages; 70 lb paper; 80 lb enamel cover. "Contemporary fiction, universal concerns, themes." Semiannually. Estab. 1987. Circ. 300.
Needs: Contemporary, historical (general), translations. Receives 12-20 unsolicited mss/month. Buys 2-3 mss/issue; 6-8 mss/year. Publishes ms 6-12 months after acceptance. Length: 3,000 words average; 1,200 words minimum; 5,000 words maximum. Sometimes recommends other markets.
How to Contact: Send complete ms with cover letter. Reports in 3-4 weeks. SASE. Photocopied submissions OK. Accepts computer printout submissions. Sample copy and fiction guidelines for $3 and SAE.
Payment: Pays $5/printed page; 1 contributor's copy.
Terms: Pays on publication for first North American serial rights. Publication copyrighted.
Advice: "Read—any and all sources available in literary reviews and national publications."

JEOPARDY (II), Literary Arts Magazine, HU 350, Western Washington University, Bellingham WA 98225. (206)676-3118. Contact: Editors. Magazine: 6x9; 108 pages; 70 lb paper; Springhill 215 cover stock; illustrations and photographs. Material published: fiction, nonfiction, interviews, poetry, photographed artwork for "all inclusive" audience. Annually. Estab. 1965. Circ. 3,000-4,000.
Needs: Adventure, confession, contemporary, ethnic, experimental, fantasy, feminist, humor/satire, literary, mainstream, prose poem, regional, contemporary romance, science fiction and translations. No long stories. Accepts 7-10 mss/year. Length: 4 pages (average 800-1,000 words).
How to Contact: Send complete ms. SASE. Simultaneous and previously published submissions OK. Accepts computer printout submissions. Sample copy $2.
Payment: Two contributor's copies. "Sometimes *Jeopardy* awards cash prizes or special recognition to winners in various categories."
Terms: Publication copyrighted.
Advice: "We are a student-funded university literary publication. Good fiction is hard to find. We are happy to look at any fiction. Sometimes, if staff is large enough, at writer's request we will comment on the work."

JEWISH CURRENTS MAGAZINE (IV), 22 E. 17th St., New York NY 10003. (212)924-5740. Editor-in-Chief: Morris U. Schappes. Magazine: 5½x8½; 48 pages. "We are a progressive monthly, broad in our interests, printing feature articles on political and cultural aspects of Jewish life in the US and elsewhere, reviews of books and film, poetry and fiction, Yiddish translations; regular columns on Israel, US Jewish community, current events, Jewish women today, secular Jewish life. Monthly themes include Holocaust and Resistance, Black-Jewish relations, Jewish Book Month, Jewish Music Month, etc. National audience, literate and politically left, well educated." Monthly. Estab. 1946. Circ. 4,000.
Needs: Contemporary, ethnic, feminist, historical (general), humor/satire, literary, senior citizen/retirement, translations. "We are interested in *authentic* experience and readable prose; Jewish themes; humanistic orientation. No religious, political sectarian; no porn or hard sex, no escapist stuff. Go easy on experimentation, but we're interested." Receives 6-10 unsolicited fiction mss/month. Accepts 0-1 ms/issue, 8-10 mss/year. Recently published work by Lou Wax, Haim Zilberman; published new writers within the last year. Length: 1,000 words minimum; 3,000 words maximum; 1,800 words average.
How to Contact: Send complete ms with cover letter. "Writers should include brief biographical information, especially their publishing histories." SASE. Reports in 2 months on mss. Publishes ms an average of 2 months to 2 years after acceptance. Sample copy $1.50 with SAE and 3 first class stamps.
Payment: 1 complimentary one-year subscription; 6 free contributor's copies.
Terms: "We readily give reprint permission at no charge." Sends galleys to author. Publication copyrighted.
Advice: "Family themes are good, but avoid sentimentality; keep the prose tight, not sprawling; matters of character and moral dilemma, maturing into pain and joy, dealing with Jewish conflicts OK. Space is increasingly a problem. Tell the truth, as sparely as possible."

THE JOURNAL (II), Creative Writing Program, Ohio State University, 164 W. 17th St., Columbus OH 43210. (614)422-4076. Editor: David Citino. Magazine: 6x9; 80 pages; illustrations; photos. "We are open to all forms of quality fiction." For an educated, general adult audience. Semiannually. Estab. 1973. Circ. 1,000.
Needs: Contemporary, erotica, ethnic, experimental, feminist gay, literary, prose poem and regional. No romance or religious/devotional. Accepts 2-12 mss/issue. Receives approximately 100 unsolicited

fiction mss each month. Publishes ms within 6 months of acceptance. Agented fiction 10%. Recently published work by Anne Brashler and Kent Meyers; published new writers within the last year. Length: 4,000 words maximum. Critiques rejected mss when there is time. Sometimes recommends other markets.

How to Contact: Send complete ms with cover letter, which should list previous publications. Reports in 2 weeks on queries; 3 months on mss. SASE. Photocopied submissions OK. "No simultaneous submissions please." Accepts computer printout submissions. Prefers letter-quality. Publishes ms 1-12 months after acceptance. Sample copy $3; fiction guidelines for SASE.

Payment: Pays $25 stipend when funds are available. Free author's copies. $3 charge for extras.

Terms: Acquires First North American serial rights. Sends galleys to author. Publication copyrighted. "All contributors are automatically eligible for the President's Award ($100 annual award)."

Advice: Mss are rejected because of "lack of understanding of the short story form, shallow plots, undeveloped characters. Cure: read as much well-written fiction as possible. Our readers prefer 'psychological' fiction rather than stories with intricate plots. Take care to present a clean, well-typed submission."

JOURNAL OF POLYMORPHOUS PERVERSITY (II), Wry-Bred Press, Inc., 10 Waterside Plaza, Suite 20-B, New York NY 10010. (212)689-5473. Editor: Glenn Ellenbogen. Magazine: 6¾x10; 24 pages; 60 lb paper; antique india cover stock; illustrations with some articles. "*JPP* is a humorous and satirical journal of psychology, psychiatry, and the closely allied mental health disciplines." For "psychologists, psychiatrists, social workers, psychiatric nurses, *and* the psychologically sophisticated layman." Semiannally. Plans special fiction issue. Estab. January, 1984.

Needs: Humor/satire. "We only consider materials that are 1) funny, 2) relate to psychology *or* behavior." Receives 10 unsolicited mss/month. Accepts 8 mss/issue; 16 mss/year. Recently published work by Kathleen Donald, Ph.D. Most writers published last year were previously unpublished writers. Length: 1,500 words average; 4,000 words maximum. Comments on rejected ms.

How to Contact: Send complete ms *in triplicate*. Reports in 1-3 months on mss. SASE. Simultaneous and photocopied submissions OK. Accepts computer printout submissions. Prefers letter-quality. Accepts disk submissions compatible with Morrow MD-11. Prefers hard copy with a disk submission. Sample copy $5. Fiction guidelines free for #10 SAE and 1 first class stamp.

Payment: 2 contributor's copies; charge for extras: $5.

Terms: Publication copyrighted.

Advice: "We will *not* look at poetry or short stories. We only want to see intelligent spoofs of scholarly psychology and psychiatry articles written in scholarly scientific languages. Take a look at *real* journals of psychology and try to lampoon their *style* as much as their content. Avoid writing in first person; rather use more quasi-scientific style. There are few places to showcase satire of the social sciences, thus we provide one vehicle for injecting a dose of humor into this often too serious area."

‡JOURNAL OF QUANTUM 'PATAPHYSICS (I,II), Box 29756, Los Angeles CA 90029. (213)662-4569. Editor: Nigey Lennon. Fiction Editor: Lionel Rolfe. Magazine: 4¼x3½; 32 pages; bond paper; self cover; illustrations; photos. "We are "pataphysical' in nature ('pataphysics being the tongue-in-cheek pseudo-science invented by French author Alfred Jarry in the 1890s). We publish a variety of fiction, essays, articles and comics along 'pataphysical lines." For readers "reasonably intellectual and open-minded, interested in the arts and current events, not afraid of strong viewpoints." Quarterly. Estab. 1987. Circ. 3,000.

Needs: "We have published a wide variety of styles and subjects. Our only real guideline is that manuscripts fit the basically irreverent style of the magazine. Each issue is loosely organized around a particular theme, so contributors should ask about future themes." Receives 5-10 mss/month. Accepts 1-5 mss/issue; 4-10 mss/year. Publishes ms within 3 months of acceptance. Recently published work by Julia Stein, Lionel Rolfe, Nigey Lennon; published new writers within the last year. Length: 500-600 words preferred; 1,000 words maximum. Publishes short shorts. Sometimes critiques rejected mss and recommends other markets.

How to Contact: Send complete mss with cover letter. Reports on queries in 1-2 weeks; on mss in 1 month. SASE. Simultaneous, photocopied and reprint submissions OK. Accepts computer printout submissions, including dot-matrix. Sample copy for $2.

Payment: Pays in contributor's copies.

Terms: Acquires one-time rights. Publication copyrighted.

Advice: "Before you waste a manuscript and an SASE, be sure you understand the *JQ'P*. Although we publish a wide variety of fiction, essays, speculative writing, etc., we are only looking for material in the spirit of the publication—that is to say, irreverent, witty, controversial, and above all, personal. If you've never seen the *JQ'P*, request a sample copy ($1.50). Feel free to send a query letter describing your manuscript—all mail is answered."

JOURNAL OF REGIONAL CRITICISM (II), Arjuna Library Press, 1025 Garner St., Box 18, Colorado Springs CO 80905. Editor: Joseph A. Uphoff, Jr. Pamphlet: size variable; number of pages variable; Xerox paper; Bristol cover stock; b&w illustrations and photos. "Surrealist and dreamlike prose poetry and very short stories to illustrate accompanying mathematical, theoretical material in the fine arts for a wide ranging audience interested in philosophical sophistication and erudite language." Variable frequency. Estab. 1979.

Needs: Adventure, contemporary, ethnic, experimental, fantasy, historical (general), horror, humor/satire, literary, mainstream, prose poem, psychic/supernatural/occult, regional, religious/inspirational, contemporary romance, science fiction. Receives 1 or fewer unsolicited fiction mss/month. Accepts 1-5 mss/issue. Publishes ms 1 month-1 year after acceptance. Recently published work by Kathryn Stewart McDonald, Dr. Joseph Raffa and Professor Jon Woodson. Short short stories preferred. Sometimes critiques rejected mss and recommends other markets.

How to Contact: Send complete ms with cover letter. Manuscript will *not* be returned. Cover letter should include goals, behind-the-scenes explanation, and biographical material or résumé, date of birth, degrees, awards, offices and publications. Reports in 2 months on mss. SASE for query. Simultaneous, photocopied and reprint submissions OK. Accepts computer printouts including dot-matrix. Sample copy, if and when available, for $1 postage.

Payment: By contract after profit; contributor's copies.

Terms: Acquires "prototype presentation rights." Publication copyrighted—limited edition procedure copyrights.

Advice: "Our dreams are not rational, but they are beautiful stories. Language need not be colorless! Free expression must nevertheless be socially and psychologically humane and responsible. Irony is dangerous but necessary. Those who do not know what surrealism is are urged to read the surrealist manifestoes of André Bréton and the literature of H.P. Lovecraft. To presevere, a sensitive person must resist the ambient persuasion that dictates a subversion of form and meaning creating inferior quality and a compromise of personal values."

K (II), 351 Dalhousie St., Brantford, Ontario N3S 3V9 Canada. Editor: G.J. McFarlane. Magazine: 7x8½; 50 pages. Has an "open theme that provides a forum for writers whose contemporary ideas establish a voice for turbulent times." Published as funds permit. Estab. 1985.

Needs: Condensed novel, confession, contemporary, erotica, experimental, feminist, humor/satire, literary, mainstream, science fiction, serialized/excerpted novel. Receives 15 unsolicited mss/month. Accepts mss "as quality and space permit." Mss published an undetermined time after acceptance. Publishes short shorts. Occasionally critiques rejected mss and recommends other markets.

How to Contact: Send complete ms with cover letter. Reports in 1 month on queries. SASE. Simultaneous, photocopied and reprint submissions OK. Accepts computer printout submissions, including dot-matrix. Sample copy $3.

Payment: Pays in contributor's copies.

Terms: Acquires one-time rights. Publication copyrighted.

KAIROS (II), A Journal of Contemporary Thought & Criticism, Box 199, Hartsdale NY 10530. Editor: Alan Mandell. Magazine: 5½x8½; 130-150 pages; 70 lb cover stock; illustrations; photos. "We have attempted to combine literary/artistic work with social and cultural criticism. Thus, *K* includes analytic essays as well as translations, poems, interviews, reviews and, we continue to hope, fiction as well. *K* has specific themes that are typically announced in forthcoming notice of each issue." Semiannually. Estab. 1981. Circ. 350.

Needs: Experimental, feminist, literary, translations. Receives 3-4 unsolicited fiction mss/month. Recently published work by Michael Stephens. Length: 2,500 words average. Publishes short shorts. "Short short stories would be most appropriate for *K* (given size/diversity of work presented, etc.)." Sometimes critiques rejected mss and recommends other markets.

How to Contact: Query with clips of published work or send complete ms with cover letter. Reports in 6-8 weeks on mss. SASE. Photocopied submissions OK. Accepts computer printouts, including dot-matrix. Sample copy for $6.

Payment: "We provide 3 copies of that issue and extras at discount rate."

Terms: Publication copyrighted.

Advice: "Short stories serve, for us, as another kind of occasion to present a *diversity* of forms—of expressions—that we seek. We will always be able to include only a very small selection of fiction, but such an inclusion is important to us."

KALEIDOSCOPE (II, IV), International Magazine of Literature, Fine Arts, and Disability, 326 Locust St., Akron OH 44302. (216)762-9755, ext. 27. Editor-in-Chief: Darshan Perusek, Ph.D. Magazine: 8½x11; 56-64 pages; non-coated paper; coated cover stock; illustrations (all media); photos. Semiannually. Estab. 1979. Circ. 1,500.

Needs: Personal experience, drama, fantasy, feminist, humor/satire, prose poem, serialized/excerpted novel. "Writers need not limit themselves to writing about being disabled." Receives 20-25 unsolicited fiction mss/month. Accepts 10 mss/year. Approximately 1% of fiction is agented. Recently published work by Kiran Nagarkar, Ellen Hunnicutt, Amber Coverdale Sumrall; published new writers within the last year. Length: 3,000 words minimum; 5,000 words maximum.

How to Contact: Query first or send complete ms and cover letter, which should include author's educational and writing background; if author is disabled, how the disability has influenced the writing. SASE. Accepts computer printout submissions. Reports in 4 weeks on queries; 8-10 weeks on mss. Sample copy $2. Guidelines for #10 SAE and 1 first class stamp.

Payment: Cash payment. 2 free contributor's copies; charge for extras: $4.

Terms: Pays on publication for first rights. Reprints are permitted with credit given to original publication. Publication copyrighted.

Advice: "Read the magazine and get fiction guidelines. Disabled writers may write on any topic; non-disabled writers must limit themselves to the theme of disability. We seek fresh and original perspectives on disability. No bias as to style, but adamantly hostile to the sentimental and the trite. The criteria for good fiction apply in every case: thought-provoking subject matter, fresh language and imagery, effective handling of technique. Minor editing to be expected."

KALLIOPE, A JOURNAL OF WOMEN'S ART (II), Florida Community College at Jacksonville, 11901 Beach Blvd., Jacksonville FL 32216. (904)646-2150. Editor: Mary Sue Koeppel. Magazine: 8¼x7¼; 76-88 pages; 70 lb coated matte paper; Bristol cover; 16-18 halftones per issue. "A literary and visual arts journal for women, *Kalliope* celebrates women in the arts by publishing their work and by providing a forum for their ideas and opinions." Short stories, poems, plays, essays, reviews and visual art. Published 3 times/year. Estab. 1978. Circ. 1,000.

Needs: "Quality short fiction by women writers." Accepts 2-4 mss/issue. Receives approximately 25 unsolicited fiction mss each month. Recently published work by Layle Silbert, Robin Merle, Robert Gentry; published new writers within the last year. Preferred length: 750-3,000 words, but occasionally publishes longer (and shorter) pieces. Critiques rejected mss "when there is time and if requested."

How to Contact: Send complete ms with SASE and short contributor's note. Reports in 2-3 months on ms. Publishes ms an average of 1-6 months after acceptance. Sample copy $4 for current issue; $2 for issues from '78-'85.

Payment: 3 free author's copies or year's subscription. $3.50 charge for extras, discount for large orders.

Terms: Acquires first rights. "We accept only unpublished work. Copyright returned to author upon request." Publication copyrighted.

Advice: "Read our magazine. The work we consider for publication will be well written and the characters and dialogue will be convincing and have strength and movement. We like a fresh approach and are interested in new or unusual forms. Make us believe your characters; give readers an insight which they might not have had if they had not read you. We would like to publish more work by minority writers." Manuscripts are rejected because "1) nothing *happens*!, 2) it is thinly disguised autobiography (richly disguised autobiography is OK), and 3) ending is either too pat or else just trails off."

‡KALLISTI (I,II), A Magazine of Alternative, Matrix Productions, Box 19566, Cincinnati OH 45219. (513)241-5974. Editor: Kenn Day. Magazine: digest-size; 44 pages; 20 lb paper; 67 lb cover; illustrations and photographs. "Forum for various counter-cultural expressions. Absurdist, magickal, philosophical, futurist, open-minded, non-sexist/racist writing." Bimonthly. "Possibly" plans special fiction issue. Estab. 1984. Circ. 1,000.

Needs: Adventure, contemporary, erotica, experimental, fantasy, feminist, gay, humor/satire, lesbian, literary, psychic/supernatural/occult, science fiction, serialized/excerpted novel, subculture. Receives 3-9 unsolicited mss/month. Accepts 1-2 mss/issue; 6-8 mss/year. Publishes ms after acceptance "as soon as space is available." Length: 600 words preferred; 300 minimum; 700 maximum (1,200 for serialized). Publishes short shorts. Sometimes critiques rejected mss and recommends other markets.

How to Contact: Query with clips of published work with cover letter. Reports in 2 weeks on queries; 6 weeks on mss. SASE for ms, not needed for query. Simultaneous, photocopied and reprint submissions OK. Accepts computer printout submissions, indluding dot-matrix. Sample copy for $1. Fiction guidelines for #10 SAE and 1 first class stamp.

Payment: Pays 3 contributor's copies.

Terms: Acquires one-time rights. Publication coyrighted.

Advice: "Open a dialogue—write to us and keep sending stuff. Listen to our critiques. We're not trying to be mean—just to improve the quality."

Kallisti: A magazine of alternatives for mature readers, published bimonthly, is a "forum for various counter-cultural expressions."

KALLISTI

P.O. Box 19566, Cincinnati, Ohio 45219

Vol. 2, Issue #3   Sept. 1988   Recommended for the mature reader $1.00

Cover art by Edison Girard.

‡KANA (II), 606 B, Walker Ave., Baltimore MD 21212. (301)377-7613. Editor: Laurie Rockefeller. Magazine: 8½x11; 32 pages; 60 lb paper; 70 lb cover; illustrations. "Any material as long as it makes sense," for a "college educated and above" audience. Semiannually. Estab. 1988. Circ. 1,000.
Needs: Adventure, confession, contemporary, ethnic, experimental, fantasy, feminist, gay, historical (general), horror, humor/satire, lesbian, literary, mainstream, psychic/supernatural/occult, regional, religious/inspirational, science fiction, senior citizen/retirement, suspense/mystery, translations, western. Does not want to see "the type of fiction that drags on without saying anything; confusing material." Receives 2-3 unsolicited mss/month. Accepts 1-2 mss/issue; 2-4 mss/year. Publishes ms 1-6 months after acceptance. Length: 500-750 words preferred; 1,000 words maximum. Publishes short shorts. Sometimes critiques rejected mss.
How to Contact: Send complete ms with cover letter. Cover letter should include "a bio, return address (on work, too), writer's philosophy on writing and/or life." Reports in 4 weeks on queries; 8 weeks on mss. SASE. Simultaneous, photocopied and reprint submissions OK "when noted as such." Accepts computer printout submissions, including dot-matrix. Sample copy for 8½x11 SAE and 2 first class stamps. Fiction guidelines for #10 SAE and 1 first class stamp.
Payment: Pays in contributor's copies. Publication not copyrighted.
Terms: All rights remain with author.
Advice: "I gear my magazine towards the public instead of the literary private sectors. I believe that the hairdresser down the street enjoys reading just as much as the professor at the university, but the material in literary magazines is often too deep for non-literature majors (or otherwise), so I keep *Kana* simple, understandable, and free to whomever wants to read it or submit to it. I believe that Steinbeck and William Carlos Williams grasped best the contemporary short story (American, anyway)."

KANSAS QUARTERLY (I, II), Kansas Quarterly Association, 122 Denison Hall, English Dept., Kansas State University, Manhattan KS 66506. (913)532-6716. Editors: Harold Schneider, Ben Nyberg, W.R. Moses and John Rees. Magazine: 6x9; 104-356 pages; 70 lb offset paper; Frankcote 8 pt. coated cover stock; illustrations occasionally; unsolicited photos rarely. "A literary and cultural arts magazine publishing fiction and poetry. Special material on selected, announced topics in literary criticism, art history, folklore and regional history. For well-read, general and academic audiences." Quarterly. Published special fiction issue last year; plans another. Estab. 1968. Circ. 1,300.
Needs: "We consider most categories as long as the fiction is of sufficient literary quality to merit inclusion, though we have no interest in children's literature. We resist translations and parts of novels, but do not absolutely refuse them." Accepts 30-50 mss/year. Limited reading done in summer. Approximately 1% of fiction is agented. Recently published work by Laurence Gonzales, Gordon Weaver and H. E. Francis. Published new writers within the last year. Length: 350-12,000 words. Sometimes rec-

ommends other markets.

How to Contact: Send complete ms with SASE. Reports in 3 months + on mss. Publishes ms an average of 18-24 months after acceptance. Sample copy $5.

Payment: 2 free author's copies and annual awards to the best of the stories published.

Terms: Acquires all rights. Sends galleys to author. "We reassign rights on request at time of republication." Sponsors awards: *KQ*/KAC (national); Seaton awards (for Kansas natives or residents). Each offers 6-10 awards from $25-$250.

Advice: "Always check a sample copy of the magazine to which you send your stories—note its editors' likes and interests. Send your story with SASE—do not appear to devalue them by asking they be discarded rather than returned."

KARAMU (II), English Dept., Eastern Illinois University, Charleston IL 61920. (217)581-5614. Editor: Peggy L. Brayfield. Magazine: 5x8; 60 pages; cover illustrations. "We like fiction that builds around real experiences, real images and real characters, that shows an awareness of current fiction and the types of experiments that are going on in it, and that avoids abstraction, sentimentality, over-philosophizing and fuzzy pontifications. For a literate, college-educated audience." Annually. Estab. 1967. Circ. 500.

Needs: Literary, contemporary. Receives approximately 20-30 unsolicited fiction mss/month. Recently published work by Chris Mazza, George W. Smyth and Bonnie McGara. Accepts 4-5 mss/issue. Published new writers within the last year. Length: 2,000-7,000 words. Critiques rejected mss when there is time.

How to Contact: Send complete ms with SASE. Accepts computer printout submissions, prefers letter-quality. Reports in 2-3 months on mss. Publishes ms an average of 1 year after acceptance. Sample copy $2.

Payment: 1 free author's copy. Half price charge for extras.

Advice: "Send for a sample copy, read it, and send a complete ms if your stories seem to match our taste. Please be patient—we sometimes get behind in our reading, especially between May and September. Mss submitted between January and June have the best chance. We feel that much of the best writing today is being done in short fiction."

‡THE KENYON REVIEW (II), Kenyon College, Gambier OH 43022. (614)427-3339. Editor: T.H. Hummer. Magazine for readers "from college on up." Quarterly. Estab. 1939. Circ. 3,500.

Needs: Condensed/excerpted novel, contemporary, ethnic, experimental, fantasy, historical, humor/satire, literary, mainstream, prose poem, science fiction, senior citizen/retirement, serialized novel, translations, western. Receives 150-200 unsolicited fiction mss/month. Accepts up to 3 mss/issue; up to 12 mss/year. Does not read mss June-August. Publishes ms 12-18 months after acceptance. 50% of fiction is agented. Length: 3-15 (typeset) pages preferred. Rarely publishes short shorts. Sometimes comments on rejected mss.

How to Contact: Query with clips of published work or send complete ms with cover letters. Reports on queries in 2 months; on mss in 1 month. SASE. Simultaneous and photocopied submissions OK. Does not accept dot-matrix computer printouts. Sample copy $6.50.

Payment: $10/page for fiction.

Terms: Pays on publication for one-time rights and option on anthology rights. Sends copy-edited version to author for approval. Publication copyrighted.

Advice: "Read several issues of our publication."

‡KID TIMES (IV), The Newspaper Just for Kids, Box 20024, Sun Valley NV 89433. (702)673-9205. Editor: Sherry Yearsley. Newspaper: tabloid size; 12 + pages; newsprint paper; illustrations and photos. "News for children (uptone—no murder, theft, etc.—educational articles, sports, etc.), for children 0-15." Monthly. Plans special fiction issue. Estab. 1988.

Needs: Adventure, fantasy, historical, humor/satire, juvenile, preschool, science fiction, sports, suspense mystery, western, young adult/teen. No fiction that deals "with the negative." Accepts 2 unsolicited fiction mss/issue. Time between acceptance and publication "depends on theme/holiday." Length:

❝ *Talent is a matter of quantity: talent doesn't write one page, it writes three hundred.* **❞**

—*Jules Renard*

800 words maximum. Publishes short shorts. Sometimes comments on rejected mss and recommends other markets.

How to Contact: Send complete ms with cover letter, which should include "what this person has published and age." Reports in 4 weeks. SASE. Simultaneous submissions OK. Accepts dot-matrix computer printouts; accepts electronic submissions via disk or modem: query for details. Sample copy $1. Fiction guidelines free.

Payment: Payment varies. "See guidelines for details."

Terms: Acquires first rights. Publication copyrighted. Sponsors contests for fiction writers. "Must be 18 years old or younger. Details are explained in each issue."

Advice: Looks for articles "on any topic that may interest children, with photos or artwork. Also need crossword puzzles, mazes, wordfinds, games, connect the dots, coloring—all with the major holiday for each issue as focus." Writers should ask themselves, "can a young person benefit by reading this in terms of more than entertainment?"

‡KIDS LIB NEWS (I,IV), Children's Liberation Movement Network, Oness Press, Box 11141, Portland OR 97211. (503)285-4848. Editor: Mycall Sunanda. Magazine: 8x11; 2-4 pages; "Xerox recycled" paper; no cover; photos. Publishes "family and natural freedom, dreams, humor, jokes, stories, plays, drawings, poems" for "parents, kids, teachers, hip or natural." Quarterly. Estab. 1985. Circ. 200.

Needs: Adventure, juvenile (5-9 years), preschool (1-4 years), prose poem, psychic/supernatural/occult, young adult/teen (10-18 years) and family nature trips. Accepts 1 ms/issue. Publishes ms within 1-2 months of acceptance. Recently published work by Mycall Sunanda, Danny Borisick and Makim Bey. Length: 200 words preferred; 5 words minimum; 500 words maximum. Sometimes critiques rejected mss and recommends other markets.

How to Contact: Query with clips of published work or send complete ms with cover letter. Reports on queries in 2-3 weeks; on mss in 2-4 weeks. Simultaneous, photocopied and reprint submissions OK. No dot-matrix computer printouts. Sample copy for $1-$2, 3x9 SAE and 1 first class stamp. Fiction guidelines for #10 SAE and 1 first class stamp.

Payment: Payment is negotiable. Free subscription to magazine and contributor's copies.

Terms: Pays on publication. Purchases first rights "or none." Publication not copyrighted.

Advice: In choosing fiction, editor considers "how much freedom seeking/finding it shares, personal growth, joy, body-games, nature-spirit! Innovative, strange and cosmicrazyness."

THE KINDRED SPIRIT, Rt. 2, Box 111, St. John KS 67576. (316)549-3933. Editor: Michael Hathaway. Tabloid: 10x13; over 24 pages; newsprint; illustrations; photos. Publishes "All types of material, no particular theme, for those interested in contemporary small press." Estab. 1982. Circ. 1,200.

Needs: Contemporary, experimental, humor/satire, literary and psychic/supernatural/occult. Receives 6 mss/month. Accepts 1 ms/issue; 4 mss/year. Publishes ms within 6-12 months of acceptance. Length: 3,500 words preferred. Publishes short shorts. Sometimes recommends other markets to writers of rejected mss.

How to Contact: Send complete ms with cover letter. Reports in 2 weeks. SASE. Photocopied submissions OK. Accepts computer printout submissions, including dot-matrix. Sample copy for $1 ($2 overseas). Fiction guidelines for #10 SAE and 1 first class stamp.

Payment: Pays 1 contributor's copy. Charge for extra copies.

Terms: Acquires first rights. Publication copyrighted.

Advice: "Be patient, courteous with editors. Never become too discouraged. If you feel a desire to write, then you were meant to write. Never give up."

KINGFISHER (II), Box 9783, N. Berkeley CA 94709. Editors: Annie Barrows, Ruthie Singer, Barbara Schultz. Magazine: 6x9; 120 pages; 60 lb paper; 80 lb cover; illustrations; photos. "*Kingfisher* sports no particular political or intellectual doctrine. We are interested in innovative short fiction primarily, but we will also consider poetry, essays and translations." Biannually. Estab. 1987.

Needs: Contemporary, experimental, literary, serialized/excerpted novel and translations. No science fiction. Receives 100 unsolicited fiction mss/month. Accepts up to 20 mss/issue; up to 40 mss/year. Recently published work by Steven Bercu, Dagoberto Gilb, Stewart O'Nan; published new writers within the last year. Length: 3,000 words average; 12,000 words maximum. Publishes short shorts. Sometimes comments on rejected mss and recommends other markets.

How to Contact: Send complete ms with cover letter, which should include short bio and list of publication credits. Reports on queries in 4 weeks; on mss in 2 months. SASE. Simultaneous, photocopied and reprint submissions OK. Accepts computer printout submissions, including dot-matrix. Sample copy: $5.

Payment: Pays in contributor's copies.

Terms: Acquires one-time rights. Publication copyrighted.

Advice: "We will continue to publish short works of fiction as long as we can find ones of the quality we require. The writer should please mention if he or she would like to receive specific reaction to his/her work. We are more than happy to help in that way."

‡KIOSK (II), English Department, S.U.N.Y. at Buffalo, 302 Clemens Hall, Buffalo NY 14260. (716)636-2570. Editors: Ted Pelton, Patrick Walters, Lisa Sheffield. Magazine: 8½x5½; 100 pages; card stock cover. "We seek innovative, non-formula fiction and poetry." Plans special fiction issue. Annually. Estab. 1986. Circ. 750.
Needs: Excerpted novel, erotica, experimental, feminist, gay, humor/satire, lesbian, prose poem and translations. "No genre or formula fiction; we seek fiction that defies categorization—lush, quirky, flippant, subversive, etc." Receives 15 mss/month. Accepts 6 mss/issue. Publishes ms within 6 months of acceptance. Recently published work by Ray Federman, Carol Berge, Tom Whalen. Length: 3,000 words preferred; 20 words minimum; 7,500 words maximum. Publishes short shorts. Sometimes critiques rejected mss; rarely recommends other markets.
How to Contact: Send complete mss with cover letter during October-February reading period. Reports in 2-3 weeks on queries; 2-3 months on mss. "Most sooner; if we keep it longer, we're considering it seriously." SASE. Simultaneous, photocopied and reprint submissions OK. Accepts computer printout submissions, including dot-matrix. Sample copy for 9x6 or larger SAE and 2 first class stamps.
Payment: Pays in contributor's copies.
Terms: Acquires one-time rights. Publication copyrighted.
Advice: "*Kiosk* was started because it seemed to us than most little mags were publishing the same type of stuff—slick, literary, polished fluff that writing programs churn out like hot dogs. If you've got a different vision of writing than others seem to be buying, then maybe this mag is for you. Literary magazine writing is exciting when editors take chances and offer a place for writers who find other avenues closed." Looks for "a writer's unique vision and care for the language. Striking, unexpected images. New forms, new thinking. A certain level of technical accomplishment."

‡LACTUCA (II), Box 621 Suffern, NY 10901. Editor: Mike Selender. Magazine: folded 8½x14; 40-60 pages; 24 lb bond; soft cover; illustrations. Publishes "poetry, short fiction and line drawings, for a general literary audience." Published 3 times/year. Estab. 1986. Circ. 250.
Needs: Adventure, condensed/excerpted novel, confession, contemporary, erotica, literary, mainstream, prose poem and regional. No "self-indulgent writing or fiction about writing fiction." Receives 30 or more mss/month. Accepts 3-4 mss/issue; 10-12 mss/year. Publishes ms within 2-6 months of acceptance. Recently published work by Douglas Mendini, Charles Kuchinski, Linda Hasselstrom; published new writers within the last year. Length: around 12-14 typewritten double-spaced pages. Publishes short shorts. Usually critiques rejected mss and recommends other markets.
How to Contact: Query first or send complete mss with cover letter. Cover letter should include "just a few brief notes about yourself. Please no long 'literary' résumés or bios. The work will speak for itself." Reports in 2 weeks on queries; 6-8 weeks on mss. SASE. Photocopied submissions OK. No simultaneous or previously published work. Accepts computer printouts, including dot-matrix. Accepts electronic submissions via "MS DOS formatted disk. We can convert most word-processing formats." Sample copy for $3.50. Fiction guidelines for #10 SAE and 1 first class stamp.
Payment: Pays 2-5 contributor's copies, depending on the length of the work published.
Terms: Acquires first North American serial rights. Sends galleys to author if requested. Publication copyrighted. Copyrights revert to authors.
Advice: "Too much of the poetry and fiction I have been reading over the past two years has been obsessed with the act of writing or life as a writer. We're not interested in this kind of writing. I place a strong emphasis on the readability of fiction. The dialogue should be clear, and the characters speaking readily discernible. It is worth making the extra revisions necessary to obtain this level of quality."

LAKE EFFECT (II), Lake County Writers Group, Oswego Art Guild, Box 315, Oswego NY 13126. (315)342-3579. Editor: Jean O'Connor Fuller, M.E. Tabloid: 11½x17; 32 pages; newsprint paper and cover; illustrations; photos. "We publish short fiction, poetry, humor, reviews, b&w art and photographs and one nonfiction piece of interest to the area each issue. Our circulation is principally upstate NY." Quarterly. Estab. 1986. Circ. 10,000.
Needs: Contemporary, fantasy, historical (general), humor/satire, literary, mainstream, regional. "We want previously unpublished, honest stories." Accepts 2-3 mss/issue. Does not read mss in August. Publishes ms within 6 months after acceptance. Recently published work by Deborah Rossen, Frederick Semken; published new writers within the last year. Length: 5,000 words maximum. Publishes short shorts. Occasionally critiques rejected mss and recommends other markets.
How to Contact: Send complete ms with cover letter, which should include biographical information on author. Reports in 2 months. SASE for ms. Photocopied submissions OK. No simultaneous submissions. Accepts computer printout submissions, including dot-matrix; "dot-matrix must be readable."

Sample copy for $2. Fiction guidelines for #10 SAE and 1 first class stamp.
Payment: $25 and 3 free contributor's copies; charge for extras.
Terms: Acquires first North American serial rights. Publication copyrighted.
Advice: "We exist primarily to give outlet to the writers of this region, but also will use good work from outside if we like it. Send us stories about human beings we can believe in, in neat, professional style. We prefer upbeat to downbeat work, but deplore sentimentality. Do not send us your death stories."

LAKE STREET REVIEW (II), Box 7188, Powderhorn Station, Minneapolis MN 55407. Editor: Kevin FitzPatrick. Magazine: 7x8½; 40 pages; good quality paper and cover stock; illustrations; photos occasionally. "An annual literary publication focusing on the writing of poets and fiction writers, both developing and established." Annually. Estab. 1976. Circ. 600.
Needs: Contemporary, ethnic, experimental, humor/satire, literary, mainstream, prose poem, science fiction. Receives 10 fiction mss/month. Accepts 5-7 mss/issue. Deadline is September 15 of each year. Publishes ms within 1 year of acceptance. Recently published work by Joe Paddock, Anne Farrer Scott, Jonathan Borden; published new writers within the last last year. Length: 4,000 words average; 500 words minimum; 4,500 words maximum. Sometimes critiques rejected mss.
How to Contact: Send complete ms. Reports on queries in 1 week; on ms "no later than 1 month after the September 15 deadline." SASE. Photocopied submissions OK. Accepts computer printout submissions, no dot-matrix. Sample copy $2. Fiction guidelines for #10 SAE and 1 first class stamp.
Payment: Pays in contributor's copies (2).
Terms: Acquires first North American serial rights. Publication copyrighted.
Advice: "Send for guidelines or purchase sample copy."

LAPIS (I, IV), LAPIS Educational Association, Inc.,3874 W. Princeton Circle, Denver CO 80236. Editor-in-Chief: Karen Degenhart. Magazine: 5½x8½; 64-80 pages; b&w illustrations. "A professional journal which publishes informative, scholarly articles about Jungian psychology, contemporary theological issues, related literary criticism, and other psycho/spiritual ideas" for an audience of psychologists, educators, poets and ministers. Published annually. Estab. 1977. Circ. 150.
Needs: "We publish little fiction"—only with Jungian or psychological-spiritual slant, rarely over 15 pages. Accepts 3-4 articles/issue. Published new writers within the last year. Publishes short shorts under 10 pages. Does not read Oct. through March. Occasionally critiques rejected mss.
How to Contact: Query first or send complete ms with SASE and brief bio. Simultaneous and photocopied submissions and previously published work OK. Accepts computer printout submissions; prefers single spaced, letter-quality. Reports in 3 weeks on queries; "indefinite" on mss. Sample copy $2. Free guidelines with #10 SASE.
Payment: 3 contributor's copies, if person joins for a year for $10 membership fee, when published.
Terms: Acquires one-time rights. Publication copyrighted.
Advice: "Query first for manuscripts over 10 pages—be sure to send enough return postage. Also, we publish in summer or fall; send submissions in spring for quicker response. We do not publish much fiction. We publish occasional short shorts with spiritual growth and exploration themes. Keep at it. *Lapis* is quite specialized."

LEFT CURVE (II), Box 472, Oakland CA 94604. (415)763-7193. Editor: Csaba Polony. Magazine: 8½x11; 96 pages; 60 lb paper; 100 pt. CIS Durosheen cover; illustrations; photos. "*Left Curve* is an artist-produced journal addressing the problem(s) of cultural forms emerging from the crises of modernity that strive to be independent from the control of dominant institutions, based on the recognition of the destructiveness of commodity (capitalist) systems to all life." Published irregularly. Estab. 1974. Circ. 1,000.
Needs: Contemporary, ethnic, experimental, historical, humor/satire, literary, prose poem, regional, science fiction, translations, political. Receives approx. 1 unsolicited fiction ms/month. Accepts approx. 1 ms/issue. Publishes ms a maximum of 6 months after acceptance. Length: 1,200 words average; 500 words minimum; 2,500 words maximum. Publishes short shorts. Sometimes comments on rejected mss or recommends other markets.
How to Contact: Send complete ms with cover letter, which should include "statement on writer's intent, brief bio., why submitting to *Left Curve*. Reports on queries in 1 month; on mss in 3 months. SASE. Accepts computer printouts, including dot-matrix. Sample copy for $5, 8½x11 envelope; 90¢ postage. Fiction guidelines for 2 first class stamps.
Payment: Pays in contributor's copies.
Terms: Acquires first rights. Publication copyrighted.
Advice: "Be honest, realistic and gorge out the truth you wish to say. Understand yourself and the world. Have writing be a means to achieve or realize what is real."

PABLO LENNIS (I, IV), The Magazine of Science Fiction, Fantasy and Fact, Manrovian Press, Fandom House, 30 North 19th St., Lafayette IN 47904. Editor: John Thiel. Magazine: 8½x11; 30 pages; standard stock; illustrations and "occasional" photos. "Science fiction, fantasy, science, research and mystic for scientists and science fiction and fantasy appreciators." Published 4-5 times/year.
Needs: Fantasy, horror, psychic/supernatural/occult, science fiction, spiritual. Receives 10 unsolicited mss/year. Accepts 3 mss/issue; 15 mss/year. Publishes ms 6 months after acceptance. Recently published work by Eugene Flinn, Archie Taylor, Martha Collins; published new writers within the last year. Length: 2,500 words average; 300 words minimum; 3,000 words maximum. Occasionally critiques rejected mss and recommends other markets.
How to Contact: "Method of submission is author's choice but he might prefer to query. No self-statement is necessary." Reports in 2 weeks. Does not accept computer printouts.
Payment: Pays in contributor's copies.
Terms: Publication not copyrighted.
Advice: "*Novel and Short Story Writer's Market* has brought in many new manuscripts, so my rate of publication has slowed down, but I don't reject frequently and then with good reasons. If you want to write a really good story, stick to materially perceived reality in setting scenes and saying something the reader would like to hear. Always have an understandable framework from which to depart imaginatively."

LETTERS MAGAZINE (II, III), Maine Writers Workshop and Mainespring Press, Box 905, RFD 1, Stonington ME 04681. (207)367-2484. Editor: Helen Nash. Magazine: 8½x11; 4+ pages; best paper. "Accepts only high quality material in all ethical fields of literature." Quarterly. Estab. 1969. Circ. 6,500.
Needs: Literary, short stories, prose poem, science fiction, poetry and mystery. "No porno, confessions, etc." Buys 5-10 mss/year. Receives 150 unsolicited fiction mss each month. Recently published work by Richard Eberhart, G. F. Bush and Jack Matthews; published new writers within the last year. Length: 500-1,000 words. Critiques rejected mss "when justified."
How to Contact: Query "with large SASE (US postage) or send one chapter with large SASE (US postage). No returns if insufficient postage." Accepts computer printout submissions; letter-quality only. Reports in 1 month on queries. Publishes ms an average of 1 year after acceptance. Sample copy for $5 with SAE and US postage. Evaluates full-length mss at usual rate.
Payment: Varies. All cash; no copies. Usual royalties for any books published.
Terms: Pays on publication for all rights. Publication copyrighted.

LIGHTHOUSE (II), Box 1377, Auburn WA 98071-1377. Editor: Tim Clinton. Magazine: 5½x8½; 56 pages; 50 lb cougar opaque paper; woodbine enamel cover; illustrations. "Timeless stories and poems for family reading—G rated." Bimonthly. Estab. 1986. Circ. 500.
Needs: Adventure, contemporary, historical, humor/satire, juvenile (5-9 years), mainstream, preschool (1-4 years), prose poem, regional, romance (contemporary, historical and young adult), senior citizen/retirement, sports, suspense/mystery, western, young adult/teen (10-18 years). Receives 180 mss/month. Accepts 15 mss/issue; 90 mss/year. Publishes ms within 2 years of acceptance. Recently published work by Margaret Shauers, Barbara Yarbrough, Patricia Elliot; published new writers within the last year. Length: 5,000 words maximum. Publishes short shorts.
How to Contact: Send complete mss, include Social Security number. Reports in 1 week on queries; in 1 month on mss. SASE. Photocopied submissions OK. Accepts computer printout submissions, including dot-matrix. Sample copy for $2. Fiction guidelines for #10 SAE and 1 first class stamp.
Payment: Pays up to $75 for stories; up to $10 for poetry.
Terms: Author copies discounted at $1.50 each. Payment on publication for first rights and first North American serial rights. Publication copyrighted.
Advice: "If there is a message in the story, we prefer it to be subtly hidden in the action. If it fits our guidelines, send it for our consideration, along with SASE with sufficient postage for return."

LILITH MAGAZINE (I, II, IV), The Jewish Women's Magazine, Suite 2432, 250 W 57th St., New York NY 10019. (212)757-0818. Editor: Susan Weidman Schneider. Fiction Editor: Julia Wolf Mazow. Magazine: 8½x11; 32 pages; 20 lb cover; b&w illustrations; b&w and color photos. Publishes work relating to Jewish feminism, for Jewish feminists, feminists and Jewish households. Quarterly. Estab.

Read the Manuscript Mechanics section to learn the correct way to prepare and submit a manuscript.

1975. Circ. 10,000.

Needs: Ethnic, feminist, lesbian, literary, prose poem, psychic/supernatural/occult, religious/inspirational, senior citizen/retirement, spiritual, translation, young adult. Nothing that does not in any way relate to Jews, women or Jewish women." Receives 15 unsolicited mss/month. Accepts 1 ms/issue; 3 mss/year. Publishes ms 2-6 months after acceptance. Recently published work by Leslea Newman, Fredelle Maynard and Marjorie Hirshen; published new writers within the last year. Publishes short shorts.

How to Contact: Send complete ms with cover letter, which should include a 2-line bio. Reports in 2 months on queries; 2-6 months on mss. SASE. Simultaneous, photocopied and reprint submissions OK. Accepts computer printout submissions, including dot-matrix. Sample copy for $4.50 and 4 first class stamps. Fiction guidelines for #10 SAE and 1 first class stamp.

Payment: Pays in contributor's copies only.

Terms: Acquires first rights. Publication copyrighted.

‡LIME (I), "Intense and Dense and No Pretense," Sub Publications, Box 6643, Cleveland OH 44101. (216)521-1982. Editor: Karen Wardrop. Co-editor: Jeff Curtis. Magazine: 5½x8½; 16-20 pages; Xerox paper; illustrations and photographs. "Our theme is intensity in life and thought—including over-reaction to anything. We publish whatever strikes our fancy." Audience is "college educated, dissatisfied, artistic, humorous." Bimonthly "or so." Plans special fiction issue. Estab. 1987. Circ. 50.

Needs: Confession, erotica, ethnic, experimental, fantasy, feminist, horror, humor/satire, lesbian, literary, prose poem, psychic/supernatural/occult, regional, romance, translations, art. "Anything is OK really, as long as it is good, rings of truth, and is intense." Receives 2-3 mss/month. Buys 1-2 mss/issue. Publishes ms 2-3 months after acceptance. Length: 500-750 words preferred; 2 words minimum; 2,000 words maximum. "The ideal is a sort of 'prose-poem' style of fiction." Sometimes critiques rejected ms.

How to Contact: Query with clips of published work or send complete ms with cover letter. Cover letter should include "personal information, background, etc." Reports in 2 weeks. SASE. Simultaneous, photocopied and reprint submissions OK. Accepts computer printout submissions, including dot-matrix. Sample copy for #10 SAE and 45¢ postage.

Payment: Free subscription to magazine and contributor's copies.

Terms: Acquires one-time rights. Publication "copyrighted just by individuals included."

Advice: "I would tell a beginning fiction writer to forget about writing fiction and instead write an autobiography, and if necessary, fictionalize from that, to make it interesting. Most people are more interesting than they realize and may come to understand that if they write about themselves. Send drawings (of anything) with your story."

LIMESTONE: A LITERARY JOURNAL (II), University of Kentucky, Dept. of English, 1215 Patterson Office Tower, Lexington KY 40506-0027. Editor: Stephen R. Whited. Fiction Editor: Rob Merritt. Magazine: 6x9; 40-70 pages; standard text paper and cover; illustrations; photos. "We publish a variety of styles and attitudes, and we're looking to expand our offering." Annually. Estab. 1981. Circ. 1,000.

Needs: Confession, contemporary, experimental, feminist, humor/satire, literary, mainstream, prose poem, regional. "We are a wee bit tired of stories about teenagers." Receives 25-50 mss/year. Accepts 5-12 mss/issue. Does not read mss June—August. Publishes ms an average of 6 months after acceptance. Recently published work by Guy Davenport, Tad Richards, R.T. Smith; published new writers within the last year. Length: 3,000-5,000 words preferred; 5,000 words maximum. Publishes short shorts. Sometimes critiques rejected mss and recommends other markets.

How to Contact: Send complete ms with cover letter, which should include "publishing record and brief bio." Reports in 1-2 weeks on queries; 6-8 weeks on mss. SASE. Simultaneous and photocopied submissions OK. Accepts computer printout submissions; no dot-matrix. Electronic submissions OK via IBM compatible disks. Sample copy for $2.

Payment: Pays 2 contributor's copies.

Terms: Rights revert to author. Publication copyrighted.

Advice: "We encourage all interested writers, but we also want to provide a forum for creative writing students looking to publish for the first time."

LININGTON LINEUP (IV), Elizabeth Linington Society, 1223 Glen Terrace, Glassboro NJ 08028. Editor: Rinehart S. Potts. Newsletter: 8½x11; 16 pages; bond paper and cover stock; illustrations and photographs. "For those interested in the publications of Elizabeth Linington (a/k/a Lesley Egan, Egan O'Neill, Anne Blaisdell, Dell Shannon)—historical fiction and detective mysteries—therefore material must relate in some way thereto." Quarterly. Plans special fiction issue. Estab. 1984. Circ. 400.

Needs: Historical (general), literary, suspense/mystery. Receives 3-4 fiction mss/month. Accepts 1 ms/issue; 4 mss/year. Publishes ms 3 months after acceptance. Charges reading fee of $1. Requires magazine subscription of $12 before reading. Publishes short shorts. Sometimes comments on rejected mss.

How to Contact: Query first. Reports in 1 month. SASE. Photocopied and reprint submissions OK.

Accepts computer printout submissions, including dot-matrix. Sample copy $3.
Payment: Free subscription to magazine.
Terms: Acquires first rights. Publication copyrighted.
Advice: "Become familiar with Miss Linington's books and continuing characters."

THE LITERARY REVIEW, An International Journal of Contemporary Writing, Fairleigh Dickinson University, 285 Madison Ave., Madison NJ 07940. (201)593-8564. Editor-in-Chief: Walter Cummins. Magazine: 9x6; 128-152 pages; illustrations; photos. "Literary magazine specializing in fiction, poetry, and essays with an international focus." Quarterly. Estab. 1957. Circ. 1,200.
Needs: Works of high literary quality only. Receives 30-40 unsolicited fiction mss/month. Approximately 1-2% of fiction is agented. Recently published Anne Brashler, Thomas E. Kennedy, Steve Yarborough; published new writers within the last year. Accepts 10-12 mss/year. Occasionally critiques rejected mss. Sometimes recommends other markets.
How to Contact: Send complete ms with SASE. "Cover letter should include publication credits." Photocopied submissions OK. Accepts computer printout submissions. Reports in 10 weeks on mss. Publishes ms an average of 12-18 months after acceptance. Sample copy $5; free guidelines with SASE.
Payment: 2 free contributor's copies; 25% discount for extras.
Terms: Acquires first rights. Publication copyrighted.
Advice: "Too much of what we are seeing today is openly derivative in subject, plot and prose style. We pride ourselves on spotting new writers with fresh insight and the ability to express it."

‡LITTLE BALKANS REVIEW (II, IV), A Southeast Kansas Literary & Graphics Quarterly, Little Balkans Press, Inc., 601 Grandview Heights Terrace, Pittsburg KS 66762. (316)231-1589 or 231-7000. Editor: Gene DeGruson. Fiction Editor: Shelby Horn. "Kansas is our theme, historical and contemporary, in poetry, fiction, nonfiction and art." General and academic audience. Quarterly. Estab. 1980. Circ. 1,200.
Needs: Adventure, contemporary, ethnic, experimental, fantasy, feminist, historical, horror, prose poem, spiritual, sports, humor/satire, literary, mainstream, prose poem, psychic/supernatural/occult, regional, science fiction, suspense/mystery, translations, western and young adult/teen. Receives 200 unsolicited mss each month. Accepts 2 mss/issue; 8 mss/year. Length: 2,500 words average; 200 words minimum; 7,000 words maximum. Occasionally critiques rejected mss.
How to Contact: Send complete ms with cover letter. "It is desirable to know womething of the personal history of the writer, since we do concentrate on this region (Southeast Kansasas), and we like to include such information in our publication." SASE. Sample copy $2.50.
Payment: 3 contributor's copies.
Terms: Acquires first rights. Publication copyrighted.
Advice: "Attempt to publish in small publications, such as ours, in order to build credibility as a writer."

LIVE LETTERS MAGAZINE, 89 Chambers Street, New York NY 10007. Editor: Ione. Estab. 1974. Circ. 2,000.
Needs: Letters, literary, feminist, gay/lesbian, humor/satire, psychic/supernatural/occult, regional, senior citizen/retirement, translations. No pornography, confessions, religious or western. Receives approximately 20 unsolicited fiction mss each month. Sometimes critiques rejected mss.
How to Contact: Send inquiries with SASE. Sample copy $3.
Payment: 2 free author's copies.
Terms: Publication copyrighted.
Advice: Most rejected mss are "not right for our magazine. Include a cover letter."

LONE STAR (II), A Magazine of Humor, Suite 103, Box 29000, San Antonio TX 78229. Editor: Lauren Barnett. "Humor publication for the general public, comedy connoisseur and professional humorist. Audience: all ages, well-educated, well-read." Published 4-6 times a year. Estab. 1983. Circ. 1,200 + .
Needs: Comics and humor/satire. "Do not want to see stories that are three pages long and take three pages before getting to the first laugh." Receives 200-500 unsolicited mss/month. Buys 1-2 mss/issue; 6-12 mss/year. Length: 800 words average; 300 words minimum; 1,000 words maximum. Occasionally critiques rejected mss.
How to Contact: Send SASE for guidelines first; then send complete ms. Reports in 2 to 3 months on queries; 3 to 4 months on mss. Publishes ms an average of 6 months after acceptance. SASE. Photocopied and "sometimes" previously published submissions OK. Inquire about prices for sample issues. Fiction guidelines for #10 SAE and 1 first class stamp.
Payment: $5-$20 and 1 free contributor's copy; variable charge for extras.
Terms: "Policy is payment on publication, but we try to pay before." Buys first rights, first North

American serial rights or one-time rights; some reprints. Publication copyrighted.

Advice: "Read the guidelines, read our publications and don't give up after one rejection. We do publish more humorous fiction now. Although we publish various styles/subjects, in general, we stay away from anything prevalent in other publications. Anything submitted to *Lone Star* is automatically considered for publication in all appropriate *Lone Star* publications."

LONG SHOT, Box 6231, Hoboken NJ 07030. Editors: Danny Shot, Caren Lee Michaelson. Magazine: 5½x8½; 116 pages; 60 lb paper; 10 pt. CIS cover; illustrations; photos. Estab. 1982. Circ. 1,500.

Needs: Adventure, confession, contemporary, erotica, ethnic, experimental, fantasy, feminist, gay, horror, humor/satire, lesbian, prose poem, psychic/supernatural/occult, science fiction, suspense/mystery, western. Receives 35 unsolicited mss/month. Accepts 1-2 mss/issue. Does not read mss in August. Publishes ms 6 months at longest after acceptance. Recently published work by Eileen Myles, Charles Bukowski, Cookie Mueller; published new writers within the last year. Publishes short shorts. Sometimes recommends other markets.

How to Contact: Send complete ms. Reports in 4-6 weeks. SASE. Simultaneous and photocopied submissions OK. Accepts computer printout submissions. Sample copy for $4 plus $1 postage.

Payment: Pays in contributor's copies.

Terms: Acquires one-time rights. Publication copyrighted.

THE LONG STORY (II), 11 Kingston St., North Andover MA 01845. (508)686-7638. Editor: R.P. Burnham. Magazine: 5½x8½; 150-200 pages; 60 lb paper; 65 lb cover stock; illustrations (b&w graphics). For serious, educated, literary people. No science fiction, adventure, romance, etc. "We publish high literary quality of any kind, but especially look for committed fiction; working class settings, left-wing themes, etc." Annually. Estab. 1983. Circ. 500.

Needs: Contemporary, ethnic, feminist and literary. Receives 30-40 unsolicited mss/month. Buys 6-7 mss/issue. Published one new writer within the last year. Length: 8,000 words minimum; 20,000 words maximum. ("To accept 20,000 word story it would have to be right down our alley—about poor, oppressed people, i.e., committed fiction.") Sometimes recommends other markets.

How to Contact: Send complete ms with a brief cover letter. Reports in 2 + months. Publishes ms an average of 3-12 months after acceptance. SASE. Photocopied submissions OK. Accepts computer printout submissions, prefers letter-quality. Sample copy for $4.

Payment: Pays in 2 free contributor's copies; $4 charge for extras.

Terms: Acquires first rights. Publication copyrighted.

Advice: "Read us first and make sure submitted material is the kind we're interested in. Send clear, legible manuscripts. We're not interested in commercial success; rather we want to provide a place for long stories, the most difficult literary form to publish in our country."

LOONFEATHER (II), Bemidji Arts Center, 426 Bemidji Ave., Bemidji MN 56601. (218)751-4869. Editors: Betty Rossi and Jeane Sliney. Magazine: 6x9; 48 pages; 60 lb Hammermill Cream woven paper; 65 lb vellum cover stock; illustrations; occasional photos. A literary journal of short prose, poetry and graphics. Mostly a market for Northern Minnesota, Minnesota and Midwest writers. Semiannually. Estab. 1979. Circ. 300.

Needs: Literary, contemporary, prose poem and regional. Accepts 2-3 mss/issue, 4-6 mss/year. Recently published work by Christian Davis, Marsh Muirhead and Jerry Hendrickson. Published new writers within the last year. Length: 600-1,500 words (prefers 1,500).

How to Contact: Send complete ms with SASE, and short autobiographical sketch. Reports in 3 months. Sample copy $2 back issues; $4 current issue.

Payment: Free author's copies.

Terms: Acquires one-time rights.

Advice: "Send carefully crafted and literary fiction. Because of increase in size of magazine, we can include more, slightly longer fiction. The writer should familiarize himself/herself with the type of fiction published in literary magazines as opposed to family magazines, religious magazines, etc."

LOST AND FOUND TIMES (II), Luna Bisonte Prods, 137 Leland Ave., Columbus OH 43214. (614)846-4126. Editor: John M. Bennett. Magazine: 8½x5½; 40 pages; good quality paper; good cover stock; illustrations; photos. Theme: experimental, avant-garde and folk literature, art. Published irregularly. Estab. 1975. Circ. 300.

Needs: Literary, contemporary, experimental, prose poem. Prefers short pieces. Accepts approximately 2 mss/issue. Recently published work by Joachim Frank, Al Ackerman, Jack Saunders. Published new writers within the last year. Sometimes recommends other markets.

How to Contact: Query with clips of published work. SASE. Accepts computer printout submissions. Reports in 1 week on queries, 2 weeks on mss. Sample copy $3.

Payment: 1 free author's copy.

Terms: Rights revert to authors.

LOUISIANA LITERATURE (II), A Review of Literature and Humanities, Southeastern Louisiana University, Box 792, Hammond LA 70402. (504)549-5022. Editor: Tim Gautreaux. Magazine: 6¾x9¾; 84 pages; 70 lb paper; card cover; illustrations; photos. "We publish literary quality fiction and essays by anyone. Essays should be about Louisiana material, but creative work can be set anywhere." Semiannually. Estab. 1984. Circ. 400 paid; 1,000 printed.
Needs: Literary, mainstream, regional. No sloppy ungrammatical manuscripts. Receives 10 unsolicited mss/month. Accepts 3 mss/issue; 6 mss/year. Does not read mss June-July. Publishes ms 6 months maximum after acceptance. Recently published work by William Caverlee and Ingrid Smith; published new writers within the last year. Length: 2,500 words preferred; 1,000 words minimum; 6,000 words maximum. Publishes short shorts. Sometimes comments on rejected mss.
How to Contact: Send complete ms. Reports in 1-2 months on mss. SASE. Photocopied submissions OK. Accepts computer printout submissions, including dot-matrix. Sample copy $4.
Payment: Pays $0-$25 and in contributor's copies.
Terms: Pays on publication for one-time rights. Publication copyrighted.
Advice: "Cut out everything that is not a functioning part of the story. Make sure everything is spelled correctly. Use relevant specific detail in every scene."

‡THE LOUISVILLE REVIEW (II), Department of English, University of Louisville, Louisville KY 40292. (502)588-6801. Editor: Sena Naslund. Magazine: 8¾x6; 100 pages; Warren's Old Style paper; cover photographs. Semiannually. Estab. 1976. Circ. 750.
Needs: Contemporary, experimental, literary, prose poem. Receives 30-40 unsolicited mss/month. Accepts 6-10 mss/issue; 12-20 mss/year. Publishes ms 2-3 months after acceptance. Recently published work by Joe Ashby Porter, John O'Shea and Richard Kostelanetz; Length: 50 pages maximum. Publishes short shorts.
How to Contact: Send complete ms with cover letter. Reports on queries in 2-3 weeks; 2-3 months on mss. SASE. Photocopied submissions OK. Accepts computer printout submissions, including dot-matrix. Sample copy for $3. Fiction guidelines for #10 SAE and 1 first class stamp.
Payment: Pays in contributor's copies.
Terms: Acquires first North American serial rights. Publication copyrighted.
Advice: Looks for "original concepts, fresh ideas, good storyline, engaging characters, a story that works."

LYRA (II), Journal of Poetry and Fiction, Lyra Society of the Arts, Inc., Box 3188, Guttenberg NJ 07093. (201)861-1941. Editors: L. Gil, I. Iturralde. Fiction Editor: Lourdes Gil. Magazine: 8½x11¼; approx. 32 pages; 70 lb paper; illustrations; photos. "Theme related to literature, art and films. Preference for French and Spanish literatures." Quarterly. Plans special fiction issue. Estab. 1987. Circ. 1,000.
Needs: Experimental, literary, prose poem, science fiction, translations, film, French and Spanish literature. Receives approx. 8 unsolicited mss/month. Accepts 1-2 mss/issue; approx. 6 mss/year. Publishes ms 6 weeks after acceptance. Recently published work by Darko Subin, Severo Sarduy, Evelyn Yoder Miller; published new writers within the last year. Length: 3,000 words average; 1,000 words minimum; 4,000 words maximum. Publishes short shorts.
How to Contact: Send complete ms with cover letter, which should include "some biographical information or short résumé. It saves time if we decide to publish it." Reports in 2 months. SASE. Photocopied submissions OK. Accepts computer printout submissions, including dot-matrix. Sample copy for $3. Fiction guidelines for #10 SAE with 1 first class stamp.
Payment: Pays in contributor's copies.
Terms: Acquires one-time rights. Publication copyrighted. Sponsors awards for fiction writers. "Send a SASE for guidelines."
Advice: "Read a sample copy and become familiar with our preferences and style. And send us several samples of your work; we like to read new authors!"

THE MACGUFFIN (II), Schoolcraft College, Department of English, 18600 Haggerty Rd., Livonia MI 48152. (313)591-6400, ext. 449. Editor: Arthur J. Lindenberg. Fiction Editor: Elizabeth Hebron. Magazine: 5½x8½; 110 pages; 60 lb paper; 110 lb cover; b&w illustrations and photos. "*The MacGuffin* is a literary magazine which publishes a range of material including poetry, nonfiction and fiction. Material ranges from traditional to experimental. We hope our periodical attracts a variety of people with many different interests." Published 3 times per year. Plans special fiction issue. Estab. 1984. Circ. 500.
Needs: Adventure, contemporary, ethnic, experimental, fantasy, historical (general), humor/satire, literary, mainstream, prose poem, psychic/supernatural/occult, science fiction, translations. No religious, inspirational, confession, romance, horror, pornography. Receives 25-40 unsolicited mss/month. Accepts 5-10 mss/issue; 10-30 mss/year. Does not read mss between July 1 and August 15. Publishes 6-24 months after acceptance. Agented fiction: 10-15%. Recently published work by Daniel

Dervin, Lawrence Pike, Jo Dereske; published new writers within the last year. Length: 2,000-2,500 words average; 400 words minimum; 4,500 words maximum. Publishes short shorts. Length: 400 words. Occasionally critiques rejected mss and recommends other markets.

How to Contact: Send complete ms with cover letter, which should include: "1. *Brief* biographical information; 2. Note that this *is not* a simultaneous submission." Reports in 4-6 weeks. SASE. Photocopied and reprint submissions OK. Accepts computer printout submissions; including dot-matrix "if readable." Sample copy for $3. Fiction guidelines free.

Payment: Pays in 2 contributor's copies.

Terms: Acquires one-time rights. Publication copyrighted.

Advice: "Be persistent. If a story is rejected, try to send it somewhere else. When we reject a story, we may accept the next one which you send us. When we make suggestions for a rewrite, we may accept the revision. There seem to be a great number of good authors of fiction, but there are far too few places for publication. However, I think this is changing. Make your characters come to life. Even the most ordinary people become fascinating if they live for your readers."

‡THE MAD ENGINEER, c/o Mosier, 4550 Flake Rd., Martinsville IN 46151. (317)342-0554. Editor: Mary Hagan. Magazine: digest size; 24 pages; illustrations; photos. Publishes "science fiction with a technical slant; short fiction (7,000 words or less); technical information or essays (innovative or unusual)." Quarterly. Plans special fiction issue. Estab. 1986. Circ. 150.

Needs: Science fiction and stories with technical slant. "No stories based on TV or movies (Star Trek, Dr. Who, etc.). Parody or satire on the above is acceptable." Receives less than 1 ms/month. Accepts 1-2 mss/issue; 4-6 mss/year. Publishes ms generally within 6 months of acceptance. Recently published work by Lee Strong, Andrew Looney. Length: 500 words minimum; 8,000 words maximum. Publishes short shorts. Sometimes critiques rejected mss.

How to Contact: Send complete mss with cover letter. Cover letter should include "short biographic information." Reports in 2 weeks on queries; in 4 weeks on mss. SASE. Photocopied and reprint submissions OK. Accepts computer printout submissions. No dot-matrix. Sample copy for 75¢.

Payment: Pays in contributor's copies.

Terms: Acquires one-time rights. Publication copyrighted.

Advice: "Just send me something. I'll never say 'no' without telling you why."

THE MADISON REVIEW (II), Department of English, White Hall, 600 N. Park St., University of Wisconsin, Madison WI 53706. Contact: Fiction Editor. Magazine: 6x9; 180 pages; illustrations. "Magazine of fiction and poetry with special emphasis on literary stories and some emphasis on midwestern writers." Published semiannually. Estab. 1978. Circ. 500.

Needs: Experimental and literary stories, prose poems, feminist and excerpts from novels. Receives 50 unsolicited fiction mss/month. Accepts 7-12 mss/issue. Recently published work by Richard Cohen, Fred Chappell and Janet Shaw. Published new writers within the last year. Length: no preference.

How to Contact: Send complete ms with cover letter and SASE. "The letters should give one or two sentences of relevant information about the writer—just enough to provide a context for the work." Reports in 8 weeks on mss. Publishes ms an average of 4 months after acceptance. "We often do not report on mss during the summer." Sample copy $4.

Payment: 2 free contributor's copies; $2.50 charge for extras.

Terms: Pays on publication for first North American serial rights. Publication copyrighted.

Advice: "We are now willing to accept chapters of novels in progress and short short fiction. Write with surgical precision—then revise. Often the label 'experimental' is used to avoid reworking a piece. If anything, the more adventurous a piece of fiction is, the more it needs to undergo revision."

THE MAGE (II, IV), A Journal of Fantasy and Science Fiction, Colgate University Student Association, Hamilton NY 13346. Editor: Richard Davis. Magazine: 8½x11; about 64 pages; good-quality paper stock and cover; b&w illustrations. "Fiction, essays, poetry, artwork and commentary within the genre of science fiction and fantasy. Emphasis is on a balance of poetry, fiction and nonfiction. We do serialize longer works of exceptional quality." Semiannually. Estab. 1984. Circ. 700, to be raised to 1,000 by 1989.

Needs: Experimental, fantasy, horror, science fiction. No sword-and-sorcery adventure or stories based on Dungeons and Dragons and its ilk; no erotica. Receives 8-10 unsolicited fiction mss/month. Accepts 6-10 mss/issue; 12-20 mss/year. Does not read mss June through August. Generally publishes ms within 3 months of acceptance. Recently published work by Patricia Anthony, Harry Dolan and Theodore Solomon. Published new writers within the last year. Length: 3,500-4,500 words average; 1,000 words minimum. Usually critiques rejected mss.

How to Contact: Query first or send complete ms with cover letter with list of previous works published. Reports in 2 weeks on queries; 3-5 weeks on mss (report time is longer if submitted just before or during the summer). SASE for ms. Simultaneous and photocopied submissions OK. Accepts

computer printouts including dot-matrix. Sample copy $3.
Payment: Pays in contributor's copies.
Terms: Acquires first North American serial rights or one-time rights. Sometimes sends galleys to author. Publication copyrighted.
Advice: "We are interested in writers who have practiced enough (even if nothing has been published) to develop a refined writing style. We are interested in presenting good writing first, but we do publish capsule reviews of new fiction. Submitting several of these to us will help a new writer develop some recognition of *The Mage*'s standards, which might help him/her when submitting a first manuscript to us."

MAGIC CHANGES (II), Celestial Otter Press, 2 S. 424 Emerald Grn. Dr., #F, Warrenville IL 60555-9269. (312)393-7856. Editor: John Sennett. Magazine: 8½x11; 110 pages; 60 lb paper; construction paper cover; illustrations; photos. "Theme: transformation by art. Material: poetry, songs, fiction, stories, reviews, art, essays, etc. For the entertainment and enlightenment of all ages." Annually. Estab. 1979. Circ. 500.
Needs: Literary, prose poem, science fiction, sports fiction, fantasy and erotica. "Fiction should have a magical slant." Accepts 8-12 mss/year. Receives approximately 15 unsolicited fiction mss each month. Recently published work by J. Weintraub, David Goodrum, Anne F. Robertson; published new writers within the last year. Length: 3,000 words maximum.
How to Contact: Send complete ms with SASE. Accepts computer printout submissions, prefers letter-quality. Accepts disk submissions compatible with IBM or Macintosh. Prefers hard copy with disk submissions. Reports in 1 month. Publishes ms an average of 5 months after acceptance. Sample copy $5. Make check payable to John Sennett.
Payment: 1-2 free author's copies. $5 charge for extras.
Terms: Acquires first North American serial rights. Publication copyrighted.
Advice: "Write about something fantastic in a natural way, or something natural in a fantastic way. We need good stories—like epic Greek poems translated into prose."

MAGICAL BLEND (II), Box 11303, San Francisco CA 94101. (415)282-9338. Editors: Michael P. Langevin, Jerry Snider. Magazine: 8½x11; 108 pages; 60 lb gloss paper; 90 lb gloss cover stock; illustrations; photos. "We believe that people's thoughts create their realities. We publish positive, uplifting material—often visionary—on a variety of themes ranging from mystical/magical/spiritual to the practical, for those interested in taking control of their lives, expanding their consciousness, focusing on the positive." Quarterly. Estab. 1980. Circ. 50,000.
Needs: Psychic/supernatural/occult, fantasy, spiritual and adventure. "We also feature specialized issues, for example: sea mammals and health. No dark or dismal portrayals of life." Accepts 1-2 mss/issue, 4-6 mss/year. Receives approximately 40 unsolicited fiction mss each month. Recently published work by Phillip K. Dick; published new writers within the last year. Length: 500-5,000 words. Critiques rejected mss when there is time. Sometimes recommends other markets.
How to Contact: Send complete ms with SASE and cover letter "indicating why this story is thought appropriate for *Magical Blend*." Reports in 5 months or longer on mss. Publishes ms an average of 6-10 months after acceptance. Sample copy $4. Guidelines for #10 SASE.
Payment: 4 free author's copies. $1.75 plus postage and handling for extras.
Terms: Acquires first North American serial rights and second serial rights. Buys reprints. Publication copyrighted.
Advice: Using less fiction than in the past. "We like fiction that takes our readers to beautiful worlds and ends happily, yet is not 'run of the mill,' trite fantasy. Share your fantasies, dreams and stories of magic with us. Mss are rejected because they are not well written, not positive or spiritual—or have too much violence or sex. Write your best original stories. Then take them apart and do them from a different angle."

THE MALAHAT REVIEW (II), University of Victoria, Box 1700, Victoria, British Columbia V8W 2Y2 Canada. (604)721-8524. Editor: Constance Rooke. Magazine: 6x9; 132 pages; photographs occasionally. Publishes fiction, poetry and reviews. Quarterly. Estab. 1967. Circ. 1,500.
Needs: Receives 100 unsolicited mss/month. Buys approximately 6 mss/issue; 25 mss/year. Publishes short shorts. Occasionally critiques rejected mss.
How to Contact: Send complete ms with cover letter. SASE (Canadian postage or IRCs). Photocopied submissions OK. Accepts computer printout submissions, including dot-matrix. Sample copy $6. Fiction guidelines free.
Payment: Pays $40 per 1,000 words; and contributor's copies.
Terms: Acquires first rights. Publication copyrighted.
Advice: "If It's good, we publish it."

MARK (II), A Journal of Scholarship, Opinion, and Literature, University of Toledo, Toledo OH 43606. (419)537-2318. Editor: Kenneth J. Bindas. Magazine: 6x9; 54 pages; acid-free paper; some illustrations; photographs. "General theme is exploration of humanity and man's effort to understand the world around him." Semiannually. Estab. 1967. Circ. 3,500.
Needs: Contemporary, ethnic, humor/satire, literary, regional, science fiction and translations. "We do not have the staff to do rewrites or heavy copyediting—send clean, legible mss only." No "typical MFA first-person narrative—we like stories, not reportage." Receives 4-5 unsolicited fiction mss/ month. Accepts 1-2 mss/issue; 2-4 mss/year. Does not read June to September. Publishes ms 6 months to 1 year after acceptance. Publishes short shorts. Occasionally critiques rejected mss and recommends other markets.
How to Contact: Send complete ms with cover letter, name, address, phone, short bio. Reports in 6 weeks. Photocopied submissions OK. Accepts computer printouts, including dot-matrix. Sample copy $3 plus 7x10 SAE with 72¢ postage.
Payment: Pays in contributor's copies.
Terms: Acquires one-time rights. Publication copyrighted.
Advice: "Beginning fiction writers should write in a style that is natural, not taught to them by others. More importantly, they should write about subjects they are familiar with. Be prepared for rejection, but good writing will always find a home."

THE MARYLAND REVIEW, Department of English, University of Maryland Eastern Shore, Princess Anne MD 21853. (301)651-2200, ext. 262. Editor: Chester M Hedgepeth. Magazine: 6x9; 100-150 pages; good quality paper stock; heavy cover; illustrations; photos "possibly." "We have a special interest in black literature, but we welcome all sorts of submissions. Our audience is literary, educated, well-read." Annually. Estab. 1986. Circ. 500.
Needs: Contemporary, humor/satire, literary, mainstream, black. No genre stories; no religious, political or juvenile material. Accepts approx. 12-15 mss/issue. Publishes ms "within 1 year" after acceptance. Recently published work by John K. Crane, David Jauss. Published new writers within the last year. Publishes short shorts. "Length is open, but we do like to include some pieces 1,500 words and under." Occasionally critiques rejected mss.
How to Contact: Send complete ms with cover letter, which should include a brief autobiography. Reports "as soon as possible." SASE. Photocopied submissions acceptable. No simultaneous submissions. Accepts computer printout submissions. Sample copy for $6.
Payment: Pays in contributor's copies.
Terms: Acquires all rights. Publication copyrighted.
Advice: "Think primarily about your *characters* in fiction, about their beliefs and how they may change. Create characters and situations that are utterly new. We will give your material a careful and considerate reading. Any fiction that is flawed by grammatical errors, misspellings, etc. will not have a chance. We're seeing a lot of fine fiction these days, and we approach each story with fresh and eager eyes. Ezra Pound's battle-cry about poetry refers to fiction as well: 'Make it New!' "

THE MASSACHUSETTS REVIEW (II), Memorial Hall, University of Massachusetts, Amherst MA 01002. (413)545-2689. Editors: Mary Heath, Fred Robinson, Paul Jenkins. Magazine: 6x9; 172 pages; 52 lb paper; 65 lb vellum cover; illustrations and photos. Quarterly.
Needs: Short stories. Published new writers within the last year. Approximately 5% of fiction is agented. Critiques rejected mss when there is time.
How to Contact: Send complete ms. No ms returned without SASE. Reports in 2 months. Publishes ms an average of 9-12 months after acceptance. Sample copy $4.50.
Payment: Pays $50 maximum.
Terms: Pays on publication for first North American serial rights. Publication copyrighted.
Advice: "Shorter rather than longer stories preferred (20-25 pages). There are too many stories about 'relationships,' domestic breakups, etc. Avoid submitting material June through October."

‡MCGUFFEY WRITER (IV), Miami University, 400A McGuffey Hall, Oxford OH 45056. (513)529-6462. Eitor Eileen Tway. Magazine; 8½x11; 16 pages; illustrations and occasionally photographs. "Child contributors, grades K-12. For children, parents, teachers." Publishes 3 issues during school year. Estab. 1977. Circ. 300.
Needs: Juvenile (5-9 years), young adult/teen (10-18 years). "We publish only children's writing: fiction, nonfiction, poetry etc. Range: K-12. We make no payment."
How to Contact: Send complete ms. "Student's name, grade level, school, and address must appear on every submitted page. A teacher, supervisor, or responsible adult must sign the initial page for verification. Typed or handwritten submissions are equally welcome as long as they are readable; however the child's original copy is preferable. Due to the limited space, excerpts may be taken from work that is longer than two double-spaced typewritten pages." Fiction guidelines and list of upcoming themes: #10

SAE and 1 first class stamp.
Advice: "Theme for Spring '89 issue (mss due Feb. 15, 1989): 'City and Country: People, Places, and Things.' "

‡MEAL, READY-TO-EAT (I), 910 Three Degree Road, Butler PA 16001. Editor: Richard Sater. Magazine: 8½x5½; 16-24 pages; Xerox paper and cover; illustrations and photographs. "Theme varies with each issue depending on material published." Monthly. Estab. 1987. Circ. 200.
Needs: Adventure, confession, contemporary, experimental, historical (general), horror, humor/satire, lesbian, literary, mainstream, prose poem, regional, romance (contemporary, historical), senior citizen/retirement, sports, suspense/mystery, western. Receives few unsolicited mss/month. Accepts one or two mss/issue. Recently published work by Patricia Henley, Marianne Boruch, Brooke Horvath. Publishes short shorts. Length: up to 4 double-spaced typed pages maximum.
How to Contact: Send complete ms with cover letter. Reports in one month on mss. SASE for ms. Photocopied submissions OK. Accepts computer printout submissions, including dot-matrix. Sample copy for 50¢, SAE and 2 first class stamps.
Payment: Pays in contributor's copies.
Terms: Acquires one-time rights. Publication copyrighted. "Post office/registered mail copyright."
Advice: "Most magazines take themselves too seriously. I've been asking writers whom I know for contributions. *Meal, Ready-To-Eat* is prepared on my word processor. I do my own editing/layout/graphics. It is Xeroxed at a local copy shop and distributed around town and by mail to interested readers. My budget is limited, but I'm attempting to put out an interesting/entertaining issue each month."

MEMPHIS STATE REVIEW (II), Dept. of English, Memphis State University, Memphis TN 38152. (901)454-4438. Editor: Sharon Bryan. Magazine: 6x9; 100 pages. National review of poetry, fiction and nonfiction. Semiannually. Estab. 1980. Circ. 1,200.
Needs: Recently published work by Fred Busch. Published new writers within the last year.
How to Contact: Send complete ms with SASE. Sample copy $3.
Payment: Annual $100 prize for best poem or best short story and 2 free contributor's copies. "We pay if grant monies are available."
Terms: Acquires first North American serial rights. Publication copyrighted.
Advice: "We're soliciting work from writers with a national reputation, and are occasionally able to pay, depending on grants received. I would prefer no cover letter."

MERLYN'S PEN (IV), The National Magazine of Student Writing, Box 1058, East Greenwich RI 02818. (401)885-5175. Editor: R. Jim Stahl. Magazine 8⅛x10⅞; 36 pages; 50 lb paper; 70 lb gloss cover stock; illustrations; photos. Student writing only—grades 7 through 10, for libraries, homes and English classrooms. Bimonthly (September-April). Estab. 1985. Circ. 14,000.
Needs: Adventure, experimental, fantasy, historical (general), horror, humor/satire, literary, mainstream, regional, romance, science fiction, suspense/mystery, western, young adult/teen. Must be written by students in grades 7-10. Receives 300 unsolicited fiction mss/month. Accepts 50 mss/issue; 250 mss/year. Publishes ms 3-12 months after acceptance. Length: 1,500 words average; 25 words minimum; 4,000 words maximum. Publishes short shorts. Responds to rejected mss.
How to Contact: Send complete ms with cover letter with name, grade and principal's name, age, home and school address, home and school telephone number, supervising teacher's name. Reports in 10-12 weeks. SASE for ms. Accepts computer printouts including dot-matrix. Sample copy $3.
Payment: Three contributor's copies, charge for extras. Each author published receives a free copy of *The Elements of Style*.
Terms: Publication copyrighted; author retains own copyright.
Advice: "Write what you *know*; write where you are."

MICHIGAN QUARTERLY REVIEW, University of Michigan, 3032 Rackham, Ann Arbor MI 48109. Editor: Laurence Goldstein. "An interdisciplinary journal which publishes mainly essays and reviews, with some high-quality fiction and poetry, for an intellectual, widely read audience." Quarterly. Estab. 1962. Circ. 1,500.
Needs: Literary. No "genre" fiction written for a "market." Receives 200 unsolicited fiction mss/month. Buys 2 mss/issue; 8 mss/year. Recently published work by Lynne Sharon Schwartz, Gloria Whelan, Ron Hansen; published new writers within the last year. Length: 1,500 words minimum; 7,000 words maximum; 5,000 words average.
How to Contact: Send complete ms with cover letter. "I like to know if a writer is at the beginning, or further along, in his or her career. Don't offer plot summaries of the enclosed story, though a background comment is welcome." SASE. Photocopied submissions OK. Accepts computer printout submissions. Prefers letter quality. Sample copy for $2 and 2 first class stamps.
Payment: Pays $8-$10/printed page.

Terms: Pays on acceptance for first rights. Publication copyrighted. Awards the Lawrence Foundation Prize of $500 for best story in *MQR* previous year.
Advice: "Read back issues to get a sense of tone; level of writing. *MQR* is very selective; only send the very finest, best-plotted, most-revised fiction."

THE MICKLE STREET REVIEW (IV), The Walt Whitman Association, 328 Mickle Blvd., Camden NJ 08103. (609)541-8250. Editor: Geoffrey M. Sill. Magazine: 5x7; 150-200 pages; cover illustrations; limited photographs. "Articles and essays on Walt Whitman, his life, works, recent studies, and poetry in the Whitman influence." Audience is largely academic, but also about 40% general. Annually. Estab. 1979. Circ. 200.
Needs: Historical, literary. "We would only consider fiction with a bent towards exemplifying Whitman influences." Receives less than 5 mss/year. Publishes ms 1 year after acceptance. Rarely critiques rejected mss. Sometimes recommends other markets.
How to Contact: Query with clips of published works. Reports in 2 months. SASE. Photocopied and reprint submissions OK. Sample copy $3.50 and SAE with 4 first class stamps.
Payment: Pays in contributor's copies; $2 charge for extras, any amount over 2.

MICROCOSM (I), New Writings in Imaginative Fiction, Quixsilver Press, Box 644, Biglerville PA 17307-0644. Editor: Bob Medcalf, Jr. Magazine: 5½x8½; 24 pages; offset paper; vellum cover stock; illustrations. Short shorts with imaginative themes and treatment, for well-read readers of imaginative fiction. Annually. Plans special fiction issue. Estab. 1096. Circ. 100.
Needs: Adventure, experimental, fantasy, horror, psychic/supernatural/occult, science fiction. Receives 10 unsolicited fiction mss/month. Accepts 12 mss/issue. Publishes ms 1 year after acceptance. Charges reading fee of $2. Length: 600 words average; 100 words minimum; 1,000 words maximum. Sometimes critiques rejected mss and recommends other markets.
How to Contact: Send complete ms with cover letter with brief publication highlights stating reading interests in the field of imaginative fiction. Reports in 2 months. SASE for ms. Simultaneous, photocopied and reprint submissions OK. Accepts computer printouts including dot-matrix. Sample copy $3.
Payment: Free subscription to magazine, contributor's copies, charge for extras.
Terms: Acquires one-time rights. Publication copyrighted.
Advice: "The beginning fiction writer can fulfill the journeyman requirements in the small press magazines if he/she diligently searches out editors willing to work with him/her on his/her beginning work. Supporting the publications that serve him or her—through subscriptions and reading fees is a requirement of this process. Send your best work. Be eager and willing to revise or rewrite new work guided by comments. Submit to other suggested markets."

MID-AMERICAN REVIEW (II), Department of English, Bowling Green State University, Bowling Green OH 43403. (419)372-2725. Contact: Robert Early, editor-in-chief. Fiction editor changes annually. Magazine: 5½x8½; 200 pages; 60 lb bond paper; coated cover stock. "We publish serious fiction and poetry, as well as critical studies in modern literature, translations and book reviews." Published biannually. Plans special fiction issue. Estab. 1981.
Needs: Experimental, traditional, literary, prose poem, excerpted novel and translations. Receives about 50 unsolicited fiction mss/month. Buys 5-6 mss/issue. Does not read June-August. Approximately 5% of fiction is agented. Recently published work by Peter Bricklebank, Joe Ashby Porter, Tricia Tunstall; published new writers within the last year. Occasionally critiques rejected mss. Sometimes recommends other markets.
How to Contact: Send complete ms with SASE. Reports in 2 months. Publishes ms an average of 3 months after acceptance. Sample copy $4.50.
Payment: $5/page up to $75; 2 free contributor's copies; $2 charge for extras.
Terms: Pays on publication for one-time rights. Publication copyrighted.
Advice: "We just want *quality* work of whatever vision and/or style. We are now looking for more translated fiction."

MIDLAND REVIEW (II), An Annual Journal of Contemporary Lit, Lit. Crit. & Art, Oklahoma State University, English Dept., Morrill Hall, Stillwater OK 74078. (405)624-6223 or 624-6138. Editor-in-Chief: Nuala Archer. Magazine: 6½x9½; 100 pages; 80 lb paper; perfect bond cover stock; illustrations; photos. "A mixed bag of quality work." For "anyone who likes to read and for those that want news that folks in Oklahoma are alive." Publishes 30-40% OSU student material." Annually. Estab. 1985. Circ. 500.
Needs: Ethnic, experimental, feminist, historical (general), horror, literary, prose poem, psychic/supernatural/occult, regional, science fiction, translations. Receives 15 unsolicited fiction mss/month. Accepts 4 mss/issue. Publishes ms 2-6 months after acceptance. Recently published work by Jene Friedemann, Steffie Corcoran, Bruce Michael Gans; published new writers within the last year. Length:

4-10 pages double-spaced, typed. Publishes short shorts of 2-4 pages.
How to Contact: Send complete manuscript with cover letter. Reports in 6-8 weeks on queries. SASE for ms. Simultaneous and photocopied submissions OK. Accepts computer printouts including dot-matrix. Sample copy for $5, 90¢ postage and 11x8 SAE. Fiction guidelines for #10 SAE and 1 first class stamp.
Payment: 1 free contributor's copy.
Terms: Publication copyrighted; copyright reverts to author.
Advice: "We want to encourage good student stories by giving them an audience with more established writers."

‡MILL HUNK HERALD MAGAZINE (I), Piece of the Hunk Publishers Inc., 916 Middle St., Pittsburgh PA 15212. Editor: Larry Evans. Magazine: 8½x11; 52 pages; newsprint stock; Southern Pride cover; illustrations; photographs. "We publish *work place* writing of any kind, for working people." Quarterly. Estab. 1979. Circ. 8,000.
Needs: Contemporary, experimental, feminist, gay, historical (general), humor/satire, lesbian, prose poem, senior citizen/retirement, work and labor. Receives 5 unsolicited mss/month. Publishes ms 2 months after acceptance. Recently published work by Eric Davin, Therese Russo, Mary Sage; published new writers within the last year. Length: 1,800 words average; 800 words minimum; 4,000 words maximum. Publishes short shorts. Occasionally critiques rejected mss and recommends other markets.
How to Contact: Send complete ms with cover letter, which should include information about the author's work history. "We like our readers to know what kind of work contributors have done." Reports in 4 weeks on mss. SASE. Simultaneous, photocopied and reprint submissions OK. Accepts computer printout submissions, including dot-matrix. Sample copy for 8½x11 SAE and 4 first class stamps. Fiction guidelines free.
Terms: Acquires one-time rights. Publication copyrighted.

MINAS TIRITH EVENING-STAR (IV), W.W. Publications, Box 373, Highland MI 48031-0373. (313)887-4703. Editor: Philip Helms. Magazine: 8½x11; 40+ pages; typewriter paper; black ink illustrations; photos. Magazine of J.R.R. Tolkien and fantasy—fiction, poetry, reviews, etc. for general audience. Quarterly. Published special fiction issue; plans another. Estab. 1967. Circ. 500.
Needs: "Fantasy and Tolkien." Receives 5 unsolicited mss/month. Accepts 1 ms/issue; 5 mss/year. Published new writers within the last year. Length: 1,000-1,200 words preferred; 5,000 words maximum. Also publishes short shorts. Occasionally critiques rejected ms.
How to Contact: Send complete ms and bio. Reports in 1 week on queries; 2 weeks on mss. SASE. Photocopied and previously published submissions OK. Accepts computer printout submissions, prefers letter-quality. Sample copy $1.
Terms: Acquires first rights. Publication copyrighted.

‡MIND IN MOTION (II), A Magazine of Poetry and Short Prose, Box 1118, Apple Valley CA 92307. (619)248-6512. Editor: Céleste Goyer. Magazine: 8½x5½; 54 pages; 20 lb paper; 50 lb cover. "We prefer to publish works of substantial brilliance that engage and encourage the readers' mind." Quarterly. Estab. 1985. Circ. 250.
Needs: Experimental, fantasy, humor/satire, literary, prose poem, science fiction. No "mainstream, romance, nostalgia, un-poetic prose; anything with a slow pace or that won't stand up to re-reading." Receives 50 unsolicited mss/month. Buys 5 mss/issue; 40 mss/year. Publishes ms 2 weeks to 3 months after acceptance. Recently published work by Robert E. Brimhall, Warren C. Miller, Michael K. White. Length: 2,000 words preferred; 250 words minimum; 3,500 words maximum. Sometimes critiques rejected mss and occasionally recommends other markets.
How to Contact: Send complete ms. "Cover letter or bio not necessary." SASE. Simultaneous (if notified) and photocopied submissions OK. Accepts computer printout submissions, including dot-matrix. Sample copy for $2.50. Fiction guidelines for #10 SAE and 1 first class stamp.
Payment: One contributor's copy when financially possible; charge for extras.
Terms: Acquires first North American serial rights. Publication copyrighted.
Advice: "We look for fiction with no wasted words that demands re-reading, and startles us continually with the knowledge that such genius exists. Send works of cosmic pressure written poetically."

‡THE MIND'S EYE (I, II), Fiction and Poetry Quarterly, Box 656, Glenview IL 60025. Editor: Gene Foreman. Magazine: 5x8; 35-45 pages; 15 lb paper; vellum cover; illustrations; photographs. Semiannually. Estab. 1986. Circ. 500.
Needs: Adventure, condensed/excerpted novel, confession, contemporary, erotica, ethnic, experimental, fantasy, feminist, gay, historical (general), horror, humor/satire, lesbian, literary, mainstream, prose poem, psychic/supernatural/occult, regional, romance (contemporary, historical, young adult), science fiction, sports, suspense/mystery, translations. Receives 50 unsolicited mss/month. Accepts 6

mss/issue; 12-24 mss/year. Publishes ms 3 months-1 year after acceptance. Length: 2,000 words average; 100 words minimum; 3,000 words maximum. Publishes short shorts. Rarely critiques rejected mss.
How to Contact: Send complete ms with cover letter. Reports in 1-2 weeks on queries; 2-4 weeks on mss. SASE. Simultaneous and photocopied submissions OK. Accepts computer printout submissions, including dot-matrix. Sample copy for $3.50. Fiction guidelines free with SAE and 1 first class stamp.
Payment: Pays in contributor's copies; charge for extras.
Terms: Acquires first rights. Sponsors annual fiction and poetry contest for subscribers.
Advice: "Read at least one past issue."

MINNESOTA INK (II), Box 9148, N. St. Paul MN 55109. (612)433-3626. Managing Editor: Valerie Hockert. Tabloid: 11x15; variable number of pages; 40 lb paper; illustrations and photographs. "A monthly publication designed to provide guidance and advice as well as inspiration for writers and other people interested in writing (e.g., the college student, the business person)." Monthly. Estab. 1987.
Needs: Adventure, contemporary, experimental, fantasy, humor/satire, mainstream, regional, romance (contemporary, historical), science fiction, senior citizen/retirement, suspense/mystery, western, young adult/teen (12-18 years). Receives about 60 unsolicited mss/month. Publishes mss "usually a couple months" after acceptance. Length: 500 words minimum; 1,500 words maximum. Sometimes critiques rejected mss.
How to Contact: Send complete ms with cover letter and biographical sketch. Reports in 1-2 months. SASE. Photocopied submissions OK. Sample copy for $2 and 9x11 SAE. Fiction guidelines for SASE.
Payment: Pays in contributor's copies.
Terms: Acquires first rights. Publication copyrighted. Sponsors contests and awards for fiction writers. "Contest announcements are published in publication."

‡THE MINNESOTA REVIEW (II), A journal of committed writing, English Dept., SUNY-Stony Brook, Stony Brook NY 11794. (516)632-7400. Editors: Helen Cooper, William J. Harris, Marlon Ross, Michael Sprinker, Susan Squier. Fiction Editor: Fred Pfeil. Magazine: 5¼x8; approximately 160 pages; some illustrations; occasional photos. "We emphasize political writing, favoring especially socialist and feminist work." Semiannually. Estab. 1960. Circ. 1,000.
Needs: Experimental, fantasy, feminist, gay, historical (general), lesbian, literary, science fiction. Receives 20 mss/month. Accepts 3-4 mss/issue; 6-8 mss/year. Publishes ms within 6-12 months of acceptance. Recently published work by Enid Dame, Ellen Gruber Garvey, John Berger. Length: 5,000-6,000 words preferred. Publishes short shorts. Sometimes critiques rejected mss and recommends other markets.
How to Contact: Send complete ms with cover letter (cover letter optional). Reports in 2-3 weeks on queries; 2-3 months on mss. SASE. Accepts computer printout submissions, including dot-matrix. Sample copy for $4. Fiction guidelines are free.
Payment: Pays in contributor's copies. Charge for extra copies.
Terms: Acquires first rights. Publication copyrighted.
Advice: "Write good stories with explicit political themes. Read back issues of *MR* for a sense of our collective taste."

MIORITA, A JOURNAL OF ROMANIAN STUDIES (IV), New Zealand Romanian Cultural Association and the Dept. FLLL, Dewey 482, University of Rochester, Rochester NY 14627. (716)275-4258. Co-Editors: Charles Carlton and Norman Simms. Magazine: 5½x8½; Xerox paper; occasional illustrations. Magazine of "essays, reviews, notes and translations on all aspects of Romanian history, culture, language and so on," for academic audience. Annually. Estab. 1973. Circ. 200.
Needs: Ethnic, historical, literary, regional and translations. "All categories contingent upon relationship to Romania." Receives "handful of mss per year." Accepts "no more than one per issue." Length: 2,000 words maximum. Occasionally critiques rejected mss.
How to Contact: Send complete ms. SASE preferred. Previously published work OK (depending on quality). Accepts computer printout submissions.
Payment: "We do not pay."
Terms: Publication copyrighted.

‡THE MIRROR-NORTHERN REPORT (I,IV), Box 269, 4732-53 Ave., High Prairie, Alberta T0G 1E0 Canada. (403)523-3706. Editor: Albert Burger. Tabloid: 14½x11½; 20-32 pages; newsprint paper; b&w illustrations; b&w photos. Publishes for a "rural—small town—native—farm" audience. Plans special fiction issue. Estab. 1986. Circ. 2,000.
Needs: Adventure, contemporary, ethnic, fantasy, feminist, historical, humor, literary, mainstream, prose poem, psychic/supernatural/occult, regional, romance, science fiction, senior citizen, sports, suspense, translations, western. Receives 10 mss/month. Accepts 1 mss/issue. Publishes ms within 1-2 months of acceptance. Length: 1,000-1,500 words preferred; 2,500 words maximum. Publishes short

shorts.
How to Contact: Send complete mss with cover letter. Reports in 1-4 weeks. SASE. Simultaneous, photocopied and reprint submissions OK. Accepts computer printout submissions, including dot-matrix. Sample copy for $1.
Payment: Pays 1¢/word.
Terms: Pays on publication for one-time rights. Publication not copyrighted.

MISSISSIPPI REVIEW, University of Southern Mississippi, Southern Station, Box 5144, Hattiesburg MS 39406. (601)266-4321. Editor: Frederick Barthelme. Managing Editor: Rie Fortenberry. "Literary publication for those interested in contemporary literature—writers, editors who read to be in touch with current modes." Semiannually. Estab. 1972. Circ. 1,500.
Needs: Literary, contemporary, fantasy, humor, translations, experimental, avant-garde and "art" fiction. No juvenile. Buys varied amount of mss/issue. Does not read mss in summer. Length: 100 pages maximum.
How to Contact: Send complete ms with SASE including a short cover letter. Accepts computer printout submissions. Sample copy $5.50.
Payment: Pays in author's copies. Charges cover price for extras.
Terms: Acquires first North American serial rights.

MISSISSIPPI VALLEY REVIEW (III), Western Illinois University, Dept. of English, Simpkins Hall, Macomb IL 61455. Editor: Forrest Robinson. Fiction Editor: Loren Logsdon. Magazine: 64 pages; original art on cover. "A small magazine, *MVR* has won 17 Illinois Arts Council awards in poetry and fiction. We publish stories, poems and reviews." Biannually. Estab. 1971. Circ. 400.
Needs: Literary, contemporary. Does not read mss in summer. Recently published work by Jack Matthews, Joseph Queenan and Rochelle Distelheim; published new writers within the last year.
How to Contact: Send complete ms with SASE. Reports in 3 months. Sample copy $3. "Do not ask for guidelines. Refer to an issue of *MVR*."
Payment: 2 free author's copies, plus one copy of the following two numbers.
Terms: Individual author retains rights.
Advice: "We prefer to receive one story at a time. Getting one's work published has always been difficult. Commitment to one's art, as well as persistence, can sustain."

THE MISSOURI REVIEW (II), 231 Arts & Science, English Dept., University of Missouri, Columbia MO 65211. (314)882-6421. Editor: Speer Morgan. Magazine: 6x9; 256 pages. Theme: fiction, poetry, essays, reviews, interviews, cartoons. "All with a distinctly contemporary orientation. For writers, and the general reader with broad literary interests. We present non-established as well as established writers of excellence. The *Review* frequently runs feature sections or special issues dedicated to particular topics frequently related to fiction." Published 3 times/academic year. Estab. 1977. Circ. 2,400.
Needs: Literary, contemporary; open to all categories except juvenile, young adult. Buys 6-8 mss/issue, 18-25 mss/year. Receives approximately 300 unsolicited fiction mss each month. Published new writers within the last year. No preferred length. Critiques rejected mss "when there is time."
How to Contact: Send complete ms with SASE. Reports in 10 weeks. Sample copy $5.
Payment: $10/page minimum.
Terms: Pays on publication for all rights. Publication copyrighted.
Advice: Awards William Peden Prize in fiction; $1,000 to best story published in *Missouri Review* in a given year.

MODERN LITURGY (IV), Resource Publications, Inc., Suite 290, 160 E. Virginia St., San Jose CA 95112. Fiction Editor: Ken Guentert. Magazine: 8½x11; 48 pages; 60 lb glossy paper and cover stock; illustrations and photographs. "*Modern Liturgy* is focused on the liturgical arts—music, visual art, architecture, drama, dance and storytelling. We use short pieces that lend themselves to religious education or preaching. Readers are professionals and volunteers who plan and organize worship for liturgically oriented churches." 10 issues/year. Estab. 1973.
Needs: Liturgical. "Storytelling should be creative. Short pieces that tell you how so-and-so came to a personal relationship with Jesus don't make it here." Receives 10 unsolicited fiction mss/month. Accepts 1 ms/issue; 9 mss/year. Length: 1,500 words average; 600 words minimum; 2,500 words maximum. Publishes short shorts.
How to Contact: Send complete ms with cover letter. Reports in 6 weeks. Sample copy $4 with 9x12 SAE and 3 first class stamps. Fiction guidelines for #10 SAE and 1 first class stamp.
Payment: Free subscription and 5 contributor's copies; charge for extras.
Terms: Acquires first rights plus right to grant non-commercial reprint permission to customers. Publication copyrighted.
Advice: "We don't publish 'short stories' in the classic literary sense, but we do publish much fictional material (stories, plays, skits humor) that is of use to worship leaders and planners."

‡THE MONOCACY VALLEY REVIEW (II), Frederick Arts Council, Box 547, Frederick MD 21701. (301)662-4190. Editor: William Heath. Fiction Editor: Janice Cole. Magazine: 8½x11; 20 pages; high-quality paper; illustrations and photographs. For readers in the "Mid-Atlantic region; all persons interested in literature." Semiannually. Estab. 1986. Circ. 250.

Needs: Adventure, contemporary, experimental, historical, humor/satire, literary, mainstream, prose poem. "We would not exclude any categories of fiction, save pornographic or obscene." Receives 10-15 unsolicited mss/month. Buys 3 mss/issue; 6 mss/year. Does not read mss Decemer-March; June-October. Publishes ms 6 weeks after acceptance. Recently published work by Ann Knox; Maxine Combs; Doris Selinsky. Length: 3,000-4,000 words preferred; no minimum; 10,000 words maximum. Sometimes critiques rejected mss.

How to Contact: Query first or ask for submission guidelines. Cover letter unnecessary. Reports in 4 weeks on queries; 1-4 months on mss. SASE. Simultaneous and photocopied submissions OK. Accepts computer printout submissions, including dot-matrix. Sample copy for $3. Fiction guidelines for #10 SAE and 1 first class stamp.

Payment: Pays $25. Free contributor's copies.

Terms: Pays on publication. Publication copyrighted.

Advice: "Be patient in receiving a response. Manuscript readings take place about eight weeks before the two publication dates (June 15 and December 15). If you submit in July, your work will likely not be read until October."

THE MONTANA REVIEW (II), Owl Creek Press, 1620 N. 45th St., Seattle WA 98103. Editor-in-Chief: Rich Ives. Magazine: 8½x5½; 200 pages; average paper quality; high quality, full-color cover; cover photo. For readers of contemporary literature. "We publish only work of literary merit. Any subject, style or approach is acceptable if the result is of lasting literary quality." Published biannually. Estab. 1979. Circ. 1,000.

Needs: Contemporary, literary, prose poem, serialized/excerpted novel and translations. "Genre is irrelevant. Quality of the writing is our only consideration." Receives 100 unsolicited fiction mss/month. Accepts 20-30mss/year. Recently published work by Raymond Carver and Irene Wanner; published several new writers in the last year. No preferred length. Occasionally critiques rejected mss. Sometimes recommends other markets.

How to Contact: Send complete ms with SASE. Simultaneous and photocopied submissions OK if stated. "Work published in magazines may be considered in book form." Accepts computer printout submissions. Prefers letter-quality. Reports in 2 months. Sample copy $5.

Advice: "Submit only to magazines you have seen and respect."

‡MONTANA SENIOR CITIZENS NEWS (II,IV), Barrett-Whitman Co., Box 3363, Great Falls MT 59403. (406)761-0305. Editor: Jack Love. Tabloid: 11x17; 40-50 pages; newsprint paper and cover; illustrations; photos. Publishes "everything of interest to seniors, except most day-to-day political items like social security and topics covered in the daily news. Personal profiles of seniors, their lives, times and reminiscences." Bimonthly. Estab. 1984. Circ. 14,000.

Needs: Historical, senior citizen/retirement, western (historical or contemporary). No fiction "unrelated to experiences to which seniors can relate." Buys 1 or fewer mss/issue; 4-5 mss/year. Publishes ms within 4 months of acceptance. Recently published work by Anne Norris, Helen Clark, Juni Dunklin. Length: 500-700 words preferred. Publishes short shorts. Length: under 500 words.

How to Contact: Send complete ms with cover letter. Reports on mss in 1 month. SASE. Simultaneous, photocopied and reprint submissions OK. Accepts computer printout submissions, including dot-matrix. Accepts electronic submission via disk or modem. Sample copy for 9x12 SAE and $1.25 postage.

Payment: Pays $10 minimum; 4¢/word maximum.

Terms: Pays on publication. Acquires first rights or one-time rights. Publication copyrighted.

THE MONTHLY INDEPENDENT TRIBUNE TIMES JOURNAL POST GAZETTE NEWS CHRONI-CLE BULLETIN (I, II), The Magazine to Which No Superlatives Apply, 2510 Bancroft Way #207, Berkeley CA 94704. Editor: T.S. Child. Magazine: 5½x7½; 8 pages; 60 lb white stock; illustrations and photos. "We use funny short stories or essays on any topic or genre. We also use cartoons and comics, spot illustration and many items that defy classification." Monthly. Estab. 1983. Circ. 500.

Needs: Humor/satire, suspense/mystery, experimental. "Due to our small size, we cannot consider any stories longer than 1,000 words." Receives 5-10 unsolicited mss/month. Accepts 1-2 mss/issue; 12-24 mss/year. Publishes ms 1 month after acceptance. Recently publishes work by Gregg Turkington, Blaster Al Ackerman and Denver Tucson; published several new writers within the last year. Length: 500 words average; 1 word minimum; 1,000 words maximum. Publishes short shorts. Length: 1-250 words. Occasionally critiques rejected mss. Sometimes recommends other markets.

How to Contact: Send complete ms with cover letter. Reports in 3 weeks on queries and mss. SASE.

Simultaneous and photocopied submissions OK. Accepts computer printout submissions, including dot-matrix. Sample copy for 50¢ or 2 first class stamps.

Payment: 3 contributor's copies. Free 2-month subscription to magazine.

Terms: Acquires one-time rights. Publication not copyrighted, "but all individual pieces can be copyrighted." Contest announcements made in magazine.

Advice: "We don't care how famous or obscure you are. All stories are judged on their own merits. Please try not to send us sensitive, slightly humorous stories with a moral; we prefer something spontaneous, twisted, hilarious. Don't rewrite humor. Spontaneity means laughter."

‡MOUNT THRUSHMORE MONUMENT (I,IV), 28 Cocks Way S.E., Medicine Hat, Alberta T1B 1R7 Canada. (403)526-8368. Editor: Kristian Moen. Newsletter: 8½x11; 20 pages; Xerox paper; color Xerox cover; illustrations; photocopied photographs. Publishes material on "political left/alternative music; articles of a non-mainstream style, original." Quarterly. Plans special fiction issue. Estab. 1987. Circ. 40-50.

Needs: Contemporary, experimental, feminist, horror, humor/satire, literary, prose poem, psychic/supernatural/occult, regional, translations, young adult/teen (10-18 years). "A slightly offbeat theme or literary style is what I am interested in. Social/political themes are preferred (that covers nearly everything). Stories of other countries, cultures and cities are also liked greatly. No mainstream romance, sci-fi, etc., though admittedly I am open to close to everything." Buys 1-2 mss/issue; 4-8 mss/year. Publishes ms 2-6 months after acceptance. Length: 300-400 words preferred; 200 words minimum; 700 words maximum. Sometimes critiques rejected mss.

How to Contact: Send complete ms with cover letter. Cover letter should include "a bit of info about the story and the author. Also, how (if accepted) you would like it printed (with a picture, large title and other minor details). Illustration accompanying the story is also appreciated." Reports in 3 weeks. SASE. Simultaneous, photocopied and reprint submissions OK. Accepts computer printout submissions, including dot-matrix. Sample copy for $1. Fiction guidelines for 50¢ postage or an IRC.

Payment: Pays 1-5 contributor's copies.

Terms: Acquires one-time rights. Sends galleys to author if desired.

Advice: Looks for "readability, originality and intelligence/wit. Be original, not verbose, and have a loose, flowing writing style. Most importantly, don't be confined to standard short-story (or poetic) rules. Have fun writing."

THE MOUNTAIN LAUREL (II), Monthly Journal of Mountain Life, Laurel Publications, Inc., Route 1, Meadows of Dan VA 24120. (703)789-7193. Editor: Susan M. Thigpen. Tabloid: 28 pages; newsprint; illustrations and photographs. "Everyday details about life in the Blue Ridge Mountains of yesterday, for people of all ages interested in folk history." Monthly. Estab. 1983. Circ. 20,000.

Needs: Historical, humor, regional. "Stories must fit our format—we accept seasonal stories. There is always a shortage of good Christmas stories. A copy of our publication will be your best guidelines as to what we want. We will not even consider stories containing bad language, sex, gore, horror." Receives approximately 40 unsolicited fiction mss/month. Accepts up to 5 mss/issue; 60 mss/year. Publishes ms 2-6 months after acceptance. Length: 500-600 words average; no minimum; 1,000 words maximum. Sometimes critiques rejected mss and recommends other markets.

How to Contact: Send complete ms with cover letter, which should include "an introduction to the writer as though he/she were meeting us in person." reports in 1 month. SASE. Simultaneous and photocopied submissions OK. Accepts computer printout submissions, including dot-matrix. Sample copy for 9x12 SAE and 5 first class stamps. Fiction guidelines for #10 SAE and 1 first class stamp.

Payment: Pays in contributor's copies.

Terms: Acquires one-time rights. Publication copyrighted.

Advice: "Tell a good story. Everything else is secondary. A tightly written story is much better than one that rambles. Short stories have no room to take off on tangents. *The Mountain Laurel* has published the work of many first-time writers as well as works by James Still and John Parris."

> **❝ It is by sitting down to write every morning that one becomes a writer. Those who do not do this remain amateurs. ❞**
>
> **—Gerald Brenan**

‡MOVING OUT (IV), Feminist Literary & Arts Journal, Box 21249, Detroit MI 48221. Contact: Margaret Kaminski, co-editor. Magazine: 8½x11; 75 pages; medium paper; heavy cover; illustrations; photos. Magazine of "material which captures the experience of women, for feminists and other humane human beings." Published semiannually. Estab. 1970. Circ. 1,000.
Needs: Feminist, lesbian and senior citizen/retirement. No male chauvinist creations. Accepts about 10-20 mss/issue. Recently published fiction by Sally Abbott. Occasionally critiques rejected mss.
How to Contact: Send complete ms with SASE. Accepts computer printout submissions. Reports in 6-12 months. Sample copy $9 (old issue $3.50); free guidelines with SASE.
Payment: 1 free contributor's copy.
Terms: Acquires first rights. Publication copyrighted.
Advice: "We like to see work explores women's aesthetics, as well as that which represents varied experiences of the poor, the handicapped, the minorities, the lonely."

‡MUSE'S MILL (I,II), Box 2117, Ashland KY 41105. (614)894-3723 (evening); (614)532-2357 (day). Editors: D. H. Spears, Cindi Griffith, Mike McDonald. Magazine: 8½x11; 36-60 pages. Publishes "short stories primarily; all types. Some articles, poems, graphics." For "nonacademic, eclectic reader." Quarterly. Estab. 1988. Circ. 500.
Needs: Adventure, condensed/excerpted novel, contemporary, ethnic, experimental, fantasy, horror, humor/satire, literary, mainstream, prose poem, psychic/supernatural/occult, romance (contemporary, historical), science fiction, serialized novel, sports, suspense/mystery, western, young adult/teen (10-18). No "graphic gratuitous sex or violence; racist or xenophobic" fiction. Receives 40 mss/month. Buys 14 mss/issue; 56 mss/year. Publishes ms within 3-6 months of acceptance. Recently published work by C.O. Lamp; Starr Lyn Butterfield, James Gish. Length: 1,500-3,000 words preferred; 50 words minimum; 5,000 words maximum. Sometimes critiques rejected mss and recommends other markets.
How to Contact: Send complete ms with cover letter, which should state previous credits. Reports on queries in 2 weeks; on mss in 9 weeks. SASE. Simultaneous, photocopied and reprint submissions OK. Accepts computer printout submissions, including dot-matrix. Accepts electronic submissions via disk. Sample copy for $5. Fiction guidelines free for SAE.
Payment: Pays $10-$100 and 1 contributor's copy.
Terms: Pays on publication for one-time rights. Offers 25% kill fee. Publication copyrighted. Sponsors awards for fiction writers.
Advice: "Many manuscripts we receive are grammatically correct but creatively barren. Read short fiction—good fiction, from Hemingway to Ellison and beyond. Don't watch TV so much. Write to acquire skills, then write with inspiration—listen to your muse. Make something happen in your stories, something or someone undergo change, growth, decline, etc. Expect it to be difficult and slow progress, but extremely satisfying."

MUSICWORKS (IV), A Triannual Magazine With Sound, Music Gallery, 1087 Queen St. W., Toronto, Ontario M6J 1H3 Canada. (416)533-0192. Editor: G. Young. Tabloid and cassette: 28 pages; Webcoat 70 paper and cover; b&w illustrations and photographs. "All aspects of contemporary sonic arts—interviews, articles, scores, visuals, sound and music on cassette." For musicians, composers, students, artists, administrators, etc. Triannually. Estab. 1978. Circ. 1,500.
Needs: Ethnic, experimental, prose poem and music-sound. No mainstream, commercial, popular fiction. Accepts less than 1 ms/issue; 1-3 mss/year, maximum. Recently published work by Paul Haines. Length: 2,000 words average; 5,000 words maximum. Occasionally critiques rejected mss.
How to Contact: Send proposal or query with clips of published work. Reports in 6 weeks. SASE or SAE and IRC for query and ms. Simultaneous, photocopied and previously published submissions OK. Accepts computer printout submissions, prefers letter-quality. Sample $3.25; with cassette $8.75.
Payment: Pays $200 maximum and 2-3 contributor's copies; charge for extras $2-$3.
Terms: Buys one time rights on publication.
Advice: "Our emphasis is on music, and we occasionally publish fiction related to experimental music."

MYSTERY TIME (I), An Anthology of Short Stories, Box 1870, Hayden ID 83835. (208)772-6184. Editor: Linda Hutton. Booklet: 5½x8½; 44 pages; bond paper; illustrations. "Annual collection of short stories with a suspense or mystery theme for mystery buffs." Estab. 1983.
Needs: Suspense/mystery only. Receives 10-15 unsolicited fiction mss/month. Accepts 10-12 mss/

year. Recently published work by Elizabeth Lucknell, Loretta Sallman Jackson, Vickie Britton. Published new writers within the last year. Length: 1,500 words maximum. Occasionally critiques rejected mss and recommends other markets.
How to Contact: Send complete ms with SASE. "No cover letters." Simultaneous, photocopied and previously published submissions OK. Accepts computer printout submissions. Prefers letter-quality. Reports in 1 month on mss. Publishes ms an average of 6-8 months after acceptance. Sample copy for $3.50. Fiction guidelines for #10 SAE and 22¢ postage.
Payment: 1/4¢/word minimum; 1¢/word maximum. 1 free contributor's copy; $2.50 charge for extras
Terms: Acquires one-time rights. Buys reprints. Publication copyrighted. Sponsors annual short story contest.
Advice: "Study a sample copy and the guidelines. Too many amateurs mark themselves as amateurs by submitting blind."

THE MYTHIC CIRCLE (I), The Mythopoeic Society, Box 6707, Altadena CA 91001. Co-Editors: Lynn Maudlin and Christine Lowentrout. Magazine: 8½x11; 50 pages; high quality photocopy paper; illustrations. "A quarterly fantasy-fiction magazine. We function as a 'writer's forum,' depending heavily on letters of comment from readers. We have an occasional section called 'Mythopoeic Youth' in which we publish stories written by writers still in high school/junior high school. We have several 'theme' issues (poetry, American fantasy) and plan more of these in the future." Quarterly. Estab. 1987. Circ. 150.
Needs: Short fantasy and prose poetry. "No erotica, no graphic horror, no 'hard' science fiction." Receives 25+ unsolicited ms/month. Accepts 19-20 mss/issue. Publishes ms 2-8 months after acceptance. Recently published work by Charles de Lint, Gwyneth Hood, Angelee Sailer Anderson; published new writers within the last year. Length: 3,000 words average. Publishes short shorts. Length: open, "though we lean heavily away from serializing." Always critiques rejected mss; may recommend other markets.
How to Contact: Send complete ms with cover letter. "We like to know if the person is very young— we give give each ms a personal response. We get many letters that try to impress us with other places they've appeared in print—that doesn't matter much to us." Reports in 2-8 weeks. SASE. Simultaneous, photocopied submissions OK. Accepts computer printout submissions, including dark dot-matrix, and IBM or MAC floppies. Sample copy $3; fiction guidelines for #10 SASE.
Payment: Contributor's copies; charges for extras.
Terms: Acquires one-time rights. Publication copyrighted.
Advice: "There are very few places a fantasy writer can send to these days. *Mythic Circle* was started up because of this; also, the writers were not getting any kind of feedback when (after nine or ten months) their mss were rejected. We give the writers personalized attention—critiques, suggestions— and we rely on our readers to send us letters of comment on the stories we publish, so that the writers can see a response. Don't be discouraged by rejections, especially if personal comments/suggestions are offered."

NAKED MAN (II), c/o Mike Smetzer, Dept. of English, University of Kansas, Lawrence KS 66045. Editor: Mike Smetzer. Magazine: 5½x8½; 36-48 pages; offset paper; ivory bristol board cover stock; illustrations on cover. "I have eclectic tastes but generally dislike work that is only clever or spontaneous work without discipline. Since *Naked Man* reflects my personal interests and tastes, writers should examine a copy before submitting." Published irregularly. Estab. 1982.
Needs: Comics, contemporary, experimental, humor/satire, literary, mainstream, prose poem and regional. Publishes ms an average of 6 months after acceptance. Recently published work by Elizabeth J. Moore, Tim Coats, Michael Pritchett. Length: no minimum; 15,000 words maximum. Occasionally critiques rejected mss "as time permits."
How to Contact: Send complete ms with SASE. Photocopied submissions OK. Accepts computer printout submissions. Prefers letter-quality. Sample copy $2.25. Subscriptions are $9 for 4 issues in U.S. and Mexico; $10.50 for other countries.
Payment: Pays in 2 contributor's copies.
Terms: Acquires first rights. Sends galleys to author. Publication copyrighted.
Advice: "Most issues of *Naked Man* will now be chapbooks. Chapbook submissions may be short stories, short novelettes, mixtures of prose and poetry, or poetry; but they should have some overall unity. No unsolicited translations, Prose length about 3,000-14,000 words. Individual pieces in collections may have previous magazine publication. The author will receive 25 of 300-500 copies printed. Copyright will be to the author. For non-subscribers there is a chapbook reading fee of $5."

NEBO (I), A Literary Journal, Arkansas Tech University, Dept. of English, Russellville AR 72801. Contact: Editor. Literary, fiction and poetry magazine: 5x8; 50-60 pages. For a general, academic audience. Semiannually. Estab. 1983. Circ. 500.
Needs: Experimental, literary, mainstream, reviews. Receives 20-30 unsolicited fiction mss/month.

Accepts 2 mss/issue; 6-10 mss/year. Does not read mss May 31-Aug 1. Published new writers within the last year. Length: 3,000 words maximum. Occasionally critiques rejected mss.
How to Contact: Send complete ms with SASE and cover letter with bio. Simultaneous and photo-copied submissions OK. Accepts computer printout submissions, prefers letter-quality. Reports in 12 weeks on mss. Publishes ms an average of 6 months after acceptance. Sample copy for $1.
Payment: 2 free contributor's copies.
Terms: Acquires one-time rights. "Rarely" buys reprints. Publication copyrighted.
Advice: "A writer should carefully edit his short story before submitting it. Write from the heart and put everything on the line. Don't write from a phony or fake perspective. Frankly, many of the manu-scripts we receive should be publishable with a little polishing. Manuscripts should *never* be submitted with misspelled words or on 'onion skin' or colored paper."

THE NEBRASKA REVIEW (II), University of Nebraska at Omaha, ASH 212, Omaha NE 68182. (402)554-2771. Editors: Arthur Homer, Richard Duggin. Magazine: 5½x8½; 72 pages; 60 lb text pa-per; chrome coat cover stock. "*TNR* attempts to publish the finest available contemporary fiction and poetry for college and literary types." Publishes 2 issues/year. Estab. 1973. Circ. 500.
Needs: Contemporary, humor/satire, literary and mainstream. Receives 20 unsolicited fiction mss/month. Accepts 3-5 mss/issue, 8 mss/year. Does not read April 1-September 1. Recently published work by Elizabeth Evans, Joan Joffe Hall and Marilyn Copley; published new writers within the last year. Length: 5,000-6,000 words average.
How to Contact: Send complete ms with SASE. Photocopied submissions OK. Reports in 1-2 months. Publishes ms an average of 4-6 months after acceptance. Sample copy $2.50.
Payment: 2 free contributor's copies plus 1 year subscription; $2 charge for extras.
Terms: Acquires first North American serial rights. Publication copyrighted.
Advice: "Don't consider us as the last place to submit your mss. Write 'honest' stories in which the lives of your characters are the primary reason for writing and techniques of craft serve to illuminate, not overshadow, the textures of those lives."

NEGATIVE CAPABILITY (II), A Literary Quarterly, 62 Ridgelawn Dr. E., Mobile AL 36608. (205)661-9114. Editor-in-Chief: Sue Walker. Managing Editor: Richard G. Beyer. Magazine: 5½x8½; 160 pages; 70 lb offset paper; 2 color/varnish cover stock; illustrations; photos. Magazine of short fic-tion, prose poems, poetry, criticism, commentaries, journals and translations for those interested in con-temporary trends, innovations in literature. Published quarterly. Estab. 1981. Circ. 1,000.
Needs: Adventure, contemporary, ethnic, experimental, fantasy, feminist, gothic/historical romance, historical (general), literary, prose poem, psychic/supernatural/occult, regional, romance (contempo-rary), science fiction, senior citizen/retirement, suspense/mystery, translations. Accepts 2-3 mss/issue, 6-10 mss/year. Does not read July-Sept. Publishes short shorts. Recently published work by A.W. Landwehr, Gerald Flaherty and Richard Moore; published new writers within the last year. Length: 1,000 words minimum. Sometimes recommends other markets.
How to Contact: Query or send complete ms. SASE. Reports in 2 weeks on queries; 6 weeks on mss. Publishes ms an average of 6 months after acceptance. Sample copy $5.
Payment: 2 free contributor's copies.
Terms: Acquires first rights, first North American serial rights and one-time rights. Sends galleys to au-thor. Publication copyrighted. Annual fiction competition. Deadline Dec. 15.
Advice: "We consider all manuscripts and often work with new authors to encourage and support. We believe fiction answers a certain need that is not filled by poetry or nonfiction."

NEW BLOOD MAGAZINE (I,II), Suite 3730, 540 W. Foothill Blvd., Glendora CA 91740. Editor: Chris Lacher. Magazine: 8½x11; 70-100 pages; 20 lb paper; gloss cover; b&w illustrations. "Of course, story counts, but *New Blood* publishes fiction considered too strong or gory to appear in today's periodi-cals; note, emphasis does not have to be on gore or grue—I just want a story that knocks me out! Fans of Clive Barker and *Fangoria* magazine, for example, will appreciate *New Blood*." Quarterly. Estab. 1986. Circ. 5,000.
Needs: Horror, gore, psychic/supernatural/occult, dark fantasy, experimental, erotica with gore or hor-ror slant, excerpted novel, suspense/mystery, translations. "I can't use sword and sorcery, unless char-acters and settings are contemporary. I will consider techno-horror, science gone mad, botanical horror, science fiction with a horror slant." Receives 200 unsolicited mss/month. Accepts 10-20 mss/issue; 45-90 mss/ year. Publishes ms 3-9 months after acceptance. Agented fiction 1%. Recently published work by Clive Barker, Gary Brandner, Ray Garton; published new writers within the last year. Length: 2,500 words average; 5,000 words maximum. Always critiques rejected mss. Sometimes recommends other markets.
How to Contact: Send complete ms with cover letter, which should include a brief bio. Reports on queries and mss "immediately." SASE. Simultaneous, photocopied and reprint submissions OK. Sam-

ple copy $4.95. Please make check payable to Chris Lacher.
Payment: Pays 1-5¢/word.
Terms: Rights revert to author on publication. Publication copyrighted.
Advice: "I see too many stories with senseless gore; involve me, show me something new. Becoming familiar with the unique type of fiction I publish by purchasing a subscription is a contributor's key to a quick sale. *New Blood* is unlike any magazine to ever appear on the newsstands, and I believe one must read *New Blood* regularly, be aware of our consistent growth, to write for us."

‡THE NEW CRUCIBLE (I), A Magazine for Man and His Environment, Box 7252, Spencer IA 51301. Editor: Garry De Young. Magazine: 8½x11; variable number of pages; 20 lb paper; soft cover; illustrations and photographs. Publishes "environmental material—includes the total human environment." Monthly. Plans special fiction issue. Estab. 1988.
Needs: "Humorous articles exposing the idiocy of religion!" Atheist. "Keep articles concise. use clear line drawings. Environmentalists must be Materialists because the environment deals with matter. Thus also evolutionists and Atheists. Keep this in mind. No religious and other superstitious drivel accepted. Manuscripts not returned. Will not accept religious or other racist or sexist material." Receives "too many" unsolicited mss/month. Charges $1/page reading fee. Length: concise preferred. Publishes short shorts. Sometimes critiques rejected mss.
How to Contact: Send complete ms with cover letter. Cover letter should include "biographical sketch of author." SASE. Simultaneous, photocopied and reprint submissions OK. Accepts computer printout submissions, including dot-matrix. Sample copy for $2, 8½x11 SAE and 4 first class stamps.
Payment: Pays in contributor's copies.
Terms: "Will discuss rights with author." Publication copyrighted.
Advice: "Be gutsy! Don't be afraid to attack the superstitionists with a vengeance. Attack those good people who remain so silent—people such as newspaper editors, so-called scientists who embrace superstition such as the Jesus myth or the Virgin Mary nonsense."

‡NEW DELTA REVIEW (I,II), English Dept./Louisiana St. University, Baton Rouge LA 70803. (504)388-2236. Editor: Leisha Jones. Fiction Editor: Gregory Fuchs. Magazine: 6x9; 75-125 pages; high quality paper; glossy card cover; illustrations; photographs possible. "No theme; all types except learned idiocy. Poetry, fiction primarily; creative reviews." Annually. "Hope to be 2/year in '89." Plans special fiction issue. Estab. 1984.
Needs: Contemporary, erotica, experimental, humor/satire, literary, mainstream, prose poem, spiritual (pagan), sports, soft porn, translations. Receives 10 mss/month. Accepts 4-8 mss/issue. Recently published work by Eve Shelnutt, Tim Parrish, Virgil Suarez; published new writers within the last year. Length: 2,500 words average; 250 words minimum; 5,000 words maximum. Publishes short shorts. Sometimes critiques rejected mss.
How to Contact: Send complete ms with cover letter. Cover letter should include "nothing long: credits, if any; who, if anyone, referred you to us." Reports on mss in 4-6 weeks. SASE. Prefers photocopied submissions. No dot-matrix. Sample copy for $4.
Payment: Pays in contributor's copies. Charge for extra copies. "We'll make a deal for a quantity."
Terms: Acquires first North American serial rights. Publication copyrighted. Sponsors awards for fiction writers. "Eyster Prize—$50 plus notice in magazine. Enclose $4 with ms submission; entrant receives free copy of latest issue."
Advice: "Each submission is read by 4-7 undergraduate and MFA students and receives a 'score' on a scale of 0 to 5. Editors have final decision. Obviously any piece scoring high has a chance for publication. There is no *a priori* criteria. Submit clean photocopies on cheap paper and let us have the copy. Enclose a #10 SASE for reply. There's no sense in all this postage and typing cost for writers hoping to break through. Also, save your wit for the submission, not the cover letter. We're not New York and glad of it."

NEW ENGLAND REVIEW AND BREAD LOAF QUARTERLY (III), NER/BLQ, Middlebury College, Middlebury VT 05753. (802)388-3711, ext. 5075. Editors: Sydney Lea, Maura High. Magazine: 6x9; 140 pages; 70 lb paper; coated cover stock; illustrations; photos. A literary quarterly publishing fiction, poetry and essays on life and the craft of writing. For general readers and professional writers. Quarterly. Estab. 1977. Circ. 2,000.
Needs: Literary. Receives 250 unsolicited fiction mss/month. Accepts 5 mss/issue; 20 mss/year. Does not read ms June-August. Recently published work by Antonio Benítez-Rojo, Philip Deaver, Lynne McFall; published new writers within the last year. Publishes ms 3-9 months after acceptance. Agented fiction: less than 5%. Publishes short shorts. Sometimes critiques rejected mss.
How to Contact: Send complete ms with cover letter. "Cover letters that demonstrate that the writer knows the magazine, and is not submitting simultaneously elsewhere, are the ones we want to read. We don't want hype, or hard-sell, or summaries of the author's intentions." Reports in 6-8 weeks on mss.

SASE. Photocopied submissions OK. Accepts computer printouts, including dot-matrix. Sample copy $4. Send #10 SAE with any inquiries.
Payment: Pays $5 per page; $10 minimum; free subscription to magazine, offprints; contributor's copies; charge for extras.
Terms: Pays on publication. Acquires first rights and reprint rights on *NER/BLQ* and Middlebury College. Sends galleys to author. Publication copyrighted.
Advice: "We look for work that combines intelligence with craft and visceral appeal. To break into the prestige or literary market, writers should avoid formulae and clichés and assume that the reader is at least as intelligent and well informed as they are."

NEW FRONTIER (IV), 421 Fairmount Ave., Philadelphia PA 19123. (215)627-5683. Editor: Sw. Virato. Magazine: 8x10; 48-60 pages; pulp paper stock; illustrations and photos. "We seek new age writers who have imagination yet authenticity." Monthly. Estab. 1981. Circ. 40,000.
Needs: New age. "A new style of writing is needed with a transformation theme." Receives 10-20 unsolicited mss/month. Accepts 1-2 mss/issue. Publishes ms 3 months after acceptance. Agented fiction "less than 5%." Recently published work by John White, Laura Anderson. Published work by new writers within the last year. Length: 1,000 words average; 750 words minimum; 2,000 words maximum. Publishes short shorts. Length: 150-500 words. Occasionally critiques rejected mss and recommends other markets.
How to Contact: Send complete ms with cover letter, which should include author's bio and credits. Reports in 2 months on mss. SASE for ms. Simultaneous, photocopied and reprint submissions OK. Accepts computer printout submissions, including dot-matrix. Sample copy for $2. Fiction guidelines for #10 SAE and 1 first class stamp.
Terms: Acquires first North American serial rights and one-time rights. Publication copyrighted.
Advice: "The new age market is ready for a special kind of fiction and we are here to serve it. Don't try to get an A on your term paper. Be sincere, aware and experimental. Old ideas that are senile don't work for us. Be fully alive and aware—tune in to our new age audience/readership."

NEW LAUREL REVIEW (II), 828 Lesseps St., New Orleans LA 70117. (504)947-6001. Editor: Lee M. Grue. Assistant Editor: George Cleveland. Magazine: 6x9; 120 pages; 60 lb book paper; Sun Felt cover; illustrations; photo essays. Journal of poetry, fiction, critical articles and reviews. "We have published such internationally known writers as Martha McFerren, Tomris Uyar and Yevgeny Yevtushenko." Readership: "Literate, adult audiences as well as anyone interested in writing with significance, human interest, vitality, subtlety, etc." Annually. Estab. 1970. Circ. 500.
Needs: Literary, contemporary, fantasy and translations. No "dogmatic, excessively inspirational or political" material. Accepts 1-2 fiction mss/issue. Receives approximately 50 unsolicited fiction mss each month. Length: about 10 printed pages. Critiques rejected mss when there is time.
How to Contact: Send complete ms with SASE. Reports in 3 months. Sample copy $4.
Payment: 2 free author's copies.
Terms: Acquires first rights. Publication copyrighted.
Advice: "We are interested in international issues pointing to libraries around the world. Write fresh, alive 'moving' work. Not interested in egocentric work without any importance to others. Be sure to watch simple details such as putting one's name and address on ms and clipping all pages together. Caution: Don't use overfancy or trite language."

NEW LETTERS MAGAZINE (I, II), University of Missouri-Kansas City, 5261 Rockhill Rd., Kansas City MO 64110. (816)276-1168. Editor: James McKinley. Magazine: 14 lb cream paper; illustrations. Quarterly. Estab. 1971 (continuation of *University Review*, founded 1935). Circ. 2,500.
Needs: Contemporary, ethnic, experimental, humor/satire, literary, mainstream, translations. No "bad fiction in any genre." Recently published work by Richard Rhodes, Jascha Kessler, Josephine Jacobsen; publshed work by new writers within the last year. Agented fiction: 10%. Also publishes short shorts. Occasionally critiques rejected mss.
How to Contact: Send complete ms with cover letter. Does not read mss May 15-October 15. Reports in 3 weeks on queries; 6 weeks on mss. SASE for ms. Photocopied submissions OK. Accepts computer printouts. Sample copy: $8.50 for issues older than 5 years; $5.50 for 5 years or less.
Payment: Honorarium—depends on grant/award money; 2 contributor's copies. Sends galleys to author.
Advice: "Seek publication of representative chapters in high-quality magazines as a way to the book contract. Try literary magazines first."

NEW MEXICO HUMANITIES REVIEW (II), Humanities Dept., New Mexico Tech, Box A, Socorro NM 87801. (505)835-5445. Editors: John Rothfork and Jerry Bradley. Magazine: 5½x9½; 100 pages; 60 lb lakewood paper; 482 ppi cover stock; illustrations; photos. Review of poetry, essays and prose of Southwest. Readership: academic but not specialized. Published 3 times/year. Estab. 1978. Circ. 600.

Needs: Literary and regional. "No formula." Accepts 40-50 mss/year. Receives approximately 30 unsolicited fiction mss/month. Recently published work by John Deming, Fred Chappell; published new writers within the last year. Length: 6,000 words maximum. Publishes short shorts. Critiques rejected mss "when there is time." Sometimes recommends other markets.
How to Contact: Send complete ms with SASE. Accepts computer printout submissions. Reports in 2 months. Publishes ms an average of 6 months after acceptance. Sample copy $3.
Payment: 1 year subscription.
Terms: Sends galleys to author. Publication copyrighted.
Advice: Mss are rejected because they are "unimaginative, predictable and technically flawed. Don't be afraid to take literary chances—be daring, experiment."

NEW MOON, A Journal of Science Fiction and Critical Feminism, Box 2056, Madison WI 53701. (608)251-3854. Editor: Janice Bogstad. "Speculative fiction, fantastic feminist fiction, reviews and criticism of such works. Copies found in university libraries, feminist and literary collections, women's studies programs." Semiannually. Estab. 1981. Circ. 600.
Needs: Experimental, fantasy, feminist, literary, prose poem, science fiction, translations. Receives 3-5 unsolicited fiction mss/month. Accepts 2-4 mss/issue; 15 mss/year. Published new writers within the last year. Length: 1,000-1,500 words average; 1,000 words minimum; 3,000 words maximum. Occasionally critiques rejected mss.
How to Contact: Query first. Cover letter should include "other interests, other publications of your work." Reports in 2 months on queries; 4 months on mss. SASE. Simultaneous, photocopied submissions and previously published work OK. "No originals." Accepts computer printout submissions. Prefers letter-quality. Sample copy $4. Fiction guidelines free for #10 SAE and 1 first class stamp.
Payment: Pays 1 contributor's copy; 60% of cover price charge for extras.
Terms: Acquires one-time rights. Publication copyrighted.
Advice: "Send photocopies only. Send clean, clear copy and advise as to turnaround time expected."

NEW ORLEANS REVIEW (II), Box 195, Loyola University, New Orleans LA 70118. (504)865-2294. Editor: John Mosier. Magazine: 8½x11; 104 pages; 60 lb Scott offset paper; 12 + King James C15 cover stock; photos. "Publishes poetry, fiction, translations, photographs, nonfiction on literature and film. Readership: those interested in current culture, literature." Published 4 times/year. Estab. 1968. Circ. 1,000.
Needs: Literary, contemporary, translations. Buys 9-12 mss/year. Length: under 40 pages.
How to Contact: Send complete ms with SASE. Does not accept simultaneous submissions. Accepts computer printout submissions. Accepts disk submissions; inquire about system compatibility. Prefers hard copy with disk submission. Reports in 1 month. Sample copy $9.
Payment: "Rates are changing."
Terms: Pays on publication for first North American serial rights. Sends galleys to author.

THE NEW PRESS (II), 87-20 166 Street, Jamaica NY 11364. (718)523-4928. Publisher: Scott Martin. Fiction Editor: Jill Heyman. Magazine: 8½x11; 20 pages; medium bond paper and cover stock; illustrations and photographs. "Poems, short stories, personal journalism. Original and entertaining." Quarterly. Estab. 1984.
Needs: Adventure, confession, ethnic, experimental, fantasy, humor/satire, literary, mainstream, prose poem, serialized/excerpted novel, spiritual, sports, translations. No pornography. Receives 10 unsolicited mss/month. Accepts 2 mss/issue; 8 mss/year. Publishes ms 6 months after acceptance. Published new writers within the last year. Length: 3,000 words maximum; 100 words minimum. Sometimes critiques rejected mss and recommends other markets.
How to Contact: Send complete ms with cover letter. Reports in 2 months. SASE. Simultaneous, photocopied and reprint submissions OK. Accepts computer printout submissions, including dot-matrix. Sample copy $2; fiction guidelines free.
Payment: Pays in contributor's copies.
Terms: Pays on publication for one-time rights.
Advice: "Show a great deal of thought input into your work."

THE NEW QUARTERLY (II, IV), new directions in Canadian writing, ELPP, University of Waterloo, Waterloo, Ontario N2L 3G1 Canada. (519)885-1212, ext. 2837. Managing Editor: Mary Merikle. Fiction Editors: Peter Hinchcliffe, Kim Jernigan. Magazine: 6x9; 80-120 pages; perfect bound cover, b&w cover photograph; photos with special issues. "We publish poetry, short fiction, excerpts from novels, interviews. We are particularly interested in writing which stretches the bounds of realism. Our audience includes those interested in Canadian literature." Quarterly. Published recent special issues on magic realism in Canadian writing and family fiction.
Needs: "I suppose we could be described as a 'literary' magazine. We look for writing which is fresh,

innovative, well crafted. We promote beginning writers alongside more established ones. Ours is a humanist magazine—no gratuitous violence, though we are not afraid of material which is irreverent or unconventional. Our interest is more in the quality than the content of the fiction we see." Receives approx. 40 unsolicited mss/month. Buys 5-6 mss/issue; 20-24 mss/year. Publishes ms usually within 6 months after acceptance. Recently published work by Sandra Birdsell, Joan Fern Shaw and Diana Kiesners; published new writers within the last year. Length: up to 20 pages. Publishes short shorts. Sometimes recommends other markets.

How to Contact: Send complete ms with cover letter, which should include a short biographical note. Reports in 1-2 weeks on queries; approx. 3 months on mss. SASE for ms. Photocopied submissions OK. Accepts computer printout submissions, no dot-matrix. Sample copy for $3.50.

Payment: Pays $100 and contributor's copies.

Terms: Pays on publication for first North American serial rights. Publication copyrighted.

Advice: "Send only one well polished manuscript at a time. Persevere. Find your own voice. The primary purpose of little literary magazines like ours is to introduce new writers to the reading public. However, because we want them to appear at their best, we apply the same standards when judging novice work as when judging that of more established writers."

The New Quarterly is a literary magazine looking for "writing which is fresh, innovative, well crafted," says editor, Kim Jernigan. "We promote beginning writers alongside more established ones. Our one firm restriction is that we publish only Canadian writers."

Cover photo by Kim and Ed Jernigan.

the new renaissance (II), 9 Heath Rd., Arlington MA 02174. Fiction Editors: Louise T. Reynolds and Harry Jackel. Magazine: 6x9; 136-144 pages; 70 lb paper; laminated cover stock; artwork; photos. "An international magazine of ideas and opinions, with a classicist position in literature and the arts. Publishes a variety of quality fiction, always well crafted, sometimes experimental. *tnr* is unique among literary magazines for its marriage of the literary and visual arts with political/sociological articles and essays. We publish the beginning as well as the established writer." Biannually. Estab. 1968. Circ. 1,500.

Needs: Literary, humor, prose poem, translations, off-beat, quality fiction and, occasionally, experimental fiction. "We don't want to see heavily plotted stories with one-dimensional characters or academic or obviously 'poetic' writing, or fiction that is self-indulgent." Buys 5-6 mss/issue, 7-12 mss/year. Receives approximately 40-60 unsolicited fiction mss each month. Requires $5.45 for 2 sample back issues or $5.20 for recent issue before reading mss. Overstocked. Suspending submissions from 7/89 through 12/90. Approximately 8-12% of fiction is agented. Recently published work by Valerie Hobbs, Marjorie Dorner, and Jeanne Schinto; published new writers within the last year. Length: 3-36 pages. Comments on rejected mss "when there is time and when we want to encourage the writer or believe we can be helpful."

How to Contact: Send complete ms with SASE of sufficient size for return or IRCs. "Inform us if multiple submission." Reluctantly accepts computer printout submissions but prefers letter-quality. Re-

ports in 4-6 months. Publishes ms an average of 16-22 months after acceptance. Sample copy $5.45 for 2 back issues, or $5 for recent issue. Current issue is $6.30.
Payment: $30-$75. 1 free author's copy. Query for additional copies.
Terms: Acquires all rights. Publication copyrighted.
Advice: "We represent one of the best markets for writers, because we publish a greater variety (of styles, statements, levels of expertise) than most magazines, small or large. Study *tnr* and then send the best manuscript you have on hand; we will read 2 manuscripts if they are 5 pages or less; 6 pages or more, send only one ms. Manuscripts are rejected because writers do not study their markets and send out indiscriminately. Fully one-quarter of our rejected manuscripts fall into this category; others are from tyro writers who haven't yet mastered their craft, or writers who are not honest with themselves or their readers, or who haven't fully thought their story through, or because writers are careless about language. Also, many writers feel compelled to 'explain' their stories to the reader instead of letting the story speak for itself, a common communication problem in the latter half of this century."

NEW VIRGINIA REVIEW (II), An anthology of literary work by and important to Virginians, 1306 East Cary St., 2A, Richmond VA 23219. (804)782-1043. Rotating guest editors. Editor 1988-89: Bob Shacochis. Magazine: 10x6½; 300+ pages; high quality paper; coated, color cover stock. "Approximately one half of the contributors have Virginia connections; the other authors are serious writers of contemporary fiction. Occasionally guest editors set a specific theme for an issue, e.g. 1986 Young Southern Writers." Annually. Estab. 1978. Circ. 2,000.
Needs: Contemporary, experimental, literary, mainstream, serialized/excerpted novel. No blue, sci-fi, romance, children's. Receives 50-100 unsolcited fiction mss/month. Accepts an average of 15 mss/issue. Does not read from April 1 to September 1. Publishes ms an average of 6-9 months after acceptance. Length: 5,000-6,500 words average; no minimum; 8,000 words maximum. Sometimes critiques rejected mss.
How to Contact: Send complete ms with cover letter, name, address, telephone number, brief biographical comment. Reports in 6 weeks on queries; up to 6 months on mss. "Will answer questions on status of ms." SASE. Photocopied submissions OK. Accepts computer printout submissions, including dot-matrix "occasionally." Sample copy $13.50 and 9x12 SAE with 5 first-class stamps.
Payment: $10/printed page; contributor's copies; charge for extras, ½ cover price.
Terms: Pays on publication for first North American serial rights. Sponsors contests and awards for Virginia writers only.
Advice: "Since we publish a wide range of styles of writing depending on the tastes of our guest editors, all we can say is—try to write good strong fiction, stick to it, and try again with another editor."

NeWEST REVIEW (II, IV), Box 394, Sub P.O. 6 Saskatoon, Saskatchewan S7N 0WO Canada. Editorial Committee: Paul Denham, Jim Sutherland, Gail McConnell, Brett Fairbairn. Fiction Editor: Edna Alford. Magazine: 56-72 pages; book stock; self cover; illustrations; photos. Magazine devoted to western Canada regional issues; "fiction, reviews, poetry for middle- to high-brow audience." Bimonthly (6 issues per year). Estab. 1975. Circ. 1,000.
Needs: Contemporary, ethnic, experimental, fantasy, feminist, gay, historical, humor/satire, literary, mainstream, science fiction. Receives 10-12 unsolicited mss/month. Buys 1 ms/issue; 10 mss/year. Recently published work by Dickinson, Farrant, Simmie; published new writers within the last year. Length: 2,500 words average; 1,500 words minimum; 5,000 words maximum. Sometimes recommends other markets.
How to Contact: "We prefer *brief* cover letters: past publications of fiction and brief instructions from the writers." Reports very promptly in a short letter. SAE, IRCs or Canadian postage. Photocopied submissions OK. No multiple submissions. Accepts computer printout submissions. Sample copy $1.50.
Payment: Pays $100 maximum.
Terms: Pays on publication for one-time rights. Publication copyrighted.
Advice: "Fiction embodies important truths inaccessible to other kinds of writing. A lot of academics who wish to be trendy claim that plot and character are not important any more. This is rubbish. If we, the readers, are to care about the people you create, you too must take them very seriously."

‡NIGHT SLIVERS (I,IV), A Journal of Nocturnal Pain, 302 N. School #19, Normal IL 61761. (309)454-7758. Editor: Kevin Kocis. Assistant Editor: Patricia Brandt. Magazine: 5½x8½; 60-80 pages; 20 lb paper; 60 lb cover; few illustrations. Publishes "short-short stories of horror and pain, like a sliver evokes pain—thus, the title." Semiannually. Estab. 1988. Circ. 200.
Needs: Experimental, fantasy, horror, literary, psychic/supernatural/occult, science fiction. "Our main interest is horror; therefore, any other fiction category must centralize around a horrific theme. We are also in literary and experimental horror, though these are difficult to write. No slasher, cannibalism, child situations, blatant religious (including satanism) and racism." Receives 30-60 unsolicited mss/month. Buys 15-20 mss/issue; 45-60 mss/year. Publishes ms 6 months-1 year after acceptance. Length:

800 words preferred; 100 words minimum; 1,000 words maximum. Publishes short shorts. Sometimes critiques rejected mss and recommends other markets.

How to Contact: Send complete ms with cover letter. Cover letter should include "informal bio, credits, interests (personal and literary)." Reports in 2 weeks on queries; 1 month on mss. SASE. Photocopied submissions OK. Sample copy for $4 and 3 first class stamps. Fiction guidelines for #10 SAE and 1 first class stamp.

Payment: Pays $5 minimum; $10 maximum. Two free contributor's copies; charge for extras.

Terms: Pays on publication for first North American serial rights. Publication copyrighted.

Advice: "Read all the literary greats—Hemingway, Updike, Steinbeck, along with the great writers of horror—Bradbury, Etchison, Matheson, Barker, King. Since there isn't a lot of time or space to produce strong characterization in a short-short, mood and feeling are important. Think about that before you write. Be brief, neat and professional."

NIGHTMARES OF REASON (II), Primal Publishing, 107 Brighton Ave., Allston MA 02134. (617)389-5193. Editor: Michael McInnis. Fiction Editors: Michael McInnis and Larry Oberc. Magazine: size varies; 80-120 pages; 20 lb bond paper; 67 lb cardstock cover; illustrations; photos. "We publish modern alternative literature, for a vast network of underground alternative-thinking people with little or no politics." Annually. Estab. 1986. Circ. 500.

Needs: Contemporary, erotica, experimental, humor/satire, literary, science fiction, serialized/excerpted novel. No "sword and sorcery fantasy; unrealistic portrayals of life and characters with soap-opera emotions." Accepts 10 unsolicited fiction mss/issue. Publishes ms 1-6 months after acceptance. Length: 2,500 words average; 10 words minimum; no maximum. Publishes short shorts. Length: 500 words. Sometimes critiques rejected mss or recommends other markets.

How to Contact: Send complete ms with cover letter, which should include "where s/he first saw magazine. Please *do not* try to describe what your writing is or should be." Reports on queries in 1-4 weeks; on mss in 1-6 months. SASE. Simultaneous, photocopied and reprint submissions OK. Accepts computer printouts, including dot-matrix. Sample copy $5.

Payment: Pays in contributor's copies.

Terms: Acquires one-time rights. Rights revert back to author upon publication. Publication copyrighted.

Advice: "Send $5. I'll send you the latest issue. After reading it, respond by sending me a manuscript and letting me know what you liked or didn't like. Or, if my magazine isn't for you, then don't respond. I plan on publishing a higher percentage of fiction to poetry. There are too few fiction markets. Don't be afraid to try non-paying/contributor copies markets."

‡NIGHTSUN, Department of English, Frostburg State University, Frostburg MD 21532. Editors-in-Chief: Doug DeMars and Barbara Wilson. Magazine: 5½x8½; 120 pages; acid free paper; varied cover stock; illustrations; photos sometimes. Magazine of "all literary forms and philosophical and literary essays for a literary and/or academic audience." Annually. Estab. 1981. Circ. 500-1,000 (varying).

Needs: Comics, contemporary, experimental, feminist, prose poem. "We are not dogmatic, but have little interest in science fiction, supernatural, etc." Receives 5 unsolicited fiction mss/month. Occasionally critiques rejected mss. Published new writers within the last year. Inquire about *theme* of each issue.

How to Contact: Send inquiry with SASE. Accepts computer printout submissions. Reporting time varies. Sample copy $6.95.

Payment: Pays 1 free contributor's copy.

Terms: Acquires one-time rights (rights revert to author after publication). Publication copyrighted.

Advice: "Try to *say* something. There is too much formal and entertainment writing."

NIMROD (II), International Literary Journal, Arts & Humanities Council of Tulsa, 2210 S. Main, Tulsa OK 74114. Editor-in-Chief: Francine Ringold. Magazine: 9x6; 120-150 pages; 60 lb white paper; illustrations; photos. "We publish 1 thematic issue and 1 open issue (which includes prize winners) each year. A recent theme was India: A Wealth f Diversity." Otherwise, we seek vigorous, imaginative, quality writing." Published semiannually. Estab. 1956. Circ. 2,000 + .

Needs: "We accept contemporary poetry and/or prose. May submit adventure, ethnic, experimental, prose poem, science fiction or translations." Receives 120 unsolicited fiction mss/month. Only one submission per author per genre. Recently published work by Gish Gen and Alvin Greenberg; published new writers within the last year. Length: 7,500 words maximum.

How to Contact: Send two photocopies of complete ms with SASE. $10 entry fee must be included. Reports in 3 weeks-3 months. Sample copy: "to see what *Nimrod* is all about, send $5.50 plus $1.50 postage. Be sure to request an awards issue."

Payment: 3 free contributor's copies.

Terms: Acquires one-time rights. Publication copyrighted.

Advice: "Read the magazine. Write well. Be courageous. No superfluous words. No clichés. Keep it

Close-up

Robley Wilson, Jr.
The North American Review

The North American Review (*NAR*) has a longstanding reputation for publishing some of the best short stories in
America. Such praise is validated by the magazine's appearance as a finalist, six times in the past ten years, in the
fiction category of the National Magazine Awards—a category it won in 1981 and 1983 against such giants as *The
New Yorker*, *Atlantic Monthly* and *Esquire*. One of editor
Robley Wilson's sources of pride in the prize derives from the fact that the stories he nomi-
nates are frequently by writers whose work has not been published prior to their appearance in
the *NAR*.

Wilson, who has been editing the magazine since 1969, said, "We are truly open to talented new writers. Half our authors are appearing in the *NAR* for the first time and half of *those*
are publishing for the first time anywhere."

Wilson writes both fiction and poetry himself. His first volume of poetry, *Kingdoms of the
Ordinary*, received the Agnes Starrett Lynch prize from the University of Pittsburgh Press in
1987 and his fourth volume of short fiction, *Terrible Kisses*, was published by Simon and
Schuster this past spring.

The *NAR* receives about 2,500 short stories per year (They must be postmarked between
January 1st and March 31st). Although the boxes of manila envelopes fill the office like excess furniture, Wilson, like many other editors, opens each one hoping for a terrific story.
What he wants is "excellent writing." He specifies some of the criteria of a good story: "Authority is the main thing—the sense that the author is trustworthy, knows the characters,
knows the world they live in. There's nothing more disheartening for me as a reader than the
feeling that I've been betrayed by a writer who either didn't do his homework or hasn't cared
enough about his story to make it truthful." And what is "truthful?" "I suppose it's the ability of an author to make the lie believable."

He has a short list of trivia he finds annoying: authors who don't read the magazine, mis-
spell his name in the cover letter, use fiber envelopes that defy the blade of "anything duller
than a machete" and insert the paper-clipped end of the manuscript in last (so the letter opener
catches the clip and flings it across the room). Other suggestions include: don't submit stories
simultaneously without warning the editors, change the printer ribbon (otherwise it appears
that you don't respect your own work), don't use second-hand envelopes.

He offers advice to new writers: "Remember that rejection doesn't mean that the manuscript isn't good; often it's not appropriate to a particular magazine." And finally, "Be patient, work hard, and be true to yourself."

—Carolyn Hardesty

tight but let your imagination flow. Read the magazine. Strongly encourage writers to send SASE for brochure. Rules are fairly explicit. Disqualification a possiblility if procedures not followed.''

‡THE NOCTURNAL LYRIC (I), Box 2602, Pasadena CA 91102-2602. (818)796-4801. Editor: Harmony Keane. Newsletter: 8½x11; 13 pages; illustrations. "We are a non-profit literary journal, dedicated to printing fiction by new writers for the sole purpose of getting read by people who otherwise might have never seen their work." Bimonthly. Estab. 1987. Circ. 100.
Needs: Adventure, contemporary, ethnic, experimental, fantasy, feminist, horror, humor/satire, literary, mainstream, psychic/supernatural/occult, romance (contemporary, historical) science fiction, serialized/excerpted novel, suspense/mystery. "We are, at the present, pretty much open to all areas of fiction, but we will give priority to fantasy/science fiction/horror/suspense and unusual, creative pieces." Receives approx. 10-20 unsolicited mss/month. Publishes ms 2-4 months after acceptance. Publishes short shorts. Length: no more than 8 double-spaced typed pages. Sometimes critiques rejected mss and recommends other markets.
How to Contact: Send complete ms with cover letter. Cover letter should include "something about the author, what areas of fiction he/she is interested in." Reports in 1 week on queries; 2-3 weeks on mss. SASE. Simultaneous, photocopied and reprint submissions OK. Accepts computer printout submissions, including dot-matrix. Sample copy for $1.25 (checks made out to Susan Ackerman, co-editor). Fiction guidelines free with #SAE and 1 first class stamp.
Terms: Publication not copyrighted.
Advice: "We are not really impressed by the stories found in current fiction magazines. They seem to be too mainstream—too ordinary. We are saddened that writers who write from their soul are frequently rejected because their material is too controversial—or not too 'commercial.' Be as original and creative as you can be—search the depths of your being for an unusual way of expressing a story that has meaning for you. This will truly impress us.''

THE NORTH AMERICAN REVIEW, University of Northern Iowa, Cedar Falls IA 50614. Editor: Robley Wilson, Jr. Publishes quality fiction. Quarterly. Estab. 1815. Circ. 4,100.
Needs: "We print quality fiction of any length and/or subject matter. Excellence is the only criterion." Reads fiction *only* from Jan. 1 to March 31. Published new writers (about 25%) within the last year. No preferred length.
How to Contact: Send complete ms with SASE. Reports in 2-3 months. Sample copy $3.
Payment: Approximately $10/printed page. 2 free author's copies. $2.50 charge for extras.
Terms: Pays on acceptance for first North American serial rights.
Advice: "We stress literary excellence and read 3,000 manuscripts a year to find an average of 35 stories that we publish. Please *read* the magazine first.''

NORTH DAKOTA QUARTERLY (II), University of North Dakota, Box 8237, University Station, Grand Forks ND 58202. (701)777-3321. Editor: Robert W. Lewis. Fiction Editor: William Borden. Magazine: 6x9; 200 pages; bond paper; illustrations; photos. Magazine publishing "essays in humanities; some short stories; some poetry." University audience. Quarterly. Estab. 1910. Circ. 600.
Needs: Contemporary, ethnic, experimental, feminist, historical (general), humor/satire and literary. Receives 15-20 unsolicited mss/month. Accepts 2 mss/issue; 8 mss/year. Recently published work by John C. Hampsey, Richard Lyons, Lucia Nevai; published new writers within the last year. Length: 3,000-4,000 words average. Sometimes critiques rejected mss.
How to Contact: Send complete ms with cover letter. "But they need not be much more than hello; please read this story; I've published (if so, best examples) . . . ." SASE. Reports in 3 months. Publishes ms an average of 6-8 months after acceptance. Sample copy $4.
Payment: 5 contributor's copies; 20% discount for extras.
Terms: Acquires one-time rights. Publication copyrighted.
Advice: "We may publish a higher average number of stories in the future—3 rather than 2. Read widely. Write, write; revise, revise.''

NORTHEAST JOURNAL (I, II), Box 217, Kingston RI 02881. (401)783-2356. Co-editors: Tina Letcher and Indu Suryanarayan. "A journal concerned with publishing a diverse selection of contemporary literature. The primary focus is on poetry, prose and reviews. Sometimes special issues are published, e.g., women's, Rhode Island poets." Annual. Estab. 1969 (under name of *Harbinger*). Circ. 600.
Needs: "Quality." Published new writers within the last year. Length: 1,000-3,000 words.
How to Contact: Send complete ms with SASE. Reports in 6 months. Sample copy with 10x12 SAE and $1 postage.
Payment: 1 free author's copy.
Advice: Amount of fiction published has "shrunk, along with our budget. Keep it short.''

‡THE NORTHERN NEW ENGLAND REVIEW (IV), Box 825, Franklin Pierce College, Rindge NH 03461. (603)899-5111. Editor: Christine Doherty. Magazine: 8 ½x11; 90 pages; good paper; heavy cover; illustrations and photos. "The *Review* only publishes material from northern New England residents (Maine, New Hampshire and Vermont) or from people with strong ties in the region. We publish quality fiction, poetry, articles and book reviews. For people who identify with the northern New England lifestyle. Also, for those who are deeply interested in humanities. A copy is sent to every college library in New England." Annually. Estab. 1973. Circ. 600.
Needs: Confession, contemporary, erotica, ethnic, experimental, fantasy, feminist, historical (general), humor/satire, literary, mainstream, prose, regional, romance, science fiction, translations. "Submissions should have that 'New England' flavor to fit in with the magazine's format. No gay or lesbian fiction or hard-core erotica." Receives 5-10 unsolicited mss/month. Accepts 3 or 4 mss/issue. Recently published work by Barry Kaplan. Length: 5,000 words minimum; 9,000 words maximum. Occasionally comments on rejected mss.
How to Contact: Send complete ms. Reports in several weeks on queries; several months on mss. SASE for ms. Photocopied submissions OK. Accepts computer printout submissions. Prefers letter-quality. Sample copy $3.50.
Payment: Pays 2 contributor's copies; $3.50 charge for extras.
Terms: Acquires first rights. Publication copyrighted.
Advice: "Saturate the market with your work. Today's magazine fiction has more pronounced emphasis on the psychological element, chiefly how man reacts to this confusing, changing world. Characters observe society and then undergo intense self-examination. As long as the submission is well written and ties in with our northern New England format in a subtle way, we will consider it. Submissions dealing with the world of academia will also be considered."

THE NORTHERN REVIEW (II, IV), University of Wisconsin-Stevens Point, 018 LRC, Stevens Point WI 54481. (715)346-3568. Editor: Richard Behm. Fiction Editor: Lawrence Watson. Magazine: 8 ½x7; 48 pages; b&w photos. "Northern themes. Upcoming 'Women in the North,' 'Canada' and 'Urban North' issues." Semiannually. Estab. 1987. Circ. 1,000.
Needs: Essays, literary, regional. Receives 25 unsolicited fiction mss/month. Accepts 4 mss/issue; 2 mss/year. Publishes ms 6-18 months after acceptance. Recently published work by Bret Lott, Jack Driscoll, Nancy Lord. Length: 2,000 words average. Publishes short shorts. Sometimes critiques rejected mss.
How to Contact: Send complete ms with cover letter. Reports in 1 month. SASE. Accepts computer printouts, including dot-matrix. Sample copy $4.
Payment: Pays in contributor's copies.
Terms: Publication copyrighted.

‡NORTHLAND QUARTERLY (II,IV), Northland Press of Winona, Suite 412, 51 E. 4th St., Winona MN 55987. (507)452-3686. Editor: Jody Wallace. Magazine: 5x8; approx. 100-125 pages; 60 lb offset paper; 10 pt cover stock; b&w illustrations; line drawings; cover photos. "Contemporary writing for discriminating reader. Short fiction, poetry, commentary and reviews. International publication, with emphasis on writers in upper-tier states and Canada. *Quarterly* features politically oriented writings, as well as regional writers and contemporary fiction from throughout US." Quarterly. Estab. 1987.
Needs: Condensed/excerpted novel, contemporary, feminist, literary, mainstream, regional, romance, serialized novel, progressive issues, political fiction. No religious, young romance. Receives 20-40 mss/month. Accepts 3-5 mss/issue. Publishes ms within 3-6 months of acceptance. Recently published work by Robert Flaum, Marcella Taylor, Robert Funge. Length: 1,500 words minimum; 4,000 words maximum. Publishes short shorts. Length: 300 words minimum. Sometimes critiques rejected mss and recommends other markets.
How to Contact: Query first, query with clips of published work or send complete ms with cover letter, which should include "general description of work, genre. Other places submitted, if any." Reports on queries in 2-3 weeks; in 3-4 weeks on mss. SASE. Simultaneous, photocopied and some reprint submissions OK. Accepts computer printout submissions, including dot-matrix. Accepts electronic submissions via disk. Sample copy for $4, 5x8 SAE and 4 first class stamps. Fiction guidelines for #10 SAE and 1 first class stamp.
Payment: Pays in contributor's copies.
Terms: Sends galleys to author if requested. Publication copyrighted. Sponsors awards for fiction writers. "Write for information."
Advice: Looks for "contemporary, adult fiction of high quality. We adopt an unprejudiced, open attitude for all manuscripts submitted, and have published world-class writers as well as the beginner."

NORTHWEST REVIEW (II), 369 PLC, University of Oregon, Eugene OR 97403. (503)686-3957. Editor: John Witte. Magazine: 6x9; 140-160 pages; coated paper; high quality cover stock; illustrations; photos. "A general literary review featuring poems, stories, essays and reviews, circulated nationally and internationally. For a literate audience in avant-garde as well as traditional literary forms; interested in the important younger writers who have not yet achieved their readership." Published 3 times/year. Estab. 1957. Circ. 1,200.
Needs: Literary, contemporary, feminist, translations and experimental. Accepts 5-10 mss/issue, 20-30 mss/year. Receives approximately 80-100 unsolicited fiction mss each month. Recently published work by Linda Norton, Barry Lopez. Published new writers within the last year. Length: "Ms longer than 40 pages is at a disadvantage." Critiques rejected mss when there is time. Sometimes recommends other markets.
How to Contact: Send complete ms with SASE. "No simultaneous submissions are considered." Accepts computer printout submissions; prefers letter-quality. Reports in 2 months. Sample copy $3.
Payment: 3 free author's copies. 40% discount.
Terms: Acquires first rights. Publication copyrighted.
Advice: "Persist. Copy should be clean, double-spaced, with generous margins. Careful proofing for spelling and grammar errors will reduce irksome slowing of editorial process." Mss are rejected because of "weak characters, lack of plot, poor execution."

NOSTOC MAGAZINE (II), Arts End Books, Box 162, Newton MA 02168. Editor: Marshall Brooks. Magazine: size varies; 60 lb book paper; illustrations; photos. Biannually. Estab. 1973. Circ. 300.
Needs: "We are open-minded." Receives approximately 15 unsolicited fiction mss each month. Published new writers within the last year. Publishes short shorts. Prefers brief word length. Frequently critiques rejected mss and recommends other markets.
How to Contact: Query. SASE for ms. Reports in 1 week on queries, 2-3 weeks on mss, ideally. Sample copy $2.50. Send SASE for catalog.
Payment: Modest payment.
Terms: Sends galleys to author. Publication copyrighted. Rights revert to author.
Advice: "We tend to publish *short* short stories that are precise and lyrical. Recently, we have been publishing *short* short story collections by one author, which are issued as a separate number of the magazine. We are always on the outlook for new material for these small collections. We publish fiction because of the high quality; quite simply, we believe that good writing deserves publication."

NOTEBOOK: A LITTLE MAGAZINE (II, IV), Esoterica Press, Box 170, Barstow CA 92312-0170. Editor: Ms. Yoly Zentella. Magazine: 5½x8½; 100 pages; bond paper; 90 lb cover stock; illustrations. "Accepting fiction and nonfiction. *Notebook*'s emphasis is on history, culture, art and literary critique and travel pieces. For ages 25-50, educated, some academia." Semiannually. Publishes special ethnic issues, e.g. Native American, Pacific, Asian. Estab. 1985. Circ. 100, "including many libraries."
Needs: Ethnic, (focusing especially on Chicano and Latino American pieces in English and Spanish), historical (Latino American, European and Muslim), humor/satire, literary, regional. "One yearly issue featured exclusively Chicano and Latino American writers, and we need black-American writers." Absolutely no explicit sex or obscenities accepted. Receives approximately 20-25 unsolicited fiction mss/month. Recently published work by Carmen M. Pursifull, Gabriela Cerda, Barbara Sheen; published new writers within the last year. Length: 2,000 words average; 2,500 words maximum. Sometimes critiques rejected mss.
How to Contact: Send complete ms with cover letter and short biography. Reports in 2 weeks on queries; 1-2 months on mss. Always SASE for ms and correspondence. Accepts computer printouts. Sample copy $5. Make checks payable to Yoly Zentella. Fiction guidelines for #10 SAE and 1 first class stamp.
Payment: 1 free contributor's copy, charges for extras.
Terms: Acquires first North American serial rights. Publication copyrighted.
Advice: "We are now planning more fiction in our issues and less poetry. We are also considering novellas for publication, appearing exclusively in one issue."

NOW & THEN (IV), Center for Appalachian Studies and Services, East Tennessee State University, Box 19180A, Johnson City TN 37614-0002. (615)929-5348. Editor: Pat Arnow. Magazine: 8½x11; 36-52 pages; coated paper and cover stock; illustrations; photographs. Publication focuses on Appalachian culture, present and past. Readers are mostly people in the region involved with Appalachian issues, literature, education." 3 issues/year. Estab. 1984. Circ. 880.
Needs: Ethnic, literary, regional, serialized/excerpted novel, prose poem, spiritual and sports. "Absolutely has to relate to Appalachian theme. Can be about adjustment to new environment, themes of leaving and returning, for instance. Nothing unrelated to region." Accepts 2-3 mss/issue. Publishes ms 3-4 months after acceptance. Recently published work by Gurney Norman, Lance Olsen, George Ella Lyon;

published new writers within the last year. Length: 3,000 words maximum. Publishes short shorts.
How to Contact: Send complete ms with cover letter. Reports in 1 month. Include "information we can use for contributor's note." SASE. Simultaneous and photocopied submissions OK. Accepts computer printout submissions, including dot-matrix. Sample copy $2.50.
Payment: Pays up to $50 per story, contributor's copies, one year subscription.
Terms: Buys first-time rights. Publication copyrighted.
Advice: "We're emphasizing Appalachian culture, which is not often appreciated because analysts are so busy looking at the trouble of the region. We're doing theme issues. Beware of stereotypes. In a regional publication like this one we get lots of them, both good guys and bad guys: salt of the earth to poor white trash. Sometimes we get letters that offer to let us polish up the story. We prefer the author does that him/herself."

NRG (II), Skydog Press, 6735 SE 78th, Portland OR 97206. Editor: Dan Raphael. Magazine/tabloid: 11x17; 20 pages; electrobrite paper; illustrations; photos. For the "educated, creative, curious." Theme is "open-ended, energized, non-linear emphasis on language and sounds"; material is "spacial, abstract, experimental." Semiannually. Estab. 1976. Circ. 400.
Needs: Contemporary, experimental, literary and prose poem. Receives 8 unsolicited mss/month. Accepts 6 mss/issue; 11 mss/year. Recently published work by Carles Brownson, Willie Smith, Virginia Lewis. Length: 1,000 words average; 3,000 words maximum. Occasionally critiques rejected mss.
How to Contact: Send complete ms with SASE and cover letter stating where you learned of magazine; list of 3-5 previous publications. See copy of magazine. Reports in 1 month. Simultaneous and photocopied submissions OK. Accepts computer printout submissions. Publishes ms an average of 1 year after acceptance. Sample copy $1.50. "Best guideline is sample copy." Fiction guidelines for SASE.
Payment: Pays in free contributor's copies only, ½ cover price charge for extras.
Terms: Acquires one-time rights.
Advice: "I'm trying to get more fiction, but am strict in my editorial bias. I don't want it to add up or be purely representational. Energy must abound in the language, or the spaces conjured. Forget what you were taught. Let the story tell you."

OAK SQUARE (II), The Short Fiction Quarterly, Oak Square Publications, Box 1238, Allston MA 02134. (617)782-5669. Publisher: Philip Borenstein. Fiction Editor: Anne E. Pluto. Magazine: 8½x7; 32-76 pages; 60 lb offset paper; card cover stock; illustrations and photographs. "*Oak Square* is a magazine of short fiction. We look for original well crafted stories by new and emerging writers. We also publish interviews, essays (non-academic, non-political), and a *small* amount of poetry." Quarterly. Estab. 1985. Circ. 500.
Needs: Contemporary, erotica, ethnic, experimental, humor/satire, literary, mainstream, prose poem, regional, serialized/excerpted novel, translations, western. No religious/inspirational, children's stories, mysteries, romances. Receives 50 unsolicited fiction mss/month. Accepts 4-10 mss/issue; 16-24 mss/year. Reads fiction January-June. Publishes ms an average of 6-12 months after acceptance. Length: 2,500 words average; 4,500 words maximum. Publishes short shorts. Sometimes critiques rejected mss; recommends other markets.
How to Contact: Send complete ms with cover letter, including "publication history if any. General comments. Send us your current phone number and address—update us when you move." Reports in 2 weeks on queries; in 3 months on mss. SASE. "We read fiction from January-June; poetry June-December." Simultaneous submissions OK. Accepts computer printout submissions including dot-matrix. Accepts electronic submissions via "Macintosh 3½" disk—MacWrite or Text only." Sample copy $3.50; fiction guidelines free.
Payment: Pays contributor's copies.
Terms: Acquires one-time rights. Sends pre-publication galleys to author when possible. Publication copyrighted.
Advice: "Although we all hold regular '9 to 5' jobs, we are all involved in fiction, either as readers or writers. We are always looking to see 'what else is out there.' We are particularly interested in the work of other '9 to 5'ers. Write about what you know—start within yourself and work outward. Don't be pretentious. Respect your readers."

OBSIDIAN II: BLACK LITERATURE IN REVIEW (II, IV), Dept. of English, North Carolina State University, Raleigh NC 27695-8105. (919)737-3870. Editor: Gerald Barrax. Fiction Editor: Linda Beatrice Brown. Magazine: 6x9; approx. 130 pages. "Creative works in English by Black writers, scholarly critical studies by all writers on Black literature in English." Published 3 times/year (spring, summer and winter). Estab. 1975. Circ. 500.
Needs: Ethnic (pan-African), feminist. No poetry, fiction or drama mss not written by Black writers. Accepts 7-9 mss/year. Published new writers within the last year. Length: 1,500-10,000 words.

How to Contact: Send complete ms in duplicate with SASE. Reports in 3 months. Publishes ms an average of 4-6 months after acceptance. Sample copy $4.
Payment: Pays in contributor's copies.
Terms: Acquires one-time rights. Publication copyrighted. Sponsors contests occasionally; guidelines published in magazine.

‡OGRE MAGAZINE (IV), peabody press, Box 322, New Holland PA 17557. Editor: Andrew Andrews. Magazine: 8½x11; number of pages varies; bond paper, vellum cover stock; b&w illustrations. Publishes "interviews with SF/fantasy authors, commentary and reviews." Plans a special fiction issue. Estab. 1979. Circ. 1,000.
Needs: Experimental, fantasy, horror, literary, science fiction. No explicit horror or sex. Receives 2-3 mss/month. Accepts 1 mss/issue; 2-4 mss/year. Publishes ms within 6 months of acceptance. Recently published work by Tony Russo. Length: 2,000 words preferred. Sometimes recommends other markets.
How to Contact: Query first. Reports in 1 week on queries; in 2 weeks on mss. SASE. Sample copy for $3. Free fiction guidelines.
Payment: Varies.
Terms: Pays on acceptance. Kill fee varies. Acquires first North American serial rights. Publication copyrighted.
Advice: Looking for "strong characterization and a well-constructed plot and milieu. Query first and send in your best work. We'll negotiate the fee. Read a lot of SF, especially the *Magazine of Fantasy & Science Fiction* and *Asimov's*."

THE OHIO REVIEW (II), Ellis Hall, Ohio University, Athens OH 45701-2979. (614)593-1900. Editor: Wayne Dodd. Magazine: 6x9; 144 pages; Warren Old Style paper; illustrations on cover. "We attempt to publish the best poetry and fiction written today. For a mainly literary audience." Triannually. Estab. 1971. Circ. 2,000.
Needs: Contemporary, experimental, literary. "We lean toward contemporary on all subjects." Receives 150-200 unsolicited fiction mss/month. Accepts 3 mss/issue. Does not read mss June 1-August 31. Publishes ms 6 months after acceptance. Agented fiction: 1%. Sometimes critiques rejected mss and/or recommends other markets.
How to Contact: Query first or send complete ms with cover letter. Reports in 6 weeks. SASE. Photocopied submissions OK. Accepts computer printouts, including dot-matrix. Sample copy $4.25. Fiction guidelines free for #10 SASE.
Payment: Pays $5/page, free subscription to magazine, 2 contributor's copies.
Terms: Pays on publication for first North American serial rights. Sends galleys to author. Publication copyrighted.
Advice: "We feel the short story is an important part of the contemporary writing field and value it highly. Read a copy of our publication to see if your fiction is of the same quality. So often people send us work that simply doesn't fit our needs."

‡OLD HICKORY REVIEW (II), Jackson Writers Group, Box 1178, Jackson TN 38302. (901)424-3277. Editor: Edna Lackie. Fiction editor: Dorothy Stanfill. Magazine: 8½x1; approx. 90 pages. "Usually two short stories and 75-80 poems—nothing obscene or in poor taste. For a family audience." Semiannually. Plans special fiction issue. Estab. 1969. Circ. 300.
Needs: Contemporary, experimental, fantasy, literary, mainstream. Receives 4-5 unsolicited fiction mss/month. Accepts 2 mss/issue; 4 mss/year. Publishes ms no more than 3-4 months after acceptance. Length: 2,500-3,000 words. Publishes short shorts. Sometimes critiques rejected mss and recommends other markets.
How to Contact: Send complete ms with cover letter, which should include "credits." Reports on queries in 2-3 weeks; on mss in 1-2 months. SASE. Photocopied submissions OK. Accepts dot-matrix computer printouts. Sample copy $1 plus 90¢ postage. Fiction guidelines free for SAE.
Payment: Pays in contributor's copies; charge for extras.
Terms: Publication copyrighted. Sponsors contests for fiction writers, "advertised in literary magazine and with flyers."
Advice: "There is too much sad and unpublishable things submitted. We are tired of war, nursing homes, abused children, etc. We are looking for things which are more entertaining. No pornographic fiction, no vile language. Our publication goes into schools, libraries, etc."

‡THE OLD RED KIMONO (II), Box 1864, Rome GA 30163. (404)295-6312. Editors: Jo Anne Starnes and Jonathan Hershey. Magazine: 8x11; 65-70 pages; white offset paper; 10 pt. board cover stock. Annually. Estab. 1974. Circ. 1,000.
Needs: Literary. "We will consider good short fiction regardless of category." Receives 20-30 mss/month. Buys 2-4 mss/issue. Does not read mss April-September. "Issue out in May every year." Re-

cently published work by Christopher Woods, Hubert Whitlow, Jeanne Cunningham. Length: 4,000-5,000 words preferred; 7,000 words maximum. Publishes short shorts. "We prefer short fiction."
How to Contact: Send complete ms with cover letter. Reports in 2 weeks on queries; 4-5 weeks on mss. SASE. Photocopied submissions OK. Accepts computer printout submissions, including dot-matrix. Sample copy for $2, 8x11 SAE and 4 first class stamps. Fiction guidelines for #10 SAE and 1 first class stamp.
Payment: Pays in contributor's copies.
Terms: Acquires first rights. Publication copyrighted.

‡ON OUR BACKS (II,IV), Entertainment for the Adventurous Lesbian, Blush Productions, 526 Castro St., San Francisco CA 94114. (415)861-4723. Editor: Susie Bright. Magazine 8½x11; 50 pages; slick paper; illustrations; photos. "Lesbian erotica, short stories, nonfiction, commentary, news clips, photos." Quarterly. Estab. 1984. Circ. 15,000.
Needs: Erotica, fantasy, humor/satire, lesbian. No "non-erotic, heterosexual" fiction. Receives 20 mss/month. Buys 3-4 mss/issue. Publishes ms within 1 year of acceptance. Recently published work by Dorothy Allison, Sarah Schulman, Pat Califia; published new writers within the last year. Length: 3,500 words preferred; 2,500 words minimum; 5,000 words maximum.
How to Contact: Query with clips of published work or send complete ms with cover letter. Include Social Security number. Reports in 6 weeks. SASE. No simultaneous submissions. Accepts computer printout submissions, including dot-matrix. Accepts electronic submissions via disk. Sample copy for $5. Fiction guidelines for #10 SAE and 1 first class stamp.
Payment: Pays $20-$100 and contributor's copies.
Terms: Pays on publication for first North American serial rights. Publication copyrighted. Sponsors awards for fiction writers.
Advice: "Ask yourself—does it turn me on? Ask a friend to read it—does it turn her on as well? Is it as well-written as any well-crafted non-erotic story? We love to read things that we don't see all the time—originality is definitely a plus!"

‡ON THE EDGE, 129 Pleasant St., No. 3, Arlington MA 02174. Editor: Cathryn McIntyre.
Needs: Short-short fiction (500-2,500 words), micro-fiction (100 words or less). Subject matter can vary but should have some contemporary relevance. Also poetry, essays, interviews and art.
How to Contact: Send complete ms. "Cover letters are not necessary and those packed with credentials are discouraged. I'm only interested in whether or not the work submitted is right for *On the Edge*."
Payment: Pays 2 contributor's copies.
Terms: All rights revert to author.
Advice: "*On the Edge* is open minded. We are open to all subjects that are presented in a creative, imaginative and intelligent way and show some relevance to contemporary life. Feel free to experiment, but don't overdo it. We're 'On' the Edge, not 'Over' it. Comments on rejections are rare. We are not comfortable assessing literary merits and therefore don't do it. A rejection from *On the Edge* means only that your work is not right for us, nothing more. If you get a rejection from *On the Edge* don't get discouraged: make a paper airplane, burn it or toss it in the waste basket and go on writing. New writers are greatly encouraged!"

OPEN MAGAZINE (II), Suite 21, 215 North Ave. W., Westfield NJ 07090. (201)654-3092. Editor: Greg Ruggiero. Fiction Editors: Editorial Board of three. Magazine: 8½x11; 50 pages; quality gloss paper; 60 lb cover stock; many illustrations and photographs. "*Open Magazine* works with uninhibited forms of writing, artwork and photography that inspire change—be they targeted at social processes or the consciousness of the individual. We are constantly restructuring, constantly trying out new ways to connect with our readers, writers and other counter-consensus publications. Verve, innovation, reader confrontation, and socio-political statement are the strengths of material we most joyfully accept." Semiannually. Estab. 1984. Circ. 1,000.
Needs: Experimental. "We are fast to accept work that pioneers form, questions the given, and risks discussing the intimate or proposing the radical. Confrontational or subtle, experimental or direct, we want intelligent work that above all else communicates to people, not to cryptians and the telepathic. Work exploring feminism, lesbian/gay experience, minority and third world culture, alternative politics and translations are always welcome." Receives 9-30 unsolicited fiction mss/month. Accepts approx. 6 mss/issue; approx. 12 mss/year. Recently published work by Barbara Ucko, Richard Royal, Greg Boyd; published new writers within the last year. Length: 200 words minimum; 5,000 words maximum. Publishes short shorts. Recommends other markets.
How to Contact: Send complete ms with cover letter which should include a bio "that extends beyond publication credits, e.g. involvements, experiences and interests that will give our readers a sense of a person." Reports in 1 week on queries; 1 month on mss. SASE. Simultaneous and photocopied submissions OK. Accepts computer printout submissions, no dot-matrix. Sample copy $5 and #10 SAE with 6

first class stamps. Fiction guidelines for SASE.
Payment: 0-$50: "dependent on grant money"; contributor's copies; charge for extras.
Terms: Acquires one-time righs. Publication copyrighted.
Advice: "*Open Magazine* publishes as an exploratory process directly involved with new modes of openness, perception and resistance. We encourage experimentation, but want to see more work drawing from common symbols and ordinary experience. We are devoted to readers and writers who believe that 'the real issue is not whether two and two make four or whether two and two make five, but whether life advances by people who love words or by people who love living.' "

‡OPEN WIDE (I), Illini Literary Society, University of Illinois, 284 Illini Union, 1401 W. Green St., Urbana IL 61801. (217)367-1746. Editor: Iris Chang. Magazine: 8½x11; 20-30 pages; glossy paper; glossy cover; illustrations; photos. "*Open Wide* is a literary magazine edited and published exclusively by University of Illinois students. We publish a wide variety of stories, ranging from slice-of-life experiences to science fiction." Semiannually. Estab. 1987. Circ. 700.
Needs: Adventure, contemporary, ethnic, experimental, fantasy, horror, humor/satire, literary, mainstream, psychic/supernatural/occult, romance, science fiction, suspense/mystery, young adult/teen. Accepts 5-10 mss/issue; 10-20 mss/year. Publishes ms within 2 months to 1 year of acceptance. Length: 2,000 words preferred; 500 words minimum; 5,000 words maximum. Publishes short shorts. Sometimes critiques rejected mss.
How to Contact: Send complete ms with cover letter, which "should include the author's full name, address and a few lines about themselves." Reports in 2 months. SASE. Simultaneous, photocopied and reprint submissions OK. Accepts computer printout submissions, including dot-matrix. "The writer should check with us first before submitting a disk." Sample copy for $1, 8½x11 SASE and $1.20 postage.
Payment: Pays in contributor's copies.
Terms: Publication copyrighted.
Advice: "We are always looking for new talent. *Open Wide* wants exciting, energetic stories that contain depth and meaning. Remember that the people who review the submissions are college students. We dislike boring, unoriginal or pretentious writing. If the story is fresh and appealing, we will publish it. Creativity and clarity are important to us, not the story topic or style."

OREGON EAST (II, IV), Hoke College Center, EOSC, La Grande OR 97850. (503)963-1787. Editor: Eric Slater. Magazine: 6x9; 80 pages; illustrations and photographs. "*Oregon East* prefers fiction about the Northwest. The majority of our issues go to the students of Eastern Oregon State College; staff, faculty and community members receive them also, and numerous high school and college libraries." Annually. Estab. 1950. Circ. 900.
Needs: Humor/satire, literary, prose poem, regional, translations. No juvenile/children's fiction. Receives 20 unsolicited mss/month. Accepts 3-6 mss/issue. Does not read April to August. Publishes ms an average of 5 months after acceptance. Recently published work by Ursula LeGuin, Madeline deFrees and George Vehn. Published new writers within the last year. Length: 2,000 words average; 3,000 words maximum. Publishes short shorts. Sometimes critiques rejected mss.
How to Contact: Send complete ms with cover letter which should include name, address, brief bio. Reports in 1 week on queries; 3 months on mss. SASE. Photocopied submissions OK. Accepts computer printout submissions, no dot-matrix. Sample copy $5; fiction guidelines for #10 SASE.
Payment: 2 contributor's copies.
Terms: Rights revert to author. Publication copyrighted.
Advice: "Follow our guidelines please! Keep trying: we have limited space because we must publish 50% on-campus material."

OTHER VOICES (II), 820 Ridge Rd., Highland Park IL 60035. (312)831-4684. Editors: Dolores Weinberg and Lois Hauselman. Magazine: 5⅞x9; 168-205 pages; 60 lb paper; coated cover stock; occasional photos. "Original, fresh, diverse stories and novel excerpts" for literate adults. Semiannually. Estab. 1985. Circ. 1,500.
Needs: Contemporary, experimental, humor/satire, literary, excerpted novel. No taboos, except ineptitude and murkiness. No fantasy, horror, juvenile, psychic/occult. Receives 45 unsolicited fiction mss/month. Accepts 20-23 mss/issue. Publishes ms approx. 3-6 months after acceptance. Agented fiction: 40%. Recently published work by Barbara Lefcowitz, Susan B. Weston; published new writers within

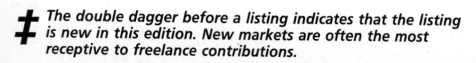

The double dagger before a listing indicates that the listing is new in this edition. New markets are often the most receptive to freelance contributions.

the last year. Length: 4,000 words average; 5,000 words maximum. Also publishes short shorts "if paired together" of 1,000 words. Only occasionally critiques rejected mss or recommends other markets.

How to Contact: Send mss with SASE or submit through agent. Cover letters "should be brief and list previous publications. Also, list title of submission. Most beginners' letters try to 'explain' the story—a big mistake." Reports in 10-12 weeks on mss. SASE. Photocopied submissions OK; no simultaneous submissions or reprints. Accepts computer printouts including dot-matrix. Sample copy $5.90 (includes postage). Fiction guidelines for #10 SAE and 1 first class stamp.

Payment: Pays in contributor's copies and modest cash gratuity.

Terms: Acquires one-time rights. Publication copyrighted.

Advice: "There are so *few* markets for *quality* fiction! We—by publishing 40-45 stories a year—provide new and established writers a forum for their work. Send us your best voice, your best work, your best best. Don't expect to earn a living at it—no matter how talented."

‡OTHER WORLDS (II), Science Fiction-Science Fantasy, Gryphon Publications, Box 209, Brooklyn NY 11228. Editor: Gary Lovisi. Magazine: 5x8; 40-60 pages; offset paper; card/color cover; illustrations and photographs. "Adventure—or action-oriented SF—stories that are fun to read." Semiannually. Estab. 1988. Circ. 300.

Needs: Science fiction. No high fantasy, sword and sorcery. Receives 10 unsolicited mss/month. Buys 4-8 mss/issue. Publishes ms 6-12 months (usually) after acceptance. Length: 3,000 words preferred; 2,000 words minimum; 5,000 words maximum. Publishes short shorts. Length: 500-1,000 words. Sometimes critiques rejected mss and recommends other markets.

How to Contact: Send complete ms with cover letter. Reports in 2 weeks on queries; 4 weeks on mss. SASE. Photocopied submissions OK. Accepts computer printout submissions, including dot-matrix. Sample copy for $4. Free fiction guidelines.

Payment: Pays in contributor's copies.

Terms: Acquires first North American serial rights. Publication copyrighted.

‡OUIJA MADNESS (III), Ouija Madness Press, Box 42212, San Francisco CA 94142. Editor: D.A. Smith. Magazine: 8½x11; 90 pages; illustrations; photos. "The wild, the wacky, the insane, contemporary themes appreciated. Make us think." Experimentation and eroticism encouraged; for everyone who thinks. Semiannually. Estab. 1980. Circ. 1,000.

Needs: Contemporary, erotica, experimental, gay, horror, humor/satire, lesbian, literary, psychic/supernatural/occult, religious/inspirational, science fiction, sports. No romance, juvenile. Receives 100 unsolicited fiction mss/month; accepts 15 fiction mss/issue. Publishes ms "in a matter of months" after acceptance. Agented fiction: 5%. Length: 5,000 words average. Publishes short stories. Sometimes comments on rejected mss and recommends other markets.

How to Contact: Send complete ms with cover letter and SASE. Reports in 2 weeks on queries; 1 month on mss. Simultaneous and photocopied submissions OK. Sample copy $3 with 9x12 SAE and 75¢ postage. Fiction guidelines free for SAE.

Payment: Pays $10-$100.

Terms: Pays on acceptance. Acquires first rights. Publication copyrighted.

OUROBOROS (II), 3912 24th St., Rock Island IL 61201-6223. Editor and Publisher: Erskine Carter. Magazine: 6x9; 76 pages; 60 lb offset paper; 80 lb cover; b&w illustrations. "We publish fiction (short stories), poetry and art for mainly college-educated audience." Semiannually. Estab. 1985. Circ. 400.

Needs: Adventure, contemporary, experimental, fantasy, historical (general), horror, humor/satire, literary, mainstream, psychic/supernatural/occult, science fiction, suspense/mystery. "We are mainly interested in stories about people, in situations of conflict or struggle. We want to see *real* characters at odds with others, themselves, their universe. No racist/right-wing/anti-minority material." Receives 40-50 unsolicited mss/month. Accepts 8-10 mss/issue; 32-40 mss/year. Publishes ms 3-12 months after acceptance. Recently published work by W. Rose, C. Lacher, Norma Blair; published new writers within the last year. Length: 2,500 words average; 3,500 words maximum. Publishes short shorts. Length: 500 words. Sometimes critiques rejected mss and recommends other markets.

How to Contact: Query first and request guidelines and a sample copy. Reports in 1 week on queries; 2 weeks on mss. SASE. Photocopied and reprint submissions OK. Accepts computer printout submissions. Sample copy for $4.25.

Payment: Pays in contributor's copies.

Terms: Rights revert to author. Sends galleys to author. Publication copyrighted. "Cash prizes are awarded on basis of reader's poll."

Advice: "The beginning writer *can* break in here and learn valuable lessons about writing and publishing. Purchase a sample copy, write something you think will grab us, then submit. Get to know the markets. Don't waste time, energy and postage without researching."

OUTERBRIDGE (II), English A-323, The College of Staten Island (CUNY), 715 Ocean Terr., Staten Island NY 10301. (212)390-7654. Editor: Charlotte Alexander. Magazine: 8½x5½; approx. 110 pages; 60 lb white offset paper; 65 lb cover stock. "We are a national literary magazine publishing mostly fiction and poetry. To date, we have had three special focus issues (the 'urban' and the 'rural' experience, 'Southern'), 2 special 10th anniversary issues and a double issue for 1986-88 with 200 pages and 73 contributors ($8). For anyone with enough interest in literature to look for writing of quality and writers on the contemporary scene who deserve attention. There probably is a growing circuit of writers, some academics, reading us by recommendations." Annually. Estab. 1975. Circ. 500-700.

Needs: Literary. "No *Reader's Digest* style; that is, very popularly oriented. We like to do interdisciplinary features, e.g., literature and music, literature and science and literature and the natural world." Accepts 8-10 mss/year. Does not read in July or August. Recently published work by William Davey, Ron Berube, Patricia Ver Ellen; published new writers within the last year. Length: 10-25 pages. Sometimes recommends other markets.

How to Contact: Query. Send complete ms with cover letter. "Don't talk too much, 'explain' the work, or act apologetic or arrogant. If published, tell where, with a brief bio." SASE. Reports in 2 weeks on queries, 2 months on mss. Sample copy $5 for annual issue.

Payment: 2 free author's copies. Charges ½ price of current issue for extras to its authors.

Terms: Acquires one-time rights. Requests credits for further publication of material used by *OB*.

Advice: "Read our publication first. Don't send out blindly; get some idea of what the magazine might want. A *short* personal note with biography is appreciated. Competition is keen. Read an eclectic mix of classic and contemporary. Beware of untransformed autobiography, but *everything* in one's experience contributes."

OWLFLIGHT (I, IV), Magazine of Science Fiction and Fantasy, Unique Graphics, 1025 55th St., Oakland CA 94608. (415)655-3024. Editor: Millea Kenin. Magazine: 8½x11; 64-80 pages; 60 lb stock; b&w, line and half tone illustrations, and b&w photos. Magazine publishes "the full range of the science fiction/fantasy genre, for readers familiar with sf/fantasy." Irregularly published. Estab. 1980. Circ. 1,500.

Needs: Fantasy, science fiction. "We do not want to see anything *not* sf or fantasy, or anything racist, sexist or pro-war." Receives 100-200 unsolicited mss/month. Buys at least 10 mss/issue. Publishes ms up to 2 years after acceptance. Recently published work by Janet Fox, Ardath Mayhar, Eric M. Heidemann; published new writers within the last year. Length: 6,000 words average; 2,500 words minimum; 8,000 words maximum (10 to 32 double-spaced pages—nothing that falls outside these limits will be considered, as different word-counting methods produce different copy-fitting results). Usually briefly critiques rejected mss. Sometimes recommends other markets.

How to Contact: "Never submit mss without querying (with SASE) for guidelines, which tell what categories are open or overstocked. Cover letter should include a brief background of the writer, but not a long credit list nor a description of an enclosed story." Reports in 1 week on requested guidelines; 2-6 weeks on mss. SASE. Simultaneous, photocopied and reprint submissions OK. State whether ms is simultaneous submission. Accepts computer printout submissions, dot-matrix only if truly near letter quality. Sample copy $2.50; check must be payable to Unique Graphics. Fiction guidelines free with sample order; otherwise free for #10 SAE and 45¢ postage.

Payment: Pays 1¢/word plus 3 free contributor's copies, charge for extras—½ cover price.

Terms: Pays on acceptance for first North American serial rights or one-time rights. If total at 1¢/word is under $10, it is paid on acceptance; if over $10, a $10 deposit is paid on acceptance with the balance paid on publication. Publication copyrighted.

Advice: "I recommend the top-down method: Send a story first to the biggest circulation, highest paying publication that is a relevant market. If it doesn't get picked out of the slush pile, send it to the relevant newsstand magazines, or original anthologies stated for commercial publicaton. If it still hasn't been accepted, send it to the small press. That's better than sticking it in a drawer. We'd love to see experimental work that stretches the limits of the genre, but not work that is outside it or work to which the sf elements are irrelevant."

OXFORD MAGAZINE (II), Bachelor Hall, Miami University, Oxford OH 45056. (513)529-5955. Editors: William Fisher and Michael Fontana. Magazine: 6x9; 85-100 pages; illustrations. "We look for first-rate quality fiction and poetry. It may be experimental and exploratory but it must be a serious investigation into the human condition." Biannually. Estab. 1985. Circ. 500-1,000.

Needs: Ethnic, experimental, feminist, gay, humor/satire, lesbian, literary, translations. Receives 20-30 unsolicited mss/month. Accepts 10 mss/issue. Does not read mss May through September. Publishes ms about 3 months after acceptance. Recently published work by Alberto Rios, Diane Wakoski and James Purdy; published new writers within the last year. Length: 2,000-3,000 words average; 4,000 words maximum. Publishes short shorts.

How to Contact: Send complete ms with cover letter, which should include a short bio or interesting

information. Reports in 3-4 months on mss. SASE. Photocopied submissions OK. Accepts computer printout submissions, including dot-matrix. Sample copy for $4, 10x12 SAE and 4 first class stamps.
Payment: Pays in contributor's copies.
Terms: Acquires one-time rights. Publication copyrighted.
Advice: "We see a lot of very well written fiction. But while a lot of it is well written, very often it is uninteresting. I suggest that young writers look for a good story to tell and then set about writing it with freshness, enthusiasm and a strong voice."

‡**P.I. MAGAZINE (II), Fact and fiction about the world of private investigators**, 755 Bronx, Toledo OH 43609. (419)382-0967. Editor: Bob Mackowiak. Magazine: 8½x11; about 50 pages; coated white paper and cover; illustrations and photographs. "All about private eyes: personality profiles and stories about professional investigators; original fiction; books, movie, video, games, etc. Audience includes private eye and mystery fans." Quarterly. Estab. 1988. Circ. 400
Needs: Adventure, humor/satire, suspense/mystery. "Principal character must be a provate detective—not a police detective, spy or school teacher who solves murders on the side. No explicit sex." Buys 2-4 mss/issue. Publishes ms 2-3 months after accpetance. Recently published work by David Martindale, Curtis Fischer. Length: 2,500 words preferred; 500 words minimum; 5,000 words maximum. Publishes short shorts. Sometimes critiques rejected ms and recommends other markets if possible.
How to Contact: Send complete ms with cover letter. Reports in 1-2 months. SASE. Simultaneous and photocopied submissions OK. Accepts computer printout submissions, including dot-matrix. Sample copy for $2.50, 1 sample copy only. "Regular single issue price via mail is $3.75."
Payment: Pays $15 minimum; $25 "or more as the magazine grows"; contributor's copies; charge for extras.
Terms: Pays on publication. Acquires one-time rights. Publication not copyrighted.
Advice: "I enjoy stories that are not necessarily murder mysteries."

"Since P.I. Magazine *includes fact and fiction about private investigators," says Bob MacKowiak, editor and publisher, "I wanted a cover that would suggest both—not a real investigator, but an obvious model, yet holding a typical 'tool of the trade,' the magnifying glass, while wearing yet another trademark, the trench coat. Female models have appeared on all the covers with 'tools' (i.e., binoculars, a gun, and case files)." Cover photographer is Mary Pencheff. Model is Ellen Hudson.*

Premier Issue
- "My toughest case"
- Great new fiction
- Book and video news

PAINTED BRIDE QUARTERLY (II), Painted Bride Art Center, 230 Vine St., Philadelphia PA 19106. (215)925-9914. Literary magazine: 6x9; 96-100 pages; illustrations; photos. Quarterly. Estab. 1975. Circ. 1,000.
Needs: Contemporary, ethnic, experimental, feminist, gay, lesbian, literary, prose poem and translations. Receives 10 unsolicited mss/week. Accepts 2 mss/issue; 8 mss/year. Published new writers within the last year. Length: 3,000 words average; 5,000 words maximum. Publishes short shorts. Occasionally critiques rejected mss.
How to Contact: Send complete ms. Reports in 3 weeks-3 months. SASE. Accepts computer printout submissions. Prefers letter-quality. Sample copy $4.

Payment: 2 contributor's copies, 1 year free subscription, 50% off additional copies.
Terms: Acquires first North American serial rights. Publication copyrighted.
Advice: "We want quality in whatever—we hold experimental work to as strict standards as anything else. Many of our readers write fiction; most of them enjoy a good reading. We hope to be an outlet for quality. A good story gives, first, enjoyment to the reader. We've seen a good many of them lately, and we've published the best of them."

PANDORA (I), 609 E. 11 Mile, #12, Royal Oak MI 48067. Editor: Meg Mac Donald. Magazine: 5½x8½; 44+ pages; offset paper; heavyweight offset cover stock; b&w illustrations; "possibly" photos. Magazine for science fiction and fantasy readers. Published 4-6 times/year. Estab. 1978. Circ. 500.
Needs: Fantasy, science fiction and sword and sorcery. "Nothing X-rated; no horror; no gratuitous violence or sex. Unless the author created the universe, she/he should not send us stories in that universe." Receives 125 unsolicited fiction mss/month. Buys 4-6 mss/issue, 20 mss/year. Publishes ms 6 months-1 year after acceptance. Recently published work by Ray Bradbury, Nina Boal, Piers Anthony, Ralph Vaughan; published many new writers within the last year. Length: 3,000 words average; 4,000 words maximum (occasional stories may be longer). Always critiques rejected mss. Sometimes recommends other markets.
How to Contact: Send complete ms with cover letter, which should include relevant publication history. Reports in 2 weeks on queries; 3-4 months on mss. Photocopied and previously published submissions OK. Accepts computer printout submissions. Prefers letter-quality. Sample copy $3.50. Free fiction guidelines with SASE.
Payment: 1-4¢/word and 1 contributor's copy.
Terms: Pays on publication for first North American serial rights, second rights or one-time rights on previously published mss. Publication not copyrighted.
Advice: "Plan to increase amount of fiction published; steering away from horror and fantasy set in mundane or contemporary society. Know your market! Read and study fiction everwhere, but know a given market well before trying to crack it. Write what your heart leads you to write, what moves you, excites you, frightens you. Above all use your gift for words as wisely as you can—don't write to hurt— write to enlighten! Good luck!"

PANGLOSS PAPERS, Box 18917, Los Angeles CA 90018. Editor: Bard Dahl. Fiction Editor: Al Schoenberg. Magazine: 7x8½; 50 pages; 20 lb bond paper; 40 lb cover stock; line drawings; offset photographs. Magazine of "satire for socially aware book readers." Quarterly. Estab. 1982. Circ. 600.
Needs: Experimental, humor/satire, literary and prose poem. No inspirational or slick fiction. Receives 25 unsolicited mss/month. Accepts 2-3 mss/issue; 8 mss/year. Recently published work by Joe Malone, Ruth Jespersen, Phyllis Green; published new writers within the last year. Length: 3,000-4,000 words average. Occasionally critiques rejected mss.
How to Contact: Send complete ms with cover letter telling "why they think their submission fits our format." Reports in 1 month. SASE. Simultaneous, photocopied and previously published submissions OK. Accepts computer printout submissions. Publishes ms an average of 1-3 months after acceptance. Sample copy $2.
Payment: 2 free contributor's copies; $1 charge for extras.
Terms: Acquires one-time rights.
Advice: "Submitting to publishers is not a lottery (the more tickets the more wins). Get outside opinions on your work, and pay attention to them."

PAPER RADIO (I,II), Loose Milk Review, Box 85302, Seattle WA 98145. Editors: N.S. Kvern and Dagmar Howard. Magazine: 8½x11; 28-36 pages; photocopied paper and cover; illustrations; high contrast b&w photographs. "We're open to anything, but it has to be short—usually less than 2,500 words, and only one or two per issue." Readers are "mostly people who are interested in avant garde, mailart, Xerox art, political, bizarre, punk, literary/experimental writing and computers." Published 3 times/ year. Estab. 1986. Circ. 500.
Needs: Erotica, experimental, fantasy, literary, prose poem, science fiction. Receives 10 unsolicited fiction mss/month. Accepts 1-2 mss/issue; 3-6 mss/year. Publishes ms an average of 2-3 months after acceptance. Length: 2,000 words average; 2,500 words maximum. Publishes short shorts. Sometimes critiques rejected mss.
How to Contact: Send complete ms with cover letter. "some autobiographical information is helpful—one or two paragraphs—and I like to know here they hear about our magazine." Reports in 3 weeks. SASE. Simultaneous or photocopied submissions OK. Accepts computer printout submissions, including dot-matrix. Sample copy $2.
Payment: Contributor's copies.
Terms: Acquires first rights, "artist can publish material elsewhere simultaneously." Publication copyrighted.

Advice: "We are devoted to the cause of experimentation and literature. The writer should attempt to make a living on his/her fiction, but we want things which are unsellable, weird, amateur or too good to sell. Beginning writers and old hands alike should write for themselves and be willing to write things which are unmarketable; this should enable them to better understand their psyches and how mutable and fascinating language is. Best to see a sample copy. Our publication is orderly in its chaos, wild and untameable in its order."

THE PARIS REVIEW (II), 541 E. 72nd St., New York NY 10021. (212)539-7085. Editor: George A. Plimpton. Managing Editor: Jeanne McCulloch. Magazine: 5¼x8½; about 240 pages; 50 lb paper; 10 pt Cls cover stock; illustrations and photographs. "Fiction and poetry of superlative quality, whatever the genre, style or mode. Our contributors include prominent, as well as little-known and previously unpublished writers. Recent issues have included the work of Raymond Carver, Elizabeth Tallent, Rick Bass, John Koethe, Sharon Olds, Derek Walcott, Carolyn Kizer, Tess Gallagher, Peter Handke, Denis Johnson, Bobbie Ann Mason, Harold Brodkey, Joseph Brodsky, John Updike, Andre Dubus, Galway Kinnell, E.L. Doctorow and Philip Levine. 'The Art of Fiction' interview series includes important contemporary writers discussing their own work and the craft of writing."
Needs: Committed work of boldness and originality, combining excellence of form and voice. Receives several hundred unsolicited fiction mss each month. Published new writers within the last year. No preferred length. Also publishes short shorts.
How to Contact: Send complete ms with SASE. Reports in 6-8 weeks on mss. Sample copy $6.50.
Payment: $100-$500. 2 free author's copies. Regular charge for extras.
Terms: Pays on publication for first North American serial rights. Sends galleys to author. Publication copyrighted.
Advice: "*The Paris Review* has the widest circulation of all the small presses. We are devoted to helping talented, original writers find larger audiences."

‡PARTING GIFTS (II), 3006 Stonecutter Terrace, Greensboro NC 27405. Editor: Robert Bixby. Magazine: 5x8; 40 pages. "High quality insightful fiction, very brief and on any theme." Semiannual. Plans special fiction issue. Estab. 1988.
Needs: "Brevity is the second most important criterion behind literary quality." Publishes ms within 1-6 months of acceptance. Length: 250 words minimum; 1,000 words maximum. Sometimes critiques rejected mss.
How to Contact: Send complete ms with cover letter. Reports in 1 day on queries; in 1-7 days on mss. SASE. Accepts computer printout submissions, including dot-matrix.
Payment: Pays in contributor's copies.
Terms: Acquires one-time rights. Publication copyrighted.
Advice: Magazine fiction today "seems to celebrate drabness and disconnection. Read the works of Jim Harrison, C.K. Williams and Janet Kauffman, all excellent writers who epitomize the writing *Parting Gifts* strives to promote."

PARTISAN REVIEW (II), 141 Bay State Rd., Boston MA 02215. (617)353-4260. Editor: William Phillips. Executive Editor: Edith Kurzweil. Magazine: 6x9; 160 pages; 40 lb paper; 60 lb cover stock. Theme is of world literature and contemporary culture: fiction, essays and poetry with emphasis on the arts and political and social commentary, for the general intellectual public; scholars. Quarterly. Estab. 1934. Circ. 8,000.
Needs: Contemporary, experimental, literary, prose poem, regional and translations. Receives 100 unsolicited fiction mss/month. Buys 2 mss/issue; 8 mss/year. Recently published work by José Donoso, Isaac Bashevis Singer, Doris Lessing; published new writers within the last year. Length: open. Publishes short shorts.
How to Contact: Send complete ms with SASE and cover letter listing past credits. Photocopied submissions OK. Accepts computer printout submissions. Prefers letter-quality. Reports in 4 months on mss. Sample copy for $5 and $1 postage.
Payment: Pays $25-$200; 1 free contributor's copy.
Terms: Pays on publication for first rights. Publication copyrighted.
Advice: "Please, research the type of fiction we publish. Often we receive manuscripts which are entirely inappropriate for our journal. Sample copies are available and this is a good way to determine audience."

PASSAGES NORTH (II), Wm. Bonifas Fine Arts Center, Escanaba MI 49829. (906)786-3833. Editor: Elinor Benedict. Tabloid: 14x11½; 24 pages; white uncoated paper; illustrations; photos. Readership: general and literary. Semiannually. Estab. 1979. Circ. 2,500.
Needs: Short fiction. "High quality is our aim. Subjects and genre are open. No excerpts of novels, unless they stand alone in a coherent way. No 'pop' or formula stories." Accepts 8-10 mss/year. Recently

published work by Gary Gildner, Ursula Hegi, Ellen Lesser; published new writers within the last year. Length: 300-5,000 words. Critiques rejected mss when there is time. Occasionally recommends other markets.

How to Contact: Send complete ms with SASE and brief letter of previous publications, awards, education. Reports in 3 weeks to several months on mss. Publishes ms an average of 3-6 months after acceptance. Sample copy $1.50. Guidelines for #10 SASE.

Payment: 3 free author's copies. $1 charge for extras. Frequent honoraria.

Terms: Copyrighted; rights revert to author on publication. Buys reprints only by request for featured writers with interviews.

Advice: "Be yourself—don't try to imitate other writers except to be aware of what they are doing best. Find your unique material and voice."

‡PASSAGES TRAVEL MAGAZINE (I, II, IV), 1110 Tower Bldg., Seattle WA 98101. (206)467-1149. Editor: Pat Glenham. Magazine: 8⅛x10⅞; 64 pages; 60 lb paper; 60 lb cover; photographs. Publishes material on "travel: US, Hawaii, Caribbean, Mexico, Canada, Asia—1989 will include some Europe. For readers 40 + age, $40,000 + income, high school and college graduate." Bimonthly. Estab. 1983. Circ. 85,000.

Needs: Adventure, contemporary, historical (general), travel. Receives 10 or more unsolicited mss/month. Number of mss bought/issue depends on quality. Publishes ms usually 2-4 months after acceptance. Recently published work by Jan Nichols, Robert Fretwell. Length: 1,000 words preferred; 500 words minimum; 1,200 words maximum. Sometimes critiques rejected mss and recommends other markets.

How to Contact: Send complete ms with cover letter and include Social Security number. Cover letter should include "biography of author. No explanation of story." Reports in 8-10 weeks. SASE. Simultaneous, photocopied and reprint submissions OK. Accepts computer printout submissions, including dot-matrix. Accepts electronic submissions via disk or modem. Sample copy and fiction guidelines free with 9x12 SAE.

Payment: Pays in contributor's copies.

Terms: Acquires one-time rights. Publication copyrighted.

Advice: Looks for writing "1) with appeal to our readership (40 + age, $40,000 + income, college-level education); 2) quality of writing; 3) universality of subject. Re-edit your own work at least three times then ask someone you trust and that has excellent English background to edit it a final time. If you don't know anyone, contact your local community college or the senior S.C.O.R.E. association for assistance."

THE PEGASUS REVIEW (I IV), Box 134, Flanders NJ 07836. (201)927-0749. Editor: Art Bounds. Magazine: 5½x8½; 6-8 pages; special paper and cover stock; illustrations. "Our magazine is a bimonthly, done entirely in calligraphy, illustrated. Each issue is based on a specific theme, for an audience appreciative of quality work." Plans special fiction issue. Estab. 1980. Circ. 200.

Needs: Humor/satire, literary, prose poem and religious/inspirational. Themes for 1989: January/February-Heroism; March/April-Faith; May/June-Love; July/August-Music; September/October-Laughter; November/December-Immortality. Send "nothing that is in bad taste." Receives 40 unsolicited mss/month. Accepts 6 mss/year. Recently published work by Slade Adamsson, Jack Brooks; published new writers within the last year. Publishes short shorts 3-3½ pages; 500 words. Themes are subject to change throughout the year, so query if in doubt. Critiques rejected mss and sometimes recommends other markets.

How to Contact: Send complete ms. SASE. Cover letter with author's background and full name—no initials. Photocopied submissions OK. Accepts computer printout submissions. Sample copy $1.50 and SAE. Fiction guidelines for SAE.

Payment: 2 contributor's copies.

Terms: Acquires one-time rights on publication. Publication copyrighted.

Advice: "Continue to read as well as write. Study your markets. Read the classics; don't overlook the contemporary writer. Catch your reader on the outset. Be brief. Magazine is done entirely in calligraphy."

PEMBROKE MAGAZINE (I, II), Box 60, Pembroke State University, Pembroke NC 28372. (919)521-4214, ext. 433. Editor: Shelby Stephenson. Fiction Editor: Stephen Smith. Magazine: 10x9; 225 pages; illustrations; photos. Magazine of poems and stories plus literary essays. Annually. Estab. 1969. Circ. 500.

Needs: Open. Receives 40 unsolicited mss/month. Publishes short shorts. Recently published work by Fred Chappell, Robert Morgan; published new writers within the last year. Length: open. Occasionally critiques rejected mss and recommends other markets.

How to Contact: Send complete ms. Reports immediately to 3 months. SASE. Accepts computer

printout submissions. Prefers letter-quality. Sample copy $3 and 10x9 SAE.
Payment: 1 contributor's copy.
Terms: Publication copyrighted.
Advice: "Write with an end for *writing*, not publication. The publication, believe it or not, will be—will out—will come about!"

‡PENNSYLVANIA ENGLISH (II), English Department, Penn State University—Behrend College, Erie PA 16563. Editor: Dean Baldwin. Fiction Editor: Chris Dubbs. Magazine: 8½x7; 100 pages; 20 lb bond paper; 65 lb matte cover. For "teachers of English in Pennsylvania at the high school and college level." Semiannually. Estab. 1975. Circ. 500.
Needs: Literary, mainstream. "Most types of genre fiction would not be suitable. We are just beginning to publish fiction." Does not read mss during the summer. Publishes ms an average of 6 months after acceptance. Length: 5,000 words maximum. Publishes short shorts. Sometimes critiques rejected mss.
How to Contact: Send 2 copies of complete ms with cover letter. Reports in 2 months. SASE. Simultaneous and photocopied submissions OK. Accepts dot-matrix computer printouts.
Payment: Pays in contributor's copies.
Terms: Acquires first North American serial rights. Publication copyrighted.

PENNSYLVANIA REVIEW, University of Pittsburgh, 526 C.L./English Dept., Pittsburgh PA 15260. (412)624-0026. Managing Editor: Deborah Pursifull. Magazine: 7x10; 70-100 pages. Magazine of fiction, poetry, nonfiction, interviews, reviews, novel excerpts, long poems for literate audience. Semiannually. Estab. 1985. Circ. 1,000.
Needs: Ethnic, experimental, feminist, gay, humor/satire, lesbian, literary, prose poem, regional, translations. "High quality!" Receives 50 unsolicited fiction mss/month. Accepts 3-5 mss/issue; 6-10 mss/year. Deadlines: Dec. 1 and March 1. Mss not read in summer months. Recently published work by Lynne Barrett and Peter Makuck; published new writers within the last year. Length: 5,000 maximum words for prose. Comments on rejected mss "rarely and only if we've had some interest."
How to Contact: Send complete ms. Reports in 1 week on queries; 6-8 weeks on ms. SASE for ms. Photocopied submissions OK. Accepts computer printout submissions. Prefers letter-quality. Sample copy $5. Fiction guidelines for #10 SAE and 1 first class stamp.
Payment: $5/page for prose; 1 contributor's copy.
Terms: Pays on publication for first North American serial rights. Publication copyrighted.
Advice: "Don't be discouraged when your work is returned to you. Returns are not necessarily a comment on the quality of the writing. Keep trying."

‡PERCEPTIONS (I), 525 Cottonwood #1, Missoula MT 59801. (406)543-5875. Editor: Temi Rose. Magazine: 4x5; 20 pages. Publishes "women's perceptions mostly," for readers of "all ages, both sexes." Published 3 times/year. Plans special fiction issue. Estab. 1983. Circ. 100.
Needs: Adventure, condensed/excerpted novel, confession contemporary, experimental, fantasy, feminist, prose poem, psychic/supernatural/occult, religions/inspirational, science fiction, suspense/mystery. Accepts 1 ms/issue. Length: four pages tops. Publishes short shorts. Critiques rejected mss "only if they ask for that."
How to Contact: Query first. Reports in 2-3 weeks on queries; in 1 month on mss. SASE. Simultaneous, photocopied and reprint submissions OK. Accepts computer printout submissions, including dot-matrix. Accepts electronic submissions via disk or modem. Sample copy for $2. Fiction guidelines free for SAE and 1 first class stamp.
Payment: Pays in contributor's copies.
Terms: Publication copyrighted. Sponsors awards for fiction writers "only occasionally."

PEREGRINE (II), The Journal of Amherst Writers and Artists, Amherst Writers and Artists, Box 1076, Amherst MA 01004. (413)253-3307. Editors: Janet Sadler, Anna Kirwan Vogel, Kathi Gleason. Magazine: 5x7; 90 pages; sturdy matte white paper; heavier cover stock; perfect bound; illustrations occasionally. "Poetry and prose—short stories, short short stories, and occasionally prose fantasies or reflections that are fiction yet are not stories." Annually.
Needs: "Most accepted pieces tend to be strong on human experience. No specific 'category' requirements. Humor is much appreciated, but it's not necessarily the focus. We don't publish children's/juvenile/'young adult' fiction, and we're not enthusiastic about gory violence, gratuitous sexism or extreme smugness." Receives 12-36 unsolicited fiction mss/month. Accepts 4-8 mss/issue. Publishes ms an average of 3-6 months after acceptance. Recently published work by Amanda Jermyn, Robert Freedman; published new writers within the last year. Length: 1,000-2,500 words preferred. Publishes short shorts. "Short pieces have a better chance of publication." Sometimes critiques rejected mss.
How to Contact: Send complete ms with cover letter, which should include brief biographical note

and list of previous publications. Reports in 3-6 months. SASE. Simultaneous and photocopied submissions OK. Accepts computer printout submissions, including dot-matrix if dark. Sample copy $4.
Payment: Contributor's copies.
Terms: All rights return to writer upon publication. Sponsors contests and awards for fiction writers. "Fiction contests are announced in issues of *Peregrine*. Cash prizes of $50-$100 offered. Write for details."
Advice: "*Peregrine* is potentially an excellent place for a beginning fiction writer to send manuscripts. When we have time, we try to respond with at least one sentence of specific comment or encouragement—although we don't always have the time. We publish on a very fine stock, have a cover by a well established artist, and include pieces by experienced, previously published writers. Experiments with very indirect time sequence are often lost on us. We'd rather read a more conventionally narrated story. But this is not a fixed rule at all, and originality counts for a great deal. We advise simultaneous submission of manuscripts because small journals cannot be fast in responding and the writer's predicament is very clear to us. We too, offer our work and wait."

PERMAFROST (II), A Literary Journal, English Dept., University of Alaska, Fairbanks AK 99775. Contact: editors. Magazine: 5½x8; 110 pages; good quality paper; b&w illustrations and photos. Magazine of "quality, contemporary fiction, poetry, essays for intelligent readers, small press audiences, writers, educators." Published semiannually. Estab. 1976. Circ. 500.
Needs: Contemporary, ethnic, experimental, feminist, gay, humor/satire, lesbian, literary, prose poem, science fiction. No "commercial, formula writing." Receives 20-30 unsolicited mss/month. Accepts 3-4 mss/issue; 6-8 mss/year. Does not read between April 15 and August 15. Recently published work by Karen Minton. Published new writers within the last year. Length: 2,500-5,000 words average; 5,000 words maximum. Also publishes short shorts of 2-10 pages. Rarely critiques rejected mss.
How to Contact: Send complete ms with cover letter. "Prefer simple letter." Reports in 2 months. SASE. Photocopied submissions OK. Accepts computer printout submissions. Prefers letter-quality. Sample copy $4.
Payment: Pays 2 contributor's copies.
Terms: All rights to author. Publication copyrighted. Send SASE for guidelines.
Advice: "*Permafrost* is a literary journal; we expect and hope to see your best work. If you write about Alaska, be sure your message is universal in scope and you are comfortable with the setting of your story. We welcome good fiction of all types."

PHOEBE (II), The George Mason Review, George Mason University, 4400 University Dr., Fairfax VA 22030. (703)323-3730. Editor: Stacey Freed. Fiction Editors: P. J. Woodside, Lawrence Roy. Magazine: 6x9; 72 pages; 80 lb quality paper; 0-5 illustrations per issue; 0-10 photographs per issue. "We publish fiction, poetry, photographs, illustrations and some reviews." Quarterly. Estab. 1972. Circ. 3,500.
Needs: Experimental, literary, mainstream, prose poem, regional, serialized/excerpted novel, translations. No romance, western, juvenile, erotica. Receives 20 mss/month. Accepts 5-7 mss/issue; 20-28 mss/year. Does not read mss June-July. Publishes ms 3-6 months after acceptance. Recently published work by Alan Cheuse, Richard Bausch, Paul Milensky. Length: 4,500 words average; 8,000 words maximum. Publishes short shorts. Sometimes comments on rejected mss.
How to Contact: Send complete ms with cover letter. Include "name, address, phone; if and where you've published previously. Brief bio." Reports in 1 week on queries; 6 weeks on mss. SASE. Photocopied submissions OK. Sample copy $3.25. Fiction guidelines for #10 SAE with 1 first class stamp.
Payment: Pays in 4 contributor's copies.
Terms: Acquires one-time rights. Publication copyrighted.
Advice: "*Phoebe* is committed to furthering the arts and particularly to helping new writers of poetry and fiction. Many of our staff are associated with the M.F.A. program in writing at George Mason University. While we are receptive to all kinds of good writing, we particularly appreciate stories that tell stories: clean, honest prose. Studying a recent issue would be helpful."

PIEDMONT LITERARY REVIEW (II), Piedmont Literary Society, Box 3656, Danville VA 24543. (804)793-0956. Editor: Olga Kronmeyer. "The theme of our publication is human expression through the written word. We publish short stories, essays and articles. Our publication is directed toward all lovers of literature regardless of their stature in life." Quarterly. Estab. 1976. Circ. 400.
Needs: Literary, contemporary, science fiction, fantasy, humor, psychic and regional. Accepts 8-12 mss/year. Receives approximately 50-100 unsolicited fiction mss each month. Length: 2,000 words maximum. Will exceed maximum if story is of highest quality. Critiques rejected mss when there is time. Sometimes recommends other markets.
How to Contact: Send complete ms with SASE. Reports in 3 months on mss. Publishes ms an average of 3-4 months after acceptance. Sample copy $2. Guidelines for #10 SASE.

Payment: 1 free author's copy. $2.50 charge for extras.
Terms: Acquires one-time rights. Seldom buys reprints.
Advice: "I have none that would guarantee publication. 'Write the truest sentence you know,' as Hemingway said. Be honest. Use the tools of fiction. An experience is not a story. To me, characters are what make a story. If I believe the characters, the plot will naturally follow."

PIG IN A PAMPHLET (II), Pig In A Poke Press, Box 81925, Pittsburgh PA 15217. (412)521-1237. Editor: Harry Calhoun. Magazine: 4¼x5½; 8-12 pages; varied cover stock; line drawings. "Literary review interested chiefly in emotionally intense but coherent poetry; also takes *very* short fiction/articles. Definitely not sewing-circle stuff, but with wide appeal for a diverse audience." Quarterly. Estab. 1982. Circ. 500.
Needs: Contemporary, erotica, experimental, fantasy, humor/satire, prose poem. No long fiction, religious themes, children's stories. Receives 50-100 unsolicited mss/month. Accepts 2 mss/issue; 8-10 mss/year. Publishes short shorts of less than 600 words. "I love well-written prose poems." Recently published work by Charles Bukowski and Robert Gregory; published new writers within the last year. Length: 1,000 words maximum. Occasionally critiques rejected mss. Frequently recommends other markets.
How to Contact: Send complete ms with cover letter. "Any info is fine." Reports in 2 weeks to 1 month. SASE. Simultaneous (if so advised) and photocopied submissions OK; "we prefer unpublished submissions but have taken (and will take) previously published on occasion." Accepts computer printout submissions. Prefers letter-quality. Sample copy $1 and 45¢ postage. Fiction guidelines for #10 SAE and 25¢ postage.
Payment: 2 free contributor's copies.
Terms: Acquires one-time rights. "All rights revert immediately back to author."
Advice: "Read the magazine—it's better than any guidelines I can give you. *Pig* tries to take some of the pomposity out of literary-magazine writing—no stuffed shirts, please."

PIG IRON (II), Box 237, Youngstown OH 44501. (216)783-1269. Editor: Jim Villani. Fiction Editor: Rose Sayre. Magazine. 8½x11; 96 pages; 60 lb offset paper; 85 pt coated cover stock; b&w illustrations; b&w 120 line photographs. "Contemporary literature by new and experimental writers." Annually. Estab. 1975. Circ. 1,000.
Needs: Literary, psychological and labor. No mainstream. Buys 1-15 mss/issue; 2-30 mss/year. Receives approximately 50 unsolicited fiction mss each month. Recently published work by Randall Silvis, Robert Fox and Gerald Haslam. Length: 8,000 words maximum.
How to Contact: Send complete ms with SASE. No simultaneous submissions. Accepts computer printout submissions. Reports in 3 months. Sample copy $2.50.
Payment: $2/printed page. 2 free author's copies. $3 charge for extras.
Terms: Pays on publication for first North American serial rights.
Advice: "Looking for works that do not ignore psychological development in character and plot/action." Mss are rejected because of "lack of new ideas and approaches. Writers need to work out interesting plot/action and setting/set. Read a lot; read for stylistic innovation. Send SASE for current themes list."

THE PIG PAPER (I, II), Pig Productions, 70 Cotton Dr., Mississauga, Ontario L5G 1Z9 Canada. (416)278-6594. Editor: Gary Pig Gold. Newsletter: 8½x11; 2 pages; 20 lb paper; illustrations and photos. "A study of the 'pop culture' its past, present and future; its reflection of—and effect on—society." Bimonthly. Estab. 1975. Circ. 1,000.
Needs: Adventure, confession, contemporary, erotica, experimental, fantasy, humor/satire, prose poem, psychic/supernatural/occult, science fiction, spiritual music. "I prefer material of a short (i.e. column) length (due to severe space restrictions), on subjects—or points of view—you'd be unlikely to read about elsewhere. Receives 10 unsolicited fiction mss/month. Accepts 5 mss/issue; 25 mss/year. Recently published work by Ace Backwords, Rev. Kenneth K. Burke, James Lord; published new writers within the last year. Length: 1,500 words average; 100 words minimum; 10,000 words maximum. Publishes short shorts. "I can serialize a longer piece over several consecutive issues." Sometimes critiques rejected mss or recommends other markets.
How to Contact: Send complete ms with cover letter, which should include "a bit about the writer (i.e. age, surroundings), and *why* they've contacted *The Pig Paper*." Reports in 3 weeks. Simultaneous, photocopied and reprint submissions OK. Accepts computer printouts, including dot-matrix. Sample copy for 9x4 envelope and 2 first class stamps.
Payment: Pays in contributor's copies.
Terms: Acquires one-time rights. Sends pre-publication galleys to author. Publication copyrighted.
Advice: Optimistic about status of magazine fiction today "because of the ever-growing size of, interaction within, and networking capabilities surrounding the (for lack of a better term) 'small press scene.'

With a little research, it'd be next to impossible *not* to find a publication somewhere that would be interested in one's material. And of course, if you simply can't uncover a suitable publication somewhere, you can always start your own. Over the years, I've (proudly) earned the reputation for a being the editor who'll publish anything—eventually. If a writer takes the time, care and trouble to write material, be it fiction or otherwise, and send it to me, odds are I'll get around to publishing it sooner or later, if only out of a sense of appreciation and obligation."

THE PIKESTAFF FORUM (II), Box 127, Normal IL 61761. (309)452-4831. Editors: Robert D. Sutherland, James Scrimgeour, James McGowan and Curtis White. Tabloid: 11½x17½; 40 pages; newsprint paper; illustrations; photos. "*The Pikestaff Forum* is a general literary magazine publishing poetry, prose fiction, drama." Readership: "General literary with a wide circulation in the small press world. Readers are educated (but not academic) and have a taste for excellent serious fiction." Published irregularly—"whenever we have sufficient quality material to warrant an issue." Estab. 1977. Circ. 1,000.
Needs: Literary and contemporary with a continuing need for good short stories or novel excerpts. "We welcome traditional and experimental works from established and non-established writers. We look for writing that is clear, concise and to the point; contains vivid imagery and sufficient concrete detail; is grounded in lived human experience; contains memorable characters and situations. No confessional self-pity or puffery; self-indulgent first or second drafts; sterile intellectual word games or five-finger exercises or slick formula writing, genre-pieces that do not go beyond their form (westerns, mysteries, gothic, horror, science fiction, swords-and-sorcery fantasy), commercially oriented mass-market stuff, violence for its own sake, racist or sexist material or pornography (sexploitation)." Accepts 1-4 mss/issue. Receives approximately 15-20 unsolicited fiction mss each month. Recently published work by Constance Pierce, Linnea Johnson; published new writers within the last year. Length: from 1 paragraph to 4,000 or 5,000 words. Critiques rejected mss when there is time.
How to Contact: Query. Send complete ms. SASE. Accepts computer printout submissions. Prefers letter-quality. Reports in 3 weeks on queries, 3 months on mss. Publishes ms up to 1 year after acceptance. Sample copy $2.
Payment: 3 free author's copies. Cover price less 50% discount for extras.
Terms: Acquires first rights. Copyright remains with author. Publication copyrighted.
Advice: "We are highly selective, publishing only 3% of the stories that are submitted for consideration. Read other authors with an appreciative and critical eye; don't send out work prematurely; develop keen powers of observation and a good visual memory; get to know your characters thoroughly; don't let others (editors, friends, etc.) define or 'determine' your sense of self-worth; be willing to learn; outgrow self-indulgence. Develop discipline. Show, don't tell; and leave some work for the reader to do. Write for the fun of it (that way there's a sure return for the investment of time and effort). Always write to achieve the best quality you can; be honest with yourself, your potential readers, and your story. Learn to become your own best editor: know when you've done well, and when you haven't done as well as you can. Remember: there's a lot of competition for the available publication slots, and editorial bias is always a factor in what gets accepted for publication. Develop a sense of humor about the enterprise."

THE PIPE SMOKER'S EPHEMERIS (I, II, IV), The Universal Coterie of Pipe Smokers, 20-37 120 St., College Point NY 11356. Editor: Tom Dunn. Magazine: 8½x11; 54-66 pages; offset paper and cover; illustrations; photos. Pipe smoking and tobacco theme for general and professional audience. Irregular quarterly. Estab. 1964.
Needs: Historical (general), humor/satire, literary, pipe smoking related. Publishes ms up to 1 year after acceptance. Length: 2,500 words average; 5,000 words maximum. Also publishes short shorts. Occasionally critiques rejected mss.
How to Contact: Send complete ms with cover letter. Reports in 2 weeks on mss. Simultaneous, photocopied submissions and reprints OK. Accepts computer printouts including dot-matrix. Sample copy for 8½x11 SAE and 6 first class stamps.
Terms: Acquires one-time rights. Publication copyrighted.

PLAINSWOMAN, Box 8027, Grand Forks ND 58202. (701)777-8043. Editor: Elizabeth Hampsten. Fiction Editor: Bjorn Benson. "A progressive publication which publishes some fiction and poetry." Readership: "Mainly women of the Plains area who want information concerning national and regional women's issues, although we have subscribers in most states, male and female." 10 times/year (February and August excluded). Estab. 1977. Circ. 600.
Needs: High quality fiction. Publishes 20 mss/year. Recently published work by Enid Shomer and Denise Panek; published new writers within the last year.
How to Contact: Send complete ms with cover letter and SASE. "Cover letter should be brief and intelligent—not get in way of story by trying to explain it." Accepts readable computer printout submissions. Prefers accepted ms sent on disk. Reports in 2 weeks-3 months. Sample copy $2.

Payment: Will pay up to 2¢/word for high quality fiction.
Terms: Buys one-time rights. Publication copyrighted.
Advice: "We will not reject a flawed manuscript if it has some merit. We often work with writers for revisions."

PLÉIADES MAGAZINE (I), Box 357, Suite D, 6677 W. Colfax, Lakewood CO 80214. (303)237-3398. Editor: Cyril Osmond. Fiction Editors: E. Whitlatch and John Moravec. Magazine: 8½x11; 30-50 pages; 30 lb paper; illustrations; b&w photographs. "We want well thought out material; no sex stories, and good poetry and prose. We want articles about national issues." Quarterly. Estab. 1984. Circ. 500.
Needs: Fantasy, historical (general), horror, literary, senior citizen/retirement, serialized/excerpted novel, suspense/mystery, western. "No sex or hippie material." Receives 50-70 unsolicited mss/month. Accepts 3 mss/issue. Publishes ms three months or less after acceptance. Recently published work by Brennan, Case, Callahan; published new writers within the last year. Length: 1,200-1,500 words average; 500-800 words minimum. Occasionally critiques rejected mss and recommends other markets.
How to Contact: Send complete ms with cover letter. Reports in 1 week on queries; 2 weeks on mss. SASE. Simultaneous submissions OK. Sample copy $1.75. Fiction guidelines for #10 SAE and 1 first class stamp.
Payment: Pays in contributor's copies.
Terms: Rights remain with author. Publication copyrighted. Offers awards and trophies for best work.
Advice: "Today's magazine fiction stinks. We want authors who can write non-stereotype material, and who are not brainwashed by a bureaucratic society. Learn to write, and take lessons on punctuation. We want shorter good fiction and articles."

‡THE PLOUGH: NORTH COAST REVIEW (II), The Firelands Writing Center, c/o Firelands College of BGSU, Huron OH 44839. (419)433-5560. Editor: Larry Smith. Fiction Editor: Andrew Bores. Publishes material of "sense of place—ecology—intercultural awareness/Ohio Writers." Annually. Estab. 1983. Circ. 500.
Needs: Humor/satire, literary, mainstream, prose poem, midwest, coming of age. "We read Sept. to Feb. 1." Recently published work by Connie Everett, Larry Smith, Andrew Hagerty. Length: 4,000 words preferred; 1,000 words minimum; 6,000 words maximum. Publishes short shorts—three per issue. Sometimes critiques rejected mss and recommends other markets.
How to Contact: Send complete ms with cover letter. "We like a short bio., 75 words, for our 'Credits' column. Don't list all your publications." Reports in February. SASE. Simultaneous and photocopied submissions OK. Sample copy for $4.
Payment: Pays in contributor's copies.
Terms: Acquires first rights and one-time rights. Publication copyrighted.
Advice: "I want to publish stories that have heart without sentimentality, stories that leave you changed. I do not appreciate minimalist fiction that exploits human character, rather than develops it. We look for sincerity and a respect for language and characters."

PLOUGHSHARES (II), Box 529, Cambridge MA 02139. (617)926-9875. Editor: DeWitt Henry. "Our theme is new writing (poetry, fiction, criticism) that addresses contemporary adult readers who look to fiction and poetry for help in making sense of themselves and of each other." Quarterly. Estab. 1971. Circ. 3,500.
Needs: Literary, prose poem. "No genre (science fiction, detective, gothic, adventure, etc.), popular formula or commercial fiction whose purpose is to entertain rather than to illuminate." Buys 20 + mss/year. Receives approximately 300-400 unsolicited fiction mss each month. Recently published work by Susanna Kaysen, Linda Bamber, Dan Wakefield; published new writers within the last year. Length: 2,000-6,000 words. Sometimes recommends other markets.
How to Contact: "Query for best time to submit and examine a sample issue." Cover letter should include "previous pubs." SASE. Reports in 3 weeks on queries, 5 months on mss. Sample copy $5. (Please specify fiction issue sample.)
Payment: $10/page to $50 maximum, plus copies. Offers 50% kill fee for assigned ms not published.
Terms: Pays on publication for first North American serial rights. Publication copyrighted.
Advice: "Be familiar with our fiction issues, fiction by our writers and by our various editors (e.g., Rosellen Brown, Tim O'Brien, Jay Neugeboren, Jayne Anne Phillips, James Allen McPherson) and more generally acquaint yourself with the best short fiction currently appearing in the literary quarterlies, and the annual prize anthologies (*Pushcart Prize, O'Henry Awards, Best American Short Stories*). Also realistically consider whether the work you are submitting is as good as or better than—in your own opinion—the work appearing in the magazine you're sending to. What is the level of competition? And what is its volume? (In our case, we accept about 1 ms in 200.) Never send 'blindly' to a magazine, or without carefully weighing your prospect there against those elsewhere. Always keep a copy of work you submit."

‡PM (I), The Pedantic Monthly, 1383 Idaho St., Santa Clara CA 95050. (408)985-9208. Editor: Erik A. Johnson. FIction Editor: Lydia Renay. Newsletter: 8½x11; 16-24 pages; 80 lb satin offset paper; b&w illustrations and photographs. "Publication is humor and satire for an educated audience, along with short fiction of most creative types." Monthly. Estab. 1986. Circ. 500.
Needs: Contemporary, fantasy, humor/satire, literary, prose poem, science fiction, serialized novel. No communist, socialist, anarchist, gay, lesbian, seditious. Receives 0-10 unsolicited mss/month. Buys 10-20 mss/year. Publishes ms 3 months at most after acceptance. Recently published work by Joe Constanza, F. R. Duplantier and June Bangham. Length: 3,500 words maximum (unless serialized). Publishes short shorts. Sometimes critiques rejected mss and recommends other markets.
How to Contact: Send complete ms with cover letter. Cover letter should include biographical information, credits, assignment availability. Reports in 3 weeks. SASE. Simultaneous, photocopied and reprint submissions OK. Accepts computer printout submissions, including dot-matrix. Accepts electronic submissions via 3½" disk for Macintosh with Word or MacWrite. Sample copy for $2.50. Fiction guidelines for #10 SAE and 1 first class stamp.
Payment: Free subscription to magazine; free contributor's copies.
Terms: Acquires first North American serial rights. Publication copyrighted.
Advice: "We look for originality in all works. In humor, we specifically look for edifying humor, that sort which can also instruct as it pokes fun; in fiction, we look for uniqueness, neologisms, daring. Be outlandish, opinionated, stylish, assertive, acerbic and creative."

‡POETRY MAGIC (I), Box 521, Potterville MI 48876. (517)645-2656. Editor: Lisa Roose-Church. Magazine: 5½x8½; over 20 pages; b&w illustrations. "Publish poetry and articles relating to poetry. Have used other themes. We will consider just about anything of high quality." Quarterly. Estab. 1988.
Needs: Contemporary, humor, prose poem. No pornography, science fiction, horror, fantasy. Receives over 100 mss/month. Accepts 1 mss/issue; 4 mss/year. Publishes ms within 2-6 months of acceptance. Recently published work by Charles Keller. Length: 50-500 words preferred; 50 words minimum; 500 words maximum. Sometimes critiques rejected mss and recommends other markets.
How to Contact: Query first, query with clips of published work or send complete ms with cover letter. Reports in 2-4 weeks. SASE. Simultaneous (if stated), photocopied and reprint submissions OK. Accepts computer printout submissions, including dot-matrix. Sample copy for $4.50. Fiction guidelines for #10 SAE and 30¢ postage.
Payment: Pays in contributor's copies.
Terms: Acquires first rights or one-time rights. Publication copyrighted.
Advice: "Correct usage of grammar, punctuation, etc. is important. We prefer fiction that is quality reading, which entices the reader for more from that author. Because we get less fiction than poetry, we are selective because our readers want to be enticed, enthralled and overwhelmed with a story. If it doesn't do this for the editor she will not accept it. Experiment and create your own style."

‡THE PORTABLE WALL (II), Basement Press, 215 Burlington, Billings MT 59101. (406)256-3588. Editor: Daniel Struckman. Fiction Editor: Gray Harris. Magazine: 6¼x9¼; 24 pages; cotton rag paper; best quality cover; line engravings; illustrations. "We consider all kinds of material. Bias toward humor." Annually. Estab. 1977. Circ. 200.
Needs: Adventure, contemporary, ethnic, experimental, feminist, historical, humor/satire, juvenile, literary, mainstream, preschool, prose poem, regional, science fiction, senior citizen, sports, translations. "We hand set all type; therefore, we favor short pieces and poetry." Receives less than 1 unsolicited ms/month. Accepts one or two mss/issue; one or two mss/year. Publishes ms 6 months to a year after acceptance. Recently published works by Gray Harris, Wilbur Wood. Length: 2,000 words preferred. Publishes short shorts. Sometimes critiques rejected mss.
How to Contact: Send complete ms with cover letter. Reports in 2 weeks on mss. SASE. Accepts computer printout submissions, including dot-matrix. Sample copy for $5.
Payment: Free subscription to magazine.
Terms: Acquires one-time rights.
Advice: "We like language that evokes believable pictures in our minds and that tells an enjoyable story."

PORTENTS (II), 12 Fir Place, Hazlet NJ 07730. (201)888-0535. Editor: Deborah Rasmussen. Magazine: 60+ pages; illustrations; photos. "Contemporary horror, dark fantasy, movie and book reviews, crossword puzzles for an adult audience." Three issues annually. Every issue has 8-10 short stories. Estab. 1986.
Needs: Horror. No poetry or science fiction. Receives 10-15 unsolicited mss/week. Accepts 9-10 mss/issue. Publishes ms 9-10 months after acceptance. Published new writers within the last year. Length: up to 3,000 words. Publishes short shorts. Critiques every rejected mss. Recommends other markets.
How to Contact: Send complete ms with cover letter. Reports in 2 weeks on queries. SASE. Photo-

copied submissions OK. Accepts computer printout submissions, including dot-matrix. Sample copy $3.50. Fiction guidelines for #10 SAE and 1 first class stamp.
Payment Pays ¹/₄¢/word.
Advice: "Keep it short, to the point and original."

PORTLAND REVIEW (I, II), Portland State University, Box 751, Portland OR 97207. Contact: Editor. "The *Review* is looking for fiction, poetry and essays that linger in the mind's eye with frightful clarity after the magazine has been put aside and the business of life resumed." Publishes 2-3 times yearly. Estab. 1955. Circ. 1,000.
Needs: "More good fiction and less bad poetry." Recently published work by Jim Carr, Wiliam Clunie; published new writers within the last year. Length: 6,000 words maximum. Occasionally critiques rejected mss.
How to Contact: Submit complete ms with personal biographical note, SASE. Photocopied submissions OK. Reports in 6 weeks. Sample copy for $4.
Payment: 1 free contributor's copy.
Terms: Acquires one-time rights. Publication copyrighted.
Advice: "We want to increase the ratio of fiction to poetry. Stick with a few magazines and let them really get to know your work."

THE POTTERSFIELD PORTFOLIO (II,IV), New Writing From Atlantic Canada, Crazy Quilt Press, 19 Oakhill Dr., Halifax Nova Scotia B3M 2V3 Canada. (902)443-9600. Editors: donalee Moulton-Barrett, Barb Cottrell, Peggy Amirault. Magazine: 8¹/₂x11; 52 pages; good quality paper; coated cover stock; illustrations; open to suggestions for photos. "All material in *The Portfolio* is written by Atlantic Canadians or those with a connection—significant—to the region." Annually. Estab. 1979.
Needs: Contemporary, ethnic, experimental, fantasy, feminist, gay, humor/satire, lesbian, literary, mainstream, prose poem, regional, science fiction. Receives 30-50 fiction mss/month. Buys 8-10 mss/issue. Recently published work by Lesley Choyce, Spider Robinson, Silver Donald Cameron; published new writers within the last year. Publishes short shorts. Sometimes comments on rejected mss and recommends other markets.
How to Contact: Send complete ms with cover letter and enough information for short bio in journal. Reports in 2 months. SASE. Simultaneous and photocopied submissions OK. Accepts computer printout submissions, including dot-matrix. Sample copy $5 (US).
Payment: Pays $25 and contributor's copies.
Terms: Pays on publication for first Canadian English-language serial rights.
Advice: "Still believe the marketplace is open to beginning writers. Tailor your fiction to a particular market—it helps to break in more quickly and avoids unnecessary rejections from publications that are not buying the type of work you're producing."

POULTRY (II, IV), A Magazine of Voice, Box 4413, Springfield MA 01101. Editors: Jack Flavin, Brendan Galvin and George Garrett. Tabloid of fiction and poetry: 8-12 pages; newspaper quality; cover photos; cartoons. Parodies contemporary poems, styles, lit-biz, contribution notes, contests, prizes, etc; for writers and readers of contemporary literature. Three or four annually. Estab. 1979. Circ. 1,000.
Needs: Humor/satire. "We want fiction that satirizes contemporary writing's foibles, pretensions, politics, etc. Make it brief and pungent. No serious fiction." Receives 10-20 unsolicited fiction mss/month. Accepts 3-4 mss/issue; 10-20 mss/year. Occasionally critiques rejected ms. Recently published work by R. H. W. Dillard, David R. Slavitt, R. S. Gwynn and Fred Chapell; published new writers within the last year. Publishes short shorts.
How to Contact: Send complete ms with SASE. Accepts computer printout submissions. Prefers letter-quality. Reports in 1 month. Sample copy for $2.
Payment: 10 free contributor's copies.
Terms: Acquires one-time rights.
Advice: "Read us; send us parodies of the things in contemporary writing and its scene that bug you the most! Make it new and funny, preferably brief. Nothing serious."

PRAIRIE FIRE (II), Manitoba Writers' Guild, Room 208, 100 Arthur St., Winnipeg, Manitoba R3B 1H3 Canada. (204)943-9066. Editor: Andris Taskans. Magazine: 6x9; 96 pages; offset bond paper; sturdy cover stock; illustrations; photos. "Essays, critical reviews, short fiction and poetry. For writers and readers interested in Canadian literature." Published 4 times/year. Estab. 1978. Circ. 1,500.
Needs: Literary, contemporary, experimental, prose poem. "We will consider work on any topic of artistic merit, including short chapters from novels-in-progress. We wish to avoid gothic, confession, religious, romance and pornography." Buys 2-3 mss/issue, 8-10 mss/year. Does not read mss in summer. Recently published work by Sandra Birdsell, George Bowering, Robert Kroetsch; published new writers within the last year. Receives 18-20 unsolicited fiction mss each month. Publishes short shorts.

Length: 5,000 maximum; no minimum; 2,000 words average. Critiques rejected mss "if requested and when there is time." Sometimes recommmends other markets.

How to Contact: Send complete ms with SASE and short bio. Reports in 2-3 months. Sample copy for $6 (Canadian).

Payment: $60 for the first page, $30 for each additional page. 1 free author's copy. $4 charge for extras.

Terms: Pays on publication for first North American serial rights. Rights revert to author on publication. Publication copyrighted.

Advice: "We are publishing more fiction, and we are commissioning illustrations. Read our publication before submitting. We prefer Canadian material. Most mss are not ready for publication. Be neat, double space. Be the best writer you can be."

THE PRAIRIE JOURNAL OF CANADIAN LITERATURE (I, II, IV), Prairie Journal Press, Box 997, Station G, Calgary, Alberta T3A 3G2 Canada. Editor: A.E. Burke. Journal: 8½x7; 50-60 pages; white bond paper; Cadillac cover stock; cover illustrations. Journal of creative writing and scholarly essays, reviews for literary audience. Semiannually. Published special fiction issue last year. Estab. 1983.

Needs: Contemporary, literary, prose poem, regional, excerpted novel, novella, typed single space on camera-ready copy. Canadian authors given preference. No romance, erotica, pulp. Receives 20-40 unsolicited mss each month. Accepts 10-15 ms/issue; 20-30 mss/year. Charges reading fee of up to $1/page "if help requested." Suggests sample issue before submitting ms. Recently published work by Nancy Ellen Russell, Carla Mobley, Patrick Quinn; published new writers within the last year. Length: 2,500 words average; 100 words minimum; 3,000 words maximum. Sometimes critiques rejected mss and recommends other markets.

How to Contact: Send complete ms. Reports in 1 month. SASE or SAE and IRC. Photocopied submissions OK. Accepts computer printout if letter quality, no dot-matrix. Sample copy $3 (Canadian) and SAE with $1.10 for postage or IRC. Include cover letter of past credits—a friendly introduction to a new acquaintance. Reply to queries for SAE with 42¢ for postage or IRC. No American stamps.

Payment: Contributor's copies.

Terms: Acquires first North American serial rights. In Canada author retains copyright.

Advice: Interested in "innovational work of quality. Beginning writers welcome. I have chosen to publish fiction simply because many magazines do not. Those who do in Canada are, for the most part, seeking formulaic writing. There is no point in simply republishing known authors or conventional, predictable plots. Of the genres we receive fiction is most often of the highest calibre. It is a very competitive field. Be proud of what you send. You're worth it."

PRAIRIE SCHOONER (II), University of Nebraska, English Department, 201 Andrews Hall, Lincoln NE 68588. (402)472-1800. Magazine: 6x9; 144 pages; good stock paper; heavy cover stock. "A general literary quarterly of stories, poems, essays and reviews for a general educated audience that reads for pleasure." Quarterly. Estab. 1927. Circ. 2,000.

Needs: Good fiction. Accepts 4-5 mss/issue. Receives approximately 150 unsolicited fiction mss each month. Recently published work by Robley Wilson, David Huddle, Jane Ann Mullen; published new writers within the last year. Length: varies.

How to Contact: Send complete ms with SASE and cover letter listing previous publications—where, when. Reports in 3 months. Sample copy for $2.

Payment: 3 free author's copies.

Terms: Acquires all rights. Publication copyrighted. Will reassign rights upon request after publication. Annual prize of $500 for best fiction, $500 for best new writer (poetry or fiction), $500 for best poetry; additional prizes, $250-$1,000.

Advice: "*Prairie Schooner* is eager to see fiction from beginning and established writers. Be tenacious. Accept rejection as a temporary setback and send out rejected stories to other magazines."

‡PRIMAVERA (II, IV), University of Chicago, 1212 E. 59th St., Chicago IL 60637. (312)324-5920. Editorial Board. Magazine: 5½x8½; 100 pages; 60 lb paper; glossy cover; illustrations; photos. Literature and graphics by women: poetry, short stories, photos, drawings. Readership: "an audience interested in women's ideas and experiences." Annually. Estab. 1975. Circ. 1,000.

Needs: Literary, contemporary, science fiction, fantasy, feminist, gay/lesbian and humor. "We dislike slick stories packaged for more traditional women's magazines. We publish only work reflecting the experiences of women, but also publish mss by men." Accepts 6-10 mss/issue. Receives approximately 40 unsolicited fiction mss each month. Recently published work by Judi Goldenberg, Chopeta C. Lyons; published new writers within the last year. Length: 25 pages maximum. Critiques rejected mss when there is time. Often gives suggestions for revisions and invites re-submission of revised ms. Occasionally recommends other markets

How to Contact: Send complete ms with SASE. Cover letter not necessary. Accepts computer print-

out submissions, "if assured it is not a multiple submission." Prefers letter-quality. Reports in 1 week—5 months on mss. Publishes ms up to 1 year after acceptance. Sample copy $5; $6 for recent issues. Guidelines for #10 SASE.
Payment: 2 free author's copies.
Terms: Acquires first rights. Publication copyrighted.
Advice: "Read the magazine. We publish a wide variety of stories. We like stories with well developed characters, interesting plots, and convincing dialogue. We like new ideas and techniques."

‡PRIMORDIAL EYE (IV), 10905 Ohio, #305, Los Angeles CA 90024. Editor: Gary J. Robinson. Magazine: 8½x5½; 80 pages; 100% cotton weave paper; card stock cover; b&w line drawings. "Specializing in fiction, poetry and art in the weird horror and fantasy genres—Lovecraftian." Quarterly. Plans special fiction issue. Estab. 1988. Circ. 100.
Needs: Experimental, fantasy, horror, science fiction, Cthulhu Mythos. No slasher/gore type horror. No cyberpunk. No high fantasy (Tolkien). No technology futuristic sci-fi (Star Wars). No stories lacking supernatural elements." Receives 45 mss/month. Buys 8-9 mss/issue; 36 mss/year. Publishes ms within 3 weeks-3 months of acceptance. Recently published work by John B. Rosenman. Length: 2,000-6,000 words preferred. Publishes short shorts. Sometimes critiques rejected mss.
How to Contact: Send complete ms with cover letter, which should include "a friendly greeting! Also mention how writer heard of us." Reports in 3 weeks. SASE. Simultaneous and photocopied submissions OK. Accepts computer printout submissions, including dot-matrix. Sample copy for $6. Fiction guidelines for #10 SAE and 1 first class stamp.
Payment: Pays ⅛¢/word and contributor's copies.
Terms: Pays on publication for first North American serial rights. Publication copyrighted.
Advice: "Most sci-fi mags are too pacifistic for me—too much soft sci-fi with lots of fiction and little science. Horror mags tend to rehash old themes—werewolves, vampires etc.—or else harp on slasher/gore themes. I am starting the *Eye* to fill the gap. Our emphasis is mood-oriented sci-fi, fantasy plus horror. What kind of moods? The moods of twilight, buried cities, forbidden magic, gates through time, and far worlds. We don't want senseless violence, but we also don't want moralistic anti-violence tales where all aliens are friendly. We just want the multiverse, with all its terrors and wonders, as human explorers find it. Our emphasis is on atmosphere, not characters. In this we are not mainstream, I suppose. Nothing offensive to women will be tolerated. Read Clark Ashton Smith! Read Jack Vance! These men are masters at creating detailed, enchanting worlds of fantasy and horror. Don't write stories (for me) about strange things happening to ordinary people; such characters anchor the story to everyday reality and disrupt the fabric of fantasy. Write about seekers after knowledge and the strange places they travel to in search of it."

PRISM INTERNATIONAL (II), E462-1866 Main Mall, University of British Columbia, Vancouver, British Columbia V6T 1W5 Canada. (604)228-2514. Editor: Janis McKenzie. Magazine: 6x9; 72-80 pages; Zephyr book paper; Cornwall, coated one side cover; photos on cover. "A journal of contemporary writing—fiction, poetry, drama and translation. *Prism's* audience is world-wide, as are our contributors." Readership: "Public and university libraries, individual subscriptions, bookstores—an audience concerned with the contemporary in literature." Published 4 times/year. Estab. 1959 Circ. 1,200.
Needs: Literary, contemporary, prose poem or translations. "Most any category as long as it is *fresh*. No overtly religious, overtly theme-heavy material or anything more message- or category-oriented than self-contained." Buys approximately 70 mss/year. Receives 50 unsolicited fiction mss each month. Published new writers within the last year. Length: 5,000 words maximum "though flexible for outstanding work." Publishes short shorts. Critiques rejected mss when there is time. Occasionally recommends other markets.
How to Contact: Send complete ms with SASE or SAE, IRC and cover letter with bio, information and publications list. "Keep it simple. US contributors take note: US stamps are not valid in Canada and your ms will not likely be returned if it contains US stamps. Send International Reply Coupons instead." Accepts computer printout submissions. Prefers letter-quality. Reports in 2-3 months. Sample copy $4.
Payment: $25/printed page, 1 free year's subscription.
Terms: Pays on publication for first North American serial rights. Publication copyrighted.
Advice: "Too many derivative, self-indulgent pieces; sloppy construction and imprecise word usage. There's not enough attention to voice and not enough invention. We are committed to publishing outstanding literary work in all genres."

PRISONERS OF THE NIGHT (II), An Adult Anthology of Erotica, Fright, Allure and ... Vampirism, MKASHEF Enterprises, Box 368, Poway CA 92064. Editor: Alayne Gelfand. Magazine: 8½x11; 150-200 pages; 20 lb paper; slick cover; illustrations. "An adult, erotic vampire anthology of original character stories and poetry. Heterosexual and homosexual situations included." Annually. Estab. 1987. Circ. approx. 1,000.

Needs: Adventure, contemporary, erotica, experimental, fantasy, feminist, gay, horror, lesbian, literary, prose poem, psychic/supernatural/occult, science fiction, suspense/mystery, western. "All stories must be vampire stories, with unique characters, unusual situations." No fiction that deals with anyone else's creations, i.e. no "Dracula" stories. Receives 10-20 unsolicited fiction mss/month. Accepts 14-20 mss/issue. Publishes ms 1-11 months after acceptance. Recently published work by Wendy Rathbone, Leo Bigley, Nancy Kilpatrick; published new writers within the last year. Length: open. Publishes short shorts. Sometimes critiques rejected mss. Recommends other markets.

How to Contact: Send complete ms with cover letter. "A short introduction of author to the editor; name, address, *some* past credits if available." Reports in 1 week on queries; 2 months on mss. SASE. Photocopied submissions OK. Accepts computer printout submissions, including dot-matrix. Accepts electronic submissions via IBM Word Perfect, disk—files no longer than 18 pages each. Sample copy $15. Fiction guidelines for #10 SAE and 1 first class stamp.

Payment: Pays 1¢/word for fiction.

Terms: Pays on publication for first North American serial rights. Publication copyrighted.

Advice: "Do not send me pornography. While graphic erotica is fine, I do not want to see cheap or tawdry sex for shock value alone. Don't use trite or overdone plots. Be original, stretch your imagination!"

PROCESSED WORLD (II), #1829, 41 Sutter St., San Francisco CA 94104. (415)495-6823. Editors: Collective. Magazine: 8½x11; 44-48 pages; 20 lb bond paper; glossy cover stock; illustrations; photos. Magazine about work, office work, computers and hi-tech (satire). Triannually. May publish special fiction issue. Estab. 1981. Circ. 4,000.

Needs: Comics, confession, contemporary, fantasy, humor/satire, literary, science fiction. Accepts 1-2 mss/issue; 3-6 mss/year. Recently published work by James Pollack. Published new writers within the last year. Length: 1,250 words average; 100 words minimum; 1,500 words maximum. Occasionally critiques rejected ms.

How to Contact: Send complete ms. Reports in 4 months. SASE. Simultaneous and photocopied submissions OK. Accepts computer printout submissions. Prefers letter-quality. Sample copy $3.

Payment: Subscription to magazine.

Terms: Acquires one-time rights.

Advice: "Make it real. Make it critical of the status quo. Read the magazine before you send us a story."

PROOF ROCK (II), Literary Arts Journal, Proof Rock Press, Box 607, Halifax VA 24558. Editor: Don R. Conner. Magazine: standard size; 40-60 pages; heavy paper; heavy cover stock; illustrations; photos. "We publish the best of what is submitted in a given period. No taboos if well done." For all segments of the literary readership. Semiannually. Published special fiction issue last year. Estab. 1982. Circ. 300.

Needs: Adventure, contemporary, erotica, experimental, fantasy, humor/satire, literary, mainstream, prose poem, psychic/supernatural, romance, translations. "Excessive sentimentality is frowned upon." Receives 8-10 unsolicited fiction mss/month. Accepts 2-4 mss/issue; 4-8 mss/year. Approximately 1% of fiction is agented. Published new writers within the last year. Length: 2,500 words maximum; 2,000 words average. Occasionally critiques rejected mss and recommends other markets.

How to Contact: Send complete ms with SASE. Simultaneous, photocopied and previously published submissions OK. Accepts computer printout submissions. Prefers letter-quality. Reports in 3 months. Publishes ms an average of 1-6 months after acceptance. Sample copy $2.50. Fiction guidelines free with #10 SAE and 1 first class stamp.

Payment: 1 free contributor's copy; $2.50 charge for extras.

Terms: Acquires one-time rights.

Advice: "Our audience is passive. We need something to stir them up. Dare to be different but not obtuse. Try something new under the sun without leaving the solar system. In other words, be original, but let your originality capture the reader rather than turn him off."

PSI (II), Suite 856, 1377 K Street NW, Washington DC 20005. Editor: A.P. Samuels. Magazine: 8½x11; 32 pages; bond paper; self cover. "Mystery and romance for an adult audience." Bimonthly. Estab. 1987.

Needs: Romance (contemporary, historical, young adult), suspense/mystery. Receives 35 unsolicited mss/month. Buys 1-2 mss/issue. Recently published work by Sharon K. Garner, Michael Riedel; published new writers within the last year. Length: 10,000 words average. Publishes short shorts. Critiques rejected mss "only on a rare occasion."

How to Contact: Send complete ms with cover letter. Reports in 2 weeks on queries; 4 weeks on mss. SASE. Accepts computer printout submissions, including dot-matrix. Accepts electronic submissions via disk.

Payment: Pays 1-4¢/word plus royalty.

Terms: Pays on acceptance for first North American serial rights. Publication copyrighted.
Advice: "Manuscripts must be for a general audience. Just good plain story telling (make it compelling). No explicit sex or ghoulish violence."

THE PUB (I, II), Ansuda Publications, Box 158J, Harris IA 51345. Editor/Publisher: Daniel R. Betz. Magazine: 5½x8½; 72 pages; mimeo paper; heavy stock cover; illustrations on cover. "We prefer stories to have some sort of social impact within them, no matter how slight, so our fiction is different from what's published in most magazines. We aren't afraid to be different or publish something that might be objectionable to current thought. *Pub* is directed toward those people, from all walks of life, who are themselves 'different' and unique, who are interested in new ideas and forms of reasoning. Our readers enjoy *Pub* and believe in what we are doing." Published 2 times/year. Estab. 1979. Circ. 350.
Needs: Literary, psychic/supernatural/occult, fantasy, horror, mystery, adventure, serialized and condensed novels. "We are looking for honest, straightforward stories. No love stories or stories that ramble on for pages about nothing in particular." Buys reprints. Accepts 4-6 mss/issue. Receives approximately 35-40 unsolicited fiction mss each month. Published new writers within the last year. Length: 8,000 words maximum. Sometimes recommends other markets.
How to Contact: Send complete ms with SASE. Accepts computer printout submissions. Prefers letter-quality. Reports in 1 month. Publishes ms an average of 6 months after acceptance. Sample copy $2.50. Guidelines for #10 SASE.
Payment: 2 free author's copies. Cover price less special bulk discount for extras.
Terms: Acquires first North American serial rights and second serial rights on reprints. Publication copyrighted.
Advice: "Read the magazine—that is *very* important. If you send a story close to what we're looking for, we'll try to help guide you to exactly what we want. We appreciate neat copy, and if photocopies are sent, we like to be able to read all of the story. Fiction seems to work for us—we are a literary magazine and have better luck with fiction than articles or poems."

PUERTO DEL SOL (I), New Mexico State University, Box 3E, Las Cruces NM 88003. (505)646-3931. Editor-in-Chief: Kevin McIlvoy. Poetry Editor: Joe Somoza. Magazine: 6x9; 200 pages; 60 lb paper; 70 lb cover stock; photos sometimes. "We publish quality material from anyone. Poetry, fiction, art, photos, interviews, reviews, parts-of-novels, long-poems." Semiannually. Estab. 1961. Circ. 1,000.
Needs: Contemporary, ethnic, experimental, literary, mainstream, prose poem, excerpted novel and translations. Receives varied number of unsolicited fiction mss/month. Accepts 8-10 mss/issue; 12-15 mss/year. Does not read mss in May-August. Recently published work by Ken Kuhlken, Susan Thornton; published new writers within the last year. Occasionally critiques rejected mss.
How to Contact: Send complete ms with SASE. Simultaneous and photocopied submissions OK. Accepts computer printout submissions. Reports in 2 months. Sample copy $4.
Payment: 3 contributor's copies.
Terms: Acquires one-time rights (rights revert to author). Publication copyrighted.
Advice: "We are open to all forms of fiction, from the conventional to the wildly experimental, as long as they have integrity and are well written. Too often we receive very impressively 'polished' mss that will dazzle readers with their sheen but offer no character/reader experience of lasting value."

‡PULPHOUSE, The Hardback Magazine of Dangerous Fiction, Box 1227, Eugene OR 97440. Editor: Kristine Kathryn Rusch. Magazine: 200-250 pages; 70 lb paper; hard cover. Quarterly. Estab. 1988. Circ. 1,250 (1,000 cloth-bound trade editions; 250 leather-bound editions).
Needs: Fantasy, horror, science fiction, speculative fiction. Requirements for fall: all horror; for winter: all speculative fiction; for spring: all fantasy; for summer: all science fiction. Recently published work by Harlan Ellison, Kate Wilhelm, Michael Bishop; published new writers within the last year. Length: 7,500 words maximum.
How to Contact: Send complete ms with cover letter "that gives publication history, work history, or any other information relevant to the magazine." SASE. Sample copy for $15.95 (cloth); $40 (leather). Fiction guidelines for #10 SAE and 1 first class stamp.
Payment: Pays 2¢-6¢/word.
Terms: Pays on acceptance for one-time anthology rights.
Advice: "*Pulphouse* is subtitled The Hardback Magazine of Dangerous Fiction. By 'dangerous,' we mean fiction that takes risks, that presents viewpoints not commonly held in the field. Although such fiction can include experimental writing, it is usually best served by clean, clear prose. We are looking for strong characterization, fast-moving plot, and intriguing settings."

PULPSMITH (II), 5 Beekman St., New York NY 10038. Editor: Harry Smith. Managing Editor: Tom Tolnay. Fiction Editor: Nancy Hallinan. Magazine: 5x7½; 300 pages (average); 50 lb Groundwood paper; 10 pt/4-color cover stock; illustrations; photos occasionally. "A modern pocket-sized version of pulp-styled pop magazines with a literary bent, for people who like to read for entertainment, and with a sense of quality." Published annually. Estab. 1981. Circ. 5,000.

Needs: Adventure, ghost, fantasy, horror, humor/satire, literary, mainstream, prose poem, science fiction, suspense/mystery and western. No women's/men's mass mag-oriented stories. Receives 200 unsolicited fiction mss/month. Buys 20 mss/issue; 60 mss/year. Submissions will be read only from Oct. 15 to May 15. Less than 5% of fiction agented. Recently published work by William John Watkins, Annie Gerard, Robert Fagan; published new writers within the last year. Length: 10,000 words maximum; 2,500 words average. Sometimes recommends other markets.

How to Contact: Send complete ms with SASE. Cover letter with credits and personal background optional. Simultaneous and photocopied submissions OK. Reports in 8 weeks on mss. Publishes ms an average of 6-20 months after acceptance. Sample copy $8; (old issues $3); writer's subscription $10/1 double-sized issue.

Payment: $35-$100 and 2 contributor's copies. $5 charge for extras.

Terms: Pays on acceptance for first North American serial rights. Rarely buys reprints. Publication copyrighted.

Advice: "Read several issues of *Pulpsmith* to get a handle on it. Submit strong writing that avoids clichews—both in language and situation, and which goes beyond the genre in which it functions."

THE P.U.N. (PLAY ON WORDS) (II), The Silly Club and Michael Rayner, Box 536-583, Orlando FL 32853. (305)898-0463. Editor: Danno Sullivan. Newsletter: 4-6 pages; cartoons. "All polite humor. Polite, meaning no foul language, sex, etc. As a joke, something like 'Child Abuse with Dr. Seuss' is OK. We have an intelligent readership. They don't mind puzzling a bit to get the joke, but they also enjoy plain silliness." Published "when possible" (average bimonthly). Estab. 1982. Circ. 250.

Needs: Humor/satire. Receives 20 unsolicited fiction mss/month. Accepts 1-3 mss/issue; 10-20 mss/year. Publishes ms "usually next issue" after acceptance. Length: short shorts, 1 page or less. Sometimes critiques rejected mss.

How to Contact: Send complete ms with cover letter. Reports in 2-3 weeks. SASE. Simultaneous, photocopied and reprint submissions OK. Accepts computer printouts, including dot-matrix. Sample copy for #10 SAE and 2 first class stamps.

Payment: Pays $1 minimum, $15 maximum; contributor's copies.

Terms: Pays on acceptance for one-time rights. Publication copyrighted

Advice: "Keep it short. Keep it obviously (even if it's subtle) funny. Above all, don't write like Erma Bombeck."

QUARRY (II), Quarry Press, Box 1061, Kingston, Ontario K7L 4Y5 Canada. (613)548-8429. Editor-in-Chief: Bob Hilderley. Magazine: 5½x8½; 120 pages; #1 book 120 paper; 160 lb Curtis Tweed cover stock; illustrations; photos. "Quarterly anthology of new Canadian poetry, prose. Also includes graphics, photographs and book reviews. We seek readers interested in vigorous, disciplined, new Canadian writing." Published special fiction issue; plans another. Estab. 1952. Circ. 1,100.

Needs: Experimental, fantasy, literary, science fiction, serialized/excerpted novel and translations. "We do not want highly derivative or clichéd style." Receives 60-80 unsolicited fiction mss/month. Buys 4-5 mss/issue; 20 mss/year. Does not read in July. Less than 5% of fiction is agented. Recently published work by Diane Schoemperlen, David Helwig, Joan Fern Shaw. Published new writers within the last year. Length: 3,000 words average. Publishes short shorts. Usually critiques rejected mss and recommends other markets.

How to Contact: Send complete ms with SAE, IRC and brief bio. Photocopied submissions OK. Accepts computer printout submissions. Prefers letter-quality. Publishes ms an average of 3-6 months after acceptance. Sample copy $5 with 4x7 SAE and 41¢ Canadian postage or IRC.

Payment: $10/page; 1 year subscription to magazine and 1 contributor's copy.

Terms: Pays on publication for first North American serial rights.

Advice: "Read previous *Quarry* to see standard we seek. Read Canadian fiction to see Canadian trends. We seek aggressive experimentation which is coupled with competence (form, style) and stimulating subject matter. We also like traditional forms. Our annual prose issue (spring) is always a sellout. Many of our selections have been anthologized. Don't send US stamps or SASE. Use IRC. Submit with brief bio."

QUARRY WEST (II), Porter College, UCSC, Santa Cruz CA 95064. (408)429-2155 or 429-2951. Editor: Kenneth Weisner. Fiction Editors: Kathy Chetkovich and Thad Nodine. Magazine: 6¾x8¼; 120 pages; 60 lb stock opaque paper; cover stock varies with cover art; illustrations sometimes; photos. Magazine of fiction, poetry, general nonfiction, art, graphics for a general audience. Semiannually. Estab. 1971. Circ. 750.

Needs: Traditional, experimental. Accepts 2-5 mss/issue; 4-10 mss/year. Length: 6,000 words maximum. Occasionally critiques rejected ms.

How to Contact: Send complete ms with SASE. Photocopied submissions OK. Reports in 6 weeks on mss. Publishes ms an average of 1-3 months after acceptance. Does not read mss July and August. Sample copy $3.50.
Payment: 2 free contributor's copies.
Terms: Acquires first North American serial rights. Publication copyrighted. Sponsors fiction contest.
Advice: "We're interested in good writing—we've published first-time writers and experienced professionals. Don't submit material you are unsure of or perhaps don't like just for the sake of publication—only show your *best* work—read the magazine for a feeling of the kind of fiction we've published. Type double-spaced and legibly."

QUARTERLY WEST (II), University of Utah, 317 Olpin Union, Salt Lake City UT 84112. (801)581-3938. Editors: Tom Hazuka, Kevin J. Ryan. Fiction Editor: Bernie Wood. Magazine: 6x9; 150 + pages; 60 lb paper; 5-color cover stock; illustrations and photographs rarely. "We try to publish a variety of fiction by writers from all over the country. Our publication is aimed primarily at an educated audience which is interested in contemporary literature and criticism." Semiannually. "We sponsor biennial novella competition." Estab. 1976. Circ. 1,000.
Needs: Literary, contemporary, translations. Buys 4-6 mss/issue, 10-12 mss/year. Receives approximately 100 unsolicited fiction mss each month. Recently published work by Andre Dubus and Chuck Rosenthal; published new writers within the last year. No preferred length. Critiques rejected mss when there is time. Sometimes recommends other markets.
How to Contact: Send complete ms. Cover letters welcome. SASE. Accepts computer printout submissions. Prefers letter-quality. Reports in 2 months; "sooner, if possible." Sample copy for $4.50.
Payment: $25-$100.
Terms: Pays on publication for first North American serial rights. Publication copyrighted.
Advice: "Write a clear and unified story which does not rely on tricks or gimmicks for its effects." Mss are rejected because of "poor style, formula writing, clichés, weak characterization. We solicit quite frequently, but tend more toward the surprises—unsolicited. Don't send more than one story per submission, but submit as often as you like."

QUEEN'S QUARTERLY (II), A Canadian Review, John Watson Hall, Queen's University, Kingston, Ontario K7L 3N6 Canada. (613)545-2667. Editors: Ms. Martha Bailey and Dr. Clive Thomson. Magazine: 6x9; 996 pages/year; 50 lb Zephyr antique paper; 65 lb Mayfair antique britewhite cover stock; illustrations. "A general interest intellectual review, featuring articles on science, politics, humanities, arts and letters. Extensive book reviews, some poetry and fiction." Published quarterly. Estab. 1893. Circ. 1,700.
Needs: Adventure, contemporary, experimental, fantasy, historical (general), humor/satire, literary, mainstream, science fiction and women's. "Special emphasis on work by Canadian writers." Buys 2 mss/issue; 8 mss/year. Recently published work by Joyce Carol Oates; published new writers within the last year. Length: 5,000 words maximum.
How to Contact: "Send complete ms—only one at a time—with SASE." Photocopied submissions OK if not part of multiple submission. Accepts computer printout submissions. Prefers letter-quality. Reports in 8 weeks. Sample copy $5.
Payment: $25-$150, 2 contributor's copies and 1-year subscription. $5 charge for extras.
Terms: Pays on publication for first North American serial rights. Sends galleys to author. Publication copyrighted.
Advice: "Don't be afraid to go over the boundaries imposed by your background, education, etc."

‡QUIMBY (I,IV), Box 281, Astor Station, Boston MA 02123. (617)723-5360. Editors: S. Thomas Svymbersky/Gerry Kaczolowski. Fiction Editor: S. Thomas Svymbersky. Magazine: 8½x11; 60 pages; 60 lb paper; 65 lb card cover; illustrations; photos. "*Quimby* is primarily a magazine of visual arts which includes interviews and articles of interest to artists. All art and writing printed must be by authors or artists living in the Boston area." Quarterly. Estab. 1985. Circ. 1,000.
Needs: Condensed/excerpted novel, contemporary, erotica, ethnic, experimental, feminist, gay, humor/satire, mainstream, prose poem, psychic/supernatural/occult, regional, suspense/mystery. "Looking for experimental fiction on any theme." Receives 10-15 mss/month. Accepts 2-3 mss/issue; 10-12 mss/year. Publishes ms within 2-4 months of acceptance. Length: 250 words minimum; 5,000 words maximum. Sometimes critiques rejected mss and recommends other markets.
How to Contact: Send complete mss with or without cover letter. Reports in 4-6 weeks on mss. SASE. Simultaneous and photocopied submissions OK. Accepts computer printout submissions, including dot-matrix. Sample copy for $3; fiction guidelines free.
Payment: Pays in contributor's copies.
Terms: Acquires one-time rights. Publication copyrighted.
Advice: "Although *Quimby* is primarily a magazine that prints visual art, we also print a few stories

each issue, and the fiction does not have to have anything to do with art. We lean towards more experimental and surrealistic themes and styles, but the main criteria is that the writing be good and the story entertaining. Authors must be from the Boston area before we will consider them, and we often ask writers to appear and read their work aloud at special events. We welcome submissions from any writers in the Boston area, but we will only print work that shows a solid grasp of the language. Besides short stories we have also printed plays and prose poems and welcome writing that is not easily categorized."

‡**QUINTESSENTIAL SPACE DEBRIS (I, IV)**, Box 42, Worthington OH 43085. Editor: Kathleen Gallagher. Fiction Editor: Michael Carroll. Newsletter: 8½x11; illustrations and photographs. "Humorous articles, anecdotes, parodies of book reviews or movie reviews, serious articles about the use of humor in science-fiction books and movies. For fans and readers of science fiction and fantasy, comic books and media." Semiannually. Plans special fiction issue. Estab. 1987. Circ. 500.
Needs: Fantasy, humor/satire, science fiction. No "Star Trek, Star Trek The Next Generation, or Dr. Who pastiches using established television and movie characters." Receives "not many" unsolicited mss/month. Publishes ms 6 months-1 year after acceptance. Publishes short shorts. Sometimes critiques rejected mss.
How to Contact: Query first or send complete ms with cover letter. Reports in 2 months on queries; 3 months on mss. SASE for query, not needed for ms. Simultaneous, photocopied and reprint submissions OK. Accepts computer printout submissions, including dot-matrix. Sample copy for 9x12 SAE and 4 first class stamps. Fiction guidelines for #10 SAE and 1 first class stamp.
Payment: Free subscription to magazine and contributor's copies.
Terms: All rights revert on publication. Publication copyrighted.
Advice: "Keep writing; keep submitting; learn from your errors; make us laugh!"

‡**THE RADDLE MOON (II)**, 9060 Ardmore Dr., Sidney, British Columbia V8L 3S1 Canada. (604)656-4045. Editor: Susan Clark. Magazine: 9x6; 140 pages; good white paper. "Publishes language-centered and 'new lyric' poetry; fiction; essays; statements concerning new poetics; nonfiction; photos and graphics." Semiannually. Plans special fiction issue. Estab. 1985. Circ. 700.
Needs: Experimental, literary, prose poem, translations. No adventure, romance or any other purely action-oriented writing. Receives 20 unsolicited fiction mss/month. Recently published work by Marja-Liisa Vartio, Alexei Remizov, Luis Dominguez. No preferred length. Publishes short shorts. Sometimes critiques rejected mss.
How to Contact: Send complete ms with cover letter, which should include "some indication that the writer has read the magazine." Reports in 8 weeks. SASE. Photocopied submissions OK. Accepts dot-matrix computer printouts. Sample copy $4.
Payment: No payment.
Terms: Publication copyrighted.
Advice: "Our chief concern is that the writer has read the magazine. While *raddle moon* will look at a broad spectrum of types of writing, it has a definite appeal for writers of experimental forms of literature, and those who like to debate such literature in essays, etc. Enclose an SASE. Don't hang back—we like to hear from you."

RAG MAG (II), Box 12, Goodhue MN 55027. (612)923-4590. Editor: Beverly Voldseth. Magazine: 5½x8½; 60 pages; varied paper quality; illustrations; photos. "We are eager to print poetry, prose and art work. We are open to all styles." Semiannually. Estab. 1982. Circ. 200.
Needs: Adventure, comics, contemporary, erotica, ethnic, experimental, fantasy, feminist, literary, mainstream, prose poem, regional. "Anything well written is a possibility. No extremely violent or pornographic writing." Receives 5 unsolicited mss each month. Accepts 1-2 mss/issue. Recently published work by Mark Bowers, Joseph Ugoretz, Graham Young; published new writers within the last year. Length: 1,000 words average; 2,200 words maximum. Occasionally critiques rejected mss. Sometimes recommends other markets.
How to Contact: Send complete ms. Reports in 2 months. SASE. Simultaneous, photocopied and previously published submissions OK. Accepts computer printout submissions. Prefers letter-quality. Single copy $3.
Payment: 1 contributor's copy; $3 charge for extras.
Terms: Acquires one-time rights. Publication copyrighted.
Advice: "Submit clean copy on regular typing paper (no tissue-thin stuff). We want fresh images, sparse language, words that will lift us out of our chairs. I like the short story form. I think it's powerful and has a definite place in the literary magazine."

RaJAH (I,II), The Rackham Journal of the Arts and Humanities, 411 Mason Hall, University of Michigan, Ann Arbor MI 48109. Fiction Editors: Patricia Armstrong, Daniel Goldberg, Juliette Grievell, Catharine Krieps, Thomas Mussio. Magazine: 6x9; approx. 100 pages; 60 lb off-white stock; 10 pt, perfect bound cover; illustrations and photos. "Our interest is in quality poetry, short fiction, essays, criticism and translations by new and established authors who are mostly graduate students at the University of Michigan, for an educated reading public." Annually. Estab. 1971. Circ. 500.

Needs: Adventure, confession, contemporary, ethnic, experimental, fantasy, feminist, historical (general), horror, humor/satire, lesbian, literary, mainstream, regional, serialized/excerpted novel, translations. No children's, pornographic or obscene fiction. Receives 2 unsolicited mss/month. Accepts approximately 1 ms/issue from author outside University of Michigan. Publishes ms no more than 2 years after acceptance. Recently published work by Gail Gilliland; published new writers within the last year. Length: 2,500 words average; 5,000 words maximum. Critiques rejected mss. Occasionally recommends other markets.

How to Contact: Send complete ms with cover letter, which should include date, brief bio, publications record (if any). Reports on mss in 6-10 months. SASE. Photocopied submissions OK. Accepts computer printout submissions, including dot-matrix. Accepts electronic submissions compatible with Apple Macintosh (preferred), or IBM compatible floppy disk using Microsoft Word. Sample copy for $1.50, 6½x9½ SAE and 95¢ postage.

Terms: Publication copyrighted.

Advice: "We are especially interested in material focusing on social issues and current culture, and we are always on the lookout for manuscripts by unpublished authors. We believe that both fiction and scholarly articles reflect that kind of work being produced by talented young people around the world. *RaJAH* is primarily a graduate student publication but accepts a limited number of manuscripts from unsolicited authors."

RAMBUNCTIOUS REVIEW (II), Rambunctious Press, Inc., 1221 W. Pratt Blvd., Chicago IL 60626. (312)338-2439. Editors: Mary Dellutri, Richard Goldman, Beth Hausler and Nancy Lennon. Magazine: 7½x10; 48 pages; b&w illustrations and photos. "Quality literary magazine publishing short dramatic works, poetry and short stories for general audience." Annually. Estab. 1984. Circ. 500.

Needs: Adventure, contemporary, erotica, ethnic, experimental, feminist, historical, humor/satire, literary, mainstream, prose poem and contemporary romance. No murder mysteries. Receives 10-20 unsolicited mss/month. Accepts 6 mss/year. Does not read June 1-August 31. Recently published work by Neal Lulops, Rod Kessler, Ronald Levitsky; published new writers within the last year. Length: 15 page maximum. Publishes short shorts. Occasionally comments on rejected mss.

How to Contact: Send complete ms. Reports in 2 months on mss. SASE. Simultaneous and photocopied submissions OK. Accepts computer printout submissions. Prefers letter-quality. Sample copy $4.

Payment: 2 contributor's copies.

Terms: Acquires first rights. Publication copyrighted.

Advice: "We sponsor a yearly fiction contest in the fall. Send SASE for details. Fiction lives—if you can grasp the essentials of fiction, you can recreate a bit of life."

THE RAMPANT GUINEA PIG (II), A Magazine of Fantasy & Subcreative Fiction, 20500 Enadia Way, Canoga Park CA 91306. Editor-in-Chief: Mary Ann Hodge. Magazine: 8½x11; 30 pages; 20 lb stock; illustrations. "Though we emphasize fantasy fiction, we also publish some poetry and material relating to the life and works of Donald K. Grundy. Our readers are literate and well read in fantasy. Many have an interest in children's literature." Published biannually. Estab. 1978. Circ. 100.

Needs: Fantasy, science fantasy and religious fantasy (Christian or otherwise). "Humorous, satire, parody and pastiche okay. All stories should be rated G or PG. No sword and sorcery/barbarian fiction, no *Star Trek* or *Star Wars* stories. I'm particularly looking for mythopoeic and subcreative fantasy, high fantasy, and stories that convey a sense of wonder and the proximity of faerie." Receives 4-8 unsolicited fiction mss/month. Prefers letter-quality or legible dot-matrix. Accepts 5-7 mss/issue; 10-14 mss/year. Recently published work by Patricia Flinn, Linda Woeltjen; published new writers within the last year. Length: 8,000 words maximum; 5,000 words average (serials may be longer); also publishes short shorts. Occasionally critiques rejected mss. Sometimes recommends other markets.

How to Contact: Send complete ms with SASE. Photocopied submissions OK. Accepts computer printout submissions. Accepts disk submissions compatible with Macintosh Plus. Reports in 6 weeks on mss. Sample copy $3, checks payable to Mary Ann Hodge. Fiction guidelines with #10 SAE and 1 first class stamp.

Payment: 2 contributor's copies. $3 charge for extras.

Terms: Pays on publication for first North American serial rights. Publication copyrighted.

Advice: "I'm publishing more fiction per issue. Read as much fantasy as you can. But don't try to clone Tolkien. Remember that tight plotting and believable characterization and dialogue are essential in fantasy. And read one or more issues of *The Rampant Guinea Pig* before submitting so you'll know the niche we occupy in the genre. At least send for the fiction guidelines. I'm always looking for humorous stories to balance the more serious ones."

‡**RANSOM (I, II)**, Box 1386, Columbia SC 29202. Editor: Alan Howard. Magazine: 5½x8; 32 pages; some illustrations. "contemporary poetry and prose." Quarterly. Estab. 1987. Circ. 200.
Needs: Contemporary, erotica, ethnic, experimental, fantasy, gay, humor/satire, lesbian, prose poem. "Fiction for *Ransom* must be very short, very tight, and a little off-beat. Also interested in short incidental pieces such as journal or letter excerpts." Receives 3-5 unsolicited mss/month. Buys 1-3 mss/issue; 4-12 mss/year. Publishes ms 6 months maximum after acceptance. Recently published work by Cliff Burns, Paul Milenski, Bennie Lee Sinclair. Length: 400 words maximum. Sometimes critiques rejected mss.
How to Contact: Send complete ms with cover letter. Reports in 4 weeks. SASE. Accepts computer printout submissions, including dot-matrix. Sample copy for $3. Fiction guidelines for #10 SAE and 1 first class stamp.
Payment: Pays in contributor's copies.
Terms: Acquires one-time rights. Publication copyrighted.
Advice: "We prefer experimental fiction, but it should be accessible."

‡**READ ME (II)**, 1118 Hoyt Ave., Everett WA 98201. (206)259-0804. Editor: Ron Fleshman. Fiction Editors: Linda McMichael and Kay Nelson. Tabloid: 11x17; over 16 pages; newsprint paper and cover; illustrations. "Entertainment and ideas in an accessible format. Fiction, articles, essays, poetry, reviews, puzzles, cartoons." For "grassroots middle America." Quarterly. Plans special fiction issue. Estab. 1988. Circ. 1,000.
Needs: Adventure, confession, contemporary, ethnic, fantasy, feminist, historical (general), horror, humor/satire, mainstream, romance (contemporary and historical), science fiction, excerpted novel, suspense/mystery, translations, western. No academic fiction. Receives approximately 100 mss/month. Buys 7 mss/issue; 30 mss/year. Publishes ms within 3-5 months of acceptance. Length: 1,500 words average; 100 words minimum; 2,500 words maximum. Publishes short shorts. Length: "Less is more—if well made." Sometimes critiques rejected mss and recommends other markets.
How to Contact: Send complete ms. Reports in 3 months. SASE. "No queries on fiction." Accepts computer printout submissions, including dot-matrix. Accepts electronic submissions via disk only PC 5¼ ASCII file. Sample copy for $1.50. Fiction guidelines for #10 SAE and 1 first class stamp.
Payment: Pays $1-$20 and contributor's copies. Charge for extra copies.
Terms: Pays on publication for first North American serial rights and one-time rights. Publication copyrighted. Some contests are planned.
Advice: "Magazine fiction reflects editor's best guess of readers' tastes and interests. Writers are the prophets, poets, saints and madmen of society and through their work, redefine and reshape the world. To clip their work to fit available space and target specific reader may be hard to accept—but that's how it works. Write for *our* readers. Be as honest as you can with yourself and fake the remainder. Don't tell the reader a story—enlist him and allow him to share the storymaking with you. Cut every word not required."

REAL FICTION (II), 298 9th Ave., San Francisco CA 94118. (415)387-3412. Editor: Genevieve Belfiglio. Co-editor: Carol Tarlen. Magazine: 5x7; 80 pages; glossy cover. "We publish a variety of serious fiction and are open to experimentation, both stylistically and thematically, as well as traditional forms and subjects, for a literary audience." Irregularly. Estab. 1982. Circ. 500.
Needs: Contemporary, erotica, ethnic, experimental, fantasy, feminist, gay, lesbian, literary, regional, serialized/excerpted novel, translations. "We don't like pornography or stories that demean women, children and people of different classes, races or religions." No science fiction, mystery, horror, romance. Receives 30 unsolicited mss/month. Accepts 10-12 mss/issue. Publishes ms 6-12 months after acceptance. Recently published work by Lisa Ruffolo, Sarah McAulay, Selby Coffin; published new writers within the last year. Length: 2,500 words average; 250 words minimum; 100,000 words maximum. Occasionally critiques rejected mss and recommends other markets.
How to Contact: Send complete ms with cover letter, which should include a description of previous publications. Reports in 2-6 weeks. SASE. Photocopied submissions OK. Accepts computer printout submissions, no dot-matrix. Sample copy for $4. Fiction guidelines for #10 SAE and 1 first class stamp.
Payment: Pays in contributor's copies.
Terms: Acquires one-time rights. Publication copyrighted.
Advice: "The best magazine fiction is in the small presses—not necessarily the academic press—but the little magazines that publish punk, women's, gay, working class, Third World and just plain good fiction. The variety and liveliness of these magazines make literature exciting, vital and relevant even in today's world of videos and rock. The mainstream magazines are boring and not as good as they were 10 years ago."

‡THE REAPER (II), Story Line Press, 325 Ocean View Ave., Santa Cruz CA 95062. (408)426-5539. "All fiction correspondence should be sent to Tom Wilhelmus, English Department, University of Southern Indiana, Evansville IN 47712." Editors: Robert McDowell and Mark Jarman. Fiction Editor: Tom Wilhelmus. Magazine: 5½x8½; 64-90 pages; 50 lb paper; enamel/80 lb cover; occasional illustrations. "Primarily interested in narrative poetry and essays about poetry, but prints fiction." Estab. 1981. Circ. 700.
Needs: Contemporary, erotica, ethnic, experimental, feminist, gay, humor/satire, lesbian, literary. Receives 25 mss/month. Accepts 1 mss/issue; 3 mss/year. Publishes ms within 1 year of acceptance. Agented fiction 5%. Recently published work by Barbara Haas, Gail Harper. No preferred word length. Publishes short shorts. Sometimes critiques rejected mss and recommends other markets.
How to Contact: Query first. Reports on queries in 2 weeks; on mss in 4 weeks. SASE. Photocopied submissions OK. No dot-matrix. Sample copy for $5, 6x9 SAE and 90¢ postage. Fiction guidelines for #10 SAE and 1 first class stamp.
Payment: Pays in contributor's copies.
Terms: Acquires one-time rights. Sometimes sends galleys to authors. Publication copyrighted. Occasionally sponsors contests for fiction writers. "Read the magazine for guidelines."

RED BASS (I, II), Red Bass Productions, 2425 Burgundy St, New Orleans LA 70117. Editor: Jay Murphy. Magazine: 8½x11; 72 pages; 60 lb offset paper; illustrations and photos. "Strongly progressive arts publication—interviews, fiction, poetry, reviews, essays that further social struggle." Irregularly. Estab. 1981. Circ. 3,000.
Needs: "We publish a variety of fiction, translations and excerpts from novels in progress—all committed to social change in one sense or another." Receives 3-5 unsolicited fiction mss/month. Accepts 1 ms/issue; 4-5 mss/year. Publishes ms in variable time after acceptance. Recently published work by Kathy Acker, James Purdy, Lucian Truscott; published new writers within the last year. Length: 1,500 words average; 500 words minimum; 3,000 words maximum. Also publishes short shorts. Sometimes critiques rejected mss and recommends other markets.
How to Contact: Send complete manuscript with cover letter. Reports in 4 weeks or more on queries; 2 months on mss. SASE for ms. Simultaneous submissions OK. Accepts computer printouts including dot-matrix. Sample copy $5.
Payment: Free contributor's copies; sometimes cash as funds allow.
Terms: Acquires first North American serial rights. Publication copyrighted.
Advice: "We plan to publish more fiction in special contexts and thematic issues. We appreciate vigorous, innovative work with integrity that also helps further critical understanding and awareness of the surrounding social, cultural, political realities."

RED CEDAR REVIEW (II), Dept. of English, Morrill Hall, Michigan State University, East Lansing MI 48825. (517)355-7570. Contact: Fiction Editor. Magazine: 8½x5½; 60-80 pages; quality b&w illustrations; good b&w photos. Theme: "literary—poetry, fiction, book reviews, one-act plays, interviews, graphics." Biannually. Estab. 1963. Circ. 400 + .
Needs: Literary, feminist, regional and humorous. Accepts 3-4 mss/issue, 6-10 mss/year. Does not read mss in summer. Published new writers within the last year. Length: 500-7,000 words.
How to Contact: Send complete ms with SASE. Reports in 2 months on mss. Publishes ms up to 4 months after acceptance. Sample copy $2.
Payment: 2 free author's copies. $2.50 charge for extras.
Terms: Acquires first rights.
Advice: "Read the magazine and good literary fiction. There are many good writers out there who need a place to publish, and we try to provide them with that chance for publication. We prefer short stories that are experimental and take risks. Make your style unique—don't get lost in the mainstream work of the genre."

THE REDNECK REVIEW OF LITERATURE (II, IV), Box 730, Twin Falls ID 83301. (208)734-6653. Editor: Penelope Reedy. Magazine: 7x10; 80 pages; offset paper; cover varies from semi-glossy to felt; illustrations; photos. "I consider *Redneck* to be one of the few—perhaps the only—magazines in the West seeking to bridge the gap between literate divisions. My aim is to provide literature from and to the diverse people in the western region. *Redneck* is not a political publication and takes no sides on such issues. Readership is extremely eclectic, including ranchers, farmers, university professors, writers, poets, activists, civil engineers, BLM conservation officers, farm wives, attorneys, judges, truck drivers." Biannually. Estab. 1975. Circ. 500.
Needs: "Publishes poetry, fiction, plays, essays, book reviews and folk pieces. *Redneck* deals strictly with a contemporary viewpoint/perspective, though the past can be evoked to show the reader how we got here. Nothing too academic or sentimental reminiscences. I am not interested in old-time wild west gunfighter stories." Receives 10 "or so" unsolicited mss/month. Receives 4-5 mss/issue. Recently

published work by Rafael Zepeda, Clay Reynolds and Gerald Haslam; published new writers within the last year. Length: 1,000 words minimum; 2,500 words maximum.
How to Contact: Send complete ms. SASE. No simultaneous submissions. Reprint submissions from established writers OK. Sample copy for $6 with $1 postage.
Payment: Contributor's copies.
Terms: Rights returned to author on publication. Publication copyrighted.
Advice: "Use strong sense of place. Give characters action, voices. Tell the truth rather than sentimentalize."

‡**REFLECTIONS (II, IV)**, Journalism Class, Box 368, Duncan Falls OH 43734. (614)674-5209. Editor: Dean Harper. Magazine: 8½x11; 32 pages; "very good" paper; "excellent" cover stock; illustrations; photos. Publishes "good wholesome stories primarily for 10-18 year olds." Estab. 1980. Circ. 1,000.
Needs: Adventure, juvenile, religious/inspirational, science fiction, senior citizen/retirement, prose poem, spiritual, sports, suspense/mystery, western, young adult/teen (10-18 years). Receives 10-20 mss/month. Accepts 1-5 mss/issue; 2-10 mss/year. Publishes ms within 1-5 months of acceptance. Recently published work by Celia and Melissa Pinson, Michelle Hurst, Natasha Snitkovsky; pulblished new writers within the last year. Length: 500 words minimum; 5,000 words maximum. Publishes short shorts. Sometimes critiques rejected mss and recommends other markets.
How to Contact: Send complete mss with cover letter. Reports in 2 weeks. SASE. Simultaneous, photocopied and reprint submissions OK. Accepts computer printout submissions, including dot-matrix. Sample copy for $2, #10 SAE and 1 first class stamp. Fiction guidelines for #10 SAE and 1 first class stamp.
Payment: Pays in contributor's copies.
Terms: Acquires one-time rights. Publication copyrighted.
Advice: "We always welcome good writing. Please avoid overuse of 'got.' Keep sending your writing. Read it first to others for opinions. Ask for suggestions from editors."

‡**THE REFORMED JOURNAL (II)**, William B. Eerdmans Publishing Co., 255 Jefferson Ave. S.E., Grand Rapids MI 49503. (616)459-4591. Editor: Mr. Jon Pott. Magazine: 8½x10¾; 32 pages; good quality offset paper; self cover. "The *R.J.* is a religious magazine of opinion in which the contributors comment on church and society from the perspective of Reformed (Calvinistic) Protestantism. Publishes personal reflection, scholarly discussions of current issues, reviews, poems, short stories. For a well-educated readership—both clergy and laity—among evangelical and mainline Christians." Monthly. Estab. 1951. Circ. 3,000.
Needs: Religious. Receives 2 mss/month. Accepts 1 mss/issue; 4-5 mss/year. Recently published work by Lawrence Dorr and Virginia Stem Owens. Publishes short shorts. Sometimes critiques rejected mss and occasionally recommends other markets.
How to Contact: Send complete mss with cover letter. Reports in 4 weeks on queries; in 2-6 weeks on mss. Photocopied submissions OK. Accepts computer printout submissions, including dot-matrix. Free sample copy.
Payment: No payment.
Terms: Publication copyrighted.

‡**RENAISSANCE FAN (I, II, IV)**, 2214 SE 53rd, Portland OR 97215. (503)235-0668. Magazine: 8½x11; 15-30 pages; illustrations and photos. "This is an amateur fanzine (fan magazine) related to science fiction and fantasy. Each issue has a theme." Readers are "science fiction and fantasy fans." Quarterly. Estab. 1988. Circ. 150.
Needs: Fantasy, science fiction. "We do not promote abuse and violence." Receives 3 unsolicited mss/month. Accepts up to 4 mss/issue. Publishes ms in next issue that relates to theme. Recently published work by Eleanor Malin, Dennis Hoggatt; published new writers within the last year. Length: 5,000 words preferred; 600 words minimum; 15,000 words maximum. Publishes short shorts. Sometimes critiques rejected mss and recommends other markets.
How to Contact: "It is best to query, but if not, find out what the themes are—a phone call is OK—no calls after 8:00 PST." Reports in weeks. SASE for ms. Simultaneous and photocopied submissions OK "must know where and when." Accepts computer printout submissions, including dot-matrix and electronic submission in ASCII, Kaypro CP/M or IBM PC. Sample copy for 9x12 SAE and 65¢. Fiction guidelines free.
Payment: Free subscription to magazine.
Terms: Acquires one-time rights. Publication copyrighted.
Advice: "Readers are not mind readers. A tree is not just a tree. It is a birch or an elm or a maple. A car is an Olds, a Ford, a Chevy, a Mustang, a Pinto, etc. Be visual—use colors, sounds, smells, tastes. Appeal to the senses. Write an active story, not just a passive one. Practice. Rewrite. Submit. Listen to what you have written. Read it aloud. Know your subject. Look at what is happening around you. An every-

day activity can be turned into a fantasy or science fiction story. Do not use two words where one will do—edit, edit, edit. Become a storyteller. Don't give up.''

RESPONSE (II, IV), A Contemporary Jewish Review, Queens College Press, 27 W. 20th St., 9th Floor, New York NY 10011. (212)675-1168. Editor: Cindy Rubin. Magazine: 6x9; 96 pages; 70 lb paper; 10 pt. CIS cover; illustrations; photos. Fiction, poetry and essays with a Jewish theme, for Jewish students and young adults. Quarterly. Estab. 1967. Circ. 2,500.
Needs: Contemporary, ethnic, experimental, feminist, historical (general), humor/satire, literary, prose poem, regional, religious/inspirational, spiritual, translations. "Nothing without some specific Jewish content." Receives 10-12 unsolicited mss/month. Accepts 5 mss/issue; 20 mss/year. Publishes ms 7-12 months after acceptance. Length: 15-20 pages (double spaced). Publishes short shorts. Sometimes critiques rejected mss and recommends other markets.
How to Contact: Send complete ms with cover letter, which include brief biography of author. Reports in 6 weeks on mss. SASE. Simultaneous and photocopied submissions OK. Accepts computer printout submissions; no dot-matrix. Free sample copy.
Payment: Pays in contributor's copies.
Terms: Publication copyrighted.

RIGHT HERE (I, II), The Hometown Magazine, Box 1014, Huntington IN 46750. (219)356-4223. Editor: Emily Jean Carroll. Magazine: 8½x11; 44-48 pages; illustrations; b&w photos. General family magazine for readers of all ages but primarily 40-plus. Bimonthly. Estab. 1984. Circ. 2,000.
Needs: Contemporary, humor/satire, mainstream, religious/inspirational, prose poem, spiritual, suspense/mystery. "We do not want fiction that has explicit sex or violence." Receives 18-20 unsolicited mss/month. Buys 1-3 mss/issue; 8-12 mss/year. Publishes ms 3-6 months after acceptance. Recently published work by Daphne Simpkins, Susan Varno, Shirley Wilcox; published new writers within the last year. Length: 2,000 words average; 1,000 words minimum; 2,500 words maximum. Occasionally critiques rejected mss and recommends other markets.
How to Contact: Send complete ms with cover letter. No queries please. "We're more interested in knowing about the writer than the writer's credits." Reports in 6-8 weeks on mss. SASE for ms. Simultaneous and photocopied submissions OK. Accepts computer printout submissions. Sample copy for $1.25. Fiction guidelines for #10 SAE and 1 first class stamp.
Payment: Pays 1¢/word-$25 maximum.
Terms: Pays on publication for first rights, first North American serial rights and one-time rights. Publication copyrighted.
Advice: "I like a story to have beginning, a middle and an end."

RIPPLES MAGAZINE (II) 1426 Las Vegas Dr., Ann Arbor MI 48103. Editor: Karen M. Schaefer. Short story and poetry magazine. Magazine: 8½x11; 50+ pages. Estab. 1973.
Needs: Contemporary, literary. No work that is superficial, weird or gratuitously obscene. No horror. Accepts 2-4 mss/issue. Recently published work by Scott Abbott, Jane Andrews and Rachel Cann. Published new writers within the last year. Length: 1,500 words minimum; 8,200 words maximum. Occasionally comments on a rejected ms.
How to Contact: Send complete ms with cover letter. "Cover letters can be helpful in evaluating the writer's overall commitment to writing. In this way, we then get a sense of the writer's willingness to correct weaknesses in the story that's been submitted." Reports in 1 week. SASE. Simultaneous and photocopied submissions OK. Accepts computer printout submissions. Writer's guidelines for #10 SAE and 1 first class stamp. Sample copy $4.75.
Payment: Pays 1 contributor's copy.
Advice: "We've noticed we are using more fiction writers than ever before, perhaps because the quality of the manuscripts has improved. Don't get discouraged. Your material may be rejected not because of its own quality, but because it simply may not fit in with the publisher's plans or previous usage record. Remember that plot and characterization are the engines that move your story along. If they are weak, your story will stall."

‡RIVERWIND (II,IV), General Studies/Hocking Technical College, Nelsonville OH 45764. (614)753-3591 (ext. 2375). Editor: Audrey Naffziger. Associate Editor: Ruth Reilly. Magazine: 6x9; 60 lb paper; cover illustrations. "College press, small literary magazine." Annually. Estab. 1975.
Needs: Adventure, contemporary, erotica, ethnic, feminist, historical (general), horror, humor/satire, literary, mainstream, prose poem, spiritual, sports, regional, translations, western. No juvenile/teen fiction. Receives 3-5 mss/month. Recently published work by Lee Martin, Roy Bentley, Kate Hancock; published new writers within the last year. Sometimes critiques rejected mss.
How to Contact: Send complete mss with cover letter. Reports on mss in 3 weeks-3 months. SASE. Photocopied submissions OK.

Payment: Pays in contributor's copies.
Advice: "Your work must be strong, entertaining. It helps if you are an Ohio/West Virginia writer. We hope to print more fiction."

ROANOKE REVIEW (II), Roanoke College, English Department, Salem VA 24153. (703)389-2351. Editor: Robert R. Walter. Magazine: 6x9; 40-60 pages. Semiannually. Estab. 1967. Circ. 300.
Needs: Receives 30-40 unsolicited mss/month. Accepts 2-3 mss/issue; 4-6 mss/year. Publishes ms 6 months after acceptance. Length: 2,500 words minimum; 7,500 words maximum. Publishes short shorts. Occasionally critiques rejected mss.
How to Contact: Send complete ms with cover letter. Reports in 1-2 weeks on queries; 8-10 weeks on mss. SASE for query. Photocopied submissions OK. Accepts computer printout submissions, including dot-matrix. Sample copy for $1.50.
Payment: Pays in contributor's copies.
Terms: Publication copyrighted.

ROHWEDDER (II, IV), International Journal of Literature & Art, Rough Weather Press, Box 29490, Los Angeles CA 90029. (213)256-5083. Editor: Hans-Jurgen Schacht. Fiction Editors: Nancy Locke and Nancy Antell. Magazine: 8½x11; 50+ pages; 20 lb paper; 90 lb cover; illustrations; photos. "Multilingual/cultural poetry and short stories. Graphic art and photography." Published 3-4 times/ year. Estab. 1986.
Needs: Contemporary, ethnic, experimental, feminist, humor/satire, literary, regional, translations. No fillers. Receives 20-50 unsolicited mss/month. Accepts 1-3 mss/issue; 6 mss/year. Publishes ms 1 month after acceptance. Length: 1,500-2,500 words average; 200 words minimum; 2,500 words maximum. Publishes short shorts. Sometimes critiques rejected mss and recommends other markets.
How to Contact: Reports in 2 weeks on queries; 2 months on mss. SASE. Photocopied submissions OK. Accepts computer printout submissions, including legible dot-matrix. Sample copy for $4.50.
Payment: Pays in contributor's copies, charges for extras.
Terms: Acquires one-time right.
Advice: "Go out as far as you have to but remember the basics: clear, concise style and form. Always enclose SASE."

ROOM OF ONE'S OWN (II), Growing Room Collective, Box 46160, Station G, Vancouver, British Columbia V6R 4G5 Canada. Editors: Gayla Reid, Jean Wilson, Jeannie Wexler, Mary Schendlinger, Robin Van Heck, Betty Wood and Eleanor Wachtel. Magazine: 5x6; 100 pages; bond paper; bond cover stock; illustrations; photos. Feminist literary: fiction, poetry, criticism, reviews. Readership: general, nonscholarly. Quarterly. Estab. 1975. Circ. 1,200.
Needs: Literary, feminist and lesbian. No "sexist or macho material." Buys 6 mss/issue. Receives approximately 40 unsolicited fiction mss each month. Approximately 2% of fiction is agented. Recently published work by Janette Turner Hospital, Anne E. Norman, Judith Monroe; published new writers within the last year. Length: 3,000 words preferred. "No critiques except under unusual circumstances."
How to Contact: Send complete ms with SASE or SAE and IRC. "Please include cover letter. State whether multiple submission or not (we don't consider multiple submissions) and whether previously published." Reports in 3 months. Publishes ms an average of 1-3 months after acceptance. Sample copy $2.75 with SASE or SAE and IRC.
Payment: $50 plus 2 free author's copies. $2 charge for extras.
Terms: Pays on publication for first rights. Publication copyrighted.
Advice: "Write well and unpretentiously." Mss are rejected because they are "unimaginative."

THE ROUND TABLE (II), A Journal of Poetry and Fiction, 375 Oakdale Dr., Rochester NY 14618. Editor: Alan and Barbara Lupack. Magazine: 6x9; 64 pages. "We publish serious poetry and fiction.' Annually. Estab. 1984. Circ. 150.
Needs: Experimental, literary, mainstream. "The quality of the fiction is the most important criterion. We would consider work in other categories if it were especially well written." Accepts 7-10 mss/year. Does not read ms July1-September 30. Published new writers within the last year. Publishes ms 9 months after acceptance. Publishes short shorts.
How to Contact: Send complete ms with cover letter. Reports usually in 2-3 months, but stories under consideration may be held longer. SASE for ms. Simultaneous submissions OK—if notified immediately upon acceptance elsewhere; photocopied submissions OK. Sample copy $4 (specify fiction issue). Fiction guidelines for 1 first class stamp.
Payment: Contributor's copy, charge for extras.
Advice: "In 1989 *TRT* will publish the second issue on the theme of 'King Arthur and His Knights' and so will only read fiction that retells or uses symbols or allusions from the Arthurian legends."

SALT LICK PRESS (II), Salt Lick Foundation, 1804 E. 38½ St., Austin TX 78722. Editor: James Haining. Magazine: 8½x11; 64 pages; 60 lb offset stock; 80 lb text cover; illustrations and photos. Irregular. Estab. 1969.

Needs: Contemporary, erotica, ethnic, experimental, feminist, gay, lesbian, literary. Receives 15 unsolicited mss each month. Accepts 2 mss/issue. Length: open. Occasionally critiques rejected mss.

How to Contact: Send complete ms with cover letter. Reports in 2 weeks on queries; 4 weeks on mss. SASE. Simultaneous, photocopied and reprint submissions OK. Accepts computer printout submissions, including dot-matrix. Sample copy $5, 9x12 SAE and 3 first class stamps.

Payment: Free contributor's copies.

Terms: Acquires first North American serial rights. Sends galleys to author. Publication copyrighted.

SAMISDAT (II), Box 129, Richford VT 05476. (514)263-4439. Editor: Merritt Clifton. Magazine: 8½x5½; 60-80 pages; offset bond paper; vellum bristol cover stock; illustrations; photos. Publication is "environmentalist, anti-war, anti-nuke, emphatically non-leftist—basically anarchist." Publishes essays, reviews, poetry and original artwork in approximately equal proportions. Audience consists of "people constructively and conscientiously engaged in changing the world." Subscribers include many secretaries, journalists, blue-collar workers and housewives "but very few bureaucrats." Quarterly. Estab. 1973. Circ. 300.

Needs: Adventure, contemporary, erotica, ethnic, experimental, fantasy, feminist, gay, historical (general), humor/satire, lesbian, literary, mainstream, prose poem, regional, science fiction, serialized/excerpted novel, sports, suspense/mystery, translations, western. "We're pretty damned eclectic if something is done well. Formula hackwork and basic ineptitude, though, won't ever hack it here. No whimsy; no self-indulgent whines about the difficulty of being a sensitive writer/artist." Receives approximately 10-100 unsolicited mss/month. Accepts 2-5 mss/issue. "We'd like to use a lot more than we're getting." Publishes ms 2-5 months after acceptance. Recently published work by Miriam Sagan, Thomas Michael McDade, Robert Swisher; published new writers within the last year. Length: 1,500-5,000 words. Publishes short shorts. Length: up to 1,000 words. Sometimes recommends other markets or critiques rejected mss.

How to Contact: Send complete ms with cover letter. "I like to know how old the author is, what he/she does for a living, and get a ballpark idea of writing experiences, but I do not want to see mere lists of credits. I also like to know why a writer is submitting here in particular." Reports in 1 week on queries and mss. SASE. Reprint submissions OK. "Does not read photocopies or multiple submissions of any kind." Accepts computer printout submissions, including dot-matrix. Sample copy $2.50.

Payment: Pays in contributor's copies.

Terms: Acquires one-time rights. Publication copyrighted.

Advice: "I'm editor, publisher, printer, distributor, and therefore I do as I damned well please. Over the past 14 years I've found enough other people who agree with me that short stories are worthwhile that my magazine manages to support itself, more or less in the tradition of the old-time radical magazines that published the now-classical short story writers. Know the factual background to your material, e.g., if writing a historical piece, get the details right."

SAN JOSE STUDIES (II), San Jose State University, One Washington Sq., San Jose CA 95152. Editor: Fauneil J. Rinn. Magazine: digest size; 112-144 pages; good paper and cover; occasional illustrations and photos. "A journal for the general, educated reader. Covers a wide variety of materials: fiction, poetry, interviews, interdisciplinary essays. Aimed toward the college-educated common reader with an interest in the broad scope of materials." Triannually. Estab. 1975. Circ. 500.

Needs: Literary, contemporary, humor, ethnic and regional. Accepts 1-2 mss/issue, 3-6 mss/year. Receives approximately 12 unsolicited fiction mss each month. Recently published work by Barbara La Porte, William Kanouse. Length: 2,500-5,000 + words. Critiques rejected mss when there is time. Sometimes recommends other markets.

How to Contact: Send complete ms with SASE. Accepts computer printout submissions. Prefers letter-quality. Reports in 2 months. Publishes ms an average of 6-12 months after acceptance. Sample copy for $5.

Payment: 2 free author's copies. Annual $100 award for best story, essay or poem.

Terms: Acquires first rights. Sends galleys to author. Publication copyrighted.

Advice: "Manuscripts read 'blind.' Name should appear *only* on cover sheet. We seldom print beginning writers of fiction. Proofread with great care. Have an interesting main character or interesting situation or both."

‡SCIENCE FICTION RANDOMLY (I, IV), Box 12705, Gainesville FL 32604. Editors: Hawk, Steve Antczak. Magazine: 8½x11; 32-48 pages; illustrations. "*SFRan* is a science fiction fanzine written by fans and intended for fans." Published "randomly"—4-6 issues per year. Plan special fiction issues/anthologies. Estab. 1987. Circ. 500.

Needs: Fantasy, horror, humor/satire, science fiction. "We publish all forms of SF, from psychological to cyberpunk. Avoid overused themes and 'tricky' endings. We would prefer instead to see more stories with well-developed characters. We are not interested in established-universe media fiction, except as parody—DO NOT send us any *Star Trek*, etc. fiction." Receives 1-2 unsolicited mss/month. Buys 4 mss/issue; 16-24 mss/year. Publishes ms average of 12 months after acceptance. Length: 3,500 words preferred; 10,000 maximum. Publishes short shorts Length: 500-1,500 words. Always critiques rejected mss and sometimes recommends other markets.

How to Contact: Send complete ms with cover letter. Cover letter should include "short bio, publishing history, or anything the author feels may be of interest." Reports in 2-3 weeks. SASE. Simultaneous, photocopied and reprint submissions OK. Accepts computer printout submissions, including dot-matrix. Accepts electronic submissions on 5¼" or 3½" disks in IBM format. Sample copy for $1. Fiction guidelines for SASE.

Payment: Pays in contributor's copies.

Terms: Acquires one-time rights. Publication copyrighted. Authors retain copyright for fiction.

Advice: "Science Fiction is the easiest field for a new writer to break into, and the way to start is through fanzines. Fanzines give writers a forum for their work and an opportunity for criticism while still perfecting their style. Many of today's best-known pros started out in fanzines, and many of them *still* write for fanzines. Read science fiction. Know the market—SFanzines, particularly *SFRan*, are very different from the typical small-press magazine. Don't send us media-based stories unless they're parodies, and DON'T send us stories with trick endings—I promise to be very, very mean to the next person who sends me a story about two space travellers who are marooned on Earth and who turn out to be Adam and Eve."

‡SCREAM MAGAZINE (II), fiction in a fantastic vein, Alternating Crimes (AC) Publishing, Box 10363, Raleigh NC 27605. (919)834-7542. Editor: Russell Boone. 8¼x10½; 76-96 pages; 24 lb bond/60 lb offset paper; 80 lb uncoated cover; illustrations and photographs. "We publish a full range of fiction from traditional to avant garde. Readers are college and professionals interested in the underground arts movement." Quarterly. Plans special fiction issue. Estab. 1985. Circ. 1,200.

Needs: Adventure, confessions, contemporary, erotica, ethnic, experimental, fantasy, feminist, gay, historical (general), horror, humor/satire, lesbian, literary, psychic/supernatural/occult, regional, science fiction, serialized/excerpted novel, suspense/mystery. No religious fiction. Receives 6-12 unsolicited mss/month. Accepts 3-5 mss/issue; 12-20 mss/year. Does not read mss in December. Publishes ms 3-6 months after acceptance. Length: 2,500 words preferred; 900 words minimum; 4,000 words maximum. Sometimes critiques rejected mss and recommends other markets.

How to Contact: Send complete ms with cover letter. Reports in 3 weeks on queries; 6 weeks on mss. SASE. Photocopied submissions OK. Accepts computer printout submissions. Sample copy for $4. Free fiction guidelines.

Payment: Pays in contributor's copes.

Terms: Acquires first North American serial rights in 1989. Publication copyrighted.

Advice: "I believe there is a 'fiction revival' on the way via the underground/small press express. The audience, the readers are out there but they can't get their fix at the general public newsstands. For the last decade (1976-1988) these discerning readers of American fiction have had to go to 'alternative bookstores' or make ther discovery by word of mouth. But all this is changing. The news agencies and booksellers have already begun picking up on this and new titles are beginning to appear at newsstands around the country. In turn, I think the mainstream publications wil begin picking up on this new mood and in the next few years open up their fiction markets. Get a recent issue of *Scream*, study it and query if there are any questions."

THE SCRIBBLER (I, II), Box 671, Madison AL 35758. (205)534-3867. Editor: Velda Crutcher. Magazine: 8½x11; 32 pages; 70 lb gloss paper; 80 lb gloss cover; illustrations; photos. Bimonthly. Plans special fiction issue. Estab. 1987.

Needs: Adventure, condensed novel, confession, contemporary, horror, humor/satire, romance (contemporary, historical, young adult), science fiction. Length: 3,000 words average; 1,000 words minimum; 4,000 words maximum. Publishes short shorts. Sometimes critiques rejected mss and may recommend other markets.

How to Contact: Send complete ms with cover letter. SASE. Photocopied and reprint submissions OK. Accepts computer printout submissions, including dot-matrix. Sample copy for SAE and 1 first class stamp. Fiction guidelines free.

Payment: Free subscription to magazine and 6 copies of issue in which work appears.

Terms: Pays on publication for first rights. Publication copyrighted.

SCRIVENER (II), 853 Sherbrooke St. W., Montreal, Quebec H3A 2T6 Canada. Editor: Andrew Burgess. Magazine: 8½x11; 40 pages; glossy paper; illustrations; b&w photos. "*Scrivener* is a creative journal publishing fiction, poetry, graphics, photography, reviews, interviews and scholarly articles. We publish the best of new and established writers. We examine how current trends in North American writing are rooted in a pervasive creative dynamic; our audience is mostly scholarly and in the writing field." Annually. Estab. 1980. Circ. 800.

Needs: Good writing. Receives 40 unsolicited mss/month. Accepts 20 mss/year. Does not read mss May 1-Sept 1. Publishes ms up to 6 months after acceptance. Recently published work by James Conway, Colin Wright, Louis Phillips; published new writers within the last year. Length: 25 pages maximum. Occasionally publishes short shorts. Often critiques rejected mss. Sometimes recommends other markets.

How to Contact: Query first. Order sample copy ($2); send complete ms with cover letter with "critical statements; where we can reach you; biographical data; education; previous publications." Reports in 4 months on queries and mss. SASE/IRC preferred but not required. Simultaneous, photocopied submissions and reprints OK. Accepts computer printouts including dot-matrix. Sample copy $3 (US in USA; Canadian in Canada). Fiction guidelines for SAE/IRC.

Payment: Sometimes pays $3-$25; provides contributor's copies; charges for extras.

Terms: Pays on publication.

Advice: "Send us your best stuff. Don't be deterred by rejections. Sometimes a magazine just isn't looking for your *kind* of writing. Don't neglect the neatness of your presentation."

‡SEARCHING SOULS MAGAZINE (I,II,IV), PSC #1, Box 2134, FAFB, WA 99011. (509)244-2722. Editor: Anthony L. Abraham. Fiction Editors: Anthony L. Abraham and Tracey Smith. Magazine: 8½x11; illustrations and photographs. "*S.S.* is looking for fiction dealing with the supernatural, surreal and macabre as told from a Christian point of view." Published irregularly. Estab. 1989.

Needs: Fantasy, horror, psychic/supernatural/occult, religious/inspirational, science fiction. "Fiction should be Christian oriented, but it is intended for open market. I am simply offering the same horror and SF/fantasy but told from a Christian perspective instead." Recently published work by Julia K. Stevens, J.F. Gonzales and Russ Miller. Length: 2,000 words preferred. Publishes short shorts. Sometimes comments on rejected mss and recommends other markets.

How to Contact: Send complete ms with cover letter. "Letter is optional." Reports in 2-3 weeks. SASE. Photocopied and reprint submissions OK. Accepts computer-printout submissions, including dot-matrix. Fiction guidelines for #10 SAE and 1 first class stamp.

Payment: Pays in contributor's copies.

Terms: Acquires first North American serial rights. Publication copyrighted.

Advice: "Submit your best work. I make personal replies to all contributors. Be open to criticism. Submit again."

THE SEATTLE REVIEW (II), Padelford Hall GN-30, University of Washington, Seattle WA 98195. (206)543-9865. Editor: Donna Gerstenberger. Consulting Editor: Charles Johnson. Magazine: 6x9. "Includes general fiction, poetry, craft essays on writing, and one interview per issue with a Northwest writer." Semiannually. Published special fiction issue. Estab. 1978. Circ. 1,000.

Needs: Contemporary, ethnic, experimental, fantasy, feminist, gay, historical, horror, humor/satire, lesbian, literary, mainstream, prose poem, psychic/supernatural/occult, regional, science fiction, excerpted novel, suspense/mystery, translations, western. "We also publish a series called Writers and their Craft, which deals with aspects of writing fiction (also poetry)—point of view, characterization, etc., rather than literary criticism, each issue." Does not want to see "anything in bad taste (porn, racist, etc.)." Receives about 50 unsolicited mss/month. Accepts about 3-6 mss/issue; about 4-10 mss/year. Reads mss all year but "slow to respond in summer." 25% of fiction is agented. Recently published work by David Milofsky, Lawson Fusao and Liz Rosenberg; published new writers within the last year. Length: 3,500 words average; 500 words minimum; 10,000 words maximum. Publishes short shorts. Sometimes critiques rejected mss. Occasionally recommends other markets.

How to Contact: Send complete ms. "If included, cover letter should list recent publications or mss we'd seen and liked, but been unable to publish." Reports in 3 months. SASE. Accepts computer printout submissions, including dot-matrix, if clearly legible. Sample copy "half-price if older than one year."

Payment: Pays 0-$100, free subscription to magazine, 2 contributor's copies; charge for extras.

Terms: Pays on publication for first North American serial rights. Copyright reverts to writer on publication; "please request release of rights and cite *SR* in reprint publications." Sends galleys to author.

Advice: "Beginners do well in our magazine if they send clean, well-written manuscripts. We've published a lot of 'first stories' from all over the country and take pleasure in discovery."

‡II CHRONICLES MAGAZINE (II, IV), Oregon Christian Arts Group, Box 42, Medford OR 97501. (503)779-4704. Editor: Mack Lloyd Lewis. Fiction Editor: Lloyd Neske. Tabloid: 11x14; 16-24 pages; Electrobrite paper and cover; illustrations and b&w photos. "General interest, Christian lifestyles publication. Interested in fiction representing a fruitful Christian walk. Doesn't have to be religious—just Christian. For southern Oregon Christians." Published 8 times/year. Plans special fiction issue. Estab. 1987. Circ. 5,000.

Needs: Adventure, contemporary, historical, humor/satire, literary, mainstream, regional, religious/inspirational. "Regardless of category, all submissions must present a biblical slant." No anti-Christian material or erotica. Receives 3-5 unsolicited fiction mss/month. Accepts 1 ms/issue; 8 mss/year. Publishes ms 2-6 months after acceptance. Recently published work by Nancy Strom and Debby De-Kenng. Length: 800 words average; 400 words minimum; 1,000 words maximum. Publishes short-shorts, 200-400 words. Sometimes critiques rejected mss.

How to Contact: Send complete ms with cover letter, which should include "brief biographical info, means of contact, publishing history." Reports in 6 weeks. SASE. Simultaneous, photocopied and reprint submissions OK. Accepts dot-matrix computer printouts. Sample copy for $1 or 9x12 SAE and 3 first class stamps. Fiction guidelines for #10 SAE and 1 first class stamp.

Payment: Pays 0-$30, free subscription to magazine and contributor's copies.

Terms: Pays on publication for one-time rights. Publication copyrighted.

Advice: Looks for fiction that is "Christian, unique, mechanically sound, precise and fast moving. Take the time to perfect the mss before submitting it. We get far too many items that are really nothing more than first drafts. Fiction writers have tended to avoid a style such as classic literature contains. They should be holding up the aged classics as examples of what they're working toward."

SEEMS (II), Lakeland College, Sheboygan WI 53081. (414)565-3871. Editor: Karl Elder. Magazine: 8½x7; 40 pages. "We publish fiction and poetry for an audience which tends to be highly literate. People read the publication, I suspect, for the sake of reading it." Published irregularly. Estab. 1971. Circ. 250.

Needs: Literary. Accepts 6-8 mss/issue. Receives approximately 10 unsolicited fiction mss each month. Recently published work by John Birchler; published new writers within the last year. Length: 5,000 words maximum. Also publishes short shorts. Critiques rejected mss when there is time.

How to Contact: Send complete ms with SASE. Accepts computer printout submissions. Prefers letter-quality. Reports in 2 months on mss. Publishes ms an average of 1-2 years after acceptance. Sample copy $3.

Payment: 1 free author's copy; $3 charge for extras.

Terms: Rights revert to author. Publication copyrighted.

Advice: "Send clear, clean copies. Read the magazine in order to help determine the taste of the editor." Mss are rejected because of "lack of economical expression, or saying with many words what could be said in only a few. Good fiction contains all of the essential elements of poetry; study poetry and apply those elements to fiction. Our interest is shifting to story poems, the grey area between genres."

‡SEQUOIA, Stanford Literary Magazine, Storke Publications Bldg., Stanford CA 94305. "Publishes poetry, prose, fiction, interviews with selected authors, b&w photography and artwork; 90% freelance; student writing welcome. *Sequoia* prints fiction and poetry to be read by those outside as well as within the Stanford community. Many of our readers are authors themselves; others are interested in our magazine because of the well-known writers and interviewees featured in past issues." Semiannually. Estab. 1887. Circ. 500.

Needs: "Literary excellence is the primary criterion. We'll consider anything but prefer literary, ethnic, avant-garde, experimental, translations and satire." Length: 8,000 words or 20 pages maximum.

How to Contact: Send complete ms with SASE. Tries to report in 3 months "during academic year." Sample copy $3.

Payment: 1-2 free author's copies. Contributor's rates on request.

Terms: Author retains rights.

Advice: "Follow your own voice. Please don't submit during the summer; we generally close down then."

‡SERENDIPITY (I,II), The Magazine of Everything, 4295 Silver Lake Rd., Pinson AL 35126-3307. (205)681-2259. Magazine: digest size; 32 pages; Mando paper; heavy cover stock; illustrations. "SF/Fantasy/Horror, with articles on anything of interest to fans of those genres." Bimonthly. Estab.

Market categories: (I) Beginning; (II) General; (III) Prestige; (IV) Specialized.

1986. Circ. 10,000.

Needs: Condensed novel, experimental, fantasy, historical (general) horror, humor/satire, mainstream, prose poem, psychic/supernatural/occult, science fiction, serialized/excerpted novel, suspense/mystery, young adult/teen, gaming. "It's got to be *good*." Receives 40 mss/month. Accepts 6 mss/issue; 36 mss/year. Publishes ms within 4 months of acceptance. Recently published work by Ada Cochran, Randy Williams, Janet P. Reedman; published new writers within the last year. Length: 1,500 words preferred; 500 words minimum; 3,500 words maximum. Sometimes critiques rejected mss and recommends other markets.

How to Contact: Send complete ms with cover letter. Cover letter should include "the address, previous credits list, a brief story description." Reports on queries in 1 month; in 2 months on mss. Photocopied submissions OK. Accepts computer printout submissions, including dot-matrix. Sample copy for $2. Fiction guidelines for #10 SAE and 1 first class stamp.

Payment: Pays 1¢-5¢/word. Acquires first North American serial rights. Publication copyrighted.

Advice: "There is an incredible market for magazine fiction in the area of the small press, of which *Serendipity* is but one example. A beginning writer has an opportunity to be published, reviewed and read by other writers. It's a great bargain. Write from the heart, and make the piece something *you* would like to read."

THE SEWANEE REVIEW (III), University of the South, Sewanee TN 37375. (615)598-1245. Editor: George Core. Magazine: 6x9; 192 pages. "A literary quarterly, publishing original fiction, poetry, essays on literary and related subjects, book reviews and book notices for well-educated readers who appreciate good American and English literature." Quarterly. Estab. 1892. Circ. 3,500.

Needs: Literary, contemporary. No translations, juvenile, gay/lesbian, erotica. Buys 10-15 mss/year. Receives approximately 100 unsolicited fiction mss each month. Does not read mss June 1-August 31. Recently published work by Andre Dubus, Helen Bell, Merrill Joan Gerber. Published new writers within the last year. Length: 6,000-7,500 words. Critiques rejected mss "when there is time." Sometimes recommends other markets.

How to Contact: Send complete ms with SASE with cover letter stating previous publications, if any. Accepts computer printout submissions. Reports in 1 month on mss. Sample copy $6 plus 50¢ postage.

Payment: $10-$12/printed page. 2 free author's copies. $3.50 charge for extras.

Terms: Pays on publication for first North American serial rights and second serial rights by agreement. Publication copyrighted.

Advice: "Send only one story at a time, with a serious and sensible cover letter. We think fiction is of greater general interest than any other literary mode."

‡SHATTERED WIG REVIEW (I, II), Shattered Wig Productions, 3322 Greenmount Ave., Baltimore MD 21218. (301)467-4344. Editor: Collective. Magazine: 8½; 40-50 pages; "average" paper; cardstock cover; illustrations and photos. "Open forum for the discussion of the political aspects of everyday life. Fiction, poetry, graphics, essays, photos." Semiannually. Estab. 1988. Circ. 300.

Needs: Confession, contemporary, erotica, ethnic, experimental, feminist, gay, humor/satire, juvenile (5-9 years), lesbian, literary, preschool (1-4 years), prose poem, psychic/supernatural/occult, regional, senior citizen/retirement, serialized/excerpted novel, translations, young adult/teen (10-18), meat, music, film, art, pickles, revolutionary practice." Does not want "anything by Ann Beattie or John Irving." Receives 15-20 unsolicited mss/month. Publishes ms 2-4 months after acceptance. Recently published work by Louise Spiegler, Al Ackerman, Jack Rice; published new writers within the last year. Publishes short shorts. Sometimes critiques rejected mss and recommends other markets.

How to Contact: Send complete ms with cover letter or "visit us in Baltimore." Reports in 4 weeks. SASE for ms. Simultaneous, photocopied and reprint submissions OK. Accepts computer printout submissions, including dot-matrix. Sample copy for $2 and SAE.

Payment: Pays in contributor's copies.

Terms: Acquires one-time rights. Publication copyrighted.

Advice: "The arts have been reduced to imploding pus with the only material rewards reserved for vapid stylists and collegiate pod suckers. The only writing that counts has no barriers between imagination and reality, thought and action. We publish any writing that addresses vital issues. Send us at least 3 pieces so we have a choice."

SHAWNEE SILHOUETTE (II), Shawnee State University, 940 Second St., Portsmouth OH 45662. (614)354-3205. Fiction Editor: Tamela Carmichael. Magazine: 5x7; 40 pages; illustrations and photos. Quarterly.

Needs: Adventure, contemporary, historical, humor/satire, literary, mainstream, regional, romance, science fiction, suspense/mystery. Receives 3 unsolicited mss/month. Accepts 8 mss/issue. Does not read mss in summer. Publishes ms an average of 3-6 months after acceptance. Published new writers within the last year. Length: 800 words average; 400 words minimum; 1,000 words maximum.

Publishes short shorts. Occasionally critiques rejected mss.
How to Contact: Send complete ms with cover letter. Reports in 3 weeks on queries. SASE. Photocopied submissions OK. Accepts computer printout submissions. Sample copy $2, 5x7 SAE and 66¢ postage.
Payment: Free contributor's copies.
Terms: Acquires one-time rights. Publication copyrighted.

‡SHMATE (II), A Journal of Progressive Jewish Thought, Box 4228, Berkeley CA 94704. Editor: Steve Fankuchen. Magazine "providing a forum for un-, mis- and under-represented social, political and literary ideas and activities for Jews and non-Jews." Quarterly. Estab. 1982. Circ. 3,500.
Needs: Comics, ethnic, experimental, fantasy, feminist, gay, historical (general), humor/satire, lesbian, literary, religious, science fiction, senior citizen/retirement, sports, political, social. Receives 8 unsolicited mss/month. Accepts 1-2 mss/issue; 4 mss/year. Published new writers within the last year. Length: 1,500 words average.
How to Contact: Send complete ms. Reports in varying number of weeks. SASE. Simultaneous and photocopied submissions OK. Accepts computer printout submissions. Sample copy $3.
Payment: Pays in contributor's copies.
Terms: Acquires "all rights legally, but informal mutual rights." Publication copyrighted.
Advice: *"Read the magazine.* Every issue is different."

SHOE TREE (I), The Literary Magazine by and for Young Writers, National Association for Young Writers, Inc., 215 Valle del Sol Dr., Sante Fe NM 87501. (505)982-8596. Editor: Sheila Cowing. Magazine: 6x9; 64 pages; 70 lb vellum/white stock; 10 pt. cover; illustrations (photos occasionally). *"Shoe Tree* is a nationwide publication dedicated to nurturing young talent. All stories, poems and artwork are done by children between the ages of 6 and 14." Published 3 times a year. Estab. 1985. Circ. 1,000.
Needs: Adventure, contemporary, fantasy, historical, horror, humor/satire, literary, mainstream, science fiction, suspense/mystery. "No formulas or classroom assignments." Receives 100-150 unsolicited mss/month. Accepts 6 fiction mss/issue; 18 mss/year. Publishes ms 3-6 months after acceptance. Published new writers within the last year. Length: 2,000 words average; 150 words minimum; 5,000 words maximum. Occasionally critiques rejected mss. Recommends other markets sometimes.
How to Contact: Send complete ms with cover letter, which should include name, address, age, school and name of teacher. Reports in 2-4 weeks on queries; 10-12 weeks on mss. SASE. Photocopied submissions OK. Accepts computer printout submissions, including dot-matrix. Sample copy $5. Fiction guidelines for #10 SAE.
Payment: 2 free contributer's copies.
Terms: Acquires all rights. Publication copyrighted. "The National Association for Young Writers sponsors three annual *Shoe Tree* contests. The contests are open to all children between the ages of 6 and 14. Categories: fiction, nonfiction and poetry. First prize in each category: $25. Deadlines: Jan. 1 (fiction); April 1 (poetry); June 1 (nonfiction). When writing for contest rules, please provide SASE."
Advice: "Because the purpose of our magazine is to nurture talented young writers, to encourage them to explore their world in words, and to help them improve their writing skills, we are very 'optimistic' toward beginning fiction writers. We look for freshness and originality. Draw on your own experiences whenever possible. Avoid formulas and stories assigned in the classroom."

SHOOTING STAR REVIEW (II, IV), 7123 Race St., Pittsburgh PA 15208. (412)731-7039. Editor: Sandra Gould Ford. Magazine: 8½x11; 32 pages; 60 lb white paper; 80 lb enamel glossy cover; illustrations; photos. "Dedicated to the African-American (Black) experience." Quarterly. Estab. 1987. Circ. 1,500.
Needs: Adventure, contemporary, experimental, literary, mainstream, regional, romance (contemporary, historical), science fiction, suspense/mystery, translations. Each issue has a different theme: "Justice" (deadline March 1, 1989); "Salute to Black Woman Writers" (deadline June 1, 1989); "Resolutions and New Beginnings" (deadline September 1, 1989); "Rhythm and Blues" (deadline November 15, 1989). Writers should send a SASE for guidelines. No juvenile, preschool, young adult fiction. Receives 10-20 unsolicited mss/month. Publishes 1-2 mss/issue. Publishes ms 4-6 months after acceptance. Length: 1,800 words preferred; 3,500 words maximum. Publishes short shorts. Length: 1,000 words or less. Sometimes critiques rejected mss and recommends other markets.
How to Contact: Send complete ms with cover letter. "We like to promote the writer as well as their work and would appreciate understanding who the writer is and why they write." Reports in 2 weeks on queries; 6-8 weeks on mss. SASE. Simultaneous, photocopied and reprint submissions OK. Accepts computer printout submissions, including dot-matrix. Accepts electronic submissions via "IBM compatible, 5¼" double sided/double density disk, ASCII non-formated modem 300 baud." Sample copy for $2. Fiction guidelines for #10 SAE and 1 first class stamp.
Payment: Pays $50 maximum or contributor's copies; charge for extras.

Close-up

Dwight Gabbard
The Short Story Review

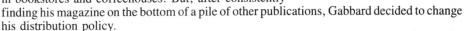

The quarterly tabloid *The Short Story Review*, actually de-
buted in 1983 as *Fiction Monthly*. Publisher/editor Dwight
Gabbard, says he started the magazine to provide a venue
for short stories which didn't have many outlets at that
time. *Fiction Monthly* was originally a monthly tabloid
printed on inexpensive paper and distributed free of charge
in bookstores and coffeehouses. But, after consistently
finding his magazine on the bottom of a pile of other publications, Gabbard decided to change
his distribution policy.

From 1985 to 1986, the magazine went through two additional name changes. Eventually
though, the name *The Short Story Review* was decided upon and publishing began on a quarterly basis.

Gabbard says his original ideal was to only print stories that would eventually get into the
O'Henry or *Best American Short Story Classic* anthology. But, he ruefully admits, they as yet
have not reached that goal. He points out though that they have had several stories anthologized and are very proud of that fact.

Gabbard says they look for five or six short stories an issue. "We have in the past solicited
stories from established writers, even paid for them. But, we are really interested in new writers. Now, everything we print comes from the 'slush pile' and contributors are paid in copies." There is an editorial board of five that meets and votes on stories to include in the magazine from the numerous submissions it receives. These stories are chosen from a total of about
2,000 manuscripts received in a year.

"The story that really stands out from the rest is the one that you get from a writer with a
professional attitude who has something to say and also has a flair for writing it," Gabbard
says. "It is really a very rare thing."

He says *The Short Story Review* gets a great deal of submissions that are "autobiographical
in nature and while it may be a very therapeutical thing to do, it isn't what we're looking for. I
think people look to writing to rescue themselves from the prosaic aspect of their lives. They
grasp at literature thinking, well, I can't be a movie actor; I can't be this or that. But, with literature, I can explore myself and work with language. And, all that is fun. It seems they're
looking to writing for a better life.

"We look for stories that have a crispness of language, where language is important to the
telling of the story and it's not *just* the story," he continues. He says there are thousands of
writers doing the same kinds of things; writing about life and death experiences common to
most people. Unless one's writing has something a little bit different, more than just an insight into these common experiences and with a punch added in, a story won't rise to the top
of the pile.

Gabbard adds that this kind of writing takes "a lot of practice. You almost have to devote
yourself to it fulltime. It's got to become your total focus and passion."

—Deborah Cinnamon

Terms: Pays on publication for first North American serial rights. Sends galleys to author upon request, if time permits. Publication copyrighted.

Advice: "*Shooting Star Review* was started specifically to provide a forum for short fiction that explores the black experience. We are committed to this art form and will make space for work that satisfies our guidelines. We welcome works on white thought on Black experience and issues."

THE SHORT STORY REVIEW (I, II), Box 882108, San Francisco CA 94188. Publisher/Editor: Dwight Gabbard. Editors: Stephen Woodhams, Catherine Jacob, Melinda Dart, Beth Overston, George Knuepfel, Eleanor Carey. Tabloid: 10x15; 16-20 pages; bookstock paper throughout. "Tabloid of short stories, interviews, book reviews." Quarterly. Published special fiction issue; plans another. Estab. 1983. Circ. 2,000.

Needs: Literary, contemporary. No romantic, science fiction or fantasy. Receives 100 unsolicited mss/month. Accepts 6 mss/quarter; 24 mss/year. Recently published work by Robert Kelly, Paul West and Fred Bonnie; published new writers in the last year. Length: 1,000-4,000 words average.

How to Contact: "Send for guidelines, include 25¢ postage on SASE." Reports in 12 weeks on mss. SASE. Photocopied submissions OK. Accepts computer printout submissions. Prefers letter-quality. Sample copy $2.50.

Payment: 3 contributor's copies, and a one year subscription.

Terms: Aquires first North American serial rights.

Advice: "Read a great deal, both the classics and contemporary literature. Be prepared to rewrite. Don't give up. We will be publishing fewer interviews and book reviews and more stories."

SIGN OF THE TIMES (II), A Chronicle of Decadence in the Atomic Age, Studio 403, Box 70672, Seattle WA 98107-0672. (206)323-6779. Editor: Mark Souder. Tabloid: 7½x11; 32 pages; book paper; 120 lb cover stock; illustrations; photos. "Decadence in all forms for those seeking literary amusement." Semiannually. Published special fiction issue last year; plans another. Estab. 1980. Circ. 750.

Needs: Comics, erotica, experimental, gay, lesbian. No religious or western manuscripts. Receives 6 unsolicited mss/month. Buys 6 mss/issue; 12 mss/year. Recently published the work by Gary Smith, Willie Smith, Ben Satterfield. Length: 3,000 words average; 500 words minimum, 5,000 words maximum. Publishes short shorts. Sometimes comments on rejected mss and recommends other markets.

How to Contact: Send complete ms with cover letter and bio. Reports in 6 weeks on mss. SASE. Photocopied submissions OK. Accepts computer printout submissions. Prefers letter-quality. Sample copy $3.50. Fiction guidelines for #10 SASE.

Payment: 0-$20, subscription to magazine, 2 contributor's copies; 1 time cover price charge for extras.

Terms: Pays on publication for first rights plus anthology in the future. Publication copyrighted.

Advice: "Write what you know and feel. We publish fiction because many magazines do not."

SILVERFISH REVIEW (IV), Silverfish Press, Box 3541, Eugene OR 97403. (503)344-5060. Editor: Rodger Moody. High quality literary material for a general audience. Published irregularly. Estab. 1979. Circ. 500.

Needs: Literary. Accepts 1-2 mss/issue.

How to Contact: Send complete ms with SASE. Reports in 1 month on mss. Sample copy $3 and $1 for postage.

Payment: 5 free author's copies.

Terms: Pays on publication; rights revert to author.

Advice: "We publish primarily poetry; we will, however, publish good quality fiction."

SING HEAVENLY MUSE! (II), Box 13299, Minneapolis MN 55414. (612)224-3209. Editor: Sue Ann Martinson. Magazine: 6x9; 125 pages; 55 lb acid-free paper; 10 pt. glossy cover stock; illustrations; photos. Women's poetry, prose and artwork. Semiannually. Estab. 1977.

Needs: Literary, contemporary, fantasy, feminist, mystery, humor, prose poem and ethnic/minority. Receives approximately 30 unsolicited fiction mss each month. "Accepts ms for consideration only in April and September." Recently published work by Helene Cappuccio, Erika Duncan, Martha Roth. Publishes short shorts. Sometimes recommends other markets.

How to Contact: Query for information on theme issues or variations in schedule. Include cover letter with "brief writing background and publications." Accepts computer printout submissions. Reports in 1-3 months on queries and mss. Publishes ms an average of 6 months after acceptance. Sample copy $3.50.

Payment: Honorarium; 2 free copies.

Terms: Pays on publication for first rights. Publication copyrighted.

Advice: "Try to avoid preaching. Look for friends also interested in writing and form a mutual support-and-criticism group."

‡**SINISTER WISDOM (IV)**, Box 3252, Berkeley CA 94703. Editor: Elana Dykewomon. Magazine: $5^7/16$x$8^1/2$; 128-144 pages; 55 lb stock; 10 pt CIS cover; illustrations; photos. Lesbian-feminist journal, providing fiction, poetry, drama, essays, journals and artwork. Quarterly. 1988 issues were on sci-fi, passing, and surviving psychiatric assault. Estab. 1976. Circ. 3,000.
Needs: Adventure, contemporary, erotica, ethnic, experimental, fantasy, feminist, historical, humor/satire, lesbian, literary, prose poem, psychic, regional, science fiction, sports, translations. No heterosexual or male-oriented fiction; nothing that stereotypes or degrades women. Receives 50 unsolicited mss/month. Accepts 25 mss/issue; 75-100 mss/year. Publishes ms 1-12 months after acceptance. Recently published work by Melanie Kaye/Kantrowitz, Adrienne Rich, Aya Blackwomon, and Gloria Anzaldúa; published new writers within the last year. Length: 2,000 words average; 500 words minimum; 4,000 words maximum. Publishes short shorts. Occasionally critiques rejected mss. Sometimes recommends other markets.
How to Contact: Send 2 copies of complete ms with cover letter, which should include a brief author's bio to be published when the work is published. Reports in 2 months on queries; 6 months on mss. SASE. Photocopied submissions OK. Accepts computer printout submissions, including dot-matrix. Sample copy $6.25; subscription $17.
Payment: Pays in contributor's copies.
Terms: Right retained by authors. Publication copyrighted.
Advice: "Read the journals to which you're submitting first."

SKYLARK (I), Purdue University, 2233 171st St., Hammond IN 46323. (219)844-0520, ext. 372. Editor: Sheila F. Binkley. Magazine: $8^1/2$x11; 140 pages; illustrations; photos. Fine arts magazine—short stories, poems and graphics for adults and children. Annually. Plans special fiction issue. Estab. 1971. Circ. 500.
Needs: Contemporary, ethnic, experimental, fantasy, feminist, historical (general), horror, humor/satire, juvenile, literary, mainstream, prose poem, psychic/supernatural/occult, regional, science fiction, serialized/excerpted novel, spiritual, sports, suspense/mystery and western. Receives 20 mss/month. Accepts 6-7 mss/issue. Recently published work by A. R. Ammons, Gerald Oosterveen and Lyn Lifshin. Published new writers within the last year. Length: 1-15 double-spaced pages.
How to Contact: Send complete ms. SASE for ms. Photocopied submissions OK. Accepts computer printout submissions. Prefers letter-quality. Sample copy $4.
Payment: 2 contributor's copies.
Terms: Acquires first rights. Publication copyrighted. Copyright reverts to author.
Advice: "Encourage submissions from children 6-18. The goal of *Skylark* is to encourage *creativity* and give beginning and published authors showcase for their work. Check for spelling errors or typos."

SLATE AND STYLE (IV) Magazine of the National Federation of the Blind Writers Division, NFB Writer's Division, 2704 Beach Drive, Merrick NY 11566. Editor: Loraine E. Stayer. Fiction Editor: Tom Stevens. Newsletter: 8x10; 25 print/Braille pages; cassette and large print. "Articles of interest to writers, and resources for blind writers. Quarterly. Estab. 1982. Circ. 60-100.
Needs: Adventure, contemporary, fantasy, humor/satire, blindness. No erotica. Does not read June, July. Length: 2,000 words average; 1,000 words minimum; 6,000 words maximum. Publishes short shorts. Critiques rejected mss only if requested. Sometimes recommends other markets.
How to Contact: Query first. Reports on queries in 2 weeks; 4 weeks on mss. Photocopied submissions OK. Sample copy $2.50 and cassette mailer if tape requested. Large print copies also available. "Sent Free Matter For The Blind. If not blind, send 2 stamps."
Payment: Pays in contributor's copies.
Terms: Acquires one-time rights. Publication not copyrighted. Sponsors contests for fiction writers.
Advice: "Planning 'showcase' publication of stories by blind writers or members of writers' division. Request that writer take responsibility of copyright permission if piece previously published. Aiming for 6,000 word length per piece. Write *Slate & Style* for details. We aren't interested in demeaning attitudes toward blindness!"

SLIPSTREAM (II, IV), Box 2071, New Market Station, Niagara Falls NY 14301. (716)282-2616. Editor: Dan Sicoli. Fiction Editors: R. Borgatti, D. Sicoli and Livio Farallo. Magazine: $8^1/2$x7; 80-120 pages; high quality paper and cover; illustrations; photos. "We use poetry and short fiction with a contemporary urban feel." Estab. 1981. Circ. 400.
Needs: Reading now for a general issue. Contemporary, erotica, ethnic, experimental, fantasy, feminist, gay, humor/satire, lesbian, literary, mainstream, prose poem and science fiction. No religious, juvenile, young adult or romance. Receives over 75 unsolicited mss/month. Accepts 2-8 mss/issue; 6-12 mss/year. Publishes short shorts. Recently published work by Gary Earl Ross, Grace B. Martin and Hal Sirowitz. Rarely critiques rejected mss. Sometimes recommends other markets.
How to Contact: Send complete ms. Reports in 2-8 weeks. SASE. Accepts computer printout sub-

missions. Sample copy $3. Fiction guidelines for #10 SASE.
Payment: 2 contributor's copies.
Terms: Acquires one-time rights on publication. Publication copyrighted.
Advice: "Writing should be honest, fresh; develop your own style. Check out a sample issue first. Don't write for the sake of writing, write from the gut as if it were a biological need. Write from experience and mean what you say, but say it in the fewest number of words."

THE SMALL POND MAGAZINE (II), Box 664, Stratford CT 06497. (203)378-4066. Editor: Napoleon St. Cyr. Magazine: 5½x8½; 42 pages; 60 lb offset paper; 65 lb cover stock; illustrations (art). "Features contemporary poetry, the salt of the earth, peppered with short prose pieces of various kinds. The college educated and erudite read it for good poetry, prose and pleasure." Triannually. Estab. 1964. Circ. 300.
Needs: "Rarely use science fiction or formula stories you'd find in *Cosmo*, *Redbook*, *Ladies Home Journal*, etc." Buys 10-12 mss/year. Longer response time in July and August. Receives approximately 50 unsolicited fiction mss each month. Length: 200-2,500 words. Critiques rejected mss when there is time. Sometimes recommends other markets.
How to Contact: Send complete ms with SASE and short vita with publishing credits. Accepts good copy computer printout submissions. Prefers letter-quality. Reports in 2 weeks-1 month. Publishes ms an average of 2-12 months after acceptance. Sample copy $2.50.
Payment: 2 free author's copies. $2/copy charge for extras.
Terms: Pays on publication for all rights. Publication copyrighted.
Advice: "Send for a sample copy first. All mss must be typed. Name and address and story title on front page, name of story on succeeding pages and paginated." Mss are rejected because of "tired plots and poor grammar; also over-long—2,500 words maximum. Don't send any writing conference ms unless it got an A or better."

‡SMILE (IV), Box 3515, Madison WI 53704. (608)258-1305. Magazine: 8½x11; 28 pages; colored cover; illustrations; photos. Publishes material on "non-mainstream politics; political theory and practice." Semiannually. Plans special fiction issue. Estab. 1987. Circ. 1,500.
Needs: "Anarchist or communist topics that deal with the psychosocial liberation from the oppressive society." Receives 2 unsolicited fiction mss/month. Length: 200 words minimum; 800 words maximum. Sometimes critiques rejected mss.
How to Contact: Query with clips of published work or send complete mss with cover letter. Simultaneous, photocopied and reprint submissions OK. Accepts computer printout submissions, including dot-matrix. Accepts electronic submissions via disk or modem. Sample copy for SAE and 6 first class stamps.
Payment: Pays in 2 contributor's copies.
Terms: "Everything printed is free to be copied by anyone." Publication is not copyrighted.

‡THE SNEAK PREVIEW (I), Box 639, Grants Pass OR 97526. (503)474-3044. Editor: Curtis Hayden. Fiction Editor: Matt Hegarty. Tabloid; 14x9¾; 24-32 pages; newsprint paper; newsprint cover; illustrations; photos. "News and arts biweekly of local events, with one page reserved for writers and poets to submit stories and poems." Biweekly. Estab. 1986. Circ. 12,500.
Needs: Adventure, condensed/excerpted novel, contemporary, experimental, historical (general), humor/satire (especially), juvenile (5-9 years), literary, mainstream, prose poem, regional, romance (contemporary, historical, young adult), science fiction, senior citizen/retirement, sports, suspense/mystery, western, young adult/teen (10-18 years). "Nothing that would offend the scruples of a small town in southern Oregon." Receives 2 unsolicited mss/month. Buys 1 ms/issue; 26 mss/year. Publishes ms within 2 weeks-6 months of acceptance. Recently published work by Leo Curzen, Cher Manuel, Garfield Price. Length: 250 words average; 200 words minimum; 300 words maximum. Sometimes critiques rejected mss and recommends other markets.
How to Contact: Query first. Reports in 2 weeks. SASE. Simultaneous, photocopied and reprint submissions OK. Accepts computer printout submissions, including dot-matrix. Accepts electronic submissions via disk or modem. Free sample copy and fiction guidelines.
Payment: Pays $10-$20 and contributor's copies.
Terms: Pays on publication for all rights. Publication not copyrighted.
Advice: "We need more people like Hunter Thompson. Everybody thinks the New-York-City-let's-get-serious-about-life-and-our-'art' is where it's at."

SNOWY EGRET (II), The Fair Press, RR #1, Box 354, Poland IN 47868. (812)829-4339. Editor: Karl Barnebey. Magazine: 8½x11; 50 pages; text paper; heavier cover; illustrations. "Literary exploration of the richness and beauty of nature and the ways man interacts with it. For those with a strong appreciation and respect for the natural world." Semiannually. Estab. 1922. Circ. 400.

Needs: Adventure, condensed/excerpted novel, experimental, humor/satire, regional, serialized novel, translations, nature writing, including 'true' stories, eye-witness accounts, descriptive sketches and traditional fiction. "We are particularly interested in fiction that celebrates the richness and beauty of nature, encourages a love and respect for the natrual world, and affirms the human connection to the environment. No works written for popular genres: horror, sci fi, romance, detective, western, etc." Receives 5 unsolicited ms/month. Buys up to 4 mss/issue; up to 8 mss/year. Publishes ms 6 months after acceptance. Recently published works by Marion Whitley, Peter Gorman and Jerry Brodgen. Length: 1,000-3,000 words preferred; 500 words minimum; 10,000 words maximum. Publishes short shorts. Length: 400-500 words. Sometimes critiques rejected mss and recommends other markets.
How to Contact: Send complete ms with cover letter. "Cover letter optional: do not query." Reports in 2 months. SASE. Simultaneous and photocopied submissions OK. Accepts computer printout submissions, including dot-matrix. Sample copy for $5, 9x12 SAE and 6 first class stamps. Fiction guidelines for #10 SAE and 1 first class stamp.
Payment: Pays $2/page. Free contributor's copy; charge for extras.
Terms: Pays on publication. Purchases first North American serial rights. Sends galleys to author. Publication copyrighted.
Advice: Looks for "honest, freshly detailed pieces with plenty of description and/or dialogue which will allow the reader to identify with the characters and step into the setting. Characters who relate strongly to nature, either positively or negatively, and who, during the course of the story, grow in their understanding of themselves and the world around them."

SONOMA MANDALA (II), Dept. of English, Sonoma State University, 1801 E. Cotati Ave., Rohnert Park CA 94928. Managing Editor: D. Jayne McPherson. Magazine: 8½x7; approx. 100 pages; bond paper; card cover stock; some illustrations; some photos. "We have no static thematic preference. We publish several short pieces (up to 2,500 words) of fiction in each issue." For campus community of a small liberal arts college and the surrounding rural/residential area. Annually. Estab. 1972. Circ. 500-1,000.
Needs: Contemporary, ethnic, experimental, fantasy, feminist, gay, humor/satire, lesbian, literary, mainstream, prose poem, translations, western, regional. Receives 10-15 unsolicited fiction mss/month. Accepts 3-5 mss/issue. Does not read ms January to September. Publishes 9-12 months after acceptance. Recently published work by Doug Levy, Gerald Rosen, Linda Heft; published new writers within the last year. Length: 1,000 words average; 2,500 words maximum. Publishes short shorts.
How to Contact: Send complete ms with cover letter. "Include info on simultaneous submissions, which we allow, if so indicated in cover letter. Always include address and telephone number, if needed." Reports in 1-3 months. SASE for ms. Photocopied submissions OK. Accepts dot-matrix computer printouts. Sample copy $4 postpaid.
Payment: 2 contributor's copies.
Terms: Pays on publication for one-time rights; rights revert to author upon publication.
Advice: "Read the literary magazines, and, if you believe in your work, keep submitting it to other publications. Especially interested in SSU and SF Bay area writers, but consider all quality submissions."

SONORA REVIEW (I), University of Arizona, Department of English, Tucson AZ 85721. (602)621-1836. Editors: Mike Magoolaghan and Heather Aronson. Fiction Editor: Melanie Bishop. Magazine: 9x6; 150 pages; 16 lb paper; 20 lb cover stock; photos seldom. *The Sonora Review* publishes short fiction and poetry of high literary quality. Semiannually. Estab. 1980. Circ. 500.
Needs: Literary. "We are open to a wide range of stories with accessibility and vitality being important in any case. We're not interested in genre fiction, formula work." Buys 4-6 mss/issue. Approximately 10% of fiction is agented. Recently published work by Ken Kalfus, Eileen Drew, Ron Hansen. Length: open, though prefers work under 25 pages. Sometimes recommends other markets.
How to Contact: Send complete ms with SASE and cover letter with previous publications. Accepts computer printout submissions. Prefers letter-quality. Reports in 2 months on mss, longer for work received during summer (May-August). Publishes ms an average of 2-6 months after acceptance. Sample copy $4.
Payment: 2 free author's copies. $2 charge for extras. Annual cash prizes.
Terms: Acquires first North American serial rights. Fall issue features fiction contest winnter: 1st prize, $100; 2nd prize $50. Submit by October 1.
Advice: "We have increased the size of the magazine at 50% and are developing more special features connecting special themes and regions. Let the story sit for several months, then review it to see if you still like it. If you're unsure, keep working on it *before* sending it out. All mss are read carefully, and we try to make brief comments if time permits. Our hope is that an author will keep us interested in his or her treatment of a subject by using fresh details and writing with an authority that is absorbing." Mss are rejected because "1) we only have space for 6-8 manuscripts out of several hundred submissions annually, and 2) most of the manuscripts we receive have some merit but are not of publishable quality. It would be helpful to receive a cover letter with all manuscripts."

‡SORE DOVE (II), Box 6332, San Mateo CA 94403. Editor Soheyl Dahi. Magazine: 12x16; 40 pages; illustrations; photos. "Aggressive, hard-ass/kick-ass attitude throughout." Audience is "anti-republican, underground, honest, no pretensions." Plans a special fiction issue. Estab. 1986. Circ. 1,000.
Needs: Confession, contemporary, erotica, ethnic, experimental, feminist, humor/satire, literary, mainstream, prose poem, translations, third world. No religious mss. Receives 20 mss/month. Accepts 12 mss/issue. Publishes ms within 3-4 months of acceptance. Recently published work by Voisard, Sotile, Bukowski, Menebroker. Length: 1,000 words average. Publishes short shorts. Sometimes critiques rejected mss and recommends other markets.
How to Contact: Query first. Reports in 2 weeks on queries; in 4 weeks on mss. SASE. Simultaneous, photocopied and reprint submissions OK. Accepts computer printout submissions, including dot-matrix. Accepts electronic submission via disk or modem. Sample copy for $3. Free fiction guidelines.
Payment: Pays in contributor's copies.
Terms: Acquires all rights. Sends galleys to author. Publication copyrighted.
Advice: "If we like it, we print it. Be honest, take chances and don't bullshit the bullshitter."

SOUNDINGS EAST (II), English Dept., Salem State College, Salem MA 01970. (617)741-6000, Ext. 2333. Advisory Editor: Claire Keyes. Magazine: 5½x8½; 64 pages; illustrations; photos. "Mainly a college audience, but we also distribute to libraries throughout the country." Biannually. Estab. 1973. Circ. 2,000.
Needs: Literary, contemporary, prose poem. No juvenile. Publishes 4-5 stories/issue. Receives 30 unsolicited fiction mss each month. Does not read April-August. Recently published work by James Brady, Terry Farish and Christina Shea. Published new writers within the last year. Length: 2,500-10,000 words. "We are open to short pieces as well as to long works." Critiques rejected mss when there is time. Sometimes recommends other markets.
How to Contact: Send complete ms with SASE between September and March. Accepts computer printout submissions. Prefers letter-quality. Reports in 2 months on mss. Sample copy $3.
Payment: 2 free author's copies.
Terms: All publication rights revert to authors.
Advice: "The writer should read a few of our issues to get a sense of the range of fiction we publish. The mss should be clean—that is, clearly typed with no hand written revisions. We seek authors with an original point of view."

SOUTH CAROLINA REVIEW (II), Clemson University, Clemson SC 29631. (803)656-3229. Editors: R.J. Calhoun, Frank Day and Carol Johnston. Managing Editor: Martin J. Jacobi. Magazine: 6x9; 132 pages; 60 lb cream white vellum paper; 65 lb cream white vellum cover stock; illustrations and photos rarely. Semiannually. Estab. 1967. Circ. 700.
Needs: Literary, contemporary, humor and ethnic. Receives approximately 50-60 unsolicited fiction mss each month. Does not read mss June-August. Recently published work by Joyce Carol Oates, Rosanne Coggeshall, Stephen Dixon. Published new writers within the last year. Critiques rejected mss when there is time.
How to Contact: Send complete ms with SASE. Accepts computer printout submissions. Reports in 2 months on mss. Sample copy $3.
Payment: Pays in contributor's copies.
Terms: Publication copyrighted.
Advice: Mss are rejected because of "poorly structured stories, or stories without vividness or intensity. The most celebrated function of a little magazine is to take a chance on writers not yet able to get into the larger magazines—the little magazine can encourage promising writers at a time when encouragement is vitally needed. (We also publish 'name' writers, like Joyce Carol Oates, Stephen Dixon, George Garrett.) Read the masters extensively. Write and write more, with a *schedule*. Listen to editorial advice when offered. Don't get discouraged with rejections. Read what writers say about writing (e.g. *The Paris Review* Interviews with George Plimpton, gen. ed.; Welty's *One Writer's Beginnings*,etc). Take courses in writing and listen to, even if you do not follow, the advice."

SOUTH DAKOTA REVIEW (II), University of South Dakota, Box 111, University Exchange, Vermillion SD 57069. (605)677-5966. Editor: John R. Milton. Magazine: 6x9; 150 + pages; book paper; glossy cover stock; illustrations sometimes; photos on cover. Literary magazine for university and college audiences and their equivalent. Emphasis is often on the West and its writers, but will accept mss from anywhere. Issues are generally fiction and poetry with some literary essays. Specific needs vary according to budget and other conditions. Quarterly. Estab. 1963. Circ. 500.
Needs: Literary, contemporary, ethnic, experimental, excerpted novel, regional and translations. "We like very well-written stories. Contemporary western American setting appeals, but not necessary. No formula stories, sports or adolescent 'I' narrator." Receives 30 unsolicited fiction mss/month. Accepts about 10-20 mss/year, more or less. Assistant editor accepts mss in June-July, sometimes August. Ap-

proximately 5% of fiction is agented. Publishes short shorts of 5 pages double-spaced typescript. Recently published work by Ed Loomis, Max Evans, Dennis Lynds; published new writers the last year. Length: 1,300 words minimum; 6,000 words maximum. (Has made exceptions, up to novella length.) Sometimes recommends other markets.

How to Contact: Send complete ms with SASE. "We like cover letters that are not boastful and do not attempt to sell the stories but rather provide some personal information about the writer." Photocopied submissions OK if not multiple submission. Reports in 1 month. Publishes ms an average of 1-6 months after acceptance. Sample copy $3.

Payment: 2-4 free author's copies depending on length of ms. $2 charge for extras.

Terms: Acquires first rights and second serial rights. Publication copyrighted.

Advice: $100 to best story published in the magazine every year or every other year. Rejects mss because of "careless writing; often careless typing; stories too personal ('I' confessional), adolescent; working-manuscript, not polished; subject matter that editor finds trivial. We are trying to use more fiction and more variety. We would like to see more sophisticated stories. Do not try to outguess editors and give them what you think they want. Write honestly. Be yourself."

SOUTHERN CALIFORNIA ANTHOLOGY (II), Master of Professional Writing Program—USC, MPW-WPH 404 USC, Los Angeles CA 90089-0031. (213)743-8255. Contact: Editors. Magazine: 5½x8½; 142 pages; semi-glossy cover stock. "The *Southern California Anthology* is a literary review that is an eclectic collection of previously unpublished quality contemporary fiction, poetry and interviews with established literary people, published for adults of all professions; of particular interest to those interested in serious contemporary literature." Annually. Estab. 1983. Circ. 1,500.

Needs: Contemporary, ethnic, experimental, feminist, historical (general), humor/satire, literary, mainstream, regional, serialized/excerpted novel. No juvenile, religious, confession, romance, science fiction. Receives 30 unsolicited fiction mss each month. Accepts 10-12 mss/issue. Does not read February-September. Publishes ms 4 months after acceptance. Length: 10-15 pages average; 2 pages minimum; 25 pages maximum. Publishes short shorts.

How to Contact: Send complete ms with cover letter or submit through agent. Cover letter should include list of previous publications. Reports on queries in 1 month; on mss in 4 months. SASE. Photocopied submissions OK. Accepts computer printout submissions, no dot-matrix. Sample copy $2.95. Fiction guidelines for #10 SAE and 1 first class stamp.

Payment: Pays in contributor's copies.

Terms: Acquires first rights. Publication copyrighted.

Advice: "The *Anthology* pays particular attention to craft and style in its selection of narrative writing."

SOUTHERN HUMANITIES REVIEW (II, IV), Auburn University, 9088 Haley Center, Auburn University AL 36849. Co-Editors: Thomas L. Wright and Dan R. Latimer. Magazine: 6x9; 96 pages; 60 lb neutral pH, natural paper, 65 lb neutral pH med. coated cover stock; occasional illustrations and photos. "We publish essays, poetry, fiction and reviews. Our fiction has ranged from very traditional in form and content to very experimental. Literate, college-educated audience. We hope they read our journal for both enlightenment and pleasure." Quarterly. Estab. 1967. Circ. 800.

Needs: Serious fiction, fantasy, feminist, humor and regional. Receives approximately 8-10 unsolicited fiction mss each month. Accepts and prints 1-2 mss/issue, 4-6 mss/year. Slower reading time in summer. Recently published work by Anne Brashler, Heimito von Doderer and Ivo Andric; published new writers within the last year. Length: 3,500-5,000 words. Critiques rejected mss when there is time. Sometimes recommends other markets.

How to Contact: Send complete ms with SASE and cover letter with an explanation of topic chosen—special, certain book, etc., a little about author if they have never submitted. Accepts computer printout submissions. Prefers letter-quality. Reports in 90 days. Sample copy $4.

Payment: 1 copy; $4 charge for extras.

Terms: Acquires first rights. Sends galleys to author. Publication copyrighted.

Advice: "Send us the ms with SASE. If we like it, we'll take it or we'll recommend changes. If we don't like it, we'll send it back as promptly as possible. Read the journal. Send a typewritten, clean copy carefully proofread. We also award annually the Hoepfner Prize of $100 for the best published essay or short story of the year. Let someone whose opinion you respect read your story and give you an honest appraisal. Rewrite, if necessary, to get the most from your story."

THE SOUTHERN REVIEW (II), Louisiana State University, 43 Allen Hall, Baton Rouge LA 70803. (504)388-5108. Editors: James Olney and Fred Hobson. Magazine: 10x6¾; 240 pages; 50 lb Warren Oldstyle paper; 65 lb #1 grade cover stock; occasional photos. A literary quarterly publishing critical essays, poetry and fiction for a highly intellectual audience. Quarterly. Published special fiction issue. Estab. 1935. Circ. 3,000.

Needs: Literary and contemporary. "We emphasize style and substantial content. No mystery, fantasy or religious mss." Buys 3-4 mss/issue. Receives approximately 100 unsolicited fiction mss each month. Approximately 17% of fiction is agented. Recently published work by Walker Percy, Maclin Bocock, Gloria Naylor. Published new writers within the last year. Length: 2,000-10,000 words. Sometimes recommends other markets.

How to Contact: Send complete ms with cover letter and SASE. "Prefer brief letters giving information on author concerning where he/she has been publshed before. Biographical info and what he/she is doing now." Accepts computer printout submissions. Prefers letter-quality. Reports in 2 months on mss. Publishes ms an average of 1-2 years after acceptance. Sample copy $5.

Payment: Pays $12/printed page. 2 free author's copies.

Terms: Pays on publication for first American serial rights. "We transfer copyright to author on request." Sends galleys to author. Publication copyrighted.

Advice: "Develop a careful style with characters in depth." Sponsors annual contest for best first collection of short stories published during the calendar year.

SOUTHWEST REVIEW (II), 6410 Airline, Southern Methodist University, Dallas TX 75275. (214)373-7440. Editor: Willard Spiegelman. Magazine: 6x9; 144 pages. "The majority of our readers are college-educated adults who wish to stay abreast of the latest and best in contemporary fiction, poetry, literary criticism and books in all but the most specialized disciplines." Quarterly. Estab. 1915. Circ. 1,600.

Needs: "High literary quality; no specific requirements as to subject matter, but cannot use sentimental, religious, western, poor science fiction, pornographic, true confession, mystery, juvenile or serialized or condensed novels." Receives approximately 200 unsolicited fiction mss each month. Recently published work by Meredith Steinbach, Ellen Akins, Michael Dorris. Length: prefers 3,000-5,000 words. Occasionally critiques rejected mss. Sometimes recommends other markets.

How to Contact: Send complete ms with SASE. Accepts computer printout submissions. Prefers letter-quality. Reports in 3 months on mss. Publishes ms 6-12 months after acceptance. Sample copy $5. Free guidelines with SASE.

Payment: Payment varies; writers receive 3 free author's copies.

Terms: Pays on publication for first North American serial rights. Sends galleys to author. Publication copyrighted.

Advice: "We have become less regional. A lot of time would be saved for us and for the writer if he looked at a copy of the *Southwest Review* before submitting. We like to receive a cover letter because it is some reassurance that the author has taken the time to check a current directory for the editor's name. When there isn't a cover letter, we wonder whether the same story is on 20 other desks around the country."

SOU'WESTER (II), English Dept., Southern Illinois University-Edwardsville, Edwardsville IL 62026-1438. (618)692-2289. Editor-in-Chief: Dickie A. Spurgeon. Magazine: 6x9; 88 pages; Warren's Olde style paper; 60 lb cover. General magazine of poetry and fiction. Published 3 times/year. Estab. 1960. Circ. 300.

Needs: Contemporary, erotica, ethnic, experimental, fantasy, feminist/lesbian, gay, literary, mainstream, regional and translations. Receives 40-50 unsolicited fiction mss/month. Accepts 3 mss/issue, 9 mss/year. Recently published work by Robert Wexelblatt, Robert Solomon; published new writers within the last year. Length: 5,000 words minimum; 10,000 words maximum. Occasionally critiques rejected mss.

How to Contact: Send complete ms with SASE. Simultaneous and photocopied submissions OK. Accepts computer printout submissions. Reports in 1 month. Publishes ms an average of 2 months after acceptance. Sample copy $1.50.

Payment: 2 contributor's copies. $1.50 charge for extras.

Terms: Acquires all rights. Publication copyrighted.

SPACE AND TIME (II, IV), 138 W. 70th St., New York NY 10023. Editor-in-Chief: Gordon Linzner. Magazine: 8½x5½; 120 pages; 20 lb paper; index cover stock; illustrations. Magazine of "fantasy fiction of all types and sub-genres (including science fiction)—the less categorizable, the better. *S&T* tends to feature new writers and odd pieces for which there are few if any other markets. Some poetry (overstocked through 1989). *S&T* attracts readers who cannot get enough of this material or who want something new and different. Because it is small, *S&T* can take chances on stories that are either too traditional or too experimental, and prides itself on its variety of styles and story types. Also well illustrated." Published semiannually. Estab. 1966. Circ. 400.

Needs: Adventure, fantasy, horror, humor/satire, psychic/supernatural/occult and science fiction. "Actually, will consider almost any type of fiction as long as it has a fantastic slant. No media clones— no tales involving characters/situations that are not your creation (*Star Trek*, et al) except for certain types of satire. No stories based on Von Daniken, etc., type cults." Receives 75-100 unsolicited fiction mss/month. Accepts 10 mss/issue, 20 mss/year. Recently published work by Phyllis Ann Karr, Mickey Zucker Reichert, Doug Beason; published new writers within the last year. Length: 12,000 words maximum. Occasionally critiques rejected mss. Sometimes recommends other markets.

How to Contact: Send complete ms with SASE. Photocopied submissions OK. Accepts computer printout submissions. Prefers letter-quality. Reports in 8 weeks. Publishes ms an average of 1-2 years after acceptance. Sample copy $5.

Payment: ½¢/word and 2 contributor's copies. Charges cover price less 40% contributor discount for extras.

Terms: Pays on acceptance for first North American serial rights. Publication copyrighted.

Advice: "For purposes of inventory re-assessment, we are not looking at any manuscripts after 12/31/88—at the moment we cannot tell when we will be an open market again—potential contributors should inquire."

SPECTRUM (II), Anna Maria College, Box 72-C, Sunset Lane, Paxton MA 01612. (617)757-4586. Editor: Robert H. Goepfert. Fiction Editor: Joseph Wilson. Magazine: 6x9; 64 pages; illustrations and photos. "An interdisciplinary publication publishing fiction as well as poetry, scholarly articles, reviews, art and photography. Submissions are especially encouraged from those affiliated with liberal arts colleges." Semiannually. Estab. 1985. Circ. 1,000.

Needs: Contemporary, experimental, historical, literary, mainstream. No western, mystery, erotica, science fiction. Receives an average of 15 unsolicited fiction mss/month. Accepts 4-6 mss/issue. Publishes ms approx. 6 months after acceptance. Length: 2,000-5,000 words preferred; 3,000 words average; 10,000 words maximum. Publishes short shorts. Sometimes critiques rejected mss and recommends other markets.

How to Contact: Send complete ms with cover letter. Reports in 6 weeks. SASE for ms. Photocopied submissions OK. Accepts computer printouts, no dot-matrix. Sample copy for $3, 7x10 SAE and 5 first class stamps. Fiction guidelines free.

Payment: Pays $20 and 2 contributor's copies.

Terms: Pays on publication for first North American serial rights. Sends pre-publication galleys to author. Publication not copyrighted.

Advice: "Our chief aim is diversity."

SPINDRIFT (II), Shoreline Community College, 16101 Greenwood Ave. North, Seattle WA 98133. (206)546-4785. Editor: Carol Orlock, advisor. Magazine: 140 pages; excellent quality paper; photographs; b&w artwork. "We look for fresh, original work that is not forced or 'straining' to be literary." Annually. Estab. around 1967. Circ. 500.

Needs: Contemporary, ethnic, experimental, historical (general), prose poem, regional, science fiction, serialized/excerpted novel, translations. No romance, religious/inspirational. Receives up to 150 mss/year. Accepts up to 20 mss/issue. Does not read during spring/summer. Publishes ms 3-4 months after acceptance. Recently published work by David Halpern, Martha Gils; published new writers within the last year. Length: 250 words minimum; 3,500-4,500 words maximum. Publishes short shorts.

How to Contact: Send complete ms and "bio, name, address, phone and list of titles submitted." Reports in 2 weeks on queries; 3 months on mss. SASE for notifiction; mss not returned. Photocopied submissions OK. Accepts computer printout submissions, including dot-matrix. Sample copy for $6, 8x10 SAE and $1 postage.

Payment: Pays in contributor's copies; charge for extras.

Terms: Acquires first rights. Publication not copyrighted.

Advice: "The tighter the story the better. The more lyric values in the narrative the better. Read the magazine, keep working on craft. Submit several pieces by December 18."

THE SPIRIT THAT MOVES US (II), Box 1585-W, Iowa City IA 52244. (319)338-0041. Editor: Morty Sklar. Publishes fiction, poetry and artwork. "We want feeling and imagination, work coming from the human experience." Semiannually. Estab. 1975. Circ. 1,500-2,000.

Needs: "SASE first to find out what our needs are." Literary and contemporary, feminist, gay/lesbian, humor, ethnic, prose poem, spiritual, sports and translations. No sensational. Buys 5-6 mss/issue and about 15 mss for special fiction issues. Receives approximately 90 unsolicited fiction mss each month. Recently published work by Jane Rule, Robert Taylor, Jr., W. D. Ehrhart; published new writers within the last year. Length: 10,000 words maximum. Critiques rejected mss when there is time.

How to Contact: Send SASE first for theme and plans. "A cover letter sort of makes the exchange more personal." Accepts computer printout submissions. Prefers letter-quality. Reports in 1 week-1 month on mss. Publishes ms an average of 6 months after acceptance. Sample copy $5 for *The Spirit That Moves Us Reader*; $3 for an issue of our choice.

Payment: Free cloth copy, 40% discount for extras; 25% on all other publications.

Terms: Pays on publication for first rights. Buys reprints for anthology issue. Publication copyrighted.
Advice: "Query first for theme with SASE. We're small but good and well-reviewed. Send the work you love best. Write from yourself and not from what you feel is the fashion or what the editor wants. This editor wants what you want if it has heart, imagination and skill. Aside from the obvious reason for rejection, poor writing, the main reason for rejection is lack of human concerns—that is, the writer seems to be concerned with style more than content. Read a copy of the magazine you'll be submitting work to. Don't rely on your writing for money unless you're in it for the money. Have time to write, as much time as you can get (be anti-social if necessary)."

SPOOFING! (I, IV), Yarns and Such, Creative With Words Publications, Box 223226, Carmel CA 93922. (408)649-5627. Editor: Brigitta Geltrich. Booklet: 8½x5½; approx. 60 pages; bond paper; illustrations. Folklore. Semiannually. Estab. 1975. Circ. varies.
Needs: Ethnic, humor/satire, juvenile (5-9 years), preschool (1-4 years), regional, young adult/teen (10-18 years), folklore. "Once a year we publish an anthology of the writings of young writers, titled: *We are Writers Too!*" No erotica, religious fiction. Receives 50-100 unsolicited fiction mss/month. Does not read mss July-August. Publishes ms 2-6 months after acceptance. Published new writers within the last year. Length: 1,000 words average. Critiques rejected mss "when requested, then we charge $20/prose, up to 1,000 words."
How to Contact: Query first or send complete ms with cover letter. "Reference has to be made to which project the manuscript is being submitted." Reports in 1 week on queries; 2 months on mss; longer on specific seasonal anthologies. SASE. Photocopied submissions OK. Accepts computer printout submissions, no dot-matrix. Accepts electronic submissions via Radio Shack Model 4/6 disk. Sample copy price varies. Fiction guidelines for #10 SAE with 2 first class stamps.
Payment: Charge for contributor's copies: 20% reduction on each copy ordered.
Terms: Acquires one-time rights. Publication copyrighted.
Advice: "Be creative with the English language, yet sincere and well informed."

SQUARE ONE (I, II), A Magazine of Fiction, Union Box 102; UW-Milwaukee, Milwaukee WI 53201. Editors: William D. Gagliani, Dennis K. Michel. Magazine: 8½x7; 75-90 pages; 20 lb white bond paper; 80 lb colored linen cover; illustrations; pen and ink drawings or any black on white. "There is no specific theme at *Square One*, but we publish only fiction and illustrations. Aimed at a general literate audience—people who *enjoy* reading fiction." Annually (currently). Estab. 1984. Circ. 250.
Needs: Open to all categories. "We like exciting stories in which things happen and characters *exist*." Receives 40-50 unsolicited fiction mss/month. Does not read mss between May and September. Accepts 6-12 mss/issue, depending on lengths; 6-12 mss/year. Publishes ms generally 1-11 months after acceptance. Recently published work by Kent Glenzer, Cheryl Sayre, David Loar; published new writers within the last year. Length: 3,000 words average; 7,500 words maximum. Publishes short shorts but not vignettes. "It is editorial policy to comment on at least 85% of submissions rejected, but please be patient—we have a very small staff."
How to Contact: Send complete ms with cover letter. "Too many letters explain or describe the story. Let the fiction stand on its own. If it doesn't, the letter won't help. We like a brief bio and some credits, but some writers get carried away. Use restraint and plain language—don't try to impress (it usually backfires)." Reports in 1-11 months on mss. SASE for ms. Simultaneous (if so labeled), photocopied and reprint submissions OK. Accepts computer printouts including dot-matrix if legible. Can accept electronic submissions via disk, but "We can *only* accept DS/DD disks—system is Kaypro 2X (CP/M), Wordstar. Upgrades likely in near future." Sample copy $3.50, 9x12 SAE, and 6 first class stamps (recent issue). Fiction guidelines for #10 SAE and 1 first class stamp. Please make checks payable to William D. Gagliani.
Payment: Two contributor's copies.
Terms: Pays on publication for one-time rights. Publication copyrighted.
Advice: "*Square One* is not a journal for beginners, despite what the name may imply. Rather, the name refers to the back-to-basics approach that we take—fiction must first and foremost be compelling. We want to see stories that elicit a response from the reader. We will give slight preference to Wisconsin writers, but will gladly consider submissions from anywhere. We must stress that, since we are currently an annual publication, contributors should expect long response lags. Our staff is small and *Square One* is a part-time endeavor. Patience is the best advice we can offer. Also, we oppose the absurdity of asking that writers subscribe to every magazine they would like to write for, especially given most writers' financial state. Check local public and college libraries and bookstores to see what's going on in the small press and literary markets, and—as a matter of dignity—consider carefully before submitting to magazines that routinely charge reading fees."

‡STAMP⊕AXE (I) Upper Ground Press, Société de Diffusion, 4484 Ave. Coloniale, Montréal, Québec H2W 2C7 Canada. (514)281-6644. Editor: Pier Lefe Bure. Magazine: size varies; 50-100 pages; plainfield 140(m) paper; silkscreened cover; illustrations and photographs. Quarterly. Plans special fiction issue. Estab. 1986.

Needs: Adventure, condensed novel, confession, contemporary, erotica, ethnic, experimental, fantasy, historical (general), horror, humor/satire, psychic/supernatural/occult, science fiction. "No conventional type of writing." Receives one or two unsolicited mss/month. Length: 1 page preferred. Publishes short shorts. Sometimes critiques rejected mss and recommends other markets.

How to Contact: Query with clips of published work or submit sample and portfolio. Reports in 2 weeks on queries; 2 months on mss. SASE. Simultaneous, photocopied and reprint submissions OK. Accepts computer printout submissions, including dot-matrix.

Payment: Pays $3 minimum; $35 maximum; contributor's copies.

Terms: Copyright reverts to the author. Publication copyrighted.

Advice: "Just go to the nearest post office and send us what you got, but please keep original manuscript. A photocopy will do it OK. If you can submit graphic artwork that goes with it, it would be great. And in case you like to express yourself (orally), you can send a cassette, for audio compilation on cassette or even for a radio broadcast. You can also insert some music in the background. We are also compiling a book object in an edition of 50: All pieces should be numbered and signed. You can submit a photocopy of your short stories, but you must put a 'hand touch' on each before sending it. If you are not familiar with this, don't be shy to ask—it would be a pleasure for me to reply."

‡STAR ROUTE JOURNAL (II), Box 1451, Redway CA 95560. (707)923-3256. Editor: May Siler Anderson. Magazine: 10³⁄₄x14¹⁄₂; 24 pages usually; newsprint paper and cover; b&w illustrations and photos. "Counter-culture—still think of ourselves as hippies—interested in environment, politics, philosophy, exploring ideas and changing consciousness. For people who are dissatisfied with pop culture and looking for new meaning." Monthly. Plans special fiction issue. Estab. 1978. Circ. 700.

Needs: Erotica, ethnic, experimental, feminist, gay, humor/satire, lesbian, literary, prose poem, science fiction, translations. Special interest: fiction having to do with hippies/1960s. Nothing "supportive of right-wing politics, racist views, militarism, mainstream conformist culture, consumerism." Receives 4-5 unsolicited fiction mss/month. "Would like to publish 1 short story/month. Plan to devote December issue to fiction and poetry." Publishes ms 1-4 months after acceptance. Recently published work by Paul Encimer, David Nokrmann and Jeff Spuck; published new writers within the last year. Length: 1,700 words average; 1,000 words minimum; 2,500 words maximum. Publishes short shorts. Sometimes comments on rejected mss and recommends other markets.

How to Contact: Send complete ms with cover letter, which should include "something about author." Reports in 3-4 weeks. SASE. Simultaneous, photocopied and reprint submissions OK. Accepts dot-matrix computer printouts. Sample copy $1. Fiction guidelines for #10 SAE and 1 first class stamp.

Payment: Pays in contributor's copies, free subscription to magazine. Charge for extras.

Terms: Acquires first rights. Publication not copyrighted "at present." Sponsors contests for fiction writers. "We publish a fiction/poetry issue every December with 1st, 2d and 3d prizes. We have essay contests 2 or 3 times a year."

Advice: "Usually everything is read by three of us and our decisions are highly subjective; either we like it or we don't. We like pieces with humor, insight, heart and imagination."

STARSONG (I, II), A Magazine of Fantasy, Science Fiction and Horror, Box 260B, St. Matthews SC 29135. (803)655-5895. Editor: Larry D. Kirby III. Magazine: 8¹⁄₂x11; 100 pages; Xeroxed paper; heavy cover stock; illustrations and photos sometimes. Quarterly. Estab. 1987. Circ. 200.

Needs: Fantasy, horror, humor/satire, prose poem, psychic/supernatural/occult, science fiction. Receives 30 unsolicited fiction mss/month. Accepts 8-12 mss/issue; 32-48 mss/year. Publishes ms 3 months after acceptance. Recently published work by Russell Lynch, Wade Tarzia, Kathleen Jurgens; published new writers within the last year. No preferred word length. Publishes short shorts. Sometimes critiques rejected mss.

How to Contact: Send complete ms with cover letter, which should include "bio." SASE. Simultaneous and photocopied submissions OK. Accepts computer printouts, including dot-matrix. Sample copy for $5; fiction guidelines for #10 SAE and 1 first class stamp.

Payment: Pays in contributor's copies.

Terms: Acquires one-time rights. Publication copyrighted.

Advice: "Larger mags won't experiment with style or subject matter. I like new ideas and particularly like new authors. Try new ideas. Experiment. Be willing to rewrite. Pay attention to your dreams. Read small press mags. By the time you change your style to match what's in the big mags, the style will change."

‡STAR-WEB PAPER, All This & Less Publishers, Box 40029, Berkeley CA 94704. Editor: Thomas Michael Fisher. Magazine: 8¹⁄₂x11, 80 pages; 60 lb bond paper; card stock; photos and drawings. Magazine of "20th-century consciousness, all types of material" for "enlightened doers of the literate world."

Relevance to world survival especially looked for." Annually. Estab. 1974.

Needs: No category limitations. Open to all subjects. Receives 10 unsolicited mss/month. Accepts 3 mss/issue; 3 mss/year. Occasionally critiques rejected mss upon request—query first; $3 reading fee.

How to Contact: Send 3-page sample and SASE. Send cover letter with ms. Reports in 1 month. Sample copy $6 postpaid. Make checks payable to editor.

Payment: Pays in 2 contributor's copies.

Terms: Copyrighted in name of authors.

Advice: "We look for language craft, not necessarily experimental. A 'plot' is not enough—how does conciousness move, how do syllables juxtapose? Check out past issues, literally, from a library or from us."

‡STELLANOVA (I), A Magazine of Fiction, Poetry, Opinion and Writing Experiments, Box 60, Poway CA 92064-0001. Editor: Douglas Nicoll. Magazine: 8½x11; 16 pages; 20 lb bond paper; linen cover. "An easygoing alternative to commercial (professional) publications." Bimonthly. Plans a special fiction issue. Estab. 1985. Circ. 150.

Needs: Adventure, contemporary, experimental, fantasy, horror (light), humor/satire, mainstream, prose poem, science fiction, suspense/mystery. Accepts 2-3 mss/issue; 12-18 mss/year. Publishes ms within 6 months after acceptance. Recently published work by Russ Miller, Tim Cadell, Tim Coats; published new writers within the last year. Length: 5,000 words maximum. Publishes short shorts. Sometimes critiques rejected mss and recommends other markets.

How to Contact: Send ms if less than 5,000 words; query if longer. "Cover letters do give additional information which might lead me to ask for other material in the future. If a story is by a 'first timer' I tend to be more careful with it." Reports on queries in 2-4 weeks; on mss in 1-2 months. SASE. Simultaneous submissions OK. Accepts computer printout submissions, including dot-matrix. Sample copy for $1.50. Fiction guidelines for #10 SAE and 1 first class stamp.

Payment: Pays in free subscription to magazine and contributor's copies.

Terms: Acquires one-time rights. Publication copyrighted.

Advice: "We look for good characterization, effective use of words and language to further the story's impact. Write the type of story you yourself would enjoy reading. Pay attention to details of character and word choice."

STONE SOUP (I), The Magazine By Children, Children's Art Foundation, Box 83, Santa Cruz CA 95063. (408)426-5557. Editor: Gerry Mandel. Magazine: 6x8¾; 48 pages; high quality paper; Sequoia matte cover stock; illustrations; photos. Stories, poems, book reviews and art by children up to age 13. Readership: children, librarians, educators. Published 5 times/year. Estab. 1973. Circ. 10,000.

Needs: Fiction by children on themes based on their own experiences, observations or special interests. No clichés, no formulas, no writing exercises; original work only. Receives approximately 500 unsolicited fiction mss each month. Accepts approx. 15 mss/issue. Published new writers within the last year. Length: 150-2,500 words. Critiques rejected mss upon request.

How to Contact: Send complete ms with cover letter. "We like to learn a little about our young writers, why they like to write, and how they came to write the story they are submitting." SASE. Accepts computer printout submissions. Prefers letter-quality. Reports in 1 month on mss. Publishes ms an average of 1-6 months after acceptance. Sample copy $4. Free guidelines with SASE.

Payment: 2 free author's copies; $2 charge for extras. Complimentary one-year subscription.

Terms: Acquires all rights. Publication copyrighted.

Advice: Mss are rejected because they are "derivatives of movies, TV, comic books; or classroom assignments or other formulas."

STORIES (II), 14 Beacon St., Boston MA 02108. Editor-in-Chief: Amy R. Kaufman. "*Stories* is a short story magazine that publishes short fiction exclusively. It is designed to encourage the writing of stories that evoke an emotional response." Quarterly. Estab. 1982.

Needs: Contemporary, ethnic, historical (general), humor/satire and literary. "Translations and sharply perceptive humor interest us; romance, mystery, fantasy, science fiction and political pieces generally do not. We will not exclude any story on the basis of genre; we wish only that the piece be the best of its genre." Buys 5-6 mss/issue. Length: 750 words minimum; 13,000 words maximum; 4,000-7,000 words average. "Editor will make every effort to assist in revising stories she feels have merit."

How to Contact: Send complete ms with SASE. Cannot answer queries. Photocopies preferred. Simultaneous submissions OK "if marked as such." Reports in 8-10 weeks on mss. Sample issue $4; 2 for $6. Free fiction guidelines with SASE.

Payment: $150 average.

Terms: Pays within 7 days of publication for first North American serial rights.

Advice: "Simplicity is achieved after a struggle, and universality is possible only to a degree, but we feel that these are the qualities most likely to evoke readers' sympathy and concern. Timelessness is another ideal we pursue, by avoiding language and subjects that are fashionable. Most writers submit half-finished work—they haven't taken themselves seriously enough. Study Strunk & White's *Elements of Style*, and emulate your favorite authors. You can't aim too high."

‡STORIES & LETTERS DIGEST (I, II), 801 S. Puget Sound Ave., Tacoma WA 98405. (206)752-9434. Editor: James Rudy Humphreys. Magazine: 5 1/2x8 1/2; 32 pages; 20 lb paper; 67 lb vellum cover; illustrations occasionally. "Publishes short fiction and letters from readers." Quarterly. Plans special fiction issue. Estab. 1988. Circ. 300.
Needs: Adventure, contemporary, experimental, fantasy, horror, humor/satire, literary, mainstream, religious/inspirational, romance (contemporary), science fiction, suspense/mystery, western. No pornographic, erotica, gay, lesbian, occult, religious "preaching." Buys 4-8 mss/issue; 16-32 mss/year. Publishes ms 3-6 months after acceptance. Length: 2,000 words preferred; 500 words minimum; 3,000 words maximum. Sometimes critiques rejected mss and recommends other markets.
How to Contact: Send complete ms with cover letter. Cover letter should include "author's bio and special writing interests." Reports in 2-3 weeks on queries; 4-6 weeks on mss. SASE. Photocopied and reprint submissions OK. Accepts computer printout submissions. Sample copy for $3. Fiction guidelines for #10 SAE and 1 first class stamp.
Payment: Pays 1/4¢/word minimum; 1/2¢/word maximum. Free contributor's copies; charge for extras.
Terms: Pays on acceptance. Purchases one-time rights. Sends galleys to author. Publication copyrighted. Plans to sponsor annual contest.
Advice: "Send me a good story. I have no restrictions on subject or style provided, in my opinion, it is not pornographic or obscene. Be yourself. Don't be afraid to be sentimental or emotional. There is nothing wrong with sentiment or emotion if it is honest, not just thrown in to manipulate the reader. I like stories that move me to the point of getting a lump in my throat. I also like stories that make me laugh."

STORYQUARTERLY (II), Box 1416, Northbrook IL 60065. (312)433-0741. Co-Editors: Anne Brashler and Diane Williams. Magazine: approximately 6x9; 130 pages; good quality paper; illustrations; photos. A magazine devoted to the short story and committed to a full range of styles and forms. Published twice yearly. Estab. 1975. Circ. 3,000.
Needs: Accepts 12-15 mss/issue, 20-30 mss/year. Receives 100 unsolicited fiction mss/month. Recently published work by Gordon Lish, Stephen Dixon and Rita Doucette. Published new writers within the last year.
How to Contact: Send complete ms with SASE. Reports in 3 months on mss. Sample copy $4.
Payment: 3 free author's copies.
Terms: Acquires one-time rights. Publication copyrighted. Copyright reverts to author after publication.
Advice: "Send one manuscript at a time, subscribe to the magazine, send SASE. Send us your best work."

‡STREAMLINES (II), Minnesota Journal of Creative Writing, Streamlines, Inc., 207 Church St. SE, Minneapolis MN 55414. (612)625-3363, 625-1595. Editor: John Seals. Fiction Editor: Leslie Worthington. Magazine: 8 1/2x11; 40 pages; 70 lb paper; Hammermill linen cover; illustrations and photos. "For writers, people interested in creative writing and in literature." Semiannually. Estab. 1979. Circ. 600.
Needs: Contemporary, ethnic, experimental, historical (general), humor/satire, literary, regional, translations. Accepts 10-12 mss/issue; 20-24 mss/year. Publishes ms 1 month after acceptance. Length: 2,500 words average; 4,000 words maximum. Publishes short shorts. Recently published work by Michael McGorrey, Michael Kennedy and Leslie Worthington. Length: 1,000 words. Occasionally critiques rejected mss.
How to Contact: Send complete ms with cover letter, which should include "name, address, phone number, brief bio; information on the author's ties to University of Minnesota, another MN college or the state in general." Reports in 1 month on queries; 4-6 months on mss. SASE. Accepts computer printouts, including dot-matrix. Sample copy $2.00 and 9x12 SAE. Free fiction guidelines for #10 SAE and 1 first class stamp.
Payment: 6 free contributor's copies.
Terms: Acquires one-time rights.
Advice: "We accept a wide range of writing, from traditional to experimental. Our main goal is to publish writing of good quality. We receive a great deal of funding from the University of Minnesota English Dept. With these ties, we are interested in receiving and publishing a wide range of creative writing."

STRUGGLE (IV), A Magazine of Proletarian Revolutionary Literature, Marxist-Leninist Party USA, Detroit Branch, Box 13261, Harper Station, Detroit MI 48213-0261. (313)824-6258. Editor: Tim Hall. Magazine: 5 1/2x8 1/2; 24-48 pages; 20 lb white bond paper; colored cover; illustrations; occasional photographs. Publishes material related to "the struggle of the working class and all progressive people against the rule of the rich—including their war policies, racism, exploitation of the workers, oppression of women, etc." Quarterly. Estab. 1985.

Needs: Contemporary, ethnic, experimental, feminist, historical (general), humor/satire, literary, prose poem, regional, science fiction, senior citizen/retirement, suspense/mystery, translations, young adult/teen (10-18). "The theme can be approached in many ways, including plenty of categories not listed here." No romance, psychic, western, erotica, religious. Receives 1-2 unsolicited fiction mss/month. "Has published three stories in past three issues. Would like more." Publishes ms 3 months or less after acceptance. Recently published work by Leo Paulson, Tim Hall, Peter Poyas; published new writers within the last year. Length: 1,000-3,000 words average; 5,000 words maximum. Publishes short shorts. Frequently critiques rejected mss.

How to Contact: Send complete ms; cover letter optional but helpful. Reports in 3 months. SASE. Simultaneous, photocopied and reprint submissions OK. Accepts computer printout submissions, including dot-matrix. Sample copy for $1.50.

Payment: Pays 2 contributor's copies.

Terms: No rights acquired. Publication not copyrighted.

Advice: "Write about the oppression of the working people, the poor, the minorities, women, and their rebellion against it—we are not interested in anything which accepts the status quo. We are not too worried about plot and advanced technique (fine if we get them!)—we would probably accept things others would call sketches, provided they sizzle with life and struggle. Just describe for us a situation in which some real people confront some problem of oppression, however seemingly minor. Observe and put down the real facts. Tidy it up later. We have increased our fiction portion of our content. We get poetry and songs all the time. We want more fiction."

SUB ROSA (II), 840 Palisade Ave., #2A, Teaneck NJ 07666. (201)836-6634. Editors: Noemie Maxwell and Nico Vassilakis. Magazine: 8½x5½; 36-40 pages; 65 lb Vellum cover; b&w illustrations. "Mostly poetry for the two years we've been in existence. We are ready now to publish short stories and plays." Published every 6 weeks. Estab. 1985. Circ. 150.

Needs: Contemporary, erotica, ethnic, experimental, fantasy, feminist, gay, historical (general), humor/satire, lesbian, literary, translations, political, prose poem, spiritual (very selectively), sports (if literary). No romance, religion, sentimental, "cute." Publishes ms up to 4 months after acceptance. Recently published work by Alan Atkinson, Duane Locke, Richard Gessner. Length: 1,000-2,500 words average; no minimum; 5,000 words maximum.

How to Contact: Send complete ms with cover letter. "We like cover letters because we are curious about the people who send us work and because we like to feel that the author has chosen *Sub Rosa* as a possible place to publish for rational or even whimsical reasons rather than as part of a statistical ploy to send to as many (unknown) magazines as possible." Reports in 2 weeks on queries; 2 months on mss. SASE. Photocopied submissions OK. Accepts computer printout submissions including dot-matrix. Sample copy $1.50. Fiction guidelines for #10 SAE and 1 first class stamp.

Payment: Pays in contributor's copies.

Terms: Acquires one-time rights.

Advice: "Our editorial choice is entirely subjective. We publish what we like. We are more likely to select work for publication if it shows a real direction away from the mainstream and toward the highly personal and the experimental. We are less likely to go for traditional themes and forms. On a more specific note, writers should avoid 'wordiness.' "

‡SUMMERFIELD JOURNAL (II),Morning Star Design Service, Box 499, Riverdale GA 30274. (404)996-7556. Editor: Darrell Bagley. Magazine: 5½x8½; 36-48 pages; high paper quality; matte card cover. "Poetry and short fiction for a general audience." Quarterly. Plans special fiction issue. Estab. 1987. Circ. 150.

Needs: Adventure, contemporary, ethnic, experimental, fantasy, feminist, historical, horror, humor/satire, juvenile, literary, mainstream, prose poem, psychic/supernatural/occult, regional, religious/inspirational, romance (contemporary, historical, young adult), science fiction, senior citizen/retirement, sports, suspense/mystery, translations, western, young adult/teen. No graphic sex and violence. Receives 30 unsolicited fiction mss/month. Accepts 6-8 mss/issue; 24-32 mss/year. Publishes ms usually in next available issue; 1-3 months. Charges reading fee of $3 (waived for subscribers). Recently published work by Roberta Ross, Dan O'Neill, James R. Shott. Length: 2,000 words maximum. Publishes short shorts. Always comments on rejected mss.

How to Contact: Request guidelines or send complete ms with cover letter. Responds in 2 weeks. SASE. Simultaneous, photocopied and reprint submissions OK. Accepts dot-matrix computer printouts "if legible." Accepts electronic submissions via disk or modem; write for requirements. Sample copy $4.50 or less. Fiction guidelines for #10 SAE and 1 first class stamp.

Payment: Pays 2 contributor's copies.

Terms: Acquires first North American serial rights. Publication copyrighted. Offers $100 award quarterly for best of issue.

Advice: "Most of what we see is very poor product; either in characterization, story line, incontinuity and/or obscurity of point. We look for a solid story line with discernible beginning, middle and end, with as good characterization as can be achieved in our limits, with that certain suspension of disbelief that draws the reader fully into the tale. Show us, don't tell us. Don't be afraid to cut out your favorite passage if it does nothing to advance your story. Don't be too proud or too disheartened to accept and act on your editor's comments and recommendations."

THE SUN (II), The Sun Publishing Company, Inc., 412 W. Rosemary St., Chapel Hill NC 27516. (919)942-5282. Editor: Sy Safransky. Magazine: 8½x11; 40 pages; offset paper; glossy cover stock; illustrations; photos. "*The Sun* is a magazine of ideas. We publish all kinds of writing—fiction, articles, poetry. Our only criteria are that the writing make sense and enrich our common space. We direct *The Sun* toward interests which move us, and we trust our readers will respond." Monthly. Estab. 1974. Circ. 10,000.

Needs: Open to all fiction. Accepts 1 ms/issue. Receives approximately 100 unsolicited fiction mss each month. Recently published work by Tillie Olsen, Susan Watkins, James Carlos Blake; published new writers within the last year. Length: 10,000 words maximum.

How to Contact: Send complete ms with SASE. Reports in 1 month. Publishes ms an average of 1-3 months after acceptance. Sample copy $3.

Payment: Up to $100 on publication, plus 2 free author's copies and a complimentary subscription.

Terms: Acquires one-time rights. Publishes reprints. Publication copyrighted.

Advice: "Nothing's necessarily 'wrong' with most rejected mss—just not what we're looking for. Helpful to read magazine first."

SUN DOG: THE SOUTHEAST REVIEW (II), English Department, 4th Floor Williams, Florida State University, Tallahassee FL 32306. (904)644-1248. Editor: Craig Stroupe. Magazine: 6x9; 60-100 pages; 70 lb paper; 10 pt. Krome Kote cover; illustrations; photos. Published biannually. Estab. 1979. Circ. 2,000.

Needs: "We want stories which are well written, beautifully written, with striking images, incidents and characters. We are interested more in quality than in style or genre." Accepts 20 mss/year. Receives approximately 60 unsolicited fiction mss each month. Reads less frequently during summer. Recently published work by Joe Straub and Padgett Powell; published new writers within the last year. Critiques rejected mss when there is time. Occasionally recommends other markets.

How to Contact: Send complete ms with SASE. Typed, double-spaced, on good bond. Clean photocopy acceptable. "Short bio or cover letter would be appreciated." Publishes ms an average of 2-6 months after acceptance. Sample copy $4.

Payment: 2 free author's copies. $2 charge for extras.

Terms: Acquires first North American serial rights which then revert to author. Publication copyrighted.

Advice: "Avoid trendy experimentation for its own sake (present-tense narration, observation that isn't also revelation). Fresh stories, moving, interesting characters and a sensitivity to language are still fiction mainstays. Also publishes winner and runners up of the World's Greatest Short Short Story Contest sponsored by the Florida State University English Department. Entries should be 250 words or less, typed double-spaced on one sheet of paper, and submitted with SASE to the World's Greatest Short Short Story Contest at the above address. Deadline for the contest is in mid-February."

SWIFT KICK (II), 1711 Amherst St., Buffalo NY 14214. (716)837-7778. Editor: Robin Kay Willoughby. Magazine: size, number of pages, paper quality, cover stock vary; illustrations; photos, b&w line art, xerographs. Specializes in unusual formats, hard-to-classify works, visual poetry, found art, etc. for " 'pataphysical, rarified audience." Published special fiction issue; plans another. Estab. 1981. Circ. 100.

Needs: Open. "If it doesn't seem to fit a regular category, it's probably what we'd like! No boring, slipshod, everyday stuff like in mass-market magazines." Receives 5 unsolicited fiction mss/month. Accepts 1-2 mss/issue. Does not read just before Christmas. Publishes ms depending on finances (6 months-1 year) after acceptance. Last published fiction by Joe Ferguson. Publishes short shorts of 1,000 words (or 1 picture). Sometimes recommends other markets.

How to Contact: Query first for longer works or send complete ms with cover letter with short work. Reports in 2-12 months. SASE ("or include reply card with OK to toss enclosed work.") Simultaneous and photocopied submissions OK. Will consider reprints of astoundingly good work (out of print). Accepts computer printouts including dot-matrix. Sample copy for $7; "sample-purchase recommended to best understand magazine's needs."

Payment: Pays in contributor's copies, (½ cover price) charge for extras.

Terms: Acquires one-time rights. Rights revert to artists/authors. Sends galleys to author if requested. Publication copyrighted.

Advice: "We always get less fiction than poetry—if a story is good, it has a good chance of publication in little mags. Editorially, I'm a snob, so don't write like anyone else; be *so* literate your writing transcends literature and (almost) literacy. Don't submit over 10 pages first time. Submit a 'grabber' that makes an editor ask for more. Don't neglect the stories in your own life for someone else's castles-in-the-air."

‡SYCAMORE REVIEW (II), Department of English, Purdue University, West Lafayette IN 47907. (317)494-3783. Editor: Henry J. Hughes. Fiction Editor: Elizabeth Stuckey-French. Magazine: 5½x8½; 100 pages; heavy, textured, uncoated paper; heavy matte uncoated cover; no unsolicited art. "Journal devoted to contemporary literature. We publish both traditional and experimental fiction, personal essay and poetry." Semiannually. Estab. 1989. Circ. 1,000.

Needs: Contemporary, experimental, historical (general), humor/satire, literary, mainstream, regional, sports, translations. "We generally avoid genre literature, but maintain no formal restrictions on style or subject matter. No science fiction, romance, children's." Publishes ms 3 months-1 year after acceptance. Length: 3,750 words preferred; 250 words minimum. Sometimes critiques rejected mss and recommends other markets.

How to Contact: Send complete ms with cover letter. Cover letter should include previous publications, address changes. Reports in 3 months. SASE. Simultaneous and photocopied submissions OK. Accepts computer printout submissions, including dot-matrix. Sample copy for $4. Fiction guidelines for #10 SAE and 1 first class stamp.

Payment: Pays in contributor's copies; charge for extras.

Terms: Acquires one-time rights. Publication copyrighted.

Advice: "We especially recommend readers to digest work from magazines like *The Indiana Review*, *Missouri Review* and *Sewanee Review* to help shape ideas concerning the status of quality magazine fiction today. The fiction writer must read voraciously. Read stories published in *The New Yorker* and read stories appearing in your community or university magazine. When you are ready to write (you are always ready) begin writing from actual experience."

‡T.W.I. (I, II), A Journal of Politics and Literature, The T.W.I. (Typing While Intoxicated) Collective, Box 19441, Washington DC 20036. (202)234-9029. Editor: Curtis Olson. Magazine: 8½x11; 50 pages; 20 lb paper; card stock; illustrations. "*T.W.I.* publishes new and unique fiction and nonfiction from the lower fringes of society and culture." Published 3-4 times per year. Plans special fiction issue. Estab. 1987. Circ. 100.

Needs: Contemporary, erotica, experimental, humor/satire, literary, prose poem. "No formula fiction. Nothing written to make money." Receives 2-4 unsolicited mss/month. Accepts 6-8 mss/year. Publishes ms 3-4 months after acceptance. Recently published work by John Calvit, Carl Zimmor, Al Poe; published new writers within the last year. Length: 8,000 words maximum. Publishes short shorts. Sometimes critiques rejected mss.

How to Contact: Query first or send complete ms with cover letter. "I like a cover letter that introduces the author, tells me a bit about them, where he/she has been published, and a bit about what is unique about the submission and what it is trying to accomplish." Reports in 2 weeks on queries; 2 month on mss. SASE for ms. Photocopied submissions OK. Accepts computer printout submissions, no dot-matrix. Sample copy for $2.

Payment: Pays in 3 contributor's copies.

Terms: Acquires first North American serial rights. Publication copyrighted.

Advice: "Most academic and magazine fiction and poetry bores me. It doesn't speak to people or to the world. I've been called a 'undergound' publisher. I guess it's true. It's in underground publications that people talk to people. That is where the future of writing is, I think (or at least, I hope). Those are two pieces of advice I give to potential contributors to *T.W.I.*: You've gotta *feel* it; and don't take yourself too seriously (but take your writing *very* seriously). *T.W.I.* is growing and changing with each issue, so our needs are constantly changing. It would probably be helpful to a contributor to write first and get our current guidelines or a copy of the latest issue."

TALES OF THE OLD WEST (IV), Bane K. Wilker's, PPG Publishing Co., Box 22866, Denver CO 80222. (303)722-9966. Editor: Keith Olsen. Magazine: 7x8½; 20-50 pages; offset stock; Vellum cover; illustrations and photos. "Our magazine deals with all aspects of the old West: cowboys, Indians, the frontier, the railroads, ranchers, gold diggers, etc. for anyone who enjoys Westerns." Quarterly. Estab. 1985. Circ. 250.

Needs: Western. Receives 25 unsolicited mss/month. Accepts 3-5 mss/issue; 12-20 mss/year. Publishes ms within 1 year after acceptance. Recently published work by Steven Levi, Phil Gulick, Bane Wilker. Published new writers within the last year. Length: 2,500 words average; 500 words mini-

mum; 5,000 words maximum. Publishes short shorts. Occasionally critiques rejected mss and recommends other markets.
How to Contact: Send complete ms with cover letter. Reports in 2-4 weeks on queries; 2 months on mss. SASE. Simultaneous, photocopied, reprint submissions OK. Accepts computer printout submissions, including dot-matrix. Sample copy $3. Subscription: $10 for 1 year; $18 for 2 years. Fiction guidelines for #10 SAE and 1 first class stamp.
Payment: Free contributor's copies.
Terms: Acquires first North American serial rights and reprint rights. Publication copyrighted. Sponsors Bane K. Wilker Westerner Awards for short fiction and poetry.
Advice: "The only requirement for writing for our magazine is a love of the West of old and what it stood for. So many writers give up after one reject. I would like to see some of the writers I reject try again. Often, the reason the piece was turned down could be corrected with a little effort."

‡THE TAMPA REVIEW (III), Humanities Division, Box 135F, University of Tampa, Tampa FL 33606. (813)253-3333, ext. 424. Editor: Richard Matthews. Fiction Editor: Andy Solomon. Magazine: 8x10; over 100 pages; bond paper; illustrations; photos. "Interested in fiction of distinctive literary quality." Annually. Estab. 1988.
Needs: Contemporary, ethnic, experimental, fantasy, historical, humor/satire, literary, mainstream, prose poem, translations. "We are far more interested in quality than in genre. No sentimental as opposed to genuinely moving, nor self-conscious style at the expense of human truth." Buys 3-7 mss/issue. Publishes ms within 2 months-1 year of acceptance. Agented fiction 60%. Recently published work by Lee K. Abbott, Lorrie Moore, Tim O'Connor. Length: 1,000 words minimum; 6,000 words maximum. Publishes short shorts "if the story is good enough." Sometimes critiques rejected mss and recommends other markets.
How to Contact: Send complete mss with cover letter, which should include brief bio and publishing record. Include Social Security number. Reports in 4 weeks. SASE. Simultaneous and photocopied submissions OK. Accepts computer printout submissions, including dot-matrix. "Letter quality preferred." Sample copy for $5, 9x12 SAE and 5 first class stamps. Fiction guidelines for #10 SAE and 1 first class stamp.
Payment: Pays $10 per printed page.
Terms: Pays on publication for first North American serial rights. Sends galleys to author. Publication copyrighted.
Advice: "There are more good writers publishing in magazines today than there have been in many decades. Unfortunately, there are even more bad ones. In T. Gertler's *Elbowing the Seducer*, an editor advises a young writer that he wants to hear her voice completely, to tell (he means 'show') him in a story the truest thing she knows. We concur. Rather than a trendy workshop story or a minimalism that actually stems from not having much to say, we would like to see stories that make us believe they mattered to the writer and, more importantly, will matter to a reader. Trim until only the essential is left, and don't give up belief in yourself. And it might help to attend a good writers conference, e.g. Wesleyan or Bennington."

‡TAPESTRY (I), Rte. 3, Box 272-D, Ripley MS 38663. Editor: Joan Cissom. Magazine: 5½x8½; 32 pages; illustrations and photographs. Monthly. Estab. 1988.
Needs: Fantasy, horror. "Publishes poems, fiction, articles on writing, interviews with pros in field, market/contact news." Recently published work by David Valentino, D.M. Vosk. Length: 3,000 words maximum. Publishes short shorts.
How to Contact; Send complete ms with cover letter. SASE. Sample copy for $2.50.
Payment: Pays $3 and 2 contributor's copies.
Terms: Pays on acceptance. Purchases one-time rights. Publication copyrighted. Sponsors contest for fiction writers. Send SASE for details.

‡TARA'S LITERARY ARTS JOURNAL (II), Anastacia Press, Box 834, Bethel Park PA 15102-9998. Editor: Stacey A. Harris. Magazine: 44 pages; glossy white paper and cover; illustrations; photos. "Religion, social issues, metaphysical." Quarterly. Estab. 1987. Circ. 300.
Needs: Ethnic, feminist, literary, psychic/supernatural/occult, prose poem, religious/inspirational, spiritual. No horror, erotica. Accepts 1 ms/issue; 4 mss/year. Publishes ms within 3 months of acceptance. Recently published work by Robert Michael Morris. Length: 1,000 words preferred; 500 words minimum; 1,500 words maximum. Will consider short shorts. Sometimes critiques rejected mss.
How to Contact: Send complete mss with cover letter which should include "bio information." Reports on mss in 1 month. SASE. Simultaneous and photocopied submissions OK. Accepts computer printout submissions, including dot-matrix. Sample copy for $2.
Payment: Pays $10 and 1 contributor copy.
Terms: Offers "entire fee" as kill fee. Acquires one-time rights. Publication copyrighted.

TERROR TIME AGAIN (I), Nocturnal Publications, 1320 Mississippi, #102, St. Paul MN 55101. Editor: Donald L. Miller. Magazine: 5x8; 53-60 pages; 20 lb paper; 67 lb cover stock; illustrations. "*Terror Time Again*'s theme is to produce terror in the reader. Material that scares the reader is our goal." Annually. Estab. 1987. Circ. 200.
Needs: Horror. No science fiction or sword and sorcery. Receives 10 unsolicited fiction mss/month. Accepts 7-10 mss/issue. Does not read September 1 to December 31. Publishes ms in October of year accepted. Recently published work by Ann Taylor, Ronald Drozdowski and Ronald Kelly; published new writers within the last year. Length: 1,000 words average; 350 words minimum; 2,000 words maximum. Publishes short shorts. Length: 350-500 words. Sometimes critiques rejected mss; recommends other markets.
How to Contact: Send complete ms with cover letter containing information about the author. Reports in 2 weeks on queries; 1 month on mss. SASE. Simultaneous, photocopied and reprint submissions OK. Accepts computer printout submissions, no dot-matrix. Sample copy $5; fiction guidelines free.
Payment: 1/4¢-1/2¢/word; contributor's copies.
Terms: Pays on publication for one-time rights. Publication copyrighted. Sponsors contests and awards for fiction writers. "*Terror Time Again* has a cover contest via *The Nightmare Express*. A cover illustration is used by an author to derive upon a story using said artwork. Interested persons need to write to me so they can find out what cover it will be. *TNE* is published every other month."
Advice: "I see a lot of new writers curbing the horror field their own way. I like that. A writer can be whatever he/she chooses, and his/her characters reveal the truth underneath. We will work with new authors. I want the readers of *Terror Time Again* to come away from a story too scared to forget the experience. Always enclose SASE."

THE TEXAS REVIEW (II), Sam Houston State University Press, Huntsville TX 77341. (713)294-1423. Editor: Paul Ruffin. Magazine: 6x9; 148-190 pages; best quality paper; 70 lb cover stock; illustrations; photos. "We publish top quality poetry, fiction, articles, interviews and reviews for a general audience." Semiannually. Estab. 1976. Circ. 700.
Needs: Literary and contemporary fiction. "We are eager enough to consider fiction of quality, no matter what its theme or subject matter. No juvenile fiction." Accepts 4 mss/issue. Receives approximately 40-60 unsolicited fiction mss each month. Recently published work by Richard Elman, Peter S. Scherman, Margaret Kingery; published new writers within the last year. Length: 500-10,000 words. Critiques rejected mss "when there is time." Recommends other markets.
How to Contact: Send complete ms with cover letter. SASE. Reports in 3 months on mss. Sample copy $3.
Payment: Free author's copies plus one year subscription.
Terms: Acquires all rights. Sends galleys to author. Publication copyrighted.
Advice: "Take a straightforward approach in submitting material, and be sure to include a SASE with sufficient postage to cover cost of return of manuscript, if desired, or a rejection/acceptance letter."

‡THEMA (II,IV), Bothomos Enterprises, Box 74109, Metairie LA 70033-4109. Editor: Virginia Howard. Magazine: 5 1/2x8 1/2; 200 pages; good paper; Grandee Strathmore cover stock; b&w illustrations. "Different specified theme for each issue—short stories, poems, b&w artwork must relate to that theme." Quarterly. Plans special fiction issue. Estab. 1988.
Needs: Adventure, contemporary, experimental, humor/satire, literary, mainstream, prose poem, psychic/supernatural/occult, regional, science fiction, sports, suspense/mystery, western. "Each issue is based on a specified premise—a different unique theme for each issue. Many types of fiction acceptable, but must fit the premise. No pornographic, scatological, erotic fiction." Publishes ms within 3-4 months of acceptance. Recently published work by Charles F. Chapman; Gail Howard; Norman McMillan. Length: 4,500 words preferred; 2,700 words minimum; 6,000 words maximum. Publishes short shorts "if very clever." Length: 300-500 words. Sometimes critiques rejected mss and recommends other markets.
How to Contact: Send complete ms with cover letter, which should include "name and address, brief introduction, specifying the intended target issue for the mss." Reports on queries in 1 week; on mss in 4-6 weeks. SASE. Photocopied submissions OK. No dot-matrix computer printouts. Sample copy for $4. Free fiction guidelines.
Payment: Pays $25.
Terms: Pays on acceptance. Purchases one-time rights. Publication copyrighted.
Advice: "A general malaise of sleaze and profanity seems to have overcome the short-story genre in many literary journals. A clever story, well-told, doesn't need that (in most cases). We need more stories told in the Mark Twain/O. Henry tradition in magazine fiction." Upcoming themes: Miz Martha say she quittin (deadline May 1, 1989); A letter to an ancient (deadline August 1, 1989).

‡**THIN ICE (II)**, 379 Lincoln Ave., Council Bluffs IA 51503. (712)322-9125. Co-editors: Kathleen Jurgens and Susan Lilas Wiggs. Magazine: digest size; 95-110 pages; 16-20 lb paper; enamel cover; b&w, pen and ink illustrations. "Horror and dark fantasy—short stories, poetry, interviews, art." Quarterly. Estab. 1987. Circ. 250.

Needs: Experimental, fantasy (dark), horror, humor/satire, literary, prose poem, psychic/supernatural/occult. No "racist, preachy, straight porn for shock value." Receives 30-60 unsolicited mss/month. Buys approx. 10 mss/issue; approx. 40 mss/year. Publishes ms 6 months-1 year after acceptance. Recently published work by J. N. Williamson, David Silva, Jeannette Hopper. Length: 2,000-4,000 words preferred; 3,000 minimum; no maximum. Sometimes critiques rejected mss and recommends other markets.

How to Contact: Send complete ms with cover letter. Cover letter should include "a personal introduction, mention a few prior 'sales' if desired (though not necessary), where the writers heard of *Thin Ice*." Reports in 1 week on queries; 4-8 weeks on mss. SASE. Photocopied and reprint submissions OK (subject to reprint rights). Accepts computer printout submissions, including dot-matrix (but prefer not to). Sample copy for $4. Fiction guidelines free with #10 SAE and 1 first class stamp.

Payment: Pays in contributor's copies.

Terms: Acquires first North American serial rights. Sends galleys to author.

Advice: "Invest in a copy of our magazine and read it from cover to cover. Get a 'feel' for the overall mood, tone, and subject matter. Don't apologize for misspellings or coffee stains on the manuscript—retype it. While we prefer informal query letters, we become quite irate when potential contributors treat us unprofessionally. We respond to all submissions personally, frequently offering editorial commentary. Always include an SASE with the correct amount of postage. Give us the full 8 weeks reponse time. Do not resort to phone calls or nasty letters of inquiry. If you're anxiety-ridden, drop us a note. We'll respond. Don't give up after a first rejection; keep trying."

Kathleen Jurgens, co-editor of Thin Ice, *explains why they chose this cover illustration by Jeanette Hopper. "Issue #1 of* Thin Ice *has a flavor of the midwest built into it," she says. "Many of the contributing writers and artists live in the midwest and the interview with David Morrell (who lives in Iowa City, Iowa) and 'Corn King,' the interview with Stephen King, encouraged us to seek a cover illustration indicative of rural America. Jeanette Hopper's style and design fit our needs exactly: clean lines, a simple yet effective design, a tonal setting—unbounded sky and fields, the stalk of wheat, the almost comical scarecrow, until you notice the skeletal hand."*

‡**THIRD WOMAN (II,IV)**, Chicano Studies Dept., Dwinelle Hall, University of California, Berkeley CA 94720. (415)642-0708 or 642-0240. Editor: Norma Alarcón Magazine: 5½x8½; 100-150 pages; standard good quality paper; glossy color cover; illustrations; photos. "Literature and the arts focusing on the work by/about U.S. Latinas, Hispanic World and Third World Women in general: poetry, narrative, drama, reviews, interviews, etc." Semiannually. Estab. 1981. Circ. 1,500.

Needs: Ethnic, feminist, translations. Receives 4 mss/month. Accepts 10 mss/year. Publishes ms within 6 months-2 years of acceptance. Recently published work by Sandra Cisneros, Luz María Umpierre. Length: 5,000-10,000 words preferred. Publishes short shorts.

How to Contact: Send complete ms with cover letter. Reports on queries in 6-8 weeks; on mss in 6 months. SASE. Simultaneous and photocopied submissions OK. Accepts computer printout submis-

sions, including dot-matrix. Free sample copy.
Payment: Pays in contributor's copies.
Terms: Acquires first rights. Sends galleys to author. Publication copyrighted. Sponsors contests for fiction writers. "Contests are occasional; please write and inquire of editor."
Advice: Looks for "aesthetic quality" in fiction submissions. "Read!"

THE THREEPENNY REVIEW (II), Box 9131, Berkeley CA 94709. (415)849-4545. Editor: Wendy Lesser. Tabloid: 11x17; 32 pages; electrobrite paper; white book stock cover; original graphic illustrations; photos. Publishes "literature and performing arts reviews, essays, fiction, poetry and other reviews for a wide-ranging audience including anyone interested in the arts." Quarterly. Estab. 1980. Circ. 8,000.
Needs: Short fiction. Receives approximately 40-60 unsolicited fiction mss each month. Accepts 3 mss/issue; 12 mss/year. Publishes short shorts. Recently published work by John Berger, Paul Bowles, Leonard Michaels, Paula Fox; published new writers within the last year. Length: 3,000-5,000 words. Sometimes recommends other markets.
How to Contact: Query or send ms with a cover letter "showing evidence of familiarity with publication; prior credits." Accepts computer printout submissions—letter-quality only. Reports in 2 weeks on queries, 2 months on mss. Sample copy $3 with 9x12 SAE and $1 postage, or $4 check. Guidelines for # 10 SASE.
Payment: Cash payment of $100.
Terms: Acquires first rights. Sends galleys to author. Publication copyrighted.
Advice: "We receive approximately 100 times as many stories as we can publish in a given quarter. Also, most of the stories we receive are either stylistically experimental without having any interesting plot or characters, or naively sentimental."

‡TIMBUKTU (II), Box 469, Charlottesville VA 22902. Editor: Molly Turner. Magazine: 8½x11; 80-100 pages; vellum paper; heavy, glossy card cover stock; illustrations; photos. "Each issue focuses on a different broad area of culture and its mythology; for instance, Africa, the American West, outer space, etc. *Timbuktu* is nationally distributed and has a diverse audience." Semiannually. Estab. 1987. Circ. 800.
Needs: Condensed/excerpted novel, experimental, humor/satire, literary, prose poem, serialized novel. "No genre stuff, no writing program formula stories—just fresh, innovative, well-written manuscripts." Receives 50 mss/month. Accepts 3-5 mss/issue; 8-10 mss/year. Publishes ms within 6 months of acceptance. Recently published work by Eberle Umbach, Sheila McMillen, Cedric Tolley. No preferred length. Publishes short shorts. Sometimes critiques rejected mss and recommends other markets.
How to Contact: Send complete ms. Reports in 1 week on queries; in 6-8 weeks on mss. SASE. Simultaneous and photocopied submissions OK. Accepts computer printout submissions, including dot-matrix. Sample copy for $4. Fiction guidelines for SAE and 1 first class stamp.
Payment: Pays in free subscription to magazine and contributor's copies.
Terms: Acquires one-time rights. Publication copyrighted.
Advice: "Cover letters generally don't contribute much—I'm only interested if the writer knows the magazine for some reason and has something interesting to say about why they chose to submit to us rather than someone else."

‡TOUCHSTONE (II), Literary Journal, Box 980579, Houston TX 77098. Magazine: 8½x5½; 40 pages; 100 lb paper; chrome cover stock; perfectbound; illustrations; photos, drawings, both camera-ready. "We publish poetry, short stories, literary criticism, interviews and reviews. We reach a liberal, well-educated audience." Quarterly. Estab. 1976. Circ. 1,000.
Needs: Contemporary, experimental, humor/satire, literary, minority viewpoints, mainstream, prose poem and translations. "No moralizing." Receives 24 unsolicited fiction mss/month. Accepts 1 mss/issue, 4 mss/year. Recently published work by Sandra Scofield, Chris Wood. Length: 750 words minimum, 3,000 words maximum, 1,500 words average.
How to Contact: Send complete ms with SASE. "We always prefer some type of cover letter. We are interested in knowing the writer's (other) occupation and recent credits, briefly stated. Writer need not summarize the enclosed story and need not tell us how well it fits our needs." Photocopied submissions OK. Accepts computer printout submissions. Prefers letter-quality. Reports in 6 weeks. Sample copy $4. Fiction guidelines for #10 SAE and 1 first class stamp.
Payment: 1 free contributor's copy; $5 charge for extras.
Terms: Acquires first rights, reverts to author upon publication. Publication copyrighted.
Advice: "Innovative form and experimental styles preferred. You can save yourself time and increase your successes by studying the publisher's work before you submit."

Close-up

Wendy Lesser
The Threepenny Review

In 1987, after seven years publishing *The Threepenny Review*, Wendy Lesser finally earned $3,500. It was the first year in which Lesser did not have to hold an outside job to support herself and her periodical, which she started in 1980 with a few subscribers, some advertising and $10,000 savings. Since 1980, Lesser has received funding from the National Endowment for the Arts, the California Arts Council, the California Council for the Humanities and other private foundations. Still, with each quarterly issue of the 28-32 page tabloid costing around $20,000 to publish, money remains tight. Nevertheless, with its circulation of 7,500, *The Threepenny Review* is now one of the ten bestselling literary magazines in the United States.

In addition to fiction, *The Threepenny Review* publishes poetry; music, dance and theater essays; interviews; political commentary; and book and television reviews. The amount of fiction Lesser publishes depends on the material she receives; Lesser also says she would like to see more social and political analysis than she currently does.

The average price Lesser pays for a contribution of any length to *The Threepenny Review* is $50, and she relies on "word of mouth" from writers whose work she has published to other writers for many of the submissions she accepts. She says the magazine, named for Bertholt Brecht's "The Threepenny Opera," continues to attract talented writers in part because "the state of American publishing is so bad that there is nowhere else to go," and admits she would have been able to attract gifted writers earlier to *The Threepenny Review* if she had been able to offer more money. "It's amazing," she says, "that people will write for as little as they do."

Despite financial problems, the periodical receives high praise from almost all quarters: *Publisher's Weekly* has described the magazine as a "serious and highly readable quarterly," and a review in the *Literary Magazine Review* has said "graphically, the magazine is striking; even the ads are beautiful."

Lesser's staff consists of two editorial assistants, one of whom is paid, an unpaid volunteer who helps with subscriptions and filing, and two proofreaders.

Lesser, who holds a PhD in English from the University of California at Berkeley, discourages the notion of *The Threepenny Review* as exclusively a West Coast publication. Draw extensively though from the work of California writers, including Leonard Michaels, Dagoberto Gilb, Robert Hass and Robert Pinsky. Issues have also included fiction by such diverse voices as Grace Paley and Elizabeth Tallent. Lesser believes well-known authors choose to submit work to her rather than to magazines with larger circulations because of *The Threepenny Review*'s reputation—and because she offers them a forum for writing that might be considered "eccentric." Although her contributors are not all well-known writers, she says, they "have faith in the character of the magazine."

—Laurie Henry

‡TRAJECTORIES (II), The Journal of Science Fiction of the Southwest,, Box 49249, Austin TX 78765. (214)272-3319 (John Manning business manager). Publisher: Richard Shannon. Managing Editor: Susan Sneller. Tabloid: 11x14½; 32+ pages; newsprint paper and cover; b&w illustrations and photos, some color. "Speculative fiction, especially science fiction and nonfiction coverage of related subculture. Include interviews, listings of events, articles and news on science. For science fiction/fantasy fans, writers and artists within field and breaking into field. Heavy college student readership." Bimonthly. Estab. 1987. Circ. over 5,000.
Needs: Science fiction, fantasy, horror, humor/satire (of SF/fantasy nature), psychic/supernatural/occult, prose poem, spiritual (if SF/fantasy in nature), serialized/excerpted novel. Does not want to see "macabre 'real life' horror, slasher stories, etc. No stories involving licensed media characters. We have made a decision to not use overly violent stories, or stories where violence and/or war are glorified or otherwise shown in positive manner." Receives 8-12 mss/month. Buys 2-3 mss/issue; 15-20 mss/year. Publishes ms within 3-9 months of acceptance. Recently published work by John Manning, C.L. Crouch, Theresa MacGarry; published new writers within the last year. Length: 2,000-5,000 words preferred; 15,000 words maximum. Publishes short shorts. Sometimes critiques rejected mss and recommends other markets.
How to Contact: Send complete ms with cover letter. Query on pieces over 15,000 words. Reports in 4-6 weeks on queries; within 2 months on mss. SASE. Simultaneous, photocopied and reprint submissions OK. Accepts computer printout submissions, including dot-matrix. Accepts electronic submission via disk or modem. "3½ inch disk, Macintosh McWrite, McPaint, Superpaint, Microsoft Word. 5½ inch disk—IBM word-processing programs." Sample copy for $1, 9x12 SAE and 4 first class stamps. Fiction guidelines for #10 SASE, also sent with sample copy if requested.
Payment: Pays $20-$125 (more on longer pieces) and contributor's copies.
Terms: Pays on publication for first North American serial rights and one-time rights. Sends galleys to author on request. Publication copyrighted.
Advice: "Though there seems to be more professional magazine markets in science fiction/fantasy than other genres, the number is still limited. They are, however, where most new SF/fantasy writers 'break in' the market. These cutting edge publications (such as *Asimov's*, *Analog* and *Omni*), are important vehicles for establishing new talent. Breaking these markets are tough, but can be done. 1. First and foremost—Join a peer critiquing writers' group. Writers' groups are invaluable in polishing form. 2. Develop thorough knowledge of genre chosen. Read *all* current professional publications of particular form and genre. 3. Continue to submit despite rejections. 4. Learn to use word processor. 5. Attend workshops, conferences on writing, and in science fiction in particular, attend science fiction conventions and go to the writers' panels and readings."

TRANSLATION (II), The Translation Center, Columbia University, 307A Mathematics Bldg., New York NY 10027. (212)854-2305. Executive Director: Diane G.H. Cook. Magazine: 6x9; 200-300 pages; coated cover stock; photos. Semiannually. Estab. 1973. Circ. 1,500.
Needs: Literary translations only. Accepts varying number of mss/year. Receives approximately 20-30 unsolicited fiction mss each month. Length: very short or excerpts; not in excess of 15 mss pages. Critiques rejected mss "rarely, because of time involved."
How to Contact: Send complete translation ms accompanied by original language text, 5-line autobiography, 5-line author's biography and SASE. Note required stating copyright clearance has been obtained. Reports in 3-6 months on mss. Single copy $9. Subscription $17.
Payment: 2 complimentary translator copies.
Terms: Acquires first North American serial rights for that volume publication only. Publication copyrighted.
Advice: "We are particularly interested in translations from the lesser-known languages. Annual awards of $1,000 for outstanding translation of a substantial part of a book-length literary work. Translator must have letter of intent to publish from a publisher. Write for description and application for awards program."

TREETOP PANORAMA (I), Rt 1, Box 160 Payson IL 62360. Editor: Jared Scarborough. Magazine: 8¾x11½; 32 pages; many illustrations. Publication is "environmental/rural, international/peace, public policy/poetic (in other words, multi-faceted)." Semiannually. Estab. 1983. Circ. 500-1,000.
Needs: Receives 1 unsolicited ms/month. Buys 1 ms/issue; 2 mss/year. Publishes ms 6-18 months after acceptance. Recently published work by Phyllis E. Ring, J. Kenneth Sieben. Length: 500 words average; 250 words minimum; 750 words maximum. Occasionally critiques rejected mss. Sometimes recommends other markets.
How to Contact: Send complete ms with cover letter. Reports in 2-3 weeks on mss. SASE. Simultaneous and photocopied submissions OK. Accepts computer printout submissions, including dot-matrix. Sample copy for $2.
Payment: Pays $2 plus contributor's copies.

Terms: Pays on publication for one-time rights. Sends galleys to author if piece has been edited. Publication copyrighted.
Advice: "Fiction is not my publication's major concern. Read a sample copy first, to ensure integration. Use compact, semi-poetic expression to shorten material. For a publication like mine, cover letters are crucial. Not only are submissions with cover letters more lkely to receive personal comments in return, but a personal touch tips me off immediately to whether or not a writer is willing to invest the necessary time when it comes to the give and take of revision (a common process with beginning and even with veteran writers)."

TRIQUARTERLY (II), Northwestern University, 1735 Benson Ave., Evanston IL 60201. (312)491-3490. Fiction Editors: Reginald Gibbons and Susan Hahn. Magazine: 6x9¼; 240+ pages; 60 lb paper; heavy cover stock; illustration; photos. "A general literary quarterly especially devoted to fiction. We publish short stories, novellas or excerpts from novels, by American and foreign writers. Genre or style is not a primary consideration. We aim for the general but serious and sophisticated reader. Many of our readers are also writers." Published 3 times/year. Estab. 1964. Circ. 5,000.
Needs: Literary, contemporary and translations. "No prejudices or preconceptions against anything *except* genre fiction (sci fi, romances, etc.)." Buys 10 mss/issue, 30 mss/year. Receives approximately 500 unsolicited fiction mss each month. Does not read May 1-Sept. 30. Approximately 10% of fiction is agented. Recently published work by Fred Pfeil, Mark Costello, Stephen Dixon; published new writers within the last year. Length: no requirement. Publishes short shorts.
How to Contact: Send complete ms with SASE. Reports in 12-14 weeks on mss. Publishes ms an average of 6-12 months after acceptance. Sample copy $4.
Payment: $100-$500, 2 free author's copies. Cover price less 40% discount for extras.
Terms: Pays on publication for first North American serial rights. Sends galleys to author. Publication copyrighted.
Advice: "Read a few recent copies of the magazine to become familiar with the kinds of fiction we publish."

‡TUCUMCARI LITERARY REVIEW (I), 3108 Bellevue Ave., Los Angeles CA 90026. Editor: Troxey Kemper. Magazine: 5½x8½; 32 pages; 20 lb bond paper; 110 lb cover; few illustrations; Xerox photographs. "Old-fashioned fiction that can be read and reread for pleasure; no weird, strange pipe dreams." Bimonthly. Estab. 1988. Circ. small.
Needs: Adventure, condensed/excerpted novel, contemporary, ethnic, historical (general), humor/satire, literary, mainstream, regional, (SW USA), senior citizen/retirement, suspense/mystery, western. No science fiction, sedition, blasphemy, fetishism, drugs/acid rock, pornography, horror, martial arts. Accepts 2 or 3 mss/issue; 12-18 mss/year. Publishes ms 2 to 4 months after acceptance. Length: 1,200-1,500 words preferred; 1,500 words maximum. Sometimes critiques rejected mss and recommends other markets.
How to Contact: Send complete ms with or without cover letter. Cover letter should include "anything pertinent to the submission." Reports in 2 weeks. SASE. Simultaneous, photocopied and reprint submissions OK. Accepts computer printout submissions, including dot-matrix. Sample copy for $1.50 plus 50¢ postage. Fiction guidelines for #10 SAE and 1 first class stamp.
Payment: Pays in contributor's copies.
Terms: Acquires one-time rights. Publication copyrighted.
Advice: "Does the work 'say something' or is it a hodgepodge of sentence fragments and paragraphs, not tied together into a story? No 'it was all a dream' endings."

TURNSTILE (II), Suite 2348, 175 Fifth Ave., New York NY 10010. Editor: Amit Shah. Magazine: 6x9; 128 pages; 55 lb paper; 10 pt cover; illustrations; photos. "Publishing work by new writers." Semiannually. Estab. 1988. Circ. 1,500.
Needs: Contemporary, experimental, fantasy, feminist, gay, humor/satire, literary, regional. No genre fiction. Receives approx. 40 unsolicited fiction mss/month. Publishes approx. 8 mss/issue. Publishes ms 3-4 months after acceptance. Recently published work by Alice Blanchard, Richard Russo, Barbara Leith; published new writers within the last year. Length: 2,000 words average; 4,000 words maximum. Publishes short shorts. Sometimes comments on rejected mss or recommends other markets.
How to Contact: Query first or send complete ms with cover letter. Reports on queries in 1-2 weeks; on mss in 4-6 weeks. SASE. Simultaneous and photocopied submissions OK. Accepts computer printouts, including dot-matrix. Sample copy for $6.50 and 9x12 SAE; fiction guidelines for #10 SAE and 1 first class stamp.
Payment: Pays in contributor's copies; charge for extras.
Terms: Acquires one-time rights. Publication copyrighted.

TV-TS TAPESTRY JOURNAL (II), International Foundation for Gender Education, Inc., Box 367, Wayland MA 01778. (617)358-2305. Editor: Merissa S. Lynn. Magazine: 11x8½; 130-150 pages; coated paper; 80 lb coated cover; illustrations; photos. "Transvestism/transsexualism fiction, nonfiction (how-to, biography, etc.), editorial and opinion, etc. For *all* persons interested in transvestism and transsexualism." Quarterly. Estab. 1978. Circ. 10,000.
Needs: Condensed novel, contemporary, historical (general), humor/satire, TVism and TSism psychology. True-to-life, tasteful, non-sexual, positive stories. "No unbelievable fantasy, fetishistic, negatives." Receives 2-5 unsolicited fiction mss/month. Accepts 1-2 mss/issue; 4-8 mss/year. Length: 3,000 words average; 5,000 words maximum. Also publishes short shorts. Occasionally critiques rejected mss and recommends other markets.
How to Contact: Send complete ms with cover letter. SASE. Simultaneous, photocopied submissions and reprints OK. Accepts computer printouts including dot-matrix. Accepts electronic submissions via IBM compatible disk, MS DOS 1.1 and 2.1. Sample copy $5.
Payment: Pays in contributor's copies.
Terms: Publication copyrighted.
Advice: "Submissions must be non-sexual and relevant to the cross-dressing/transsexual theme. We are more interested in what the writer has to say than the quality of the writing. If the writer has a valuable message to our readers, we will help the writer with editing and rewriting. *Tapestry* is a non-profit tax exempt journal designed to provide education and support. Submitted items should be positive and informative."

TWISTED, 22071 Pineview Dr., Antioch IL 60002. (312)395-3085. Editor: Christine Hoard. Magazine: 8½x11; 96 pages; 60 lb paper; 67 lb cover; illustrations; photos. "Emphasis on contemporary horror and fantasy, anything on the dark side of reality." For readers of horror, "weird," fantasy, etc. Published irregularly. Estab. 1985. Circ. 150.
Needs: Fantasy, horror, prose poem, psychic/supernatural/occult, science fiction. "No hard science fiction, no sword and sorcery. Graphic horror or sex scenes OK if tastefully done. Sexist-racist writing turns me off." Receives approx. 12 unsolicited fiction mss/month. Accepts 10 mss/issue. Publishes ms 2 months to 2 years after acceptance. Recently published work by David Bruce, Joe Faust, Kathleen Jurgens; published new writers within the last year. Length: 2,000 words average; 200 words minimum; 5,000 words maximum. Sometimes critiques rejected mss and recommends other markets.
How to Contact: Query first. "Cover letters not necessary." Reports in 2 weeks on queries; 2 months on mss. SASE for query and ms. Photocopied submissions OK. Accepts computer printouts including dot-matrix. Sample copy $4. Fiction guidelines for #10 SAE and 1 first class stamp.
Payment: Pays in contributor's copies.
Terms: Acquires first rights. Publication copyrighted.
Advice: "Right now we are overstocked. Best to query first. Try to be original and avoid rehashing formula stories. Look into smaller press magazines. They are open to more experimental work and work by new writers."

2 AM MAGAZINE (I, II, IV), Box 6754, Rockford IL 61125-1754. (815)397-5901. Editor: Gretta M. Anderson. Magazine: 8½x11; 60 or more pages; 60 lb offset paper; 70 lb offset cover; illustrations; photos occasionally. "Horror, science fiction, fantasy stories, poetry, articles and art for a sophisticated adult audience." Quarterly. Summer fiction issue planned. Estab. 1986. Circ. 1,000.
Needs: Experimental, fantasy, horror, humor/satire, prose poem, psychic/supernatural/occult, science fiction, suspense/mystery. No juvenile. Receives 400 unsolicited mss/month. Buys 12-14 mss/issue; 50 mss/year. Publishes ms an average of 6-9 months after acceptance. Recently published work by J. N. Williamson, Elizabeth Engstrom, Leonard Carpenter; published new writers within the last year. Length: 1,800 words average; 500 words minimum; 5,000 words maximum. Publishes short shorts. Sometimes critiques rejected mss and recommends other markets.
How to Contact: Send complete ms with cover letter (cover letter optional). Reports in 4 weeks on queries; 6-10 weeks on mss. SASE. Simultaneous, photocopied and reprint submissions OK. Accepts computer printout submissions, no dot-matrix. Sample copy $4.95 and $1 postage. Fiction guidelines for #10 SASE.
Payment: ½¢/word minimum, negotiable maximum; 1 contributor's copy; 40% discount on additional copies.
Terms: Pays on acceptance for one-time rights with non-exclusive anthology option. Sends prepublication galleys to author. Publication copyrighted.
Advice: "Publishing more pages of fiction, more sf, some sword and sorcery and mystery, as well as horror. Put name and address on manuscript, double-space, use standard ms format. Pseudonym should appear under title on 1st manuscript page. True name and address should appear on upper left on 1st ms page."

TYRO MAGAZINE (I), For Discriminating Readers and Developing Writers, 194 Carlbert Street, Sault Ste. Marie, Ontario P6A 5E1 Canada. (705)253-6402. Editor: Stan Gordon. Magazine: 5½x8½; approx. 110 pages; bond paper; firm card cover; some illustrations; photographs. Published "to provide a forum and practice medium for writers to try out almost any type of short fiction. We also publish some poetry and nonfiction, and how-to articles on writing." Special fiction issue planned. Bimonthly. Estab. 1984. Circ. 500.
Needs: Adventure, condensed novel, confession, contemporary, ethnic, experimental, fantasy, historical (general), horror, humor/satire, juvenile (5-9 years), literary, mainstream, preschool (0-4 years), prose poem, psychic/supernatural, regional, religious/inspirational, romance (contemporary, historical, young adult), science fiction, senior citizen/retirement, serialized/excerpted novel, spiritual, sports, suspense/mystery, young adult/teen (10-18 years). No "wildly experimental or legally dangerous" material. Receives about 40 unsolicited mss/month. Accepts 8-12 mss/issue; 60-80 mss/year. Publishes ms 2 months after acceptance. Recently published work by David Sandstad, Stephen Flocks and Robert Peterson. Published new writers within the last year. Length: 500 words minimum; 5,000 words maximum. Publishes short shorts. Usually critiques rejected mss. Sometimes recommends other markets.
How to Contact: Send complete ms with cover letter. Reports in 2 weeks on queries; 3-4 weeks on mss. SASE for ms. Simultaneous and photocopied submissions OK. Accepts computer printout submissions, including dot-matrix. Sample copy $5. Free fiction guidelines.
Payment: Offers awards of over 10¢/word for the best fiction in each issue.
Terms: Writers retain all rights.
Advice: "Short fiction must be trim and active; everything must advance the story."

THE UNCOMMON READER (I,II), 1220 Taransay, Henderson KY 42420. (502)827-3878. Editor: Louis B. Hatchett, Jr. Fiction Editors: Aija Baltzersen and Celia Greenman. Magazine: 8½x11; 40 pages; will consider illustrations and photographs. "Theme: intelligent, irreverent, earthy humor. Types of material published: sarcastic, cynical points of view; prefers above combined with strong plots." Biannually. Estab. 1986. Circ. 1,200.
Needs: Adventure, historical (general), humor/satire, literary, mainstream, suspense/mystery, Larry Semon (historical biographies of), English translations of French and German westerns (circa 1870-1918). "Don't send stories written in present tense; don't send stories with sex in them at all. Don't send any experimental fiction." Receives 1,000 unsolicited fiction mss/month. Accepts 12 mss/issue; 24 mss/year. Publishes ms 6 months to a year after acceptance. Recently published work by Leon McNamara, David Woodbury, Jane Jeffries; published new writers within the last year. Length: 5,000 words average; 2,500 words minimum; 6,000 words maximum. "We will critique manuscripts for a $10 fee."
How to Contact: Send complete ms with cover letter, brief biographical information; writer must be a subscriber to be published. Reports in 3 weeks on queries; 2 months on mss. SASE. Simultaneous, photocopied and reprint submissions OK. Accepts computer printout submisions, no dot-matrix. Sample copy $4.95 and 12x9 SAE with $1 postage. Fiction guidelines 25¢ with #10 SAE and 1 first class stamp.
Payment: Pays $10.
Terms: Pays on publication for one-time rights.
Advice: "We are nearly always broke and so we had to go from a quarterly mag to a biannual mag. Just study what has been pubilshed by master writers (say, Raymond Chandler) and figure out what made their writing 'work' on the page. Then try out some of their techniques."

UNIVERSITY OF PORTLAND REVIEW (II), University of Portland, 5000 N. Willamette Blvd., Portland OR 97203. (503)283-7144. Editor-in-Chief: Thompson M. Faller. Magazine: 8x5; 40-55 pages. "Magazine for the college-educated layman of liberal arts background. Its purpose is to comment on the human condition and to present information in different fields with relevance to the contemporary scene." Published semiannually. Established 1948. Circ. 1,000.
Needs: "Only fiction that makes a significant statement about the contemporary scene will be employed." Receives 4 unsolicited mss/month. Accepts 2-3 mss/issue, 4-6 mss/year. Published new writers within the last year. Length: 1,500 words minimum; 3,500 words maximum; 2,000 words average. Sometimes recommends other markets.
How to Contact: Send complete ms with SASE. Reports in 3 weeks on queries; 6 months on mss. Publishes ms up to 1 year after acceptance. Sample copy 50¢.
Payment: 5 contributor's copies. 50¢ charge for extras.
Terms: Pays on publication for all rights. Publication copyrighted.
Advice: "Send manuscript in line with guidelines."

UNIVERSITY OF WINDSOR REVIEW, University of Windsor, Windsor, Ontario N9B 3P4 Canada. Editor: Joseph A. Quinn. Fiction Editor: Alistair MacLeod. Biannually. Estab. 1965.
Needs: Literary, contemporary. Buys 4-8 mss/year. Receives 4-8 unsolicited fiction mss each month. Length: no requirement.
How to Contact: Send complete ms with SAE, IRC. Reports in 6 weeks.
Payment: $25 Canadian funds.
Terms: Publication copyrighted.

UNKNOWNS (I, II), Abri Publications, Suite 1, 1900 Century Blvd., Atlanta GA 30345. (404)636-3145. Publisher: Julia B. Davidson. Editor: Christine Puckett. Magazine: 11x8; 70-100 pages; good quality paper; excellent cover stock; few illustrations. Quarterly collection of short fiction and poems. Estab. 1973. Circ. 500.
Needs: Short fiction and poems that combine simplicity and beauty of language with dramatizations of ageless truth. "Please write for an audience whose tastes are traditional and for whose reading time there is much competition." Also offers criticism service; write for fee information. Recently published work by Carl Freeman, Walter Duenning, Eva Blake; published new writers within the last year. Length: 2,700-2,800 words. Sometimes recommends other markets.
How to Contact: Send complete ms with cover letter. SASE. Reports as soon as possible. Publishes ms an average of 1 year after acceptance. Sample copy $5; postage $1.
Payment: 1 contributor's copy.
Terms: Acquires first rights (all rights revert to author). Publication copyrighted.
Advice: "Become craftsmen in private before trying to become artists in public. Learn all you can about publishing in general. Write for the enjoyment and benefit of readers, and think about how your work can affect civilization."

UNMUZZLED OX (III), Unmuzzled Ox Foundation Ltd., 105 Hudson St., New York NY 10013. Editor: Michael Andre. Tabloid. "Magazine about life, for an intelligent audience." Quarterly. Estab. 1971. Circ. 20,000.
Needs: Contemporary, literary, prose poem and translations. No commercial material. Receives 10-15 unsolicited mss/month. Buys 1-5 mss/issue. Occasionally critiques rejected mss.
How to Contact: "Cover letter is significant." Reports in 1 month. SASE. Sample copy $7.50.
Payment: Generally in copies.
Terms: Publication copyrighted.

THE UNSPEAKABLE VISIONS OF THE INDIVIDUAL (III, IV), Box 439, California PA 15419. (412)938-8956. Editors: Arthur and Kit Knight. Magazine: Specializes in beat generation-oriented fiction for "well educated—above average literacy." Annually. Estab. 1971. Circ. 2,000.
Needs: Confession, contemporary, erotica, literary, prose poem, excerpted novel, autobiographical fiction, e.g., Jack Kerouac. Receives 10-15 unsolicited mss/month. Buys 2 mss/issue. Length: 2,000-3,000 words average. Occasionally comments on rejected mss.
How to Contact: Send complete ms. Reports in 3 months maximum. SASE. Photocopied submissions OK. Accepts computer printout submissions. Sample copy $3.50.
Payment: 2 copies plus $10.
Terms: Pays on publication for first rights. Publication copyrighted.
Advice: "See a sample copy."

‡US1 (II), US1 Poets' Cooperative, 21 Lake Dr., Roosevelt NJ 08555. (609)448-5096. Editor: rotating board. Magazine: 8½x11; 60 pages; good paper. Publishes poetry and fiction. Annually. Estab. 1973.
Needs: "Any. No badly written, simple-minded stories." Publishes ms within 3 months of acceptance. Recently published work by Alice Mattison. Publishes short shorts. Sometimes critiques rejected mss.
How to Contact: Query first. Reports on queries in 1 week. SASE. Photocopied submissions OK. Sample copy for $2.50.
Payment: Pays in contributor's copies.
Terms: Acquires one-time rights. Copyright "reverts to author."
Advice: "Query to see if we're reading."

VALLEY GRAPEVINE (I, IV), Seven Buffaloes Press, Box 249, Big Timber MT 59011. Editor/Publisher: Art Cuelho. Theme: "poems, stories, history, folklore, photographs, ink drawings or anything native to the Great Central Valley of California, which includes the San Joaquin and Sacramento valleys. Focus is on land and people and the oil fields, farms, orchards, Okies, small town life, hobos." Readership: "Rural and small town audience, the common man with a rural background, salt-of-the-earth. The working man reads *Valley Grapevine* because it's his personal history recorded." Annually. Estab. 1978. Circ. 500.

Needs: Literary, contemporary, western and ethnic (Okie, Arkie). No academic, religious (unless natural to theme), gay/lesbian or supernatural material. Receives approximately 4-5 unsolicited fiction mss each month. Length: 2,500-10,000 (prefers 5,000) words.
How to Contact: Query. SASE for query, ms. Reports in 1 week. Sample copy available to writers for $4.75.
Payment: 1-2 author's copies.
Terms: Acquires first North American serial rights. Returns rights to author after publication, but reserves the right to reprint in an anthology or any future special collection of Seven Buffaloes Press. Publication copyrighted.
Advice: "Buy a copy to get a feel of the professional quality of the writing. Know the theme of a particular issue. Some contributors have 30 years experience as writers; most 15 years. Age does not matter; quality does."

‡VALLEY WOMEN'S VOICE (II,IV), Feminist Newsjournal, 321 Student Union, University of Massachusetts, Amherst MA 01002. (413)545-2436. Newspaper: 16 pages. "Feminist analysis, feminist poetry, stories, health articles, revolution-visionary-action oriented." For women readers. Monthly. Estab. 1979. Circ. 5,000.
Needs: Ethnic, feminist, lesbian, prose poem, spiritual, women's sports. Any subject "as long as it is feminist." Receives 3-10 mss/month. Recently published work by Roni D. Ginsberg; published new writers within the last year.
How to Contact: Send complete ms with cover letter. "Cover letter should include short biographical statement which provides a context for work submitted." SASE. Simultaneous, photocopied and reprint submissions OK. Accepts computer printout submissions, including dot-matrix. Sample copy for $1.
Payment: No payment.

‡VAR TUFA (I,II), Box 1472, Upland CA 91735. (714)981-2736 or (714)946-1013. Editor: Bill Batchelor. Associate Editor: Justin Gorman. Tabloid: 16 pages; newsprint paper; illustrations; photos. Published "to display reality in such a context people think it is fake. *Var Tufa* is limited to an alternative audience (it's our own fault, typos and bad language take from our credibility and limit our audience)." Quarterly. Estab. 1986. Circ. 3,500.
Needs: Erotica, horror, humor/satire, psychic/supernatural/occult. "Basically anything that is good. We have very high standards." Accepts 1-3 mss/year "from friends." Publishes short shorts. Sometimes critiques rejected mss and recommends other markets.
How to Contact: Send complete ms with cover letter. "Talk to us; we are pretty easy to deal with." SASE. Photocopied submissions OK. No dot-matrix computer printout submissions. Free sample copy and fiction guidelines.
Payment: "We pay with magazines and T shirts."
Terms: "We know a lot of our material is reprinted. We just ask that proper acknowledgment is credited." Publication not copyrighted.
Advice: "The 'underground' punk rock literary world is in dire need of something except poetry. We are very poor college students with no money. We publish and pay for *Var Tufa* on our own. It takes a lot of time and effort and we basically lose our shirts. To make a living and write solely what you want to write are two fine notions that do not equate. We have an established network, we have a reputation. Don't expect money—write to have other people comment. The best thing is when somebody you don't know from a place you have never been takes the time, effort and money to tell you his/her reaction. Good or bad, it is a real high to have one person's perspective changed by what you have written."

‡THE VILLAGE IDIOT (II), an irregular periodical, Mother of Ashes Press, Box 66, Harrison ID 83833. Editor: Judith Shannon Paine. Magazine: Format varies; illustrations; photos. *The Village Idiot* publishes poetry, pictures and stories. "Well-written stories are preferred, but that criteria can be overlooked if the fiction 'breathes.' " For literate audience. Published irregularly. Estab. 1970. Circ. 100.
Needs: Adventure, confession, contemporary, erotica, ethnic, experimental, fantasy, feminist, gay, historical (general), humor/satire, lesbian, literary, mainstream, prose poem, romance (contemporary and historical), science fiction, senior citizen/retirement, suspense/mystery, translations, western. "Subject matter is not so important as style. The magazine has a bias in favor of a literal method of story telling; no stream-of-consciousness and none of this writing that seems to work at obscuring the story's action and/or intent. Most important is that the fiction 'breathe.' " No novels, preteen, occult, religious. Publishes ms up to 1 year after acceptance. Recently published work by Ruth Jespersen, Walt Franklin, William Harrel; published new writers within the last year. Length: 2,000-3,000 words average; 100 words minimum; 5,000 words maximum. Occasionally critiques rejected mss.
How to Contact: Send complete ms with SASE. Reports 3 months maximum. Photocopied submissions OK. Accepts computer printouts, including dot-matrix. Sample copy $4.
Payment: Nominal cash payment "at the whim of the press" and contributor's copies (2 if the second

one is requested).
Terms: Acquires one-time rights (copyright for author). Publication coyrighted.
Advice: "Be the most critical, mean editor on the block before you submit copy for consideration."

VINTAGE NORTHWEST (I, IV), Northshore Senior Center (Sponsor), Box 193, Bothell WA 98041. (206)487-1201. Editors: volunteer editorial board. Magazine: 7x8½; 60 pages; illustrations. "We are a senior literary magazine, published by and for seniors. All work done by volunteers except printing." For "all ages who are interested in our seniors' experiences." Winter and summer. Estab. 1980. Circ. 500.
Needs: Adventure, comedy, condensed novel (1,000 words maximum), fantasy, historical, humor/satire, inspirational, prose poem, senior citizen/retirement, suspense/mystery. No religious or political mss. Receives 2-3 unsolicited mss/month. Accepts 2 mss/issue. Recently published work by Virginia Vahey, Jean W. Immerwahr, Mary Louise R. O'Hara; published new writers within the last year. Length: 1,000 words maximum. Occasionally critiques rejected mss.
How to Contact: Send complete ms. SASE. Simultaneous, photocopied and previously published submissions OK. Accepts computer printout submissions. Sample copy for $2. Fiction guidelines with SASE.
Payment: Pays 1 free contributor's copy.
Terms: Publication copyrighted.
Advice: "Our only requirement is that the author be over 50 when submission is written."

‡VIRGIN MEAT FANZINE (I), In The Tomb, 5247 W. L10, Quartz Hill CA 93536. (805)943-5604. Editor: Steve Blum. Digest: 4x5; 20 pages; Xerox paper; illustrations. "Gothic and underground music with odd short stories, comix and reviews (music)." Published "about once every 3 months." Plans a special fiction issue. Estab. 1987. Circ. over 150.
Needs: Erotica, experimental, horror, humor/satire, prose poem, psychic/supernatural/occult, underground music. Receives 1 ms/month. Accepts 2 mss/issue. Publishes ms within 1-2 months of acceptance. Published new writers within the last year. Length: 2,000 words maximum. Publishes short shorts. Sometimes critiques rejected mss and recommends other markets.
How to Contact: Send complete ms with cover letter. Reports in 1 week. Simultaneous, photocopied and reprint submissions OK. Accepts computer printout submissions, including dot-matrix. Accepts electronic submissions via Commodore 64 disk. Free sample copy.
Payment: Pays in contributor's copies.
Terms: Acquires one-time rights. Publication not copyrighted.
Advice: Publishes fiction because "readers express interest."

VIRGINIA QUARTERLY REVIEW (III), 1 W. Range, Charlottesville VA 22903. (804)924-3124. Editor: Staige Blackford. "A national magazine of literature and discussion. A lay, intellectual audience, people who are not out-and-out scholars but who are interested in ideas and literature." Quarterly. Estab. 1925. Circ. 4,500.
Needs: Literary, contemporary, feminist, romance, adventure, humor, ethnic, serialized novels (excerpts) and translations. "No gay/lesbian or pornography." Buys 3 mss/issue, 20 mss/year. Length: 3,000-7,000 words.
How to Contact: Query or send complete ms. SASE. Reports in 2 weeks on queries, 2 months on mss. Sample copy $5.
Payment: $10/printed page. Offers Emily Clark Balch Award for best published short story of the year.
Terms: Pays on publication for all rights. "Will transfer upon request."
Advice: "Because of the competition, it's difficult for a nonpublished writer to break in."

VISIBILITIES (IV), Box 1258, Peter Stuyvesant Station, New York NY 10009-1258. (212)473-4635. Editor: Susan T. Chasin. Magazine: 8x11; 32+ pages; coated paper; heavy coated cover stock; illustrations and photographs. "We are an international magazine by and for lesbians." Bimonthly. Estab. 1987. Circ. 5,000.
Needs: Lesbian. No "violence, sexist, racist, agist, etc." Accepts 1 ms/issue. Length: 1,300 words average; 1,000 words minimum; 1,500 words maximum. Publishes short shorts. Sometimes critiques rejected mss.
How to Contact: Send complete ms with cover letter, which should include "just basics; name, address, telephone and how you heard about us." Reports in 2 weeks on queries; 2 months on mss. SASE. Accepts computer printout submissions, no dot-matrix. Sample copy $2.25; fiction guidelines for #10 SASE.
Payment: Contributor's copies; charge for extras.
Terms: Acquires first North American serial rights. Publication copyrighted.
Advice: "We are looking for life-affirming fiction—which tell us how people can live healthy, produc-

tive lives as lesbians. This does not preclude stories about painful experiences—but tell us how your characters survive and keep going.''

VOICES IN THE WILDERNESS (II), Box 4486, Salem MA 01970. (617)745-8164. Editors: Hal Miller, Lynn-Marie Marcotte, Christian Smith. Magazine: 8½x11; 28 pages; 50-70 lb paper; 80 lb cover stock; line art. "Alternative forms of Christian witness, home churches, social/political change." Bimonthly. Estab. 1986. Circ. 1,500.
Needs: Humor/satire, religious, political. No "devotional fiction." Accepts 3 mss/issue. Publishes ms an average of 4-6 months after acceptance. Recently published work by Ken Rolph, Lynn-Marie Marcotte. Length: 1,000 words minimum; 2,500 words maximum. Publishes short shorts. Sometimes critiques rejected mss.
How to Contact: Send query or complete ms with cover letter, which should tell "why we should use the ms." Reports in 2 weeks on queries; 3 months on mss. SASE. Simultaneous and photocopied submissions OK. Accepts computer printout submissions, including dot-matrix. Accepts electronic submissions via IBM PC compatible disk, ASCII text file. Sample copy $3.
Payment: Free subscription to magazine; contributor's copies.
Terms: Acquires first rights. Publication copyrighted.
Advice: "We look for integrity in fiction—a genuine expression of the author's experience or understanding—which somehow fits our editorial purpose. Clearly, a knowledge of the overall tone of our publication is essential."

‡WASHINGTON DC PERIODICAL (II), Chow Chow Productions, Box 39074, Washington DC 20016. (202)363-2968. Editor: Gordon. Fiction Editor: Sara W. Tabloid: 11x14; 16-24 pages; newsprint paper and cover; illustrations; photos. "Anything goes if it strikes our fancy. Mostly a guide to alternative media (such as music, theater, art, comics, books, etc.). Generally speaking, audience is 15-35, art/progressive/college-high school students." May publish a special edition for fiction writers. Estab. 1984. Circ. 10,000.
Needs: Confession, experimental, fantasy, feminist, gay, horror, humor/satire, lesbian, literary, psychic/supernatural/occult, science fiction, serialized/excerpted novel. "We're pretty negative about a lot of things and enjoy things that are able to piss someone off." Length: "short."
How to Contact: Send complete mss with cover letter. SASE. Simultaneous, photocopied and reprint submissions OK. Accepts computer printout submissions, including dot-matrix. Sample copy for $1.
Payment: Free subscription to magazine (if requested).
Terms: "Author retains all copyrights of their own material. We put a copyright notice in paper to protect any rights." Publication copyrighted.
Advice: "Readers should be aware that the *WDC Period* is a free monthly tabloid that's evolved from what was once a 'punk fanzine.' I guess what this means to them is that while I wouldn't assume there's any prestige (from a writer's viewpoint) in being included in our publication, they will have the opportunity to have their work published and read. We've evolved/matured throughout the years we've been publishing, so it's hard to tell what roads we'll be taking in '89. Anyone who is interested in being published in a paper such as ours should definitely do so, but not expect anything (unless they include return postage)."

WASHINGTON REVIEW (II, IV), Friends of the Washington Review of the Arts, Box 50132, Washington DC 20004. (202)638-0515. Fiction Editor: Jeff Richards. "We publish fiction, poetry, articles and reviews on all areas of the arts. We have a particular interest in the interrelationships of the arts and emphasize the cultural life of the DC area." Readership: "Artists, writers and those interested in cultural life in this area." Bimonthly. Estab. 1975. Circ. 10,000.
Needs: Literary. Accepts 1-2 mss/issue. Receives approximately 50-100 unsolicited fiction mss each month. Length: Prefers 2,000 words or less. Critiques rejected mss when there is time.
How to Contact: Send complete ms with SASE. Reports in 2 months. Publishes ms an average of 6 months after acceptance. Sample copy for tabloid-sized SASE.
Payment: Author's copies plus small payment whenever possible.
Terms: Pays on publication for first North American serial rights. Publication copyrighted.
Advice: "Edit your writing for redundant adjectives. Make sure everything makes sense: the plot, character, motivation. Try to avoid clichés."

WEBSTER REVIEW (II), Webster University, 470 E. Lockwood, Webster Groves MO 63119. Editor/Publisher: Nancy Schapiro. Magazine: 5½x8½; 104 pages; 60 lb white paper; 10 pt. C15 black ink varnish cover stock; illustrations; photos on cover only. "We're interested in quality contemporary fiction and in translations of international fiction." Semiannually. Estab. 1974. Circ. 1,500.
Needs: Literary, contemporary stories, translations, prose poems and excerpted novels. "Not interested in popular (i.e., nonserious) work." No pornographic, sentimental or *Star Wars*-type science fiction.

Accepts 4 mss/issue, 8 mss/year. Receives approximately 40 unsolicited fiction mss each month. Recently published work by A. D. Nauman, Leslie Johnson, Tatiana Stavron; published new writers within the last year. No preferred length. Publishes short shorts. Sometimes critiques rejected mss.
How to Contact: Send complete ms with SASE. Simultaneous and photocopied submissions OK. Accepts computer printout submissions. Prefers letter-quality. Reports in 1 month. Free sample copy.
Payment: 2 free author's copies. No charge for extras.
Terms: Acquires first rights. Publication copyrighted.
Advice: "The competition is stiff so a writer should master his craft before attempting to publish. Don't send us unsuitable work (amateurish, slick, pop or sentimental stuff). Include SASE for report on work even if you don't want work returned—and a *big* enough envelope if you do. The short story seems to me to be the most exciting form of writing being done."

WEIRDBOOK (II), Box 149, Amherst Branch, Buffalo NY 14226. Editor: W. Paul Ganley. Magazine: 8½x11; 64 pages; self cover; illustrations. "Latter day 'pulp magazine' along the lines of the old pulp magazine *Weird Tales*. We tend to use established writers. We look for an audience of fairly literate people who like good writing and good characterization in their fantasy and horror fiction, but are tired of the clichés in the field." Annually. Estab. 1968. Circ. 1,000.
Needs: *Presently overstocked*. Psychic/supernatural, fantasy, horror and gothic (not modern). No psychological horror; mystery fiction; physical horror (blood); traditional ghost stories (unless original theme); science fiction; swords and sorcery without a supernatural element; or reincarnation stories that conclude with 'And the doctor patted him on . . . THE END!' " Buys 8-12 mss/issue. Length: 15,000 + words maximum. Sometimes recommends other markets.
How to Contact: Send complete ms with SASE. Reports in 3 months on mss. Sample copy $5.75. Guidelines for #10 SASE.
Payment: 1¢ word minimum and 1 free author's copy.
Terms: Pays on publication ("part on acceptance only for solicited mss") for first North American serial rights plus right to reprint the entire issue.
Advice: *Currently overstocked*. "Read a copy and then some of the best anthologies in the field (such as DAW's 'Best Horror of the Year,' Arkham House anthologies, etc.) Occasionally we keep mss longer than planned. When sending a SASE marked 'book rate' (or anything not first class) the writer should add 'Forwarding Postage Guaranteed.' "

WEST BRANCH (II), Dept. of English, Bucknell University, Lewisburg PA 17837. Editors: K. Patten and R. Taylor. Magazine: 5½x8½; 96-120 pages; good quality paper; illustrations; photos. Fiction and poetry for readers of contemporary literature. Biannually. Estab. 1977. Circ. 500.
Needs: Literary, contemporary, prose peom and translations. No science fiction. Accepts 3-6 mss/issue. Recently published work by Ingrid Hughes, Molly Best Tinsley, Daniel Curley; published new writers within the last year. No preferred length.
How to Contact: Send complete ms with cover letter, "with information about writer's background, previous publications, etc." SASE. Reports in 6 weeks on mss. Sample copy $2.
Payment: 2 free author's copies and one-year subscription; cover price less 20% discount charge for extras.
Terms: Acquires first rights. Publication copyrighted.
Advice: "Narrative art fulfills a basic human need—our dreams attest to this—and storytelling is therefore a high calling in any age. Find your own voice and vision. Make a story that speaks to your own mysteries. Cultivate simplicity in form, complexity in theme. Look and listen through your characters."

WEST COAST REVIEW (II), West Coast Review Publishing Society, % English Dept., Simon Fraser University, Burnaby, British Columbia V5A 1S6 Canada. (604)291-4287. Magazine: 6x9; 80 pages, focusing on "contemporary poetry, short fiction, drama and reviews." Quarterly. Estab. 1966. Circ. 700.
Needs: Contemporary, experimental, literary, prose poem, serialized/excerpted novel (possibly) and translations (possible if translator arranges for all necessary permissions). Receives 10-20 unsolicited fiction mss/month. Accepts 2-3 mss/issue, 8-10 mss/year. Less than 10% of fiction is agented. Recently published work by John Mills, Daphne Marlatt, David McFadden; published new writers within the last year. Length: 250 words minimum; 5,000 words maximum.
How to Contact: Send complete ms with SAE, IRC. "Photocopies acceptable with assurances that

Read the Manuscript Mechanics section to learn the correct way to prepare and submit a manuscript.

they are not under consideration elsewhere." Accepts computer printout submissions. Prefers letter-quality. Include a short biographical note. Reports in 2-3 months on mss. Publishes ms an average of 1-12 months after acceptance. Sample copy $4 (Canadian) with 8x11 SAE and 68¢ postage (IRC).
Payment: Approx. $10/page and 1-year subscription; $2.50 charge for extras.
Terms: Pays on acceptance for first rights. Publication copyrighted.
Advice: "Read several issues of the *Review* before submitting. Send standard, professional submissions."

WHAT (II), Conman Publications, Box 338, Station J, Toronto, Ontario M4J 4Y8 Canada. Editor: Jason Sherman. Tabloid: 11x17; 16 pages; newsprint; illustrations and photos. "To create new audiences for established and beginning/lesser-known writers of poetry, fiction, drama and criticism by making such writing available on a free basis and in large quantity, and by inviting the participation of readers through a letters/commentary section." Bimonthly. Estab. 1985. Circ. 10,000.
Needs: "Submissions are judged on the basis of the quality of the writing, regardless of the nature of the content/subject matter." Receives 10 unsolicited mss/month; accepts 1 ms/issue; 6 mss/year. Publishes ms 2-4 months after acceptance. Recently published work by Günter Grass, Liliana Heker, Julio Cortazar; published new writers within the last year. Length: 2,000 words average; no minimum; 3,000 words maximum, but will serialize if longer. Publishes short shorts. Comments on most rejected mss and sometimes recommends other markets.
How to Contact: Send complete ms with cover letter, which should include "where the reader heard of or saw the magazine; whether the reader has read the magazine (and thus feels feels his or her work is suitable for it); list of prior and/or forthcoming publications." Reports on queries in 2 weeks; on mss in 2 months on average. SASE or IRC. Simultaneous, photocopied and reprint submissions OK. Accepts computer printout submissions, including dot-matrix. Accepts electronic submissions "but query first." Sample copy $2.
Payment: Pays $100 for short story; $25-$50 for short shorts.
Terms: Acquires first North American serial rights or one-time rights. Publication copyrighted.
Advice: "Much of what we see is written to fill a specific formula, which means it is devoid of any passion the author might have otherwise put into the work. Guidelines and generalizations are fine as they go, but taken too seriously they hurt the material. Read us before you send us your work."

WHETSTONE (II), English Dept., University of Lethbridge, Lethbridge, Alberta T1K 3M4 Canada. (403)329-2490. Contact: Editor. Magazine: approximately 6x9; 48-64 pages; superbond paper; pen or pencil sketches; photos. Magazine publishing "poetry, prose, drama, prints, photographs and occasional music compositions for a university audience." Twice yearly. Estab. 1971. Circ. 200.
Needs: Experimental, literary and mainstream. "Interested in works by native writers/artists. Interested in multi-media works by individuals or collaborators. Yearly writing contest with cash prizes." Receives 1 unsolicited fiction ms/month. Accepts 1 ms/issue, 2 mss/year. Does not read May through August. Published new writers within the last year. Length: 12 double-spaced pages maximum.
How to Contact: Send complete ms with SASE, or SAE with IRC and cover letter with author's background and experience. Simultaneous and photocopied submissions OK. Accepts computer printout submissions. Prefers letter-quality. Reports in 5 months on mss. Publishes ms an average of 3-4 months after acceptance. Sample copy $3 and 10½x7½ or larger SAE and 2 Canadian first class stamps or IRCs.
Payment: 1 free contributor's copy.
Terms: Acquires no rights. Publication copyrighted.
Advice: "We seek good writing. Avoid moralizing."

WHISKEY ISLAND MAGAZINE, University Center 7, Cleveland State University, Cleveland OH 44115. (216)687-2056. Fiction Editor: Jeff Erdie. Magazine with no specific theme of fiction, poetry, photography. Published 2 times/year. Estab. 1978. Circ. 2,500.
Needs: Receives 5-10 unsolicited fiction mss/month. Acquires 3-4 mss/issue. Length: 5,000 words maximum; 2,000-3,000 words average.
How to Contact: Send complete ms with SASE. No simultaneous, photocopied or previously published submissions. Reports in 2 months on mss. Sample copy $2.50.
Payment: 2 free contributor's copies.
Terms: Acquires one-time rights. Publication copyrighted.
Advice: "Please include brief bio."

THE JAMES WHITE REVIEW (II, IV), A Gay Men's Literary Quarterly, The James White Review Association, 3356 Traffic Station, Minneapolis MN 55403. (612)291-2913. Editor: Collective of 3. Tabloid: 26x17; 16 pages; illustrations; photos. "We publish work by *male* gay writers—any subject for primarily gay and/or gay sensitive audience." Quarterly. Estab. 1983. Circ. 2,500.
Needs: Contemporary, experimental, gay, humor/satire, literary, prose poem, translations. No por-

nography. Receives 15 unsolicited fiction mss/month. Accepts 4 mss/issue; 16 mss/year. Publishes ms 3 months or sooner after acceptance. Recently published work by Robert Patrick and Richard Hall. Published new writers within the last year. Length: 22 pages, double spaced. Sometimes critiques rejected mss. Recommends other markets "when we can."
How to Contact: Send complete ms with cover letter with short bio. SASE. Reports in 2-3 months. SASE for ms. Photocopied submissions OK. Sample copy $2. Fiction guidelines $1.
Payment: 3 contributor's copies.
Terms: Acquires one-time rights; returns rights to author. Publication copyrighted.

THE WHITE WALL REVIEW, 63 Gould St., Toronto, Ontario M5B 1E9 Canada. Editor: Changes annually. Magazine: 5³/₄x8³/₄; 150 pages; Zephyr Antique paper; soft cover, glossy; two-tone illustrations; b&w photographs. Book of poetry, prose, art, plays, music and photography. Publishes both Ryerson Polytechnical Institute and professional writers. For Toronto and/or university audience. Annually. Estab. 1975. Circ. 400.
Needs: "No content 'requirements.' " Published new writers within the last year. Must be reasonably short. Nothing "spawning hate, prejudice or obscenity." Accepts 100 + mss/book. Recently published work by Gaetan Charlebois, Tony Cosier, Laurie Kruk; published new writers within the last year.
How to Contact: Send complete ms with cover letter. "The cover letter should contain important information about why the writer is submitting to our publication, where he/she saw our information and some biographical information." Reports on mss "when accepted." SASE or SAE and IRC for ms. Simultaneous, photocopied and previously published submissions OK "if no conflict of interest (providing description forthcoming)." Accepts computer printout submissions. Prefers letter-quality. Sample copy $5 and SAE (8¹/₂x11), plus $1 for postage and handling.
Payment: Pays 1 contributor's copy. Acquires first or one-time rights.
Advice: "Keep it *short*. We look for creativity but not to the point of obscurity."

‡**WHITE WALLS, A Magazine of Writings by Artists**, White Walls, Inc., Box 8204, Chicago IL 60680. Editors: Timothy Porges and Laurie Palmer. "Writings, documentation and projects by visual artists (i.e., painters, sculptors, performance artists, photographers, graphic artists)." For "artists, critics, museum professionals and others interested in contemporary art." Published three times/year. Estab. 1978. Circ. 800.
Needs: Experimental. Authors should be practicing visual artists. Recently published work by David Sedaris, Jay Leibold, Joe Scanlan; published new writers within the last year. Occasionally critiques rejected mss.
How to Contact: Send ms or project proposal accompanied by slides or photographs of artwork, plus résumé. Reports in 3 weeks. SASE. Photocopied submissions OK. Accepts computer printout submissions. Prefers letter-quality. Sample copy for $5.
Payment: Pays $5/page ($15 minimum) and 5 contributor's copies; 40% discount off cover price for extras.
Terms: Pays on publication for all rights. Publication copyrighted.

‡**THE WICAZO SA REVIEW (IV), A Journal of American Indian Studies**, Eastern Washington University, Indian Studies, MS25-188, Cheney WA 99004. (509)359-2871. Editor: Elizabeth Cook-Lynn. Magazine: 8¹/₂x11; 50 pages. Publishes material relating to "Indian studies—all types, including scholarly research and reviews, for an academic audience." Plans special fiction issue. Estab. 1985. Circ. 300-500.
Needs: American Indian. "We wish to publish the creative works of American Indian writers. This is an academic journal devoted to the development of Indian studies topics. We want fiction *by* American Indians, not *about* American Indians." Recently published work by Elizabeth Cook-Lynn and Ralph Salisbury. Publishes short shorts.
How to Contact: Send complete ms with cover letter. Reports in 3 months. SASE. Sample copy for $4.
Payment: No payment.
Terms: Acquires first rights. Publication copyrighted.
Advice: "Very little of magazine fiction today appeals to the ethnicity and the cultural diversity of America in any realistic way. Know the body of work which is now called Contemporary American Indian Fiction—the N. Scott Momaday, Simon Ortiz, Leslie Silko work, the criticism which is emerging from this development, the journals and collections which publish in this field."

WIDE OPEN MAGAZINE (II), Wide Open Press, 116 Lincoln St., Santa Rosa CA 95401. (707)545-3821. Editors: Clif and Lynn Simms. Magazine: 8¹/₂x11; 48 pages; 60 lb paper and cover. Magazine is concerned with finding "solutions to problems, political, social, economic, moral and personal." Quarterly. Estab. 1984. Circ. 500.

Needs: Adventure, contemporary, ethnic, experimental, fantasy, feminist, gay, historical (general), horror, humor/satire, lesbian, mainstream, psychic/supernatural/occult, science fiction, senior citizen/ retirement, suspense/mystery, western. No "religious, children's, vignettes or character studies without plot." Receives 40 unsolicited mss/month. Buys 3 mss/issue; 12 mss/year. Publishes ms 1-3 months after acceptance. A $5 reading fee should accompany each prose submission. This fee will be refunded for all works that we accept for publication. Recently published work by Dan Morra, Mary Whitenack, Phyllis I. Nelson; published new writers within the last year. Length: 2,500 words maximum. Publishes short shorts. Sometimes critiques rejected mss and recommends other markets.
How to Contact: Send complete ms. "We want no clips or bios, please. Let the work stand on its own." Reports in 3 months. SASE. Photocopied and reprint submissions OK. Accepts computer print-out submissions, including dot-matrix. Sample copy $6. Fiction guidelines for #10 SASE and 1 first class stamp.
Payment: Pays $5-$25; 1 contributor copy; charges $6 for extras.
Terms: Pays on publication for one-time rights. Publication copyrighted.
Advice: "We find most magazine fiction today of very poor quality. It is too often esoteric and unfeeling, leaving the reader with the reaction 'who cares?' We love stories about real people in real situations. We believe publications are dropping fiction because their editors select low-quality fiction that they cannot sell to readers."

THE WIDENER REVIEW (III), Widener University, 14th and Chesnut Sts., Chester PA 19013. (215)499-4266. Fiction editor: Michael Clark. Magazine: 5¼x8½; 80 pages. Fiction, poetry, book reviews for general audience. Annually. Estab. 1984. Circ. 250.
Needs: Contemporary, experimental, literary, mainstream, regional, serialized/excerpted novel. Receives 40 unsolicited mss/month. Publishes 3-4 mss/issue. Does not read mss in summer. Publishes ms 3-9 months after acceptance. Length: 1,000 words minimum; 5,000 words maximum. Occasionally critiques rejected mss.
How to Contact: Send complete ms with cover letter. Reports in 3 months on mss. SASE for ms. No simultaneous or photocopied submissions or reprints. Accepts computer printouts, including dot-matrix. Sample copy $3. Fiction guidelines for #10 SAE and 1 first class stamp.
Payment: Pays in contributor's copies; charge for extras.
Terms: Acquires first serial rights. Publication copyrighted.

THE WILLIAM AND MARY REVIEW (II), The College of William and Mary, Williamsburg VA 23185. Editor: William Clark. Magazine: 100 page; graphics; photography. "We publish high quality fiction, poetry, essays, interviews with writers and art. Our audience is primarily academic." Annually. Estab. 1962. Circ. 5,500.
Needs: Literary, contemporary and humor. Receives approximately 90 unsolicited fiction mss each month. Accepts 9 mss/issue. Recently published work by Paul Wood, W.S. Penn and Dana Gioia; published new writers within the last year. Length: 7,000 words maximum. Usually critiques rejected mss.
How to Contact: Send complete ms with SASE and cover letter with name, address and phone number. "Cover letter should be as brief as possible." Reports in 2 months. Fiction department closed in June, July and August. Sample copy $5.
Payment: 5 free author's copies.
Terms: Acquires first rights. Publication copyrighted.
Advice: "We want original, well written stories. Staff requests names be attached separately to individual works. Page allotment to fiction will rise in relation to quality fiction received. The most important aspect of submitting ms is to be familiar with the publication and the types of material it accepts. For this reason, back copies are available."

WILLOW SPRINGS (II, III), Box 1062, Eastern Washington University, Cheney WA 99004. (509)458-6424. Editor: Gillian Conoley, Fiction Editor: Paulette Carstons. Semiannually. Estab. 1977. Circ. 900.
Needs: Parts of novels, short stories, literary, prose poems and translations. Receives 50 unsolicited mss/month. Accepts 3-4 mss/issue; 6-8 mss/year. Recently published work by David Russell Young, William Van Wert, Susan Wheeler; published new writers within the last year. Length: 5,000 words maximum. Rarely critiques rejected mss.
How to Contact: Send complete ms with SASE. Photocopied submissions OK. No simultanious submissions. Reports in 2-3 months on mss. Publishes ms an average of 1-6 months after acceptance. Sample copy for $4.
Payment: 2 contributor's copies.
Terms: Acquires first North American rights.

Advice: "We hope to attract good fiction writers to our magazine, and we've made a commitment to publish 4 stories per issue. We like fiction that exhibits a fresh approach to language. Our most recent issues, we feel, indicate the quality and level of our commitment."

WIND MAGAZINE, Rt. 1, Box 809K, Pikeville KY 41501. (606)631-1129. Editor: Quentin R. Howard. Magazine: 8½x5½; 86+ pages. "Literary journal with stories, poems, book reviews from the small presses and some university presses. Readership is students, literary people, professors, housewives and others." Published irregularly. Estab. 1971. Circ. 500.
Needs: Literary and regional. "No restriction on form, content or subject." Recently published work by Anabel Thomas, Peter LaSalle and Mary Clearman Bleu; published new writers within the last year. Length: no minimum; 5,000 words maximum. Critiques rejected mss when there is time.
How to Contact: Send complete ms with SASE. Photocopied submissions OK. Accepts computer printout submissions. Prefers letter-quality. Reports in 1 month. Publishes ms an average of 1 year after acceptance. Sample copy $2.50.
Payment: Free author's copies. $1.50 charge for extras.
Terms: Acquires first rights. Publication not copyrighted.
Advice: "We're constantly looking for beginning fiction writers. Diversity is one of our major editorial goals. No multiple submissions please. We have no taboos, but set our own standards on reading each ms."

WISCONSIN ACADEMY REVIEW (II, IV), Wisconsin Academy of Sciences, Arts & Letters, 1922 University Ave., Madison WI 53705. (608)263-1692. Editor-in-Chief: Patricia Powell. Magazine: 8½x11; 64-80 pages; 75 lb coated paper; coated cover stock; illustrations; photos. "The *Review* reflects the focus of the sponsoring institution with its editorial emphasis on Wisconsin's intellectual, cultural, social and physical environment. It features short fiction, poetry, essays and Wisconsin-related book reviews for well-educated, well-traveled people interested in furthering regional arts and literature and disseminating information about sciences." Quarterly. Publishes annual fiction issue. Estab. 1954. Circ. 2,000.
Needs: Experimental, historical (general), humor/satire, literary, mainstream, prose poem. "Author must have lived or be living in Wisconsin or fiction must be set in Wisconsin." Receives 5-6 unsolicited fiction mss/month. Accepts 1-2 mss/issue; 8-10 mss/year. Published new writers within the last year. Length: 1,000 words minimum; 4,000 words maximum; 3,000 words average.
How to Contact: Send complete ms with SAE and state author's connection to Wisconsin, the prerequisite. Photocopied submissions OK. Accepts computer printout submissions. Prefers letter-quality. Publishes ms an average of 6 months after acceptance. Sample copy $2. Fiction guidelines for SAE and 1 first class stamp.
Payment: 5 contributor's copies.
Terms: Pays on publication for first rights. Publication copyrighted.

WISCONSIN REVIEW(II), Box 158, Radford Hall, University of Wisconsin, Oshkosh WI 45901. (414)424-2267. Editor: Erin L. McGath. Magazine: 6x9; 60-100 pages; illustrations. Literary prose and poetry. Triquarterly. Estab. 1966. Circ. 2,000.
Needs: Literary and experimental. Receives 30 unsolicited fiction mss each month. Published new writers within the last year. Length: up to 5,000 words. Publishes short shorts. Critiques rejected mss when there is time. Occasionally recommends other markets.
How to Contact: Send complete ms with SASE and cover letter with bio notes. Reports in 1-2 months. Publishes ms an average of 1-2 months after acceptance. Sample copy $2.
Payment: Pays in contributor's copies.
Terms: Acquires first rights. Publication copyrighted.
Advice: "We look for well-crafted work with well developed characters and plots and meaningful situations."

‡WITNESS TO THE BIZARRE (I), Box 2825, Poughkeepsie NY 12603. (914)473-9609. Editor: Melinda Jaeb. Magazine: digest size; 50 pages; 20 lb paper; heavy cover stock; illustrations on cover. "Horror—only the bizarre—sci/fi, gothic, soft gore. For persons who are bored with the spaceman stories." Quarterly. Estab. 1988. Circ. 200+.
Needs: Fantasy, horror, psychic/supernatural/occult, science fiction, suspense/mystery. "Nothing murderous, hard porn, fantasy with mumbo-jumbo names, galactica, fantasy set in a futuristic world." Receives 15 unsolicited mss/month. Accepts 15 mss/issue; 40 mss/year. Publishes ms 4-8 months after acceptance. Published new writers within the last year. Length: 1,500 words preferred; 500 words minimum; 15,000 words maximum. Publishes short shorts. Always critiques rejected mss; sometimes recommends other markets.
How to Contact: Send complete ms with cover letter, "brief description of writer's writing history,

where they heard about us; interesting cover letters that are personalized are enjoyed." Reports in 3 weeks on queries; 2 weeks on mss. SASE. No simultaneous submissions. Photocopied submissions OK. Sample copy for $4. Fiction guidelines for #10 SAE and 1 first class stamp.

Payment: Pays in 2 contributor's copies.

Terms: Acquires first North American serial rights. Publication copyrighted. Sponsors awards for fiction writers. "At end of year, a survey is conducted for all regular readers for the most memorable and bizarre story. The prize is $50."

Advice: "I want material that overrides *The Twilight Zone*, and the dime-a-dozen galactica and alien-orientated magazines. I want things that are really impossible possibilities. The coined phrase of 'you must know someone' to get a story published isn't true as far as *Witness* is concerned. I *always* critique mss, along with notes praising the work, or recommendations for other markets. No writer will *ever* be hurt, embarrassed or frustrated by *Witness*'s rejection slips, because we are encouraging and personal. As writers, we know what it's like out there!"

THE WOOSTER REVIEW (II), The College of Wooster, Wooster OH 44691. (216)263-2000, ext. 2255. Editor/Adviser: Steven Moore. Magazine: 6x9; 112 pages; standard quality. "We like to publish fiction that is accessible to a wide audience. Since our staff is undergraduates, we tend to publish fiction with plots, characters, beginnings, middles and ends. We shy away from the avant-garde and the too sexy. Our readership is collegiate and high school, plus interested writers/contributors and parents." Semiannually. Plans special fiction issue. Estab. 1984. Circ. 1,000.

Needs: Contemporary, fantasy, humor/satire, literary, mainstream, prose poem, science fiction, suspense/mystery. No Robbe-Grillet. Receives 20 unsolicited mss/month. Accepts 6-7 mss/issue; 12-15 mss/year. Slow to respond in summer. Publishes ms 6 months after acceptance. Recently published work by Joseph Bruchac, Barney Bush, Steve Crow; published new writers within the last year. Length: 2,000 words average; 300 words minimum; 3,000 words maximum. Publishes short shorts. Occasionally critiques rejected mss. Sometimes recommends other markets.

How to Contact: Send complete ms with cover letter, which should include biographical information. Reports in 1 week on queries; 2 months on mss. SASE. Photocopied submissions OK. Accepts computer printout submissions, including dot-matrix. Sample copy $2. Fiction guidelines for #10 SAE and 1 first class stamp.

Payment: Pays in 3 contributor's copies.

Terms: Acquires first rights. Publication copyrighted. "The Donaldson Prize for Fiction is $300 cash prize for the best short story published in *The Wooster Review* during a calendar year."

Advice: *The Wooster Review* exists as a part of the creative writing program at The College of Wooster. The magazine is therefore part of our curriculum and helps introduce students to contemporary writing, both fiction and poetry. We know that having our student writers read, discuss and evaluate submissions to the magazine can only help make them better writers."

THE WORCESTER REVIEW, Worcester Country Poetry Association, Inc., 6 Chatham St., Worcester MA 01609. Editor: Rodger Martin. Magazine: 6x9; 60-100 pages; 60 lb white offset paper; 10 pt C15 cover stock; illustrations and photos. "We like high quality, creative poetry, artwork and fiction. Critical articles should be connected to New England." Semiannually. Estab. 1972. Circ. 1,000.

Needs: Literary, prose poem. "We encourage New England writers in the hopes we will publish at least 30% New England but want the other 70% to show the best of writing from across the US." Receives 10-20 unsolicited fiction mss/month. Accepts 2-4 mss/issue. Publishes ms an average of 6 months to 1 year after acceptance. Less than 10% of fiction is agented. Recently published work by Debra Friedman, Carol Glickfeld. Length: 2,000 words average; 1,000 words minimum; 4,000 words maximum. Publishes short shorts. Sometimes critiques rejected mss and recommends other markets.

How to Contact: Send complete ms with cover letter. Reports in 2 weeks on queries; 2-3 months on mss. SASE. Simultaneous submissions OK if other markets are clearly identified. Accepts computer printout submissions, including dot-matrix. Sample copy $4; fiction guidelines free.

Payment: 2 contributor's copies and honorarium if possible.

Terms: Acquires one-time rights. Publication copyrighted.

Advice: "Send only one short story—reading editors do not like to read two by the same author at the same time. We will use only one. We generally look for creative work with a blend of craftsmanship, insight and empathy. This does not exclude humor. We won't print work that is shoddy in any of these areas."

‡WORD & IMAGE (I), The Illustrated Journal, 3811 Priest Lake Dr., Nashville TN 37217. (615)361-4733. Editor: Joanna Long. Magazine: 7x8½; 48-64 pages; 22 lb paper; 60 lb cover; illustrations and photographs. "Strongly visual—usually up-beat material—well-crafted but not obscure or 'arty.' General interest stories and poetry, some nonfiction. No sensational or 'porn.' " Semiannually. Estab. 1986. Circ. 500.

Needs: Condensed/excerpted novel, contemporary, fantasy (occasionally), historical (general—"We feature a history topic in each issue,") humor/satire, literary ("if not obscure,") prose poem, regional, religious/inspirational, romance (historical), senior citizen/retirement. *"Word & Image* is a nonprofit press committed to helping senior citizens and other worthy causes. It is produced by an inter-genera-tional writer's workshop. We meet at the local senior citizen center. I am volunteer teacher, editor, writ-er, etc. We're trying to expand our readership beyond local interest. No mss that ignore a storyline." Re-ceives 4-5 unsolicited mss/month. Accepts 3-4 mss/issue; 6-8 mss/year. Length: 1,500-2,500 words preferred; 600-700 words minimum; 3,500 words maximum. Publishes short shorts. Sometimes cri-tiques rejected mss and recommends other markets.
How to Contact: Send complete ms with cover letter or contact Donelson-Hermitage Writers' Work-shop, Senior Citizens' Center, Donelson, TN 37214. Cover letter should include "brief bio info." Re-ports in 2-3 weeks. SASE. Photocopied and reprint submissions OK. Accepts computer printout sub-missions, including dot-matrix. Sample copy for $3. Retail price: $4.50/copy; $7 for year's subscrip-tion. Fiction guidelines for #10 SAE and 1 first class stamp.
Payment: 1 contributor's copy; charge for extras: $3 each.
Terms: Acquires one-time rights. Publication copyrighted.
Advice: "Write from the heart (or right brain). Let it rest awhile—then revise coldly and objectively (from left brain). Give your mss the best appearance possible before sending it to *Word & Image*. (But I have accepted less-than-professional-looking copy.) It's the story you tell that really counts."

WORLD HUMOR AND IRONY MEMBERSHIP SERIAL YEARBOOK: WHIMSY (IV), World Hu-mor and Irony Membership (WHIM), English Department, Arizona State University, Tempe AZ 85287. (602)965-7592. Editor: Don L.F. Nilsen. Co-Editor: Alleen Pace Nilsen. Magazine: 8½x11; 350 pages; 20 lb bond paper; cover stock varies; illustrations and photographs. "We have an international and inter-disciplinary audience interested in humor. All contributions must deal with humor, comedy, irony, jokes, laughter, puns, sarcasm, satire, smiling, whimsy or wit. You must attend the annual WHIM con-ference in order to have your material considered." Annually. Estab. 1983. Circ. 1,000.
Needs: Humor/satire. Accepts 15 mss/issue. Publishes ms 1 year after acceptance. Length: 1,000 words average; 500 words minimum; 1,500 words maximum. Publishes short shorts.
How to Contact: Present at annual WHIM conference. Reports in 1 week. SASE. Accepts computer printout submissions, including dot-matrix. Sample copy $10.
Payment: None.
Terms: "We hold the copyright; however, rights revert to the author for reprinting." Sends pre-publica-tion galleys to author. Publication copyrighted.
Advice: Publishes short stories "because of our dedication to humor studies."

WRIT MAGAZINE (II), 2 Sussex Ave., Toronto, Ontario M5S 1J5 Canada. (416)978-4871. Editor: Ro-ger Greenwald. Assoc. Editor: Richard M. Lush. Magazine: 6x9; 96 pages; Zephyr laid paper; cover stock varies; cover illustrations. "Literary magazine for literate readers interested in the work of new writers." Annually. Publishes occasional special fiction issues. Estab. 1970. Circ. 700.
Needs: Literary, short stories, short shorts, parts of novels, translations. Accepts 10-15 mss/year. Does not read mss in summer. Recently published fiction by Austin Alexis, Mark Gillingham and John Lo-wry; published new writers in the last year. Length: 300-20,000 words. Critiques rejected mss "when there is time. Sometimes recommends other markets."
How to Contact: Send complete ms with SASE (Canadian stamps or IRCs) and brief biographical note on author and/or translator, and a phone number. Translators must send copy of original text. Ac-cepts computer printout submissions if letter quality. Reports in 8-12 weeks. Sample copy $6.
Payment: 2 free author's copies. Negotiates charge for extras.
Terms: Acquires first North American serial rights. Copyright reverts to author.
Advice: "Look at your target magazine before submitting."

THE WRITERS' BAR-B-Q (II), Sangamon Writers, Inc., 924 Bryn Mawr, Springfield IL 62703. (217)525-6987. Fiction Editors: Tim Osburn, Becky Bradway, Gary Smith, Bill Gorden, Katherine Costa, Gael Cox Carnes. Magazine: 8½x11; 80-110 pages; slick cover stock with full-page photo; illus-trations and photos. *"The Writers' Bar-B-Q* is a fiction magazine that is looking for unpretentious, fun, exciting writing. A good story with purpose and well-drawn characters is more important to us than clever phrasing. We want writing that shows the author cares, and has something to say." Semiannually. Estab. 1987. Circ. 1,000.
Needs: Adventure, contemporary, erotica, ethnic, experimental, fantasy, feminist, gay, historical (general), horror, humor/satire, lesbian, literary, mainstream, psychic/supernatural/occult, regional, science fiction, serialized/excerpted novel, suspense/mystery, translations. "Display a strong personal voice, a unique view of the world, and a sense of commitment and caring toward the characters and sub-ject. Contemporary, thoughtful sci-fi, horror and detective are encouraged, along with more main-

stream, contemporary work. We are looking for inventiveness, humor and insight. No formulas—whether they be genre formulas or academic formulas. Work that is sexist, racist or homophobic should not be mailed!" Receives 50-100 unsolicited fiction mss/month. Accepts 15-20 mss/issue; 30-40 mss/year. Publishes ms 6 months to 1 year after acceptance. Recently published work by Lowry Pei, Nolan Porterfield, Mameve Medwed; published new writers within the last year. Length: 500-15,000 words. Publishes short shorts. Sometimes critiques rejected mss.

How to Contact: Send complete ms with cover letter, which should include "a sense of who the writer is—a list of publications is fine, but personality is more fun." Reports in 4 weeks on queries; in 6-12 weeks on mss. SASE. Simultaneous, photocopied and reprint submissions OK. Accepts computer printout submissions, including dot-matrix. Accepts electronic submissions via disk. "We have an Epson MS-DOS and a Kaypro CP M. No Apple." Sample copy $5; subscription $10. Fiction guidelines for #10 SASE.

Payment: 3 contributor's copies.

Terms: Acquires first rights. Rights revert upon publication. Publication copyrighted.

Advice: "The editors of the *Bar-B-Q* come from a maligned area of the country—the Midwest—which is filled with talented authors who suffer under the cliché of Midwesterners as backwoods, illiterate hicks. We want to provide a place where wonderful, unconventional, supposedly unmarketable writing can be found. We want Midwestern and other silenced stories to be discovered."

‡THE WRITERS' BLOC (I), Box 212, Marysville OH 43040. (513)642-8019. Editor: Deborah Holland. Chapbook: 6x8½; 40 pages; 16 lb stock; 20 lb cover; illustrations. "We are a showcase for writers of all genres, as long as the work is in good taste. We publish both short stories and essays. We will sometimes take a character sketch if it is extremely well written. Our audience consists of writers trying to break into print and those who share the love of writing." Quarterly. Estab. 1985. Circ. 300.

Needs: Adventure, contemporary, experimental, historical (general), juvenile (5-9 years), literary, mainstream, psychic/supernatural/occult, romance (contemporary), science fiction, suspense/mystery, young adult/teen (10-18 years). No erotica. Receives 40-60 unsolicited mss/month. Accepts 4-6 mss/issue; 16-24 mss/year. Publishes ms 3-6 months after acceptance. Recently published work by Kenneth Schulze; published new writers within the last year. Length: 2,000-3,000 words average; 6,000 words maximum. Publishes short shorts. Length: 750-1,000 words. Almost always critiques rejected mss. Sometimes recommends other markets.

How to Contact: Send complete ms with cover letter, which should include the author's credits. Reports in 6-12 weeks on queries; 6-16 weeks on mss. SASE. Simultaneous and photocopied submissions OK. Accepts computer printout submissions. Sample copy for $3. Fiction guidelines for #10 SAE and 1 first class stamp.

Payment: Pays in contributor's copies.

Terms: Acquires one-time rights. Publication copyrighted. "We sponsor one contest per year for subscribers only. Deadline is December 1st of each year."

Advice: "Let the story speak for itself; don't tell the reader what he should notice on his own. Try to send us something new, or at least something old with a new twist. I've pretty much had my fill of stories about writers. We make personal comments on each ms to help our contributors."

‡WRITERS' EXCHANGE (I), General Publications, Inc., Box 2368, Columbia MD 21045. (301)381-9295. Editor: D. Binning. Newsletter: 8½x11; 20-30 pages; 20 lb paper; 60 lb cover stock. "Publication's aim: To be a writers' support group by mail. We are looking for subscribers and contributing editors." Bimonthly. Estab. 1987. Circ. 100-200.

Needs: "All genres, no poetry, also looking for articles on the craft of writing."

Advice: "We are a paid subscription newsletter. The subscribers are beginning and semi-pro writers. For the annual subscription fee of $45, we professionally critique a writer's work at G.P.I., publish it in the newsletter, distribute newsletter to other subscribers as well as agents and book/magazine editors, and the subscribers critique the work through evaluation forms in the newsletter. We collect and redirect critiques back to the author. The above work can be fiction or nonfiction. In addition we publish articles on what it is like being a writer, how to get published, how to write better, etc. These articles we pay $10 per and give priority to our subscribers."

WRITERS' FORUM (II), University of Colorado at Colorado Springs, Colorado Springs CO 80933-7150. Editor: Dr. Alex Blackburn. "Ten to fifteen short stories or self-contained novel excerpts published once a year along with 25-35 poems. Funded by grants from National Endowment for the Arts, Coordinating Council for Literary Magazines, University of Colorado, McGraw Hill and others. Highest literary quality only: mainstream, avant-garde, with preference to western themes. For small press enthusiasts, teachers and students of creative writing, commercial agents/publishers, university libraries and departments interested in contemporary American literature."

Needs: Literary, contemporary, ethnic (Native American, Chicano, not excluding others) and regional

(West). No "sentimental, over-plotted, pornographic, anecdotal, polemical, trendy, disguised autobiographical, fantasy (sexual, extra-terrestrial), pseudo-philosophical, passionless, placeless, undramatized, etc. material." Accepts 10-15 mss/issue. Receives approximately 40 unsolicited fiction mss each month and will publish new as well as experienced authors. Recently published fiction by Thomas E. Kennedy, Anthony Bukoski, Rita LaSalle; published new writers within the last year. Length: 1,500-10,000 words. Critiques rejected mss "when there is time and perceived merit."

How to Contact: Send complete ms and letter with relevant career information with SASE. Accepts computer printout submissions. Prefers letter-quality. Reports in 3-5 weeks on mss. Publishes ms an average of 6 months after acceptance. Sample back copy $5.95 to *NSSWM* readers. Current copy $5.95.

Payment: 1 free author's copy. Cover price less 60% discount for extras.

Terms: Acquires one-time rights. Rights revert to author. Publication copyrighted.

Advice: "Read our publication. Be prepared for constructive criticism. We especially seek submissions that show immersion in place (trans-Mississippi West) and development of credible characters. Turned off by slick 'decadent' New York-ish content. Probably the TV-influenced fiction is the most quickly rejected. Our format—a 5½x8½ professionally edited and printed paperback book—lends credibility to authors published in our imprint."

WRITERS GAZETTE (I, II), Trouvère Company, Rt. 2, Box 290, Eclectic AL 36024. Editor: Brenda Williamson. Magazine: 8½x11; 36+ pages; 20 lb bond paper; illustrations; photos sometimes. For writers, by writers, about writing. Quarterly. Estab. 1983.

Needs: Adventure, contemporary, fantasy, horror, humor/satire, literary, mainstream, prose poem, psychic/supernatural, religious/inspirational, romance (contemporary, gothic/historical), science fiction, spiritual, suspense/mystery and western. Wants to see a "definite story—fictitious." Buys 16-20 mss/year. Recently published work by Barbara Bell, Carol Garelick; published beginning writers within the last year. Length: 2,500 words maximum; 700 words average.

How to Contact: Send complete ms with cover letter. "I like to have knowledge about a writer's success with stories, not how many, but more if they have sold before or this would be their first time." SASE. Simultaneous, photocopied and reprint submissions OK. Reports in 4-8 weeks on ms. Sample copy $4. Fiction guidelines for #10 SAE and 1 first class stamp.

Payment: Varies. Contributor's copy, cash—$1-$30—or subscription.

Terms: "Pays on acceptance and for first, second or one-time rights." Publication copyrighted.

Advice: "Try the bizarre and unbelievable and making it into a realistic story."

WRITERS' HAVEN JOURNAL (I,II), Writers' Bookstore & Haven, 3341 Adams Ave., San Diego CA 92116. (619)282-3363. Editor: Nancy J. Painter. Magazine: 8½x7; 28 pages; bond paper; yellow matte cover stock; illustrations. "About and for writers, featuring articles on the art and craft of writing, personal writing experience with the writing world, news of writers, fiction, poetry, illustrations, columns and announcements." Monthly. Estab. 1984. Circ. 350.

Needs: Fiction and articles about writers, writing, publishing, etc. Receives 15-20 unsolicited fiction mss/month. Accepts 2-3 mss/issue; 30 mss/year. Publishes mss 1-4 months after acceptance. Recently published work by Stanley Field, Bob Chatelle, Leif Fearn; published new writers within the last year. Length: 1,250 words average; no minimum; 1,300 words maximum. Rarely critiques rejected ms. Occasionally recommends other markets.

How to Contact: Send complete ms with cover letter. Reports in 6 weeks. SASE. Simultaneous and photocopied submissions OK. Accepts computer printout submissions, including dot-matix. Sample copy $1.50.

Payment: Pays in contributor's copies. "$10 on acceptance for cover story (fiction about writers, writing)."

Terms: Rights remain with author. Publication not copyrighted.

Advice: "We're interested in who the writers are—do they write full time?—Have other projects underway,—published? More focused toward writers in fiction situations than in the past. Would like interviews with writers who have been published nationally."

> **❝ I never desire to converse with a man who has written more books than he has read. ❞**
>
> **—Samuel Johnson**

WRITERS-IN-WAITING NEWSLETTER (I), Bjo's Enterprises, 837 Archie St., Eugene OR 97402. (503)688-5400. Editor: Bjo Ashwill. Newsletter: 8½x11; 8-16 pages; 20 lb bond paper; clip art. "For beginning writers. Nonfiction limited to how-to articles on fiction and poetry writing. Short stories, plays and poems." Bimonthly. Estab. 1986. Circ. 40.
Needs: Adventure, contemporary, ethnic, experimental, feminist, historical, humor/satire, literary, mainstream, romance, suspense/mystery, western. Receives 10 unsolicited fiction mss/month. Accepts 2 mss/issue. Publishes ms an average of 2-4 months after acceptance. Length: 200 words minimum; 2,400 words maximum. Publishes short shorts. Sometimes comments on rejected mss.
How to Contact: Send complete ms with cover letter. "Keep it simple and specific. Specify if work is for Work-in-Progress column or not. Items in WIP columns are critiqued in the newsletter." Reports in 2 weeks on queries; in 1 month on mss. SASE. Simultaneous, photocopied and reprint submissions OK. Accepts computer printout submissions, including dot-matrix. Accepts electronic submissions via IBM with Perfect Link compatible modem software. Sample copy $2 with #10 SASE. Fiction guidelines for #10 SASE.
Payment: Contributor's copies.
Terms: Acquires first rights or one-time rights. Publication copyrighted. Sponsors contests for fiction writers—query for details.
Advice: "The purpose of my newsletter is to be helpful and optimistic toward the beginning writer. I want to publish first timers."

‡WRITERS NEWSLETTER (I), Writers Studio, 1530 7th St., Rock Island IL 61201. (309)788-3980. Editor: Betty Mowery. Newsletter: 8½x11; 8-9 pages. "Anything of help to writers." Bimonthly. Estab. 1968. Circ. 385.
Needs: Adventure, contemporary, experimental, historical (general), humor/satire, mainstream, prose poem, regional, religious/inspiration, romance, spiritual, suspense/mystery. "Also, articles, fiction, nonfiction and poetry manuscripts from young authors K-12, for young author page. Please state age on manuscript." No erotica. Receives about 12 mss/month. Buys or accepts up to 6 mss/issue. Publishes ms within 3 months of acceptance. Recently published work by David R. Collins, Evelyn Witter, Chris Walkowicz; published new writers within the last year. Length: 500 words maximum. Publishes short shorts. Length: 200 words.
How to Contact: Send complete ms. Reports in 1 week. SASE. Simultaneous, photocopied and reprint submissions OK. Accepts computer printout submissions, including dot-matrix. Sample copy for 75¢ and #10 SAE.
Payment: Pays in contributor's copies.
Terms: Acquires first rights.
Advice: "Just send a manuscript, but first read a copy of our publication to get an idea of what type of material we take. Please send SASE. If not, manuscripts *will not* be returned. Be sure name and address is on the manuscript."

WRITERS' RENDEZVOUS (I), 3954 Mississippi St., Suite 8, San Diego CA 92104. (619)296-2758. Editor: Karen Campbell. Newsletter: 8½x11; approx. 24 pages; bond paper; no cover; line drawings. "Writer-oriented, publish only work relating to freelance writing and penpalling." Quarterly. Plans special fiction issue. Estab. 1986. Circ. 100.
Needs: Contemporary, feminist, humor/satire, literary, mainstream, religious/inspirational, serialized/excerpted novel, suspense/mystery, translations, writing. No fiction "not related to writing/penpalling." Receives approx. 10 unsolicited fiction mss/month. Publishes approx. 2 mss/issue; approx. 10 mss/year. Publishes ms 6 weeks-1 year after acceptance. Recently published work by Bettye Griffin, Jan McDaniel, Linda Hutton; published new writers within the last year. Length: 750 words average; 1,500 words maximum. Publishes short shorts. Sometimes comments on rejected mss and recommends other markets.
How to Contact: Send complete ms with cover letter. Reports in 2-4 weeks. SASE. Simultaneous, photocopied and reprint submissions OK. Accepts computer printouts, including dot-matrix "with true descenders only." Sample copy for $3, #10 SAE and 3 first class stamps; fiction guidelines for #10 SAE and 1 first class stamp.
Payment: Pays in contributor's copies.
Terms: Acquires one-time rights. Publication not copyrighted. Sponsors contests for fiction writers. "SASE for guidelines; $2 entry fee. Cash prize."
Advice: "Proofread. Then proofread again. Then ask a friend or teacher to proofread. Use your dictionary—both for spelling and meaning. Read the guidelines carefully. And, if you want cash for your work,

be sure you aren't submitting to markets which pay copies. (I've had several acceptances fall through when I advised the author of our non-payment policy)."

‡WRITING PURSUITS (I), Twin Falls Chapter of Idaho Writer's League, 1863 Bitterroot Dr., Twin Falls ID 83301. (208)734-0746 (evenings). Editor: Bill White. Newsletter: 8x11; 2-5 pages; illustrations. Newsletter for writers. Monthly except July and August. Estab. 1986. Circ. approximately 100.
Needs: Literary, regional, suspense/mystery, humor/satire and western. No erotica, gay, lesbian, religious or occult fiction. Accepts 1 ms/issue; 10 mss/year. Publishes ms within 1-2 months of acceptance. Length: 500 words maximum. Sometimes critiques rejected mss and recommends other markets.
How to Contact: Query first. Reports in 1-2 weeks. SASE. Photocopied submissions OK. Accepts computer printout submissions, including dot-matrix; also electronic submissions via disk or modem. Sample copy for 50¢ or #10 SAE and 1 first class stamp. Fiction guidelines for #10 SAE and 1 first class stamp.
Payment: Pays in free subscription to newsletter and contributor's copies.
Terms: Acquires first rights. Publication copyrighted. Sponsors yearly contest for fiction writers—inquire with SASE.
Advice: "Be persistent. Study a sample of our publication. Make your story exciting."

‡WRITTEN WORD (I), Poetry and Short Stories, 7617 North Ridge Dr., Citrus Hts. CA 95610. (916)725-2736. Editor: Joe Seerfeld. Newsletter: 8x10½; 10-15 pages; graphics. "*W.W.* is mainly an alternative literary forum with short stories and poetry. Originality is the theme." Monthly. Estab. 1987. Circ. 50+.
Needs: Adventure, erotica, fantasy, horror, humor/satire, juvenile (5-9 years), literary, preschool (0-4 years), psychic/supernatural/occult, suspense/mystery, political. No "sexist or racist material. No boring, redundant pieces that would be better suited for *The New Yorker*." Receives 20+ unsolicited mss/month. Accepts 10 mss/issue; 100 mss/year. Publishes ms 3-4 weeks after acceptance. Length: 200 words preferred; 300 words maximum. Sometimes recommends other markets.
How to Contact: Send complete ms with cover letter. Simultaneous, photocopied and reprint submissions OK. Accepts computer printout submissions, including dot-matrix. Sample copy for 50¢. Fiction guidelines free.
Payment: Pays in contributor's copies.
Terms: Acquires one-time rights. Publication not copyrighted.
Advice: "I actually lose money on this venture, but the beauty of a new issue transcends the money loss and headaches. I have seen many other literary 'zines and hundreds of works by unknowns that glow next to the crap in *Playboy*, *New Yorker*, *Esquire* or any other 'bigtime' magazine. The new era of fiction writer, whether they be a beatnik/punk cross or a Chandler clone, have the tools for great storytelling. To me, short stories are the true feeling of fiction. To fit a feeling into 2 or 3 paragraphs is a very difficult thing, which can be a quite beauitful if done properly and creatively. Anybody who has the patience and guts to sit down and create something deserves recognition. Send 'em in!"

WYOMING, THE HUB OF THE WHEEL (II), A Journal for Universal Spokesmen, Willow Bee Publishing House, Box 9, Saratoga WY 82331. (307)326-5214. Editor: Lenore A. Senior. Fiction Editor: Dawn Senior. Magazine: 6x9; 100 pages average; 60 lb paper; 10 pt CIS cover; illustrations; photographs. "Themes: Peace (from International Peace to Personal Peace), The Human Race, Positive Relationships (Between People, Youth & Age, People & Nature), The Human Spirit and all its Possibilities." Semiannually. Estab. 1985. Circ. 300.
Needs: Contemporary, ethnic, experimental, literary, prose poem, regional, translations. No violence, sex, religious materials or writing in any way racist or sexist. Receives 15 unsolicited fiction mss/month. Publishes 2-6 mss/issue. Publishes mss 6-18 months after acceptance. Recently published work by Rochelle Lynn Holt, Elizabeth Follin-Jones. Length: 2,500 words maximum. Publishes short shorts. Sometimes comments on rejected mss or recommends other markets.
How to Contact: Send complete ms with cover letter, which should include a short bio. Reports on queries in 2-3 weeks; on mss in 6-8 weeks. SASE. Simultaneous, photocopied and reprint submissions OK. Accepts computer printouts, including dot-matrix. Sample copy for $5. Fiction guidelines for #10 SAE and 45¢ postage.
Payment: Pays 1 contributor's copy. Contributor discounts also available.
Terms: Acquires one-time rights. Publication copyrighted.
Advice: "We look for fiction of emotional and psychological depth and clear, understandable, yet subtle language that is sensitive to the reader's intelligence, imagination and sense of the exquisite mystery of existence. Beginners' best hope of achieving excellence is to look deeply into their own experience and honestly draw from those elements of it that best contain the universal within the unique and particular."

XAVIER REVIEW (I, II), Xavier University, Box 110C, New Orleans LA 70125. (504)486-7411, ext. 481. Editor: Thomas Bonner, Jr. Magazine of "poetry/fiction/nonfiction/reviews (contemporary literature) for professional writers/libraries/colleges/universities." Published semiannually. Estab. 1980. Circ. 500.
Needs: Contemporary, ethnic, experimental, historical (general), literary, Latin-American, prose poem, Southern, religious, serialized/excerpted novel, translations. Receives 30 unsolicited fiction mss/month. Buys 2 mss/issue; 4 mss/year. Length: 10-15 pages. Occasionally critiques rejected mss.
How to Contact: Send complete ms. SASE. Sample copy $3.
Payment: 2 contributor's copies.
Terms: Publication copyrighted.

THE YALE REVIEW (II), Yale University Press, 1902A Yale Station, New Haven CT 06520. (203)432-0499. Editor: Kai Erikson. Associate Editor: Penelope Laurans. Managing Editor: Wendy Wipprecht. "A general interest quarterly; publishes literary criticism, original fiction and poetry, cultural commentary, book reviews for an informed general audience." Quarterly. Estab. 1911. Circ. 6,000.
Needs: Literary and contemporary. Buys 4-8 mss/year. Less than 1% of fiction is agented. Length: 3,000-5,000 words.
How to Contact: Send complete ms with SASE. Reports in 2 months. Publishes ms up to 1 year after acceptance. Sample copy $7.
Payment: Approximately $100. 1 free author's copy; $3 charge for extras.
Terms: Makes assignments on a work-for-hire basis. Pays on publication for first North American serial rights.

YELLOW SILK (II): Journal of Erotic Arts, Verygraphics, Box 6374, Albany CA 94706. Editor/Publisher: Lily Pond. Magazine: 8⅜x10⅞; 52 pages; matte coated stock; glossy cover stock; 4-color illustrations; photos. "We are interested in nonpornographic erotic literature: joyous, mad, musical, elegant, passionate and beautiful. 'All persuasions; no brutality' is our editorial policy. Literary excellence is a priority; innovative forms are welcomed, as well as traditional ones." Published quarterly. Estab. 1981. Circ. 13,000.
Needs: Comics, erotica, ethnic, experimental, fantasy, feminist/lesbian, gay, humor/satire, literary, prose poem, science fiction and translations. No "blow-by-blow" descriptions; no hackneyed writing except when used for satirical purposes. Nothing containing brutality. Buys 4-5 mss/issue; 16-20 mss/year. Recently published work by William Kotzwinkle, Gary Soto. Published new writers within the last year. Length: no preference. Occasionally critiques rejected ms.
How to Contact: Send complete ms with SASE and include short, *personal* bio notes. No queries. No pre-published material. No simultaneous submissions. Name, address and phone number on each page. Photocopied submissions OK. Accepts computer printout submissions. Prefers letter-quality. Reports in 6-8 weeks on mss. Publishes ms up to 2 years after acceptance. Sample copy $5.
Payment: 3 contributor's copies plus minimum of $10 per prose item.
Terms: Pays on publication for all periodical and anthology rights for one year following publication, at which time rights revert back to author; and non-exclusive reprint and anthology rights for the duration of the copyright. Publication copyrighted.
Advice: "Read, read, read! Including our magazine—plus Nabokov and Nin, and Rimbaud, Virginia Woolf, William Kotzwinkle, James Joyce. Then send in your story! Trust that the magazine/editor will not rip you off—they don't. As they say, 'find your own voice,' then trust it. Most manuscripts I reject appear to be written by people without great amounts of writing experience. It takes years (frequently) to develop your work to publishable quality; it can take many re-writes on each individual piece. I also see many approaches to sexuality (for my magazine) that are trite and not fresh. The use of language is not original, and the people do not seem real. However, the gems come too, and what a wonderful moment that is. Please don't send me anything with blue eye shadow."

Z MISCELLANEOUS (II), Again & Again Press, Box 20041, New York NY 10028. Editor: Charles Fabrizio. Magazine: 8½x11; 100 pages; 70 lb paper; 80 lb cover stock; illustrations. "Publishes work that enables the reader to reassess the familiar, discover the new, and learn about the different." Quarterly. Estab. 1987. Circ. 300.
Needs: Contemporary, ethnic, fantasy, horror, humor/satire, literary, mainstream, science fiction. "We welcome original, well crafted stories that present clearly defined characters, a logical progression of events, and a coherent plot." No confessions, romance, religious, political or pornography. Receives approx. 50-75 unsolicited fiction mss/month. Accepts 10-15 mss/issue; 60-75 mss/year. Publishes ms an average of 2-4 months after acceptance. Recently published work by Kathryn Machan Aal, Bruce Boston and Will Inman; published new writers within the last year. Length: 2,000 words maximum. Publishes short shorts. Sometimes critiques rejected mss.
How to Contact: Send complete ms with cover letter. (Cover letter optional.) Reports in 6 weeks.

SASE. Photocopied submissions OK. Accepts computer printout submissions, no dot-matrix. Sample copy $3.50; fiction guidelines for #10 SASE.

Payment: $10 maximum; tearsheets of work.

Terms: Pays on acceptance for first rights. Publication copyrighted. "An Achievement Award In Fiction, chosen by the magazine's staff, is selected from the stories published in each issue and carries a payment of $10. The works so cited are eligible for the Annual Achievement In Fiction Award, which is determined by the magazine's subscribers and carries a payment of $50."

Advice: "Editorial comments/suggestions are meant to help a writer achieve the full potential of their work. You may, and have every right to, disagree with the editor's opinion. But editors and writers should be allies, not adversaries."

‡ZOIKS! (I,II,IV), It Isn't Just for Breakfast Anymore, 604 Dixie Trail, Raleigh NC 27067. (919)821-1336. Editor: Skip Elsheimer. Fiction Editor: Joe Corey. Magazine; illustrations and photos. "*Zoiks!* is interested in new ideas and new ways of thinking. Or at least using old ideas in a new way. Exploring the world through cynicism." Bimonthly. Plans special fiction issue. Estab. 1986.

Needs: Experimental, humor/satire, prose poem, psychic/supernatural/occult, translations, underground literature, conspiracy-oriented fiction. "I'm interested in anything that will make you question your surroundings. No fiction that is pretentious, lacking humor." Receives 2-3 unsolicited mss/month. Accepts 1-2 mss/issue; 6-12 mss/year. Recently published work by Joe Corey, Skip Elsheimer, Karen Bartlett; published new writers within the last year. Publishes short shorts. Sometimes criitiques rejected mss or recommends other markets.

How to Contact: Query first with clips of published work or send complete ms with cover letter, which should include "address. Should tell something about the author." Reports in 3 weeks. Simultaneous, photocopied and reprint submissions OK. Accepts computer submissions, including dot-matrix. Accepts electronic submissions via Macintosh 800K. Sample copy for 50¢.

Payment: Pays in contributor's copies; charges for extras at cost.

Terms: Publication not copyrighted. Work belongs to the author.

Advice: "I feel that magazine fiction is too industry oriented. Everyone should have a shot at getting published. Express *yourself*! Not the style of another famous author."

ZONË (II), A Feminist Journal for Women and Men, Box 803, Brookline Village MA 02147. (617)524-7920. Editor: Richard Waring. Fiction Editor: Peter Fong. Magazine: 6x9; 132 pages; 60 lb high quality paper; 100 lb glossy cover stock; illustrations; photos. Magazine's focus is "new forms of femininity and masculinity; ethnic, philosophical mix; gay/straight; feminism in translation." Audience: "politically/sexually aware; feminists—both women and men; serious popular literature addicts." Published annually. Estab. 1983. Circ. approximately 1,000.

Needs: Contemporary, ethnic, experimental, feminist, gay, historical, lesbian, literary, prose poem, science fiction, spiritual, translations, veteran's, handicapped. "Nothing meant for the more commercial outlets." Receives 50 unsolicited mss/month. Recently published work by P. B. Parris, Nicolette de Csipkay, Pamela Uschuk; published new writers within the last year. Length: 2,500 words or under average; 500 words minimum; 3,000 words maximum. Rarely accepts above 10 pages. Occasionally critiques rejected mss.

How to Contact: Query first or send complete ms. "Unless author knows our theme, query is best initial contact." Reports in 1 week on queries; 3 months on mss. SASE. Photocopied submissions OK. Accepts computer printout submissions. Prefers letter-quality. Accepts disk submissions compatible with Compugraphic. Prefers hard copy with disk submission. Sample copy $5.50.

Payment: 1 contributor's copy.

Terms: Acquires one-time rights. Publication copyrighted.

Advice: "We have gone from publishing two stories per issue to accepting three stories. Be language conscious. Write about what you know—imaginatively—using common words in new ways."

ZYZZYVA (II, IV), The Last Word: West Coast Writers and Artists, Suite 1400, 41 Sutter St., San Francisco CA 94104. (415)982-3440. Editor: Howard Junker. Magazine: 6x9; 136 pages; Starwhite Vicksburg smooth paper; graphics; photos. "Literate" magazine. Quarterly. Estab. 1985. Circ. 3,000.

Needs: Contemporary, experimental, literary, prose poem. West Coast writers only. Receives 200 unsolicited mss/month. Buys 5 fiction mss/issue; 20 mss/year. Agented fiction: 10%. Recent issues have included Salvatore La Puma, Gina Berriault, Juan Felipe Herrera; published new writers within the last year. Length: varies.

How to Contact: Send complete ms. "Cover letters are of minimal importance." Reports in 2 weeks on mss. SASE. No simultaneous submissions or reprints. Accepts computer printouts, including dot-matrix. Sample copy $8. Fiction guidelines on masthead page.

Payment: Pays $25-$100.

Terms: Pays on acceptance for first North American serial rights. Publication copyrighted.

Advice: "Keep the faith."

Foreign little/literary magazines

The following is a list of little/literary journals published in countries outside the U.S. and Canada that accept or buy short fiction in English (or in the universal languages of Esperanto or Ido) by North American writers.

Before sending a manuscript to a foreign publication with which you are unfamiliar, it's a good idea to query the magazine's editors first for their needs and interests in short stories, and to request a sample copy. All foreign correspondence must include international reply coupons (IRCs) or foreign postage stamps to ensure an answer to your query or the return of your manuscript. You might find it less expensive to send a photocopy of your manuscript and tell the editor not to return it if it is not accepted. Then enclose just one IRC for a response.

‡**ACUMEN**, 6, The Mount, Furzeham, Brixham, Devon TQ5 8QY England. Fiction Editor: Patricia Oxley. Circ. 500. "Literary magazine with an emphasis on poetry. I use 2-4 short stories/year (2 issues) which are around 1,500 words, have a clear statement and are written in a literary style. Writers paid in extra copies of *Acumen*. Writers receive copies of the issue containing their work. Send sufficient IRCs to cover return postage. Make sure name and address are on manuscript (not just covering letter or, worse still, on outside of envelope.)"

AMMONITE, Suite 5, Somdor House, Station Road, Gillingham Dorset SP8 4QA England. Publishes 6 stories/year. Publishes science fiction, fantasy and mythical fiction. Pays in copies. "Buy a sample copy." ($2.50 including postage.)

AQUARIUS, Flat 3, 114 Sutherland Ave., Maida-Vale, London W9 England. Fiction Editor: Sean Glackin. Circ. 5,000. Publishes five stories/issue. Interested in humor/satire, literary, prose poem and serialized/exerpted novels. "We publish prose and poetry and reviews." Payment is by agreement. "We only suggest changes. Most stories are taken on merit." Price in UK £2 50p. plus postage and packing; in US $8 plus $3 postage.

‡**ARGO**, Museum of Modern Art, 30 Pembroke St., Oxford OX1 1BP England. Fiction Editors: Hilary Davies and David Constantine. Circ. 800. Averages 1 short story/issue. Magazine published 3 times/year. "Predominantly a poetry magazine, we nevertheless regularly publish fiction (short stories) of all types. Payment: about $6 and 2 copies; plus chance to purchase reduced price subscription and complimentary subscription for friend." Stories "should not be over long (about 5,000 words upper limit). Otherwise judged on merit."

‡**AUGURIES**, 48 Anglesey Road, Alverstoke, Gosport, Hampshire P012 2EQ England. Editor: Nik Morton. Circ. 100. Averages 25-30 stories/year. "Science fiction and fantasy, maximum length 4,000 words." Pays £2 per 1,000 words plus complimentary copy. "Buy back issues, then try me!" Sample copy $3.

BACK BRAIN RECLUSE, Chris Reed, 16 Somersall Lane, Chesterfield, Derbyshire S40 3LA England. Fiction Editor: Chris Reed. Circ. 250-300. Averages 30 stories/year. "*Back Brain Recluse* is a *prose* magazine. No genre restrictions, though tendencies to 'new wave'/avant-garde science fiction/fantasy/horror." Pays in copies. "Contributors advised to consult submissions guidelines available for two IRCs. Samples $4 (cash only please)."

BOUNDARY MAGAZINE, 23 Kingsley Rd., Runcorn, Cheshire WA7 5PL England. Fiction Editor: R.J.Darlington. Circ. 250. Publishes 20 pieces/issue; 3 issues per year. "A duplicated magazine which accepts poetry, prose, articles and artwork. Short stories—max. 1,500 words. Pays 1 contributor's copy. "Submissions must be accompanied with a large SASE; no sexist or racist material accepted."

‡**BRAVE NEW WORD**, Box 88, Clifton Hill, Victoria 3068 Australia. Fiction Editor: Helen Murnane. Circ. 300-1,500. Publishes 60 mss/year. "We publish contemporary Australian short stories and poetry. We would consider a small amount of international writing." Writers receive either 2 copies or a small payment. Enclose SASE.

CENTRAL COAST COURIER, Box 44, Oxford, Tasmania 7190 Australia. Fiction Editor: J.C. Read. Circ. 1,000. Local newspaper publishing general fiction and poetry on a bimonthly basis. Pays nominal fee; sends contributor's copy where possible. Maximum word length for short stories: 1,500 words. Also uses summaries of novels.

‡**CONTRAST**, Box 3841, Cape Town 8000 South Africa. Editor: Geoffrey Haresnape. Circ. 1,000. Averages 6-8 short stories/year. "A literary journal of Southern Africa; emphasis on publishing short stories (max 6,500 words), poetry and literary articles." No payment—contributor's copies sent. "Include self-addressed envelope."

‡**CORPUS JOURNAL**, 76 Iveson Drive, Leeds, West Yorkshire LS16 6NL England. Editor: Patricia Khan. Circ. 500. Averages 12 short stories/year. Published quarterly. "*Corpus Journal* is a Yorkshire-based quarterly magazine containing poetry, artworks and short stories from all over the UK and abroad. Its sister publications—Unibird Publications and Unibird Minibooks—feature anthologies by writers previously printed in *Corpus Journal*. There is no payment for any work published, but writers do receive a copy of the issue in which their work appears. "Well-written and non-political short stories of less than 2,500 words are preferred; humorous pieces are especially welcomed and are given priority. An SAE or 3 IRCs should be enclosed for return of manuscripts."

‡**CREATIVE FORUM**, Bahri Publications Pvt Limited., 57 Santnagar, Box 7023, New Delhi 110065 India. Fiction Editor: U.S. Bahri. Circ. 1,800. Publishes 8-12 stories annually. "We accept short stories only for our journal, *Creative Forum*. Novels/novellas accepted if suitable subsidy is forthcoming from the author." Pays in copies. Manuscripts should be "neatly typed and not beyond 200 A4 size sheets."

‡**CRITICAL QUARTERLY**, Department of English, The University of Manchester, M13 9PL England. Editor: Maureen Duffy. Circ. 3,000. Averages 80,000 words/year. Publishes literary fiction. Writers receive copies of the issue in which their work appears. Pays £30/thousand words. "Submit with SASE or envelope with IRCs if return required."

CROSSCURRENT (II), A Multicultural and Multilingual Review, Outrigger Publishers, Box 1198, Hamilton New Zealand. Editor-in-Chief: Norman Simms. "Concerned with interaction of multi-cultural and multilingual societies, particularly in the Asia-Pacific rim countries, for intelligent, imaginative readers with cosmopolitan tastes."

‡**DADA DANCE MAGAZINE**, 3FR/47 Forrest Road, Edinburgh EH1 2QP Scotland. Fiction Editor: Dee Rimbaud. "We are Scotland's alternative literature magazine: we are looking for work that is unusual, bizarre, underground, psychedelic, poetic, erratic, erotic (not porn). Anything that is born from genius. There is no payment—unless you consider prestige. Send an IRC—or, before you do that, buy a copy, available for £5."

‡**DARK HORIZONS (II)**, British Fantasy Society, 56 Mickle Hill, Little Sandhurst, Camberley, Surrey GU17 8QU England. Editor: Jon Harvey. 1 or 2 stories/issue. Magazine of dark fantasy, heroic fantasy, film fantasy, fact and fiction for fantasy fans.

EDINBURGH REVIEW, 22 George Square, Edinburgh EH3 Scotland. Circ. 2,000. Publishes 16 stories/year. "An international journal of ideas and literature. Interested in all stories, especially the experimental and unorthodox." Pays for published fiction and provides contributor's copies. "We take 10 weeks to give a decision. We are especially interested in translations and interviews of some length."

‡**FIKCJE**, Silesian Science Fiction Club, 40-956 Katowice, skr pocz 502 Poland. Editor: Piotr Kasprowski. Averages around 350 pages of fiction/year. "*Fikcje* is a monthly; one issue every year is of triple volume. It contains, usually, some reviews, reports from recent conventions and the bibliography of sf published in Poland. As fiction, we use short stories mainly, also a novel in the triple issue." Writers are not paid, but receive two copies of the issue in which their work appears. Fiction "should be good and written in some easily translatable language: English—yes, Japanese—no. Short stories should not exceed 15 pages."

FORESIGHT (IV), 44 Brockhurst Rd., Hodge Hill, Birmingham B36 8JB England. Editor: John Barklam. Fiction Editor: Judy Barklam. Magazine including "new age material, world peace, psychic phenomena, research, occultism, spiritualism, mysticism, UFOs, philosophy, etc. Shorter articles required on a specific theme related to the subject matter of *Foresight* magazine." Sample copy for 30p and 25p postage.

‡**FORUM FABULATORUM**, Cort Adelersgade 5, 2.tv., DK-1053 Copenhagen K Denmark. Fiction Editor: Morten Sorensen. Circ. 250. Publishes 60,000-80,000 words of fiction annually. "*Forum Fabulatorum* is a fiction magazine devoted to 'fantastic literature,' by which is meant fantasy, horror and science fiction, although other kinds of non-naturalist prose and poetry are welcomed. Prints both 'name' authors and beginners, and both conventional and avant-garde material. Typically, *Forum Fabu-*

latorum pays around Danish kroner 150 for a story with first Danish rights; all contributors receive at least two free copies of the issue where they appear. Concentrate on psychological, philosophical and perhaps supernatural content; avoid hard science fiction, pulp and formula fiction. Stylistic innovation encouraged." English language submissions welcomed.

FRANK (II), An International Journal of Contemporary Writing and Art, 31 rue Colonel Delorme, 93100 Montreuil France. Editor: David Applefield. "Eclectic, serious fiction—all styles, voices—and translations, novel extracts" for literary international audience. "Send your best work, consult a copy of the journal before submitting." Recently published work by Hubert Selby, Raymond Carver, Stephen Dixon and A.I. Bezzerides." Sample copy $7.

GOING DOWN SWINGING, Box 64, Corburg Victoria 3058 Australia. Fiction Editor: Kevin Brophy. Circ. 500. Publishes approx. 80 pages of fiction/year. "We publish short stories, prose poetry, poetry and prose reviews. We try to encourage young or new writers as well as established writers. Interested in experimental writing. Writers not paid as we can't afford it. Writers receive a copy of the issue they are published in. Send ms and SASE with a short biographical note."

GRANTA, 44a Hobson St., Cambridge CB1 1NL England. Editor: Bill Buford. US office: 250 W. 57th St., New York NY 10107. U.S. Editor: Anne Kinard. "Paperback magazine (256 pages) publishing fiction and cultural and political journalism: fiction (including novellas and works-in-progress), essays, political analysis, journalism, etc."

GYPSY (II), Die Sympathische Alternative, Vergin Press, Petersbergstrasse #5, Bechtolsheim 6509 West Germany. Editor: Belinda Subraman. Fiction Editor: S. Ramnath. Seeks "the best writing and art from all genres for an intelligent and creative audience." Circ. 1,000. "Any category will be considered. Quality is the main criteria." Pays in copies. Sample copy $4. "No clichés, no abstractions, no judgments, sparse adjectives. Surprise the reader and give him/her an experience. Write about real people and real things."

HARRY'S HAND, %Jackson's Arm Press, 115 Westcott St., Holderness Road, Hull HU8 8LZ England. Fiction Editor: Michael Blackburn. Circ. 200. Publishes 4-5 stories/year. "*HH* is a review of new poetry, fiction, articles and reviews; looks for the more innovative and out-of-the-way material." Writers paid in copies only. "All submissions to be accompanied by IRCs. No ms more than 3,000 words can be considered unless it's a real knockout."

‡HECATE, Box 99, St. Lucia Q4037 Australia. Fiction Editor: Carole Ferrier. Circ. 2,000. Publishes 5-6 stories annually. "Socialist feminist; we like political stories (broadly defined)." Writers receive $6/page and 5 copies. "We only rarely publish non-Australian writers of fiction."

‡HRAFNHOH, 32 Strŷd Ebeneser, Pontypridd Mid Glamorgan CF37 5PB Wales. Fiction Editor: Joseph Biddulph. Circ. 100-200. "Only poetry published to date, mostly connected with Biddulph surname studies, with a little explicitly Christian literature. I could use the following, however: 1. short story with strong historical base in pottery industry, Trenton, New Jersey, particularly about immigrants from North Staffordshire, England; 2. fictionalized incident in Primitive Methodist history. No payment but as many free copies as needed. Free copy of any of my other (mostly linguistic) publications if wanted. Be brief, use a lot of local colour and nature description: write in a controlled, resonant prose, perhaps a rather old-fashioned, Victorian style if possible, avoiding modern North American idiom. Please provide sources in footnotes."

‡IDO-VIVO, 10 Heol Salop, Penarth, De Morgannwg CF6 HG Wales. Fiction Editor: Nic Ap Glyn. Circ. 200. Publishes 10 short stories (approximately) annually. Publication "entirely written in the international language Ido." Writers not paid for published fiction; receive copies of the issue in which work appears if requested. Writers "would have to learn the language first. Would consider translating short stories from a national language into Ido."

‡IKARIE XB, Jaroslav Olša, Jr., Anhaltova 41/987, 169 00, Prague 6 Czechoslovakia. Editors: Ivan Adamovič and Jaroslav Olša, Jr. Circ. 500. Averages 30 short stories/year. "We are interested in good quality SF—no fantasy please. *IKARIE XB* is a semi-professional magazine published 3-4 times yearly, each issue publishing more than 75,000 words." Authors receive copies of their publications.

‡INKSHED, 387 Beverly Road, Hull HU5 1LS England. Fiction Editor: Sue Wilsea. Circ. 200. Publishes approx. 10 stories/year. "Small press poetry/fiction magazine. Any type of fiction used up to 2,000 words." Writers receive a complimentary copy. "Just keep it neat, typed, well-spaced with name and address on front sheet."

IRON MAGAZINE (II), Iron Press, 5 Marden Ter., Cullercoats, North Shields, Tyne & Wear NE30 4PD England. Editor: Peter Mortimer. Circ. 800. Publishes 14 stories/year. "Literary magazine of contemporary fiction, poetry, articles and graphics." Pays approx. £10/page. No simultaneous submissions. Five poems, two stories per submission maximum. Sample copy for $4 (no bills-no checks). "Please see magazine before submitting and don't submit to it before you're ready!"

LA KANCERKLINIKO (IV), 51 rue Mondenard, F-33000 Bordeaux France. Fiction Editor: Laurent Septier. Circ. 300 ± . Publishes ± 40 pages of fiction annually. "An esperanto magazine which appears 4 times annually. Each issue contains 32 pages. *La Kancerkliniko* is a political and cultural magazine. General fiction, science fiction, etc. Short stories or very short novels." "The short story (or the very short novel) must be written only in esperanto, either original or translation from any other language."

‡LINQ (II), Literature in North Queensland, English Language and Literature Association, English Dept., James Cook University of North Queensland, Townsville 4811 Australia. Editor: Elizabeth Perkins. Magazine of articles, stories, poems, reveries on literature, history, for academic and general audience.

‡LUNA (I,II), Luna Collective, Box 36, East Melbourne, Victoria, Australia 3002. Contact: Editorial collective. "We publish poetry and short stories of a consistently high quality." Circ. 500. Publishes as funds permit. Pays 2 copies.

MARGIN, a quarterly magazine for imaginative writing and ideas, 20 Brook Green, London W6 7BL England. Fiction Editor: Robin Magowan. Circ. 2,000. Publishes 8-12 short stories or extracts from novels/year. "Arts quarterly including politics, fine arts, literature, architecture, etc. Fiction should be adventurous in its approach both to writing and content." Writers receive 4 free copies plus $25/page. "Read two or three issues of *margin* before submitting. We are also interested in good obsessive prose."

‡MATRIX, Box 1198, Hamilton New Zealand. Fiction Editor: Norman Simms. Publishes 6-8 short stories annually. "Short, concise stories, well-written with a point." Writer receives 1 free copy. "First subscribe at $15 per year."

MEANJIN, University of Melbourne, Parkville, Victoria 3052 Australia. Fiction Editors: Jenny Lee and Gerald Murnane. Circ. 3,000. "*Meanjin*'s emphasis is on publishing a wide range of writing by new and established writers. Our primary orientation is toward Australian writers, but material from overseas sources is also published." Writer receives approx. $50 per 1,000 words and 2 copies. "Please submit typed manuscript and enclose return addressed envelope with IRCs."

‡MOMENTUM, %Christine Stace, 31 Alexandra Rd., Wrexham, Clwyd LL13 7SL Wales. Fiction Editor: Jeff Bell. Circ. 300. Publishes an average of 18 stories annually. "*Momentum*: A 'middle-of-the-road' general interest mag with some verse, specializing in new writers—within those parameters anything goes, but no way-out extremes of fantasy or cult stuff, etc. Fiction only. Published 3 times a year (50 page edition)." Writers receive 1 contributor's copy. "Type fairly legibly, 2500 words maximum and a rough word count is welcome, one side of a sheet please. Address (and name) on copy. Politics *not* barred."

‡NEW HOPE INTERNATIONAL, 20 Werneth Avenue, Gee Cross, Hyde, Cheshire SK14 5NL England. Editor: Gerald England. Circ. 500. Publishes 1-4 stories annually. Publishes "mainly poetry. Fiction used must be essentially literary but not pretentious. Only short fiction used (max 2,000 words). Would use more fiction but the standard submitted (in comparison to the poetry) has been rather poor." Payment: 1 complimentary copy. Guidelines available for IRC. Sample copy: $3.

‡NIEUWE KOEKRAND, Box 14767, 1001 LG Amsterdam Holland. Fiction Editor: Johan Van Leeuwen. Circ. 2,000. Publishes 2-3 pages of fiction/issue. "*Nieuwe Koekrand* is basically considered a hardcore/punk magazine but often goes beyond that. It also includes articles on writers/fiction/moviews/politics/art/comics/horror. Fiction we use is horror and political satire. Writers don't get paid. I put in 50% of the money to get the magazine published. Others put in their efforts and energy. Don't expect too much response on getting stuff published. In case you send in something, make sure it's not over 5,000 words (approximately)."

‡NINTH DECADE, 12 Stevenage Rd., London SW6 6ES England. Fiction Editor: Ian Robinson. Circ. 600. Averages 3 fiction titles/year. "*Ninth Decade* is an avant-garde literary magazine publishing poetry, fiction, reviews, essays. Most material is solicited. Fiction should be innovative, avant-garde. No surrealism." Pays in copies.

‡**NNIDNID: SURREALITY**, 3 Vale View, Ponsanooth, Truro, Cornwall England. Fiction Editor: Tony Shiels. Circ. 500-650. Publishes 5 or 6 short stories annually. "*Nnidnid: Surreality* is an irregular publication (sometimes issued in the form of an audio cassette) devoted to the current manifestations of the International Surrealist Movement. Any prose fiction submitted should be strictly surreal in content, style and intention. We have published work by Gascoyne, Roditi, Soupault, etc. Writers are unpaid, but will receive two free copies of the issue in which their work appears. Potential contributors should understand the meaning of 'surreality,' should *be* surrealists (we instantly detect fakes!). We prefer stories of rather less than 2,500 words. Unsolicited manuscripts must be accompanied by a self-addressed envelope and an IRC."

NORTHERN PERSPECTIVE, Box 40146, Casuarina 5792 Australia. Fiction Editor: Dr. Barry Bannister. Circ. 1,000. Publishes about 200 pages of fiction annually. "Publishes short stories, poems, book reviews. *Northern Perspective* is a liberal arts/literary magazine." Writers are paid and receive contributor's copies. "Strive for 'form' and style in short story; image in poetry."

‡**ORE**, 7 The Towers, Stevenage, Herts SG1 1HE England. Fiction Editor: Eric Ratcliffe. Published 2-3 times/year. Prints mainly poetry and a little fiction relative to myth and legend. Contributors receive 1 free copy of the issue in which their work appears and may order extra copies at half price. Sample copy £1.40 (£1.60 including postage).

‡**OUTRIDER, Journal of Multicultural Literary**, Box 210 Indooroopilly, Queensland 4068 Australia. Fiction Editor: Manfred Jurgensen. Circ. 1,000. Publishes approx. 20 short stories plus other prose features annually. "*Outrider* aims to extend the concept of Australian literature. It publishes literary prose, poetry and articles dealing wth literature in Australia. Translated works are welcome." Pays $10/1,000 words. "We expect a professional presentation of manuscripts (enclose self-addressed stamped envelope!). There are no restrictions on what we publish, provided it is good writing."

PANURGE (I), 22 Belle Grove West, Newcastle-on Tyne NE2 4LT England. Fiction Editor: David Almond. Circ. 1,000. Published twice/year. perfectbound, 120 pages. "Dedicated to short fiction by new and up-and-coming names. Each issue features several previously unpublished names. We seek work that shows vitality of language, command of form, an individual approach. We pay 1 month after publication and send 1 contributor's copy. Overseas subscription £7. Sample copy £3.50."

‡**PEACE AND FREEDOM**, 17 Farrow Rd., Whaplode Drove, Spalding, Lincs. PE12 OTS England. Fiction Editor: Paul Rance. Circ. 500 + . Publishes around a dozen short stories annually. "A mixture of poetry, art, short stories, music and general features. *P and F* has a general humanism slant, as the title suggests, but good literature is judged purely as literature. Anything which is inventive, compelling, compassionate and literate will stand a chance of acceptance. Any racist, sexist, American-Russian tirades will be instantly returned." Pays in copies. "A sample copy of *P and F* costs $2 (75p SAE UK) and is advisable." Subscription—$7 (£3 UK) for 4 issues. "If we have a lot of work to read, of equal merit, then the work sent in by subscribers will be chosen first. No stories over 1,000 words, please."

PRINTED MATTER (II), Tokyo English Literature Society (TELS), %The Second Story, Nakajima Bldg., 1-26-7 Umegaoka, Setagaya-Ku, Tokyo 154 Japan. Editor-in-Chief: Richard Evanoff. Circ. 300-500. Bimonthly magazine. "Pay attention to presentation of manuscript: punctuation, spelling, age of typewriter ribbon, etc. Cut anything in your story that you're not absolutely sure about."

‡**RASHI**, Box 1198, Hamilton New Zealand. Editor: Norman Simms. Circ. 100. Averages 3 or 4 short stories/year. "Jewish Studies and Culture. All kinds of short fiction—usually 200-1,500 words." Pays in copies. "Remember limitations of space, and special thematic concerns."

SCARP (II), %School of Creative Arts, University of Wollongong, Box 1144, Wollongong 2500 Australia. Editor: Ron Pretty. Circ. 1,000. Publishes 15,000-20,000 words of fiction annually. Published twice a year. "We look for fiction in a contemporary idiom, even if it uses a traditional form. Preferred length: 1,000-3,000 words. We're looking for energy, impact, quality." Payment: $20 (Australian) per 1,000 words; contributor's copies supplied. "Submit to reach us in April and/or August. Include SASE. In Australia the beginning writer faces stiff competition—the number of paying outlets is not increasing, but the number of capable writers is."

‡**SEPIA (I), Poetry & Prose Magazine**, Kawabata Press, Knill Cross House, Higher Anderton Rd., Millbrook, Nr Torpoint, Cornwall England. Editor-in-Chief: Collin David Webb. "Magazine for those interested in modern un-clichéd work."

SLOW DANCER (II), Flat 4, 1 Park Valley, The Park, Nottingham NG7 1BS England. Fiction Editors: John Harvey and Jennifer Bailey. Circ. 500. Annually. Reading period November 1-April 30. Averages 2-3 short stories per issue. Pays 5 contributor's copies. Back numbers from Alan Brooks, Box 149a, RFD 1, Lubec, ME 04652 for $2. Submissions must be sent to UK.

‡SMOKE (II), Windows Project, 22 Roseheath Dr., Halewood, Liverpool L26 9UH England. Contact: Dave Ward. Magazine of poetry, fiction, art, long poems, collages, concrete art, photos, cartoons. "N.B. Fiction up to 2,000 words."

SOCIAL ALTERNATIVES, %Dept. of Government, University of Queensland, St. Lucia, Queensland 4067 Australia. Fiction Editor: Reba Gostand. Circ. 3,000. Publishes 2-3 stories in each quarterly issue. "The journal is socio-political, but stories of any theme or style will be considered. The criterion is excellence." Pays writers "if we have money—we usually don't." Writers receive one contributor's copy. Send "3 copies of story, immaculately presented so no sub-editing is necessary. SASE for return."

STAND MAGAZINE, 179 Wingrove Rd., Newcastle Upon Tyne, NE4 9DA England. Contact: Jon Silkin. Circ. 4,500. Averages 16-20 stories/year. "*Stand* is an international quarterly publishing poetry, short stories, reviews, criticism and translations." Payment: £30 per 1,000 words of prose on publication; contributor's copies. "Read copies of the magazine before submitting. Enclose sufficient IRCs for return of mss/reply. No more than 6 poems or 2 short stories at any one time." Sponsors biennial short story competition: First prize: $1,500. Send 2 IRCs for information.

‡STARKINDLER, GPO Box 652E, Melbourne 3001 Australia. Editor: Michael Green. Circ. 200+. Publishes about 65,000 words (4 issues of 40 pages/year)/year. "*Starkindler* publishes fantasy, the fantastic, speculative and science fiction, artwork, poetry, critical work, and anything else that takes our fancy. Maximum length: 4,500 words." Contributors receive a complimentary copy of the issue in which their work appears. "Work should be typed double-spaced on white paper. (The more legible the better). Please enclose a SASE if you'd like your story back."

STRIDE, 37 Portland St., Newtown, Exeter, Devon EX1 2EG England. Contact: Rupert Loydell. Circ. 750+. Poetry, fiction, articles, art, interviews, criticism, reviews, music, long poems, collages, concrete art. Pays in copies. "Send us neat, typed ms with name, address on every sheet and return postage. We are interested in *new* writing. We publish paperbacks of prose and poetry too and are considering novel mss." Sample copy £2 plus 50¢ postage.

STUDIO: A JOURNAL OF CHRISTIANS WRITING (II), 2/724 East St., Albury 2640 Australia. Fiction Editor: Paul Grover. Circ. 300. Averages 20-30 stories/year. "*Studio* is a magazine striving for excellence, because God himself is true excellence. Our magazine contains short stories, poems and occasional articles relating Christian views of literary ideas." Pays in copies. Sample copy $8. Subscription $33 for four issues (one year).

TEARS IN THE FENCE (II), 38 Hod View, Stourpaine, Nr. Blandford Forum, Dorset DT11 8TN England. Editor: David Caddy. A magazine of poetry, fiction and graphics, "blended with a conservation section to develop the concepts of ecology and conservation beyond their present narrow usage." Pays £7.50 per story plus complimentary copy of the magazine. Sample copy $4.

VERANDAH, Victoria College, %TAS 336, Glentferrie Rd., Hawthorn, Victoria 3144 Australia. Circ. 1,000. Publishes 6-8 stories annually. "*Verandah* is an annual publication published by TAS (Toorak Association of Students and Victoria College). *Verandah* is edited by students of Victoria College who are majoring in writing and literature. We publish contemporary fiction (no science fiction), poetry and nonfiction and graphics. No pay for published fiction. Writers and artists receive 2 copies of each issue. Mss should be "typed, presented on A4-sized paper, double-spaced and, if author wants ms returned, a stamped, self-addressed envelope with sufficient postage must be included. We accept submissions from late February to mid-July, and *Verandah* is published in October."

VIGIL (II), (formerly *Period Piece & Paperback*), Vigil Publications, Suite 5, Somdor House Station Rd., Gillingham, Dorset SP8 4QA England. Editor: John Howard. Magazine: 8½x5¼; 44 pages; illustrations. "Simply the enjoyment of varied forms of poetry and literature with an informed view of poetic technique." Plans special fiction issue. Estab. 1979. Circ. 250. Needs: experimental, literary, regional, c. 1,500 words. Pays in contributor's copies. Contributor guidelines available for IRC. "Most of the stories we receive are banal or lacking in honesty. Well structured, vibrantly expressed work is a delight when it arrives. Freshness and originality must always find an audience."

WESTERLY, c/o University of Western Australia, Nedlands, Western Australia 6009 Australia. A quarterly of poetry, prose and articles of a literary and cultural kind, giving special attention to Australia and Southeast Asia.

‡WORKS, 12 Blakestones Rd., Slaithwaite, Huddersfield HD7 5UQ England. Fiction Editors: D. Hughes and A. Stewart. Circ. 200 + . 60% + of content is fiction. "52 pages speculative and imaginative fiction (SF) with poetry, illustrated. Published quarterly. Price: £1.25 or £4.50 subscription. Sterling only. Enclose IRC." Pays in copies. "All manuscripts should be accompanied by a SASE. Usual maximum is 4,500 words."

‡THE WORLD OF ENGLISH, Box 1504, Beijing China. Fiction Editor: Chen Yu-lun. Circ. 300,000 + . "We welcome contributions of short articles that would cater to the interest of our reading public, new and knowledgeable writings on technological finds, especially interesting stories and novels, etc. We can only pay in our currency which regrettably is inconvertible." Write for sample copy.

‡THE WRITERS' ROSTRUM (I), 14 Ardbeg Rd., Rothesay, Bute PA20 0NJ Scotland. Fiction Editor: Jenny Chaplin. Circ. 1,000. Publishes approx. 15 short stories annually. "My magazine *The Writers' Rostrum* has been described as 'cosy' and being like 'tea and cream buns on a Sunday afternoon.' From this, you will gather that I refuse to publish anything that is in any way controversial, political or obscene. Short stories are on such topics as family life, friendship, telepathy and other aspects of the supernatural. Also seasonal topics: beauties of nature, etc. Writers in Britain receive cheque (£1-£3) on publication, together with a copy of the particular issue in which their work appears. Writers abroad receive complimentary copy and a year's free subscription to *TWR*. Keep to the required wordage, 900 words maximum. If at all possible, study the magazine. Always send SASE and/or IRC. Where possible, I will suggest other UK markets, since my main aim is to help handicapped/beginners/retired people get started on the craft of writing and see their work."

WRITING WOMEN, 10 Mistletoe Road, Newcastle Upon Tyne NE2 2DX England. Circ. 700-800. Publishes 12 stories per year. "We publish work by new and established women writers. Stories should be not more than 3,000 words. We pay £10 per 1,000 words." Contributors receive 2 copies of the issue in which they appear. "We can take 2-3 months to reach a decision."

ZELOT (II), Solliveien 37, 1370 Asker Norway. Editor: Ragnar F. Lie. Fantasy, humor/satire and science fiction. Free sample copy.

Little/literary magazines/'88-'89 changes

The following literary magazines appeared in the 1988 edition of *Fiction Writer's Market* but are not in the 1989 edition of *Novel and Short Story Writer's Market*. Those publications whose editors did not respond to our request for an update of their listings may not have done so for a variety of reasons—they may be out of business, for example, or they may be overstocked with submissions. Note that literary magazines from outside the U.S. and Canada appear at the end of this list.

Agada (did not respond)
The Agincourt Irregular (out of business)
AKA:Writer (did not respond)
The Alchemist (did not respond)
Amateur Writers Journal (did not respond)
ambergris (suspending publication for 1 year)
The Americas Review (did not respond)
Apocalypso (did not respond)
Applause (see listing for Creative Spirit)
Atlantis (did not respond)
Aurora (did not respond)
Aztec Peak (out of business)

B-City (did not respond)
Ba Shiru (did not respond)
Balcones (moved; no forwarding address)
Before the Sun (asked to be deleted)
Bibliophilos (did not respond)
Bitch (did not respond)
Bizarre Confessions (asked to be deleted)
Black Ice (asked to be deleted)
Black Mountain Review (out of business)
The Black Scholar (did not respond)
Blatant Artifice (did not respond)

The Blotter (out of business—may resume publication)
Blueline (did not respond)
Bogus Review (did not respond)
Both Sides Now (did not respond)
Bottomfish (did not respond)
Box 749 (did not respond)
Breakthrough (out of business)
Caribbean Review (asked to be deleted)
Cerberus (asked to be deleted)
Channels (did not respond)
Children's Album (did not respond)
Chimera Connections (out of business)

Clock Radio (did not respond)
Communities: Journal of Cooperation (did not respond)
Confrontation/Change Review (did not respond)
Corona (did not respond)
Cottonwood (did not respond)
The Creative Urge (asked to be deleted)
Creative Years (out of business)
The Crescent Review (did not respond)
Critique (did not respond)
Croton Review ("on hiatus")
Crowdancing Quarterly (did not respond)
Cryptogram Detective (did not respond)
Cumberland (did not respond)
Cutting Edge Quarterly (did not respond)
Dimension (did not respond)
Ellensburg Anthology (did not respond)
Empty Calories (moved; no forwarding address)
Event (did not respond)
Ex G Radio Club Bulletin (did not respond)
Explorations '88 (did not respond)
Expresso Tilt (did not respond)
(F.)lip (did not respond)
Facet (out of business)
Fag Rag (did not respond)
Fantasies and Realities (asked to be deleted)
The Fiddlehead (did not respond)
Fireweed (did not respond)
Footsteps (asked to be deleted)
Great River Review (did not respond)
HA Magazine (moved; no forwarding address)
Handicap News (did not respond)
Happiness Holding Tank (did not respond)
The Idaho (did not respond)
Image Magazine (did not respond)
Inky Trails Publications (out of business)
Kennebec: A Portfolio of Maine Writing (did not respond)
Late Knocking (did not respond)
Latin American Literary Review (did not respond)
The Limberlost Review (did not respond)
Lionsong (asked to be deleted)
Maelstrom Review (out of business)
Mati (did not respond)
Metrosphere (did not respond)

Midwest Arts & Literature (did not respond)
Mirage (did not respond)
The Mystic Muse (did not respond)
New America (did not respond)
New England Sampler (did not respond)
New Pathways (did not respond)
The New Southern Literary Messenger (asked to be deleted)
Nexus (responded too late to be included)
No Idea Magazine (did not respond)
North American Mentor Magazine (out of business)
North Country Anvil (did not respond)
Off Main Street (responded too late to be included)
Ohio Renaissance Review (did not respond)
Oikos (did not respond)
One Shot (no more fiction)
Orim (asked to be deleted)
Oyez Review (did not respond)
Phoenix Rising (did not respond)
Pinchpenny (did not respond)
Poetry Motel (did not respond)
Potboiler (did not respond)
Ptolemy/The Browns Mills Review (did not respond)
Quixote (did not respond)
Rafale (did not respond)
Re: Artes Liberales (did not respond)
Review, Latin American Literature and Art (did not respond)
RFD (did not respond)
Rhino (no more fiction)
Ridge Review (did not respond)
Sagewoman Magazine (did not respond)
St. Andrews Review (did not respond)
Salome: A Journal of the Performing Arts (did not respond)
Scandinavian Review (did not respond)
Second Coming (did not respond)
Senior Scribes (out of business)
Sidewinder (asked to be deleted)
The Signal (did not respond)
The Silver Apple Branch (did not respond)
Sojourner (did not respond)
Southeastern Front (did not respond)
Spectrum (did not respond)
Spitball (did not respond)

SPWAO Showcase (did not respond)
Stardate (did not respond)
Striking Sci Fi (did not respond)
Studia Mystica (did not respond)
Sunrust (did not respond)
Sycophant (did not respond)
Ten Million Flies Can't be Wrong (did not respond)
Tightrope (did not respond)
Time to Pause (out of business)
Toyon (asked to be deleted)
Unveiling (did not respond)
Viaztlan (did not respond)
Vintage '45 (did not respond)
Voyageur (moved; no forwarding address)
Wascana Review (did not respond)
Which Dr? (out of business)
Whispering Wind Magazine (overstocked)
Woman of Power (did not respond)
Women's Quarterly Review (did not respond)
Working Classics (did not respond)
Stephen Wright's Mystery Notebook (did not respond)
The Yale Literary Magazine (asked to be deleted)

Foreign little/literary magazines

Antigruppo (did not respond)
Cencrastus (responded too late to be included)
Diliman Review (did not respond)
Global Tapestry Journal (responded too late to be included)
Hat Magazine/Alternative Times Magazine (did not respond)
Indian Literature (did not respond)
Jennings (out of business)
Kunapipi (did not respond)
Magazing (did not respond)
Marang (did not respond)
New Outlook (did not respond)
Okike (did not respond)
Prospice (did not respond)
Quadrant (did not respond)
SF Spectrum Publications (did not respond)
Trapani Nuova (did not respond)
Untold (did not respond)
Words International (did not respond)

Commercial Periodicals

The one constant in the magazine fiction market is change. Unlike those magazines listed in the Little/Literary section, the primary focus of most commercial magazines is not on fiction. In fact, fiction is usually the first thing sacrificed to allow space for advertising or nonfiction material. On the other hand, the addition of fiction is also one of the first improvements made when magazines upgrade their formats.

While the needs of specific magazines have changed, overall the need for good short fiction is as strong as ever. This year we've added almost 40 new markets, including a few which do focus on fiction, such as *American Accent Short Story Magazine*, *Magazine of Fantasy and Science Fiction* and *Modern Short Story*. We've included these "fiction only" magazines in the commercial section because they pay writers for their work as do all the publications listed in this section.

Most of the specialized markets listed last year have returned this year, such as *American Trucker*, *Bowbender* and *Student Lawyer*, and we've added several more, especially in the sport and fitness field. These magazines use only one or two stories each issue and look for stories aimed specifically at their audiences. We've also added many new religious magazine markets including several for teens and young adults. While we lost some city and town regional publications, we've added regional magazines covering larger geographic areas— some state-wide, such as *Oh! Idaho* and some for certain sections of the country, such as *Northwest*.

Some notable prestige markets have opted not to be included this year, including *Esquire*, *New Age Journal* and *YM*, because they've filled their fiction needs, no longer accept fiction or are in the process of changing their formats. (To find out more about those listings not continued from last year, see the new Additional Listings pages at the end of each section).

We have added, however, a number of well-known markets this year, including the leading humor magazine, *National Lampoon*. Markets known for their support of fine fiction, such as *Atlantic Monthly* and *The New Yorker*, also list in this section. (For more on prestigious markets for short stories see Gayle Feldman's article, "Is There a Short Story Boom?" included in this edition). While breaking into these markets is difficult, most are willing to look at the work of beginning writers, as long as the material is professionally presented.

Quality counts

We cannot emphasize enough the need for professionally presented manuscripts in the commercial magazine market. Editors still complain of shoddily typed submissions filled with typos, grammatical errors and crossed-out mistakes. No matter how talented the writer, if a submission is unreadable, it is usually returned or tossed out unread.

No matter how clean a manuscript may be, however, there is no substitute for quality writing. Most editors are glad to look at work by new writers, because the deciding factor is always the quality of the piece, not what the writer has done before. Again and again the editors listed here echo what the editors of *Highlights* say, "We accept a story on its merit whether written by an unpublished or experienced writer."

All editors, regardless of what type of fiction they handle, look for realistic dialogue, well-developed plots and solid characterization. Many say they also seek subjects that are original and appropriate for their audience. Editors looking for certain genres of fiction also ask that writers have a familiarity with their particular fields.

Religious magazines, for example, often ask that stories display an understanding of church doctrine, but plots must seem natural and writers should always avoid preaching. Moral values should be present, but should be well-integrated into the plot. These editors also advise writers not to be afraid of real-life or even controversial issues. "Don't write what you think will feel sweet or appealing to this audience," says Michael Lerner, editor of *Tikkun*, "but, rather, that which will provoke, bring to life and engage them."

Even editors of magazines for children and teenagers warn writers to avoid overdone plots and to be willing to tackle modern-day issues. "We look for stories with a teen perspective, with references to *current* trends, language, issues, etc.," says Karen Christianson, associate editor of *TQ*.

In science fiction and fantasy, writers must be especially careful not to repeat old plot ideas. Familiarity with the classics of the genre is expected, but editors complain that many writers copy what they've read or seen recently on television or at the movies. "Keep up with what's being printed in the science fiction/fantasy field, so that rehashes of other people's ideas are not being submitted," says Patrick Lucien Price, editor of *Amazing Stories*.

Although experimental fiction offers the opportunity to dispense with some of the standard rules of popular fiction, writers working in this field must also submit work of the highest quality. "Don't be afraid to stretch the medium," says *Splash* Editor, Jordan Crandall, "as long as you've already *learned the rules* of the medium."

Editors advise writers to do two things that will help improve the quality of their writing— read and write. Many say they feel writers have not read enough fine writing or the classics in their particular fields. Others say beginning writers, in particular, should write every day and never give up submitting their work because of a few rejections. Experienced writers should also write regularly and should occasionally try different types of writing to remain fresh and original.

Some trends

In addition to quality and professionalism, a number of editors this year note a trend toward shorter submissions. Many have revised their listings to include "short-shorts," fictional pieces less than 500 words. They also warn against submitting novella-length manuscripts— short stories are generally no more than 3,000 words. Science fiction and mystery markets are especially open to the shortening trend.

This year we've eliminated the terms "men's" and "women's" fiction, because the distinctions have become so blurred they not longer apply. Traditional men's fiction, action-adventure and some erotica, is no longer restricted to what is considered men's magazines. While the traditional women's magazine market continues to be an excellent outlet for fiction, for some time now it has not been restricted to romance and problem stories as in the past. In fact, many magazines catering to a mainly female audience now actively seek adventure, mystery and humor.

We've increased the number of teen and children's magazines and have also seen a growth in magazines aimed at other age groups, such as senior citizens and adults over age 30. Other growth areas include religious, regional and science fiction sections.

Many new magazines point to trends that may influence future fiction markets. For example, a number of magazines for women in their 40s have made recent debuts, such as *Lears* and *Quarante*. There are also a number of new upbeat, unisex fashion magazines on the market, such as *In Fashion* and *Details*. These magazines are not listed in the book this year, because they have *not* developed a need for fiction, but keep an eye on these markets as they grow. Watch newsstands and The Markets column in *Writers Digest* for the most recent market trends. Also note that bookstores are carrying more magazines now and many offer a highly varied selection.

To find markets in this section for particular categories of fiction, such as fantasy and western, please check the fiction subject index located just before the Markets Index at the back of the book.

Here's the ranking system we've used to categorize the listings in this section.

I   Periodical encourages beginning or unpublished writers to submit work for consideration and publishes new writers frequently;

II   Periodical publishes work by established writers and occasionally by new writers of exceptional talent;

III   Magazine does not encourage beginning writers; prints mostly writers with substantial previous publication credits and a very few new writers;

IV   Special-interest or regional magazine, open only to writers on certain topics or from certain geographical areas.

ABORIGINAL SF (II, IV), Box 2449, Woburn MA 01888-0849. Editor: Charles C. Ryan. Tabloid: 8½x11; 64 pages; 50 lb paper; 60-80 lb cover; 4-color illustrations; photos. *"Aboriginal SF* is looking for good science fiction stories. While 'hard' science fiction will get the most favorable attention, *Aboriginal SF* also wants good action-adventure stories, *good* space opera, humor and science fantasy, for adult science fiction readers." Bimonthly. Estab. 1986. Circ. 18,000-20,000.
Needs: Science fiction. Original, previously unpublished work only. "No fantasy, sword and sorcery, horror, or Twilight-Zone type stories." Receives 120-140 unsolicited mss/month. Buys 5-8 mss/issue; 30-50 mss/year. Publishes ms 4 months to 1 year after acceptance. Agented fiction 5%. Recently published work by Harlan Ellison, Frederik Pohl, Ben Bova; published new writers within the last year. Length: 2,500 words minimum; 4,500 words maximum. Publishes short shorts "no shorter than 1,500-2,000 words for fiction. Jokes may be 50-150 words." Sometimes comments on rejected mss.
How to Contact: Send complete ms with cover letter. Reports on mss in 4-10 weeks. SASE. Good quality photocopied submissions OK. Accepts computer printout submissions, including dot-matrix "if very legible." Sample copy for $3 plus 50¢ postage and handling. Fiction guidelines for #10 SAE and 1 first class stamp.
Payment: Pays "$250 flat" and 2 contributor's copies.
Terms: Pays on publication for first North American serial rights and non-exclusive reprint and foreign options. Publication copyrighted.
Advice: "Stories with the best chance of acceptance will make unique use of science ideas, have lively, convincing characters, an ingenious plot, a powerful and well integrated theme, and use an imaginative setting. We recommend you read *Aboriginal SF* to obtain an idea of the type of stories we publish, and we also recommend you read other SF publications. Watching science fiction on television or at the movies will not provide adequate experience or background to write a good science fiction story."

ACTION, Dept. of Christian Education, Free Methodist Headquarters, 901 College Ave., Winona Lake IN 46590. (219)267-7161. Editor: Vera Bethel. Sunday school take-home paper for children in grades 4-5-6. Magazine: 5¼x8¼; 8 pages; uncoated paper; full-color illustrations; b&w photos. Weekly. Estab. 1970. Circ. 35,000.
Needs: Juvenile. "We buy fiction involving kids aged 10-14 in school and play situations wherein some conflict must be solved in a manner suggesting positive attitudes and growth. Readers are pre-teens; have young teen interests. Need urban settings in fiction." Buys 1 ms/issue, 52 mss/year. Receives approximately 100 unsolicited fiction mss each month. Published new writers within the last year. Length: 1,000 words.
How to Contact: Send complete ms with SASE. Reports in 1 month on mss. Free sample copy, free fiction guidelines with 6x9 SASE.
Payment: $35; 2 free author's copies. 10¢ charge for extra.
Terms: Pays on publication for simultaneous, first, second serial (reprint) and one-time rights.
Advice: Rejects mss because of "predictable, yet unbelievable (unreal) characters."

AIM MAGAZINE (I, II), 7308 S. Eberhart Ave., Chicago IL 60619. (312)874-6184. Editor: Ruth Apilado. Fiction Editor: Mark Boone. Newspaper: 8½x11; 48 pages; slick paper; photos and illustrations. "Material of social significance: down-to-earth gut. Personal experience, inspirational." For "high school, college and general public." Quarterly. Published special fiction issue last year; plans another. Estab. 1973. Circ. 10,000.
Needs: Open. No "religious" mss. Receives 25 unsolicited mss/month. Buys 15 mss/issue; 60 mss/

year. Recently published work by Jules Archer, Abigail Ann Martin, Dawn Zapletal; published new writers within the last year. Length: 800-1,000 words average. Publishes short shorts. Sometimes comments on rejected mss.

How to Contact: Send complete ms. SASE with a cover letter and author's photograph. Simultaneous submissions OK. Accepts computer printout submissions. Sample copy for $3 with SAE (8x11½) and 65¢ postage. Fiction guidelines for #10 envelope and 1 first class stamp.

Payment: Pays $15-$25.

Terms: Pays on publication for first rights.

Advice: "Search for those in your community who are making unselfish contributions to their community and write about them. Write from the heart. Think! Rewrite! Keep a dictionary close by."

alive now! (I, II), The Upper Room, Box 189, Nashville TN 37202-0189. (615)340-7218. Editor: Mary R. Coffman. Magazine of devotional writing and visuals for young adults. Bimonthly. Estab. 1971. Circ. 75,000.

Needs: Religious/inspirational. Buys 4 mss/issue; 12 mss/year. Length: 10 words minimum; 300 words maximum.

How to Contact: Send complete mss with SASE. Photocopied and previously published submissions OK. Accepts computer printout submissions. Prefers letter-quality. Reports in 1 month on mss. Sample copy free. Fiction guidelines free. Enclose SASE.

Payment: Pays $5-$25; 12 contributor's copies.

Terms: Pays on publication for first rights, one-time rights, newspaper and periodical rights. Occasionally buys reprints. Publication copyrighted.

ALOHA, The Magazine of Hawaii and the Pacific (IV), Davick Publishing Co., 828 Fort St. Mall, Suite 640, Honolulu HI 96813. (808)523-9871. Editor: Cheryl Tsutsumi. Magazine about the 50th state. Upscale demographics. Bimonthly. Estab. 1979. Circ. 75,000.

Needs: "Only fiction that illuminates the Hawaiian experience. No stories about tourists in Waikiki or beachboys or contrived pidgin dialogue." Receives 3-4 unsolicited mss/month. Length: 2,500 words average.

How to Contact: Send complete ms. Reports in 2 months. Publishes ms up to 1 year after acceptance. SASE. Photocopied submissions OK. Accepts computer printout submissions. Letter-quality only. Sample copy $2.95.

Payment: 10¢/word minimum.

Terms: Pays on publication for all rights. Publication copyrighted.

Advice: "Submit only fiction that is truly local in character. Do not try to write anything about Hawaii if you have not experienced this culturally different part of America."

AMAZING STORIES (II), TSR, Inc., Box 110, Lake Geneva WI 53147. (414)248-3625. Editor: Patrick L. Price. Magazine: digest-sized 5³/₁₆x7⅝; 164 pages; 5 pt Dombook paper; 9 pt federal cover stock; illustrations; rarely photos. Magazine of science fiction and fantasy fiction stories for adults and young adults. Bimonthly. Published special fiction issue last year; plans another. Estab. 1926. Circ. 13,000.

Needs: Fantasy, horror, science fiction. "We publish about 75% science fiction to 25% fantasy with only 2 or 3 horror pieces per year." No "cyberpunk or futilistic SF; no high or heroic fantasy; no hack-n-slach or teen exploitation horror." Receives 1,000 unsolicited fiction mss/month. Buys 10 mss/issue; 60 mss/year. Does not read mss between Thanksgiving and New Years. Approximately 5% of fiction is agented. Recently published work by Sheila Finch, Gregory Benford, Robert Silverberg; published new writers within the last year. Length: 500 words minimum; 20,000 words maximum. Publishes short shorts of 250 words. Occasionally critiques rejected mss.

How to Contact: Send complete ms with cover letter (list other professional credits in SF, fantasy or horror). SASE. Photocopied submissions OK. Accepts computer printout submissions. Prefers letter-quality. Reports in 2 months on mss. Publishes ms 9-24 months after acceptance. Sample copy $2.50. Fiction guidelines free with #10 SASE.

Payment: Pays 6¢-8¢/word.

Terms: Pays on acceptance for first rights. Sends prepublication galleys to author. Publication copyrighted.

Advice: "We are interested in all forms of science fiction (militaristic, hard, soft, speculative), but we do place a very strong emphasis on characterization, as we wish to see how the protagonists deal with a problem posed by the writer's scientific extrapolation. The same holds true for fantasy. For fantasy, we are extremely interested in contemporary fantasy and in ethnic fantasy or cultural fantasy of non-European traditions. Keep up with what's being printed in the sf/fantasy magazines, so that rehashes of other people's ideas are not being submitted."

‡AMERICAN ACCENT SHORT STORY MAGAZINE (I), Box 80270, Las Vegas NV 89180. (702)648-2669. Editor/Publisher: Marvin Gelbart. Fiction Editor: Carol Colina. Magazine: 5⅛x7¼; 176 pages; newsprint paper; 70 lb coated cover; some illustrations. "A forum for introducing new authors to the reading public—all genres." Monthly. Estab. 1988.
Needs: Adventure, contemporary, fantasy, historical, humor/satire, literary, mainstream, romance (contemporary), science fiction, suspense/mystery. Buys approx. 10 mss/issue. Length: 4,000 words preferred; 1,000 words minimum; 5,000 words maximum. Sometimes critiques reject mss.
How to Contact: Send complete ms with cover letter. Reports in 8-10 weeks. SASE. Simultaneous and photocopied submissions OK. Sample copy for $2.25; fiction guidelines free with a #10 SASE.
Payment: Pays $50 minimum; $250 maximum; contributor's copies.
Terms: Pays on publication for first North Amercian serial rights or other rights. Publication copyrighted.
Advice: "We feel that the first step to becoming a writer is to learn the craft. We suggest that the beginner learn proper manuscript form. In our guidelines we state, 'Your manuscript reveals your professionalism. When you submit a manuscript or query letter, you send a representation of yourself. It is your job interview. Make it work for you.' All stories accepted for publication are automatically entered in our contest."

AMERICAN DANE (II,IV), The Danish Brotherhood in America, 3717 Harney, Box 31748, Omaha NE 68131. (402)341-5049. Editor: Pamela K. Dorau. Magazine: 8¼x11; 20-28 pages; 40 lb paper; slick cover; illustrations and photos. "The *American Dane* is the official publication of the Danish Brotherhood. Corporate purpose of the Danish Brotherhood is to promote and perpetuate Danish culture and traditions and to provide Fraternal benefits and family protection." Estab. 1916. Circ. 8,900.
Needs: Ethnic. "Danish!" Receives 4 unsolicited fiction mss/month. Accepts 1 ms/issue; 12 mss/year. Reads mss during August and September only. Publishes ms up to one year after acceptance. Length: 1,000 words average; 3,000 words maximum. Publishes short shorts.
How to Contact: Query first. SASE. Simultaneous submissions OK. Accepts computer printout submissions, including dot-matrix. Sample copy for $1 and 9x12 SAE with 54¢ postage. Fiction guidelines free for 4x9½ SAE and 1 first class stamp.
Payment: Pays $15-$50.
Terms: Pays on publication for first rights. Publication not copyrighted.
Advice: "Think Danish!"

THE AMERICAN NEWSPAPER CARRIER (II), Box 15300, Winston-Salem NC 27113. (919)725-3400. Editor: Marilyn H. Rollins. Newsletter: 9x12; 4 pages; slick paper; b&w illustrations and photos. "A motivational newsletter publishing upbeat articles—mystery, humor, adventure and inspirational material for newspaper carriers (younger teenagers, male and female)." Monthly. Estab. 1927.
Needs: Adventure, comics, humor/satire, inspirational, suspense/mystery and young adult/teen. No erotica, fantasy, feminist, gay, juvenile, lesbian, preschool, psychic/supernatural or serialized/excerpted novel. Receives approximately 12 unsolicited mss/month. Buys 1 ms/issue; 12 mss/year. "About all" of fiction is agented. Published new writers within the last year. Length: approximately 1,000 words average; 800 words minimum; 1,200 words maximum. Publishes short shorts of 1,000 words. Rarely critiques rejected mss.
How to Contact: Send complete ms. Reports in 1 month. Publishes ms 3-6 months after acceptance. SASE. Accepts computer printout submissions. Free sample copy and fiction guidelines with #10 SAE and 1 first class stamp for each.
Payment: Pays $25.
Terms: Pays on acceptance for all rights.
Advice: "We prefer that stories concern or refer to newspaper carriers. Well-written upbeat stories—happy and humorous—are rare."

AMERICAN SQUAREDANCE (IV), Burdick Enterprises, Box 488, Huron OH 44839. (419)433-2188. Editors: Stan and Cathie Burdick. Magazine: 5x8½; 100 pages; 50 lb offset paper; glossy, 60 lb cover stock; illustrations; photos. Magazine about square dancing. Monthly. Estab. 1945. Circ. 24,000.
Needs: Adventure, fantasy, historical, humor/satire, romance, science fiction and western. Must have square dance theme. Buys 2+ mss/year. Length: 2,500 words average. Publishes short stories of 1,000 words average.

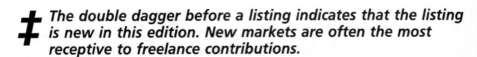

The double dagger before a listing indicates that the listing is new in this edition. New markets are often the most receptive to freelance contributions.

How to Contact: Send complete ms with SASE and cover letter with bio. Reports in 2 weeks on queries. Publishes ms within 6 months after acceptance. Free sample copy. Free fiction guidelines.
Payment: Pays $1/column inch minimum; free magazine subscription or free contributor's copies.
Terms: Pays on publication for all rights. Publication copyrighted.

AMERICAN TRUCKER (II), American Trucker Marketing, Box 9159, Brea CA 92622. (714)528-6600. Editor: Tom Berg. Magazine. 8¼x10¾; 64-96 pages; 60 lb cover stock; illustrations and photographs. "Directed toward owner-operator drivers. Focuses on 'glamour' trucks, trucking-related articles, industry news, technical information, trucking-related humor; for owner-operator truck drivers." Monthly.
Needs: Adventure, contemporary, humor/satire. Fiction must relate to truck drivers. Receives 10-50 unsolicited fiction mss/month. Accepts 0-1 mss/issue; 10 mss/year. Publishes ms 2-10 months after acceptance. Length: 2,500-5,000 words average; 2,000 words minimum; 6,000 words maximum. Publishes short shorts. Length: 500 words. Sometimes critiques rejected mss and recommends other markets.
How to Contact: Query first; query with clip or send complete work. Reports in 2 weeks on queries or mss. SASE. Photocopied submissions OK. Accepts computer printout submissions, including dot-matrix. Sample copy $2; fiction guidelines free.
Payment: $150-300 and contributor's copies.
Terms: Pays on publication for first North American serial rights. Sends pre-publication galleys to author if requested. Publication copyrighted.

AMÉRICAS (IV), Organization of American States, Washington DC 20006. Editor: Edgardo Costa Reis. Managing Editor: Catherine Healy. Magazine: 64 pages; 50 lb glossy paper; heavy glossy cover stock; b&w illustrations; photos. Magazine of cultural articles on Latin America and the Caribbean for a general audience. Bimonthly. Estab. 1949. Circ. 75,000.
Needs: Latin American and Caribbean themes. "We publish one short story per issue, for a total of six per year. These are winners of our short story contest, announced in January/February issue. New guidelines to appear in January/February issue for contest." Published new writers within the last year. Publishes short shorts, 1,000-1,700 words.
How to Contact: Enter short story contest.
Payment: $100-$500; 4 contributor's copies; no charge for extras up to 20 copies; $2.50/copy if more than 20 requested.
Terms: Acquires one-time rights.
Advice: "As an official publication of the OAS, we cover hemisphere culture."

ANALOG SCIENCE FICTION/SCIENCE FACT (II), Davis Publications, Inc., 380 Lexington Ave., New York NY 10017. (212)557-9100. Editor: Stanley Schmidt. Magazine: 7⅜x5³⁄₁₆; 192 pages; illustrations (drawings); photos. "Well-written science fiction based on speculative ideas and fact articles on topics on the present and future frontiers of research. Our readership includes intelligent laymen and/or those professionally active in science and technology." Thirteen times yearly. Published special fiction issue. Estab. 1930. Circ. 100,000.
Needs: Science fiction and serialized novels. "No stories which are not truly science fiction in the sense of having a plausible speculative idea *integral to the story*." Buys 4-8 mss/issue. Receives 300-500 unsolicited fiction mss/month. Publishes short shorts. Approximately 30% of fiction is agented. Recently published work by Poul Anderson, Roger MacBride Allen, Michael F. Flynn; published new writers within the last year. Length: 2,000-80,000 words. Critiques rejected mss "when there is time." Sometimes recommends other markets.
How to Contact: Send complete ms with SASE. Cover letter with "anything that I need to know before reading the story, e.g. that it's a rewrite I suggested or that it incorporates copyrighted material. Otherwise, no cover letter is needed." Query with SASE only on serials. Accepts computer printout submissions. Prefers letter-quality. Reports in 1 month on both query and ms. Free guidelines with SASE. Sample copy for $2.50.
Payment: 5¢-8¢/word.
Terms: Pays on acceptance for first North American serial rights and nonexclusive foreign rights. Sends galleys to author. Publication copyrighted.
Advice: Mss are rejected because of "inaccurate science; poor plotting, characterization or writing in

Market categories: (I) Beginning; (II) General; (III) Prestige; (IV) Specialized.

general. We literally only have room for 1-2% of what we get. Many stories are rejected not because of anything conspicuously *wrong*, but because they lack anything sufficiently *special*. What we buy must stand out from the crowd. Fresh, thought-provoking ideas are important. Familiarize yourself with the magazine—but don't try to imitate what we've already published."

ANGUS JOURNAL (IV), Angus Productions, Inc., 3201 Frederick, St. Joseph MO (800)821-5478. Editor: Jim Cotton. Magazine: 8x11;140 pages; slick paper. Publishes material related to "Angus beef cattle and the beef industry." Monthly. Circ. 15,000
Needs: Western, young adult/teen (10-18 years), cattle. "*Must* be related to ranching/farming with Angus theme or background." Publishes ms 6 months after acceptance. Length: 2,000 words average; 5,000 words maximum. "Might" publish short shorts. Always comments on rejected mss.
How to Contact: Send complete ms with cover letter (include payment expected) or submit through agent. Reports in 2 weeks. SASE. Simultaneous, photocopied and reprint submissions OK. Accepts computer printouts, including dot-matrix. Sample copy for 10x12 SAE and $2 postage.
Payment: Pays $100-$300.
Terms: Pays on acceptance for one-time rights. Publication copyrighted.
Advice: "Writer must be able to transport readers away and enhance their belief in our way of life (Angus cattle). We expect knowledge of our area—no sentimental clap-trap. Grit but tasteful."

‡**ANIMAL PRESS (II,IV)**, Box 441, Lakeside CA 92040. (619)561-9025. Editor: Ginger Julian. Tabloid: 12 pages; newsprint paper. Publishes "strictly animal stories, for animal lovers." Monthly. Estab. 1987. Circ. 55,000.
Needs: Special interest: animals. "Stories must be upbeat and positive—no sob stories or poor-animal stories. Writing must have personality with emphasis on animal(s), not people. No stories written in the first person from an animal." Receives 1-2 unsolicited fiction mss/month. Publishes ms 1-2 months after acceptance. Recently published work by Shirley Wells, Blue Cinder. Length: 800 words preferred; 600 words minimum; 1,000 words maximum. Publishes short shorts. Length: 400-500 words.
How to Contact: Query with sample of writing, "whether published or not." Reports in 1-2 months. SASE. Photocopied submissions OK. Accepts dot-matrix computer printouts; accepts electronic submissions via IBM disk. Sample copy $2.
Payment: $25 and contributor's copies. "Most stories are donated, but if very good, will buy."
Terms: Payment is on publication. Buys first rights. Publication copyrighted.
Advice: Looks for fiction that is "well written and interesting."

‡**ARETE (I,II), Forum for Thought**, 405 W. Washington St., Suite 418, San Diego CA 92130. (619)237-0074. Fiction/Poetry Editor: Erica Lowe. Magazine. Published 8 times/year. Estab: 1988. Circ. 20,000.
Needs: Adventure, condensed/excerpted novel, contemporary, ethnic, experimental, feminist, gay, historical, horror, humor/satire, lesbian, literary, mainstream, prose poem, regional, religious/inspirational, science fiction, senior citizen/retirement, sports, suspense/mystery, translations. Receives 500 unsolicited fiction mss/month. Buys 2-3 fiction mss/issue; 24 fiction mss/year. Publishes ms 2-5 months after acceptance. Agented fiction 10%. Length: 3,500 words preferred; 1,000 words minimum; 6,000 words maximum.
How to Contact: Send complete ms with cover letter. Reports in 6-8 weeks on mss. SASE preferred. Accepts photocopied and simultaneous submissions, "as long as we know." Accepts dot-matrix computer printout submissions. Sample copy for $2.95. Fiction guidelines for SAE.
Payment: Pays $300 minimum; $2,500 maximum.
Terms: Pays on acceptance for first North American serial rights. Sends pre-publication galleys to author "if requested."

ART TIMES (II), A Cultural and Creative Journal, CSS Publications, Inc., 7484 Fite Rd., Saugerties NY 12477. (914)246-6944. Editor: Raymond J. Steiner. Magazine: 12x15; 20 pages; Jet paper and cover; illustrations; photos. "Arts magazine covering the disciplines, for over 40, affluent, arts-conscious, literate audience." Monthly. Estab. 1984. Circ. 15,000.
Needs: Adventure, contemporary, ethnic, fantasy, feminist, gay, historical, humor/satire, lesbian, literary, mainstream, science fiction. "We seek quality, literary pieces. No violence, sexist, erotic, juve-

Read the Manuscript Mechanics section to learn the correct way to prepare and submit a manuscript.

nile, racist, romantic, political, etc." Receives 25-30 mss/month. Buys 1 ms/issue; 11 mss/year. Publishes ms within 14-16 months of acceptance. Recently published work by Judith Jones, Winifred Elze, Lisa Schuchter; published new writers within the last year. Length: 1,500 words maximum. Publishes short shorts.

How to Contact: Send complete ms with cover letter. Reports in 6 months. SASE. Simultaneous and photocopied submissions OK. Accepts computer printout submissions, including dot-matrix; also electronic submissions via disk or modem. Sample copy for $1.50, 9x12 SAE and 3 first class stamps. Fiction guidelines for #10 SAE and 1 first class stamp.

Payment: Pays $15, free subscription to magazine (one year); six contributor's copies.

Terms: Pays on publication for first North American serial rights. Kill fee $10. Publication copyrighted.

‡**ARTHRITIS TODAY (II), Publication of the Arthritis Foundation**, Arthritis Foundation, 1314 Spring St. NW, Atlanta GA 30309. (404)872-7100. Editor: Cindy T. McDaniel. Magazine: 52+ pages; 45 lb coated paper; 70 lb coated cover; color illustrations and photos. Publishes material relating to "better living with arthritis; general health and the older years." Estab. 1987. Circ. 700,000.

Needs: Adventure, historical, humor/satire, senior citizen/retirement, health/arthritis. "Fiction should appeal to an older audience; direct reference to arthritis is not required, but might increase chances of acceptance." Receives 6-8 unsolicited mss/month. Buys 1 ms/issue; 4-5 mss/year. Publishes ms up to 1 year after acceptance. Recently published work by Charles Nicholson, Lorraine Jolian Cazin, Dianne Gloe. Length: 1,000-2,500 words preferred. Publishes short-shorts. Length: 250-500 words. Sometimes critiques rejected mss and recommends other markets.

How to Contact: Query with clips of published work or submit complete ms with cover letter. Reports in 6 weeks. SASE preferred. Simultaneous, photocopied and reprint submissions OK. Accepts dot-matrix computer printouts. Sample copy and fiction guidelines free.

Payment: Pays $250 minimum; $750 maximum; contributor's copies.

Terms: Pays on acceptance for one-time rights, plus unlimited reprint rights in any Arthritis Foundation publication. Offers 25% kill fee. Publication copyrighted.

Advice: Looks for "quality and readability; relevance to subject matter. Become familiar with the book—know the type article we print. Don't send articles that are clearly irrelevant or aimed at the wrong audience."

Terry Lee created this cover illustration for Issaac Asimov's Science Fiction Magazine which is published 13 times per year. Lee made a clay sculpture of the alien to serve as a model for the painting.

ISAAC ASIMOV'S SCIENCE FICTION MAGAZINE (II), Davis Publications, Inc., 380 Lexington Ave., New York NY 10017. Editor: Gardner Dozois. Magazine: 5³/₁₆x7³/₈, (trim size); 192 pages; 29 lb newspaper; 70 lb to 8 pt CIS cover stock; illustrations; rarely photos. Magazine consists of science fiction and fantasy stories for adults and young adults. 13 issues a year. Estab. 1977. Circ. 120,000.

Needs: Science fiction and fantasy. No horror or psychic/supernatural. Buys 10 mss/issue. Publishes short shorts. Receives approximately 800 unsolicited fiction mss each month. Approximately 30% of fiction is agented. Recently published work by Harlan Ellison, Lucius Shepard, Ben Bora, Connie Willis and Robert Silverberg, Isaac Asimov; published new writers in the last year. Length: up to 20,000 words. Critiques rejected mss "when there is time." Sometimes recommends other markets.
How to Contact: Send complete ms with SASE. Photocopied submissions OK. Accepts letter-quality computer printout submissions only. Reports in 1-2 months on mss. Publishes ms 6-12 months after acceptance. Free fiction guidelines with #10 SASE. Sample copy $2.
Payment: 6¢-8¢/word for stories up to 7,500 words, 5¢/word for stories over 12,500, $450 for stories between those limits.
Terms: Pays on acceptance for first North American serial rights plus specified foreign rights, as explained in contract. Very rarely buys reprints. Sends galleys to author. Publication copyrighted.
Advice: We are "looking for character stories rather than those emphasizing technology or science. New writers will do best with a story under 10,000 words. Every new science fiction or fantasy film seems to 'inspire' writers—and this is not a desirable trend. We consider every submission. We published several first stories last year. Be sure to be familiar with our magazine and the type of story we like; workshops and lots of practice help."

THE ASSOCIATE REFORMED PRESBYTERIAN MAGAZINE (II), The Associate Reformed Presbyterian, Inc., 1 Cleveland St., Greenville SC 29601. (803)232-8297. Editor: Ben Johnston. Magazine: 8½x11; 32-48 pages; 50 lb offset paper; illustrations; photos. "We are the official magazine of our denomination. Articles generally relate to activities within the denomination—conferences, department work, etc., with a few special articles that would be of general interest to readers. We have resumed our annual contest for writers of children's stories; write for details." Monthly. Estab. 1976. Circ. 7,000.
Needs: Adventure, contemporary, juvenile, religious/inspirational, spiritual, suspense/mystery, young adult/teen. "Stories should portray Christian values. No retelling of Bible stories or 'talking animal' stories. Stories for youth should deal with resolving real issues for young people." Receives 10-15 unsolicited fiction mss/month. Buys 1 ms/some months; 6-8 mss/year. Publishes ms within 1 year after acceptance. Recently published work by Margaret Woolington, Anita Burke Creel, Elizabeth Howard; published new writers within the last year. Length: 300-750 (children); 1,250 words maximum (youth). Sometimes critiques rejected mss. Occasionally recommends other markets.
How to Contact: Query and cover letter preferred. "We need to know whether a writer is submitting a contest entry or just a free-lanced story on speculation." Reports in 6 weeks on queries and mss. Simultaneous submissions OK. Sample copy $1.50; fiction guidelines for #10 SAE and 1 first class stamp.
Payment: Pays $20-$50 and contributor's copies.
Terms: Buys first rights.
Advice: "Know your market."

ATLANTA SINGLES MAGAZINE, Sigma Publications, 3423 Piedmont Dr. NE, Suite 320, Atlanta GA 30305. (404)239-0642. Editor: Margaret Anthony. Magazine: 8½x11; 80 pages; 50 lb paper; 80 lb cover; illustrations; photographs. "Magazine for singles; publishes mostly nonfiction work by local writers. Occasional fiction, but not often." Bimonthly. Estab. 1977. Circ. 15,000.
Needs: Contemporary, humor/satire, single life. No sci-fi, erotica. Receives 20-25 unsolicited mss/month. Accepts up to 3-5 mss/year. Publishes ms 3-6 months after acceptance. Length: 1,500 words average; 1,000 words minimum; 2,500 words maximum. Sometimes critiques rejected mss and recommends other markets.
How to Contact: Query first or send complete ms with cover letter. "Include a short bio, areas of interest in cover letter." Reports in 1 month. SASE. Simultaneous, photocopied and reprint submissions OK. Accepts computer printout submissions, including dot-matrix. Sample copy for $2. Fiction guidelines free.
Payment: Pays $100-300.
Terms: Pays on publication for one-time rights. Publication copyrighted.
Advice: "Submit any and everywhere—if it's good, there is room for your material."

THE ATLANTIC ADVOCATE (I, II, IV), University Press of New Brunswick Ltd., Box 3370, Fredericton, New Brunswick E3B 5A2 Canada. (506)452-6671. Editor: H. P. Wood. Magazine: 8¼x10⅞; 56 pages; coated offset paper and cover; illustrations; photos. Magazine of the Atlantic Provinces of Canada—Nova Scotia, New Brunswick, Prince Edward Island and Newfoundland. For "audience 35 years and over." Monthly. Estab. 1956. Circ. 30,000 (approximately).
Needs: Historical (general), humor/satire, and regional. Nothing "offensive or in poor taste." Receives 2-3 unsolicited mss/month. Buys 4-5 mss/year. Published new writers within the last year. Length: 1,000-1,200 words average; 1,500 words maximum. Occasionally comments on rejected mss.
How to Contact: Query first. Reports in 1-2 weeks on queries; 3-4 weeks on mss. Accepts computer

printout submissions. Prefers letter-quality. Sample copy for $1.75. Fiction guidelines free.
Payment: Pays 8¢/word minimum; 10¢/word maximum, with contributor's copies; charge for extras.
Terms: Pays on publication for first North American serial rights. Publication copyrighted.
Advice: "Mss should focus on the Atlantic Provinces of Canada."

ATLANTIC MONTHLY (II), 8 Arlington St., Boston MA 02116. (617)536-9500. Editor: William Whitworth. Senior Editor: Michael Curtis. General magazine for the college educated with broad cultural interests. Monthly. Estab. 1857. Circ. 440,000.
Needs: Literary and contemporary. "Seeks fiction that is clear, tightly written with strong sense of 'story' and well-defined characters." Buys 15-18 stories/year. Receives approximately 1,000 unsolicited fiction mss each month. Published new writers within the last year. Preferred length: 2,000-6,000 words.
How to Contact: Send cover letter and complete ms with SASE. "Grudgingly" accepts computer printout submissions. Prefers letter-quality. Reports in 2 months on mss.
Payment: $2,500/story.
Terms: Pays on acceptance for first North American serial rights. Publication copyrighted.
Advice: "Read magazine with great care and write well." When making first contact, "cover letters are sometimes helpful, particularly if they cite prior publications or involvement in writing programs. Common mistakes: excessive cuteness, too lengthy a list of prior publications."

ATLANTIC SALMON JOURNAL (IV), The Atlantic Salmon Federation, 1435 St. Alexandre #1030, Montreal Quebec H3A 2G4 Canada. (514)842-8059. Editor: Terry Davis. Magazine: 8½x11; 48-56 pages; 140 lb stock; 140 lb cover; illustrations; photographs. Conservation of Atlantic salmon: History, research, angling, science and management articles for conservationists, biologists, anglers and politicians. Quarterly. Estab. 1952. Circ. 20,000.
Needs: Historical (general), humor/satire. Receives 2-3 unsolicited mss/month. Buys 2 mss/issue. Publishes ms 2-6 months after acceptance. Length: 2,000-3,000 words average; 1,500 words minimum; 3,000 words maximum. Publishes short shorts.
How to Contact: Query with clips of published work or send complete manuscript with cover letter. Reports in 4-6 weeks on queries; 6-8 weeks on mss. SASE. Simultaneous submissions OK. Accepts computer printout submissions, no dot-matrix. Accepts electronic submissions via IBM floppy diskette, Wordstar or Wordperfect. Sample copy for 9x12 SAE and 51¢ postage. Fiction guidelines for #8 or #10 SAE and 39¢ postage.
Payment: Pays $50-$350 and contributor's copies.
Terms: Pays on publication for first rights or first North American serial rights. Publication copyrighted.

BAKERSFIELD LIFESTYLE MAGAZINE (II), American Lifestyle Communications Inc., 123 Truxtun Ave., Bakersfield CA 93301. Editor: Steve Walsh. Magazine: 8½x11; 64-112 pages; slick paper; slick cover stock; illustrations; photos. City magazine for general audience. Monthly. Estab. 1981.
Needs: Condensed novel, science fiction, senior citizen/retirement and suspense/mystery. Receives 25-30 unsolicited mss/month. Buys 1-2 mss/issue. Published new writers within the last year. Length: 1,000-1,500 words average. Occasionally comments on rejected mss.
How to Contact: Send complete ms. SASE and cover letter with summary of story. Simultaneous, photocopied and previously published submissions OK. Accepts computer printout submissions. Prefers letter-quality. Sample copy for $5.
Payment: Pays $10+.
Terms: Pays on publication. Publication copyrighted.
Advice: "Although many publishers have decided to make their publication a widely targeted and specialized one, I feel that magazines are the mother of American fiction and therefore have a responsibility to continue publishing fiction in some capacity. Know the beginning and ending of your story before you start, and slant the location and characters of your story to the special interest of the publication you are trying to sell."

BALTIMORE JEWISH TIMES (II, IV), 2104 N. Charles St., Baltimore MD 21218. (301)752-3504. Magazine: 160 pages a week, average; illustrations; photos. Magazine with subjects of interest to Jewish readers. Weekly. Estab. 1918. Circ. 19,000.
Needs: Contemporary Jewish themes only. Receives 7-10 unsolicited fiction mss/month. Buys 10-15 mss/year. Length: 3,500 words maximum (or 6-15 typed pages). Occasionally critiques rejected mss.
How to Contact: Send complete ms. Simultaneous, photocopied and previously published submissions OK "on occasion." Accepts computer printout submissions. Prefers letter-quality. Reports in 2 months on mss. Sample copy $2 and legal-size envelope.
Payment: Pays $35-$150.
Terms: Pays on publication. Publication copyrighted.

Close-up

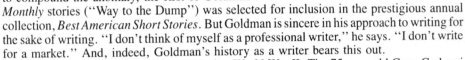

E.S. Goldman
Writer

E.S. Goldman is something of an anomaly among today's writers. He views writing as "something you ought to be able to do, just like you ought to be able to paint a little and maybe play a musical instrument."

That may seem odd, coming from a man whose fiction appeared three times in *Atlantic Monthly* in one year. And, to compound the anomaly, the first of Goldman's *Atlantic Monthly* stories ("Way to the Dump") was selected for inclusion in the prestigious annual collection, *Best American Short Stories*. But Goldman is sincere in his approach to writing for the sake of writing. "I don't think of myself as a professional writer," he says. "I don't write for a market." And, indeed, Goldman's history as a writer bears this out.

Goldman's writing "career" began during World War II. The 75-year-old Cape Cod resident served on a U.S. Navy mine sweeper during the war, and actually sold, using a pseudonym, his first piece of fiction then—a short story to the now-defunct *Adventure* magazine.

After the war, he worked in advertising and eventually built up his own agency. Throughout his career he continued his avocational writing, concentrating on what he *wanted* to write, rather than on writing for markets. And he was always writing something.

Goldman sold his business in 1961, when he retired "for the first time." Finding himself in need of something to do, he turned to writing and wrote a musical comedy. "I liked to write short things," he says. "When it came to doing anything fully-rounded, I found that I wanted to revise endlessly and could never finish a more complex work." Despite that problem, Goldman completed a novel in 1962. It appeared to be headed for publication until it was rejected after he cut it to fit a publisher's specifications.

After moving to Massachusetts from New York, he went into business again, this time with his artist-wife. When he sold that business, he found himself at loose ends and once again he turned to writing. (He had managed to publish a collection of poetry in the interim.)

"At this point," Goldman says, "my family expected me to write a memoir of my father's life." A veteran of the Spanish-American War who lived to be 99, his father lived "an interesting life." Plagued by the prospect of endless revision, Goldman was hesitant to tackle the project until his son suggested a word processor would help him overcome the problem. And, indeed, it did. Goldman went to work on another novel in 1981. "I took that musical I wrote in the '60s and converted it to a novel, *Big Chocolate Cookies*." The novel was published in 1988 by John Daniel, a California publisher and is now in its second printing and is optioned for a film.

But how, with Goldman's low-key approach, did this success come about? The novel sale was the result of a "mutual connection" as he puts it. His first sale to *Atlantic Monthly* wasn't really due to a direct effort on his part. Instead, "Francis Johnson, a retired English teacher, sent the first one in for me—not an agent. The editor, Michael Curtis, called me and said he liked the story and to send him another. So I sent him another, which was bought and published first. And he said again, 'Send me anything you have.'"

Currently, in addition to another novel, Goldman is trying to write enough stories for a collection. Writers who seek success in the mainstream market might do well to consider his advice: "Stop wanting to be published and start writing for the joy of writing."

—*Michael A. Banks*

BAY & DELTA YACHTSMAN (II, IV), Recreation Publications, Alameda Marina, 2019 Clement Ave., Alameda CA 94501. (415)865-7500. Editor: Bill Parks. Tabloid for upper-middle to upper-income audience. Monthly. Estab. 1966. Circ. 30,000.
Needs: Adventure, comics, condensed novel, fantasy, historical, humor/satire, literary, psychic/supernatural/occult, romance (historical), science fiction, senior citizen/retirement and suspense/mystery. "We look for stories relevant to power and sail boats over 30'; a Northern California slant or tie is important. No heavy dialogue, youth-oriented fiction." Receives 12 + unsolicited mss/month. Buys 2-3 mss/issue; 32 mss/year. Recently published work by Charles Doane. Published new writers within the last year. Length: 2,500-3,000 words; 2,000 words minimum; 4,000 words maximum.
How to Contact: Send complete ms. Reports in 3 weeks. SASE. Accepts computer printout submissions. Prefers letter-quality. Free sample copy.
Payment: Open.
Terms: Pays on publication for one-time rights. Publication copyrighted.
Advice: "Our readers prefer fun-to-read material."

‡BECKETT BASEBALL CARD MONTHLY (IV), Statabase, 3410 Mid Court, Suite 110, Carrollton TX 75006. (214)991-6657. Editor: Dr. James Beckett. Fiction Editor: Fred Reed. Magazine: 8½x11; 96 pages; coated glossy paper; 10 pt Sterling cover; 12 illustration; 100 + photographs. "Collecting baseball cards is a leisure-time avocation. It's wholesome and something the entire family can do together. We emphasize its positive aspects. For card collectors and sports enthusiasts, 6-60." Monthly. Estab. 1984. Circ. 220,000 paid.
Needs: Humor/satire, juvenile (5-9 years), sports, young adult/teen (10-18 years). "Sports hero worship; historical fiction involving real baseball figures; fictionalizing specific franchises of national interest such as the Yankees, Dodgers or Mets." No fiction that is "unrealistic sportswise." Publishes ms 4-6 months after acceptance. Length: 1,500 words average; 2,500 words maximum. Publishes short shorts. Sometimes comments on rejected mss or recommends other markets "if we feel we can help the reader close the gap between rejection and acceptance."
How to Contact: Send complete ms with cover letter. Include Social Security number. Reports in 6 weeks. SASE. Will consider reprints "if prior publication is in a very obscure or very prestigious publication." Accepts dot-matrix computer printouts; accepts electronic submissions via IBM ASCII files. Sample copy $3. Fiction guidelines free.
Payment: Pays $80 minimum; $400 maximum.
Terms: Pays on acceptance for first rights. Publication copyrighted.
Advice: "Fiction must be baseball oriented and accessible to both pre-teenagers and adults; fiction must stress redeeming social values; fictionalization must involve the heroes of the game (past or present) or a major-league baseball franchise with significant national following. The writer must have a healthy regard for standard English usage. A prospective writer must examine several issues of our publication prior to submission. Our publication is extremely successful in our genre, and our writers must respect the sensitivities of our readers. We are different from other sports publications and a prospective writer must understand our distinctiveness to make a sale here."

BIKE REPORT (I, IV), Bikecentennial, Box 8308, Missoula MT 59807. (406)721-1776. Editor: Daniel D'Ambrosio. Magazine on bicycle touring: 8½x11; 24 pages; coated paper; self cover; illustrations and b&w photos. 9 times yearly. Estab. 1974. Circ. 15,000.
Needs: Adventure, fantasy, historical (general), humor/satire, regional and senior citizen/retirement with a bicycling theme. Buys variable number mss/year. Published new writers within the last year. Length: 2,000-3,000 words average; 1,000 words minimum; 2,500 words maximum. Publishes short shorts. Occasionally comments on a rejected ms.
How to Contact: Send complete ms with SASE. Reports in 6 weeks on mss. Simultaneous, photocopied and previously published submissions OK. Accepts computer printout submissions. Prefers letter-quality. Prefers hard copy with disk submission. Sample copy for $1, 9x12 SAE and 60¢ postage. Fiction guidelines free for #10 SAE and 1 first class stamp.
Payment: Pays 3¢/word.
Terms: Pays on publication for first North American serial rights. Publication copyrighted.

BIRD TALK, Fancy Publications, Box 6050, Mission Viejo CA 92690. (714)855-8822. Editor: Karyn New. General pet bird magazine, consumer oriented, "for cage bird owners." Monthly. Circ. 150,000.
Needs: Pet bird-centered theme. Buys 1 ms/year. Length: 2,000-3,000 words. Must be labeled fiction.
How to Contact: Query first or send complete ms. SASE always. Photocopied submissions OK. Reports in 2 weeks on queries, 2 months on mss. Sample copy $3.50. Free writer's guidelines with SASE. No simultaneous submissions.
Terms: Buys one-time rights. Publication copyrighted.

‡BLACK BELT (II), Rainbow Publications, Inc., 1813 Victory Place, Burbank CA 91504. (818)843-4444. Executive Editor: Jim Coleman. Magazine: 132 pages. Emphasizes "martial arts for both practitioner and layman." Monthly. Circ. 110,000.
Needs: Martial arts-related; historical and modern-day. Buys 3-5 fiction mss/year. Publishes ms 3-5 months after acceptance.
How to Contact: Query first. Reports in 1 month. Photocopied submissions OK. Accepts computer printout submissions, "prefers letter quality."
Payment: Pays $100 minimum; $175 maximum.
Terms: Pays on publication for first North American serial rights, retains right to republish.

THE B'NAI B'RITH INTERNATIONAL JEWISH MONTHLY (IV), 1640 Rhode Island Ave. NW, Washington DC 20036. (202)857-6645. Editor: Marc Silver. Magazine: 8⅛x10⅞; 48-56 pages; coated stock; illustrations; photos. Subjects of Jewish interest—politics, culture, lifestyle, religion—for a Jewish family audience. 10 times annually. Estab. 1886.
Needs: Contemporary, ethnic, historical (general), humor/satire. No immigrant memoirs; holocaust memoirs. Receives 2 unsolicited mss/month. Buys 2 mss/year. Publishes ms 6 months-1 year after acceptance. Length: 2,500 words average; 1,000 words minimum; 5,000 words maximum. Occasionally critiques rejected mss. Recommends other markets.
How to Contact: Reports in 1 month on queries; 6 weeks on mss. Include cover letter and SASE. Accepts computer printout submissions. Accepts electronic submissions via disk or modem. Sample copy $1.
Payment: Pays $100-$750.
Terms: Pays on publication for first North American serial rights. Sends galleys to author. Publication copyrighted.
Advice: "A writer who submits a manuscript without a cover letter doesn't seem to have an awareness of/interest in our publication. Cover letters should include a sentence or two or biographical information (publishing credits) and an introduction to the story."

BOSTON REVIEW (II), Boston Critic Inc., 33 Harrison Ave., Boston MA 02111. Publisher/Editor: Margaret Ann Roth. "A bimonthly magazine of the arts and culture." Tabloid: 11x17; 24-32 pages; jet paper. Estab. 1975. Circ. 10,000.
Needs: Contemporary, ethnic, experimental, humor/satire, literary, mainstream, prose poem, regional, serialized/excerpted novel, sports and translations. Receives 100 plus unsolicited fiction mss/month. Buys 4-6 mss/year. Recently published work by Joyce Carol Oates, Yasunari Kawabata, Christopher Coe. Length: 3,000 words maximum; 2,000 words average. Publishes short shorts. Occasionally critiques rejected mss.
How to Contact: Send complete ms with cover letter and SASE. "You can almost always tell professional writers by the very thought-out way they present themselves in cover letters. But even a beginning writer should find some link between the work (its style, subject, etc.) and the publication—some reason why the editor should consider publishing it." Simultaneous and photocopied mss OK. Accepts computer printout submissions. Reports in 2-3 months on mss. Publishes ms an average of 4 months after acceptance. Sample copy $3.
Payment: $50-$200 and 2 contributor's copies.
Terms: Pays on publication for first rights. Publication copyrighted.
Advice: "We believe that original fiction is an important part of our culture—and that this should be represented by the *Boston Review*. We have embarked on a more vigorous fiction program—including a special effort to work with new writers."

BOWBENDER (II, IV), Canada's Archery Magazine, Box 912, Carstairs, Alberta T0M 0N0 Canada. (403)337-3023. Editor: Kathleen Windsor. Magazine: 8¼x10⅞; 48 lb pages; 57 lb gloss stock; 80 lb gloss cover; illustrations; photos. "We publish material dealing with hunting, wildlife, conservation, equipment, nature and Olympic team coverage etc., for outdoorsmen, especially hunters and competitive archers." Published 5 times/year. Estab. 1984. Circ. 25,000.
Needs: Adventure, sports, western. "Might publish fiction if it concerned (bow)hunting, archery or traveling in the Canadian outdoors." Does not want to see anything veering off the topic of archery in Canada. Publishes ms within 1 year after acceptance. Recently published work by James Richey; published new writers within the last year. Length: 2,250 words average; 1,000 words minimum; 3,000 words maximum.
How to Contact: Query first or send complete manuscript with cover letter, which should include a brief autobiography (archery) to be included in the magazine. Reports in 1 week on queries; 2 weeks on mss. SASE for ms. Photocopied submissions OK. Accepts computer printout submissions, including dot-matrix. Sample copy for $2.50 (Canadian), 9x12 SAE and $1.12 (Canadian postage). Fiction guidelines for #10 SAE and 34¢ (Canadian), 39¢ (U.S.) postage.

Payment: Pays $300 maximum. (Roughly 10¢/word depending on regularity of submission, quality photo complement etc.) Free contributor's copies; charge for extras.
Terms: Pays on publication for first North American serial rights, or first Canadian if requested and acceptable. Publication copyrighted.
Advice: "Fiction remains a "big" maybe. Write for guidelines and review a sample copy first."

BOWHUNTER MAGAZINE (IV), The Magazine for the Hunting Archer, Cowles Magazines, Inc., 2245 Kohn Rd., Box 8200, Harrisburg, PA 17105. (717)540-8192. Editor: M.R. James. Executive Editor: Dave Caufield. Magazine. 8¼x10¾; 150 pages; 75 lb glossy paper; 150 lb glossy cover stock; illustrations and photographs. "We are a special interest publication for people who hunt with the bow and arrow. We publish hunting adventure and how-to stories. Our audience is predominantly male, 30-50, middle income." Bimonthly. Circ. 230,000.
Needs: Bowhunting, outdoor adventure. "Writers must expect a very limited market. We buy only one or two fiction pieces a year. Writers must know the market—bowhunting—and let that be the theme of their work. No 'me and my dog' types of stories; no stories by people who have obviously never held a bow in their hands." Receives 1-2 unsolicited fiction mss/month. Buys 1-2 mss/year. Publishes ms 3 months to 2 years after acceptance. Length: 2,000 words average; 500 words minimum; 3,000 words maximum. Publishes short shorts. Length: 500. Sometimes critiques rejected mss and recommends other markets.
How to Contact: Query first or send complete ms with cover letter. Reports in 2 weeks on queries; 6 weeks on mss. Accepts computer printout submissions, including dot-matrix "if legible." Sample copy for $2 and 8½x11 SAE with appropriate postage. Fiction guidelines for #10 SAE and 1 first class stamp.
Payment: $25-250; free subscription to the magazine, if requested; contributor's copies, if requested up to 6; charge for extras, half price over 6.
Terms: Pays on acceptance for first North American serial rights. Publication copyrighted.
Advice: "We have a resident humorist who supplies us with most of the 'fiction' we need. But if a story comes through the door which captures the essence of bowhunting and we feel it will reach out to our readers, we will buy it. Despite our macho outdoor magazine status, we are a bunch of English majors who love to read. You can't bull your way around real outdoor people—they can spot a phony at 20 paces. If you've never camped out under the stars and listened to an elk bugle and try to relate that experience without really experiencing it, someone's going to know. We are very specialized; we don't want stories about shooting apples off people's heads or of Cupid's arrow finding its mark. James Dickey's *Deliverance* used bowhunting metaphorically, very effectively . . . while we don't expect that type of writing from everyone, that's the kind of feeling that characterizes a good piece of outdoor fiction."

BOYS' LIFE (III), For All Boys, Boy Scouts of America, Magazine Division, 1325 Walnut Hill Lane, Box 152079, Irving TX 75015-2079. (214)580-2000. Editor: William B. McMorris. Fiction Editor: William E. Butterworth IV. Magazine: 8x11; 68 pages; slick cover stock; illustrations; photos. "*Boys' Life* covers Boy Scout activities and general interest subjects for ages 8 to 18, Boy Scouts, Cub Scouts and others of that age group." Monthly. Estab. 1911. Circ. 1,500,000.
Needs: Adventure, contemporary, humor/satire, science fiction, suspense/mystery, western, young adult and sports. "We publish short stories aimed at a young adult audience and frequently written from the viewpoint of a 10- to 16-year-old boy protagonist." Receives approximately 100 unsolicited mss/month. Buys 12-18 mss/year. Recently published work by Donald J. Sobol, Maureen Crane Wartski, Rabod Rodgers; published new writers within the last year. Length: 1,000 words minimum; 3,000 words maximum; 2,500 words average. "Very rarely" critiques rejected ms.
How to Contact: Send complete ms with SASE. "We'd much rather see manuscripts than queries." Simultaneous and photocopied submissions OK. Accepts dot-matrix printout submissions; prefers letter-quality. Reports in 2 weeks on mss. For sample copy "check your local library." Writer's guidelines available; send SASE.
Payment: Pays $500 and up, "depending on length and writer's experience with us."
Terms: Pays on acceptance for one-time rights. Publication copyrighted.
Advice: "*Boys' Life* writers understand the reader. They treat them as intelligent human beings with a thirst for knowledge and entertainment. We tend to use many of the same authors repeatedly because their characters, themes, etc., develop a following among our readers."

BREAD (II), Church of the Nazarene, 6401 The Paseo, Kansas City MO 64131. (816)333-7000. Editor: Karen De Sollar. Magazine: 8½x11; 34 pages; illustrations; photos. Christian leisure reading magazine for junior and senior high students. Monthly.
Needs: Adventure and how-to stories on Christian living. Themes should be school and church oriented. Adventure stories wanted, but without sermonizing. Buys 25 mss/year. Does not read in summer. Recently published work by Alan Cliburn and Betty Steele Everett; published new writers within the last year.

How to Contact: Send complete ms with SASE. Reports in 6 weeks on mss. Free sample copy and guidelines for SASE.
Payment: Pays 3½¢/word for first rights and 3¢/word for second rights.
Terms: Pays on acceptance for first rights and second serial rights. Accepts simultaneous submissions. Byline given.
Advice: "Our readers clamor for fiction."

BUFFALO SPREE MAGAZINE (II, IV), Spree Publishing Co., Inc., 4511 Harlem Rd., Buffalo NY 14226. (716)839-3405. Editor: Johanna V. Shotell. Fiction Editor: Gary L. Goss. "City magazine for professional, educated and above-average income people." Quarterly. Estab. 1967. Circ. 21,000.
Needs: Literary, contemporary, feminist, mystery, adventure, humor and ethnic. No pornographic or religious. Buys 10 mss/issue, 40 mss/year. Length: 1,800 words maximum.
How to Contact: Send complete ms with SASE. Reports within 3 to 6 months on ms. Sample copy for $2 with 9x12 SASE and $2.40 postage.
Payment: $50-$125; 1 free author's copy.
Terms: Pays on publication for first rights.

CAMPUS LIFE MAGAZINE (II), Christianity Today, Inc., 465 Gundersen Drive, Carol Stream IL 60188. (312)260-6200. Senior Editor: James Long. Magazine: 8¼x11¼; 100 pages; 4-color and b&w illustrations; 4-color and b&w photos. "General interest magazine with a religious twist. Not limited strictly to Christian content. Articles on skateboarding and forgiveness, videogames and divorce, Frisbees and self-worth, etc., for high school and college age readers." Monthly. Plans special fiction issue. Estab. 1942. Circ. 200,000.
Needs: Condensed novel, fantasy, humor/satire, prose poem, science fiction, serialized/excerpted novel, and young adult. Prefers "realistic situations. We are a Christian magazine but are *not* interested in sappy, formulaic, sentimentally religious stories. We *are* interested in well crafted stories that portray life realistically, stories high school and college youth relate to. Nothing contradictory of Christian values. If you don't understand our market and style, don't submit." Receives 30 unsolicited fiction mss/ month. Buys 10 mss/year. Reading, response time slower in summer. Published new writers within the last year. Length: 1,000-3,000 words average, "possibly longer." Publishes short shorts.
How to Contact: Query with clips of published work and SASE. Simultaneous, photocopied and previously published submissions OK. Reports in 4-6 weeks on queries. Sample copy $2 and 9½x11 envelope.
Payment: Pays $250-$400, "generally"; 2 contributor's copies.
Terms: Pays on acceptance for one-time rights.
Advice: "A good realistic story generally captures high readership in *Campus Life*. Read the magazine—understand our purpose, style, and stance. Perfect your craft. Ask us for sample copy with fiction story. Fiction communicates to our reader. We want to encourage fiction writers who have something to say to or about young people without getting propagandistic."

CANADIAN BIKER MAGAZINE, Western Biker Publications, Ltd., Box 4122, Station A, Victoria, British Columbia V8X 3X4 Canada. (604)384-0333. Editor: Len Creed. Magazine: 8x10½; 68 pages; gloss and newsprint paper; glossy cover; illustrations; photos. Publishes material on motorcycles and motorcycling. Published every 6-7 weeks. Estab. 1980. Circ. 20,000.
Needs: "We are overstocked on fiction at present and fiction gets low priority to articles."

‡CANADIAN MESSENGER (IV), Apostleship of Prayer, 661 Greenwood Ave., Toronto, Ontario M4J 4B3 Canada. (416)466-1195. Editors: Rev. F.J. Power, S.J.; Alfred De Manche. Magazine: 7x10; 24 pages; glossy paper; self cover; illustrations; photos. Publishes material with a "religious theme or a moral about people, adventure, heroism, humor, for Roman Catholic adults." Monthly. Estab. 1891. Circ. 17,000.
Needs: Religious/inspirational. "Stories should leave a moral or faith message." Receives 10 mss/ month. Buys 1 ms/issue. Publishes ms within 1-1½ years of acceptance. Length: 500 words minimum; 1,500 words maximum.
How to Contact: Send complete ms with cover letter. Reports on mss in "a few" weeks. SASE. Accepts computer printout submissions, including dot-matrix. Sample copy for $1. Fiction guidelines for $1 and 7½x10½ SAE.
Payment: Pays 2¢/word.
Terms: Pays on acceptance for first North American rights. Publication copyrighted.

CAPE COD COMPASS (III,IV), Quarterdeck Communications, Inc., 60 I Munson Meeting Way, Chatham MA 02633. (617)945-3542. Editor-in-Chief: Andrew Scherding. Managing Editor: Donald Davidson. Magazine: 9x11; 180 pages; high gloss stock; heavy cover; illustrations; photos. "The publication has a strictly regional focus on Cape Cod (Massachusetts) and the islands of Nantucket, Martha's Vineyard and Cuttyhunk. Any fiction submissions must revolve around this regional focus." Quarterly. Estab. 1946. Circ. 25,000.

Needs: Condensed novel, contemporary, fantasy, historical, humor/satire, literary, mainstream, regional, serialized/excerpted novel. Receives 3-4 unsolicited mss/month. Buys 1 mss/issue; 4 mss/year. Publishes ms 6 months to 1 year after acceptance. Agented fiction 30%. Length: 3,000 words average; 2,000 words minimum; 6,000 words maximum.

How to Contact: Send complete manuscript with cover letter. Reports in 1 month on queries. Photocopied submissions OK. Accepts computer printout submissions, including dot-matrix. Sample copy $4. Fiction guidelines free.

Payment: Pays $250-$500; contributor's copies, charge for extras.

Terms: Pays on acceptance for first rights. Sends galleys to author. Publication copyrighted.

Advice: "We have no prejudice whatsoever to a writer's past experience, although we will not assign a piece to a novice. All that matters is the manuscript itself."

CAPPER'S (II), Stauffer Communications, Inc., 616 Jefferson, Topeka KS 66607. (913)295-1108. Editor: Nancy Peavler. Magazine: 24-48 pages; newsprint paper and cover stock; photos. A "clean, uplifting and nonsensational newspaper for families from children to grandparents." Biweekly. Estab. 1879. Circ. 400,000.

Needs: Serialized novels. "We accept only novel-length stories for serialization. No fiction containing violence or obscenity." Buys 2-3 stories/year. Receives 2-3 unsolicited fiction mss each month. Recently published work by Cleoral Lovell, Ellie Watson McMasters, Betty Jarmusch; published new writers within the last year. Sometimes recommends other markets.

How to Contact: Send complete ms with SASE. Cover letter and/or synopsis helpful. Reports in 5-6 months on ms. Sample copy 75¢.

Payment: $150-$200 for one-time serialization. Free author's copies (1-2 copies as needed for copyright).

Terms: Pays on acceptance for second serial (reprint) rights and one-time rights.

Advice: "Be patient. Send SASE. Copy your work before sending—mss do get lost!"

‡CAREER FOCUS, COLLEGE PREVIEW, JOURNEY, VISIONS (IV), Communications Publishing Group, Inc., 3100 Broadway, 225 Penn Tower, Kansas City MO 64111. Editor: Georgia Clark Groves. Associate Fiction Editor: Beryl Rayford-Saibu. Magazines: 70 pages; 50 lb paper; gloss enamel cover; 8x10 or 5x7 (preferred) illustrations; camera ready mat, photographs. *Career Focus*, "For Today's Professionals" includes career preparation, continuing education and upward mobility skills for advanced college students and college graduates. Published every two months. *College Preview*, "For College-Bound Students" is designed to inform and motivate Black and Hispanic high school students on college preparation and career planning. Semiannually. *Journey*, "A Success Guide for College and Career-Bound Students" is for Asian American high school and college students who have indicated a desire to pursue higher education through college, vocational/technical or proprietary schools. Semiannually. *Visions*, "A Success Guide For Career-Bound Students" is designed for Native American students who want to pursue a higher education through college, vocational/technical or proprietary schools. Semiannually.

Needs: Adventure, condensed/excerpted novel, contemporary, ethnic, experimental, historical (general), humor/satire, prose poem, romance (contemporary, historical, young adult), science fiction, sports, suspense/mystery. Receives 2-3 unsolicited mss/month. Buys 2-4 mss/year. After acceptance of ms, time varies before it is published. Length: 1,000 words minimum; 4,000 words maximum. Publishes short shorts. Does not usually comment on rejected ms.

How to Contact: Query with clips of published work (include social security number) or send copy of resume and when available to perform. Reports in 1-2 weeks. SASE. Simultaneous, photocopied and reprint submissions OK. Sample copy and fiction guidelines for 9x10 SASE.

Payment: Pays $100 minimum; $400 maximum.

Terms: Pays on acceptance. Acquires first rights and second serial (reprint) rights. Publication copyrighted.

Advice: "Today's fiction market is geared toward stories that are generated from real-life events because readers are more sophisticated and aware of current affairs. But because everyday life is quite stressful nowadays, even young adults want to escape into science fiction and fairytales. Fiction should be entertaining and easy to read. Be aware of reader audience. Material should be designed for status-conscious young adults searching for quality and excellence. Do not assume readers are totally unsophisticated and avoid casual mention of drug use, alcohol abuse or sex. Avoid overly ponderous, overly cute writing styles. Query describing the topic and length of proposed article. Include samples of published work if possible. Must be typed, double spaced on white bond paper (clean copy only)."

CAT FANCY (IV), Fancy Publications, Box 6050, Mission Viejo CA 92690. (714)855-8822. Editor-in-Chief: Linda W. Lewis. General cat and kitten magazine, consumer oriented for cat and kitten lovers. Published monthly. Circ. 250,000.
Needs: Cat-related themes only. Receives approximately 60 unsolicited fiction mss/month. Accepts 12 mss/year. Approximately 20% of fiction agented. Length: 3,000 words maximum. Sometimes recommends other markets.
How to Contact: Send complete ms with SASE. Simultaneous and photocopied submissions OK. Reports in 2 months. Publishes ms 2-10 months after acceptance. Sample copy $3. Free fiction guidelines with SASE.
Payment: 5¢/word and 2 contributor's copies. $3 charge for extras.
Terms: Rarely buys reprints. Publication copyrighted.
Advice: "Stories should focus on a cat or cats, not just be about people who happen to have a cat. No anthropomorphism."

CATHOLIC FORESTER (I, II, III), Catholic Order of Foresters, 425 W. Shuman Blvd., Naperville IL 60566. (312)983-4920. Editor: Barbara Cunningham. Magazine: 8¼x10¾; 36 pages; 45 lb paper and 60 lb cover stock; illustrations; photos. "No special theme but we want interesting, lively stories and articles. No true confessions type, no dumb romances. People who have not bothered to study the art of writing need not apply." Bimonthly. Estab. 1884. Circ. 160,000.
Needs: Adventure, contemporary, ethnic, feminist, humor/satire, mainstream, regional, senior citizen/retirement, sports, suspense/mystery. Receives 200 unsolicited fiction mss/month. Buys approximately 4 mss/issue; 25 mss/year. "Publication may be immediate or not for 4-5 months." Agented fiction: 5%. Recently published work by John Keefauver, Eileen Curtis; published new writers within the last year. Length: 2,000 words average; 3,000 words maximum. Also publishes short shorts. Occasionally critiques rejected mss. Sometimes recommends other markets.
How to Contact: Send complete ms. "Cover letters extolling the virtue of the story do not help—manuscripts stand or fall on their own merit. I do not accept queries anymore—too many problems in authors misunderstanding 'speculation.' " SASE for ms. Simultaneous, photocopied submissions and reprints OK. Sample copy for 8½x11 SAE and 73¢ postage. Fiction guidelines for #10 SASE.
Payment: Pays 5 cents minimum; and one contributor's copy. Author may request more copies—no charge.
Advice: "I enjoy a short, friendly cover letter but do not appreciate a long letter telling me the author's personal history, past credits, a complicated synopsis of the story enclosed, and his/her opinion of it. The only thing that counts is the quality and suitability of the story itself. Also, many writers ask for comments on their stories and want to be told why the stories were rejected. We understand how they feel and are sympathetic, but to explain all the things wrong with a story, or why we can't use it, or how they could improve it is much too time-consuming. In many cases we would just be acting as a teacher, and editors really don't have time to also be teachers. I do make short comments occasionally on rejection slips but cannot go into great detail. Before submitting a story, act out some of your scenes to see if they make sense—speak your dialogue aloud to assure that it is realistic. Ask yourself "is this how people really talk to each other?" Also, every rejection doesn't mean that the editor thinks the story is bad. It may just simply not fit the publication's readers, or that our space is limited."

CAVALIER MAGAZINE (II), Dugent Publishing Corp., 2355 Salzedo St., Coral Gables FL 33134. (305)443-2378. Editor: Douglas Allen. Fiction Editor: M. DeWalt. Magazine: 8½x11; 103 pages; 60 lb paper; laminated cover stock; illustrations; photos. Sexually oriented, sophisticated magazine for single men aged 18-35. Published special fiction issue last year; plans another. Monthly. Estab. 1952. Circ. 250,000.
Needs: Adventure, horror, and erotica. No material on children, religious subjects or anything that might be libelous. Buys 3 mss/issue. Receives approximately 200 unsolicited fiction mss each month. Recently published work by Janris Manley, Dillon McGrath, Wayne Rogers; published new writers within the last year. Length: 1,500-3,000 words. Critiques rejected mss "when there is time." Sometimes recommends other markets.
How to Contact: Send complete ms with SASE. A cover letter is not necessary except if ms is a multiple submission or there's special information. Accepts computer printout submissions. Prefers letter-quality. Reports in 3-6 weeks on mss. Sample copy for $3. Free fiction guidelines with SASE.
Payment: $200-$300. Offers 50% kill fee for assigned mss not published.
Terms: Pays on publication for first North American serial rights. Publication copyrighted.
Advice: Mss are rejected because writers "either don't know our market or the manuscripts are too long or too short. Length and erotic content are crucial (erotica in *every* story). Fiction is often much sexier and more imaginative than photos. If you are a poor speller, grammarian or typist, have your work proofread. Ask for our guidelines and follow them. Occasionally sponsors contests . . . watch publication."

‡CHANGES, For Adult Children, U.S. Journal Inc., 3201 SW 15th St., Deerfield Beach FL 33442. (305)360-0909. Editorial Coordinator: Andrew Meacham. Managing Editor: Jeffrey Laign. Magazine: 8½x11; 72 pages; slick paper; glossy cover; illustrations; photos. "Fiction often deals with recovery from dysfunctional families. Readers are children of alcoholics and other dysfunctional families." Bimonthly. Estab. 1986. Circ. 60,000.
Needs: Quality, professional fiction, typed, double-spaced." Receives 30 mss/month. Buys 1-3 mss/ issue. Publishes ms within several months of acceptance. Agented fiction 5%. Recently published work by Deborah Shouse, Susan Weston. Length: 2,000 words maximum. Publishes short shorts. Sometimes critiques rejected mss and recommends other markets.
How to Contact: Query with clips of published work or send complete ms with cover letter which should include Social Security number and "a short professional bio." Reports in 6 weeks. SASE. Simultaneous submissions OK. Accepts computer printout submissions, including dot-matrix. Sample copy for SAE. Fiction guidelines for #10 SAE and 1 first class stamp.
Payment: Pays 15¢/word.
Terms: Pays on publication for first North American serial rights. Publication copyrighted.
Advice: "Too much of the fiction we read is superficial and imitative. We're looking for bold new writers who have something to say. Write daily; read everything; proofread manuscripts; nothing turns us off more that typos and grammar errors; write about what you know."

CHESAPEAKE BAY MAGAZINE (II, IV), Chesapeake Bay Communications, Inc., 1819 Bay Ridge Ave., Annapolis MD 21403. (301)263-2662. Editor: Betty Rigoli. Magazine: 8½x11½; 88 pages; coated stock paper; coated cover stock; illustrations; photos. "*Chesapeake Bay Magazine* is a regional publication for those who enjoy reading about the Bay and its tributaries. Most of our articles are boating-related. Our readers are yachtsmen, boating families, fishermen, ecologists, anyone who is part of Chesapeake Bay life." Monthly. Estab. 1971. Circ. 32,000.
Needs: Fantasy, mystery, adventure, humor and historical. "Any fiction piece *must* concern the Chesapeake Bay. Only stories done by authors who are familiar with the area are accepted. No general type stories with the Chesapeake Bay superimposed in an attempt to make a sale." Buys 1 ms/issue, 8 mss/ year. Receives approximately 3 unsolicited fiction mss each month. Recently published work by Gilbert Byron and Arline Chase. Published new writers within the last year. Length: 1,250-3,000 words. Publishes short shorts. Critiques rejected mss "when there is time." Recommends other markets.
How to Contact: "Query or send ms, including cover letter with bio information to indicate familiarity with our publication. SASE always. Reports in 1 month on queries, 2 months on mss. Publishes ms an average of 12-14 months after acceptance. Sample copy $2. Free fiction guidelines with SASE.
Payment: Pays $85-$125. 2 free author's copies.
Terms: Pays on publication for all rights or first North American serial rights. Publication copyrighted.
Advice: "Make sure you have knowledge of the area. Send only material that is related to our market. All manuscripts must be typed, double-spaced, in duplicate. Our readers are interested in any and all material about the Chesapeake Bay area. Thus we use a limited amount of fiction as well as factual material. Work must be fairly short, or have clear break-points for serialization."

CHIC (II), Larry Flynt Publications, 9171 Wilshire Blvd., Suite 300, Beverly Hills CA 90210. Executive Editor: Doug Oliver. Article Editor: Allan MacDonell. Magazine: 100 pages; illustrations; photos. "Men's magazine, for men and women." Monthly. Estab. 1976. Circ. 100,000.
Needs: Erotica. Receives 20-30 unsolicited mss/month. Buys 1 ms/issue; 12 mss/year. Publishes ms 1-6 months after acceptance. Published new writers within the last year. Length: 3,500 words average; 3,000 words minimum; 4,000 words maximum. Occasionally critiques rejected mss. Recommends other markets.
How to Contact: Send complete manuscript with cover letter, which should include "writer's name, address, telephone number and whether the manuscript has been or is being offered elsewhere." Reports in 4-6 weeks. SASE for ms. Photocopied submissions OK. Accepts computer printout submissions, including dot-matrix. Fiction guidelines free for SASE.
Payment: Pays $500.
Terms: Pays on acceptance for all rights. Publication copyrighted.
Advice: "Readers have indicated a desire to read well-written erotic fiction, which we classify as a good story with a sexual undercurrent. The writer should read several published short stories to see the general tone and style that we're looking for. The writer should keep in mind that the first requirement is that the story be a well-written piece of fiction, and secondarily that it deal with sex; we are not interested in 'clinically descriptive' sex accounts. Due to limited space, writers should keep their stories within the word-length requirements as the time necessary to and possible ill effects of cutting longer pieces bode against their acceptance."

CHICKADEE (II), The Magazine for Young Children from OWL, Young Naturalist Foundation, 56 The Esplanade, Suite 306, Toronto, Ontario M5E 1A7 Canada. (416)868-6001. Editor: Janis Nostbakken. Magazine: 8½x11¾; 32 pages; glossy paper and cover stock; illustrations and photographs. "*Chickadee* is created to give children under nine a lively, fun-filled look at the world around them. Each issue has a mix of activities, puzzles, games and read-aloud stories." Monthly except July and August. Estab. 1979. Circ. 160,000.
Needs: Juvenile. No fantasy, religious or anthropomorphic material. Buys 1 ms/issue; 10 mss/year. Recently published work by Marilyn Pond, Janet Novak, Elsie Mitchell; published new writers within the last year. Length: 200 words minimum; 800 words maximum; 500 words average. Recommends other markets.
How to Contact: Send complete ms and cover letter with $1 to cover postage and handling. Reports in 2 months. Publishes ms an average of 1 year after acceptance. Sample copy for $2.50. Free fiction guidelines for SAE.
Payment: Pays $25-$350; 1 free contributor's copy; $1.25 charge for extras.
Terms: Pays on publication for all rights. Occasionally buys reprints. Publication copyrighted.
Advice: "We are looking for shorter stories that contain a puzzle, mystery, twist or tie-in to a puzzle that follows on the next spread. Make sure the story has a beginning, middle and an end. This seems simple, but it is often a problem for new writers."

CHILD LIFE, The Benjamin Franklin Literary & Medical Society, Inc., Box 567, 1100 Waterway Blvd., Indianapolis IN 46206. (317)636-8881. Editor: Steve Charles. Juvenile magazine for youngsters ages 7-9. Looking for adventure, humor, contemporary situations, folk and fairy tales and stories that deal with an aspect of health, nutrition, exercise (sports) or safety.
Needs: Juvenile. No adult or adolescent fiction. Length: 1,200 words maximum.
How to Contact: Send complete ms with SASE. Reports in 8-10 weeks. Sample copy 75¢. Free writer's guidelines with SASE.
Payment: Approximately 8¢/word for all rights. Publication copyrighted.
Terms: Pays on publication.

This cover was assigned to George Sears, a frequent contributor to Children's Digest. *He also illustrates "Tim Tyme," a regular cartoon feature in the magazine. The editor, Elizabeth Rinck, comments, "We felt that Tim, the 'star' of the cartoon, was an ideal cover subject." Illustration used by permission of* Children's Better Health Institute, Benjamin Franklin Literary & Medical Society.

What Happened in 1769? Find Out With Tim Tyme!

CHILDREN'S DIGEST (II), Children's Better Health Institute, Box 567, 1100 Waterway Blvd., Indianapolis IN 46206. Editor: Elizabeth A. Rinck. Magazine: 6½x9; 48 pages; reflective and preseparated illustrations; color and b&w photos. Magazine with special emphasis on health, nutrition, exercise and safety for 8-10-year-olds.
Needs: "Realistic stories, short plays, adventure and mysteries. Humorous stories are highly desirable. We especially need stories that *subtly* encourage readers to develop better health or safety habits.

Stories should not exceed 500 words." Receives 40-50 unsolicited fiction mss each month. Recently published work by Sharen Liddell, Linell Wohlers, Mary Magers; published new writers within the last year.
How to Contact: Send complete ms with SASE. A cover letter isn't necessary unless an author wishes to include publishing credits and special knowledge of the subject matter. Sample copy 75¢. Queries not needed. Reports in 10 weeks. Free guidelines with SASE.
Payment: Pays approximately 8¢/word with 2 free author's copies.
Terms: Pays on publication for all rights. Publication copyrighted.
Advice: "We try to present our health-related material in a positive—not a negative—light, and we try to incorporate humor and a light approach wherever possible without minimizing the seriousness of what we are saying. Fiction stories that deal with a health theme need not have health as the primary subject but should include it in some way in the course of events. Most rejected health-related manuscripts are too preachy or they lack substance. Children's magazines are not training grounds where authors learn to write 'real' material for 'real' readers. Because our readers are not experienced readers and frequently have limited attention spans, it is very important that we offer them well written stories."

CHILDREN'S PLAYMATE, The Benjamin Franklin Literary & Medical Society, Inc., Box 567, 1100 Waterway Blvd., Indianapolis IN 46206. (317)636-8881. Editor: Elizabeth A. Rinck. Magazine: 6½x9; 48 pages; preseparated and reflective art; b&w and color illustrations. Juvenile magazine for children ages 5-7 years.
Needs: Juvenile with special emphasis on health, nutrition, safety and exercise. No adult or adolescent fiction. Receives approximately 150 unsolicited fiction mss each month. Recently published work by Catherine Deverell, Stephanie Sammartino McPherson, Ann Devendorf; published new writers within the last year. Length: 700 words or less. Indicate word count on material.
How to Contact: Send complete ms with SASE. Accepts computer printout submissions. Prefers letter-quality. Reports in 8-10 weeks. Sample copy for 75¢.
Payment: Approximately 8¢/word.
Terms: Pays on publication for all rights. Publication copyrighted.
Advice: "Stories should be kept simple and entertaining. Study past issues of the magazine—be aware of vocabulary limitations of the readers. Stories or articles must be interesting for the target age of the readers." Rejects mss because "we receive thousands of manuscripts every year and have space to publish only about 30 stories a year."

CHRISTIAN LIVING FOR SENIOR HIGHS (IV), David C. Cook Publishing Co., 850 N. Grove, Elgin IL 60120. (312)741-2400. Editor: Anne E. Dinnan. A take-home Sunday school paper: 8½x11; 4 pages; Penegra paper and cover; full color illustrations and photos. For senior high classes. Weekly.
Needs: Christian spiritual. Writers work mostly on assignment. "Each piece must present some aspect of the Christian life without being preachy. No closing sermons and no pat answers. Any topic appropriate to senior high is acceptable." Buys 5-10 mss/year. Recently published work by Peg Ratliff, Randy Fishell, Rus Murphy; published new writers within the last year. Length: 900-1,200 words.
How to Contact: Send complete ms with SASE. No queries please. Cover letter with brief bio, religious credentials and experience with senior highs. Reports in 2 months on mss. Free guidelines with SASE.
Payment: Pays $100-$125.
Terms: Pays on acceptance for all rights.
Advice: "You've got to know kids and be aware of the struggles Christian kids are facing today. Don't write about how things were when you were a teenager—kids don't want to hear it."

‡CHRISTMAS (IV), The Annual of Christmas Literature and Art, Augsburg Fortress, 426 S. 5th St., Box 1209, Minneapolis MN 55440. (612)330-3300. Editor: Gloria Bengtson. Fiction Editor: Jennifer Huber. Magazine: 10⅜x13¾; 64 pages; illustrations and photographs. "Christmas—its history, celebration, traditions, music, customs, literature. For anyone who observes Christmas, especially its religious significance." Annually. Estab. 1931.
Needs: Ethnic, historical (general), literary, mainstream, prose poem, religious/inspirational, Christmas. No romance, horror, gay, lesbian. Receives 60-90 unsolicited mss/month. Buys 2-3 mss/issue. Publishes ms 1-3 years after acceptance. Length: 5,000 words preferred.
How to Contact: Send complete ms with cover letter. Reports in 2 weeks on queries; 4-6 weeks on mss. SASE. Simultaneous and reprint submissions OK. Sample copy for $7.95. Fiction guidelines for #10 SAE and 1 first class stamp.
Payment: Pays $150 minimum; $300 maximum. Free contributor's copies; charge for extras. Pays on acceptance. Purchases all rights, first rights or one-time rights. Publication copyrighted.

‡CHRYSALIS (II), Journal of the Swedenborg Foundation, The Swedenborg Foundation, 139 E. 23rd St., New York NY 10010. (212)673-7310. Send mss to: Rt. 1, Box 184, Dillwyn VA 23936. (804)983-3121. Editor-in-Chief: Carol S. Lawson. Fiction Editor: Phoebe Loughrey. Magazine: 7½x10; 96 pages; archival paper; coated cover stock; illustrations; photos. "A literary magazine centered around one theme per issue (e.g., 'Wise Woman: A Human Process' and 'Aspects of African Spirit' and 'Tree of Knowledge'). Publishes fiction, articles, poetry, book and film reviews for intellectually curious readers interested in spiritual topics." Triannually. "Would like to publish special fiction issues, but we need more writers!" Estab. 1985. Circ. 1,000.
Needs: Adventure, contemporary, experimental, historical (general), literary, mainstream, science fiction, spiritual, sports, suspense/mystery. No religious, juvenile, preschool. Receives 40 mss/month. Buys 2-3 mss/issue; 6-9 mss/year. Publishes ms within 9 months of acceptance. Recently published work by Virgil Livingston, A.D. McIntyre, Daniel Matokot; published new writers within the last year. Length: 1,500 words minimum; 2,500 words maximum. Publishes short shorts. Sometimes critiques rejected mss and recommends other markets. Does not accept reprinted or inpress material.
How to Contact: Query first and send SASE for guidelines. Reports in 2 weeks on queries; in 1 month on mss. SASE. Photocopied submissions OK. Accepts computer printout submissions, including dot-matrix, "prefers letter quality." Sample copy for $5. Fiction guidelines for #10 SAE and 1 first class stamp.
Payment: Pays $75-$250, free subscription to magazine and 5 contributor's copies.
Terms: Pays on publication for one-time rights. Sends galleys to author. Publication copyrighted.
Advice: Looking for "1. *Quality*; 2. appeal for our audience; 3. relevance to/illumination of an aspect of issue's theme."

THE CHURCH HERALD (II), 6157 28th St. SE, Grand Rapids MI 49506. (616)957-1351. Editor: John Stapert. Managing Editor: Jeffrey Japinga. Magazine: 8½x11; 60 pages. "We deal with religious themes and other reflections of a faith in God for a general audience, most members of the Reformed Church in America." Monthly. Estab. 1944. Circ. 50,000.
Needs: Prose poem, religious/inspirational, spiritual. Length: 1,200-1,500. Sometimes critiques rejected mss and may recommend other markets. Recently published work by Louis Lotz, James Schoop.
How to Contact: Send complete ms with cover letter. Reports in 1 month on queries; 6 weeks on mss. SASE. Simultaneous, photocopied and reprint submissions OK. Accepts computer printout submissions, including dot-matrix.
Payment: Pay varies according to length.
Terms: Pays on acceptance for all rights, first rights, first North American serial rights and one-time rights. Publication copyrighted.
Advice: "Take your time; one good submission is better than ten lousy ones."

THE CHURCH MUSICIAN (IV), The Sunday School Board of the Southern Baptist Convention, 127 9th Ave. N., Nashville TN 37234. (615)251-2961. Editor: William M. Anderson Jr. "*The Church Musician* is for church music leaders in local churches—music directors, pastors, organists, pianists, choir coordinators, and members of music councils and/or other planning committees or groups. Music leaders read the magazine for spiritual enrichment, testimonials, human interest stories and other materials related to music programs in local churches." Monthly. Estab. 1950. Circ. 20,000.
Needs: Categories related to church music. Receives 1-2 unsolicited fiction mss each month. Length: 750-2,000 words.
How to Contact: Send complete ms with SAE. Reports in 2 months on ms. Free sample copy with SAE and 30¢ postage. No simultaneous submissions.
Payment: Maximum 5¢ per word.
Terms: Pays on acceptance for all rights. Publication copyrighted.
Advice: "Avoid mushy sentiment when writing. It must be believable and, of course, practical." Many mss are rejected because they are "too long, too general, too sweet and sentimental, shallow."

CITY PAPER (II), 800 N. Charles St., Baltimore MD 21201. (301)539-5200. Editor: Phyllis Orrick. Tabloid: 70-80 pages; newsprint paper; illustrations; photos. "Alternative weekly newspaper serving Baltimore metro area." For 18-44 year-old educated audience. Estab. 1977. Circ. 90,000.
Needs: Adventure, confession, ethnic, experimental, historical, humor/satire, literary, mainstream. No inspirational, ideological, romance, pornography. Receives 40 unsolicited fiction mss/month. Buys 10-15 mss/year. Publishes ms 1-2 months after acceptance. Recently published work by Stephen Killduff; published new writers within the last year. Length: 500 words minimum. Occasionally critiques rejected mss.
How to Contact: Send complete ms with cover letter with basic bio. Reports in 6-12 weeks. SASE. Accepts computer printouts. Sample copy for SAE and $5 postage.
Payment: Pays $100-$500 and contributor's copies.
Terms: Pays on publication for first rights. Publication copyrighted.

CLUBHOUSE (II), Your Story Hour, Box 15, Berrien Springs MI 49103. (616)471-3701. Editor-in-Chief: Elaine Meseraull. Magazine: 6x9; 32 pages; 60 lb offset paper; self cover stock; illustrations and some photos. "A Christian magazine designed to help young people feel good about themselves. Our primary goal is to let them know there is a God and that He loves kids. Stories are non-moralistic in tone and full of adventure." Readers are "children 9-14 years old. Stories are selected for the upper end of the age range. Primary audience—kids without church affiliation." Published 6 times/year. Estab. 1951 under former name *The Good Deeder*. Circ. 15,000.

Needs: Adventure, contemporary, historical (general), religious, young adult/teen. No Christmas stories that refer to Santa, elves, reindeer, etc. No Halloween/occult stories. Receives 250+ unsolicited fiction mss/month. Buys 6 mss/issue, 40 mss/year. Reads mss in March-April only. Published new writers within the last year. Length: 1,000-1,200 words. Occasionally critiques rejected mss. Occasionally recommends other markets.

How to Contact: Send complete ms. SASE always. Simultaneous and photocopied submissions and previously published work OK. Accepts computer printout submissions. Prefers letter-quality. Reports in 2 months on queries and mss. Publishes ms 6-18 months after acceptance. Free sample copy with 6x9 SAE and 3 first class stamps. Free fiction guidelines with #10 SAE and 1 first class stamp.

Payment: Pays $25-$35 and contributor's copies.

Terms: Pays on acceptance for any rights offered. Buys reprints. Publication copyrighted.

Advice: "Especially interested in stories in which children are responsible, heroic, kind, etc., not stories in which children are pushed into admitting that a parent, sibling, friend, etc., was right all along. I want upbeat, fun, exciting stories. Do not mention church, Sunday School, etc., just because this is a Christian magazine. General tone of the magazine is warmth, not criticism. Remember that a story should follow a plot sequence and be properly wrapped up at the end. Most stories I reject involve kids who have regrettable turns of behavior which they finally change, appeal to a too-young age group, are preachy, are the wrong length or lack sparkle. Fiction can be more exact than truths, because details can be fashioned to complete the plot which might by necessity be omitted if the account were strictly factual."

COBBLESTONE: The History Magazine for Young People (IV), Cobblestone Publishing, Inc., 20 Grove St., Peterborough NH 03458. (603)924-7209. Editor-in-Chief: Carolyn P. Yoder. History magazine for children (ages 8-14): 7x9; 48 pages; 4-color covers; illustrations; b&w photos. Monthly with a national distribution.

Needs: Adventure, historical, regional and biographical fiction, reminiscences, plays and retold folk tales. *Must* relate to month's theme. Published new writers within the last year. Length: 500-1,500 words.

How to Contact: Simultaneous and previously published submissions OK. Accepts computer printout submissions. Publishes ms an average of 6 weeks after acceptance. Sample copy $3.95, enclose 7½x10½ (or larger) SASE. Free guidelines with SASE.

Payment: Pays 10-15¢/word.

Terms: Pays on publication. Buys all rights. Buys reprints. Makes work-for-hire assignments.

Advice: "Request an editorial guideline sheet that explains the upcoming issue themes and gives query deadlines. Prefer queries to unsolicited manuscripts." Rejects mss because "it appears that many writers do not obtain our guidelines before submitting fiction. In addition, we receive much fiction that is predictable and *too* juvenile for our readers. We publish fiction (usually one story per issue) as it pertains to the issue's theme. Fiction offers diversity, especially to a history magazine. Write as much as possible. Don't give up. Be true to your own style; don't try to write like other writers. Look to other writers for inspiration."

‡THE COMPANION OF ST. FRANCIS AND ST. ANTHONY (II), Conventual Franciscan Friars, Box 535, Postal Station F, Toronto, Ontario M4Y 2L8 Canada. (416)924-6349. Editor-in-Chief: Friar Philip Kelly, OFM Conv. Magazine. Publishes material "emphasizing religious and human values and stressing Franciscan virtues—peace, simplicity, joy." Monthly. Estab. 1936. Circ. 10,000.

Needs: Adventure, humor, mainstream, religious. Canadian settings preferred. Receives 50 unsolicited fiction mss/month. Buys 2 mss/issue, but "backlogged right now." Does not read mss in summer. Time varies between acceptance and publication. Length: 800 words minimum; 1,000 words maximum. Publishes short shorts, 200 words preferred.

How to Contact: Send complete mss. Reports in 3 weeks to 1 month on mss. SASE with "cash to buy stamps" or IRC. Sample copy and fiction guidelines free.

Payment: Pays 6¢/word (Canadian funds).

Terms: Pays on acceptance for first North American serial rights.

‡COMPUTOREDGE (IV), San Diego's MicroComputer Magazine, The Byte Buyer, Inc., Box 83086, San Diego CA 92138. (619)573-0315. Editor: Dan Gookin. Assistant Editor: Tina Berke. Magazine: 8½x11; 100 pages; newsprint paper; 50 lb bookwrap cover; illustrations and photos. Publishes material relating to "personal computers from a human point of view. For new users/shoppers." Biweekly. Estab. 1983. Circ. 65,000 + .

Needs: Confession, feminist, humor/satire, science fiction, computers. *"Really* has to speak to our audience/readership; new computer user /first-time shopper; new and enthusiastic about computing." Receives 0-3 unsolicited fiction mss/month. Buys 3 fiction mss/year. Publishes ms 1 month-9 months after acceptance. Recently published work by Alan Russel and Kent Patterson. Length: 300 words minimum; 1,200 words maximum.

How to Contact: Send complete ms with cover letter. Include Social Security number and phone number. Reports in 1 month. SASE. Photocopied and reprint submissions OK. Accepts dot-matrix computer printouts if near letter quality. Electronic submission of *accepted* mss encouraged. Sample copy for 9x12 SAE and $1.50 postage; writer's guidelines for #10 SAE and 1 first class stamp.

Payment: Pays 5¢-10¢/word.

Terms: Pays on publication for first rights or first North American serial rights. Offers $15 kill fee. Publication copyrighted.

Advice: Magazine fiction today is "too trendy. Reader should be able to come away from article moved, enlightened, edified. Submit in a professional manner an article/story that's well proofed and edited. Bring *yourself* into your writing!"

CORNERSTONE MAGAZINE (II), Jesus People USA, 4707 N. Malden, Chicago IL 60640. (312)989-2080. Editor: Dawn Herrin. Magazine about "the faith of the ages in the culture of today with social issues, interviews with musicians and artists, investigative reporting and fiction for the 18-35 age group." Bimonthly. Estab. 1972. Circ. 95,000.

Needs: Comics, condensed novel, contemporary, experimental, fantasy, humor/satire, literary, mainstream, prose poem, religious/inspirational, science fiction. No erotic or romance. Receives 20-60 unsolicited ms/month. Accepts 1 mss/issue; 4-6 mss/year. Recently published work by Robert Morgan. Published new writers within the last year. Length: 2,500-3,000 words average; 2,000 words minimum; 3,500 words maximum.

How to Contact: Query first or send complete ms. Reports in 4-5 weeks on queries; 1-2 months on mss. SASE. Accepts computer printout submissions, prefers letter-quality. Accepts disk submissions compatible with Kaypro II (C/PM). Sample copy $1.75. When asking for a sample copy or fiction guidelines, send a 9x12 SAE with 4 first class stamps. Address query or ms to Sarah Darden, Assistant Editor.

Payment: Pays $50-250.

Terms: Pays on publication for first rights. Publication copyrighted.

Advice: "We're looking for fiction which expresses a Christian world view in highly original ways. The sky's the limit."

CORVETTE FEVER MAGAZINE (II, IV), Prospect Publishing Co., Inc., Box 44620, Ft. Washington MD 20744. (301)839-2221. Editor-in-Chief: Patricia E. Stivers. "General magazine: 8½x11; 72 pages; coated paper; 60 lb coated cover stock; illustrations; photos. About Corvettes covering history of the car, restorations, stock and customizing, how-to articles on maintenance and repair, and coverage of the Corvette culture that surrounds the car. Corvette owners mainly are 25 to 45 years of age with incomes ranging from $25,000-$55,000 average. Majority are male. All have a keen loyalty to the Corvette." Bimonthly. Estab. 1978. Circ. 35,000.

Needs: Adventure and humor/satire. "Must deal with Corvettes." Receives 2-3 unsolicited fiction mss/month. Accepts 1 ms/issue, 6-8 mss/year. Published new writers within the last year. Length: 800-1,200 words.

How to Contact: Send complete ms with SASE. Photocopied submissions OK. Reports in 2 months. Sample copy $2. Free fiction guidelines with SASE.

Payment: 10¢/word.

Terms: Pays on publication (within 60 days) for first rights and second serial rights (second rights can be nonexclusive). Publication copyrighted.

Advice: Likes to see "good humor or satire that laughs with the Corvette owner but not at him. Generally using less" fiction than previously.

COSMOPOLITAN MAGAZINE (III), The Hearst Corporation, 224 W. 57th St., New York NY 10019. (212)649-2000. Editor: Helen Gurley Brown. Fiction Editor: Betty Kelly. Associate Fiction Editor: Gail Greiner. "Most stories include male-female relationships, traditional plots, characterizations. Readers are single career women (18-34)." Monthly. Circ. just under 3 million.

Needs: Contemporary, romance, mystery and adventure. "Stories should include a romantic relationship and usually a female protagonist. The characters should be in their 20s or 30s (i.e. the same ages as our readers). No highly experimental pieces. Upbeat endings." Buys 1 short story plus a novel or book excerpt/issue. Approximately 90% of fiction is agented. Length: short shorts (1,500 words); longer (2,000-4,000 words). Occasionally recommends other markets.

How to Contact: Send complete ms with SASE. Accepts computer printout submissions. Free guidelines with #10 SASE. Publishes ms 6-18 months after acceptance. Reprint submissions OK.

Payment: Pays $750-$2,000.

Terms: Pays on acceptance for first North American serial rights.

Advice: "It is rare that unsolicited mss are accepted. We tend to use agented, professional writers. The majority of unsolicited short stories we receive are inappropriate for *Cosmo* in terms of characters used and situations presented, or they are just not well written. Research the magazine you are submitting to."

COUNTRY WOMAN (IV), Reiman Publications, Box 643, Milwaukee WI 53201. (414)423-0100. Editor: Ann Kaiser. Managing Editor: Kathleen Pohl. Magazine. 8½x11; 68 pages; excellent quality paper; excellent cover stock; illustrations and photographs. "Articles should have a rural theme and be of specific interest to women who live on a farm or ranch, or in a small town or country home, and/or are simply interested in country-oriented topics." Bimonthly. Estab. 1971. Circ. 450,000.

Needs: "Profiles of country women—ordinary women who are doing unusual things, told in a light, conversational style with plenty of direct quotes and illustrated with bright, clear, candid color photos. No negative or unwholesome subject matter." Photo/feature package payment—$150 average. Also need: crafts, decorating, nostalgia, inspirational articles, poetry (short—25 lines max, traditional style) and fiction. "Fiction must be upbeat, heartwarming and focus on a country woman as central character. Many of our stories and articles are written by our readers! We publish 1 fiction story per issue, 6-8 profiles per issue. If good material comes in, we will buy it!" All articles/stories—750-1,000 words.

How to Contact: Query first. Reports in 2-3 months. Include cover letter and SASE. Simultaneous, photocopied and reprint submissions OK. Accepts computer printout submissions, including dot-matrix "but not preferred." Sample copy and writer's guidelines for $2 and SASE. Guidelines for #10 SASE.

Payment: $90-$125.

Terms: Pays on acceptance for one-time rights. Publication copyrighted.

Advice: "Read our magazine and become familiar with the type of material we publish."

CRICKET MAGAZINE (II), Carus Corporation, Box 300, Peru IL 61354. (815)224-6643. Editor: Marianne Carus. Magazine: 7x9; 64 pages; groundwood paper; #1 enamel cover stock; illustrations; photos. Magazine for children, ages 6-12. Monthly. Estab. 1973. Circ. 110,000.

Needs: Juvenile, including literary, contemporary, science fiction, historic fiction, fantasy, western, mystery, adventure, humor, ethnic and translations. No adult articles. Buys 10-20 mss/year. Receives approximately 500 unsolicited fiction mss each month. Approximately 1-2% of fiction is agented. Length: 500-1,500 words.

How to Contact: Do not query first. Send complete ms with SASE. List previous publications. Reports in 3 months on mss. Publishes ms 6-24 months after acceptance. Sample copy $2. Free guidelines with SASE.

Payment: Up to 25¢/word; 2 free author's copies. $1.25 charge for extras.

Terms: Pays on publication for first North American serial rights and one-time rights. Sends edited mss for approval. Buys reprints. Publication copyrighted.

Advice: "Do not write *down* to children. Write about subjects you are familiar with which have been well researched. Children *need* fiction and fantasy. Carefully study several issues of *Cricket* before you submit your manuscript." Published new writers within the last year. Sponsors contests for children, ages 6-12.

CRUSADER MAGAZINE (II), Calvinist Cadet Corps, Box 7259, Grand Rapids MI 49510. (616)241-5616. Editor: G. Richard Broene. Magazine: 8½x11; 24 pages; 50 lb white paper and cover stock; illustrations; photos. Magazine to help boys ages 9-14 discover how God is at work in their lives and in the world around them. 7 issues/year. Estab. 1958. Circ. 12,000.

Needs: Adventure, comics, confession, ethnic, juvenile, religious/inspirational, science fiction, spiritual and sports. Receives 60 unsolicited fiction mss/month. Buys 3 mss/issue; 18 mss/year. Recently published work by Sigmund Brouwer, Alan Cliburn and Betty Steele Everett. Length: 800 words minimum; 1,500 words maximum; 1,200 words average. Publishes short shorts.

How to Contact: Send complete ms and SASE with cover letter including theme of story. Simultaneous, photocopied and previously published submissions OK. Accepts computer printout submissions. Prefers letter-quality. Reports in 3 weeks on mss. Publishes ms 4-11 months after acceptance. Free sample copy with a 9x12 SAE and 3 first stamps. Free fiction guidelines with #10 SAE and 1 first class stamp.

Payment: Pays 2-5¢/word; 1 free contributor's copy.

Terms: Pays on acceptance for one-time rights. Buys reprints.

Advice: "On a cover sheet list the point your story is trying to make. Our magazine has a theme for each issue, and we try to fit the fiction to the theme."

DAUGHTERS OF SARAH (II, IV), 3801 N. Keeler, Box 416790, Chicago IL 60618. (312)736-3399. Editor: Reta Finger. Magazine: 8½x5½; 40 pages; illustrations and photos. "Christian feminist publication dealing with Christian theology, history, women and social issues from a feminist point of view." Bimonthly. Estab. 1974. Circ. 6,000.
Needs: Historical, religious/inspirational, feminist and spiritual (Christian feminist). "No subjects unrelated to feminism from Christian viewpoint." Receives 15-20 unsolicited fiction mss/month. Buys 10-15 mss/year. Recently published work by Letha Scanzoni, Virginia Mollenkott; published new writers within the last year. Length: 1,800 words maximum. Publishes short shorts. Occasionally critiques rejected mss "if related and close to acceptance."
How to Contact: Cover letter stating why ms was written; biography of author. Query first with description of ms and SASE. Simultaneous, photocopied and previously published submissions OK "but won't pay." Accepts computer printout submissions. Prefers letter-quality. Reports in 2 weeks on queries. Publishes "most" ms 3-12 months after acceptance. Sample copy for $2.50.
Payment: Pays $15/printed page; 3 free contributor's copies. Offers kill fee of one-half stated fee.
Terms: Pays upon acceptance for first North American serial or one-time rights.
Advice: "Make sure topic of story fits with publication. We get many stories that are either Christian stories, women's stories, Christian women's stories, but not necessarily feminist."

DIALOGUE (I, II), The Magazine for the Visually Impaired, Dialogue Publications, Inc., 3100 Oak Park Ave., Berwyn IL 60402. (312)749-1908. Editor-in-Chief: Bonnie Miller. Magazine: 9x11; 235 pages; matte stock; glossy cover; illustrations. Publishes information on blind-related technology and human interest articles for blind, deaf-blind and visually impaired adults. Quarterly. Estab. 1961. Circ. 50,000.
Needs: Adventure, contemporary, humor/satire, literary, mainstream, regional, senior citizen/retirement, suspense/mystery. No erotica, religion, confessional or experimental. Receives approximately 10 unsolicited fiction mss/month. Buys 3 mss/issue, 12 mss/year. Publishes ms an average of 6 months after acceptance. Recently published work by Phyllis Campbell, Rudy Makoul; published new writers within the last year. Length: 1,500 words average; 500 words minimum; 2,000 words maximum. Publishes short shorts. Occasionally critiques rejected mss. Sometimes recommends other markets.
How to Contact: Query first or send complete ms with SASE. Also send statement of visual handicap. Reports in 2 weeks on queries; 6 weeks on mss. Photocopied and reprint submissions OK. Accepts computer printout submissions; including dot-matrix. Sample copy for $5 and #10 SAE with 1 first class stamp; free to visually impaired. Fiction guidelines free.
Payment: Pays $5-$35 and contributor's copy.
Terms: Pays on acceptance for first rights. Publication copyrighted. "All fiction published in *Dialogue* automatically enters the Victorin Memorial Award Contest held annually. One winner per year.
Advice: "Study the magazine. This is a very specialized field. Follow submission procedures. Remember the SASE!"

THE DISCIPLE (II,IV), Journal of the Christian Church (Disciples of Christ), Christian Board of Publication, Box 179, St. Louis MO 63166. (314)231-8500. Editor: James Merrell. Magazine: 7¾x10½; 64 pages; coated cover stock; line art illustrations; 4 color and b&w photographs. Inspirational material; primarily feature articles for adult Christians. Monthly. Estab. 1974. Circ. 55,000.
Needs: Mainstream, religious/inspirational. This is primarily a denominational publication. Receives 50 unsolicited fiction mss/month. Accepts 10 mss/issue; 120 mss/year. Publishes ms up to 6 months after acceptance. Length: 2,500 words average. Publishes short shorts. Length: 1,000 words.
How to Contact: Query first. Reports in 2 weeks. SASE. Simultaneous submissions OK. Accepts computer printout submissions, including dot-matrix. Sample copy for $1.50 and 8½x11 SASE. Fiction guidelines for #10 SAE and 1 first class stamp.
Payment: $10-$35, contributor's copies; charge for extras.
Terms: Pays on publication for first rights and one-time rights. Publication copyrighted.
Advice: "It will be difficult but not impossible to be published. Do not submit materials to any publication without first becoming familiar with the style and content. (It is a waste of your time and the publisher's.) Do not ask for favors and do not forget a SASE."

DISCOVERIES (II), Nazarene Publishing House, 6401 The Paseo, Kansas City MO 64131. Editor: Molly Mitchell. Story paper. 5½x8¼; 8 pages; illustrations; color photos. "Committed to reinforce the Bible concept taught in Sunday School curriculum, for ages 8 to 12 (grades 3 to 6)." Weekly.
Needs: Religious, puzzles. Buys 1-2 stories and 1-2 puzzles/issue. Publishes ms 1-2 years after acceptance. Length: 400-800 words. Publishes short shorts.

How to Contact: Send complete ms with cover letter and SASE. Send for free sample copy and fiction guidelines with SASE.
Payment: 3.5¢/word.
Terms: Pays on acceptance for first rights.
Advice: "Stories should vividly portray definite Christian emphasis or character building values, without being preachy. Stories need to be shorter because size of story paper is smaller."

DOG FANCY, Fancy Publications, Box 6050, Mission Viejo CA 92690. (714)855-8822. Editor-in-Chief: Linda W. Lewis. General dog and puppy magazine, consumer oriented, "for dog and puppy lovers." Monthly. Circ. 150,000.
Needs: Dog-centered theme. Receives approximately 40 unsolicited fiction mss/month. Buys 12 mss/year. Length: 3,000 words maximum.
How to Contact: Query first or send complete ms. SASE always. Photocopied submissions OK. Reports in 2 weeks on queries, 6 weeks on mss. Publishes ms an average of 6 months after acceptance. Sample copy $3. Free fiction guidelines with SASE.
Payment: 5¢/word and 2 contributor's copies. $3 charge for extras.
Terms: Publication copyrighted. Buys reprints.
Advice: "Must be about dogs (and people), candid; first person is preferable. Include *brief* cover letter. Write to style of publication so that no re-write is necessary. Please no stories written 'by the dog' or talking dogs. Dog and dog's experiences must be focus of article; dog shouldn't be incidental character in a 'people' story. We are always especially interested in Christmas fiction—something heartwarming for the season, though not necessarily specifically Christmassy in theme."

DRAGON MAGAZINE (IV), The Monthly Adventure Role-Playing Aid, Dragon Publishing, Box 110, Lake Geneva WI 53147. (414)248-3625. Editor: Roger E. Moore. Magazine: 8½x11; 104 pages; 50 penn. plus paper; 80 lb northcote cover stock; illustrations; rarely photos. "*Dragon* contains primarily nonfiction—articles and essays on various aspects of the hobby of fantasy and science fiction role-playing games. Fiction is used occasionally if the story has relevance to fantasy gaming. Readers are mature teens and young adults; over half our readers are under 18 years of age." Monthly. Estab. 1976. Circ. 85,000.
Needs: "It's not essential for a fiction writer to be involved or familiar with role-playing games, but it helps. The gaming approach to fantasy is somewhat different than the so-called 'traditional' fantasy genre." Receives 50-60 unsolicited fiction mss/month. Buys 5-8 mss/year. Approximately 5% of fiction is agented. Recently published work by Nina Kiriki Hoffman, Bruce Boston, Robert Frazier; published new writers within the last year. Length: 1,500 words minimum; 8,000 words maximum; 3,000-4,000 words average. Occasionally critiques rejected mss.
How to Contact: Cover letter with short plot synopsis, estimated word length, SASE. List only credits of professionally published materials. Query with clips of published work and SASE. Photocopied submissions OK. Accepts computer printout submissions. Prefers letter-quality. Reports in 2-3 weeks on queries. Publishes ms 6-12 months after acceptance. Sample copy for $4.50. Free fiction guidelines for #10 SAE and 1 first class stamp.
Payment: Pays 5-8¢/word; 2 free contributor's copies; $2 charge for extras.
Terms: Pays on publication (or by prior arrangement, in advance) for all or first rights. Publication copyrighted.
Advice: "Know the basic principles of fantasy and science fiction role-playing games to develop a feel for the specific sort of fantasy we're interested in. Fiction is a nice complement to our gaming articles."

DRUMMER (II, IV), Desmodus, Inc., Box 11314, San Francisco CA 94101. (415)978-5377. Editor: A.F. DeBlasse. Associate Editor: Tim Barrus. Magazine: 8½x11; 100 pages; 80 lb ultrabrite paper; glossy full-color cover; illustrations and photos. "Gay male erotica, fantasy and mystery with a leather, SM or other fetish twist." Monthly. Estab. 1975. Circ. 23,000.
Needs: Adventure, erotica, fantasy, gay, horror, humor/satire, science fiction, suspense/mystery, western. "Fiction must have an appeal to gay men." Receives 20-30 unsolicited fiction mss/month. Accepts 4-5 mss/issue. Publishes ms 2-3 months after acceptance. Agented fiction 10%. Publishes short shorts.
How to Contact: Send complete ms with cover letter. SASE. Photocopied submissions OK; reprints OK "only if previously in foreign or very local publications." Accepts computer printouts, including dot-matrix. Accepts electronic submissions compatible with IBM PC. Sample copy for $5. Fiction guidelines for #10 SAE and 2 first class stamps.
Payment: Pays $50-$200, free contributor's copies and "possible subscription to magazine for frequent contributor."
Terms: Pays on publication for first North American serial rights. Publication copyrighted. Sponsors "infrequent" fiction contests.
Advice: Desmodus, Inc., also publishes *DungeonMaster*, *Mach* and *FQ* magazines. Write for details.

‡EASYRIDERS MAGAZINE (II), Entertainment for Adult Riders, Box 3000, Aurora Hills CA 91301. Fiction Editor: Mark Williamson. Magazine: 8½x10⅞; 118 pages; 50 lb coated paper; 70 lb coated cover stock; illustrations; photos. Men's magazine with bike-related material: how-to's, travel, new equipment information, and fiction for adult men who own or desire to own expensive custom motorcycles, and rugged individualists who own and enjoy their choppers and the good times derived from them. Monthly. Circ. 300,000.
Needs: Adventure. Should be bike-oriented, but doesn't have to dwell on the fact. "We are only interested in hard-hitting, rugged fiction that depicts bikers in a favorable light, and we're strongly inclined to favor material with a humorous bent." Recently published work by John Watson, Jody Via, Carl Kohler; published new writers within the last year. Length: 1,500-2,500 words. Publishes short shorts to 1,500 words.
How to Contact: Send complete ms with SASE and cover letter. Reports in 3 weeks on mss. Sample copy $2.95.
Payment: Pays 10-15¢/word; payment depends on quality, length and use in magazine.
Terms: Pays on acceptance for first rights. Sends galleys to author on paperback books.
Advice: "Gut level language accepted; dope or sex scenes OK but are not to be graphically described. As long as the material is directly aimed at our macho intelligent male audience, there should be no great problem breaking into our magazine. Before submitting material, however, we strongly recommend that the writer observe our requirements and study a sample copy."

‡THE ENSIGN (II,IV), Of The Church of Jesus Christ of Latter-day Saints, The Corporation of the President of the Church of Jesus Christ of Latter-day Saints, 50 East North Temple, Salt Lake City, UT 84150. (801)240-2950. Editor: Jay M. Todd. Fiction Editor: Giles Florence. Magazine: 8¼x10½; 80 pages; standard paper; color and b&w illustrations and photos. "Material should inspire, edify, instruct, inform and/or entertain our primarily LDS readers." Monthly. Estab. 1971. Circ. 500,000.
Needs: Contemporary, historical (general), humor, literary, mainstream, prose poem, regional, religious/inspirational, spiritual, sports. No erotica, gay, lesbian, occult. Receives 10 mss/month. Buys 2 mss/year. Publishes ms within 6 months- 5 years of acceptance. Recently published work by Jack Weyland (a professional writer, published widely in LDS market); Caren Llewellyn (an amateur). Published new writers within the last year. Length: 2,000 words preferred; 500 words minimum; 5,000 words maximum. Sometimes recommends other markets.
How to Contact: Send complete ms with cover letter; include social security number. Reports in 2 months. SASE. Simultaneous and photocopied submissions OK. Sample copy for $1 and 8½x11 SAE. Fiction guidelines for #10 SAE.
Payment: Pays $100-$400 and contributor's copies. Charge for extra copies.
Terms: Pays on acceptance for all rights "but writer can receive permission to republish by contacting us. Pay on acceptance serves as kill fee if not published." Sends prepublication copy to author. Publication copyrighted. Sponsors contests "usually, once a year. We have no contest for 1989, however. Writer's guidelines and rules are included in our July issue."
Advice: Looking for fiction that is "well-written, appealing to LDS readers. Review previous two years of the magazine."

EQUILIBRIUM, EVERYONE'S ENTERTAINMENT (II), The Magazine of Balance, Eagle Publishing Productions, Box 162, Golden CO 80401. Editor: Gary Eagle. Magazine: 8½x13½; 20 pages; bond and glossy paper; semi-hard cover; many illustrations and photos. "*Equilibrium* deals with the subject of balance and "having fun with opposites. It is an entertainment magazine for everyone." Quarterly. Plans special issue. Estab. 1984. Circ. 15,000.
Needs: Adventure, condensed novel, confession, contemporary, erotica, ethnic, experimental, fantasy, feminist, historical, horror, humor/satire, juvenile (5-9 years), literary, mainstream, preschool (1-4 years), psychic/supernatural/occult, regional, religious/inspirational, romance (contemporary, historical, young adult), senior citizen/retirement, serialized/excerpted novel, suspense/mystery, translations, western, young adult/teen (10-18). "The article doesn't necessarily have to be on opposites or balance because we sometimes pair two articles of two authors up with each other for a balance effect." Receives 50 unsolicited mss/month. Accepts 30 mss/issue; 120 mss/year. Length: 1,200 words maximum. Publishes short shorts.
How to Contact: Query first; then send complete ms with cover letter, which should be "double spaced and typed on 8½x11 paper with a query stating why our readers would enjoy reading their article. Tell a little about the article quickly." Reports in 10 weeks on queries; 3 months on mss (minimum). SASE. Simultaneous, photocopied and reprint submissions OK. Accepts computer printout submissions; no dot-matrix. Sample copy for $3 and 9x14 SAE with four first class stamps. Fiction guidelines for #10 SAE and 2 first class stamps.
Payment: Pays $20-$500; contributor's copies; charge for extras.

Terms: Pays on publication for one time or second serial rights. Publication copyrighted. Sponsors awards for fiction writers. "Just send in your article (should be on opposites or balance) and indicate that you'd like to enter the Writer's Sweepstakes. Letters are intended for publication and will be used for such. Queries may and will be published 'as is.' "
Advice: "Writers should write an article on opposites (extremes) or even do a very short one. Sketches are very nice to have. Humorous ones are good!"

ESSENCE (II), 1500 Broadway, New York NY 10036. (212)642-0600. Editor-in-Chief: Susan L. Taylor. Fiction/Senior Editor: Elsie Washington. General interest magazine with historical, how-to, humor, fashion, career, food, interior design, financial, health, education, beauty, and travel subjects for black women. Monthly. Estab. 1970. Circ. 900,000.
Needs: Romance, adventure, humor, fantasy, feminist, experimental, and condensed and serialized novels. Buys 3 mss/year. Length: 1,500-2,000 words.
How to Contact: Send complete ms with SASE. Typed and double-spaced. Reports in 3 months on mss. Sample copy $1.50. Free guidelines with query and SASE.
Payment: Pay varies.
Terms: Pays on acceptance. 25% kill fee. Buys second serial rights for serialized novels.
Advice: "We're looking for fiction that teaches and inspires—stories about contemporary black people, the challenges they face, their joys and sorrows."

EVANGEL, Dept. of Christian Education, Free Methodist Headquarters, 901 College Ave., Winona Lake IN 46590. (219)267-7161. Editor: Vera Bethel. Sunday School take-home paper for distribution to young adults who attend church. Fiction involves young couples and singles coping with everyday crises, making decisions that show growth; ages 25-35. Magazine: 8½x5½; 8 pages; 2-color illustrations; b&w photos. Weekly. Estab. 1896. Circ. 35,000.
Needs: Religious/inspirational. "No fiction without any semblance of Christian message or where the message clobbers the reader." Buys 1 ms/issue, 52 mss/year. Receives approximately 75 unsolicited fiction mss each month. Recently published work by C. Ellen Watts and Ralph Filicchia; published new writers within the last year. Length: 1,000-1,200 words.
How to Contact: Send complete ms with SASE. Reports in 1 month on ms. Free sample copy and free fiction guidelines with 6x9 SASE.
Payment: $45; 2 free author's copies. 10¢ charge for each extra.
Terms: Pays on publication for simultaneous, first, second serial (reprint), first North American serial and one-time rights.
Advice: "Choose a contemporary situation or conflict and create a good mix for the characters (not all-good or all-bad heroes and villains). Don't spell out everything in detail; let the reader fill in some blanks in the story. Keep him guessing." Rejects mss because of "unbelievable characters and predictable events in the story."

FACES (II,IV), The Magazine About People, Cobblestone Publishing, Inc. 20 Grove St., Peterborough NH 03458. (603)924-7209. Editor-in-Chief: Carolyn P. Yoder. Magazine covering world cultures for 8- to 14-year-olds; 7x9; 36 pages; 4-color covers; illustrations; b&w photos. 10 times/year.
Needs: Each issue deals with a specific theme. Editors consider "retold legends, folktales, stories from around the world relating to the theme." Length: 1,500 words maximum.
How to Contact: Query first. "Send ideas/suggestions in outline form." SASE. Sample copy $3.75; enclose 7½x10½ (or larger) SASE. Guidelines provide list of upcoming themes; free with SASE.
Payment: Pays 10-15¢/word.
Advice: "All manuscripts are reviewed by the American Museum of Natural History in New York before being accepted. Writers are encouraged to study recent back issues for content and style."

FAMILY MAGAZINE (II), The Magazine for Military Wives, Box 4993, Walnut Creek CA 94596. (415)284-9093. Editor: Janet A. Venturino. Magazine: 80 pages; glossy paper; 80 lb glossy cover stock; illustrations; photos. Magazine with stories of interest to military wives. Audience: high school-educated married women. Published 10 times/year. Estab. 1958. Circ. 550,000 worldwide.
Needs: Contemporary. No "singles" stories. Receives 100 unsolicited mss/month. Buys 12-20 mss/year. Published new writers within the last year. Length: 1,000-3,000 words.
How to Contact: Send complete ms. Reports in 2 months. SASE. Simultaneous and photocopied submissions OK. Accepts computer printout submissions. Prefers letter-quality. Publishes ms an average of 1 year after acceptance. Sample copy $1.25. Fiction guidelines for SASE.
Payment: Pays $75-$300; 1 contributor's copy; $1.25 charge for extras.
Terms: Pays on publication for first rights. Publication copyrighted.
Advice: "Good quality still jumps out as a pearl among swine."

FIRST HAND (II, IV), Experiences for Loving Men, First Hand Ltd., Box 1314, Teaneck NJ 07666. (201)836-9177. Editor: Lou Thomas. Magazine: digest size; 130 pages; illustrations. "Half of the magazine is made up of our readers' own gay sexual experiences. Rest is fiction and columns devoted to health, travel, books, etc." Monthly. Estab. 1980. Circ. 60,000.
Needs: Erotica, gay. "Should be written in first person." No science fiction or fantasy. Erotica should detail experiences based in reality. Receives 75-100 unsolicited mss/month. Buys 6 mss/issue; 72 mss/ year. Publishes ms 9-18 months after acceptance. Recently published work by John Hoff, Robert Allison, Julian Biddle; published new writers within the last year. Length: 3,000 words preferred; 2,000 words minimum; 3,750 words maximum. Sometimes critiques rejected mss.
How to Contact: Send complete ms with cover letter. Reports in 4-6 weeks on mss. SASE. Accepts computer printout submissions; no dot-matrix. Sample copy for $4. Fiction guidelines for #10 SAE and 1 first class stamp.
Payment: Pays $100-$150.
Terms: Pays on publication for all rights or first North American serial rights. Publication copyrighted.
Advice: "Cover letters are a must. Should include writer's name, address, telephone and social security number and should advise on use of pseudonym if any. Also whether he is selling all rights or first North American serial rights. Avoid the hackneyed situations. Be original. We like strong plots."

FIVE GREAT ROMANCES, WORLD'S GREATEST LOVE STORIES (II), Digest Publishing. 158 Linwood Plaza, Ft. Lee NJ 07024. (201)592-7002. Editor: Lynn Lauber. Magazine, 144 pages. Romance fiction—stories of approx. 16,000 words. Readers are primarily women 30 + years. Bimonthly. Circ. 500,000 (for 2 magazines).
Needs: Romance—contemporary and historical. Receives 20 unsolicited fiction mss/month. Accepts 5 mss/issue. Sometimes critiques rejected mss and recommends other markets.
How to Contact: Send complete ms with cover letter. Reports in 1 month. SASE. Simultaneous submissions OK. Accepts computer printout submissions, including dot-matrix. Fiction guidelines for #10 SAE and 1 first class stamp.
Payment: $400 maximum.
Terms: Pays on publication for first rights. Publication copyrighted.

FLING (II), Relim Publishing Co., Inc., 550 Miller Ave., Mill Valley CA 94941. (415)383-5464. Editor: Arv Miller. Magazine: 8½x11; 84 pages; slick paper and cover; color illustrations; mostly color photos. "Sex-type publication for young males 18-34 who like photos of very busty young models. They also like to read sex-type stories of bosomy heroines." Bimonthly. Estab. 1957. Circ. 100,000.
Needs: Erotica, fantasy. "Much of the text material in *Fling* deals with sex in combination of busty females." No historicals, mysteries, westerns, plotless stories. Receives 2 dozen unsolicited mss/month. Buys 2-3 mss/issue; 12-15 mss/year. Publishes 2-12 months after acceptance. Published new writers within the last year. Length: 4,000 average; 2,000 words maximum. Occasionally critiques rejected mss.
How to Contact: Send complete ms with cover letter. Reports in 2-6 weeks. SASE for ms. No electronic or photocopied submissions. Sample copy $5. Fiction guidelines for SAE and 25¢ postage.
Payment: Pays $135-$200.
Terms: Pays on acceptance for first rights. Publication copyrighted.
Advice: "Read a copy of *Fling*, plus study the fiction requirement sheet. Fiction gives *Fling* a special department we feel is necessary. There is a new aspect of sensuality that can be explored by readers. Know exactly what *Fling* wants in the way of story. Or, in some cases, query editor about story ideas. *Fling* has very specific requirements in fiction that must be clearly understood by potential author. While the men's sophisticate market is big, *Fling* needs stories that are tailor-made, not the usual 'sex-mag' submissions. Most authors forget *Fling* needs a lot of emphasis on descriptions of female characters, particularly 'big-bosom' descriptions."

THE FLYFISHER (IV), Federation of Flyfishers, 1387 Cambridge Dr., Idaho Falls ID 83401. (208)523-7300. Editor: Dennis Bitton. Magazine: 8½x11; 64 pages; 70 lb glossy stock; self cover; b&w; illustrations; color and b/w photos. Magazine for fly fishermen. "We only publish material directly related to fly fishing." Quarterly. Estab. 1967. Circ. 10,000.
Needs: Fiction related to fly fishing only. Accepts 1 ms/issue, 4 mss/year. Published new writers within the last year. Length: 1,000 words minimum; 2,500 words maximum; 2,000 words average (preferred).
How to Contact: Query first with SASE. Reports in 1 month on queries and mss. Sample copy $3 with 9x12 SAE and 10 first class stamps. Free fiction guidelines with #10 SAE and 1 first class stamp.
Payment: Pays $50-$175.
Terms: Pays on publication for first North American serial rights and one-time rights. Publication copyrighted.
Advice: "See a current issue of the magazine. Write like you talk. Be brief, be honest."

FLYFISHING NEWS, VIEWS AND REVIEWS (II,IV), Bitton Inc., 1387 Cambridge, Idaho Falls, ID 83401. (207)523-7300. Editor: Dennis G. Bitton. Newspaper tabloid: 16 pages; good newsprint; b&w illustrations; b&w photos. Publishes information on flyfishing and all related subjects, flyfishermen and women. Bimonthly. Estab. 1986. Circ. 5,000.
Needs: Adventure, condensed novel, confession, historical, humor, regional. "All as flyfishing topics." Receives 20 unsolicited mss/month. Accepts 2 mss/month; 12 mss/year. Length: 1,500-2,000 words average; 250 words minimum; 4,000 words maximum. Occasionally critiques rejected mss. Recommends other markets.
How to Contact: Query first. Reports in 2 weeks. SASE.
Payment: Pays $50-$250 and 5 contributor's copies. Charge for extras.
Terms: Pays 2-3 weeks after publication for one-time rights. Publication copyrighted.
Advice: "I want to see all good flyfishing fiction. Write like you talk."

THE FRIEND MAGAZINE (II), The Church of Jesus Christ of Latter-day Saints, 50 E. North Temple, Salt Lake City UT 84150. (801)531-2210. Editor: Vivian Paulsen. Magazine: 8½x10½; 50 pages; 40 lb coated paper; 70 lb coated cover stock; illustrations, photos. Publishes for 3-11 year-olds. Monthly. Estab. 1971. Circ. 210,000.
Needs: Adventure, ethnic, some historical, humor, mainstream, religious/inspirational, nature. Length: 1,000 words maximum. Publishes short shorts. Length: 250 words.
How to Contact: Send complete ms with cover letter. Reports in 6-8 weeks. SASE. Photocopied submissions OK. Accepts computer printout submissions, including dot-matrix. Sample copy for 9½x11 SAE and 76¢/postage.
Payment: Pays 8¢/word.
Terms: Pays on acceptance for all rights. Publication copyrighted.
Advice: "The *Friend* is particularly interested in stories with substance for tiny tots. Stories should focus on character-building qualities and should be wholesome without moralizing or preaching. Boys and girls resolving conflicts is a theme of particular merit. Since the magazine is circulated worldwide, the *Friend* is interested in stories and articles with universal settings, conflicts, and character. Other suggestions include rebus, picture, holiday, sports, and photo stories, or manuscripts that portray various cultures. Very short pieces (up to 250 words) are desired for younger readers and preschool children; the *Friend* is particularly interested in stories with substance for tiny tots. Appropriate humor is a constant need."

GALLERY MAGAZINE, Montcalm Publishing Corporation, 401 Park Avenue South, New York NY 10016. (212)779-8900. Editor: Marc Lichter. Fiction Editor: John Bowers. Magazine: 112 pages; illustrations and photographs. Magazine for men, 18-34. Monthly. Estab. 1972. Circ. 425,000.
Needs: Adventure, erotica, humor/satire, literary, mainstream, suspense/mystery. Receives 100 unsolicited fiction mss/month. Accepts 1 mss/issue. Publishes ms 2-3 months after acceptance. Less than 10% of fiction is agented. Length: 1,500-3,000 words average; 1,000 words minimum; 3,500 words maximum. Publishes short shorts. Sometimes critiques rejected mss and recommends other markets.
How to Contact: Send complete ms. Reports in 2 months. SASE. Photocopied submissions OK. Accepts computer printout submissions, including dot-matrix. Sample copy $5. Fiction guidelines for #10 SAE and 1 first class stamp.
Payment: $400-$1,000, contributor's copies.
Terms: Pays 50% on acceptance/50% on publication. Buys first North American serial rights. Publication copyrighted.

GEM (II), G&S Publications, Inc., 1472 Broadway, New York NY 10036. (212)840-7224. Editor: Will Martin. Men's sophisticate magazine: 8x11; 64 pages; "good" quality paper; illustrations; photos. Estab. 1961. Circ. 100,000.
Needs: Erotica (but not pornography), humor/satire and men's fiction and articles. Buys 3-4 mss/month; 35-40 mss/year. Length: 1,000 words minimum; 2,500 words maximum; 2,000 words average. Occasionally critiques rejected mss.
How to Contact: Send complete ms with SASE. No simultaneous submissions; photocopied submissions OK. Sample copy for $5.
Payment: Pays $40 (for short-shorts, 400-500 words) to $100; 1 free contributor's copy if requested.
Terms: Payment is usually on assignment to a specific issue for all rights. Publication copyrighted.

THE GEM (II), Churches of God, General Conference, Box 926, Findlay OH 45839. (419)424-1961. Editor: Marilyn Rayle Kern. Magazine: 6x9; 8 pages; 50 lb uncoated paper; illustrations (clip art). "True-to-life stories of healed relationships and growing maturity in the Christian faith for senior high students through senior citizens who attend Churches of God, General Conference Sunday Schools." Weekly. Estab. 1865. Circ. 7,700.

Needs: Adventure, feminist, humor, mainstream, religious/inspirational, senior citizen/retirement. Nothing that denies or ridicules standard Christian values. Receives 30 unsolicited fiction mss/month. Buys 1 ms every 2-3 issue; 20-25 mss/year. Publishes ms 4-12 months after submission. Length: 1,500 words average; 1,000 words minimum; 1,700 words maximum.

How to Contact: Send complete ms with cover letter ("letter not essential, unless there is information about author's background which enhances story's credibility or verifies details as being authentic"). Reports in 6 months on mss. SASE for ms. Simultaneous, photocopied submissions and reprints OK. Accepts computer printouts including dot-matrix if "correspondence quality." Can use Kaypro 2 or 4 disks written with Perfect Writer, Wordstar, or NewWord, or Victor 900 disks written with Victor Writer or Benchmark. Sample copy free with 4x9 SAE and 1 first class stamp. Fiction guidelines for "one 4x9 SAE will accommodate guidelines plus one sample copy for one stamp. If more than one sample copy is desired along with the guidelines, will need 2 oz. postage."

Payment: Pays $10-$15 and contributor's copies. Charge for extras (postage for mailing more than one).

Terms: Pays on publication for one-time rights.

Advice: "Competition at the mediocre level is fierce. There is a dearth of well written, relevent fiction which wrestles with real problems involving Christian values applied to the crisis times and 'passages' of life. Humor which puts the daily grind into a fresh perspective which promises hope for survival is also in short supply. Write from your own experience. Avoid religious jargon and stereotypes. Conclusion must be believable in terms of the story—don't force a 'Christian' ending. Avoid simplistic solutions to complex problems. Reader should care enough about the characters and be interested enough in the plot to keep reading when story is 'continued on page 6.' Listen to the story-telling art of Garrison Keillor on 'Prairie Home Companion' National Public Radio program. Feel how very particular experiences of small town life in Minnesota become universal."

GENT (II), Dugent Publishing Corp., Suite 204, 2355 Salzedo St., Coral Gables FL 33134. (305)443-2378. Editor: Bruce Arthur. "Men's magazine designed to have erotic appeal for the reader. Our publications are directed to a male audience, but we do have a certain percentage of female readers. For the most part, our audience is interested in erotically stimulating material, but not exclusively." Monthly. Estab. 1959. Circ. 175,000.

Needs: Contemporary, psychic/supernatural, science fiction, horror, erotica, mystery, adventure and humor. *Gent* specializes in "D-Cup cheesecake," and fiction should be slanted accordingly. "Most of the fiction published includes several sex scenes. No fiction that concerns children, religious subjects or anything that might be libelous." Buys 3 mss/issue, 36 mss/year. Receives approximately 30-50 unsolicited fiction mss/month. Approximately 10% of fiction is agented. Length: 2,000-3,500 words. Critiques rejected mss "when there is time."

How to Contact: Send complete ms with SASE. Reports in 1 month on mss. Publishes ms an average of 6 weeks after acceptance. Sample copy $5. Free fiction guidelines with legal-sized SASE.

Payment: $125-$175. Free author's copy.

Terms: Pays on publication for first North American serial rights. Publication copyrighted.

Advice: "Since *Gent* magazine is the 'Home of the D-Cups,' stories and articles containing either characters or themes with a major emphasis on large breasts will have the best chance for consideration. Study a sample copy first." Mss are rejected because "there are not enough or ineffective erotic sequences, plot is not plausible, wrong length, or not slanted specifically for us."

GENTLEMAN'S COMPANION (I), Gentleman's Companion, Inc., Box 447, Voorhees NJ 08003. (212)564-0112. Editor: Harvey George. Magazine: 8½x11; 96 pages; 50 lb coated paper; 80 lb cover stock; illustrations; photos. Men's magazine, sexually oriented material of a heavily erotic nature, geared to swinging concepts. Monthly. Published special fiction issue. Estab. 1976. Circ. 175,000.

Needs: Erotica, fantasy. No non-erotic fiction. Receives 20 unsolicited fiction mss/month; accepts 2 fiction mss/issue. Publishes ms 6 weeks to 6 months after acceptance. Length: 1,000-2,500 words.

Payment: Payment is negotiable.

How to Contact: Send complete ms with cover letter. SASE. Reports in 1 month on queries. Sample copy $3.95 and 8½x11 SAE with 2 first class stamps. Fiction guidelines for $3.95 and 8½x11 SAE with 2 first class stamps.

Terms: Pays on publication. Acquires all rights. Publication copyrighted.

GOLF JOURNAL (II), United States Golf Assoc., Golf House, Far Hills NJ 07931. (201)234-2300. Editor: Robert Sommers. Managing Editor: George Eberl. Magazine: 36-40 pages; good paper; self cover stock; illustrations and photos. "The magazine's subject is golf—its history, lore, rules, equipment and general information. The focus is on amateur golf and those things applying to the millions of American golfers. Our audience is generally professional, highly literate, and knowledgeable; presumably they read *Golf Journal* because of an interest in the game, its traditions, and its noncommercial aspects."

Published 8 times/year. Estab. 1949. Circ. 175,000.
Needs: Humor. "Fiction is very limited. *Golf Journal* has had an occasional humorous story, topical in nature. Generally speaking, short stories are not used. Golf jokes will not be used." Buys 10-12 mss/year. Published new writers within the last year. Length: 1,000-2,000 words. Recommends other markets. Critiques rejected mss "when there is time."
How to Contact: Send complete ms with SASE. Reports in 2 months on mss. Free sample copy with SASE.
Payment: $500-$1,000. 1-10 free author's copies.
Terms: Pays on acceptance. Publication copyrighted.
Advice: "Know your subject (golf); edit your copy thoroughly; familiarize yourself first with the publication." Rejects mss because "fiction usually does not serve the function of *Golf Journal*, which, as the official magazine of the United States Golf Association, deals chiefly with nonfiction subjects."

GOOD HOUSEKEEPING (II), 959 Eighth Ave., New York NY 10019. Editor: John Mack Carter. Fiction Editor: Naome Lewis. Magazine: 8x10; approximately 250 pages; slick paper; thick, high-gloss cover; 4-color illustrations, b&w and color photos. Homemaking magazine of informational articles, how-to's for homemakers of all ages. Monthly. Circ. 20 million.
Needs: Contemporary, romance and mother-child stories. Buys 2 short stories/issue. Approximately 75% of fiction is agented. Length: 1,000-4,000 words.
How to Contact: Query or send complete ms. SASE always. Accepts computer printout submissions. Prefers letter-quality. Reports in 6-8 weeks on both queries and mss. Publishes ms an average of 6 months after acceptance.
Payment: Pays standard magazine rates.
Terms: Pays on acceptance for first North American serial rights.
Advice: Most fiction is solicited. "The old standard needs restating: Know the market to which you are submitting."

GUIDE MAGAZINE, International Northwest Edition, One in Ten Publishing, Box 23070, Seattle WA 98102. (206)323-7374. Contact: Editor. "We publish humor pieces, fiction, poetry, feature stories and interpretive essays examining personalities, politics, science fiction, current events, the arts and indeed the whole of culture as it relates to gay life." Monthly. Estab. 1986. Circ. 11,000.
Needs: Adventure, condensed novels, ethnic, experimental, historical, horror, humor, mainstream, romance, science fiction, serialized novel, mystery/suspense, western. "All fiction must relate to experience of gay people. No erotica nor porn." Buys 7 fiction mss/year. Length: 800 words minimum; 3,000 words maximum.
How to Contact: Send complete ms. SASE. Simultaneous, photocopied and reprint submissions OK. Accepts computer printout submissions, including dot-matrix. Accepts electronic submissions via 5¼" disks formatted with MS/DOS files stored in ASCII or WordPerfect. Send hard copy with electronic submissions. Sample copy for 9x12 SAE and $1 postage. Writer's guidelines for #10 SAE and 1 first class stamp.
Payment: Pays 0-$30.
Terms: Pays on publication for first North American serial rights, second serial (reprint) rights, simultaneous rights, or makes work-for-hire assignments. Publication copyrighted.
Advice: "Well researched and intellectually challenging pieces get top priority."

‡THE GUIDE (II,IV), to the Gay Northeast, Box 593, Boston MA 02199. (617)266-8557. Editor: French Wall. Magazine: 8x10; 104-136; newsprint; 60 lb cover stock; photos. "Gay liberation and sex positive information, articles and columns; radical political and radical religious philosophies welcome. Audience is primarily gay men, some lesbians, bar crowd and grassroots politicos." Monthly. Estab. 1981. Circ. 22,000.
Needs: Adventure, erotica, ethnic, experimental, fantasy, feminist, gay, historical (general), humor/satire, lesbian, regional, religious/inspirational romance (contemporary, historical and young adult), science fiction, senior citizen, spiritual, sports, suspense/mystery. "Focus on empowerment—avoidance of 'victim' philosophy appreciated." Receives 1 ms/month. Publishes ms within 3-6 months of acceptance. Length: 1,200 words average; 500 words minimum; 5,000 words maximum. Publishes short shorts. Sometimes critiques rejected mss.
How to Contact: Query first. "Demonstrable commitment to gay liberation helps." Reports in 2-4 weeks. SASE; include cover letter and phone number. Simultaneous and photocopied submissions OK. Accepts computer printout submissions, including dot-matrix. Sample copy for 9x13 SAE and 6 first class stamps.
Payment: Pays $30-$120.
Terms: Pays on acceptance for all rights or first rights. Publication copyrighted.
Advice: Gay fiction writers have few (if any) places to be published in the US Northeast and Eastern

Canada. *The Guide*'s format and extensive distribution in this area makes it an excellent vehicle for writers anxious to be read. *The Guide* has multiplied its press run fourfold in the past years and is committed to continued growth in this region. The creative, politically aware, and culturally diverse audience we reach makes the addition of fiction to the magazine exciting to both us and our writers and readers. We're looking for shorter pieces than we've generally received."

GUYS, First Hand Ltd., Box 1314, Teaneck NJ 07666. (201)836-9177. Editor: Lou Thomas. Magazine: digest size; 160 pages; illustrations; photos. "Fiction and nonfiction for today's gay man. Fiction is of an erotic nature, and we especially need short shorts and novella-length stories." Bimonthly. Estab. 1988.
Needs: Should be written in first person. No science-fiction or fantasy. Erotica should be based on reality. Buys 7 mss/issue; 42 mss/year. Publishes ms 9-18 months after acceptance. Recently published work by Kevin Esser, Guy Willard, Dirk Hannam; published new writers within the last year. Length: 3,000 words average; 2,000 words minimum; 3,750 words maximum. For novellas: 7,500-8,600 words. Publishes short shorts. Length: 750-1,250 words. Sometimes critiques rejected mss and recommends other markets.
How to Contact: Send complete ms with cover letter; should include writer's name, address, telephone and soc. sec. number and whether he is selling all rights of First North American Serial Rights. Reports in 4-6 weeks on mss. SASE. Accepts computer printout submissions, no dot-matrix. Sample copy for $4.50. Fiction guidelines for #10 SAE and 1 first class stamp.
Payment: Pays $100-150. $75 for short shorts (all rights); $250 for novellas (all rights).
Terms: Pays on publication for all rights or first North American serial rights. Publication copyrighted.

HADASSAH MAGAZINE (IV), 50 W. 58th St., New York NY 10019. Executive Editor: Alan M. Tigay. Senior Editor: Zelda Shluker. General interest magazine: 8½x11; 48-70 pages; coated and uncoated paper; slick, medium weight coated cover; drawings and cartoons; photos. Primarily concerned with Israel, the American Jewish community, Jewish communities around the world and American current affairs. Monthly except combined June/July and August/September issues. Circ. 375,000.
Needs: Ethnic (Jewish). Receives 20-25 unsolicited fiction mss each month. Recently published fiction by Sylvia Rothchild and Lore Segal; published new writers within the last year. Length: 3,000 words maximum. Also publishes short stories 1,500-2,000 words.
How to Contact: Send complete ms with SASE. Accepts computer printout submissions. Reports in 6 weeks on mss. "Not interested in multiple submissions or previously published articles."
Payment: Pays $300 minimum. Offers $100 kill fee for assigned mss not published.
Terms: Pays on publication for U.S. publication rights. Publication copyrighted.
Advice: "Write fresh and look inside yourself. Stories on a Jewish theme should be neither self-hating nor schmaltzy."

HANG GLIDING MAGAZINE (IV), US Hang Gliding Association, Box 500, Pearblossom CA 93553. (805)944-5333. Editor-in-Chief: Gil Dodgen. Magazine: 8½x11; 54 pages; 60 lb paper; 70 lb cover; illustrations; b&w and 4-color photos. "For hang glider pilots. Publishes stories, technical articles, competition reports and features about hang gliding." Monthly. Estab. 1971. Circ. approx. 9,000.
Needs: Adventure, comics, experimental, fantasy, historical, horror, humor/satire, science fiction and suspense/mystery. "Fiction must relate strongly to the sport of hang gliding." Occasionally critiques rejected mss.
How to Contact: Query with clips of published work, or send complete ms. SASE always. Reports in 1 month. Free sample copy for 8½x11 SAE and $1.07 postage.
Payment: "Negotiable—varies with the quality of the work and our needs at the time." Up to 4 free contributor's copies.
Terms: Pays on publication for all rights (usually). Publication copyrighted.
Advice: "Learn to hang glide, read the magazine. No erotica."

HARPER'S MAGAZINE (II, III), 666 Broadway, 11th Floor, New York NY 10012. (212)614-6500. Editor: Lewis H. Lapham. Magazine: 8x10¾; 80 pages; illustrations. Magazine for well educated, widely read and socially concerned readers, college-aged and older, those active in political and community affairs. Monthly. Circ. 164,000.
Needs: Contemporary and humor. Stories on contemporary life and its problems. Receives approximately 300 unsolicited fiction mss/month. Published new writers within the last year. Length: 1,000-5,000 words. Also publishes short shorts.
How to Contact: Query to managing editor, or through agent. Reports in 6 weeks on queries.
Payment: Pays $500-$1,000. Negotiable kill fee.
Terms: Pays on acceptance for rights, which vary on each author and material. Sends galleys to author. Publication copyrighted.

Advice: Mss are rejected because of "poor writing and petty concerns—often they are too long (over 25 pages)." Buys very little fiction but *Harper's* has published short stories traditionally.

HARVEY FOR LOVING PEOPLE, Harvey Shapiro Inc., Box 2070, Cherry Hill NJ 08003. (212)564-0112. Editor: Harvey Shapiro. Managing Editor: Jack Sharp. Magazine dedicated to the enrichment of loving relationships between couples, offering sexually informative material in graphically erotic manner about swingers' lifestyles. "Our readership consists of people interested in highly informative sex-related information." Monthly. Estab. 1979. Circ. 200,000.
Needs: Lesbian and heterosexual erotica. No material accepted that is not sexually oriented. Buys 2-3 mss/issue. Length: 1,000-2,000 words.
How to Contact: Send mss with SASE. Reports in 1 month.
Payment: $50-$200.
Terms: Pays on publication for all rights.
Advice: Send SASE. "We reserve the right to edit. Stay within the Meese Commission guidelines."

HI-CALL (II), Gospel Publishing House, 1445 Boonville Ave., Springfield MO 65802. (417)862-2781. Editor: Sinda S. Zinn. Take-home Sunday school paper for teenagers (ages 12-17). Weekly. Estab. 1936. Circ. 95,000.
Needs: Religious/inspirational, western, mystery/suspense, adventure, humor, spiritual and young adult, with a strong but not preachy Biblical emphasis. Receives approximately 100 unsolicited fiction mss/month. Published new writers within the last year. Length: up to 1,500 words.
How to Contact: Send complete ms with SASE. Simultaneous and previously published submissions OK. Accepts computer printout submissions. Prefers letter-quality. Reports in 3-6 months on mss. Free sample copy and guidelines.
Payment: Pays 2-3¢/word. Offers 100% kill fee for assigned mss not published.
Terms: Pays on acceptance for one-time rights.
Advice: "Most manuscripts are rejected because of shallow characters, shallow or predictable plots, and/or a lack of spiritual emphasis. Send seasonal material approximately one year in advance."

HIGH ADVENTURE (II), General Council Assemblies of God (Gospel Publishing Co.), 1445 Boonville, Springfield MO 65802. (417)862-2781, ext. 1497. Editor-in-Chief: Johnnie Barnes. Magazine: 8⅝x11⅛; 16 pages; lancer paper; self cover; illustrations; photos. Magazine for adolescent boys. "Designed to provide boys with worthwhile, enjoyable, leisure reading; to challenge them in narrative form to higher ideals and greater spiritual dedication; and to perpetuate the spirit of the Royal Rangers program through stories, ideas and illustrations." Quarterly. Published special fiction issue; plans another. Estab. 1971. Circ. 84,000.
Needs: Adventure, historical (general), religious/inspirational, suspense/mystery and western. Published new writers within the last year. Length: 1,200 words minimum. Publishes short shorts to 1,000 words. Occasionally critiques rejected mss.
How to Contact: Send ms with SASE. Include social security number. Simultaneous, photocopied and previously published submissions OK. Reports in 6 weeks on mss. Free sample copy; free fiction guidelines for 9x12 SASE.
Payment: 2¢/word (base) and 3 contributor's copies.
Terms: Pays on acceptance for first rights and one-time rights. Publication copyrighted.
Advice: "Read the magazine; know the readership; give attention to writing style; be accurate."

HIGH TIMES (II), Trans High Corp., 211 E. 43rd St., New York NY 10017. (212)972-8484. Editor: Steven Hager. Magazine: 8½x11; 100 pages; glossy paper; illustrations; photos. Publishes "drug-related" material for "counter-culture" readers. Monthly. Plans special fiction issue. Circ. 300,000.
Needs: Adventure, experimental, fantasy, science fiction, serialized/excerpted novel. No stories about "my drug bust." Receives 16 unsolicited mss/month. Buys 5 mss/year. Publishes ms 6-8 months after acceptance. Recently published work by John Shirley, William Gibson; published new writers within the last year. Length: 2,000-4,000 preferred. Publishes short shorts.
How to Contact: Send complete ms with cover letter. Reports in 1 month on queries; 6 weeks on mss. SASE. Simultaneous, photocopied and reprint submissions OK. Accepts computer printout submissions, including dot-matrix. "Call John Holmstrom for modem information." Sample copy for $5. Fiction guidelines free.
Payment: Pays $200-$600 and contributor's copies.
Terms: Pays on publication. Purchases negotiable rights. Publication copyrighted.

HIGHLIGHTS FOR CHILDREN, 803 Church St., Honesdale PA 18431. (717)253-1080. Editor-in-Chief: Walter B. Barbe, Ph.D. Address fiction to: Kent L. Brown, Jr., Editor. Magazine: 8½x11; 42 pages; newsprint paper; coated cover stock; illustrations; photos. Published 11 times/year. Circ. 1.9 million.

Needs: Juvenile (ages 2-12). Unusual stories appealing to both girls and boys; stories with good characterization, strong emotional appeal, vivid, full of action. "Begin with action rather than description, have strong plot, believable setting, suspense from start to finish." Length: 900 words maximum. "We also need easy stories for very young readers (600 words)." No war, crime or violence. Buys 6-7 mss/issue. Receives 600-800 unsolicited fiction mss/month. Also publishes rebus (picture) stories of 150 words or under for the 3-4 year old child. Critiques rejected mss occasionally, "especially when editors see possibilities in story."

How to Contact: Send complete ms with SASE and include a rough word count and cover letter "with any previous acceptances by our magazine; any other published work anywhere." Accepts computer printout submissions. Prefers letter-quality. Reports in 2 months on mss. Free guidelines with SASE.

Payment: Pays 8¢ and up per word.

Terms: Pays on acceptance for all rights. Sends galleys to author. Publication copyrighted.

Advice: "We accept a story on its merit whether written by an unpublished or an experienced writer. Mss are rejected because of poor writing, lack of plot, trite or worn-out plot, or poor characterization. Children *like* stories and learn about life from stories. Children learn to become lifelong fiction readers by enjoying stories." Sponsors occasional contests. Write for information.

ALFRED HITCHCOCK'S MYSTERY MAGAZINE (I, II), Davis Publications, Inc., 380 Lexington Ave., New York NY 10017. (212)557-9100. Editor: Cathleen Jordan. Mystery fiction magazine: 5¹/₁₆x7³/₈; 160 pages; 30 lb newsprint paper; 60 lb machine-/coated cover stock; illustrations; photos. Published 13 times/year. Estab. 1956. Circ. 225,000.

Needs: Mystery and detection. No sensationalism. Number of mss/issue varies with length of mss. Published new writers within the last year. Length: up to 14,000 words. Also publishes short shorts.

How to Contact: Send complete ms and SASE. Accepts computer printout submissions. Reports in 2 months. Free guideline sheet for SASE.

Payment: 5¢/word on acceptance.

THE HOME ALTAR (II), Meditations for Families with Children, Box 590179, San Francisco, CA 94159-0179. Editor: M. Elaine Dunham. Magazine: 5¹/₄x7¹/₄; 64 pages; newsprint paper; coated 4-color cover stock; b&w illustrations and photos. "*The Home Altar* is a magazine of daily devotions. For each day, there is a designated Bible reading, a short story (fiction or nonfiction) which reflects the central message of the biblical passage, and a concluding prayer." Readers are "primarily Lutheran (ELCA) families—with children between 6 and 14 years of age." Quarterly. Estab. 1940. Circ. 82,000.

Needs: Juvenile (5-9 years) and religious/inspirational. "No unsolicited manuscripts are accepted for publication in *The Home Altar*. All writing is done on assignment, to reflect specific Bible readings and themes." Accepts 0-90 mss/issue; approximately 200 mss/year. Publishes ms an average of 6 months to 1 year after acceptance. Length: 150 words average; 125 words minimum; 170 words maximum. Publishes short shorts. Length: 150 words. Sometimes critiques rejected mss.

How to Contact: Query with clips of published or unpublished work. Reports on queries in 3 months; on mss in 2 weeks. Photocopied submissions OK. Accepts computer printout submissions, including dot-matrix "but only on our manuscript forms." Sample copy and fiction guidelines free.

Payment: $10 per "story"; contributor's copies.

Terms: Pays on acceptance for all rights. Publication copyrighted.

Advice: "We're trying to serve a diverse group of readers—children of all ages as well as adults. A well written story often has several levels of meaning and will touch people of different ages and experiences in different ways. Write stories in which children are the protagonists. Keep your sentences short. Use inclusive language when referring to human beings or to God."

HOME LIFE (II), The Sunday School Board of the Southern Baptist Convention, 127 9th Ave. N., Nashville TN 37234. (615)251-2271. Editor: Charlie Warren. A Christian family magazine: 8¹/₈x11; 66 pages; coated paper; separate cover stock; illustrations; photos. "Top priorities are strengthening and enriching marriage; parenthood; family concerns and problems; and spiritual and personal growth. Most of our readers are married couples and parents between the ages of 25-50. They read it out of denominational loyalty and desire for Christian growth and discipleship." Monthly. Estab. 1947. Circ. 725,000.

Needs: Contemporary, prose poem, religious/inspirational, spiritual, humor and young adult. "We do not want distasteful, risqué or raunchy fiction. Nor should it be too fanciful or far-fetched." Buys 1-2 mss/issue, 12-24 mss/year. Receives approximately 800 unsolicited fiction mss/month. Does not critique rejected mss. Recently published work by June Rae Woods, Edith Lanstrom, Betty Steele Everett; published new writers within the last year. Length: 750-2,500 words. Publishes short shorts of 500 + words. Recommends other markets.

How to Contact: Query or send complete ms. SASE always. Simultaneous submissions OK. Accepts computer printout submissions; prefers letter-quality. Reports in 2 weeks on queries, 1 month on mss. Publishes ms 12-20 months after acceptance. Sample copy for $1.

Payment: Up to 5¢/word for unsolicited mss. 3 free author's copies.
Terms: Pays on acceptance for all rights, first rights and first North American serial rights. Rarely buys reprints. Publication copyrighted.
Advice: "We publish fiction to communicate Christian values."

"The December cover photo was chosen because it captured both the warmth of Christmas and the religious aspects of the holiday," explains Charlie Warren, editor of Home Life. "Our target [audience] is Christian families and the family pictured appears to be a healthy Christian family."

Cover photo by Jim Whitmer.

HOOF BEATS (IV), World's Largest Standardbred Publication, U.S. Trotting Association, 750 Michigan Ave., Columbus OH 43215. (614)224-2291. Executive Editor: Dean A. Hoffman. Magazine: 150 pages; illustrations and photographs. "All material must pertain to racing or breeding of harness horses." Audience is owners, breeders, trainers of harness horses. Monthly. Circ. 26,000.
Needs: Receives 2 unsolicited fiction mss/month. Accepts 4 mss/year. Publishes ms an average of 6 months after acceptance. Publishes short shorts. Sometimes critiques rejected ms; recommends other markets.
How to Contact: Query first with "story ideas and background of author." Reports in 1 week on queries; 2 weeks on mss. Photocopied and reprint submissions OK. Accepts computer printout submissions, including dot-matrix. Sample copy free.
Payment: $100-$300.
Terms: Pays on publication for first rights. Publication copyrighted.
Advice: "Be persistent. Don't write on speculation, query editors first. Don't simultaneous submit. Know the publication to which you're submitting an article."

HORSE ILLUSTRATED, Fancy Publications, Box 6050, Mission Viejo CA 92690. (714)855-8822. Editor: Jill-Marie Jones. "General all-breed horse magazine for horse lovers of all ages but mainly women riding for show and pleasure. All material is centered around horses; both English and Western riding styles are profiled." Monthly. Estab. 1982. Circ. 110,000.
Needs: Adventure, comics, suspense/mystery and western. "Must concern horses. Liberal—nothing unsuitable to a younger audience, although we do not want mss aimed directly at young readers." Receives 3-5 unsolicited mss/month. Buys 5-6 mss/year. Recently published work by M.J. Miller; published new writers within the last year. Length: 1,500-2,000 words average; 1,000 words minimum; 2,500 words maximum. Occasionally critiques rejected mss.
How to Contact: Query first or send complete ms. Reports in 1 month on queries; 2 months on mss. SASE. Photocopied submissions OK. Accepts computer printout submissions. Prefers letter-quality. Publishes ms 4-10 months after acceptance. Sample copy $3.25. Free fiction guidelines for SASE.
Payment: $50-$150; 2 contributor's copies; $2 charge for extras ("free if request is for a reasonable number of copies").
Terms: Pays on publication for one-time rights. Publication copyrighted.

Advice: "Write about adult women—*no* little girl and wild stallion or cowboy and Indian stories, please—and their horses. It must be a believable, interesting story that they can identify with."

HOT SHOTS (IV), Sunshine Publishing Company, Inc., 7366 Convoy Court, San Diego CA 92111. (619)278-9058. Editor: Chuck Edwards. Magazine: digest sized; 132 pages; pulp/coated paper; coated 4-color cover; photographs. "Adult erotica, real-life fantasies, and true reader experience. Explicit fiction about 18-35-year-old males only, for gay males." Monthly. Plans special fiction issue. Estab. 1986. Circ. 100,000.
Needs: Confession, erotica, gay. No subjugation, rape, S&M, bestiality, incest, excessive raunch. Receives 4-5 unsolicited fiction mss/month. Accepts 10-12 mss/issue; 120-150 mss/year. Publishes ms 4 months after acceptance. Length: 3,000 words average; 2,500 words minimum; 4,000 words maximum. Publishes short shorts. Sometimes critiques rejected mss.
How to Contact: Send complete ms with cover letter. Reports in 1 month. Accepts computer printout submissions, no dot-matrix. Accepts electronic submissions via disk convertible to ASCII format. Requires hard copy also. Sample copy $4. Fiction guidelines free.
Payment: $75-$250; contributor's copies.
Terms: Pays on publication for all rights. Publication copyrighted.
Advice: "Keep all sexual activity between fictional characters within the realm of possibility for a real persona with a similar level of experience. Do not over-exaggerate physical characteristics. Erotica is hot, not raunchy. We want stimulating fiction, not comedy. The overall tone of *Hot Shots* is always fun, upbeat, compassionate."

HUMPTY DUMPTY'S MAGAZINE (II), Children's Better Health Institute, Benjamin Franklin Literary & Medical Society, Inc., 1100 Waterway Blvd., Box 567, Indianapolis IN 46206. Editor: Christine French Clark. Magazine: 6½x9⅛; 48 pages; 35 lb paper; coated cover; color, 2-color, or b&w illustrations; rarely photos. Children's magazine stressing health, nutrition, hygiene, exercise and safety for children ages 4-6. Monthly, except bimonthly February-March, April-May, June-July and August-September.
Needs: Juvenile health-related material and material of a more general nature. No inanimate talking objects. Rhyming stories should flow easily with no contrived rhymes. Buys 3-5 mss/issue. Receives 250-300 unsolicited fiction mss/month. Published new writers within the last year. Length: 600 words maximum.
How to Contact: Send complete ms with SASE. Reports in 8-10 weeks. Sample copy 75¢. Editorial guidelines with SASE. No queries.
Payment: Pays 8¢/word for stories plus 2 author's copies (more upon request).
Terms: Pays on publication for all rights. (One-time book rights returned when requested for specific publication.) Publication copyrighted.
Advice: "In contemporary stories, characters should be up-to-date, with realistic dialogue. We're looking for health-related stories with unusual twists or surprise endings. We want to avoid stories and poems that 'preach.' We try to present the health material in a positive way, utilizing a light humorous approach wherever possible." Most rejected mss "are too wordy. Stories should not exceed 600 words. Many manuscripts are rejected because they are too similar to previously published material. Cover letters should be included only if they give pertinent information—list of credits, bibliography, or mention of any special training or qualifications that make author an authority."

HUSTLER (IV), Larry Flynt Publications, Suite 300, 9171 Wilshire Blvd., Beverly Hills CA 90210-5530. (213)858-7100. Editor: Tim Conaway. Fiction Editors: Allan MacDonnell, Michael DiGregorio. Magazine: 100 pages; illustrations; photos. "Men's magazine, for men and women." Monthly. Estab. 1976. Circ. 1 million.
Needs: Erotica. Receives 20-30 unsolicited mss/month. Buys 1 ms/issue; 12 mss/year. Publishes ms 1-6 months after acceptance. Length: 3,500 words average; 3,000 words minimum; 4,000 words maximum. Occasionally critiques rejected mss. Recommends other markets.
How to Contact: Send complete ms with cover letter which should include "writer's name, address, telephone number, and whether the manuscript has been or is being offered elsewhere." Reports in 4-6 weeks on ms. SASE for ms. Photocopied submissions OK. Accepts computer printout submissions, including dot-matrix. Sample copy and fiction guidelines free.
Payment: $500.
Terms: Pays on acceptance for all rights. Publication copyrighted.
Advice: "Readers have indicated a desire to read well written erotic fiction, which we classify as a good story with a sexual undercurrent. The writer should read several published short stories to see the general tone and style that we're looking for. The writer should keep in mind that the first requirement is that the story be a well written piece of fiction, and secondarily that it deal with sex; we are not interested in

'clinically descriptive' sex accounts. Due to limited space, writers should keep their stories within the word-length requirements as the time necessary to and possible ill effects of cutting longer pieces bode against their acceptance."

HUSTLER LETTERS (IV), Larry Flynt Publications, 9171 Wilshire Blvd., Third Floor, Beverly Hills CA 90210-5530. (213)858-7100. Editor: Tim Conaway. Fiction Editor: Michael DiGregorio. Magazine: 100 pages; illustrations; photos. "Men's magazine, for men and women." Monthly. Estab. 1985. Circ. 105,000.
Needs: Erotica. Receives 20-30 unsolicited mss/month. Buys 2 mss/issue; 24 mss/year. Publishes ms 1-6 months after acceptance. Length: 3,500 words average; 3,000 words minimum; 4,500 words maximum. Occasionally critiques rejected mss.
How to Contact: Send complete ms with cover letter, which should include "writer's name, address, telephone number and whether the manuscript has been or is being offered elsewhere." Reports in 4-6 weeks on ms. SASE for ms. Photocopied submissions OK. Accepts computer printout submissions. Fiction guidelines free.
Payment: $500.
Terms: Pays on acceptance for all rights. Publication copyrighted.
Advice: "Readers have indicated a desire to read well written erotic fiction, which we classify as a good story with a sexual undercurrent. The writer should read several published short stories to see the general tone and style that we're looking for. The writer should keep in mind that the first requirement is that the story be a well written piece of fiction, and secondarily that it deal with sex; we are not interested in 'clinically descriptive' sex accounts. Due to limited space, writers should keep their stories within the word-length requirements as the time necessary to and possible ill effects of cutting longer pieces bode against their acceptance."

IDEALS MAGAZINE (II), Ideals Publishing Corp., Nelson Place at Elm Hill Pike, Nashville TN 37214. (615)885-8270. Vice President of Publishing: Patricia Pingry. Magazine: $8^7/16$x$10^7/8$; 80 pages; 60 lb Cougarpaper; 12 pt CI-S cover; illustrations; photos. *Ideals* is a family-oriented magazine with issues corresponding to seasons and based on traditional values. Published 8 times a year. Estab. 1944.
Needs: Seasonal, inspirational, spiritual, or humorous short, short fiction or prose poem. Beginning new policy of one short story per issue. Length: about 2,000 words.
How to Contact: Send complete ms with SASE. Reports in 8-12 weeks on mss.
Payment: Varies.
Terms: Pays on publication for one-time rights.
Advice: "Familiarize yourself with *Ideals* before submitting. We publish fiction that is appropriate to the theme of the issue and to our audience. Manuscript should be clean and stylistically correct."

IN TOUCH (II, IV), Wesleyan Press, Box 50434 Indianapolis IN 46250-0434. (317)576-8144. Editor: Angelyn Lively. Magazine: $8^1/2$x11; 32 pages; offset paper and cover stock; illustrations; photos. Publication for teens, ages 13-18. Monthly in weekly parts.
Needs: *True* experiences and Christian testimonies told in fiction style, humorous fiction, C.S. Lewis-type allegories and spiritual. Receives 100 unsolicited fiction mss/month. Recently published work by Betty Steele Everett, Muriel Larson, Blain and Penny Bargo; published new writers within the last year. Length: 500-1,200 words.
How to Contact: Send complete ms with SASE. "Queries are not encouraged." Accepts computer printout submissions; prefers letter-quality. Reports in 1-3 weeks on mss. Publishes ms 6-9 months after acceptance.
Payment: Pays 4¢/word, 2¢/word on reprints.
Terms: Pays on acceptance. Byline given and brief autobiographical sketch. Buys reprints.
Advice: "Send SASE for writer's guide before submitting. We are only using true events written in fiction style, humor and allegories. Most religious fiction is unrealistic."

IN TOUCH FOR MEN (IV), 7216 Varna St., North Hollywood CA 91605. (818)764-2288. Editor: Bob Stanford. Magazine: 8x$10^3/4$; 100 pages; glossy paper; coated cover; illustrations and photographs. "*In Touch* is a magazine for gay men. It features five nude male centerfolds in each issue, but is erotic rather than pornographic. We include fiction, articles, interviews, humor, cartoons, media comment."

Market categories: (I) Beginning; (II) General;
(III) Prestige; (IV) Specialized.

Monthly. Estab. 1973. Circ. 70,000.
Needs: Adventure, confession, contemporary, erotica, ethnic, experimental, fantasy, gay, historical, horror, humor, literary, regional, romance (contemporary, historical, young adult), science fiction, suspense/mystery, translations, western. All characters must be over 18 years old. Stories must have an explicit erotic content. No heterosexual or internalized homophobic fiction. Buys 3 mss/month; 36 mss/year. Publishes ms 3 months after acceptance. Length: 2,500 words average; no minimum; 3,500 words maximum. Sometimes critiques rejected mss and recommends other markets.
How to Contact: Send complete ms with cover letter, name, address and social security number. Reports in 1 week on queries; 2 months on mss. SASE. Simultaneous, photocopied and reprint submissions, if from local publication, OK. Accepts computer printout submissions, including dot-matrix. Sample copy $4.95. Fiction guidelines free.
Payment: $25-$75 (except on rare occasions for a longer piece).
Terms: Pays on acceptance for one-time rights. Publication copyrighted.
Advice: "Fiction is one of the most popular features of our magazine."

IN TOUCH TALKS (II), In Touch International Inc., 7216 Varna St., N. Hollywood CA 91605. Editor: Bob Stanford. Magazine: 5½x8½; 100 pages; coated paper; glossy cover; illustrations and photographs. "Writers and readers describe their true-life sexual experiences for a gay male audience." Quarterly. Estab. 1987.
Needs: Erotica, gay. "*I.T.T.* consists entirely of true-life sex experiences, plus a section of humor called 'Uncle Peter's Laff Trax.' " Receives 40-50 unsolicited fiction mss/month. Accepts 30 + mss/issue; 180 + mss/year. Publishes ms approximately 2 months after acceptance. Length: 750 + words. "Approximately 3 double-spaced typewritten pages, but may be shorter, no longer, however." Publishes short shorts. Sometimes critiques rejected mss; sometimes recommends other markets.
How to Contact: Send complete ms with cover letter. Reports in 1 month. SASE. Simultaneous, photocopied and reprint submissions OK. Accepts computer printout submissions, including dot-matrix. Sample copy $2.95; fiction guidelines free.
Payment: $25, 1 free contributor's copy.
Terms: Pays on acceptance for first North American serial rights. Publication copyrighted.
Advice: "There are few markets but good writers can make sales if very active."

INDIAN LIFE MAGAZINE (II, IV), Intertribal Christian Communications, Box 3765, Station B, Winnipeg, Manitoba RAW 3R6 Canada. (204)661-9333. Editor: George McPeek. Magazine: 8½x11; 24 pages; newsprint paper and cover stock; illustrations; photos. A nondenominational Christian magazine written and read mostly by North American Indians. Bimonthly. Estab. 1979. Circ. 50,000.
Needs: Adventure, confession, ethnic (Indian), historical (general), juvenile, men's, religious/inspirational, women's, and young adult/teen. Receives 2-3 unsolicited mss/month. Buys 1 ms/issue; 4-5 mss/year. Published new writers within the last year. Length: 1,000-1,200 words average. Publishes short shorts of 600-900 words. Occasionally comments on rejected mss.
How to Contact: Query first, send complete manuscript (with cover letter; bio and published clips), or query with clips of published work. Reports in 1 month on queries; in 2 months on mss. IRC or SASE ("US stamps no good up here"). Accepts computer printout submissions. Prefers letter-quality. Sample copy $1 and 8½x11 SAE. Fiction guidelines for $1 and #10 SAE.
Payment: 2¢-4¢/word and 5 contributor's copies; 50¢ charge for extras.
Terms: Pays on publication for first rights. Publication copyrighted.
Advice: "Keep it simple with an Indian viewpoint at about a 5th grade reading level. Read story out loud. Have someone else read it to you. If it doesn't come across smoothly and naturally, it needs work."

INSIDE (II), The Magazine of the Jewish Exponent, Jewish Federation, 226 S. 16th St., Philadelphia PA 19102. (215)893-5700. Editor-in-Chief: Jane Biberman. Magazine: 175-225 pages; glossy paper; illustrations; photos. Aimed at middle- and upper-middle-class audience, Jewish-oriented articles and fiction. Quarterly. Estab. 1980. Circ. 80,000.
Needs: Contemporary, ethnic, humor/satire, literary and translations. No erotica. Receives approximately 10 unsolicited fiction mss/month. Buys 1-2 mss/issue, 4-8 mss/year. Published new writers within the last year. Length: 1,500 words minimum; 3,000 words maximum; 2,000 words average. Occasionally critiques rejected mss.
How to Contact: Query first with clips of published work. Reports on queries in 3 weeks. SASE. Accepts computer printouts, no dot-matrix. Simultaneous and photocopied submissions OK. Sample copy $3. Free fiction guidelines with SASE.
Payment: $100-$600.
Terms: Pays on acceptance for first rights. Sometimes buys reprints. Sends galleys to author. Publication copyrighted.
Advice: "We're looking for original, avant-garde, stylish writing."

INSIDE KUNG FU, The Ultimate in Martial Arts Coverage (II, IV), Unique Publications, 4201 Vanowen Pl., Burbank CA 91505. (818)845-2656. Editorial Director: Dave Cater. Magazine of martial arts history, technique, philosophy, theory, training methods, and self defense (especially Chinese arts). Audience: mostly men, sports-oriented, ages 18-35. Monthly. Estab. 1973. Circ. 130,000.
Needs: "Want Chinese-flavored fiction, rather than Japanese (as in *Shogun*, etc.). No movie plots, please. We do not accept mundane, personal, diary-type writing." Receives 2 unsolicited fiction mss/month. Buys 1 ms/issue, 10 mss/year. Length: 1,000 words minimum; 4,000 words maximum; 2,000 words average, photographs with text expected. Usually critiques rejected mss.
How to Contact: Send complete ms with SASE. Accepts computer printout submissions. Prefers letter-quality. Reports in 4-6 weeks on mss. Publishes ms 3-9 months after acceptance. Sample copy $2.
Payment: $75-$150 and 2 contributor's copies.
Terms: Pays on publication for first North American serial rights. Publication copyrighted.
Advice: "We encourage manuscript submissions and will give personal attention to each."

INSIDE TEXAS RUNNING (II, IV), The Tabloid Magazine that Runs Texas, 9514 Bristlebrook, Houston TX 77083. (713)498-3208. Publisher/Editor: Joanne Schmidt. Specialized tabloid for Texas joggers/runners—novice to marathoner, bicycling, aerobics and general fitness. Monthly. Estab. 1977. Circ. 10,00; over all readers 30,000.
Needs: Historical, humor/satire, literary and serialized/excerpted books on running and general fitness. "Nothing sexually explicit—we're family oriented." Texas-oriented mss preferred. Buys 1 ms/issue. Length: 300 words minimum; 2,000 words maximum. Occasionally critiques rejected mss.
How to Contact: Query only. "We're overrun with too much to read. Not accepting mss at this time." Simultaneous, photocopied and previously published submissions OK. Reports in 4 weeks. Sample copy $1.50. Free fiction guidelines with SASE.
Payment: $25-$75.
Terms: Pays on acceptance for one-time rights. Publication copyrighted.
Advice: "If a writer has something useful and original to convey, editors will want to buy his work. Period. A writer should ask himself if he, as a reader, would find the story worth reading. Too many writers can't look beyond their own experiences and relate very boring personal incident, which they disguise as fiction."

INSIGHTS (II, IV), NRA News for Young Shooters, National Rifle Association of America, 1600 Rhode Island Ave. NW, Washington DC 20036. (202)828-6059. Editor: Brenda K. Dalessandro. Magazine: 8 1/8x10 7/8; 24 pages; 60 lb Midset paper and cover; illustrations and photos. "*InSights* publishes educational yet entertaining articles, teaching young hunters and shooters ways to improve their performance. For boys and girls ages eight to 20." Monthly. Estab. 1981. Circ. 46,000.
Needs: Hunting or competition shooting. No "anti-hunting, anti-firearms." Receives 5-10 unsolicited mss/month. Accepts 1 ms/issue; 12 mss/year. Publishes ms an average of 1 month to 1 year after acceptance. Recently published work by Jim Mize, Jim Ottman, Connie Mertz. Length: 1,000 words minimum; 1,500 words maximum. Publishes short shorts. Sometimes critiques rejected ms; occasionally recommends other markets.
How to Contact: Query with clips of published work and cover letter. Reports in 1 month on query; 6-8 weeks on mss. SASE. Photocopied submissions OK. Accepts computer printout submissions, including dot-matrix. Sample copy and fiction guidelines free.
Payment: $100 maximum.
Terms: Pays on acceptance. Publication copyrighted.
Advice: "Writing is an art but publishing is a business—a big business. Any writer who understands his market place has an edge over a writer who isn't familiar with the publications that want his kind of writing."

JACK AND JILL, The Benjamin Franklin Literary & Medical Society, Inc., 1100 Waterway Blvd., Box 567, Indianapolis IN 46206. (317)636-8881. Editor: Steve Charles. Children's magazine of articles, stories and activities many with a health, safety, exercise or nutritional-oriented theme, ages 6-8 years. Monthly except February/March, April/May, June/July, August/September. Estab. 1938.
Needs: Science fiction, mystery, sports, adventure, historical fiction and humor. Health-related stories with a subtle lesson. No religious subjects. Length: 500-1,500 words.
How to Contact: Send complete ms with SASE. Reports in 10 weeks on mss. Sample copy 75¢. Free fiction guidelines with SASE.
Payment: 8¢/word.
Terms: Pays on publication for all rights.
Advice: "Try to present health material in a positive—not a negative—light. Use humor and a light approach wherever possible without minimizing the seriousness of the subject."

THE JEWISH MONTHLY, B'nai B'rith International, 1640 Rhode Island Ave. NW, Washington DC 20036. (202)857-6645. Editor: Marc Silver. Jewish general interest magazine that publishes occasional short stories; journalistic articles (political, cultural, sociological), and book reviews. Family audience. Monthly. Estab. 1886. Circ. 200,000.
Needs: Ethnic, historical, humor, literary and religious. Receives 2 unsolicited mss/month. Buys 2 mss/year. Length: 3,000 words average; 1,000 words minimum; 5,000 words maximum. Occasionally critiques rejected mss.
How to Contact: Send complete ms. Reports in 1 month. Publishes ms 3-9 months after acceptance. SASE. Photocopied submissions OK. Sample copy $1.
Payment: 10-20¢/word; 2 contributor's copies.
Terms: Pays on publication for first North American serial rights. Publication copyrighted.

JIVE, BLACK CONFESSIONS, BLACK ROMANCE, BRONZE THRILLS (I, II), Sterling's Magazines/ Lexington Library, 355 Lexington Ave., New York NY 10017. (212)391-1400. Editor: Nathasha Brooks. Magazine: 8½x11; 72 pages; newsprint paper; glossy cover; 8x10 photographs. "We publish stories that are ultra romantic and have romantic lovemaking scenes in them. Our audience is basically young and in high school and college. However, we have a significant audience base of divorcees and housewives. The age range is from 18-49." Bimonthly (*Jive* and *Black Romance* in odd-numbered months; *Black Confessions* and *Bronze Thrills* in even-numbered months). Estab. 1962. Circ. 100,000.
Needs: Confession, romance (contemporary, young adult), spiritual. No "stories that are stereotypical to black people, ones that do not follow the basic rules of writing, or ones that are too sexual in content and lack a romantic element." Receives 200 or more unsolicited fiction mss/month. Buys 12 mss/issue; 144 mss/year. Publishes ms an average of 3-6 months after acceptance. Recently published work by Francis Ray, Nancy Bulk, Jean Newsome; published new writers within the last year. Length: 12-15 pages. Always critiques rejected mss; recommends other markets.
How to Contact: Query with clips of published work or send complete ms with cover letter. "I'd prefer a combination of the two. A cover letter should include an author's bio, professionally, and what he or she proposes to do. Of course, address and phone number." Reports in 3-6 months. SASE. Simultaneous and photocopied submissions OK. "Please contact me if simultaneosly submitted work has been accepted elsewhere." Accepts computer printout submissions, including dot-matrix. Sample copy for 9x12 SAE and 5 first class stamps; fiction guidelines for #10 SAE and 2 first class stamps.
Payment: $75-$100.
Terms: Pays on publication for first rights or one-time rights. Publication copyrighted.
Advice: "My four magazines are a great starting point for new writers. I accept work from beginners as well as established writers. In fact, I prefer the newer writers because they can be molded and will take more criticism and advice. They will look at my comments and do the rewrite and resubmit their work. My first suggestion is that any writer who wants to submit work to us should spell my name correctly. Please study and research black culture and lifestyles if you are not a black writer. Stereotypical stories are not acceptable. Set the stories all over the world and all over the USA—not just down south. We are not looking for 'the runaway who gets turned out by a sweet-talking pimp' stories. We are looking for stories about ruthless female characters. It is very important to write some storylines about 'the bitch goddess.' Any writer should not be afraid to communicate with me if he or she is having some difficulty with writing a story. I am available to help at any stage of the submission process. Also, writers should practice patience. Not hearing from me is a good sign. If I do not contact the writer, that means that the story is being read or is being held on file for future publication. If I get in touch with the writer, it usually means a rejection or a request for revision and resubmission. Do the best work possible and don't let rejection slips send you off 'the deep end.' Don't take everything that is said about your work so personally. We are buying all of our work from freelance writers. We have a need for stories with high school aged characters."

JOCK MAGAZINE (II,IV), Klinger International Inc., Suite 210, 7715 Sunset Blvd., Los Angeles CA 90046. (213)850-5353. Editor: Robert Leighton. Magazine. 8x10⅞; 100 pages; coated paper; 80 lb cover stock; illustrations and photographs. "Heavy gay sexual. All stories in first person." Monthly. Has published special fiction issue. Estab. 1985. Circ. 125,000.
Needs: Erotica, gay. Gay erotic stories only. Receives 50-75 unsolicited fiction mss/month. Accepts 8-10 mss/issue; 120 mss/year. Publishes ms 3-4 months after acceptance. Recently published work by Michael Hill, Forrest Hooper, Brad Turbo; published new writers within the last year. Length: 2,000 words average; 1,500 words minimum; 2,500 words maximum. Publishes short shorts. Sometimes critiques rejected mss and recommends other markets.
How to Contact: Send complete ms with cover letter. Reports in 2 weeks on queries; 1 month on mss. SASE. Photocopied submissions OK. Accepts computer printout submissions, including dot-matrix. Sample copy $6; fiction guidelines free with SASE.
Payment: $75-$100.

Terms: Pays on publication for first rights and first North American serial rights. Publication copyrighted.
Advice: "There should be a distinct clarity of the writer's name and address (name on check) and the desired byline. Many writers use only their byline and bark when they get a check they can't cash. An emphasis on safe sex is important. Unusual ideas and off-beat characters catch an editor's attention. Will save a story and fix if problems are minor and style is fresh."

JUGGLER'S WORLD (IV), International Juggler's Association, Box 443, Davidson NC 28036. (704)892-1296. Editor: Bill Giduz. Fiction Editor: Ken Letko. Magazine: 8½x11; 44 pages; 70 lb paper and cover stock; illustrations and photos. For and about jugglers and juggling. Quarterly.
Needs: Historical (general), humor/satire, science fiction. No stories "that don't include juggling as a central theme." Receives "very few" unsolicited mss/month. Accepts 2 mss/year. Publishes ms an average of 6 months to 1 year after acceptance. Length: 1,000 words average; 500 words minimum; 2,000 words maximum. Publishes short shorts. Sometimes critiques rejected mss.
How to Contact: Query first. Reports in 1 week. Simultaneous and photocopied submissions OK. Accepts computer printout submissions, including dot-matrix. Accepts electronic submissions via IBM compatible disk. Sample copy $2.
Payment: $25-$50, free subscription to magazine, 5 contributor's copies.
Terms: Pays on acceptance for first rights. Publication copyrighted.

JUNIOR TRAILS (I, II), Gospel Publishing House, 1445 Boonville Ave., Springfield MO 65802. (417)862-2781. Elementary Editor: Cathy Ketcher. Magazine: 8½x11; 4 pages; 36 lb coated offset paper; coat and matte cover stock; art illustrations; photos. A Sunday School take-home paper of nature articles and fictional stories that apply Christian principles to everyday living for 9-12 year old children. Weekly. Estab. 1954. Circ. 70,000.
Needs: Contemporary, religious/inspirational, spiritual, sports and juvenile. Adventure stories are welcome. No Biblical fiction or science fiction. Buys 2 mss/issue. Publishes short shorts. Recently published work by Betty Lou Mell, Miriam Gautier and Dorothy Rustebakke. Published new writers within the last year. Length: 1,000-1,800 words.
How to Contact: Send complete ms with SASE. Accepts computer printout submissions. Reports 6-8 weeks on mss. Free sample copy and guidelines.
Payment: 2½-3¢/word. 3 free author's copies.
Terms: Pays on acceptance for first rights.
Advice: "Know the age level and direct stories relevant to that age group. Since junior-age children (grades 5 and 6) enjoy action, fiction provides a vehicle for communicating moral/spiritual principles in a dramatic framework. Fiction, if well done, can be a powerful tool for relating Christian principles. It must, however, be realistic and believable in its development. Make your children be children, not overly mature for their age."

KID CITY (II), (formerly *The Electric Company*), Children's Telelvision Workshop, 1 Lincoln Plaza, New York NY 10023. (212)595-3456. Editor: Maureen Hunter-Bone. Magazine: 8½x11; 32 pages; glossy cover; illustrations; photos. General interest for children 6-10 "devoted to sparking kids' interest in reading and writing about the world around them." Published 10 times/year. Estab. 1974. Circ. 260,000.
Needs: Adventure, fantasy, juvenile (6-10 years), science fiction. Publishes ms 6 months "at least" after acceptance. Length: 600-750 words average; 1,000 words maximum.
How to Contact: Send complete ms with cover letter. Reports in 1-2 months on mss. SASE. Photocopied submissions OK. Accepts computer printout submissions, including dot-matrix. Sample copy $1.50 and 9x12 SAE with 75¢ postage. Writers' guidelines free for 9x12 SAE with 75¢ postage.
Payment: Pays $200-$400 and contributor's copies.
Terms: Pays on acceptance for all rights (some negotiable). Publication copyrighted.
Advice: "We look for bright and sparkling prose. Don't talk down. Don't stereotype. Don't use cutesy names, animals or plots. No heavy moralizing or pat dilemmas. Be original. Write about what you know."

KINDERGARTEN LISTEN (IV), Beacon Hill Press, Box 419527, Kansas City MO 64141. (816)931-1900 or (816)333-7000 (editorial). Editor: Jan Sawyer. Fiction Editor: Lisa Ham. Tabloid: 4 page story paper; 8½x11; newsprint; newsprint cover; b&w and 4 color illustrations; 4 color photos. "Stories cover a 2-year topic cycle available upon request. Readers are kindergarten 4s, 5s and early 6s." Weekly. Estab. 1981. Circ. 45,000.
Needs: Contemporary, prose poem, religious/inspirational, spiritual, Christian topic themes. Recently published work by Barbara Kraus, Donna Colwell Rosser, V. J. Luckery. Length: 200 words minimum; 400 words maximum. Sometimes critiques rejected mss and recommends other markets.

Close-up

Lisa Ham
Kindergarten LISTEN

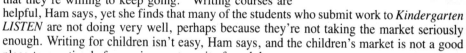

"I've got several writers who started out doing really poorly," says Lisa Ham. "And I tried to offer suggestions when they did submit. They've probably seen 100 pink slips, and they still try to learn from the last one and they try it again. Those kind of writers we really need; people who want so much to contribute to the children's market that they're willing to keep going." Writing courses are helpful, Ham says, yet she finds that many of the students who submit work to *Kindergarten LISTEN* are not doing very well, perhaps because they're not taking the market seriously enough. Writing for children isn't easy, Ham says, and the children's market is not a good place to practice before going on to write for adults.

Ham is the first reader of the 20-50 stories that come in the mail to *Kindergarten LISTEN* each month. The first thing she does is check the word count and return stories longer than 400 words and those that are obviously inappropriate for the weekly Sunday School take-home paper. Stories Ham finds of interest are also read by another editor and by *Kindergarten LISTEN*'s editorial director. Those stories which are accepted are filed to be published at the correct time in the magazine's recently updated two-year cycle of themes.

Above all, Ham looks for realism in stories—stories "that don't portray children or parents as too good or too bad." A common "problem" story Ham sees is what she calls the Beaver Cleaver story, where "the child is perfect and speaks well and acts well and shares well."

Sharing is a subject that writers seem to find particularly difficult to work with, in part because "sharing is not necessarily something that comes without parental guidance," Ham says. "A lot of stories we get lack that adult guidance—the child comes up with things on his own that the average 4-year-old child could not do." Not infrequently, Ham says, "if we purchase a story, we have to write in an adult's inference that the child should share—some kind of urging on the adult's part instead of having the child come up with an idea on his own."

Since *Kindergarten LISTEN* is connected with the Church of the Nazarene, it's important that writers not deal with subjects involving dice, card playing or movies, Ham says. She's also bothered by stories relating to children in obviously unsafe situations and who in general lack parental supervision. Ham gets little mail from children—but one story about a single father and his son—in which there was no mother at home to take care of the child—did anger conservative readers. Ham asserts the importance of ministering to children from divorced families, however, as well as to children of different racial and economic backgrounds. She says also that since most of the stories are read to children by their parents, she likes to receive fiction that will not only reach children but will also "subtly instruct the adult reading the story about the proper way to handle things."

To writers interested in selling stories to *Kindergarten LISTEN*, Ham urges, "know the subject matter, the children's abilities, their interests. Read about them and read popular texts for the age group and then just write and write and write. It takes time, but it can be done—and it is very rewarding."

—*Laurie Henry*

How to Contact: Query first "if unfamiliar with 2-year topic cycle." or send complete mss. Writers must include SASE for each submission. Reports in 3 weeks on queries; in 1 month on mss. SASE. Photocopied submissions OK. Accepts computer printout submissions, including dot-matrix. Accepts electronic submissions via disk or modem in ASCII text only. Sample copy and fiction guidelines for 8 ½x11 SAE and 1 first class stamp.

Payment: Pays $10-$12 minimum and $17 maximum, with contributor's copies (4 each purchase). Charge for extra copies.

Terms: Pays on acceptance for all rights, first rights or one-time rights (as specified by author).

Advice: "A majority of submissions we've received lately are of poor quality. Dialogue and actions of main child characters are unrealistic to the young age group our magazine ministers to. Actions and dialogue of parent characters is often too unrealistic as well. They're either too good to be true or very stilted in actions and speech. Because today's children are growing up in a rough world, we seek to help them deal with a variety of situations from divorce to the simple worries of a young child, like being left with a new babysitter. We seek to portray fictional children finding real solutions in the love and guidance of Christ, assisted by parent and other adult figures. Too many submissions appear to come from writers who don't take the children's market seriously or view it as an easy area to write prose for. In fact, children's stories require research and realism, and much effort in writing and rewriting. Writers have to know the audience well, not just guess or try to recall what it was like to be a Pre-K kid. Few writers can relate well enough to produce good manuscripts without these efforts." Criteria used in choosing fiction: "(1) Does it relate to our theme titles for the 2-year cycle (2) Is the story interesting to children (3) Does it assist them in understanding some vital area of the Christian life, God's love, etc. (4) Is it realistic in portrayal of all characters (5) Does it flow naturally and make for good reading (6) Does the story line progress logically (7) Does it include any inappropriate references to parent behavior, an accepted practice or doctrine of the Church of the Nazarene. Ex: We've had a hair-raising number of writers portraying scenes where children are left unattended in shopping malls or some other public place—which is highly inappropriate parental behavior considering the abduction situation that has terrorized our country's parents and families. The portrayal shows little insight on the writer's part."

LADIES' HOME JOURNAL (III), (Published by Meredith Corporation), 100 Park Ave., New York NY 10017. Editor-in-Chief: Myrna Blyth. Fiction/Books Editor: Mary Lou Mullen. Magazine: 190 pages; 34-38 lb coated paper; 65 lb coated cover; illustrations and photos.

Needs: Book mss and short stories, *accepted only through an agent*. Return of unsolicited material cannot be guaranteed. Publishes short shorts of 3,500 words approximately.

How to Contact: Cover letter with ms (credits). Publishes ms 4-12 months after acceptance.

Terms: Rarely buys reprints.

Advice: "Our readers like stories, especially those that have emotional impact. We are using fiction every month, whether it's an excerpt from a novel or a short story. Stories about relationships between people—husband/wife—mother/son—seem to be subjects that can be explored effectively in short stories. Our reader's mail and surveys attest to this fact: Readers enjoy our fiction, and are most keenly tuned to stories dealing with children. Fiction today is stronger than ever. Beginners can be optimistic; if they have talent, I do believe that talent will be discovered."

‡LADYS CIRCLE (II), Lopez Publications, 105 East 35th St., New York NY 10016. (212)689-3933. Fiction Editor: Mary Bemis. Magazine. "A lot of our readers are in Midwestern states." Monthly. Estab. 1963. Circ. 300,000.

Needs: Confession, ethnic, historical, humor/satire, juvenile, mainstream, religious/inspirational, romance (contemporary, historical, young adult), senior citizen/retirement, young adult/teen. Receives 100 unsolicited fiction mss/month. Buys 3-4 fiction mss/issue; about 6-7 fiction mss/year. Time between acceptance and publication "varies, usually works 2 months ahead." Length: 3,000 words preferred; 1,000 words minimum; 3,000 words maximum. Accepts short shorts "for fillers." Sometimes critiques rejected ms.

How to Contact: Query first. Reports in up to 3 months on queries. SASE. Simultaneous, photocopied and reprint submissions OK. Accepts electronic submissions via disk or modem. Sample copy for $1.95; fiction guidelines for SAE.

Payment: Pay varies, depending on ms.

Terms: Pays on publication for first North American serial rights. Publication copyrighted.

LATTER-DAY WOMAN MAGAZINE (II), 547 W, 9460 S. #126, Sandy UT 84070. (801)255-5239. Fiction Editor: Marsha Newman. Magazine: 5⅜x8⅜; 48-64 pages; slick 60 lb paper; 70 lb cover; mostly b&w illustrations; approx. 4 color photos per issue, 1 or 2 b&w photos. "Our purpose is to offer inspiration and support to help women cope with challenges. We explore today's issues with an uplifting, reassuring perspective. Theme: to help overcome feelings of isolation and discouragment for Christian women, mainstream women, mostly mothers juggling many roles. Age range 20-up. Largest concentration between age 35-60." Bimonthly. Estab. 1986. Circ. 15,000.

Needs: Humor/satire, literary, mainstream, religious/inspirational. "We want stories dealing with women and their problems, written in a convincing, realistic fashion. They must leave the reader with a sense of warmth or comfort or humorous identification." Receives approx. 25 unsolicited fiction mss/month. Accepts 2 mss/issue; 12 mss/year. Length: 700 words average; 1,250 words maximum. Publishes short shorts. Sometimes critiques rejected mss and may recommend other markets.

How to Contact: Send complete ms—no cover letter required. Reports in 3 months. SASE. Simultaneous, photocopied and reprint submissions OK. Accepts computer printout submissions, including dot-matrix. Fiction guidelines for #10 SASE.

Payment: 5¢/word.

Terms: Pays on publication for first rights. Sends pre-publication galleys to author. Publication copyrighted.

Advice: "Our readers love fiction. We don't receive nearly enough of it. We quickly print any fiction of exceptional quality and short length that comes our way. Many insights can be shared in a non-preachy way thru fiction and feedback from our readers assures us of their enthusiasm for a good story. We prefer that stories make a point, give a fresh insight, leave a feeling of completion."

LEFTHANDER MAGAZINE (II, IV), Lefthanders International, Box 8249, Topeka KS 66608. (913)234-2177. Editor: Suzan Ireland. Magazine: 32 pages; 70 lb gloss paper and cover; illustrations; photos. "We accept fiction for juvenile insert, ages 9-15, which has some connection to lefthandedness." Bimonthly. Estab. 1975. Circ. 23,000.

Needs: Children/young teen (9-15); special interest: lefthandedness. Buys 3 fiction mss/year. Publishes ms 2 months after acceptance. Published new writers within the last year. Length: 750-1,000 words average. Occasionally critiques rejected mss.

How to Contact: Query first. Reports in 3 weeks on queries; 3 weeks on mss. SASE. Accepts computer printouts including dot-matrix. Sample copy $2. Fiction guidelines free for #10 SAE and 1 first class stamp.

Payment: Pays $40-$75.

Terms: Pays on publication for all rights. Publication copyrighted.

LIGHTED PATHWAY (II), Church of God Publishing House (Pathway Press), 922 Montgomery Ave., Cleveland TN 37311. (615)476-4512. Editor: Marcus V. Hand. Magazine: 8½x11; 28 pages; b&w photos. Christian, evangelical, youth inspiration magazine (ages 15-25) with at least two fiction short stories per issue. Monthly. Estab. 1929. Circ. 26,000.

Needs: Adventure, contemporary, feminist, historical (general), humor/satire, juvenile, religious/inspirational and young adult. "Real life problems, no profanity." Receives 1-24 unsolicited fiction mss/month. Buys 2 (minimum) mss/issue; 24 (minimum) mss/year. Published new writers within the last year. Length: 800-1,200 words preferred; 1,500 words maximum. Occasionally critiques rejected mss.

How to Contact: Query first or send complete ms. SASE always. Simultaneous and previously published submissions OK sometimes. Accepts computer printout submissions. Prefers letter-quality. Reports in 3 weeks on queries and mss. Free sample copy and fiction guidelines with SASE.

Payment: 2-5¢/word; 3 contributor's copies. 75¢ charge for extras.

Terms: Pays on acceptance for first North American serial rights and one-time rights. Publication copyrighted.

Advice: "Study a sample. Make story exciting."

LIGUORIAN (I, IV), "A Leading Catholic Magazine", Liguori Publications, 1 Liguori Dr., Liguori MO 63057. (314)464-2500. Editor-in-Chief: Norman J. Muckerman, CSS.R. Managing Editor: Francine M. O'Connor. Magazine: 5x8½; 64 pages; b&w illustrations and photographs. "*Liguorian* is a Catholic magazine aimed at helping our readers to live a full Christian life. We publish articles for families, young people, children, religious and singles—all with the same aim." Monthly. Estab. 1913. Circ. 500,000.

Needs: Religious/inspirational, young adult and senior citizen/retirement (with moral Christian thrust), spiritual. "Stories submitted to *Liguorian* must have as their goal the lifting up of the reader to a higher Christian view of values and goals. We are not interested in contemporary works that lack purpose or are of questionable moral value." Receives approximately 25 unsolicited fiction mss/month. Buys 4-5 mss/year. Recently published work by Mitch Finley, Sharon Helgens and Louis G. Miller, CSS.R. Published new writers within the last year. Length: 1,500-2,000 words preferred. Also publishes short shorts. Occasionally critiques rejected mss "if we feel the author is capable of giving us something we need even though this story did not suit us." Occasionally recommends other markets.

How to Contact: Send complete ms with SASE. Accepts computer printout submissions; prefers letter-quality. Accepts disk submissions compatible with TRS-80 Model III. Prefers hard copy with disk submission. Reports in 6 weeks on mss. Sample copy for $1.25; free fiction guidelines..

Payment: 7-10¢/word and 6 contributor's copies. Offers 50% kill fee for assigned mss not published.
Terms: Pays on acceptance for all rights. Publication copyrighted.
Advice: "First read several issues containing short stories. We look for originality and creative input in each story we read. Since most editors must wade through mounds of manuscripts each month, consideration for the editor requires that the market be studied, the manuscript be carefully presented and polished before submitting. Our publication uses only one story a month. Compare this with the 25 or more we receive over the transom each month. Also, many fiction mss are written without a specific goal or thrust, i.e., an interesting incident that goes nowhere is *not a story*. We believe fiction is a highly effective mode for transmitting the Christian message and also provides a good balance in an unusually heavy issue."

LIVE, Assemblies of God, 1445 Boonville, Springfield MO 65802. (417)862-2781. Editor: John Maempa. A Sunday School take-home paper for adults containing stories and articles of believable characters working out their problems according to Bible principles. Weekly. Circ. 192,000.
Needs: Religious/inspirational, prose poem and spiritual. No controversial stories about such subjects as feminism, war or capital punishment. Buys 2 mss/issue. Recently published work by Betty Steele Everett, C. Ellen Watts, Joyce E. Kelley; published new writers within the last year. Length: 1,000-2,000 words.
How to Contact: Send complete ms with SASE. Social Security number must be included. Free sample copy and fiction guidelines only with SASE.
Payment: 3¢/word (first rights); 2¢/word (second rights).
Terms: Pays on acceptance for one-time rights.
Advice: "Closely study needs of a given publisher (what he has published) and match with the story in question."

LIVING WITH TEENAGERS (II), Baptist Sunday School Board, 127 9th Ave. North, Nashville TN 37234. (615)251-2273. Editor: Jimmy Hester. Magazine: 10⅜x8⅛; 50 pages; illustrations; photos. Magazine especially designed "to enrich the parent-teen relationship, with reading material from a Christian perspective" for Southern Baptist parents of teenagers. Quarterly. Estab. 1978. Circ. 50,000.
Needs: Religious/inspirational, spiritual and parent-teen relationships. Nothing not related to parent-teen relationships or not from a Christian perspective. Buys 2 mss/issue. Receives approximately 50 unsolicited fiction mss/month. Published new writers within the last year. Length: 600-1,200 words (short shorts).
How to Contact: Cover letter with reason for writing article; credentials for writing. Query with clips of published work or send complete ms. SASE always. Reports in 2 months on both queries and mss. Free sample copy with 9x12 SAE and proper postage.
Payment: 5¢/published word. 3 free author's copies.
Terms: Pays on acceptance for all and first rights. Publication copyrighted.
Advice: Mss are rejected most often because "subject is inappropriate, the events and characters are unrealistic. Sometimes a fictitious story can communicate a principle in the parent-youth relationship quite well."

LLAMAS MAGAZINE (IV), The International Camelid Journal, Clay Press Inc., Box 100, Herald CA 95638. (209)748-2620. Editor: Cheryl Dal Porto. Magazine: 8½x11; 112+ pages; glossy paper; 80 lb glossy cover stock; illustrations and pictures. For llama owners and lovers. 8 issues/year. Estab. 1979. Circ. 5,000.
Needs: Adventure, historical, humor/satire. Receives 15-25 unsolicited fiction mss/month. Accepts 1-4 mss/issue; 6-12 mss/year. Publishes ms usually 3-4 months after acceptance. 15% of fiction is agented. Length; 2,000-3,000 words average. Publishes short shorts. Length: 300-1,000 words. Sometimes critiques rejected mss.
How to Contact: Send query to: Susan L. Jones, *Llamas* Asst. Editor, Box 1038, Dublin, Ohio 43017. Reports in 1 month. Reprint submissions OK. Accepts computer printout submissions, including dot-marix. Accepts electronic submissions via Apple 2 disk. Fiction guidelines free.
Payment: $25-$500, free subscription to magazine, contributor's copies.
Terms: Pays on publication for first rights, first North American serial rights and one-time rights. Sends pre-publication galleys to author if requested. Publication copyrighted.

‡LOLLIPOPS, LADYBUGS AND LUCKY STARS (II), Good Apple, Inc., Box 299, Carthage IL 62321. (217)357-3981. Editor: Cindy Stansbery. Newspaper: 11x16; 32 pages; illustrations. "Preschool-2nd grade publication for teachers and their students. All educational material. Short stories, poems, activities, math, gameboards." 5 times/year. Estab. 1980. Circ. 16,000.
Needs: Preschool-grade 2. Submissions cover all areas of the curriculum. Seasonal materials considered. Receives 30-40 unsolicited mss/month. Number of fiction mss bought varies per issue.

How to Contact: Query first or write for guidelines and a free sample copy. Reports in 1 week on queries. SASE for ms. Accepts computer printouts including dot-matrix. Send for free sample copies and guidelines.
Payment: Depends on story.
Terms: Pays on publication for all rights. Publication copyrighted.

THE LOOKOUT (II), Standard Publishing, 8121 Hamilton Ave., Cincinnati OH 45231. (513)931-4050. Editor: Mark A. Taylor. Magazine: 8½x11; 16 pages; newsprint paper; newsprint cover stock; illustrations; photos. "Conservative Christian magazine for adults and young adults." Weekly. Estab. 1894. Circ. 140,000 + .
Needs: Religious/inspirational. No predictable, preachy material. Taboos are blatant sex, swear words and drinking alcohol. Receives 50 unsolicited mss/month. Buys 1 ms/issue; buys 45-50 mss/year. Published new writers within the last year. Length: 1,200-2,000 words.
How to Contact: Send complete ms with SASE. Accepts computer printout submissions. Prefers letter-quality. Reports in 2 months on ms. Simultaneous, photocopied and reprint submissions OK. Publishes ms 2-12 months after acceptance. Sample copy 50¢. Free guidelines with #10 SASE.
Payment: 5-6¢/word for first rights. 4-5¢/word for other rights. Free author's copies.
Terms: Pays on acceptance for one-time rights. Buys reprints.
Advice: "No queries please. Send us a believable story which is inspirational and helpful but down to earth."

THE LUTHERAN JOURNAL, Outlook Publications, Inc., 7317 Cahill Rd., Minneapolis MN 55435. (612)941-6830. Editor: Rev. A.U. Deye. A family magazine providing wholesome and inspirational reading material for the enjoyment and enrichment of Lutherans. Quarterly. Estab. 1936. Circ. 136,000.
Needs: Literary, contemporary, religious/inspirational, romance (historical), senior citizen/retirement and young adult. Must be appropriate for distribution in the churches. Buys 2-4 mss/issue. Length: 1,000-2,500 words.
How to Contact: Send complete ms with SASE. Accepts computer printout submissions. Free sample copy with SASE (59¢ postage).
Payment: $10-$25. 6 free author's copies.
Terms: Pays on publication for all and first rights.

‡LUTHERAN WOMAN TODAY (IV), Published by: Augsburg Fortress, Box 1209, Minneapolis, MN 55440. LWT editorial offices: 8765 West Higgins Rd., Chicago IL 60631. (380)312-2743. Editor: Nancy Stelling. Fiction Editor: Sue Edison-Swift. Magazine: 5⅜x8⅜; 48 pages; 40 lb paper; illustrations; photos. Publishes solicited and freelance theological articles, fiction, good devotional pieces, articles of interest to women. "A magazine for women of the Evangelical Lutheran Church in America 'for growth in faith and mission.' " Monthly. Estab. 1988. Circ. 300,000.
Needs: Faith-related-to-life, religious/inspirational, advocacy/peace and justice, feminist. "We look for short (700-1,000 words), well written work of special interest to Christian women." Receives 10-15 mss/month. Buys 5-10 mss/year. Publishes ms within 1 year of acceptance. Recently published work by Carol Bly, Joyce Ditmanson. Length: 700 words average; 1,200 words maximum. Publishes short shorts. Length: 350 words.
How to Contact: Send complete ms with cover letter which should include name, address, phone, word count, *rights offered*. Reports on queries in 3 months; on mss in 2 months. SASE. Accepts computer printout submissions, including dot-matrix. Sample copy for $1 and 5x7 SAE. Fiction guidelines for #10 SAE and 1 first class stamp.
Payment: Pays per printed page.
Terms: Pays on acceptance for first rights and one-time rights. Sometimes offers kill fee. Publication copyrighted.

M.A. TRAINING, Rainbow Publications, 1813 Victory Place, Burbank CA 91504. (818)843-4444. Editor: William Groak. Magazine: 88 pages; illustrations. "*M.A. Training* is a magazine limited to self-training aspects of martial arts." Quarterly. Estab. 1973. Circ. 75,000.
Needs: Self-training techniques, some fiction pertaining to the arts, workout routines, history. No erotica, and anything else that does not pertain to our focus." Receives 5-10 unsolicited mss/month. Buys 2-3 ms/issue; 6 mss/year. Length: 1,500 + words. Occasionally critiques rejected mss. Recommends other markets.
How to Contact: Query first or call 1-800-423-2874. Reports in 2-4 weeks on queries and mss. SASE for query and ms. Simultaneous and photocopied submissions OK. Accepts computer printouts, including dot-matrix. Sample copy free with SASE. Fiction guidelines free.
Payment: Pays $75-$150.

Terms: Pays on publication for first North American serial rights. Publication copyrighted.
Advice: "As a martial arts magazine, we need stories that will satisfy our core readership, but also some that could interest non-martial artists. Fiction not only gives the reader a break, but also provides a change in terms of what issues can be addressed and how they can be presented."

MADEMOISELLE MAGAZINE, Condé Nast Publications, Inc., 350 Madison Ave., New York NY 10017. (212)880-8690. Fiction Editor: Eileen Schnurr. Fashion magazine for women from ages 18-34 with articles of interest to women; beauty and health tips, features, home and food, fiction. Audience interested in self-improvement, curious about trends, interested in updating lifestyle and pursuing a career. Monthly. Estab. 1935. Circ. 1.1 million.
Needs: Literary and contemporary short stories. Publishes 1-2 ms/issue, 12-20 mss/year. Recently published work by Maxine Kawui, Mary Gordon, Kelly Cherry; published new writers within the last year. Length: 7-25 pages.
How to Contact: Send complete ms with SASE. Reports in 3 months. Publishes ms up to a year after acceptance. Free fiction guidelines with SASE.
Payment: $1,000 minimum for short shorts; $1,500 for short stories.
Terms: Pays on acceptance for first North American serial rights.
Advice: "We are particularly interested in stories of relevance to young single women, and we continue in the *Mademoiselle* tradition of publishing fiction of literary quality. Be sure to see the listing in Contest and Awards section for guidelines for *Mademoiselle's* Fiction Writers Contest."

THE MAGAZINE FOR CHRISTIAN YOUTH! (II), The United Methodist Publishing House, 201 8th Avenue S., Nashville TN 37202. (615)749-6463. Editor: Christopher B. Hughes. Magazine: 8½x11; 52 pages; slick, matte finish paper. "*The Magazine for Christian Youth!* tries to help teenagers develop Christian identity and live their faith in contemporary culture. Fiction and nonfiction which contributes to this purpose are welcome." Monthly. Estab. 1985. Circ. 45,000.
Needs: Adventure, contemporary, ethnic, fantasy, humor/satire, prose poem, religious/inspirational, science fiction, spiritual, suspense/mystery, translations, young adult/teen (10-18 years). "Don't preach; but story should have a message to help teenagers in some way or to make them think more deeply about an issue. No Sunday School lessons, like those found in curriculum." Receives 50-75 unsolicited mss/month. Buys 1-2 mss/issue; 12-24 mss/year. Publishes ms 9-12 months after acceptance. Length: 700-2,000 words. Publishes short shorts.
How to Contact: Send complete ms with cover letter. Reports in 3-6 months. SASE. Simultaneous and reprint submissions OK. Accepts computer printouts, including dot-matrix. Sample copy and fiction guidelines free for #10 SASE.
Payment: Pays $1.50 minimum, 4¢/word.
Terms: Pays on acceptance for first North American serial rights or one-time rights. Publication copyrighted.
Advice: "Get a feel for our magazine first. Don't send in the types of fiction that would appear in Sunday School curriculum just because it's a Christian publication. Reflect the real world of teens in contemporary fiction."

‡MAGAZINE OF FANTASY AND SCIENCE FICTION (II), Box 56, Cornwall CT 06753. (203)672-6376. Publisher/Editor: Edward Ferman. Magazine: illustrations on cover only. Publishes "science fiction and fantasy. Our readers are age 13 and up who are interested in science fiction and fantasy." Monthly. Plans special fiction issue. Estab. 1949.
Needs: Fantasy and science fiction. Receives "hundreds" of unsolicited fiction submissions/month. Buys 8 fiction mss/issue ("on average"). Time between acceptance and publication varies. Length: 10,000 words maximum. Publishes short shorts. Critiques rejected ms, "if quality warrants it." Sometimes recommends other markets.
How to Contact: Send complete ms with cover letter. Reports in 6-8 weeks. SASE. Simultaneous, photocopied and reprint submissions OK. Accepts computer printout submissions; prefers letter-quality. Sample copy for $3 or $5 for 2. Fiction guidelines for SAE.
Payment: Pays 5¢/word.
Terms: Pays on acceptance for first North American serial rights; foreign, option on anthology if requested. Publication copyrighted.

MAINE LIFE (I), Atlantic Publishing Group, 1 Auburn Center, Suite 203, Auburn ME 04210. (207)783-4374. Managing Editor: Lisa Rodrique. Magazine: 8x10¾; 80-96 pages; glossy paper; varied cover stock; illustrations; photos. "Theme is found in the title of our magazine—*Maine Life*, past, present and future. The people and places of Maine emphasize the contemporary. Our readers are people who love Maine and its unique environment, what it was like and especially what it is like now." Published 6 times/year. Estab. 1945. Circ. 30,000.

Needs: "Upbeat or innovative material that will capture the interest of a young, professional readership welcome." Buys 1-2 mss/year. Receives 2-3 unsolicited fiction mss each month. Publishes short shorts. Length: 1,000-4,000 words.
How to Contact: Send complete ms with SASE with cover letter stating "why the writer feels the story pertains to our magazine." Reports ASAP. Free sample copy with SASE.
Payment: Varies with each article.
Terms: Pays on publication for first rights.
Advice: "Discard pretention. Write as you would speak. Write from personal experience, using people you've actually known or met as characters. If writing comes hard, begin by writing anything at all, then revise."

MANSCAPE (II, IV), First Hand Ltd., Box 1314, Teaneck NJ 07666. (201)836-9177. Editor: Lou Thomas. Magazine: digest sized; 130 pages; illustrations. "Magazine is devoted to gay male sexual fetishes; publishes fiction and readers' letters devoted to this theme." Monthly. Estab. 1985. Circ. 60,000.
Needs: Erotica, gay. Should be written in first person. No science fiction or fantasy. Erotica must be based on real life. Receives 25 unsolicited fiction mss/month. Accepts 7 mss/issue; 84 mss/year. Publishes ms an average of 9-18 months after acceptance. Recently published work by Marty Rubin, Rick Jackson, Jay Shaffer; published new writers within the last year. Length: 3,000 words average; 2,000 words minimum; 3,750 words maximum. Sometimes critiques rejected ms.
How to Contact: Send complete ms with cover letter. SASE. Accepts computer printout submissions, no dot-matrix. Sample copy $3.50; fiction guidelines for #10 SASE.
Payment: $100-$150.
Terms: Pays on publication for all rights or first North American serial rights. Publication copyrighted.

MANSCAPE 2 (II, IV), First Hand Ltd., Box 1314, Teaneck NJ 07666. (201)836-9177. Editor: Lou Thomas. Magazine: 8½x11; 100 pages; illustrations and photos. "Magazine is devoted to gay male sexual fetishes; publishes fiction and readers' letters along this line." Bimonthly. Estab. 1985. Circ. 60,000.
Needs: Erotica, gay. Should be written in first person. No science fiction or fantasy. Erotica must be based in reality. Receives 15-20 unsolicited fiction mss/month. Accepts 7 mss/issue; 42 mss/year. Publishes ms an average of 9-18 months after acceptance. Recently published work by Marty Rubin, Jay Shaffer, Jack Ricardo; published new writers within the last year. Length: 3,000 words average; 2,000 words minimum; 3,750 words maximum. Sometimes critiques rejected ms; recommends other markets.
How to Contact: Send complete ms with cover letter; should include writer's name, address, telephone and soc. sec. number and should advise on use of pseudonym if any. Also whether he is selling all rights of First North American Serial Rights. SASE. Accepts computer printout submissions, no dot-matrix. Sample copy $4.50; fiction guidelines for #10 SASE.
Payment: $100-$150.
Terms: Pays on publication for all rights or first North American serial rights. Publication copyrighted.

MATURE LIVING (II), Sunday School Board of the Southern Baptist Conv., MSN 140, 127 Ninth Ave. N., Nashville TN 37234. (615)251-2191. Editor: Jack Gulledge. Magazine: 8½x11; 48 pages; nonglare paper; slick cover stock; illustrations; photos. "Our magazine is Christian in content and the material required is what would appeal to 60+ age group (mainly Southern Baptists): inspirational, instructional, nostalgic, humorous. Our magazine is distributed mainly through churches (especially Southern Baptist churches) that buy the magazine in bulk and distribute it to members in this age group." Monthly. Estab. 1977. Circ. 350,000.
Needs: Contemporary, religious/inspirational, humor, gardening tips, prose poem, spiritual and senior citizen/retirement. Avoid all types of pornography, drugs, liquor, horror, science fiction and stories demeaning to the elderly. Buys 1 ms/issue. Recently published work by Burndean N. Sheffy, Pearl E. Trigg, Joyce M. Sixberry; published new writers within the last year. Length: 425-1,475 words (prefers 900).
How to Contact: Send complete ms with SASE. Reports in 6 weeks on mss. Publishes ms an average of 1 year after acceptance. Sample copy $1. Free guidelines with SASE.
Payment: $21-$73; 3 free author's copies. 85¢ charge for extras.
Terms: Pays on acceptance. First rights 15% less than all rights, reprint rights 25% less. Rarely buys reprints. Publication copyrighted.
Advice: Mss are rejected because they are too long or subject matter unsuitable. "Our readers seem to enjoy an occasional short piece of fiction. It must be believable, however, and present senior adults in a favorable light."

MATURE YEARS (II), United Methodist Publishing House, 201 Eighth Ave. S., Nashville TN 37202. (615)749-6438. Editor: John P. Gilbert. Magazine: 8½x11; 96 pages; good paper; illustrations and pho-

tos. Magazine "helps persons in and nearing retirement to appropriate the resources of the Christian faith as they seek to face the problems and opportunities related to aging." Quarterly. Estab. 1953.
Needs: Religious/inspirational, nostalgia, prose poem, spiritual (for older adults). "We don't want anything poking fun at old age, saccharine stories or anything not for older adults." Buys 3-4 mss/issue, 12-16 mss/year. Needs at least one unsolicited fiction ms each month. Published new writers within the last year. Length: 1,000-1,800 words.
How to Contact: Send complete ms with SASE and Social Security number. Reports in 2 months on mss. Usually publishes ms 12-18 months after acceptance. Free sample copy with 10 1/2x11 SAE and 67¢ postage.
Payment: 4¢/word.
Terms: Pays on acceptance for all and first rights. Publication copyrighted.
Advice: "Practice writing dialogue! Listen to people talk; take notes; master dialogue writing! Not easy, but well worth it! Most inquiry letters are far too long. If you can't sell me an idea in a brief paragraph, you're not going to sell the reader on reading your finished article or story."

McCALL'S (II), The McCall's Publishing Co., 230 Park Ave., New York NY 10169. (212)551-9500. Editor: Elizabeth Sloan. Fiction Editor: Helen DelMonte. General women's magazine for "intelligent, active, energetic, involved women, interested in all facets of family life as well as the world around them." Monthly. Estab. 1876. Circ. 5,000,000.
Needs: "We're looking for stories with some action and adventure. Always interested in strong family stories, love stories, stories with an element of humor. Would welcome a mystery with appeal for women. Suspense."
How to Contact: Send complete ms with SASE. Reports in 1-2 months on ms. Free guidelines with SASE. "We're interested in learning about previous publications. *Don't* tell us what may have inspired the story. If some other editor has recommended *McCall's*, tell us."
Payment: $1,500-$3,000.
Terms: Pays on acceptance for first North American serial rights. Publication copyrighted.
Advice: "Fiction writers should stay tuned to the vibrations of contemporary life if their fiction is to have the vitality we look for. Read *several* issues of the magazine to get a sense of the kinds of stories we publish. Don't try to typecast us on the basis of one issue. We still see too many stories that are totally inappropriate. Try for a fresh approach. Work on characterization. It's essential to make the reader *care* for your characters. Make something happen. Give your story a discernible point. We see many well written stories that leave us wondering what the story was all about."

MERIDIAN MAGAZINE (IV), Canada's Magazine for the 55 Plus, Troika Publishing Inc., Box 13337, Kanata, Ontario K2K 1X5 Canada. (613)592-5623. Magazine: 8 1/2x11; 24-32 pages; glossy 100 lb paper; 120 lb cover stock; illustrations and photos. "*Meridian* promotes a positive view of aging and publishes information and entertainment articles, for people 55 years old and older." Bimonthly. Estab. 1985. Circ. 25,000.
Needs: Humor/satire, senior citizen/retirement. Receives 40-50 unsolicited fiction mss/month. Accepts 2-3 mss/year. Publishes ms an average of 6 months to 1 year after acceptance. Length: 700 words average; 200 words minimum; 1,000 words maximum. Publishes short shorts. Length: 500 words.
How to Contact: Send complete ms with cover letter, or send "curriculum vita of writer." Reports in 1 month on queries; 10 weeks on mss. SASE. Simultaneous and photocopied submissions OK. Accepts computer printout submissions, including dot-matrix. Sample copy for $3 and 8 1/2x11 SAE and 3 IRCs. Fiction guidelines for #10 SAE and IRC.
Payment: $5-$30 Canadian funds, charge for extra copies.
Terms: Pays on publication for first rights. Publication copyrighted.

MESSENGER OF THE SACRED HEART (II), Apostleship of Prayer, 661 Greenwood Ave., Toronto, Ontario M4J 4B3 Canada. (416)466-1195. Editors: Rev. F.J. Power, S.J., and Alfred DeManche. Magazine: 7x10; 24 pages; coated paper; selfcover; illustrations; photos. Magazine for Canadian and U.S. Catholics interested in developing a life of prayer and spirituality; stresses the great value of our ordinary actions and lives." Monthly. Estab. 1891. Circ. 15,000.
Needs: Religious/inspirational. Stories about people, adventure, heroism, humor, drama. No poetry. Buys 1 ms/issue. Length: 750-1,500 words. Recommends other markets.
How to Contact: Send complete ms with SAE or IRC. Rarely buys reprints. Reports in 1 month on mss. Sample copy $1.50.
Payment: 2¢/word. 3 free author's copies.
Terms: Pays on acceptance for first North American serial rights.
Advice: "Develop a story that sustains interest to the end. Do not preach, but use plot and characters to convey the message or theme. Aim to move the heart as well as the mind. Before sending, cut out unnecessary or unrelated words or sentences. If you can, add a light touch or a sense of humor to the story. Your ending should have impact, leaving a moral or faith message for the reader."

McCall's *magazine, with more than 5 million readers, is known as one of the leading women's magazines. Backlogged last year with fiction submissions, the magazine is now accepting fiction manuscripts again. Fiction Editor Helen DelMonte looks for "stories with some action and adventure," as well as family stories, humorous stories and mysteries. This emphasis on variety reflects the trend in the market for women's fiction toward action-oriented, suspense and adventure. Cover reprinted with permission from McCall's magazine © copyright 1989 by the Working Woman/McCall's Group.*

METRO SINGLES LIFESTYLES (II), Metro Publications, Box 28203, Kansas City MO 64118. (816)436-8424. Editor: Robert L. Huffstutter. Fiction Editor: Earl R. Stonebridge. Tabloid: 36 pages; 30 lb newspaper stock; 30 lb cover; illustrations; photos. "Positive, uplifting, original, semi-literary material for all singles: widowed, divorced, never-married, of all ages 18 and over." Bimonthly. Estab. 1984. Circ. 25,000.
Needs: Humor/satire, literary, prose poem, religious/inspirational, romance (contemporary), special interest, spiritual, single parents. No erotic, political, moralistic fiction. Receives 2-3 unsolicited mss/month. Buys 1-2 mss/issue; 12-18 mss/year. Publishes ms 2 months after acceptance. Length: 1,500 words average; 1,200 words minimum; 4,000 words maximum. Publishes short shorts. Recently published work by Jerry P. Watson, James Rudy Humphries, Lynn Weitzel; published new writers within the last year. Length: 1,200. Occasionally critiques rejected mss. Recommends other markets.
How to Contact: Send complete ms with cover letter. Include short paragraph/bio listing credits (if any), current profession or job. Reports in 3 weeks on queries. SASE. Accepts computer printout submissions, including dot-matrix. Sample copy $2.
Payment: Pays $25-$50, free subscription to magazine and contributor's copies.
Terms: Payment on publication. Publication copyrighted.
Advice: "A question I ask myself about my own writing is: will the reader feel the time spent reading the story or article was worth the effort? Personally, I enjoy stories and articles which will create a particular emotion, build suspense, or offer excitement or entertainment. We prefer 1,000 to 2,000 words short story or feature. Features accompanied by photos receive special attention."

MICHIGAN MAGAZINE (IV), The Magazine of the Detroit News, 615 W. Lafayette, Detroit MI 48231. (313)222-2620. Editor: Beaufort Cranford. Magazine: 10x11½; 24-40 pages; Roto paper; illustrations; photos. Michigan authors or themes for broad audience. Weekly.
Needs: Adventure, condensed novel, contemporary, historical, horror, humor/satire, literary, mainstream, regional, science fiction, serialized/excerpted novel, suspense/mystery. Receives "several dozen" unsolicited mss/month. Buys dozen mss/year. Recently published work by Thomas Sullivan, Cynthia Vann, Beaufort Cranford; published new writers within the last year. Length: 1,500 words average; 3,000 words maximum. Also publishes short shorts.
How to Contact: Send complete ms with cover letter. Reports in 2-4 weeks on mss. Simultaneous, photocopied submissions and reprints OK. Accepts computer printouts including dot-matrix. Sample copy for $1 and SAE; writers guidelines free.
Payment: Pays $200-350.
Terms: Pays on publication for first rights. Publication copyrighted.
Advice: "Have someone copy edit for basic spelling and grammatical mistakes."

MIDDLE EASTERN DANCER (II), The International Monthly Magazine of Middle Eastern Dance & Culture, Box 1572, Casselberry FL 32707-1572. (407)788-0301. Editor: Karen Kuzsel. Fiction Editor: Tracie Harris. Magazine: 8½x11; 36 pages; 60 lb stock; enamel cover; illustrations; photos. "Our theme is Middle Eastern dance and culture. We run seminar listings, professional directory, astrology geared to dancers, history, interviews, poetry, recipes, reviews of movies, clubs, shows, records, video, costuming, personal beauty care, exercise and dance choreography." Monthly. Estab. 1979. Circ. 2,500.
Needs: No fiction that does not relate to Middle-Eastern dance or culture. Receives 1 unsolicited ms/month. Publishes ms within 4 months after acceptance. Recently published work by Alan Fisher, George Blenkins; published new writers within the last year. Charges $10 if comments are desired. Occasionally critiques rejected mss. Recommends other markets.
How to Contact: Send complete ms with cover letter, which should include "background in Middle Eastern dance or culture, why they came to write this story and how they know of the magazine." Reports in 1 month on queries. SASE. Photocopied and reprint submissions OK; "if not to other Middle Eastern Dance and culture publication." Accepts computer printout submissions, including dot-matrix. Sample copy for $1, 9x12 SAE and 75¢ postage.
Payment: Pays $10-$25 and 2 contributor's copies.
Terms: Pays on acceptance for one-time rights. Publication copyrighted.
Advice: "Stick strictly to Middle Eastern dance/culture and don't write about subject ideas unless well familiar with it."

MIDSTREAM (II,IV), A Monthly Jewish Review, Theodor Herzl Foundation, 515 Park Ave., New York NY 10022. (212)752-0600. Editor: Murray Zuckoff. Magazine: 8½x11; 64 pages; 50 lb paper; 65 lb white smooth cover stock. "We are a Zionist journal; we publish material with Jewish themes or that would appeal to a Jewish readership." Monthly. Estab. 1955. Circ. 10,000.
Needs: Historical (general), humor/satire, literary, mainstream, translations. Receives 15-20 unsolicited mss/month. Accepts 1 mss/issue; 10 mss/year. Publishes ms 6-18 months after acceptance. 10% of

fiction is agented. Recently published work by I. B. Singer, Anita Jackson, Enid Shomer. Length: 2,500 words average; 1,500 words minimum; 3,000 words maximum. Sometimes critiques rejected mss.
How to Contact: Send complete ms with cover letter, which should include "address, telephone, identification or affiliation of author; state that the ms is fiction." Reports in 1-2 weeks. SASE. Photocopied submissions OK. Accepts computer printout submissions; no dot-matrix. Sample copy for 9x12 SAE. Fiction guidelines for #10 SASE.
Payment: Pays 5¢/word and contributor's copies.
Terms: Pays on publication for first rights. Sends prepublication galleys to author. Publication copyrighted.
Advice "Always include a cover letter and double space."

MILITARY LIFESTYLE (II), Downey Communications, Inc., 1732 Wisconsin Ave. NW, Washington DC 20007. (202)944-4000. Editor: Hope M. Daniels. Magazine: 8½x11; 80-100 pages; coated paper; illustrations and photos. Monthly magazine for military families worldwide. Ten issues per year. Estab. 1969. Circ. 520,000.
Needs: Contemporary. "Fiction must deal with lifestyle or issues of particular concern to our specific military families audience." Receives 50 unsolicited mss/month. Buys 1-2 mss/issue; 10-15 mss/year. Publishes ms 2-6 months after acceptance. Recently published work by Colin Cobb, Judy Covington; published new writers within the last year. Length: 1,800 words average. Generally critiques rejected mss. Recommends other markets if applicable.
How to Contact: Send complete ms with cover letter, which should include info on writer and writing credits and history. Reports in 6-8 weeks on mss. SASE. Photocopied submissions OK. Accepts computer printout submissions, including dot-matrix. Sample copy for $1.50, 9x12 SAE and 4 first class stamps. Fiction guidelines for #10 SASE and 1 first class stamp.
Payment: Pays $300 minimum and 2 free copies.
Terms: Pays generally on publication unless held more than 6 months; then on acceptance for first North American serial rights. Publication copyrighted.
Advice: "Fiction is slice-of-life reading for our audience. Primarily written by military wives or military members themselves, the stories deal with subjects very close to our readers: prolonged absences by spouses, the necessity of handling child-raising alone, the fear of accidents while spouses are on maneuvers or in dangerous situations, etc. The important point: Target the material to our audience—military families—and make the characters real, empathetic and believable. Read your copy over as an objective reader rather than as its author before submission. Better yet, read it aloud!"

MILWAUKEE MAGAZINE (IV), Quad/Graphics, 312 E. Buffalo St., Milwaukee WI 53202. (414)273-1101. Editor: Judith Woodburn. Magazine: 8x11; 150-250 pages; glossy cover stock; illustrations; photos. "Regional material/issues related to Milwaukee business, arts, entertainment and personalities" for 46 yr. median age; college-plus education and $45,000 income. Monthly. Circ. 50,000.
Needs: Contemporary, feminist, literary, mainstream, regional. "We prefer (strongly) to use Wisconsin writers, and we publish fiction only as part of annual contest." No overt romances, no thinly-veiled historical treatises, no quaint reminiscences. "*All* must have regional Wisconsin flavor, or be linked to this city or region in integral way—such as being written by a Wisconsin author. Buys 1 fiction mss/year. Publishes ms 3 months after acceptance. Published new writers within the last year. Length: 5,000 words. Very rarely critiques rejected ms.
How to Contact: Accepts ms only in September/October for fiction contest. Simultaneous and photocopied submissions OK. Accepts computer printouts including dot-matrix. Sample copy $3.25.
Payment: Pays $500.
Terms: Pays on publication for one-time rights. Sends galleys to authors. Publication copyrighted.
Advice: Check August issue of each year for fiction contest details.

THE MIRACULOUS MEDAL, The Central Association of the Miraculous Medal, 475 E. Chelten Ave., Philadelphia PA 19144. (215)848-1010. Editor: Rev. Robert P. Cawley, C.M. Magazine. Quarterly.
Needs: Religious/inspirational. Receives 25 unsolicited fiction mss/month; accepts 2 mss/issue; 8 mss/year. Publishes ms up to two years or more after acceptance.
How to Contact: Query first with SASE. Sample copy and fiction guidelines free.
Payment: Pays 2¢/word minimum.
Terms: Pays on acceptance for first rights. Publication copyrighted.

‡MODERN SHORT STORIES (I), Entertaining Stories for Fiction Lovers, Claggk Inc., 500B Bi-county Blvd., Farmingdale NY 11762. (516)293-3751. Editor: Glen Steckler. Magazine: Digest-sized; supercalendered paper, 60 lb cover stock; illustrations; photographs. Publishes "a variety of fiction for audiences of all ages." Bimonthly. Estab. 1988.
Needs: Adventure, confession, contemporary, erotica, experimental, fantasy, historical, horror, hu-

mor/satire, mainstream, psychic/supernatural/occult, regional, religious/inspirational, romance (contemporary, historical, young adult), science fiction, sports, suspense/mystery, western. Receives 500-1,000 unsolicited fiction mss/month. Buys 12-15 fiction mss/issue. Publishes mss 4 months to 1 year after acceptance. Length: 1,000-5,000 words preferred. Publishes short shorts "on rare occasions." Sometimes critiques rejected ms.

How to Contact: Send complete mss with cover letter. Reports in 1-3 weeks. SASE required. Photocopied submissions OK. Accepts dot-matrix computer printouts. Sample copy $2; fiction guidelines free.

Payment: Pays $10 minimum; $50 maximum.

Terms: Pays on acceptance for first rights and first anthology rights. Publication copyrighted.

Advice: "There is not enough space devoted to fiction today—tv has tended to replace it. However, we feel the demand is there and that is our reason for publishing *Modern Short Stories*."

THE MODERN WOODMEN (II), Modern Woodmen of America, Mississippi River at 17th St., Rock Island IL 61201. (309)786-6481. Editor: Gloria Bergh. Fiction Editor: Sandy Howell. Magazine: 8½x11; 24 pages; 50 lb paper; self cover; illustrations and photos. "We want articles that appeal to families, emphasize family interaction, for the family audience including all age groups from children to the elderly." Quarterly. Circ. 350,000.

Needs: Adventure, contemporary, historical (general), juvenile (5-9 years), mainstream, senior citizen/retirement, young adult/teen (10-18 years). Receives approx. 35 unsolicited fiction mss/month. Accepts 1-2 mss/month; 12-24 mss/year. Length: 1,200 words preferred. Sometimes critiques rejected mss, "but very seldom."

How to Contact: Send complete ms with cover letter. Reports in up to 2 months. SASE. Simultaneous, photocopied and reprint submissions OK. Accepts computer printout submissions, including dot-matrix. Sample copy for 8½x11 SAE with 2 first class stamps. Fiction guidelines for #10 SASE.

Payment: $50 and up.

Terms: Pays on acceptance for one-time rights.

Advice: "A well written short story is a drawing card to interest our readers."

MOMENT MAGAZINE (II, IV), 3000 Connecticut Ave. NW, Suite 300, Washington DC 20008. (202)387-8888. Publisher/Editor: Hershel Shanks. Magazine: 8½x11; 64 pages; 60 lb coated paper; 80 lb cover stock; illustrations and photos. Modern, historical magazine publishing material on intellectual, cultural and political issues of interest to the Jewish community. Audience is college-educated, liberal, concerned with Jewish affairs. Monthly. Estab. 1975. Circ. 30,000.

Needs: Contemporary, ethnic, historical, religious, excerpted novel and translations. "All fiction should have Jewish content. No sentimental stories about 'Grandma' etc. Do not encourage Holocaust themes." Receives 60-80 unsolicited fiction mss/month. Buys 0-1 ms/issue, 2-3 mss/year. Published new writers in the past year. Length: 2,000 words minimum; 4,000 words maximum; 3,000 words average. Publishes short shorts. Occasionally recommends other markets.

How to Contact: Cover letter with bio. Query first or send complete ms. SASE always. Photocopied submissions OK. No multiple submissions. Accepts computer printout submissions, prefers letter-quality. Reports in 1 month on queries; 1-2 months on mss. Publishes ms 1-12 months after acceptance. Sample copy $2.95. Free fiction guidelines for #10 SAE and 1 first class stamp.

Payment: Varies.

Terms: Pays on publication for first rights. Publication copyrighted.

Advice: "We caution against over-sentimentalized writing which we get way too much of all the time. Query first is helpful; reading stories we've published a must."

‡THE MOUNTAIN (I,II), Thomas Shaw Publications, Inc., Box 1010, 110 W. Center St., Galax VA 24333. (703)236-7112. Editor: Lynn Webb. Fiction Editor: Kathie Pini. Magazine: 8½x11; 60 + pages; 60 lb gloss paper; 80 lb gloss cover stock; illustrations and photographs. "Our theme is mountainous. We publish all types of material of high literary quality. Readers are 35-80 years. Very educated." Bimonthly. Estab. 1988. Circ. 3,800.

Needs: Adventure, contemporary, experimental, feminist, historical (general), humor/satire, literary, mainstream, prose poem, regional, senior citizen/retirement, serialized novel, suspense/mystery. "We are particularly interested in serializing novels, especially from new and unpublished writers. We would like to keep a novel going at all times. Though we are small and new, and our payment is low, we are just starting promotional campaigns, and as we grow we'll take our contributors with us." No religious, syrupy romances, fiction that seems to do nothing but entertain. Receives about 50 unsolicited mss/month; accepts "2-4 short stories, 1-2 humor" mss/month; about 30 mss/year. Publishes ms an average of 3-18 months after acceptance. Recently published Jules Archer, Garry Barker, Pat McManus. Length: 3,000-3,500 words average; 20,000 words maximum. Sometimes critiques rejected mss and recommends other markets.

How to Contact: Send complete ms with cover letter: "information about the writer. We like to know why a writer is interested in our magazine." Reports on queries in 1-8 weeks; on mss in 1-3 months, sometimes longer. SASE. Simultaneous, photocopied and previously published submissions OK. Sample copy $3.50; fiction guidelines free.
Payment: Pays $50-$800 and contributor's copies.
Terms: Pays on publication. Buys first North American serial rights. Publication copyrighted.
Advice: "Please send a cover letter. Please send a neat, clean manuscript. We prefer impressionistic fiction. We like well developed plots and strong characterization. No cardboard characters, please. We like stories that are realistic and make our readers look at life in a new and different way. Don't give up. We love new writers. We're new too. We want to grow together."

MY FRIEND (II), A Magazine for Children, Daughters of St. Paul, 50 St. Paul's Ave., Boston MA 02130. (617)522-8911. Editor: Sister Anne Joan. Magazine: 8½x11; 32 pages; smooth, glossy paper; smooth, glossy cover stock; illustrations; photos. Magazine of "religious truths and positive values for children in a format which is enjoyable and attractive. Each issue contains Bible stories, lives of saints and famous people, short stories, science corner, contests, projects, etc." Monthly during school year (September-June). Estab. 1979. Circ. 16,000.
Needs: Juvenile, prose poem, religious/inspirational, spiritual (children), sports (children). Receives 8-10 unsolicited fiction mss/month. Accepts 3-4 mss/issue; 30-40 mss/year. Recently published work by Virginia L. Kroll, Dorothy Baughman, Kay Gibson; published new writers within the past year. Length: 500 words minimum; 700 words maximum; 600 words average.
How to Contact: Send complete ms with SASE. Simultaneous, photocopied and previously published submissions OK. Accepts computer printout submissions. Reports in 1-2 months on mss. Publishes ms an average of 1 year after acceptance. Free sample copy for 10x14 SAE and 60¢ postage.
Payment: 6 free contributor's copies.
Advice: "We prefer child-centered stories in a real-world setting which teach positive values. Children enjoy fiction. They can relate to the characters and learn lessons that they might not derive from a more 'preachy' article. Generally, we accept only stories that teach wholesome, positive values."

NA'AMAT WOMAN, Magazine of Pioneer Na'amat USA, The Women's Labor Zionist Organization of America, 200 Madison Ave., New York NY 10016. (212)725-8010. Editor: Judith A. Sokoloff. Magazine covering a wide variety of subjects of interest to the Jewish community—including political and social issues, arts, profiles; many articles about Israel; and women's issues. Fiction must have a Jewish theme. Readers are the American Jewish community. Published 5 times/year. Estab. 1926. Circ. 30,000.
Needs: Contemporary, literary, feminist. Receives 10 unsolicited fiction mss/month. Buys 3-5 fiction mss/year. Length: 1,500 words minimum; 3,000 words maximum. Also buys nonfiction.
How to Contact: Query first or send complete ms with SASE. Photocopied submissions OK. Accepts computer printout submissions. Prefers letter-quality. Reports in 3 months on mss. Free sample copy for 9x11½ SAE and 71¢ postage.
Payment: Pays 8¢/word; 2 free contributor's copies. Offers kill fee of 25%.
Terms: Pays on publication for first and first North American serial rights; assignments on work-for-hire basis.
Advice: Submit "good writing. No maudlin nostalgia or romance; no hackneyed Jewish humor and no poetry."

‡NATIONAL LAMPOON (II), 155 Avenue of the Americas, New York NY 10013. (212)645-5040. Editor: Larry Sloman. Magazine. "We publish humor and satire." Bimonthly. Estab. 1970. Circ. 250,000.
Needs: "We do satire and humor on all things in the world around us." Receives 200 unsolicited fiction mss/month. Buys 2 mss/issue. Publishes ms 2-3 months after acceptance. Length: 1,000 words preferred; 500 words minimum; 2,000 words maximum. Publishes short shorts.
How to Contact: Query first. Reports in 1-2 months. SASE preferred. Simultaneous and photocopied submissions OK. Accepts dot-matrix computer printout submissions. Accepts electronic submissions via disk or modem. Fiction guidelines free.
Payment: Payment is negotiated.
Terms: Pays on publication for first North American serial rights and anthology rights. Offers varying kill fee. Publication copyrighted.

NATIONAL RACQUETBALL MAGAZINE (IV), Florida Trade Publications, Inc., Suite B, 400 Douglas Ave., Punedin FL 34698. (813)736-5616. Editor: Sigmond Brouwer. Magazine with news, current events, and fitness dealing with the sport of racquetball. Monthly. Estab. 1981. Circ. 40,000.
Needs: Call editor *before* submitting ms. "We take *very* little fiction."

How to Contact: Send complete ms with SASE. Photocopied submissions OK with SASE.
Payment: Pays $50-$300.
Terms: Pays on publication for all rights. Publication copyrighted.

NEW ALASKAN (IV), R.W. Pickrell Agency, Rt. 1, Box 677, Ketchikan AK 99901. (907)247-2490. Tabloid sized; 24-32 pages; newsprint paper; newsprint cover stock; illustrations; photos. Magazine with both fiction and nonfiction dealing with the history and lifestyle of Southeast Alaska. Monthly. Estab. 1964. Circ. 6,000.
Needs: Adventure, humor, preschool, regional and senior citizen/retirement. "We accept only stories dealing with Southeast Alaska." Buys 12 mss/year. Publishes short shorts. Almost 100% of fiction is agented. Published new writers within the last year. Length: 1,000-5,000 words.
How to Contact: Send complete ms with SASE. Reports in 4 months on mss. Sample copy $1.50 with 8x13 or larger SAE with 66¢ postage.
Payment: 1½¢/word.
Terms: Pays on publication for first, second serial (reprint) and one-time rights. Buys reprints.
Advice: "We publish fiction to diversify editorial material."

NEW ENGLAND SENIOR CITIZEN/SENIOR AMERICAN NEWS (II), Prime National Publishing Corp., 470 Boston Post Rd., Weston MA 02193. (617)899-2702. Editor-in-Chief: Eileen DeVito. Tabloid: 10x16; 16-32 pages; newsprint paper; illustrations; b&w photos. Tabloid newspaper for senior citizens. "We publish articles of particular interest to seniors." Monthly. Estab. 1970.
Needs: Adventure, entertainment, travel, comics, contemporary, ethnic, historical (general), humor/satire, mainstream, suspense/mystery and western. Receives about 15-25 unsolicited fiction mss/month. Buys 6-12 mss/issue. Published new writers within the last year. Length: 600 words minimum; 1,200 words maximum.
How to Contact: Send complete ms with SASE. "We publish first rights only." Accepts computer printout submissions. Prefers letter-quality. Reports in 6 months on mss. Sample copy 50¢.
Payment: $25-$100.
Terms: Pays on publication for all rights. Publication copyrighted.
Advice: "Writers forget to put their names and addresses directly on their manuscripts and forget to double-space their lines of typing, which we require; also, to list number of words therein."

NEW METHODS (IV), The Journal of Animal Health Technology, Box 22605, San Francisco CA 94122-0605. (415)664-3469. Editor: Ronald S. Lippert, Aht. Newsletter ("could become magazine again"): 8½x11; 4-6 pages; 20 lb paper; illustrations; photos "rarely." Network service in the animal field educating services for mostly professionals in the animal field; e.g. animal health technicians. Monthly. Estab. 1976. Circ. 5,608.
Needs: Animals: adventure, condensed novel, contemporary, experimental, historical, mainstream, regional, science fiction, western. No stories unrelated to animals. Receives 4 unsolicited fiction mss/month. Buys one ms/issue; 12 mss/year. Published new writers within the last year. Length: open. "Rarely" publishes short shorts. Occasionally critiques rejected mss. Recommends other markets.
How to Contact: Query first with theme, length, expected time of completion, photos/illustrations, if any, biographical sketch of author, all necessary credits or send complete ms. Report time varies. SASE for query and ms. Simultaneous and photocopied submissions OK. Accepts printouts, including dot-matrix. Sample copy $2 for *NSSWM* readers with #10 SAE and 2 first class stamps. Fiction guidelines free for #10 SAE and 2 first class stamps.
Payment: Varies.
Terms: Pays on publication for one-time rights. Publication copyrighted.
Advice: Contests: theme changes but is generally the biggest topics of the year in the animal field. "Emotion, personal experience—make the person feel it. We are growing."

NEW YORK RUNNING NEWS (IV), New York Road Runners Club, 9 East 89 St., New York NY 10128. Editor: Raleigh Mayer. Magazine: 8x11; 80 + pages; illustrations; b&w and color photos. "Regional running magazine, local event coverage and membership (NY Road Runners Club) profiles, for serious and recreational runners, and road racers." Bimonthly. Estab. 1958. Circ. 40,000.
Needs: "Only running-related" fiction. Receives "several dozen" unsolicited fiction mss/month. Accepts "one or less" ms/issue. Publishes ms 1-6 months after acceptance. Length: 1,000 words average; 500 words minimum; 1,500 words maximum. Publishes short shorts. Length: 500 words. Occasionally critiques rejected mss.
How to Contact: Send complete ms with cover letter. Reports in "a few" weeks. SASE. Photocopied and reprint submissions OK. Accepts computer printout submissions, including dot-matrix. Sample copy $2.50 and 2 first class stamps. Fiction guidelines for #10 SASE.
Payment: $50-$150; charges for extra copies.

Terms: Pays on publication for first rights. Publication copyrighted.
Advice: "Anything well done is publishable. Be funny. Be sophisticated. Be natural."

THE NEW YORKER (III), The New Yorker, Inc., 25 W. 43rd St., New York NY 10036. (212)840-3800. Editor: Robert Gottlieb. A quality magazine of interesting, well-written stories, articles, essays and poems for a literate audience. Weekly. Estab. 1925.
Needs: Publishes 2 mss/issue.
How to Contact: Send complete ms with SASE. Reports in 6-8 weeks on mss.
Payment: Varies.
Terms: Pays on acceptance.
Advice: "Be lively, original, not overly literary. Write what you want to write, not what you think the editor would like."

NOAH'S ARK (II, IV), A Newspaper for Jewish Children, Suite 250, 8323 Southwest Freeway, Houston TX 77074. (713)771-7143. Editors: Debbie Israel Dubin and Linda Freedman Block. Tabloid: 4 pages; newsprint paper; illustrations; photos. "All material must be on some Jewish theme. Seasonal material relating to Jewish holidays is used as well as articles and stories relating to Jewish culture (charity, Soviet Jewry, ecology), etc." for Jewish children, ages 6-12. Monthly Sept.-June. Estab. 1979. Circ. 450,000.
Needs: Juvenile (6-12 years); religious/inspirational; young adult/teen (10-12 years); ages 6-12 Jewish children. "Newspaper is not only included as a supplement to numerous Jewish newspapers and sent to individual subscribers but is also distributed in bulk quantities to religious schools; therefore all stories and articles should have educational value as well as being entertaining and interesting to children." Receives 10 unsolicited mss/month. Buys "few mss but we'd probably use more if more appropriate mss were submitted." Published new writers within the last year. Length: 600 words maximum.
How to Contact: Send complete ms with SASE. "The cover letter is not necessary; the submission will be accepted or rejected on its own merits." Simultaneous, photocopied submissions and reprints OK. Accepts computer printouts including dot-matrix. Sample copy for #10 envelope and 1 first class stamp. "The best guideline is a copy of our publication."
Payment: Varies; contributor's copies.
Terms: Pays on acceptance for one-time rights. Publication copyrighted.
Advice: "Our newspaper was created by two writers looking for a place to have our work published. It has grown in only 10 years to nearly 1 million readers throughout the world. Beginners with determination can accomplish the impossible."

THE NORTH AMERICAN VOICE OF FATIMA (II), Barnabite Fathers, 1023 Swan Rd., Youngstown NY 14174-0167. (716)754-7489. Editor: Rev. Paul M. Keeling, C.R.S.P. Marian Magazine fostering devotion to Mary, the Mother of God. Bimonthly. Estab. 1961. Circ. 3,000.
Needs: Religious/inspirational. Recently published work by Starlette L. Howard. Length: 1,000 words average.
How to Contact: Send complete ms with SASE. Reports in 1 month on mss. Sample copy free.
Payment: 2¢/word.
Terms: Pays on publication.

NORTHCOAST VIEW (II), Blarney Publishing, Box 1374, Eureka CA 95502. (707)443-4887. Editors: Scott K. Ryan and Damon Maguire. Magazine; 11x14½; 56 pages; electrabrite, 38 lb paper and cover; illustrations; photos. "Entertainment, recreation, arts and news magazine, open to all kinds of fiction." For Humboldt County, ages 18-75 and others. Monthly. Plans anthology in future. Estab. 1982. Circ. 22,500.
Needs: Open to most subjects. Adventure, condensed novel, contemporary, erotica, ethnic, experimental, fantasy, historical (local, general), horror, humor/satire, literary, psychic/supernatural/occult, regional, science fiction, suspense/mystery, translations. No romances. Receives 30-50 unsolicited mss/month. Buys 1-2 mss/issue; 12-20 mss/year. Publishes ms 1-3 months after acceptance. Length: 2,500 words average; 250 words minimum; 5,000 words maximum.
How to Contact: Send complete ms with cover letter (background info or bio if published). Reports in 3-6 months on mss. SASE. Simultaneous, photocopied submissions and reprints (sometimes) OK. Accepts computer printouts. No dot-matrix. Sample copy $1. Fiction guidelines for #10 SAE and 1 first class stamp.
Payment: Pays $5-$150.
Terms: Pays on publication for all rights. Publication copyrighted.

NORTHEAST, the Sunday Magazine of the Hartford Courant, 285 Broad St., Hartford CT 06115. (203)241-3700. Editor: Lary Bloom. Magazine: 11½x10; 32-100 pages; illustrations; photos. "A regional (New England, specifically Connecticut) magazine, we publish stories of varied subjects of interest to our Connecticut audience" for a general audience. Weekly. Published special fiction issue last summer and a special college writing issue for fiction and poetry. Estab. 1981. Circ. 300,000.
Needs: Contemporary and regional. No children's stories or stories with distinct setting outside Connecticut. Receives 60 unsolicited mss/month. Buys 1 ms/issue. Publishes short shorts. Recently published work by Wally Lamb, Ken Chowder, June B. Wassell. Published new writers within the last year. Length: 750 words minimum; 3,500 words maximum.
How to Contact: Send complete ms with SASE. Reports in 3 weeks. Simultaneous and photocopied submissions OK. No reprints or previously published work. Accepts computer printout submissions. Prefers letter-quality. Free sample copy and fiction guidelines with 12x10 or larger SASE.
Payment: $250-$600.
Terms: Pays on acceptance for one-time rights. Publication copyrighted.
Advice: "We are committed to providing a vehicle for quality stories."

‡NORTHWEST MAGAZINE (I, II, IV), The Sunday Oregonian Magazine, 1320 SW Broadway, Portland OR 97210. (503)221-8228. Editor: Jack Hart. Magazine: 10¼x11½; 24-36 pages; illustrations; photos. Weekly. Plans a special fiction issue. Circ. 400.000.
Needs: Contemporary, experimental fantasy, humor/satire, literary mainstream, prose poem, young adult, science fiction. Receives 20-30 mss/month. Buys 30-40 mss/year. "We don't run fiction every week. Publishes ms within 1-3 months of acceptance. Agented fiction 5%. Recently published work by Jack Estes, Robert Sheckley; published new writers within the last year. Length: 2,000 words preferred. Publishes short shorts. Sometimes critiques rejected mss and recommends other markets.
How to Contact: Send complete mss with cover letter. Reports in 1 week. SASE. Photocopied submissions OK. Accepts computer printout submissions, including dot-matrix. Accepts electronic submission via disk or modem. Sample copy and fiction guidelines for SAE.
Payment: Pays $150-$300 and contributor's copies.
Terms: Pays on acceptance for one-time rights. Offers kill fee. Sends galleys to author. Publication copyrighted. Sponsors awards for fiction writers.

NUGGET (II), Dugent Publishing Corp., Suite 204, 2355 Salzedo St., Coral Gables FL 33134. (305)443-2378. Editor: Jerome Slaughter. A newsstand magazine designed to have erotic appeal for a fetish-oriented audience. Bimonthly. Estab. 1956. Circ. 100,000.
Needs: Offbeat, fetish-oriented material should encompass a variety of subjects. Most of fiction includes several sex scenes. No fiction that concerns children or religious subjects. Buys 3 mss/issue. Approximately 5% of fiction is agented. Length: 2,000-3,500 words.
How to Contact: Send complete ms with SASE. Reports in 1 month on ms. Sample copy $5. Free guidelines with legal-sized SASE.
Payment: $125-$200. Free author's copy.
Terms: Pays on publication for first rights.
Advice: "Keep in mind the nature of the publication, which is fetish erotica. Subject matter can vary, but we prefer fetish themes."

‡OCEAN SPORTS INTERNATIONAL (II, IV), Box 1388, Soquel CA 95073. Editor: Joe Grassadonia. Magazine: 8½x11; 96 pages; glossy paper and cover; illustrations; color/b&w photos. Articles on ocean sports of all kinds for ocean people and general audience. Quarterly. Estab. 1981. Circ. 45,000.
Needs: Adventure, historical (general), humor/satire, literary, sports, special interest: water related. No experimental. Plans to buy 1 or 2 mss/issue. Publishes ms 3-6 months after acceptance. Recently published work by James Houston and Fred Van Dyke. Length: 2,000 words average; 1,000 words minimum; 4,000 words maximum. Occasionally comments on rejected mss if requested. Recommends other markets if requested.
How to Contact: Send complete ms with cover letter with SASE. Reports in 2 weeks on mss. SASE for query and ms. Simultaneous, photocopied submissions and reprints OK with rights obtained. Accepts computer printouts including dot-matrix if readable. Sample copy $3. Fiction guidelines for #10 SAE and 1 first class stamp.
Payment: Pays 5¢-10¢/word, plus contributor's copies; $2.20 charge for extras.
Terms: Pays on publication for first rights within 2 months. Publication copyrighted.
Advice: "There are many markets open to the right *kind* of fiction. Particularly fiction of specific readership: shorts, regional, parent/children, etc. A good query letter helps. Remember that we're looking for stories on ocean sports, risk and survival, high adventure and stories on relationships with the ocean/water. Remember also that editors have little time, so if you call or write, be prepared, conscious of time and specific."

‡OH! IDAHO (IV), The Idaho State Magazine, Peak Media, Box 925, Hailey ID 83333. Editor: Colleen Daly. Magazine: 80-96 pages; high quality paper; some illustrations and photographs. Publishes material on "Idaho, for Idahoans and people across the nation." Quarterly. Estab. 1988. Circ. 20,000.
Needs: Humor/satire. "Must relate specifically to Idaho, without being denigrating to the potato state. Easy on the peeve, long on the humor. Adventure—stories with information in a fictional format." Receives 4-5 unsolicited mss/month. Publishes ms 6 months after acceptance. Length: 1,200 words preferred. Sometimes critiques rejected mss and recommends other markets.
How to Contact: Query with clips of published work. Include social security number with ms. Reports in 4-6 weeks on queries. SASE. Simultaneous, photocopied and reprint submissions OK. Accepts dot-matrix computer printouts if legible. Accepts electronic submissions via Word Perfect or MS-DOS ASCII only. Sample copy for $3. Guidelines for #10 SAE and 1 first class stamp.
Payment: Pays 10¢/word.
Terms: Pays on publication. Purchases first North American serial rights. Publication copyrighted.
Advice: "All articles must relate specifically to Idaho and should convey all or part of this idea: Idaho is a beautiful place to live and vacation in, there are many fun and interesting activities here and the people of Idaho are fascinating. Articles should be timeless, upscale and positive. The subject matter should focus on all facets of Idaho and/or her people."

OMNI (II), Penthouse International, 1965 Broadway, New York NY 10023. Fiction Editor: Ellen Datlow. Magazine: 8½x11; 114-182 pages; 40-50 lb stock paper; 100 lb Mead off cover stock; illustrations; photos. Magazine of science and science fiction with an interest in near future; stories of what science holds, what life and lifestyles will be like in areas affected by science for a young, bright and well-educated audience between ages 18-45. Monthly. Estab. 1978. Circ. 1,000,000.
Needs: Science fiction, contemporary, fantasy and technological horror. No sword and sorcery or space opera. Buys 30 mss/year. Receives approximately 400 unsolicited fiction mss/month. Approximately 5% of fiction is agented. Recently published work by Harlan Ellison, Robert Silverberg, Pat Cadigan. Length: 2,000 words minimum, 12,000 words maximum. Critiques rejected mss that interest me "when there is time." Sometimes recommends other markets.
How to Contact: Send complete ms with SASE. Accepts computer printout submissions, prefers letter-quality. Reports within 3 weeks on mss. Publishes ms 3-24 months after acceptance.
Payment: Pays $1,250-$2,000; 2 free author's copies.
Terms: Pays on acceptance for first North American serial rights with exclusive worldwide English language periodical rights and nonexclusive anthology rights. Publication copyrighted.
Advice: "In 1988 Kate Wilhelm's "Forever Yours, Anna" won the Nebula Award and George RR Martin's "The Pear-shaped Man" won the Bram Stoker Award. Beginning writers should read a lot of the best science fiction short stories today. We are looking for strong, well-written stories dealing with the next 100 years. Don't give up on a market just because you've been rejected several times. If you're good, you'll get published eventually. Don't ever call an editor on the phone and ask why he/she rejected a story. You'll either find out in a personal rejection letter (which means the editor liked it or thought enough of your writing to comment) or you won't find out at all (most likely the editor won't remember a form-rejected story)." Mss are rejected because "they rehash old ideas, are poorly written or are trite."

ON THE LINE (II), Mennonite Publishing House, 616 Walnut Ave., Scottdale PA 15683-1999. (412)887-8500. Editor: Virginia A. Hostetler. Magazine: 7x10; 8 pages; illustrations; b&w photos. "A religious take-home paper with the goal of helping children grow in their understanding and appreciation of God, the created world, themselves and other people." For children ages 10-14. Weekly. Estab. 1970. Circ. 11,000.
Needs: Adventure and religious/inspirational for older children and young teens (10-14 years). Receives 50-100 unsolicited mss/month. Buys 1 ms/issue; 52 mss/year. Length: 750-1,000 words.
How to Contact: Send complete ms with cover letter noting whether author is offering first-time or reprint rights. Reports in 1 month. SASE. Simultaneous, photocopied and previously published work OK. Accepts computer printout submissions. Prefers letter-quality. Sample copy and fiction guidelines free.
Payment: Pays on acceptance for one-time rights. Publication copyrighted.
Advice: "Write and write some more before submitting. We believe in the power of story to entertain, inspire and challenge the reader to new growth. Know children, the readers of our publication, their thoughts, feelings and interests. Be realistic with characters and events in the fiction. Stories do not need to be true, but need to *feel* true."

THE OTHER SIDE (III), 300 W. Apsley St., Philadelphia PA 19144. (215)849-2178. Editor: Mark Olson. Fiction Editor: Barbara Moorman. Magazine of justice rooted in discipleship for Christians with a strong interest in peace, social and economic justice. Monthly. Estab. 1965. Circ. 40,000.
Needs: Contemporary, ethnic, experimental, feminist, humor/satire, literary, mainstream, prose poem, spiritual and suspense/mystery. Receives 30 unsolicited fiction mss/month. Buys 6 mss/year.

Length: 1,500 words minimum; 5,000 words maximum; 3,500 words average.
How to Contact: Send complete ms with SASE. Photocopied submissions OK. "Simultaneous submissions and pre-published material *strongly* discouraged." Accepts computer printout submissions. Accepts disk submissions compatible with IBM PC. Reports in 6-8 weeks on mss. Publishes ms 3-9 months after acceptance. Sample copy for $3.
Payment: Pays $50-$250; free subscription to magazine; 5 free contributor's copies.
Terms: Pays on acceptance for all or first rights; assignments on work-for-hire basis. Publication copyrighted.

OUI MAGAZINE (II), 6th Floor, 300 W. 43rd St., New York NY 10036. (212)397-5200. Editor: Richard Kidd. Magazine: 8x11; 112 pages; illustrations; photos. Magazine for college-age males and older. Monthly. Estab. 1972. Circ. 1 million.
Needs: Contemporary, fantasy, lesbian, men's, mystery and humor. Buys 1 ms/issue; 12 mss/year. Receives 200-300 unsolicited fiction mss/month. Published new writers within the last year. Length: 1,500-3,000 words.
How to Contact: Cover letter with author background, previous publications, etc. Send complete ms with SASE. Accepts computer printout submissions. Prefers letter-quality. Reports in 6-to-8 weeks on mss.
Payment: Pays $250 and up.
Terms: Pays on publication for first rights. Publication copyrighted.
Advice: "Many mss are rejected because writers have not studied the market or the magazine. We want writers to take chances and offer us something out of the ordinary. Look at several recent issues to see what direction our fiction is headed."

OUR FAMILY (II, IV), Box 249, Battleford, Saskatchewan S0M 0E0 Canada. (306)937-7772. Editor: N. Gregoire. Magazine: 8½x11; 40 pages; illustrations; photos. Magazine primarily for Catholic families who want information, inspiration and encouragement in Christian living. Monthly. Estab. 1949. Circ. 14,000.
Needs: Religious/inspirational, senior citizen/retirement and spiritual. "The material we use must have Christian content and values. No science fiction or adult sex stories." Buys 1 ms/month. Recently published work by Arthur Stilwell, Helen Taylor Friesen, Mary Hilbert; published new writers within the last year. Length: 1,000-3,000 words. Recommends other markets.
How to Contact: Send complete ms with SAE and IRC or personal check. (U.S. stamps cannot be used in Canada.) Accepts computer printout submissions. Prefers letter-quality. Reports in 1 month after receipt of the ms. Publishes ms 4-6 months after acceptance. Sample copy $2.50. Free Fiction Requirement Guide with SAE and 43¢ for postage.
Payment: 7-10¢/word for original ms. Lesser payment for reprint. 2-4 free author's copies. $1 charge for extras.
Terms: Pays on acceptance for simultaneous, second serial (reprint) and first North American serial rights. Buys reprints.
Advice: "Base your story on an actual Christian experience, a personal experience or one you have come to know. We reject a good number of stories simply because they have no Christian dimension."

OUTLAW BIKER (II, IV), Outlaw Biker Enterprises, 450 7th Ave. #2305, New York NY 10123. (212)564-0112. Publisher/Editor: Casey Exton. Magazine: 8½x11; 96 pages; 50 lb color paper; 80 lb cover stock; illustrations; photos. Publication for hard-core bikers, their partners and for tattoo enthusiasts. Monthly. Published special fiction issue on Vietnam. Special issue 3 times/year, *Tattoo Review*. Estab. 1984. Circ. 225,000.
Needs: Adventure, bikers. Receives 20 unsolicited mss/month. Accepts 3 fiction mss/issue. Publishes ms 4 months after acceptance. Published new writers within the last year. Length: 2,500 words minimum; 3,000 words maximum. Critiques rejected mss.
How to Contact: Send complete ms with cover letter. SASE very important. Reports on queries in 1 month. Simultaneous, photocopied and reprint submissions OK. Sample copy $3.50.
Payment: Pays $50-$180.
Terms: Pays on publication for all rights. Publication copyrighted.
Advice: "Timely biker events with photos used constantly. Photos do not have to be professionally taken. Clear snapshots of events with the short story usually accepted. Send to: Casey Exton Attention."

PALOUSE JOURNAL (II, IV), North Country Book Express, Box 9632, Moscow ID 83843. (208)882-0888. Editor: Tim Steury. Tabloid: 11x17; 24-40 pages; 34 lb stock; illustrations; photos. "We are a regional general interest magazine, for an educated, literate audience." Bimonthly. Estab. 1981.
Needs: Regional. "We will consider good writing of any sort, mostly with some 'hook' to our region." Buys 1 ms/issue at most; 2-6 mss/year. Published new writers within the last year. Length: 2,500 words

maximum. Will consider short shorts as columns, up to 1,000 words. Occasionally critiques rejected mss. Occasionally recommends other markets.

How to Contact: Send complete ms with cover letter. Reports in 2-3 months on mss. SASE. Photocopied submissions OK. Accepts computer printout submissions, including dot-matrix, "if good quality." Accepts MS DOS WordStar submissions. Sample copy $1. Writers' guidelines for 9x12 and 3 first class stamps.

Payment: Pays $25 for a short-short, $100 for a full feature story.

Terms: Pays on publication for first North American serial rights. Publication copyrighted.

Advice: "We look for good clean writing, a regional hook and relevance. Manuscripts are often rejected because writer is obviously not familiar with the magazine and story lacks regional flavor."

PEN SYNDICATE FICTION (I), Box 15650, Washington D.C. 20003. (202)543-6322. Director: Caroline Marshall. Program, established by the NEA, to promote short fiction through syndication. Submissions selected sent to newspapers and regional magazines. Accepts submissions *only in the month of January*. Estab: 1982.

Needs: "Tight, well-plotted stories, unpublished or published in publications of less than 2,000 circulation.' Receives 1,800 mss per reading period. Length: no more than 2,500 words.

How to Contact: *Submissions accepted in January only*. Send two copies, brief bio and SASE. Decisions made in April. Include cover sheet with author, title and number of words.

Payment: $500 for rights to selected story; $100 per publication by participating newspapers.

Terms: Pays $500 on return of contract; $100 within 60 days of newspaper publication. Realistic possible potential: $1,000.

PENNSYLVANIA SPORTSMAN (II), Northwoods Publications, Inc., Box 5196, Harrisburg PA 17110. (717)233-4797. Editor: Lou Hoffman. Magazine for field sports audience: 8½x11; 96 pages; 30 lb coated paper; 70 lb cover stock; illustrations; photos. Estab. 1959. Circ. 52,000.

Needs: Hunting- and fishing-related stories. Receives 6 unsolicited mss/month. Buys 1-2 mss/issue; 6-14 mss/year. Published new writers within the year. Length: 1,000-1,200 words average. Occasionally critiques rejected mss.

How to Contact: Query first. Reports in 2 months on queries. SASE. Simultaneous submissions OK "if not within our audience." Accepts computer printout submissions. Prefers letter-quality. Does not read mss summer or winter. Sample copy $1 with 9x12 SAE and $1.25 postage.

Payment: $30-$75.

Terms: Pays on publication for all rights. Publication copyrighted.

PENNYWHISTLE PRESS (II), Gannett Co., Inc., Box 500-P, Washington DC 20044. Editor: Anita Sama. Magazine: tabloid size; 8 pages; newsprint paper; illustrations; photos. Education and information for children ages 6-12. Weekly. Estab. 1981. Circ. 2.5 million.

Needs: Juvenile (5-9 years), (long) prose poem, young adult/teen (10-14 years). No talking animals, poorly spelled and unprofessional mss. Receives "hundreds" of unsolicited fiction mss/month. Accepts 20 mss/year. Published new writers within the last year. Length: 450 words for 5-7 year olds; 850 words for older children.

How to Contact: Send complete ms with cover letter with SASE. *No* queries. No simultaneous submissions accepted. "We do not accept previously published manuscripts." Sample copy 50¢.

Payment: Varies.

Terms: Pays on acceptance.

PENTHOUSE (II), Penthouse International, Ltd., 1965 Broadway, New York NY 10023. (212)496-6100. Fiction Editor: Gwen Given. A men's entertainment magazine featuring "high quality sophisticated articles of interest to men between the ages of 18-34." Exposés, humor, profiles and interviews. Monthly. Estab. 1965. Circ. 3,000,000.

Needs: Contemporary, psychic/supernatural/occult, science fiction, horror, erotica, western, adventure and first serial excerpts from novels. No stories with women's point of view, plotless sexual encounters or extreme avant-garde fiction. Buys 12 mss/year. Receives approximately 400 unsolicited fiction mss/month. Recently published work by William F. Buckley, Jr. and James Michener; published new writers within the last year. Length: 3,000-6,000 words.

How to Contact: Send ms with SASE. Reports in 1 month on mss. Sample copy for $5.

Terms: Pays on acceptance for exclusive first English language rights and sometimes world rights. Publication copyrighted.

Advice: "Send us well-written stories, neatly typed and of interest to our audience. We are always looking for new fiction talent." Many mss are rejected because they are "not right for our audience; characters are not fully developed; they are too short. Take more time to consider who the readers of the particular magazine you submit to are."

PILLOW TALK (II), 801 2nd Ave., New York NY 10017. Editor: Mario Almonte. Magazine: digest-sized; 98 pages; illustrations; photos. Quarterly letters magazine.

Needs: "We are in need of approximately 40 short letters per issue in length of no more than four manuscript pages, and five long letters of approximately 10 manuscript pages." Published new writers within the last year. Recommends other markets.

How to Contact: In general, "we assign the majority of the material to writers who have proven reliable, but often we receive excellent unsolicited material, and encourage unsolicited mss."

Terms: *Pillow Talk* pays $5 per page for short letters, and $75 for long ten-page letters. Pays on publication.

Advice: "Our guidelines for *PillowTalk* are simple: Good characterization, believable plots and the sex should be a natural outgrowth of a relationship. No S&M, incest, homosexuality, anal sex or sex-crazed women and 'studs.' No sex for its own sake; let's have a little romance."

PLAYBOY MAGAZINE (III), Playboy Enterprises, Inc., 919 N. Michigan Ave., Chicago IL 60611. (312)751-8000. Fiction Editor: Alice K. Turner. Magazine: 8½x11; 250 pages; glossy cover stock; illustrations; photos. Entertainment magazine for a male audience. Monthly. Estab. 1953. Circ. 4,250,342.

Needs: Literary, contemporary, science fiction, fantasy, horror, sports, western, mystery, adventure and humor. No pornography or fiction geared to a female audience. Buys 1-3 mss/issue; 25 mss/year. Receives approximately 1,200 unsolicited fiction mss each month. Recently published work by Andre Dubus, Joseph Neller, Bret Easton Ellis; published new writers within the last year. Length: 1,000-10,000 (average 6,000) words. Also publishes short shorts of 1,000 words. Critiques rejected mss "when there is time." Recommends other markets "sometimes."

How to Contact: Send complete ms with SASE and cover letter with prior publication information. Reports in 6-8 weeks on mss. Free guidelines with SASE.

Payment: $5,000 minimum; $2,000 minimum for short-shorts.

Terms: Pays on acceptance for all rights. Publication copyrighted.

Advice: "Writers should take a close look at *Playboy* to see the kind and quality of fiction we publish."

PLAYGIRL MAGAZINE (II), 801 Second Ave., New York NY 10017. (212)986-5100. Fiction Editor: Mary Ellen Strote. Magazine: 8x10; 120 pages; 40 lb paper; 60 lb cover stock; illustrations; photos. Magazine for today's young women ages 18-40, average age 26, featuring entertainment, fiction, beauty and fashion, current events, sex and health. Monthly. Estab. 1973. Circ. 800,000.

Needs: Feminist, excerpted novel. "No gay, juvenile, murder, mystery, graphic sex." Receives approximately 200 unsolicited fiction mss/month. Buys 1 ms/issue. Approximately 40% of fiction is agented. Recently published work by Lewis Nordan, Sharon Sheehe Stark, Kurt Rheinheimer; published new writers within the last year. Length: 1,000 words minimum; 5,000 words maximum; 3,500 words average. Publishes short shorts. Occasionally critiques rejected mss.

How to Contact: Send complete ms with SASE. Simultaneous, photocopied and previously published submissions OK. Accepts computer printout submissions. Prefers letter-quality. Reports in 6-8 weeks on mss. Publishes ms an average of 3-6 months after acceptance. Sample copy from Customer Service Department; $6 includes postage and handling.

Payment: $500 minimum and 1-2 contributor's copies.

Terms: Pays on acceptance for one-time magazine rights in the English language. Occasionally buys reprints. Publication copyrighted.

Advice: "Know your market. Keep trying! Make your stories *emotional*."

POCKETS (II), Devotional Magazine for Children, The Upper Room, Box 189, 1908 Grand Ave., Nashville TN 37202. (615)340-7333. Editor-in-Chief: Janet M. Bugg. Magazine: 7x9; 32 pages; 50 lb white econowrite paper; 80 lb white coated, heavy cover stock; color and 2-color illustrations; some photos. Magazine for children ages 6-12, with articles specifically geared for ages 8 to 11. "The magazine offers stories, activities, prayers, poems—all geared to giving children a better understanding of themselves as children of God." Published monthly except for January. Estab. 1981. Estimated circ. 65,000.

Needs: Adventure, contemporary, ethnic, fantasy, historical (general), juvenile, religious/inspirational and suspense/mystery. "All submissions should address the broad theme of the magazine. Each issue will be built around several themes with material which can be used by children in a variety of ways. Scripture stories, fiction, poetry, prayers, art, graphics, puzzles and activities will all be included. Submissions do not need to be overtly religious. They should help children experience a Christian lifestyle that is not always a neatly wrapped moral package, but is open to the continuing revelation of God's will. Seasonal material, both secular and liturgical, is desired. No violence, horror, sexual and racial stereotyping or fiction containing heavy moralizing." Receives approximately 120 unsolicited fiction mss/month. Buys 2-3 mss/issue; 22-33 mss/year. Publishes short shorts. A peace-with-justice theme will run

throughout the magazine. Approximately 50% of fiction is agented. Recently published work by Peggy King Anderson. Length: 600 words minimum; 1,500 words maximum; 1,200 words average.
How to Contact: Send complete ms with SASE. Photocopied and previously published submissions OK, but no simultaneous submissions. Accepts computer printout submissions. Reports in 2 months on mss. Publishes ms 12-18 months after acceptance. Sample copy $1.70. Free fiction guidelines and themes with SASE. "Strongly advise sending for themes before submitting."
Payment: 7¢/word and up and 2-5 contributor's copies. $1.70 charge for extras; 25¢ each for 10 or more.
Terms: Pays on acceptance for newspaper and periodical rights. Buys reprints.
Advice: "Do not write *down* to children." Rejects mss because "we receive far more submissions than we can use. If all were of high quality, we still would purchase only a few. The most common problems are overworked story lines and flat, unrealistic characters. Most stories simply do not 'ring true', and children know that. Each issue is theme-related. Please send for list of themes. Include SASE."

PORTLAND MONTHLY MAGAZINE (II), 578 Congress St., Portland ME 04101. (207)773-5250. Editor: Colin Sargent. Magazine: 68 pages; 60 lb paper; 80 lb cover stock; illustrations and photographs. "City lifestyle magazine—style, business, real estate, controversy, fashion, cuisine, interviews, art." Estab. 1986. Circ. 22,000.
Needs: Contemporary, historical, literary, mainstream, regional, suspense/mystery. Receives 20 unsolicited fiction mss/month. Buys 1 mss/issue; 12 mss/year. Publishes short shorts. Recently published work by Frederick Barthelme, Diane Lefer, Dan Domench. Length: 3 double-spaced typed pages.
How to Contact: Send complete ms with cover letter. Reports in 6 weeks. SASE. Accepts computer printout submissions. Sample copy $2.
Terms: Pays on publication for first North American serial rights. Publication copyrighted.
Advice: "We publish ambitious short fiction featuring everyone from Frederick Barthelme to newly discovered fiction by Edna St. Vincent Millay."

‡PRIME TIME SPORTS AND FITNESS (I, II), GND Prime Time Publishing, Box 6091, Evanston IL 60204. (312)864-8113. Fiction Editor: Joy Keifer. Magazine "covering racquet and health club sports and fitness." Monthly. Circ. 35,000.
Needs: Erotica (if related to fitness club), fantasy (related to fitness), humor/satire, religious (no "God-is-my-sheperd," but "body-is-God's-temple" is okay), romance (related to fitness). "No raunchy or talking down exercise stories, upbeat is what we want." Buys 10 fiction mss/year. Length: 500 words minimum; 2,500 words maximum.
How to Contact: Send complete ms. Photocopied submissions OK. No dot-matrix computer printout submissions. Sample copy for SAE and 3 first-class stamps; writer's guidelines for #10 SASE.
Payment: Pays $20-$150.
Terms: Pays on publication for all rights, but will assign back to author. Publication copyrighted.

PRIME TIMES (II), National Association for Retired Credit Union People, Inc., (NARCUP), Editorial Offices: Suite 120, 2802 International Ln., Madison WI 53704. Executive Editor: Joan Donovan. Magazine: medium sized; 40 pages; illustrations; photos. Editorial slant is toward redefining the mid-life transition and promoting a dynamic vision of the prime-life years. Each edition revolves loosely around a theme—for example, stress management and preventive health help, second careers, unique problems of the midlife or "bridge" generation. The short story may sketch relational conflicts and resolutions between prime-life men and women, or with their children, parents, etc., or place them in situations that try their spirits and revalidate them. Fiction that is not targeted to this group but of excellent quality and broad general appeal is also very welcome. Staff will review adventure, ethnic, science fiction, fantasy, mainstream and humorous fiction as well. No sentimental romances or nostalgia pieces, please. Quarterly. Estab. 1979. Circ. 75,000.
Needs: Literary, contemporary, romance, adventure, humor, ethnic, travel. Buys 2 mss/year. Approximately 10% of fiction is agented. Recently published work by Ethan Canin. Length: 2,500-4,000 words. Shorter lengths preferred.
How to Contact: Send complete ms. SASE always. Accepts computer printout submissions. Prefers letter-quality. Reports in 4-6 weeks on queries and mss. Publishes ms 6-12 months after acceptance. Free sample copy with 9x12 SASE (5 first class stamps). Free guidelines with SASE.
Payment: $150-$750. 3 free author's copies; $1 charge for each extra.
Terms: Pays on publication for first North American serial rights and for second serial (reprint) rights.
Advice: "We may feature fiction only once or twice yearly, now, instead of regularly. Quality is *everything*. Readers favor the short stories we've featured on positive human relationships. We are very happy to feature second-serial work as long as it hasn't appeared in another *national* 'maturity market' publication. *Always* request a publication's writer's guidelines before submitting. Write with emotional integrity and imagination."

‡PRIVATE LETTERS (I,II), 801 2nd Ave., New York NY 10017. Editor: Mario Almonte. Magazine; digest-sized; 98 pages; illustrations; photographs. Quarterly letters magazine.

Needs: Erotica, written in letter form. "We use approximately 40 short letters per issue of no more than four double-spaced manuscript pages and five long letters of about 10 double-spaced manuscript pages." Recently published work by J. Paul Sutter, Diana Shamblin, Jack Macy; published new writers last year. Recommends other markets.

How to Contact: Send complete mss. "The majority of the material is assigned to people whose writing has proven consistently top-notch. They usually reach this level by sending us unsolicited material which impresses us. We invite them to send us some more on spec, and we're impressed again. Then a long and fruitful relationship is hopefully established. We greatly encourage unsolicited submissions."

Payment: Pays $5 per page for short letters; $75 for long (7-10 page) letters.

Terms: Pays on acceptance.

Advice: "If you base your writing on erotic magazines other than our own, then we'll probably find your material too gross. We want good characterization, believable plots, a little romance, with sex being a natural outgrowth of a relationship. (Yes, it can be done. Read our magazine.) No S&M, incest, homosexuality, anal sex or sex-crazed women and macho, women-conquering studs. Portray sex as an emotionally charged, romantic experience—not an animalistic ritual. *Never* give up, except if you die. In which case, if your haven't succeeded as a writer yet, you probably never will. (Though there have been exceptions.)"

PURPOSE (II), Mennonite Publishing House, 616 Walnut Ave., Scottdale PA 15683-1999. (412)887-8500. Editor: James E. Horsch. Magazine: 5⅜x8⅜; 8 pages; illustrations; photos. "Magazine discipleship—how to be a faithful Christian in the midst of tough everday life complexities. Use story form to present models and examples for Christians interested in exploring faithful discipleship." Weekly. Estab. 1969. Circ. 19,250.

Needs: Historical, religious/inspirational. No militaristic/narrow patriotism or racism. Receives 100 unsolicited mss/month. Buys 3 mss/issue; 40 mss/year. Publishes short shorts. Published new writers within the last year. Length: 800 words average; 350 words minimum; 1,200 words maximum. Occasionally comments on rejected ms.

How to Contact: Prefer full manuscript. Will respond to query. Reports in 6 weeks on queries and mss. Simultaneous, photocopied and previously published work OK. Accepts computer printout submissions. Prefers letter-quality. Sample copy free with 6x9 SAE and 2 first class stamps. Writer's guidelines free with sample copy only.

Payment: Up to 5¢/word for stories and up to $1 per line for poetry and 2 contributor's copies.

Terms: Pays on acceptance for one-time rights. Publication copyrighted.

Advice: Many stories are "situational—how to respond to dilemmas. Write crisp, action moving, personal style, focused upon an individual, a group of people, or an organization. The story form is an excellent literary device to use in exploring discipleship issues. There are many issues to explore. Each writer brings a unique solution. Let's hear them. The first two paragraphs are crucial in establishing the mood/issue to be resolved in the story. Work hard on this."

ELLERY QUEEN'S MYSTERY MAGAZINE (II), Davis Publications, Inc., 380 Lexington Ave., New York NY 10017. (212)557-9100. Editor: Eleanor Sullivan. Magazine: digest sized; 160 pages. Magazine for lovers of mystery fiction. Published 13 times/year. Estab. 1941. Circ. 350,000.

Needs: "We accept only mystery, crime and detective fiction." Buys 10-15 mss/issue. Receives approximately 250 unsolicited fiction mss each month. Approximately 50% of fiction is agented. Recently published work by Clark Howard, Antonia Fraser, Joe Gores; published new writers within the last year. Length: up to 9,000 words. Critiques rejected mss "only when a story might be a possibility for us if revised." Sometimes recommends other markets.

How to Contact: Send complete ms with SASE. Cover letter should include publishing credits and brief biographical sketch. Reports in 1 month or sooner on mss. Publishes ms 6-12 months after acceptance. Free fiction guidelines with SASE. Sample copy for $2.

Payment: 3¢ per word and up.

Terms: Pays on acceptance for first North American serial rights. Occasionally buys reprints. Publication copyrighted.

Advice: "Read the magazine; know what we publish. Originality of a writer's work and an awareness of what has been published help. We have Department of First Stories and usually publish at least one first story an issue—i.e., the author's first published fiction. We select stories that are fresh and of the kind our readers have expressed a liking for. In writing a detective story, you must play fair with the reader re clues and necessary information. Otherwise you have a better chance of publishing if you avoid writing to formula."

R-A-D-A-R (II), Standard Publishing, 8121 Hamilton Ave., Cincinnati OH 45231. (513)931-4050. Editor: Margaret Williams. Magazine: 12 pages; newsprint; illustrations; a few photos. "*R-A-D-A-R* is a take-home paper, distributed in Sunday school classes for children in grades 3-6. The stories and other features reinforce the Bible lesson taught in class. Boys and girls who attend Sunday school make up the audience. The fiction stories, Bible picture stories and other special features appeal to their interests." Weekly. Estab. 1978.

Needs: Fiction—The hero of the story should be an 11- or 12-year-old in a situation involving one or more of the following: history, mystery, animals (preferably horses or dogs), prose poem, spiritual, sports, adventure, school, travel, relationships with parents, friends and others. Stories should have believable plots and be wholesome, Christian character-building, but not "preachy." No science fiction. Receives approximately 75-100 unsolicited mss/month. Recently published work by Betty Lou Mell, Betty Steele Everett; published new writers within the last year. Length: 900-1,000 words average; 400 words minimum; 1,200 words maximum. Publishes short shorts.

How to Contact: Send complete ms. Reports in 2 weeks on queries; 6-8 weeks on mss. SASE for ms. No simultaneous submissions; photocopied and reprint submissions OK. Accepts computer printout submissions; no dot-matrix. Reports in 6-8 weeks. Free sample copy and guidelines.

Payment: 3¢ a word. Free contributor's copy.

Terms: Pays on acceptance for first rights. Publication copyrighted.

Advice: "Send for sample copy, guidesheet, and theme list. Follow the specifics of guidelines. Keep your writing current with the times and happenings of our world."

‡RADIANCE (II), The Magazine for Large Women, Box 31703, Oakland CA 94604. (415)482-0680. Editor: Alice Ansfield. Fiction Editors: Alice Ansfield and Lisa Zimmerman. Magazine: 8½x11; 48-52 pages; glossy/coated paper; 70 lb cover stock; illustrations; photos. "Theme is to encourage women to live fully now, whatever their body size. To stop waiting to live or feel good about themselves until they lose weight. Health, emotional well-being, cultural views of body size, poetry/art, profiles, book reviews, lots of ads for services/products for large women, etc." Audience is "large women (size 16 and over) from all walks of life, all ages, ethnic groups, education levels and lifestyles. Feminist, fashion, emotionally supportive magazine." Quarterly. Estab. 1984. Circ. 35,000.

Needs: Adventure, contemporary, erotica, ethnic, fantasy, feminist, historical, humor/satire, mainstream, preschool, prose poem, science fiction, spiritual, sports, suspense, young/adult/teen. "Would prefer fiction to have in it a larger-bodied character; living in a positive, upbeat way. Our goal is to empower women." Receives 30-50 mss/month. Buys 4 mss/year. Publishes ms within 1 year of acceptance. Recently published work by Jean Gonick. Length: 1,800 words preferred; 800 words minimum; 2,500 words maximum. Publishes short shorts. Sometimes critiques rejected mss and recommends other markets.

How to Contact: Query with clips of published work and send complete mss with cover letter. Reports in 1-2 months. SASE. Simultaneous, photocopied and reprint submissions OK. Accepts computer printout submissions, including dot-matrix. Sample copy for $1.50. Fiction guidelines for #10 SAE and 1 first class stamp.

Payment: Pays $50-$100 and contributor's copies.

Terms: Pays on publication for one-time rights. Sends galleys to the author if requested. Publication copyrighted.

Advice: "Read our magazine before sending anything to us. Know what our philosophy and points of view are before sending a manuscript. Look around within your community for inspiring, successful and unique large women doing things worth writing about. We will do more fiction in the future, as we grow and have more space for it. At this time, prefer fiction having to do with a larger woman (man, child). Read our magazine. Know our point of view."

RANGER RICK MAGAZINE (II), National Wildlife Federation, 1412 16th St. NW, Washington DC 20036-2266. (703)790-4278. Editor: Gerald Bishop. Fiction Editor: Betty Blair. Magazine: 8x10; 48 pages; glossy paper; 60 lb cover stock; illustrations; photos. "*Ranger Rick* emphasizes conservation and the enjoyment of nature through full-color photos and art, fiction and nonfiction articles, games and puzzles, and special columns. Our audience ranges in ages from 6-12, with the greatest number in the 7 to 10 group. We aim for a fourth grade reading level. They read for fun and information." Monthly. Estab. 1967. Circ. 800,000 + .

Needs: Fantasy, mystery, adventure, science fiction and humor. "Interesting stories for kids focusing directly on nature or related subjects. Fiction that carries a conservation message is always needed, as are adventure stories involving kids with nature or the outdoors. Moralistic 'lessons' taught children by parents or teachers are not accepted. Human qualities are attributed to animals only in our regular feature, 'Adventures of Ranger Rick.' " Receives about 75 unsolicited fiction mss each month. Buys about 6 mss/year. Recently published fiction by Judy Braus. Length: 900 words maximum. Critiques rejected mss "when there is time."

How to Contact: Query with sample lead and any clips of published work with SASE. Reports in 3 weeks on queries, 2 months on mss. Publishes ms 8-12 months after acceptance, but sometimes longer. Free sample copy. Free guidelines with legal-sized SASE.

Payment: $500 maximum/full-length ms.

Terms: Pays on acceptance for all rights. Very rarely buys reprints. Sends galleys to author. Publication copyrighted.

Advice: "For our magazine, the writer needs to understand kids and that aspect of nature he or she is writing about—a difficult combination! Read past issues to learn preferred style and approach; write naturally with no affectation; keep reader in mind at all times without being condescending." Mss are rejected because they are "contrived and/or condescending—often overwritten. Some mss are anthropomorphic, others are above our readers' level. We find that fiction stories help children understand the natural world and the environmental problems it faces. Beginning writers have a chance equal to that of established authors *provided* the quality is there. We are dealing more directly with nature now."

RECONSTRUCTIONIST (II), Federation of Reconstructionist Congregations & Havurot, Church Rd. and Greenwood Ave., Wyncote PA 19095. (215)887-1988. Editor: Jacob Staub. Magazine: 8½x11; 32 pages; illustrations; photos. Review of Jewish culture—essays, fiction, poetry of Jewish interest for American Jews. Published 8 times/year. Estab. 1935. Circ. 9,000.

Needs: Ethnic. Receives 10 unsolicited mss/month; buys 15 mss/year. Publishes ms 1-2 years after acceptance. Recently published work by Myron Taube, Lev Raphael. Published new writers within the last year. Length: 2,500 words average; 3,000 words maximum. Publishes short shorts. Recommends other markets.

How to Contact: Send complete ms with cover letter. Reports in 6-8 weeks. SASE for mss. Photocopied submissions OK. Accepts computer printouts including dot-matrix. Sample copy free.

Payment: Pays $25-$36 and contributor's copies.

Terms: Pays on publication for first rights. Publication copyrighted.

REDBOOK (II), The Hearst Corporation, 224 W. 57th St., New York NY 10019. (212)262-8284. Editor: Annette Capone. Fiction Editor: Deborah Purcell. Magazine: 8x10¾; 150-250 pages; 34 lb paper; 70 lb cover; illustrations; photos. "*Redbook*'s readership consists primarily of American women 25-44 years of age. Most are married, have children and also work outside the home. *Redbook* readers are well-educated, progressive in their attitudes toward the roles and opportunities open to them as women, and are concerned with larger social issues as well as with their homes, their personal relationships and their health and appearance." Monthly. Publishes special fiction issue each August. Estab. 1903. Circ. 4,100,000.

Needs: "*Redbook* takes fiction very seriously, which may be why *Redbook* is one of the few magazines to win the National Magazine Award for fiction *twice*. We generally publish three to four fiction pieces in every issue, except in August, when our special fiction issue features five to six stories. We are looking for fiction that will appeal to active, thinking, contemporary women. Stories need not be about women exclusively; we also look for fiction reflecting the broad range of human experience. We are interested in new voices and buy approximately a quarter of our stories from unsolicited submissions. But standards are high: Stories must be fresh, felt and intelligent; no straight formula fiction, pat endings, highly oblique or symbolic stories without conclusions." Receives up to 3,000 unsolicited fiction mss each month. Recently published work by Dominick Dunne, Alice Hoffman, Susan Kenney; published new writers within the last year. Length: up to 22 ms pages for short stories, up to 9 pages for short shorts.

How to Contact: Send complete ms with 8x11 SASE. No queries, please. Reports in 10-12 weeks. Free guidelines for submission available on request with SASE. Sample copy for $3.25 by mail; $1.50 pick up in person.

Terms: Pays on acceptance. Buys first North American serial rights. Publication copyrighted.

Advice: "We are looking for intelligently humorous stories (not anecdotes); stories of mystery or psychological suspense with particualr attention paid to strong characterizations; topical stories; stories featuring a male protagonist and/or told from the male point of view; stories about women in uniquely challenging situations. Whatever the theme, superior craftsmanship is of paramount importance: Pay keen attention to plotting, character development and a strong and engaging storyline; character sketches and mood or slice-of-life pieces are better suited to other markets. Submit seasonal material nine to 12 months before the appropriate issue." Sponsors Short Story Contest for unpublished writers 18 years of age and up. See March issue of *Redbook* for complete rules.

‡REFORM JUDAISM (II), Union of American Hebrew Congregations, 838 5th Ave., New York NY 10021. (212)249-0100, ext. 400. Editor: Aron Hirt-Manheimer. Managing Editor: Joy Weinberg. Fiction Editor: Steven Schnur. Magazine: 8½x11; 32 or 48 pages; illustrations; photos. "We cover subjects of Jewish interest in general and Reform Jewish in particular, for members of Reform Jewish congrega-

tions in the United States and Canada." Quarterly. Estab. 1972. Circ. 280,000.
Needs: Humor/satire, religious/inspirational. Receives 30 unsolicited mss/month. Buys 3 mss/year. Publishes ms 3 months after acceptance. Length: 1,000 words average; 700 words minimum; 2,000 words maximum. Sometimes recommends other markets.
How to Contact: Send complete ms with cover letter. Reports in 3 weeks. SASE for ms. Simultaneous and photocopied submissions OK. Accepts computer printout submissions, including dot-matrix. Sample copy for $1 and SAE. Fiction guidelines for SAE.
Payment: Pays 10¢/word.
Terms: Pays on publication for first North American serial rights. Publication copyrighted.

RELIX MAGAZINE (IV), Music for the Mind, Box 94, Brooklyn NY 11229. Editor: Toni A. Brown. Magazine: 54 pages; coated paper; 70 lb cover stock; illustrations; photos. "Classic rock publication focusing on psychedelic '60s—Grateful Dead, etc. Have other fiction project in works focusing on rock fiction-futuristic. For 18-40 year old audience." Bimonthly. Estab. 1974. Circ. 25,000.
Needs: Music—Rock 'n Roll. "Want fiction—futuristic rock or fantasy—music related a must." Receives 5 mss/month. Buys 3 mss/year. Length: 2,000 words preferred. Publishes short shorts. Length: 250 words. Sometimes critiques rejected mss.
How to Contact: Send complete ms with cover letter. Reports in 1 year. SASE. Simultaneous submissions OK. Accepts computer printout submissions, including dot-matrix. Sample copy for $3. Fiction guidelines for #10 SAE and 1 first class stamp.
Payment: Pays $1.75/column inch.
Terms: Pays on publication for all rights. Publication copyrighted.

ROAD KING MAGAZINE (I), William A. Coop, Inc., Box 250, Park Forest IL 60466. (312)481-9240. Magazine: 5³⁄₄x8; 48-88 pages; 55 lb enamel paper; 55 lb enamel cover stock; illustrations; photos. "Quarterly leisure-reading magazine for long-haul, over-the-road professional truckers. Contains short articles, short fiction, some product news, games, puzzles and industry news. Truck drivers read it while eating, fueling, during layovers and at other similar times while they are en route."
Needs: Western, mystery, adventure and humor. "Remember that our magazine gets into the home and that some truckers tend to be Bible belt types. No erotica or violence." Buys 1 ms/issue; 4 mss/year. Receives 200 unsolicited fiction mss each year. Published new writers within the last year. Length: 1,200 words.
How to Contact: Send complete ms with SASE. Reports in 3-6 months on mss. Publishes ms 1-2 months after acceptance. Sample copy with 6x9 SAE and 56¢ postage.
Payment: $400 maximum.
Terms: Pays on acceptance for all rights. Publication copyrighted.
Advice: "Don't phone. Don't send mss by registered or insured mail or they will be returned unopened by post office. Don't try to get us involved in lengthy correspondence. Be patient. We have a small staff and we are slow." Mss are rejected because "most don't fit our format . . . they are too long; they do not have enough knowledge of trucking; there is too much violence; they are not really short stories, nothing happens. Our readers like fiction. We are a leisure reading publication with a wide variety of themes and articles in each issue. Truckers can read a bit over coffee, in the washroom, etc., then save the rest of the magazine for the next stop."

THE ROSE ARTS MAGAZINE (II), 336 SE 32nd Ave., Portland OR 97214. (503)231-0644. Editor: Terry Hammond. Magazine: 8½x10³⁄₄; 40+ pages; Catalina paper and cover; illustrations; photos. "*The Rose Arts Magazine* is dedicated to the promotion of arts and artists, gives attention also to broad cultural themes, and offers a platform for feature articles, creative writing, essays, fiction and historical perspectives." Bimonthly. Estab. 1986. Circ. 10,000.
Needs: Adventure, contemporary, erotica, ethnic, experimental, fantasy, feminist, gay, historical (general), humor/satire, lesbian, literary, psychic/supernatural/occult, regional, romance (contemporary, historical), science fiction, suspense/mystery, translations. Receives 20 unsolicited mss/month. Buys 0-1 ms/issue; 2-6 mss/year. Publishes ms 1-4 months after acceptance. Recently published work by Larry Stolte, W. Sean Roberts, Lesley Conger; published new writers within the last year. Length: 2,000-2,500 words average; 1,000 words minimim; 3,000 words maximum. Sometimes critiques rejected mss.
How to Contact: Send complete ms with cover letter, which should include brief, informal introduction of author and piece. Reports in 1-2 weeks on queries; 2-6 weeks on mss. SASE. Photocopied submissions OK. Accepts computer printout submissions, including dot-matrix. Sample copy for $1. Fiction guidelines free.
Payment: Pays 2¢/word minimum (generous number of copies provided for cost of postage only).
Terms: Pays on publication for one-time rights. Publication copyrighted.
Advice: "I welcome submissions by beginning writers and am willing to work on a piece with an author by making suggestions for a second draft if necessary according to our standards of quality."

ST. ANTHONY MESSENGER (II), St. Anthony Messenger, 1615 Republic St., Cincinnati OH 45210. Editor: Norman Perry, O.F.M. Magazine: 10¾x8; 56 pages; illustrations; photos. "*St. Anthony Messenger* is a Catholic family magazine which aims to help its readers lead more fully human and Christian lives. We publish articles which report on a changing church and world, opinion pieces written from the perspective of Christian faith and values, personality profiles, and fiction which entertains and informs." Monthly. Estab. 1893. Circ. 400,000.

Needs: Contemporary, religious/inspirational, romance, senior citizen/retirement and spiritual. "We do not want mawkishly sentimental or preachy fiction. Stories are most often rejected for poor plotting and characterization; bad dialogue—listen to how people talk; inadequate motivation. Many stories say nothing, are 'happenings' rather than stories." No fetal journals, no rewritten Bible stories. Receives 50-60 unsolicited fiction mss/month. Buys 1 ms/issue; 12 mss/year. Recently published work by Mary Anne McCarthy, Patricia White, Lin Nowicki. Published new writers within the last year. Length: 2,500-3,000 words. Critiques rejected mss "when there is time." Sometimes recommends other markets.

How to Contact: Send complete ms with SASE. Accepts computer printout submissions. Prefers letter-quality. Reports in 6 weeks on mss. Publishes ms up to 1 year after acceptance. Free sample copy and guidelines with #10 SASE.

Payment: 14¢/word maximum; 2 free author's copies; $1 charge for extras.

Terms: Pays on acceptance for first North American serial rights. Publication copyrighted.

Advice: "We publish one story a month and we get 500 or 600 a year. Stick to published word length. Read guidelines and look at back issues to see what we *do* publish. Plots and characters have to be real. Too many offer simplistic 'solutions' or answers. Fiction entertains but can also convey a point in a very telling way just as the Bible uses stories to teach."

ST. JOSEPH'S MESSENGER AND ADVOCATE OF THE BLIND (II), Sisters of St. Joseph of Peace, 541 Pavonia Ave., Jersey City NJ 07306. (201)798-4141. Magazine: 8½x11; 16 pages; illustrations; photos. For Catholics generally but not exclusively. Theme is "religious—relevant—real." Quarterly. Estab. 1903. Circ. 30,000.

Needs: Contemporary, humor/satire, mainstream, religious/inspirational, romance, and senior citizen/retirement. Receives 30-40 unsolicited fiction mss/month. Buys 3 mss/issue; 20 mss/year. Recently published work by Alan Cliburn. Published new writers within the last year. Length: 800 words minimum; 1,800 words maximum; 1,500 words average. Occasionally critiques rejected mss.

How to Contact: Send complete ms with SASE. Simultaneous, photocopied and previously published submissions OK. Publishes ms an average of 1 year after acceptance. Free sample copy with #10 SAE and 1 first class stamp. Free fiction guidelines with SASE.

Payment: $10-$25 and 2 contributor's copies.

Terms: Pays on acceptance for one-time rights.

Advice: Rejects mss because of "vague focus or theme. Write to be read—keep material current and of interest. *Do not preach*—the story will tell the message. Keep the ending from being too obvious. Fiction is the greatest area of interest to our particular reading public."

SAN GABRIEL VALLEY MAGAZINE (IV), Miller Books, 2908 W. Valley Blvd., Alhambra CA 91803. (213)284-7607. Editor: Joseph Miller. Magazine: 5¼x7¼; 48 pages; 60 lb book paper; vellum Bristol cover stock; illustrations; photos. "Regional magazine for the Valley featuring local entertainment, dining, sports and events. We also carry articles about successful people from the area. For upper-middle class people who enjoy going out a lot." Bimonthly. Published special fiction issue last year; plans another. Estab. 1976. Circ. 3,000.

Needs: Contemporary, inspirational, psychic/supernatural/occult, western, adventure and humor. No articles on sex or ERA. Receives approximately 10 unsolicited fiction mss/month. Buys 2 mss/issue; 20 mss/year. Published new writers within the last year. Length: 500-2,500 words. Also publishes short shorts. Recommends other markets.

How to Contact: Send complete ms with SASE. Accepts computer printout submissions. Reports in 2 weeks on mss. Sample copy $1 with 9x12 SASE.

Payment: 5¢/word; 2 free author's copies.

Terms: Payment on acceptance for one-time rights. Publication copyrighted.

Advice: "Write a good story with positive attitudes." Mss are rejected because "they do not relate to our region or readers."

SATURDAY EVENING POST (I, II), Benjamin Franklin Literary and Medical Society, 1100 Waterway Blvd., Indianapolis IN 46202. (317)636-8881. Editor: Dr. Cory Servaas, M.D. Senior Editor: Ted Kreiter. Magazine with articles on general interest, health care, personalities and book reviews for conservative middle-aged, middle-income, college-educated audience. Published 9 times/year. Estab. 1728. Circ. 700,000.

Needs: Religious/inspirational, adventure and humor. No explicit sex, profanity, perversion, ethnic humor or anti-traditional family life. Buys very few unsolicited mss. Length: average of 2,500 words.
How to Contact: Send complete ms with SASE. Reports in 1-8 weeks.
Payment: Pays average of $250.
Terms: Pays on publication for all rights.
Advice: "We want positive stories about romance, family and love, people winning out in the end. Humor has a better chance. Keep it simple."

SCHOLASTIC SCOPE (II), Scholastic, Inc., 730 Broadway, New York NY 10003. Magazine: 8½x11; 22-28 pages; pulp paper stock; glossy cover; illustrations and photos. National publication on subjects of general and human interest; profiles of teenagers who have overcome obstacles or done something unusual; short stories and plays for teens. Weekly. Circ. 1,100,000.
Needs: Stories about the problems of teens (drugs, prejudice, runaways, failure in school, family problems, etc.); relationships between people in family; job and school situations. No crime stories. Recently published work by Norma Fox Mazer and Julius Lester. Published new writers within the last year. Length: 400-2,000 words.
How to Contact: Send complete ms with SASE. Sample copy for $1.75.
Payment: Pays $125 minimum.
Terms: Acquires all rights.
Advice: "Strive for directness, realism and action in dialogue rather than narrative. Characters should have depth. Avoid too many coincidences and random happenings."

SCORE (IV), Canada's Golf Magazine, Canadian Controlled Media Communications (CCMC), 287 MacPherson Ave., Toronto Ontario M4V 1A4 Canada. (416)928-2909. Managing Editor: John Gordon. Magazine: 8½x10⅞; 80 pages; 60 lb coated paper stock and cover; b&w & color photos. "Golf: players, events, travel (as golf destinations), equipment, technical, instruction, humor, fiction, etc." For "over 25, upper income, socially active, those usually belonging to private or semi-private golf clubs." Published 8 times/year. Estab. 1981. Circ. 171,000 +.
Needs: Golf related. No adventure or science fiction. Receives approximately 8 unsolicited fiction mss/month. Buys 0-2 mss/issue; 4-9 mss/year "depending on their caliber and our editorial needs." Does not read mss September-December. Publishes ms 1½-6 months after acceptance. Length: 800-1,500 words average; 1,700 words maximum. Occasionally critiques rejected mss.
How to Contact: Query with clips of published work or send complete ms with cover letter with resumé, published references, full name, address, phone number, reasons why writer wishes to work with *Score* and some indication writer is familiar with magazine." Reports in 1 month. SAE and IRC for query and ms. Simultaneous submissions OK. Accepts computer printouts, no dot-matrix. Sample copy for $2, 9x12 SAE and 65¢ postage (no US stamps). Fiction guidelines for #10 SAE and 65¢ postage.
Payment: Pays $175-$500 (Canadian).
Terms: Pays on publication for all rights. Publication copyrighted.
Advice: "Writers of fiction must have a solid foundation in researching their subjects (as far as possible) in order to make it *good* fiction rather than just fantasy. Writers wishing to work for *Score* must have a background in the game of golf, whether they write technical material or fiction. Writing is also obviously very competitive, so writers just breaking in will have to not only show their knowledge, they will have to have a firm fluency in the basics of presentations: grammar, usage, spelling, typing, etc. and introductory letters. You have only one chance to make a first impression, and that's quite often what catches the editor's eye, or sends the query into limbo. Golf lends itself to various facets of fiction writing. It also breaks up what can become an annoying continuum of technical/instructional material. Decide exactly what you have to write before you contact us. If you have a half-baked idea we are not going to finish it for you. Make us aware that you have taken the trouble to familiarize yourself with *Score* before you write to us, and present yourself well."

SCREW MAGAZINE (II), The Sex Review, Milky Way Productions, Box 432, Old Chelsea Station, New York NY 10011. (212)989-8001. Editor: Al Goldstein. Fiction Editor: Manny Neuhaus. Tabloid: 56 pages; pulp paper; 2-color pulp cover stock; illustrations; photos. Humor, sex, satire, parody, first-person erotica stories for adult males. Weekly. Estab. 1968. Circ. 150,000.
Needs: Confession, erotica, ethnic, experimental, feminist, gay, humor/satire, lesbian. Nothing non-sexual. Receives 5-15 unsolicited fiction mss/month. Buys 1-3 mss/issue. Publishes ms 1-6 months after acceptance. Length: 1,300 words average; 1,000 words minimum; 2,500 words maximum. Occasionally critiques rejected mss. Recommends other markets.
How to Contact: Send complete ms with cover letter. Reports in 1-2 months. Photocopied submissions OK. Accepts computer printouts including dot-matrix. Sample copy and fiction guidelines free.
Payment: Pays $40-$150; contributor's copies.
Terms: Pays on publication for all rights. Publication copyrighted.

SEACOAST LIFE (II, IV), American Marketing Systems/AMS Publishing Ltd., Box 594, North Hampton NH 03862. (603)964-9898. Fiction Editor: Kathleen J. Hargreaves. Magazine: 8¹/₂x11; 126 pages; coated freesheet paper; 65 lb coated cover stock; 4-color illustrations, 50/issue; 4-color photographs, 75/issue. "Lifestyle, reflecting southern Maine, seacoast New Hampshire and northeast Massachusetts. We publish fiction each issue plus regional events, investigative journalism, recipes, business, health, fashion, people articles, for an upscale, well-educated audience 25-50." Quarterly. Estab. 1985. Circ. 20,000.
Needs: Adventure, condensed novel, contemporary, fantasy, humor/satire, literary, mainstream, regional, science fiction, senior citizen/retirement, serialized/excerpted novel, suspense/mystery, translations. No radical fiction, i.e. homosexual, pornographic, etc. Receives 2-3 unsolicited fiction mss/month. Accepts 1 mss/issue; 5 mss/year (we also publish a holiday issue). Publishes ms 90-180 days after acceptance. Length: 1,500-3,000 words average. Sometimes critiques rejected ms.
How to Contact: "Must be regional in order to submit—northern Massachusetts, coastal New Hampshire, southern Maine." Send complete ms with cover letter, writer's bio. Reports in 2 weeks. SASE. Simultaneous and photocopied submissions OK. Accepts computer printout submissions, including dot-matrix. Sample copy $2.50 and 9x12 SAE with $2.40 postage. Fiction guidelines for #10 SAE and 40¢ postage.
Payment: Varies; charge for copies.
Terms: Pays 30 days after publication. Rights purchased negotiated with each individual writer. Publication copyrighted.
Advice: "Our readership is highly educated, critical of shabby work and loves good fiction. Our readers love to read. Send manuscripts which are clear and easy to read. We will read all submissions and reply to all writers."

SEEK (II), Standard Publishing, 8121 Hamilton Ave., Cincinnati OH 45231. Editor: Eileen H. Wilmoth. Magazine: 8¹/₂x5¹/₂; 8 pages; newsprint paper; art and photos in each issue. "Inspirational stories of faith-in-action for Christian young adults; a Sunday School take-home paper." Weekly. Published special fiction issue last year; plans another. Estab. 1970. Circ. 75,000.
Needs: Religious/inspirational. Buys 150 mss/year. Published new writers within the last year. Length: 500-1,200 words.
How to Contact: Send complete ms with SASE. Accepts computer printout submissions. Prefers letter-quality. Reports in 4-6 weeks on mss. Publishes ms an average of 1 year after acceptance. Free sample copy and guidelines.
Payment: 2¹/₂-3¢/word.
Terms: Pays on acceptance. Buys reprints.
Advice: "Write a credible story with Christian slant—no preachments; avoid overworked themes such as joy in suffering, generation gaps, etc. Most mss are rejected by us because of irrelevant topic or message; unrealistic story; or poor character and/or plot development. We use fiction stories that are believable."

‡SENIOR LIFE MAGAZINE (IV), 1420 E. Cooley Dr., Suite 200L, Colton CA 92324. (714)824-6681. Editor: Bobbi Mason. Magazine: 8¹/₂x10³/₄; 48 pages; 47 lb paper; 50 lb cover; illustrations and photos. "For readers age 50 + ; subjects vary widely." Monthly. Estab. 1979. Circ. 30,000.
Needs: Adventure, condensed novel, historical, humor/satire, literary, inspirational, senior citizen/retirement, sports, suspense/mystery, western, nostalgia, holidays, family scenarios/reunions, RV camping, moving/relocating, trains (collectors or small steamers). No erotica, food, travel, health, political, gay/lesbian/feminist, psychic. Receives "too many" unsolicited fiction mss/month. Buys 6 fiction mss/year. Length: 400-800 words preferred. "The shorter the better; space is tight."
How to Contact: Query first; "please state 'up front' required/requested fee." Reporting time "depends on load." SASE. Simultaneous, photocopied (if clear) and reprint submissions OK. No dot-matrix computer printouts. Accepts electronic submissions via disk or modem; query for details. Sample copy $2.50.
Payment: Pays $10-$50 (with art and photos); 1 contributor's copy. Free subscription to magazine on request.
Terms: Pays on publication. Publication copyrighted.
Advice: "Write tight. Space is limited. Enclose SASE. Prefer name, address and phone on all pieces sent, i.e. each page of manuscript, each sketch, graph or photo."

ROD SERLING'S THE TWILIGHT ZONE MAGAZINE (II), TZ Publications, Third Floor, 401 Park Ave. South, New York NY 10016-8802. Editor-in-Chief: Tappan King. Magazine: 8¹/₂x11; 104-116 pages; 96 pp of b&w and a color section; color/slick cover; 10-15 full page illustrations; photos. "A magazine devoted to imaginative and speculative fiction. We're always on the lookout for originality, strong writing, and strong, vivid characters." Bimonthly. Estab. 1981. Circ. 150,000.

Close-up

Sara London
Seventeen

William Milliot

When Sara London reads or talks about fiction, she doesn't dwell on dos and don'ts. She poses questions—the kind that writers must ask. "There may be plenty of plot and characterization, and a lot of good work," she says, "but finally what is the story about?"

Working in *Seventeen*'s New York City office, London receives about 300 fiction manuscripts per month. As fiction editor, she does most of the reading except when an intern works in the office. "I take manuscripts home almost nightly and always on weekends. I do a lot of reading for the one manuscript that is a great surprise and a wonderful piece for us," she says.

London looks for stories "that are accessible and appealing to a teenage audience, but also challenging, sophisticated, literary." *Seventeen* stories must have distinctive characterizations; credible dialogue; and freshly handled plots, settings and subjects.

One difficulty in selecting stories for *Seventeen* is the wide range of readers' ages—from 13 to 21, with most of them between 15 and 18. Readers are not easily engaged and are very intelligent, London says. "They enjoy stories with some degree of complexity and depth. I often get a story, a nice story, but there's no complexity there or no real depth of character."

London likes short stories that portray a change: obvious or subtle. "There has to be some change that has been effected over the course of the story," she says. "How did the events affect the narrator or the protagonist?"

As for changes in the magazine, perceptive writers will notice a trend toward publishing stories of different lengths. In some issues, *Seventeen* will be publishing a few short short stories rather than the usual one story per issue, and the summer novelette has been discontinued. London is interested in short short stories of about 1,500 words in addition to stories of any genre in the 3,000-word range. She is also looking for mystery stories.

London was accustomed to editing novel-length fiction at Charles Scribner's Sons when she joined *Seventeen* about two years ago. Prior to moving to New York City, she worked as managing editor of the literary magazine *The Iowa Review*.

London knows (and never forgets) that fiction is difficult to write and revise. "I very much sympathize with writers who feel they don't know what to do with a story, and it has something wrong with it," she says. "Try to be objective. Ask yourself some very basic questions about what you've done: Is the story about too many things? What is the theme here?" She adds, "I find a lot of prose that is impressive, but the story doesn't work, and so it is getting a coherent unified story that seems to be the most difficult part."

London spends numerous hours editing writers' work. "Almost every story that we publish has gone through one or two revisions at least. I don't find polished finished manuscripts in the mail. I wish I did," she says. "What I will find is something that shows wonderful promise or is just about there, so I will work very hard with the writer to get the story to the point where it is in the best shape it can possibly be in. The best stories come from writers who are working the hardest," she says, those willing to revise their work and to ask questions about the stories they're writing.

—Paula Deimling

Needs: Fantasy, horror, science fiction and surrealism. "Characterizations are important. No cheap horror, sword-and-sorcery or Tolkien rip-offs." Receives 800 unsolicited fiction mss/month. Buys 8-10 mss/issue. Approximately 25% of fiction is agented. Length: short-short to 6,000 words. Seldom critiques rejected mss.

How to Contact: Send complete ms with SASE. No queries please. Simultaneous and photocopied submissions OK. Reports in 4-6 months on mss. Publishes ms 2-12 months after acceptance. Free fiction guidelines for legal-sized SAE and 22¢ postage. Sample copy for $2.50.

Payment: Pays $150-$800; 2 free contributor's copies. Buys reprints "only in exceptional cases."

Terms: Pays one-half on acceptance and one-half on publication. Publication copyrighted.

Advice: "We're interested in fantastic fiction of every kind, from the strange and supernatural to the science fictional and the surreal. We're *not* particularly interested in formula fiction. Show me believable people caught up in remarkable situations. I'm looking for exceptional writing quality, and stories that move the reader deeply."

SEVENTEEN (II), Triangle Communications, 850 3rd Ave., New York NY 10022. (212)759-8100. Fiction Editor: Sara London. Magazine: 8½x11; 125-400 pages; 40 lb coated paper; 80 lb coated cover stock; illustrations; photos. A service magazine with fashion, beauty care, pertinent topics such as trends in dating, attitudes, experiences and concerns during the teenage years. Monthly. Estab. 1944. Circ. 1.7 million.

Needs: High-quality fiction on topics of interest to teenage girls. The editors look for fresh themes and well paced plots. Buys 1 ms/issue. Receives 300 unsolicited fiction mss/month. Approximately 25% of fiction is agented. Published new writers within the last year. Length: approximately 1,500-3,000 words. Also publishes short shorts.

How to Contact: Send complete ms with SASE and cover letter with relevant credits. Reports in 2 months on mss. Free guidelines with SASE.

Payment: Pays $700-$1,000.

Terms: Pays on acceptance for one-time rights. Publication copyrighted.

Advice: "Respect the intelligence and sophistication of today's teenage reader. *Seventeen* remains open to the surprise of the new voices. Our commitment to publishing the work of new writers remains strong; we continue to read every submission we receive. We believe that good fiction can move the reader toward thoughtful examination of her own life as well as the lives of others—providing her ultimately with a fuller appreciation of what it means to be human." Co-sponsors annual teen fiction contest. Rules are announced each year in October issue.

SHOFAR (I, II, IV), For Jewish Kids On The Move, Senior Publications, Ltd., 43 Northcote Dr., Melville NY 11747. (914)634-9423. Editor: Gerald H. Grayson, PhD. Magazine: 8½x11; 32-48 pages; 60 lb paper; 80 lb cover; illustration; photos. Audience: Jewish children in fourth through eighth grades. Monthly (October-May). Estab. 1984. Circ. 10,000.

Needs: Adventure, contemporary, ethnic, fantasy, humor, juvenile (5-9 years), prose poem, religious/inspirational, spiritual, sports, suspense/mystery, translations, young adult/teen (10-18 years), Jewish. Receives 12-24 unsolicited mss/month. Buys 3-5 mss/issue; 24-40 mss/year. Recently published work by Phyllis R. Emert, Ellen Frankel, Alan Key; published new writers within the last year. Length: 750-1,000 words. Occasionally critiques rejected mss. Recommends other markets.

How to Contact: Send complete ms with cover letter. Reports in 6-8 weeks on ms. SASE. Simultaneous, photocopied and reprint submissions OK. Accepts computer printout submissions, including dot-matrix. Sample copy for 9x12 SAE and 5 first class stamps. Fiction guidelines for 3½x6½ SAE and 1 first class stamp.

Payment: Pays 7¢/word.

Terms: Pays on publication for first North American serial rights. Publication copyrighted.

Advice: "Know the magazine and the religious-education needs of Jewish elementary school age children. If you are a Jewish educator, what has worked for you in the classroom? Write it out; send it on to me; I'll help you develop the idea into a short piece of fiction. A beginning fiction writer eager to break into *Shofar* will find an eager editor willing to help."

THE SINGLE PARENT (IV), Journal of Parents Without Partners, Parents Without Partners, Inc., 8807 Colesville Rd., Silver Spring MD 20910. (301)588-9354. Magazine: 8½x11; 48 pages; 40 lb glossy paper; 60 lb cover stock; illustrations; photos. Publication for divorced, separated, widowed or

Read the Manuscript Mechanics section to learn the correct way to prepare and submit a manuscript.

never-married parents and their children. Published 6 times/year. Estab. 1965. Circ. 145,000.
Needs: Short stories for *children only*, not adults. Stories should deal with issues that children from
one-parent families might face. Buys 1 ms/issue. Published new writers within the last year. Length:
1,000 words maximum.
How to Contact: Query letter before sending manuscript. Send complete ms with SASE (10x10 ma-
nila envelope; 60¢ postage). Reports within 3 months.
Payment: Pays up to $50; 2 free contributor's copies.
Terms: Pays on publication.
Advice: "Upbeat, problem-solving themes preferred."

SINGLELIFE MAGAZINE (II), Single Life Enterprises, Inc., 606 W. Wisconsin Ave., Suite 706, Milwaukee WI 53203. (414)271-9700. Editor: Leifa Botrick. Magazine: 8x11; 82 pages; slick paper; illustrations; photos. "Material deals with concerns of single persons of 24-60 age group." Primarily a nonfiction magazine. Bimonthly. Estab. 1982. Circ. 25,000.
Needs: Humor/satire, literary, travel, relationships, self-help, seasonal food and entertaining. Receives 50 unsolicited mss/month. Recently published work by Deborah Shouse, Jonathan Lowe, Bret
Rauschenbusch. Publishes ms 2-4 months after acceptance. Length: 1,000 words minimum; 3,500
words maximum. Also publishes short shorts. Occasionally critiques rejected mss.
How to Contact: Send complete ms. Reports in 3-6 weeks, "depends on production schedule." SASE
for ms. Simultaneous, photocopied and reprint submissions OK. Accepts computer printouts including
dot-matrix. Accepts electronic submissions via disc or modem. Sample copy $3.50. Fiction guidelines
for SAE and 1 first class stamp.
Payment: Pays $50-$150 and contributor's copies.
Terms: Pays on publication for one-time rights. Publication copyrighted.

‡**SKYLINE (IV)**, New York Skyline Publications, Inc., 857 Carroll St., Brooklyn NY 11215. (212)807-
5511. Editor: William J. Lawrence. Magazine: 8½x11; 32 pages; photographs. Publishes material "on
and about the city of New York, for an upscale, literate, professional" audience. Bimonthly. Plans special fiction issue. Estab. 1988.
Needs: Adventure, ethnic, fantasy, historical, humor/satire, literary, prose poem. "*Skyline* attempts to
string history of New York City into context with issues of concern to New Yorkers today." Receives 20-
30 unsolicited mss/month. Buys 5-6 mss/issue. Publishes ms 1-3 quarters after acceptance. Agented fiction 25%. Length: 2,000-3,000 words preferred; 2,500 words average. Publishes short shorts. Sometimes critiques rejected mss and recommends other markets.
How to Contact: Query with clips of published work. Reports in 2 weeks on queries; 3 weeks on mss.
SASE. Simultaneous and photocopied submissions OK. Accepts computer printout submissions, including dot-matrix. Accepts electronic submissions via disk. Sample copy for $5.
Payment: Pays $100 minimum; $1,500 maximum. Charge for extras.
Terms: Pays on acceptance. Acquires first North American serial rights and one-time rights. Sends gal-
leys to author. Publication copyrighted.
Advice: Looking for fiction that is "specific to New York City; readable, literate and informative about
an interesting topic on or about the city. Each issue of *Skyline* is on a specific general topic such as art,
culture, transportation, etc."

‡**SOUTHERN MAGAZINE (II, IV)**, 201 E. Markham St., Little Rock AR 72201. (501)375-4114. Editor: Linton Weeks. Fiction Editor: Donovan Webster. Magazine: 8x10⅞; 84 pages; coated paper; glossy
cover; illustrations and photographs. "Fiction must have a Southern subject, slant or feel. Beyond this
criterion, each story is judged on its own merit. Our readership is college educated, primarily in its 40s,
and has a household income of about $50,000 annually. The readership is 50% male." Monthly. Estab.
1986. Circ. 280,000.
Needs: Adventure, excerpted novel, contemporary, humor/satire, literary, mainstream, regional, romance (contemporary), sports, suspense/mystery. Receives 250 unsolicited mss/month. Buys 1 ms/is-
sue; 12 mss/year. Publishes ms usually 2-6 months after acceptance. Agented fiction 25%. Recently
published work by Walker Percy, William Price Fox, Bobbie Ann Mason. Length: 4,500 words preferred. Publishes short shorts. Sometimes critiques rejected mss and occasionally recommends other
markets.
How to Contact: Send complete ms with cover letter or submit through agent. Reports in 1-6 weeks on
queries. SASE. Simultaneous, photocopied and reprint submissions OK. Accepts computer printout
submissions, including dot-matrix. Sample copy for $4, 9x12 SAE and 1 first class stamp. Fiction
guidelines for #10 SAE and 1 first class stamp.
Payment: Pays $600 minimum. Free contributor's copies.
Terms: Pays on acceptance. Acquires first North American serial rights. Sends galleys to authors. Publication copyrighted.

Advice: "Writers expecting to be published in *Southern Magazine* must remember to tell a story with a story. To the editors of *Southern Magazine*, there is no such thing as experimental fiction; there is fiction that works and fiction that doesn't."

SPLASH (II), Crandall Enterprises, Inc., 561 Broadway, 4B, New York NY 10012. (212)966-3218. Editor: Jordan Crandall. Magazine: 9½x13; 116 pages; 80 lb matte paper; 100 lb glossy cover. "*Splash* is a publication devoted to the arts, fashion and contemporary culture. We use mainly nonfiction material but are expanding our fiction section. For fiction, a sophisticated or literary style is necessary." Published 5 times/year. Estab. 1984. Circ. 30,000.
Needs: Contemporary, experimental, fantasy, humor/satire, literary. "We are rather open to the content or subject of a piece, but its style must fit in with the *Splash* format. We need avant-garde writing, nothing mainstream. Experimental, surreal, absurd and strongly literate pieces are encouraged. First person writing is *not* encouraged unless a marked objectivity is maintained. No confessional/romance type of things, nothing maudlin, polemical, obvious or sentimental." Receives about 35 unsolicited mss/months. Buys 2-3 mss/issue; 10-15 mss/year "would like to use more." Publishes ms 1-6 months after acceptance. Published new writers within the last year. Length: under 1,000 words preferred; 1,700 words maximum. Publishes short shorts. Sometimes critiques rejected mss.
How to Contact: Query with clips of published work or send complete ms with cover letter (the latter is preferred). "Cover letter may be brief, stating topics of interest with a brief introduction about the writer." Reports in 3-4 weeks. SASE. Simultaneous and photocopied submissions OK. Accepts computer printout submissions, including dot-matrix. Sample copy for $3 US, $8 international. Writer's guidelines for #10 SAE and 1 first class stamp.
Payment: Pays $50-$350.
Terms: Pays on acceptance for first rights. Publication copyrighted.
Advice: "A succinct style of writing is the best. Say as much in as few words as possible. Don't be obvious, don't condescend to the reader, don't hammer away at a point. Don't be afraid to stretch the medium—as long as you've already *learned the rules* of the medium. In other words, no one should try to write experimental fiction unless they can also write mainstream. Experimental style should be a preference, and *not* something to use because one doesn't know correct grammar and form."

SPORTS AFIELD (II, IV), Hearst Magazine, 250 W. 55th St., New York 10019. (212)262-8835. Editor: Tom Paugh. Magazine: 11x8; 128 pages minimum; "the best paper"; 70 lb cover stock; illustrations; photos. "This is an outdoor magazine: hunting, fishing, camping, boating, conservation, etc." for men and women who take an active interest in their sport. Monthly. Estab. 1887. Circ. 542,000.
Needs: Adventure, humor/satire when related to hunting and fishing, sports (fishing, hunting, camping). No old-fashioned me-and-Joe yarns. Receives 20 unsolicited mss/week. Buys a few mss each year. Publishes ms up to 2 years after acceptance. Agented fiction: 5%. Recently published work by Paul Quinnett, Harry Middleton, Larry Chandler. Length: 2,500 words or less. Also publishes short shorts of 200-250 words.
How to Contact: Query first; include name, address, a little background and credits, *brief* synopsis of story. Reports in 1 month on queries and mss. SASE for query. Accepts computer printouts including dot-matrix.
Payment: Pays $850.
Terms: Pays on acceptance for first rights. Publication copyrighted.
Advice: "Fiction is a very tough market—and not just in the outdoor field. Know the market."

STANDARD (II, IV), Nazarene International Headquarters, 6401 The Paseo, Kansas City MO 64131. (816)333-7000. Editor: Sheila Boggess. Magazine: 8½x11; 8 pages; illustrations; photos. Inspirational reading for adults. Weekly. Estab. 1936. Circ. 177,000.
Needs: Religious/inspirational, spiritual. Receives 350 unsolicited mss/month (both fiction and nonfiction). Accepts 60 mss/year. Publishes ms 9-24 months after acceptance. Recently published work by Betty Steele Everett, Allen Wright, C. Ellen Watts; published new writers within the last year. Length: 1,000 words average; 300 words minimum; 1,500 words maximum. Also publishes short shorts of 300-350 words.
How to Contact: Send complete ms with name, address and phone number. Reports in 1-2 months on mss. SASE. Simultaneous and photocopied submissions OK but will pay only reprint rates. Accepts computer printouts and electronic media in ASCII. Sample copy and guidelines for SAE and 1 first class stamp.
Payment: Pays 3.5¢/word; 2¢/word (reprint); contributor's copies.
Terms: Pays on acceptance for one-time rights. Publication copyrighted.
Advice: "Too much is superficial; containing the same story lines. Give me something original, humorous, yet helpful. I'm also looking for more stories on current social issues. Make plot, characters realistic. Contrived articles are quick to spot and reject."

A science fiction and fantasy magazine for young adults, Starwind, *looks for "science fiction that shows hope for the future and protagonists who interact with their environment rather than let themselves be manipulated by it."*

An Interview with
HARLAN ELLISON

JACK WILLIAMSON
Passage to Saturn

JEFF DUNTEMANN
Whale Meat

LARRY BLANKENSHIP
Blue Moon of Kentockwei

Cover art by Georgia Mase.

STARWIND (I), Starwind Press, Box 98, Ripley OH 45167. (513)392-4549. Editor: David F. Powell. Magazine: 8½x11; 64 pages; 60 lb offset paper and cover; b&w illustrations; line shot photos. "Science fiction and fantasy for young adults (teen to 25 or so) with interest in science, technology, science fiction and fantasy." Quarterly. Estab. 1974. Circ. 2,000.

Needs: Fantasy, humor/satire, science fiction. "We like SF that shows hope for the future and protagonists who interact with their environment rather than let themselves be manipulated by it." No horror, pastiches of other authors, stories featuring characters created by others (i.e. Captain Kirk and crew, Dr. Who, etc.). Receives 50 + unsolicited mss/month. Buys 4-6 mss/issue; 16-24 mss/year. Publishes ms between 4 months-2 years after acceptance. Recently published work by Barbara Myers, Allen Byerle, Kurt Hyatt; published new writers within the last year. Length: 3,000-8,000 words average; 2,000 words minimum; 10,000 words maximum. Occasionally critiques rejected mss.

How to Contact: Send complete ms. Reports in 6-8 weeks. SASE for ms. Photocopied submissions OK. Accepts computer printouts including dot-matrix. Accepts electronic submissions via disk for the IBM PC or PC compatible; MacIntosh; word processors: Multimate, WordStar, MacWrite, or ASCII. Sample copy $3.50; issue #2-4 $2.50. Fiction guidelines free for #10 SAE and 1 first class stamp.

Payment: Pays 1-4¢/word and contributor's copies.

Terms: Pays 25% on acceptance; 75% on publication. "25% payment is kill fee if we decide not to publish story." Rights negotiable. Sends galleys to the author. Publication copyrighted.

Advice: "I certainly think a beginning writer can be successful if he/she studies the publication *before* submitting, and matches the submission with the magazine's needs. Get our guidelines and study them *before* submitting. Don't submit something *way over* or *way under* our word length requirements. Be understanding of editors; they can get swamped very easily, *especially* if there's only one editor handling all submissions. Be professional. Type your manuscript on typing paper, with a minimum of erasures and editorial notes. You don't need to write a synopsis of your story in your cover letter—the story should be able to stand on its own. Read a lot of the type of fiction you plan to write (in our case, science fiction). Also try to read books about writing (Writer's Digest Books has published quite a few!)"

STORY FRIENDS (II), Mennonite Publishing House, 616 Walnut Ave., Scottdale PA 15683. (412)887-8500. Editor: Marjorie Waybill. Sunday school publication which portrays Jesus as a friend and helper. Nonfiction and fiction for children 4-9 years of age. Weekly.

Needs: Juvenile. Stories of everyday experiences at home, in church, in school or at play, which provide models of Christian values. Length: 300-800 words.

How to Contact: Send complete ms with SASE. Seasonal or holiday material should be submitted 6 months in advance. Free sample copy.

Payment: Pays 3-5¢/word.

Terms: Pays on acceptance for one-time rights. Buys reprints. Not copyrighted.

Advice: "It is important to include relationships, patterns of forgiveness, respect, honesty, trust and caring. Prefer exciting yet plausible short stories which offer different settings, introduce children to wide ranges of friends and demonstrate joys, fears, temptations and successes of the readers."

STRAIGHT (II), Standard Publishing Co., 8121 Hamilton Ave., Cincinnati OH 45231. (513)931-4050. Editor: Carla Crane. Publication helping and encouraging teens to live a victorious, fulfilling Christian life. Distributed through churches and some private subscriptions. Magazine: 6½x7½; 12 pages; newsprint paper and cover; illustrations (color); photos. Quarterly in weekly parts. Estab. 1951. Circ. 75,000.
Needs: Contemporary, religious/inspirational, romance, spiritual, mystery, adventure, and humor—all with Christian emphasis. "Stories dealing with teens and teen life, with a positive message or theme. Topics that interest teenagers include school, family life, recreation, friends, church, part-time jobs, dating and music. Main character should be a 15- or 16-year old boy or girl, a Christian and regular churchgoer, who faces situations using Bible principles." Buys 1-2 mss/issue; 75-100 mss/year. Receives approximately 100 unsolicited fiction mss/month. Less than 1% of fiction is agented. Recently published work by Alan Cliburn, Betty Steele Everett, Teresa Cleary; published new writers within the last year. Length: 800-1,200 words. Recommends other markets.
How to Contact: Send complete ms with SASE with cover letter (experience with teens, especially preferred from new writers). Accepts computer printout submissions. Reports in 1 month on mss. Publishes ms an average of 1 year after acceptance. Free sample copy and guidelines with SASE.
Payment: 2-3½¢/word.
Terms: Pays on acceptance for first and one-time rights. Buys reprints. Publication copyrighted.
Advice: "Get to know us before submitting, through guidelines and sample issues (free with an SASE). And get to know teenagers. A writer must know what today's teens are like, and what kinds of conflicts they experience. In writing a short fiction piece for the teen reader, don't try to accomplish too much. If your character is dealing with the problem of prejudice, don't also deal with his/her fights with sister, desire for a bicycle, or anything else that is not absolutely essential to the reader's understanding of the major conflict."

THE STUDENT (I, II), A Christian Collegiate Magazine, Student Ministry Department of the Baptist Sunday School Board, 127 Ninth Ave., North, Nashville TN 37234. (615)251-2788. Magazine: 8¼x11; 50 pages; uncoated paper; coated cover stock; illustrations; photos. Magazine for Christians and nonChristians about life and work with Christian students on campus and related articles on living in dorm setting, dating life, missions activities, Bible study, and church ministry to students. Monthly. Estab. 1922. Circ. 40,000.
Needs: Adventure, humor, comics, confession, contemporary, ethnic, and religious/inspirational. Does not want to see mss "without purpose or without moral tone." Receives approximately 25 unsolicited fiction mss/month. Buys 1-2 mss/issue; 12-24 mss/year. Published approximately 10 new writers within the last year. Length: 300 words minimum (or less, depending on treatment); 1,000 words maximum; 750 words average.
How to Contact: Cover letter with bio and description of published works. Query first with SASE. Simultaneous, photocopied and previously published submissions OK. Reports in 3 weeks on queries; 6 weeks on mss. Sample copy 61¢. Free fiction guidelines with SASE.
Payment: 4¢/word and 3 contributor's copies.
Terms: Pays on publication for all rights, first rights, one-time rights, and assignments for work-for-hire basis. Publication copyrighted.
Advice: "Fit writing to format and concept of the piece. View many issues of the magazine before you write. Our readers demand fiction which conveys our message in an interesting way."

STUDENT LAWYER (II, IV), American Bar Association, 750 N. Lake Shore Dr., Chicago IL 60611. (312)988-6048. Editor: Sarah Hoban. Magazine: 8½x10¾; 48 pages; glossy paper and cover; illustrations; photos. "Magazine for law students as part of their Law Student Division/ABA membership. Features legal aspects, trends in the law, social/legal issues, and lawyer profiles." Monthly (September-May). Circ. 35,000.
Needs: "All stories have to have a legal/law/lawyer/law-school element to them. No science fiction." Buys 1 full-length or 2-3 short humorous pieces/year. Recently published work by Lowell Komie. Length: 1,000-3,000 words. Sometimes recommends other markets.
How to Contact: Send complete ms with SASE. Accepts computer printout submissions. Reports in 1 month on mss. Publishes ms 1-6 months after acceptance. Sample copy $3; contact Order Fulfillment at above address.
Payment: $75-$500.
Terms: Pays on acceptance for first rights. Buys very few reprints.

Advice: Rejects mss because "usually, the stories are of mediocre quality. Because we favor nonfiction pieces, the fiction we do publish has to be outstanding or at least very original. Keep trying—and *know* the magazine you're submitting to."

SUNDAY JOURNAL MAGAZINE,*The Providence Journal-Bulletin*, 75 Fountain St., Providence RI 02902. (401)277-7349. Editor: Doug Cumming. Magazine: 10x11½; 28 pages; coated newsprint paper; illustrations; photos. "Magazine which has appeared weekly for 40 years in the *Providence Sunday Journal*." Circ. 280,000.
Needs: Regional. No explicit sex or graphic violence. Recently published fiction by Jincy Willet, Daniel Asa Rose and Ann Hood; published new writers within the last year.
How to Contact: Query with clips of published work and brief cover letter. SASE.
Payment: $175 minimum; $400 maximum.
Terms: Buys one-time rights. Publication copyrighted. Sponsors short-story contest for New England writers. Deadline: June 1, 1989.
Advice: "Condensation and distillation are what distinguish good short fiction. This is especially true in our limited space."

SUNSHINE MAGAZINE (II), Henrichs Publications, Box 40, Sunshine Park, Litchfield IL 62056. Magazine. 5¼x7¼; 48 pages; matte paper and cover stock; illustrations. "To promote good will for the betterment of our society. We publish short, non-denominational, inspirational material." Monthly. Estab. 1924. Circ. 60,000.
Needs: Adventure, historical (general), humor, juvenile (5-9 years), preschool (0-4 years), senior citizen/retirement. No fiction that is lengthy, fantasy, sexual, specifically religious, violent or dealing with death, drugs, divorce or alcohol. Receives 500 unsolicited fiction mss/month. Buys 12 mss/issue; 140 mss/year. Publishes ms within a year of acceptance. Recently published work by Janice L. Brown, Roderick Wilkinson, Vivyan Connolly; published new writers within the last year. Length: 750 words average; 100 words minimum; 1,250 words maximum. Publishes short shorts. Sometimes critiques rejected ms and recommends other markets.
How to Contact: Send complete ms with SASE and cover letter with name, address, rights offered. Reports in 2 months on mss. SASE. Photocopied submissions OK. Accepts computer printout submissions, including dot-matrix. Sample copy 50¢ or 6x8 SAE with 2 first class stamps. Fiction guidelines with #10 SASE.
Payment: $10-$100, contributor's copies; charge for extras.
Terms: Pays on acceptance for first North American serial rights. Publication copyrighted.
Advice: "Beginning writers are more than welcome to submit to *Sunshine*. Don't get discouraged—just keep trying. We can use only about 5% of what we receive."

SURFING MAGAZINE (IV), Western Empire, Box 3010, San Clemente CA 92672. (714)492-7873. Editor: David Gilovich. Magazine: 8x11; 140 pages; 50 lb free sheet paper; 80 lb cover stock; photos. Magazine covering "all aspects of the sport of surfing for young, active surfing enthusiasts." Monthly. Estab. 1964. Circ. 92,000.
Needs: Surfing-related fiction. Receives 2 unsolicited mss/month. Buys 3 mss/year. Length: 2,000-3,000 words average. Occasionally critiques rejected mss. Also publishes short shorts.
How to Contact: Cover letter with background on surfing. Query first. Reports in 2 weeks. SASE. Photocopied submissions OK. Accepts computer printout submissions. Prefers letter-quality. Free sample copy and fiction guidelines.
Payment: 15-20¢/word.
Terms: Pays on publication for one-time rights. Publication copyrighted.
Advice: "Establish yourself as a *Surfing* general contributor before tackling fiction."

SWANK MAGAZINE (II, IV), Broadway Publishing Company, 888 7th Ave., New York NY 10106. Editor: W.B. Gerard. Magazine: 8½x11; 116 pages; 20 lb paper; 60 lb coated stock; illustrations; photos. "Men's sophisticate format. Sexually-oriented material. Presumably our reader is after erotic material." Monthly. Estab. 1952. Circ. 350,000.
Needs: High-caliber erotica. "Fiction always has an erotic or other male-oriented theme; also eligible would be mystery or suspense with a very erotic scene. Writers should try to avoid the cliches of the genre." Buys 1 ms/issue, 12 mss/year. Receives approximately 30 unsolicited fiction mss each month. Published new writers within the last year. Length: 1,500-2,750 words.
How to Contact: Send complete ms with SASE and cover letter, which should list previous publishing credits. No simultaneous submissions. Accepts computer printout submissions. Prefers letter-quality. Reports in 6 weeks on mss. Sample copy $5 with SASE.
Payment: $250-$400. Offers 25% kill fee for assigned ms not published.
Terms: Buys first North American serial rights. Publication copyrighted.

Advice: "Research the men's magazine market." Mss are rejected because of "typical, overly simple storylines and poor execution. We're looking for interesting stories—whether erotic in theme or not—that break the mold of the usual men's magazine fiction. We're not only just considering strict erotica. Mystery, adventure, etc. with erotica passages will be considered."

'TEEN MAGAZINE (II), Petersen Publishing Co., 8490 Sunset Blvd., Los Angeles CA 90069. Editor: Roxanne Camron. Magazine: 100-150 pages; 34 lb paper; 60 lb cover; illustrations; photos. "The magazine contains fashion, beauty and features for the young teenage girl. The median age of our readers is 16. Our success stems from our dealing with relevant issues teens face, printing recent entertainment news and showing the latest fashions and beauty looks." Monthly. Estab. 1957. Circ. 1 million.
Needs: Romance, adventure, mystery, humor, and young adult. Every story, whether romance, mystery, humor, etc., must be aimed for teenage girls. The protagonist should be a teenager, preferably female. No experimental, science fiction, fantasy or horror. Buys 1 ms/issue; 12 mss/year. Publishes short shorts. Recently published work by Janet Dagon, Ralph Vaughan, Dee Gee Lester; published new writers within the last year. Length: 2,500-4,000 words.
How to Contact: Send complete ms and short cover letter with SASE. Reports in 10 weeks on mss. Generally publishes ms 3-5 months after acceptance. Sample copy for $2.50. Free guidelines with SASE.
Payment: Pays $100.
Terms: Pays on acceptance for all rights.
Advice: "Try to find themes that suit the modern teen. We need innovative ways of looking at the age-old problems of young love, parental pressures, making friends, being left out, etc. '*TEEN* would prefer to have romance balanced with a plot, re: a girl's inner development and search for self. Mss must be typed neatly and double spaced. Handwritten mss will not be read."

‡TEEN POWER, Scripture Press Publications, Inc., Box 632, Glen Ellyn IL 60138. (312)668-6000. Editor: Mark Oestreicher. Magazine: 5³⁄₈x8³⁄₈; 8 pages; non-glossy paper and cover; illustrations and photographs. "Teen Power publishes mostly fiction with a conservative Christian slant—must have some sort of spiritual emphasis for young teens (11-14 years); many small town and rural; includes large readerships in Canada, England and other countries in addition to U.S." Estab. 1966. Circ. 80,000.
Needs: Adventure, humor/satire, religious/inspirational, young adult/teen (10-18 years). "All must have spiritual emphasis of some sort." Receives approx. 50-75 unsolicited mss/month. Buys 1 ms/issue; about 50 mss/year. Publishes ms at least one year after acceptance. Recently published work by Alan Cliburn, Betty Steele Everett, Chris Lutes. Length: 1,000 preferred; 250 words minimum; 1,100 words maximum. Publishes short shorts. Length: 300-500 words. Sometimes critiques rejected mss and recommends other markets.
How to Contact: Send complete ms with cover letter. Reports in 1 month. SASE. Simultaneous, photocopied and reprint submissions OK. Accepts computer printouts, including dot-matrix. Sample copy and fiction guidelines for #10 SAE and 1 first class stamp.
Payment: Pays $20 minimum; $120 maximum; and contributor's copies.
Terms: Pays on acceptance. Purchases first rights and one-time rights. Publication copyrighted.
Advice: "We look for spiritual emphasis (strong but not preachy); writing style; age appropriateness; creativity in topic choice and presentation. A writer for Teen Power must know something about young teens and what is important to them, plus have a working knowledge of basic Christian doctrine, and be able to weave the two together."

TEENS TODAY (II), Church of the Nazarene, 6401 The Paseo, Kansas City MO 64131. (816)333-7000. Editor: Karen DeSollar. Sunday school take-home paper: 8¹⁄₂x11; 8 pages; illustrations; photos. For junior and senior high students involved with the Church of the Nazarene who find it interesting and helpful to their areas of life. Weekly. Circ. 60,000.
Needs: Contemporary, religious/inspirational, romance, humor, juvenile, young adult, and ethnic. "Nothing that puts teens down or endorses lifestyles not in keeping with the denomination's beliefs and standards." Buys 1-2 mss/issue. Published new writers within the last year. Length: 1,000-1,500 words.
How to Contact: Send complete ms with SASE. Reports in 6 weeks on mss. Publishes ms 8-10 months after acceptance. Free sample copy and guidelines with SASE.
Payment: Pays 3¹⁄₂¢/word and 3¢/word on second reprint.
Terms: Pays on acceptance for first and second serial rights. Buys reprints.
Advice: "Study sample copies. Don't be too juvenile."

‡TEXAS CONNECTION MAGAZINE (IV), Box 541805, Dallas TX 75220. (214)470-4090. Editor: Alan Miles. Magazine: 8¹⁄₂x11; 132 pages; book offset paper; 100 lb enamel cover; illustrations and photographs. "Adult erotica, for adults only." Monthly. Estab. 1985. Circ. 10,000.
Needs: Erotica, erotic cartooning, sexual fantasy, feminist, gay, humor/satire, lesbian. Receives 20-30

unsolicited mss/month. Buys 2-3 mss/issue. Publishes ms 2-3 months after acceptance. Length: 1,750 words preferred; 1,000 words minimum; 2,500 words maximum.

How to Contact: Send complete ms with cover letter. Cover letter must state writer/author's age (18 yrs. minimum). Reports in 1 week. SASE for ms, not needed for query. Simultaneous, photocopied, and reprint submissions OK. Accepts computer printout submissions, including dot-matrix. Sample copy for $7.50. Free fiction guidelines.

Payment: Pays $25 minimum; $200 maximum. Free subscription to magazine. Free contributor's copies.

Terms: Pays on publication. Purchases all rights on some, first rights on most. Publication copyrighted.

Advice: "We publish an adult, alternative lifestyle magazine that is (uniquely) distributed both in the adult store market and mass-market outlets (convenience stores) throughout 5 states: Texas (main), Oklahoma, Arkansas, Louisiana, New Mexico. We are, of course, interested in fresh, erotic fiction only."

‡TIKKUN (III), A Bimonthly Jewish Critique of Politics, Culture and Society, Institute for Labor and Mental Health, 5100 Leona St., Oakland CA 94619. (415)482-0805. Editor: Michael Lerner. Fiction Editors: Rosellen Brown and Marvin Hoffman. Magazine: 8x11; 96 pages; high quality paper. "*Tikkun* was created two years ago as the liberal alternative to *Commentary Magazine* and the voices of Jewish conservatism, but is not aimed just at a Jewish audience. Readers are intellectuals, political activists, Washington policy circles, writers, poets." Bimonthly.

Needs: Condensed/excerpted novel, contemporary, feminist, gay, historical (general), humor/satire, lesbian, literary, mainstream, translations, Jewish political. "No narrowly Jewish fiction. At least ½ of our readers are not Jewish. Or anything that is not of highest quality." Receives 150 unsolicited mss/month. Buys 1 ms/issue. Publishes ms 6-9 months after acceptance. Agented fiction 50%. Recently published work by Amos Oz, Lynne Sharon Schwartz, E.M. Broner. Length: 4,000 words preferred. Publishes short shorts. Almost always critiques rejected mss.

How to Contact: Send complete ms with cover letter. Reports in 2-3 months. SASE. Accepts computer printout submissions, including dot-matrix. Sample copy for $7.

Payment: Pays $100 minimum; $250 maximum.

Terms: Pays on publication for first rights. Publication copyrighted.

Advice: Looks for creativity, sensitivity, intelligence, originality, profundity of insight. Read *Tikkun*, at least 3-4 issues worth, understand the kinds of issues that interest our readers, and then imagine yourself trying to write fiction that delights, surprises and intrigues this kind of an audience. Do not write what you think will feel sweet or appealing to this audience—but rather that which will provoke, bring to life and engage them."

TOUCH (II), Calvinettes, Box 7259, Grand Rapids MI 49510. (616)241-5616. Editor: Joanne Ilbrink. Magazine: 8½x11; 24 pages; 50 lb paper; 50 lb cover stock; illustrations; photos. "Our purpose is to lead girls into a living relationship with Jesus Christ. Puzzles, poetry, crafts, stories, articles, and club input for girls ages 9-14." Monthly. Circ. 15,000.

Needs: Adventure, ethnic, juvenile and religious/inspirational. "Articles must help girls discover how God is at work in their world and the world around them." Receives 50 unsolicited fiction mss/month. Buys 3 mss/issue; 30 mss/year. Usually does not read during February, March, September and October. Recently published work by Ida Mae Petsock. Published new writers within the last year. Length: 900 words minimum; 1,200 words maximum; 1,000 words average.

How to Contact: Send complete ms with 8x10 SASE. Prefers no cover letter. Simultaneous, photocopied and previously published submissions OK. Reports in 1 month on mss. Free sample copy for 8x10 SASE. Free guidelines.

Payment: Pays 3¢/word.

Terms: Pays on acceptance for simultaneous, first or second serial rights.

Advice: "Write for guidelines and theme update and submit manuscripts in advance of deadline. In fiction often the truths we choose to convey can be done with short stories."

TORSO, The New Era In All-Male Erotica, Mavety Media Group, 462 Broadway, New York NY 10013. (212)966-8400. Editor: Joseph Mauro. Fiction Editor: Stan Leventhal. Magazine: 96 pages; illustrations; photos. "Gay male erotica: photos, stories, columns, etc." Monthly. Estab. 1981. Circ. 150,000.

Needs: Erotica. "No minors, illegal drugs, S&M, scat, water sports." Receives 35 unsolicited mss/month. Buys 3 mss/issue; 36 mss/year. Publishes ms up to 1 year after acceptance. Length: 5,000 words preferred. Publishes short shorts. Sometimes critiques rejected mss and recommends other markets.

How to Contact: Send complete ms with cover letter. Reports in 1 week. SASE. Photocopied submissions OK. Accepts computer printout submissions. Sample copy for $6. Fiction guidelines for #10 SAE and 1 first class stamp.

Payment: Pays $75-$100.
Terms: Pays on publication for first rights. Publication copyrighted.
Advice: "Read a whole bunch of gay erotica stories—then start writing them."

TQ (TEENQUEST) (II), Good News Broadcasting Co., Box 82808, Lincoln NE 68501. (402)474-4567. Managing Editor: Barbara Camito. Magazine: 8½x11; 48 pages; illustrations; photos. "*TQ* is designed to aid the spiritual growth of young teen Christian readers by presenting Biblical principles." 11 issues/year. Estab. 1946. Circ. 70,000.
Needs: Religious/inspirational, regional, romance, adventure, fantasy, science fiction and mystery. "Stories must be grounded in Biblical Christianity and should feature teens in the 14-17 year range." Buys 3-4 mss/issue; 35-40 mss/year. Receives 50-60 unsolicited fiction mss/month. Recently published work by Nancy Rue, Stephen Bly, Marian Bray, Scott Pinzon; published new writers within the last year. Length: up to 2,000 words.
How to Contact: Send complete ms with SASE and cover letter. Accepts computer printout submissions. Prefers letter-quality. Reports in 2 months. Publishes ms 6-24 months after acceptance. Free sample copy and guidelines for 9x12 SASE.
Payment: 4-7¢/word for unassigned fiction. More for assignments. 3¢/word for reprints.
Terms: Pays on acceptance for first or reprint rights. Buys reprints. Publication copyrighted.
Advice: "The most common problem is that writers don't understand the limitations of stories under 2,500 words and try to cram a 6,000-word plot into 2,000 words at the expense of characterization, pacing, and mood. We feel that fiction communicates well to our teenage readers. They consistently rank fiction as their favorite part of the magazine. We get hundreds of stories on 'big issues' (death, drugs, etc). Choose less dramatic subjects, that are important to teenagers and give us a new storyline that has a Biblical emphasis, but isn't preachy. Before you try to write for teens, get to know some—talk to them, watch their TV shows, read their magazines. You'll get ideas for stories and you'll be able to write for our audience with accurate and up-to-date knowledge." Teen fiction writers under age 20 may enter annual contest.

TRAILER BOATS MAGAZINE (II, IV), Poole Publications Inc., 20700 Belshaw Ave., Box 5427, Carson CA (902)749-5427. Editor-in-Chief: Chuck Coyne. Magazine: 100 pages; high paper quality; 80 lb cover stock. "Our magazine covers boats of 26 feet and shorter, (trailerable size limits) and related activities; skiing, fishing, cruising, travel, racing, etc. We publish how-to articles on boat and trailer maintenance, travel, skiing, boat tests and evaluations of new products." Audience: owners and prospective owners of trailerable-size boats. Monthly. Estab. 1971. Circ. 65,000.
Needs: Adventure, contemporary, fantasy, humor/satire, science fiction, and suspense/mystery. "Must meet general guidelines of the magazine regarding boats and related activities." Receives very few unsolicited fiction mss/month. Buys 1-3 mss/year. Published new writers within the last year. Length: 200 words minimum; 1,000 words maximum. Publishes short shorts of 500 words. Occasionally critiques rejected mss. Sometimes recommends other markets.
How to Contact: Query first with SASE. Accepts computer printout submissions. Prefers letter-quality. Reports in 1 month on queries; 4-6 weeks on mss. Publishes ms 1-6 months after acceptance. Free general guidelines. Sample copy $1.50.
Payment: 7-10¢/word.
Terms: Pays on publication for all rights. Publication copyrighted.
Advice: "In our case, knowing the audience is of prime importance. Our readership and experience with fiction is limited. We are a consumer magazine with an audience of dedicated boaters. My suggestion is to know the audience and write for it specifically."

TRISTATE MAGAZINE (IV), The Cincinnati Enquirer, 617 Vine St., Cincinnati OH 45201. Editor: Alice Hornbaker. Magazine: Sunday supplement, 10x12; slick paper; illustrations and photographs. Weekly. Circ. 350,000.
Needs: Stories on any subject, but must have "local tri-state [Ohio, Kentucky, Indiana] base." Receives "few" unsolicited fiction mss/month; accepts about 4 stories/year. Length: 1,000 words. Sometimes critiques rejected mss.
How to Contact: Query first. Reports on queries in 1 month. SASE for query and/or guidelines. Simultaneous submissions OK. Accepts computer printouts, including dot matrix "if near letter quality." Sample copy and fiction guidelines for SAE.
Payment: "$200 maximum. Usually $100."
Terms: Pays on publication for first rights. Publication copyrighted.
Advice: "Write tight. Start off with a bang. Get right into it."

TURTLE MAGAZINE FOR PRESCHOOL KIDS (I, II), Children's Better Health Institute, Benjamin Franklin Literary & Medical Society, Inc., 1100 Waterway Blvd., Box 567, Indianapolis IN 46206. Editorial Director: Beth Wood Thomas. Magazine of picture stories and articles for preschool children 2-5 years old.
Needs: Juvenile (preschool). Receives approximately 75 unsolicited fiction mss/month. Length: 8-24 lines for picture stories; 500 words for bedtime or naptime stories. Special emphasis on health, nutrition, exercise, and safety. Also has need for humorous and anthropomorphic animal stories.
How to Contact: Send complete ms with SASE. Reports in 8-10 weeks on mss. No queries. Send SASE for Editorial Guidelines. Sample copy, 75¢.
Payment: 8¢/word (approximate). Payment varies for poetry and activities.
Terms: Pays on publication for all rights. Publication copyrighted.
Advice: "Keep it simple and easy to read. Vocabulary must be below first grade level. Be familiar with past issues of the magazine. Mss should be checked thoroughly before submission for misspelled words, errors in grammar, and suitability of subject matter and vocabulary for the preschooler."

VERDICT MAGAZINE (I, IV), Journal of the Southern California Defense Counsel, 123 Truxton Ave., Bakersfield CA 93301. (805)325-7124. Editor: Steve Walsh. Magazine: 8½x11; 48 pages; slick paper; 70 lb Tahoe cover; clip art illustrations. "The magazine is geared to lawyers who specialize in insurance defense law. It is a trade publication that focuses on their work, legal cases and lifestyles." Quarterly. Estab. 1973. Circ. 5,000.
Needs: Law. Receives 10 unsolicited mss/month. Buys 2 mss/issue. Publishes ms 6 months-1 year after acceptance. Length: 2,000 words average. Publishes short shorts. Occasionally critiques rejected mss. Recommends other markets.
How to Contact: Send complete ms and cover letter with brief description of submitted ms. SASE. Simultaneous and photocopied submissions OK. Accepts computer printout submissions, including dot-matrix. Sample copy for $5 or 11x14 SAE and 10 first class stamps.
Payment: Pays $10.
Terms: Pays on publication for one-time rights. Publication copyrighted.

VIRTUE (II), The Christian Magazine for Women, Virtue Ministries, Inc., Box 850, Sisters OR 97759. (503)549-8261. Editor: Becky Durost Fish. Magazine: 8⅛x10⅞ 80 pages; illustrations; photos. Christian women's magazine featuring food, fashion, family, etc., aimed primarily at homemakers— "real women with everyday problems, etc." Published 8 times/year. Estab. 1978. Circ. 110,000.
Needs: Condensed novel, contemporary, humor, religious/inspirational, romance. "Must have Christian slant." Buys 1 ms/issue; 8 mss/year (maximum). Publishes short shorts. Published new writers within the last year. Length: 1,200 words minimum; 2,500 words maximum; 2,000 words average.
How to Contact: Accepts computer printout submissions. Prefers letter-quality. Reports in 6-8 weeks on ms. Sample copy $3 with 9x13 SAE and 90¢ postage. Free fiction guidelines with SASE.
Payment: 10¢/published word.
Terms: Pays on publication for first rights or reprint rights. Publication copyrighted.
Advice: "Send us descriptive, colorful writing with good style. *Please*—no simplistic, unrealistic pat endings. There are three main reasons *Virtue* rejects fiction: 1) The stories are not believable, 2) writing is dull, and 3) the story does not convey a Christian message."

VISION (II,IV), Box 7259, Grand Rapids MI 45910. (616)241-5616. Editor: Dale Dieleman. Magazine: 8½x11; 16-20 pages; 60 lb paper; 60 lb cover; photos. *Vision*'s readers are young adults in their 20s in the U.S. and Canada. Bimonthly. Circ. 3,500.
Needs: Stories exploring values, lifestyles, relationships as young adults in workplace, campus, social settings—cultural, ethnic variety a plus. Christian perspective but no preachy, pious platitudes. Length: 1,500 words maximum.
How to Contact: Send ms plus SASE for return. Reports in 1 month on mss. Simultaneous submissions OK (specify other submission periodicals). Sample copy for 9x12 and 56¢ postage.
Payment: Pays $35-$75.
Terms: Pays on acceptance. Publication copyrighted.
Advice: "We'd like to publish more fiction—it all depends on quality."

VISTA (II), Wesley Press, Box 50434, Indianapolis IN 46953. (317)842-0444. Editor: Becky Higgins. Magazine: 8½x11; 8 pages; offset paper and cover; illustrations; photos. "*Vista* is our adult take-home paper and is published in conjunction with the Enduring Word Series adult Sunday school lesson." Weekly. Estab. 1906. Circ. 50,000.
Needs: Humor/satire, religious/inspirational, senior citizen/retirement, young adult/teen. "We are not looking for "Sunday Soap Opera," romance, stories with pat or easy outs, or incidents that wouldn't feasibly happen to members of your own church." Receives 100 unsolicited mss/month. Buys 1 mss/is-

sue; 50 mss/year. Publishes ms 10 months after acceptance. Length: 500 words minimum; 1,300 words maximum. Sometimes critiques rejected mss.

How to Contact: Send complete ms with cover letter. Reports in 2 weeks. SASE. Simultaneous, photocopied and reprint submissions OK. Accepts computer printout submissions, including dot-matrix. Sample copy for 9x12 SAE.

Payment: Pays $10-60.

Terms: Pays on acceptance for one-time rights.

Advice: "Use the official password: John Wesley. Manuscripts for all publications must be in keeping with early Methodist teachings that people have a free will to personally accept or reject Christ. Wesleyanism also stresses a transformed life, holiness of heart and social responsibility."

Vision uses stories exploring values, lifestyles and relationships of young adults in the workplace, campus and social settings.

Cover photo credits: Stirix Pix, Robert Settles, Camerique.

‡VOLLEYBALL MONTHLY MAGAZINE (I, II), Straight Down Inc., Box 3137, San Luis Obispo CA 93403. (805)541-2294. Editor: Jon Hastings. Fiction Editor: Dennis Steers. Magazine: 8½x11; 64-112 pages; 60 lb paper; 70 lb cover; illustrations and photographs. For "young and enthusiastic players of volleyball." Monthly. Estab. 1982. Circ. 45,000.

Needs: Volleyball. Receives 5 unsolicited mss/month. Buys 3 to 5 fiction mss/year. Publishes ms 3 months after acceptance. Length: 1,500 words preferred; 750 words minimum; 3,000 words maximum. Sometimes critiques rejected mss.

How to Contact: Send complete ms with cover letter. Reports in 2 weeks on queries; 3 weeks on mss. SASE. Simultaneous submissions OK. Accepts dot-matrix computer printout submissions. Free sample copy and fiction guidelines.

Payment: Pays $50-$300, subscription to magazine, contributor's copies.

Terms: Pays on publication for first rights. Publication copyrighted.

WAG MAGAZINE (II), Titan Publishing Inc., Box 1747, 291 Woodlawn Rd. W., Unit 7, Guelph, Ontario N1H 7A1 Canada. (519)763-5058. Editor: Karen Mantel. Magazine. 5⅛x7⅛; 160 pages; uncoated stock paper; coated 80 lb litho cover stock; illustrations. "Publication dedicated to the preservation and promotion of humorous writing and other creative forms of humor in North America. It incorporates the best work of contemporary and class writers, poets and cartoonists, and publishes writing of enduring quality that transcends regional geography, culture and politics." Bimonthly. Estab. 1989. Circ. 25,000.

Needs: Humor/satire. Accepts 6-8 mss/issue. Publishes ms 3-4 months after acceptance. Length: 3,500 words average. Publishes short shorts. Length: 1,200-1,500 words.

How to Contact: Query first. Reports on queries in 2 months. SASE. Simultaneous, photocopied and reprint submissions OK. Accepts computer printout submissions, including dot-matrix. Fiction guide-

lines for 8x10 SAE and Canadian postage or International Reply Coupons.
Payment: $50-$500.
Terms: Pays on publication for first North American serial rights. Publication copyrighted.
Advice: "In terms of volume, there are more magazines published today than there were forty years ago. They are just smaller and less well known. One must cast one's net out farther, and expect fewer fish in the beginning. Read Mark Twain, O. Henry, S.J. Perleman, Thorne Smith, Ludwig Bemelmans, James Thurber, Woody Allen, Dan Greenberg, Tom Robbins, Leo Rosten, Joey Slinger, Stephen Leacock, Jack Douglas, and anyone else you may know who writes like they do. Then send us material of a similar ilk."

THE WASHINGTONIAN (IV), Washington Magazine Co., Suite 200, 1828 L St. NW, Washington DC 20036. (202)296-3600. Editor: John A. Limpert. General interest, regional magazine. Magazine: 8¼x10⅞; 300 pages; 40 lb paper; 80 lb cover; illustrations; photos. Monthly. Estab. 1965. Circ. 153,184.
Needs: Short pieces, must be set in Washington. Receives 8-10 unsolicited fiction mss/month. Buys 3 fiction mss/year. Length: 1,000 words minimum; 10,000 words maximum. Occasionally critiques rejected mss.
How to Contact: Send complete ms with SASE. Simultaneous and photocopied submissions OK. Reports in 2 months on mss. Sample copy for $3.
Payment: $100-$2,000. Negotiates kill fee for assigned mss not published.
Terms: Pays on publication for first North American rights. Publication copyrighted.

THE WAVE PRESS (II), Catalyst Communications Enterprises, 95 Tussel Lane, Scotch Plains NJ 07076. (201)382-8450. Editors: Jason Mark Moskowitz and Michael E. Napoliello Jr. Tabloid: 16x9¾; 30 + pages; newsprint Jet stock; illustrations; photos. "We want articles that reflect the essence of a conversation amongst good and concerned friends." Weekly. Estab. 1982. Circ. 50,000.
Needs: Adventure, contemporary, experimental, fantasy, horror, humor/satire, literary, psychic/supernatural/occult, regional, science fiction, suspense/mystery. Receives 100 + unsolicited mss/month. Buys 5 mss/issue; 54 mss/year. Publishes 2-4 weeks after acceptance. Agented fiction 10%. Recently published work by Marc Stuarts, Skot Davis. Published new writers within the last year. Length: 1,000-2,000 words average; 100 words minimum; 6,500 words maximum. Publishes short shorts. Occasionally critiques rejected mss. Recommends other markets.
How to Contact: Query first or, submit through agent. Reports in 2 weeks on queries; 2 months on mss. SASE for ms. Simultaneous and photocopied submissions OK. Accepts computer printout submissions, including dot-matrix. Accepts electronic submissions compatible with IBM PC, send via Hayes modem at 300/1200 baud rate. Query first. Sample copy for $2 and 8½x11 SAE and 4 first class postage stamps.
Payment: Pays $10-150. Sometimes offers free subscription to magazine instead of payment, "depending on time of year/budget."
Terms: Pays on acceptance for first rights, first North American serial rights, or one-time rights. Publication is copyrighted.
Advice: "Send for a copy. Read it. Smell it. Bathe with it. Read it again. Feel it. Learn it. Then, look at your own work and say, 'Would this fit in here?' If yes, please send it soon."

WEE WISDOM MAGAZINE (II), Unity School of Christianity, Unity Villiage MO 64065. (816)524-3550-ext 397. Editor: Judy Gehrlein. Magazine: 48 pages; 45 lb pentair suede stock; 80 lb Mountie matte cover; illustrations; photos (very seldom). "We publish material designed to meet needs of today's children in an entertaining, positive way. For children through 12. 10 issues per year. Estab. 1893. Circ. 175,000.
Needs: Adventure, contemporary, fantasy, juvenile (5-9 years), preschool, (0-4 years), young adult/teen (10-13). No violence or religious denominational. Receives 150 unsolicited mss/month. Buys 6 mss/issue; 60 mss/year. Publishes ms 6 months to 1 year after acceptance. Recently published work by Bette Killion, Shirley Mozelle, Barbara Gaal Luty. "Many of our writers are previously unpublished." Length: 500-800 words.
How to Contact: Send complete ms with SASE and "short, informative" cover letter. Reports in 4-6 weeks on mss. Photocopied submissions OK. Accepts computer printout submissions, no dot-matrix. Sample copy and fiction guidelines free.
Payment: Pays 4¢ per word.
Terms: Pays on acceptance for first rights. Publication copyrighted.
Advice: "Grab the readers in the first few lines. Write with verbs—not adjectives. Help the child see the wisdom within him and help him see how to use it."

‡WEIRD TALES (I,IV), The Unique Magazine, Terminus Publishing Company, Inc., Box 13418, Philadelphia PA 19101. Editors: George Scithers, Darrell Schweitzer and John Betancourt. Magazine: 6½x9½; 140 pages; acid-free book paper; pen and ink illustrations. "This is a professional fantasy-fiction and horror-fiction magazine." Quarterly. Estab. 1923. Circ. 11,000 +.
Needs: Fantasy, horror, psychic/supernatural/occult. "Writers should be familiar with the fantasy/horror genres; the three editors are well read in the field and want fresh ideas, rather than tired old retreads. To paraphrase Ursula K. LeGuin, 'If you want tos23write it, you gotta read it!'" Receives 150-200 unsolicited fiction mss/month. Buys 12-20 fiction mss/issue; 48-80 mss/year. Publishes ms usually less than 1 year after acceptance. Agented fiction 15%. Recently published work by Gene Wolf, Ramsey Campbell and Nancy Springer. Length: 20,000 words maximum. Publishes short shorts. Always comments on rejected mss.
How to Contact: Send complete ms with cover letter, which should include "date, return address." Reports in 1 week. SASE. Accepts photocopied submissions. Accepts dot-matrix computer printouts "if as good as typewritten pages." Sample copy $4.50. Fiction guidelines for #10 SAE and 1 first class stamp.
Payment: Pays 3¢-7¢/word, depending on length of story, plus 2 contributor's copies.
Terms: Pays on acceptance for first North American serial rights. Sends galleys to author. Publication copyrighted.
Advice: "The science fiction/fantasy/horror short fiction field seems to be doing fine these days; there have been several new professional magazines started, and the audience seems to be responding well to them. We are looking forward to the SF/F/H market expanding still further. *Weird Tales* is a revival of a famous old 'pulp' magazine, published in the original format, but with new fiction by many top writers and talented newcomers to the field. Basically, we're trying to make this *Weird Tales* as it would be today had it continued uninterrupted to the present. Know the field. Know manuscript format. Be familiar with the magazine, its contents and its markets."

WESTERN PEOPLE (II), Western Producer Publications, Box 2500, Saskatoon, Saskatchewan S7K 2C4 Canada. (306)665-3500. Editor: Keith Dryden. Managing Editor: Liz Delahey. Magazine: 8½x11; 16 pages; newsprint paper and cover stock; illustrations; photos. "*Western People* is for and about western Canadians, a supplement of the region's foremost weekly agricultural newspaper. Includes fiction, nonfiction (contemporary and history) and poetry. Readership is mainly rural and western Canadian." Weekly. Published special fiction issue last year; plans another. Estab. 1978. Circ. 130,000.
Needs: Contemporary, adventure, humor and serialized novels. Buys 50 mss/year. Publishes short shorts. Published new writers within the last year. Length: 750-2,500 words (unless for serialization).
How to Contact: Send complete ms with SAE, IRC (or $1 without IRC). Reports in 3 weeks on mss. Free sample copy with 9x12 SAE, IRC. Free general guidelines with legal-sized SAE, IRC.
Payment: $150 maximum (more for serials).
Terms: Pays on acceptance for first and first North American serial rights.
Advice: "The story should be lively, not long, related in some way to the experience of rural western Canadians. We believe our readers enjoy a good story, particularly when it has some relevance to their own lives. Although most of the stories in *Western People* are nonfictional, we offer variety to our readers, including fiction and poetry. Write about what could happen, not what did happen. We find that beginning writers try to fictionalize actual events with a result that is neither fish nor fowl."

THE WISCONSIN RESTAURATEUR, Published: Wisconsin Restaurant Association, 122 W. Washington, Madison WI 53703. (608)251-3663. Editor: Jan LaRue. Magazine: 8½x11; 80 pages; 80 lb enamel cover stock; illustrations; photos. Published for foodservice operators in the state of Wisconsin and for suppliers of those operations. Theme is the promotion, protection and improvement of the foodservice industry for foodservice students, operators and suppliers. Monthly except December/January combined. Estab. 1933. Circ. 4,000.
Needs: Literary, contemporary, feminist, science fiction, regional, western, mystery, adventure, humor, juvenile and young adult. "Only exceptional fiction material used. No stories accepted that put down persons in the foodservice business or poke fun at any group of people. No off-color material. No religious, no political." Buys 1-2 mss/issue, 12-24 mss/year. Receives 15-20 unsolicited fiction mss/month. Published new writers within the last year. Length: 500-2,500 words. Critiques rejected mss "when there is time."
How to Contact: Send complete ms with SASE. Accepts computer printout submissions. Reports in 1 month. Free sample copy with 8½x11 SASE. Free guidelines with SASE.
Payment: $2.50-$20. Free author's copy. 50¢ charge for extra copy.
Terms: Pays on acceptance for first rights and first North American serial rights. Publication copyrighted.
Advice: "Make sure there is some kind of lesson to be learned, a humorous aspect, or some kind of moral to your story." Mss are rejected because they are not written for the restaurateur/reader.

WITH MAGAZINE (II, IV), Faith & Life Press and Mennonite Publishing House, Box 347, Newton KS 67114. (316)283-5100. Editor: Susan Janzen. Magazine: 8½x11; 24 pages; 60 lb uncoated paper and cover; illustrations; photos. "Our purpose is to help teenagers understand the issues that impact them and to help them make choices that reflect Mennonite-Anabaptist understandings of living by the Spirit of Christ. We publish all types of material—fiction, nonfiction, poetry, prose poem, spiritual, sports, features, 'think' pieces, etc." Monthly. Estab. 1968. Circ. 6,500.

Needs: Contemporary, ethnic, humor/satire, literary, mainstream, religious, translations, young adult/teen (13-18 years). "We accept issue-oriented pieces as well as religious pieces. No religious fiction that gives 'pat' answers to serious situations." Receives about 50 unsolicited mss/month. Buys 1-2 mss/issue; 18-20 mss/year. Publishes ms up to 1 year after acceptance. Recently published work by Alan Cliburn, Marilyn Anderson and Sharon Roberts; published new writers within the last year. Length: 1,500 words preferred; 1,000 words minimum; 2,000 words maximum. Publishes short stories. Length: 800-1,000 words. Sometimes critiques rejected mss and recommends other markets.

How to Contact: Send complete ms with cover letter, which should include short summary of author's credits and what rights they are selling. Reports in 2-3 weeks on queries; 3 months on mss. SASE. Simultaneous, photocopied and reprint submissions OK. Accepts computer printout submissions, including dot-matrix. Accepts electronic submissions via DOS (IBM compatible) disk, preferably in Wordstar. Sample copy for $1.25 with 9x12 SAE and 85¢ postage. Fiction guidelines for #10 SAE and 1 first class stamp.

Payment: Pays 2¢/word for reprints; 4¢/word for first rights. Supplies contributor's copies; charge for extras.

Terms: Pays on acceptance for first or one-time rights. Publication copyrighted.

Advice: "Write with a teenage audience in mind, but don't talk down to them. Treat the audience with respect. Don't expect to make a sale with the usual 'I've-got-a-problem-give-it-all-to-Jesus-and-everything-will-turn-out-fine' story. Real life isn't always like that and teens will perceive the story as unbelievable. Do include ethnic minorities in your stories; our audience is both rural and urban."

WOMAN'S DAY (II), 1515 Broadway, New York NY 10036. (212)719-6492. Editor-in-Chief: Ellen R. Levine. Fiction Editor: Eileen Herbert Jordan. A strong service magazine geared to women, with a wide variety of well written subjects (foods, crafts, beauty, medical, etc.). Publishes 15 issues/year. Estab. 1939. Circ. 7½ million; readership 17 million.

Needs: Literary, contemporary, fantasy, women's. No violence, crime or totally male-oriented stories. Length: 2,000-3,000 words average.

How to Contact: Send complete ms with SASE. Free guidelines with SASE.

Payment: Pays top rates.

Terms: Pays on acceptance for first North American serial rights. Publication copyrighted. Occasionally buys reprints.

Advice: "Read the magazine and keep trying."

WOMAN'S WORLD (II), The Woman's Weekly, Heinrich Bauer, N.A., Box 6700, Englewood NJ 07631. (201)569-0006. Editor-in-Chief: Dennis Neeld. Fiction Editor: Mary McHugh. Magazine: 9x11⅜; 56 pages; super calendar paper and cover stock; illustrations; photos. Service magazine for women, lower to middle income, ages 18-80. Includes both career and family oriented stories. Weekly. Estab. 1981.

Needs: Mainstream romance (contemporary), suspense/mystery. "No science fiction, graphic language, explicit sex, gruesome or grotesque stories." Receives 500-600 unsolicited fiction mss/month. Buys 2 mss/issue; 104 mss/year. Approximately 10% of fiction is agented. Recently published work by Sheila Stroup, Jessie Gunn Stephens, P.J. Platz, Jane Berlin; published new writers within the last year. Length: 4,500 words for short stories; 1,600 words for mini-mysteries. Occasionally critiques rejected mss.

How to Contact: Send complete ms *with SASE*. Simultaneous and photocopied submissions OK. Reports in 1-2 months on mss. Publishes ms an average of 4 months after acceptance. Fiction guidelines for SASE.

Payment: $500 (for mysteries)-$1,000 (for romances).

Terms: Pays on acceptance for first North American serial rights. Publication copyrighted.

Advice: "Read several issues and send for guidelines before submitting stories. Our prime interest is stories with a romance theme and positive resolution. Prepare your mss carefully, using standard form—neat, clean, no or very few typos—editors won't ruin their eyes and waste their time on illegible, illiterate, careless writers. I'm not interested in 'generic' 'TV' stories, but in ones where the author's vision shines through. Also—*SASE*—I cannot emphasize this too strongly. SASE for *everything*—a query or *any* request, as well as with your mss."

WONDER TIME (II), Beacon Hill, Press of Kansas City, 6401 Paseo, Kansas City MO 64131. (816)333-7000. Editor: Evelyn Beals. Magazine: 8¼x11; 4 pages; self cover; color illustrations; photos. Hand-out story paper published through the Church of the Nazarene Sunday school; stories should follow outline of Sunday school lesson for 6-7 year olds. Weekly. Circ. 45,000.
Needs: Religious/inspirational and juvenile. Stories must have controlled vocabulary and be easy to read. No fairy tales or science fiction. Buys 1 ms/issue. Receives 50-75 unsolicited fiction mss/month. Approximately 25% of fiction is agented. Published new writers within the last year. Length: 300-550 words. Also publishes short shorts. Recommends other markets.
How to Contact: Send complete ms with SASE. Reports in 6 weeks on mss. Publishes ms an average of 1 year after acceptance. Free sample copy and curriculum guide with SASE.
Payment: Pays 3½¢/word.
Terms: Pays on acceptance for first rights. Buys reprints. Publication copyrighted.
Advice: "Control vocabulary. Study children to know what children are interested in; stories should deal with children's problems of today and must be tastefully handled." Mss may be rejected because they "do not correlate with the Sunday school lessons."

WYOMING RURAL ELECTRIC NEWS (WREN) (II), Wyoming Rural Electric Association, Suite 101, 340 W. B St., Casper WY 82601. (307)234-6152. Editor: Gale Eisenhauer. Magazine: 8½x11; 24 pages; 50 lb paper; illustrations; photos. Magazine for Wyoming people who use rural electric power. Publishes a variety of material: features on Wyoming people, places, historicals, short fiction and some poetry; energy and conservation material pertinent to readers. Monthly. Published special fiction issue last year; plans another. Circ. 38,500.
Needs: Adventure, ethnic, historical (general), humor/satire, literary, regional, romance (historical), senior citizen/retirement, western and energy. "Fiction must appeal in one form or another to our audience of rural Wyomingites." Receives approximately 6 unsolicited fiction mss/month. Buys 1 ms/issue (maximum); approximately 11 mss/year. Published new writers within the last year. Length: 750 words minimum; 2,000 words maximum; 1,600 words average. Occasionally critiques rejected mss.
How to Contact: Send complete ms with SASE. Simultaneous and photocopied submissions OK. "We prefer not to use previously published work but will if it is exactly something we are looking for." Accepts computer printout submissions. Prefers letter-quality. Reports in 3 months on mss. Publishes ms 2-4 months after acceptance. Free sample copy with 8½x11 SASE and 45¢ postage. Free fiction guidelines with SASE.
Payment: Pays $10-$25, "with a possibility of higher pay in special circumstances."
Terms: Pays on publication for first rights or one-time rights. Rarely buys reprints.
Advice: "We are publishing fewer short stories, less fiction—more features."

YANKEE MAGAZINE (II, III), Yankee, Inc., Dublin NH 03444. Editor: Judson D. Hale. Fiction Editor: Edie Clark. Magazine: 6x9; 176+ pages; glossy paper; 4-color glossy cover stock; illustrations; 4-color photos. Entertaining and informative New England regional on current issues, people, history, antiques, crafts for general reading audience. Monthly. Estab. 1935. Circ. 1,000,000.
Needs: Literary. Fiction is to be set in New England or compatible with the area. No religious/inspirational, formula fiction or stereotypical dialect, novels or novellas. Buys 1 ms/issue; 12 mss/year. Recently published work by Andre Dubus, H. L. Mountzovres, David Huddle; published new writers within the last year. Length: 2,000-4,000 words. Publishes short shorts up to 1,500 words. Recommends other markets.
How to Contact: Send complete ms with SASE and previous publications. "Cover letters are important if they provide relevant information: previous publications or awards; special courses taken; special references (e.g. 'William Shakespeare suggested I send this to you . . . . ')" Reports in 3-6 weeks on mss.
Payment: $1,000.
Terms: Pays on acceptance; rights negotiable. Sends galleys to author.
Advice: "Read previous 10 stories in *Yankee* for style and content. Fiction must be realistic and reflect life as it is—complexities and ambiguities inherent. Our fiction adds to the 'complete menu'—the magazine includes many categories—humor, profiles, straight journalism, essays, etc.—and our readers tell us: They like our fiction. Listen to the advice of any editor who takes the time to write a personal letter. Go to workshops; get advice and other readings before sending story out cold." Fiction prize of $600 awarded to best story published in *Yankee* each year.

YOUNG AMERICAN (II), America's Newspaper for Kids, Box 12409, Portland OR 97212. (503)230-1895. Editor: Kristina T. Linden. Magazine: 10½x13. 16-32 pages; newsprint paper and cover; illustrations; photos. "Our focus is on children, and they are taken seriously. Articles are intended to inform and entertain. We are particularly interested in stories about newsworthy kids." Biweekly. Plans special fiction issue. Estab. 1983. Circ. 1,500,000 in early 1988.
Needs: Short (1,000 words) fiction pieces—fantasy, humor, mystery, prose poem, sports. No sex, vio-

lence, gore or religion. Receives more than 50 mss/month. Buys 4-6 mss/issue, 120 mss/year. Published new writers within the last year. Length: Up to 1,000 words.

How to Contact: Queries, clips, cover letters discouraged. Finished work encouraged. Reports within 4 months. No simultaneous submissions. SASE with mss. Sample copy available for $1.50. Guidelines available with SASE.

Payment: 7¢/word.

Terms: Pays on publication for first North American rights. May also purchase reprint rights of articles published in *Young American*. Publication copyrighted.

Advice: "Speak to the kids, not down to them. Read some of the books that are popular with the younger set. You may be surprised of the level of sophistication of kids today. Now looking at longer fiction for serialization. Treat writing like a job, not a hobby."

THE YOUNG CRUSADER, National Woman's Christian Temperance Union, 1730 Chicago Ave., Evanston IL 60201. (312)864-1396. Editor-in-Chief: Mrs. Rachel Bubar Kelly. Managing Editor: Michael C. Vitucci. "Character building material showing high morals and sound values; inspirational, informational nature articles and stories for 6-12 year olds." Monthly. Estab. 1887. Circ. 10,000.

Needs: Juvenile. Stories should be naturally written pieces, not saccharine or preachy. Buys 3-4 mss/issue; 60 mss/year. Length: 600-800 words.

How to Contact: Send complete ms with SASE. Reports in 6 months or longer on mss. Free sample copy with SASE.

Payment: Pays ½¢/word and free author's copy.

Terms: Pays on publication. "If I like the story and use it, I'm very lenient and allow the author to use it elsewhere."

YOUNG JUDAEAN (IV), Hadassah Zionist Youth Commission, 50 W. 58th St., New York NY 10019. (212)355-7900, ext. 452. Editor: Mordecai Newman. Magazine: 8½x11; 16 pages; illustrations. "*Young Judaean* is for members of the Young Judaea Zionist youth movement, ages 9-12." Quarterly. Estab. 1910. Circ. 4,000.

Needs: Children's fiction including adventure, ethnic, fantasy, historical, humor/satire, juvenile, prose poem, religious, science fiction, suspense/mystery, and translations. "All stories must have Jewish relevance." Receives 10-15 unsolicited fiction mss/month. Publishes ms up to 2 years after acceptance. Buys 1-2 mss/issue; 10-20 mss/year. Length: 500 words minimum; 1,500 words maximum; 1,000 words average.

How to Contact: Send complete ms with SASE. Photocopied submissions OK. Reports in 3 months on mss. Sample copy for 75¢. Free fiction guidelines.

Payment: Pays 5¢/word up to $50; 2 free contributor's copies; 75¢ charge for extras.

Terms: Pays on publication for first rights. Publication copyrighted.

Advice: "Stories must be of Jewish interest—lively and accessible to children without being condescending."

YOUNG SALVATIONIST/YOUNG SOLDIER (II, IV), The Salvation Army, 799 Bloomfield Ave., Verona NJ 07044. (201)239-0606. Editor: Capt. Robert Hostetler. Magazine: 8x11; 16 pages (*Young Salvationist*), 8 pages (*Young Soldier*); illustrations; photos. Christian emphasis articles for youth members of the Salvation Army. Monthly. Estab. 1984. Circ. 50,000.

Needs: Religious/inspirational, young adult/teen. Receives 40 unsolicited mss/month. Buys 1-3 ms/issue; 11-30 mss/year. Publishes ms 3-4 months after acceptance. Length: 1,200 words preferred; 750 words minimum; 1,500 words maximum. Publishes short shorts. Sometimes critiques rejected mss and recommends other markets.

How to Contact: Query first or query with clips of published work then send complete ms. Reports in 1-2 weeks on queries; 2-3 weeks on mss. SASE. Simultaneous, photocopied and reprint submissions OK. Accepts computer printout submissions, including dot-matrix. Sample copy for 30¢ and 8½x11 SAE and 2 first class stamps. Fiction guidelines for #10 SAE with 1 first class stamp.

Payment: Pays 3¢-5¢/word.

Terms: Pays on acceptance for all rights, first rights, first North American serial rights, and one-time rights. Publication copyrighted.

Foreign commercial periodicals

The following commercial magazines located in the United Kingdom, Europe, Australia and South Africa are paying markets for short fiction in English by North American writers. Query first and follow fiction guidelines carefully. Always enclose proper return postage (IRCs or foreign postage stamps—see Manuscript Mechanics). You might find it less expensive to send a photocopy of your manuscript and tell the editor not to return it if it is not accepted. Then enclose just one IRC for a response.

ANIMAL WORLD, RSPCA, Causeway, Horsham, West Sussex RH12 1HG England. Editor: Elizabeth Winson. Circ. 30,000. Publishes approximately 40 stories/year. "For readers up to 17. Fact and fiction, mainly animal-welfare oriented. Covers all aspects of animal life (wild, domestic, pets). Includes puzzles, competitions and full-color poster center spread." Pays up to £18 per article. "Articles should be no longer than 1,000 words. No anthropomorphism is accepted. Style and technical accuracy are particularly important."

‡AUSTRALIAN PLAYBOY, 200 Crown St., Darlinghurst NSW 2010 Australia. Fiction Editor: Peter Olszewski. Circ. 50,000. Publishes 12 pieces of fiction/year. "Adult men's magazine. Strong contemporary fiction but not too avant-garde." Writers paid $AUS150/1,000 words. "Keep length to 2,000-3,000 words. Double space manuscript. Be original, be good."

BLUE JEANS MAGAZINE, D. C. Thomson, Albert Square, Dundee DD1 9QJ Scotland. Fiction Editor: Allyson Bean. Circ. 250,000 weekly. Publishes 52-60 stories/year. "Teenage magazine, age group 12-16. Romantic/funny stories about adolescence." Pays for published fiction and provides contributor's copies. "Keep it down-to-earth. Make your characters believable and real. Try to remember what it's like being a teenager! Approx. 1,500 words."

ENCOUNTER, 44 Great Windmill St., London W1V 7PA England. Circ. 20,000. Averages 10 stories/year. Pays and sends 1 contributor's copy. "No mss returned unless accompanied by IRCs. Read the magazine first!"

‡FAIR LADY (III), National Magazine, Box 1802, Cape Town 8000 South Africa. Editor: Liz Butler. "Women's glossy magazine with regular fashion, features, beauty, cooking, parenting section, competitions, fiction, book reviews, interviews (especially celebrity, serious articles in general on self-help, and current affairs) for a very broad spectrum of population, including men. More interested in quality writing than ever." Sample copy 35 Rand.

‡FANTASY TALES, The Paperback Magazine of Fantasy and Terror, Robinson Publishing, 11 Shepherd House, Shepherd St., London W1Y 7LD England. Fiction Editor: David A. Sutton. Circ. 10,000. Publishes 12-15 stories (twice yearly). "*Fantasy Tales* is a digest-size pulp magazine that publishes fantasy, horror and some science fiction. Authors inlcude Clive Barker, Ramsey Campbell, Charles L. Grant, Robert Bloch, etc. We are looking for well-written contemporary urban horror and stories in the *Weird Tales* tradition." Writers are paid and receive a complimentary copy. "We are not interested in run-of-the-mill plotting. If you expect a reply, ensure you enclose self-addressed envelope and three IRCs. (US stamps *don't* work in Britain)."

‡HORSE & PONY MAGAZINE, Bretton Court, Bretton, Peterborough, Cambs England. Circ. 50,000. Publishes fiction in every issue (26 issues/year). "*Horse & Pony* caters for horse-lovers, mainly within the 11-16 age range. Stories with a pony/teenage theme and appeal considered. Maximum 2,000 words."

INTERZONE, 124 Osborne Rd., Brighton BN1 6LU England. Editors: David Pringle and Simon Ounsley. Circ. 14,000. Publishes 5-6 stories per issue; publishes 6 times/year. "We're looking for intelligent science fiction in the 2,000-7,000 word range." Pays £30 per 1,000 words on publication and 2 free copies of magazine. "Please read our magazine before submitting."

‡ISRAEL-AL, 17 Borgrashov St., Tel Aviv, Israel. Fiction Editor: Orna Fraser. Circ. 250,000. Publishes fiction related to tourism. Pays 15¢/word.

‡**JUST SEVENTEEN**, 52-55 Carnaby St., London W1 England. Fiction Editor: Jacqui Deevoy. Circ. 300,000. Publishes approx. 100 short stories/year. Publication "aimed at 12-18 year old girls. Varied fiction. Topics include anything a teenage girl can relate to." Writers "paid about 2 weeks after publication: £100 per 1,000 words. Writers receive free copy of magazine." Length: about 1,500 words. Style: "not too corny."

KNAVE (II), Box 312, Witham, Essex CM8 3SZ England. Editor: Rupert Metcalf. Circ. 160,000. 13 issues/year. "We are a male interest magazine. We publish one short story (1,500-2,000 words) per issue, preferably erotic." Pays £200 for first British rights on publication. Contributor's copies are sent. Sample copy £1.50.

‡**MONTHLY LIFE**, Box 3445, Lagos Nigeria. Fiction Editor: Cyprian Ekwenski. Circ. 50,000. Publishes 12 stories/year. "*Monthly Life* is a general-interest family magazine with a bias for stories and features that are relevant to the young and not-so-young members of the family. Writers are paid in Naira (Nigerian currency) but arrangements could be made to pay in Pound Sterling for outstanding stories." Authors receive contributor's copies. "The writer should concentrate on romance-type stories with an explosively ironic twist. Length: 1,200 words."

MY WEEKLY, 80 Kingsway East, Dundee DD4 8SL Scotland. Editor: Sandy Monks. "*My Weekly* is a widely read magazine aimed at 'young' women of all ages. We are read by busy young mothers, active middle-aged wives and elderly retired ladies." Fiction (romance and humor) "should deal with real, down-to-earth themes that relate to the lives of our readers. Our rates compare favourably with other British magazines. Complete stories can be of any length from 1,500 to 4,000 words. Serials from 3 to 10 installments."

‡**NOVA SF**, Perseo Libri srl, Box 1240, I-40100 Bologna Italy. Fiction Editor: Ugo Malaguti. Circ. 5,000. "Science fiction and fantasy short stories, stories and short novels." Pays $100-$600 depending on length. "No formalities required, we read all submissions and give an answer in about 6 weeks. Buys first Italian serial rights on stories."

OVERSEAS! (II), Panoramastrasse 49, Leimen 6906 West Germany. Editorial Director: Charles L. Kaufman. "*Overseas!* is published for the US military personnel stationed in Europe. It is the leading military magazine in Europe, specifically directed to males ages 18-35." Needs very short tourist, travel-in-Europe, or military-related humor for Back Talk humor page. Also need cartoons.

PATCHES, Courier Buildings, Albert Square, Dundee DDI 9QJ Scotland. Fiction Editor: Judey Paris. Publishes material of general interest to teenage readership, normally with a strong romantic interest. Writers paid for published fiction.

PEOPLE'S FRIEND, 80 Kingsway East, Dundee Scotland. Fiction Editor: S. Matheson. Circ. 566,000. Averages 200 stories/year. Writers are paid for published fiction. "Writers should study the publication before submitting material. Stories can be anything from 1,000 up to 3,000 words in length."

‡**PERSONALITY**, Republican Press (PTY) Ltd., Box 32083 Mobeni Durban 4060 South Africa. Editor: John Gardiner. "Family magazine concentrating on interesting people for a middle-to-upper-income group with a bias toward married women."

R&R ENTERTAINMENT DIGEST (IV), R&R Werbe GmbH, Kolpingstrasse 1, Leimen 6906 West Germany. Editor: Marji Hess. Monthly entertainment guide for military and government employees and their families stationed in Europe "specializing in travel in Europe, audio/video/photo information, music and the homemaker scene. Generally we do not publish any fiction. However, best chances are with first-person stories with a tie to travel in Europe or, better yet, celebrating American holidays in Europe." Sample copy for IRC.

‡**REALITY MAGAZINE**, Z75 Orwell Road, Rathgar, Dublin 6 Ireland. Fiction Editor: Fr. Kevin H. Donlon. Circ. 30,000. Publishes an average of 11 short stories annually. Pays £25/piece. "Be clear, brief, to the point and practical."

SCHOOL MAGAZINE, Box A242, Sydney South NSW 2000 Australia. Fiction Editor: Anna Fienberg. Circ. 350,000. Publishes 80 stories/year. "Literary magazine for 8-11 year olds (much like *Cricket*). All types of stories—real life, fantasy, sci-fi, folk tales." Pays $112/1,000 words on acceptance—one use only. Two free copies. "Study *Cricket* and take out subscription to *School Magazine* (Government Printer, Box 75, Pyrmont 7000, NSW Australia)."

SIMPLY LIVING (III), Otter Publications Pty/Ltd., Box 124, Terrey Hills, 2084 Australia. Editor: Mr. Richard Jones. Bimonthly magazine covering the environment, peace, animal, spiritual, natural health and social issues. 2,000 word limit. "Simultaneous submissions OK if we are informed of Australian mags submitted to. Humor particularly welcome. Prefer non-USA topics but all considered." Sample copy for U.S. $7.

‡SUPERBIKE, Link House, Dingwall Ave., Croydon CR9 2TA England. Editor: Tony Middlehurst. Circ. 42,500 (monthly). Publishes approximatley 6 fiction pieces/year. "Monthly motorcycle magazine catering to enthusiasts—concentrating on larger machines (200cc +). Drag racing, sports, road tests, etc. Also touring stories and fiction—obviously motorcycle oriented. 2,500 words max." Writers paid on publication. Looks for "double-spaced type—neat manuscripts! Good spelling. Humorous!"

‡TRUE ROMANCES, Argus Consumer Publications Ltd., 12-18 Paul St., London EC2A 4JS England. Managing Editor: Veronica Dunn. Fiction Editor: Rosie Burston. Publishes approx. 150 stories annually. "Romantic situations for 17-21 age group, teenage to first relationships/first love/engagement perhaps funny, off-beat. Young and trendy. Warmth, passion, not explicit sex. Sex only within confines of a love relationship, not casual. 1st person, male or female point of view, dialogue lively and up-to-the-minute, colloquial." Length: 1,500-6,000 words. "Bear in mind their way of life—e.g. not a lot of money, possibly unemployed or at college, therefore no going out to dinner. Takeaway, burger bar, going for a drink or to a film OK. Sad or thoughtful endings also welcome, not everything ends happy ever after. Avoid death, illness, dead parents, living with auntie."

TRUE STORY, 12-18 Paul St., London EC2A 4JS England. Managing Editor: Veronica Dunn. Fiction Editor: Rosie Burston. Circ. approx. 90,000. Approx. 144 complete stories published annually. Publishes love stories. "Age-group 21-25, romance, love, relationship problems, weddings, first baby, moving house, living together, getting over first relationship, meeting new men. First person, 1,500 to 6,000 words." Writers are paid for published fiction; also receive copies of their work. "Use plenty of up-to-date dialogue, lively style." "We have tip sheets we send to new writers if they ask for one."

WOMAN'S OWN, IPC Magazines, King's Reach Tower, Stamford Street, London SE1 9LS England. Fiction Editor: Susan Oudot. Circ. 1,055,286. Publishes weekly serials or stories. "A magazine attractive to the younger woman, with an extrovert editorial style. Fiction is usually blockbuster serials or short stories by established writers. Also TV-related material." Writers paid for published fiction and receive two copies of the magazine. Rates vary. Writers "should send in their work via an agent as we don't consider unsolicited work, or enter our annual short story competition, which is usually announced late October/November, from which a winning story and five runners up are selected and later reprinted in the magazine."

‡WOMAN'S REALM, 1 PC Magazines, King's Reach Tower, Stamford Street, London SE1 9LS England. Fiction Editor: Sally Bowden. Circ. 620,000. Publishes 50-60 stories and 9 serials/year. Appeals to practical, intelligent, family—minded women, age 23 upwards. High standard of writing required. Originality important. Writers paid for published work. "Nearest US equivalent to our kind of fiction is probably *Redbook*. Length should be 1,200-4,000 words."

WOMAN'S STORY (II), Argus Consumer Publications Ltd., 12-18 Paul St., London EC2A 4JS England. Managing Editor: Veronica Dunn. Fiction Editor: Rosie Burston. Circ. Approximately 60,000. Approximately 144 stories published annually. "Publishes a wide range of love stories including humorous, first- or third-person, single, divorcée, second marriage, perhaps with kids, career/home conflicts, 20s-30s. Stories narrated by men also welcome. Avoid doom and gloom. Length: 1,500-6,000 words." Writers paid for published fiction. "Write for tip sheet."

Commercial periodicals/'88-'89 changes

The following commercial magazines appeared in the 1988 edition of *Fiction Writer's Market* but are not in the 1989 edition of *Novel and Short Story Writer's Market*. Those publications whose editors did not respond to our request for an update of their listings may not have done so for a variety of reasons—they may be out of business, for example, or they may be overstocked with submissions. Note that commercial publications outside the U.S. and Canada appear at the end of this list.

Ararat (did not respond)
Currents (did not respond)
Echelon (out of business)
Esquire (asked to be deleted)
Family Circle (asked to be deleted)
Gambling Times (did not respond)
Georgia Journal ("no fiction at this time")
Impressions (did not respond)
L.A. West (no fiction except at Christmas)
Leaatherneck (no more fiction)
Midcontinental (asked to be deleted)
New Age Journal (no more fiction)

The New American Land (out of business)
New Era Magazine (asked to be deleted)
Options (overstocked)
Shining Star (did not respond)
Stallion Magazine (out of business)
Turn-On Letters (asked to be deleted)
U(University) Magazine (did not respond)
Uncensored Letters (asked to be deleted)
Western Living (asked to be deleted)
White Wolf Magazine (asked to be deleted)

YM (asked to be deleted)

Foreign commercial periodicals

Cleo Magazine (no more fiction)
Commando (did not respond)
Dolly (asked to be deleted)
Femina (asked to be deleted)
It Magazine (did not respond)
Jackie (did not respond)
Living & Loving (did not respond)
19 Magazine (did not respond)
Woman (no more unsolicited fiction)

Writers interested in submitting work to commercial publishers are finding fewer markets for their work each year. In recent years a series of mergers, buy-outs and takeovers has resulted in a sharp decrease in the number of large commercial publishing outlets. This trend hits fiction writers hardest, especially those whose work is new, literary or experimental. Not only has the number of markets declined, but also profitability is fast becoming the determining factor in publishing decisions, sometimes at the expense of originality and variety.

Yet this same trend—consolidation of the major publishing houses—has been a boon for small publishers. The small presses are thriving by doing what they do best—filling the void in the market left open by their larger commercial counterparts. Unlike the major firms, small presses do not need blockbusters with initial press runs of 10,000 and 20,000 books to make a profit. Much lower overhead and production costs enable many small publishers to "stay afloat" with press runs of 5,000 books or less.

One factor that has contributed to the increasing profitability of small press runs is the advancement in production technology. A decade ago many small presses had to contract out for all production services—typesetting, layout, etc. Desk top publishing has changed forever the way small publishers produce books. Much of the production work (pre-press) can be done inhouse and by one person. In addition to the savings in time and money, expanded production capabilities have also meant more attractive, professional-looking books. In turn, these factors have led to increased sales and a new respectability for small press books.

Writers whose work might be considered too risky for the commercial publisher or a title which might not have mass market appeal, may do well with a small publisher. The advances, if there are any, are small, but successful small publishers keep books in the bookstores for much longer periods of time than do commercial publishers. This can actually mean higher profits for the author in the long run.

One advantage to working with a small publisher has little to do with money. Most authors whose books were published by a small press say they received more attention and care from editors than they would have had they gone to a larger house. A reason for this is stability— editors at the large New York publishers tend to change jobs once every two or three years. Another reason is many small publishers are also writers. Many started by publishing their own books and built a business by helping to publish the work of friends and other writers. They are, therefore, particularly sensitive to the importance of the writer/editor relationship.

Strategies for success

While many small publishers founded their businesses more to support new writing than to build fortunes, marketing is becoming more and more important. Several have found that by working together in associations such as COSMEP, small press publishers can learn about new technology from each other and share ideas on marketing and other subjects.

By banding together, small presses are able to take advantage of better distribution networks, cooperative advertising and other group marketing plans. This group effort has given rise to a number of small press wholesalers, distributors and other businesses who provide services to the group that would be too costly for individual small publishers.

Independent booksellers have also formed trade associations in recent years and have begun to build a strong working relationship with the small press. Chain bookstores have also begun to recognize the importance of small presses, especially in providing books for highly specialized audiences. Other market strategies used by small publishers include direct mail advertising and sales to libraries and university bookstores.

Writers who publish with small presses are often expected to do more marketing of their own books. Small publishers cannot afford large publicity tours or extensive national advertising. They rely heavily on authors and are usually open to any suggestions or help with marketing plans. In exchange, authors have the opportunity to be involved with all aspects of publishing their books.

Building publication credits

While most small publishers accept unsolicited submissions and many even encourage new writers, most editors say literary magazines are the first place they look for new talent. Publication, even in a small journal, gives the writer experience and demonstrates to the small press editor that you are familiar with the editing and publication process.

Although few literary journals pay top rates and many only pay in copies, the exposure generated can help your career. Editors listed prestige magazines such as *The Paris Review*, *The North American Review* and *The Threepenny Review*, as must-see publications, but many said they also read several less well-known publications. Genre publishers have their own lists of specialized magazines.

Fiction publication in commercial magazines can also be a plus. Even publication of non-fiction articles and participation in writing workshops and conferences build your readership and can enhance your marketability—something small press publishers appreciate. Mention publications in your cover letter—but note, of course, there's no substitute for talent.

Submitting to small presses

As with larger publishers, professionalism counts. Show you've done your homework by not sending inappropriate submissions. Cave Books, for example, receives manuscripts for all sorts of adventure, horror and other stories, but rarely receives the type of story outlined in the needs section of its listing—books with cave themes or settings.

Since many small presses are highly specialized, it's important to obtain a catalog or a flyer first to find out what types of books the press publishes. Visit a local college library or independent bookstore to look for the publisher's books. For publishers listed in this book, check the small press subject index located before the main index. Keep in mind, however, the categories are broad—although both Seal Press and New Victoria Publishers publish feminist fiction, their approaches may be quite different.

Even though these publishers are small and are often owner-operated, manuscripts must be submitted in the same manner acceptable to major houses. Manuscripts must be typed neatly, proofread and free of most errors. Never send your only copy and always use an SASE—many of these publishers cannot otherwise afford to return submissions.

Here are the codes we've used to classify the small presses:

> I *Publisher encourages beginning or unpublished writers to submit work for consideration and publishes new writers frequently;*
> II *Publisher accepts work by established writers and by occasional new writers of unusual talent;*
> III *Publisher does not encourage beginning, unagented writers; publishes mainly writers with extensive previous publication credits and a very few new writers;*
> IV *Special-interest or regional publisher open only to writers on certain subjects or from certain geographical areas.*

‡ACADIA PUBLISHING CO. (II,IV), Subsidiary of World Three, Inc., Box 170, Bar Harbor ME 04609. (207)288-9025. President: Frank J. Matter, Fiction Editor: Wendy Copson. Estab. 1980. "Small independent publisher with grand plans." Publishes hardcover and paperback originals and reprints. Books: offset printing; case, paperback or spiral binding; line art, photo, 4-color illustrations; average print order: 2,500; first novel print order: 2,000. Published new writers within the last year. Plans 2 first novels this year. Averages 6 total titles, 2 fiction titles each year. Sometimes comments on rejected mss; $50 charge for critiques.
Needs: Historical, juvenile (5-9 yrs.) including: animal and historical; young adult/teen (10-18 years): historical. No erotica, ethnic, gay, romance, science fiction.
How to Contact: Accepts unsolicited mss. Query first or submit complete ms with cover letter. SASE. Cover letter should include Social Security number. Reports on queries in 2 weeks; on mss in 2 months. Simultaneous and photocopied submissions OK, if good. Accepts computer printout submissions, including dot-matrix.
Terms: Pays standard royalties. Advance is negotiable. Sends galleys to author. Publishes within 12-18 months of acceptance. "We will produce a work under contract. Rate depends on condition of the manuscript, final quality required, etc. We are very selective (2-3 titles a year)." Subsidy titles "do not bear our imprint." Book catalog: for #10 SAE and 1 first class stamp.
Advice: "We like quality regardless of the author's past publishing history. Please, do not send a manuscript in its 'working stage.' We need to see what you *can do*—not what you only think you can do. Please be professional, neat and reasonable. Research, research, research. This is a very competitive business and each work we publish can make or break us. If the work is right we will work with the author so that we both win."

ADVOCACY PRESS (IV), Box 236, Santa Barbara CA 93102. Publisher: Mindy Bingham. Estab. 1983. Small publisher with 3-5 titles/year. Hardcover and paperback originals. Books: perfect or Smythe-sewn binding; illustrations; average print order: 20,000 copies; first novel print order: 10,000. Plans 2 first novels this year; 2 fiction titles/year.
Needs: Juvenile (5-9 years); preschool/picture book. Wants only feminist/nontraditional messages to boys or girls—picture books. Recently published *Father Gander Nursery Rhymes*, by Dr. Doug Harch (picture book); *Minou*, by Mindy Bingham (picture book).
How to Contact: No unsolicited mss; will not return them. Submit outline/synopsis with SASE. Reports in 6 weeks on queries. Simultaneous submissions OK. No photocopies. Accepts computer printouts, including dot-matrix.
Terms: Pays in royalties of 5% minimum; 10% maximum. Sends pre-publication galleys to the author. Book catalog free on request.
Advice: "We are looking for fictional stories for children 4-8 years old that give messages of self sufficiency for little girls; little boys can nurture and little girls can be anything they want to be, etc. Looking for talented writers/artists."

ALASKA NATIVE LANGUAGE CENTER (IV), University of Alaska, Box 900111, Fairbanks AK 99775-0120. (907)474-6577. Editor: Lorraine B. Elder. Estab. 1972. Small education publisher limited to books in and about Alaska native languages. Generally nonfiction. Publishes hardcover and paperback originals. Books: 60 lb book paper; offset printing; perfect binding; photos, line art illustrations; average print order: 500-1,000 copies. Averages 6-8 total titles each year.
Needs: Ethnic. Publishes original fiction only in native language and English by Alaska native writers.
How to Contact: Does not accept unsolicited mss. Photocopied submissions OK. Accepts computer printout submissions, including dot-matrix. Electronic submissions via ASCII for modem transmissions or Macintosh compatible files on 3½" disk.
Terms: Does not pay. Sends galleys to author.

ALYSON PUBLICATIONS, INC. (II), 40 Plympton St., Boston MA 02118. (617)542-5679. Subsidiary is Carrier Pigeon Distributors. Fiction Editor: Sasha Alyson. Estab. 1977. Medium-sized publisher specializing in lesbian- and gay-related material. Publishes paperback originals and reprints. Books: paper and printing varies; trade paper, perfect bound binding; average print order: 8,000; first novel print order: 6,000. Published new writers within the last year; plans 4 first novels this year. Averages 15 total titles, 8 fiction titles each year. Average first novel print order 6,000 copies.

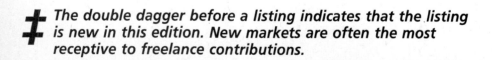

The double dagger before a listing indicates that the listing is new in this edition. New markets are often the most receptive to freelance contributions.

Needs: "We are interested in all categories; *all* materials must be geared toward lesbian and/or gay readers." Recently published *Goldenboy*, by M. Nava; *The Crystal Curtain*, by S. Bayer; *Boys' Town*, by A Bosch.

How to Contact: Query first with SASE. Reports in 3 weeks on queries; 2 months on mss. Photocopied submissions OK but not preferable. Prefers letter-quality.

Terms: "We prefer to discuss terms with the author." Sends galleys to author. Book catalog for SAE and 37¢ postage.

Advice: "We're getting more top-quality mss—I think because we're better known."

AMERICAN ATHEIST PRESS (IV), Gustav Broukal Press, Box 140195, Austin TX 78714-0195. (512)458-1244. Editor: Robin Murray-O'Hair, Estab. 1960. Paperback originals and reprints. Books: bond and other paper; offset printing; perfect binding; illustrations "if pertinent." Averages 6 total titles/year. Occasionally critiques or comments on rejected mss.

Needs: Contemporary, humor/satire, literary, science fiction. No "religious/spiritual/occult."

How to Contact: Query with sample chapters and outline. SASE. Reports in 6 weeks on queries; 2 months on mss. Simultaneous and photocopied submissions OK. Accepts computer printout submissions, including dot-matrix. Accepts electronic submissions via IBM-PC/Word-Perfect on disk.

Terms: Pays 6-11% royalties and subscription to magazine. Writers guidelines free for SASE, #9 and 1 first class stamp. Book catalog free on request.

Advice: "We only publish fiction which relates to Atheism; we receive many queries for general interest fiction, which we do not publish."

AND BOOKS (IV), 702 S. Michigan, South Bend IN 46618. (219)232-3134. Editorial Director: Emil Krause. Estab. 1977. Publishes paperback originals and reprints, primarily nonfiction. Occasionally comments on rejected mss. Occasionally recommends other markets. Averages 10-15 titles/year.

Needs: Historical, regional. "No romance, please."

How to Contact: SASE. Simultaneous and photocopied submissions OK. Accepts computer printout submissions, including dot-matrix. Reports in 1 month on queries.

Terms: Pays 5-10% royalties and 10 author copies. Writer's guidelines and book catalog for SASE.

Advice: "Send mss that will sell. Consider your market and how it will be reached. We sell mainly through book stores and are a general reading market."

‡ANDROGYNE, 930 Shields St., San Francisco CA 94132. (415)586-2697. Contact: Ken Weichel. Estab. 1971. "Independent press working within the cultural coincidence of San Francisco." Publishes books and a periodical, *Androgyne*. Publishes paperback originals. Averages 3 total titles, 1 fiction title each year. Average first novel print order 500 copies.

Needs: Contemporary, experimental, and literary.

How to Contact: Does not accept unsolicited mss. Query. Reports in 1 month on queries; 2 months on mss. Simultaneous and photocopied submissions OK. Accepts computer printout submissions; prefers letter-quality.

Terms: Pays in author's copies (10%). See magazine for writer's guidelines. Free book catalog.

ANNICK PRESS LTD. (IV), 15 Patricia Ave., Willowdale, Ontario M2M 1H9 Canada. (416)221-4802. Publisher of children's books only. Publishes hardcover and paperback originals. Books: offset paper; full-color offset printing; perfect and library binding; full-color illustrations; average print order: 9,000; first novel print order: 7,000. Plans 18 first picture books this year. Averages approximately 20 titles each year, all fiction. Average first picture book print order 2,000 cloth, 9,000 paper copies. Occasionally critiques rejected ms.

How to Contact: "Annick Press publishes only work by Canadian citizens or residents." Does not accept unsolicited mss. Query with SASE. Free book catalog.

Terms: Sends galleys to author.

Advice: "Publishing more fiction this year, because our company is growing. But our publishing program is currently full."

ANOTHER CHICAGO PRESS (II), Box 11223, Chicago IL 60611. Senior Editor: Barry Silesky. Fiction Editor: Sharon Solwitz. Estab 1976. Small literary press, non-profit. Books: offset printing; perfect

---

Market categories: (I) Beginning; (II) General;
(III) Prestige; (IV) Specialized.

binding, occasional illustrations; average print order 2,000. Averages 2 total titles, 1 fiction title each year. Published new writers within the last year. Occasionally critiques or comments on rejected ms.
Needs: Literary. No inspirational religious fiction. Recently published *Curtains*, by James McManus (short fiction collection).
How to Contact: Does not accept or return unsolicited mss. Query first for books, then submit outline/synopsis and sample chapters. SASE. Agented fiction 10%. Reports in 3-6 weeks on queries; 8-12 weeks on mss. Simultaneous and photocopied submissions OK. Accepts computer printout submissions, but prefers letter quality.
Terms: Advance: $100 negotiable; honorarium depends on grant/award money. Sends galleys to author.
Advice: "Our main enterprise is the publication, bi-annually, of *ACM (Another Chicago Magazine)*. We publish novels and collections of short stories and poetry only occasionally, as our funds and time permit—and then probably only by solicitation."

ANOTHER WAY (IV), 400 East Las Palmas Dr., Fullerton CA 92635. (714)969-2346. President: Carrie Teasdale. Estab. 1985. Small, 2-person publisher. Publishes paperback originals. Published new writers within the last year. Plans 4 first novels this year. Averages about 4 total titles, 2 fiction titles each year.
Needs: Looking for practical new age fiction. Will not review manuscripts again until 1990.
How to Contact: Does not accept or return unsolicited mss. Query first. SASE. Reports on queries in 1 month. Sends pre-publication galleys to author.
Advice: "Query only publishers with an expressed interest in your type of fiction. We get too many inappropriate submissions. We are *not* interested in descriptive, experiential works—we're looking for solutions, how-to's, *practical* writings."

ANSUDA PUBLICATIONS (II), Box 158J, Harris IA 51345. Fiction Editor: Daniel Betz. Estab. 1978. One-man operation on part-time basis, "planning to someday expand into a full-time business." Publishes paperback originals. Books: mimeo paper; mimeo printing; index stock covers with square spine binding; illustrations on cover; average print order varies. Plans 1-2 first novels this year. Averages 3-5 total titles, 1 fiction title each year. Occasionally critiques rejected mss.
Needs: Fantasy, horror, literary, mainstream, psychic/supernatural, short story collections and suspense/mystery. "Interested mostly in fantasy, horror, psychic and supernatural. No romance, juvenile, experimental, translations or science fiction." Recently published *Motherland*, by Martin DiCarlantonio.
How to Contact: Query first or submit outline/synopsis and 1-2 sample chapters. SASE always. Photocopied submissions OK. Accepts computer printout submissions, prefers letter-quality. Reports in 1 day on queries, 1-8 weeks on mss. Publishes ms an average of 1 year after acceptance.
Terms: Pays in royalties by arrangement and 5 author's copies. Writer's guidelines and book catalog for #10 SASE.
Advice: "We appreciate neat copy. If photocopies are sent, we like to be able to read dark letters and to read all of the story. We try to work closely with the author through the period from first submission to publication."

APPLEZABA PRESS, Box 4134, Long Beach CA 90804. Editorial Director: Shelley Hellen. Estab. 1977. "We are a family-operated publishing house, working on a part-time basis. We plan to expand over the years." Publishes paperback originals. Averages 1 fiction title each year.
Needs: Contemporary, literary, experimental, faction, feminist, gay, lesbian, fantasy, humor/satire, translations, and short story collections. No gothic, romance, confession, inspirational, satirical, black humor or slapstick. Recently published *Flight of Freedom*, by F.N. Wright.
How to Contact: Accepts unsolicited mss. Submit complete ms with SASE. No simultaneous submissions; photocopied submissions OK. Accepts computer printout submissions, prefers letter-quality. Reports in 2 months. Publishes ms 2-3 years after acceptance.
Terms: Pays in author's copies and 8-15% royalties; no advance. Free book catalog.
Advice: "Write legibly. Cover letter with previous publications, etc. is OK. Each book, first or twentieth, has to stand on its own. If a first-time novelist has had shorter works published in magazines, it makes it somewhat easier for us to market the book. We publish only book-length material."

Read the Manuscript Mechanics section to learn the correct way to prepare and submit a manuscript.

ARIADNE PRESS (I), 4817 Tallahassee Ave., Rockville MD 20853. (301)949-2514. President: Carol Hoover. Estab. 1976. Shoestring operation—corporation with 4 directors who also act as editors. Publishes hardcover and paperback originals (may enter paperback field). Books: 50 lb alkaline paper; offset printing; Smythe-sewn binding. Average print order 1,000; average first novel print order 1,000. Plans 1 first novel this year. Averages 1 total title each year; only fiction. Sometimes critiques rejected mss. "We comment on selected mss of superior writing quality, even when rejected."
Needs: Adventure, contemporary, fantasy, feminist, historical, humor/satire, literary, mainstream, suspense/mystery, war. Looking for "Literary-mainstream" fiction. No short stories, no science fiction or horror. Recently published *The Lattice*, by Henry Alley (mainstream/literary).
How to Contact: Accepts unsolicited mss. Query first. SASE. 5% of fiction is agented. Reports in 1 month on queries; 2 months on mss. Simultaneous and photocopied submissions OK. Accepts computer printout submissions, no dot-matrix.
Terms: Pays royalties of 10%. No advance. Sends pre-publication galleys to author. Writer's guidelines not available. List of books in stock for #10 SASE.
Advice: "We exist primarily for non-established writers. Try large, commercial presses first."

ARSENAL PULP PRESS (II), 1150 Homer St., Vancouver, British Columbia V6B 2X6 Canada. (604)687-4233. Imprints include Tillacum Library, Pulp Press, Arsenal Editions. Editors: Stephen Osborne, Linda Field. Estab. 1972. Small, co-operative publisher. Publishes hardcover and paperback originals. Books: 60 lb deluxe book paper; offset printing; perfect binding; occasional illustrations; average print order: 500-1,000; first novel print order: 500-1,000. Plans 1 first novel this year. Averages 8 total titles, 3 fiction titles each year. Average first novel print order 1,000-2,000 copies. Occasionally critiques rejected ms.
Needs: Contemporary, experimental, literary, short story collections, translations. "We are an open-minded organization always on the lookout for new, fresh works." No romance, supernatural/occult or religious. Recently published *The Promise*, by W. Campbell (short stories); *The Lost Tribe*, By Don Austin (short stories); *Momentum*, by Marc Diamond (contemporary); *Hardwired Angel*, by Nora Abercrombie and Cannas Jane Dorsey (contemporary). Published new writers within the last year.
How to Contact: Accepts unsolicited mss. Submit outline/synopsis and sample chapters or complete ms with SASE or SAE and IRC. Simultaneous and photocopied submissions OK. Accepts computer printout submissions; prefers letter-quality.
Terms: Pays in royalties of 10% minimum, 15% maximum; offers $30 average advance. Sends galleys to author. Subsidy publishes. "Approximately 20-30% of our titles are funded or partially funded by grants."
Advice: "Publishing of first novels depends entirely on quality of work. Publishing more fiction this year as an objective, being a literary house. We are looking for new, fresh talent. We have a 3-day novel contest, held annually on Labor Day weekend and actively encourage new writers."

ARTE PUBLICO PRESS (II, IV), University of Houston, Houston TX 77004. (713)749-4768. Publisher: Dr. Nicolas Kanellos. Estab. 1979. Small press devoted to the publication of contemporary U.S. Hispanic literature. Publishes paperback originals and occasionally reprints. Average print order 2,000-5,000; first novel print order 2,500-5,000. Sometimes critiques rejected mss.
Needs: Contemporary, ethnic, feminist, literary, short story collections. Recently published *A Shroud in the Family*, by Lionel Garcia (satire); *This Migrant Earth*, by Rolando Hinojosa; and *Taking Control*, by Mary Helen Ponce (short stories).
How to Contact: Accepts unsolicited mss. Submit outline/synopsis and sample chapters or complete ms with cover letter. 1% of fiction is agented. Accepts computer printout submissions, including dot-matrix.
Terms: $1,000 average advance; 25 author's copies. Sends pre-publication galleys to author. Book catalog free on request.
Tips: "All fiction, all paperback."

ARTIFACTS PRESS (I, II), Oswego Art Guild, Box 315, Oswego NY 13126. (315)342-3579. Director: Carlos Steward. Estab. 1984. Art press for limited edition artist's books, literature, nonfiction and children's titles. Publishes hardcover originals and reprints. Average print order 500-1,000; average first novel print order 500-1,000. Averages 2-4 total titles/year; 1 fiction title.
Needs: Experimental, feminist, gay, juvenile (5-9 years, including: animal, easy-to-read, fantasy, contemporary), lesbian, literary, preschool/picture book, psychic/supernatural/occult, short story collection. Looking for non-traditional fiction. No mainstream fiction. Recently published *Herland*, collection (literary); *In the Deep, Dark Jungle*, by Lisa McLaughlin (children); and *Whispery Secret*, by Lois Hobart (children).
How to Contact: Accepts unsolicited submissions. Submit complete ms with cover letter. 50% of fiction is agented. SASE. Reports in 1 month on ms. Photocopied submissions OK. Accepts computer

printout submissions, including dot-matrix.

Terms: Pays in royalties, author's copies, honorarium; depends on grant/award money. "We will submit grant applications for consideration for writers we are interested in. This material should reach us by 1/15 and 6/30 yearly. We also have a writer-in-residence program for 1-4 months residency in Oswego for a maximum of $7,500. Leigh Wilson is current resident working on a first novel."

Advice: "For our organization we consider only the highest quality, non-traditional material. Send the entire ms. Multiple submissions will not be considered for any reason."

BALANCE BEAM PRESS, INC. (I), 12711 Stoneridge Rd., Dayton MN 55327. (612)427-3168. President/Fiction Editor: Mary Ellis Peterson. Estab. 1982. One-woman operation on part-time basis. Publishes paperback originals. Books: letter press printing; perfect binding; b&w illustrations; first novel print order: 300. "Current plans include only poetry and short stories; these could change." Averages 2 total titles each year—currently only anthologies. Occasionally critiques rejected mss; query first.

Needs: Currently publishing work dealing with alternatives to nuclear/militaristic society/future. I am planning an anthology of writing, poetry, short stories, humor, fantasy, science fiction, etc., dealing with fears and concerns, but more important, with possible alternatives and solutions. Also interested in new age fiction."

How to Contact: Query first with SASE and cover letter with outline or synopsis. Reports in 1 month. Simultaneous and photocopied submissions OK, but say so. Accepts computer printout submissions.

Terms: Pays in royalties of 10% minimum "or may cost share with larger percentage of net profits going to author." Sends galleys to author. Book catalog for #10 SASE.

Advice: Recent trends include "nuclear concerns, children, one title dealing with adoption of disabled and multiracial children. I am very excited about bringing out the work of new authors. We regard the author/editor relationship as a team. Keep trying and be flexible. Think through who your market is, and be able to tell a publisher what contacts, networks, etc. you have or could develop to assist in marketing."

BANK STREET PRESS, 24 Bank St., New York NY 10014. (212)255-0692. Publisher: Mary Bertschmann. Estab. 1985. Small independent publisher with plans to expand. Publishes hardcover and paperback originals. Books: Spring Hill offset white paper; printing varies; perfect binding; illustrations; average print order: 500-1,000; first novel print order: 700. Published new writers within the last year; plans 1 first novel this year. Averages 4 total titles/year; 2 fiction titles/year.

Needs: Only aesthetically oriented books.

How to Contact: Query first in writing. SASE for query. No agents. Reports in 3 weeks on queries; 6 weeks on mss.

Terms: To be determined eventually. Sends galleys to author.

BANNED BOOKS (I, II), Subsidiary of Edward-William Publishing Co., Box 33280, #231, Austin TX 78764. Senior Editor: Tom Hayes. Estab. 1985. Small press with plans to expand. Publishes paperback originals. Books: 60 lb acid-free paper; sheet-fed offset printing; perfect binding; illustrations; average print order: 2,000; first novel print order: 2,000. Plans 10 first novels this year. Averages 12 total titles, 10 fiction titles each year. Critiques or comments on rejected ms.

Needs: Erotica, fantasy, gay, humor/satire, lesbian, science fiction, short story collections. Looking for "all forms of fiction for the gay/lesbian market with the exception of poetry collections." Recently published *Mountain Climbing in Sheridan Square*, by Stan Leventhal (short story collection); *Skiptrace*, by Antoinette Azolakov; *Kite Music*, by Gary Shellhart.

How to Contact: Accepts unsolicited mss. Submit complete ms with cover letter. SASE. Reports in 3 weeks on queries; 3 months on mss. Simultaneous and photocopied submissions OK. Accepts computer printout submissions, including dot-matrix (very clear only).

Terms: Pays in royalties of 10% minimum; 15% maximum; 10 author's copies. Sends galleys to author. Writer's guidelines free for #SASE.

Advice: "Study the market before submitting. We get far too much "over the transom" that is of no interest to us. Much time and expense could be avoided if the author really read the entries in Novel/& Short Story Writer's Market before sending it out."

‡BARLOW PRESS (I,II), Box 5403, Helena MT 59604. (406)449-7310. Fiction Editor: Russell B. Hill. Estab. 1987. One-person publishing/printing company which produces titles both by offset and letterpress (hand-set) printing. Publishes hardcover and paperback originals and reprints. Books: acid-free letterpress stock (i.e. Mohawk, Superfine); usually letterpress printing, occasionally offset, hand-sewn binding with end papers, heavier cover stock, sometimes leather; woodcuts, line-art plates or one-color artwork. Average print order: 500-1,000 letterpress; 2,000-3,000 offset. Publishes 2 total titles/year; plans 0-1 first fiction title this year. Sometimes critiques rejected mss.

Needs: Adventure, contemporary, historical, humor/satire, literary, mainstream, regional, short story.

How to Contact: Query first. Accepts unsolicited mss. Send complete mss with cover letter and SASE. Reports in 2 months. Simultaneous and photocopied submissions OK. Accepts dot-matrix computer printouts and electronic disk submissions.
Terms: Payment by individual arrangement, depending on the book. Publishes ms 6 months-2 years after acceptance. Rarely subsidy, but "publication by Barlow Press usually involves a joint effort—Barlow Press contributes the time and expenses, author contributes mss, with particular terms of reimbursement subject to negotiation."
Advice: "Frankly, a publisher like Barlow Press can't compete with larger publishers for manuscripts they want, and we encourage authors to submit material to potentially lucrative publishers first. But we are convinced too many manuscripts deserve one more reading, one more potential outlet. We don't publish most manuscripts we read, but we have never regretted reading a manuscript. And because Barlow Press handles every publication by individual arrangement with the author, we aren't shy about proposing to edit manuscripts to fit our needs."

BARN OWL BOOKS (I, IV), Box 7727, Berkeley CA 94707. (415)524-8621. Imprints include Amazon Press. Publisher: Gina Covina. Estab. 1983. Two-person small publisher; "author participation in publishing process encouraged." Publishes paperback originals. Books: quality paperback standard paper; offset litho printing; perfect binding; illustrations "if appropriate"; average print order: 2,000-5,000; first novel print order: 2,000. Averages 1 total title/year. Occasionally critiques or comments on rejected ms.
Needs: Contemporary, ethnic, feminist, gay, lesbian, literary, regional.
How to Contact: Accepts unsolicited mss. Query first. SASE. Reports in 1 month on queries; 2 months on mss. Photocopied submissions OK. Accepts computer printout submissions, no dot-matrix.
Terms: Pays royalties of 7% minimum; 12% maximum. Sends galleys to authors.

FREDERIC C. BEIL, PUBLISHER, INC. (II), 414 Tattnall St., Savannah GA 31401. Imprints include The Sandstone Press. President: Frederic C. Beil III. Estab. 1983. General trade publisher. Publishes hardcover originals and reprints. Books: acid-free paper; letterpress and offset printing; Smyth-sewn, hardcover binding; illustrations; average print order: 2,000; first novel print order: 2,000. Plans 2 first novels this year. Averages 10 total titles, 2 fiction titles each year.
Needs: Historical, literary, regional, short story collections, translations. Recently published fiction by Peter Taylor, Madison Jones, Samuel Hynes.
How to Contact: Does not accept unsolicited mss. Query first. Reports in 1 week on queries. Accepts computer printout submissions, including dot-matrix.
Terms: Payment "all negotiable." Sends galleys to author. Book catalog free on request.
Advice: "Publishing more fiction—hardcover only."

BILINGUAL REVIEW PRESS (II, IV), Hispanic Research Center, Arizona State University, Tempe AZ 85287. (602)965-3867. Editor: Gary Keller. Estab. 1974. Publishes hardcover and paperback originals. Books: 55 lb acid-free paper; sheet fed printing; illustrations when appropriate; average first novel print order: 2,000-4,000 depending on sales potential. Published new writers within the last year. Plans 4 first novels this year. Averages 15 total titles, 10 fiction titles each year. Publishes also in Spanish. Occasionally critiques rejected mss.
Needs: Ethnic, historical, literary, short story collections, and translations. U.S. Hispanic themes only. "We will publish up to 12-15 good novels per year on U.S. Hispanic life if the material is available." Recently published *The Ultraviolet Sky*, by Alma Villanueva and *Death of an Anglo*, by Alejandro Morales.
How to Contact: Query first with SASE and adequate description of ms or table of contents, sample chapter. Simultaneous and high-quality photocopied submissions OK. Reports in 1 month on queries. Publishes ms an average of 1 year after acceptance.
Terms: Pays in standard royalty of 10% with an average of $300 advance. Must return advance if book is not completed or is unacceptable. Subsidy publishes less than 10% of total books. "We occasionally subsidy publish a scholarly book. We never subsidy publish fiction, poetry or any books in the trade market." Free book catalog.
Advice: "A strong market is developing for U.S. Hispanic fiction. Double space all manuscripts! Send original plus 1 copy, or 2 high quality copies. We do not publish literature about tourists in Latin America and their perceptions of the native culture."

BkMk PRESS (I, II), 107 Cockefair Hall, UMKC, 5216 Rockhill Rd. #204, Kansas City MO 64110. (816)276-2558. Fiction Editor: Dan Jaffe. Estab. 1971. Publishes hardback and paperback originals. Books: standard paper; offset printing; perfect and case binding; average print order: 1,000; averages 6 total titles; 1 fiction title each year.
Needs: Contemporary, ethnic, experimental, historical, literary and translations. "We are new to fic-

tion publishing but we plan to print one collection or anthology of short stories per year."
How to Contact: Query first with SASE. Reports in 3-4 months on queries.
Terms: Pays in royalties (approximately 10%, adjustable by contract); provides author's copies and $50 payment. Sends galleys to author. Free book catalog.

BLACK HAT PRESS (II), Subsidiary: *Rag Mag*, Box 12, Goodhue MN 55027. (612)923-4590. Editor: Beverly Voldseth. Estab. 1982. Books: 70 lb paper; offset printing; saddle-stitch binding; illustrations; average print order 250. 2 poetry books/year. Occasionally comments on rejected ms.
Needs: Contemporary, ethnic, literary, regional. No "porno/violent, poorly written, non-tension, nothing-happens sort of thing."
How to Contact: Query first for book length ms. SASE. Simultaneous and photocopied submissions OK for prose poetry, art. Include brief bio.
Terms: "Payment in copies."
Advice: "We don't do novels"

BLACK HERON PRESS (I, II), P.O. Box 95676, Seattle WA 98145. Editor: Jerry Gold. Estab. 1984. One-person operation; no immediate plans to expand. Publishes paperback and hardback originals. Average print order: 1,000; first novel print order: 500-1,500. Averages 2 fiction titles each year. Occasionally critiques or comments on rejected mss.
Needs: Adventure, contemporary, erotica, experimental, gay, humor/satire, lesbian, literary, mainstream, science fiction, suspense/mystery. Adventure/moral *dilemma*. Vietnam war novel—literary. "We don't want to see fiction written for the mass market. If it sells to the mass market fine, but we don't see ourselves as a commercial press."
How to Contact: Will not accept unsolicited manuscripts until 1989. Reports in 2 months on queries, and 3 months on mss. Simultaneous and photocopied submissions OK.
Terms: "Payment schedule uncertain."
Advice: "I prefer a query, but I'll look at an unsolicited ms anyway. One that I am planning to publish came complete with a one-paragraph cover letter. A query letter should tell me: 1) number of words, 2) number of pages, 3) is ms available on floppy disk, 4) have parts of novel been published? 5) where? If you're going to submit to *Black Heron*, make the work as good as you can. I'm a good editor but I don't have the time to solve major problems with a manuscript. Occasionally I get a ms in which I can tell that the author was careless. I resent this."

BLACKBERRY BOOKS, RR 1, Box 228, Nobleboro ME 04555. (207)729-5083. Contact: Gary Lawless. Estab. 1974. Two-person small press publishing poetry and fiction. Publishes paperback originals and reprints. Average print order: 1,500. Plans 0 first novels this year. Averages 8 total titles each year; 2 fiction titles each year.
Needs: Recently published *Spoon Handle* and *The Weir* both by Ruth Moore and *The Enchanted* by Elizabeth Coatsworth.
How to Contact: Not accepting unsolicited mss until 1989.
Terms: Pays royalties of 10%.

BLIND BEGGAR PRESS, Box 437, Bronx NY 10467. Imprint: LampLight Editions. Fiction Editors: Gary Johnston, C.D. Grant. Estab. 1975. Small press with plans to expand. Publishes paperback originals. Plans to publish first novels "dependent upon budget." Averages 2-3 total titles each year; "no fiction titles thus far." Average print order 2,000 copies. Occasionally critiques rejected ms.
Needs: Ethnic (Third World), experimental, juvenile (animal, easy-to-read, fantasy, historical), preschool/picture book, short story collections, translations and young adult/teen (historical).
How to Contact: Query first with SASE. Reports in 1 month on queries; 2 months on mss. Simultaneous and photocopied submissions OK. Publishes ms 12-18 months after acceptance.
Terms: Pays in author's copies (10-15% of run). "If author wishes to pay all or part of production costs, we work out individual arrangements directly." Book catalog free on request.
Advice: Recent trends include ethnic historical (biographies, political history, etc.). In first novels interested in high quality, relevancy to Third World readers. "Within two years we plan to publish children's books, short stories and *maybe* a small novel."

‡**BLOOD & GUTS PRESS**, 2076 Westwood Blvd., Los Angeles CA 90025. (213)475-2700. Owners/editorial contact: Patricia and Craig Graham. Publishes hardcover originals. Books: average print order 250-1,000; also publishes signed, numbered hardcover editions. Publishes 3-5 fiction titles/year.
Needs: Mainstream fiction, science fiction, suspense/mystery. Publishes novels and short story collections. Recently published *Killer Inside Me*, by Jim Thompson (mystery); *Ray Bradbury Reviewed*, by Ray Bradbury and William F. Nolan.
How to Contact: Query first with SASE. Accepts unsolicited manuscripts. Reports in 1-6 months on

queries. Simultaneous and photocopied submissions OK. Accepts dot-matrix computer printout submissions.

Terms: Pays negotiable advance. Sends prepublication galleys to author. Publishes ms up to 1 year after acceptance.

Advice: "Because we also own the Vagabond Books bookstore, we have a lot of authors in to sign their works. We tend to seek out authors who we know can write what we're looking for. Occasionally, I'll get a query that grabs me and I'll follow it up."

BOOKMAKERS GUILD INC. (IV), 9655 W. Colfax Ave., Lakewood CO 80215. (303)772-7322. Publisher: Barbara J. Ciletti. Estab. 1981. "We publish fiction and nonfiction for children and young adults (particularly high-quality, educational material in the language arts and natural sciences); books on social issues for adults. Publishes hardcover and paperback originals. Books: 60-80 lb matte paper; web offset printing. smythe-sewn or perfect binding; b&w and full-color illustrations; average print order: 5,000-7,000. Plans 1 first novel this year. Averages 6-8 total titles/year; 2-4 fiction titles/year.

Needs: Adventure, juvenile including easy-to-read, literary, short story collections, young adult/teen (10-18 years) including historical and problem novels. "We look for material containing classic mythopoeic elements, allegory, etc. No thrillers, romance, pre-school fantasy or picture books. No fiction for adults unless uniquely literary."

How to Contact: Accepts unsolicited mss. Query first. Submit outline/synopsis and 3 sample chapters. Reports in 1 month on queries; 2 months on mss. Simultaneous submissions OK. Accepts computer printout submissions, including dot-matrix.

Terms: Pays 8-15% royalties; $1,000 average advance, negotiable (only for exceptional works); 20 author's copies. Sends galleys to author. Writers guidelines for SASE; book catalog free on request.

Advice: "We do not encourage first novelists. We have not, to date, published any previously unpublished fiction writers. This has occurred by circumstance, not by design. We believe that fiction requires a strong central message and a comprehensive understanding of the English language."

BOOKS FOR ALL TIMES, INC., Box 2, Alexandria VA 22313. Publisher/Editor: Joe David. Estab. 1981. One-man operation. Publishes hardcover and paperback originals. Books: 60 lb paper; offset printing; perfect binding; average print order: 1,000. "No plans for new writers at present." Has published 1 fiction title to date. Occasionally critiques rejected mss.

Needs: Contemporary, literary and short story collections. "No novels at the moment; hopeful, though, of someday soon publishing a collection of quality short stories. No popular fiction or material easily published by the major or minor houses specializing in mindless entertainment. Only interested in stories of the Victor Hugo or Sinclair Lewis quality." Recently published *The Fire Within*, by Joe David (literary); *Glad You Asked!*, by Joe David (non-fiction).

How to Contact: Query first with SASE. Simultaneous and photocopied submission OK. Reports in 1 month on queries.

Terms: Pays negotiable advance. "Publishing/payment arrangement will depend on plans for the book." Book catalog free on request.

Advice: Interested in "controversial, honest books which satisfy the reader's curiosity to know. Read Victor Hugo, Fyodor Dostoyevsky, etc., and if you can, emulate them!"

BOTTOM DOG PRESS (IV), Firelands College, Huron OH 44839. (419)433-5560. Dr. Larry Smith, Editor/Publisher. Estab. 1984. Four-person part-time operation assisted by grants from Ohio Arts Council. Publishes paperback originals. Books: fine paper; saddle or perfect binding; cover art illustrations; average print order: 1,500 fiction. Averages 3 total titles, 1-2 fiction titles each year. Always critiques or comments on rejected mss.

Needs: Literary, mainstream. Recently published *Best Ohio Fiction* collection (160 pp) with work by Jack Matthews, Robert Flanagan, Philip F. O'Conner, Robert Fox. Published new writers within the last year.

How to Contact: Accepts unsolicited mss. Submit complete ms with cover letter. SASE. Reports on queries in 2 weeks; 2 months on mss. Accepts computer printout submissions, no dot-matrix.

Terms: Pays royalties of 10-15% minimum and 20 author's copies. Sends galleys to author. Has done 2 books co-operatively—50/50. Book catalog free on request.

Advice: "We do an 'Ohio Writers series' specializing in chapbook collection of stories or novellas—emphasis on sense of place and strong human characters." All submissions must fall within the 35,000 word limit.

BREAKWATER BOOKS, LTD. (II), 277 Duckwork St., Box 2188, St. John's Newfoundland A1C 6E5 Canada. (709)722-6680. President: Clyde Rose. Estab. 1973. Publishes hardcover and paperback originals and reprints. Books: offset printing; perfect sewn and spiral binding; illustrations; average print order: 1,000. Number of titles: 3 in 1987.

Needs: Literary, historical, ethnic (Canadian), juvenile and young adult. Recently published *January, February, June or July*, by Helen Porter; *Fanny for Change*, by Jean Hayes Feather.
How to Contact: Query or submit complete ms with SASE. Simultaneous and photocopied submissions OK. Reports in 2 months on queries, 6 months on mss.
Terms: Negotiable; no advance, free book catalog.
Advice: "Get magazine publishing experience first, and seek good editorial advice before submitting to a publisher."

BRIGHT RING PUBLISHING (IV), Box 5768-F, Bellingham WA 98227. (206)734-1601. Editor: Mary Ann F. Kohl. Estab. 1985. One-person, full-time, plans to expand to children's fiction. Publishes paperback originals. Books: offset printing; perfect binding; b&w illustrations; average print order: 3,000-5,000. Averages 1 title each year. Sometimes critiques rejected mss.
Needs: Juvenile (5-9 yrs.), easy-to-read, preschool/picture book (also 2-9 years). "Should encourage independent/creative thinking. Possibly with a theme of 'art.' No real requirements—looking at all children's books. Nothing trendy or commercial, no scary monsters or anything too 'sappy.' "
How to Contact: Accepts unsolicited ms. Submit complete ms with cover letter. SASE. Reports in 2 weeks on queries; 6 weeks on mss. Simultaneous submissions and photocopied submissions OK. Accepts computer printout submissions, including dot-matrix.
Terms: Pays royalties of 10-15% or in author's copies. Book catalog for #10 SASE or IRC.

‡BRYANS & BRYANS (I) (Book Packager and Editorial Consultant), Box 121, Fairfield CT 06430. (203)454-2051. President: John B. Bryans. Fiction Editor: James A. Bryans. Arranges publication of paperback originals (packages). Books: paperback/mass market. Critiques mss: $50 charge "for 2-page evaluation only when this has been agreed upon in advance. Often I will offer comments and criticism at no charge where we, based on a query, have encouraged submission."
Needs: Adventure contemporary, historical, horror, humor/satire, literary, mainstream, regional romance (contemporary, historical). Upcoming titles (1989) include: *The Hucksters of Holiness*, by Ron Gorton (contemporary social thriller); *Cincinnati* (historical with romance elements); *Baton Rouge* (historical with romance elements); and *Portland*, by Lee Davis Willoughby.
How to Contact: Does not accept unsolicited mss. Query first. SASE. Agented fiction 80%-90%. Reports in 3 weeks on queries; 2 months on mss. Electronic submissions OK via Macintosh disk.
Terms: Pays in royalties of 6% minimum; 10% maximum. Negotiable advance.
Advice: "Send us a letter, max. 2 pages, describing the project and giving pertinent background info on yourself. Include an SASE and we will reply to let you know if we find the idea intriguing enough to see 3 sample chapters (the *first* three) and a detailed synopsis."

BURNING BOOKS (IV), 690 Market St., Suite 1501, San Francisco CA 94104. (415)788-7480. Publisher: Kathleen Burch, Michael Sumner, Melody Sumner. Estab. 1979. Three-person part-time operation. Publishes paperback originals. Books: acid-free paper; offset and letterpress printing; spiral or signature sewn binding; illustrations; average print order: 1,000-3,000. Averages 1 title/year; 1 fiction title every 2 years. Will provide detailed critique of ms for $100.
Needs: Literary. No "commercially inspired" fiction. Recently published *The Guests Go In To Supper*, a new music anthology with John Cage, Robert Ashley, Yoko Ono, Laurie Anderson, Charles Amirkhanian, Michael Peppe and K. Atchley.
How to Contact: Does not accept unsolicited mss. Query first. Reports on queries in 6 weeks.
Terms: Pays in author's copies. Sends galleys to author. Book catalog free on request.

CADMUS EDITIONS (III), Box 687, Tiburon CA 94920. (707)431-8527. Editor: Jeffrey Miller. Estab. 1979. Emphasis on quality literature. Publishes hardcover originals and paperback originals. Books: Approximately 50% letterpress; 50% offset printing; perfect and case binding; average print order: 2,000; first novel print order: 2,000. Averages 3-5 total titles, 3 fiction titles each year.
Needs: Literary. Recently published *The Wandering Fool*, by Yunus Emre, translated by Edovard Roditi and Guzin Dino; *The Hungry Girls*, by Patricia Eakins; *Zig-Zag*, by Richard Thornley.
How to Contact: Does not accept or return unsolicited mss. Query first. SASE. Photocopied submissions OK.
Terms: Royalties negotiated per book. Sends galleys to author.

‡CANADIAN STAGE & ARTS PUBLICATIONS (I, IV), 263 Adelaide St. W, 5th Floor, Toronto, Ontario M5H 1Y2 Canada. Editor: Patricia Michael. Children's Literature Editor: Diane England. Estab. 1966. "Small press, slowly expanding. Canadian themes mostly—centered on the arts at present." Books: 50 or 60 lb stock (matte) or art paper; offset web printing; perfect bound or saddle-stitched binding; illustrations in children's line; average print order: 1,000-5,000. Averages 1-2 total titles.
Needs: Arts/culture, juvenile, literary. "Emphasis on Canadian authors. To date almost all titles have

been nonfiction (exception being a poetry book, children's line). These themes have priority, but always interested in a good story if fiction. No American themes. Would *encourage* art (performing or visual) subjects. Authors should have literary weight." Recently published *Image in the Mind: CBC radio drama 1944-1954*, by N. Alice Frick (docu-account of radio drama days at the Canadian Broadcasting Corp.); *The Amazing Lumberjack*, by Rabbi Gottesman (children's).

How to Contact: Submit outline/synopsis and 1 sample chapter. SASE. Reports in 4 weeks on queries; 6 weeks on mss. Simultaneous and photocopied submissions OK.

Terms: Pays 10% royalties, depends on grant/award money. Sends prepublication galleys to author. Publishes ms up to 1 year (depends on editing process) after acceptance. "Many books are subsidy published. Also, with Canadian content, government grants may be available."

Advice: "Would appreciate writers who query us with works suitable to small press budgets and marketing schemes—also those with Canadian themes. Artistic subjects receive most attention, but we are also planning biographies and other nonfiction for the future. Most writers have been known by us in some capacity. Most unsolicited manuscripts have been totally inappropriate. A solid storyline, honest approach and dedication to subject as a literary work will catch our interest. Nothing *too* esoteric though (must have market appeal)."

CARAVAN PRESS (II), 15445 Ventura Bl. #279, Sherman Oaks CA 91403. (818)377-4301. Publisher: O.S. Lewis. Estab. 1979. "Small three-person publisher with expansion goals." Publishes hardcover and paperback originals, especially poetry collections. Recently published *Litany*, by Scott Sonders (poems). Plans 1-2 novels this year. Averages 6 total titles. Occasionally critiques or comments on rejected ms; fee varies.

Needs: Erotica, historical, humor/satire, literary, short story collections. List for novels filled for next year or two.

How to Contact: Accepts unsolicited mss. Query through agent only. SASE. Agented fiction 90%. Reports in 2 months on queries. Simultaneous and photocopied submissions OK. Accepts computer printout submissions, including dot-matrix.

Terms: Payment rate is "very variable." Sends galleys to author. Subsidy publication rate "varies."

Advice: "Be competent, be solvent. Know who you are. Target your market."

CARLTON BOOKS (IV), Box 5052, Evanston IL 60204. (312)328-0400. Contact: Graham Carlton. Estab. 1985. Midsize independent publisher with plans to expand. Publishes hardcover and paperback originals and reprints.

Needs: Erotica, suspense/mystery.

How to Contact: Does not accept or return unsolicited ms. Query first. SASE.

CARNIVAL ENTERPRISES (IV), Box 19087, Minneapolis MN 55419. Editor: Rosemary Wallner. Estab. 1981. Number of titles: 200 trade and library editions (Carnival Press Books imprint for Raintree Publishers Group and other publishers). "*Not* a publishing company; a production and design firm for book series. Carnival presents projects and stories to publishers and retail firms coupled with the work of prominent juvenile illustrators."

Needs: Résumés only with SASE, along with short samples of writing in the juvenile fiction and nonfiction areas. "No adult or adolescent fiction."

How to Contact: Send résumé, SASE plus sample of work for files. No unsolicited mss, please!"

Terms: "Varies from client to client; flat fees usually for toy company accounts, advance and royalty for publishing accounts."

CARPENTER PRESS (I, II), Box 14387, Columbus OH 43214. Editorial Director: Robert Fox. Estab. 1973. One-man operation on part-time basis. Publishes paperback originals. Books: alkaline paper; offset printing; perfect or saddle stapled binding; illustrations sometimes; average print order: 500-2,500; first novel print order: 1,000.

Needs: Contemporary, literary, experimental, science fiction, and fantasy. "Literary rather than genre science fiction and fantasy." Recently published *Song for Three Voices*, by Curt Johnson (novel); and the 10th anniversary first novel contest winner, *The Three-Week Trance Diet*, by Jane Pirto. "Do not plan to publish more than one book/year including chapbooks, and this depends upon funding, which is erratic. Contemplating future competitions in the novel and short story."

How to Contact: Accepts unsolicited mss. Query. SASE. Simultaneous and photocopied submissions OK. Accepts computer printout submissions. Letter-quality only. Reports promptly.

Terms: Pays in author's copies or 10% royalties. "Terms vary according to contract." No cash advance. Free book catalog with #10 SASE.

Advice: "Don't try to impress us with whom you've studied or where you've published. Read as much as you can so you're not unwittingly repeating what's already been done. I look for freshness and originality. I wouldn't say that I favor experimental over traditional writing. Rather, I'm interested in seeing how recent experimentation is tying tradition to the future and to the work of writers in other countries. Our books should be read before submitting. We encourage first novelists."

‡CATBIRD PRESS (II), 44 N. 6th Ave., Highland Park NJ 08904. (201)572-0816. Publisher: Robert Wechsler. Estab. 1987. Small independent trade publisher. Publishes hardcover and paperback originals and reprints. Books: acid-free paper; offset printing; cloth/paper binding; illustrations (where relevant). Average print order: 3,000; first novel print order: 2,000. Plans 1 first novel this year. Averages 5 total titles, 1-2 fiction titles each year.
Needs: Contemporary, ethnic, experimental, humor/satire (specialty); literary, mainstream, short story collections, translations (specialty Czech, French and German read in-house). Recently published *Catapult*, by Vladimír Páral, translated by William E. Harkins (Czech, literary but popular).
How to Contact: Accepts unsolicited mss. Submit outline/synopsis with sample chapters. SASE. Reports in 2 weeks on queries; 4-6 weeks on mss. Simultaneous and photocopied submissions OK.
Terms: Pays royalties of 7½% minimum; 15% maximum. Average advance: $1,000; offers negotiable advance. Pays in 10 author's copies. Sends prepublication galleys to author. Publishes ms approx. 1 year after acceptance. Some subsidy publishing; terms depend on particular book. Writer's guidelines for #10 SAE with 1 first class stamp.
Advice: "We are a new publisher interested in quality fiction particularly of a humorous nature. We are definitely interested in unpublished novelists who combine a sense of humor with a true knowledge of and love for literature, a lack of ideology, care for craft, and self-criticism (falling out of love with one's words)."

‡CAVE BOOKS (IV), Subsidiary of Cave Research Foundation, 756 Harvard Ave., St. Louis MO 63130. (314)862-7646. Editor: Richard A. Watson. Estab. 1957. Small press. Publishes hardcover and paperback originals and reprints. Books: acid free paper; various methods printing; binding sewn in signatures; illustrations; average print order: 1,500; first novel print order: 1,500. Averages 4 total titles. Number of fiction titles varies each year. Critiques or comments on rejected ms.
Needs: Adventure (cave exploration). Needs any realistic novel with caves as central theme. "No gothics, romance, fantasy or science fiction. Mystery and detective OK if the action in the cave is central and realistic. (What I mean by 'realistic' is that the author must know what he or she is talking about.)"
How to Contact: Accepts unsolicited mss. Submit complete ms with cover letter. Reports in 1 week on queries; 1 month on mss. Simultaneous and photocopied submissions OK. Accepts computer printouts.
Terms: Pays in royalties of 10%. Sends galleys to author. Book catalog free on request.
Advice: Encourages first novelists. "We would like to publish more fiction, but we get very few submissions. Why doesn't someone write a historical novel about Mammoth Cave, Carlsbad Caverns, . . .?"

‡CHELSEA GREEN PUBLISHING CO., One Court St., Box 283, Chelsea VT 05038. (802)685-3108. Editor: Michael Moore. Estab. 1985. "Small independent trade publisher with plans to expand." Publishes hardcover and paperback originals. Averages 8-10 total titles, 1-2 fiction titles each year.
Needs: Serious fiction only . . . no genre fiction (ie. romance, spy, sci fi) or mainstream." Recently published *The Automotive History of Lucky Kellerman*, by Steve Heller (literary); *The Eight Corners of the World*, by Gordon Weaver (lit/comedy).
How to Contact: Query first. Prefers no unsolicited submissions. SASE.
Terms: Royalties to trade standards; advances on royalties negotiable.

‡CHILD WELFARE LEAGUE OF AMERICA (IV), 440 First St. NW, Suite 310, Washington DC 20001. (202)638-2952. Director of Publications: Susan Brite. Estab. 1920. Nonprofit association with publishing arm. Publishes hardcover and paperback originals. Books: average print order 3,000. Publishes 1 or 2 fiction titles/year.
Needs: Recently published *Floating*, by Mark Krueger, PhD (stories about youth-care workers in residential homes for children).
How to Contact: Query first with SASE.
Terms: Payment varies. Book catalog free.

‡CHINA BOOKS (IV), 2929 24th St., San Francisco CA 94110. (415)282-2994. Editorial Director: Foster Stockwell. Estab. 1959. "Publishes books about China or things Chinese." Publishes hardcover and paperback originals. Books: letterpress, offset printing; perfect binding; b&w illustrations; average print order: 5,000. Published new writers within the past year. Plans 1 first novel this year. Averages 12 total titles, 1 fiction title each year. Sometimes critiques rejected mss.

Needs: Ethnic, subjects relating to China. Recently published *Lapse of Time*, by Wang Angi (collection of short stories and novella).
How to Contact: Query first or submit outline/synopsis and 2 sample chapters. No agented fiction. Reports in 2 weeks on queries; in 1 month on mss. Simultaneous and photocopied submissions OK.
Terms: Pays royalties 5% minimum; 8% maximum. Sends galleys to author. Publishes ms 1 year after acceptance. Subsidy publishes 1%/year. Writer's guidelines and book catalog free on request.

CINCO PUNTOS PRESS (IV), 2709 Louisville, El Paso, TX 79930. (915)566-9072. Co-Director: Bobby Byrd. Fiction Editor: Lee Merrill Byrd. Estab. 1985. Two-person operation specializing in Southwest literature. Publishes paperback originals. Books: perfect binding; illustrations; average print order: 1,750. Averages 4 total titles each year; 1 fiction title each year.
Needs: Regional. Recently published *Sonalchi*, by Pat Carr (short story collection).
How to Contact: Query first. SASE.
Terms: Pays in royalties. Sends pre-publication galleys to author.
Advice: "Interested in focus on the Southwest or in how the book relates to Hispanic, Indian, Anglo culture here."

CLARITY PRESS (I, II, IV), Ste 469, 3277 Roswell Rd NE, Atlanta GA 30505. Contact: Editorial Committee, Fiction. Estab. 1984. Small press publishing fiction and nonfiction on political, social, minority issues and human rights. Books: 120 M paper; offset printing; perfect binding; illustrations where necessary or enhancing; average print order: 2,000; first novel print order: 1,000. Plans 1 first novel this year. Averages 3 total titles/year. Occasionally critiques or comments on rejected ms.
Needs: Ethnic, literary, social commentary. Short stories for anthology. Query a necessity. Recently published *The Invisible Women of Washington*, by Diana G. Collier, (social issues).
How to Contact: Accepts unsolicited mss. Query is a necessity. SASE. Reports in 6 weeks. Simultaneous and photocopied submissions OK. Accepts computer printout submissions, including dot-matrix.
Terms: Authors paid by individual arrangement.
Advice: "We are interested only in novels concerning political, minority or human rights issues. Mss not preceded by query letter will be returned."

‡CLEIS PRESS (I,II,IV), Box 14684, San Francisco CA 94114. Co-editor: Frederique Delacoste. "Midsize independent women's press. Publishes paperback originals and reprints." Books: offset 50 lb paper; offset printing; perfect binding; illustrations in some books; average print order: 3,000-5,000; first novel print order: 3,500. Published new writers within the past year. Averages 4 total titles, 1 fiction title each year. Sometimes critiques rejected mss.
Needs: Feminist, lesbian, literary, translations. "Particularly interested in translations of women's fiction. No mainstream, genre fiction." Recently published *Unholy Alliances*, edited by Louise Rafkin (fiction collection).
How to Contact: Submit outline and 1 chapter. SASE. Reports on queries in 1 month; on mss in 3 months. Simultaneous and photocopied submissions OK "with letter of explanation." Accepts computer printout submissions, including dot-matrix "only if NLQ."
Terms: Pays negotiable royalties. Sends pre-publication galleys to author. Publishes 6-12 months after acceptance. Writer's guidelines and book catalog for #10 SAE and 2 first class stamps.
Advice: Publishing more fiction than in the past. "We encourage new women writers."

CLIFFHANGER PRESS (II), Box 29527, Oakland CA 94604-9527. (415)763-3510. Editor: Nancy Chirich. Estab. 1986. Publishes paperback and hardcover originals. Books: 60 lb text stock paper; offset printing; perfect binding; average print order: 2,000; first novel print order: 2,000. Published new writers within the last year; plans 8 first novels this year (1989). Averages 4 total titles per year, all fiction.
Needs: Suspense/mystery. "Need mystery/suspense (75,000 words approximately); heavy on the American regional or foreign background. No grossly hardboiled detectives and no spies." (Send SASE for guidelines for specific needs.) Recently published *Death in a Small Southern Town*, by Robert L. McKinney; *The Mystic Policeman*, by James Patrick O'Neill; *The Case of the Johannisberg Riesling*, by Gerry Maddren.
How to Contact: Please first send for writer's guidelines and book catalog, free on request for SASE. We prefer query first with outline/synopsis and 2-3 sample chapters. SASE. If sample appears to be our style, we will request complete ms. Reports in 2 weeks on queries; approx. 6-8 weeks on mss. Simultaneous and photocopied submissions OK, but please let us know. Accepts computer printout submissions, but no dot-matrix or justified type.
Terms: No advances. Pays royalties of 8% minimum; 15% maximum. Sends galleys to author.
Advice: "Author must be able to accept editorial suggestions with grace. Our motto is 'we can work it out.' If manuscript is accepted, there is something there, so no *drastic* substantive changes would be anticipated."

CLOTHESPIN FEVER PRESS (I), 5529 N. Figueroa, Los Angeles CA 90042. (213)254-1373. Publisher: Jenny Wrenn. Fiction Editor: Carolyn Weathers. Estab. 1986. Small two-person operation with plans to expand. Books: Tahoe suede coated or other high quality/high rag content paper; offset or letterpress printing; handsewn, comb or saddlestitched binding; graphics of 2 or 3 colors, photos etc., average print order: 250-500 copies. Averages 2 total titles, 0-1 fiction title each year.

Needs: Experimental, feminist, lesbian, literary, short story collections. "Looking for literary work by lesbian writers. No male stories by male writers." Recently published *Shitkickers and Other Texas Stories*, by Carolyn Weathers. "We will be publishing an anthology of prose and poetry by predominately unpublished lesbian writers this year."

How to Contact: Accepts unsolicited mss. Query first with cover letter that includes summary or topic plus sample short story or chapter. SASE. Reports in 3 weeks on queries; 3 months on mss. Simultaneous and photocopied submissions OK. Accepts computer printout submissions, including dot-matrix.

Terms: Pays 2 author's copies. Sends galleys to author. "We would consider subsidy publishing." Writer's guidelines free for SASE. Book catalog on request.

Advice: "A writer should be open to rewrite suggestions that a publisher might suggest without taking offense. Spelling and correct grammar should be strived for above all. Keep writing and rewriting but don't despair if you think your work is unmarketable. Keep in mind that the right publisher for you may be hard to find."

‡CONARI PRESS (II), 713 Euclid Ave., Berkeley CA 94708. (415)527-9915. Editor: Mary Jane Ryan. Estab. 1979. Publishes paperback originals and reprints. Books: 60-70 lb paper; web printing; perfect binding; average print order: 5,000; first novel print order 2,500. Averages 5 total titles, 1-2 fiction titles each year.

Needs: Literary. "Looking for high quality literary fiction."

How to Contact: Accepts unsolicited mss. Submit complete ms with cover letter. SASE. Agented fiction 10%. Reports in 3 months. Simultaneous and photocopied submissions OK. Accepts computer printout submissions, including dot-matrix.

Terms: Pays royalties 6½% minimum; 10% maximum. Average advance is negotiable. Provides 10 author's copies. Sends galleys to author. After acceptance ms is published within a year. Book catalog on request.

CONFLUENCE PRESS INC. (II), Spalding Hall, Lewis-Clark State College, Lewiston ID 83501. (208)799-2336. Imprint is Blue Moon Press. Fiction Editor: James R. Hepworth. Estab. 1976. Small trade publisher. Publishes hardcover originals and reprints; paperback originals and reprints. Books: 60 lb paper; photo offset printing; Smythe-sewn binding; average print order: 1,500-5,000 copies. Published new writers this year. Averages 10 total titles/year. Critiques rejected mss for $25/hour.

Needs: Contemporary, historical, literary, mainstream, short story collections, translations. "Our needs favor serious fition, 1 novel and 1 short fiction collection a year, with preference going to work set in the contemporary western United States." Recently published *A Charge of Angels*, by L.D. Clark (fiction); and *The Other Side of the Story*, by Richard Shelton (short fiction).

How to Contact: Query first. SASE for query and ms. Agented fiction 50%. Reports in 6-8 weeks on queries and mss. Simultaneous and photocopied submissions OK. Accepts computer printouts; letter-quality only.

Terms: Pays in royalties of 10% minimum; 15% maximum; advance is negotiable; payment depends on grant/award money. Sends galleys to author. Book catalog for 6x9 SASE.

Advice: "We are currently looking for short novels."

‡CORKSCREW PRESS (IV), 2815 Fenimore Rd., Silver Spring MD 20902. (301)933-0407. President: Richard Lippman. Estab. 1988. "Just getting started with first book, but plan to expand *rapidly*." Publishes paperback originals. Published new writers within the past year. Plans 2 first novels this year. Averages 3 total titles each year. Sometimes comments on rejected mss.

Needs: Humor.

How to Contact: Accepts unsolicited mss. Submit outline/synopsis with 2 sample chapters. SASE. Reports in 1 month. Simultaneous and photocopied submissions OK. Accepts computer printout submissions, including dot-matrix.

Terms: Pays negotiable royalties. Offers negotiable advance. Provides 25 author's copies. Sends galleys to author. Book catalog for #10 SAE and 1 first class stamp.

‡COTEAU BOOKS (IV), Thunder Creek Publishing Co-operative Ltd., 209-1945 Scarth St., Regina, Saskatchewan S4P 2H2 Canada. (306)352-5346. Managing Editor: Shelley Sopher. Estab. 1975. Small, independent publisher; focus on first-time published works. Publishes hardcover and paperback originals. Books: #2 offset or 60 lb hi-bulk paper; offset printing; perfect and smythe-sewn binding; 4 color illustrations; average print order: 1,500-3,000; first novel print order: approx. 1,500. Published

Close-up

George Benington
Coyote Love

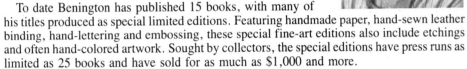

Unlike many one-person publishing operations, Coyote Love was not started by a writer. George Benington is a photographer and started his press with as much an interest in the art of the book as with a love of fine writing.

To date Benington has published 15 books, with many of his titles produced as special limited editions. Featuring handmade paper, hand-sewn leather binding, hand-lettering and embossing, these special fine-art editions also include etchings and often hand-colored artwork. Sought by collectors, the special editions have press runs as limited as 25 books and have sold for as much as $1,000 and more.

Benington sometimes publishes a less expensive edition also featuring fine printing and binding, but without the more painstaking work, such as hand-coloring. He also always publishes an offset edition in press runs of 500 to 1,000 books at a much lower selling price.

Publishing books in this way—special editions and concurrent offset editions—Benington says he can both produce fine art and give authors the exposure they deserve. "I feel strongly that if I do a book that costs $200 a copy, only wealthy collectors and special (library) collections will buy it and that's *not* the reason I publish books. I publish them to get the authors read by the public at large.'

Benington publishes a lot of poetry, because short works are easier and less expensive to produce. Yet he is always looking for good short fiction. Most of the fiction he finds best suited to his press have been either "adult fables" or monographs.

"I read a lot of literary magazines and sometimes I will contact authors to solicit their work. When I get a query letter, I'm very interested in the publication credits. If I see a publication credit from a magazine whose editorial policy I respect, I'm going to be much more interested."

He says publication in a literary magazine, or winning an award in a writing contest, means someone else felt strongly about the author's work. "It's like already having a first reader.

"I can't imagine getting a book published without being published first somewhere else." Beginning writers should start by sending their work to small magazines, then larger ones, to build a list of publication credits, says Benington.

Proper presentation and professionalism also count. "The more professional the presentation the better. If I read a manuscript and find three typos in the first page, I really wonder how professional the writer is and how much self esteem the person has."

It's harder for Benington to describe the qualities he looks for within a piece of fiction. "This may sound strange, but I look for writing that gives me goose bumps—that raises the hair on the back of my neck—work that is stirring. I don't mean sensationally so, but that it has a presence.

"I like contemporary fiction by and large." Benington looks for writing that is "life-affirming—something that speaks of the human condition, both in the contemporary world and throughout time."

—Robin Gee

new writers within the last year. Plans 1 first novel this year. Publishes 8-9 total titles, 5-6 fiction titles each year. Sometimes comments on rejected mss.

Needs: "We do first novels of unpublished writers, or writers who have published in another genre; dealing with Canadian/prairie issues by Canadian, and preferably western writers." No young adult, science fiction. Recently published *Valley of Flowers*, by Veronica Eddy Brock (semi-autobiographical).

How to Contact: Query first, then submit complete ms with cover letter. SASE. Agented fiction 10%. Reports on queries in 2 weeks; on mss in 6-8 weeks. Photocopied submissions OK. Accepts dot-matrix computer printout submissions "if they are in good shape."

Terms: "We're a co-operative who receives subsidies from the Canadian, provincial and local governments. We do not accept payments from authors to publish their works." Sends galleys to author. Publishes ms 1-2 years after acceptance. Book catalog free.

Advice: "We publish first-time collections, novels and poetry collections, as well as literary interviews and children's books. This is part of our mandate."

COUNCIL FOR INDIAN EDUCATION (I,IV), 517 Rimrock Rd., Billings MT 59102. (406)252-7451. Editor: Hap Gilliland. Estab. 1963. Small, non-profit organization publishing Native American materials for schools. Publishes hardcover and paperback originals. Books: offset printing; perfect bound or saddle stitched binding; b&w illustrations; average print order; 1,500; first novel print order: 1,500. Published new writers within the last year; plans 3 first novels this year. Averages 5 total titles, 4 fiction titles each year. Usually critiques rejected ms.

Needs: Adventure, ethnic, historical, juvenile (historical, adventure and others), preschool/picture book, regional, western, young adult/teen (easy-to-read, and historical). Especially needs "short novels, and short stories accurately portraying American Indian life past or present—fast moving with high interest." No sex emphasis. Recently published *Fire Mate*, by Olga Cossi (junior novel).

How to Contact: Accepts unsolicited mss. Submit complete ms with SASE. Reports in 3 months. Simultaneous and photocopied submissions OK. Accepts computer printout submissions.

Terms: 10% of wholesale price or 1½¢/word. Sends galleys to author. Free writer's guidelines and book catalog.

Advice: Mostly publishes original fiction in paperback. "Be sure material is culturally authentic and good for the self-concept of the group about whom it is written. If you write about minorities, make sure they are true to the culture and way of life, and that you don't downgrade any group."

COYOTE LOVE PRESS (II), 294 Spring St., Portland ME 04102. (207)774-8451. Managing Editor: George B. Benington. Estab. 1982. "Small press which publishes when there is money enough and work worth publishing: one-man studio handpress and offset." Publishes hardcover and paperback originals. Books: highest quality paper; illustrations. Averages 2 total titles, 1 fiction title each year.

Needs: Contemporary, experimental, literary and short story collections. No "romance, light or trashy fiction." Recently published *Three American One-Act Monologues*, by Dan Domench (short stories); and *The Wildman*, by Martin Steingesser.

How to Contact: Query first with SASE. Reports in 3 weeks on queries; 6 weeks on mss. Simultaneous and photocopied submissions OK.

Terms: Pays 10% of press run; royalties depend on grant/award money.

CREATIVE ARTS BOOK CO. (II), 833 Bancroft Way, Berkeley CA 94710. (415)848-4777. Imprint: Black Lizard. Editorial Production Manager: Peg O'Donnell. Estab. 1975. Small independent trade publisher. Publishes hardcover originals and paperback originals and reprints. Average print order: 2,500-10,000; average first novel print order: 2,500-10,000. Published new writers within the last year. Plans 3 first novels this year. Averages 30-40 total titles; 20 fiction titles each year.

Needs: Contemporary, erotica (literary), feminist, historical, literary, regional, short story collections, suspense/mystery (Black Lizard Crime Fiction), translations, western. Recently published *California Childhood: Recollections and Stories of the Golden State*, edited by Gary Soto.

How to Contact: Accepts unsolicited ms. Submit outline/synopsis and 3 sample chapters (approx. 50 pp). SASE (IRC). 50% of fiction is agented. Reports in 2 weeks on queries; 1 month on mss. Simultaneous and photocopied submissions OK. Accepts computer printout submissions.

Terms: Pays royalties of 6-10%; average advance of $500-1,000; 10 author's copies. Sends galleys to author. Writers guidelines and book catalog for SASE or IRC.

CREATIVE WITH WORDS PUBLICATIONS (II, III), Box 223226, Carmel CA 93922. Editor-in-Chief: Brigitta Geltrich. Estab. 1975. One-woman operation on part-time basis. Books: bond and stock paper; mimeographed printing; saddle stitch binding; illustrations; average print order varies. Publishes paperback anthologies of new and established writers. Averages 3-4 anthologies each year. Critiques rejected mss; $10 for short stories; $20 for longer stories, folklore items.

Needs: Humor/satire, juvenile (animal, easy-to-read, fantasy). "Editorial needs center on folkloristic items (according to themes): tall tales and such for biannual anthologies." Needs short stories appealing to general public; "tales" of folklore nature, appealing to all ages, poetry and prose written by children. Prose not to exceed 1,000 words.
How to Contact: Accepts unsolicited mss. Query first; submit complete ms with SASE and cover letter. Photocopied submissions OK. Accepts computer printout submissions, prefers letter-quality. Reports in 1 month on queries; 2 months on mss. Publishes ms 1-6 months after acceptance. Writer's guidelines and catalog sheet (2 oz.) for SASE.
Terms: Pays in 20% reduced author copies.
Advice: "Our fiction appeals to general public: children-senior citizens. Follow guidelines and rules of *Creative With Words* publications and not those the writer feels CWW should have. We only consider fiction along the lines of folklore or seasonal genres. Be brief, sincere, well-informed and proficient!"

CREATIVITY UNLIMITED PRESS (II), 30819 Casilina, Rancho Palos Verdes CA 90274. (213)377-7908. Contact: Rochelle Stockwell. Estab. 1980. One-person operation with plans to expand. Publishes paperback originals and self-hypnosis cassette tapes. Books: perfect binding; illustrations; average print order: 1,000. Averages 1 title (fiction) each year. Average first novel print order 1,000 copies.
Needs: Recently published *Insides Out*, by Shelley Stockwell (plain talk poetry).
Advice: Write for more information.

THE CROSSING PRESS (II), Box 1048, Freedom CA 95019. Editor: Elaine Gill. Editor, Gay Literature and Literature: John Gill. Publishes paperback and hardcover originals. Books: 50-55 lb offset paper; offset printing; perfect and hardbound binding; illustrations sometimes; average print order: 5,000; first novel print order: 3,500-5,000. Published new writers last year. Estab. 1966.
Needs: Literary, contemporary, cookbooks, feminist, gay/lesbian, herbal books, women's health.
How to Contact: Query with SASE.
Terms: Standard royalty contracts.
Advice: "We are publishing more fiction and more paperbacks. Don't submit first work before showing to very critical friends. Do the necessary research in library to see which publisher would possibly be interested in your work."

DAN RIVER PRESS (I,II), Conservatory of American Letters, Box 88, Thomaston ME 04861. (207)354-6550. President: Robert Olmsted. Fiction Editor: R.S. Danbury III. Estab. 1976. Publishes hardcover and paperback originals. Books: 60 lb offset paper; offset printing; perfect (paperback); hand-sewn (cloth) binding; illustrations; average print order: 1,000; first novel print order: 1,000. Published new writers within the past year. Averages 13-17 total titles; 3 fiction titles each year.
Needs: Adventure, contemporary, experimental, fantasy, historical, horror, humor/satire, literary, mainstream, military/war, psychic/supernatural/occult, regional, science fiction, short story collections; western. "We want good fiction that can't find a home in the big press world. No mindless stuff written flawlessly."
How to Contact: Accepts unsolicited mss. Reports in 2 weeks. Simultaneous and photocopied submissions OK, plain paper only. Accepts computer printout submissions, including dot-matrix.
Terms: Pays royalties of 10%. Sends galleys to author. After acceptance, publication "depends on many things (funding, etc.). Probably in six months once funding is achieved." Writer's guidelines for #10 SAE and 2 first class stamps. Book catalog for 6x9 SAE and 2 first class stamps.
Advice: "Submit to us (and any other small press) only when you have exhausted all hope for big press publication. Then, do not expect the small press to be a big press. We lack the resources to do things like 'promotion,' 'author's tours.' These things either go undone or are done by the author. When you give up on marketability of any novel submitted to small press, adopt a different attitude. Become humble, as you get to work on your second/next novel, grow, correct mistakes and develop an audience."

DANCING BEAR PRODUCTIONS (I,II), Box 733, Concord MA 01742. Imprints include Bear Dance Cards, Clips From Bear's Home Movies. Editor/Publisher: Craig Ellis. Fiction Editors: Criag Ellis and Nancy Lundy. Estab. 1983. "Very small, for now." Publishes paperback originals. Books: acid free paper; illustrations when appropriate; average print order: 1-1,000 for first run. Averages 2-6 total titles each year; 1-3 fiction titles.
Needs: Erotica, experimental, fantasy, humor/satire, juvenile (animal, fantasy, contemporary), literary, preschool/picture book, science fiction, short story collections, translations, young adult (10-18 years; fantasy/science fiction). Recently published *Doing and Undoing* and *Game of Spirit*, by Jonathan Strong; and *Two High School Stories* and *Drawings*, by Fielding Dawson (novellas/experimental).
How To Contact: Must query first. No unsolicited mss." SASE. Reports in 1 month on queries; 6 months on mss. Simultaneous and photocopied submissions OK.
Terms: Payment is negotiable/usually percentage of print-run.
Advice: "Just beginning. Have concentrated on poetry/drama. Expect to put out more fiction."

JOHN DANIEL AND COMPANY, PUBLISHERS (I, II), Box 21922, Santa Barbara CA 93121. (805)962-1780. Fiction Editor: John Daniel. Estab. 1980/reestablished 1985. Small publisher with plans to expand. Publishes paperback originals. Books: 55-65 lb book text paper; offset printing; perfect bound paperbacks; illustrations sometimes; average print order: 2,000; first novel print order: 2,000. Plans 2 first novels this year. Averages 10 total titles, 3-4 fiction titles each year. Critiques rejected ms.
Needs: "I'm open to all subjects (including nonfiction)." Literary, mainstream, short story collections. No pornographic, exploitive, illegal, or badly written fiction. Recently published *The Sea Child*, by Leslie G. Cady; *Big Chocolate Cookies*, by E. S. Goldman; *In My Father's House*, by Nancy Huddleston Packer; published new writers within the last year.
How to Contact: Accepts unsolicited mss. Query first. SASE. Submit outline/synopsis and 2 sample chapters. Reports in 3 weeks on queries; 2 months on mss. Simultaneous and photocopied submissions OK. Accepts computer printouts, including dot-matrix.
Terms: Pays in royalties of 10% of net minimum. Sends galleys to author.
Advice: Encourages first novelists. "As an acquiring editor, I would never sign a book unless I were willing to publish it in its present state. Once the book is signed, though, I, as a developmental editor, would do hard labor to make the book everything it could become. Read a lot, write a lot, and stay in contact with other artists so you won't burn out from this, the loneliest profession in the world."

MAY DAVENPORT PUBLISHERS (I, II, IV), 26313 Purissima Rd., Los Altos Hills CA 94022. (415)948-6499. Editor/Publisher: May Davenport. Estab. 1975. One-person operation with independent sub-contractors. Publishes hardcover and paperback originals. Books: 65-80 lb paper; off-set printing; perfect binding/saddle stitch/plastic spirals; line drawing illustrations; average print order 500-3,000; average first novel print order: 3,000. Plans 1-3 first novels this year. Averages 3-5 total titles/year (including coloring books/reprints); 2-5 fiction titles/year. Sometimes critiques rejected mss.
Needs: "Always looking for children's fiction, easy enough to capture the attention of the tv-oriented children of today. Must be geared towards the junior-high level, yet still interesting enough for remedial senior high students' reading level." No adult vocabulary, life style, problems. Recently published *Comic Tale #1*, anthology, May Davenport, editor (short plays and poetry); *Comic Tale #3—Green Horn Danny*, by Wilma Thompson; *Darby's Rainbow*, by James C. McCoy.
How to Contact: Accepts unsolicited mss. Query first with SASE. 2% of fiction is agented. Reports in 2-3 weeks. Simultaneous and photocopied submissions OK. Accepts computer printout submissions, including dot-matrix.
Terms: Pays royalties of 10-15%; no advance. Sends galleys to author. "Partial subsidy whenever possible in advance sales of 3,000 copies, which usually covers the printing and binding costs only. The authors are usually teachers in school districts who have a special book of fiction or textbook relating to literature." Writer's guidelines free with your SASE.
Advice: "Single titles of short fiction of unknown authors do not sell. So reprinting earlier children's books into new anthologies, into new coloring books to be 'color and read' comic strips for newspaper syndication interest me as a publisher. Hardcovers are usually run off with the paperbacks—only bound separately. Personal tip: Combat illiteracy by creating material which will motivate children/young adults to enjoy words and actions. Write a play for this junior/senior high age? They will read anything which they think they can participate in dramatically for themselves. So why not first plays? Try writing entertaining plays for jr./sr. high students to read and to perform."

DAWNWOOD PRESS (II, IV), Suite 2650, Two Park Ave., New York NY 10016. (212)532-7160. Telex: 666156. FAX: 212-213-2495. President: Kathryn Drayton. Fiction Editor: John Welch. Estab. 1984. Publishes hardcover originals. Books: 60 lb Lakewood-white paper; offset litho printing; adhesive case binding; average print order: 5,000. Averages 1 fiction title each year.
Needs: Contemporary. "Our needs are taken care of for the next 2 years." No experimental. Recently published *Headaches for History Buffs*, by Paul Kuttner (history); *Tough Questions . . . Amazing Answers*, by Paul Kuttner (non-trivia about science, sports, entertainment, places, literature, art, music).
How to Contact: Does not accept unsolicited mss. Submit through agent only. Reports in 2 weeks on queries; 2 weeks on mss. Simultaneous and photocopied submissions OK.
Terms: Advance negotiable. Sends galleys to author.
Advice: "Same advice since Dickens's days: Tell a story from the opening sentence in easily understood English, and if you must philosophize do so through action and colloquial dialogue."

DOUBLE M PRESS (II), 16455 Tuba St., Sepulveda CA 91343. (818)360-3166. Publisher: Charlotte M. Stein. Estab. 1975. Small independent press with plans to expand. Publishes hardcover and trade paperback originals. Buys juvenile mss with illustrations. Books: 60 lb white or ivory paper; web press printing; perfect binding; graphics and photographs; average first novel print order 1,000 copies.
Needs: Juvenile (fantasy, historical, contemporary), preschool, inspirational, and young adult (fantasy, historical, problem novels). "We are interested in work that deals with the problems of growth and

solving contemporary situations in a 'positive' manner. No degradation, violence, or exploitation of the characters. Strong in imagination."
How to Contact: Accepts unsolicited mss. Query first with outline/synopsis and 2 sample chapters. Reports in 2 weeks on queries; 2 months, if possible, on mss. Photocopied submissions OK. Publishes ms usually within 1 year after acceptance.
Terms: Pays in royalties of 8% minimum. "We do not pay advances."
Advice: "Master the techniques of your craft. Do not submit poorly typed ms. Check spelling. We did not publish any new books in 1988 but are gearing up to publish at least 3 titles in 1989."

‡**DRAGON'S DEN PUBLISHING (II, IV)**, 11659 Doverwood Drive, Riverside CA 92505. Imprints include Little Dragon and Double Dragon. President: G. Michael Short. Fiction Editor: Daryl David. Estab. 1988. Small, full-time press. Publishes hardcover and paperback originals. Books: usually hardcover binding; cover artwork only; average print order 1,000; first novel print order 500-1,000. Plans 1 first novel this year. Sometimes comments on rejected mss; charges $5.
Needs: Fantasy, historical, horror, psychic/supernatural/occult, science fiction, short story collections, spiritual, suspense/mystery, young adult (fantasy/science fiction). Needs "novels dealing with the paranormal, extraordinary, etc.; also fantasy (especially sword and sorcery); historical novels dealing with the war periods; realistic horror (e.g. dealing with devil worshippers, witchcraft, voodoo, etc.)." No "fiction giving ESP a bad name; make-overs of Conan; unbelievable horror (such as *Nightmare on Elm Street* or *Friday the 13th*)."
How to Contact: Accepts unsolicited mss. Submit outline/synopsis and 3 sample chapters with SASE. Agented fiction 10%. Reports in 3-4 weeks on queries; 3-4 months on mss. Photocopied submissions OK.
Terms: Pays in royalties of 10-20%. Publishes ms 6-9 months after acceptance. Subsidy publishes "only at author's request upon receipt of rejection. Author pays 50% of production cost." Writer's guidelines free for #10 SASE. "Our Double Dragon imprint holds an annual contest for fantasy novels only. Entries may be any length between novella and novel length (no more than 100,000 words). Must be previously unpublished. Top two entries receive: A royalty shared sixty-forty; publication and author's copies."
Advice: "A cover letter is a must! We need to know the author's background. A résumé is not necessary for fiction. We enourage agented work. Keep cover letters short (no more than a page if possible) but sweet. Do not include your synopsis in your cover letter; keep it separate."

‡**THE DRAGONSBREATH PRESS (IV)**, 10905 Bay Shore Dr., Sister Bay WI 54234. Editor: Fred Johnson. Estab. 1973. One-man operation on part-time basis. Publishes paperback and hardback originals in small editions as handmade books. Books: varied paper; letterpress printing hand binding; illustrations.
Needs: Contemporary, literary, experimental, erotica, science fiction, fantasy, and humor/satire. "NO NOVELS, but rather single short stories."
How to Contact: "We are not currently accepting any unsolicited mss." Query and when requested send complete ms with SASE. Simultaneous and photocopied submissions OK. Accepts computer printout submissions. Prefers letter-quality. Reports in 1 month on queries, 2 months on mss. "Always include a cover letter and SASE."
Terms: Negotiates terms. No advance. "Since we are a small press, we prefer to work cooperatively, sharing the work and expenses between the author and the press. We are not a 'vanity press'."
Advice: "This is a small press working with the book as an art form producing handmade limited-edition books combining original artwork with original writing. Since we work with hand-set type and have limited time and money, we prefer shorter writing suited to handwork and illustrating. We are not a typical publishing house; books would have limited distribution, mainly to art and book collectors. We are now also looking for regional (Wisconsin) writing for a yearly regional magazine the press has begun publishing entitled *The Door County Alamanak*. Always include cover letter with brief description of story."

THE ECCO PRESS (II), 26 W. 17th St., New York NY 10011. (212)645-2214. Managing Editor: Lee Ann Chearneyi. Editor: Daniel Halpern. Estab. 1970. Small publisher. Publishes hardcover and paperback originals and reprints. Books: acid-free paper; offset printing; Smythe-sewn binding; occasional illustrations. Averages 25 total titles, 10 fiction titles each year. Average first novel print order 3,000 copies.
Needs: Literary and short story collections. "We can publish possibly one or two original novels a year." No science fiction, romantic novels, western (cowboy). Recently published: *The Assignation*, by Joyce Carol Oates (stories); *In the Music Library*, by Ellen Hunnicutt; *A Distant Episode*, by Paul Bonles.
How to Contact: Accepts unsolicited mss. Query first especially on novels with SASE. Photocopied

submissions OK. Accepts computer printout submissions, prefers letter-quality. Reports in 2 to 3 months, depending on the season.

Terms: Pays in royalties. Advance is negotiable. Writer's guidelines for SASE. Book catalog free on request.

Advice: "We are always interested in first novels and feel it's important that they be brought to the attention of the reading public."

EDEN PRESS (II), 31A Westminster Ave., Montréal, Québéc H4Y 1Y8 Canada. (514)488-2088. Imprints include Eden Entertainment, Occasion Books. Editor: Lynette Stokes. Estab. 1976. "Medium-sized independent publisher of mostly trade but sometimes scholarly books. Just starting to publish fiction this year." Books: paper depends on size and quality of the book; either perfect (for paperbacks) or Smythe-sewn (for hardcover) binding; average print order: 5,000-15,000. Published new writers within the last year. Plans 2 first novels this year. Averages 20 total titles/year; 4 fiction titles/year. Critiques rejected ms.

Needs: Humor/satire, suspense/mystery. Looking for "humor combined preferably with mystery." No short stories, literary, romance, poetry, autobiography. Recently published *The 7th Year of the Manna Bird*, by Lou Vertolli and Frederick Biro (humor/detective); and *The Competition*, by Robert Assels (humor).

How to Contact: Accepts unsolicited mss. Query first. Submit outline/synopsis and 2 sample chapters. SASE (IRC). Reports in 6 weeks on queries; 3-4 months on mss. Simultaneous and photocopied submissions OK. Accepts computer printout submissions, including dot-matrix. Accepts electronic submissions via IBM compatible disk, 3.1 DOS or more.

Terms: Pays 10% maximum royalties; negotiable advance; 10 author's copies. Sends galleys to author. "Terms are standard." Book catalog free on request.

Advice: "We do not accept work that requires us to do masses of rewriting in-house."

‡THE EIGHTH MT. PRESS (II), 624 SE 29th Ave., Portland OR 97214. (503)233-3936. Puslisher: Ruth Gundle. Estab. 1984. One-person operation on part-time basis. Publishes paperback originals. Books: acid-free paper, perfect binding; average print order: 5,000. Averages 2 total titles, 1 fiction title, each year.

Needs: Ethnic, feminist, gay, lesbian, literary, short story collections. Recently published *Cows and Horses*, by Barbara Wilson (feminist/literary).

How to Contact: Accepts unsolicited mss. Query first. SASE. Reports on queries in 2 weeks; on mss in 3 weeks.

Terms: Pays royalties of 8% minimum; 10% maximum. Sends galleys to author. Publishes ms within 1 year of acceptance.

Advice: Encourages first novelists.

‡ESOTERICA PRESS (I, II, IV), Also publishes *Notebook: A Little Magazine*, Box 170 Barstow CA 92312-0170. Editor: Ms. Yoly Zentella. Estab. 1983. Two-person operation on a part-time basis. Publishes paperback originals. Books: 50 lb white/neutral paper; offset printing; saddle stitch binding; black and white illustrations and photos; average print order: 200-300; first novel print order: 150-200. Plans more than 1 first novel this year. Averages 1-2 total titles each year. Sometimes comments on rejected ms.

Needs: Contemporary, ethnic (especially Chicano), historical, juvenile (5-9, including: historical), literary, short story collections, translations (Spanish-English/English-Spanish), young adult/teen (10-18 years, including: historical); women's issues. Looking for "fiction, nonfiction based on Latino-American experience, Black-American, Arab-American. No erotic, mystery, frivolity."

How to Contact: Accepts unsolicited mss with SASE. Submit complete ms with cover letter. SASE (IRC) necessary for return of ms. Agented fiction 1%. Reports in 2-3 months on mss. Simultaneous and photocopied submissions OK. Accepts computer printout submissions, including dot-matrix.

Terms: Provides author's copies. Contract is negotiable. Profits of book are split author/publisher. Sends pre-publication galleys to author. Publishes ms 6 months to 1 year after acceptance. Writer's guidelines and book catalog for #10 SAE and 1 first class stamp.

Advice: Publishing "more fiction. If you think it's good, submit it!"

EXILE PRESS (I), 765 Sunset Pky., Novato CA 94947-4875. (415)883-2132. Editor/Publisher: Dr. L. W. Hedley. Estab. 1983. Small independent publisher. Publishes paperback originals and reprints. Books: 60 lb bookstock paper; offset printing; perfect binding; illustrations; average print order: 500 + . Published new writers within the last year; plans books of short stories. Averages 3 titles each year, all fiction. Average first print order 500-1,000 copies. Occasionally critiques rejected ms.

Needs: Collections of short stories. Contemporary, experimental, satire and literary. No "religious, academic kitsch, westerns, gothic, science fiction, pornography or political propaganda." Recently published *Monkey*, by Rod Moore (novella); *Fiction 1986; The Way Things Are*, by Phillip Corwin (stories); *Imaginary People & Other Strangers*, by Layle Silbert (stories); *XYZ & Other Stories*, by Leslie Woolf Hedley; and *Poore Hunter*, by Lance Hazzard (novel).

How to Contact: Accepts unsolicited mss. Submit complete ms with SASE. Does not work through agents. Reports in 2 months. Simultaneous and photocopied submissions OK. Accepts computer printout submissions, prefers letter-quality. Highly selective.

Terms: Pays in 12 or more author's copies. "The number of copies to author depends on size of book and of the edition." Free book catalog.

Advice: "*Innovative* is the key word. Break away from all institutional approaches and find your own language. Work, work, read, read, listen to human beings around you and learn every day. Don't be afraid to be different."

FABER AND FABER, INC. (I, II), 50 Cross St., Winchester WA 01890. Editor: Betsy Uhrig. Small trade house which publishes literary fiction and collections. Published new writers within the last year. Averages 5-10 total titles each year. Submit proposal and sample chapters—enclose SASE for reply.

Needs: Recently published *Adele At the End of the Day*, by Tom Marshall; *The Monkey King*, by Timothy Mo.

How to Contact: "Prefer query and one or two sample chapters with SASE for reply. Require synopsis/description—cannot consider ms without this. Many beginning writers make the mistake of submitting entire ms without even a cover letter."

Advice: Looking for "more fiction, more paperbacks due to increasing popularity/acceptance of paperback originals. Use a word processor if at all possible."

FASA CORPORATION (II, IV), 1026 West Van Buren, Chicago IL 60607. Editor: L. Ross Babcock III. "Company responsible for science fiction/fantasy adventure games, to include adventures, scenarios, game designs and novels, for an audience high school age and up." Published new writers within the last year.

Needs: Adventure, fantasy, science fiction. Publishes ms an average of 4-8 months after acceptance. Occasionally critiques or comments on rejected ms. Recommends other markets. Recently published fiction by William H. Keith, Jr., Michael A. Stackpole, Bob Charrette.

How to Contact: Query first. Reports in 2-6 weeks on queries; 2-6 weeks on mss. Simultaneous and photocopied submissions OK. Accepts computer printout submissions, including dot-matrix. Accepts electronic submissions via IBM ASCII or MacIntosh disks.

Terms: Pays on publication for all rights. Sends galleys to author. Publication copyrighted.

Advice: "Be familiar with our product and always ask about suitability before plunging into a big piece of work that I may not be able to use."

THE FEMINIST PRESS AT THE CITY UNIVERSITY OF NEW YORK, 311 East 94 St., New York NY 10128. (212)360-5790. Publisher: Florence Howe. Estab. 1970. "Nonprofit, tax-exempt, education organization interested in changing the curriculum, the classroom and consciousness." Publishes hardcover and paperback reprints. "We use a fine quality paper, perfect bind our books, four color covers; and some cloth for library sales if the book has been out of print for some time; we shoot from the original text when possible. We always include a scholarly and literary afterword, since we are introducing a text to a new audience; average print run: 4,000." Publishes no original fiction. Averages 12 total titles/year; 4-6 fiction titles/year (reprints of feminist classics only).

Needs: Contemporary, ethnic, experimental, feminist, gay, historical, lesbian, literary, regional, science fiction, short story collections, translations, women's.

How to Contact: Accepts unsolicited mss. Query first. Submit outline/synopsis and 1 sample chapter. SASE (IRC). Reports in 2 weeks on queries; 2 months on mss. Simultaneous and photocopied submissions OK. Accepts computer printout submissions including dot-matrix.

Terms: Pays royalties of 10% of net sales; $100 advance; 10 author's copies. Sends galleys to author. Book catalog free on request.

FICTION COLLECTIVE INC. (II), % Department of English, Brooklyn College, Brooklyn NY 11210. Co-Directors: Ronald Sukenick and Curtis White. Estab. 1974. "The Fiction Collective is an expanding cooperative of 42 writers dedicated to the publication of quality fiction. We publish hardcover and paperback originals. We encourage new writers of contemporary and experimental fiction. The Collective is primarily interested in new fiction and all that term implies." Average first novel print order 2,000-2,500 copies.

Needs: Contemporary, literary, and experimental fiction. Recently published: *Plane Geometry*, by R. M. Berry; *Heroes and Villains*, by Jerry Bumpus; and *The Endless Short Story*, by Ronald Sukenick.

How to Contact: Accepts unsolicited mss "only if we have first responded in the affirmative to an author's query." Query with SASE and brief sample materials. Photocopied submissions OK. Reports in 2 months on queries, 6 months on mss. Send queries to Fiction Collective Manuscript Central, Publications Center, Dept. of English, University of Colorado, Boulder, Colorado 80309. Publishes ms 12-15 months after acceptance.

Terms: Pays 10% royalties plus 35 copies of the book (upon publication) after production costs have been met. "The Collective is a nonprofit writers' cooperative. The Collective makes editorial decisions. Books are published with assistance from NEA and NYSCA. If a manuscript is accepted for publication, then the author shares in editorial decisions." No advance. Free book catalog available by writing to *Brooklyn* office.

Advice: "Manuscripts are chosen for publication wholly on the basis of artistic merit, free of commercial considerations, tending toward innovative fiction. Since commercial publishers are often not willing to take the risk of publishing first novels regardless of their quality, this is one area to which the Collective is committed. Query first, rather than sending manuscripts without having first queried us. Once a book has been accepted, it is much easier to promote the book if the author provides us with information that can be used for publicity and is generally cooperative and interested in helping to promote his or her book."

FIREBRAND BOOKS (II), 141 The Commons, Ithaca NY 14850. (607)272-0000. Contact: Nancy K. Bereano. Estab. 1985. Publishes quality trade paperback originals and reprints. Plans 2 first novels in 1989. Averages 6-8 total titles each year.
Needs: Feminist, lesbian.
How to Contact: Accepts unsolicited mss. Submit outline/synopsis and sample chapters or send complete ms with cover letter. SASE. Reports in 2 weeks on queries; 2 months on mss. Simultaneous and photocopied submissions OK with notification. Accepts computer printouts.
Terms: Pays royalties.

FLORICANTO PRESS (I, II, IV), Suite 830, 16161 Ventura Blvd., Encino CA 91436. Editor: Roberta Cabello-Argandoňa. Estab. 1984. Publishes hardcover and paperback originals. Books: 60 lb paper; offset printing; hard or soft binding; occasionally illustrations; average print order: 5,000. Plans 2-4 first novels this year. Averages 5-7 total titles, 1-4 fiction titles each year. Publishes La Mujer Latina series fiction and nonfiction titles on Latin women.
Needs: Ethnic; juvenile (5-9 years) including: animal, easy-to-read, fantasy, historical, sports, spy/adventure, contemporary; literary; regional; translations. Needs works related to Latinos/Hispanics in the U.S. Recently published *Maravilla*, by Laura del Fuego (novel).
How to Contact: Does not accept unsolicited mss. Query first or submit outline/synopsis and sample chapters. SASE. Reports in 5 weeks on queries; 4 months on mss. Simultaneous and photocopied submissions OK. Accepts computer printout submissions, including dot-matrix if good quality.
Terms: Pays in royalties of 5% minimum. Sends galleys to author. Writer's guidelines free for SASE. Book catalog free on request.

FOUR WALLS EIGHT WINDOWS, Box 548, Village Station, New York NY 10014. (212)463-0316. Co-Publishers: John Oakes/Dan Simon. Estab. 1986. "We are a small independent publisher." Publishes hardcover and papberback originals and paperback reprints. Books: quality paper; paper or cloth binding; illustrations sometimes; average print order: 3,000-5,000; first novel print order: 3,000-5,000. Averages 9 total titles/year; approximately 3-4 fiction titles/year.
Needs: Contemporary, experimental, literary, detective/mystery, mainstream, short story collections, translations. Recently published *School for Fools*, by Sasha Sokolov; *X in Paris*, by Michael Brodsky; *Familiarity is the Kingdom of the Lost*, by Dugmore Boetie; published new writers within the last year.
How to Contact: "Query letter accompanied by sample chapter and SASE is best. Useful to know if writer has published elsewhere, and if so, where." Accepts unsolicited mss. Submit outline/synopsis and 1 sample chapter. SASE (IRC). 30% of fiction is agented. Reports in 2 months on mss. Simultaneous and photocopied submissions OK. Accepts computer printout submissions, including dot-matrix.
Terms: Pays standard royalties; advance varies. Sends galleys to author. Book catalog free on request.
Advice: "We believe in close cooperation between author and publisher."

GARBER COMMUNICATIONS, INC. (IV), Multimedia Publishers/Consultants, 5 Garber Hill Rd., Blauvelt NY 10913. Imprint: Spiritual Fiction. Associate Publisher: Patricia Abrams. Estab. 1958. Midsize independent publisher with plans to expand. Publishes hardcover and paperback originals and reprints. Published new writers within the last year. Plans to publish 4 first novels this year. Publishes 10 total titles each year; approx. 3-4 fiction titles/year.
Needs: "Spiritual fiction is our genre." Recently published *Legend*, by Barry Maher and *Hypatia: New Foe With an Old Face*, by Charles Kingsley.
How to Contact: Does not accept or return unsolicited mss. Query first. SASE. 20% of fiction is agented. Reports in 1 month. Photocopied submissions OK.

Terms: Pays royalties of 6-10%; advance of $250. Send pre-publication galleys to author. Writer's guidelines for #10 SASE; book catalog free on request.

GAY SUNSHINE PRESS AND LEYLAND PUBLICATIONS (IV), Box 40397, San Francisco CA 94140. (415)824-3184. Editor: Winston Leyland. Estab. 1970. Publishes hardcover and paperback originals. Books: natural paper; perfect bound binding; illustrations; average print order: 5,000-10,000; first novel: 5,000-10,000. Number of titles: 10 in 1988, 10 in 1987, 10 in 1986.
Needs: Literary, experimental and translations—all gay material only. "We desire fiction on gay themes of *high* literary quality and prefer writers who have already had work published in literary magazines. We also publish erotica—short stories and novels." Recently published *Stand by Your Man*, by Jack Fritscher.
How to Contact: "Do not send an unsolicited manuscript." Query letter with SASE. Reports in 3 weeks on queries, 2 months on mss.
Terms: Negotiates terms with author. Sends galleys to author. Royalties or outright purchase.
Advice: "We continue to be interested in receiving queries from authors who have manuscripts of high literary quality. We feel it is important that an author know exactly what to expect from our press (promotion, distribution etc.) before a contract is signed. Before submitting a query or manuscript to a particular press, obtain critical feedback from knowledgeable people on your manuscript, e.g. a friend who teaches college English. If you alienate a publisher by submitting a manuscript shoddily prepared/typed, or one needing very extensive re-writing, you will surely not get a second chance with that press."

GOOSE LANE EDITIONS (I, II), Fiddlehead Poetry Books, 248 Brunswick St., Fredericton, New Brunswick E3B 1G9 Canada. (506)454-8319. Editor: Peter Thomas. Estab. 1981. Publishes hardcover and paperback originals and hardcover and paperback reprints. Books: illustrations sometimes, average print order: 2,000; first novel print order: 1,500. Plans 1 first novel this year. Averages 10 total titles, 1-3 fiction, each year. Sometimes critiques rejected mss.
Needs: Adventure, contemporary, ethnic, experimental, historical, literary, short story collections. Recently published *A Spy in My House*, by Kenneth Langdon (suspense/spy); *Leaping Up, Sliding Away*, by Kent Thompson (short stories); and *After Six Days* by Keith Harrison (contemporary).
How to Contact: Accepts unsolicited mss; send complete work; no "samples." Query first. SASE. Reports in 6 weeks. Simultaneous and photocopied submissions OK. Accepts computer printout submissions, including dot-matrix.
Terms: "*Only mss from Canada, because of government funding policy.*" Pays royalties of 8% minimum; 12% maximum. Average advance: $250, is negotiable. Sends galleys to author. Writers guidelines for 9x12 SAE and IRCs.

GRAYWOLF PRESS (III), Box 75006, St. Paul MN 55175. (612)222-8342. Publisher: Scott Walker. Estab. 1974. Growing small press, nonprofit corporation. Publishes hardcover and paperback originals and paperback reprints. Books: acid-free quality paper; offset printing; hardcover and soft binding; illustrations occasionally; average print order: 3,000-10,000; first novel print order: 2,000-3,000. Averages 12-16 total titles, 6-8 fiction titles each year. Occasionally critiques rejected ms.
Needs: Literary, and short story collections. Recently published *The Book of Seeing With One's Own Eyes*, by Sharon Doubiago; *Blood Line*, by David Quammen; and *Family: Stories From the Interior*, edited by Geri Giebel Chavis.
How to Contact: Query with SASE. Reports in 2 weeks. Simultaneous and photocopied submissions OK.
Terms: Pays in royalties of 7½% minimum, 10% maximum; negotiates advance and number of author's copies. Sends galleys to author. Writer's guidelines for SASE. Free book catalog.
Advice: Publishing "less fiction, more creative nonfiction, essays, etc."

‡THE GREEN STREET PRESS (I), Box 1957, Cambridge MA 02238. (508)374-9923. Fiction Editor: Michael Hutcheson. Estab. 1984. Three-person small press with plans to expand. Publishes hardcover and paperback originals and reprints. Books: acid free, high quality paper; average print order: 6,000 copies (paperback); first novel print order: 2,500 copies (hardcover). Plans 2 first novels this year. Averages 10 total titles, all fiction. Occasionally critiques or comments on all rejected mss.
Needs: Contemporary, experimental, literary, regional, short story collections, translations. Recently published *The Lieutenant*, by André Dubus (reprint); *Into the Silence*, edited by Andre Dubus (anthology); *The Shallow Grass*, by Tom Horn (reprint).
How to Contact: Accepts unsolicited mss. Submit outline/synopsis and 2 sample chapters with SASE. Reports in 1 month on queries; 4-6 months on mss. Simultaneous and photocopied submissions OK. Accepts computer printout submissions, including dot-matrix. Accepts electronic submissions via Apple MacIntosh compatible systems.
Terms: Pays royalties of 10% minimum; 15% maximum. Average advance $1,000. Sends galleys to

author.

Advice: "I think the most hopeful sign for unpublished fiction writers is the growing acceptance of original paperback publication. The lower financial stakes of this approach may make pubilshers more willing to take a chance with an unpublished writer. The cover letter is a ritualistic form of communication, but an important one. It should be straightforward, honest, and avoid displays of hubris."

GREEN TIGER PRESS (II), 1061 India St., San Diego CA 92101. Contact: Editorial Committee. Estab. 1971. Publishes picture books, greeting cards, calendars, posters and stationery products. Published new writers within the last year. Buys 10% agented fiction. Encourages new writers. Averages 10-12 titles/year.
Needs: Specific interest in imaginative fiction for children lending itself to illustration. "We look for manuscripts containing a romantic, visionary or imaginative quality, often with a mythic feeling where fantasy and reality co-exist. We also welcome nostalgia and the world of the child themes. We do not publish science fiction. Since we are a visually oriented house, we look for manuscripts whose texts readily conjure up visual imagery." Recently published *Winner Friends of American Writers*, by John Hay (juvenile award).
How to Contact: Query or submit complete ms or outline/synopsis and sample chapters with SASE or submit through agent. Simultaneous and photocopied submissions OK. Reports in 1 month on queries, 3-4 months on mss. Publishes ms 12-18 months after acceptance.
Terms: Payment is usually on a royalty basis.

GUERNICA EDITIONS (III, IV), 316 Avenue de Carignan, Montréal, Québec H1N 2Y5 Canada. Editor: Antonio D'Alfonso. Fiction Editor: Umberto Claudio. Estab. 1978. Publishes hardcover and paperback originals. Books: offset printing; perfect/sewn binding; average print order: 1,000; average first novel print order: 1,000. Plans to publish 1 first novel this year. Publishes 8-10 total titles each year.
Needs: Contemporary, ethnic, literary. Looking for novels about women and ethnic subjects. No unsolicited works. Recently published *Devour Me Too* by Dacia Mariani; *Talking It Out (the October Crisis)*, by Francis Sinard.
How to Contact: Does not accept or return unsolicited mss. Query first. IRC. 100% of fiction is agented. Reports in 6 months. Photocopied submissions OK. Accepts computer printout submissions, including dot-matrix. Electronic submissions via IBM WordPerfect disks.
Terms: Pays royalty of 10% and 10 authors copies. Book catalog for SAE and 50¢ postage.
Advice: "Publish with a publisher whose works resemble yours." Publishing "more hardcovers and more pocket books."

‡MAX HARDY—PUBLISHER (IV), Box 28219, Las Vegas NV 89126-2219. (702)368-0379. Contact: Max Hardy. Estab. 1976. Publishes paperback originals. Books: offset printing; perfect binding; illustrations; average print order: 2-3,000; first novel print order: 3,000. Averages 6 total titles each year. Occasionally critiques rejected ms.
Needs: Publishes fiction on bridge only. Recently published *The Mexican Contract*: by Allan De Serpa (novel); and *Everything's Jake with Me*, by Don Von Elsner (anthology).
How to Contact: Accepts unsolicited mss. Submit complete ms. Simultaneous and photocopied submissions OK.
Terms: Pays in royalties of 10% maximum. "Author pays all expenses; receives 80% of all returns until he recovers 150%—then revert to royalties." Free book catalog.
Advice: "We encourage first novelists. Of our 30 + titles we have 5 novels and 2 anthologies. We consider fiction on bridge only."

HEART OF THE LAKES PUBLISHING (IV), Empire State Books, Box 299, 2989 Lodi Road, Interlaken NY 14847-0299. (607)532-4997. Imprint: Windswept Press. Editorial Contact Person: Walter Steesy. Estab. 1976. We publish material relating to NY state history and regional studies. Publishes hardcover and paperback originals and hardcover reprints. Books: paper varies; offset printing; perfect and case binding; illustrations; average print order: 1,000; first novel order: 1,000-3,000. Plans 1-2 novels this year. Averages 20-30 titles, 3-5 fiction titles each year. Occasionally critiques or comments on rejected ms.
Needs: Historical, juvenile (5-9 yrs.) historical, regional—New York State. Published new writers within the last year.
How to Contact: Accepts unsolicited mss. Query first or submit outline/synopsis and 1-2 sample chapters. Reports in 1 week on queries. Simultaneous and photocopied submissions OK. Accepts computer printout submissions, including dot-matrix. Accepts electronic submissions via MS-DOS, ASCII file.
Terms: Pays royalties. Provides 10 author's copies. Sends galleys to author.
Advice: "Windswept Press is a new imprint which includes material of non-New York subject matter. Some of the books under this imprint will be author supported."

HERITAGE PRESS (II, IV), Box 18625, Baltimore MD 21216. (301)383-9330. President: Wilbert L. Walker. Estab. 1979. One-man operation, full-time basis; uses contractual staff as needed. Publishes hardcover originals. Books: 60 lb white offset paper; offset printing; sewn hardcover binding; average print order: 2,000; first novel print order: 1,000. Averages 2 total titles, 1-2 fiction titles each year.
Needs: Ethnic (black). Interested in "fiction that presents a balanced portrayal of the black experience in America, from the black perspective. No fiction not dealing with blacks, or which views blacks as inferior. Recently published *Stalemate at Panmunjon* (the Korean War), and *Servants of All*, by Wilbert L. Walker.
How to Contact: Does not accept unsolicited mss. Query first with SASE. Simultaneous and photocopied submissions OK. Reports in 2 weeks on queries, 2 months on mss. Publishes ms an average of 9 months after acceptance.
Terms: Must return advance if book is not completed or is unacceptable. "We plan to subsidy publish only those works that meet our standards for approval. No more than 1 or 2 a year. Payment for publication is based on individual arrangement with author." Book catalog free on request.
Advice: "Write what you know about. No one else can know and feel what it is like to be black in America better than one who has experienced our dichotomy on race." Would like to see new ideas with broad appeal. "First novels must contain previously unexplored areas on the black experience in America. We regard the author/editor relationship as open, one of mutual respect. Editor has final decision, but listens to author's views."

‡HICKMAN SYSTEMS (IV), New Age Books, 4 Woodland Lane, Kirksville MO 63501. Contact: Irene Hickman. Estab. 1983. Small independent press. Publishes hardcover and paperback originals; hardcover and paperback reprints. Average print order: 2,000-3,000 copies; first novel print order: 2,000 copies. Averages 2 titles/year. Occasionally comments on rejected ms.
Needs: Psychic/supernatural, inspirational, special interest: new age, hypnotherapy, reincarnation. No ethnic, horror, science fiction. Recently published *Free Spirit*, by Antoinette May (historical with reincarnation theme).
How to Contact: Accepts unsolicited mss. Query. SASE for query and ms. Reports in 1 month on queries; 6 weeks on mss. Simultaneous and photocopied submissions OK. No dot-matrix. Accepts computer printouts.
Terms: Pays in royalties of 10%; advance is negotiable. Sends galleys to author. Book list free on request.
Advice: "Editor/author partnership is for the purpose of producing the best book possible. I edit very carefully and submit all editorial changes to the author for approval. Keep writing and writing and writing."

LAWRENCE HILL BOOKS, an imprint of Chicago Revew Press, 642 W. 227 St. #3, Riverdale NY 10463. Estab. 1973. Publishes hardcover and paperback originals and reprints. Averages 12-15 total titles.
Needs: Literary and translations. No genres (in general): romance, science fiction (in particular). Recently published *Prophecy and Politics*, by Grace Halsell; and *My Friend the Enemy*, by Uri Avnery; *Assata: An Autobiography*, by Assata Shakur.
How to Contact: Query first with SASE. Reports in 1 month on queries. Publishes ms 6-18 months after acceptance.
Terms: Pays in royalties. Book catalog for #10 SASE.
Advice: "Send query letters before complete ms."

HOMESTEAD PUBLISHING (I, II), Box 227, Moose WY 83012. (406)538-8960. Editor: Carl Schreier. Estab. 1980. Regional publishers for the Rocky Mountains, midsize firm. Publishes hardcover and paperback originals and reprints. Books: natural stock to enamel paper; web, sheet-feed printing; perfect or smythe-sewn binding; b&w or 4-6 color illustrations; average print order: 10,000; first novel print order: 2,000-5,000. Plans 1-2 first novels this year. Averages 8-10 total titles; 1-2 fiction each year. Sometimes critiques rejected mss.
Needs: Adventure, historical, juvenile (animal, historical), literary, preschool/picture book, short story collection, western, young adult/teen (10-18 years, historical). Looking for "good quality, well written and contemporary" fiction. Recently published *The Great Plains: A Young Reader's Journal*, by Bullock (children's natural history-adventure).
How to Contact: Accepts unsolicited mss. Query first. SASE. Agented fiction 0%. Reports in 1 month. Sends galleys to author. Simultaneous and photocopied submissions OK. Accepts computer printout submissions, including dot-matrix.
Terms: Pays royalties of 6% minimum; 10% maximum. Provides 6 author's copies. Subsidy publishes "occasionally, depending on project."

INTERNATIONAL MARINE PUBLISHING CO. (II, IV), 21 Elm St., Camden ME 04843. (207)236-4837. Jonathan Eaton, Managing Editor. Estab. 1969. Small, independent, specialty publisher in the nautical book market, with plans to expand. Publishes hardcover and paperback originals. Books: offset or cameron printing; casebound or perfectbound binding; illustrations "when appropriate"; average print order: 5,000; first novel print order: 5,000. Plans 1 first novel this year. Averages 25 total titles, 1 fiction title each year. Occasionally critiques or comments on rejected ms.
Needs: Nautical. Recently published *The Captain Nemo Cookbook Papers*, by Hal Painter (series of humorous vignettes woven around boats and with unifying plot).
How to Contact: Accepts unsolicited mss. Query first with outline/synopsis or submit complete ms and 2-3 chapters. Reports in 6 weeks on queries. Simultaneous and photocopied submissions OK. Accepts computer printout submissions, including dot-matrix.
Terms: Pays royalties of 10% minimum; 15% maximum. Advance is negotiable. Sends galleys to author.
Advice: "We published our first fiction title this year. We're open to more."

INTERTEXT (III), 2633 E. 17th Ave., Anchorage AK 99508. Imprint: Larchwood Books, Devon Editions. Editor: Sharon Ann Jaeger. Estab. 1982. Independent publisher. Publishes hardcover and paperback originals. Books: pH-neutral paper; offset printing; smythe-sewn and perfect bound binding; illustrations sometimes-occasionally do 4-color covers; average print order: 1,000; first novel print order: 1,000. "We publish writers of excellence only, whether novices or veterans." Averages 1-3 titles each year. No longer able to critique rejected mss. No longer takes on first-timers.
Needs: Literary, short story collections and translations. "We are presently concentrating on poetry, translations and literary criticism, together with selected (and solicited) titles in the fine arts."
How to Contact: Query by first-class mail with sample chapter and SASE. Do not send unsolicited complete mss. Reports in 2 months on queries; 6 months on mss. Simultaneous queries and photocopied submissions OK.
Terms: Pays 10% royalties after all costs of printing, promotion and distribution are met. Sends galleys to author. Writer's guidelines for SASE.
Advice: "A novel has to be very extraordinary indeed—truly compelling, with exquisite craftsmanship and a powerful and poetic style—for us to consider it. Get a variety of experience. Learn about people. Don't be (or at least sound) self-centered. Revise, revise, revise. We are not a market for the beginning writer, but would recommend to new writers to revise ruthlessly, to cut all unnecessary exposition—to make things *happen*, more 'show' than 'tell.' "

INVERTED-A, INC. (II), 401 Forrest Hill, Grand Prairie TX 75051. (214)264-0066. Editors: Amnon Katz or Aya Katz. Estab. 1977. A small press which evolved from publishing technical manuals for other products. "Publishing is a small part of our business." Publishes paperback originals. Books: bond paper; offset printing; illustrations; average print order: 250; first novel print order: 250. Publishes 2 titles a year, in recent years mostly poetry, fiction is now about every other year. Also publishes a periodical *Inverted-A, Horn*, which appears irregularly and is open to very short fiction as well as excerpts from unpublished longer fiction. Comments on rejected mss.
Needs: "We are interested in justice and freedom approached in a positive and romantic perspective." Recently published *The Few Who Count*, by Aya Katz (novel); and *Damned in Hell*, by A.A. Wilson (novella).
How to Contact: Submit query with sample. SASE. Reports in 6 weeks on queries; 3 months on mss. Simultaneous and photocopied submissions OK. Accepts computer printouts including dot-matrix. Accepts electronic submissions via modem or ASCII file on a PC MSDOS diskette. Sends galleys to author. For current list send SAE and 1 first class stamp.
Advice: "Deal with more than personal problems. Project hope."

ION BOOKS (II), Box 111327, Memphis TN 38111-1327. Imprint: Raccoon Books. President: David Spicer. Fiction Editor: Phyllis Tickle. Estab. 1977. Midsize independent publisher with plans to expand. Publishes hardcover originals and "occasionally" paperback originals. Books: 60 or 70 lb offset paper; offset printing; smythe-sewn binding; cover illustrations only; average print order: 3,000; average first novel print order: 3,000. Plans 1 first novel this year. Publishes 6-9 total titles each year; 1-2 fiction titles. Sometimes critiques rejected mss.
Needs: Adventure, contemporary, erotica, ethnic, experimental, juvenile (5-9 years; easy-to-read), literary, short story collections, suspense/mystery. High-quality literary fiction. No porn, writing about writing. Recently published *Hershel and the Beast*, by Steven Stern (juvenile).
How to Contact: Does not accept unsolicited mss. Query first with outline/synopsis and sample characters. SASE. Reports in 1 week on queries; 1-2 months on mss. Accepts computer printout submissions.

Close-up

Madeline Wikler
Kar-Ben Copies

When Judye Groner and Madeline Wikler decided to self-publish a Passover book they created for their own children, they had no idea they were starting what would become a full-time publishing operation, producing eight to 10 titles a year. "We started on the classic route where most people usually go under," says Wikler, illustrator of the book and now co-editor of Kar-Ben copies.

"We did a 5,000 printing of that little book and to our amazement they all sold." In fact, with distribution help from a local supermarket chain, friends, relatives and bookstore mailings, the book sold so well over three years, it became clear they'd discovered a niche in the market. "We found a real need for nonsexist, nondidactic books of Jewish interest for very young children," says Wikler. "And people started coming to us with their manuscripts."

Wikler now works with 52 authors and illustrators and Kar-Ben Copies has more than 70 books in print. Despite the rapid growth, Groner and Wikler, along with an office manager and a warehouse supervisor, run their operation from a small office in Groner's home. "While we're small, we're probably the largest for what we do," says Wikler. "And because we're small, we don't have to sell 100,000 copies of a title to stay afloat. We can also do only the books we like."

Wikler looks for books aimed at young readers, but that covers subjects once considered too mature or sophisticated for children under age 10. Religious celebration and holiday books, such as those for Hanukkah, Passover and Shabbat, are the backbone of their line, but Kar-Ben Copies also publishes books dealing with a variety of everyday subjects. Controversial subjects, such as interfaith marriage, divorce and illness, are not taboo if they are handled in a manner suitable to the young child. "We look for things done for older kids which we can do on a younger level, such as biographies and good renditions of Bible stories," says Wikler.

What Wikler and Groner do not want to see are anthropomorphic characters—talking candles, etc. "We don't want derivative Christmas stories, either—stories that are really Christmas stories in which the author has changed three words to make it a Hanukkah story—no Hanukkah trees.

"We don't like preachy books," adds Wikler. "It's fine if there's a message, but the message needs to come through the story not in a moral at the end."

Unlike many other publishers, Wikler and Groner read every submission, about 300 to 400 manuscripts each year. "We have a very clear focus. We occasionally get young adult novels and we do look at them, but we have not decided to branch into this area yet."

Kar-Ben Copies books are distributed to both secular and Jewish bookstores, as well as to libraries in Jewish schools, temples and to synagogue giftshops. Wikler makes use of direct mail and other advertising, but appreciates help from authors with ideas on marketing their own books.

Whenever possible, Groner and Wikler visit trade shows and writers conferences, promoting books, of course, but also meeting writers and artists. For writers, Wikler has this advice: "Write honest, clear, nonphony, nonmoralizing prose at an appropriate language level for the audience. For our type of book, we like to see the entire manuscript, rather than just a query. Don't send illustrations (they like to match writers to artists) and ALWAYS include a SASE."

—Robin Gee

Terms: Pays royalties of 10-15%, advance of $250 and 10 author's copies. Sends pre-publication galleys to author. Writers guidelines for #10 SAE and 1 first class stamp. Book catalog free on request.
Advice: Publishing less fiction now than in the past, and more hardcovers.

ITALICA PRESS (IV), #641, 625 Main St., New York NY 10044. (212)935-4230. Publishers: Eileen Gardiner and Ronald G. Musto. Estab. 1985. Small independent publisher. Publishes paperback originals and reprints. Books: 50-60 lb natural paper; offset printing; smythe-sewn binding; illustrations; average print order: 1,000. "First time translators published. We would like to see translations of well-known Italian writers in Italy who are not yet translated for an American audience." Publishes 6 total titles each year; 3 fiction titles. Sometimes critiques rejected mss.
Needs: Translations from Italian. Looking for "six novels over next two years—particularly translations of 20th Century Italian literature." Recently published *Family Chronicle*, by Vasco Pratolini; and *The Wooden Throne*, by Carlo Sgorlon; *Woman at War*, by Dacia Maraini.
How to Contact: Accepts unsolicited mss. Query first. Reports in 3 weeks on queries; 2 months on mss. Simultaneous and photocopied submissions OK. Accepts computer printout submissions, including dot-matrix. Electronic submissions via Macintosh or IBM-PC disk.
Terms: Pays in royalties of 5-15% and 10 author's copies. Sends pre-publication galleys to author. Book catalog free on request.

‡JAYELL ENTERPRISES (IV), Box 2616, Dearborn MI 48124. (313)565-9687. President: James L. Limbacher. Estab. 1983. One-person operation on a part-time basis; also produces TV cable programs. Publishes paperback originals. Books: average print order: 1,000; first novel print order 1,000. Averages 1 fiction title each year. Sometimes comments on rejected mss; $50 charge for critiques.
Needs: Historical. No "badly written, amateurish works."
How to Contact: Accepts unsolicited mss. Query first. Reports in 3 weeks on queries; in 1 month on mss. Photocopied submissions OK. Accepts computer printout submissions, including dot-matrix.
Terms: Pays royalties of 25% minimum. Provides 6 author's copies. Sends galleys to author.
Advice: Publishing "less fiction. nonfiction sells better. Paperbacks are cheaper."

‡THE JEWISH PUBLICATION SOCIETY (III,IV), 1930 Chestnut St., Philadelphia Pa 19103. (215)564-5925. Editor-in-chief: Sheila F. Segal. Estab. 1888. Small, nonprofit educational institution devoted to Jewish culture. Publishes hardcover and paperback originals and reprints. Published new writers within the past year. Plans 2-3 first novels this year. Averages 15-20 total titles, including juveniles, 2-3 fiction titles each year. Sometimes comments on rejected mss.
How to Contact: Sometimes accepts unsolicited mss. Query first. Reports on queries in 1-2 weeks; on mss in 2-3 months. Photocopied submissions OK. Accepts computer printout submissions, including dot-matrix.
Terms: Pays royalties. Advance negotiable. Provides 10 author's copies. Sends galleys to author. Publishes ms "approximately 1 year from the time it goes into production." Book catalog free on request.

KAR-BEN COPIES, INC. (II), 6800 Tildenwood La., Rockville MD 20852. (301)984-8733. President: Judye Groner. Estab. 1974. Small publisher specializing in juvenile Judaica. Publishes hardcover and paperback originals. Books: 70-80 lb patina paper; offset printing; perfect and case binding; 2-4 color illustrations; average print order: 5,000-10,000. Averages 8-10 total titles, 6-8 fiction titles each year. Published new writers within the last year.
Needs: Juvenile (3-10 years). Recently published *The Big Sukkah*, by Peninnah Schram; *The Yanov Torah*, by Erwin Herman; *My Mommy is a Rabbi*, by Mindy Portnoy.
How to Contact: Accepts unsolicited mss. SASE. Submit outline/synopsis and sample chapters or complete ms with cover letter. SASE. Reports in 1 week on queries; 1 month on mss. Simultaneous and photocopied submissions OK. Accepts computer printouts including dot-matrix.
Terms: Pays in royalties of 5% minimum; 10% maximum; average advance: $500; 12 author's copies. Sends galleys to author. Writer's guidelines free for SASE. Book catalog free on request.

‡KITCHEN TABLE: WOMEN OF COLOR PRESS (II, IV), Box 908, Latham NY 12110. Publisher: Barbara Smith. Estab. 1981. "Independent press with several paid employees, very good distribution." Publishes paperback originals. Books: 50 lb stock paper; offset/web press printing; perfect binding; some b&w graphic elements/designs; average print order: 5,000; first novel print order: 3,000. "All of our books are trade paperbacks, a few of which are bound for libraries." Averages 2 total titles each year; 1 fiction title every two years. Occasionally critiques rejected ms.
Needs: Ethnic, feminist, lesbian, literary, short story collections. Needs for novels include novels by women of color—authors that reflect in some way the experiences of women of color. "We are looking for high quality, politically conscious writing and would particularly like to hear from American Indian

women fiction writers." Has published *Cuentos: Stories by Latinas*, edited by Alma Gómez, Cherríe Moraga; Mariana Romo-Carmona (short story anthology with selections in both English and Spanish).
How to Contact: Accepts unsolicited mss. Query first. Submit outline/synopsis and 3 sample chapters. SASE. Reports in 1 month on queries; 6 months on mss. Simultaneous and photocopied submissions OK.
Terms: Pays in royalties of 8% minimum; 10% maximum and 10 author's copies. Sends galleys to author. Book catalog for 2 first class stamps.
Advice: "One of the most common mistakes that our press tries to address is the notion that the first work a writer publishes should be a book as opposed to a submission to a periodical. Periodicals serve as a very valuable apprenticeship for a beginning writer. They should submit work to appropriate literary and other kinds of journals that publish fiction. By appropriate I mean appropriate for the kind of writing they do. Getting published in periodicals gives the writer experience and also creates a 'track record' that may interest the prospective book publisher."

KNIGHTS PRESS (II, IV), Box 454, Pound Ridge NY 10576. (203)322-7381. Publisher: Elizabeth G. Gershman. Estab. 1983. Small press publishing only gay male fiction. Publishes trade paperback originals. Published new writers in the last year. Plans 6 first novels this year. Averages 12 total titles, 12 fiction titles each year.
Needs: "Fiction must have a gay theme (not lesbian or non-gay). We publish on merit, not category." No erotica. Recently published *Seth*, by Ray Wood; *Gods and Lovers*, by Paul Jeffers; *The Wrong Apple*, by David Rees.
How to Contact: Accepts unsolicited mss. Query first. SASE. Agented fiction: 25%. Reports in 3 weeks on queries; 3 months on mss. No simultaneous submissions. Photocopied submissions OK. Accepts computer printouts.
Terms: Pays in royalties of 10% minimum; average advance: $500. Sends galleys to author. Writer's guidelines free for #10 SASE and 1 first class stamp. Book catalog free on request.
Advice: "Write about people, places, events you know. Then plot, plot, plot. Story must have a positive gay lifestyle or relationship. Present manuscript in best possible form—double spaced, correct spelling and punctuation; minimum typos; proofread. Consider that a book costs money to buy and to produce. Would *you* spend your money to read your submission? Would you spend thousands of dollars to produce it? If you wouldn't, neither would the book buyer or the publisher."

KNOLL PUBLISHING CO., INC. (II),831 W. Washington Blvd., Ft. Wayne IN 46802. (219)426-1926 or (219)422-7774. Publisher: Joseph Laiacona. Estab. 1986. Small, independent, human potential publisher. Publishes paperback originals and reprints. Books: Offset printing; perfect binding; illustrations; average print order: 3,000. Averages 4 total titles, 1 fiction title each year. Sometimes comments on rejected mss.
Needs: Psychic/supernatural/occult, religious/inspirational. Looking for mss on "human potential only."
How to Contact: Does not accept or return unsolicited mss. Submit outline/synopsis with 1 sample chapter. Reports on queries in 2 weeks; on mss in 2 months. Simultaneous and photocopied submissions OK. Accepts computer printouts, including dot-matrix.
Terms: "Wildly negotiable." Provides 10 author's copies. Sends galleys to author. Book catalog free.

KRUZA KALEIDOSCOPIX, INC. (IV), Box 389, Franklin MA 02038. (617)528-6211. Editor/President: J.A. Kruza. Fiction Editor: R. Burbank. Estab. 1976. Publishes hardcover and paperback originals. Books: 60-80 lb coated paper; offset printing; saddle and perfect binding; illustrations; average print order: 10,000. Averages 12 total titles each year. Sometimes critiques rejected mss.
Needs: Historical (nautical); juvenile (5-9 yrs.) including: animal, lesson teachings about work ethic, historical. "Stories for children, ages 3-7, with problem and characters who work out solution to problem, i.e. work ethic." Recently published *A Candle For Boo*, by Beth Cox (children's giant story); *The Greedy Dinosaur*, by Terry Barnhill (dino gets stuck in mud); and *The Long Sleep*, by Dorothy L. Blackman (bear loses reading glasses that he must earn back).
How to Contact: Accepts and returns unsolicited mss. Submit complete ms with cover letter. SASE. Reports in 3 weeks on queries; 3 months on mss. Simultaneous and photocopied submissions OK. Accepts computer printout submissions, no dot-matrix.
Terms: Pays in royalties of 3% minimum; 5% maximum, "or flat fee, depending on strength of story. Length of royalties are usually limited to a specific time, usually 4 to 7 years." Provides 10 author's copies. Writer's guidelines for #10 SAE with 1 first class stamp.

‡KUBICEK & ASSOCIATES (I,II), Box 30269, 320 N. 26th St., Lincoln NB 68503-0269. (402)435-4607. President: David Kubicek. Estab. 1988. "We're a small company (3 people) with ambitious plans for expansion over the next few years." Publishes hardcover and paperback originals. Books: offset white, normally 60 lb paper; photo offset printing; usually perfect and case binding; illustrations (depending on book); average print order: 1,500-2,500; first novel print order: 1,500 "unless it's an exceptional novel." Published new writers within the last year. Plans 1 first novel and 1 picture book by previously unpublished writers this year. Plans 5 total titles, 3 fiction titles this year. Sometimes critiques rejected mss.

Needs: Fantasy, historical, horror, juvenile (5-9 years, including animal, fantasy, historical, contemporary), mainstream, psychic/supernatural/occult, regional (midwest), science fiction, short story collections, suspense/mystery, westerns, young adult/teen (10-18 years, including fantasy/science fiction, historical, romance). No romance (the genre—we like to see some romance in our books, when it's done intelligently), pornography, sword and sorcery. Recently published *The Pelican in the Desert: And Other Stories of the Family Farm*, edited by David Kubicek (anthology of short stories); *Dark Eyes*, by David Kubicek (science fiction novel); and *October Dreams*, edited by David Kubicek (anthology of horror/supernatural stories).

How to Contact: Accepts unsolicited mss. Query first with outline/synopsis and 1-3 sample chapters. Include social security number with submission. Agented fiction 0%. Reports on queries in 3-4 weeks; on mss in 4-6 weeks. Photocopied submissions OK. No dot-matrix computer printouts.

Terms: Pays royalties of 10-15%; at least 10 author's copies; discount on additional copies. Sends galleys to author. Publishes ms 9-18 months after acceptance. "Since our budget isn't large to publish every book we'd like to, we may offer to publish a book if the author pays printing/binding costs; we will market it and receive a percentage (30-40%) of sales." Writers guidelines and book catalog for #10 SAE and 1 first class stamp.

Advice: "Our marketing program is flexible; if we find something we like and think we can sell it, we'll publish it. Our interests range from genre like science fiction to mainstream. We like writing that creates a strong mood and evokes an emotional reaction from the readers, writing by writers who enjoy working with the language."

LAPIS EDUCATIONAL ASSOCIATION, INC. (II, IV), 3874 W. Princeton Circle, Denver CO 80236. Editor and Director: Karen Degenhart. Estab. 1977. One-person operation on part-time basis; nonprofit organization's biennial journal is main publication. Journal: regular paper; offset printing; staple binding; b&w illustrations; average print order: 100-200.

Needs: Contemporary, literary, religious/inspirational, psychology; some feminist, alternative lifestyles; and psychic/supernatural/occult with psychological slant. "Jungian psychology and informed Christianity-related topics are the focus." Rarely publishes fiction; some poetry. Also "contemporary issues in ministry, and theology, including New Age and Native American spirituality."

How to Contact: Accepts unsolicited mss. Query with SASE. Simultaneous and photocopied submissions OK. Accepts computer printout submissions. Reports in 2 weeks on queries, "indefinite" on mss.

Terms: "We do not pay. Authors must be fee-paying members of this association to be published but may join after submitting ms. Members pay a $10 yearly fee (and receive 3 copies of the issue they are published in) if they are selected to be published. Don't have to join to submit ms." No advance.

Advice: "The few fiction titles we've published are about psychological and spiritual life journeys. We do not publish any novels. We regard the author/editor relationship as a personal friendship and creative endeavor."

LIBERTY PRESS, INC. (IV), Box 50421, Austin TX 78763. (512)495-9843. Editors: Lynn Burson and Tom Doyal. Estab. 1986. Publishes paperback originals and reprints. Books: perfect binding; average print order: 2,500; first novel print order: 1,000. Published new writers within the last year. Plans at least 3 first novels this year. Averages 8 total titles, 4 fiction titles each year.

Needs: Special requirement for all categories: significant lesbian or gay content. Adventure, erotica, fantasy, gay, historical, humor/satire, lesbian, literary, mainstream, religious/inspirational, contemporary and historical romance, science fiction, short story collections, suspense/mystery, western. Looking for "mystery/suspense (lesbian/gay content); lesbian erotica; contemporary and historical romances (lesbian/gay romance); literary novels (lesbian/gay content). We publish no work that has negative stereotypes of gay/lesbian persons." Recently published *The Heir*, by John Preston (gay male erotica); *The Rose-Bearer*, by Lizabeth May (lesbian contemporary romance); *The Holy Spirit Dance Club*, by Joseph Puccia (gay literary novel with spiritual subtext).

How to Contact: Accepts unsolicited mss. Submit outline/synopsis and 3 or more sample chapters. SASE. Reports in 1 month on queries; 6-8 weeks on mss. Photocopied submissions OK if clear and dark. Accepts computer printout submissions, if clear and dark.

Terms: Pays royalties of 10% minimum; 15% maximum. Average advance: $150, $100 for first work, $300 for previously published writers. Writer's guidelines not available. Book catalog free.

Advice: "Manuscripts must have significant, *positive* lesbian/gay content."

LIBRA PUBLISHERS, INC. (II), 3098C Clairemont Dr., Suite 383, San Deigo CA 92117. (619)581-9449. President: Wiliam Kroll. Estab. 1960. Small independent publisher. Hardcover and paperback originals. Books: 60 lb offset paper; offset printing; hardcover-smythe sewn binding, paperback-perfect binding; illustrations occasionally; average print order: 3,000; first novel print order: 1,000 +. Has published fiction by a previously unpublished writer within the last year. Plans 3 first novels this year. Averages approximately 15 titles/year, 3-4 fiction titles/year.
Needs: "We consider all categories." Recently published *All God's Children*, by Alex La Perchia (inspirational); *Seed Of The Divine Fruit*, by Enrico Rinaldi (multi-generational about founding of Atlantic City); *Caveat Emptor*, by William Attias (racist takeover of a city).
How to Contact: Accepts unsolicited mss. Submit complete ms with cover letter. SASE. Reports in 1 week on queries; 2-3 weeks on mss. Simultaneous and photocopied submissions OK. Computer printout submissions OK.
Terms: Pays 10%-40% royalties. Sends galleys to author. Publishes ms 6-12 months after acceptance. Book catalog for SASE and 5 first class stamps.
Advice: "*Libra* publishes nonfiction books in all fields, specializing in the behavioral sciences. We also publish two professional journals: Adolescence and Family Therapy. We have published fiction on a royalty basis but because of the difficulty in marketing works by unknown writers, we are not optimistic about the chances of offering a standard contract. However, we shall continue to consider fiction in the hope of publishing on a standard basis books that we like and believe have good marketing potential. In addition, our procedure is as follows: Manuscripts we do not consider publishable are returned to the author. When we receive manuscripts which we feel are publishable but are uncertain in terms of marketability, we suggest that the author continue to try other houses. If they have already done so and are interested in self-publishing, we offer two types of services: (1) We provide editing, proofreading, book and cover design, copyrighting, and production of the book; copies are then shipped to the author. (2) We provide these services plus promotion and distribution. In all cases, the problems and risks are spelled out."

LIBRARY RESEARCH ASSOCIATES, INC. (IV), RD. 5, Box 41, Dunderberg Rd., Monroe NY 10950. Imprints include Lloyd-Simone Publishing Co., Willow Tree Press and Criminal Justice Press. Editorial Director: Matilda A. Gocek. Estab. 1968. Publishes hardcover and paperback originals. Books: 50 lb paper; narrow web offset printing; perfect bound hardcover binding; b&w half-tones, line drawings; average print order: 3,500; first novel print order: 1,500. Published 2 new writers within the last year.
Needs: New York State based, fictional biographies or historical events. Recently published fiction by Janet Dempsey.
How to Contact: Accepts unsolicited mss. Submit outline/synopsis and sample chapters with SASE. No simultaneous submissions; photocopied submissions OK. Accepts computer printout submissions, prefers letter-quality. Reports in 10 weeks. Publishes ms 12-14 months after acceptance.
Terms: Pays in royalties; no advance. Sends galleys to author. Book catalog for #10 SASE.
Advice: "There is a gradual return to a good story line less dependent upon violence and explicit sex. I am looking to develop our line of Empire State Fiction. Fictionalized biographies based on fact would be welcomed, particularly of women in New York, any period. Prepare clean, double-spaced manuscripts—one-page outline or abstract is most helpful. I want to develop *new authors* so I work willingly with them." Publishing less fiction because it's "hard to generate sales."

LINCOLN SPRINGS PRESS (II), Box 269, Franklin Lakes NJ 07417. Editor: M. Gabriel. Estab. 1987. Small, independent press. Publishes poetry, fiction, photography, high quality. Publishes paperback originals. Books: 65 lb paper; offset printing; perfect binding; average print order: 1,000. Published new writers within the last year. "Prefers short stories, but will publish first novels if quality high enough." Averages 4 total titles/year; 2 fiction titles.
Needs: Contemporary, ethnic, experimental, feminist, historical, literary, short story collections. No "romance, Janet Dailey variety." Recently published *The Crazy Aunt and Other Stories*, by James T. McCartin (collection of short stories); *Ellis Island: Then & Now*, by Sharon Spencer and Dennis Toner (photographs and vignettes).
How to Contact: Accepts unsolicited mss. Query first with 1 sample chapter. SASE. Reports in 2 weeks-3 months. Simultaneous and photocopied submissions OK. Accepts computer printouts, including dot-matrix.
Terms: Authors receive royalties of 5% minimum; 15% maximum "after all costs met." Provides 10 author's copies. Sends galleys to author. Book catalog for SASE.

LINTEL (II), Box 8609, Roanoke VA 24014. Editorial Director: Walter James Miller. Estab. 1977. Two-person organization on part-time basis. Books: 90% opaque paper; photo offset printing; perfect binding; illustrations; average print order: 1,000; first novel print order: 1,200. Publishes hardcover and paperback originals. Occasionally comments on rejected mss.

Needs: Experimental, short fiction, feminist, gay, lesbian, psychic/supernatural/occult, and regional. Recently published second edition (fourth printing) of *Klytaimnestra Who Stayed at Home*, mythopoeic novel by Nancy Bogen.
How to Contact: Accepts unsolicited mss. Query with SASE. Simultaneous and photocopied submissions OK. Accepts computer printout submissions. Prefers letter-quality. Reports in 1 month on queries, 2 months on mss. Publishes ms from 6-8 months after acceptance.
Terms: Negotiated. No advance. Sends galleys to author. Free book catalog.
Advice: "Lintel is devoted to the kinds of literary art that will never make The Literary Guild or even the Book-of-the-Month Club: that is, literature concerned with the advancement of literary art. We still look for the innovative work ignored by the commercial presses. We consider any ms on its merits alone. We encourage first novelists. Be innovative, advance the *art* of fiction, but still keep in mind need to reach reader's aspirations as well as your own. Consistent misspelling errors, errors in grammar and syntax can mean only rejection."

LOFT PRESS (II), 42 Sherman Ave., Glens Falls NY 12801. Editor: Jean Rikhoff. Estab. 1981. Published new writers within the last year. Small press for chapbooks. Publishes novellas and new writers "as well as established writers such as William Bronk, William Kennedy." Average print order: 1,000.
Needs: Contemporary, ethnic, experimental, feminist, gay, literary, mainstream, suspense/mystery, short stories, translations, nonfiction of general interest, regional (Adirondacks). Publishes ms an average of 3-6 months after acceptance. Sometimes critiques rejected mss and recommends other markets.
How to Contact: Send complete ms with cover letter. Reports in 2 months on queries. SASE. Simultaneous and photocopied submissions OK. Accepts computer printout submissions. Sample copy for $4. Fiction guidelines free.
Terms: Acquires one-time rights. Publication copyrighted. Payment as well as 50 copies for acceptance. Average advance is $200.
Advice: "Send us a legible ms. You'd be surprised what we get."

LOLLIPOP POWER BOOKS (II), Box 277, Carrboro NC 27510. (919)376-8152. Contact: Judy Hogan, Carolina Wren editor. Estab. 1970. Now children's division of the Carolina Wren Press, publishes non-sexist, multi-racial "alternative" children's books. Publishes paperback originals. Buys juvenile mss with or without illustrations. Averages 1 title (fiction) each year. Average first book run 2,500 copies. Usually critiques rejected ms "unless completely inappropriate submission for our purpose."
Needs: Juvenile. "We are currently looking for well written stories with strong plots which deal with issues of race or sex-role stereotyping or with contemporary family problems, especially divorce. We would like to see ms about a realistic black child or family or ms dealing with handicapped children."
How to Contact: Query first for author guidelines and book catalog with SASE. Reports in 2 weeks on queries; 6 weeks on mss. Simultaneous and photocopied submissions OK. Publishes ms from 6-12 months after acceptance.
Terms: Pays 10%.
Advice: "Know what the publisher's specialty is. Though we want books with a strong message, we also want strong and appealing characters, and plots which children will want to return to again and again."

LTD. EDITION PRESS (I, II), 4725 Conowingo Rd., Darlington MD 21034. (301)836-3715. Imprint: Penny Paper Novels. Publisher: Fern Smith-Brown. Estab. 1980. "Small publishers, but we are expanding every year." Publishes paperback and hardcover originals and "tabloid size novels distributed through motels, convenience stores and various businesses." Books: tabloid newsprint paper; web offset print; minimal illustrations; average print order: 20,000-100,000 for Penny Paper Novels. Plans 24 first novels this year; "most of our writers are new, having published only short stories." Publishes 30 total titles each year; all fiction. Sometimes critiques rejected ms.
Needs: Adventure, historical, romance (contemporary, historical), gothics, suspense/mystery, western. Wants to see "fast moving, easy to read novels suitable for men and women from all walks of life. Nothing any member of a family can't read. 25,000 words preferred. No explicit sex or violence." Recently published *The Siege of Canton*, by Jack P. Jones (western novel); *Run, Amanda, Run*, by Charles S. Roberts (romance); *A Texas Eligy*, by Don Johnson.
How to Contact: Submit complete ms with cover letter. SASE. Reports in 6 weeks. Simultaneous submissions OK.
Terms: "We purchase manuscript outright. Amount depends on manuscript and how much editing is required. Differs with each ms and author." Writer's guidelines for #10 SAE and 1 first class stamp. Book catalog not available but we will send sample of published Penny Paper Novels for perspective writers to peruse if 9x12 SASE is sent.
Advice: "While our pay is low, we are an excellent place for new writers to start. We have the readers

and we take the time to guide and lend tips. We're a good place to sharpen their craft! Penny Paper Novels are intended for a 'quick read' in a fast-paced society."

LUCKY HEART BOOKS (I), *(formerly Salt Lick Press)*, Subsidiary of Salt Lick Foundation, 1804 E. 38½ St., Austin TX 78722. Imprint: Lucky Heart Books. Editor/Publisher: James Haining. Estab. 1969. Small press with significant work reviews in several national publications. Publishes paperback originals and reprints. Books: offset/bond paper; offset printing; stitch, perfect bound; illustrations; average print order: 500; first novel print order: 500. Sometimes comments on rejected mss.
Needs: Open to all fiction categories.
How to Contact: Accepts unsolicited mss. SASE. 1% of fiction is agented. Reports in 2 weeks on mss. Photocopied submissions OK. Accepts computer printout submissions, including dot-matrix.
Terms: Pays 10 author's copies. Sends pre-publication galleys to author.

MAGNIFICAT (IV), Subsidiary of AMDG Corp., 315 Main St., Box 365, Avon NJ 07717. (201)988-8915. Publisher: Stephen Dunham. Estab. 1986. Publishes hardcover and paperback originals. Books: 50 lb cream-white 360 PPI paper; cameron or web printing; perfect or casebound binding; illustrations sometimes; average print order: 5,625; first novel print order: 5,000. Published new writers within the last year. Plans 2 first novels this year. Averages 8 total titles, 2 fiction titles each year. Sometimes critiques rejected mss.
Needs: Religious/inspirational. "We do not need any fiction submissions through the end of 1989." Recently published *A Convenant with Life*, by Clifford Blair (spy/adventure, religious); *The Ananias Precedent*, by Floyd Allen (contemporary religious); and *Angels Get No Respect*, by Cecil Bauer et al (humor, short stories).
How to Contact: Accepts unsolicited mss. Query. Reports in 2 weeks on queries; 2 months on mss. Simultaneous and photocopied submissions OK. Accepts computer printouts, including dot-matrix.
Terms: Pays in royalties of 5% minimum; 8% maximum. Writer's guidelines for #10 SAE and 1 first class stamp. Book catalog for 9x12 SAE with 73¢ postage.
Advice: "A common mistake is not writing with a particular audience in mind. Yes, writing should be done so as to be accessible to anyone interested, but many writers write for no one in particular and then run it up the flag pole to see if anyone salutes—and may have no audience. Have your audience and market in mind, and write for them, and submit your work to the publishers who reach that audience."

MAINESPRING PRESS (II), Maine Writers Workshop, Box 905, R.F.D, Stonington ME 04681. Also publishes *Letters* Magazine. (207)367-2484. Editor: Helen Nash. Midsize independent publisher. Publishes hardcover and paperback originals. Books: 20 lb paper; photo offset printing; perfect binding; average print order: 2,000-5,000; first novel print order: 3,000. Published new writers within the last year; plans 1 first novel this year. Averages 3 total titles, 1 fiction title each year. Average first novel print order 5,000 copies. Always critiques good rejected ms; sometimes charges to critique more than 1 sample chapter. Query first on complete book.
Needs: Contemporary, faction, historical, literary, and science fiction. Recently published *Born to Die*, by H.G. Woods; *Truth Fairy*, by G. F. Bush; *Pearls from My Oyster*, by G. F. Bush.
How to Contact: Accepts unsolicited mss with large SASE (US funds). Submit outline/synopsis and first, middle and last chapters to 50 pages. Complete ms on request. Reports in 1 month. No simultaneous submissions; legible photocopied submissions OK. Accepts computer printout submissions, no dot-matrix.
Terms: Pays in royalties of 10% minimum, 15% maximum; seldom an honorarium but always cash, not copies, for all rights. Writer's guidelines for SASE.
Advice: "We encourage first novels of quality."

McDONALD PUBLISHING COMPANY, INC., RD2, Box 1162, Hemlock Road, Columbia NJ 07832. (201)496-4441. Imprint: Shoe Tree Press. Publisher/Editor: Joyce McDonald. Estab. 1984 as Shoe Tree Press. "Small independent publisher, two-person operation, full-time, with plans to expand." Publishes hardcover and paperback original reprints. Books: generally 70 lb vellum paper; offset printing; reinforced binding; and perfect for softcover; occasionally uses illustrations for middle years books; average print order: 2,500-5,000. First novel print order: 2,500. Published new writers within the last year; plans 2 novels this year. Averages 3 fiction titles each year. Rarely critiques or comments on rejected mss.
Needs: Literary, short story collections, mainstream, horror, contemporary, young adult, middle years fiction. No formula or genre fiction please. Recently published *Summer Captive*, by Penny Pollock (young adult).
How to Contact: We no longer accept unsolicited manuscripts. Please query. SASE. Agented fiction 33%. Reports in 2-4 weeks on queries; 10-12 weeks on mss. Simultaneous and photocopied submissions OK. Accepts computer printout submissions, including dot-matrix.

Terms: Pays in royalties 10% hardcover; 6% softcover. Advance varies and is negotiable. Sends galleys to author.

Advice: "Don't get caught up in trying to follow 'market trends.' Write about what you know, and write it from the heart."

‡MELIOR PUBLICATIONS (IV), Division of Futurepast: The History Company, N. 10 Post, Suite 550, Box 1905, Spokane WA 99210-1905. (509)455-5617. Vice President: Barbara Greene Chamberlain. Estab. 1986. Small independent press, mostly nonfiction but interested in quality fiction of a historical or regional nature. Books: acid-free book stock; photo offset printing on cut-sheet press; hardcover, smythe-sewn or perfect binding; illustrations sometimes; first novel print order: "probably 2,500." Plans 1 first novel this year. Publishes 4-5 total titles/year; bringing out first fiction title this year. Sometimes critiques rejected mss.

Needs: Historical, regional. "Well-written historical or regional (Pacific Northwest) works are the only ones we're currently considering. Strong *stories* get our attention. We especially welcome good women's history and ethnic history, but it has to be a good story, not a soapbox." Recently published *Fireweed: An American Saga*, by Nellie Burton Picken (historical/regional).

How to Contact: Accepts unsolicited mss. Submit outline/synopsis, 5 sample chapters and cover letter with SASE. Reports on queries in 1 month; on mss in 4-6 months. Simultaneous and photocopied submissions OK. Accepts dot-matrix computer printouts if "readable."

Terms: Royalties negotiated on individual basis. Sends galleys to author. Publishes ms 9 months-1 year after acceptance. Writer's guidelines for #10 SAE and 1 first class stamp; book catalog for 9x12 envelope and 65¢ postage.

Advice: "We are just bringing out our first fiction—the future depends a great deal on the quality and quantity of submissions. We encourage first novelists if they're willing to put time into rewrites, accept some coaching and editing, and understand that the demands of the marketplace as well as literary value must be part of our decision-making process. We're eager to develop ongoing relationships with writers. We recognize that we can't compete with New York royalties and advances, but feel that the personal attention we give to each and every title more than makes up for this for a first novelist. Do market research—do works of this type do well? What's the audience? Be realistic—we're a small press and probably won't do a first print run of 20,000 and send you to Donahue and Oprah. Above all, write well, with vivid power and imagination—set us on fire."

METAMORPHOUS PRESS (IV), 3249 NW 29th Ave., Portland OR 97210. Publisher: David Balding. Fiction Editor: Anita Sullivan. Estab. 1982. General trade book publisher and distributor to the trade for other publishers with compatible titles. Publishes hardcover and paperback originals and paperback reprints. Books: white 55 lb paper; sewn, case, perfect or paper binding; average print order: 2,000-5,000; first novel print order: 2,000. Published new writers within the last year. Plans 2 first novels this year. Averages 12 total titles, 2 fiction titles each year. Sometimes critiques rejected mss.

Needs: Humor/satire, juvenile (animal, easy-to-read, fantasy, historical, sports, spy/adventure, contemporary), young adult/teen (problem novels). "We look for works that respect the notion that we create our own reality. Works that generally provide the reader tools to gain better control over their personal lives work well for us."

How to Contact: Accepts unsolicited mss. Query first with outline. SASE. Reports in 3 months on queries; 6 months on mss. Simultaneous and photocopied submissions OK. Accepts computer printout submissions, including dot-matrix.

Terms: Pays royalties of 10% minimum; 15% maximum. Pays in 10 author's copies. Sends galleys to author. Subsidy publishes 10% of books. "Author can increase royalty percent by contributing toward the production cost." Book catalog free on request.

Advice: "Publishing more fiction in an attempt to diversify, but careful to be consistent with statement of purpose. Our editorial staff is a resource to the author. Our policy is to have the author centrally involved to maintain their high energy for their work."

METIS PRESS, INC. (IV), Box 25187, Chicago IL 60625. Estab. 1976. Small collective of volunteers, part time. Publishers of paperback originals. Books: 50 lb offset paper; offset printing; perfect binding; some line-art illustrations; average print order: 2,000; first novel print order: 2,000. Encourages new writers. No poetry.

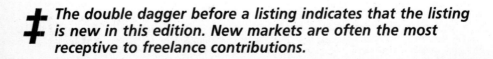

The double dagger before a listing indicates that the listing is new in this edition. New markets are often the most receptive to freelance contributions.

Needs: Feminist and lesbian. Especially needs novels and short stories with lesbian content. Recently published *Bernice: A Comedy in Letters*, by Georgia Jo Ressmeyer; and *The Secret Witch*, by Linda J. Stem (children's).

How to Contact: Query or "enclose a synopsis with short section of work; this is preferred to entire manuscript. We'll inquire further if interested." SASE with query, ms. Publishes ms 12-18 months after acceptance.

Terms: Pays in royalties, by outright purchase and in author's copies. Sends galleys to author. Free book catalog.

Advice: Noticeable trends include "short stories, new writers, Midwest voice and humor. All fiction we publish is original. We publish first novels not over 250 pages in print with lesbian content."

MICAH PUBLICATIONS (II), 255 Humphrey St., Marblehead MA 01945. (617)631-7601. Imprints include Kol, Echad, A Whole Global Anthology Series. Literary and General Editor: Roberta Kalechofsky. Estab. 1975. Publishes paperback originals and reprints. Books: 55 lb glatfelter paper; offset printing; paper binding, hardcover for scholarly works; illustrations; average print order: 1,000; first novel print order: 500. Averages 3 total titles each year. Occasionally critiques rejected mss.

Needs: Historical (specific), literary, religious, short story collections, anti-vivisection literature. Recently published *Bodmin, 1349*, by Roberta Kalechafsky.

How to Contact: Submit outline/synopsis and sample chapters (about 30 pages) with SASE. Simultaneous and photocopied submissions OK. Reports in 3 months on mss.

Terms: Pays in royalties of up to 30% and 15 author's copies. Sends galleys to author if requested. "Our arrangements are flexible and subject to specific requirements of each book or what kind of cooperation the author can make towards advertising, printing (production) or distributing his/her work. We do not accept money or subsidies of any kind, but we will accept work—for instance, if the author can typeset his/her ms or do art work for it, and we fully expect him or her to undertake a portion of the work in trying to sell, advertise or promote the book—in return for which our royalties are high." Book catalog free on request.

Advice: "Please don't be *slick*; don't send me formula or workshop-inspired fiction. Know your craft, but don't let craft be your dominant guide. We are publishing less fiction because of uninteresting submissions and slick proposals. We definitely encourage first novelists. Our greatest problem in dealing with new writers, is that they have illusions about fame and publishing, which are hard to eradicate. I think that writers should do hard research in publishing and consider publishing their own novels or their works of poetry. With computers and new printing technology, any writer can publish his or her own work."

MILKWEED EDITIONS, Box 3226, Minneapolis MN 55030. (612)332-3192. Editor: Emilie Buchwald. Estab. 1980—*Milkweed Chronicle*/1984—*Milkweed Editions*. Small press with emphasis on literary and visual arts work. Publishes hardcover and paperback originals. Books: book text quality—acid free paper; offset printing; perfect or hardcover binding; illustrations in all books; average print order: 2,000; first novel print order depends on book. Averages 8 total titles/year. Number of fiction titles "depends on mss."

Needs: Contemporary, experimental, literary. Looking for excellent writing. No romance, mysteries, science fiction. Recently published *Spillville* by Hampi and Sorman; *Ganado Red*, by Susan Lowell.

How to Contact: Accepts unsolicited mss. Submit outline/synopsis and 2 sample chapters. SASE. Reports in 3 weeks on queries; 2 months on mss. Simultaneous and photocopied submissions OK. Accepts computer printouts. No dot-matrix. "Please send for guidelines. Enclose SASE."

Terms: Authors are paid in royalties of 10% minimum; 20% maximum; advance is negotiable; 10 author's copies. Sends galleys to author. Book catalog for SASE or IRC and 2 first class stamps.

Advice: "Read good contemporary fiction; find your own voice. Do not send us pornographic work, or work in which violence is done to women or children or men."

MILLERS RIVER PUBLISHING CO. (IV), Box 159, Athol MA 01331. Owner: Allen Young. One person operation on part-time basis; New England regional interest. Publishes paperback originals. Books: Glatfelter 60 lb paper; offset printing; perfect binding; illustrations; average print order: 2,000; first novel print order: 1,000. Averages 2 total titles, 1 fiction title each year. Critiques or comments on rejected ms.

Needs: Regional (New England setting). Recently published *Summer for Joey*, by Lyle Glazier.

How to Contact: Accepts unsolicited mss. SASE. Query first, or submit outline/synopsis and 2 sample chapters. No phone queries. Reports in 1 month on queries; 1 month on mss. Simultaneous and photocopied submissions OK. Accepts computer printouts including dot-matrix.

Terms: Pays in royalties of 5% minimum; 10% maximum; average advance: $300; advance is negotiable. Sends galleys to author. Subsidy—will consider and negotiate. Book catalog for #10 SASE and 39¢ postage.

MINA PRESS (II), Box 854, Sebastopol CA 95472. (707)829-0854. Fiction Editors: Mei Nakano, Adam David Miller. Estab. 1982. Three-person part-time operation. Publishes hardcover and paperback originals. Books: offset printing; paper binding; average print order: 2,000; first novel print order: 2,500. Plans 3 first novels this year. Averages 1-5 total titles each year. Occasionally critiques rejected ms.
Needs: Ethnic, feminist, gay, juvenile (contemporary), lesbian, science fiction, and easy-to-read (teen). "No works that glorify war; no gratuitous violence; nothing racist, sexist, ageist." Recently published *Riko Rabbit*, by Mei Nakano (folk children's); *Is a Mountain Just a Rock*, by Gregory Uba (early teen initiation); *Quadrille for Tigers*, by Christine Craig (poetry).
How to Contact: Accepts unsolicited mss. Query first. Submit complete ms with SASE. Reports in 3 months. Simultaneous and photocopied submissions OK. Accepts computer printout submissions; prefers letter-quality.
Terms: Pays in royalties of 10% maximum; 10 author's copies; no advance. Sends galleys to author. Writer's guidelines and book catalog for SASE.
Advice: "We encourage new writers. We regard the author/editor relationship as one of close collaboration on all aspects/phases of publication. Determine your market and send ms to publisher who most fits it."

MISTY HILL PRESS (II), 5024 Turner Rd., Sebastopol, CA 95472. (707)823-7437. Managing Editor: Sally S. Karste. Estab. 1985. One person operation on a part-time basis. Publishes paperback originals. Books: illustrations; average print order: 2,000; first novel print order: 500-1,000. Plans 1 first novel this year. Publishes 1 title each year. Sometimes critiques rejected mss; $15/hour charge for critiques.
Needs: Juvenile (historical). Looking for "historical fiction for children, well researched for library market." Recently published *Trails to Poosey*, by Olive R. Cook (historical fiction); *Tales Fledgling Homestead*, by Joe Armstrong (nonfiction portraits).
How to Contact: Accepts unsolicited mss. Submit outline/synopsis and sample chapters. Reports within weeks. Simultaneous and photocopied submissions OK. Accepts computer printout submissions, no dot-matrix.
Terms: Pays royalties of 5%. Sends prepublication galleys to author. Writer's guidelines and book catalog for SASE.
Advice: "We specialize in well designed and illustrated quality paperbacks."

MOGUL BOOKS & FILMWORKS, Box 2773, Pittsburgh PA 15230. Editor: Vincent Risoli. Estab. 1982. One person operation on part-time basis. Publishes hardcover and paperback originals. Plans 1 first novel this year. Publishes 1 novel "every year or two."
Needs: Gay, lesbian. "No coming-out books." Recently published *Ex-The Unknown*, by Vinnie Robinson (gay fiction).
How to contact: Accepts unsolicited mss. SASE. Reports in 2 weeks on queries; 6 weeks on mss. Photocopied submissions OK.
Terms: Sends pre-publication galleys to author.
Advice: "Will be publishing a New York playwright's first novel within two years. When we accept a mss, we try to compensate for our publishing inadequacies compared with large publishers by regarding the relationship with the author the best we know how."

MOSAIC PRESS (II, IV), Fine Miniature Books, 358 Oliver Rd., Cincinnati OH 45215. (513)761-5977. Publisher: Miriam Irwin. Estab. 1977. Publishes hardcover originals in miniature format. Books: acid-free archival paper; litho or letter press printing; hardbound, cloth, leather or half-leather binding; illustrations; average print order: 2,000. Plans to publish 2 new authors this year. Averages 8 total titles, 2 fiction titles each year. Occasionally buys juvenile mss with or without illustrations.
Needs: Comics, historical, humor/satire, juvenile (animal, historical, picture book, sports), literary, regional, religious/inspirational, romance, and young adult (historical, sports). "Our books are short (3,500 words maximum). No fantasy, science fiction or occult." Recently published *Scrimshaw*, by Carolyn G. Orr.
How to Contact: Accepts unsolicited mss. Query first or submit complete ms. SASE always. Simultaneous and photocopied submissions OK. Accepts computer printout submissions. Reports in 2 weeks on queries; 2 weeks on mss. Publishes ms an average of 2 years after acceptance.
Terms: Pays in outright purchase of $50 and 5 author's copies. "We also do subsidy publishing of private editions. Negotiable arrangements." Book catalog $3. Free writer's guidelines with SASE.
Advice: "We want a good topic, beautifully written, in very few words; no full-length novel submissions. Regarding the author/editor relationship, the writer should trust editor; editor should trust designer. Read the publisher's stated purpose carefully."

MOTHER COURAGE PRESS (II), 1533 Illinois St., Racine WI 53405. (414)634-1047. Estab. 1981. Small feminist press. Publishes paperback originals. Books: perfect binding; sometimes illustrations; average print order: 5,000; first novel print order: 5,000. Plans 2 first novels this year. Averages 6 total titles, 2 fiction titles each year.
Needs: Adventure, contemporary, feminist, humor/satire, lesbian, romance (lesbian), science fiction, suspense/mystery. "Need strongly feminist or women oriented, or humanist; nothing written by men." Recently published *News*, by Heather Conrad (political, humanist feminist); and *Night Lights*, by Bonnie Arthur (lesbian romance).
How to Contact: Accepts unsolicited mss. Query first then submit outline/synopsis and 2 sample chapters. SAE. Agented fiction 10%. Reports in 6 weeks on queries; 3 months on mss. Simultaneous and photocopied submissions OK. Accepts computer printout submissions, including dot-matrix. Accepts electronic submissions via Macintosh.
Terms: Pays in royalties of 10% minimum; 15% maximum. Average advance: $250. Sends galleys to author. Writer's guidelines not available. Book catalog free on request.
Advice: "Write a good query letter, including, the plot of the novel, main characters, possible markets, etc."

THE NAIAD PRESS, INC. (I, II, IV), Box 10543, Tallahassee FL 32302. (904)539-9322. Imprint: Volute Books. Editorial Director: Barbara Grier. Estab. 1973. Books: 55 lb offset paper; Cameron belt; perfect binding; illustrations seldom; average print order: 12,000; first novel print order: 12,000. Published new writers within the last year. Publishes 19 total books/year.
Needs: Lesbian fiction, all genres. Recently published *The Finer Grain*, by Denise Ohio; *Heavy Gilt*, by Dolores Klaich; *We Walk the Back of the Tiger*, by Patricia A. Murphy.
How to Contact: Query first only. SASE for query, ms. No simultaneous submissions; photocopied submissions OK "but we prefer original mss." Reports in 1 week on queries, 2 months on mss. Publishes ms 6-8 months after acceptance.
Terms: Pays 15% royalties using a standard recovery contract. Occasionally pays 7½% royalties against cover price. "Seldom gives advances and has never seen a first novel worthy of one. Believes authors are investments in their own and the company's future—that the best author is the author that produces a book every 12-18 months forever and knows that there is a *home* for that book." Book catalog for legal-sized SASE.
Advice: "We publish lesbian fiction primarily and prefer honest work (i.e., positive, upbeat lesbian characters). Lesbian content must be accurate . . . a lot of earlier lesbian novels were less than honest. No breast beating or complaining." New imprint will publish reprints and original fiction. "Our fiction titles are becoming increasingly *genre* fiction, which we encourage. Original fiction in paperback is our main field, and its popularity increases. First novels are where the world is . . . really. Don't be a smart aleck. Send a simple letter, who, what, why, where, when, about yourself and a single page with at most a 2 paragraph precis of your book . . . not how good but WHAT IT IS ABOUT. Remember that no editor has time to waste, and the more accurate your self-description is, the more chance you have of getting a reader who will READ your book. Include telephone numbers, day and evening if possible. Get your homework done, be sure you are sending out the best book you can produce. Publishers are not sitting around waiting to help you write your book. Make it VERY easy for the editor to deal with you. The concise, smart, savvy, self-serving author wins the glass doughnut . . . every time."

‡THE NAUTICAL & AVIATION PUBLISHING CO. OF AMERICA INC. (II), Suite 314, 101 W. Read St., Baltimore MD 21203. (301)659-0220. Assistant Editor: Kevin Lavey. Fiction Editors: Kevin Lavey, Jan Snouck-Hurgronje. Estab. 1979. Small publisher interested in quality military history and literature. Publishes hardcover originals and reprints. Averages 10 total titles, 1-4 fiction titles each year. Sometimes comments on rejected mss.
Needs: Military/war. Looks for "novels with a strong military history orientation." Recently published *South to Java*, by Adm. William P. Mack and William Mack, Jr., (historical fiction); *The Captain*, by Hartog (reprint); *Greenmantle*, by John Buchan (reprint).
How to Contact: Accepts unsolicited mss. Query first or submit complete mss with cover letter, SASE necessary for return of mss. Agented fiction "miniscule." Reports on queries in 2-3 weeks, on mss in 3 weeks. Simultaneous and photocopied submissions OK. Accepts computer printout submissions, including dot-matrix.
Terms: Pays royalties of 15%. Advance negotiable. After acceptance publishes ms "as quickly as possible—next season." Book catalog free on request.
Advice: Publishing more fiction. Encourages first novelists. "We're interested in good writing—first novel or last novel. Keep it historical, put characters in a historical context. Professionalism counts. Know your subject. *Convince us.*"

‡**NEW DIRECTIONS (I, II)**, 80 Eighth Ave., New York NY 10011. (212)255-0230. Fiction Editor: Peter Glassgold. Midsize independent publisher with plans to expand. Publishes hardcover and paperback originals and reprints. Average print order: 1,000 hardback; 3,000 paperback. Sometimes critiques rejected mss.
Needs: "Mostly avant-garde; look at everything, including poetry." Recently published *The Hedgehog*, by H.D.; *A Tree Within*, by Octavio Paz.
How to Contact: Query first with outline/synopsis and sample chapters. Accepts unsolicited mss. SASE. Reports in 6-8 weeks on queries; 3-4 months on mss. Photocopied submissions OK. Accepts dotmatrix computer printout submissions.
Terms: Pays in royalties. Offers advance. Sometimes sends prepublication galleys to author. Publishes ms at least 1 year after acceptance, "depends on type of book."
Advice: "Try to get published in a literary magazine first to establish a writing reputation and for the experience."

NEW RIVERS PRESS, 1602 Selby Ave., St. Paul MN 55104. Editorial Director: C.W. Truesdale. Fiction Editor: C.W. Truesdale. Estab. 1968. Plans 4 fiction titles in 1989.
Needs: Contemporary, literary, experimental, translations. "No popular fantasy/romance. Nothing pious, polemical (unless very good other redeeming qualities). We are interested in only quality literature and always have been (though our concentration in the past has been poetry)."
How to Contact: Query. SASE for query, ms. Photocopied submissions OK. Reports in 2 months on queries, within 2 months of query approval on mss. "No multiple submissions tolerated."
Terms: Pays in 100 author's copies; also pays in royalties; no advance. Minnesota Voices Series pays authors $500 cash plus 15% royalties on list price for second and subsequent printings. Free book catalog.
Advice: "We are not really concerned with trends. We read for quality, which experience has taught can be very eclectic and can come sometimes from out of nowhere. We are interested in publishing short fiction (as well as poetry and translations) because it is and has been a great indigenous American form and is almost completely ignored by the commercial houses. Find a *real* subject, something that belongs to you and not what you think or surmise that you should be doing by current standards and fads."

NEW SEED PRESS (II, IV), Box 9488, Berkeley CA 94709. (415)540-7576. Editor: Helen Chetin. Estab. 1971. Publishes paperback originals in Spanish/English and Chinese/English, and English only. Books: 70 lb paper; typeset printing; saddle-stitched binding; b&w line art or halftone. Average print order: 2,000-3,000. Encourages new writers.
Needs: Feminist, ethnic, regional, juvenile (historical, contemporary), and young adult (historical, problem novels, easy-to-read teen). "No adult fiction that is not appropriate for children." Recently published *Green March Moons*, by Mary Tallmountain, a Koyukon Alaskan.
How to Contact: Query first. SASE always. Simultaneous and photocopied submissions OK. Accepts computer printout submissions. Reports in 2 weeks on queries, 1 month on mss.
Terms: Pays in royalties and by outright purchase. Sends galleys to author. Book catalog legal-sized SASE.
Advice: "As we are a feminist collective, we discourage writers from sending us 'apolitical animal-type stories' whose intent is to avoid rather than confront issues. We publish children's books free from stereotyping with content that is relative to today's happenings, stories with active female characters who take responsibility for their lives, stories that challenge assumptions about the inferiority of women and Third World peoples."

NEW VICTORIA PUBLISHERS, Box 27, Norwich VT 05055. (802)649-5297. Editor: Claudia Lamperti. Publishes trade paperback originals. Averages 3-4 titles/year.
Needs: Adventure, erotica, ethnic, fantasy, lesbian, historical, humor, feminist, mystery, romance, science fiction and western. Looking for "strong feminist characters, also strong plot and action. We will consider most anything if it is well written and appeals to a lesbian/feminist audience." Recently published *Lesbian Stages* and *Grey Magic*, by Sarah Dreher (mystery/plays); *Promise of the Rose Stone*, by Claudia McKay (fantasy); *All Out*, by Judith Alguire (sports romance novel).
How to Contact: Submit outline/synopsis and sample chapters. SASE. Reports in 2 weeks on queries; 1 month on mss. Photocopied submissions OK.
Terms: Pays royalties of 10%.
Advice: "We would particularly enjoy a humorous novel."

NIGHT TREE PRESS (II, IV), The Gorge Road, Rt. 46, R.D. 2, Box 140-G, Boonville NY 13309. (315)942-6001. Publisher: Gregg Fedchak. Estab. 1985. "One person full-time, another part-time." Paperback originals. Books: 60 lb paper; perfect bound softcover; regional photographs, line drawings, prints; average print order: 1,000 copies; first novel print order: 1,000 copies. Plans 1 first novel this year. Averages 1 total title/year.

Needs: Adventure, historical, humor/satire, literary, regional, short story collections. "Within each category, fiction *must* be strictly regional in nature; the far north country of New York State." Recently published *The Way To Heron Mountain*, by Ed Zahniser; *Lost River*, by Roger Sheffer.

How to Contact: Query first. SASE. Reports in 1-3 weeks. Simultaneous and photocopied submissions OK. Accepts computer printouts, including dot-matrix.

Terms: Pays in author's copies; 10% of total press run and/or individual author negotiations. Book catalog free on request.

Advice: "We are looking for first novels and short story collections by serious, professional authors who can bring the experience of our region to life. Night Tree wants to be their first break. We *prefer* first novelists and short story authors of exceptional ability to established ones. If the very small presses can't be a first-time fiction writer's home, then we have little reason to exist. Please understand the market that your publisher is trying to reach. There is intelligent marketing and stupid marketing. The former is easy to learn, and must be learned, because the latter always results in failure for the beginning fiction writer. In the future Night Tree will probably be publishing more fiction, because that's the niche commercial publishers have left open."

NORTH POINT PRESS (III), Box 6275, Albany CA 94706. (415)527-6260. Editor-in-Chief: Jack Shoemaker. Editor: Thomas Christensen. Estab. 1980. Publishes hardcover and paperback originals and reprints. Books: acid-free paper; sewn binding; illustrations; average print order: 5,000; first novel print order: 5,000. Averages 30 total titles, 6 fiction titles each year. Buys 50% agented fiction.

Needs: Contemporary, experimental, literary, short story collections, and translations. Especially needs serious and experimental. No "genre" fiction written for a "market." Recently published *Dusk and Other Stories*, by James Salter; *The Ideal Bakery*, by Donald Hall; and *On Nature*, edited by Daniel Halpern. Chances for fiction not good.

How to Contact: Query first with SASE. No unsolicited mss. Photocopied submissions OK. Reports in 1 month on queries; 6 months on mss. Publishes ms 8 months-3 years after acceptance.

Terms: Royalty payment varies; advance negotiable. Sends galleys to author. Must return advance if book is not completed or is unacceptable.

Advice: "Chances for acceptance of fiction here continue to diminish. We receive about 4,000 submissions a year, few appropriate for our publishing program. No block letter computer printouts. Type. We encourage first novels and published new writers last year."

‡THE OVERLOOK PRESS, 12 W. 21st St., New York NY 10010. (212)675-0585. Estab. 1972. Small-staffed, full-time operation. Publishes hardcover and paperback originals and reprints. Averages 30 total titles; 7 fiction titles each year. Occasionally critiques rejected mss.

Needs: Adventure, contemporary, ethnic, experimental, fantasy, historical, humor/satire, juvenile (fantasy, historical, sports, contemporary), literary, psychic/supernatural/occult, science fiction, translations. No romance or horror. Recently published *The Book of Rowing*, by D. C. Churbuck (sports); *Sweet Death*, by Claude Tasdat (novel); *The Universe, and Other Fictions*, by Paul West (short stories).

How to Contact: Query first or submit outline/synopsis and 3 sample chapters with SASE. Allow up to 6 months for reports on queries and mss. Simultaneous and photocopied submissions OK.

Terms: Vary.

OWL CREEK PRESS (III), 1620 N. 45th St., Seattle WA 98103. (206)633-5929. Also publishes *The Montana Review*. Editor: Rich Ives. Estab. 1979. Small independent literary publisher with plans to expand. Publishes hardcover and paperback originals. Books: photo offset printing; sewn or perfect binding; illustrations sometimes; average print order: 1,000; first novel print order: 1,000. Plans 3-4 short fiction collections/novels in next year or two. Averages 7 total titles, 0-3 fiction titles each year. Occasionally critiques rejected ms.

Needs: Contemporary, literary, short story collections, and translations. "Literary quality is our only criteria." No formula fiction.

How to Contact: Accepts unsolicited mss. "We recommend purchase of sample issue ($3 back issue, $5 current) of *The Montana Review* to determine our interests." Submit outline/synopsis and 1-3 sample chapters with SASE. Reports in 2 months. Simultaneous (if stated) and photocopied submissions OK. Accepts computer printout submissions (if clear copy). Publishes ms 3-18 months after acceptance.

Terms: Payment depends on grant/award money. Possible payment in royalties of 10% minimum, 20% maximum; author's copies, 10% of run minimum. Book catalog for SASE.

Advice: "We are expanding in all areas. The number of fiction titles in the next 2-3 years will depend on grants, sales and the quality of submissions. We ignore trends. Subject is irrelevant. Our *only* criterion is quality of the writing itself. Write to last—ignore fads and 'market advice'; good writers create their own markets."

‡PADRE PRODUCTIONS (II), Box 3113, Pismo Beach CA 93449. (805)473-1947. Imprints include Bear Flag Books, Channel X series, The Press of MacDonald and Reinecke. Editor/Publisher: Lachlan P. MacDonald. Fiction Editor: Mack Sullivan. Estab. 1974. Small independent publisher. Publishes hardcover and paperback originals and paperback reprints. Books: 60 lb book paper; offset printing; hardcover and perfect binding; average print order: 3,000; first novel print order: 3,000. Plans 1 novel per year. Averages 8-12 total titles, 1 fiction title each year. Buys 5% agented fiction. Occasionally critiques rejected ms.
Needs: Contemporary, literary, regional and short story collections. "Overstocked on juveniles." Accepts short stories for Channel X anthology. Juveniles must run 160 pages, for 8-14 year-old readers, both male and female protagonists. No romances, fantasy, sci-fi, or westerns. Recently published *Chrona*, by Aaron Carob (fantasy); and *Joel in Tananar*, by Robert M. Walton (juvenile fantasy).
How to Contact: Accepts unsolicited mss (include length and subject). Query first with SASE. Reports in 1 month. Simultaneous and photocopied submissions OK. Accepts computer printout submissions, prefers letter-quality. Publishes ms 1-4 years after acceptance.
Terms: Pays in royalties of 6% minimum; 12% maximum. Sends galleys to author. Advance is negotiable. No subsidy publishing; "we package and produce books for self-publishers and small publishers, however." Writer's guidelines and book catalog free for #10 SASE.
Advice: "California-based historical fiction welcome." Published less fiction this year. "We encourage writers of short-short stories."

PAPIER-MACHE PRESS (IV), 795 Via Manzana, Watsonville CA 95076. (408)726-2933. Editor/Publisher: Sandra Martz. Estab. 1984. One person operation on a part-time basis. Publishes anthologies and paperback originals. Books: 60-70 lb offset paper; perfect binding; photographs; average print order: 3,000-6,000 copies. Published new writers within the last year. Publishes 2-3 total titles/year; 2-3 fiction titles/year.
Needs: Contemporary, experimental, feminist, short story collections, women's. Recently published fiction by Mary Ann Ashley, Marisa Labozetta, Sandra Redding.
How to Contact: Query first. SASE. Reports in 4 weeks on queries; 3 months on mss. Simultaneous and photocopied submissions OK. Accepts computer printouts, including dot-matrix.
Terms: Honorarium—depending on circumstances. Pays 1-2 author's copies. Some potential for co-publishing with authors.
Advice: "Always query first to make sure you understand what the current needs are. Indicate with your manuscript whether or not you are open to revision suggestions. Always indicate on original submission if this is a simultaneous submission or a previously published work. We can handle either, but only if we know in advance."

PATH PRESS, INC. (II), Suite 1040, 53 W. Jackson, Chicago IL 60604. (312)663-0167. Editorial Director: Herman C. Gilbert. "Small independent publisher which specializes in books by, for and about Black Americans and Third World Peoples." Averages 8 total titles, 4 fiction titles each year. Occasionally critiques rejected ms.
Needs: Ethnic, historical, sports, and short story collections. Needs for novels include "black or minority-oriented novels of any genre, style or subject." Recently published *Brown Sky*, by David Covin (a novel of World War II); *Congo Crew*, by William Goodlett (a novel set in Africa during 1960-61); published new writers within the last year.
How to Contact: Accepts unsolicited mss. Query first or submit outline/synopsis and 5 sample chapters with SASE. Reports in 1 month on queries; 2 months on mss. Simultaneous and photocopied submissions OK. Accepts computer printout submissions.
Terms: Pays in royalties of 10% minimum; 15% maximum. No advance.
Advice: "Deal honestly with your subject matter and with your characters. Dig deeply into the motivations of your characters, regardless how painful it might be to you personally."

PAYCOCK PRESS (II), Box 30906, Bethesda MD 20814. (301)656-5146. Imprint: *Gargoyle Magazine*. Editor/Publisher: Richard Peabody, Jr. Estab. 1976. Small independent publisher with international distribution. Publishes paperback originals and reprints. Books: 55 lb natural paper; offset printing; perfect binding; illustrations sometimes; average print order: 1,000; first novel print order: 1,000. Number of titles: 1 in 1988. Encourages new writers. Occasionally comments on rejected mss. "Recently started producing audio tapes of music/spoken-word material."
Needs: Contemporary, literary, experimental, humor/satire and translations. "No tedious AWP resumé-conscious writing or NEA-funded minimalism. We'd be interested in a good first novel that deals with the musical changes of the past few years." Recently published *The Love Letter Hack*, by Michael Brondoli (contemporary/literary); *Natural History*, by George Myers, Jr. (poems and stories); and a fiction triptych, *Fiction/82*, *Fiction/84* and *Fiction 86*, "which features short stories and novel excerpts by 67 authors. Over 15,000 submissions were considered for those 3 volumes."

How to Contact: Accepts unsolicited mss. Query with SASE. No simultaneous submissions; photocopied submissions OK. Accepts computer printout submissions. Prefers letter-quality. Reports in 1 week on queries, 1 month on mss.
Terms: Pays in author's copies—10% of print run plus 50% of all sales "after/if we break even on book." Sends galleys to author. No advance.
Advice: "Keep trying. Many good writers simply quit. Many mediocre writers keep writing, eventually get published, and become better writers. If the big magazines won't publish you, try the small magazines, try the local newspaper. Always read your fiction aloud. If you think something is *silly*, no doubt we'd be embarrassed too. Write the kind of stories you'd like to read and can't seem to find. We are more concerned with *how* a novelist says what he/she says, than with *what* he/she says. We are more interested in *right now* than in books about the '50s, '60s, '70s, etc. We are publishing more in anthology format, and encourage first novelists."

PEACHTREE PUBLISHERS, LTD. (II), 494 Armour Circle NE, Atlanta GA 30324. (404)876-8761. Executive Editor: Margaret Quinlan. Estab. 1977. Small, independent publisher specializing in general interest publications, particularly of Southern origin. Publishes hardcover and paperback originals and hardcover reprints. Published new writers within the last year; plans 2 first novels this year. Averages 20 total titles, 4 fiction titles each year. Average first novel print order 10,000-15,000 copies.
Needs: Contemporary, literary, mainstream, regional, and short story collections. "We are primarily seeking Southern fiction: Southern themes, characters, and/or locales." No science fiction/fantasy, children's/young adult, horror, religious, romance, historical or mystery/suspense. Recently published *Any Cold Jordan*, by David Bottoms; *Angel Child*, by Mark Steadman; *After the Storm*, by Judith Richards; and *The Widow's Mite and Other Stories*, by Ferrol Sams (all mainstream).
How to Contact: Accepts unsolicited mss. Query, submit outline/synopsis and 50 pages, or submit complete ms with SASE. Reports in 1 month on queries; 3 months on mss. Simultaneous and photocopied submissions OK. Accepts computer printout submissions, prefers letter-quality.
Terms: Pays in royalties. Sends galleys to author. Free writer's guidelines and book catalog.
Advice: "We encourage original efforts in first novels."

PENTAGRAM PRESS (II), 212 N. 2nd St., Minneapolis MN 55401. (612)340-9821. Fiction Editor: Michael Tarachow. Estab. 1974. One-person letterpress shop; presswork, design and distribution are all handled in-house. Publishes hardcover and paperback originals. Books: various handmade and mouldmade papers; letterpress printing; sewn binding; illustrations; average print order: 123-242. "Fiction *is* seldom published; poetry and typography are the main emphasis." Averages 2-5 total titles, 0-1 fiction title each year.
Needs: Adventure, experimental, literary. "We're committed for next 3 years; writers should *always* query with SASE before sending actual mss." Recently published: *Ninja*, by John Jacob; *The Master*, by Tom Clark; and *A Man in Stir*, by Theodore Enslin.
How to Contact: Query first with SASE. Reports in 1-2 weeks on queries.
Terms: Payment arrangements variable. Book catalog free on request.

PERIVALE PRESS (I, II), 13830 Erwin St., Van Nuys CA 91401. (818)785-4671. President: Lawrence P. Spingarn. Estab. 1968. One-man midsize operation, part time. Books: 50-60 lb cover paper; offset printing; perfect paper bound binding; illustrations on cover only; average print order: 1,200; first novel print order: 500-1,000. Buys 5% agented fiction. Encourages new writers. Occasionally comments on rejected mss.
Needs: Contemporary, mainstream, literary, experimental, ethnic (any), erotica, regional (West), and translations. No adventure, mystery, spy, historical, war, gothic, romance, confession, gay/lesbian, psychic, religious, science fiction, horror or juvenile. Novellas up to 100 pages in typescript; no limitation on genres or styles. Publishes one per year. Recently published *Rice Powder*, by Sergio Galindo (novella of Mexico); *Mountainhouse*, by Pat McDermid; and *Fire & Water*, by Elisabeth Stevens (stories).
How to Contact: Does not accept unsolicited mss. Query (include publishing credits) with SASE. Simultaneous and photocopied submissions OK. Reports in 6 weeks on queries, 2 months on mss. Publishes ms 6-12 months after acceptance.
Terms: Pays 10-12½% in royalties. Sends galleys to author. No advance. Subsidy publishes 20% of total books. Author pays cost of printing and gets contract which stipulates that this amount, usually about $1,800, will be returned from sales within 2 years. Free book catalog and writer's guidelines with SAE and 1 first class stamp.
Advice: "Place stories first, even in literary magazines, before submitting ms to publisher. Novels should appeal to a college-educated audience. We foresee the publication of more serious novels of a less sensational kind in the next few years. On translated work, get clearance from original publisher before submitting. Writer should consider a subsidy plan whereby his investment is returned through sales; he

should also agree to making personal appearances (lectures, TV shows, etc.) if we offer contract." Publishing more original fiction in paperback "particularly novellas if subsidized by author under returnable arrangement. We want first novels but author must promote his/her work via readings, appearances, etc. to overcome problem of being unknown."

PERSEVERANCE PRESS (I, II, IV), Box 384, Menlo Park CA 94026. Editor: Meredith Phillips. Estab. 1979. One-person press publishing only mysteries. Publishes trade paperback originals. Books: 55 lb paper; offset litho printing; perfect binding; average print order: 2,000; first novel print order: 2,000. Plans 1 or 2 first novels this year. Averages 2-3 total titles each year, all fiction. Occasionally critiques rejected ms.
Needs: "Mysteries only, of the old-fashioned sort: whodunits, puzzlers, 'village cozies,' suspense thrillers, etc., with no gratuitous violence, excessive gore, or exploitive sex." No romance novels, historicals, horror, occult. Recently published *Murder Once Done*, by Mary Lou Bennett (first novel) and *Revolting Development*, by Lora Smith.
How to Contact: Accepts unsolicited complete mss "reluctantly." Submit outline/synopsis and 3 sample chapters with SASE. Reports in 1 month. Simultaneous (if noted) and photocopied submissions OK.
Terms: Pays in royalties of 10% (net receipts); 10 author's copies. Sends galleys to author. Writer's guidelines for SASE.
Advice: "We are delighted to find new novelists. We ask for revisions if necessary, and do as much substantive editorial work as required—working with the author till it's right. The quality of material is rising and we are publishing more. We regard the author/editor relationship as open, honest, cooperative, professional."

PERSPECTIVES PRESS (II, IV), Box 90318, Indianapolis IN 46290-0318. (317)872-3055. Publisher: Pat Johnston. Estab. 1981. Small operation expanding to become *the* publisher of fiction and nonfiction materials related to adoption and infertility. Publishes hardcover originals and paperback originals. Books: offset printing; smyth sewn cloth, perfect bound and saddle stitched binding; average print order: 3,000; first novel print order: 2,000. Published new writers within the last year; plans 1 first novel this year. Averages 2-6 total titles, 1 fiction title each year. Critiques or comments on rejected mss.
Needs: Submissions for adults or children but must have adoption or infertility as the theme. Recently published *The Miracle Seekers*, by Mary Martin Mason.
How to Contact: Query first. SASE. Reports in 2 weeks on queries; 1 month on mss. Simultaneous and photocopied submissions OK. Accepts computer printouts.
Terms: Pays in royalties of 5% minimum; 15% maximum. Advance negotiable. Sends galleys to author. Book catalog for #10 SAE and 45¢ postage.

PIKESTAFF PUBLICATIONS, INC. (I, II), Box 127, Normal IL 61761. (309)452-4831. Imprints include The Pikestaff Press: Pikestaff Fiction Chapbooks; *The Pikestaff Forum*, general literary magazine. Editorial Directors: Robert D. Sutherland and James R. Scrimgeour. Estab. 1977. Small independent publisher with plans to expand gradually. Publishes hardcover and paperback originals. Books: paper varies; offset printing; b&w illustrations; average print order: 500-2,000. "One of the purposes of the press is to encourage new talent." Occasionally comments on rejected mss.
Needs: Contemporary, literary, and experimental. "No slick formula writing written with an eye to the commercial mass market or pure entertainment that does not provide insights into the human condition. Not interested in heroic fantasy (dungeons & dragons, swords & sorcery); science-fiction of the space-opera variety; westerns; mysteries; love-romance; gothic adventure; or pornography (sexploitation)." Recently published fiction by Constance Pierce and Linnea Johnson.
How to Contact: Query or submit outline/synopsis and sample chapters (1-2 chapters). SASE always. "Anyone may inquire; affirmative responses may submit ms." No simultaneous or photocopied submissions. Accepts computer printout submissions, prefers letter-quality. Reports in 1 month on queries, 3 months on mss. Publishes ms within 1 year after acceptance.
Terms: Negotiates terms with author. Sends galleys to author.
Advice: "Have fictional characters we can really *care* about; we are tired of disembodied characters wandering about in their heads unable to relate to other people or the world about them. Avoid too much TELLING; let the reader participate by leaving something for him or her to do. Yet avoid vagueness, opaqueness, personal or 'private' symbolisms and allusions. Here we regard the relationship between the writer and editor as a cooperative relationship—we are colleagues in getting the book out. The writer has an obligation to do the best self-editing job of which he or she is capable; writers should not rely on editors to make their books presentable. Don't give up easily; understand your reasons for wanting the work published (personal satisfaction? money? fame? to 'prove' something? to 'be a novelist'? etc.) Ask yourself honestly, Should it be published? What can it provide for a reader that makes it worth part of

that reader's *lifetime* to read? Be prepared for shocks and disappointments; study contracts carefully and retain as many rights and as much control over the book's appearance as possible. Be prepared to learn how to be your own best promoter and publicist."

PINEAPPLE PRESS (II), P.O. Drawer 16008, Sarasota FL 34239. (813)952-1085. Executive Editor: June Cussen. Estab. 1982. Small independent trade publisher. Publishes hardcover and paperback originals and paperback reprints. Books: book quality paper; offset printing; smythe sewn hardcover perfect bound paperback binding; illustrations occasionally; average print order: 5,000; first novel print order: 2,000-5,000. Published new writers within the last year. Averages 8-10 total titles each year. Occasionally critiques rejected ms.
Needs: Contemporary, experimental, historical, environmental, regional, how-to and reference. Recently published *The Paper Boat*, by Dan Bentley-Baker (a first novel).
How to Contact: Prefers query, outline or one-page synopsis with sample chapters and SASE. Then if requested, submit complete ms with SASE. Reports in 6 weeks. Simultaneous and photocopied submissions OK. Accepts computer printout submissions, prefers letter-quality.
Terms: Pays in royalties of 7½% minimum; 15% maximum. Sends galleys to author. Advance is not usually offered. "Basically, it is an individual agreement with each author depending on the book." Book catalog sent if label and 45¢ stamp enclosed.
Advice: "We publish both Florida regional books and general trade fiction and nonfiction. Quality first novels will be published. We regard the author/editor relationship as a trusting relationship with communication open both ways. Learn all you can about the publishing process and about how to promote your book once it is published."

‡PIPPIN PRESS. 229 East 85th Street, Gracie Station Box 92, New York NY 10028. (212)288-4920. Publisher: Barbara Francis. Estab. 1987. "Small, independent children's book company, formed by the former editor-in-chief of Prentice Hall's juvenile division." Publishes hardcover originals. Books: 135-150 GSM offset-semi-matte (for picture books) paper; offset, sheet-fed printing; smythe-sewn binding; full color, black and white line illustrations and half tone, b&w and full color photographs. Averages 8-10 titles for first 2 years; will average 10-12. Sometimes comments on rejected mss.
Needs: Juvenile (5-9 yrs. including animal, easy-to-read, fantasy, humorous, spy/adventure). "I am interested in humorous novels for children of about 7-12 and in picture books with the focus on humor."
How to Contact: Accepts unsolicited mss. Query first or submit outline/synopsis and 2 sample chapters. SASE. Reports in 2-3 weeks on queries; 3 months on mss. Simultaneous submissions OK. Accepts computer printout submissions, no dot-matrix.
Terms: Pays royalties. Sends galleys to author. Publication time after ms is accepted "depends on the amount of revision required, type of illustration, etc."

POCAHONTAS PRESS, INC. (II, IV), Manuscript Memories, 2805 Wellesley Court, Blacksburg VA 24060. (703)951-0467. Editorial contact person: Mary C. Holliman. Estab. 1984. "One-person operation on part-time basis, with several part-time colleagues. Subjects not limited, but stories about real people are preferred. Main intended audience is youth—young adults, ages 10-18." Books 70 lb white offset paper; offset litho printing; perfect binding; illustrations; average print order 3,000-5,000. Averages 4 total titles, 2-3 fiction and 2 poetry titles each year. Usually critiques or comments on rejected mss.
Needs: Contemporary, ethnic, historical, sports, regional, translations, western. "I will treat a short story as a book, with illustrations and a translation into Spanish or French and also Chinese someday." No fantasy or horror. Recently published *From Lions to Lincoln*, by Fran Hartman; and *Mountain Summer*, by Bill Mashburn.
How to Contact: Accepts unsolicited mss. Query first. Reports in 1 month on queries; 1-2 months on manuscripts. Simultaneous, photocopied submissions OK. "If simultaneous, I would need to know up front what other options the author is considering." Accepts computer printout submissions, including dot-matrix.
Terms: Pays royalties of 10% maximum. $50 advance negotiable. Sends galleys to author. "I will to subsidy publish—but expect book and author to meet the same qualifications as a regular author, and will pay royalties on all copies sold as well as pay back the author's investment as books are sold."
Advice: "Get an unbiased, non-friend editor and follow his or her suggestions. Understand that the author *must* be involved in selling the book; if he/she is not willing to help sell, don't expect too much from publisher. Beginning writers seem to think that all they have to do is get the book into bookstores—and they have no conception at all as to how hard that is, and that that's only the *beginning* of selling the book. I'm really looking for long short stories about real people and places, to be published with copious illustrations."

‡PORCÉPIC BOOKS (II,IV), Press Porcépic Ltd., Subsidiaries include Softwords and Tesseract Books, Suite 235, 560 Johnson St., Victoria, B.C. V8W 3C6 Canada. (604)381-5502. Managing Editor: Gerry Truscott. Estab. 1971. "Small, literary press; new SF Imprint—Tesseract Books; Canadian authors only." Publishes hardcover and paperback originals. Books: 60 lb paper; offset printing; perfect binding; photographs and color illustrations in children's books; average print order: 2,000. Published new writers within the past year. Plans 1 first novel this year. Averages 4 total titles, 3 fiction titles each year. Sometimes comments rejected mss.
Needs: Contemporary, experimental, fantasy, feminist, literary, mainstream, science fiction, short story collections, translations. "Literary science fiction; speculative fiction; experimental fiction. No romance." Recently published *Fires of the Kindred*, by Robin Skelton (speculative fiction); *Tesseracts2*, edited by Phyllis Gotlieb and Douglas Barbour (literary science fiction collection); *Flights of Magic*, by John Steffler (Shawn Steffler, illustrator) (juvenile 5-8).
How to Contact: Accepts unsolicited mss. Query first or submit outline/synopsis and 3 chapters. "We prefer a query first." SASE for return of mss. Agented fiction 20%. Reports on queries in 2 weeks; on mss in 14 weeks. Simultaneous and photocopied submissions OK. Accepts computer printout submissions, including dot-matrix (prefers letter quality).
Terms: Pays royalties of 10%. Average advance: $300. Sends galleys to author. Publishes mss 10 months after acceptance. "We do *not* subsidy publish with authors. We receive a Canada Council Grant for publishing works by Canadian authors." Book catalog free on request.
Advice: "We are publishing more fiction and less poetry and nonfiction. This is mainly because we are currently launching our SF line; Tesseract Books. Most of our books are trade paperbacks. A summary of the whole work is always appreciated. We also find the following helpful: an outline of the characteristics of the book which make it especially promotable; any relevant marketing information regarding the manuscript and the author's ability to promote it."

PORCUPINE'S QUILL, INC. (III), 68 Main St., Erin, Ontario, N0B 1T0 Canada. (519)833-9158. Contact: Ann Reatherford. Estab. 1974. Small press. Publishes hardcover and paperback originals and occasional paperback reprints. Books: 70 lb Zephyr antique paper; offset on Heidelberg Kord 64 printing; paper, occasional hand hardcover binding; illustrations; average print order: 750; first novel print order: 750. Averages 7 total titles, 4 fiction titles each year.
Needs: Contemporary, fantasy, historical, literary, and young adult/teen (historical). Recently published *Flying a Red Kite*, by Hugh Hood.
How to Contact: Accepts unsolicited mss, but prefers query first. Reports in 2 weeks. Simultaneous and photocopied submissions OK. Accepts computer printout submissions.
Terms: Pays in royalties of 5% minimum; 10% maximum; 10 author's copies. Sends proofs to author. Free book catalog.
Advice: "We are publishing more fiction and occasional art books, and published new writers last year."

PRAIRIE JOURNAL PRESS (II, IV), Prairie Journal Trust, Box 997, Station G, Calgory, Alberta T3A 3G2 Canada. Editorial contact person: A. Burke. Estab. 1983. Small-press non-commercial literary publisher. Publishes paperback originals. Books: bond paper; offset printing; stapled binding; b&w line drawings. Average 2 total titles or anthologies/year. Occasionally critiques or comments on rejected ms if requested.
Needs: Experimental. No romance, horror, pulp, erotica, magazine type, children's, adventure, formula, "western." Recently published *Prairie Journal Fiction*, *Prairie Journal Fiction II* (anthologies of short stories) and *Solstice*, (short fiction on the theme of aging).
How to Contact: Accepts unsolicited mss. Query first and send IRCs and $3 for sample copy, then submit 1 or 2 stories. Submit outline/synopsis and 1-2 stories with SASE (IRC). Reports in 2 weeks. Photocopied submissions OK. Accepts computer printout submissions, no dot-matrix.
Terms: Pays 1 author's copy; honorarium depends on grant/award. Book catalog free on request to institutions; SAE with IRC for individuals. "No U.S. stamps!"
Advice: "We wish we had the means to promote more new writers."

THE PRAIRIE PUBLISHING COMPANY, Box 2997, Station C, Winnipeg, Manitoba R3C 4B5 Canada. (204)885-6496. Publisher: Ralph Watkins. Estab. 1969. Buys juvenile mss with illustrations. Books: 60 lb high-bulk paper; offset printing; perfect binding; line-drawings illustrations; average print order: 2,000; first novel print order: 2,000.
How to Contact: Query with SASE or SAE, IRC. No simultaneous submissions; photocopied submissions OK. Reports in 1 month on queries, 6 weeks on mss. Publishes ms 4-6 months after acceptance.
Terms: Pays 10% in royalties. No advance. Free book catalog.
Advice: "We work on a manuscript with the intensity of a Max Perkins of Charles Scribner's Sons of

New York. A clean, well-prepared manuscript can go a long way toward making an editor's job easier. On the other hand, the author should not attempt to anticipate the format of the book, which is a decision for the publisher to make. In order to succeed in today's market, the story must be tight, well written and to the point. Do not be discouraged by rejections."

PRESS GANG PUBLISHERS (II, IV), 603 Powell St., Vancouver, British Columbia V6A 1H2 Canada. (604)253-2537. Estab. 1974. Feminist press, 2 full-time staff, 1 half-time staff. Publishes paperback originals and reprints. Books: paperback paper; offset printing; perfect binding; average print order: 2,000; first novel print order: 1,500. Plans 3 first novels this year. Sometimes critiques rejected mss.
Needs: Contemporary, erotica, ethnic (native women especially), feminist, humor/satire, lesbian, literary, regional (priority), science fiction, short story collections, suspense/mystery. Looking for "feminist, mystery/suspense, short stories." No children's/young adult/teen. Recently published *Not Vanishing* (poetry/prose) by Native American activist and writer Chrystos.
How to Contact: Accepts unsolicited mss. Query first. SASE (IRC). Reports in 2 weeks on queries; 4-6 weeks on mss. Simultaneous and photocopied submissions OK. Accepts computer printout submissions, including dot-matrix. Accepts AT compatible discs.
Terms: Pays 10% royalties. Sends galleys to author. Book catalog free on request.

‡THE PRESS OF MACDONALD AND RENECKE (II,III), Padre Productions, Box 3113, Pismo Beach CA 93449. (805)473-1947. Publisher: Lachlan P. MacDonald. Fiction Editor: Mack Sullivan. Estab. 1974. "Literary imprint of a small independent press." Publishes hardcover and paperback originals. Books: book paper; offset printing; Smyth casebound and perfect binding; illustrations; average print order: 3,000-5,000; first novel print order: 3,500. Publishes fiction by a previously unpublished writer "every 2-3 years." Plans 1 first novel this year. Averages 6 total titles, 1-2 fiction titles each year. Sometimes comments on rejected mss.
Needs: Fantasy, historical, humor/satire, literary, mainstream, short story collections. Currently overstocked. No mystery, suspense, western, religious, military, adventure, romance categories. Recently published *Chrona*, by Aaron Conob (fantasy); *Joel in Tananar*, by Robert M. Walton (juvenile).
How to Contact: Accepts unsolicited mss. Submit outline/synopsis and sample chapters (1-2). SASE. Agented fiction 5%. Reports on queries in 2 weeks; on mss in 2 months. Simultaneous and photocopied submissions OK.
Terms: Pays in royalties. Sends galleys to author. "Unfortunately, it may be years" before publication after acceptance. Writer's guidelines for SASE. Book catalog for 6x9 SAE.
Advice: Publishing less fiction than in the past. "Buyers prefer big-list promotional titles/videos! Demonstrate a following by documenting publication in literary magazines, general magazines or anthologies."

‡PRIMAL PUBLISHING (I,II), 107 Brighton Ave., Allston MA 02134. (617)389-5193. Editor: Michael McInnis. Estab. 1986. One-person operation on part-time basis. Publishes paperback originals. Books: standard 20 lb paper; offset printing; perfect bound; some illustrations; average print order 200-2,000; first novel print order: 200-2,000. Averages 1 total title, 1 fiction title each year.
Needs: Contemporary, erotica, experimental, gay, lesbian, literary, science fiction. "Have already chosen manuscripts for the next few years." No "cliché romance, soap opera lifestyles or new age spiritualism."
How to Contact: Accepts unsolicited mss. Submit complete ms with cover letter. SASE. Reports in 1-3 months. Simultaneous submissions OK. Accepts computer printout submissions, including dot-matrix.
Terms: Pays in author's copies (25% of print run). Sends galleys to author. Publishes ms 1 year after acceptance. "Author is given option to buy back an additional 25% of print run at cost."
Advice: "Keep it tight. It's gotta hit in the gut, but keep the brain active as well. Violence and sex are okay. Definitely look for things with punk sensibilities."

‡PROPER TALES PRESS (II), Box 789, Station F, Toronto, Ontario M4Y 2N7 Canada. Subsidiaries include Cops Going for Doughnuts Editions; Proper Tales Blind Date. Editor: Stuart Ross. Estab. 1979. "One-masochist operation in all-too-rare spare time." Books: 20 lb bond or 70 lb bond/plainfield paper; photocopy, offset printing; perfect, saddlestitched binding; b&w line drawings. Published new writers within the past year. Plans 2 or fewer first novels this year. Averages 2-7 total titles, 3 fiction titles each

> **❝ A novelist must preserve a childlike belief in the importance of things which common sense considers of no great importance. ❞**
>
> **—W. Somerset Maugham**

year. Sometimes comments on rejected mss.

Needs: Experimental, faction, feminist, gay, horror, lesbian, literary, science fiction, short story collections, suspense/mystery. "I'm open to appropriate submissions—surrealism, avant-garde, hardboiled nun stories, demento-primitivo. No illiterate fiction; 'mainstream'; religious; pompous shit."

How to Contact: Accepts unsolicited mss. Submit complete ms with cover letter (no longer than 60 pages). SASE necessary. Reports on queries in 1-25 weeks; on mss in 1-100 weeks. Simultaneous and photocopied submissions OK. Accepts computer printout submissions, including dot-matrix (if the ribbon's dark).

Terms: Pays in 10% of print run. Sends galleys to author. Publishes 1-100 weeks after acceptance. Writer's guidelines and book catalog for 6x9 SASE and 2 first class stamps.

Advice: "Read *Lucky Daryl*, by James Tate and Bill Knott."

‡PULP PRESS BOOK PUBLISHERS (I), Subsidiary of Arsenal Pulp Press Ltd. Imprints include Tillacum Library, Arsenal Editions, 1150 Homer St. Vancouver, B.C. V6B 2X6 Canada. (604)687-4233. Manager: Brian Lam. Fiction Editor: Linda Field. Estab. 1972. Small literary publisher. Publishes paperback originals. Books: 80 lb paper; offset printing; perfect binding; average print order: 1,000; first novel print order: 750. Published new writers within the past year. Plans 1 first novel this year. Averages 7 total titles, 2-3 fiction titles each year. Sometimes comments on rejected mss.

Needs: Contemporary, feminist, literary, short story collections. "We are looking for well-written literary material, largely regardless of genre. No romance, westerns, thrillers." Recently published *Torque*, by J. Michael Yates (short fiction); *Prelude*, by D.M. Fraser (short fiction); *Starting Small*, by James Dunn (novel).

How to Contact: Accepts unsolicited mss. Query first. Agented fiction 5%. Reports on queries in 2 weeks; on mss in 2 months. Photocopied submissions OK. Accepts computer printout submissions, including dot-matrix.

Terms: Pays royalties of 15% of net. Average advance: $100. Sends galleys to author. Publishes ms 6 months-1 year after acceptance. Occasionally publishes books on a subsidy basis—0-10%. Book catalog for 9x11½ SAE and 2 IRCs.

Advice: "We are always on the lookout for good material, regardless of publishing experience."

‡Q.E.D. PRESS OF ANN ARBOR, INC. (I), Box 4312, Ann Arbor MI 48106. (313)994-0371. Imprint: ProForma Books. Fiction Editor: Dan Fox. Estab. 1985. Publishes hardcover and paperback originals. Books: cloth binding; average print order: 1,000; first novel print order: 500. Published new writers within the last year. Plans 2 first novels this year. Publishes 8 titles each year, 2 fiction titles. Sometimes critiques rejected mss.

Needs: Literary. Recently published *Half Dozen Dutch*, by Tom Broos; *Found Time: An Anti-Novel*, by Mike Gallatin.

How to Contact: Does not accept or return unsolicited mss. Query first or submit outline/synopsis with 1 sample chapter. SASE. Agented fiction 0%. Reports on queries in 1 month; on mss in 3 months. Simultaneous and photocopied submissions OK. Accepts dot-matrix computer printouts.

Terms: Pays in royalties of 6-12% and approx. 25 author's copies. Sends galleys to author. Publishes ms 6 months after acceptance. Subsidy publishes 15% of mss. Writer's guidelines and book catalog for #10 SAE and 1 first class stamp.

‡QUARRY PRESS (I,II), Box 1061, Kingston, Ontario, K7L 4Y5 Canada. (613)548-8429. Managing Editor: Linda Bussière. Estab. 1965. Small independent publisher with plans to expand. Publishes paperback originals. Books: Rolland tint paper; offset printing; perfect binding; illustrations; average print order: 1,200; first novel print order 1,200. Published new writers within the past year. Plans 1 first novel this year. Averages 12 total titles, 2-4 fiction titles each year. Sometimes comments on rejected mss.

Needs: Experimental, feminist, historical, literary, short story collections. Recently published *Mona's Dance*, by Ann Diamond; *Hockey Night in Canada*, by Diane Schoemperlen; *Open Windows: Canadian Short-Short Stories*.

How to Contact: Accepts unsolicited mss. Query first. SASE for query and ms. No agented fiction. Reports in 4 months. Simultaneous and photocopied submissions OK. Accepts computer printout submissions, including dot-matrix.

Terms: Pays royalties of 7% minimum; 10% maximum. Advance: negotiable. Provides 5-10 author's copies. Sends galleys to author. Publishes ms 6-8 months after acceptance. Book catalog free on request.

Advice: Publishing more fiction than in the past. Encourages first novelists.

RANGER ASSOCIATES, INC. (II), 600 Washington Court, Guilderland NY 12084. (518)456-6401. Director of Publications: Sharon M. Lane. Estab. 1979. Small press with plans to expand; presently considers approximately 50 submissions per year, selecting 4-5 for publication. Publishes hardcover and paperback originals and reprints. Books: 50 lb paper; offset printing; perfect binding; illustrations; average print order: 5,000; first novel print order: 3,000. Plans 3-4 first novels this year. Averages 5 total titles, 1 fiction title each year. Usually critiques rejected ms.

Needs: Adventure, historical and war. Accepts short stories from freelancers. Novel needs include military/historical. No erotica. Recently published *Goodness Gracious*, by Harry Levitt (juvenile); *The Pestilence Plot*, by Betty Patterson (adventure/terrorism); and *A Special Breed of Man*, by Ed Edell (Vietnam war).

How to Contact: Query with SASE. Reports in 6 weeks on queries; 2-3 months on mss. Simultaneous and photocopied submissions OK. Accepts computer printout submissions, prefers letter-quality. Disk submissions OK with IBM or MacIntosh. Prefers hard copy with disk submissions.

Terms: Individual arrangements with authors. Sends galleys to author. Pays in royalties of 5% minimum, 7% maximum; 25 author's copies; honorarium. Subsidy arrangement: copyright to author; author agrees to market book; author receives proportion of books related to subsidy, e.g., if author subsidizes at 50% of manufacturing costs, author receives 50% of books. Book catalog for SASE.

Advice: "Rewrite, review, rewrite. Let someone you dislike read your manuscript; rewrite once more before submitting. Query letters reflect on the author—correct grammar, neatness and briefness count. Will publish first novels if good enough. Novelist must be willing to promote his/her own work in every way possible. Small presses cannot afford to publish without *very* active author promotions."

‡READ 'N RUN BOOKS (I), Subsidiary of Crumb Elbow Publishing, Box 294, Rhododendron OR 97049. (503)622-4798. Imprints are Elbow Books, Research Centrex. Publisher: Michael P. Jones. Estab. 1978. Small independent publisher with three staff. Publishes hardcover and paperback originals and reprints. Books: special order paper; offset printing; "usually a lot" of illustrations; average print order: varies. Published new writers within the last year. Plans 1 first novel this year. Averages 10 titles, 2 fiction titles each year. Sometimes comments on rejected ms; $75 charge for critiques depending upon length. May be less or more.

Needs: Adventure, contemporary, ethnic, experimental, fantasy, feminist, historical, horror, humor/satire, juvenile (animal, easy-to-read, fantasy, historical, sports, spy/adventure, contemporary), literary, mainstream, military/war, preschool/picture book, psychic/supernatural/occult, regional, religious/inspirational, romance (contemporary, historical), science fiction, short story collections, spiritual, suspense/mystery, translations, western, young adult/teen (easy-to-read, fantasy/science fiction, historical, problem novels, romance, sports, spy/adventure). Looking for fiction on "historical and wildlife" subjects. "Also, some creative short stories would be nice to see for a change. No pornography."

How to Contact: Accepts unsolicited ms. Query first. Submit outline/synopsis and complete ms with cover letter. SASE. Agented fiction 1%. Reports in 2 weeks on queries; 1-2 months on mss. Simultaneous and photocopied submissions OK. Accepts computer printout submissions, including dot-matrix.

Terms: Provides 5 + author's copies (negotiated). Sends galleys to author. Publishes ms 6-12 months after acceptance. Subsidy publishes two books or more/year. Terms vary from book to book. Writer's guidelines for 45¢ postage. Book catalog for SASE or IRC and $1.25 postage.

Advice: Publishing "more hardcover fiction books based on real-life events. They are in demand by libraries. Submit everything you have—even artwork. Also, if you have ideas for layout, provide those also. If you have an illustrator that you're working with, be sure to get them in touch with us."

‡RED ALDER BOOKS (IV), Imprint: Pan-Erotic Review, Box 2992, Santa Cruz CA 95063. (408)426-7082. Editorial Contact Person: David Steinberg, owner. Estab. 1974. Small, independent publisher. Publishes hardcover and paperback originals. Books: offset printing, case/perfect binding; some illustrations; average print order: 5,000. Published new writers within the past year. Averages 1 total title, 1 fiction title each year. Sometimes comments on rejected mss.

Needs: "Quality-conscious, provocative erotica only." Erotica, feminist, lesbian, literary, short story collections. "Short stories only." No pornography, cliché sexual stories." Recently published *Erotic by Nature*, by Steinberg, editor (collection of erotic stories, poems, photographs).

How to Contact: Accepts and returns unsolicited mss. Query first. SASE for query and ms. Reports on queries in 2 weeks; on mss in 4-6 weeks. Simultaneous and photocopied submissions OK. Accepts computer printout submissions, including dot-matrix.

Terms: Pays royalties of 8% minimum. Sends galleys to author.

Advice: Publishing more fiction than in the past.

‡RED DEER COLLEGE PRESS (I,IV), Box 5005, Red Deer, Alberta T4N 5H5 Canada. (403)342-3321. Managing Editor: Dennis Johnson. Estab. 1975. Publishes hardcover and paperback originals. Books: offset paper; offset printing; hardcover/perfect binding; average print order: 1,000-4,000; first novel print order 1,500. Plans 1 first novel this year. Averages 4-8 total titles, 1 fiction title each year. Sometimes comments on rejected mss.

Needs: Contemporary, experimental, literary, short story collections. No romance, sci-fi, gay, feminist.

How to Contact: Does not accept unsolicited mss. Query first or submit outline/synopsis and 2 sample chapters. SASE for query and for ms. Agented fiction 10%. Reports in 1 month on queries; in 3 months on mss. Simultaneous and photocopied submissions OK. Accepts computer printout submissions, including dot-matrix.

Terms: Pays royalties of 8% minimum; 10% maximum. Advance is negotiable. Sends galleys to author. Publishes ms 1 year after acceptance. Book catalog for 8½x11 SASE and IRC.

Advice: Expanding output of press. Study market and publishers' needs. Offer concrete ideas for promoting a title. Be willing to rewrite. Final manuscripts must be submitted on Mac disk in MS Word 3.1. Absolutely *no* unsolicited mss. Query first. Canadian authors only."

‡RE/SEARCH PUBLISHING (I,II), 20 Romolo, Suite B, San Francisco CA 94133. (415)362-1465. Editors: V. Vale and A. Juno. Estab. 1980. Two-person operation, small independent publisher. Publishes paperback originals of non-fiction and paperback reprint classics. Books: 50 lb paper; sewn & stitched binding; photos & other illustrations; average print order: 5,000-7,000. Averages 3-5 total titles per year. Occasionally critiques or comments on rejected ms.

Needs: Experimental, science fiction or *roman noir*. No realism.

How to Contact: Accepts unsolicited mss. Query first. SASE. Reports in 1 month on queries; 1 month on mss. Simultaneous and photocopied submissions OK. Accepts computer printout submissions, including dot-matrix.

Terms: Pays 8% of press run. Book catalog on request.

ROWAN TREE PRESS (II), 124 Chestnut St., Boston MA 02108. (617)523-7627. Editor: Nadya Aisenberg. Fiction Editors: Nadya Aisenberg, Jean Pedrick, Cornelia Veenendaal. Estab. 1980. Small general trade publishing house. Publishes paperback originals and reprints. Books: acid-free, 50-60 lb vellum paper; offset print; perfect binding; illustrations; average print order: 1,500-2,000; first novel print order: 1,500-2,000. Publishes 3 total titles each year; 1 fiction title. Sometimes critiques rejected ms.

Needs: Contemporary, literary, biography, travel, memoir, short story collections and suspense/mystery. No political or religious fiction.

How to Contact: Accepts unsolicited mss. Submit complete ms with cover letter. SASE. 10% of fiction is agented. Reports in 2 week on queries; 2 months on mss. Accepts computer printout submissions, no dot-matrix.

Terms: Pays royalties of 7½% and 10 author's copies. Sends pre-publication galleys to author. Book catalog free on request.

S.O.C.O. PUBLICATIONS, RD #1, Box 71, Ward Road, Mohawk NY 13407. (315)866-7445. Editor: Carol Ann Vercz. Estab. 1975. Publishes paperback originals. Books: 60 lb good grade of book paper; sheet fed printing; perfect binding; average print order: 1,000; first novel print order: 1,000. Published new writers within the last year. Plans 1-4 first novels this year. Averages 1-4 total titles/year. Sometimes critiques rejected ms; charges fee of $50/ms.

Needs: Adventure, fantasy, historical, humor/satire, mainstream, romance (contemporary, historical), science fiction, suspense/mystery, young adult/teen (fantasy/science fiction, historical, romance, sports, spy/adventure).

How to Contact: Accepts unsolicited mss. Submit.

Terms: Pays royalties on retail price. Sends galleys to author. Book catalog free on request.

Advice: "Keep writing; stick with your project and see it through."

ST. JOHN'S PUBLISHING, INC. (II), 6824 Oaklawn Ave., Edina MN 55435. (612)920-9044. Editor-in-Chief: Lee Francis. Estab. 1986. Small independent publisher, growth oriented. Publishes paperback originals and reprints. Books: printing subcontracted; average print order: 5,000; first novel print order: 5,000. Published new writers within the last year. Plans 1 first novel this year. Average less than 6 fiction titles/year. Rarely critiques rejected ms.

Needs: Literary, religious/inspirational, short story collections, suspense/mystery, translations. No romance. Recently published *The Krasnodar Affair: A Story of Crisis, World Peace, and Disarmament*, by Donald E. Montgomery (techno-thriller with a universal message/purpose).

How to Contact: Does not accept unsolicited mss. Query first with synopsis. SASE (IRC). Reports in 3 weeks on queries; 6 weeks on mss. Simultaneous and photocopied submissions OK. Accepts computer printout submissions, including dot-matrix.

Terms: Pays standard royalties; no advance. Sends galleys to author. Book catalog for 9x12 SAE with 2 first class stamps or IRCs.

Advice: "Our ratio of nonfiction to fiction is 2:1, as of our first year in publication. Strive for writing clarity, superior structure, and subject timeliness. Avoid offensive language, trivial plots, and limited appeal efforts. First have a few friends read the ms for readiness."

SAMISDAT (II), Box 129, Richford VT 05476. Imprint: *Samisdat Magazine*. Editor/Publisher: Merritt Clifton. Estab. 1973. Publishes paperback originals. Books: standard bond paper; offset printing; saddle-stitch or square back binding; illustrations sometimes; average print order: 300-500. Encourages new writers. "Over 60% of our titles are first books—about 1 first novel per year." Comments on rejected mss.
Needs: Literary, feminist, gay, lesbian, and regional. Recently published *An American Love Story*, by Robert Swisher (novel).
How to Contact: Query or submit complete ms. SASE always. Reports in 1 week on queries; time varies on mss.
Terms: No advance. Free book catalog with SASE. "Our author payments for books are a paradox: At this writing, we've published over 200 titles over the past 15 years, about 85% of which have earned the authors a profit. On the other hand, we've relatively seldom issued royalty checks—maybe 20 or 30 in all this time, and all for small amounts. We're also paradoxical in our modus operandi: Authors cover our cash expenses (this comes to about a third of the total publishing cost—we're supplying equipment and labor) in exchange for half of the press run, but we make no money from authors, and if we don't promote a book successfully, we still lose." Publishes ms from 2-6 months after acceptance.
Advice: "We do not wish to see *any* book-length ms submissions from anyone who has not already either published in our quarterly magazine, *Samisdat*, or at least subscribed for about a year to find out who we are and what we're doing. We are not a 'market' engaged in handling books as commodities and are equipped to read only about one novel submission per month over and above our magazine submission load. Submissions are getting much slicker, with a lot less guts to them. This is precisely the opposite of what we're after. Read the magazine. Submit stories or poems or chapters to it. When familiar with us, and our subscribers, query about an appropriate book ms. We don't publish books except as special issues of the magazine, and blind submissions stand absolutely no chance of acceptance at all. Go deep. Involve your characters with the outside world, as well as with each other. Use the most compact structure possible, bearing in mind that fiction is essentially drama without a stage."

SANDPIPER PRESS (IV), Box 286, Brookings OR 97415. (503)469-5588. Owner: Marilyn Reed Riddle. Estab. 1979. One person operation specializing in low-cost large-print 18 pt. books. Publishes paperback originals. Books: 70 lb paper; saddle stitch binding, 64 page maximum; leatherette cover binding; b&w sketches or photos; average print order 1,000-1,500; no novels. Averages 1 title every 2 years. Occasionally critiques or comments on rejected mss.
Needs: Rod Serling type short-short stories. Short story collections. Also nonfiction/true stories of rising above handicaps (no bragging or preachy or Pollyanna); but helpful and unusual ways of earning a living for handicapped people, etc. Going beyond "What I can't do now, to what I *can* do now. Will publish anthology in 1989."
How to Contact: Does not accept unsolicited mss. Query first or submit outline/synopsis. SASE. Reports in 1 month on queries; 1 month on mss. Simultaneous and photocopied submissions OK. Accepts computer printout submissions, including dot-matrix.
Terms: Pays 2 author's copies and $10. Publisher buys story and owns copyright. Author may buy any number of copies at 40% discount and postage. Book catalog for #10 SAE and 1 first class stamp.
Advice: "Watch *Twilight Zone* on TV. *Not* scary stories but irony, leading us up the garden path and over the cliff. Morality-play type with surprise ending. The good guys should win. Most interested in ways to earn a living with serious physical handicap. This one nearly full. Areas not yet covered include blind, deaf, AIDS. All must be true first-person accounts."

SCOJTIA PUBLISHING COMPANY, INC. (II), 6457 Wilcox Station, Box 38002, Los Angeles CA 90038. Imprint: The Lion. Managing Editor: Patrique Quintahlen. Estab. 1986. "Small independent publisher plans to expand, ten-member operation on full-time basis." Publishes hardcover and paperback originals and reprints. Books: 50-60 lb weight paper; perfect bound; artists on staff for illustrations; average print order: 1,000-15,000; first novel print order: 1,000. Published new writers within the last year. Averages 5 total titles/year; 2 fiction titles/year. Offers editorial/publishing services for a fee. Query for details.
Needs: Adventure, contemporary, ethnic, experimental, fantasy, historical, humor/satire, juvenile (animal, easy-to-read, fantasy, historical, sports, spy/adventure, contemporary), literary, mainstream, preschool/picture book, romance (contemporary, historical), science fiction, suspense/mystery, western, young adult/teen (easy-to-read, fantasy/science fiction, historical, problem novels, romance, sports, spy/adventure). "Looking for contemporary romance novels, science fiction." No horror, gore, erotica, gay, occult, novels. No sexism, racism, or pornography.
How to Contact: Accepts unsolicited mss. Query first. Submit outline/synopsis with 3 sample chap-

ters. SASE (IRC). 50% of fiction is agented. Reports in 4 months on queries; in 6 months on mss. Photo-copied submissions OK. Accepts computer printout submissions, no dot-matrix. Accepts disk submissions from Macintosh Plus.

Terms: Pays royalties of 7-10%; average advance $1,000-$3,000; advance is negotiable; advance is more for agented ms; 50 author's copies. Sends galleys to author. Subsidy publishes 5% of books each year. Subsidy publishes books of poetry only, 50-150 pages. Subjects: love, psychology, philosophy, new male/female relationships, family. Book catalog for $1.

Advice: "To save time and expense, it is recommended that authors learn as much as possible about not simply their writing craft, but also the very art of publishing. I recommend studying self publishing at some point after the author has completed several works, learning the actual book making process, book design, marketing, sales, distribution, and publishing and the money saving typesetting advantages of today's word processing and computer options. This advice is to speed the process of 'submission-to-publication' process between author and small press operations. This is valuable in respect to new un-published authors, but the classical submissions methods of ms to major publishers still remains an im-portant option to the author with a book with commercial value, for literary works of the highest quality Small presses are the proven markets for success to the literary author."

SCORE PUBLICATIONS, 491 Mandana Blvd., #3, Oakland CA 94610. (415)268-9284. Publishers: Laurie Schneider and Crag Hill. Estab. 1983. "Small press/3 people, part-time." Publishes chapbooks. Books: offset printing; staple binding; illustrations; average print order: 150 +. Averages 0-1 fiction ti-tles each year. Occasionally critiques or comments on rejected ms.

Needs: Experimental.

How to Contact: Accepts unsolicited mss. Query first with a short (1-2 page) sample from ms. We publish only non-traditional forms, writers *must* query." Reports in 3 weeks on queries; 6 weeks on mss. Simultaneous and photocopied submissions OK. Accepts computer printout submissions, no dot-ma-trix.

Terms: Pays in author's copies. Sends galleys to author if requested. Book catalog and writer's guide-lines free for #10 SASE and 1 first class stamp.

Advice: "*Score* publishes only experimental fiction. That is, stories or texts that no traditional press or magazine would want. Our focus is on non-traditional poetry. We publish a magazine three times a year, several pamphlets, and an occasional chapbook. We cannot work with full-length manuscripts."

SEA FOG PRESS, INC. (II), Box 210056, San Francisco CA 94121-0056. (415)221-8527. President: Rose Evans. Estab. 1984. Small one-person press. Publishes hardcover and paperback originals. Occa-sionally critiques rejected ms.

Needs: Contemporary, ethnic, feminist, juvenile (animal, historical, contemporary), religious/inspira-tional, translations, war (anti-war theme) and young adult/teen (historical, problem novels). "We are mainly interested in books that promote reverence for life, including animal welfare, animal rights, dis-abled achievement and disabled rights, social justice, peace, and reverence for human life." Recently published *Friends of All Creatures*, by Rose Evans; *The Whale's Tale*, by Deborah Evans Smith (chil-dren's).

How to Contact: Accepts unsolicited mss. Query first or submit outline/synopsis and 3 sample chap-ters with SASE. Reports in 2 weeks on queries. Simultaneous and photocopied submissions OK. Ac-cepts computer printout submissions. Prefers letter-quality.

Terms: Negotiates royalties and advance. Free writer's guidelines and book catalog.

Advice: "We are willing to publish a first novel if we like the manuscript."

SEAL PRESS (IV), 3131 Western Ave., Seattle WA 98121. President: Faith Conlon. Estab. 1976. Publishes hardcover and paperback originals. Books: acid-free paper; offset printing; perfect or cloth binding; average print order: 4,000. Averages 8-10 total titles, including 4-5 fiction, each year. Some-times critiques rejected ms "very briefly."

Needs: Ethnic, feminist, lesbian, literary, short story collections, women's/feminist. "We publish women only. Work must be feminist, non-racist, non-homophobic." Recently published *Girls, Visions & Everything*, by Sarah Schulman; *Sisters of the Road*, by Barbara Wilson (feminist mystery); and *Two Women in One*, by Nawal El-Saadawi. "A recent development is "International Women's Crime" (sub-series of "Women in Translation")—a feminist mystery series translated from other languages."

How to Contact: "Sometimes" accepts unsolicited mss. Query first. SASE. Reports in 1-2 months. Accepts "readable" computer printouts.

Terms: "Standard publishing practices; do not wish to disclose specifics." Sends galleys to author. Book catalog for SAE and 45¢ postage.

SECOND CHANCE PRESS AND THE PERMANENT PRESS (II), R.D.#2 Noyac Rd., Sag Harbor NY 11963. (516)725-1101. Editor: Judith Shepard. Estab. 1977. Mid-size, independent publisher.

Publishes hardcover originals and reprints. Books: 5½x8½ hardcover and trade paperbacks; average print order: 3,000; first novel print order: 3,000. Plans to publish 5 first novels this year. Averages 12 total titles; 10 fiction titles each year.
Needs: Adventure, contemporary, ethnic, experimental, historical, literary, mainstream, supsense/ mystery. "I like novels that have a unique point of view and have a high quality of writing." No gothic, romance, horror, science fiction, pulp. Recently published *The Pacifist*, by Donald Wetzel (autobiography); and *The Last to Die*, by William Herrick (war adventure); *Tho Dwell by a Churchyard*, by Berry Fleming; published new writers within the last year.
How to Contact: Query first. SASE. Agented fiction: 10%. Reports in 2 weeks on queries; 2 months on mss. Simultaneous and photocopied submissions OK. Accepts computer printouts.
Terms: Pays in royalties of 10% minimum; 15% maximum of net sales. Sends galleys to author. Advance to $1,000. Sends galleys to author. Book catalog for $2.
Advice: "Be as thorough in your submissions and covering all bases as you, presumably, have been in writing your book."

SEVEN BUFFALOES PRESS (II), Box 249, Big Timber MT 59011. Editor/Publisher: Art Cuelho. Estab. 1975. Publishes paperback originals. Averages 4-5 total titles each year.
Needs: Contemporary, short story collections, "rural, American Hobo, Okies, American Indian, Southern Appalachia, Arkansas and the Ozarks. Wants farm and ranch based stories." Recently published *Rig Nine*, by William Rintoul (collection of oilfield short stories).
How to Contact: Query first with SASE. Photocopied submissions OK. Reports in 1 week on queries; 2 weeks on mss.
Terms: Pays in royalties of 10% minimum; 15% on second edition or in author's copies (10% of edition). No advance. Free writer's guidelines and book catalog for SASE.
Advice: "There's too much influence from TV and Hollywood; media writing I call it. We need to get back to the people; to those who built and are still building this nation with sweat, blood, and brains. More people are into it for the money; instead of for the good writing that is still to be cranked out by isolated writers. Remember, I was a writer for 10 years before I became a publisher."

SILVERLEAF PRESS, INC. (I, II), Box 70189, Seattle WA 98107. Editor: Ann Larson. Estab. 1985. Publishes paperback originals. Books: 50 lb book stock; offset printing; perfect binding; no illustrations; average print order: 1,600; first novel print order: 1,600. Published new writers within the last year. Plans 1-2 first novels this year. Averages 2 total titles/year; 2 fiction titles/year. Sometimes critiques or comments on rejected mss.
Needs: Feminist, humor/satire, lesbian, short story collections. "Must be feminist or lesbian." Recently published *Crossing the Mainstream: New Fiction by Women Writers*, (short story collection).
How to Contact: Accepts unsolicited mss. Submit complete ms with cover letter. SASE (IRC). Reports in 2-3 months. Photocopied submissions OK. Accepts computer printout submissions, including dot-matrix.
Terms: Pays negotiable royalties and advance; author's copies. Sends galleys to author. Book catalog free on request.
Advice: "Try the small presses—they are more likely to give you a chance."

SLOUGH PRESS (I, II), Box 1385, Austin TX 78767. Editor: Jim Cole. Estab. 1973. One person operation on a part-time basis. Publishes hardcover and paperback originals. Books: 60 lb paper; offset printing; perfect binding; illustrations; average print order: 500-1,000; first novel print order: 1,000. Published new writers within the last year. Publishes 1 first novel every 5 years. Averages 5 total titles/ year; 2 fiction titles/year. Sometimes critiques rejected mss; charges fee of $5/hour.
Needs: Erotica, literary, short story collections. No genre fiction. Recently published *Horseplayer*, by Frank Cotolos; *Colleen and Other Stories*, by Ivan Reyes.
How to Contact: Submit outline/synopsis and sample chapters. SASE (IRC). Reports in 1 month. Simultaneous and photocopied submissions OK. Does not accept computer printout submissions.
Terms: Pays in author's copies or percentage of profits; depends on grant/award money. "Some titles of poetry and fiction we require that the author pre-purchase, at a discount, a certain number of copies. We have used numerous methods of finance from grants, contests, loans from bank or 'fat cats' or friends, author pre-purchase of books, etc. We want to get quality work published and are open to suggestions. Chapbook fiction contest." Writer's guidelines and book catalog for $1.
Advice: "Publishing more fiction, because we like fiction and we have the hope it will sell better than essays or poetry. We're interested in fiction which presents alternative values, and presents non-middle class, non-straight lifestyles. We like books which present unusual, but not necessarily SF, worlds. We hate blind submissions. Advise writers to familiarize themselves with at least one title at a library before sending manuscripts, because if we're busy and getting snowballed with submissions, we will mail them back, rejected, perhaps, after reading the first paragraph."

‡AARON SMIRNOFF BOOKS, 400 Parkdale Ave., "C" Box 3942, Ottawa, Ontario K1Y 4P2 Canada. Editor: Sean McGoldrick. Estab. 1980. Independent publisher—"growing." Publishes paperback and hardcover originals and reprints. Averages approximately 3 titles/year. Sometimes comments on rejected mss.
Needs: Juvenile (5-9 years, including animal and historical), literary, romance (historical), western, young adult teen (10-18 years, historical).
How to Contact: Accepts unsolicited mss. Does not always return unsolicited mss. "Material sent is author's responsibility, not ours." Submit outline and first, third and last chapters.
Terms: Makes individual arrangment with author. Prepublication galleys sent to author "if requested with good reason." Publishes ms an average of 2-3 years after acceptance. Writer's guidelines for SAE and 2 first class stamps (or IRC—2 oz first class).

THE SMITH (II), 5 Beekman St., New York NY 10038. Editor: Harry Smith. Managing Editor: Tom Tolnay. Estab. 1964. Books: 50 lb bookmark paper for offset and 80 lb vellum for letterpress printing; perfect binding; often uses illustrations; average print order: 1,000; first novel print order: 1,000.
Needs: *Extremely* limited book publishing market—currently doing only two books annually, and these are of a literary nature, usually essays or poetry.

SOHO PRESS, 1 Union Square, New York NY 10003. (212)243-1527. Publisher: Juris Jurjevics. Publishes hardcover and trade paperback originals. Averages 10 titles/year.
Needs: Adventure, ethnic, historical, mainstream, mystery/espionage, suspense. "We do novels that are the very best in their genres." Recently published *Men*, by M. Diehl (novel); *High Crimes*, by John Westermann (suspense); and *Houses of Ivory*, by Hart Wegner; published new writers within the last year.
How to Contact: Submit query or complete ms with SASE. Reports in 2 weeks on queries; 1 month on mss. Photocopied and simultaneous submissions OK.
Terms: Pays royalties of 10% minimum; 15% maximum on retail price. For trade paperbacks pays 7½% royalties to 10,000 copies; 10% after. Offers advance. Book catalog free on request.
Advice: "There aren't any tricks (to writing a good query letter)—just say what the book is. Don't analyze the market for it. Don't take writing courses too seriously, and *read* the best people in whatever genre you are working. We are looking for those who have taught themselves or otherwise mastered the craft."

SPACE AND TIME (IV), 138 W. 70th St. (4-B), New York NY 10023-4432. Book Editor: Jani Anderson. Estab. 1966—book line 1984. Two-person operation on part-time basis. Publishes paperback originals. Books: 50 lb Lakewood white 512PPi paper; offset Litho printing; perfect binding; illustrations on cover and frontispiece; average print order: 1,000; first novel print order: 1,000. Averages 1-2 total titles; 1-2 fiction titles each year. Critiques or comments on rejected ms.
Needs: Fantasy, horror, psychic/supernatural/occult, science fiction. Wants to see cross-genre material, such as horror-western, sf-mystery, occult-spy adventure, etc. Does not want anything *without* some element of fantasy or sf (or at least the 'feel' of same). Recently published *The Wall*, by Ardath Mayhar (horror-mystery); *Vanitas*, by Jeffrey Ford (sci-fantasy-horror); *The Maze of Peril*, by John Eric Holmes (fantasy).
How to Contact: Accepts unsolicited mss. Query first or submit outline/synopsis and 2 sample chapters. Reports in 4-6 weeks on queries; 3-4 months on mss. Simultaneous and photocopied submissions OK. Prefer photocopies.
Terms: Pays in royalties of 10% based on cover price and print run, within 60 days of publication (additional royalties, if going back to press). Average advance $100, negotiable. Sends galleys to author. Book catalog free on request.
Advice: "We are actively interested in publishing new authors."

THE SPEECH BIN, INC. (IV), 231 Clarksville Rd., Box 218, Princeton Junction NJ 08550-0218. (609)799-3935. Senior Editor: Jan J. Binney. Estab. 1984. Small independent publisher and major national and international distributor of books and material for speech-language pathologists, audiologists, special educators and caregivers. Publishes hardcover and paperback originals. Averages 6-10 total titles/year. "No fiction at present time, but we are very interested in publishing fiction relevant to our specialties."
Needs: "We are most interested in seeing fiction, including books for children, dealing with individuals experiencing communication disorders, other handicaps, and their families and caregivers, particularly their parents, or family members dealing with individuals who have strokes, physical disability, hearing loss, Alzheimer's and so forth."
How to Contact: Accepts unsolicited mss. Query first. SASE (IRC). 10% of fiction is agented. Reports in 4-6 weeks on queries; 1-3 months on mss. Simultaneous and photocopied submissions OK. Ac-

cepts computer printout submissions, including dot-matrix.
Terms: Pays royalties of 8% + . Sends galleys to author. Writer's guidelines for #10 SASE. Book catalog for 9x12 SAE with 3 first class stamps.
Advice: "We are most interested in publishing fiction about individuals who have speech, hearing and other handicaps."

SPINSTERS/AUNT LUTE BOOK CO. (IV), Box 410687, San Francisco CA 94141. (415)558-9655. Editors: Sherilyn Thomas and Joan Pinkross. Estab. 1978. Moderate size women's publishing company growing steadily. Publishes paperback originals and reprints. Books: 55 lb acid free natural paper; photo offset printing; perfect binding; illustrations when appropriate; average print order: 5,000. Plans 3 first novels this year. Averages 6 total titles, 3-5 fiction titles each year. Occasionally critiques rejected ms.
Needs: Feminist, lesbian. Wants "full-length quality fiction—thoroughly revised novels which display deep characterization, theme and style. We *only* consider books by women. No books by men, or books with sexist, racist or ageist content." Recently published fiction by Gloria Anzaldúa, Sandi Hall, Anne Cameron.
How to Contact: Accepts unsolicited mss. Query or submit outline/synopsis and 3 sample chapters with SASE. Reports in 1 month on queries; 2 months on mss. No simultaneous submissions without specific permission; photocopied submissions OK. Accepts computer printout submissions. Prefers letter-quality. Disk submissions OK with Morrow Designs MDII system. Prefers hard copy with disk submission.
Terms: Pays in royalties of 8% minimum, 12% maximum (after 10,000) plus 25 author's copies; unlimited extra copies at 50% discount. Free book catalog.
Advice: "Our recent titles are primarily feminist and/or lesbian. We would publish more fiction if we could get excellent manuscripts. Get in a writers' group for critical feedback. Know publisher's market before submitting. Query professionally."

SPIRITUAL FICTION PUBLICATIONS (II, IV), Subsidiary of Garber Communications, Inc., 5 Garber Hill Rd., Blauvelt NY 10913. (914)359-9292. Editor-in-Chief: Bernard J. Garber. Fiction Editor: Patricia Abrams. Midsize publisher. Averages 4-5 titles each year. Average first novel print order 1,000 copies paperback; 300 copies cloth.
Needs: Psychic/supernatural/occult, historical, religious/inspirational. No science fiction. Recently published *Legend*, by Barry Maher.
How to Contact: Does not accept unsolicited mss. Query first or send 1-2 page outline plus SASE. Reports in 1 month on queries.
Advice: "Read what we have published. We accept first novels if they are good."

SQUARE ONE PUBLISHERS (II), Box 4385, Madison WI 53711. (608)255-8425. Director: Lyn Miller-Lachman. "We publish book-length young adult (ages 14-18) fiction that examines controversial issues in a realistic and compelling way, with a special emphasis upon relationships among young people of different cultures and teenagers who become involved in political and social issues. Our audience includes young adults—young people who are impatient with stereotypes and who feel themselves to be different in some way." Books: 60 lb paper; offset printing; perfect binding; first novel print order: 5,000-6,000.
Needs: Young adult/teen (10-18). Plans two fiction titles this year. No formula fiction; no fiction that reinforces racial or sex stereotypes or glorifies war. Recently published *Cassandra Robbins, Esq.*, by Pat Costa Viglucci; *Center Stage Summer*, by Cynthia K. Lukas; and *The Twenty-Six Minutes*, by Robert Hawks; published new writers within the last year. Occasionally critiques or comments on rejected ms.
How to Contact: Accepts unsolicited mss. Send complete ms with cover letter, which should include a history of a manuscript's submission elsewhere, especially if the manuscript was deemed "too controversial." SASE. Reports in 1 month on queries; 2-3 months on mss. Simultaneous and photocopied submissions OK "with notification in cover letter." Accepts computer printout submissions, including dot-matrix.
Terms: Pays 5-6% royalties of cover price. Writers guidelines for SAE and 1 first class stamp. Sends galleys to author.
Advice: "Be honest to yourself as a writer and as a person. Too many authors write superficial, unimaginative material because they think it will sell, and too often they leave out honest, compelling material because it might be seen as too shocking or disturbing, thereby jeopardizing the sale of the manuscript. The only way that great fiction exists is if people fight for it. It would be a good idea to look at some of the books we've published too—they're available in most libraries. Check publishers' catalogs and read the kind of books they're publishing."

STAR BOOKS, INC., 408 Pearson St., Wilson NC 27893. (919)237-1591. President: Irene Burk Harrell. Estab. 1983. "Small but growing" publisher. Publishes paperback originals. Books: offset paper;

offset printing; perfect binding. some illustrations; average print order: 1,000; first novel print order: 1,000. Plans 1 first novel this year. Averages 5-6 total titles, 1 fiction title each year. Sometimes comments on rejected mss, "comment no charge; critique $1 per ms page, $25 minimum."

Needs: Religious/inspirational, young adult/teen. "Strongly and specifically Christian." Recently published *The Bridge*, by Ralph Filicchia (contemporary inner-city); *And Now I See*, by Clyde Bolton (Biblical novel); and *Light at Haypark*, by Marie Denison (contemporary).

How to Contact: Accepts unsolicited mss. Submit complete ms with cover letter. SASE for ms. Reports on queries in 2 weeks. Photocopied submissions OK. Accepts computer printout submissions, including dot-matrix (if legible).

Terms: Pays royalties of 8% minimum; 15% maximum. Sends galleys to author. Publishing of ms after acceptance "depends on our situation." "*Sometimes*, (not always) we need author to buy prepub copies (at 50% off list) to help with first printing costs." Guidelines for #10 SAE and 1 first class stamp. Book catalog for #10 SAE and 2 first class stamps.

Advice: "Make sure that for us the book is in line with Biblical principles and powerful enough to cause the reader to make an initial commitment of his/her life to Jesus Christ, or if the reader is already a Christian, to strengthen his/her walk with Him."

STATION HILL PRESS (II, III), Barrytown NY 12507. (914)758-5840. Imprints include Open Book, Pulse, Artext, Clinamen Studies and Contemporary Artists Series. Publishers: George Quasha and Susan Quasha. Estab. 1978. Publishes paperback and cloth originals. Averages 10-15 total titles, 5-7 fiction titles each year.

Needs: Contemporary, experimental, literary, translations, and new age. Recently published *Operas and Plays*, by Gertrude Stein; *Narrative Unbound*, by Donald Ault.

How to Contact: Query first with SASE before sending ms. No unsolicited mss. Reports in 4-6 weeks on queries; 4 months on mss.

Terms: Pays in author's copies (10% of print run) or by standard royalty, depending on the nature of the material. Occasional subsidy publishing. "Co-venture arrangements are possible with higher royalty." Book catalog free on request.

STILL POINT PRESS (II), 4222 Willow Grove Rd., Dallas TX 75220. (214)352-8282. Editor/Publisher: Charlotte T. Whaley. Estab. 1984. Small independent publisher, producing a few books each year. Publishes hardcover originals. Books: acid-free Warrens olde style, 60 lb paper; letterpress, offset, photocomposition printing; cloth (Roxite B grade) case binding; photos, engravings, drawings; average print order: 2,000 trade editions; 300 limited editions.

Needs: Recently published *O. Henry's Texas Stories*, edited by Marian McClintock and Michael Simms.

How to Contact: No unsolicited mss considered.

Terms: Individual arrangement with author, depending on the book. Sends galleys to author. Pays in royalties of 10% minimum, 15% maximum; 6 author's copies; contingent advance.

Advice: "Query. We regard author/editor relationships a friendly, collaborative effort. Strive hard for quality."

STORMLINE PRESS, INC. (I,II, IV), Box 593, Urbana IL 61801. (217)328-2665. Publisher: Raymond Bial. Estab. 1985. Independent literary press. Publishes hardcover and paperback originals. Books: best quality, usually acid-free paper; commercial printing—all graphics in duotone printing; perfect bound and clothbound binding; illustrations photographs and original artwork; average print order: 1,000-1,500; first novel print order: 1,000-1,500. Plans 1 first novel this year. Averages 4-5 total titles; 1 fiction title each year. Occasionally critiques or comments on rejected ms "on serious works only."

Needs: Ethnic, humor/satire, literary, mainstream, short story collections. "Serious literary works only. We are only interested in novels, collections of short stories and novellas that accurately and sensitively portray rural and small town life." No genre fiction, or anything that was written primarily for its commercial value. Recently published *People of Gumption and Other Stories*, by Fran Lehr (short stories).

How to Contact: Accepts mss during November and December only. Submit complete ms with cover letter. SASE. "We urge that you write for guidelines (enclose SASE)." Reports in 2 weeks on queries; 1 month on mss. Accepts computer printout submissions, including dot-matrix, although letter-quality much preferred.

Terms: Pays royalties of 10% minimum; 15% maximum. Pays 25 author copies. Payment depends on grant/award money. Authors are generally paid 15% royalties once the production costs of the book have been met. Book catalog free on request.

Advice: "We are interested in works of the highest literary quality which also make for enjoyable reading. It is difficult, if not nearly impossible to get book length manuscripts published these days. Of those manuscripts published most are quickly forgotten within a few months or a few years. Only a precious few writers are sufficiently talented to stand the test of time. Therefore, I recommend that you not consider writing unless your work cries to be published and read."

STUDIA HISPANICA EDITORS (IV), Box 7304, UT Station, Austin TX 78713. Attention: Luis Ramos-Garcia. (512)471-9113 (request to speak to Dave Oliphant). Imprints include Prickly Pear Press. Fiction Editor: Luis Ramos-Garcia. Estab. 1978. Small independent publisher (a group operation on part-time basis). Publishes paperback originals. Books: 60-70 lb off-white paper; offset printing; perfect binding; illustrations; average print order: 500-1,000. Averages 2 total titles, 1 fiction title each year.
Needs: Contemporary, ethnic, literary, regional, short story collections and translations. Especially needs regional novels and novel translations. No horror or science fiction. Recently published *Tales from Austin* and *A South American Trilogy*, edited by L.A.R.G.; *From the Threshold: Contemporary Peruvian Fiction in Translation* (short stories); and *Five Rolls of Plus-X: an Urban Photography Vision of Peru*.
How to Contact: Does not accept unsolicited mss. Query with SASE. Reports in 3 weeks. No simultaneous submissions; photocopied submissions OK. Accepts computer printout submissions, prefers letter-quality.
Terms: "Author pays for all expenses except salaries, design (inside and cover). We keep 25% of published books and deliver the rest to author(s). Fifty percent of all expenses should be paid in advance and 50% upon notice of release." Sends galleys to author. Book flyers for SASE.
Advice: "Our recent title lists are moving towards Texas and Latin American fiction—more regional (southwest) and international interest."

SUN & MOON PRESS (III), 6148 Wilshire Blvd., Suite 115, Los Angeles CA 90048. (213)857-1115. Imprint: New American Fiction series. Subsidiary of the Contemporary Arts Educational Project, Inc. Publisher: Douglas Messerli. Senior Editor: Ann Klefstad. Estab. 1979. Publishes hardcover and paperback originals and reprints. Books: acid-free high quality paper; offset printing; perfect and Smythe-sewn binding; average print order: 3,000; first novel print order: 1,500. Averages 15 total titles, 10 fiction titles each year. Occasionally critiques "if quality ms."
Needs: Contemporary, experimental, literary, mainstream, short story collections, translations.
How to Contact: Submit complete ms with SASE. Photocopied submissions OK. Reports in 1 month on mss.
Terms: Pays in royalties of 10%. Sends galleys to author. Book catalog for 39¢ postage.
Advice: Publishing more fiction in paper and cloth; have new line, New American Fiction Series. Published new writers last year.

SUNSTONE PRESS (IV), Box 2321, Santa Fe NM 87504-2321. (505)988-4418. Fiction Editor: Marcia Muth. Estab. 1971. Midsize publisher. Publishes paperback originals. Plans 2 first novels this year. Averages 16 total titles; 2-3 fiction titles each year. "Sometimes" buys juvenile mss with illustrations. Average first novel print order 2,000 copies.
Needs: Western. "We have a Southwestern theme emphasis." No science fiction, romance or occult. Recently published *Apache: The Long Ride Home*, by Grant Gall (Indian/Western); *Border Patrol*, by Cmdr. Alvin E. Moore and *The Last Narrow Gauge Train Robbery*, by Robert K. Swisher, Jr.; published new writers within the last year.
How to Contact: Accepts unsolicited mss. Query first or submit outline/synopsis and 2 sample chapters with SASE. Reports in 2 weeks. Simultaneous and photocopied submissions OK. Accepts computer printout submissions, including dot-matrix. Publishes ms 9-12 months after acceptance.
Terms: Pays in royalties, 10% maximum, and 10 author's copies.
Advice: "Look at what publisher wants, i.e. don't send fiction that is clearly indicated as being outside the scope of the editorial needs."

TALON BOOKS LTD., 201/1019 E. Cordova St., Vancouver, British Columbia V6A 1M8 Canada. (604)253-5261. President: Karl Siegler. Estab. 1970. Literary press specializing in Canadian drama. Publishes paperback originals. Averages 10 total titles, 3 fiction titles each year. Average print order: 2,000. Sometimes critiques or comments on rejected mss.
Needs: Contemporary, feminist, gay, lesbian, literary. No romance, adventure, American-related. Recently published *Under the House*, by Leslie Hall Pinder; *Cambodia: A Book for People Who Find Television too Slow*, by Brian Fawcett; and *In the Shadow of the Vulture*, by George Ryga.
How to Contact: Does not accept unsolicited mss.
Terms: Pays royalties of 5% minimum; 15% maximum and $200 average amount; 10 free copies, sends to author's list for promotional copies. Book catalog for 9x12 SAE and 64¢ Canadian postage or international reply coupons.

Advice: "We encourage new writers but we need something to work with; i.e., we prefer a writer who has published in periodicals, is known in academic circles, or has some similar basis for marketing and promotion."

TEAL PRESS (II), Box 4098, Santa Fe NM 87502-4098. (505)989-7861. Editor: Robert Jebb. Estab. 1983. Small press publishing 2-4 titles per year. Publishes hardcover and paperback originals. Books: acid-free paper; offset printing; Smythe-sewn binding; average print order: 1,500; first novel print order: 1,500. Published new writers within the last year.
Needs: Contemporary and literary. Especially needs "serious novels that deal with the diversity, complexity of our age." Recently published *Portrait of Little Boy in Darkness*, by Daniel McGuire and *Through an Eastern Window* by Jack Huber.
How to Contact: Not seeking mss, 1988-89. Announcing program to promote the novella. Look for announcements in literary publications or write to Teal Press for details.
Terms: Pays in royalties of 10% minimum.

THIRD WORLD PRESS, 7524 S. Cottage Grove Ave., Chicago IL 60619. (312)651-0700. Assistant Editor: Dana L. Reid. Estab. 1967. Small independent publisher with plans to expand. Publishes paperback originals. Plans 2 first novels this year. Averages 10 total titles, 3 fiction titles each year. Average first novel print order 15,000 copies.
Needs: Ethnic, historical, juvenile (animal, easy-to-read, fantasy, historical, contemporary), preschool/picture book, science fiction, short story collections, and young adult/teen (easy-to-read/teen, fantasy/science fiction, historical). "We primarily publish nonfiction, but will consider fiction by and about Blacks."
How to Contact: Accepts unsolicited mss. Query or submit outline/synopsis and 1 sample chapter with SASE. Reports in 6 weeks on queries; 5 months on mss. Simultaneous and photocopied submissions OK. Accepts computer printout submissions. Prefers letter-quality.
Terms: Individual arrangement with author depending on the book, etc.

THISTLEDOWN PRESS (II, IV), 668 East Place, Saskatoon, Saskatchewan S7J 2Z5 Canada. (306)244-1722. Editor-in-Chief: Paddy O'Rourke. Estab. 1975. Publishes hardcover and paperback originals. Books: quality stock paper; offset printing; Smythe-sewn binding; occasionally illustrations; average print order 1,500-2,000; first novel print order: 1,250-1,500. Plans 1 first novel and 3 collections of stories. Publishes 12 titles/year, 4 or 5 fiction. Occasionally critiques rejected mss.
Needs: Literary, experimental, short story collections. "We *only* want to see Canadian-authored submissions. We will *not* consider multiple submissions."
How to Contact: No unsolicited mss. Query first with SASE. Photocopied submissions OK. Reports in 2 months on queries. Recently published *Medieval Hour in the Author's Mind*, by Ernest Hekkenan; *The Fungus Garden*, by Brian Brett; *Forms of Captivity and Escape*, by J. J. Steinfeld.
Advice: "We are primarily looking for quality writing that is original and innovative in its perspective and/or use of language. Thistledown would like to receive queries first before submission—perhaps with novel outline, some indication of previous publications, periodicals your work has appeared in. We publish Canadian authors only. We are continuing to publish more fiction and are looking for new fiction writers to add to our list. Familiarize yourself with some of our books before submitting a query or manuscript to the press."

THRESHOLD BOOKS, RD 3, Box 1350, Dusty Ridge Rd., Putney VT 05346. (802)254-8300. Director: Edmund Helminski. Estab. 1981. Small independent publisher with plans for gradual expansion. Publishes paperback originals. Books: 60 lb natural paper; offset litho printing; sew-wrap binding; average print order: 2,500. Averages 2-3 total titles each year. Occasionally critiques rejected ms.
Needs: Spiritual literature and translations of sacred texts. Recently published *I Come From Behind KAF Mountain*, by Murat Yagan (autobiographical), and *The Sandstone Papers*, by Marty Glass.
How to Contact: Accepts unsolicited mss. Query first, submit outline/synopsis and sample chapters or complete ms with SASE. Reports in 6 weeks. Simultaneous and photocopied submissions OK. Accepts computer printout submissions, prefers letter-quality. Publishes ms an average of 18 months after acceptance.
Terms: Pays in royalties of 10% of net. Sometimes sends galleys to author. Book catalog free on request.
Advice: "We are still small and publishing little fiction." Publishing "less fiction, more paperbacks due to our particular area of concentration and our size."

‡TIDE BOOK PUBLISHING COMPANY, Box 101, York Harbor ME 03911. Subsidiary of Tide Media. President: Rose Safran. Estab. 1979. Independent, small publisher. Publishes paperback originals. Averages 1 title each year. Occasionally critiques rejected mss.

Needs: Contemporary, contemporary romance, feminist, historical, humor/satire, literary, mainstream, regional. Needs women's novels with a social service thrust; contemporary. No gothic, trash.
How to Contact: Query first; submit outline synopsis and 1-2 sample chapters with SASE. Simultaneous submissions OK. Accepts computer printout submissions, prefers letter-quality. Reports in 1 month.
Terms: Pays in 100 author's copies. Considering cost plus subsidy arrangements—will advertise.

TIMES EAGLE BOOKS (IV), Box 11735, Portland OR 97211. Fiction Editor: Mark Hurst. Estab. 1971. "Small operation on part-time basis." Specialized publisher limited to contributors from West Coast region. First novel print order: 2,500. Plans 2 first novels this year. Averages 2 titles/year, all fiction.
Needs: Contemporary. "Graphic descriptions of teenage life by West Coast youth, such as Bret Easton Ellis's *Less than Zero*.
How to Contact: Does not accept or return unsolicited mss. Query first in one paragraph. Reports in 2 weeks.
Terms: Pays 10-15% royalties.
Advice: "Times Eagle Books prefers first novelists."

TIPTOE LITERARY SERVICE (IV), Box 206-OH, Naselle WA 98638. (206)484-7722. Publisher: A. Grimm-Richardson. Estab. 1985. Small publisher, books under 75 pages and booklets. Publishes paperback originals. Books: xerographic paper; photocopy print; saddle stitch binding; line drawings/sketches & graphs; average print order: limited 1st edition 250 press run. Has recently published first time author. Plans 1 first novelette this year. Publishes 3 total titles each year; 1 fiction title. Sometimes critiques rejected mss.
Needs: Currently overstocked. Recently published *Something Fishy at The Panama Canal*, by Meldeau Dampfer (faction); and *Effie's Bytes*, by Lou Lazer (computer science fiction).
How to Contact: Does not accept unsolicited mss. Query first. SASE. No agented fiction. Reports on queries in 3 weeks. Simultaneous and photocopied submissions OK. Accepts computer printout submissions, including dot-matrix.
Terms: "Private arrangement with local writer associates, usually barter." Book catalog free on request to foreign addresses; otherwise for #10 SAE with 1 first class stamp.
Advice: "Still a 'new' business—plans for a mix of categories, fiction one-third. We will be stressing our Writer Guide pamphlets for the next year."

THE TRANSLATION CENTER (II), 307A Mathematics, Columbia University, New York NY 10027. (212)854-2305. Managing Editor: Diane G.H. Cook. Editors: Frank MacShane, William Jay Smith, Lane Dunlop. Estab. 1972. Publishes paperback originals. Books: 6x9; perfect bound; high-quality paper. Averages 2 total titles/year.
Needs: Translations.
How to Contact: Accepts unsolicited ms. Submit complete ms with cover letter and SASE. Photocopied submissions OK. Accepts computer printouts including dot-matrix.
Terms: Pays in 2 translator's copies.

TRIPLE 'P' PUBLICATIONS INTERNATIONAL (II), Box 1321, Kendall Square, Cambridge MA 02142. (617)437-1856. Subsidiaries include *Persuasion Magazine* and *The Kiosk Newsletter*. Editorial Manager: Eugene FPC de Mesne. Fiction Editor: Monica Selwyn-Jones. Estab. 1974. Independent publisher with expansion plans. Publishes hardcover and paperback originals. Books: Velum/mottled paper (depending on type of book published); offset printing from print-set mock-ups; hardbound binding (unless paperback when card stock is used); illustrations infrequently; average print and first novel order 250 copies (first ed.). Plans 4 first novels this year. Averages 3-4 total titles, 3-4 fiction titles each year. Buys 60% agented fiction.
Needs: Adventure, fantasy, horror, historical, historical romance, literary, psychic/supernatural/occult, regional ("must be solid entertainment"), science fiction, short story collections; feminist, gay, and lesbian ("if done subtly with emphasis on plot"). Needs "the unusual, bizarre, suspense story, with definable characters, and tight plots, set in different periods of history. No melodramas. We do *not* want fiction that conforms to life, but rather, fiction that gives the reader an unusual view of human struggle and coping with situations that arise. No pat solutions or trite romance mush will be considered. Also, no religion or political harangues, please." Recently published *Impressions of a Night Person*; *Wild Child in Heaven*; *Silverthaw*; *Rally Round the Moon* (all by Julian Ocean).
How to Contact: Query to editorial manager with SASE, brief outline, business-like letter only. Simultaneous and photocopied submissions OK. Accepts computer printout submissions. Prefers letter-

quality. Reports in 4-6 weeks on queries. Publishes ms an average of 6 months after acceptance.
Terms: Negotiates advance. Sends galleys to author to check.
Advice: "We find authors write a story as though it is going to be the cinema or television hit of the year. We want word stories, not visual scripts. For novels: write a novel, not a screen-play or television script barely disguised as a novel. Novels are work stories, vivid and vibrant . . . that come alive when the reader reads it. Moreover, the story will stay with the reader a lifetime . . . ."

TURNSTONE PRESS (II), 607-100 Arthur St., Winnipeg, Manitoba R3B 1H3 Canada. (204)947-1555. Managing Editor: Marilyn Morton. Books: offset paper; usually photo direct printing; perfect binding; average first novel print order: 2,000. Published new writers within the last year. Estab. 1976. Publishes paperback originals. Averages 8 total titles/year. Occasionally critiques rejected ms.
Needs: Experimental and literary. "We will be doing only 2-3 fiction titles a year. Interested in new work exploring new narrative/fiction forms." Recently published *Agassiz Stories*, by Sandra Birdsell and *Shutter Speed*, by Larry Krotz.
How to Contact: Send SASE or SAE and IRC. Photocopied submissions OK. Reports in 1 month on queries; 2-4 months on mss.
Terms: "Like most Canadian literary presses, we depend heavily on government grants which are not available for books by nonCanadians. Do some homework before submitting work to make sure your subject matter/genre/writing style falls within the publishers area of interest." Pays in royalties of 10%; 10 (complimentary) author's copies. Book catalog free on request.

ULTRAMARINE PUBLISHING CO., INC. (III), Box 303, Hastings-on-the-Hudson NY 10706. (914)478-2522. Publisher: Christopher P. Stephens. Estab. 1973. Small publisher. "We have 150 titles in print. We also distribute for authors where a major publisher has dropped a title." Encourages new writers. Averages 15 total titles, 12 fiction titles each year. Buys 90% agented fiction. Occasionally critiques rejected ms.
Needs: Experimental, fantasy, mainstream, science fiction, and short story collections. No romance, westerns, mysteries.
How to Contact: Accepts unsolicited mss. Submit outline/synopsis and 2 sample chapters with SASE. Prefers agented ms. Reports in 6 weeks. Simultaneous, photocopied submissions OK. Accepts computer printout submissions. Publishes ms an average of 8 months after acceptance.
Terms: Pays in royalties of 10% minimum; advance is negotiable. Free book catalog.
Advice: "We encourage first novelists."

UNDERWOOD/MILLER (III), 515 Chestnut St., Columbia PA 17512. (717)684-7335. Imprint: Brandywyne Books. Publisher: Chuck Miller. Estab. 1976. Publishes hardcover originals and reprints. Books: acid free paper; offset printing; Smythe-sewn binding; illustrations; average print order 1,000. Averages 12 total titles, 10 fiction titles each year.
Needs: Open. Recently published fiction by Philip K. Dick.
How to Contact: Query first with SASE. Simultaneous and photocopied submissions OK. Reports on queries in 1 month.
Terms: Pays in royalties of 10% minimum; negotiable advance. Sometimes sends galleys to author. Book catalog free on request.

UNICORN PUBLISHING HOUSE, INC., 1148 Parsippany Blvd., Parsippany NJ 07054. (201)334-0353. Associate Juvenile Editor: Heidi K. L. Corso. Estab. 1978. Midsize independent publisher with plans to expand. Publishes hardcover originals and reprints. Books: 100 lb paper; Web press printing; Smythe-sewn binding; illustrations. Publishes 25 total titles.
Needs: Adventure, juvenile (animal, easy-to-read), fantasy, preschool/picture book. Recently published *Peter Pan* by Barrie (children's); *Antique Fairy Tales* (children's); *Treasures of Chanukah*.
How to Contact: Accepts unsolicited mss. Query first. Submit outline/synopsis and 3 sample chapters with SASE. Reports a maximum of 3 months on queries; 3 months on mss. Simultaneous and photocopied submissions OK. Accepts computer printout submissions, including dot-matrix.
Terms: Payment is negotiable.

UNIVERSITY EDITIONS (I, II), 59 Oak Lane, Spring Valley, Huntington WV 25704. Imprint: Aegina Press. Managing Editor: Ira Herman. Estab. 1983. Independent publisher presently expanding. Publishes paperback originals and reprints. Books: 50 lb library-weight paper; litho offset printing; most are perfect bound; illustrations; average print order: 500-1,000; first novel print order: 500-1,000. Published new writers within the last year; plans 10 first novels this year. "We strongly encourage new writers." Averages 20 total titles, approximately 12 fiction titles each year. Often critiques rejected ms.
Needs: Adventure, contemporary, ethnic, experimental, faction, fantasy, feminist, historical, romance, horror, humor/satire, juvenile (all types), literary, mainstream, regional, science fiction, short

story collections, translations and war. "Historical, literary, and regional fiction are our main areas of emphasis." Recently published *Birth Pains*, by Roberta Shapiro (novel); *Uncle Wooley*, by August Keating (novel); *Feeling Free*, by Jack Welch (novel); published new writers within the last year.
How to Contact: Accepts unsolicited mss. "We depend upon manuscripts that arrive unsolicited." Query or submit outline/synopsis and 3 or more sample chapters or complete ms. "We prefer to see entire manuscripts; we will consider queries and partials as well." SASE for queries, mss. Reports in 1 week on queries; 1 month on mss. Simultaneous and photocopied submissions OK. Accepts computer printout submissions, prefers letter-quality.
Terms: Payment is negotiated individually for each book. Sends galleys to author. Depends upon author and subject. Subsidy publishes most new titles.
Advice: "We attempt to encourage and establish new authors. Editorial tastes in fiction are eclectic. We try to be open to any type of fiction that is well written. We are publishing more fiction now that the very large publishers are getting harder to break into. We publish softcovers primarily, in order to keep books affordable."

THE UNIVERSITY OF ARKANSAS PRESS (I), Fayetteville AR 72701. (501)575-3246. Director: Miller Williams. Acquisitions Editor: James Twiggs. Estab. 1980. Small university press. Publishes hardcover and paperback originals. Averages 30 total titles, 2 short fiction titles each year. Average print order 500 cloth and 2,000 paper copies.
Needs: Literary, mainstream, novels and short story collections, and translations. Recently published *All My Trials*, by John William Corrington and *Transferences*, by James Twiggs.
How to Contact: Accepts unsolicited mss. Query first with SASE. Simultaneous and photocopied submissions OK "if very clean." Accepts computer printout submissions, no dot-matrix without sample first. Reports in 2 weeks on queries. Publishes ms an average of 1 year after acceptance.
Terms: Pays in royalties of 10%; 10 author's copies. Writer's guidelines and book catalog free for 9x12 SASE.
Advice: "We are looking for fiction written with energy, clarity and economy. Apart from this, we have no predisposition concerning style or subject matter. The University of Arkansas Press does not respond to queries or proposals not accompanied by SASE."

UNIVERSITY OF ILLINOIS PRESS (I), 54 E. Gregory, Champaign IL 61820. (217)333-0950. Senior Editor: Ann Lowry Weir. Estab. 1918. Not-for-profit university press. Publishes clothbound originals. Books: acid free paper; cloth binding; average print order: 1,500-2,000. Number of titles: 4 per year. Encourages new writers who have journal publications. Occasionally comments on rejected mss.
Needs: Contemporary, literary, and experimental. "No novels." Recently published *Tumbling* by Kermit Moyer; *The Trojan Generals Talk*, by Phillip Parotti; *Water into Wine*, by Helen Norris, and *Playing with Shadows*, by Gloria Whelan.
How to Contact: Accepts unsolicited mss. Query or submit complete ms. SASE for query, ms. Simultaneous and photocopied submissions OK. Accepts computer printout submissions. Reports in 1 week on queries, 2-4 months on mss.
Terms: Pays 7½% net of all copies sold. No advance. Free book catalog.
Advice: "We do not publish novels, and we have no outlet for individual short stories. We publish collections of short fiction by authors who've usually established their credentials by being accepted for publication in periodicals, generally literary periodicals."

VÉHICULE PRESS (IV), Box 125, Place du Parc Station, Montréal, Québec H2W 2M9 Canada. Imprint: Signal Editions for poetry. Publisher/Editor: Simon Dardick. Estab. 1973. Small publisher of scholarly, literary and cultural books. Publishes hardcover and paperback originals. Books: good quality paper; offset printing; perfect and cloth binding; illustrations; average print order: 1,000-3,000. Averages 7 total titles/year.
Needs: Feminist, literary, regional, short story collections, translations—"*by Canadian residents only.*" No romance or formula writing. "We do not accept novels at this point."
How to Contact: Query first or send sample chapters; SASE or SAE and IRC ("no US stamps, please"). Reports in 2 weeks on queries, 2 months on mss.
Terms: Pays in royalties of 10% minimum, 12% maximum; "depends on press run and sales. Sends galleys to author. Translators of fiction can receive Canada Council funding, which publisher applies for." Book catalog for 9x12 SASE.
Advice: "Our only fiction titles at this point are short story collections. Quality in almost any style is acceptable. We believe in the editing process.

W.W. PUBLICATIONS (IV), Subsidiary of A.T.S., Box 373, Highland MI 48031-0373. (313)887-4703. Also publishes *Minas Tirith Evening Star*. Editor: Philip Helms. Estab. 1967. One-man operation on part-time basis. Publishes paperback originals and reprints. Books: typing paper; offset printing; sta-

pled binding; black ink illustrations; average print order: 500 + ; first novel print order: 500. Averages 1 title (fiction) each year. Occasionally critiques rejected mss.
Needs: Fantasy, science fiction, and young adult/teen (fantasy/science fiction). Novel needs: "Tolkien-related mainly, some fantasy."
How to Contact: Accepts unsolicited mss. Submit complete ms with SASE. Reports in 1 month. Simultaneous and photocopied submissions OK. Accepts computer printout submissions, prefers letter-quality.
Terms: Individual arrangement with author depending on book, etc.; provides 5 author's copies. Free book catalog.
Advice: "We are publishing more fiction and more paperbacks. The author/editor relationship: a friend and helper."

WATERFRONT PRESS (IV), 52 Maple Ave., Maplewood NJ 07040. (201)762-1565. President: Kal Wagenheim. Estab. 1982. Two persons, active part-time small press. Hardcover originals and reprints; paperback originals and reprints. Books: standard trade and textbook formats, illustrations occasionally; average print order: 1,000-1,500; first novel print order: 500-1,000. Averages 4 total titles/year; 1 or 2 fiction titles/year. Occasionally critiques rejected mss.
Needs: Ethnic, translations. "Our main focus is Puerto Rico and Hispanics in the US. We may consider other Caribbean nations." Recently published *The Labyrinth*, by Enrique A. Laguerre (translation from Spanish of book first published 1959); and *La Charca*, by Manuel Zeno-Gandia (translation from Spanish of 19th century novel).
How to Contact: Does not accept unsolicited mss. Query first or submit outline/synopsis and sample chapters. SASE for query and ms. Reports in 1 month on queries; 2 months on mss. Simultaneous and photocopied submissions OK. Accepts computer printouts including dot-matrix if legible.
Terms: Pays in royalties of 10% minimum; 15% maximum; $250-500 advance; advance is negotiable. Sends galleys to author. "On a few occasions, with books of great merit, we have co-published with author, who provided part of costs (in cases where our budget did not permit us to proceed quickly with the project)."
Advice: "We will endorse or support grant applications made by writers to foundations, if we believe the work has merit."

‡WATERMARK PRESS, INC. (I,II,IV), 149 N. Broadway, Suite 201, Wichita KS 67202. (316)683-3007. Editor: Gaylord L. Dold. Estab. 1988. Regional independent publisher, planning to expand. Publishes hardcover originals. "New line in spring, 1989, high quality cover." Plans to publish 2 first novels this year.
Needs: Literary. "We need quality literary manuscripts, short story collections, with a regional theme, novels but no genre work, mystery etc."
How to contact: Accepts unsolicited mss. Query first. Reports on queries in 1 month. Simultaneous and photocopied submissions OK.
Terms: Pays 7% royalty. Sends prepublication galleys to author. Publishes ms an average of 1 year after acceptance.
Advice: "We are currently planning to publish three works of fiction for spring 1989. Two of the manuscripts are from new writers who have never before published fiction. These manuscripts were received through previous contacts. We encourage absolutely new writers, established—in fact, the only criterion is the quality of the manuscript itself. No computer printouts."

WESTGATE PRESS (IV), Subsidiary of The Westgate Group, 8 Bernstein Blvd., Center Moriches NY 11934. (516)878-2901. Assistant Editor: Loraine Chandler. Estab. 1981. "Independent press with a semi-pro status, soon to be 'very in demand.'" Publishes paperback originals. Books: variable good-quality and specialty stocks paper; offset printing; perfect binding; illustrations; average print order 1,000-5,000; first novel print order: 1,000. Plans 1 first novel this year. Publishes 4-5 total titles each year; 1-2 fiction titles. Sometimes critiques rejected mss.
Needs: Psychic/supernatural/occult, short story collections. Serious metaphysical topics only as related to New Age topics. No porno, sectarian religion, contemporary surface material, one-sided theories, etc.
How to Contact: Does not accept or return unsolicited mss. Query first with outline/synopsis and 3 sample chapters. SASE. No agented fiction. Reports on queries in 1 week; 2 weeks on mss. Simultaneous and photocopied submissions OK. Accepts computer printout submissions, including dot-matrix.
Terms: Pays royalties of 5-10%, negotiable advance. Sends pre-publication galleys to author. Writer's guidelines free for SASE; book catalog for #10 SASE.
Advice: "Please! Please! Give us something truly unique! Don't be afraid of controversy or of shattering outdated hypothesis. Give us a genuinely moving blend of the macabre and the metaphysical!"

‡WINDRIVER PUBLISHING COMPANY INC., 6309 North O'Connor Rd., Suite 100, Irving TX 75039-3510. (214)869-7625. Imprints include: WindRiver Books (adult), The Magic Lantern (children's). VP/Editorial, Fiction Editor: Vicki Crow. Estab. 1986. "Midsize publisher (8 persons)—we will grow!" Publishes hardcover and paperback (trade paper only) originals. Books: 60-80 lb paper (varies by book); contract printing (such companies as Braun-Brumfield/R.R. Donnelly, etc.); smyth (hardcover), notch-adhesive (softcover) and saddle (childrens—24 page) binding; sometimes illustrations; average print order: varies from 2-3,000 up; first novel print order: 2-3,000 up. Published new writers within the last year. Plans 3 first novels. Averages 10 total titles, 3-4 fiction titles each year. Sometimes comments on rejected ms.
Needs: Mystery, mainstream, childrens. "We prefer mystery, but accept nearly all types except romance and/or sex." Recently published *Message of the Locust*, by Marcum/Meyers (mystery/adventure); *The Conquerors*, by Poole (historical); *The Golden Carousel*, by Crow (mainstream).
How to Contact: Query first. Box 111003, Carrollton TX 75011-1003. SASE (we will always return a manuscript, but prefer return postage). Very little agented fiction. Reports in 1 week on queries; 1-2 months on mss. Simultaneous and photocopied submissions OK. Accepts dot-matrix computer printout submissions (but DO NOT LIKE).
Terms: Royalty varies. Advance varies. Publishes ms about 1 year after acceptance.
Advice: "We have not been big in fiction before now, so we are treading a rather new and somewhat strange land. But, if it is a good book, we are interested. Everybody has to start somewhere. Stephen King did. Louis L'Amour did. All a new writer really needs is an editor willing to look at his or her work. We will and I hope we never change, no matter how big we get. We have had good luck with new writers. With few (and I mean few) exceptions, they have been a great bunch. Clear, concise queries and some really good manuscripts, well presented. We've had to turn down a lot of good stories simply because they weren't right for us, not because they were bad books. Don't be afraid to try. At the worst, we'll say no. At the best, we'll say yes. Remember: we prefer mysteries."

THE WOMAN SLEUTH MYSTERY SERIES (II), Subsidiary of The Crossing Press, Freedom, CA, 307 W. State St., Ithaca NY 14850. (607)273-4675; (607)273-2325. Series Editor: Irene Zahava. Publishes paperback originals and reprints. Books: 5x7 inch trade paperbacks; average print order: 5,000-7,500. Plans 2 first novels this year. Publishes 2-4 total titles/year.
Needs: Feminist, lesbian, suspense/mystery. Looking for "mystery novels, written by women, featuring strong female main character(s)—a womansleuth who is either a professional or amateur detective." No romance/mystery, if it's primarily romance. Recently published *Murder in the English Department*, by Valerie Miner (mystery); *She Came Too Late*, by Mary Wings, (mystery); *The Woman Sleuth Anthology: Contemporary Mystery Fiction by Women*; edited by Irene Zahava.
How to Contact: Accepts unsolicited ms. Submit outline/synopsis and 3-4 sample chapters. SASE (IRC). Reports in 2 weeks on queries; 1 month on mss. Photocopied submissions OK. Accepts computer printout submissions, including dot-matrix. Also send short stories for forthcoming volumes of *Woman Sleuth Anthology*—open deadline for stories.
Terms: Pays 7-10% royalties; negotiable advance. Sends galleys to author. Writer's guidelines for #10 SASE. Book catalog free on request (write to Crossing Press, Box 1048, Freedom CA 95019).
Advice: "Proofread your work carefully before sending it. If chapter one has many typos, ungrammatical sentences, etc.—I won't be enthusiastic about tackling chapter two."

WOMEN'S PRESS (I, II, IV), 229 College St., Toronto, Ontario M5T 1R4 Canada. (416)598-0082. Estab. 1972. Publishes paperback originals. Book: web coat paper; web printing; perfect binding; average print order: 2,000; first novel print order: 1,500. Plans 2 first novels this year. Averages 8 total titles each year. Sometimes "briefly" critiques rejected ms.
Needs: Contemporary, experimental, feminist, historical, juvenile and adolescent (fantasy, historical, contemporary), lesbian, literary, preschool/picture book, short story collections, mysteries, women's and young adult/teen (problem novels). Nothing sexist, pornographic, racist. Recently published *Imaging Women, an Anthology* (20 writers); *Never No Matter What*, by Maryleak Otto (children's book); *The Aerial Letter*, by Nicole Brossard (feminist essay).
How to Contact: Submit complete ms with SAE and "Canadian NB. stamps or a check. Our mandate is to publish Canadian women or landed immigrants." Reports in 3 months. Simultaneous or photocopied submissions OK. Accepts computer printout submissions. Prefers letter-quality.
Terms: Pays in royalties of 10% maximum. Sends galleys to author. Advance is negotiable. Free book catalog.
Advice: "We have so far published 4 novels and 2 collections of short stories. Our three adult novels have all been first novels. A translated work of fiction from Québec was published in 1985 and we plan more translations. We encourage first novelists. We edit very carefully. We can sometimes suggest alternative publishers."

WOODSONG GRAPHICS INC. (II), Box 238, New Hope PA 18938. (215)794-8321. Editor: Ellen Bordner. Estab. 1977. "Small publishing firm dedicated to printing quality books and marketing them creatively." Publishes paperback and hardcover originals. Books: standard or coated stock paper; photo offset printing; GBC or standard binding; illustrations; average print order: 5,000; first novel print order; 2,500. Averages 6-8 total titles each year. "Sometimes" buys juvenile mss with illustrations. Occasionally critiques rejected mss.
Needs: Adventure, contemporary, gothic/historical and contemporary romance, historical (general), humor/satire, juvenile (animal, easy-to-read, fantasy, historical, picture book, spy/adventure, contemporary), literary, mainstream, psychic/supernatural/occult, science fiction, suspense/mystery, war, western, and young adult (easy-to-read/teen, fantasy/science fiction, historical, problem novels, spy/adventure). No deviant sex of any kind or pornography.
How to Contact: Accepts unsolicited mss. Query first or submit complete ms. SASE always. Simultaneous and photocopied submissions OK. Accepts computer printout submissions, prefers letter-quality. Reports in 3 weeks on queries, longer on mss. "We do everything possible to get replies out promptly, but do read everything we're sent . . . and that takes time." Publishes ms 6-12 months after acceptance.
Terms: Pays in royalties; negotiates advance. Sends galleys to author. "Arrangements will depend totally on the author and manuscript."
Advice: "If first novels are good, we have no problem with them, and we're always happy to look. Along with queries, send at least a few pages of actual ms text, since quality of writing is more important than topic where fiction is concerned. If you believe in what you've written, stick with it. There is so much good material that we must reject simply because we can't afford to do everything. Others must have the same problem, and it's a matter of being on the right desk on the right day to finally succeed."

WORD BEAT PRESS (I), Box 22310, Flagstaff AZ 86002. Estab. 1982. Publishes hardback and trade paperback originals. Publishes four short story anthologies, collections or novellas a year, average print order: 1,000. Only accepting work through established agents.

WYRICK & COMPANY, 1A Pinckney St., Box 89, Charleston SC 29402. (803)772-0881. Editor-in-Chief: Charles L. Wyrick, Jr. Publishes hardcover and trade paperback originals and reprints. Averages 8-12 titles/year.
Needs: Adventure, ethnic, experimental, humor, mainstream. "We seek exemplary works of fiction, particularly those by southern writers. We welcome submissions by unpublished authors. We are not normally interested in sci-fi, western or romance." Recently published *The Secret at Robert's Roost*, by Mary M. Tallent; published new writers within the last year.
How to Contact: Submit outline/synopsis with a "clear, concise" cover letter and sample chapters or complete ms. SASE. Reports in 2-3 weeks on queries; 4-6 weeks on mss. Simultaneous and photocopied submissions OK.
Terms: Pays royalties of 8-12% on retail price. Average advance: $250.
Advice: "By publishing quality works of fiction and nonfiction, Wyrick & Company hopes to sell to knowledgeable readers of all ages—those who seek well written, well designed and well produced books of all types. Overemphasis by major houses and the media on blockbusters has created a greater, rather than a lesser, opportunity for small and medium-sized publishers to find and publish tomorrow's great books."

YANARIA PRESS (IV), 503 South Boston, Galion OH 44833. Editor/Publisher: R. Nathaniel Waldbauer. Assistant Editor: Patricia Stewart Weber. Two-person operation on part-time basis. Estab. 1986. Publishes paperback originals. Books: 20 lb bond paper; offset and photocopy printing; saddlestitched binding; b&w pen-and-ink illustrations; average print order: 1,500. Published new writers within the last year. Averages 4 titles/year, all fiction. Occasionally critiques rejected mss.
Needs: Adventure, fantasy, horror, science fiction, short story collections. "At this time, I am only accepting short stories for various anthologies." Recently published *World of Yanaria* (anthology); *Timelane* (anthology); *Marewon*, by L. Craig and P.S. Weber.
How to Contact: Accepts unsolicited mss. Submit complete ms with cover letter. SASE. Reports in 4 weeks on queries; 8-12 weeks on mss. Photocopied submissions OK. Accepts computer printout submissions.
Terms: Average advance: 1¢/word. Provides two author's copies. Writer's guidelines for #10 SASE and 65¢ postage.
Advice: "As a new publishing enterprise, I'm focusing more on SF/fantasy/horror anthologies, as well as some 'shared-universe' anthologies, using stories to 12,000 words. Read the guidelines!"

YITH PRESS (I, IV), 1051 Wellington Rd., Lawrence KS 66044. (913)843-4341. Subsidiary: *Eldritch Tales Magazine*. Editor/Publisher: Crispin Burnham. Estab. 1984. One-man operation on part-time basis. Publishes paperback originals and reprints. Books: offset printing; perfect binding; illustrations; average print order: 500-1,000. Averages 1-2 titles each year. Average first novel print order 500-1,000 (depending pre-publication orders). Occasionally critiques rejected ms.

Needs: Fantasy and horror. Accepts short stories for collections only. Novels needs include "anything in the supernatural horror category." No "mad slasher or sword and sorcery."

How to Contact: Accepts unsolicited mss. Submit complete ms with SASE. Reports in 2 months. Simultaneous and photocopied submissions OK. Accepts computer printout submissions. Prefers letter-quality. Disk submissions OK with MacIntosh II system.

Terms: Individual arrangement with author depending on the book. Sends galleys to author. Pays in royalties of 25% minimum; 35% maximum.

Advice: "Be original, don't try to be the next Lovecraft or Stephen King. Currently, I plan to publish one or two books/year, along with *Eldritch Tales*. The author/editor relationship should be give and take on both sides. I will try *not* to rewrite the author's work. If I feel that it needs some changes then I'll suggest them to the author. We are currently on hold with the book line as we are trying to get *Eldritch Tales* out on a quarterly schedule. Any potential submitter should send a card to inquire as to status."

YORK PRESS, Box 1172, Fredericton, New Brunswick E3B 5C8 Canada. (506)458-8748. Editorial Director: Dr. S. Elkhadem. Estab. 1975. Midsize independent publisher with plans to expand. Publishes hardcover and paperback originals. Publishes in English exclusively. Number of titles: 50 in 1988. Average first novel print order 1,000 copies.

Needs: Contemporary, experimental, and translations by established writers. "No mss written mainly for entertainment, i.e., those without literary or artistic merit." Recently published *Modern Egyptian Short Stories* and *Three Contemporary Egyptian Novels*, translated and edited by Saad El-Gabalawy; and Michel Butor's *Description of San Marco*, translated by Barbara Mason.

How to Contact: Accepts unsolicited mss, "although an initial query is appreciated." Query with SASE or SAE and IRC. No simultaneous submissions; photocopied submissions OK. Reports in 1 week on queries, 1 month on mss.

Terms: Pays 5-10% in royalties; no advance. Free book catalog.

Advice: "We are devoted to the promotion of scholarly publications; areas of special interest include general and comparative literature, literary criticism and creative writing of an experimental nature."

ZEPHYR PRESS (I), 13 Robinson St., Somerville MA 02145. Subsidiary of Aspect, Inc. Editors: Ed Hogan, Miriam Sagan, Leora Zeitlin, Hugh Abernethy. Estab. 1980. Small press with part-time staff of 3. Publishes hardcover and paperback originals. Books: acid free paper; offset printing; Smythe-sewn binding; illustrations sometimes; average print order: 1000-1,500; first novel print order: 1,000-1,500. Averages 2 total titles, 1-2 fiction titles each year. $12 reading fee for all mss submitted; written critique with all responses.

Needs: Contemporary, ethnic, experimental, feminist/lesbian, gay, historical, humor/satire, literary, mainstream, regional, science fiction, short story collections. "We in general seek fiction or short stories by less-established writers." Recently published *Two Novels*, by Philip Whalen, and *The St. Veronica Gig Stories*, by Jack Pulaski.

How to Contact: Accepts unsolicited mss. Query first with SASE recommended. Accepts computer printout submissions. Prefers letter-quality. Reports in 2-4 weeks on queries.

Terms: Pays in author's copies of 10% of print (1st edition); 20% royalties on publisher's net (subsequent editions, if any). Sends galleys to author by arrangement. "There can be some flexibility of terms, based on mutual arrangements, if desired by author and publisher." Book catalog for SASE.

Advice: "Seek well qualified feedback from press and/or professionally established writers before submitting manuscripts to publishers. We are especially interested in first novels. We encourage first novelists if they truly feel they are ready. We regard the author/editor relationship as one of close cooperation, from editing through promotion."

> 66 *The legend that characters run away from their authors—taking up drugs, having sex operations and becoming president—implies that the writer is a fool with no knowledge or mastery of his craft. The idea of authors running around helplessly behind their cretinous inventions is contemptible.* 99
>
> —*John Cheever*

Foreign small presses

The following small presses in countries outside the U.S. and Canada will consider novels or short fiction collections by North American writers. Most of these markets do not pay. Always include proper return postage (IRCs or foreign stamps) to ensure a response or the return of the manuscript. (See Manuscript Mechanics.)

‡**ALBATROSS BOOKS PTY LTD**, Box 320, Sutherland 2232 Australia. Fiction Editor: Ken Goodlet. Publishes 4 fiction titles annually. "We are Christian publishers for the general market and publish children's, teenage and adult fiction." Author's royalty is 10% of the retail sales (Australian dollar sales) and 15% of net receipts (on US and other foreign currency sales). "While it should reflect a Christian world view, this may be either implicit or explicit. We envisage the reader as not necessarily Christian but expecting a gripping, well written story."

‡**ARLINGTON BOOKS PUBLISHERS LTD.**, 15-17 King St., St. James's, London SW1Y 6QU England. Fiction Editor: Peter Danckwerts. Publishes 6-8 fiction titles annually. "Romances, thrillers, general fiction. We are a general publisher with a large health and beauty list. Only a small minority of our books are fiction." Writers receive royalty payment every six months. A modest advance against royalties is paid upon signature of the contract, and another advance is paid upon publication. "Only submit a manuscript in what you consider to be its finished form, neatly typed without spelling mistakes. Neat presentation and wide margins help to make the manuscript more readable. If you use a computer or word processor, run the book through a spelling checker before printing out. Don't expect a rapid answer; we may want three or four opinions before replying. Return postage is appreciated."

‡**ASHTON SCHOLASTIC LTD.**, Private Bag 1, Penrose, Auckland New Zealand. Fiction Editor: Penny Scown. Publishes 15 fiction titles annually. "Educational publishing with a focus on books for the teaching of language arts and children's liteature for all ages." Pays royalties. "Do not 'write down' to children—write the story you want to tell using the best language—i.e., most appropriate vocabulary, letting the story only dictate the length."

‡**BIBLIOTECA DI NOVA SF, FUTURO, GREAT WORKS OF SF**, Perseo LIbri srl, Box 1240, I-40100 Bologna Italy. Fiction Editor: Ugo Malaguti. "Science fiction and fantasy; novels and/or collections of stories." Pays 7% royalties on cover price; advance: $800-$1,000 on signing contract. Buys Italian book rights; other rights remain with author. "While preferring published writers, we also consider new writers."

‡**BLOODAXE BOOKS LTD.**, Box 1SN, Newcastle Upon Tyne NE99 1SN England. Editor: Neil Astley. Publishes 1-3 novels or story collections/year. "We are primarily a poetry publisher, and publish very little fiction in any form. The only fiction we are interested in seeing is 'literary' fiction." Writers are paid an agreed fee, half on signature of contract, half on publication. Royalties thereafter. "Send an explanatory letter beforehand together with a SAE."

‡**EASTERN CARIBBEAN INSTITUTE (ECI) (IV)**, Box 1338, Frederiksted, Virgin Islands 00841. Editor/President: S.B. Jones-Hendrickson, PhD. Estab. 1982. Small press with plans to expand. Publishes hardcover originals and paperback originals. Regional. Needs for novels include Caribbean issues and settings. No religious. Query with SASE. Reports in 1 week on queries; 1 month for mss.

EXCESS PRESS (IV), 4 Bower St., Maidstone, Kent ME16 8SD England. Subsidiary: *Excess* magazine. Editor: Paul Buck. One-man operation, part-time. Contemporary, sexuality, experimental, language-centered, literary and translations. "If you believe in what you're doing, you'll persevere despite all the odds against you."

‡**FOURTH ESTATE**, Classic House, 113 Westbourne Grove, London W2 4UP England. Editor: Giles O'Bryen. Publishes 6 books/year. "Small general publisher. Modern fiction, mostly young writers. Strong storyline but often a new or different way of telling it." Writers paid advance against royalties. "Submit only a synopsis and sample chapter in the first instance."

GMP PUBLISHER LTD., Box 247, London N15 6RW England. Editor: Richard Dipple. Publishes 10 story collections or novels yearly. "Gay publishing house specialising in books for or by gay men, though we do also publish some books of interest to women and/or by women authors. We hope that many of our titles also reach a wider audience." Pays royalties. "We're particularly interested in authors who use a word processor and can supply material on disk. This is particularly true with writers sending in work from abroad."

HANDSHAKE EDITIONS, Atelier A2, 83 rue de la Tombe Issoire, 75014 Paris France. Editor: Jim Haynes. Publishes 4 story collections or novels/year. "Only face-to-face submissions accepted. More interested in 'faction' and autobiographical writing." Pays in copies. Writers interested in submitting a manuscript should "have lunch or dinner with me in Paris."

‡**HARD ECHO PRESS LTD.**, 171 The Mall, Onehunga AK6 New Zealand. Fiction Editor: Warwick Jordan. Publishes approx. 2-5 fiction titles annually. "Small, independent press. Interested in publishing small editions of novels which are experimental and current in their approach. Am particularly interested in doing handcraft (i.e. letterpress) limited editions for established writers, or publishing work they would prefer to not submit to major publishers, or which their publishers can't handle." Pays 10% royalty on retail sales, paid when publisher receives payment. "Include SASE; must be typed ms; not interested in short stories unless they are particularly brilliant; prefer shorter (100-200 pages) novels."

HEMKUNT, Publishers A-78 Naraina Industrial Area Ph.I, New Delhi India 110028. Managing Director: G.P. Singh. "We would be interested in novels, preferably by authors with a published work. Would like to have distribution rights for US, Canada and UK beside India."

JOURNEYMAN, 97 Ferme Park Rd., Crouch End, London, N8 95A England. US Address: Kampmann & Company, 9 E. 40th St., New York NY 10016. Editor: Peter Sinclair. Publishes 6-10 novels or story collections/year. Socialist and feminist fiction. Pays royalties. "Take account of the type of fiction we publish first, and then write asking us if we would be interested to see a manuscript."

‡**KARNAC HOUSE**, 300 Westbourne Park Road, London W11 1EH England. Fiction Editor: Amon Saba Saakana. Publishes 3-4 fiction titles annually. "An Afro-Caribbean publishing company concerned with global literary concerns of the Afrikan community, whether in North and South America, the Caribbean, Afrika or Europe. We rarely pay advances, and if so, very small, but pay a royalty rate of 8-10% on the published price of the book. We look for innovative work in the areas outlined above and work which attempts to express the culture, language, mythology—ethos—of the people. We look for work which tries to break away from standard English as the dominant narrative voice."

KAWABATA PRESS (II), Knill Cross House, HR Anderton Rd., Millbrook, Torpoint, Cornwall PL10 1DX England. Fiction Editor: C. Webb. "Mostly poetry—but prose should be realistic, free of genre writing and clichés and above all original in ideas and content." Writers receive half of profits after print costs are covered. "Write first with outline."

‡**KINGSWAY PUBLICATIONS**, Lottbridge Drove, Eastbourne, E. Sussex BN23 6NT England. Managing Editor: Elizabeth Gibson. Publishes 10-12 fiction titles annually. Publishes "Christian books; children's books. Books on leadership, discipleship, devotional, biography, music, the church, currrent issues from a Christian perspective. A few works of fiction." Payment varies "according to whether writer has an agent or not, and whether we negotiate contract directly or through a US publisher. Submit one sample chapter, double-spaced, typed with adequate margins and a synopsis. Allow 6-8 weeks for response. The writer should understand the international market. Do not send anything on millenium, new age or astrology."

‡**THE MALVERN PUBLISHING CO. LTD.**, 32 Old Street, Upton-Upon-Severn, Worcs. WR8 OHW England. Fiction Editor: Cintia Stammers. Publishes 12 stories/year. "Full length adult fiction—60,000-80,000 words." Pays in royalties. "No science fiction or fantasy."

MAROVERLAG, Riedingerstrasse 24, D-8900, Augsburg West Germany. Editor: Benno Käsmayr. Publishes 4-6 novels or story collections/year. Publishes "exciting American authors in excellent translations; e.g. Charles Bukowski, Jack Kerouac, William Burroughs, Paul Bowles, Gerald Locklin." Writers paid for published fiction. "Please include SAE and postage."

‡**MORRIGAN PUBLICATIONS**, 84 IM Avenue, Bath, Avon BA2 1AN England. Fiction Editor: Les Escott. Publishes 4 fiction titles annually. Publishes "1,000 copies of which 250-300 are signed limited editions." Writers receive "advance on contract and publication, and royalties of 10-12.5%. If no advance paid, then increased royalties (usually 15%) on ltds and 10% on trade. Just send the manuscript with return postage. No hard SF or sword and sorcery (unless if are exeptionally high standard)."

‡**NEW ORCHARD EDITIONS**, Stanley House, Fleets Land, Poole BH15 3AJ United Kingdom. Fiction Editor: David Graves. Publishes 5 fiction titles annually. Publishes "crime, mystery, war." Pays royalties of 10% of retail price. "Submit a good synopsis/outline first!"

‡**RIMU**, Box 1198, Hamilton New Zealand. Fiction Editors: Theola Wyllie et al. Publishes 1-2 fiction titles annually. "Small house selling high-quality fiction and normal commercial/trade line. Best sub-

jects on/by third/fourth world. But quality counts." Payment "by negotiation. Because of our small and remote situation, cost sharing often used. Write first with proposal and sample of work."

‡SETTLE PRESS (WIGMORE), 32 Savile Row, London WIX 1AG England. Fiction Editors: Mrs. M. Carter, Mr. D. Settle. Publishes 10 + fiction titles annually. "Political and contemporary thrillers (often with film potential). Books with a strong storyline, from love stories to psychological overtones, animal stories." Writers paid on royalty basis. "Send a synopsis plus information on author. We will consider carefully."

‡TRANSWORLD PUBLISHERS, Level 1,20 Young Street, Neutral Bay, N.S.W. 2089 Australia. Editor: Jacqueline Kent. "Mass-market fiction with strong plots and characters; some literary fiction under our Black Swan paperback imprint; some children's. Greater interest, at present, in adventure drama/character drama than science fiction or fantasy. Give us a synopsis and sample chapter first. Evaluation normally takes between four and six weeks."

‡UNIVERSITY OF QUEENSLAND PRESS, Box 42, St. Lucia, Queensland 4060 Australia. Fiction Editor: D'Arcy Randall. Publishes 14 + fiction titles and 4 young adult titles annually. "UQP publishes literary fiction with Australian content or relevance to Australian cultural life." Pays royalties. "Send brief biography, synopsis and sample chapters plus IRC to fiction editor."

WOLFHOUND PRESS, 68 Mountjoy Sq., Dublin Ireland. Publisher: Seamus Cashman. Estab. 1974. Publishes hardcover and paperback originals and reprints. Plans 3 first novels this year. Occasionally critiques rejected mss. Needs contemporary, experimental, juvenile, literary and short story collections. "Query first; submit outline/synopsis and 3 sample chapters with SAE, IRCs." Pays royalties or negotiable contract.

Small press/'88-'89 changes

The following small presses appeared in the 1988 edition of *Fiction Writer's Market* but are not in the 1989 edition of *Novel and Short Story Writer's Market*. Those presses whose editors did not respond to our request for an update of their listings may not have done so for a variety of reasons—they may be out of business, for example, or they may be overstocked with submissions. Note that small presses from outside the U.S. and Canada appear at the end of this list.

Abbey Press (asked to be deleted)
Alaska Nature Press-Publishers (did not respond)
Andromeda Press (out of business)
Arrowood Books (did not respond)
Borealis Press (asked to be deleted)
Circa Press (asked to be deleted)
First East Coast Theatre and Publishing Company (did not respond)
Fjord Press (asked to be deleted)
Frog in the Well (did not respond)
Gay Presses of New York (asked to be deleted)
Griffon House Publications (did not respond)
Grunwald & Radcliffe Publishers (did not respond)
Heroica Books (asked to be deleted)
Kav Books (out of business)

Lowery Publishing and Productions Corp. (did not respond)
Mey-House Books (did not respond)
Middle Coast Publishing (did not respond)
National Press (did not respond)
Nerve Press (did not respond)
North Country Press (did not respond)
Ommation Press (did not respond)
Parable Press (did not respond)
The Perigee Press (did not respond)
Randall House Publications (not accepting mss by writers outside denomination)
Routledge, Chapman & Hall (did not respond)
St. Luke's Press (asked to be deleted)
San Diego Publishing Company (subsidy)
Second Coming Press (did not respond)

Shameless Hussy Press (asked to be deleted)
Shining Knight Press (did not respond)
Stabur Press (did not respond)
Swallow's Tale Press (did not respond)
Swamp Press (did not respond)
Third Woman Press (did not respond)
Thunder Creek Publishing Cooperative (moved; no forwarding address)
Sherry Urie (asked to be deleted)
John Westburg (not accepting manuscripts)
George Whittell Memorial Press (did not respond)
Yankee Books (no more fiction)

Foreign small press
Aquila Publishing (U.K.), Ltd. (did not respond)
Poplar Press (did not respond)
Spectre Press (did not respond)
The Vanitas Press (responded too late to be included)

Commercial Publishers

People continued to read more fiction than ever last year; individual publishers are enjoying record profits; and forecasters are predicting these trends will continue. In 1983, a Gallup poll found 39% of the books purchased by its study group were fiction—by last year, 44% of the books were fiction. This growth has an effect—generally positive—on the individual fiction writer. It means new writers are still in demand!

If you're interested in submitting to listings in this section—especially if you don't ever plan to submit to small presses—you should take a good look at the literary agent section on page 599. Every year, a few more commercial publishers change their listings to reflect the fact that they no longer consider unsolicited manuscripts or even query letters from unpublished writers, but will look only at work submitted by literary agents. Another reason why you should think of finding an agent is that publishing houses today are in such flux with takeovers and changes in editors, that submitting through an agent is likely to offer greater stability than submitting on your own.

Consolidation

Random House's purchase of Crown Books for a rumored price of more than $100 million links Random with Waldenbooks, the biggest bookseller in the U.S.—and makes Random House the largest publisher in the country. The move is probably a good one for Random House and Crown, but even publishers worry that anything that diminishes the number of independent publishing houses is a setback for most writers. Two percent of the nation's publishers are now responsible for 75% of the titles published in the country, and the top 30% are responsible for 99%.

Major book combinations have been Random House Inc., which in addition to Crown owns Alfred A. Knopf, Times Books, Pantheon and Ballantine; Bantam Doubleday Dell, owned by the German Bertelsmann company, which includes Delacorte Press; Simon & Schuster, which owns Prentice-Hall and Pocket Books; Viking Penguin, which is owned by Pearson and includes E.P. Dutton and NAL; and the Putnam and Berkley publishing groups, owned by MCA. In addition, the Hearst Corporation owns William Morrow and Avon Books; and Rupert Murdoch owns Harper & Row and Salem House. Yet another publishing combination, Macmillan, Inc., which also includes Charles Scribner Sons and Atheneum Publishers, was acquired by Robert Maxwell, the English publisher.

Harper & Row also picked up the Zondervan Corporation, a major publisher of religious books; Random House bought Vanguard Press, the independent publishing house that published the first books of Saul Bellow, Dr. Seuss and Joyce Carol Oates. The 32-year-old firm Lyle Stuart was sold to Carol Management Corporation in the fall of 1988. However. Carol Communications' plans to establish Birch Lane Press as a general fiction and nonfiction house go against the general trend in which one publishing company buys another, sells off assets and takes over the company's backlist.

Even authors who command million-dollar advances may not really be benefiting by all the takeovers. When one publishing house acquires another, the two houses are usually not allowed to bid against one another in an auction. For not-yet-published and midlist authors, there is another problem: the decrease in the number of independent publishers means a decrease in the number of independent voices with the power to accept a manuscript for publication. Both writers and publishers worry this trend may ultimately lead to an increased homogeneity in what is published by the major houses.

Bestsellers and big advances

One hundred twelve mass-market paperback titles, topped by horror, glitz and romance, published last year had in-print figures of at least 1 million copies. There were 254 trade paperback bestsellers, up from 193 titles the previous year; and a record 52 hardcover fiction books sold 100,000 or more copies during the year. While the top 15 hardcover fiction sales last year included 13 writers whose work had appeared on previous bestselling fiction lists, two—Scott Turow (*Presumed Innocent*) and Tom Wolfe (*The Bonfire of the Vanities*)—were new to the list and set sales records for their publishers.

Top-selling fiction writers received more money than ever for their work—between $10.1 million and $11.6 million to Mary Higgins Clark for five books; $9 million to Barbara Taylor Bradford for 3 books; $2.75 million, plus $1.4 million contingent on sales, to Clive Cussler for 2 books—for example. Lesser-known writers must expect much smaller advances (usually $5,000 average). In fact, some of those huge advances are made at the expense of less well-known writers of category, literary and midlist fiction. Only by holding advances and royalties down for other fiction manuscripts, are publishers able to finance these blockbusters. Publishers sometimes do pay big money to little-known writers, however: Fawcett paid $500,000 for *Fire Arrow*, for example, a first novel by Franklin Allen Leib last year, hoping to get in on the ground floor with a talented writer.

Mass-market paperbacks and hard/soft deals

Except for the bestsellers, mass-market paperbacks have not been doing well lately, with unsold books being returned at a rate as high as 40%. Reasons for these poor sales include the great growth in hardcover sales, and the rising prices of the paperbacks themselves; the pricing ratio between hardcovers and paperbacks used to be about 8:1 or 10:1 but is now more like 4:1 or 3:1. Nevertheless, more and more publishers who traditionally published only hardcover books are now acquiring paperback houses as well. This is due to the new trend in publishing, under which a book is acquired at the same time by a hardcover and a softcover house under the same corporate ownership.

The major push for these hard/soft deals comes from the big-name authors and their agents, rather than from the publishers themselves. In a conventional publishing arrangement, the author has to share reprint rights—the money earned from the sale of paperback rights—with the hardcover house, but in a hard-soft deal, the author keeps the entire paperback advance.

This means more money for bestselling authors, but it also means more risks for publishers, who are not now guaranteed profits by selling a hardcover books' rights to a separate paperback publisher. Some industry insiders worry hard/soft deals might make publishers leery of acquiring a book which is considered a little risky—on which they might lose money in both hardcover and paperback editions.

Trade paperbacks

Three years after the launch of Vintage Contemporaries, trade paperback imprints still offer outstanding opportunities for writers of contemporary and literary fiction, although some publishers feel the market is becoming crowded and are taking a wait-and-see attitude toward expanding their lines. Penguin, for example, decided to cut back its Contemporary American Fiction series to 20 titles in 1988.

Most publishers are not cutting back, however. Vintage Contemporaries scheduled around a dozen titles for 1988, and Collier Fiction, Macmillan's new trade paperback series, will publish six titles a season; Bantam New Fiction planned to publish 8-10 titles in 1988, bolstered by the strong sales for the six initial titles, especially Glenn Savan's *White Palace* (70,000 copies), and Ann Hood's *Somewhere Off the Coast of Maine* (55,000 copies), which were heavily pushed by Waldenbooks. And in the fall of 1988, Dell introduced the Delta Fiction line of novels, expecting to present 12 books a year (6 originals and 6 chosen from either Delta's own backlist or from other houses' lists). Booksellers have been guardedly optimistic about the continued success of these series—fewer have been taking on a publisher's entire series, with more attention being given to the individual books themselves.

Science fiction and fantasy

It was a record year for science fiction publishing—the third in a row, with the total number of books published rising by 12% from the year before. Putnam/Berkley/Ace led in sales, followed by Tor and Ballantine/Del Rey; DAW Books also had its most successful year to date. A record 177 publishers produced science fiction and fantasy books last year, and publishers predict this year will prove a record-breaker too.

Trends in the field include more humor and satire, and an increase in the number of women who are writing and publishing science fiction. Science fiction is becoming more and more professional and less and less "fannish," as larger companies want to make money in the genre. The writers who began the cyberpunk trend—the subgenre dealing with a future of computer networks and computer-brain connections combined with a kind of rock 'n' roll sensibility—three years ago have for the most part moved on to different things. In fantasy, editors are findings more plots set in the real world—magic intruding on realistic characters rather than on fantasy figures. Tor will be introducing the new Tor Doubles—back-to-back novellas, noting that some of science fiction's best work has been done as novellas, but they've been difficult to package for an audience mostly looking for long novels.

It remains to be seen whether readers will continue to support this intense productivity in the science fiction/fantasy fields—some publishers worry that there may be a period of glut in the future. Some publishers also see a kind of stratification appearing in the field: more copies of fewer titles have been selling, and some publishers are even cutting back in their lines. Tor Books is cutting at least 25% of its mass market list next year, and St. Martin's will be dropping its science fiction mass-market program and publishing less hardcover science fiction.

Romance

Harlequin launched its new Harlequin Historical line in July with plans to publish two new books each month, set for the most part in North America, the British Commonwealth, France or other "accessible" countries. Otherwise, series romance increasingly seems to be emphasizing traditional values—according to a Waldenbooks survey, nearly 64% of romance novel readers consider realism more important than sensuality—while at the same time developing a strong romantic suspense subgenre, as seen in the popularity of the Intimate Moments line. Readers have also responded favorably to romances with 'new age' themes, such as psychic phenomena and time travel. Characters in general are getting older, reflecting the aging of the baby boom generation.

Children's books

As the baby-boom generation continues to reproduce, children's books continue their tremendous popularity—and that's good news for writers. There are more children's bookstores than ever (over 350 specialty children's bookstores now in the country), and parents are buying books for their children in record numbers. Also children are taking a greater interest in reading—according to a Waldenbooks' survey, 75% of 5-13 year old readers would rather read than watch TV. Books for the intermediate age group (9-12) are doing particularly well, led by the Babysitter's Club and Sweet Valley Twins series. Dinosaurs are "out" this year (although Waldenbooks reports an increased interest in books about farm animals), as are books about licensed characters like the Smurfs. Readers are currently requesting more basic, traditional books, and sales are stronger than they have been in 10 years. The only real problem seen in the children's book industry right now is that there are so many new titles being published that booksellers have trouble stocking them all and choosing among the many good titles available.

How to submit

Accept the fact that placing a novel may take as much time as writing one, but editors insist that quality fiction will eventually get published. If you haven't sent a book-length manuscript out before, check the Manuscript Mechanics section on page 131 before mailing your novel or story collection. Always query before you send out a complete manuscript, and spend as much time on your proposal letter as you would on writing a page of your book. Remember your chances of publishing improve if you have magazine publication credits, or if you have an agent working for you.

Submit work to contests and try to make contact with editors at writing conferences. Study publishers' catalogues, and direct your query letter to a particular person—not just "Fiction Editor." Editors are always frustrated when writers submit manuscripts that don't meet their needs at all. But don't give up! The writers who eventually are published are often simply the most persistent.

Check the category index on page 636 to get an idea of possible publishers for your type of fiction. We've used the following ranking system to help you find appropriate markets for your manuscript:

> I   *Publisher encourages beginning or unpublished writers to submit work for consideration, and publishes new writers frequently;*
> II   *Publisher accepts work by established writers and by occasional new writers of unusual talent;*
> III   *Publisher does not encourage beginning or unagented writers; publishes mainly writers with previous credits;*
> IV   *Special-interest or regional publisher open only to writers on certain subjects or from certain geographical areas.*

ACCENT BOOKS (II), A Division of Accent Publications, Box 15337, Denver CO 80215. (303)988-5300. Executive Editor: Mary B. Nelson. Estab. 1975. Growing midsize independent publisher of Christian books. Publishes paperback originals. Books: type of paper varies; established book printers; average print order varies. Published new writers within the last year. Averages 18-24 total titles, 4-6 fiction titles this year. Occasionally critiques rejected mss.
Needs: "Only Christian books in these categories: contemporary, mystery/romance and frontier romance. We will look at any Christian novel in these areas. All must have strong, evangelical, Christian storylines showing how Christ makes a difference in a person's life." Recently published *Storm at Daybreak*, by B.J. Hoff (contemporary mystery/romance); *Colorado Lady*, by Mary Langer Smith (frontier romance).
How to Contact: Does not accept unsolicited mss. Submit outline/synopsis and 3-4 sample chapters with SASE. Reports in 5 weeks on queries, 90 days on mss. Simultaneous submissions and clear photocopied submissions accepted. Accepts computer printout submissions if letter-quality. No dot-matrix.
Terms: Pays royalties. Sends galleys to author. Writer's guidelines for SASE; book catalog for 6x9 SASE with 60¢ postage.
Advice: "We are looking for fiction with a solid evangelical message written with an evident command of plot and character development. We encourage and accept new writers. We're looking for quality writers. We like a personal, privileged and pleasant relationship with authors. We foresee conservative, planned growth in both fiction and nonfiction in a wider number of subject areas."

ACE CHARTER BOOKS, Berkley Publishing Group, 200 Madison Ave., New York NY 10016. (212)686-9820. Estab. 1977. Publishes paperback originals and reprints. See Berkley Publishing Group.

‡ANTIOCH CHILDREN'S BOOKS (IV), 888 Dayton St., Yellow Springs OH 45387. (513)767-7379. Associate Editor: Linda King. Fiction Editor: Corey Slabitt. Estab. 1926. Midsize independent publisher with plans to expand. Publishes paperback originals and reprints. "24 pages is our usual length for our children's line." Books: average print order: 10,000-50,000. Plans 4-6 first novels this year. Averages 20 total titles/year.
Needs: Juvenile (4-12 years) including animal, easy-to-read, fantasy, historical, sports, spy/adventure and contemporary. "Most of our novels are generated in-house, but subjects and themes dealing with children is what we look for. We do not want to see anything unrelated to the juvenile field." Recently published *Away in the Manger* (a Christmas story); and *Teddy Bear's First Thanksgiving*, by Jill Wolf.
How to Contact: Accepts unsolicited mss. Query first. SASE. Reports on queries in 2 weeks; on mss in 4 weeks. Simultaneous submissions OK.
Terms: Payment varies. Sends galleys to author. Publishes mss 3-4 months after acceptance.

APPLE BOOKS, Scholastic, Inc., 730 Broadway, New York NY 10003. (212)505-3000. Senior Editor: Regina Griffin. Children's imprint. See Scholastic Inc.
Needs: "Apple books are generally contemporary. There are no restrictions as to length or subject matter, but all Apple Books are geared toward the capacities and interests of 8-12 year olds." Recently published *The Friendship Pact*, by Susan Beth Pfeffer; and *The Baby-sitters Club*, by Ann M. Martin.
How to Contact: Accepts unsolicited mss. Submit outline/synopsis and 3 sample chapters. Reports in 2 weeks on queries; 6 weeks on mss. Single submissions only. Accepts computer printout submissions. Prefers letter-quality.
Terms: Pays in royalties.

ARCHWAY PAPERBACKS, 1230 Avenue of the Americas, New York NY 10020. (212)698-7000. Senior Editor: Patricia McDonald. Published by Pocket Books. Imprints: Minstrel Books (ages 8-12); and Archway (ages 11 and up). Publishes paperback originals and reprints.
Needs: Young adult (girls' novels, suspense/adventure, adventure, thrillers, young readers (short, 80 pages and up), animals, theme— friends, adventure, mystery, family, etc.). Recently published *Is There Life After Boys*, by Linda Lewis: *Who Needs a Bratty Brother* by Linda Gandosch; *Hobie Hanson, You're Weird*, by Jamie Gilson.
How to Contact: Submit query first with outline; SASE "mandatory."
Advice: "Look at previously published novels in Archway series and Minstrel Books."

ATHENEUM BOOKS FOR CHILDREN (II), Imprint of the Macmillan Children's Book Group, 866 Third Ave., New York NY 10022. (212)702-7894. Editorial Director: Jonathan J. Lanman. Fiction Editors: Gail Paris or Marcia Marshall (especially sf/fantasy). Midsize imprint of large publisher/corporation. Publishes hardcover originals. Books: illustrations for picture books, some illustrated short novels; average print order: 6,000-7,500; first novel print order: 6,000. Published new writers within the last year. Plans 3 first novels this year. Averages 70 total titles, 55 fiction titles each year. Very rarely critiques rejected mss.
Needs: Juvenile (animal, fantasy, historical, sports, adventure, contemporary), preschool/picture book, young adult/teen (fantasy/science fiction, historical, problem novels, sports, spy/adventure, mystery). No "paperback romance type" fiction. Recently published *The Good-bye Book*, by Judith Viorst (3-6, picture book); *Tree by Leaf*, by Cynthia I. Voigt (9-13, pre-teen "problem"); and *Maudie in the Middle*, by Phyllis Reynolds Naylor (7-11, pre-teen illustrated novel).
How to Contact: Accepts unsolicited mss "if novel length, we want outline and 3 sample chapters." SASE. Agented fiction 40%. Reports in 3-4 weeks on queries; 6-8 weeks on mss. Simultaneous submissions OK "if we are so informed"; photocopied submissions OK "if clear and legible." Accepts computer printout submissions, including dot-matrix if dark and clear.
Terms: Pays in royalties of 10% minimum; 12% maximum. Average advance: $3,000 "along with advance and royalties, authors standardly receive ten free copies of their book and can purchase more at a 40% discount." Sends galleys to author. Writer's guidelines for #10 SAE and 1 first class stamp. Book catalog for 9x12 SAE and 6 first class stamps.
Advice: "We publish all hardcover originals, occasionally an American edition of a British publication. Our fiction needs have not varied in terms of quantity—of the 60-70 titles we do each year, 50-60 are fiction in different age levels. Our Spring 1988 list consisted of approximately 8 books for those be-

✝ *The double dagger before a listing indicates that the listing is new in this edition. New markets are often the most receptive to freelance contributions.*

tween 3 and 8, one of which was nonfiction; 11 books for ages 7-12 (4 nonfiction); 4 for the 10-14 level (2 nonfiction); and 5 for 10, 11 and up (1 nonfiction). We are less interested in specific topics or subject matter than in overall quality of craftsmanship. First, know your market thoroughly. We publish only children's books, so caring for and *respecting* children is of utmost importance. Also, fad topics are dangerous, as are works you haven't polished to the best of your ability. (Why should we choose a 'jewel in the rough' when we can get a manuscript a professional has polished to be ready for publication.) The juvenile market is not one in which a writer can 'practice' to become an adult writer. In general, be professional. We appreciate the writers who take the time to find out what type of books we publish by visiting the libraries and reading the books. Neatness is a pleasure, too.''

AUGSBURG PUBLISHING HOUSE, Box 1209, Minneapolis MN 55440. (612)330-3432. Editor: Roland Seboldt. Estab. 1850. Publishes paperback originals.
Needs: Religious/inspirational short stories for young readers (grades 8-12); for young teens ages 12-15, youth ages 15-17, adults. Recently published *Everybody Needs a Friend*, by Barbara Degrotte-Sorensen (for girls); *The Friendship Olympics*, by David Sorenson (for boys); *It Takes Two*, by Steve Swanson; and *Playing for Life*, by Nate Aaseng (short stories for young teens).
How to Contact: Query or submit complete ms or submit outline/synopsis and sample chapters with SASE. Simultaneous and photocopied submissions OK. Reports in 6 weeks on queries.
Terms: Pays 10% in royalties and offers $500 advance. Free book catalog with SASE.
Advice: "We are looking for short stories with life-related problems and Christian themes."

AVALON BOOKS (II, IV), 401 Lafayette St., New York NY 10003. See Thomas Bouregy & Co., Inc. Small category line.

AVON BOOKS (II), The Hearst Corporation, 105 Madison Ave., New York NY 10016. (212)481-5600. Imprints include Avon, Camelot and Flare. Estab. 1941. Large paperback publisher. Publishes paperback originals and reprints. Averages 300 titles a year.
Needs: Fantasy, historical romance, mainstream, occult/horror, science fiction, medical thrillers, intrigue, war, western and young adult/teen. No poetry, mystery, short story collections, religious, limited literary or esoteric nonfiction. Recently published *Through A Glass Darkly*, by Karleen Koen (historical); and *Vale of the Vole*, by Piers Anthony (fantasy/science fiction).
How to Contact: Query letters only. SASE to insure response.
Terms: Vary. Book catalog for SASE. Sponsors Flare Novel competition.

BAEN BOOKS (II), 260 5th Ave., New York NY 10001. (212)532-4111. Baen Science Fiction, Baen Fantasy. Publisher and Editor: Jim Baen. Assistant Editor: Toni Weiskopf. Consulting Editor: Josepha Sherman. Estab. 1983. Independent publisher; books are distributed by Simon & Schuster. Publishes hardcover and paperback originals and paperback reprints. Published new writers within the last year. Plans 8-12 first novels this year. Averages 600 fiction titles each year. Occasionally critiques rejected mss.
Needs: Fantasy and science fiction. Interested in science fiction novels (generally "hard" science fiction) and fantasy novels "that are not rewrites of last year's bestsellers." Recently published *The Paladin*, by C. J. Cherryh (fantasy); *The Man-Kzin Wars*, by Larry Niven (science fiction); and *The White Bull*, by Fred Saberhagen (science fiction).
How to Contact: Accepts unsolicited mss. Submit ms or outline/synopsis and 3 consecutive sample chapters with SASE. Reports in 2-3 weeks on partials; 4-8 weeks on mss. Will consider simultaneous submissions, "but grudgingly and not as seriously as exclusives." Accepts letter-quality computer printout submissions.
Terms: Pays in royalties; offers advance. Sends galleys to author. Writer's guidelines for SASE.
Advice: "We are publishing more—our line is healthy and growing. We encourage first novelists. Keep an eye and a firm hand on the overall story you are telling. Style is important but less important than plot. We like to maintain long-term relationships with authors."

BALLANTINE BOOKS, 201 E. 50th St., New York NY 10022. Subsidiary of Random House. Senior Editor: Pamela D. Strickler. Publishes originals (general fiction, mass-market, trade paperback and hardcover). Averages over 120 total titles each year.
Needs: Major historical fiction and women's contemporary. Manuscripts can be submitted unsolicited

Market categories: (I) Beginning; (II) General; (III) Prestige; (IV) Specialized.

to Pamela D. Strickler.
How to Contact: Submit outline/synopsis and complete ms. SASE required. Photocopied submissions OK. Reports in 2 months on queries; 4-5 months on mss.
Terms: Pays in royalties and advance.

BALLANTINE/EPIPHANY BOOKS (II), 201 E. 50th St., New York NY 10022. (212)572-1699. Division of Random House. Publicist: Carol Fass. Editor: Toni Simmons. Estab. 1983. Imprint includes Ballantine/Epiphany Hardcover. Publishes hardcover and paperback originals and paperback reprints. Books: offset printing; average print order: 30,000. Published new writers within the last year. Averages 13 total titles, 20% fiction titles each year. Average first novel print order 30,000 copies.
Needs: Religious/inspirational. "Novels must have inspirational qualities of a Christian nature." No fantasies. No Christian romances. Recently published *The River Line*, by Charles Morgan; *Poppy*, by Barbara Larriva.
How to Contact: Query; submit outline/synopsis, 3 sample chapters and SASE. Reports in 4-6 weeks on queries and mss. Simultaneous and photocopied submissions OK. Accepts computer printout submissions; prefers letter-quality.
Terms: Offers negotiable advance. Sends galleys to author. Writer's guidelines for #10 SASE. Book catalog for 9x12 SAE and 40¢ postage.
Advice: "Read some novels published by the publishing company to which you intend to submit a manuscript. Find an author you particularly admire and read all of his/her books! Common mistake is to try to describe a lengthy novel in a brief query letter without including a synopsis! It's impossible to assess a novel from a writer's brief description. It also looks amateurish when a writer states that he/her work is copywritten and when he/she states an expected advance. And never call an editor to query him/her about your manuscript!"

BANTAM BOOKS, INC. (II), Division of Bantam Dell Doubleday Publishing Group, 666 5th Ave., New York NY 10103. (212)765-6500. Imprints include Skylark, New Age, Loveswept, Sweet Dreams, Sweet Valley High, Spectra, Bantam New Fiction and Starfire. Estab. 1945. Complete publishing: hard-cover, trade, mass market. Number of titles: Plans 600 for 1988.
Needs: Contemporary, literary, adventure, mystery, spy, historical, western, war, gothic, romance, feminist, gay/lesbian, ethnic, psychic/supernatural, religious/inspirational, science fiction, fantasy, horror, humor/satire, and young adult. Recently published *Doctors*, by Erich Segal; *A Brief History of Time* Steven Hawkings.
How to Contact: Submit through agent. No unsolicited material accepted. Simultaneous and photocopied submissions OK. Reports on queries as soon as possible.
Terms: Individually negotiated; offers advance.

BANTAM SPECTRA BOOKS (II, IV), Subsidiary of Bantam Doubleday Dell Publishing Group, 666 5th Ave., New York NY 10103. (212)765-6500. Vice-President and Publisher: Lou Aronica; Senior Editors: Amy Stout, Betsy Mitchell; Pat LoBrutto. Assistant Editor: Janna Silverstein. Estab. 1985. Large science fiction, fantasy and speculative fiction line. Publishes hardcover originals and paperback originals and reprints. Plans to publish 2 first novels in 1989. Averages 66 total titles each year, all fiction.
Needs: Fantasy, literary, science fiction. Needs for novels include novels that attempt to broaden the traditional range of science fiction and fantasy. Strong emphasis on characterization. Especially well written traditional science fiction and fantasy will be considered. No fiction that doesn't have at least some element of speculation or the fantastic. Recently published *Triumph of the Darksword*, by Margaret Weis and Tracy Hickman (epic fantasy); *Return to Eden*, by Harry Harrison (speculative fiction); *Great Sky River*, by Gregory Benford.
How to Contact: Query first. "We prefer to see query letters first, including a couple of paragraphs summarizing the story, along with background on the author listing previous writing credits, if any." SASE. Agented fiction 90%. Reports in 3-4 weeks on queries; 6-8 weeks on mss. Photocopied submissions OK. Accepts computer printouts, including dot-matrix, "only very dark and very readable ones."
Terms: Pays in royalties; negotiable advance. Sends galleys to author.
Advice: "With the merging of Bantam with Doubleday and Dell, we have created a hardcover science fiction and fantasy imprint called Foundation with Doubleday. The list presently includes authors such as Isaac Asimov, Parke Godwin, Lewis Shiner and Sheri S. Tepper. We are always looking for first nov-

Read the Manuscript Mechanics section to learn the correct way to prepare and submit a manuscript.

elists. Don't pay much attention to current trends, just write what really comes from the heart. We work very closely with our writers on both development of their fiction and long-term career goals."

‡BART BOOKS (II), 155 E. 34th St., New York NY 10016. (212)696-9141. Publisher: Norman Goldfind. Independent mass-market line. Estab. 1985. Publishes paperback originals and reprints. Books: newsprint paper; offset printing; perfect binding; average print order: 25,000. Published new writers within the last year. Plans 2 first novels this year. Averages 60 total titles, 36 fiction titles each year.
Needs: Adventure, contemporary, historical, horror, humor/satire, mainstream, romance (historical), suspense/mystery. Recently published *The Final Four*, by Roy H. Parker (suspense); *Ayra*, by Elizabeth McHee (historical); and *Shadow Lives*, by Betty Benson (psychological).
How to Contact: Does not accept unsolicited mss. Query first. SASE. Agented fiction 90%. Reports in 4 weeks on queries; 12 weeks on mss. Simultaneous and photocopied submissions OK.
Terms: Pays royalties of 6% minimum; 10% maximum. Average advance: $1,500 or negotiable. Sends galleys to author. Publishes ms 12-18 months after acceptance. Writer receives ½ of advance on signing of contract; ½ on publiclation. Book catalog for #10 SAE with 1 first class stamp.

THE BERKLEY PUBLISHING GROUP (III), Subsidiary of G.P. Putnam's Sons, 200 Madison Ave., New York NY 10016. (212)951-8800. Imprints are Berkley, Jove, Charter, Ace, Second Chance at Love, Pacer. Editor-in-Chief: Ed Breslin. Fiction Editors: Damaris Rowland, Jayne Pliner, Natalee Rosenstein, Ginger Buchanan, Mercer Warriner, Hillary Cige, Jim Morris. Nonfiction: Trish Todd. Large commercial category line. Publishes paperback originals and hardcover and paperback reprints. Books: paperbound printing; perfect binding; average print order: "depends on position in list." Plans approx. 10 first novels this year. Averages 1,180 total titles, 1,000 fiction titles each year. Sometimes critiques rejected mss.
Needs: Fantasy, horror, humor/satire, literary, mainstream, psychic/supernatural/occult, religious/inspirational, romance (contemporary, historical), science fiction, short story collections (by established authors, but rarely), suspense/mystery, war, western, young adult/teen (problem novels). We are looking for strong horror and contemporary romance/mainstream fiction titles. "Because we are a mass market publishing house, we publish a vast array of genres. We do not do erotica or short story collections, except for the rare collection by an established author." Recently published *The Gamble*, by LaVyrle Spencer (historical romance); *Red Storm Rising*, by Tom Clancy (fiction/military); and *Twilight Eyes*, by Dean Koontz (horror).
How to Contact: Accepts no unsolicited mss. Submit through agent only. Agented fiction 98%. Reports in 1 month on mss. Simultaneous and photocopied submissions OK. Accepts computer printout submissions, including dot-matrix.
Terms: Pays royalties of 4% minimum; 10% maximum. Provides 25 author's copies. Sends galleys to author. Writer's guidelines and book catalog not available.
Advice: "We do some work with first novelists, but the titles are few in comparison to our large list. And those authors we have published have submitted brilliant work. Aspiring novelists should keep abreast of the current trends in publishing by reading the New York Times Bestseller Lists, trade magazines for their desired genre and *Publisher's Weekly*. And most importantly, get an agent. Only then, will your work be considered priority."

BERKLEY/ACE SCIENCE FICTION (II), Berkley Publishing Group, 200 Madison Ave., New York NY 10016. Editor-in-Chief: Susan Allison. Estab. 1948. Publishes paperback originals and reprints. Number of titles: 15/month. Buys 85-95% agented fiction.
Needs: Science fiction and fantasy. No other genre accepted. No short stories. Recently published *The Cat Who Walks Through Walls*, by Robert Heinlein; *Neuromancer*, by William Cribson.
How to Contact: Submit outline/synopsis and 3 sample chapters with SASE. No simultaneous submissions; photocopied submissions OK. Reports in 2 months minimum on mss. "Queries answered immediately if SASE enclosed." Publishes ms an average of 18 months after acceptance.
Terms: Standard for the field. Sends galleys to author.
Advice: "Good science fiction and fantasy are almost always written by people who have read and loved a lot of it. We are looking for knowledgeable science or magic, as well as sympathetic characters with recognizable motivation. We need less fantasy and more science fiction. In science fiction, we are looking for solid, well-plotted SF: good action adventure, well-researched hard science with good characterization and books that emphasize characterization without sacrificing plot. In fantasy, again, we are looking for all types of work, from high fantasy to sword and sorcery." Submit fantasy and science fiction to Susan Allison, Ginjer Buchanan, Beth Fleisher and Susan Stone.

BETHANY HOUSE PUBLISHERS (II), 6820 Auto Club Rd., Minneapolis MN 55438. (612)829-2500. Fiction lines include: Prairie Love Stories, The Stonewyck Trilogy, The Starlight Trilogy, George MacDonald Classics, Canadian West, The Zion Chronicles. Editorial Director: Carol Johnson. Acquisitions:

Sharon Madison. Estab. 1956. Midsize independent religious publisher with plans to expand; publishing in a variety of categories from theological to fiction. Publishes paperback and hardcover originals. Books: type of paper varies; offset printing; average print order: 20,000; first novel print order average: 15,000. Published new writers within the last year.

Needs: Religious/inspirational, adventure, mystery, regional, romance (historical and young adult), gothic and juvenile. Recently published *Love Takes Wing*, by Janette Oke (prairie romance); and *Key to Zion*, by Bodie Thoene (historical); *Code of Honor*, by Sandy Dengler (historical).

How to Contact: Query or submit outline/synopsis and 2-3 sample chapters with SASE. Simultaneous and photocopied submissions OK. Accepts computer printout submissions. Prefers letter-quality. No disks. Reports in 1 month on queries, 6 weeks on mss. Publishes ms an average of 1 year after acceptance.

Terms: Pays in royalties. Sends galleys to author. Free book catalog and fiction guidelines with 8½x11 SASE.

Advice: "Prairie romances are *very* strong in our line; next are gothic romances, then historical fiction. We look at everything that is submitted; a first novel has a chance with us, especially if it has series possibilities. We do *not* recommend an agent—this puts an unnecessary barrier between publisher and author (chances for misunderstanding, mistrust). Send queries and proposals around till you have raised some interest; work with the editor to fit it to a publisher's needs."

‡BLACKTHORNE PUBLISHING, INC. (I,II), 1340 Hill St., El Cajon CA 92020. (619)588-2055. Editorial contact person: Steve Schanes. Fiction Editor: John Stephenson. Estab. 1984. Publishes comic books, paperback originals and reprints. Books: 50 lb white stock paper; cold web printing; squarebound binding; illustrations. Average print order: 10,000; first novel print order: 10,000. Published new writers within the past year. Plans 5 first novels this year. Averages 40 fiction titles each year. Sometimes critiques rejected mss.

Needs: Adventure, horror, humor/satire, juvenile, fantasy, spy/adventure, mainstream, preschool/picture book, science fiction, short story collections. Looking for "science fiction and fantasy." No romance. Recently published *Twisted Tales*, by Bruce Jones (horror); *Star Wars*, by Len Wein (space opera); *Salimba*, by Steve Perry (adventure).

How to Contact: Accepts unsolicited mss. Submit complete mss with cover letter. SASE. Agented fiction 5%. Reports in 6 weeks. Simultaneous and photocopied submissions OK. Accepts computer printout submissions, including dot-matrix.

Terms: Pays negotiable royalties and advance. Provides 25 author's copies. Sends galleys to author. Publishes ms within 3-9 months of acceptance. Book catalog on request.

Advice: Encourages first novelists.

JOHN F. BLAIR, PUBLISHER (II, IV), 1406 Plaza Dr., Winston-Salem NC 27103. (919)768-1374. President: Margaret Couch. Editor: Stephen Kirk. Estab. 1954. Small independent publisher. Publishes hardcover and paperback originals. Books: acid free paper; offset printing; casebound or softbound; illustrations; average print order 2,500-5,000. Number of titles: 8 in 1988. Encourages new writers. Occasionally comments on rejected mss.

Needs: Contemporary, literary, ethnic and regional. Generally prefers regional material dealing with southeastern U.S. No confessions or erotica. "We do not limit our consideration of manuscripts to those representing specific genres or styles. Our primary concern is that anything we publish be of high literary quality." Recently published *Being a Boy*, by Paxton Davis (autobiography); *The Hatterask Incident*, by John D. Randall (novel).

How to Contact: Query or submit with SASE. Simultaneous and photocopied submissions OK. Accepts computer printout submissions. Prefers letter-quality. Reports in 1 month on queries, 3 months on mss. Publishes ms 1-2 years after acceptance. Free book catalog.

Terms: Pays 10% standard royalties, 7% on paperback royalties. Royalties can go as high as 15% by special arrangement. Sends galleys to author. Must return advance if book is not completed or is not acceptable.

Advice: "We are primarily interested in serious adult novels of high literary quality. Most of our titles have a tie-in with North Carolina or the Southeastern United States. Please enclose a cover letter and outline with the manuscript. We prefer to review queries before we are sent complete manuscripts. Queries should include an approximate word count. We find that beginning writers often neglect to research the field, and so may expend their energies in addressing themselves to publishers that are not likely to be receptive to their kind of material."

BOGIE'S MYSTERY BOOKS (III, IV), Subsidiary of Paperjacks, 210 Fifth Ave., 7th Floor, New York NY 10010. (212)889-7726. Packagers/Editors: Bill and Karen Palmer. Estab. 1988. Imprint line (mysteries only) of midsize independent publisher. Publishes hardcover reprints and paperback originals.

Published new writers within the last year. Published 8 first novels in 1988. Averages 24 titles each year, all fiction. Rarely comments on rejected ms. "We're looking for fast-moving Playfair whodunits; private eyes; and amateur sleuths. No mysteries involving drugs, child prostitution or pornography, graphic sex and violence, mutilations." Recently published *Death on the Rocks*, by Michael Allegretto; *Mission Bay Murder*, by Philip Carlton Williams; *Robak's Fire*, by Joe Hensley.

How to Contact: Accepts unsolicited mss. Submit outline/synopsis with 3 sample chapters or complete ms with cover letter. "Beginning authors often send poorly written letters, which are taken as an example of their writing ability. The letter should be professional, as should the ms." SASE. Agented fiction 90%. reports in 2-4 weeks on queries; 4-8 weeks on mss. Good quality photocopied submissions OK. Accepts computer printout submissions, including dot-matrix if good copies (only NLQ, dark).

Terms: Pays royaltiesof 6-8% minimum. Offers negotiable advance. Provides 10 author's copies. Sends galleys to author. Book catalog for SASE.

Advice: "Encourages first novelists if they are exceptionally talented and are willing to work with the editors and make changes where requested. The work should be professional, well-written, and literate with an interesting storyline (preferably something the author knows about). Writers should edit their work and check spelling and grammatical errors."

BOOKCRAFT, INC., 1848 W. 2300 South, Salt Lake City UT 84119. (801)972-6180. Editorial Manager: Cory H. Maxwell. Publishes hardcover originals. Books: #60 stock paper; sheet-fed and web press; average print order: 5,000-7,000; 3,000 for reprints. Published new writers within the last year. Encourages new writers. "We are always open for creative, fresh ideas."

Needs: Contemporary, historical, western, romance and religious/inspirational. Recently published *Lady of Mystery*, by Susan Evans McCloud; *Hostage*, by Herbert Harker; and *A Love that Endures*, by Barbara E. Snedecor.

How to Contact: Query, submit outline/synopsis and sample chapters, or submit complete ms with SASE. Photocopied submissions OK. Reports in 2 months on both queries and mss.

Terms: Pays royalties; no advance. Sends galleys to author. Free book catalog and writer's guidelines.

Advice: "Read our fiction. Our market is the membership of The Church of Jesus Christ of Latter-Day Saints (Mormons), and all stories must be related to the background, doctrines or practices of that church. No preaching, but tone should be fresh, positive and motivational. No anti-Mormon works. The amount of fiction we publish has remained the same the last three or four years. We publish little in the way of paperback; given regional nature of our market, it is difficult to price paperbacks competitively."

THOMAS BOUREGY & COMPANY, INC., 401 Lafayette St., New York, NY 10003. Editor: Barbara J. Brett. Imprint: Avalon Books. Publishes hardcover originals. Average print order for all books (including first novels): 2,500. Averages 60 titles/year. Buys very little agented fiction. Recently published *Warm Winter Love*, by Constance Walker (romance); *A Kiss for the Captain*, by D. L. Hepler (career romance); *Web of Danger*, by Alma Blair (mystery romance).

Needs: "Avalon Books publishes wholesome, young-adult romances, adventures and westerns that are sold to libraries throughout the country. Intended for family reading, our books are read by adults as well as teenagers, and their characters are all adults: The heroines of the romances are all young (early through mid-twenties) single (no divorces or widows, please!) women, and the heroes of the westerns range in age from late twenties to early thirties. There is no graphic sex in any of our novels; kisses and embraces are as far as our characters go. The heroines of the romances and the heroes of the westerns and adventures should all be looking forward to marriage at the end of the book. Currently, we publish five books a month: two romances, one mystery romance, one career romance and one adventure. All the romances are contemporary; all the westerns are historical. The important action in all our novels takes place over a short period of time, ranging from days to no longer than a year." Books range in length from a minimum of 35,000 words to a maximum of 50,000 words.

How to Contact: Submit the first chapter and a brief, but complete, summary of the book, or submit complete manuscript. Publishes very little agented fiction. Enclose ms-size SASE. Reports in about three months.

Terms: $500 for the first book and $600 thereafter, against the first 3,500 copies sold. (Initial run is 2,500.) A royalty of 10% is paid on any additional sales. The first half of the advance is paid upon signing of the contract; the second on publication.

Advice: "Avoid the old stereotypes of character and plot. We are looking for believable stories about contemporary people. We encourage new writers. Send SASE for a copy of our tip sheet."

BRADBURY PRESS, INC. (I, II), Affiliate of Macmillan, Inc., 866 3rd Ave., New York NY 10022. (212)702-9809. Editor: Barbara Lalicki. Publishes juvenile hardcover originals. Books: excellent quality paper printing and binding; full color or black-and-white illustrations—depends on what the book needs. Number of titles: 30 in 1988. Encourages new writers. Seldom comments on rejected mss.

Needs: Juvenile and young adult: contemporary, adventure, science fiction. Recently published *The

Riddle and the Rune, by Grace Chetwin, *Hattie and the Fox*, by Mem Fox; and *Oma and Bobo*, by Amy Schwartz.
How to Contact: Query first on novels. Send complete picture book ms with SASE. No simultaneous submissions; photocopied submissions OK. Reports in 3 months on mss.
Terms: Pays royalty based on retail price. Advance negotiable.
Advice: "Write with sureness; include good detail."

BRANDEN PUBLISHING CO., (I, II), Subsidiary of Branden Press, 17 Station St., Box 843, Brookline Village MA 02147. (617)734-2045. Imprint: I.P.L. President: Adolpho Caso. Estab. 1967. Publishes originals and hardcover and paperback originals and reprints. Books: 55-60 lb acid free paper; case or perfect binding; illustrations; average print order: 5,000. Published new writers within the last year. Plans 5 first novels this year. Averages 15 total titles, 5 fiction titles each year.
Needs: Adventure, contemporary, ethnic, historical, literary, mainstream, military/war, romance, short story collections, suspense/mystery, translations. Looking for "contemporary, fast pace, modern society." No porno, experimental, horror. Recently published *The Will of God*, by Paul Walkosky (mystery); *A Lady A Peacemaker*, by Russell Ramsey (mainstream/women); and *Sarah Deale*, by Joan King (historical).
How to Contact: Does not accept unsolicited mss. Query first with vita. SASE. Agented fiction 20%. Reports in 1 week on queries. Accepts computer printout submissions, including dot-matrix.
Terms: Pays royalties of 10% minimum. Advance negotiable. Provides 10 author's copies. Sends galleys to author. Publishes ms "several months" after acceptance. Writer's guidelines for 4x9 SAE with 1 first class stamp. Book catalog for 4x9 SAE with 1 first class stamp.
Advice: "Publishing more fiction because of demand. Do not oversubmit; try single submissions; do not procrastinate if contract is offered."

‡GEORGE BRAZILLER, INC. (III), 60 Madison Ave., New York NY 10016. (212)889-0909. Estab. 1955. Publishes hardcover originals and paperback reprints. Books: cloth binding; illustrations sometimes; average print order 4,000, average first novel print order: 3,000. Buys 10% agented fiction. Averages 25 total titles, 6 fiction titles each year. Occasionally critiques rejected mss.
Needs: Art, feminist, literary, poetry, short story collections and translations. Recently published *Confessions of a Good Arab*, by Yoram Kaniuk (literary); and *The Carpanthians*, by Janet Frame (literary); and *A Revolutionary Woman*, by Sheila Fugard.
How to Contact: Query first with SASE. Photocopied submissions OK. Reports in 2 weeks on queries. Publishes ms an average of 1 year after acceptance.
Terms: Negotiates advance. Must return advance if book is not completed or is not acceptable. Sends galleys to author. Free book catalog on request with oversized SASE.
Advice: "We are publishing art, poetry, fiction, nonfiction— more paperbacks and nonfiction."

BRIDGE PUBLISHING, INC. (III, IV), 2500 Hamilton Blvd., South Plainfield NJ 07080. (201)754-0745. Editor: Raymond Stanbury. Estab. 1981. Midsize independent publisher of Christian literature. Publishes cloth and paperback originals and reprints. Averages 20 total titles/year.
Needs: "We want quality, literary Christian fiction, written in the style of Frederick Buechner, John Cheever, and John Updike. *No* 'genre' fiction (romance, biblical novels, gothics, sci-fi, etc.). We want well written fiction that shows believable characters struggling to 'work out their salvations' in believable situations. Books that exhibit real human drama and stylistic craftsmanship." Recently published *Getting Them Sober*, by Toby Drews; *Help for the Battered Woman*, by Dr. Lydia Savina; and *The Teen Sex Survival Manual*, by Watkins.
How to Contact: Accepts unsolicited mss. Submit complete ms with cover letter. SASE required. Reports in 1 month. Simultaneous or photocopied submissions OK. Accepts computer printouts, including dot-matrix.
Terms: No longer offers self/cooperative publishing services. Writer's guidelines free for #10 SASE and 1 first class stamp. Book catalog for $2.
Advice: "While we are not generally accepting fiction, we will consider manuscripts of exceptional merit. Authors must already have material published and/or other books published by reputable publishers. The work must be written from a biblical Christian worldview but does not necessarily need to be explicitly religious in nature. Only completed manuscripts will be considered."

BROADMAN PRESS (II), 127 9th Ave. N., Nashville TN 37234. (615)251-2433. Editorial Director: Harold S. Smith. Religious publisher associated with the Southern Baptist Convention. Publishes hardcover and paperback originals. Books: offset paper stock; offset printing; perfect Smyth sewn binding; illustrations possible; average print order: depends on forecast. Average number of titles: 3/year.
Needs: Adventure, historical, religious/inspirational, humor/satire, juvenile, and young adult. Will accept no other genre. Recently published: *In Search of a Quiet Place*, by Phyllis C. Gobbell (adult); *Deci-*

sion at Brushy Creek, by Ruby C. Tolliver (juvenile/youth); and *To Make All Things New*, by Caryl Porter.

How to Contact: Query, but decision is not made until ms is reviewed. No simultaneous submissions; photocopied submissions OK. Reports in 2 months on queries and mss.

Terms: Pays 10% in royalties; no advance. Sends galleys to author if requested.

Advice: "We publish very few fiction works, but we encourage first novelists. We encourage a close working relationship with the author to develop the best possible product."

CAMELOT BOOKS (II), Imprint of Avon Books, (Division of the Hearst Corporation), 105 Madison Ave., New York NY 10016. (212)481-5609. Editorial Director: Ellen E. Krieger. Estab. 1961. Publishes paperback originals and reprints for middle-grade juvenile list. Books: 6-10 line drawings in a few of the younger books. No color. Published new writers within the last year. Plans 30 novels this year.

Needs: Juvenile (fantasy—"very selective," contemporary—"selective"). Looking for "contemporary, humorous, books about real kids in real-life situations." No "science fiction, animal stories, picture books." Recently published *Search for Grissi*, by Mary Francis Shura (contemporary fiction); *Count Dracula, Me and Norma D*, by Jessica Hatchigan (contemporary fiction); and *Richard and the Vratch*, by Beatrice Gormley (fantasy, contemporary fiction).

How to Contact: Accepts unsolicited mss. Submit complete ms with cover letter (preferred) or outline/synopsis and 3 sample chapters. Agented fiction 75%. Reports in 3-4 weeks on queries; 6-10 weeks on mss. Simultaneous and photocopied submissions OK. Accepts computer printout submissions, including dot-matrix.

Terms: Royalties and advance negotiable. Sends galleys to author. Writer's guidelines for #10 SAE and 1 first class stamp. Book catalog for 9x11 SAE and 98¢ postage.

CAROLRHODA BOOKS, INC. (II), Lerner Publications Co., 241 1st Ave. N, Minneapolis MN 55401. (612)332-3344. Submissions editor: Rebecca Poole. Estab. 1969. Midsize children's hardcover publisher. Publishes hardcover originals. Books: Vellum or matte paper depending on type of illustration; sheetfed printing; reinforced school and library binding; illustrations every spread; average print order: 5,000 copies; first novel print order: 5,000. Published new writers within the last year. Buys 5% agented fiction. Averages 25-35 total titles, 2-3 fiction titles, not counting picture books, each year.

Needs: Juvenile (easy-to-read, historical, spy/adventure, contemporary, humor, biography, nature-oriented nonfiction). Needs include novels for ages 7-10 and 10-13; no problem novels. Recently published *Walking the Road to Freedom: A Story About Sojourner Truth*, by Jeri Ferris (biography); and *Wild Boars*, by Darrel Nicholson (nature-oriented nonfiction).

How to Contact: Reviews unsolicited mss. Submit outline/synopsis and 3 sample chapters for nonfiction, complete ms for fiction, both with SASE. Reports in 1 month on queries; 3 months on mss. Simultaneous and photocopied submissions OK. Accepts computer printout submissions if close to letter-quality. Publishes ms an average of 18 months after acceptance. Sends galleys to author.

Terms: Variable. Individual arrangement with author depending on the book. Writer's guidelines for #10 SAE with 25¢ postage.

Advice: "Most of our fiction is in the form of picture books. Our emphasis is on quality rather than trend. Submissions are improving in quality, but we're still not getting publishable novels for 7-10- and 10-13 year-olds. Be sure *not* to send us adult material, problem novels, or forget SASE. Make sure easy-to-read material is short, no more than 10-15 double-spaced typewritten pages, and indeed easy to read. Research your appropriate market carefully to avoid wasted effort. Write what you want to write or that which is begging to come out of you onto paper, not what you will sell in a particular market. Marketing of your manuscript comes after the creation, not before. Expect a slower response between April and August."

CARROLL & GRAF PUBLISHERS, INC. (III), 260 5th Ave., New York NY 10001. (212)889-8772. Contact: Editor. Estab. 1983. Publishes hardcover and paperback originals and paperback reprints. Plans 5 first novels this year. Averages 80 total titles, 45 fiction titles each year. Average first novel print order 20,000 copies. Occasionally critiques rejected mss.

Needs: Adventure, contemporary, erotica, experimental, fantasy, science fiction, literary, mainstream, suspense/mystery and war. No romance.

How to Contact: Does not accept unsolicited mss. Query first or submit outline/synopsis and sample chapters. SASE. Reports in 2 weeks. Photocopied submissions OK. Accepts computer printout submissions, no dot-matrix.

Terms: Pays in royalties of 6% minimum; 15% maximum; advance negotiable. Sends galleys to author. Free book catalog on request.

Advice: Publishing more fiction than in the past. Encourages first novels.

CHILDRENS PRESS (II), Division of Regensteiner Publishing Enterprises, Inc., 544 N. Cumberland Ave., Chicago IL 60656. (312)693-0800. Vice President, Editorial: Fran Dyra. Estab. 1946. Publishes hardcover originals. Published new writers within the last year. Averages 125-150 total titles, 40 fiction titles each year.
Needs: Juvenile (easy-to-read, picture books, biographies (historical and contemporary) for middle and junior high grades. Recently published *Your Body and How It Works*, (intermediate level); *Picture Stories Biographies*, (intermediate level).
How to Contact: Query first if long ms (more than 5 ms pages or series idea); or submit outline/synopsis and sample chapters or complete ms with SASE. Simultaneous submissions and photocopied submissions OK. Do not send original artwork. Reports in 3 months.
Terms: Occasionally pays in royalties of 5% minimum; negotiates advance. Generally makes outright purchase of $500 minimum; 6 author's copies. Occasionally subsidy publishes. Offers 25% of sale price for subsidiary rights. Free writer's guidelines; free book catalog on request.
Advice: "Have started trade sales primarily to museums and teacher-supply bookstores. Need authors who can write social studies materials for our Enchantment of the World series (128 page books, 6th-grade reading level). Also need writers for our Cornerstones of Freedom series (48 pages, 4th grade reading level). Looking for action-packed stories for young readers who have second- or third-grade reading skills."

THE CHILD'S WORLD, INC. (II), Box 989, Elgin IL 60121. (312)741-7591. President: Jane Buerger. Estab. 1968. Publishes hardcover and paperback originals. Published new writers within the last year. Number of titles: approximately 50/year.
Needs: Supplemental books for school and library market. Juvenile: concept books, sports, animal, spy/adventure, historical, fantasy/science fiction and easy-to-read. "All of our titles are for the juvenile market. Most are only 32 pages." Recently published *Magic Castle Readers*, a 27 book series by Jane Belk Moncure; 5 Dinosaur books by Janet Riehecky, the Polka-Dot Puppy Series.
How to Contact: Submit complete ms with SASE. Simultaneous and photocopied submissions OK. Reports in 4 months on queries.
Terms: Pays by outright purchase of $400-$700; no advance. Free book catalog.
Advice: "Be persistent. Only submit manuscripts for preschool — grade 2."

CITADEL PRESS (II), Lyle Stuart Inc., 120 Enterprise Ave., Secaucus NJ 07094. (201)866-4199. Vice President: Allan J. Wilson. Estab. 1942. Publishes hardcover and paperback originals and paperback reprints. Averages 65 total titles, 8-10 fiction titles each year. Occasionally critiques rejected mss.
Needs: No religious, romantic or detective. Recently published *The Rain Maiden*, by Jill M. Phillips and *Human Oddities*, by Martin Monestiere.
How to Contact: Accepts unsolicited mss. Query first with SASE. Reports in 6 weeks on queries; 2 months on mss. Simultaneous and photocopied submissions OK.
Terms: Pays in royalties of 10% minimum; 15% maximum; 12-25 author's copies. Advance is more for agented ms; depends on grant/award money.

CLARION BOOKS (II): A Houghton Mifflin Company, 52 Vanderbilt Ave., New York NY 10017. (212)972-1190. Editor/Publisher: James C. Giblin. Estab. 1965 "as the children's book division of Seabury Press; 1979 as a new children's book imprint of Houghton Mifflin Company." Midsize children's book imprint of a major publishing company. Publishes hardcover originals and paperback reprints from its own backlist. Number of titles: 40 in 1988. Average print order: 6,000-7,000. Published new writers within the last year. Buys 10-15% agented fiction. Comments on rejected mss "only if we're encouraging a revision."
Needs: Juvenile and young adult: adventure, suspense and humorous contemporary stories for ages 8-12 and 10-14; "fresh, personal stories that capture our attention, and that we think young readers would enjoy." Recently published *Always and Forever Friends*, by C. S. Adler; *Saying Good-bye to Grandma*, by Jane Resh Thomas; *December Stillness*, by Mary Downing Hahn. Especially interested in humorous stories for ages 8 to 12.
How to Contact: Accepts unsolicited mss. Query on mss of more than 50 pages. SASE. "We like queries to be straightforward—no dramatic teaser openings—and to contain a description of the story, plus any relevant writing credits. It's good if they can be kept to a page, or at most two pages." Reluctantly considers simultaneous submissions; photocopied submissions OK. Accepts computer printout submissions. Reports in 2 weeks on queries, 8 weeks on mss. Publishes ms 12-18 months after acceptance.
Terms: Pays 5% royalties on picture books; 10% on other books; offers $2,000-$3,500 advances. Writer must return advance if book is not completed or is not acceptable. Free book catalog and guidelines.
Advice: "I really believe that the best novels come out of the author's self-knowledge of his or her own experience and background. Don't send us imitations of other writers' successes. We're always open to

first novelists in the hope that they'll become regular contributors to our list. We've noticed a return to lighter stories from the heavier problem novels of recent years. Attend a writer's workshop or critique group in order to study the structure of successful novels" Publishing "more middle grade fiction, less young adult fiction, because paperback originals seem to have covered that market. More paperback reprints from our backlist because bookstores like them."

‡CONTEMPORARY BOOKS (IV), 180 N. Michigan Ave., Chicago IL 60657. (312)782-9181. Imprint: Congdon & Weed. Associate Publisher: Nancy J. Crossman. Estab. 1977. Mostly nonfiction adult trade publisher. Publishes hardcover and paperback originals and reprints. Published new writers within the last year. Averages 120 total titles, 1-2 fiction titles each year.
Needs: "Sports only."
How to Contact: Accepts unsolicited mss. Query first. SASE. Report in 3 weeks on queries; 3 months on mss. Simultaneous and photocopied submissions OK.
Terms: Pays royalties.

DAVID C. COOK PUBLISHING COMPANY, 850 N. Grove, Elgin IL 60120. (312)741-2400. Imprint: Chariot Books. Managing Editor: Catherine L. Davis. Estab. 1875. Publishes hardcover and paperback originals. Published new writers within the last year. Number of fiction titles: 35-40 juvenile. Encourages new writers.
Needs: Religious/inspirational, juvenile and young adult: sports, animal, spy/adventure, historical, Biblical, fantasy/science fiction, picture book and easy-to-read. Recently published *Jeremy, Barnabas and the Wonderful Dream*, by Joni Earickson Tada; *Mystery of the Laughing Cat*, by Elspeth Campbell Murphy; *Mystery Rider at Thunder Ridge*, by David Gillett.
How to Contact: Query with SASE. All unsolicited mss are returned unopened. Simultaneous and photocopied submissions OK. Accepts computer printout submissions. Reports in 3 months on queries.
Terms: Royalties vary ("depending on whether it is trade, mass market or cloth" and whether picture book or novel). Offers advance. Free writer's guidelines with SASE.
Advice: "Chariot Books publishes books for toddlers through teens which help children better understand their relationship with God, and/or the message of God's book, the Bible."

CRITIC'S CHOICE PAPERBACKS (I, II), Subsidiary of Lorevan Publishers, Inc., 31 East 28 St., New York NY 10016. (212)685-1550. Editor-in-Chief: Stanley L. Reisner. Estab. 1985. Publishes paperback originals and reprints. Books: mass market paperbacks; average print order: 50,000. Published new writers within the last year. Plans 6 first novels this year. Averages 72 total titles, 70 fiction titles each year. Sometimes comments on rejected mss.
Needs: Adventure, horror, historical romance, war, western. Looks for novels of 70,000 + words. Recently published *Moonslasher*, by Doug Hawk (horror); *Fatal Memory*, by Bruce Forrester (thriller).
How to Contact: Query first or submit outline/synopsis and 3 sample chapters. SASE. Agented fiction: 25%. Reports in 4-6 weeks on queries; 8-10 weeks on mss. Simultaneous and photocopied submissions OK. Accepts computer printout submissions.
Terms: Pays royalties of 4% minimum; 6% maximum. Average advance: $1,000. Book catalog for #10 SAE with 1 first class stamp.

CROSSWAY BOOKS (II), Division of Good News Publishers, 9825 W. Roosevelt Rd., Westchester IL 60153. (312)345-7474. Managing Editor: Ted Griffin. Estab. 1938. Midsize independent religious publisher with plans to expand. Publishes paperback originals. Book: illustrations sometimes; average print order 3,000-5,000. Plans 4 first novels this year. Buys 50% agented fiction. Averages 25 total titles, 4-5 fiction titles each year.
Needs: Contemporary, adventure, fantasy, juvenile (fantasy, animal), literary, religious/inspirational, science fiction and young adult (fantasy/science fiction). "All fiction published by Crossway Books must be written from the perspective of historic orthodox Christianity. It need not be *explicitly* Christian, but it must understand and view the world through Christian principle. For example, our books *Taliesin* and *Merlin* take place in a pre-Christian era, but Christian themes (e.g., sin, forgiveness, sacrifice, redemption) are present. We are *eager* to discover and nurture Christian novelists." No sentimental, didactic, "inspirational" religious fiction; heavy-handed allegorical or derivative (of C.S. Lewis or J.R.R. Tolkien) fantasy. Recently published *Merlin* by Stephen R. Lawhead; and *This Present Darkness*, by Frank Peretti.
How to Contact: Send query with synopsis and sample chapters. Accepts computer printout submissions. Prefers letter-quality. Reports in 3 weeks to 4 months on queries. Publishes ms 1-2 years after acceptance.
Terms: Pays in royalties and negotiates advance. Book catalog for $1 postage.
Advice: "Publishing a higher quality of writing as we develop a wider reputation for excellent Christian fiction. Christian novelists—you must get your writing *up to standard*. The major reason novels in-

formed by a Christian perspective do not have more presence in the market is because they are inferior. Sad but true. I believe Crossway can successfully publish and market *quality* Christian novelists. Also read John Gardner's *On Moral Fiction*. The market for fantasy/science fiction continues to expand (and genre fiction in general). There are more attempts lately at Christian science fiction and fantasy, though they generally fail from didacticism or from being overly derivative."

CROWN PUBLISHERS, INC. (II), 225 Park Ave. S., New York NY 10003. (212)254-1600. Imprints include Crown, Crown Juvenile Books, Harmony Books, Orion Books, Pagent Books, Clarkson N. Potter, Inc. Crown Executive Editor: Jane O'Shea Wade; Editorial Director: Peter Guzzardi; Harmony Books Editor-in-Chief: Betty Prashker. Sr. Editors: Mark Gompertz, Lisa Hely, Barbara Grossman, Harriet Bells, Nancy Novograd, and David Allender. Managing Editor: Laurie Stark. Estab. 1936. Large independent publisher of fiction and nonfiction. Publishes hardcover and paperback originals and reprints. Magazine: 50 lb paper; offset printing; hardcover binding; sometimes illustrations; average print order: 15,000. Plans 4 first novels this year. Averages 250 total titles, 26 fiction titles each year. Average first novel print order 15,000 copies. Occasionally critiques rejected mss.
Needs: Adventure, contemporary, historical, horror, humor/satire, literary, mainstream, romance (historical, contemporary), science fiction, war, juvenile and young adult (fiction for ages 8-12, young adult, picture books). Needs for novels: genre. Recently published *Herb N' Lorna*, by Eric Krast (love story); *Spirit of the Hills,* by Dan O'Brien (tale of murder and revenge); *Cape Ann*, by Faith Sullivan.
How to Contact: Query first or submit outline/synopsis and 3 sample chapters; send complete ms for picture books; send complete mss are returned unread. SASE. Reports in 3-4 months. Photocopied submissions OK; no simultaneous submissions for children's books.
Terms: Pays advance against royalty; terms vary and are negotiated per book. Book catalog for SASE.
Advice: Publishing "more fiction; more hardcovers. Because we're receiving higher-quality fiction."

DAW BOOKS, INC. (I, IV),1633 Broadway, New York NY 10019. Publisher: Donald A. Wollheim. Editor-in-Chief: Betsy Wollheim. Senior Editor: Sheila Gilbert. Estab. 1971. Publishes paperback originals, hardcover reprints and hardcover originals. Books: illustrations sometimes; average print and first novel order vary widely. May publish as many as 6 or more first novels a year. Averages 60 total titles, all fiction, each year. Occasionally critiques rejected mss.
Needs: Fantasy, science fiction and horror only.
How to Contact: Submit complete ms with SASE. Usually reports in 8-12 weeks of mss, but in special cases may take longer.
Terms: Pays an advance against royalities. Sends galleys to author (if there is time).
Advice: "We strongly encourage new writers. In 1988, we published first novels by six new authors and are currently working with more than a dozen additional new authors whose first novels we plan to publish in 1989 and 1990. We like a close and friendly relationship with authors. We are publishing more fantasy than previously, but we are looking for more *serious* fantasy and especially need science fiction. To unpublished authors: Try to make an educated submission and don't give up."

DEL REY BOOKS, Subsidiary of Ballantine Books, 201 E. 50 St., New York NY 10022. (212)572-2677. Estab. 1977. Publishes hardcover originals and paperback originals and reprints. "In 1988 we published 5 novels by authors who had never published novels before." Plans 4-5 first novels this year. Publishes 120 titles each year, all fiction. Sometimes critiques rejected mss.
Needs: Fantasy, science fiction. Fantasy must have magic as an intrinsic element to the plot. No flying-saucer, Atlantis, or occult novels. Recently published *The Smoke Ring*, by Larry Niven (science fiction/hardcover original); *Guardians of the West*, by David Eddings (fantasy/hardcover original); and *Foundation and Earth*, by Isaac Asimov (science fiction/paperback reprint).
How to Contact: Accepts unsolicited mss. Submit complete manuscript with cover letter or outline/synopsis and 3 consecutive sample chapters. Address science fiction to SF editor; fantasy to fantasy editor. Reports in 2 weeks on queries; 10 months on ms. Photocopied submissions OK. Computer printout submissions OK, including dot-matrix.
Terms: Pays in royalties; "advance is competitive." Sends pre-publication galleys to author. Writer's guidelines for #10 SAE and 1 first class stamp.
Advice: Has been publishing "more fiction and more hardcovers, because the market is there for them. Read a lot of science fiction and fantasy, such as works by Anne McCaffrey, David Eddings, Larry Niven, Arthur C. Clarke, Terry Brooks, Frederik Pohl, Barbara Hambly. When writing, pay particular attention to plotting (and a satisfactory conclusion) and characters (sympathetic and well-rounded)—because those are what readers look for."

DELACORTE/DELL BOOKS FOR YOUNG READERS (II, III, IV), Subsidiary of Doubleday, 245 E. 47 St., New York NY 10017. (212)605-3000. New imprint: is Young Yearling Books, for readers around 6 years old. Editors: Bebe Willoughby, Michelle Poploff. Large publisher specializing in young adult and middle-age fiction. titles each year. Occasionally critiques or comments on rejected ms.

Needs: Fantasy, juvenile, young adult. "We are looking for quality fiction—all categories possible." No romance of the formula type. Recently published *Fade*, by Robert Cormier; *Beans on the Roof*, by Betsy Byars; *Cal Cameron by Day, Spiderman by Night*, by Ann Cosum (winner of Delacorte fiction contest).

How to Contact: Query first. Unsolicited manuscripts not accepted. Fiction is agented.

Terms: Pays in royalties; advance is negotiable. Send galleys to author. Book catalog free on request.

Advice: "We are publishing more fiction than in the past. The market is good. We encourage first YA novelists for our contest and published new writers last year. We are primarily interested in quality."

DELL PUBLISHING, 666 Fifth Avenue, New York NY 10103. (212)765-6500. Imprints include Delacorte Press, Delacorte Juvenile, Delta, Dell, Laurel, Laurel-Leaf and Yearling. Estab. 1922. Publishes hardcover and paperback originals and paperback reprints.

Needs: See below for individual imprint requirements.

How to Contact: Reports in 3 months. Photocopied and simultaneous submissions OK. Please adhere strictly to the following procedures: 1. Send *only* a 4-page synopsis or outline with a cover letter stating previous work published or relevant experience. Enclose SASE. 2. *Do not* send ms, sample chapters or artwork. 3. *Do not* register, certify or insure your letter. Dell is comprised of several imprints, each with its own editorial department. Please review carefully the following information and direct your submissions to the appropriate department. Your envelope must be marked: Attention: (One of the following names of imprints), Editorial Department—Proposal.

DELACORTE: Publishes in hardcover; looks for top-notch commercial fiction; historical romance. Recently published *Firefly Summer*, by Maeve Binchy; and *Zoya*, by Danielle Steel. 35 titles/year.

DELTA: Publishes trade paperbacks; will be publishing original fiction; looks for useful, substantial guides (nonfiction). 20 titles/year.

DELL: Publishes mass-market paperbacks; rarely publishes original nonfiction; looks for family sagas, historical romances, sexy modern romances, adventure and suspense thrillers, psychic/supernatural, horror, war novels, fiction and nonfiction. Not currently publishing original mysteries or science fiction. 200 titles/year.

DELACORTE JUVENILE: Publishes in hardcover for children and young adults, grades K-12. 40 titles/year. "We prefer complete mss for fiction."

LAUREL-LEAF: Publishes originals and reprints in paperback for young adults, grades 7-12. 48 titles/year.

YEARLING: Publishes originals and reprints in paperback for children, grades K-6. 75 titles/year.

Terms: Pays 6-15% in royalties; offers advance. Sends galleys to author. Book catalog for 8½x11 SASE plus $1.30 postage (Attention: Customer Service).

Advice: "Don't get your hopes up. Query first only with 4-page synopsis plus SASE. Study the paperback racks in your local drugstore. We encourage first novelists. We also encourage all authors to seek agents."

DEMBNER BOOKS (II), Division of Red Dembner Enterprises, 80 8th Ave., New York NY 10011. Editor: S. Arthur Dembner. Fiction Editor: Therese Eiben. Publishes hardcover originals. Books: quality consignment stock paper; sheet and web printing; hardcover binding; illustrations rarely; average print order: 5,000-10,000; first novel print order: 3,000-5,000. Published new writers within the last year.

Needs: Mystery/suspense and literary. "We are prepared to publish a limited number of well-written, nonsensational works of fiction." Recently published *In Siberia It Is Very Cold*, by Lester Goldberg; and *Haunt of the Nightingale*, by John Riggs.

How to Contact: Submit outline/synopsis and sample chapters with SASE. Simultaneous and photocopied submissions OK.

Terms: Offers negotiable advance. Sends galleys to author.

Advice: Encourages first novelists. "Library sales are up; general sales to bookstores are down. Have patience and forbearance. Those who make it big on a first novel are a very not-so-select few. The randomness of publishing success stories is one of the hardest things about being a writer (and editor, I must add)."

DIAL BOOKS FOR YOUNG READERS (II), Subsidiary of New American Library, 2 Park Ave., New York NY 10016. (212)725-1818. Imprints include Pied Piper Books, Easy to Read Books. Editor: Arthur Levine. Estab. 1961. Trade children's book publisher, "looking for picture book mss and novels." Publishes hardcover originals. Plans 1 first novel this year. Averages 50-60 titles, all fiction. Occasionally critiques or comments on rejected ms.

Needs: Juvenile (1-9 yrs.) including: animal, fantasy, spy/adventure, contemporary, easy-to-read; young adult/teen (10-18 years) including: fantasy/science fiction, historical, problem novels, literary fiction, sports, spy/adventure. Recently published *Horrible Holidays*, by Audrey Wood (easy-to-read);

Flossie & the Fox, by Patricia McKissack (picture book); and *The Gold Cadillac*, by Mildred Taylor (novel).

How to Contact: Accepts unsolicited mss. Submit outline/synopsis and sample chapters or complete ms with cover letter. SASE. Agented fiction 50%. Reports in 3-4 weeks on queries. Simultaneous and photocopied submissions OK. Accepts computer printout submissions, including dot-matrix.

Terms: Pays in royalties. Writer's guidelines free for #10 SAE and 1 first class stamp. Book catalog for 9x12 SAE and $1.92 postage.

Advice: "We are publishing more fiction books than in the past, and we publish only hardcover originals, most of which are fiction. At this time we are particularly interested in both fiction and nonfiction for the middle grades, and innovative picture book manuscripts. We also are looking for easy-to-reads for first and second graders. Plays, collections of games and riddles, and counting and alphabet books are generally discouraged. Before submitting a manuscript to a publisher, it is a good idea to request a catalog to see what the publisher is currently publishing. As the 'Sweet Valley High' phenomenon has loosened its stranglehold on YA fiction, we are seeing more writers able to translate traditional values of literary excellence and contemporary innovation into the genre. Find a bookstore that sells quality books for children and visit constantly; read not only all the Dial books you can get your hands on, but as many books by other fine houses as possible. Your work will be better, and we will be more favorably inclined toward it, if it shows a familiarity with contemporary children's books as well as the 'classics.' "

DODD, MEAD & COMPANY, INC., 71 Fifth Ave., New York NY 10003. (212)627-8444. Fiction Editor: Cynthia Vartan. Mystery Editor: Margaret Norton. Estab. 1839. Publishes hardcover and trade paperback reprints. Published new writers within the last year. Number of fiction titles: 30-40.

Needs: High quality mysteries.

How to Contact: Submit synopsis and 2 sample chapters or entire manuscript. SASE. All manuscripts should be typed, double-spaced. Dot-matrix unacceptable. Reports in 1-3 months.

Terms: Pays in royalties; offers advance.

DORCHESTER PUBLISHING CO., INC. (II), Leisure Books, 276 Fifth Ave., New York NY 10001. (212)725-8811. Imprint: Leisure Books. Editor: Tracey Lubben. Estab. 1982. Publisher of mass market paperbacks. Publishes paperback originals and reprints. Books: photo offset printing; average print order varies. Receptive to first novels. Published new writers within the last year. Averages 150 total titles, mostly fiction. Buys 20% agented fiction.

Needs: Horror, romance (historical, minimum length 90,000 words), science fiction. "At present, Dorchester is looking for historical romance and horror." No juvenile, contemporary romance, gothic or romantic suspense. "Publishes 1 or 2 SF mss/year or occasional nonfiction book, but these are usually agented." Recently published *Fangs*, by Richard Forsythe (horror); and *Summer Storm*, by Catherine Hart (historical romance).

How to Contact: Query first or submit outline/synopsis and 3 sample chapters with SASE. No unsolicited mss. "*Nothing* will be returned without SASE." Reports in 3 weeks on queries; 6 weeks on mss. Simultaneous and photocopied submissions OK from agents only. Letter-quality computer printouts only. Publishes ms usually within 2 years after acceptance.

Terms: Pays in royalties of 4%. Advance is negotiable. Must return advance (minus 10% which author retains) if book is not completed or is unacceptable. Sends galleys to author.

Advice: "We are concentrating heavily on horror and historical romance. *Learn to spell*! Learn the difference between *its* and *it's*. And most important, don't get discouraged by all those rejection slips—if you're any good, you'll get published sooner or later. We encourage first novelists. Our relationship with authors is 'a limited partnership with limitless possibilities.' "

DOUBLEDAY Books, Division of Bantam Doubleday Dell Publishing Group, 666 Fifth Ave., New York NY 10103. (212)765-6500. Estab. 1897. Publishes hardcover originals.

Needs: Doubleday is not able to consider unsolicited queries, proposals or manuscripts unless submitted through a bona fide literary agent, except that we will consider fiction for science fiction imprints and westerns. Send copy of complete ms (60,000-80,000 words) to Crime Club Editor, Science Fiction Editor or Western Editor as appropriate. Sufficient postage for return via fourth class mail must accompany ms.

How to Contact: Reports in 2-6 months."

Terms: Pays in royalties; offers advance.

DOUBLEDAY CANADA LIMITED (III,IV), 105 Bond St., Toronto, Ontario M5B 1Y3 Canada. (416)340-0777. Imprint: Dell Distributing. Estab. 1936. Large commercial *Canadian* publisher. Publishes hardcover originals (Doubleday) and paperback reprints (Dell). Book: offset or high bulk paper; offset printing; perfect or sewn binding. Plans "one at most" first novels this year. Publishes 20-40 total titles each year, 10-15 fiction titles.

Needs: Mainstream, humor/satire, literary, mysteries, commercial fiction, literary fiction, suspense, science fiction, juvenile. Recently published *Road to the Top*, by Aird, Novack and Westcott (business); *Death on Prague*; by John Reeves (mystery); *My Father's House*, by Sylvia Fraser (autobiography).
How to Contact: Accepts unsolicited mss. Query or send outline and chapters with cover letter. SASE (IRC) necessary for return of mss. "Please do *not* send SASE with US stamps!" 90% of fiction is agented. Reports on queries in up to 3 weeks; on ms in up to 2 months. Simultaneous and photocopied submissions OK. Accepts computer printout submissions, no dot-matrix.
Terms: Pays standard royalties, negotiable advance and 10 author's copies. Sends prepublication galleys to author.
Advice: "Think about marketability. Research the publishing house you plan to submit your work to."

‡DOUBLEDAY-FOUNDATION BOOKS (II), Subsidiary of Bertelsmann, 666 Fifth Ave., New York NY 10103. (212)492-8971. Editors: Patrick LoBrutto and Lou Aronica. Estab. 1987. Publishes hardcover originals and reprints. Published new writers within the last year. Plans 1 first novel this year. Averages 18 total titles, all fiction each year. Sometimes critiques rejected mss.
Needs: Fantasy, horror, science fiction, short story collections. Needs "SF, fantasy mainly. Horror in very limited amounts. No unimaginative, lousy fiction." Recently published *Faerie Tale*, by Ray Feist (fantasy); *Shadows 10*, by Charles L. Grant (ed.) (original horror anthology); and *Last Fall*, by Bruce Stolbov (sf 1st novel).
How to Contact: Accepts unsolicited mss. Query first. SASE. Agented fiction 80-90%. Reports in 2 months. Simultaneous and photocopied submissions OK.
Terms: Pays royalties of 6-10%; offers negotiable advance. Sends galleys to author. Publishes ms within 18-24 months after acceptance. Writer's guidelines and book catalog free.
Advice: Publishing more fiction than in the past due to market demand. Encourages first novelists—"a tradition in SF field."

E.P. DUTTON (III), 2 Park Ave., New York NY 10016. Division Of New American Library. Imprints include Dial Books for Young Readers, Pied Piper Books, Easy-to-Read Books, Very First Books, Unicorn Paperbacks, Lodestar Books and Obelisk. Editor-in-Chief: Joyce Engelson. Juvenile: Ann Durell. Artbook Editor: Cy Nelson. Publishes hardcover and paperback reprints in the Obelisk line. Books: illustrations sometimes. Published new writers within the last year.
Needs: Contemporary, experimental, humor/satire, literary, juvenile, picture books, suspense/mystery, war, young adult and translations. No gothics, romance or poetry.
How to Contact: Accepts unsolicited mss for juvenile books. Query before sending adult mss. Reports in 8 weeks on queries. SASE required for response.
Terms: Rates vary individually; offers advance. Sends galleys to author.
Advice: "Do not overlook literary magazines and journals. They are often receptive and have more time to supply feedback. Literary agents are very helpful. What we and the public want is the exceptionally good first novel. We work closely with the author."

EAKIN PRESS (II, IV), Box 23069, Austin TX 78735. (512)288-1771. Imprint: Nortex. Editor: Edwin M. Eakin. Estab. 1978. Publishes hardcover originals. Books: old style (acid free); offset printing; case binding; illustrations; average print order 2,000; first novel print order 5,000. Plans 2 first novels this year. Averages 40 total titles each year.
Needs: Juvenile. Specifically needs historical fiction for school market, juveniles set in Texas for Texas grade schoolers. Recently published *Powderhorn Passage*, by Tom Townsend; and *Spirit of Iron*, by Janice Shefelman.
How to Contact: Accepts unsolicted mss. First send query or submit outline/synopsis and 2 sample chapters. SASE. Agented fiction 5%. Simultaneous and photocopied submissions OK. Accepts computer printout submissions. Prefers letter quality. Reports in 3 months on queries.
Terms: Pays 10-15% in royalties; average advance: $1,000. Send galleys to author. Publishes ms 1-1½ years after acceptance. Writers guidelines for #10 SAE and 1 first class stamp. Book catalog for 75¢.
Advice: Juvenile fiction only with strong Texas theme. Just beginning category of adult fiction. We receive around 600 queries or unsolicited mss a year."

PAUL S. ERIKSSON, PUBLISHER (II), 208 Battell Bldg., Middlebury VT 05753. (802)388-7303. Editor: Paul S. Eriksson. Estab. 1960. Publishes hardcover and paperback originals.
Needs: Mainstream. Recently published *The Headmaster's Papers*, by Richard A. Hawley; and *Norman Rockwell's Greatest Painting*, by Hollis Hodges (novel).
How to Contact: Query first. Photocopied submissions OK. Publishes ms an average of 6 months after acceptance.
Terms: Pays 10-15% in royalties; advance offered if necessary. Free book catalog.
Advice: "Our taste runs to serious fiction."

‡M. EVANS & CO., INC. (II),216 E. 49th St., New York NY 10017. (212)688-2810. Contact: Editors. Westerns Editor: Sara Ann Freed. Publishes paperback originals. Books: average print order: 5,000-10,000. Publishes 4-6 titles each year, all fiction.
Needs: Western, young adult/teen (10-18 years). "We only want to see young adult and westerns. We are thinking of adding historical romance to our line, but have not yet made that decision."
How to Contact: Accepts unsolicited mss. Query first with outline/synopsis and 3 sample chapters. SASE. Agented fiction: 100%. Reports on queries in 3-5 weeks. Simultaneous and photocopied submissions OK. Accepts computer printout submissions, no dot-matrix.
Terms: Pays in royalties and offers advance; amounts vary. Sends galleys to author. Publishes ms 5-6 months after acceptance.

FARRAR, STRAUS & GIROUX (II), 19 Union Sq. W., New York NY 10003. Imprints include Michael DiCapua Books, Sunburst Books, Hill & Wang. Children's Books Publisher: Stephen Roxburgh. Editor-in-Chief: Margaret Ferguson. Number of titles: 40 in 1988. Published new writers within the last year. Buys juvenile mss with illustrations. Buys 50% agented fiction.
Needs: Children's picture books, juvenile novels, nonfiction. Recently published *Sweet Creek Holler*, by Ruth White; *Dear Mili*, by Maurice Sendak; *The Incredible Painting of Felix Clousseau*, by Jon Agee.
How to Contact: Submit outline/synopsis and 3 sample chapters, summary of ms and any pertinent information about author, author's writing, etc. No simultaneous submissions; photocopied submissions OK. Reports in 1 month on queries, 3 months on mss. Publishes ms 18-24 months after acceptance.
Terms: Pays in royalties; offers advance. Free book catalog with #10 SASE.
Advice: "Study our list before sending something inappropriate. Publishing more hardcovers—our list has expanded."

FAWCETT (I, II, III), Division of Random House/Ballantine, 201 E. 50th St., New York NY 10022. (212)751-2600. Imprints include Ivy, Crest, Gold Medal, Columbine and Juniper. Executive Editor: Barbara Dicks. Editor-in-Chief: Leona Nevler. Estab. 1955. Major publisher of mass market and trade paperbacks. Publishes paperback originals and reprints. Prints 160 titles annually. Encourages new writers. "Always looking for *great* first novels."
Needs: Historical, suspense, occult, adventure, mysteries. Recently published *The Omega Command*, by John Land; *Mid-town South*, by Christopher O'Brian; *The Incense Tree*, by Jacqueline La Tourette.
How to Contact: Query with SASE. Send outline and sample chapters for adult mass market. If ms is requested, simultaneous and photocopied submissions OK. Accepts computer printout submissions. Prefers letter-quality. Reports in 1 month on queries, 3 months on mss.
Terms: Pays usual advance and royalties.
Advice: "Gold Medal list consists of 5 original paperbacks per month—usually 4 are novels."

FEARON EDUCATION (II), Subsidiary of David S. Lake Publishers, 500 Harbor Blvd., Belmont CA 94002. (415)592-7810. Imprints include: Fearon Teacher Aids, Lake Books. Editorial & Promotional Director: Carol Hegarty. Estab. 1954. Special-education publishers with a junior high, high school, and adult basic education audience—focusing mainly on high interest/low level fiction and vocational and life skills materials. Publishes paperback originals and reprints. Books: 3 lb book set paper; offset printing; perfect or saddlewired binding, line art illustrations, average print order: 5,000. Published 20 fiction titles in 1988.
Needs: Adventure, contemporary, ethnic, historical, regional, romance, science fiction, short story collections, suspense/mystery, western, young adult/teen. "Our fiction appears in series of short novellas, aimed at new literates and high school students reading no higher than a fifth-grade level. All are written to specification. It's a hard market to crack without some experience writing at low reading levels. Manuscripts for specific series of fiction are solicited from time to time, and unsolicited manuscripts are accepted occasionally." Recently published *A Question of Freedom*, by Lucy Jane Bledsoe (adventure novella—one of series of eight); *Just for Today*, by Tana Reiff (one novella of series of seven life-issues stories); and *The Everett Eyes*, by Bernard Jackson & Susie Quintanilla (one of twenty in a series of extra-short thrillers).
How to Contact: Submit outline/synopsis and sample chapters. SASE. Reports in 1 month. Simultaneous and photocopied submissions OK.
Terms: Authors usually receive a predetermined project fee. Book catalog for 9x12 SAE with 4 first class stamps.

FLARE BOOKS (II), Imprint of Avon Books, Div. of the Hearst Corp., 105 Madison Ave., New York NY 10016. (212)481-5609. Editorial Director: Ellen Krieger. Estab. 1981. Small, young adult line. Publishes paperback originals and reprints. Published new writers within the last year. Plans 2-3 first novels this year. Averages 30 titles, all fiction each year.

Needs: Young adult (easy-to-read [hi-lo], problem novels, romance, spy/adventure.) "very selective." Looking for contemporary fiction. No historical, science fiction/fantasy, heavy problem novels. Recently published *Breaking Up Is Hard To Do*, by Bruce and Carol Hart; *Maybe By Then I'll Understand*, by Jane McFann; and *Baby Sister*, by Marilyn Sachs (all contemporary).

How to Contact: Accepts unsolicited mss. Submit complete ms with cover letter (preferred) or outline/synopsis and 3 sample chapters. Agented fiction 75%. Reports in 3-4 weeks on queries; 6-10 weeks on mss. Simultaneous and photocopied submissions OK. Accepts computer printout submissions, including dot-matrix.

Terms: Royalties and advance negotiable. Sends galleys to author. Writer's guidelines for #10 SAE and 1 first class stamp. Book catalog for 9x12 SAE with 98¢ postage. "We run a young adult novel competition each year."

FOUR WINDS PRESS (II), Subsidiary of Macmillan Publishing Co., 866 Third Ave., New York NY 10022. (212)702-2000. Editor-in-Chief: Cynthia Kane. Estab. 1966. A children's trade book imprint. Publishes hardcover originals. Books: 3 piece binding; books for children ages 3-12 usually illustrated; average print order 6,000-10,000; first novel print order: 6,000. Published new writers within the last year. Plans 1 first novel this year. Publishes 24 total titles each year, 12 fiction titles. Sometimes critiques rejected ms.

Needs: Picture book manuscripts for ages 5-8, especially minimal word mss; middle grade and young adult novels about family situations; YA fiction with a strong, original voice. No adult books. Recently published *Step Into the Night*, by Joanne Ryder; *How's Business*, by Alison Prince (juvenile 8-12 years); and *Return to Morocco*, by Norma Johnston (young adult).

How to Contact: Accepts unsolicited mss. Submit complete ms with cover letter. SASE. 75% of fiction is agented. Reports in 8 weeks. Simultaneous and photocopied submissions OK. Accepts computer printout submissions, including dot-matrix.

Terms: Pays royalties, negotiable advance and author's copies. Book catalog free on request.

Advice: "For children's books, study books that are currently being published. Length, vocabulary, subject matter are usually determined by the age group for which the book is intended."

GEMSTONE BOOKS (I, II), Imprint of Dillon Press, 242 Portland Ave. S., Minneapolis MN 55415. (612)333-2691. Fiction Reader: Karin Snelson. Estab. 1966. "Dillon Press is a juvenile book publisher, both of fiction and educational nonfiction titles." Publishes hardcover and paperback originals. Books: type of paper varies; offset lithography; Smythe and sidesewn binding; illustrations; average print order: 5,000. Published new writers within the last year. Averages 40 total titles, 10 fiction titles each year.

Needs: Juvenile (8-12): mystery; historical; adventure; contemporary, stories about Hispanics, Asians, Blacks; juvenile (8-11) historical fiction based on actual events. No problem novels. No picture books. Recently published *Mr. Z and the Time Clock*, by Bonnie Pryor and *A Gift for Tia Rosa*, by Karen Taha.

How to Contact: Accepts unsolicited mss. Prefer complete ms with SASE. Reports in 6 weeks. Simultaneous and photocopied submissions OK. Accepts computer submissions; prefers letter-quality.

Terms: Negotiable. Sends galleys to author. Book catalog for 9x12 SASE with 90¢ postage.

Advice: "We stress quality in all aspects of our editorial and production work. We are expanding our fiction imprint, Gemstone Books."

DAVID R. GODINE, PUBLISHER, INC. (I, II), 300 Massachusetts, Boston MA 02115. (617)536-0761. Imprint: Nonpareil Books (trade paperbacks). President: David R. Godine. Editorial Director: William B. Goodman. Manuscript submissions: Andre Bernard. Juvenile ms submissions: Audrey Bryant. Estab. 1970. Books: acid free paper; sewn binding; illustrations; average print order: 4,000-5,000; first novel print order: 3,500-6,500. Small independent publisher (10-person staff). Publishes hardcover and paperback originals and reprints. Published new writers within the last year. Comments on rejected mss "if of particular interest."

Needs: Contemporary, literary, mystery, collecting, historical, food and wine and juvenile. Recently published *Out On the Marsh*, by David Updike; *Life: A User's Manual*, by Georges Perec; *Casey at the Bat*, illustrated by Barry Moser.

How to Contact: Accepts unsolicited mss with self-addressed, stamped book envelope. Query with outline/synopsis. "We prefer query letters—include publishing history, complete outline of story, and SASE. Do not call to follow up on submission." Simultaneous and photocopied submissions OK. Accepts computer printout submissions; letter-quality only.

Terms: Standard royalties; offers advance. Sends galleys to author. Free book catalog.

Advice: "Keep trying. Remember that every writer now published has been rejected countless times at the beginning. We publish less fiction these days—economic reality."

‡GOSPEL PUBLISHING HOUSE, Subsidiary of Assemblies of God General Council, 1445 Boonville Ave., Springfield MO 65802-2894. (417)862-2731. Book Editor: Glen Ellard. Publishes hardcover originals, trade-paperback originals and mass-market paperback originals. Averages 18 titles/year.
Needs: Adventure, fantasy, historical, humor, juvenile, mystery, religious and young adult. Recently published *Mystery at Pier Fourteen*, by Betty Swinford (juvenile Christian); *The Adventures of Heart Longing*, by Julie Klassen (juvenile Christian); and *Grace Comes Home*, by Darlene Stauffer (juvenile Christian).
How to Contact: Query or submit outline/synopsis and sample chapters. Receives approx. 360 queries and mss from writers each year. Agented fiction 10%. 90% of books bought come from first-time authors. Reports in 2 months. Simultaneous submissions OK. Accepts computer printout submissions, no dot-matrix.
Terms: Pays royalties of 10% on retail price. Publishes ms approx. 18 months after acceptance. Book catalog and writer's guidelines free.
Advice: "Gospel Publishing House is owned and operated by the Assemblies of God. Therefore, the doctrinal viewpoint of all books published is required to be compatible with our denominational position."

GREENLEAF CLASSICS, INC. (II, IV), Box 20194, San Diego CA 92120. Editorial Director: Douglas Saito. Estab. 1961. Publishes paperback originals. Prints 450 new titles annually. "We usually publish a dozen or more first novels a year."
Needs: Erotica. No science fiction, fantasy, mysteries, satire, memoirs, period pieces, gay fiction or occult themes.
How to Contact: Query (requesting guidelines) or submit complete ms with SASE. No simultaneous, computer or photocopied submissions. Reports in 1 week on queries, 1 month on mss.
Advice: "Our needs are very specific, and the average writer will not know those needs without receiving our guidelines. Don't waste time submitting until you've received them."

GROSSET & DUNLAP, INC. (III), A Division of the Putnam & Grosset Group, 200 Madison Ave., 11th Floor, New York NY 10016. Editor-in-Chief: Bernette Ford.
Needs: Juvenile, preschool/picture book. Queries only. "Include such details as length and intended age group and any other information that you think will help us to understand the nature of your material. Be sure to enclose a stamped, self-addressed envelope for our reply. We can no longer review manuscripts that we have not asked to see, and they will be returned unread."

HARCOURT BRACE JOVANOVICH (III), 1250 Sixth Ave., San Diego CA 92101. Imprints include HBJ Children's Books and Gulliver Books. Director: Willa Perlman. Senior Editor, HBJ Children's Books: Bonnie V. Ingber. Editors, HBJ Children's Books: Diane D'Andrade and Allyn Johnston. Senior Editors, Gulliver Books: Elinor Williams and Elizabeth Van Doren. Associate Editor, all imprints: Karen Grove. Publishes hardcover originals and paperback reprints. Averages 75 titles/year. Published new writers within the last year.
Needs: Young adult fiction, nonfiction for all ages, picture books for very young children, mystery. Recently published *Elbert's Bad Word*, by Audrey Wood, illustrated by Don and Audrey Wood; *In the Beginning*, by Virginia Hamilton, illustrated by Barry Moser; *A Sudden Silence*, by Eve Bunting.
How to Contact: Unsolicited mss currently accepted *only* by HBJ Children's Books, not by Gulliver Books, Jane Yolen Books or Voyager Books. Send to "Manuscript Submissions, HBJ Children's Books." SASE. For picture books, send complete ms; for novels, send outline/synopsis and 2-4 sample chapters. Photocopied submissions OK. No simultaneous submissions. No phone calls. Responds in 6-8 weeks.
Terms: Terms vary according to individual books; pays on royalty basis. Writers' guidelines for #10 SASE; catalog for 9x12 SASE.
Advice: "Familiarize yourself with the type of book published by a company before submitting a manuscript; make sure your work is in line with the style of the publishing house. Research the market your work will reach; make yourself familiar with the current children's book field."

HARLEQUIN ENTERPRISES, LTD. (II, IV), 225 Duncan Mill Rd., Don Mills, Ontario M3B 3K9 Canada. (416)445-5860. Imprints include Harlequin Romances, Harlequin Presents, Harlequin American Romances, Superromances, Temptation, Intrigue and Regency, Silhouette, Worldwide Library, Gold Eagle. Editorial Director: Star Helmer. Estab. 1949. Publishes paperback originals and reprints. Books: newsprint paper; web printing; perfect binding. Published new writers within the last year. Number of titles: averages 670/year. Buys 80% agented fiction.
Needs: Romance and heroic adventure. Will accept nothing that is not related to the desired categories.
How to Contact: Send outline and first 50 pages (2 or 3 chapters) or submit through agent with IRC and SASE (Canadian). Absolutely no simultaneous submissions; photocopied submissions OK. Re-

ports in 1 month on queries; 2 months on mss. Publishes ms 12-18 months after acceptance.
Terms: Offers royalties, advance. Must return advance if book is not completed or is unacceptable. Sends galleys to author.
Advice: "The quickest route to success is to follow directions for submissions: query first. We encourage first novelists. Before sending a manuscript, read as many Harlequin titles as you can get your hands on. It's very important to study the style and do your homework first." Authors may send manuscript for Romances and Presents to Karin Stoecker, senior editor; Superromances: Marsha Zinberg, senior editor; Temptation: Lisa Boyes, senior editor, Regencys: Marmie Charndoff, editor to the Canada address. American Romances and Intrigue: Debra Matteucci, senior editor, Harlequin Books, 300 E. 42 Street, 6th Floor, New York, NY 10017. Silhouette submissions should also be sent to the New York office, attention Karen Solem. Gold Eagle and Worldwide Library query letters should be addressed to Randall Toye, editorial director, at the Canada address. "The relationship between the novelist and editor is regarded highly and treated with professionalism."

‡HARMONY BOOKS (II), Subsidiary of Crown Publishers, 225 Park Ave. So., New York NY 10003. (212)254-1600. Assistant Editor: Mary Ellen O'Neill. Publishes paperback originals.
Needs: Historical and literary fiction. Also publishes in serious nonfiction, history, biography, personal growth, media and music fields.
How to Contact: Accepts unsolicited mss. Query first with outline/synopsis and 2-3 sample chapters. SASE. Agented fiction: 75%. Simultaneous and photocopied submissions OK. Accepts dot-matrix computer printouts.
Terms: Pays royalties and advance; amounts negotiable. Sends galleys to authors.

HARPER & ROW JUNIOR BOOKS GROUP (II), 10 E. 53rd St., New York NY 10022. (212)207-7044. Imprints include Charlotte Zolotow Books; T.Y. Crowell, Lippincott Junior Books. Publisher: Elizabeth Gordon. Editors: Charlotte Zolotow, Nina Ignatowicz, Marilyn Kriney, Barbara Fenton, Laura Geringer, Robert O. Warren and Antonia Markiet. Publishes hardcover originals and paperback reprints. Number of titles: *Harper—Cloth*: 98 in 1988; *Harper—Trophy* (paperback): 93 in 1988; *Crowell*: 24 in 1988; *Lippincott*: 38 in 1988.
Needs: Picture books, easy-to-read, middle-grade, teenage and young adult novels; fiction, fantasy, animal, sports, spy/adventure, historical, science fiction, problem novels and contemporary. Recently published *Say Goodnight Gracie*, by Julie Reece Deaver (ages 12 and up), *Dinosaur Bob and His Adventures with The Family Lazzardo*, by William Joyce, (ages 4-8); *Glaciers, Revised Edition*, by Wendell V. Tangborn, (ages 4-8); and *Summer Stories*, by Nola Thacker, (ages 8-12).
How to Contact: Query; submit complete ms; submit outline/synopsis and sample chapters; submit through agent. SASE for query, ms. Please identify simultaneous submissions; photocopied submissions OK. Reports in 2-3 months.
Terms: Average 10% in royalties. Royalties on picture books shared with illustrators. Offers advance. Book catalog for self-addressed label.
Advice: "Write from your own experience and the child you once were. Read widely in the field of adult and children's literature. Realize that writing for children is a difficult challenge. Read other young adult novelists as well as adult novelists. Pay attention to styles, approaches, topics. Be willing to rewrite, perhaps many times. We have no rules for subject matter, length or vocabulary but look instead for ideas that are fresh and imaginative. Good writing that involves the reader in a story or subject that has appeal for young readers is also essential. One submission is considered by the four imprints."

HARPER & ROW PUBLISHERS, INC. (III), 10 E. 53rd St., New York NY 10022. (212)207-7000. Editorial Director: Loraine Chandley Estab. 1817. Publishes hardcover originals. Averages 608 first novels/year.
Needs: Harper & Row will review only mss and proposals submitted by agents or those works submitted upon recommendation of someone known by one of Harper's editors. Recently published *An American Childhood*, by Annie Dillard; *Perestroika*, by Mikhail Gorbachev.

HARVEST HOUSE PUBLISHERS (IV), 1075 Arrowsmith, Eugene OR 97402. (503)343-0123. Manuscript Coordinator: LaRae Weikert. Editor-in-Chief: Eileen L. Mason. Estab. 1974. Midsize independent publisher with plans to expand. Publishes hardcover and paperback originals and reprints. Books: 40 lb ground wood paper; offset printing; perfect binding; average print order 10,000; first novel print order: 10,000-15,000. Averages 50 total titles, 4 fiction titles each year.
Needs: Christian living, contemporary issues, humor, Christian preschool/picture books, religious/inspirational, Christian romance (contemporary, historical). Especially seeks inspirational, romance/historical, mystery. Recently published *The Gift*, by Dennis Hensley/Holly Miller; *When Hearts Awaken*, by June Masters Bacher.
How to Contact: Accepts unsolicited mss. Query first or submit outline/synopsis and 2 sample chap-

ters with SASE. Reports on queries in 2-8 weeks; on mss in 6-8 weeks. Simultaneous and photocopied submissions OK.
Terms: Pays in royalties of 14%-18%; 10 author's copies. Sends galleys to author. Writer's guidelines for SASE. Book catalog for 8½x11 SASE.
Advice: Publishing less fiction than in the past. "See writer's guidelines."

HERALD PRESS (II), Division of Mennonite Publishing House, 616 Walnut Ave., Scottdale PA 15683. (412)887-8500. General Book Editor: S. David Garber. Denominational publisher with full line of religious books. Publishes hardcover and paperback originals. Books: acid free paper; offset printing; squareback adhesive bound paperback; illustrations in juveniles; average print order: 5,000; first novel print order 3,500. Published 4 new writers in the last year. Number of fiction titles: 4-6 per year.
Needs: Religious/inspirational, juvenile and young adult. Recently published *The Splendid Vista*, by Esther Loewen Vogt (adult); and *The Mysterious Passover Visitors*, by Ann Bixby Herold (juvenile).
How to Contact: Accepts unsolicited mss. Query or submit outline/synopsis and 2 sample chapters with SASE. No simultaneous submissions; photocopied submissions OK. Accepts computer printout submissions. Prefers letter-quality. Accepts disk submissions compatible with CP/M. Prefers hard copy with disk submissions. Reports in 4 weeks on queries, 6 weeks on mss.
Terms: Pays 10-15% in royalties; 12 free author's copies; no advance. Sends printouts to author. Book catalog 50¢.
Advice: "We are happy to consider book proposals from Christian authors of adult and juvenile fiction. We like to reflect a Christian response to social issues such as poverty and peacemaking." First novels "no problem if the quality is excellent." Usually publishes original fiction in trade paperback rather than hardcover.

HOLIDAY HOUSE, INC.(I, II), 18 E. 53rd St., New York NY 10022. (212)688-0085. Editor: Margery Cuyler. Estab. 1935. Small independent publisher. Books: high quality printing; occasionally reinforced binding; illustrations sometimes; average print order: 7,500; first novel print order depends on novel. Publishes hardcover originals and paperbacks. Published new writers within the last year. Number of titles: 39 hardcovers in 1987; 5 paperbacks in 1987.
Needs: Contemporary, literary, adventure, humor and animal stories for young readers—preschool through high school. Recently published *Ten Kids, No Pets*, by Ann M. Martin; *Pick of the Litter*, by Mary Jane Auch; *The Pike River Phantom*, by Betty Ren Wright. "We're not in a position to be too encouraging, as our list is tight, but we're always open to good 'family' novels and humor."
How to Contact: "We prefer query letters for novels; complete mansuscripts for shorter books and picture books." Simultaneous and photocopied submissions OK as long a covering letter mentions that other publishers are looking at the same material. Accepts computer printout submissions. Prefers letter-quality. Reports in 4 weeks on queries, 6-8 weeks on mss.
Terms: Advance and royalties are flexible, depending upon whether the book is illustrated. Sends galleys to author.
Advice: "We have received an increasing number of manuscripts, but the quality has not improved vastly. This appears to be a decade in which publishers are interested in reviving the type of good, solid story that was popular in the '50s. Certainly there's a trend toward humor, family novels, novels with school settings, biographies and historical novels. Problem-type novels and romances seem to be on the wane. We are always open to well-written manuscripts, whether by a published or nonpublished author. Submit only one project at a time."

HOLLOWAY HOUSE PUBLISHING COMPANY (II), 8060 Melrose Ave., Los Angeles CA 90046 (213)653-8060. Imprints include Mankind Books, Melrose Square and Heartline Books. Executive Editor: Raymond Friday Locke. Editors: Peter Stone, Tony Stately. Estab. 1960. Midsize independent publisher of varying interests, publishes black experience books, history, games and gambling books. Publishes paperback originals and reprints. Book: offset printing; paper binding; some illustrations; average print order: 20,000 to 30,000; first novel print order: 15,000. Published new writers within last year. Plans 6 first novels this year. Publishes 30-40 titles each year, 15-25 fiction titles.
Needs: Adventure, contemporary, ethnic, experimental, fantasy, historical, horror, literary, mainstream, romance (historical), science fiction, suspense/mystery, war, western. "We are looking for more 'literary' type books than in the past; books that appeal to young professionals. No books dealing with 'street action' about pimps, whores, dope dealing, prisons, etc." Recently published *A Mississippi Family*, by Barbara Johnson (fiction); *Diva*, a first novel by the award-winning playwright Stanley Bennet Clay; *Secret Music*, by Odie Hawkins (memoirs); also a Jessie Jackson bio, by Eddie Stone.
How to Contact: Accepts unsolicited mss. Submit outlline/synopsis and 3 sample chapters or complete ms with cover letter. SASE. 50% of fiction is agented. Reports in 3 weeks on queries; 2 months on mss. Simultaneous submssions and photocopied submissions OK "if they are legible." Accepts computer printout submissions.

Terms: Pays 5½-8½% royalties, advance of $1,000, more for agented mss and nonfiction. Sometimes sends galleys to author. Writer's guidelines and book catalog for #10 SASE.

Advice: Publishing fewer Heartline Romances "as the contemporary romance market seems to have bottomed out, at least for us. Study the market; we do not publish poetry, short story collections, juvies, etc. but not a week goes by that we don't get at least one submissions of each. If you send second-generation copies or dot-matrix check and see if *you* can read it before you expect us to. Neatness, spelling, etc. counts!"

HENRY HOLT & COMPANY (II), 115 W 18th St., 6th Floor, New York NY 10011. (212)886-9200. Imprint includes Owl (paper). Publishes hardcover originals and reprints and paperback originals and reprints. Averages 50-60 total titles, ¼ to ⅓ of total is fiction each year.

Needs: Adventure, contemporary, erotica, ethnic, fantasy, feminist, gay, historical, humor/satire, juvenile (5-9 years, including animal, easy-to-read, fantasy, historical, sports, spy/adventure, contemporary), literary, mainstream, psychic/supernatural/occult, romance (contemporary, historical), suspense/mystery, translations, war, western, young adult/teen (10-18 years including easy-to-read, fantasy/science fiction, historical, problem novels, romance, sports, spy/adventure). Recently published *American Blood*, by John Nichols; *Innocence*, by Penelope Fitzgerald; *A Yellow Raft in Blue Water*, by Michael Doris; *Age of Consent*, by Joanne Greenberg.

How to Contact: Accepts queries; no unsolicited mss. Agented fiction 100%.

Terms: Pays in royalties of 10% minimum; 15% maximum; advance. Sends galleys to author. Book catalog free on request.

Advice: "We encourage first novelists and published new writers last year."

‡HORIZON PUBLISHERS & DIST., INC. (III, IV), 50 S. 500 West, Box 490, Bountiful UT 84010-0490. (801)295-9451. President: Duane S. Crowther. Estab. 1971. "Midsize independent publisher with in-house printing facilities, staff of 30+. Publishes hardcover and paperback originals and reprints. Books: 60 lb offset paper; hardbound, perfect and saddlestitch binding; illustrations; average print order: 3,000; first novel print order: 3,000. Published new writers within the last year. Plans 2 first novels this year. Averages 25-30 total titles; 1-3 fiction titles each year.

Needs: Adventure, historical, humor/satire, juvenile, literary, mainstream, military/war, religious/inspirational, romance (contemporary and historical); science fiction, spiritual, young adult/teen (romance, spy/adventure). "Religious titles are directed only to the LDS market. General titles are marketed nationwide." Looking for "good quality writing in saleable subject areas. Will also consider well-written books on social problems and issues, (divorce, abortion, child abuse, suicide, capital punishment, homosexuality)." Recently published *The Doomsday Factor*, by Anderson (religious science fiction); *Popular Girls*, by Aviatt (college romance); and *The Feather of the Owl*, by Dalton (life after death).

How to Contact: Accepts unsolicited mss. Query first or submit outline/synopsis and 3 sample chapters or complete ms. SASE. Include social security number with submission. Reports in 2-4 weeks on queries; 10-12 weeks on mss. Simultaneous and photocopied submissions OK if identified as such. Accepts computer printout submissions, including dot-matrix. Accepts electronic submissions.

Terms: Pays royalties of 6% minimum; 12% maximum. Provides 10 author's copies. Sends page proofs to author. Publishes ms 3-9 months after acceptance. "We are not a subsidy publisher but we do job printing, book production/for private authors and book packaging." Writer's guidelines for #10 SAE and 1 first class stamp.

Advice: Encourages "only those first novelists who write very well, with saleable subjects. Please avoid the trite themes which are plaguing LDS fiction such as crossing the plains, conversion stories, and struggling courtships that always end in temple marriage. While these themes are important, they have been used so often that they are now frequently perceived as trite and are often ignored by those shopping for new books. In religious fiction we hope to see a process of moral, spiritual, or emotional growth presented. Some type of conflict is definitely essential for good plot development (man against man, man against nature, or man against self). Watch your vocabulary too—use appropriate words for the age group for which you are writing."

HOUGHTON MIFFLIN COMPANY (III), 2 Park St., Boston MA 02108. (617)725-5000. Subsidiary: Ticknor and Fields Inc. Contact: Fiction Editor. Publishes hardcover and paperback originals and paperback reprints. Averages 150 (includes children's) total titles, 45 fiction titles each year. Buys 70-80% agented fiction.

Needs: Contemporary, literary, mainstream, suspense/mystery. No religious, gothic, occult or westerns. Recently published *Emperor of the Air*, by Ethan Canin; *Mama Day*, by Gloria Naylor.

How to Contact: Write to Coordinator of Submissions. Query first; submit outline/synopsis with SASE. Simultaneous and photocopied submissions OK, but no default-mode dot matrix. Reports in 1 month on queries; 2 months on mss. Publishes ms an average of 1 year after acceptance.

Terms: Pays in royalties on sliding scale of 10-12-15%; pays advance. Must return advance if book is not completed or is unacceptable.

‡IRON CROWN ENTERPRISES, INC., 108 Fifth St. SE, Charlottesville VA 22901. (804)295-3918. Editor: John D. Ruemmler. Estab. 1980. "Growing independent publishers of gamebooks expanding into sci fi and fantasy fiction." Publishes paperback originals. Books: offset printing; adhesive paper binding; 4-color covers, 1-color illustrations inside; average print order: 5,000-10,000 (some up to 50,000); first novel print order: 25,000-50,000. Published new writers within the last year. Plans 2-10 first novels this year. Averages 45 total titles, 12 fiction titles each year. Sometimes comments on rejected mss.
Needs: Fantasy and science fiction. Recently published *Murder at The Diogenes Club*, by G. Lientz (interactive mystery); *Return to Deathwater*, by C. Norris (interactive fantasy); and *A Spy in Isengard*, by Terry Amthor (interactive fantasy).
How to Contact: Accepts unsolicited mss. Query first. SASE. Reports in 2-4 weeks on queries; 1-2 months on mss. Simultaneous and photocopied submissions OK. Computer printout submissions OK, including dot-matrix. Accepts electronic submissions.
Terms: Pays royalties of 2% minimum; 4% maximum. Average advance: $1,000. Provides 25 author's copies. Publishes ms 2-8 months after acceptance. Writer's guidelines for #10 SAE with 1 first class stamp. Book catalog for SASE.
Advice: "We publish only paperback originals, most of it either FRP (gaming) oriented or interactive fiction. We hope to begin publishing paperback originals in fantasy and sci fi fiction in 1989. We still get a lot of letters and manuscripts from writers who have no idea what we're looking for. Take courses and join a club or group if they help to keep you writing. And hang on to your job until you make your first million!"

JAMESON BOOKS (I, II, IV), Jameson Books, Inc., The Frontier Library, 722 Columbus St., Ottawa IL 61350. (815)434-7905. Editor: Jameson G. Campaigne, Jr. Estab. 1986. Publishes hardcover and paperback originals and reprints. Books: free sheet paper; offset printing; average print order: 10,000; first novel print order: 5,000. Plans 6-8 novels this year. Averages 12-16 total titles, 4-8 fiction titles each year. Occasionally critiques or comments on rejected mss.
Needs: Very well-researched western (frontier pre-1850). No romance, sci-fi, mystery, et al. Recently published *Wister Trace*, by Loren Estelman; *Buckskin Brigades*, by L. Ron Hubbard; *One-Eyed Dream*, by Terry Johnston.
How to Contact: Does not accepted unsolicited mss. Submit outline/synopsis and 3 consecutive sample chapters. SASE. Agented fiction 50%. Reports in 2 weeks on queries; 8-20 weeks on mss. Simultaneous and photocopied submissions OK. Accepts computer printouts, including quality dot-matrix.
Terms: Pays royalties of 5% minimum; 15% maximum. Average advance: $1,500. Sends galleys to author. Book catalog for 6x9 SASE.
Advice: "Read deeply in your area."

JOY STREET BOOKS, 34 Beacon St., Boston MA 02108. (617)227-0730. Imprint of Little Brown and Co. Children's Books Editor-in-chief: Melanie Kroupa. Publishes hardcover and quality paperback originals. Published new writers within the last year. Number of titles: 24 in 1988. Sometimes buys juvenile mss with illustrations.
Needs: General fiction, juvenile: sports, animal, mystery/adventure, realistic contemporary fiction, picture books and easy-to-read. Recently published *The Arizona Kid*, by Ron Koertge; *The Girl in the Box*, by Ouida Sebestyen; *Alias Madame Doubtfire*, by Anne Fine. Very interested in first novels.
How to Contact: Prefers query letter with sample chapters. SASE. Accepts simultaneous submissions; photocopied submissions OK.
Terms: Pays variable advances and royalties.
Advice: "Books for young adults should show superior storytelling with strong characterization and convincing action and plot development."

KEEPSAKE (II), (formerly *Crosswinds*), Subsidiary of Harlequin/Silhouette, 300 E. 42nd St., 6th Floor, New York NY 10017. Senior Editors: Carolyn Marino and Nancy Jackson. Romance fiction for young adults. Publishes paperback originals. Published new writers within the last year. Average 24 titles each year, all fiction.
Needs: Quality romance fiction for young adults. Also supernatural mysteries for young adults. Recently published *Masquerade*, by Janice Harrell; *Boy Crazy*, by Bebe Faas Rice; *Broken Date*, by R. L. Stine.
How to Contact: Accepts unsolicited mss. Submit complete ms with cover letter. SASE. Reports in 6 weeks. Photocopied submissions OK. Accepts computer printout submissions, no dot-matrix. No multiple submissions.

Terms: Pays royalties of 6% and 10 author's copies. Sends printouts to author. Writer's guidelines for SASE.
Advice: "We are now acquiring manuscripts—young adult romances and young adult supernatural mysteries—for our German market."

ALFRED A. KNOPF (II), 201 E. 50th St., New York NY 10022. Senior Editor: Ashbel Green. Estab. 1915. Publishes hardcover originals. Number of titles: 49 in 1988. Buys 75% agented fiction. Published 9 new writers within the last year.
Needs: Contemporary, literary, mystery and spy. No western, gothic, romance, erotica, religious or science fiction. Recently published *Breathing Lessons*, by Anne Tyler; *Blue Belles*, by Andrew Vachss.
How to Contact: Submit complete ms with SASE. Simultaneous and photocopied submissions OK. Reports in 1 month on mss. Publishes ms an average of 1 year after acceptance.
Terms: Pays 10-15% in royalties; offers advance. Must return advance if book is not completed or is unacceptable.
Advice: Publishes book-length fiction of literary merit by known and unknown writers. "Don't submit manuscripts with matrix type."

KNOPF BOOKS FOR YOUNG READERS (II), 201 E. 50th St., New York NY 10022. Subsidiary of Random House, Inc. Editor-in-Chief: Janet Schulman. Publishes hardcover and paperback originals and reprints. New paperback imprints include Dragonfly Books (picture books), Bullseye (middle-grade fiction) and Borzoi Sprinters (YA fiction). Averages 50 total titles, approximately 20 fiction titles each year.
Needs: "High-quality" adventure, contemporary, humor and nonfiction. "Young adult novels, picture books, middle group novels." Recently published *The Adventures of Pinnochio*, by Carlo Collodi, illustrated by Roberto Innocenti; *Lulu and the Flying Babies*, by Posy Simmonds; *No More Saturday Nights*, by Norma Klein (YA).
How to Contact: Query with outline/synopsis and 2 sample chapters with SASE. Simultaneous and photocopied submissions OK. Reports in 6-8 weeks on mss.
Terms: Sends galleys to author.
Advice: Note new paperback line.

LEISURE BOOKS (II), A Division of Dorchester Publishing Co., Inc., Suite 1008, 276 Fifth Ave., New York NY 10001. (212)725-8811. Editor: Tracey J. Lubben. Address submissions to Audrey LeFehr, assistant editor. Mass-market paperback publisher—originals and reprints. Books: newsprint paper; offset printing; perfect binding; average print order: variable; first novel print order: variable. Published new writers within the last year. Plans 25 first novels this year. Averages 150 total titles, 145 fiction titles each year. Comments on rejected ms "only if requested ms requires it."
Needs: Faction, fantasy, historical, horror, romance (historical), western. Looking for "historical romance (90,000 words), horror novels (80,000 words), western series books." Recently published *Wilder Shores of Love*, by Sandra DuBay (romance); *The Summoning*, by Dana Reed (horror); and *Track of the Snake/Day of the Scorpion*, by Gene Shelton (western).
How to Contact: Accepts unsolicited mss. Query first. SASE. Agented fiction 70%. Reports in 4 weeks on queries; 2 months on mss. Simultaneous and photocopied submissions OK.
Terms: Offers negotiable advance. Payment depends "on category and track record of author." Sends galleys to author. Publishes ms 18 months after acceptance. Writer's guidelines and book catalog for #10 SASE.
Advice: Encourages first novelists "if they are talented and willing to take direction, *and* write the kind of category fiction we publish. Read our catalog and find out what kind of books we publish—mass-market category fiction."

LITTLE, BROWN AND COMPANY, INC. (II, III), 34 Beacon St., Boston MA 02108. (617)227-0730. Imprints include Little, Brown, Joy Street, New York Graphic Society. Medium-size house. Publishes adult and juvenile hardcover and paperback originals. Published new writers in the last year. Averages 100-125 total titles/year. Number of fiction titles varies. Occasionally critiques rejected mss.
Needs: Open. No science fiction. Recently published *Children of the Arbat*, by Anatoli Rybakov; *The Five Bells and Bladebone*, by Martha Grimes; *The Truth About Lorin Jones*, by Alison Lurie.
How to Contact: Does not accept unsolicited mss. Query editorial department first; "we accept submissions from authors who have published before, in book form, magazines, newspapers or journals. No submissions from unpublished writers." Reports in 4-6 months on queries. Simultaneous and photocopied submissions OK.
Terms: "We publish on a royalty basis, with advance." Writer's guidelines free. Book catalog for SASE.

Close-up
Tracey Lubben
Leisure Books

Editors do *and* don't like surprises. It depends on the type of "surprise" that you send them.

At Leisure Books, the best surprises are books that "give us something that's unusual, that we haven't seen before in the historical romance and horror categories," says managing editor Tracey Lubben.

Editors Alicia Condon, Audrey LaFehr and Lubben prefer query letters with detailed synopses, which should be addressed to LaFehr. "Explain the plot, what happens and how it ends," says Lubben.

Leisure editors are looking for historical romances and horror novels and manuscripts for a series of western novels. Occasionally the company also publishes fantasy and science fiction.

The three editors publish 12 titles each month, usually including at least one title by a previously unpublished author. "We're very open to first-time authors," Lubben says, emphasizing that Leisure is a good place for romance and horror writers to get a start. "We enjoy working with them and developing them. It benefits us; it benefits authors."

For writers of horror novels, finding a unique story to cater to readers' expectations is crucial. "You have to stick within certain guidelines and with what's scary, and then come up with new twists and something that's interesting." For instance, Leisure's *Slime* takes the blob theme in a new direction with nuclear waste as the antagonist.

"Keep the story believable at all times," Lubben says. "You're dealing with fantastic genres here, especially horror, but you've got to back up every plot movement that you make."

That advice also applies to the romances that Leisure editors buy. "We see a lot of plot jumps that are exciting and fast paced, but you wouldn't believe them for a second."

Readers have specific expectations, and editors don't want to disappoint them. "especially in category fiction, readers expect a hero and heroine, a lot of conflict between them, and that they'll live happily ever after."

Lubben tells writers not to be discouraged by form letter rejection slips from Leisure or other publishers. If a publisher says no, send that manuscript to other publishers. "That's the business. If you're serious about being a writer, it's something you have to accept."

Begin a second book even as you're trying to sell the first one, Lubben advises. "Most of the time, a writer really improves from the first book to the second, and from the second to the third book, and we can see that."

What surprises Lubben as she deals with writers? Query letters with typographical errors, and published writers worrying whether the company is promoting their books. A publisher wants to sell books as much as the author does, she says. Concentrate on developing fresh plots and characters, writing well, and finally proofreading. Those things, more than author tours, build a writer's career.

—Paula Deimling

LITTLE, BROWN & CO. CHILDREN'S BOOKS (II), Trade Division; Children's Books, 34 Beacon St., Boston MA 02108. Editorial Department. Contact: John G. Keller, publisher; Maria Modugno, editor-in-chief; Karen Klockner, Senior Editor; Stephanie Owens Lurie, managing editor. Books: 70 lb paper; sheet-fed printing; illustrations. Published new writers within the last year. Sometimes buys juvenile mss with illustrations "if by professional artist." Buys 60% agented fiction.
Needs: Middle grade fiction and young adult. Recently published *The Shadow Club*, by Neal Shusterman; *Dump Days*, by Jerry Spinelli.
How to Contact: Will accept unsolicited mss. "Query letters for novels are not necessary."
Terms: Pays on royalty basis. Must return advance if book is not completed or is unacceptable. Sends galleys to author. Publishes ms 1-2 years after acceptance.
Advice: "We are looking for trade books with bookstore appeal. Young adult 'problem' novels are no longer in vogue, but there is now a dearth of good fiction for that age group. We are looking for young children's (ages 3-5) books that might be adapted to unusual toy/book formats. We encourage first novelists. New authors should be aware of what of what is currently being published. I recommend they spend time at the local library familiarizing themselves with new publications."

LODESTAR BOOKS (II), An imprint of E.P. Dutton, 2 Park Ave., New York NY 10016. (212)725-1818. Editorial Director: Virginia Buckley. Senior Editor: Rosemary Brosnan. Young adult and middle-age imprint of juvenile department of trade publisher bought by New American Library in 1985. Publishes hardcover fiction for ages 12-17, ages 10-14 and ages 8-12. Books: 50 or 55 lb antique cream paper; offset printing; hardcover binding; illustrations sometimes; average print order: 5,000-6,000; first novel print order 5,000. Only nonfiction picture books. Published new writers within the last year. Number of titles: approximately 20-24 annually, 10 fiction titles annually. Buys 50% agented fiction.
Needs: Contemporary, humorous, sports, mystery/supernatural, adventure, fantasy, sports, spy/adventure, contemporary, for middle-grade and young adult. Recently published *The Honorable Prison*, by Lyll Becerra de Jenkins (YA first novel set in South America); *Blue Tights*, by Rita Williams-Garcia (YA first novel, contemporary); *Park's Quest*, by Katherine Paterson (YA contemporary).
How to Contact: "Can query, but prefer complete ms." SASE. Simultaneous and photocopied submissions OK. Accepts computer printout submissions. Prefers letter-quality. Reports in 2-4 months. Publishes ms an average of 1 year after acceptance.
Terms: Pays 8-10% in royalties; offers negotiable advance. Sends galleys to author. Free book catalog.
Advice: "We are looking to add to our list more books about black, Hispanic, Native American, and Asian children, in particular. We encourage first novelists. Publishing fewer YA novels. They are difficult to find and difficult to sell reprint rights. Middle grade does better in terms of subsidiary rights sales."

LOUISIANA STATE UNIVERSITY PRESS (II), French House, Baton Rouge LA 70893. (504)388-6294. Executive Editor: Ms. Beverly Jarrett. Fiction Editor: Martha Hall. Estab. 1935. University press—medium size. Publishes hardcover originals. Average print order: 1,500-2,500; first novel print order: 2,000. Averages 50 total titles, 4 fiction titles/year.
Needs: Contemporary, literary, mainstream, short story collections. No science fiction and/or juvenile material. Recently published *I Am One Of You Forever*, by Fred Chappell; and *In the Dutch Mountains*, by Cees Nooteboom.
How to Contact: Does not accept unsolicited mss. Query first. Reports in 2-3 months on queries and mss. Simultaneous and photocopied submissions OK. No computer printouts.
Terms: Pays in royalties, which vary. Sends pre-publication galleys to the author.
Advice: Encourages first novelists.

LOVESWEPT (I, II), Bantam Books, 666 5th Ave., New York NY 10103. (212)765-6500. Associate Pubisher: Carolyn Nichols. Administrative Editor: Susann Brailey. Imprint estab. 1982. Publishes paperback originals. Plans several first novels this year. Averages 72 total titles each year.
Needs: "Contemporary romance, highly sensual, believable primary characters, fresh and vibrant approaches to plot. No gothics, regencies or suspense. Check with editorial assistant for trend-setting titles recommended by the editors."
How to Contact: Query with SASE; no unsolicited mss. "Query letters should be no more than two to three pages. Content should be a brief description of the plot and the two main characters."
Terms: Pays in royalties of 6%; negotiates advance.
Advice: "Read extensively in the genre. Rewrite, polish, and edit your own work until it is the best it can be—before submitting."

MACMILLAN OF CANADA (II), A Division of Canada Publishing Corporation, 29 Birch Ave., Toronto, Ontario M4V 1E2 Canada. (416)963-8830. Editorial Assistant: S. Girvan. Estab. 1905. Publishes hardcover and trade paperback originals and paperback reprints. Books: average print order: 4,000-

5,000; first novel print order: 2,000. Plans 1 first novel this year. Averages 35 total titles, 8-10 fiction titles each year. Rarely comments on rejected mss.

Needs: Literary, mainstream, short story collection, suspense/mystery. Recently published *The Victory of Geraldine Gull*, by Joan Clark; *Memory Board*, by Jane Rule; and *Adele at the End of the Day*, by Tom Marshall.

How to Contact: Accepts unsolicited mss. Query first or submit outline/synopsis with 2-3 sample chapters. SASE for return of ms. Agented fiction 90%. Reports in 3 weeks on queries; 1-2 months on mss. Simultaneous and photocopied submissions OK. Accepts computer printout submissions, including dot-matrix.

Terms: Pays royalties of 8% minimum; 15% maximum; advance negotiable. Provides 10 author's copies. Sends galleys to author. Book catalog for 9x12 SASE.

Advice: Does not encourage first novelists, "but we do consider unsolicited manuscripts."

MACMILLAN CHILDREN'S BOOKS, Macmillan Publishing Co., 866 Third Ave., New York NY 10022. (212)702-4299. Imprints include Four Winds Press, Alladin Books, and Collier Books. Estab. 1919. Large children's trade list which has been expanding. Publishes hardcover originals.

Needs: Juvenile submissions.

How to Contact: Accepts unsolicited mss. Send complete ms with SASE. Reports in 6-8 weeks. No simultaneous submissions; photocopied submissions OK. Accepts computer printout submissions. Prefers letter-quality.

Terms: Pays in royalties; negotiates advance. Free book catalog.

MACMILLAN PUBLISHING CO., INC. (III), 866 3rd Ave., New York NY 10022. (212)702-2000. Contact: Fiction Editor. Fiction imprints include Collier Books, The Free Press, Bradbury and Schimer. Publishes hardcover and paperback originals and paperback reprints. Recently published *Good Hearts*, by Reynolds Price; *The Mustache*, by Emmanuael Carrère; *Spirit Lost*, by Nancy Thayer.

How to Contact: Submit through agent or brief query.

Terms: Pays in royalties; offers advance. Free book catalog.

MARGARET K. McELDERRY BOOKS (I, II), Imprint of the Macmillan Children's Book Group, 866 3rd Ave., New York NY 10022. (212)702-7855. Publisher: Margaret K. McElderry. Division estab. at Atheneum Publishers 1971. Publishes hardcover originals. Books: high quality paper; offset printing; cloth binding; illustrations; average print order: 7,500-10,000; first novel print order: 6,000. Published new writers within the last year. Number of titles: 24 in 1988. Buys juvenile and YA mss, agented or non-agented.

Needs: All categories (fiction and nonfiction) for juvenile and young adult: picture books, contemporary, literary, adventure, mystery, science fiction and fantasy. "We will consider any category. Results depend on the quality of the imagination, the artwork and the writing." Recently published *Memory*, by Margaret Mahy; *False Face*, by Welwyn Wilton Katz; and *I Have a Friend*, by Keiko Narahashi.

How to Contact: Accepts unsolicited mss. Prefers query rather than complete ms. "We feel it is also helpful for us to receive a sample chapter along with the query letter." SASE for query, ms. Simultaneous submissions OK only if so indicated (and preferably *not*); photocopied submissions must be clear and clean. Accepts computer printout submissions. Prefers letter-quality. Reports in 2 weeks on queries, 6-8 weeks on mss. Publishes ms an average of 1 year after acceptance.

Terms: Pays in royalties; offers advance.

Advice: "Imaginative writing of high quality is always in demand; also picture books that are original and unusual. We are looking for nonfiction and for easy-to-read books for beginners. Beginning picture-book writers often assume that texts for the very young must be rhymed. This is a misconception, and we are more than willing to consider picture-book manuscripts that are written in prose. We continue to publish primarily picture books and fiction for the middle grades and some for young adults."

MERCURY HOUSE (III), Box 640, Forest Knolls CA 94933. (415)488-4005. Executive Editor: Alev Lytle. Publisher: William Brinton. Submissions Editor: Carol Pitts. Small, independent publisher of quality fiction and nonfiction. Publishes hardcovers and some paperback originals and reprints. Averages 20 titles annually. 25% of books from first-time authors.

Needs: Contemporary, experimental, literary fiction and translations. Quality fiction and nonfiction only.

How to Contact: No unsolicited mss. Submit query letter, 2 sample chapters, synopsis and SASE. Reports in 2 months. Book catalog for 10x12 SAE. Simultaneous submissions OK.

‡MODERN PUBLISHING (II), A Division of Unisystem, Inc., 155 East 55th St., New York NY 10022. (212)826-0850. Imprint: Honey Bear Books. Contact: Kathy O'Hehir, editorial director. Fiction Editors: Jennifer Daniel, Cythia Lechan. Estab. 1973. "Mass-market juvenile publisher; list mainly consists of picture, coloring and activity, and novelty books for ages 2-8 and board books." Publishes hardcover and paperback originals, and Americanized hardcover and paperback reprints from foreign markets. Average print order: 50,000-100,000 of each title within a series. Published new writers within the last year. "85% of our list first novels this year." Averages 100 + total titles each year. Sometimes comments on rejected mss.

Needs: Juvenile (5-9 yrs, including animal, easy-to-read, fantasy, historical, sports, spy/adventure and contemporary), preschool/picture book, young adult/teen (easy-to-read).

How to Contact: Accepts unsolicited mss. Submit complete ms. SASE. Agented fiction 5%. Reports in 2 months. Simultaneous and photocopied submissions OK.

Terms: Pays by work-for-hire or royalty arrangements. Advance negotiable. Publishes ms 7-12 months after acceptance.

Advice: "We publish picture storybooks, board books, coloring and activity books, bath books, shape books and any other new and original ideas for the children's publishing arena. We gear our books for the preschool through third-grade market and publish series of four to six books at a time. Presently we are looking for new material as we are expanding our list and would appreciate receiving any new submissions. We will consider manuscripts with accompanying artwork or by themselves, and submissions from illustrators who would like to work in the juvenile books publishing genre and can adapt their style to fit our needs. However, we will only consider those projects that are written and illustrated for series of four to six books. Manuscripts must be neatly typed and submitted either as a synopsis of the series and broken-down plot summaries of the books within the series, or full manuscripts for review with a SASE."

WILLIAM MORROW AND COMPANY, INC. (II), 105 Madison Ave., New York NY 10016. Imprints include Arbor House, Beech Tree Books, Silver Arrow, Quill, Perigord, Greenwillow Books, Lothrop, Lee & Shepard and Fielding Publications (travel books), and Morrow Junior Books. Publisher, Morrow Adult: James D. Landis. Estab. 1926. Approximately one fourth of books published will be fiction.

Needs: "Morrow accepts only the highest quality submissions" in contemporary, literary, experimental, adventure, mystery, spy, historical, war, romance, feminist, gay/lesbian, science fiction, horror, humor/satire and translations. Juvenile and young adult divisions are separate. Recently published works by Michael Chabon, William Boyd, Elmore Leonard.

How to Contact: Submit through agent. All unsolicited mss are returned unopened. "We will only accept queries, proposals or mss when submitted through a literary agent." Simultaneous and photocopied submissions OK. Accepts computer printout submissions. Prefers letter-quality. Reports in 2-3 months.

Terms: Pays in royalties; offers advance. Sends galleys to author. Free book catalog.

Advice: "The Morrow divisions of Morrow Junior Books, Greenwillow Books, and Lothrop, Lee and Shepard handle juvenile books. We do 5-10 first novels every year and about ¼ titles are fiction. Having an agent helps to find a publisher. Morrow Junior Books not accepting unsolicited mss."

‡MORROW JUNIOR BOOKS (III), 129 W. 56th Street, New York NY 10019. (212)889-3050. Editor-In-Chief: David L. Reuther. Published new writers within the last year; plans 1 first novel this year. Averages 55 total titles each year.

Needs: Juvenile (5-9 years, including animal, easy-to-read, fantasy (little), spy/adventure (very little), preschool/picture book, young adult/teen (10-18 years, including historical, sports).

How to Contact: Does not accept unsolicited fiction mss.

Terms: Authors paid in royalties. Books published 12-18 months after acceptance. Book catalog free on request.

Advice: "Our list is very full at this time. No unsolicited manuscripts."

THE MYSTERIOUS PRESS (III), 129 W. 56th St., New York NY 10019. (212)765-0923. Imprint: Penzler Books. Publisher: Otto Penzler. Editor-in-Chief: William Malloy. Editors: Sara Ann Freed and Edward Strosser. Estab. 1976. Small independent publisher, publishing only mystery and suspense fiction. Publishes hardcover originals and paperback reprints. Books: hardcover (some Smythe sewn) and paperback binding; illustrations rarely. 110 titles scheduled for 1988. Published new writers within the last year. Average first novel print order 5,000 copies. Critiques "only those rejected writers we wish particularly to encourage."

Needs: Suspense/mystery. Recently published *The Big Nowhere*, by James Ellroy; *The Silver Ghost*, by Charlotte MacLeod; *Trust Me On This*, by Donald E. Westlake.

How to Contact: Agented material only.

Terms: Pays in royalties of 10% minimum; offers negotiable advance. Sends galleys to author. Buys hard and softcover rights. Book catalog for SASE.

Advice: "We have a strong belief in the everlasting interest in and strength of mystery fiction. Don't talk about writing, do it. Don't ride band wagons, create them. Our philosophy about publishing first novels is the same as our philosophy about publishing: the cream rises to the top. We are looking for writers with whom we can have a long term relationship. *Carolina Skeletons*, by David Stout, is a first novel published this year. A good editor is an angel, assisting according to the writer's needs. My job is to see to it that the writer writes the best book he/she is capable of, *not* to have the writer write *my* book. Don't worry, publishing will catch up to you; the cycles continue as they always have. If your work is good, keep it circulating and begin the next one, and keep the faith. Get an agent.''

NAVAL INSTITUTE PRESS (II, IV), Book publishing arm of US Naval Institute, Annapolis MD 21402. Fiction Editor: Deborah Guberti Estes. Estab. 1873. Nonprofit publisher with area of concentration in naval and maritime subjects. Publishes hardcover originals. Averages 25 total titles, 1 fiction title each year. Average first novel print order: 15,000 copies.
Needs: Adventure (naval and maritime), historical (naval) and war (naval aspects). "We are looking for exceptional novels written on a naval or maritime theme." Recently published *Hunt for Red October*, by T. Clancy (naval adventure, contemporary); *Flight of the Intruder*, by Stephen Coonts.
How to Contact: Accepts unsolicited mss. Prefers to receive outline/synopsis and 2 sample chapters. Reports in 6 weeks. Simultaneous and photocopied submissions OK. Accepts computer printout submissions; prefers letter-quality.
Terms: Pays in royalties of 14% of net sales minimum; 21% maximum; 6 author's copies; offers negotiable advance. Sends galleys to author. Free writer's guidelines and book catalog.
Advice: "Fiction must be on a naval or maritime theme and exceptionally well written."

NEW AMERICAN LIBRARY (III), 1633 Broadway, New York NY 10019. (212)397-8000. Imprints include Onyx, Signet, Mentor, Signet Classic, Plume, Plume Fiction, DAW, Meridian. Contact: Michaela Hamilton, executive editor (hardcover); Arnold Dolin, editor-in-chief, Plume (trade paperback); Maureen Baron, editor-in-chief, Signet/Onyx Books (mass-market). Estab. 1948. Publishes hardcover and paperback originals and paperback reprints. Published new writers within the last year.
Needs: "All kinds of commercial and literary fiction, including mainstream, historical, Regency, New Age, western, thriller, science fiction, fantasy, gay. Full length novels and collections." Recently published *Misery*, by Stephen King: *Small Sacrifices*, by Ann Rule; and *Blood Run*, by Leah Ruth Robinson.
How to Contact: Queries accepted with SASE. "State type of book and past publishing projects." Agented mss only. Simultaneous and photocopied submissions OK. Reports in 3 months.
Terms: Pays in royalties and author's copies; offers advance. Sends galleys to author. Free book catalog.
Advice: "Write the complete manuscript and submit it to an agent or agents."

NEW READERS PRESS (IV), Publishing division of Laubach Literacy International, Box 131, Syracuse NY 13210. (315)422-9121. Acquisitions Editor: Kay Koschnick. Estab. 1959. Publishes paperback originals. Books: 55A Warner's Old Style paper; offset printing; paper binding; 6-12 illustrations per fiction book; average print order: 7,500; first novel print order: 5,000. Fiction titles may be published both in book form and as read-along audio tapes. Plans 4 first novels this year. Averages 30 total titles, 4-8 fiction titles each year.
Needs: High-interest, low-reading-level materials for adults and older teens with limited reading skills. Short novels (Sundown Books) of 12,000-15,000 words, written on 3rd-grade level, "should address serious questions that are part of adult life. We will also accept mystery, romance, adventure, science fiction, sports or humor if characters are well-developed, situations realistic, and plot developments believable." Accepts short stories for textbooks, only in collections of 8-20 very short stories (2 to 6 pages each) of same genre. Will accept collections of one-act plays that can be performed in a single class period (45-50 min.) with settings than can be created within a classroom. Short stories and plays can be at 3rd-5th grade reading level. All material must be suitable for classroom use in public education, i.e., little violence and no explicit sex. "We will not accept anything at all for readers under 16 years of age."
How to Contact: Accepts unsolicited mss. Query first or submit outline/synopsis and 3 sample chapters. SASE. Reports in 1 month on queries; 3 months on mss. Photocopied submissions OK. Accepts computer printout submissions, prefers letter-quality to dot-matrix.
Terms: Pays royalties of 5% minimum, 7.5% maximum on gross sales. Average advance: $200. "We may offer authors a choice of a royalty or flat fee. The fee would vary depending on the type of work." Book catalog, authors' brochure and guidelines for short novels free.
Advice: "Most of our fiction authors are being published for the first time. It is necessary to have a sympathetic attitude toward adults with limited reading skills and an understanding of their life situation. Direct experience with them is helpful."

‡NEWMARKET PRESS (II), 18 E. 48th St., 15th Floor, New York NY 10017. (212)832-3575. Imprint: Newmarket Medallion (mass-market paperback). Fiction Editor: Teresa Burns. Estab. 1980. Midsize independent publisher with plans to expand. Publishes hardcover and paperback originals. Books: average print order: 15,000.

Needs: "Anything; primarily child care and parenting." No pornography. Recently published *Stolen Goods*, by Susan Dworkin.

How to Contact: Accepts unsolicited mss. Query first with outline/synopsis. SASE. Most fiction is agented. Reports on queries in 6-10 weeks. Simultaneous and photocopied mss OK. Accepts dot-matrix computer printouts.

Terms: Pays royalties and advance; advance is negotiable. "Almost always" sends galleys to author. Publishes ms "usually 1 or 2 seasons" after acceptance.

Advice: Publishing less fiction than in the past. "Never established as a fiction house." Encourages first novelists "if they show potential and are willing to work at making their writing better. Be aware of what we publish."

W.W. NORTON & COMPANY, INC. (II), 500 5th Ave., New York NY 10110. (212)354-5500. For unsolicited mss contact: Liz Malcolm. Estab. 1924. Midsize independent publisher of trade books and college textbooks. Publishes hardcover originals. Published new writers within the last year. Occasionally comments on rejected mss.

Needs: High-quality fiction (preferably literary). No occult, science fiction, religious, gothic, romances, experimental, confession, erotica, psychic/supernatural, fantasy, horror, juvenile or young adult. Recently published *God's Snake*, by Irini Spanidou (literary); *Agents of Innocence*, by David Ignatius (suspense).

How to Contact: Submit outline/synopsis and sample chapters (of which one is the first). Simultaneous and photocopied submissions OK. Accepts computer printout submissions. Prefers letter-quality. Reports in 6-8 weeks. Packaging and postage must be enclosed to ensure safe return of materials.

Terms: Graduated royalty scale starting at 7½% or 10% of net invoice price, in addition to 25 author's copies; offers advance. Free book catalog.

Advice: "We will occasionally encourage writers of promise whom we do not immediately publish. We are principally interested in the literary quality of fiction manuscripts. A familiarity with our current list of titles will give you an idea of what we're looking for. Chances are, if your book is good and you have no agent you will eventually succeed; but the road to success will be easier and shorter if you have an agent backing the book. We encourage the submission of first novels."

ODDO PUBLISHING CO. (II), 819 Redwine Rd., Box 68, Fayetteville GA 30214. (404)461-7627. Imprints: Read: Read, Explore, and Develop. Managing Editor: Charles W. Oddo. Midsize independent publisher with plans to expand. Publishes hardcover and paperback originals. Books: 80 lb matte coated paper; library binding; color illustrations; average print order 5,000; first novel print order 3,500. Would consider buying juvenile mss with illustrations. Prefers not to work with agents.

Needs: Short children's supplementary readers. Recently published *Bobby Bear and The Kite Contest*, by Marilue; *Bobby Bear and Uncle Sam's Riddle*, by Dr. Lee Mountain; *Bobby Bear's Birthday*, by Rae Oetting.

How to Contact: Accepts unsolicited mss. Submit complete ms with SASE. "Information provided in query letter should include brief summary of plot. Beginning writers tend not to send manuscripts prepared in a neat and organized manner. Also, many provide their own illustrations as a package with the scripts. In most cases the illustrations detract from the manuscript." Reports in 3-4 months on mss. Will consider simultaneous submissions.

Terms: Pays in royalties for special mss only. "We judge all manuscripts independently and pay by outright purchase accordingly." Send $1.25 for book catalog and postage cost.

Advice: "Send simultaneous submissions to as many publishers as possible. Do not be discouraged with rejections. The 'No's' far outnumber the 'Yes's.'"

‡OMEIGA BOOKS (II), Byron Preiss Visual Publications, 24 W. 25th St., New York NY 10010. (212)645-9870. Imprint of Lynx, produced by Byron Preiss. Executive Editor: David M. Harris. Estab. 1987. "Omeiga is a science-fiction line of Lynx Books, a new mass-market paperback publisher, and specializes in series." Publishes paperback originals. Books: newsprint paper; offset printing; perfect binding; average print order: 50,000; first novel print order: 40,000. Plans 1-2 first novels this year. Averages 8 total titles, all fiction, each year. Sometimes critiques rejected mss.

Needs: "Truly extraordinary novels that might have trouble finding a home elsewhere." Fantasy, science fiction. We are looking for originality as well as commercial appeal, and we have a strong bias in favor of series. We also commission some books. If it is a formula or an imitation, don't send it."

How to Contact: Accepts unsolicited ms. Query first or submit outline/synopsis with 2 sample chapters. SASE for ms. Agented fiction 95%. Reports in 4-8 weeks on queries; 8-10 weeks on mss. Simultaneous and photocopied submissions OK. Accepts computer printout submissions, including dot-matrix.

Terms: Pays royalties of 2% minimum; 6% maximum. Average advance: $5,000; advance is negotiable. Sends galleys to author if time permits. Publishes ms 6-10 months after acceptance.

Close-up

David Harris
Omeiga Books

Andrew Porter

"Literary values in science fiction are making a very strong comeback," says David Harris, executive editor of Omeiga Books, a new science fiction imprint packaged by Byron Preiss Visual Publications for Lynx Books. "For a long time it was said science fiction is a literature of ideas. Character, plotting and style were less important, because we were talking about science. This is no longer the case. We now expect the same amount of polish from a science fiction writer as from someone writing a mainstream novel."

Polished writing is one quality Harris looks for when selecting manuscripts. He also looks for stories that can be developed into an ongoing series. In fact both Omeiga and its parent company, Lynx, specialize in series fiction. And science fiction and fantasy are especially suited to series treatment, notes Harris.

"We're looking for stories that are too big to be covered in a single volume. Our science fiction series generally take between three and six volumes to tell the complete story." Harris explains that while each book must stand alone as a novel, it may take several volumes to tell the overall story of a character's development and the development of the world in which it takes place.

Writers must be mindful of this when querying Omeiga. "Ideally we think in terms of three to six books, but a series could be from two to 100 books," says Harris. "We would need an outline—not just of a specific book—but also of what will happen throughout the series. We need to know where the story will go."

Omeiga will usually negotiate the entire series, if it is to be done by a single author, under one contract. Advances for each book, however, are spread out over time, providing an almost steady income during the course of the series. The company has found science fiction audiences are more likely to be interested in a second book if they know the characters, but Harris says he is interested in single-volume stories as well.

Much of the work Omeiga buys is through agents. It was not planned this way, says Harris, but he has found most of the best work is agented and he tends to work with established writers. "But we do look at unagented material. We look at everything that comes in. I love to discover new people and most of the unagented submissions we've published were by people who were new—we've published a number of first novels already. It's always a thrill."

The science fiction field is becoming increasingly competitive, says Harris. He looks at several established magazines in the field regularly to keep up with trends and to keep an eye out for new writers. Some of the magazines he reads include *Analog Science Fiction/Science Fact*, *Aboriginal SF* and *Isaac Asimov's Science Fiction Magazine*. There are several excellent smaller magazines around, says Harris, that he does not have time to read. It's great to be published in these, but "you have to let me know you are available. Send a copy of your story or write and let me know you have a story in one of these books (magazines)."

Keeping up-to-date is especially important in science fiction, says Harris. "I'd like to see more new ideas. I get a lot of submissions that are essentially retellings of classic or popular stories. Tell me a story that is important to you. You have to have the skill, of course—an understanding of the structure of narrative—but it's the commitment to telling a new story or putting on a new slant on a story that is most important."

—Robin Gee

Advice: "More science fiction is indeed being published than in the past. This makes it somewhat easier to break in, but it does not mean that it is, in fact, easy. The science-fiction boom was fed by a number of movies and television shows, and, except for a few well-established novelists, has passed its peak. That is, more books are being published, but the total number of copies sold is not rising. We encourage first novelists in exactly the way we encourage all novelists—if they are talented, but not yet ready to write for us, we try to provide a small amount of editorial guidance (our time is the major limitation here). In our other operations we have published a number of first novels by writers who have come to our attention through their short fiction. After all, second novelists come exclusively from the ranks of first novelists. However, people with no publication credits at all will have a harder time of it with us. Don't oversell yourself. If you're a genius, the work will show it and you don't have to tell me. If you aren't, telling me you are won't help your case."

‡ORCHARD BOOKS (I,II), Subsidiary of Franklin Watts, Inc., 387 Park Ave. S., New York NY 10016. (212)686-7070. Publisher: Norma Jean Sawacki. Estab. 1986. "Orchard books is a children's trade and library imprint of Franklin Watts, Inc., publishing high quality fiction for the youngest readers through young adult." Publishes hardcover originals. Published new writers within the last year. Plans 5 first novels this year. Averages 60 total titles, all fiction titles, each year. Average print order: 7,500. Sometimes critiques rejected ms.
Needs: Fantasy, feminist, historical, juvenile (animal, easy-to-read, fantasy, historical, sports, spy/adventure, contemporary), regional, young adult/teen (easy-to-read, fantasy/science fiction, contemporary, historical, sports, spy/adventure). "We are always interested in new voices, serious or comic, that express insights valuable to children and young adults in original and graceful ways. We are especially interested in novels for the middle grades. And in genre novels that somehow transcend the traditional limits of their specific form." Recently published *Borrowed Children*, by George Ella Lyon; *The Village by the Sea*, by Paula Fox; *A Thief in the Village*, by James Berry (middle grade).
How to Contact: Accepts unsolicited mss. SASE. Agented fiction 50%. Reports in 4 weeks on queries; 12 weeks on mss. Accepts computer printout submissions, including dot-matrix.
Terms: Pays royalties of 7% minimum; 10% maximum. Advance is negotiable. Provides 10 author's copies. Sends galleys to author. Publishes ms 1-2 years after publication, depending on necessity for illustration. Writer's guidelines for SASE.
Advice: "Our list is about half novels—middle grade to young adult, and half picture books. We are always interested in finding new talent."

PAGEANT BOOKS, Subsidiary of Crown Publishing Group, 225 Park Ave. S., New York NY 10003. (212)254-1600. Editors: Karen V. Haas and Carrie Feron. A new mass market category fiction paperback publisher, marketed and distributed by Waldenbooks. Publishes paperback originals. Plans approx. 72 first novels each year. Averages 144 titles, all fiction, each year.
Needs: Adventure—male oriented, fantasy, horror, romance (contemporary, historical, regency), science fiction, espionage thrillers, mystery, western. No illustrated, UFO's, experimental, verse, generational sagas, general fiction.
How to Contact: Accepts unsolicited mss. Submit cover letter, outline/synopsis and 3 sample chapters or 50 pages. Cover letter should state "which category the novel fits into and a brief synopsis (1-2 paragraphs)." Send romances to Carrie Feron; other mss to Karen V. Haas. SASE. Agented fiction 75%. Reports in 6-8 weeks on outlines; 10-14 weeks on mss. Photocopied submissions OK. Accepts computer printout submissions, no dot-matrix.
Terms: Offers negotiable advance. Sends page proofs to author.
Advice: Encourages first novelists. "Before you write, have a good, solid background understanding of American and British literature and of the literature past and present of the category in which you are writing. Always double-space and proofread. The appearance of a manuscript, especially by a new writer, says a lot about the author."

PANTHEON BOOKS (III), Subsidiary of Random House, 201 E. 50th St., New York NY 10022. (212)572-2404. Estab. 1950. "Small but well-established imprint of well-known large house." Publishes hardcover and trade paperback originals and trade paperback reprints. Plans 1-2 first novels this year. Averages 90 total titles, 25 fiction titles each year.
Needs: Pantheon no longer accepts unsolicited fiction. Recently published *Blue Eyes, Black Hair*, by Marguerite Duras; *A Friend From England*, by Anita Brookner; and *Once in Europa*, by John Berger.
How to Contact: Agented fiction 100%.

‡PAPERJACKS BOOKS (I,II), 210 Fifth Ave., 7th Floor, New York NY 10010. (212)889-7726. Editorial Director: Jim Connor. Estab. 1962. Publishes paperback originals and reprints. Published new writers within the last year. Plans 10-12 first novels this year. Averages 120 total titles each year. Sometimes comments on rejected mss.

Needs: Adventure, contemporary, ethnic, experimental, feminist, historical, horror, humor/satire, literary, mainstream, military/war, psychic/supernatural/occult, regional, religious/inspirational, romance (historical), spiritual, suspense/mystery, western. Recently published *Fast Friends*, by Ruth Smith and Sharon Lloyd; *Midnight Affair*, by Nan Ryan; *Jade and Fire*, by Raymond Barnett (reprint).
How to Contact: Accepts unsolicited mss. Query first with outline/synopsis and 3 sample chapters. SASE. Agented fiction: 80%. Reports on queries in 1-2 months. Simultaneous and photocopied submissions "if readable" OK. Accepts dot-matrix computer printouts.
Terms: Pays in royalties and advance; advance is negotiable. Sends galleys to author. Publishes ms within 18 months of acceptance.
Advice: "Don't give up your day job."

PELICAN PUBLISHING COMPANY (IV), Box 189, 1101 Monroe St., Gretna LA 70053. Associate Editor: Dean Shapiro. Executive Editor: James Calhoun. Estab. 1926. Publishes hardcover reprints and originals. Books: hardcover and paperback binding; illustrations sometimes. Published new writers within the last year. Buys juvenile mss with illustrations. Comments on rejected mss "infrequently."
Needs: Juvenile and young adult fiction, especially with a regional focus. "Our adult fiction is *very* limited." Recently published *Belizaire The Cajun*, by Glen Pitre, edited by Dean Shapiro (1988); *The Over-the-Hill Ghost*, by Ruth Calif (1988).
How to Contact: Prefers query. May submit complete ms or outline/synopsis and 2-3 sample chapters with SASE. No simultaneous submissions; photocopied submissions only. ::Not responsible if writer's only copy is sent." Reports in 4-12 weeks on queries; varies on mss. Publishes ms 12-18 months after acceptance.
Terms: Pays 10% in royalties; 10 free author's copies; advance considered. Sends galleys to author. Free list of titles and writer's guidelines. with SASE.
Advice: "Research the mareket carefully. Order and look through publishing catalogs to see if your work is consistent with their lists."

PHILOMEL BOOKS (II), 51 Madison Ave., New York NY 10010. (212)689-9200. Subsidiary of The Putnam Publishing Group. Editors: Patricia Lee Gauch, Paula Wiseman. Publishes hardcover originals and paperback reprints. Books: variable paper; offset printing; reinforced bindings; full color illustrations; average print order: 10,000-15,000; first novel print order: 6,000. Averages 30 total titles each year. "Critiques only if we feel there is some reason to from our point of view."
Needs: Juvenile (animal, nonfiction, historical, picture book, fantasy) and young adult (of more literary variety). "We are not closed to any kind of subject matter, but it must be very well written, fresh and original." Recently published work: *A White Romance*, by Virginia Hamilton; *Miracle at Clements Pond*, by Patricia Pendergraft.
How to Contact: Query first with SASE. Accepts computer printout submissions. Prefers letter-quality. Reports in 2 weeks on queries; 6 weeks on mss.
Terms: Payment arrangement varies. Sends galleys to author.
Advice: "Philomel is devoted to quality children's and young-adult books. Emphasize beautiful and simple language and make sure your story has substance. We do fiction and nonfiction, picture books and some paperbacks, all of them definitely 'up market.' If they are good enough for Philomel, we publish first novels, but we publish mostly established authors. Do not send unsolicited manuscripts. Don't send 'blind' query letters." Publishing less fiction than in the past.

POCKET BOOKS (II), Division of Simon & Schuster, 1230 Avenue of the Americas, New York NY 10020. (212)698-7000. Imprints include Washington Square Press, Poseidon and Star Trek. Vice President/Editorial Director: William Grose. Publishes paperback originals and reprints. Published new writers within the last year. Averages 300 titles each year. Buys 90% agented fiction. Sometimes critiques rejected mss.
Needs: Contemporary, literary, faction, adventure, mystery, spy, historical, western, gothic, romance, literary, military/war, mainstream, suspense/mystery, feminist, ethnic, erotica, psychic/supernatural, fantasy, horror and humor/satire. Recently published *A Cannibal in Manhattan*, by Tama Janowitz; *Stinger*, by Robert R. McCammon (horror); *Lover Man*, by Dallas Murphy (mystery).
How to Contact: Query with SASE. No unsolicited mss. Reports in 6 months on queries only. Publishes ms 12-18 months after acceptance.
Terms: Pays in royalties and offers advance. Sends galleys to author. Writer must return advance if book is not completed or is not acceptable. Free book catalog.

POINT BOOKS, Scholastic, Inc., 730 Broadway, New York NY 10003. (212)505-3000. Senior Editor: Regina Griffin. Estab. 1984. Young adult imprint. Publishes paperback originals. Published new writers within the last year.
Needs: Young adult/teen (10-18 years). No romance. Recently published *Fallen Angels*, by Walter

Dean Myers; *Born into Light*, Paul Samuel Jacobs; *Oh, Brother*, by Johnneice Marshal Wilson.
How to Contact: Query first. SASE.
Advice: "Query letters should describe the genre of the book (mystery, sci-fi, etc.), give a brief plot description, and tell about the writer's background (i.e. have they published anything; taken writing courses, etc.). One common mistake I see is that I get letters that go on and on about the marketing possibilities, but neglect to describe the book at all. That makes me feel I'm dealing with someone who wants to be a 'writer,' but doesn't really take writing seriously enough. We like to publish fiction by previously unpublished writers, if we can. We are expanding our hardcover program and our paperback middle-reader line."

POPULAR LIBRARY (II), Subsidiary of Warner Communictions, Inc., 666 5th Ave., 9th Floor, New York NY 10144. (212)484-3145. Executive Editor: Jeanne Tiedge. Large commercial fiction imprint. Publishes paperback originals. Published new writers within the last year. Plans 2 first novels this year. Publishes 60 titles each year, all fiction.
Needs: Male adventure, fantasy, horror, mainstream, romance (contemporary, historical), science fiction, military/war, western. Recently published *Sweet Starfire*, by Jayne Ann Krentz (futuristic); *Wild Nights*, Ann Miller (contemporary); *Frontier Fires*, by F. Roseanne Bittner (historicl saga); *Survivor of Nam*, by Donald Elotnick.
How to Contact: Does not accept unsolicited mss. Query first. 95% of fiction agented. Reports in 1 month. Photocopied submssions OK "if it's neat." Accepts computer printout submissions, including dot-matrix.
Terms: Terms vary with author's experience. Author always sees page proofs.

POSEIDON PRESS (II), 1230 Avenue of the Americas, New York NY 10020. (212)698-7290. Distributed by Simon & Schuster. Publisher: Ann E. Patty. Senior Editor: Kathleen Mooney. Estab. 1981. Hardcover and quality trade paper. Books: paper varies; offset printing; illustrations; average print order varies; first novel print order: 5,000-7,500. Recently published *Inheritance*, by Judith Michael; and *Bad Behavin*, by Mary Gaitskill. Averages 20 total titles, 10-12 fiction titles (3 first novels) each year. Does "not critique rejected ms by unsolicited authors unless work merits it."
Needs: General fiction and nonfiction, commercial and literary.
How to Contact: Query first. No unsolicited manuscripts or sample chapters. Photocopied submissions OK. Reports in 2 months.
Terms: Payment varies, according to content of book.

CLARKSON N. POTTER, INC., 225 Park Ave. S., New York NY 10003. Distributed by Crown Publishers, Inc. Vice President Editorial Director: Carol Southern.
Needs: Illustrated fiction, biography, humor/satire and juvenile.
How to Contact: Prefers submissions through an agent. Simultaneous and photocopied submissions OK. Accepts computer printout submissions.
Terms: Pays 6-12% in royalties on hardcover; 6-7½% in royalties on paperback; offers $5,000 up in advance.

PRENTICE-HALL BOOKS FOR YOUNG READERS (II), A Division of Simon & Schuster, Inc., Juvenile Publishing Division, 1230 Avenue of the Americas, New York NY 10020. (212)698-7000. Manuscript Coordinator: Rose Lopez. Publishes hardcover originals and paperback originals and reprints. Books: offset printing; illustrations on most titles; average print order: 10,000. Published new writers within the last year. Number of titles: 30 hardcover children's books and 15 children's paperbacks/year.
Needs: Juvenile, picture books, humor, mystery, "high-quality middle-grade fiction," and "imaginative nonfiction." Recently published *Over in the Meadow*, by Paul Galdone (picture book); *Waiter,There's a Fly In My Soup!*, by Charles Keller, illustrations by Lee Lorenz (humor); *Who Let Muddy Boots Into The White House?*, by Robert Quackenbush (biography).
How to Contact: Agented or solicited mss only.
Terms: Pays in royalties; offers advance. Sends galleys to author.

PRESIDIO PRESS (IV), 31 Pamaron Way, Novato CA 94947. (415)883-1373. Editors: Adele Horwitz, Joan Griffin. Estab. 1976. Small independent general trade—specialist in military. Publishes hardcover originals. Books: 20 lb regular paper, average print order: 5,000. Published new writers within the last year. Publishes at least one military fiction book per list. Averages 15 total titles each year. Critiques or comments on rejected ms.
Needs: Historical with military background, war.
How to Contact: Accepts unsolicited mss. Query first or submit 4 sample chapters. SASE. Reports in 2 weeks on queries; 3 months on mss. Simultaneous and photocopied submissions OK. Accepts computer printouts.

Terms: Pays in royalties of 15% minimum; advance: $1,000 average. Sends galleys to author. Book catalog free on request.
Advice: "Think twice before entering any highly competitive genre; don't imitate; do your best. Have faith in your writing and don't let the market disappoint or discourage you."

PRICE STERN SLOAN, INC. (II), 360 N. La Cienega Blvd., Los Angeles CA 90048. (213)657-6100. Subsidiaries/Divisions are Wonder Books, Troubador, Serendipity, Doodle Art, HPBooks, Contact: Editorial Dept. Estab. 1962. Midsize independent, expanding. Publishes hardcover originals and paperback originals and reprints. Books: perfect or saddle-stitched binding; illustrations. Averages 200 total titles each year.
Needs: Humor/satire, juvenile (series, easy-to-read, humor, educational), adult trade nonfiction. No adult fiction. Recently published *Shopaholics* (adult trade); *My Grandmother's Cookie Jar* (juvenile fiction); and *How Old Is Old?* (juvenile fiction). Also publishes "self-help, cookbooks, automotive books, photography and gardening."
How to Contact: Query only. Submit outline/synopsis and sample pages. SASE required. Reports in 2 months on queries. Simultaneous and photocopied submissions OK. Accepts computer printouts including dot-matrix.
Terms: Terms vary.

G.P. PUTNAM'S SONS (III), The Putnam Publishing Group, 200 Madison Ave., New York NY 10016. (212)576-8900. Imprints include Perigee, Philomel, Platt and Munk, Coward McCann, Grosset and Dunlap Pacer. Publishes hardcover originals. Published new writers within the last year.
Needs: Recently published fiction by Stephen King, Lawrence Sanders, Alice Hoffman.
How to Contact: Does not accept unsolicited mss.

RANDOM HOUSE, INC., 201 E. 50th St., New York NY 10022. (212)751-2600. Imprints include Pantheon Books, Panache Press at Random House, Vintage Books, Times Books, Villard Books and Knopf. Publishes hardcover and paperback originals. Rarely comments on rejected mss.
Needs: Adventure, contemporary, historical, literary, mainstream, short story collections, suspense/mystery. "We publish fiction of the highest standard." Authors include James Michener, Robert Ludlum, Mary Gordon.
How to Contact: Query with SASE. Simultaneous and photocopied submissions OK. Reports in 4-6 weeks on queries, 2 months on mss.
Terms: Payment as per standard minimum book contracts.

RANDOM HOUSE, INC./JUVENILE DIVISION (III), 201 E. 50th St., New York NY 10022. (212)751-2600. Imprints include Happy House and Knopf. Managing Editor: Regina Abend. "Large mass market *juvenile* publisher (division of a multi-faceted publishing house)—some licensed characters." Publishes hardcover and paperback originals. Books: various kinds of paper, binding and printing; color illustrations. Published new writers within the last year. Number of titles: 200 in 1988 (includes Random House and Knopf imprints).
Needs: Juvenile. Recently published Stepping Stone Books (ages 7-9, 64 pages, fiction); and Just Right Books (ages 2-5, picture books, 3 levels).
How to Contact: "At present, we are only reviewing mss from published authors and agents." Publishes ms 12-18 months after acceptance.
Terms: Sends galleys to author on longer books.
Advice: "Much work is generated in-house, or freelancers are commissioned for flat fee. No first novels (or any novels) published in several years. Some of our books still feature licensed characters."

RESOURCE PUBLICATIONS, INC. (I, IV), Suite 290, 160 E. Virginia St., San Jose CA 95112. (408)286-8505. Book Editor: Kenneth Guentert. Estab. 1973. "Independent book and magazine publisher focusing on imaginative resources for celebration." Publishes paperback originals. Published third novel ever last year. Averages 12-14 total titles, 2-3 fiction titles each year.
Needs: Story collections for storytellers. "Novels dealing with contemporary religious issues or mythical themes would be considered. No evangelical pieces." Recently published *BreakThrough: Stories of Conversion*, by Andre Papineau (biblical stories); *Joanna, the Pope*, by Daniel Panger (historical); and *One Perfect Lover*, by Matthew Ignoffo (Biblical).
How to Contact: Query first or submit outline/synopsis and 1 sample chapter with SASE. Reports in 2 weeks on queries; 6 weeks on mss. Photocopied submissions OK "if specified as *not* simultaneous." Accepts computer printout submissions. Prefers letter-quality. Accepts disk submissions compatible with CP/M, IBM system. Prefers hard copy with disk submissions.
Terms: Pays in royalties of 8% minimum, 10% maximum; 10 author's copies. "We do not subsidy publish. We do require that the author purchase a small portion of the first press run."

RICHARDSON & STEIRMAN (I, II), 246 Fifth Ave., New York NY 10001. (212)213-1203. President: Stewart Richardson. Fiction Editors: Hy Steirman and Stewart Richardson. Estab. 1984. Publishes hardcover and paperback originals. Books: offset printing; high quality paper; case binding; average first novel print order; 4,000-10,000. Plans 2 first novels this year; 30 total titles, 5-6 fiction titles. Occasionally critiques rejected ms "if author has talent."
Needs: Adventure and suspense novels. No domestic novels or partial mss.
How to Contact: Query. Reports in 3 weeks on queries; 1 month or more on mss. No simultaneous submissions. Computer printout submissions OK. Prefers letter-quality. Disk submissions OK with IBM. Sends galleys to author.
Terms: Pays in royalties of 10% minimum, 15% maximum; advance is more for agented ms. Book catalog for $3.
Advice: "Every writer begins with a first novel. We are interested in real talent, with writing that creates a world in which characters live—atmosphere and originality. What makes novels work is the growth, decline, triumph or *change* in characters you care about. The autobiographical novel doesn't work unless the author sees his fictional creation from a distance, so to speak. We will publish books of quality in adventure, suspense, in the sense of Hammond Innes, Helen MacInnes, Graham Greene's 'entertainments,' and writers who can tell a story like the late Desmond Bagley and the live John Gardner (now 007's creator.) We are also interested in 'scenario' fiction. We publish books of contemporary affairs—*Mikhail Gorbachev*, etc. We don't have facilities to handle a lot of unsolicited manuscripts. We prefer a synopsis of a work of fiction envisioned to be at least 75,000 words long. Submissions will be read within four to five weeks."

ST. MARTIN'S PRESS, 175 5th Abve., New York NY 10010. (212)674-5151. Imprint: Joan Kahn. Chairman and CEO: Thomas J. McCormack. Publishes hardcover and paperback reprints and originals.
Needs: Contemporary, literary, experimental, faction, adventure, mystery, spy, historical, war, gothic, romance, confession, feminist, gay, lesbian, ethnic, erotica, psychic/supernatural, religious/inspirational, science fiction, fantasy, horror and humor/satire. No plays, children's literature or short fiction. Recently published *The Silence of the Lambs*, by Thomas Harris; *Little Saigon*, by T. Jefferson Parker; *The Shell Seekers*, by Rosamunde Pilcher.
How to Contact: Query or submit complete ms with SASE. Simultaneous (if declared as such) and photocopied submissions OK. Reports in 2-3 weeks on queries, 4-6 weeks on mss.
Terms: Pays standard advance and royalties.

‡ST. PAUL BOOKS AND MEDIA (I), Subsidiary of Daughters of St. Paul, 50 St. Paul's Ave., Jamaica Plain, Boston MA 02130. (617)522-8911. Children's Editor: Sister Anne Joan, fsp. Estab. 1934. Roman catholic publishing house. Publishes hardcover and paperback originals. Averages 20 total titles, 5 fiction titles each year. Sometimes comments briefly on rejected mss.
Needs: Juvenile (animal, easy-to-read, fantasy, historical, contemporary), preschool/picture book, young adult/teen (historical, problem novels). All fiction must communicate high moral and family values. "Our fiction needs are entirely in the area of children's literature. We are looking for bedtime stories, historical and contemporary novels for children. Would like to see characters who manifest faith and trust in God." Does not want "material with an ideological bent contrary to Catholic church teachings; characters' lifestyles not in conformity with Catholic teachings (e.g. divorce is understandable, but no divorce and remarriage)."
How to Contact: Does not accept unsolicited mss. Query first. SASE. Reports in 2 weeks. Accepts dot-matrix computer printouts.
Terms: Pays royalties of 8% minimum; 12% maximum. Provides negotiable number of author's copies. Publishes ms approx. 1 year after acceptance. Writer's guidelines for #10 SAE and 1 first class stamp; book catalog for 9x11½ SAE and 3 first class stamps.
Advice: Publishing more fiction than in the past. "Recognized a dearth of juvenile fiction appropriate for Catholics and other Christians."

SCHOLASTIC, Scholastic, Inc., 730 Broadway, New York NY 10003. (212)505-3000. Executive Editor for romance books: Ann Reit. Publishes a variety of books (paperback originals and reprints) for children and young adults, under the following imprints:
POINT BOOKS: Senior Editor: Brenda Bowen. Estab. 1984. A paperback line of young adult fiction for readers aged 12-up. Not restricted as to length, setting or subject matter. Most Point novels have contemporary settings, and take as their central characters young adults between the ages of 13-20. No romances. Include SASE.
APPLE BOOKS: Senior Editor: Brenda Bowen. Estab. 1981. A paperback line of juvenile fiction for readers aged 8-11. Not restricted to setting or subject matter, but most Apples are "slim novels" (between 128-200 pages), and all are geared to the capabilities and interests of readers 8-12. Single submissions only. Include SASE.

Scholastic also publishes original paperback books for its school book clubs: TAB BOOK CLUB (TEEN AGE BOOK CLUB) (Grades 7-12) Contact: Greg Holch.
How to Contact: Query first or submit outline/synopsis and 3 sample chapters with SASE. Simultaneous and photocopied submissions OK. Accepts computer printout submissions.

CHARLES SCRIBNER'S SONS (II), Subsidiary of Macmillan, 866 3rd Ave., New York NY 10022. (212)702-2000. Editors: Edward Chase, Susanne Kirk. Publisher and Editor-in-Chief: Robert Stewart. Estab. 1846. Publishes hardcover originals and paperback reprints of its own titles. Number of titles: over 100 last year. Does not comment on rejected mss.
Needs: Contemporary, adventure, mystery, spy, feminist, horror, humor/satire.
How to Contact: Submit outline/synopsis and sample chapter with SASE or submit through agent. "Go to writing workshops. Most important, find an agent." Reports in 2 months on queries. Does not accept unsolicited mss, only queries.
Terms: Pays in royalties; offers advance. Sends galleys to author.

CHARLES SCRIBNER'S SONS, BOOKS FOR YOUNG READERS, Division of Macmillan Publishing Co., 866 Third Ave., New York NY 10022. (212)702-7885. Editorial Director: Clare Costello. Publishes hardcover originals. Averages 20-25 total titles, 8-13 fiction titles each year.
Needs: Juvenile (animal, easy-to-read, fantasy, historical, picture book, sports, spy/adventure, contemporary, ethnic, science fiction) and young adult (fantasy/science fiction, romance, historical, problem novels, sports, spy/adventure). Recently published *The Giver*, by Lynn Hall (young adult contemporary fiction); *How Do You Know It's True?*, by David and Marymae Klein (young adult nonfiction); and *Welcome to Grossville*, by Alice Fleming (intermediate contemporary fiction).
How to Contact: Submit complete ms with SASE. Simultaneous and photocopied submissions OK. Reports in 8-10 weeks on mss.
Terms: Free book catalog free on request. Sends galleys to author.
Advice: "Stories about contemporary children, their problems and experiences are doing well for us in today's market. We encourage first novelists."

SEAL BOOKS (McCLELLAND/BANTAM, INC.) (I, II, IV), 105 Bond St., Toronto, Ontario M5B 1Y3 Canada. (416)340-0777.. Editorial Director: Susan Rutledge. Estab. 1977. Canada's largest mass market paperback publisher. Publishes paperback originals and reprints. Averages about 40 total titles, about 30 fiction titles each year.
Needs: Adventure, contemporary, horror, mainstream, suspense/mystery, Needs for novels: "fiction that will appeal to mass market and to a Canadian readership." Recently published *The Handmaid's Tale*, by Margaret Atwood; *FORD*, by Robert Lacey.
How to Contact: Submit outline/synopsis and 4 sample chapters. Reports in 2 months. Simultaneous and photocopied submissions OK. Accepts computer printout submissions. Prefers letter quality.
Terms: Pays in royalties; advance.
Advice: Publishes work by Canadian citizens or landed immigrants only.

SECOND CHANCE AT LOVE (II, IV), 200 Madison Ave., New York NY 10016. (212)686-9820. Subsidiary of Berkley Publishing Group. Editor: Hillary Cige. Estab. 1981. Commercial category line. Publishes paperback originals. Plans "many" first novels this year. Publishes 24 titles each year, all fiction. Open to unagented mss/writers.
Needs: Contemporary romance. No gothic, suspense, mystery or historicals. Recently published *Gambler's Lady*, by Cait Logan; *All That Jazz*, by Carole Buck.
How to Contact: "Please call in 1989 to find out when we are buying new mss."
Terms: Advance against royalties. Sends galleys to author. Free writer's guidelines with SASE.
Advice: "Study the books published in our line along with our guidelines and *target* submissions to our needs. We are willing to publish first novels that are of high quality. Category romance remains a good place for new writers to get published. But prospective authors must read the genre, know the genre, and be able to deliver something fresh and original within the framework of our guidelines."

SIERRA CLUB BOOKS, 730 Polk St., San Francisco CA 94109. (415)776-2211. Editor-in-Chief: D. Moses. Estab. 1892. Midsize independent publisher. Publishes hardcover and paperback originals and paperback reprints. Averages 20-25 titles, 1-2 fiction titles each year.

Market categories: (I) Beginning; (II) General; (III) Prestige; (IV) Specialized.

Needs: Contemporary (conservation, environment).
How to Contact: Query only with SASE. "We will only deal with queries; we are not staffed to deal with mss." Simultaneous and photocopied submissions OK. Accepts computer printout submissions. Prefers letter-quality. Reports in 6 weeks on queries.
Terms: Pays in royalties. Free book catalog for SASE.
Advice: "Only rarely do we publish fiction. We will consider novels on their quality and on the basis of their relevance to our organization's environmentalist aims."

SILHOUETTE BOOKS (II, IV), 6th Floor, 300 E. 42nd St., New York NY 10017. (212)682-6080. Imprints include Silhouette Romances, Silhouette Special Edition, Silhouette Desire, Silhouette Intimate Moments, Harlequin Historicals, Crosswinds (Young Adult). Vice President and Executive Editor: Karen Solem. Senior Editor and Editorial Coordinator: Isabel Swift. Senior Editors: Tara Hughes, Leslie J. Wainger, Leslie Kazanjian. Editor: Lucia Macro. Historicals: Associate Editors: Eliza Shallcross, Tracy Farrell. Crosswinds: Senior Editors: Nancy Jackson, Carolyn Marino. Estab. 1979. Publishes paperback originals. Published 10-20 new writers within the last year. Buys agented and unagented adult romances and young adult fiction. Number of titles: 312/year. Occasionally comments on rejected mss.
Needs: Contemporary romances, adult and young adult, historical romances. Recently published *A Crime of the Heart*, by Cheryl Reavis; *A Touch of Spring*, by Annette Broadrick; *Silver Noose*, by Patricia Gardner Evans; *The Name of the Game*, by Nora Roberts.
How to Contact: Submit query letter with brief synopsis and SASE. No unsolicited or simultaneous submissions; photocopied submissions OK. Accepts computer printout submissions. Prefers letter-quality. Publishes ms 9-24 months after acceptance.
Terms: Pays in royalties; offers advance (negotiated on an individual basis). Must return advance if book is not completed or is unacceptable.
Advice: "Study our published books before submitting to make sure that the submission is a potential Silhouette." Added new line of historical romances last year.

‡SILVER ARROW BOOKS (II), 105 Madison Ave., New York NY 10024. (212)889-3050. Imprint of William Morrow & Co., Publisher: Sherry Arden. Fiction Editor: Jennifer Williams. Estab. 1988. "Small press with big company (William Morrow) backing." Publishes hardcover originals. Publishes new writers. Averages 10-15 total titles each year.
Needs: Contemporary, historical, literary, mainstream, supsense/mystery. No paperback genre fiction. Will publish *Splinters*, by Erica Heller, in 1989.
How to Contact: Please send query first. Almost all agented fiction.

SIMON & PIERRE PUBLISHING COMPANY LIMITED (II), Box 280, Adelaide St. Postal Stn., Toronto, Ontario M5C 2J4 Canada. Imprints includes Bastet Books, Canplay Series, Canadian Theatre History Series, The Canadian Dramatist, and Drama for Life. Contact: Editors. Estab. 1972. Publishes hardcover and paperback originals. Books: 55 lb hi bulk web printing; perfect binding; line drawings; average print order 2,000. Averages 10-12 titles/year.
Needs: Contemporary, literary, mystery, spy, historical, humor/satire, juvenile, young adult and translations. No romance, erotica, horror, science fiction, or poetry. Recently published *The Blackbird Song*, by Pauline Holdstock; and *Welcome to America, Mr. Sherlock Holmes*, by Christopher Redmond.
How to Contact: Query, submit complete ms, submit outline/synopsis and sample chapter or submit through agent with SASE (Canadian stamps) or IRCs. Simultaneous and photocopied submissions OK. Reports in 1 month on queries, 4 months on mss.
Terms: Pays in royalties; small advance. Sends galleys to author. Free book catalog.
Advice: "We prefer Canadian authors. Include with submissions: professional résumé listing previous publications, detailed outline of proposed work and sample chapters. We publish novelists who are good at proofing themselves and not afraid of being involved in their own marketing, but the fiction must be based on a current topics or themes."

SIMON & SCHUSTER, 1230 Avenue of the Americas, New York NY 10020. (212)698-7000. Imprints include Pocket Books, Linden Press.
Needs: General adult fiction, mostly commercial fiction.
How to Contact: Agented material 100%.

GIBBS SMITH, PUBLISHER (II), Box 667, Layton UT 84041. (801)544-9800. Imprints: Peregrine Smith Books. Editorial Director: Madge Baird. Estab. 1969. Publishes hardcover and paperback originals and reprints. Books: illustrations as needed; average print order 5,000. Publishes 25 + total titles each year, 5-6 fiction titles.
Needs: Adventure, contemporary, experimental, humor/satire, literary, short story collections, translations and nature. Literary works exhibiting the social consciousness of our times. Recently published

Fall Out of Heaven, by Alan Cheuse; *Best of the West*, edited by Thomas (short story collection); and *Girl From Cardigan*, by Leslie Norris (short stories).

How to Contact: Query first. SASE. 60% of fiction is agented. Reports in 3 weeks on queries; 10 weeks on mss. Simultaneous and photocopied submissions OK. Accepts computer printout submissions, including dot-matrix.

Terms: Pays 7-15% royalties. Sends galleys to author. Writers guidelines for #10 SASE; book catalog for 9x6 SAE and 56¢ postage.

Advice: "Our foremost criteria is the literary merit of the work."

STANDARD PUBLISHING (II, IV), 8121 Hamilton Ave., Cincinnati OH 45231. (513)931-4050. Director: Mark Plunkett. Estab. 1866. Independent religious publisher. Publishes paperback originals and reprints. Books: offset printing; paper binding; b&w line art; average print order: 7,500; first novel print order: 5,000-7,500. Published new writers in the last year. Number of titles: averages 18/year. Rarely buys juvenile mss with illustrations. Occasionally comments on rejected mss.

Needs: Religious/inspirational and easy-to-read. "Should have some relation to moral values or Biblical concepts and principles." Katie Hooper Series, by Jane Sorenson; Wheeler Series, by Dan Schantz.

How to Contact: Accepts unsolicited mss. Query or submit outline/synopsis and 2-3 sample chapters with SASE. "Query should include synopsis and general description of perceived market." Accepts computer printout submissions. Prefers letter-quality. Reports in 1 month on queries, 12 weeks on mss. Publishes ms 12-24 months after acceptance.

Terms: Pays varied royalties and by outright purchase; offers varied advance. Sends galleys to author. Free catalog with SASE.

Advice: Publishes fiction with "strong moral and ethical implications." First novels "should be appropriate, fitting into new or existing series. We're dealing more with issues."

STARBLAZE EDITIONS (IV), Subsidiary of The Donning Company, 5659 Virginia Beach Blvd., Virginia Beach VA 23502. (804)461-8090. Fiction Editor: Jean Campbell. Estab. 1974. Midsize independent publisher with plans to expand. Publishes hardcover and trade paperback originals and reprints. Books: acid free paper; perfect, hardbound binding; illustrations; average print order: 20,000. Averages 40-50 total titles, 10 fiction titles each year. Sometimes critiques rejected mss.

Needs: Looking for "fantasy, science fiction, and to some degree, horror novels. We are concentrating on more established writers at the moment." Recently published *An Edge in My Voice*, by Harlan Ellison (collection); *The Harp of the Grey Rose*, by Charles deLint (fantasy novel); and *Myth Nomer and Im-Pervections*, by Robert Asprin (fantasy novel).

How to Contact: Accepts unsolicited mss. Query first. "Writers need to list their writing experience in a cover letter. Since we publish very select list of titles, we seldom publish first novels unless they are exceptional." SASE. Reports in 1-2 weeks on queries; 3-4 months on mss. Simultaneous "but tell us" and photocopied submissions OK. Accepts computer printout submissions, including dot-matrix if readable.

Terms: Pays royalties of 8% minimum; 15% maximum. Provides 10 author's copies. Sends galleys to author. Writer's guidelines free for #10 SAE with 1 first class stamp. Book catalog for $1.

Advice: "Within Starblaze, we created the Starblaze Classics, a series of oversize editions of classic science fiction and fantasy lavishly illustrated by well-known artists. We are currently re-evaluating our line in regard to the ratio between graphic novels, art books and standard fiction. In science fiction and fantasy, know the field. Try the many workshops offered at conventions every month around the country."

STEMMER HOUSE PUBLISHERS, INC. (III), 2627 Caves Rd., Owings Mills MD 21117. (301)363-3690. Imprint includes International Design Library, Victoria and Albert Museum Introductions to the Decorative Arts. Editor: Barbara Holdridge. Estab. 1975. Independent publishing house. Publishes hardcover originals. Books: acid free paper; offset printing; Smythe sewn binding; illustrations occasionally; average print order 3,000-5,000; first novel print order 4,000. Number of titles: averages 20/year, 0-1 fiction titles.

Needs: Literary and historical novels. No fantasy, detective or science fiction. Recently published *Paradise*, by Dikkon Eberhart (6th century A.D.); *The Fringe of Heaven*, by Margaret Sutherland (contemporary); and *Naked in Deccan*, by Venkatesh Kulkarni (contemporary).

How to Contact: Accepts unsolicited mss. Query first with SASE. Agented fiction: 50%. Simultaneous and photocopied submissions OK if well reproduced. Reports in 2 weeks on queries, 4 weeks on mss, depending on backlog. Publishes ms 1-2 years after acceptance.

Terms: Pays 10% in royalties; offers small advance upon publication. Sends galleys to author. Book catalog free for SASE.

Advice: Publishing "less fiction, since we find little of the quality we require. Trend today seems to be less literate work. Write to be read 50 years from today. Don't tell us how good the novel is. Perfect your grammar and spelling. Most writers seem to have read the latest paperback and swear to write something 'just as good'—but it's most often not even as competent." Interested in "literary quality rather than trendy or genre material. We plan to continue trying to find worthwhile fiction, including first novels, on a long-term basis. Send a cogent query letter, not coy, not a teaser, not self-pitying. We have been overwhelmed with unsolicited, unsuitable submissions and cannot keep up with them. If we cannot cope any better in the future, we will begin returning them unread."

‡STODDART (III), Subsidiary of General Publishing, 34 Lesmill Rd., Toronto, Ontario M3B 2T6 Canada. (416)445-3333. Managing Editor: Donald G. Bastian. "Largest Canadian-owned publisher in Canada, with a list that features nonfiction primarily." Publishes hardcover and paperback originals and reprints. Plans 2 first novels this year. Averages 50-60 total titles, 8 fiction each year.
Needs: Adventure, suspense/mystery, young adult/teen (10-18 years). Looking for "quality commercial fiction with international potential." Recently published *The Sounding*, by Peter Goddard (light suspense); *Winter Palace*, by Dennis Jones (high-level suspense); and *A Dream Like Mine*, by M.T. Kelly (literary).
How to Contact: Submit outline/synopsis and 2-3 sample chapters. SASE. Agented fiction 50%. Reports in 4-6 weeks on queries; 2-3 months on mss. Simultaneous and photocopied submissions OK. Accepts computer printout submissions, including dot-matrix.
Terms: Pays royalties of 10% minimum; 15% maximum for hardcover. Advance is negotiable. Sends galleys to author. Publishes ms up to 2 years after acceptance.
Advice: "Fiction accounts for about 10% of the list. The amount we do depends on quality and marketability, co-publishing arrangements in US etc., and foreign language sales potential." Encourages first novelists, "but they should be realistic. Don't expect to make a living on it. Presentation is very important. Clear-typed, open spacing. Typos can easily turn readers away from a potentially good book."

LYLE STUART/IRMA HELDMAN BOOKS (I, II), Subsidiary of Lyle Stuart Inc., 275 Central Park West, New York NY 10024. (212)877-6834. Imprint: Citadel Press. Editorial contact person: Irma Heldman. Estab. 1986. Publishes hardcover originals. Published new writers within the last year.
Needs: Suspense/mystery, contemporary, mainstream, adventure. Recently published *St. John's Baptism, a Detective Novel*, by Wiliam Babula; *Silver Spoon Murders*, by D. W. Smith; *Lost Daughter*, by Michael Cormany. Needs novel-length manuscripts, 60,000 words and up.
How to Contact: Accepts unsolicited mss. Submit complete ms. "I find query letters misleading at best." SASE "*stamps only:* no money orders, checks or cash." Simultaneous and photocopied submissions OK. Accepts computer printout submissions.
Terms: Advance is negotiable. Sends galleys to author. Book catalog free on request.
Advice: "Any manuscript, once accepted, will be very thoroughly edited by myself. Don't try to be like anybody else. Be yourself and draw on what you know to create."

‡SUMMIT BOOKS (II,III), Subsidiary of Simon & Schuster, 1230 Avenue of the Americas, New York NY 10020. (212)698-7500. President and Editor-in-Chief: James Silverman. Estab. 1976. Midsize independent publisher with plans to expand. Publishes hardcover originals. Books: average print order: 3,000-200,000. Plans 1 first novel this year. Averages 30-35 total titles each year.
Needs: Contemporary, feminist, historical (occasionally), satire, literary, mainstream, suspense/mystery, translations.
How to Contact: Does not accept unsolicited mss. Unagented authors should query first. SASE. Agented fiction 99%. Reports on queries in 8-12 weeks. Simultaneous and photocopied submissions OK. Does not accept dot-matrix computer printouts.
Terms: Pays in royalties and advance; advance is negotiable. Sends galleys to author. Publication time after ms is accepted varies.
Advice: "Our editorial staff is too small to critique writers, and it is sometimes hard to tell exactly what is wrong (or right) with a novel in the time we would have to do it. Get an agent."

SWEET DREAMS, Cloverdale Press, 133 5th Ave., New York NY 10003. (212)420-1555. Editor: Ellen Steiber.Estab. 1981. Book packager. Publishes paperback originals.
Needs: Young adult romance. Recently published *More Then Friends*, by Janice Boies; *Hand-me-Down Heart*, by Mary Schulz; and *Rocky Romance*, by Sharon Dennis-Wyath.
How to Contact: Query first with SASE. Simultaneous and photocopied submissions OK. Accepts computer printout submissions. Prefers letter quality. Reports in 1 month on queries; 2 months on mss.
Terms: Negotiated. Free writer's guidelines for SASE.
Advice: Interested in "contemporary fiction with realistic protagonists and situations. We do publish first novels."

TAB BOOK CLUB (TEEN AGE BOOK CLUB) (II), Scholastic Inc., 730 Broadway, New York NY 10003. Contact: Greg Holch. See listing for Scholastic Inc. Published new writers within the last year. **Needs:** "We will be publishing less teenage fiction. We are not publishing standard teenage romances. A book has to be unique, different, and of high literary quality." **How to Contact:** Send "a query letter and the first 20 pages of the manuscript." **Advice:** "I personally prefer humorous, light novels that revolve around a unique premise. We publish mass-market entertainment reading, not educational books."

TEXAS MONTHLY PRESS (III), Box 1569, Austin TX 78767. (512)476-7085. Subsidiary of Mediatex, Inc. Director and Editor-in-Chief: Scott Lubeck. Fiction Editor: Stephen Harrigan. Estab. 1978. Publishes hardcover and paperback originals and reprints (60,000 word minimum). Books: 60 lb paper; offset printing; sewn or perfect binding; average first novel print order: 2,500-3,000. Plans 1 first novel this year. Averages 22 total titles, 1 fiction title, each year. **Needs:** "Interested in serious fiction of all sorts, particularly novels set in Texas or the Southwest." Recently published *A Flatland Fable*, by Joe Commer; *Baby Houston*, by June Arnold. **How to Contact:** Query first or submit outline/synopsis with SASE. Simultaneous and photocopied submissions OK. Accepts computer printout submissions. Prefers letter-quality. Accepts disk submissions compatible with Osborne, Lanier, Xerox, IBM. Prefers hard copy with disk submissions. Reports in 2 weeks on queries; 1 month on mss. **Terms:** Pays royalties on net. **Advice:** Now publishing fiction reprint series in trade paperback editions.

THORNDIKE PRESS (IV), Subsidiary of Senior Service Corp., Box 159, Thorndike ME 04986. (800)223-6121. Editorial Assistant: Jamie Knobloch. Estab. 1979. Midsize independent publisher, of large print reprints. Publishes hardcover and paperback large print *reprints*. Books: alkaline paper; offset printing; Smythe-sewn library binding; average print order: 4,000. Publishes 88 total titles each year, 80 fiction titles. **Needs:** *No fiction that has not been previously published*. Recently published *Beloved*, by Toni Morrison; *Secret for a Nightingale*, by Victoria Holt; *Legacy*, by James Michener. **How to Contact:** Accepts unsolicited mss. Submit complete published book or galley. SASE. Reports in 5-6 months. Simultaneous and photocopied submissions OK. **Terms:** Pays 10% in royalties; advance of $2,000; advance is negotiable. Book catalog for 8 ½x11 SAE with 39¢ postage. **Advice:** "Be very professional."

THREE CONTINENTS PRESS (II, IV), 1636 Connecticut Ave. N.W., Washington DC 20009. (202)332-3885. Fiction Editor: Donald Herdeck. Estab. 1973. Small independent publisher with expanding list. Publishes hardcover and paperback originals and reprints. Books: library binding; illustrations; average print order: 1,000-1,500; first novel print order: 1,000. Averages 15 total titles, 6-8 fiction titles each year. Average first novel print order: 1,000 copies. Occasionally critiques ("a few sentences") rejected mss. **Needs:** "We publish original fiction only by writers from Africa, the Caribbean, the Middle East, Asia and the Pacific. No fiction by writers from North America or Western Europe." Recently published *Kaidara*, by Mamadou Bah, translated by Daniel Whitman; *Fountain and Tomb* by Naguib Mahfous, translated by James Kennison. **How to Contact:** Query with outline/synopsis and sample pages and SAE, IRC. State "origins (non-Western), education, previous publications." Reports in 1 month on queries; 2 months on mss. Simultaneous and photocopied submissions OK. Computer printout submissions OK. **Terms:** "We are not a subsidy publisher, but do a few specialized titles a year with subsidy. In those cases we accept grants or institutional subventions. Foundation or institution receives 20-30 copies of book and at times royalty on first printing. We pay royalties twice yearly (against advance) as a percentage of net paid receipts." Royalties of 5% minimum, 10% maximum; 10 author's copies; offers negotiable advance, $300 average. Depends on grant/award money. Sends galleys to author. Free book catalog. **Advice:** "Mss should be professionally edited, clean, clear. Amateur, poorly thought out or imitative work is all too common."

TICKNOR & FIELDS (I, II), Affiliate of Houghton-Mifflin, 52 Vanderbilt Ave., New York NY 10017. (212)687-8996. Estab. 1979. Publishes hardcover originals. **Needs:** Open to all categories, but selective list of only 15 titles a year. **How to Contact:** Query letters only; no unsolicited mss accepted. No simultaneous submissions (unless very special); photocopied submissions OK. Reports in 8 weeks on ms. **Terms:** Pays standard royalties. Offers advance depending on the book. Free book catalog with SAE and first class stamps.

TOR BOOKS (II), 49 W. 24th St., New York NY 10010. Imprints include Tor Horror and Aerie books. Managing Editor: Martha Schwartz. Editor-in-Chief: Beth Meacham. Estab. 1980. Publishes paperback originals and reprints; also has hardcover trade list of approximately 30 titles a year. Books: 5 point Dombook paper; offset printing; Bursel and perfect binding; few illustrations. Averages 200 total titles, all fiction, each year.
Needs: Adventure, fantasy, horror, mainstream, science fiction, suspense and young adult (fantasy/science fiction). Recently published *The God Game*, by Andrew Greeley; *Cat Magic*, by Whitley Streiber; and *Speaker for the Dead*, by Orson Scott Card.
How to Contact: Agented mss preferred. Buys 75% agented fiction. Photocopied submissions OK. Publishes ms a maximum of 2 years after acceptance.
Terms: Pays in royalties and advance. Writer must return advance if book is not completed or is unacceptable. Sends galleys to author. Free book catalog on request.

‡TROLL ASSOCIATES (II), Watermill Press, 100 Corporate Drive, Mahwah NJ 07430. (201)529-4000. Editorial Contact Person: M. Frances. Estab. 1968. Midsize independent publisher. Publishes hardcover originals, paperback originals and reprints. Published new writers within the last year (juvenile fiction). Averages 100-300 total titles each year.
Needs: Adventure, historical, juvenile (5-9 yrs. including: animal, easy-to-read, fantasy), preschool/picture book, young adult/teen (10-18 years) including: easy-to-read, fantasy/science fiction, historical, romance (ya), sports, spy/adventure
How to Contact: Accepts and returns unsolicited mss. Query first. Submit outline/synopsis and sample chapters. Reports in 2-3 weeks on queries. Accepts dot-matrix computer printout submissions.
Terms: Pays royalties. Sometimes sends galleys to author. Publishes ms 6-18 months after acceptance.

‡TSR, INC., Box 756, Lake Geneva WI 53147. (414)248-3625. Imprints include the Drangonlance® series, Forgotten Realms™ series, Buck Rogers™ books, ™ Books. Contact: Book Department. Estab. 1974. "We publish original paperback novels and interactive game books. TSR publishes games as well, including the Dungeons & Dragons® role-playing game. Books: standard paperbacks; offset printing; prefect binding; b&w (usually) illustrations; average first novel print order: 75,000. Averages 20-30 titles each year, mostly fiction.
Needs: "We most often publish character-oriented fantasy and science fiction, and some horror. We do fewer interactive books each year, so we really aren't looking for new ones at present. We work with authors who can deal in a serious fashion with the genres we concentrate on and can be creative within the confines of our work-for-hire contracts. Recently published *Spellfire*, by Ed Greenwood; *Stormblade*, by Nancy Varian Berberick; *Bimbos of the Death Sun*, by Sharyn McCrumb.
How to Contact: "TSR no longer accepts unsolicited or unagented manuscripts. Contact with the TSR Book Department should be initiated through an agent. Because most of our books are strongly tied to our other products, we expect our writers to be very familiar with those products."
Terms: Pays royalties of 3%-4% of cover price. Offers advances. Sometimes sends galleys to authors. "Commissioned work, with the exception of our ™ Books line, are written as work-for-hire, with TSR, Inc., holding all copyrights.
Advice: "With the huge success of our Dragonlance® trilogies and Forgotten Realms™ books, we expect to be working even more closely with TSR-owned fantasy worlds. We also plan an extensive line of Buck Rogers™ books. Be familiar with our line and have your agent contact us about accepting a proposal."

TYNDALE HOUSE PUBLISHERS (II, IV), 336 Gundersen Dr., Wheaton IL 60187. (312)668-8300. Editor-in-Chief: Dr. Wendell C. Hawley. Estab. 1960. Privately owned religious press. Publishes hardcover and paperback originals and paperback reprints. Plans 6 first novels this year. Averages 87 total titles, 15-20 fiction titles each year. Average first novel print order: 5,000-10,000 copies.
Needs: Religious/inspirational.
How to Contact: Accepts unsolicited mss. Submit complete ms. Reports in variable number of weeks. Simultaneous and photocopied submissions OK. Publishes ms an average of 1 year after acceptance.
Terms: Pays in royalties of 10% minimum; negotiable advance. Must return advance if book is not completed or is unacceptable. Sends galleys to author. Free writer's guidelines. Free book catalog on request.
Advice: "We are publishing less fiction."

UNIVERSITY OF GEORGIA PRESS (II), Terrell Hall, Athens GA 30602. (404)542-2830. Flannery O'Connor Short Fiction Award Editor: Charles East. Estab. 1938. Midsize university press with editorial program focusing on scholarly nonfiction. Publishes hardcover and paperback originals and reprints.
Needs: Short story collections. No novellas or novels. Recently published *Silent Retreats*, by Philip F.

Close-up

Alice Harron Orr
Walker & Company

"In order to function effectively as a kind of discovery house," says Alice Harron Orr, editor of Walker's mystery-suspense and regency romance novel lines, "we need to have a strong volume of submissions to choose from. One of my major goals has been to increase that volume, so I've attended a lot of writers' conferences, and I talk to local writers' organizations." Orr says the results of her publicity efforts have been "what you would expect"—the majority of manuscripts she sees are not in line with Walker's list or are not ready for publication. "Then, however, there are the occasional gems," she adds. "And the greater the number of submissions, the more gems you're going to find."

Orr is particularly pleased when such a gem comes from a new author. "There are a number of larger houses that no longer accept unagented material," she says, "but at Walker, we encourage both agented and unagented submissions, by both previously published and unpublished writers."

Creating characters and a plot that balance with and complement each other is a key to writing compelling popular fiction, Orr says. The protagonist should be someone the reader will admire and want to identify with—and the key to that is creating strong motivations for the character. As far as plot is concerned, the worst thing that can occur in a manuscript is "when the reader can look at what the character is involved with and say 'who cares.' Something significant has to be at stake." Orr also emphasizes the importance of the villain. "The drive that has made him do all these awful things has to be believable," she says. "A writer must be careful not to create villains who are more like cartoons than real people."

Orr encourages writers of regency romances (which generally take place between 1805 and 1811) to read texts, biographies and journals of the period as research, and points writers to a special regency romance issue of *Fiction Writer's Magazine* for help. But a greater danger than historical inaccuracy, she says, is a tendency by writers "to get carried away with the research and let it overwhelm the story. Historical details are meant to flavor the story and create an atmosphere within which that story happens. It is always the story itself which is most important."

Walker has added suspense to its mystery line, "which means we've opened up the list to the entire spectrum of the genre—whodunits, psychological thrillers, police procedurals—everything in between," Orr says. "That means we have a much more diversified line than we have had in the past." One subgenre in which Orr is *not* interested is romantic suspense, saying, "romantic suspense as such is pretty much considered passé by most houses, with the exception, of course, of established greats in the field like Phyllis Whitney."

The most common problem writers face when submitting to Walker is "failure to understand that this is a business, and professionalism is the order of the day," Orr says. "The same kind of behavior that would be appropriate or inappropriate in any business setting is equally so in publishing. When an author submits a manuscript he ir she is well advised to think of that process as if he or she were applying for a job. Study the field you're attempting to enter, sharpen your specific skills, and make the best presentation you can. Don't make personal references in your cover letter; don't send a manuscript that's anything less than your best shot."

—Laurie Henry

Deaver; *The Purchase of Order*, by Gail Galloway Adams.
How to Contact: Short story collections are considered only in conjunction with the Flannery O'Connor award competition. Next submission period is June 1-July 31, 1989. *Manuscripts cannot be accepted at any other time. Competition information for SASE.*
Terms: The Flannery O'Connor Award carries a $500 cash award plus standard royalties. Free book catalog.

VESTA PUBLICATIONS, LTD (II), Box 1641, Cornwall, Ontario K6H 5V6 Canada. (613)932-2135. Editor: Stephen Gill. Estab. 1974. Midsize publisher with plans to expand. Publishes hardcover and paperback originals. Books: bond paper; offset printing; paperback and sewn hardcover binding; illustrations; average print order; 1,200; first novel print order; 1,000. Plans 7 first novels this year. Averages 18 total titles, 5 fiction titles each year. Negotiable charge for critiquing rejected mss.
Needs: Adventure, contemporary, ethnic, experimental, faction, fantasy, feminist, historical, humor/satire, juvenile, literary, mainstream, preschool/picture book, psychic/supernatural/occult, regional, religious/inspirational, romance, science fiction, short story collections, suspense/mystery, translations, war, and young adult/teen. Recently published *Sodom in her Heart*, by Donna Nevling (religious); *The Blessings of a Bird*, by Stephen Gill (juvenile); and *Whistle Stop and Other Stories*, by Ordrach.
How to Contact: Accepts unsolicited mss. Submit complete ms with SASE or SAE and IRC. Reports in 1 months. Simultaneous and photocopied submissions OK. Accepts computer printout submissions. Disk submissions OK with CPM/Kaypro 2 system.
Terms: Pays in royalties of 10% minimum. Sends galleys to author. "For first novel we usually ask authors from outside of Canada to pay half of our printing cost." Free book catalog.
Advice: "We published new writers last year. Don't be discouraged; keep trying."

VIKING PENGUIN, INC. (III), 40 W. 23rd St., New York NY 10010. Imprints include Viking (hardcover adult and juvenile) and Penguin Books (trade paperback). Estab. 1925. Number of fiction titles: averages 100/year.
Needs: Open.
How to Contact: Submissions accepted only through agent or through intermediary to specific editor. No unsolicited query letters, proposals or manuscripts.
Terms: Amount and type of advance payment and royalty scale depend on the individual situation.

VILLARD BOOKS (II, III), Random House, Inc., 201 E. 50th St., New York NY 10022. (212)572-2720. Editorial Director: Peter Gethers. Fiction Editors: Diane Reverand, Alison Acker, Heather Lehr (asst.). Estab. 1983. Imprint specializes in commercial fiction and nonfiction. Publishes hardcover and trade paperback originals. Published new writers within the last year. Plans 2 first novels this year. Averages 30 total titles, approx. 10-15 fiction titles each year. Sometimes critiques rejected mss.
Needs: Strong commercial fiction and nonfiction. Adventure, contemporary, historical, horror, humor/satire, literary, mainstream, romance (contemporary and historical), suspense/mystery, women's. Special interest in mystery, thriller, and literary novels. Recently published *The Life of Helen Alone*, by Karen Lawrence (literary); *Pattern Crimes*, by William Bayer (thriller); and *Carnival of Spies*, by Robert Moss (thriller).
How to Contact: Accepts unsolicited mss. Submit outline/synopsis and 1-2 sample chapters. Agented fiction: 95%. Reports in 2-3 weeks. Simultaneous and photocopied submissions OK. Accepts electronic submissions, no dot-matrix.
Terms: "Depends upon contract negotiated." Sends galleys to author. Writer's guidelines for 8½x11 SAE with 1 first class stamp. Book catalog free on request.
Advice: "Most fiction published in hardcover."

WALKER AND COMPANY (II), 720 5th Ave., New York NY 10019. Editors: Jacqueline Johnson, Alice Harron Orr, Sally Paynter, Peter Rubie, Amy Shields, Susan Suffes, William Thorndike. Midsize independent publisher with plans to expand. Publishes hardcover and paperback originals and reprints. Average first novel print order: 4,000-5,000. Number of titles: averages 250/year. Published many new writers within the last year. Occasionally comments on rejected mss.
Needs: Nonfiction, mystery, regency romance, quality male adventure, western, young adult and horror fiction.
How to Contact: Submit outline and chapters as preliminary. Query letter should include "a concise description of the story line, including its outcome, word length of story, writing experience, publishing credits, particular expertise on this subject and in this genre. Common mistakes: sounding unprofessional (i.e. too chatty, too braggardly). Forgetting SASE." Buys 50% agented fiction. Photocopied submissions OK, "but must notify if multiple submissions." Accepts computer printout submissions; must be letter-quality. Reports in 1-2 months. Publishes ms an average of 1 year after acceptance.

Terms: Negotiable (usually advance against royalty). Must return advance if book is not completed or is unacceptable.
Advice: Publishing more fiction than previously, "exclusively hardcover. Manuscripts should be sophisticated. As for mysteries, we are open to all types, including suspense novels. In fact, the line has been renamed Walker Mystery-Suspense. We favor strong plot and compelling action. We are always looking for well written western novels. While we publish some of the traditional 'revenge' westerns, we like to publish historical 'explorations' about any aspect of the West. Character development is most important in all Walker fiction. We have been actively soliciting submissions to all divisions."

WARNER BOOKS (II), Subsidiary of Warner Publishing, Inc., 666 Fifth Ave., New York NY 10103. (212)484-2900. Imprints include Popular Library, Mysterious Press. Contact: editorial dept. for specific editors. Estab. 1961. Publishes hardcover and paperback originals. Published new writers within the last year. Averages approx. 500 titles/year. Sometimes critiques rejected mss.
Needs: Adventure, contemporary, fantasy, horror, mainstream, preschool/picture book, romance (contemporary, historical, regency), science fiction, suspense/mystery, war, western, "We are continuing to publish romances, mainstream novels, science fiction, men's adventure, etc. No historicals that are not romances, Civil War novels, young adult." Recently published *Silk Lady*, by Gwen Davis (commercial women's fiction); *Lost*, by Gary Devon (suspense); and *Desire in Disguise*, by Rebecca Brandewyne (historical romance).
How to Contact: Accepts unsolicited mss "but we prefer not to." Query first. Agented fiction 85-90%. Reports in 4-6 weeks on queries; 6-8 weeks on mss. Simultaneous submissions "but we prefer exclusive submissions"; and photocopied submissions "of high quality" OK.
Terms: Varies for each book. Writer's guidelines free on request.
Advice: "Continuing a strong, varied list of fiction titles. We encourage first novelists we feel have potential for more books and whose writing is extremely polished. Be able to explain your work clearly and succinctly in query or cover letter. Read books a publisher has done already—best way to get a feel for publisher's strengths. Read *Publisher's Weekly* to keep in touch with trends and industry news."

‡WEST END GAMES OF PENNSYLVANIA, INC. (II, IV), RD 3, Box 2345, Honesdale PA 18431. Editorial Director: Bill Slavicsek. Fiction Editors: Douglas Kaufman, Wargame & Boardgame and Paranoia editor; Jonatha Ariadne Caspian, Multipath and Ghostbusters editor; Bill Slavicsek, Star Wars editor. Estab. 1978. "West End is an adventure game publisher expanding into multipath and fiction." Publishes hardcover and paperback originals. Books: 60 lb paper, offset perfect binding; illustrations; average print order varies: 10,000 to 100,000 (multipath novels are on high end). Published new writers within the last year. Plans 1-4 first novels this year. Averages 12-16 total titles/year, all fiction. Sometimes comments on rejected mss.
Needs: "All of our fiction has a roleplaying, multipath or boardgame application." Adventure, fantasy, historical, humor/satire, juvenile (fantasy and/or spy/adventure), military/war, preschool/picture book, science fiction, suspense/mystery, young adult/teen (fantasy/science fiction, historical and/or spy/adventure). "We are publishing 4-6 multipath books a year in the *Star Wars* series, and 1-6 roleplaying adventures in each of three lines: Star Wars, Paranoia and Ghostbusters. Other multipath and roleplaying lines may come up, but are not definite. No erotica, experimental, sports, regional, religious, spiritual." Recently published *The Star Wars Sourcebook*, by Bill Slavicsek and Curtis Smith, (an omnibus of Star Wars vehicles, alien lore, character backgrounds, and more); *Alpha Complexities*, by Edward S. Bolme, (a roleplaying adventure for the *Paranoia* roleplaying game); *Star Wars Campaign Pack*, by Paul Murphy (a compendium of advice and adventure outlines to help the novice or experienced gamemaster).
How to Contact: Does not accept usolicited mss. Query first; enclose SASE (IRC) for answer to query or return of ms. Agented fiction 10%. Reports in 3 weeks on queries; 3 months on mss. No simultaneous submissions. Photocopied submissions OK. "We accept dot-matrix if the typeface has descenders; we do not accept electronic submissions."
Terms: "We pay advances averaging $500 + ; the advance is negotiable." Publishes ms 6-18 months after acceptance. "When possible we buy all rights; occasionally we pay royalties of 1-3% on retail." Writer's guidelines are available for #10 (IRC) and 1 first class stamp. Book catalog for 9x12 (IRC) and 2 first class stamps.
Advice: "West End is publishing more, and more various, interactive fiction (both roleplaying and multipath) than we have in the past. We are doing hardcovers for the roleplaying lines, and large-format perfectbound paperbacks, because we find that these resources are referred to again and again by our gamers, and they want materials that have an extended shelf life. We are publishing mulitpath paperbacks beause we think the genre is new and innovative—and here to stay. We are always interested in new authors. The roleplaying industry is both young and small, and the requirements of the genre(s) it encompasses are fairly welldefined. A writer has a much better chance here of getting feedback on his or her work. Then, too, we have the possiblitiy of discovering the next Gary Gygax or Tracey Hickman. Since

West End does a great deal of business in licensed products, knowing the lines we produce is a must. The consistent tone and humor of our products sets us apart in the industry. Read what we have already published. Research our materials carefully before you submit anything. We can help work out the mechanics of the roleplaying or mulitpath systems if your ideas are innovative and your writing is strong.''

WESTERN PRODUCER PRAIRIE BOOKS (II), Subsidiary of Saskatchewan Wheat Pool, 2310 Millar Ave., Box 2500, Saskatoon, Saskatchewan S7K 2C4 Canada. (306)665-3548. Imprint: Concordia International Youth Fiction Series (translations of foreign young adult novels). Editorial Director: Jane McHughen. Estab. 1954. Midsize publisher with plans to expand line of juvenile and young adult fiction. Publishes paperback originals and reprints. Books: 60 lb hi-bulk paper; traditional offset printing; perfect bound paperback binding; b&w illustrations (if warranted); average print order: 5,000; first novel print order: 3,000. Published new writers within the last year. Plans 1 first novel this year. Averages 20 total titles, 2 fiction titles each year. Sometimes critiques rejected mss.
Needs: Juvenile (fantasy, historical, sports, contemporary), young adult/teen (fantasy, historical, problem novels, sports). Looking for juvenile and young-adult novels appealing to 8 to 14 year olds. Recently published *A Question of Courage*, by Irene Morck.
How to Contact: Accepts unsolicited mss. Submit outline/synopsis and 3-4 sample chapters. SASE. Agented fiction: very little. Reports in 1 month on queries; 2-3 months on mss. Simultaneous (as long as we are notified) and photocopied submissions OK. Accepts computer printout submissions, including dot-matrix.
Terms: Pays in royalties of 10% minimum; 12.5% maximum. Offers average advance: $1,000. Sends galleys to author. Writer's guidelines and book catalog free on request.
Advice: "Interested in expanding paperback juvenile and young adult fiction list. Very active in selling editions to countries outside of Canada."

WESTERN PUBLISHING COMPANY, INC., 850 3rd Ave., New York NY 10022. (212)753-8500. Imprint: Golden Books. Juvenile Editor-in-Chief: Eric Suben. Estab. 1907. High-volume mass market and trade publisher. Publishes hardcover and paperback originals. Number of titles: averages 160/year. Buys 20-30% agented fiction.
Needs: Juvenile: adventure, mystery, humor, sports, animal, easy-to-read picture books, and "a few" nonfiction titles. Recently published *Little Critter's Bedtime Story*, by Mercer Mayer; *Cyndy Szokeves' Mother Goose Rhymes*; and *Spaghetti Manners*, by Stephanie Calmsenson, illustrated by Lisa MaCue Karsten.
How to Contact: Send a query letter with a description of the story and SASE. Unsolicited mss are returned unread. Publishes ms an average of 1 year after acceptance.
Terms: Pays by outright purchase or royalty.
Advice: "Read our books to see what we do. Call for appointment if you do illustrations, to show your work. Do not send illustrations. Illustrations are not necessary; if your book is what we are looking for, we can use one of our artists."

ALBERT WHITMAN & COMPANY (II), 5747 W. Howard, Niles IL 60648. (312)647-1358. Senior Editors: Ann Fay and Abby Levine. Editor-in-Chief: Kathleen Tucker. Estab. 1919. Small independent juvenile publisher. Publishes hardcover originals. Books: paper varies; printing varies; library binding; most books illustrated; average print order: 7,500. Published several new writers in the last year. Average 20-26 total titles/year. Number of fiction titles varies.
Needs: Juvenile (2-12 years including easy-to-read, fantasy, historical, adventure, contemporary, mysteries, picture-book stories). Primarily interested in picture book manuscripts. Recently published *Where's Chimpy?*, by Berniece Rabe (with photographs by Diane Schmidt). *Spiffen, a Tale of a Tidy Pig*, by Mary Ann Schwartz (illustrated by Lynn Munsinger).
How to Contact: Accepts unsolicited mss. Submit outline/synopsis and 1-3 sample chapters; complete ms for picture books. SASE. "Half or more fiction is not agented." Reports in 3 weeks on queries; 8 weeks on mss. Simultaneous and photocopied submissions OK. ("We prefer to be told.") Accepts computer printouts including dot-matrix.
Terms: Payment varies. Royalties, advance; number of author's copies varies. Some flat fees. Sends galleys to author. Writer's guidelines free for SASE. Book catalog for 9x12 SASE and 85¢ postage.

‡WILDSTAR BOOKS/EMPIRE BOOKS (II, IV), Subsidiary of The Holy Grail Co., Inc., 26 Nantucket Pl., Scarsdale NY 10583. (914)961-2965. Vice President: Ralph Leone. Estab. 1986. Packager of Empire Books. Imprint: Wildstar (with Lynx Communications). Publishes paperback originals. Publishes new writers within the last year. Averages 40 fiction titles each year. Sometimes critiques rejected mss.
Needs: Horror, psychic/supernatural/occult, romance (contemporary, historical), suspense/mystery, western. Looking for romance, horror, new age, occult, western, mystery and thriller. Recently published 22-book series *American Regency*; *Wildstar* for Warner Books (romance); 12-book series,

Americans Abroad, Empire for St. Martin's (romance); 18-book series, *Horror, Empire* for Pageant Books (horror).
How to Contact: Accepts unsolicited mss. Query first. SASE. Agented fiction 80%. Reports in 3 weeks on queries; 3 months on mss. Photocopied submissions OK. Accepts computer printout submissions, including dot-matrix.
Terms: Pays in royalties: "depends on deal we make with publisher." Advance negotiable. Provides author's copies. Sends galleys to author. Publishes ms generally within 18 months after acceptance.
Advice: "Short and to the point—not cute or paranoid—is best tone in a query letter."

WINSTON-DEREK PUBLISHERS (II), Box 90883, Nashville TN 37209. (615)321-0535, 329-1319. Imprints include Scythe Books. Senior Editor: Marjorie Staton. Estab. 1978. Midsize publisher. Publishes hardcover and paperback originals and reprints. Books: 60 lb old Warren style paper; litho press; perfect and/or sewn binding; illustrations sometimes; average print order 3,000-5,000 copies; first novel print order 2,000 copies. Published new writers within the last year. Plans 3 first novels this year. Averages 35-50 total titles, 10-12 fiction titles each year; "90% of material is from freelance writers; each year we add 15 more titles."
Needs: Gothic, historical, juvenile (historical), psychic, religious/inspirational, and young adult (easy-to-read, historical, romance) and programmed reading material for middle and high school students. "Must be 50,000 words or less. Novels strong with human interest. Characters overcoming a weakness or working through a difficulty. Prefer plots related to a historical event but not necessary. No science fiction, explicit eroticism, minorities in conflict without working out a solution to the problem. Down play on religious ideal and values." Recently published *With Wings of an Eagle*, by James H. Goodman; *The Banana Horse*, by Velma Armstrong; *The Good Jude*, by Jim Lynch.
How to Contact: Submit outline/synopsis and 3-4 sample chapters with SASE. Simultaneous and photocopied submissions OK. Accepts computer printout submissions. Prefers letter-quality. Reports in 4-6 weeks on queries; 6-8 weeks on mss. Must query first. Do not send complete ms.
Terms: Pays in royalties of 10% minimum, 15% maximum; negotiates advance. Book catalog on request for $1 postage.
Advice: "Stay in the mainstream of writing. The public is reading serene and contemplative literature. Authors should strive for originality and a clear writing style, depicting universal themes which portray character building and are beneficial to mankind."

WORLDWIDE LIBRARY (II), Subsidiary of Harlequin Books Library, 225 Duncan Mill Rd., Don Mills, Ontario Canada. (416)445-5860. Imprints are Worldwide Library Science Fiction; Worldwide Library Mysteries; Gold Eagle Books. Senior Editor: Feroze Mohammed. Estab. 1979. Large commercial category line. Publishes paperback originals and reprints. Published new writers within the last year. Averages 90 total titles, all fiction, each year. Sometimes critiques rejected msa.
Needs: Adventure, suspense/mystery. Looking for "men's action-adventure series and writers; mystery; future fiction." Recently published *Red Danube*, by Carl A. Posey (espionage); *The Case of the Fragmented Woman*, by Cleo Jones (mystery); and *Storm*, by Ian Slater (adventure).
How to Contact: Accepts unsolicited mss. Query first or submit outline/synopsis and sample chapters. "Try to establish the category or genre in which your novel fit." SASE. Agented fiction 95%. Reports in 10 weeks on queries; 16 weeks on mss. Simultaneous and photocopied submissions OK. Accepts computer printout submissions including dot-matrix.
Terms: Advance and royalties; work for hire. Publishes ms 1-2 years after acceptance.
Advice: "Publishing more fiction, but in very selective areas. As a genre publisher, we are always on the lookout for new talent, especially in the men's adventure area. Do your homework. Be familiar with what we publish. If you are interested in writing for one of our men's adventure series in the Gold Eagle imprint, study a number of the books in that series before contacting us."

YEARLING (II, III), 666 5th Ave., New York NY 10103. (212)765-6500. See Dell Publishing Co., Inc. Publishes originals and reprints for children grades K-6. Most interested in humorous upbeat novels, mysteries and family stories. 60 titles a year. "Will, regrettably, no longer consider unsolicited material at this time."
Terms: Sends galleys to author.

ZEBRA BOOKS (II), 475 Park Ave. S, New York NY 10016. (212)889-2299. Editorial Director: Leslie Gelbman. Estab. 1975. Publishes hardcover reprints and paperback originals. Averages 200 total titles/year.
Needs: Contemporary, adventure, English-style mysteries, historical, war, Vietnam novels, gothic, saga, romance, thrillers and horror. No science fiction. Recently published *Passions Wild and Free*, by Janelle Taylor; *Outlaws*, by George Z. Higgins; and *The Carlton Club*, by Katherine Stone.
How to Contact: Query or submit complete ms or outline/synopsis and sample chapters with SASE.

Simultaneous and photocopied submissions OK. Address women's mss to Leslie Gelbman and male adventure mss to Wally Exman. Reports in 3-5 months.
Terms: Pays royalties and advances. Free book catalog.
Advice: "Put aside your literary ideals, be commercial. We like big contemporary women's fiction; glitzy career novels, espionage and horrors. Work fast and on assignment. Keep your cover letter simple and to the point. Too many times, 'cutesy' letters about category or content turn us off some fine mss. More involved with family and historical sagas. But please do research. We buy many unsolicited manuscripts, but we're slow readers. Have patience."

CHARLOTTE ZOLOTOW BOOKS (II), 10 E. 53rd St., New York NY 10022. (212)207-7044. "Editor works mainly with authors she has edited over the years." See Harper & Row Junior Books Group.

Foreign commercial publishers

Commercial publishers are often interested in fiction submissions from U.S. and Canadian residents. These are all paying markets. Query the press of your choice first for a catalog or their guidelines to be sure your manuscript is appropriate for their needs. And always include proper postage (IRCs or foreign stamps) with any foreign correspondence to ensure a response or the return of your manuscript. (See Manuscript Mechanics.)

ANGUS & ROBERTSON UK LTD., Bay Books, 16 Golden Sq., London W1R 4BN England. "Small UK publisher with some independent publishing and acting as marketing/scouting office for major Australian publishing house." Australian adventure, ethnic, juvenile (sports, spy/adventure, contemporary), psychic/supernatural/occult, film, theatre, health, language/linguistics and humor.

ATMA RAM AND SONS, 1376 Lothian Road, Kashmere Gate, Delhi 110006 India. Fiction Editor: Ish Kumar Puri. Publishes 30 books/year. Modern themes but not science fiction. Regular royalties are paid on the published prices of the books. "Works of fiction should be in the theme of current affairs, nuclear warfare, romance etc."

THE BLACKSTAFF PRESS (I), 3 Galway Park, Dundonald BT16 0AN Northern Ireland. Editor: Hilary Parker. Midsize, independent publisher, wide range of subjects. Publishes hardcover and paperback originals and reprints. Contemporary, ethnic (Irish), historical, humor/satire, literary, short story collections, political thrillers and feminist. "Be patient."

THE BODLEY HEAD (III), 32 Bedford Square, London WC1B 3EL England. Fiction Editors: Derek Johns, Caroline Upcher, Jill Black. Approximately 25 fiction titles/year. "We publish general fiction and nonfiction, of a literary and popular nature; mainly English but some American novels; some crime fiction too." Offers annual Georgette Heyer Prize for a Historical Novel. Pays advances and royalties, usually through agents. "We prefer a preliminary letter with a synopsis of the work and some sample writing; we ask for the entire work only when we think it relevant to our list." Publishing "rather more fiction" now than in the past.

MARION BOYARS PUBLISHERS INC., 26 E. 33rd St., New York NY 10016. *All manuscripts to 24 Lacy Road London SW15 1NL England*. Fiction Editor: Marion Boyars. "Compact independent publisher."

‡COLLINS PUBLISHERS AUSTRALIA, 55 Clarence St., Sydney NSW 2000 Australia. Publisher: Lisa Highton. Publishes 100 + titles/year. "Collins Publishers Australia is part of the International Collins Group. We operate independently from London, and our fiction list is all published straight into paperback. We have a formal mass-market list and a B format list/trade paperback imprint for more literary work. All work submitted should clearly have an Australian focus." Writers paid on a royalty basis. "Please send an outline and sample chapters only initially."

‡HALLMARK PUBLISHING LTD., Gopala Prabhu Rd., Box 3541 Cochin-682 035 India. President: Prof. Dr. M. V. Pylee. Managing and Editorial Director: C. I. Ooommen. Publishers of trade paperbacks and educational books. Looking for folktales, adventure, novel and short fiction anthologies. Accepts unsolicited mss, simultaneous and photocopied submissions and computer printouts (prefers letter quality). Reports in 2 months. Pays in royalties of 10% maximum. No advance. "We also produce books for self publishers and small press with marketing and distribution support."

HEADLINE BOOK PUBLISHING PLC, 79 Great Titchfield St., London W1P 7FN England. Editorial Director: Susan J. Fletcher. Averages approximately 200 titles/year. Mainstream publisher of popular fiction (and nonfiction) in hardcover and mass-market paperback. Pays advance against royalties. "Send a synopsis and *curriculum vita* first, and return postage."

MICHAEL JOSEPH LTD., The Penguin Group, 27 Wrights Lane, London W8 5TZ England. Contact: Fiction Editor. General publisher of adult fiction and nonfiction. Publishes hardcover originals and some trade paperback originals and reprints, not mass market." Needs: Adventure, contemporary, historical, humor, literary, mainstream, regional, suspense/mystery and war.

MILLS & BOON, Eton House, 18-24 Paradise Road, Richmond, Surrey TW9 1SR England. Publishes 250 fiction titles/year. Modern romantic fiction, historical romances and doctor/nurse romances. "We are happy to see the whole manuscript or 3 sample chapters and synopsis."

‡MY WEEKLY STORY LIBRARY, D.C. Thomson and Co., Ltd., 22 Meadowside, Dundee Scotland. Fiction Editor: Mrs. D. Hunter. Publishes 48 35,000-word romantic novels/year. "Cheap paperback story library with full-colour cover. Material should not be violent, controversial or sexually explicit." Writers are paid on acceptance. "Send the opening two chapters and a synopsis."

‡NIOBA UITGEVERS, Maarschalk Gerardstraat 6, 2000 Antwerpen Belgium. Fiction Editor: Peter De Greef. Averages 50 fiction titles/year. "We have mainly novels and poetry. Our catalog contains only really literary books. We are also interested in gay literature." Writers receive 10% royalties on the retail price. "Please send only typed copies. Our judgment will take about two months."

ORIENT PAPERBACKS, A division of Vision Books Pvt Ltd., Madarsa Rd., Kashmere Gate, Delhi 110 006 India. Editor: Sudhir Malhotra. Publishes 10-15 novels or story collections/year. "We are one of the largest paperback publishers in S.E. Asia and publish English fiction by authors from this part of the world." Pays royalty on copies sold.

‡PETER OWEN LIMITED, 73 Kenway Road, London SW5 0RE England. Fiction Editor: Michael Levien. Publishes 20-30 titles/year. "General list trade books—art, belles-lettres, biography and memoirs, theatre, etc., publishing literary fiction, European and other foreign writers in translation, US novelists. Writers receive advance on royalties: half on delivery of mss, half on publication. "Study our list; send in the first instance a synopsis plus possibly 2 sample chapters, with IRCs sufficient to cover their possible return. We do not undertake to return unsolicited mss."

‡PAGODA BOOKS, 7g Great Titchfield Street, London W1P 7FN England. Fiction Editor: Susan Pinkus. "Principally nonfiction. Considering new fiction imprint for 1989." Pays advance against royalties. "Please submit clearly typed copy, together with return airmail postage."

PANDORA PRESS (II), 15-17 Broadwick St., London W1V 1FP England. Fiction Editor: Kate Figes. Small imprint in large firm. Averages 40 total titles/year; 13 fiction titles. Needs: Feminist, gay, lesbian, literary, suspense/mystery and translations. Pays 7½%-10% royalties, negotiable advance, average £1,500; advance is more for agented mss. "Most novelists ought to be less precious about their work and able to accept criticism."

RAJPAL AND SONS, Kashmere Gate, Delhi 110 006 India. Editor: Vishwa Nath. Publishes 24 novels or story collections/year. "A century-old publishing house, we publish in Hindi and English, the latter as Orient paperbacks. Fiction is a major line, which includes translations." Pays on royalty basis. Fiction "has to be interesting reading, with sufficient sales potential."

‡SIDGWICK & JACKSON LTD., 1 Tavistock Chambers Bloomsbury Way, London WC1A 2SG England. Fiction Editor: Oliver Johnson. Publishes 24 titles/year. "Quali-pop, commercial fiction—particularly women's fiction, historical novels, thrillers. No short stories." Pays advance and royalties. "Please send synopsis with manuscript/extract. Please think of potential appeal for the *British* market."

SPHERE BOOKS (III), 27 Wrights Lane, London W8 5T2 England. Editorial Director: Barbara Boote. Publishes paperback originals and reprints. General mass-market genre fiction. "Get a name for an editor at a company to send material into. Ensures a slightly better chance of being read and considered properly."

VIRAGO PRESS, Centro House, 20-23 Mandela St., London NW1 0HQ England. Fiction Editors: Ruth Petrie; Lynn Knight (Virago Modern Classics). Published 52 novels and short story collections last year (10 by North American Writers; 3 Canadian). "This includes reprint novels (Virago Modern Classics), new fiction and fiction for younger readers (aged 13 +) in our Upstarts series." Looking for "books for the general and educational market which highlight all aspects of women's lives." Writers receive advance and royalties and subsidiary-rights earnings. "Virago accepts both manuscripts via agents and unsolicited manuscripts. Writers wishing to submit a manuscript for consideration should, in the first instance, send a synopsis and about three sample chapters."

‡**VISION BOOKS PVT LTD.**, Madarsa Rd., Kashmere Gate, Delhi 110006 India. Fiction Editor: Sudhir Malhotra. Publishes 25 titles/year. "We are a large multilingual publishing house publishing fiction and other trade books." Pays royalties. "A brief synopsis should be submitted initially. Subsequently, upon hearing from the editor, a typescript may be sent."

‡**WALKER BOOKS/JULIA MACRAE BOOKS/NICK HERN BOOKS**, 87 Vauxhall Walk, London SE11 5HJ England. Editors: Julia MacRae, Delia Huddy, Jill Evans, Nick Hern, Anne Carter, David Lloyd, Wendy Boase. Publishes 150 story collections annually. "Walker Books: Children's, board books, picture books, junior fiction, teenage fiction. Julia MacRae Books: picture book, junior fiction, teenage fiction, music and general adult books." Nick Hern Books: theatre, plays and literary books. Writers are paid by royalties. "Walker Braes and Julia MacRae Books welcome manuscripts and reply to all letters regarding potential authors. Please send typed manuscripts to the editorial secretary."

‡**WEIDENFELD AND NICOLSON LTD.**, 91, Clapham High St., London SW4 7TA England. Fiction Editors: Juliet Gardiner, Allegra Houston, Malcolm Gerratt. Publishes approx. 30 titles/year. "We are an independent publisher with a well established fiction list. Authors include, or have included, V. Nabokov, J.G. Farrell, Olivia Manning, Edna O'Brien, Margaret Drabble, Richard Powers, John Hersey, Penelope Gilliatt, Charlotte Vale Allen. We publish literary and commercial fiction: sagas, historicals, crime." Pays by advance. Royalties are set against advances. "Send a covering letter, a detailed synopsis and some sample pages such as the first chapter. Do not send the whole typescript unless invited. Please enclose return postage if possible and retain photocopies of all material sent."

‡**THE WOMEN'S PRESS**, 34 Great Suton St., London EC1V 0DX England. Publishes approx. 30 titles/year. "Women's fiction, written by women. Centered on women. Theme can be anything—all themes may be women's concern—but we look for political/feminist awareness, originality, wit: fiction of ideas. Includes genre fiction sf, crime, and teenage list *Livewire*." Writers receive royalty, including advance. Writers should ask themselves, "is this a manuscript which would interest a feminist/political press? We tend to ask ourselves whether a ms has a special appeal on our list as distinct from a mainstream house."

Commercial publishers/'88-'89 changes

The following commercial publishers appeared in the 1988 edition of *Fiction Writer's Market* but are not in the 1989 edition of *Novel and Short Story Writer's Market*. Those presses whose editors did not respond to our request for an update of their listings may not have done so for a variety of reasons—they may be out of business, for example, or they may be overstocked with submissions. Note that commercial publishers from outside the U.S. and Canada appear at the end of this list.

Abingdon Press (asked to be deleted)
Academy Chicago Press (did not respond)
Beufort Books (asked to be deleted)
T.Y. Crowell (did not respond)
Dillon Press (see Gemstone Books)
Gulliver Books (see Harcourt Brace Jovanovich)
Heartfire Romance (did not respond)
Lippincott Junior Books (did not respond)

Peregrine Smith (see Gibbs Smith)
Signet (did not respond)
SOS Publications (did not respond)
Stein and Day Publishers (bankrupt)
Vanguard Press (asked to be deleted)
Washington Square Books (did not respond)
Wordspinner Press (did not respond)

Foreign commercial publishers

Cambridge University Press (did not respond)
Transworld Publishers Pty Ltd (did not respond)

Special Markets

This section provides a place for fiction markets that really don't fit into any other category in the book. Most of the listings are of particular interest to writers of comic books, graphic novels and publications like *Mad Magazine*, in which the story cannot really be separated from the artwork that accompanies it. As *Mad* editors remind writers, "Remember! No straight text pieces! *Mad* is a visual magazine."

Some of these publications pay very well—others are really more similar to listings in the little/literary magazine category and don't pay, but can be good places for beginners to send their work. Beginning writers of graphic forms will find Allen McKenzie's *How to Draw and Sell Cartoon Strips* (North Light Books) especially useful.

The popularity of graphic novels—which are even more popular in Europe where they account for as much as 10% of total book sales—continues to rise, and the books are being read by older and more sophisticated readers all the time. If you're unfamiliar with graphic novels, you might want to read two of the best, which were published in 1986: Art Spiegelman's *Maus* (Pantheon), a chilling memoir of Hitler's Germany; and, on a lighter note, Frank Miller's *The Dark Knight Returns* (Warner), concerning the adventures of an updated, somewhat insane version of Batman.

The number of audio-visual listings remains small this year—producers have generally been disappointed by the sales of romance videos, thought last year to be a growing market. Still, writers should certainly not ignore the opportunities provided by this mixed bag of unusual markets. Stories bought by the BBC World Service, for example, are broadcast by radio all over the world. And science fiction writers may want to consider *Scifant*, similar in many respects to many other "fanzines" except that it is published only on microfiche, because microfiche, as editor Paul Doerr says, "are the libraries of the future and the future is now." For a more comprehensive list of audio-visual producers, see *Audio-Visual Marketplace* (R.R. Bowker Co.).

Comics and Graphic Novels

‡AIRCEL PUBLISHING, 298 Elgin St., Suite 102, Ottawa, Ontario K2P 1M3 Canada. (613)563-4237. Editor: Mike Charbonneau. Estab. 1985. Publishes comic books; series (3/month); limited editions (approx. 4/year); graphic novels (3/year). Newsprint/mando paper; laser separation printing; saddlestitch binding; pen-and-ink/paint illustrations. Average print order: 10,000-30,000.
Needs: Adventure, fantasy, mystery, horror, science fiction, social parody, subculture genre. Themes: outer space, future science, teenage, alternative lifestyles, social commentary, past history. Recently published *Elflord*, *Samurai*, *Dragonforce*, *Warlocks*, *Warlock 5* and *China Sea*.
How to Contact: Accepts unsolicited mss. Send query letter with samples or photocopy of story/character outline. "Rough outline and character sketch (approx. 1,000 words)." Interested in samples from writers who illustrate their own work. Reports in 4-6 weeks. Simultaneous and photocopied submissions OK. Sample copy for $1.

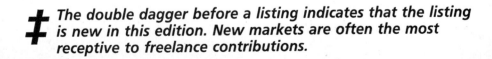 **The double dagger before a listing indicates that the listing is new in this edition. New markets are often the most receptive to freelance contributions.**

Terms: Writers receive royalties or one-time payment depending on project. Pays on publication. Copyrights for author.
Advice: "Writers should be very confident that their work is of high calibre, as the comic book market is very unstable at the current moment, thus limiting the number of acceptances by many companies."

‡CARTOONS, Petersen Publishing, 8490 Sunset Blvd., Los Angeles CA 90069. (213)854-2222. Editor: Dennis Ellefson. Estab. 1947. Publishes comic books (6/year). Newsprint; web offset printing; saddlestitch binding.
Needs: Automotive humor.
How to Contact: Send query letter with samples or call. Interested in samples from writers who illustrate their own work. Reports in 4 weeks. Photocopied submissions OK. Sample copies available.
Terms: One-time payment of $100 minimum; $250 maximum. Pays on acceptance for all rights. Does not copyright for author.

COMICO THE COMIC COMPANY (II), 1547 DeKalb Street, Norristown PA 19401. (215)277-4305. Editor-in-Chief: Diana Schutz. Estab. 1982. Publishes paperback originals and reprint comic books: 45 lb Baxter stock (70 lb for graphic novels) paper; web offset printing; stapled or squarebound binding; always illustrations. Averages 8 comic books/month.
Needs: Adventure, contemporary, fantasy, historical, horror, psychic/supernatural/occult, romance (contemporary), science fiction, suspense/mystery, war, western, women's, young adult/teen (10-18 years including fantasy/science fiction, historical, spy/adventure). Recently published *Grendel*, by Matt Wagner (monthly comic book: horror/suspense); *Jonny Quest*, by William Messner-Loebs (monthly comic: new stories and art based on Hanna-Barbera cartoon); *Rio*, by Doug Wildey (western genre graphic novel).
How to Contact: Accepts unsolicited mss. Submit outline/synopsis. SASE. Reports in 6 months. Simultaneous submissions OK. Accepts computer printout submissions.
Terms: "Terms are negotiated *separately* and *privately* in each individual case." Per page rate plus royalties.
Advice: "Publishing more limited series and graphic novels. We are a small company, but one that is renowned within the comic book industry for our high production values and top quality writing. We have embarked on a forward trend and are continuing to grow, through slow and careful expansion of our line of titles."

ECLIPSE COMICS (I, II), Box 1099, Forestville CA 95436. (707)887-1521. Editor-in-Chief: Catherine Yronwode. Comic books. "Adventure and super-heroic serial comics; will select promising concepts for development into full script submissions." For discriminating comic book fans. "We publish as many adventure and super-heroic series as our schedule permits." Circ. 35,000-85,000 per issue; 20 issues per month.
Needs: Adventure, fantasy, horror, humor/satire, psychic/supernatural/occult, romance, science fiction, suspense/mystery, western. Special needs: moody, romantic, character-oriented pieces with overtones of humanism, morality, political, opinion, philosophical speculation and/or social commentary. No sexually explicit material. Buys 150 mss (mostly from established comic writers). Publishes ms 1 month after acceptance. Recently published work by Bruce Jones, Chuck Dixon and Timothy Truman; published new writers in the past year. Length: 8-11 pages.
How to Contact: Send adventure superhero scripts featuring Eclipse characters. Reports in 1 month on mss. SASE for query and ms. Simultaneous submissions (also queries) and photocopied submissions OK. Accepts computer printouts, but no dot-matrix. Sample copy $1.75. Fiction guidelines for #10 SAE and 1 first class stamp.
Payment: Pays $30/page.
Terms: Pays on acceptance for first North American serial rights and second serial reprint rights; exclusive rights to sell material to South American or European markets (with additional payments).
Advice: "85% of the stories in these anthologies have downbeat twist endings of the kind popularized by O. Henry and the EC comic books of the 1950s. The other 15% start off in that mold but lead to an unexpected upbeat resolution." Looks for "anything topical but not trendy; anything with realistic human relationships portrayed."

Read the Manuscript Mechanics section to learn the correct way to prepare and submit a manuscript.

‡EMERALD CITY COMIX & STORIES, Wonder Comix, Box 95402, Seattle WA 98145-2402. (206)523-1201. Editor: N. Osmar. Estab. 1987. Tabloid: 11x17; 12-24 pages; newsprint paper and cover; illustrations and photos. Average print order: 7,000. Quarterly.
Needs: Adventure, contemporary, experimental, fantasy, humor/satire, mainstream, prose poem, science fiction, serialized novel, sports, suspense/mystery. "We publish prose, poetry and comics—looking for high quality, well-written fiction—fantasy, SF, mainstream, etc., all OK." Recently published work by Jerome Gold, David Dawson and Margaret Collins. Length: 500-4,000 words.
How to Contact: Send complete ms with cover letter. Reports on queries in 5-6 weeks; on mss in 2-3 months. Photocopied submissions OK. Sample copy for $1.25; writer's guidelines for #10 SAE.
Terms: Pays in contributor's copies. Acquires one-time rights. Publication copyrighted.
Advice: "Short pieces have the best chance of being published. Writing quality is more important than theme or subject matter. Feel free to submit several pieces at once."

‡ETERNITY COMICS, INC., Malibu Graphics., Inc., 2635 Lavery Ct., #11, Newbury Park CA 91320. (805)499-3015. Creative Director: Tom Mason. Editor: Chris Ulm. Estab. 1986. Publishes comic books; series (15/month); graphic novels (8/year). Newsprint paper; web offset printing; saddlestich binding. Average print order: 5,000-20,000. 120 + titles published annually.
Needs: Adventure, mystery, horror. "We're always looking for new writers. Script length varies according to individual projects." Recently published *Ninja High School*, *Dinosaurs for Hire* and *Ex-Mutants*.
How to Contact: Accepts unsolicited submissions. Send query with samples. Interested in samples from writers who illustrate their own work. Reports in 6 weeks. Simultaneous and photocopied submissions OK. Sample copies for $2.50.
Terms: Pays in royalties and offers advance. "Payment varies according to individual projects." Pays on publication; rights purchased "depend on project." Does not copyright for author.
Advice: "Read what is already being published, particularly by Eternity, before submitting any material."

‡FANTAGRAPHIC BOOKS, 1800 Bridgegate St., Suite 101, Westlake Village CA 91361. Publisher: Gary Groth. Estab. 1976. Publishes comic books; series (15/month); limited editions (8/year); graphic novels (3/year). Groundwood paper; offset printing; saddlestitch binding; illustrations. Average print order: 12,000. 9 titles published annually.
Needs: Adventure, fantasy, romance, mystery, horror, science fiction, social parodies, animals, "superbly executed graphic narration regardless of genre, including historical, factual commentary." Recently published *Yahoo*, *Usagh Yojimbo* and *Love & Rockets*.
How to Contact: Accepts unsolicited submissions. Send complete ms with cover letter or send query letter with résumé and samples. Prefers to work with writer/artists. Reports in 1 month. Simultaneous and photocopied submissions OK. Sample copies available.
Terms: Pays royalties of 4% minimum; 8% maximum. Pays on publication for first rights. Copyrights for author.
Advice: "Please present only *polished*, high-standard work. While we are interested in talented, innovative and experimental amateurs and newcomers to comics, we do not have time for novices or beginners. Sorry. Good luck."

‡FANTASY FRONTIERS, Magazine of Creative Comic and Ideas, Fantasy Frontiers Publishing, Box 555, Ely NV 89301. (702)289-2091. Editor: Robert Tomlinson. Estab. 1986. Magazine: 8½x11; 36-44 pages; 20 lb paper; 60 lb cover stock; illustrations; photos occasionally. Average print order: 500.
Needs: Adventure, experimental, fantasy, horror, humor/satire, psychic/supernatural/occult, science fiction. "We publish all types of material from illustrated stories (comic) to political discussions to movie reviews to original fiction. Theme is the promotion of comics and ideas." Recently published work by Jeff Schultz, Richard Dengrove and Joseph Shea. Length: 250-1,500 words preferred.
How to Contact: Send complete ms with cover letter. Reports in 2-4 weeks. Simultaneous and photocopied submissions OK. Sample copy $2.25; writers guidelines for #10 SAE and 1 first class stamp.
Terms: Pays in contributor's copies. Acquires one-time rights. Publication copyrighted.
Advice: "It must be quality work, fit size requirements for the issue, and I must like it. Don't send your first drafts for consideration."

❝ I write books to find out about things. ❞
—Rebecca West

HEROES, Blackbird Comics, Box 3211, Austin TX 78764. (512)282-2065. Publisher: John Nordland II. Estab. 1985. Publishes comic books; series (bimonthly); limited editions. Comics: 60-70 lb paper; offset printing; saddle-stitch binding; average print order: 5,000-10,000. Semiannually.

Needs: Adventure, fantasy, romance, mystery, horror, science fiction. Looking for themes on outer space, future science, alternative lifestyles. Recently published *Heroes*; *Spare Parts*; *PSIBERTEX* and *Just Friends*.

How to Contact: Accepts unsolicited submissions. Send complete ms with cover letter; or send query letter with samples. Also interested in samples from writers who illustrate their own work. Reports on queries in 3-4 weeks. Simultaneous and photocopied submissions OK.

Terms: One-time payment, depends on length. "75% of net is split between creators for original work as per contract." Pays on publication for first rights, "occasionally 2nd print rights." Does not copyright for author. Sample copy for SASE with $2 postage.

Advice: "I'm interested in 'people stories' regardless of genre. An exciting plot with depth of character is of paramount importance. I also prefer a more realistic approach to fantasy and prefer stories that have only a few 'fetish' elements and otherwise are realistic."

JUDY (II), D.C. Thomson and Co. Ltd., Albert Square, Dundee DD1 9QJ Scotland. Editor: Jim Davie. Around 1,300 pages published annually of picture-story scripts, each page about 8 frames. Weekly comic for young schoolgirls around 8-10 years old.

Needs: Mainly serious picture-stories with a few humorous cartoon-style strips and general features.

Terms: Writer's work paid for on acceptance. Copies of the issues concerned will be sent on request.

Advice: "Study the publication and send for our leaflet, 'Writing to Earn.' "

MAD (IV), EC Creations, 485 Madison Ave., New York NY 10022. (212)752-7685. Editors: John Ficarra/Nick Meglin. Magazine: 48 pages; illustrations; occasional photos. "Although we are a 'fiction' magazine, we never publish straight prose pieces. *MAD* is a visual magazine and writers should submit art notes accompanying their submissions. *MAD* appeals to an extremely wide audience, especially young people." Published every 6 weeks. Estab. 1952. Circ. "around one million."

Needs: Humor/satire. Write for specific needs. Nothing "bland." Receives "lots" of unsolicited mss each month. Buys "lots" of mss/issue. Publishes ms 4-12 months after acceptance.

How to Contact: Query first. SASE. Fiction guidelines for SAE.

Payment: Pays $300-$550/*MAD* page.

Terms: Pays on acceptance for all rights. Publication copyrighted.

Advice: "Write on anything or everything that catches your fancy and is funny. Especially prized are articles on current hot trends (topics might be rock videos, computers, etc.). Send us a paragraph or two explaining the premise of your article with 3 or 4 examples of how you intend to carry it through, describing the action and visual content of each example. Rough sketches are welcomed but not necessary. Remember! No straight text pieces! *MAD* is a visual magazine! You can include more than one idea in a submission. Each is judged on its own merit. Have fun! Don't be afraid to be stupid and don't self-edit yourself because *you* don't think it's what *you* think *we're* looking for. Sometimes *we* don't know what we're looking for until we see it! Make us earn our money as editors."

MARVEL COMICS (II, IV), 387 Park Ave. S, New York NY 10016. (212)576-9200. Imprints include Marvel, Epic Star Comics and Marvel Books. Editor-in-Chief: Tom DeFalco. Estab. 1939. Largest comic book publisher in the world. Publishes comic books, magazines, graphic novels and storybooks. Encourages new writers. Averages 600-800 total titles (fiction) each year.

Needs: Comic book material featuring superheroes, adventure, fantasy, horror, humor/satire, psychic/supernatural/occult, science fiction, romance, juvenile, western and young adult/teen (fantasy/science fiction, spy/adventure).

How to Contact: Accepts unsolicited mss. Submit short outline/synopsis with SASE to the editor of the appropriate comic magazine. Photocopied submissions preferred. Reports in 6 months. Publishes ms from 6 months to 6 years after acceptance.

Terms: "Payments, royalties, incentives and benefits vary with format and type of work." Pays on acceptance.

Advice: "Read our comics and study our established characters before you attempt a submission."

NBM, 35-53 70th St., Jackson Heights NY 11372. (718)458-3199. Publisher: Terry Nantier. Estab. 1976. Publishes comic strips and classic reprints (8/year); graphic novels (12/year). Graphic novels: 60 lb offset white paper; offset printing; paperback binding; average print order: 5,000-7,000. 20 titles published annually.

Needs: Adventure, fantasy, mystery, horror, science fiction, social parodies. Looking for themes on outer space, future science, teenage. "high need for graphic novels, preferably 46-64 pages." Recently published *A Treasury of Victorian Murder*; *The Mercenary*; and *Corto Maltese*.

How to Contact: Send query letter with résumé, samples and 1 page synopsis. Also interested in samples frm writers who illustrate their own work. Reports in 4 weeks. Simultaneous and photocopied submssions OK.
Terms: Pays royalties of 10%; advance: negotiable. Pays on publication for all rights. Copyrights for author.
Advice: "Write for catalog."

‡NOVA (I IV), EDC-Animation Association, Box 515942, Dallas TX 75251. (214)234-8107. Editor: Kelli Wakefield. Magazine: 8½x11; 40-50 pages; Xerox-type paper; soft cover; illustrations. Publishes "animation programs centering around adult-themed foreign animation (Japanese, French). Not R or X rated, but mature style and themes for any age group. For anyone interested in art style, general animation." Semiannually. Has published and plans to publish a special fiction issue. Estab: 1982. Circulation: 250.
Needs: Animation, adventure, fantasy, horror, humor/satire, prose poem, psychic/supernatural/occult, science fiction. 'Fiction stories set in an established animation program universe (Robotech, Real Ghostbusters) and from author-created universes with animation-like style and pacing. No Star Wars, Star Trek, Dr. Who—unless cross over type with animation theme." Receives 2-3 unsolicited fiction mss/month. Publishes 1-2 fiction mss/month. Recently published work by Chris Todd, Pat Muson-Sites, Kenneth Mays. Length: 500-1,000 words. Publishes short shorts. Comments on rejected mss if requested. Will forward to related publishers with permission.
How to Contact: Query first. SASE. Photocopied and reprinted submissions are OK. Accepts dot-matrix; no electronic submissions. Sample copy for $5; fiction guidelines for #10 envelope and 25¢.
Payment: Pays in contributor's copies. Charges for extras.
Terms: Pays on publication. Publication is copyrighted.
Advice: "Be creative and/or original in expanding on known universes. Create your own animated-type universe and characters. Have illustrations ready or allow us to find an artist."

STARBLAZE GRAPHICS (IV), Subsidiary of The Donning Company/Publishers, 5659 Virginia Beach Blvd., Norfolk VA 23502. (804)461-8090. Assistant Editor: Mary Gray. Executive Editor: Jean Campbell. Estab. 1974. Midsize independent publisher with plans to expand. Publishes hardcover and trade paperback originals. Books: acid free paper; web printing; perfect binding; comics style illustrated graphics albums, 72-120 pp., average print order: 10,000-25,000; first novel print order: 10,000. Averages 20-30 total titles, 5 graphic novels each year.
Needs: Entertaining, well-told science fiction and fantasy that is enhanced by being in graphic format. "We are looking for graphic novels that will go beyond the standard comic book conventions and reach the wider reading public. We are not particularly interested in super heroes, nor do we want action-oriented stories that slight character development." Recently published *Thieves' World Graphics*, by Robert Asprin & Lynn Abbey; *Buck Godot-Zap Gun for Hire*, by Phil Foglio (science fiction); and *Duncan & Mallory: The Bar None Ranch*, by Robert Asprin & Mel White (fantasy).
How to Contact: Please query first. SASE. Reports in 3-4 weeks on queries; 1 month on mss. Simultaneous "but please let us know if you sell elsewhere" and photocopied submissions OK. Accepts computer printout submissions, including dot-matrix "if we can read them."
Terms: Pays royalties of 8% minimum; 15% maximum. Offers 10 author's copies. Writer's guidelines for # SAE and 1 first class stamp. Book catalog for $1.
Advice: "Publishing more graphic albums now than in the past; market is opening up beyond the comics field. This is a very specialized field which almost demands experience (comic books, adaptations). Make sure your research on markets is *up-to-date*. Behave in as professional a manner as possible. Don't take rejection personally; there are many reasons why a manuscript may not be suitable for a particular publisher."

Audiovisual Producers

‡BBC WORLD SERVICE, Bush House, London England. Contact: BBC Short Story Producer. Produces material for "25 million English speakers, worldwide."
Needs: Radio. "We broadcast a weekly short story from a listener overseas. Twelve-and-a-half minutes or 2,000 words." Purchases approx. 40 fiction mss from writers each year.
How to Contact: Query with samples or submit completed script. Responds in 2 weeks-1 month. "We may hold 'possible' material longer." No previously produced material. Writers' guidelines available for SAE with IRCs.
Terms: Offers outright purchase of £55.50. Purchases broadcast rights for 2 years.

Advice: "Material must be original. No rules for writing, but suggest people listen to the programme to see the kind of radio fiction we broadcast. Typed mss only."

CAEDMON (II), 1995 Broadway, New York NY 10023. (212)580-3400. Editor: John Wynne. Estab. 1952. Produces fiction for children.
Needs: Audio cassettes and tapes. Plans to buy 15 fiction scripts during the next year. "Manuscripts geared for preschoolers or infants/toddlers."
How to Contact: Query first. Reports in 3 months. Simultaneous and photocopied submissions OK. Accepts computer printouts, including dot-matrix.
Terms: Pays royalties. Buys all rights.
Advice: "Looking for professional, creative queries with accurate subject information."

‡DEBORAH HUTCHISON PRODUCTIONS, 7797 Torreyson Dr., Los Angeles CA 90046. (213)850-1859. Contact: Deborah Hutchison. Estab. 1987. Produces material for television and film.
Needs: "Good stories. Mystery, comedy, true stories, etc."
How to Contact: Submit synopsis/outline or completed script. No previously produced material. Responds in 4-6 weeks.
Terms: Determines rights purchased after ms is reviewed. "Each individual case handled differently."

‡SCIFANT (I), Box 398, Suisun CA 94585. Editor: Paul Doerr. Magazine: 8½x11; 98 pages (*microfiche only*); illustrations and photos. "We publish science fiction, fantasy, horror, space fiction and space high technology." Monthly.
Needs: Adventure, experimental, fantasy, historical (general), horror, humor/satire, romance, science fiction, serialized/excerpted novel, suspense mystery. Receives 50 + unsolicited mss/month. Buys 30 + mss/issue. Publishes ms 2 months - 1 year after acceptance. Publishes short shorts. Length: ½ page and up. Occasionally critiques rejected mss and recommends other markets.
How to Contact: Send complete ms with cover letter. Ms must be *single spaced* with margins no greater than ½" and proofread (camera ready). Reports in 1 month. SASE. Simultaneous, photocopied and reprint submissions OK. Prefers letter quality computer printout submissions. Accepts electronic submissions via Apple II. Fiction guidelines for #10 SAE and 1 first class stamp. Sample copy $3. (Copy is in microfiche.)
Payment: Payment schedule on spec sheet.
Terms: Pays % of sales. Publication copyrighted.
Advice: "Send me something! What worse can happen than a rejection slip, some advice and the cost of some stamps? What have you to lose? If you never try, you'll never make it, certainly. Would like to see more fiction on topics of WW III and space colonization."

‡TENTRA ARTNET BBS, Garage Music Co., Box 63 Rockaway Park, New York NY 11694. Editor: Andy Anderson. Electronic bulletin board.
Needs: Adventure, contemporary, erotica (maybe), ethnic, experimental, fantasy, feminist, historical (left-wing Labor), humor/satire, literary, mainstream, prose poem, regional, science fiction, senior citizen/retirement, serialized novel, sports, suspense/mystery, translations, western, young adult/teen (10-18 years). Length: 500-5,000 words.
How to Contact: Send complete ms with cover letter or telephone voice line (718)945-115 or BBS data line (718)945-1127—8 bit word, no parity, 1 stop bit.
Terms: Pays $5-$25 on acceptance for all rights.
Advice: "We invite writers to log onto our system without charge to find what we're all about."

Special markets/'88-'89 changes

The following special markets appeared in the 1988 edition of *Fiction Writer's Market* but are not in the 1989 edition of *Novel and Short Story Writer's Market*. Those markets whose editors did not respond to our request for an update of their listings may not have done so for a variety of reasons—they may be out of business, for example, or they may be overstocked with submissions.

Cutting Edge (did not respond)
Dimestore Stories Presents (did not respond)

Embassy Cassette (did not respond)
Story Cards (out of business)

Story Series (did not respond)
Surplus Wyvern Press Postcard

Contests and Awards

This section is one of the fastest growing sections in the book. We've added this year more than 60 new listings for contests, awards, fellowships and grants. For writers just starting out, as well as for published authors looking for more outlets for their work, these markets offer a challenging (and often lucrative) alternative to submitting work for publication only.

Although several contests offer publication in a literary magazine or a book contract as part of the prize, the markets are not restricted by many of the considerations involved in publishing decisions. When selecting a manuscript for publication, editors must weigh content needs, article mix, timing, tone and length, against the quality of the piece under consideration. Contests and awards, however, offer writers the opportunity to have their works judged on quality alone, once a few basic entry requirements are met.

Many of the contests and award programs listed here do offer some award money. Some offer hundreds, even thousands of dollars, but don't overlook modest prizes or contests offering a plaque or certificate. Prestigious awards, such as the Irma Simonton Black Children's Book Award, offer no money, but can enhance your reputation and help increase the sales of your book.

There are contests for almost every type of fiction (and nonfiction) writing. Contests open to specific fiction forms include those for short stories, novellas and novels. This year we've added several contests for writers from certain states and a number of English-speaking countries, especially Australia, England and New Zealand.

Organizations interested in promoting certain kinds of writing, genres or topics also sponsor contests. Among the organizations whose listings we've added this year are the Crime Writers' Association, the Connecticut Writers League, the Japan-United States Friendship Commission and the Sierra Club.

Other opportunities for writers listed here can help support a writer while he or she is working on a manuscript. Fellowships, residencies and grants provide money, time and sometimes work space and lodging, so that writers can work without the pressure of day-to-day financial concerns. Some of these involve short-term residencies at universities or writers' colonies.

State arts councils, seeking to promote the literary arts in their state, offer fellowships and grant programs that can run into the thousands of dollars for writers living within the state. This year we've added contests and grants sponsored by art councils in Alaska, Idaho, New York and Wyoming.

Choosing a contest

Not all contests, awards and fellowships are for everyone. Some are open to all writers, such as the *Mademoiselle* Fiction Writers Contest or The Flannery O'Connor Award for Short Fiction. Others are restricted to previously published authors, members of sponsoring groups, writers who live in a specific state, region or country or writers in a particular age group.

Some contests are open to previously unpublished submissions, some to published works only and some are open to both. If you want to submit to a contest for published works, be sure to check what publication dates are acceptable—many require the work be published only in the year prior to the contest.

With all contests, it is important to obtain a copy of the submission requirements. Many require entry forms and a fee. Usually, the fees are necessary to offset the cost of administration, judges' fees and prizes. Yet beware of contests requiring fees almost as large as their prizes (a contest whose award is $25, may not be worth a $5 or $10 submission fee).

Although most of the contests and awards listed here are open to submissions directly from writers, a few require work be submitted only by the publisher. Don't assume, however, that your publisher knows about the contest. Feel free to let your editor know about the contest and that you would like to be nominated.

Coding system for contests and awards

The Roman numeral coding system in this section is different from that used in other parts of the book. A new or unpublished writer is eligible to enter those contests ranked I (and some IVs), while a writer with a published (usually including self-published) book may enter most contests ranked I and II (and again, some IVs). Entrants for contests ranked III must be nominated by someone who is not the writer (usually the publisher or editor).

> I *Contest for unpublished fiction, usually open to both new and experienced writers;*
> II *Contest for published (usually including self-published) fiction, which may be entered by the author;*
> III *Contest for published fiction, which must be nominated by an editor, publisher or other nominating body;*
> IV *Contest limited to residents of a certain region, of a certain age or to writing on certain themes or subjects.*

‡**ACT 1 CREATIVITY CENTER FELLOWSHIP (I)**, ACTS Institute, Inc., Kansas City MO 64111. (816)753-0208. Contact: Charlotte Platshy. Award: Residency at the ACT 1 Writers/Artists Colony at the ACT 1 Creativity Center, Horseshoe Bend Resort Area. Receives approx. 20 applications/year. Judge: "a professional." Application fee $10. No deadlines—open admissions policy.

JANE ADDAMS PEACE ASSOCIATION CHILDREN'S BOOK AWARD (II), Jane Addams Peace Association/Women's International League for Peace and Freedom. Chair: Jean Gore, 980 Lincoln Place, Boulder CO 80302. "To honor the writer of the children's book that most effectively promotes peace, social justice, world community and the equality of the sexes and all races." Annual competition for short stories, novels and translations. Award: certificate. Competition receives approx. 50-100 submissions. Judges: committee. Guidelines for SASE. Deadline April 15, for books published during previous year.

AIM MAGAZINE **SHORT STORY CONTEST (I)**, Box 20554, Chicago IL 60619. (312)874-6184. Contact: Ruth Apilado and Mark Boone, publisher and fiction editor. Estab. 1984. Contest likely to be offered annually if money is available. "To encourage and reward good writing in the short story form. The contest is particularly for new writers." Unpublished submissions. Award: $100 plus publication in fall issue. "Judged by *Aim*'s editorial staff." Contest rules for SASE. "We're looking for compelling, well-written stories with lasting social significance."

ALABAMA STATE COUNCIL ON THE ARTS INDIVIDUAL ARTIST FELLOWSHIP (II, IV), #1 Dexter Ave., Montgomery AL 36130. (205)261-4076. Randy Shoults. "To provide assistance to an individual artist." Annual grant/fellowship. Award: $2,500 and $5,000 grants. Competition receives approximately 30 submissions annually. 1989 judges: independent peer panel. Entry forms or rules for SASE. Deadline May 1, 1989. Two year Alabama residency required.

✝ *The double dagger before a listing indicates that the listing is new in this edition. New markets are often the most receptive to freelance contributions.*

‡ALASKA STATE COUNCIL ON THE ARTS LITERARY ARTS FELLOWSHIPS (I, IV), Alaska State Council on the Arts, 619 Warehouse Ave., #220, Anchorage AK 99501-1682. (907)279-1558. Contact: Christine D'Arcy. "Open-ended grant award, non-matching, to enable creative writers to advance their careers as they see it." Biannual competition for stort stories and novels. Award: $5,000 per writer. Competition receives approx. 45 submissions. Judges: panel of Alaskan writers. Next award offered in 1990. "Alaskan writers only are eligible to apply."

‡EDWARD F. ALBEE FOUNDATION FELLOWSHIP (I), Edward F. Albee Foundation, Inc., 14 Harrison St., New York NY 10013. (212)266-2020. Contact: Carl Capotorto. Provides one-month residencies for writers and artists at the William Flanagan Memorial Creative Persons Center (better known as "The Barn") in Montauk, on Long Island, New York. 24 residencies per year, June-September. Award for writers of novels, story collections and translators. Receives approx. 50 applications for each residency. Judges: several writers. Guidelines for SASE. Deadline April 1, 1989. Write for official guidelines.

ALBERTA NEW FICTION COMPETITION (I, IV), Alberta Culture and Multiculturalism in cooperation with Doubleday Canada Ltd. of Toronto, 12th Floor, CN Tower, Edmonton, Alberta T5J 0K5 Canada. Contact: Ruth B. Fraser, director. Biennial award. To encourage the development of fiction writers living in the province of Alberta. The competition is open to all writers who are residents of the province of Alberta. Deadline December 31, 1989. No SASE is necessary. Brochures and further information available. Award: $4,000; of this, $2,500 is an outright award given by Alberta Culture and $1,500 is an advance against royalties given by Doubleday. Three categories of submission: full-length novel from 60,000-100,000 words; short story collection totalling approximately 60,000 words; novella/short story combination totalling 60,000 words.

THE ALBERTA WRITING FOR YOUNG PEOPLE COMPETITION (I, IV), Alberta Culture and Multiculturalism in cooperation with Doubleday Canada Ltd. and Allarcom/Superchannel. 12th Floor, CN Tower, 10004-104 Avenue, Edmonton, Alberta T5J 0K5 Canada. Contact: Ruth Bertelsen Fraser, director. Bienniel award (even years). The competition is designed to direct Alberta's writers to the challenging world of writing for juveniles. Unpublished submissions. Entry deadline: Dec. 31. The competition brochure and/or further information will be sent upon request. Award: $4,500 prize; an outright award of $2,000 from Alberta Culture and Multiculturalism, a $1,000 advance against royalties from Doubleday Canada Ltd. and a $1,500 12-month option for motion picture/television rights from Allarcom/Superchannel. "We have 2 categories: book mss for young adults (up to age 16) averaging 40,000 words in length; and book mss suitable for younger readers (8-12 years) running between 12,000 and 20,000 words."

THE NELSON ALGREN AWARD FOR SHORT FICTION (I), *Chicago Tribune*, 435 N. Michigan Ave., Chicago IL 60611. (312)222-3232. Contact: Nadia Cowen, Nelson Algren coordinator. Formerly sponsored by *Chicago Magazine*. Annual award. To recognize an outstanding, unpublished short story, minimum 2,500 words; maximum 10,000 words. Awards: $5,000 first prize; three runners-up receive $1,000 awards. Publication of four winning stories in the *Chicago Tribune*. Deadline: Entries are accepted only from October 15th-February 1. No entry fee. A poster bearing the rules of the contest will be sent to writers who inquire.

***AMELIA MAGAZINE* AWARDS (I)**, The Reed Smith Fiction Prize; The Willie Lee Martin Short Story Award; The Cassie Wade Short Fiction Award; The Patrick T. T. Bradshaw Fiction Award; and four annual genre awards in science fiction, romance, western and fantasy/horror. 329 "E" St., Bakersfield CA 93303. (805)323-4064. Contact: Frederick A. Raborg, Jr., editor. Estab. 1984. Annually. "To publish the finest fiction possible and reward the writer; to allow good writers to earn some money in small press publication. *Amelia* strives to fill that gap between major circulation magazines and quality university journals." Unpublished submissions. Length: The Reed Smith—3,500-5,000 words; The Willie Lee Martin—3,500-5,000 words, The Cassie Wade—3,500 words; The Patrick T. T. Bradshaw—25,000 words; the genre awards—science fiction, 5,000 words; romance, 3,000 words; western, 5,000 words; fantasy/horror, 5,000 words. Award: "Each prize consists of $200 plus publication and two con-

Market categories: (I) Beginning; (II) General; (III) Prestige; (IV) Specialized.

tributor's copies of issue containing winner's work. The Reed Smith Fiction Prize offers two additional awards of $100 and $50, and publication; Bradshaw Book Award: $300 plus publication, 2 copies. Deadline: The Reed Smith Prize—September 1; The Willie Lee Martin—March 1; The Cassie Wade—June 1; The Patrick T. T. Bradshaw—February 15; Amelia fantasy/horror—February 1; Amelia western—April 1; Amelia romance—October 1; Amelia science fiction—December 15. Entry fee: $5. Bradshaw Award fee: $10. Contest rules for SASE. Looking for "high quality work equal to finest fiction being published today."

AMERICAN FICTION 89 (I), Wesley Press/American Fiction, English Dept., Springfield College, 263 Alden St., Springfield MA 0ll09 (413)788-3254. Editors: Michael C. White. To "recognize unpublished stories by both *known* and *unknown* writers." Annual competition for short stories. Award: $500 first prize, publication, 2 copies. Competition received 550 submissions in 1987. Editor:Michael C. White, Alan Davis, guest judge. Entry fee: $7.50. Guidelines in *AWP Newsletter* and *Poets and Writers*. Submit only after ads appear. Unpublished submissions. 10,000 word limit.

AMERICAN HEALTH BODY STORY CONTEST (I), *American Health* Magazine, 80 Fifth Ave., New York NY 10011. (212)242-2460. Body Story Editor: Allegra Holch. Annual award for unpublished short stories. Award: $2,000 and publication in *American Health*. Receives approximately 700 entries for each award. Judge: Mark Haris. Entry guidelines for SASE. Deadline March 1, 1989. "For the best account—fact or fiction—of an intense physical experience. A detailed story is not enough. We're looking for creative writers who can capture the body's triumphs and trials with imagination, sensitivity, style and humor."

‡AMERICAN LITERARY TRANSLATIONS ASSOCATION GREGORY RABASSA PRIZE FOR FICTION (I, IV), Box 830688, University of Texas Dallas, Richardson TX 75083-0688. Contact: Sheryl St. Germain. Award for "exceptionally well executed translations from any foreign language into English." Biannually. "One year the award is the Gregory Rabassa Prize for Fiction and the next it is the Richard Wilbur Prize for Poetry." Award: Publication of manuscript by University of Missouri Press. Judges: Committee of distinguished translators. Guidelines for SASE. Previously unpublished submissions. "The submitted manuscript must be a complete translation of an entire book of poems or an entire book (not excerpted) work of fiction. The translator must have permission for publication in the United States."

SHERWOOD ANDERSON SHORT FICTION PRIZE (I), *Mid-American Review*, Dept. of English, Bowling Green State University, Bowling Green OH 43403. (419)372-2725. Contact: Robert Early, editor. Award frequency is subject to availability of funds. "To encourage the writer of quality short fiction." Unpublished material. Award: $200. No deadline. No entry fee. "Winners are selected from stories published by the magazine, so submission for publication is the first step."

CHARLES ANGOFF AWARDS (I), *The Literary Review*, Fairleigh Dickinson University, Madison NJ 07940. (201)593-8564. Walter Cummins, editor-in-chief. "To recognize the 4 or 5 best contributions of each volume year." Annual award for short stories, poetry or essays. Award: $100. Judges are the *Review*'s editors and advisory board. Prerequisite to consideration: publication in *TLR* during a volume year.

ARIZONA AUTHORS' ASSOCIATION ANNUAL LITERARY CONTEST (I), Annual Literary Contest, 3509 E. Shea Blvd., Suite 117, Phoenix AZ 85028. (602)996-9706. Contact: Dorothy Tegeler. Estab. 1981. Annually. "To encourage AAA members and all other writers in the country to discipline themselves to write regularly, steadily for competition and publication." Unpublished submissions. Award: "Cash prizes totalling $1,000 for winners and honorable mentions in short stories, essays and poetry. Winning entries are published in the *Arizona Literary Magazine*." Deadline: July 29. Entry fee: $4 for poetry, $6 for essays and short stories. Contest rules for SASE. Looking for "strong concept; good, effective writing, with emphasis on the subject/story."

ARIZONA COMMISSION ON THE ARTS CREATIVE WRITING FELLOWSHIPS (I,IV), 417 West Roosevelt St., Phoenix AZ 85003. (602)255-5882. Public Information Officer: Tonda Gorton. Fellow-

Read the Manuscript Mechanics section to learn the correct way to prepare and submit a manuscript.

ships awarded in alternate years to fiction writers and poets. Four awards of $4,000. Judges: in-state and out-of-state writers/editors. Guidelines for SASE. Next deadline for fiction writers: 1989. Arizona poets and writers over 18 years of age only.

ARKANSAS ARTS COUNCIL INDIVIDUAL ARTIST FELLOWSHIP (I,IV), Suite 200, 225 E. Markham, Little Rock AR 72201. (501)371-2539. Director of Programs: Suzanne Davidson. Grant offered every year for literature. Includes short stories, novels, story collections, plays and poetry. Award: $5,000 maximum fellowship. Competition receives approx. 30 submissions. Judge: individual juror. Guidelines for SASE. Arkansas artists only.

ASF TRANSLATION PRIZE (I, IV), American-Scandinavian Foundation, 127 E. 73rd St., New York NY 10021. Contact: Publishing office. Estab. 1980. Annual award. Competition includes submissions of poetry, drama, literary prose and fiction translations. To encourage the translation and publication of the best of contemporary Scandinavian poetry and fiction and to make it available to a wider American audience. Submissions must have been previously published in the original Scandinavian language. No previously translated material. Original authors should have been born within past 100 years. Deadline for entry: June 1. Competition rules and entry forms available with SASE. Award: $1,000 and publication in *Scandinavian Review*.

ASTED/PRIX MARIE-CLAIRE DAVELUY (I,IV), Association pour l'avancement des sciences et des techniques de la documentation, 3839 rue Saint-Denis, Montréal, Québec Canada. (514)849-1889. President: Michèle Ouellette. Contest for young people from 15-20 years old, French speaking and living in Canada. Annual "competition for all kinds of literary productions." Award: $700 (first prize); $300 (second prize). Judge: a committee. Deadline: summer. "Only young people from 15 to 20 years old, French speaking and living in Canada are eligible."

THE ATHENAEUM LITERARY AWARD (II, IV), The Athenaeum of Philadelphia, 219 S. 6th St., Philadelphia PA 19106. Contact: Literary Award Committee. Annual award. To recognize and encourage outstanding literary achievement in Philadelphia and its vicinity. Submissions must have been published during the preceding year. Deadline: December. Nominations shall be made in writing to the Literary Award Committee by the author, the publisher or a member of the Athenaeum, accompanied by a copy of the book. Judged by committee appointed by Board of Directors. Award: A bronze medal bearing the name of the award, the seal of the Athenaeum, the title of the book, the name of the author and the year. The Athenaeum Literary Award is granted for a work of general literature, not exclusively for fiction. Juvenile fiction is not included.

AVON FLARE YOUNG ADULT NOVEL COMPETITION (I, IV), *Avon Books*, 105 Madison Ave., New York NY 10016. (212)481-5609. Ellen E. Krieger, Editorial Director, Books for Young Readers. "To discover, encourage, and develop young writing talent." Biannual award for novels "about 30,000 to 50,000 words." Award: Publication of the novel under the Avon/Flare imprint for an advance against royalties. Competition receives approximately 400-500 submissions annually. Judges are the Avon editorial staff. Entry forms or rules for SASE. Deadline August 31, 1989. Contest restricted to writers who were no younger than 12 and no older than 18 years of age as of December 31, 1988. With your manuscript include letter with your name, address, telephone number, age and short description of your novel."

AWP AWARD SERIES IN SHORT FICTION (I), The Associated Writing Programs, c/o Old Dominion University, Norfolk VA 23508. Annual award. The AWP Award Series was established in cooperation with several university presses in order to make quality short fiction available to a wide audience. Only book-length manuscripts are eligible. Manuscripts previously published in their entirety, including self-publishing, are not eligible. Submissions dates: manuscripts postmarked between January 1-February 29. Awards judged by distinguished writers in each genre. Contest/award rules and entry forms available for SASE. Award: The winning manuscript in short fiction is published by the University of Missouri Press. Carries a $1,000 honorarium. $10 submission fee with ms.

AWP AWARD SERIES IN THE NOVEL (I), The Associated Writing Programs, c/o Old Dominion University, Norfolk VA 23508. Annual award. The AWP Award Series was established in cooperation with several university presses in order to publish and make fine fiction available to a wide audience. Only book-length manuscripts are eligible. Manuscripts previously published in their entirety, including self-publishing, are not eligible. Submission dates: manuscript postmarked between January 1-February 29. Awards judged by distinguished writers in each genre. Contest/award rules available for SASE. Winning novel will be published by the University of Iowa Press. Carries a $1,000 honorarium. In addition, AWP tries to place mss of finalists with participating presses. $10 submission fee with ms.

EMILY CLARK BALCH AWARDS (I), *The Virginia Quarterly Review*, 1 West Range, Charlottesville VA 22903. Editor: Staige D. Blackford. Annual award. To recognize distinguished short fiction by American writers. For stories published in *The Virginia Quarterly Review* during the calendar year. Award: $500.

MILDRED L. BATCHELDER AWARD (II), Association for Library Service to Children/American Library Association, 50 E. Huron St., Chicago IL 60611. (312)944-6780. To encourage international exchange of quality children's books by recognizing U.S. publishers of such books in translation. Annual competition for translations. Award: citation. Judge: Mildred L. Batchelder award committee. Guidelines for SASE. Deadline December, 1989. Books should be U.S. trade publications for which children, up to and including age 14 are potential audience.

‡H.E. BATES SHORT STORY COMPETITION (I), Northampton Borough Concil, Bedford Rd., Northampton England. Contact: Leisure Manager. "An arts service." Annual competition for short stories. Award: £50. Competition receives approx. 200 submissions. Entry fee £1.20. Guidelines for SASE. Deadline: August. Word length: 2,000 words.

BELLAGIO CENTER RESIDENCY (I), Rockefeller Foundation, 1133 Avenue of the Americas, New York NY 10036. (212)869-8500. Manager: Susan E. Garfield. Award 4- to 5-week residency in northern Italy for scholars and artists (including writers). Residencies for authors of short stories, novels and story collections. Judges: committee of Foundation officers. Guidelines for SASE. Writers should submit applications 1 year prior to preferred dates. "Competition is most intense for May through September. Each scholar or artist is provided with a private room and a bath, and with a study in which to work. At dinner and over aperitivi, scholars in residence have the opportunity to meet participants in international conferences that are scheduled concurrently. The Foundation does not provide financial assistance to scholars in residence, nor does it contribute ordinarily to travel expenses. Write for application."

GEORGE BENNETT FELLOWSHIP (I), Phillips Exeter Academy, Exeter NH 03833. (603)772-4311. Coordinator, Selection Committee: Charles Pratt. "To provide time and freedom from monetary concerns to a person contemplating or pursuing a career as a professional writer." Annual award for writing residency. Award: A stipend ($5,000 at present), plus room and board for academic year. Competition receives approximately 100 submissions. Judges are a committee of the English department. Entry fee $5. SASE for application form and guidelines. Deadline for submission of manuscript is December 1 annually.

BEST OF BLURBS CONTEST (I), Writer's Refinery, Box 47786, Phoenix AZ 85068-7786. (602)944-5268. President: Libbi Goodman. "Compose a blurb for the back cover of a hypothetical novel. It's the blurb that sells the book, so write in your most dramatic and exciting style. Who knows, you may want to write what's between the covers as well." Annual award for blurbs for novels. Award: Engraved wall plaque/certificate of merit. Judges are a panel of professional writers. Entry forms for SASE. Deadline: September 30 of each year. No entry fee.

IRMA SIMONTON BLACK CHILDREN'S BOOK AWARD (II), Bank Street College, 610 W. 112th St., New York NY 10025. (212)663-7200, ext. 254. Publications Director: Williams Hooks. Annual award. "To honor the young children's book published in the preceding year judged the most outstanding in text as well as in art. Book must be published the year preceding the May award." Award: Press luncheon at Harvard Club, a scroll, and seals by Maurice Sendak for attaching to award book's run. Entry deadline: January 15. No entry fee. "Write to address above. Usually publishers submit books they want considered, but individuals can too. No entries are returned."

‡JAMES TAIT BLACK MEMORIAL PRIZES (III, IV), Department of English Literature, University of Edinburgh, Edinburgh EH8 9JX Scotland. Contact: W.W. Robson. "Two prizes are awarded: one for the best work of fiction, one for the best biography or work of that nature, published during the calendar year." Annual competition for short stories, novels and story collections. Award: £1,000 each. Competition receives approx. 100 submissions. Judge: Professor W.W. Robson, Masson Professor of English Literature. Guidelines for SASE. Deadline December 31, 1989. Previously published submissions. "Eligible works are those written in English, originating with a British publisher, and first published in Britain in the year of the award. Works should be submitted by publishers."

THE BLACK WARRIOR REVIEW LITERARY AWARD (III, II), Box 2936, Tuscaloosa AL 35487. (205)348-4518. Editor: Jeff Mock. "Award is to recognize the best fiction published in *BWR* in a volume year." Competition is for short stories and novel chapters. Award: $500. Competition receives approximately 1,500 submissions. Prize awarded by an outside judge. SASE.

THE BLUE MOUNTAIN CENTER (I), Blue Mountain Lake NY 12812. (518)352-7391. Director: Harriet Barlow. "To provide a peaceful and comfortable environment in which guests are able to work, free from the distractions and demands of normal daily life." Residencies for established writers. Award: residencies are for 1 month between June 15 and October 15. Send SASE for guidelines. Application deadline. March 1. Write for brochure.

‡**BOARDMAN TASKER PRIZE (II)**, 56 St. Michael's Ave., Bramhall, Stockport, Cheshire SK7 2PL United Kingdom. Contact: Mrs. D. Boardman. "To reward a book which has made an outstanding contribution to mountain literature. A memorial to Peter Boardman and Joe Tasker, who disappeared on Everest in 1982." Award: £1,000. Competition receives approx. 15 submissions. Judges: a panel of 3 judges elected by trustees. Guidelines for SASE. Deadline: August 1, 1989. Previously published submissions. Limited to works published or distributed in the UK for the first time between November 1, 1988 and October 31, 1989. Publisher's entry only. "May be fiction, nonfiction, poetry or drama. Not an anthology. The prize is not primarily for fiction though that is not excluded. Subject must be concerned with mountain environment. Previous winners have been books on expeditions, Himalayan experiences, a biography of a mountaineer."

BOOKS IN CANADA AWARD FOR FIRST NOVELS, (III, IV), Books in Canada, 366 Adelaide St. E, Toronto, Ontario M5A 3X9 Canada. (416)363-5426. Contact: Doris Cowan, editor. Annual award. "To promote and recognize Canadian writing." Award: $1,000. No entry fee. Submissions are made by publishers. Contest is restricted to first novels in English published in Canada in the previous calendar year.

‡**BOOTS ROMANTIC NOVEL OF THE YEAR**, 2A Rye Walk, Ingatestone, Essex CM4 9Al England. Contact: Eileen Huckbody, Award Organiser, Romantic Novelists' Association. "To publish good romantic fiction and therefore raise the prestige of the genre." Annual competition for novels. Award £5,000. Competition receives approx. 100 submissions. Judges: a panel of experienced writers. Deadline: Sept. 1-Dec. 15, 1989. Previously published submissions. For novels "published in the U.K. only. A modern or historical (before 1950) romantic novel. "Two copies of each entry are required. They may be hardback or paperback. Only novels written in English and published in the U.K. during the relevant year are eligible. Authors must be domiciled in UK or temporarily living abroad whilst in possession of British passport."

‡*BOSTON GLOBE*-**HORN BOOK AWARDS (II)**, *Boston Globe* Newspaper, *Horn Book* Magazine, Promotion Department, 135 Morrissey Blvd., Boston MA 02107. Contact: Stephanie Loer, children's book editor. Annual award. "To honor most outstanding children's fiction, picture and nonfiction books published within the U.S." Previously published material from July 1-June 30 of following year. Award: $500 first prize in each category; silver plate for the 2 honor books in each category. Entry deadline: May 1. No entry fee. Entry forms or rules for SASE.

‡**THE F.G. BRESSANI PRIZE (II, IV)**, Italian Cultural Centre Society, 3075 Slocan Street, Vancouver, B.C. V5M 3E4 Canada. (604)430-3337. Contact: The Literary Committee. Prize "to promote excellence in writing from an ethnic minority viewpoint, to increase appreciation and understanding of Canada's cultural diversity, and to honour an important historical figure F.G. Bressani, the first Italian missionary in Canada." Award granted biannually. Competition for novels and story collections. Award: $500 in prose and poetry categories. Also offers prizes fo $250 each for prose and poetry books written in Italian. (Prizes awarded in cooperation with the Istituto Italiano de Cultura.) "Up to now we've received 28 publications." Judges: "knowledgeable people in our community." Guidelines for SASE. Deadline: 1990. Published submissions. Prize "available to Canadian citizens or landed immigrants to Canada. Books must be written from a viewpoint of any of Canada's ethnic minority groups."

BUMBERSHOOT WRITTEN WORKS COMPETITION (I), Seattle's Arts Festival, Box 9750, Seattle WA 98109-0750. (206)622-5123. Contact: Judith Roehe. Annual award for short stories. Award: Six awards of $150 for poetry or literary prose. Winners published in Bumbershoot arts magazine, *Ergo!* Judges are professional writers/publishers/literary bookshop managers. Entry forms or rules for SASE. Deadline mid-April.

‡**BUNTING INSTITUTE FELLOWSHIP (I)**, Mary Ingraham Bunting Institute of Radcliffe College, 34 Concord Ave., Cambridge MA 02138. (617)495-8212. "Fellowship programs are designed to support women who wish to pursue independent study in academic and professional fields, and in the creative arts. Applications will be judged on the significance and quality of the project proposal, and on the difference the fellowship might make in the applicant's career." Annual award for creative writing. Award: $19,400 for one year. Competition receives 600 total applicant pool. Judges: distinguished academics and professionals from a variety of disciplines. Entry fee $35. Guidelines for SASE. Deadline: October

2, 1989. Previously published or unpublished submissions. "Office or studio space, auditing privileges and access to libraries and other resources of Radcliffe College and Harvard University are provided. Residence in the Boston area and participation in the Institute community are required during the fellowship appointment. Fellows are expected to present their work in progress at public colloquia. Women scholars, professionals, creative writers and musicians, with receipt of doctorate or appropriate terminal degree at least two years prior to appointment, or with equivalent professional experience (i.e., publication, group or solo show) are eligible."

BURNABY WRITERS' SOCIETY ANNUAL COMPETITION (I, IV), 6450 Gilpin St., Burnaby, British Columbia V5G 2J3 Canada. (604)435-6500. Annual competition to encourage creative writing in British Columbia. "Category varies from year to year." Award: $100, $50 and $25 prizes. Receives 400-600 entries for each award. Judge: "independent recognized professional in the field." Entry fee $5. Contest requirements for SASE. Deadline April 30. Open to British Columbia authors only.

BUSH ARTIST FELLOWSHIPS (I, IV), The Bush Foundation, E-900 First Nat'l Bank Building St. Paul MN 55101. (612)227-0891. Contact: Sally Dixon, program director. To provide artists of exceptional talent time to work in their chosen art forms. Annual grant. Award: Stipend maximum of $25,000 for 6-18 months, plus a production and travel allowance of $6,240. Competition receives approximately 350 submissions. Judges are writers, critics and editors from outside MN, SD or ND. SASE. Applicants must be at least 25 years old, and Minnesota, South Dakota or North Dakota residents for 12 of 36 months preceding deadline. Students not eligible.

BYLINE MAGAZINE LITERARY AWARDS (I,IV), Box 130596, Edmond OK 73013. (405)348-3325. Exec. editor/publisher: Marcia Preston. "To encourage our subscribers in striving for high quality writing." Annual award for short stories. Award: $250 cash in each category—fiction and poetry. Judges are published writers not on the *Byline* staff. Entry fee $5 for stories; $2 for poems. Postmark Deadline December 1. "Entries should be unpublished and not have won money in any previous contest. Winners announced in February issue and published in March issue with photo and short bio. Open to subscribers only."

‡CALIFORNIA WRITERS' ROUNDTABLE ANNUAL WRITING CONTESTS (I), The Los Angeles Chapter, Women's National Book Association, 11684 Ventura Blvd., Suite 807, Studio City CA 91604-2652. Contact: Lou Carter Keay. Annual competition for short stories. Award: $150 first prize; $75 second prize; $25 third prize. If less than 6 entries are received, the contest will be canceled and entry fees and entries returned to the author. Entry fee $5 to nonmembers of Women's National Book Association. Guidelines for SASE. Deadline: 1989. Previously unpublished submissions. 3,000 word limit. "Manuscripts must be typed, on standard paper, 8½x11 inches. Margins of one inch on all sides. The title of short story must appear on each page, all pages numbered. Send 3 copies of the short story. Include a small envelope with a card containing the author's name, address and phone number, along with the title of short story. Do not put the name of author on the manuscript itself. If you wish one copy of your manuscript returned, include a SASE."

JOHN W. CAMPBELL MEMORIAL AWARD FOR THE BEST SCIENCE-FICTION NOVEL OF THE YEAR; THEODORE STURGEON MEMORIAL AWARD FOR THE BEST SF SHORT FICTION (II, III), Center for the Study of Science Fiction, English Dept., University of Kansas, Lawrence KS 66045. (913)864-3380. Professor and Director: James Gunn. "To honor the best novel and short science fiction of the year." Annual competition for short stories and novels. Award: a trophy. Competition receives approx. 50-100 submissions. Judges: two separate juries. Deadline Dec. 31. For previously published submissions. "Ordinarily publishers should submit work, but authors have done so when publishers would not. Send for list of jurors."

CANADA COUNCIL AWARDS (III, IV), Canada Council, 99 Metcalfe St., Box 1047, Ottawa, Ontario K1P 5V8 Canada. (613)598-4365. The Canada Council sponsors the following awards, for which no applications are accepted. *Canada-Australia Literary Prize*: 1 prize of $3,000, awarded in alternate years to an Australian or Canadian writer for the author's complete work; *Canada-French Community of Belgium Literary Prize*: 1 prize of $2,500, awarded in alternate years to a Canadian or Belgian writer on the basis of the complete works of the writer; *Canada-Italy Literary Prize*: awarded for the annual translation of a work of literature of both countries into the language of the other country. English and French works are translated alternately into Italian, followed by the author's visit to Italy to publicize the translation. Italian works are translated alternately into English and French, followed by the author's visit to Canada to publicize the translation; *Canada-Switzerland Literary Prize*: 1 prize of $2,500, awarded in alternate years to a Canadian or Swiss writer for a work published in French during the preceding 8 years.

CANADA COUNCIL GOVERNOR GENERAL'S LITERARY AWARDS (III, IV), Canada Council, Box 1047, 99 Metcalfe St., Ottawa, Ontario K1P 5V8 Canada. (613)598-4365. Contact: writing and publishing section. "Awards of $5,000 each are given annually to the best English-language and best French-language Canadian work in each of the six categories: children's literature (text and illustration), drama, fiction, poetry, nonfiction and translation." All literary works published by Canadians during the preceding year are considered. Canadian authors, illustrators and translators only.

CANADIAN AUTHORS ASSOCIATION LITERARY AWARD (FICTION) (II, IV), Canadian Authors Association, Suite 104, 121 Avenue Road, Toronto M5R 2G3 Ontario, Canada. (416)926-8084. Contact: Executive Director. Annual award. "To honor writing that achieves literary excellence without sacrificing popular appeal." For novels published during the previous calendar year. Award: $5,000 plus silver medal. Entry deadline: December 31 of calendar year. No entry fee. Entry forms or rules for SASE. Restricted to full-length novels. Author must be Canadian or Canadian landed immigrant. CAA also sponsors the Air Canada Award, literary awards as above in poetry, nonfiction and drama, and the Bicky Metcalf Awards for children's literature.

CANADIAN FICTION MAGAZINE **CONTRIBUTOR'S PRIZE (IV)**, Box 946, Station F, Toronto, Ontario M4Y 2N9 Canada. Contact: Geoffrey Hancock, editor-in-chief. Annual award. To celebrate the best story published by *CFM* in either French or English during the preceding year. Contributors must reside in Canada or be Canadians living abroad. All manuscripts published in *CFM* are eligible. Deadline: August 15. Award: $500, public announcement, photograph. "Looking for contemporary creative writing of the highest possible literary standards."

CANADIAN LIBRARY ASSOCIATION BOOK OF THE YEAR FOR CHILDREN AWARD (III,IV), Canadian Library Association, 200 Elgin Street, Ottawa, Ontario K2P 1L5 Canada. (613)232-9625. To encourage the writing in Canada of good books for children up to and including age 14. Annual competition for short stories and novels for children. Award: a specially designed medal. Competition receives approx. 10-20 submissions/year. Judging: CLA Book of the Year Award Committee. Guidelines for SASE. Deadline Februrary 1, 1989. Book must have been published in Canada during the last year and its author must be Canadian citizen or a landed immigrant. Nominations are generally made by CLA membership—a call for nominations is posted in the Association's newsletter in October. "Although the award is sponsored by the Canadian Library Association, it is the Canadian Association of Children's Librarians (a section of Canadian Association of Public Libraries which in turn is a division of CLA) which staffs the Award Committee, selects the winner and administers the award."

RAYMOND CARVER SHORT STORY CONTEST (I), Dept. of English, Humboldt State University, Arcata CA 95521. Contact: Coordinator. Annual award for previously unpublished short stories. For authors living in United States only. Deadline: November. Entry fee $5. SASE for rules. Send 2 copies of story; author's name on separate title page only. "Don't be discouraged by the technicalities of submitting manuscripts etc.; write for writing's sake."

CCL STUDENT WRITING CONTEST (I,IV), Conference on Christianity and Literature, Department of English, Baylor University, Waco TX 76798. (817)755-1768. Contact: Daniel Taylor, Department of English, Bethel College, 3900 Bethel Drive, St Paul MN 55112. Annual award. "To recognize excellence in undergraduate writing." Unpublished submissions. First-prize winner sometimes published in *C&L*. Award: $75, $50 and $25 awarded in book certificates. Deadline: February 15. Looking for "excellence in artistic achievement and reflection of writer's Christian premises." Contect open to all regularly enrolled undergraduate students. Entries will not be returned. Winners will be announced in summer issue of *Christianity and Literature*.

CHILD STUDY CHILDREN'S BOOK AWARD (III, IV), Child Study Children's Book Committee at Bank St. College, 610 W. 112th St., New York NY 10025. Contact: Anita Wilkes Dore, Committee Chair. Annual award. "To honor a book for children or young people which deals realistically with problems in their world. It may concern social, individual and ethical problems." Only books sent by publishers for review are considered. No personal submissions. Books must have been published within current calendar year. Award: Certificate and cash prize.

‡THE CHILDREN'S BOOK AWARD (II), Federation of Children's Book Groups, 22 Beacon Brow, Bradford W. Yorkshire BD6 3DE England. Award "to promote the publication of good quality books for children." Annual award for short stories, novels, story collections and translations. Award: "scrapbook of children's writing and drawings and unique glass bowl—engraved." Competition received 450 submissions in 1987. Judges: hundreds of children. Guidelines for SASE. Deadline December 31, 1989. Published and previously unpublished submissions (first publication in UK). "The book should be suitable for children up to 14 years of age."

THE CHRISTOPHER AWARD (II), The Christophers, 12 E. 48th St., New York NY 10017. Contact: Ms. Peggy Flanagan, awards coordinator. Annual award. "To encourage creative people to continue to produce works which affirm the highest values of the human spirit in adult and children's books." Published submissions only. "Award judged by a grassroots panel and a final panel of experts. Juvenile works are 'children tested.' " Award: Bronze medallion. Examples of books awarded: *Dear Mr. Henshaw*, by Beverly Cleary (ages 8-10); *Sarah, Plain and Tall* by Patricia MacLachlan (ages 10-12).

CINTAS FELLOWSHIP (I, IV), Cintas Foundation/Arts International Program of I.I.E., 809 U.N. Plaza, New York NY 11217. (212)984-5564. Contact: Rebecca A. Abrams. "To foster and encourage the professional development and recognition of talented Cuban creative artists. *Not* intended for furtherance of academic or professional study, nor for research or writings of a scholarly nature." Annual competition for authors of short stories, novels, story collections and poetry. 10 awards of $10,000 each. Fellowship receives approx. 120 applicants/year. Judges: selection committees from each field. Guidelines for SASE. Deadline: March 1 of each year. Previously published or unpublished submissions. Limited to artists of Cuban lineage *only*. "Awards are given to artists in the following fields: visual arts, literature, music composition, and architecture."

‡CITY OF REGINA WRITING AWARD (I, IV), City of Regina Arts Commission, Saskatchewan Writers Guild, Box 3986, Regina, Saskatchewan S4P 3R9 Canada. (306)757-6310, "To enable a writer to work for 3 months on a specific writing project; to reward merit in writing." Annual competition for short stories, novels and story collections. Award: $3,300. Competition receives approx. 21 submissions. Judges: selection committee of SWG. Guidelines for SASE. Deadline: March 17, 1989. Unpublished submissions. "Grant available only to residents of Regina for previous year."

COLORADO COUNCIL ON THE ARTS & HUMANITIES CREATIVE FELLOWSHIP (I, II, IV), 770 Pennsylvania Street, Denver CO 80203. (303)866-2617. Director, Individual Artist Programs: Daniel Salazar. To provide both recognition and significant financial support to Colorado's outstanding individual artists and to provide a forum and secure an audience for the promotion of their work. Award presented on rotating basis. Award: 8 fellowships of $4,000 each. Competition receives 250 entries/year. Judges: peer panels. Guidelines available for SASE. For either previously published or unpublished manuscripts. Colorado residents only.

COLUMBIA MAGAZINE EDITORS AWARDS (I), *Columbia; a Magazine of Poetry and Prose*, Writing Division, 404 Dodge Hall, Columbia University NY 10027. Contact: Fiction Editors. Annually. Short stories and sections of novels, unpublished. Deadline: April 1. Entry fee $5, made payable to *Columbia Magazine*. SASE for rules/entry forms. "Submissions can be no more than 25 pages; include SASE. First prize is $350; second prize is $150; both include publication."

COMMONWEALTH CLUB OF CALIFORNIA (II, IV), California Book Awards, 595 Market St., San Francisco CA 94105. (415)543-3353. Contact: Michael J. Brassington, executive director. Main contest established in 1931. Annually. Purpose: "To encourage California writers and honor literary merit." Requirements: For books published during the year of the particular contest. Three copies of book and a completed entry form required. Awards: Gold and silver medals. Judged by jury of literary experts. "Write or phone asking for the forms. Either an author or publisher may enter a book. We usually receive over 200 entries."

CONNECTICUT COMMISSION ON THE ARTS ARTIST GRANTS (I, IV), 227 Lawrence St., Hartford CT 06106. (203)566-4770. Senior Program Associate: Linda Dente. To support the creation of new work by a creative artist *living in Connecticut*. Biannual competition for the creation or completion of new works in literature, i.e. short stories, novels, story collections, poetry and playwriting. Award: $5,000. Judges: peer professionals (writers, editors). Guidelines available August, 1989. Deadline October, 1989. Writers may send either previously published or unpublished submissions. Writers may submit up to 25 pages of material. Connecticut residents only.

‡CONNECTICUT WRITERS LEAGUE ANNUAL WRITING CONTEST (II), Box 10536, West Hartford CT 06110. Contact: Ruth Lucas, editor. Estab. 1982. Annual award. "To encourage writing. Winners are published in the annual publication, *The Connecticut Writer*, produced by the Connecticut Writers League." Unpublished submissions. Award: "Recent prizes were $100 for 1st place in poetry and fiction; 2nd place, $75 each in above categories. A contest committee screens the manuscripts; final selections are made by judges outside the Connecticut Writers League. Interested persons should send for guidelines with SASE in the early spring." Entry fee: $3.

**CONSEIL DE LA VIE FRANCAISE EN AMÉRIQUE/PRIX CHAMPLAIN (The Champlain Prize)
(II)**, Conseil de la vie française en amérique, 59, Rue d'Auteuil, Québec G1R 4C2 Canada. Prix Champlain estab. 1957. Annual award. To encourage literary work in novel or short story in French by Francophiles living outside Québec and in the US or Canada. "There is no restriction as to the subject matter. If the author lives in Quebec, the subject matter must be realted to French-speaking people living outside of Quebec." For previously published or contracted submissions, published no more than 3 years prior to award. Deadline Dec. 31. Author must furnish 4 examples of work, curriculum vita, address and phone number. Judges: 3 different judges each year. Award: $1,500 in Canadian currency. The prize will be given alternately; one year for fiction, the next for nonfiction. Next fiction award in 1989.

‡*COTTON BOLL* SHORT STORY CONTEST (I), *Cotton Boll/The Atlanta Review*, Box 76757, Atlanta GA 30358-0703. Annual competition for short stories. Entry fee $3/story. Guidelines for SASE. Deadline: July 15, 1989. Previously unpublished submissions. Word length: 1,500-3,000 words. "Each story must be submitted in triplicate with the name and address of the author on only one copy. Entry will not be returned so author should retain copies. Since entry will not be returned, no SASE is necessary for return of manuscript; however, if author wishes contest results, he or she should enclose SASE marked 'Contest Winners.' "

‡COUNCIL FOR WISCONSIN WRITERS ANNUAL WRITING CONTEST (III, IV), Box 55322, Madison WI 53705. President: Lynn Entine. "To recognize excellence in Wisconsin writing published during the year in 10 categories." Annual competition for short stories and novels. Award: $200-300 for 1st place. Competition receives between 5 and 80 entries, depending on category. Judges: qualified judges from other states. Entry fee $7/member; $10/nonmember. Guidelines for SASE. Previously published submissions. Wisconsin residents only. Official entry form (available in November) required. Deadline: mid-January.

‡COUNCIL FOR WISCONSIN WRITERS PAULETTE CHANDLER AWARD (IV), Box 55322, Madison WI 53705. President: Lynn Entine. "To provide support for a Wisconsin short story writer or poet on the basis of ability and need." Alternate years competition for short stories (1989 next). Award: $1,500. Competition receives approx. 75 submissions. Judges: the *CWW* board and qualified Wisconsin or other judges. Guidelines for SASE. Either published or previously unpublished submissions. Wisconsin residents only. Official entry form required. Deadline: mid-January.

‡CRIME WRITERS' ASSOCIATION AWARDS (III, IV), Box 172, Tring Herts HP23 5LP England. Six awards. Annual award for crime novels. Competition receives varied amount of submissions. Deadline October 1. Published submissions in UK in current year. Writer must be nominated by UK publishers.

***CROSS-CANADA WRITERS' MAGAZINE* EDITORS' PRIZE (I)**, (formerly WQ Editors' Prize), Box 277, Station F, Toronto, Ontario M4Y 2L7 Canada. Contact: Ted Plantos, editor. Annual award. "To encourage and publicize the best in new Canadian and international fiction writing." Unpublished submissions, under 3,000 words. Award: Over $1,500 in cash and book prizes, plus publication of the 1st and 2nd prize winners in *Cross-Canada Writers' Magazine*. Entry deadline: June 30 each year. Details are announced in Nos. 1 & 2 of annual volume (winter and spring issues.) Entry fees are nominal. "Stories must demonstrate excellent handling of characterization, setting, plot and dialogue. Theme and approach must be absorbing and original."

‡DALY CITY POETRY AND SHORT STORY CONTEST (I), Daly City CA 94015. (415)992-3179. Contact: Ruth Hoppin, Contest Organizer. "To recognize and reward excellence in writing; encourage poets and writers; promote cultural activities." Annual competition for short stories. Award: 1st: $25, runner-up: $10; honorable mention: $5. "We receive about 50 stories in the contest, 500 poems." Judges: "a qualified judge, usually a teacher of creative writing." Entry fee $2/story. Deadline: January 2 postmark. Unpublished submissions. Open to all writers. 300 words maximum. "Send 2 copies of story; type, double-spaced photocopieds acceptable. Computer printouts OK. Name, address, telephone on cover sheet only. Awards ceremony In February. Attendance not required."

DEEP SOUTH WRITERS CONFERENCE ANNUAL COMPETITION (I), DSWC Inc., English Dept., University of Southwestern Louisiana, Box 44691, Lafayette LA 70504. (318)231-6908. Contact: John Fiero, director. Annual awards. "To encourage aspiring, unpublished writers." Unpublished submissions. Award: Certificates and cash plus possible publication of shorter works. Contest rules and addition to mailing list for SASE. Deadline: July 15.

DELACORTE PRESS ANNUAL PRIZE FOR AN OUTSTANDING FIRST YOUNG ADULT NOVEL (I), Delacorte Press, Department BFYR (Books for Young Readers), 1 Dag Hammarskjold Plaza, New York NY 10017. (212)605-3000. Contact: George Nicholson, vice president and editorial director, BFYR. Estab. 1983. Annual award. "To encourage the writing of contemporary young adult fiction and publish first novelists." Unpublished submissions; fiction with a contemporary setting in the United States or Canada that will be suitable for ages 12-18. Award: Contract for publication of book; $1,500 cash prize and a $6,000 advance against royalties. Deadline: December 31. Contest rules for SASE.

DELAWARE STATE ARTS COUNCIL (I, IV), 820 N. French St., Wilimington DE 19801. (302)571-3540. John Gatti, coordinator. "To help further careers of established, emerging and professional artists." Annual award for Delaware residents only. Award: $5,000 for established professional; $2,000 for emerging professional. Judges are out-of-state professionals in each division. Entry forms or rules for SASE. Deadline March 25, 1989.

DORLAND MOUNTAIN ARTS COLONY, INC. (I), Box 6, Temecula CA 92390. (714)676-5039. Contact: Admissions committee. "To provide uninterrupted time for creativity in a natural environment. The Colony is located on a 300-acre nature preserve." Residencies for authors of short stories, novels, translations and story collections. Award: residency for 1-2 months. Judges: admissions committee review panel. $150/month cottage fee requested. Guidelines for SASE. Deadline: March 1 and September 1 annually. "Four to seven residents can be accommodated at one time. Composers, writers and painters live in studio cottages of simple construction, consisting of kitchen, bathroom, living- and work-area. Residents learn to use woodstoves and kerosene lamps for their heat and evening light."

‡JOHN DOS PASSOS PRIZE FOR LITERATURE (III,IV), Longwood College, Farmville VA 23901. (804)392-9371. "The John Dos Passos Prize for Literature annually commemorates one of the greatest of 20th century American authors by honoring other writers in his name." Award: a medal and $1,000 cash. "The winner, announced each fall in ceremonies at the college, is chosen by an independent jury charged especially to seek out American creative writers in the middle stages of their careers—men and women who have established a substantial body of significant publication, and particularly those whose work demonstrates one or more of the following qualities, all characteristics of the art of the man for whom the prize is named: an intense and original exploration of specifically American themes; an experimental tone; and/or writing in a wide range of literature forms." Application for prize is by nomination only.

EATON LITERARY ASSOCIATES' LITERARY AWARDS PROGRAM (I), Eaton Literary Associates, Box 49795, Sarasota FL 34230. (813)355-4561. Lana L. Bruce, editorial director. Biannual award for short stories and novels. Award: $2,500 for best book-length ms, $500 for best short story. Competition receives approximately 2,000 submissions annually. Judges are 2 staff members in conjunction with an independent agency. Entry forms or rules for SASE. Deadline is March 31 for short stories; August 31 for book-length mss.

***EDMONTON JOURNAL*'S LITERARY AWARDS (I,IV)**, *Edmonton Journal*, Box 2421, Edmonton, Alberta T5J 2S6 Canada. (403)429-5100. Contact: Dennis L. Skulsky, manager, human resources and community relations. Annual award "to recognize novice writers in our circulation area; promote writing and reading; establish good-will in the community." SASE for guidelines. Unpublished submissions. Award changes annually.

EYSTER PRIZES (I, IV), *The New Delta Review*, LSU/Dept. of English, Baton Rouge LA 70803. (504)388-5922. Gregory Fuchs, editor. "To honor author and teacher Warren Eyster, who has served as advisor to *New Delta Review* predecessors *Manchac* and *Delta*." Annual award for short stories. Award: $50 and 2 free copies of our publication. Competition receives approximately 75 submissions/year. Judges are writers and faculty members from LSU not directly connected with *The New Delta Review*. Entry forms or rules for SASE. Deadline October 15.

FICTION NETWORK COMPETITION (I), Box 5651, San Francisco CA 94101. (415)391-6610. Jay Schaefer, Editor. "To find short fiction for syndication to newspapers." Annual award for short stories. Award: $1,500. Competition receives approximately 3,000 submissions. Outside judges. "Requirements (length, entry fee, etc.) change each year; writers must send SASE in March for rules, or see Spring issue of *Fiction Network*."

FINE ARTS WORK CENTER IN PROVINCETOWN FELLOWSHIP (I), Box 565, Provincetown MA 02657. (617)487-9960. Contact: Writing Coordinator. "Fellowship is to aid writers who have completed their formal education, but who have yet to firmly establish their careers." Writing residency offered annually. Award: an apartment and stipend, from October 1 to May. "We choose 8 fellows out of 400 applicants yearly." Judged by writing committee of the Fine Arts Work Center. Application fee $20. Applications for SASE.

‡ROBERT L. FISH MEMORIAL AWARD (II), Mystery Writers of America, 236 West 27th St. #600, New York NY 10001-5906. (212)255-7005. Estab. 1984. Annually. "To encourage new writers in the mystery/detective/suspense short story—and, subsequently, larger work in the genre." Previously published submissions published the year prior to the award. Award: $500. Judged by the MWA committee for best short story of the year in the mystery genre. Deadline: December 1. Looking for "a story with a crime that is central to the plot that is well written and distinctive."

DOROTHY CANFIELD FISHER AWARD (III), Vermont Congress of Parents and Teachers, 131 Main St., Montpelier VT 05602. Contact: Betty Lallier, chairperson. Estab. 1957. Annual award. "To encourage Vermont schoolchildren to become enthusiastic and discriminating readers and to honor the memory of one of Vermont's most distinguished and beloved literary figures." Publishers send the committee review copies of books to consider. Only books of the current publishing year can be considered for next year's award. Master list of titles is drawn up in late February or March each year. Children vote each year in the spring and the award is given before the school year ends. Award: illuminated scroll. Submissions must be "written by living American authors, be suitable for children in grades 4-8, and have literary merit. Can be nonfiction also."

FLORIDA ARTS COUNCIL/LITERATURE FELLOWSHIPS (I,IV), Division of Cultural Affairs, Dept. of State, The Capitol, Tallahassee FL 32399-0250. (904)487-2980. Director: Mr. Chris Doolin. "To allow Florida artists time to develop their artistic skills and enhance their careers." Annual award for fiction or poetry. Award: $5,000. Competition receives approximately 100 submissions/year. Judges are review panels made up of individuals with a demonstrated interest in literature. Entry forms for SASE. Entry restricted to practicing, professional writers who are legal residents of Florida and have been living in the state for 12 consecutive months at the time of the deadline.

FOSTER CITY ANNUAL WRITERS CONTEST (I), Foster City Committee for the Arts, 650 Shell Blvd., Foster City CA 94404. Contact: Ted Lance, contest chairman. Annually. "To foster and encourage aspiring writers." Unpublished submissions. Award: 1st prize in each of four categories $300. Ribbons for honorable mention in each category. The four catagories are short stories, poetry, humor and children's stories. "Contest begins in April and usually closes in August. Dates are announced." Entry fee: $5. Contest rules for SASE. Looking for short stories (3,000 words maximum).

FOUNDATION FOR THE ADVANCEMENT OF CANADIAN LETTERS AUTHOR'S AWARDS (II,IV), In conjunction with Periodical Marketers of Canada (PMC), 6 Adelaide St. E, 5th Floor, Toronto, Ontario M5C 1H6 Canada. (416)367-8760. Awards, Coordinators: Sheryll Reid, Paddy Bateman. "To recognize outstanding Canadian writing and design." Annual award for short stories, novels. 1989 competition judged by an independent panel. Deadline is July 15, 1989. "Must be published in a Canadian 'mass market' publication."

FRIENDS OF AMERICAN WRITERS AWARDS (III, IV), Friends of American Writers, 755 N. Merrill, Park Ridge IL 60068. Chairman: Jane Lederer. To encourage high standards and to promote literary ideals among American writers. Annual award for prose writing. Awards: $1,200 (1st prize) and $750 (2nd prize). Competition receives 50 entries. Judges: a committee of 18. Deadline December 15. Manuscripts must have been published during current year. Limited to midwestern authors who have previously published no more than 3 books and have not received a major literary award or to story with a midwestern locale. Two copies of the book are to be submitted to awards chairman by the publisher of the book.

GOLD MEDALLION BOOK AWARDS (III,IV), Evangelical Christian Publishers Association, Suite 106, 950 W. Southern, Tempe AZ 85282. Award to "encourage excellence in evangelical Christian book publishing." Annually. Judges: "at least five judges chosen from among the ranks of evangelical leaders and book-review editors." Entry fee $75 for ECPA member publishers; $200 for non-member publishers. Deadline January 1, 1990. For books published between 11-1-88 and 10-31-89. Publishers submit entries. Contest breaks down into 19 categories.

‡GOODMAN FIELDER WATTIE BOOK AWARD (III,IV), Goodman Fielder Wattie Ltd., Book Publishers Association of New Zealand (BPANZ), Box 44146, Auckland 2, New Zealand. Contact: Gerard Reid, executive director. "To recognize excellence in writing and publishing books by New Zealanders. This is not a category award. Fiction/nonfiction/childen's etc. are all included." Award: 1st NZ$18,000;

2nd: NZ$7,000; 3rd: NZ$4,000. Competition receives approx. 80-90 submissions. Judges: panel of 3 selected annually by the BPANZ—1 writer, 1 book trade person and 1 other. Entry fee NZ$65. Guidelines for SASE. Deadline: April 5, 1989. "Writer must be New Zealander or resident of New Zealand and its former Pacific territories. Must be submitted by publisher. Fuller details available from BPANZ."

‡LES GRANDS PRIX DU *JOURNAL DE MONTRÉAL* (I,IV), Union des écrivains québécois, 1030 rue Cherrier, #510, Montréal, Québec H2L 1H9 Canada. (514)526-6653. "To support the development of the literature of Québec and assure the public recognition of its authors." Annual award for novels and story collections. Award: $1,500 (Canadian). Judges: 5 judges, nominated by the *Journal de Montréal* and the Union des écrivains québécois. Guidelines for SASE. Deadline: June 10, 1989. For books published within the 12 months preceding June 1. Writers must have published at least 3 books and must submit 6 copies of the work to be considered. Write for rules and entry form (in French).

GREAT LAKES COLLEGES ASSOCIATION NEW WRITERS AWARDS (II), Great Lakes Colleges Association, Albion College, Albion MI 49224. Contact: James W. Cook, director—or after July 1, 1989, contact Paul Loakides. Annual award. "To recognize new young writers, promote and encourage interest in good literature." For books published "during the year preceding each year's February 28 deadline for entry, or the following spring." Award judged by critics and writers in residence at Great Lakes Colleges Association colleges and universities. Entry form or rules for SASE. Award: "Invited tour of up to 12 Great Lakes Colleges (usually 7 or 8) with honoraria and expenses paid. Entries in fiction (there is also a poetry section) must be first novels or first volumes of short stories already published, and must be submitted (four copies) *by publishers only*—but this may include privately published books."

GREAT PLAINS STORYTELLING & POETRY READING CONTEST (I), Box 438, Walnut IA 51577. (712)366-1136. Contact: Robert Everhart, director. Estab. 1976. Annual award. "To provide an outlet for writers to present not only their works, but also to provide a large audience for their presentation live by the writer." Previously published or unpublished submissions. Award: 1st prize $75; 2nd prize $50; 3rd prize $25; 4th prize $15; and 5th prize $10. Entry deadline: day of contest, which takes place over Labor Day Weekend. Entry fee: $5. Entry forms or rules for SASE.

THE GREENSBORO REVIEW LITERARY AWARDS (I), Dept. of English, UNC-Greensboro, Greensboro NC 27412. (919)334-5459. Editor: Jim Clark. Annually. Unpublished submissions. Award: $250. Deadline: September 15. Contest rules for SASE.

‡GUARDIAN CHILDREN'S FICTION AWARD (III, IV), The Guardian, 119 Farringdon Rd., London EC1R 3ER England. Contact: Stephanie Nettell, children's books editor. "To recognize an outstanding work of children's fiction—and gain publicity for the field of children's books." Annual competition for fiction. Award: £500. Competition receives approx. 100 submissions. Judges: four eminent children's writers plus children's books editor of the *Guardian*. Deadline: December 31. "British or Commonwealth authors only; published in UK in previous year; not picture books. Awarded every March for book published in previous year."

HACKNEY LITERARY AWARDS (I), Birmingham Southern College, Box A-3, Birmingham AL 35254. (205)226-4921. Contact: Doris Whisenhunt. Annual award for previously unpublished short stories, poetry and novel. Deadline for submitting a novel—must be postmarked on or before November 24, 1989. Deadline for submitting short stories or poetry—must be postmarked on or before December 31, 1989. No entry fee. Rules/entry form for SASE.

HAMBIDGE CENTER FOR CREATIVE ARTS AND SCIENCES (I), Box 339, Rabun Gap GA 30568. (404)746-5718. Executive Director: R. Pierotti. Two-week to two-month residencies are offered to writers, visual artists, composers, historians, humanists and scientists. "Center is open from May through October. It is located on 600 acres of quiet woods and streams in north Georgia. Private cottages as well as communal housing available for those who qualify. For application forms send SASE to Executive Director. Once application forms are returned to the Center it takes about 2 months processing time. No deadline."

DRUE HEINZ LITERATURE PRIZE (II), The Howard Heinz Endowment and the University of Pittsburgh Press, University of Pittsburgh Press, 127 North Bellefield Ave., Pittsburgh PA 15260. (412)624-4110. Annual award. "To support the writer of short fiction at a time when the economics of commercial publishing make it more and more difficult for the serious literary artist working in the short story and novella to find publication." Manuscripts must be unpublished in book form. The award is open to writers who have published a book-length collection of fiction or a minimum of three short stories or novellas in commercial magazines or literary journals of national distribution. Award: $7,500 and publication by the University of Pittsburgh Press. Request complete rules of the competition before submitting a manuscript. Entry deadline: August 31. Submissions will be received only during the months of July and August.

‡HEMINGWAY DAYS SHORT STORY COMPETITION (I), Hemingway Days Festival, Box 4045, Key West FL 33041. (305)294-4440. "To honor excellence in unpublished short fiction." Annual competition for short stories. Award: $1000—1st; $500—2nd; $250—3rd. Competition receives approx. 400-600 submissions. Judges: panel led by Lorian Hemingway, granddaughter of Ernest Hemingway and journalist based out of Seattle, WA. Entry fee $10/story. Guidelines for SASE. Deadline: July 10, 1989. Unpublished submissions. "Open to anyone so long as the work is unpublished. No longer than 2,500 words."

ERNEST HEMINGWAY FOUNDATION AWARD (II), PEN American Center, 568 Broadway, New York NY 10012. Contact: John Morrone, coordinator of programs. Annual award. "To give beginning writers recognition and encouragement and to stimulate interest in first novels among publishers and readers." Novels must have been published during calendar year under consideration. Deadline December 31. Entry form or rules for SASE. Award: $7,500. "The Ernest Hemingway Foundation Award is given to an American author of the best first-published booklength work of fiction published by an established publishing house in the US each calendar year."

‡THE O. HENRY AWARDS (III), Doubleday, 666 Fifth Avenue, New York NY 10103. Contact: Sally Arteseros, senior editor. Annual award. To honor the memory of O. Henry with a sampling of outstanding short stories and to make these stories better known to the public. These awards are published by Anchor Books/Doubleday every spring. Previously published submissions. "All selections are made by the editor of the volume, William Abrahams. No stories may be submitted."

GEORGETTE HEYER HISTORICAL NOVEL PRIZE (I), The Bodley Head and Transworld Publishers, (Corgi Books). The Bodley Head, 32 Bedford Square, London WC1B 3EL England. Jill Black, editor. For an outstanding full-length historical novel, which should be set pre-1939 and have a minimum length of 40,000 words. Annual award for novels. Award: £5,000 and hardback and paperback publication plus royalties. Judges are appointed by The Bodley Head and Corgi Books. Entry forms for SASE.

***HIGHLIGHTS FOR CHILDREN* (I,IV)**, 803 Church St., Honesdale PA 18431. Editor: Kent L. Brown, Jr. "To honor quality stories (previously unpublished) for young readers." Stories: up to 900 words for beginning readers (to age 8) and for more advanced readers (ages 9 to 12). No minimum word length. No entry form necessary. To be submitted between January 1 and March 31 to "Fiction Contest" at address above. Three $750 awards. No violence or crime. Non-winning entries returned in June if SASE is included with manuscript. Write for information.

‡THE ALFRED HODDER FELLOWSHIP (II), The Council of the Humanities, Princeton University, 122 E. Pyne, Princeton NJ 08544. "This fellowship is awarded for the pursuit of independent work in the humanities. The recipient is usually a writer or scholar in the early stages of his or her career, a person "with more than ordinary learning" and with "much more than ordinary intellectual and literary gifts." Traditionally, the Hodder Fellow has been a humanist outside of academia. Candidates for the Ph.D. are not eligible. Annual competition for short stories, novels, story collections and translations. Award: $34,000. The Hodder fellow spends an academic year in residence at Princeton working independently. Judges; Princeton Committee on Humanistic studies. Guidelines for SASE. Deadline November 15, 1989. "Applicants must submit a résumé, a sample of previous work (10 page maximum, not returnable), and a project proposal of 2 to 3 pages. Letters of recommendation are not required."

THEODORE CHRISTIAN HOEPFNER AWARD (I), *Southern Humanities Review*, 9088 Haley Center, Auburn University AL 36849. Contact: Thomas L. Wright or Dan R. Latimer, co-editors. Annual award. "To award the authors of the best essay, the best short story and the best poem published in *SHR* each year." Unpublished submissions to the magazine only. Award judged by editorial staff. Award: $100 for the best short story. Only published work in the current volume (4 issues) will be judged.

HOHENBERG AWARD (I), *Memphis State Review*, Dept. of English, Memphis State University, Memphis TN 38152. (901)454-4438. Contact: Sharon Bryan, editor. Estab. 1982. Annual award. "To encourage writing of outstanding merit." Unpublished submissions. Award: $100. Judged by a review panel. No entry fee. For entry submit fiction for publication in *Memphis State Review*.

HONOLULU MAGAZINE/PARKER PEN COMPANY FICTION CONTEST (I,IV), *Honolulu* Magazine, 36 Merchant St., Honolulu HI 96813. (808)524-7400. Brian Nicol, editor. "We do not accept fiction except during our annual contest, at which time we welcome it." Annual award for short stories. Award: $1,000 and publication in the March issue of *Honolulu* Magazine. Competition receives approximately 200 submissions. Judges: panel of well-known writers. Rules for SASE. Deadline December 9, 1989. "Stories must have a Hawaii theme, setting and/or characters. Author should enclose name and address in separate small envelope. Do not put name on story."

‡IDAHO COMMISSION ON THE ARTS AWARDS (I, IV), The Alexander House, 304 W. State St., Boise ID 83720. (208)334-2119. Public Information Officer: Patricia Thornton. "The Idaho Commission on the Arts offers funding to writers in several categories: Idaho Writer-in-Residence, biannually; Fellowships and Apprenticeships, annually; and Sudden Opportunity Assistance Program, bi-monthly. Grants and awards are not limited to fiction writing and all applicants must be residents of the State of Idaho."

ILLINOIS ARTS COUNCIL SPECIAL ASSISTANCE GRANT AND ARTIST'S FELLOWSHIP (I,IV), 100 W. Randolph St. (10-500), Chicago IL 60657. (312)917-6750. Communication Arts Coordinator: Alan Leder. "Grant is for project completion or to help defray the costs of attending workshops, seminars or conferences. The fellowships are awarded to Illinois artists of exceptional talent to enable them to pursue their artistic goals. Annually. Grants for up to $1,500 (average is $500). Fellowships are for set amounts of $15,000, $10,000 and $5,000. Arts Council receives over 200 + fellowship applicants, approx. 30 Special Assistance applicants. Judges: "Grants are evaluated by staff and panel consultants. Fellowships are evaluated by professional out-of-state writers and scholars." Guidelines available, SASE not required. The Special Assistance Grant is an open-deadline program available throughout the year until funds are used up. Fellowship deadline is September 1st each year. Submissions may be either previously published or unpublished. Only Illinois writers are eligible. Fellowship limits submission to 30 pages of fiction or 15 pages of poetry.

ILLINOIS STATE UNIVERSITY NATIONAL FICTION COMPETITION (I), Illinois State University Fiction Collective, English Department, Illinois State University, Normal IL 61761. Curtis White, series editor. Annual award for novels, novellas and story collections. Award: publication. Competition receives approximately 150 submissions each year. Judges different each year. Entry fee $10. Entry forms or rules for SASE.

INSTITUTE FOR HUMANE STUDIES FELIX MORLEY MEMORIAL PRIZES (II,IV), Institute for Humane Studies, George Mason University, 4400 University Drive, Fairfax VA 22030. (703)323-1055. Contact: Morley Prize Secretary. Award to "discover good college-aged writers who reflect an interest in the classical liberal tradition of private property and free exchange." Annually for short stories. Award: $2,500 (1st prize); $1,500 (2nd prize); $1,000 (3rd prize); $500 (five runners up). Competition receives 250 entries/year. Judges: review committee of 19. Write for application. Deadline June 15, 1989. Submissions should have been previously published in student or other publications. For college-aged writers from U.S. or abroad.

INTERNATIONAL JANUSZ KORCZAK LITERARY COMPETITION (II, IV), International Center for Holocaust Studies Anti-Defamation League of B'nai B'rith, 823 United Nations Plaza, New York NY 10017. (212)490-2525. Contact: Dr. Dennis B. Klein, director. Biannually, for published novels, novellas, translations, short story collections. "Books for or about children which best reflect the humanitarianism and leadership of Janusz Korczak, a Jewish and Polish physician, educator and author." Deadline: January, even years. SASE for rules/entry form.

‡INTERNATIONAL LITERARY CONTEST (I), Writer's Refinery, Box 47786, Phoenix AZ 85068-7786. Contact: Libbi Goodman, contest director. Annual award for fiction, poetry and essays. Unpublished submissions. Deadline November 30.

INTERNATIONAL READING ASSOCIATION CHILDREN'S BOOK AWARDS (II), Sponsored by IRA/Institute for Reading Research, 800 Barksdale Rd., Box 8139, Newark DE 19714-8139. (302)731-1600. Annual award. To encourage an author who shows unusual promise in the field of children's books. Two awards will be given for a first or second book in two categories: one for literature for older children, 10-16 years old; one for literature for younger children, 4-10 years old. Submissions must have been published during the calendar year prior to the year in which the award is given. Award: $1,000 stipend. Entry deadline: December 1. No entry fee. Contest/award rules and awards flyer for SASE. To enter the contest, the author or publisher should send 10 copies of the book to Walter Barbe, 823 Church Street, Honesdale PA 18431.

IOWA ARTS COUNCIL LITERARY AWARDS (I, IV), Iowa Arts Council, State Capitol Complex, Des Moines IA 50319. (515)281-4451. Grants Officer: Julie Bailey. Estab. 1984. "To give exposure to Iowa's fine poets and fiction writers." Unpublished submissions by legal residents of Iowa only. Award: 1st prize, $1,000; 2nd prize, $500. Deadline: varies. Contest rules for SASE.

IOWA SCHOOL OF LETTERS AWARD FOR SHORT FICTION, THE JOHN SIMMONS SHORT FICTION AWARD (I), Iowa Writers' Workshop, 436 English-Philosophy Building, The University of Iowa, Iowa City IA 52242. Annual award for short story collections. To encourage writers of short fiction. Entries must be at least 150 pages, typewritten, and submitted between Aug. 1 and Sept. 30. Stamped, self-addressed return packaging must accompany the manuscript. Rules for SASE. Two awards: $1,000 each, plus publication of winning collections by University of Iowa Press the following fall. Iowa Writer's Workshop does initial screening of entries; finalists (about 6) sent to outside judge for final selection. "A different well known writer is chosen each year as judge. Any writer who has not previously published a volume of prose fiction is eligible to enter the competition for these prizes. Revised manuscripts which have been previously entered may be resubmitted."

JOSEPH HENRY JACKSON AWARD (I, IV), The San Francisco Foundation, 685 Market St., Suite 910, San Francisco CA 94105. Contact: Adrienne Krug, assistant coordinator. Annual competition "to award the author of an unpublished work-in-progress of fiction (novel or short stories), nonfiction or poetry." Unpublished submissions only. Applicant must be resident of northern California or Nevada for 3 consecutive years immediately prior to the deadline date. Age of applicant must be 20 through 35. Deadline: January 15. Entry form and rules available after November 1 for SASE. Award: $2,000 and award certificate.

‡JAPAN-UNITED STATES FRIENDSHIP COMMISSION PRIZE FOR THE TRANSLATION OF JAPANESE LITERATURE (I, IV), The Donald Keene Center of Japanese Culture, Columbia University, 407 Kent Hall, Columbia University, New York NY 10027. (212)280-5036. Contact: Victoria Lyon-Bestor. "To encourage fine translations of Japanese literature and to award and encourage young translators to develop that craft." Annual competition for translations only. Award: $2,000. Competition receives approx. 10 submissions. Judges: a jury of writers, literary agents, critics and scholar/translators. Guidelines for SASE. Previously published or unpublished submissions. "Translators must be American citizens."

JAPANOPHILE SHORT STORY CONTEST (I, IV), *Japanophile*, Box 223, Okemos MI 48864. (517)349-1795. Contact: Earl R. Snodgrass, editor. Estab. 1972. Annually. "To encourage quality writing on Japan-America understanding." Prefers unpublished submissions. Stories should involve Japanese and non-Japanese characters. Award: $100 plus possible publication. Deadline: Dec. 31. Entry fee: $5. Send $4 for sample copy of magazine. Contest rules for SASE.

KANSAS QUARTERLY/KANSAS ARTS COMMISSION AWARDS (I), *Kansas Quarterly*, 122 Denison Hall, Dept. of English, Kansas State University, Manhattan KS 66506. Contact: Editors. Annual awards. "To reward and recognize the best fiction published in *Kansas Quarterly* during the year from authors anywhere in the US or abroad. Anyone who submits unpublished material which is then accepted for publication becomes eligible for the awards." No deadline; material simply may be submitted for consideration at any time. To submit fiction for consideration, send it in with SASE. Award: Recognition and monetary sums of $300, $200, $100, $50. "Ours are not 'contests'; they are monetary awards and recognition given by persons of national literary stature." Fiction judges recently have included Lee Zacharias, Fred Chappell, R. V. Cassill, David Bradley, and James B. Hall.

‡EZRA JACK KEATS MEMORIAL FELLOWSHIP (I), Ezra Jack Keats Foundation (funding); Awarded through the Kerlan Collection CLRC, 109 Walter Library, 117 Pleasant St., S.E., Minneapolis MN 55455. (612)624-4576. Annual award for writer or illustrator of children's books. Award: $1,500. Judges: committee of 5 members from different colleges at the University of Minnesota and Minnesota Library Association. SASE for news release and application form. Deadline: May 1. Published or previously unpublished submissions. Children's literature only. Writers not nominated; letters of recommendation required for application, though.

ROBERT F. KENNEDY BOOK AWARDS (II, IV), 1031 31st St., NW, Washington DC 20007. (202)333-1880. Contact: Ms. Caroline Croft. Endowed by Arthur Schlesinger, Jr., from proceeds of his biography, *Robert Kennedy and His Times*. Annual award. "To award the author of a book which most faithfully and forcefully reflects Robert Kennedy's purposes." For books published during the calendar year. Award: $2,500 cash prize awarded in the spring. Looking for "a work of literary merit in fact or fiction that shows compassion for the poor or powerless or those suffering from injustice." Deadline: January 5, 1990.

KENTUCKY ARTS COUNCIL, AL SMITH ARTISTS FELLOWSHIPS (I, IV), Berry Hill, Frankfort KY 40601. (502)564-3757. "To encourage and support the professional development of Kentucky artists." Writing fellowships offered every other year in fiction, poetry, playwriting. Award: $5,000. Competition received approximately "110 submissions in 1988 in all writing categories." Judges are out-of-state panelists (writers, editors, playwrights, etc.) of distinction. Entry forms or rules "even without SASE." Next appropriate deadline for writers is July 1, 1990.

‡LOUISA KERN FUND GRANT (I), University of Washington, Creative Writing, GN-30, Seattle WA 98195. (206)543-9865. "The Louisa Kern Fund has as its 'primary purpose and interest . . . to provide funds and to encourage and assist the training and development of persons interested in the field of literary endeavors and, in particular, the field of creative writing.' In the words of the enabling bequest, 'I wish to make it clear that formal educational training, while desirable, is not required as the sole aim of this trust." Annual competition for short stories, novels and story collections. Award: $2,500. Competition receives approx. 195 submissions. Judges: 3 faculty members (2 in creative writing program and 1 from outside program). Guidelines for SASE. Deadline April 1, 1989. Previously published or unpublished submissions. Preference given to Northwest writers. "Applicants for the grant should send a letter of application by April 1 of the year in which they hope for support. Read guidelines before applying."

AGA KHAN PRIZE (I), *Paris Review*, 541 E. 72nd St., New York NY 10021. Annual award. For the best short story received during the preceding year. Unpublished submissions with SASE. Deadline: June 1. Award judged by the editors. Award: $1,000 and publication. Unpublished short story (1,000-10,000 words). Translations acceptable.

LAWRENCE FELLOWSHIP (I), University of New Mexico, Dept. of English Language and Literature, Albuquerque NM 87131. (505)277-6347. Contact: Prof. Gene Frumkin, chairperson. Annually. Fellowship, for writers of unpublished or previously published fiction, poetry, drama. (June-August residency at D.H. Lawrence Ranch, $2,100 stipend). Deadline: January 31. $10 processing fee. SASE for return of materials. Write for rules, application form.

LETRAS DE ORO SPANISH LITERARY PRIZES (I, IV), American Express and the Graduate School of International Studies, University of Miami, Box 248123, Coral Gables FL 33124. (305)284-3266. "The *Letras de Oro* Spanish Literary Prizes were created in order to reward creative excellence in the Spanish language and to promote Spanish literary production in this country. *Letras de Oro* also serves to recognize the importance of Hispanic culture in the United States." Annual award for novels, story collections, drama, essays and translations of Spanish or Latin American into English. The prizes are $2,500 cash. The jury will consist of five members: a writer, an academician, an editor, a literature critic and a journalist. Deadline October 12.

‡LITERARY LIGHTS, SHORT STORY CONTESTS (II), Box 25809, Seattle WA 98125. Contact: Contest Editor. To "encourage and foster new writers." Award granted at completion of each contest for short stories. Award: cash prize and possible publication. Number of entries vary depending on theme of the contest. Entry fee $5. Guidelines for SASE. Deadline January 30, 1989, March 30, 1989, September 30, 1989 and November 11, 1989. Unpublished submissions. "Each contest has a theme and maximum word length."

LITERATURE AND BELIEF WRITING CONTEST (I,IV), Center for the Study of Christian Values in Literature, 3134 JKHB, Brigham Young University, Provo UT 84602. (801)378-2304. Director: Jay Fox. Award to "encourage affirmative literature in the Judeo-Christian tradition." Annual competition for short stories. Award $150 (1st place); $100 (2nd place). Competition receives 200-300 entries. Judges: BYU faculty. Guidelines for SASE. Deadline May 15, 1989. Unpublished submissions, up to 25 pages.

LOFT-MCKNIGHT WRITERS AWARDS (I,IV), The Loft, 2301 E. Franklin Ave., Minneapolis MN 55406. (612)341-0431. Susan Broadhead, executive director. "To give Minnesota writers of demonstrated ability an opportunity to work for a concentrated period of time on their writing." Annual award for creative prose. $7,500 per award; four awards. Competition receives approximately 275 submissions/year. Judges are out-of-state judges. Entry forms or rules for SASE. "Applicants must send for and observe guidelines."

LOS ANGELES TIMES BOOK PRIZES (III), L.A. *Times, Book Review*, Times Mirror Square, Los Angeles CA 90053. (213)972-7777. Contact: Jack Miles, book editor. Annual award. "To recognize finest books published each year." For books published between August 1 and July 31. Award: $1,000 cash prize plus a handmade, leather-bound version of the winning book. Entry is by nomination; *Times* reviewers nominate. No entry fee.

LOUISIANA LITERARY AWARD (II, IV), Louisiana Library Association (LLA), Box 3058, Baton Rouge LA 70821. (504)342-4928. Contact: Chair, Louisiana Literary Award Committee. Annual award. "To promote interest in books related to Louisiana and to encourage their production." Submissions must have been published during the calendar year prior to presentation of the award. (The award is presented in March or April.) Award: Bronze medallion and $250. Entry deadline: publication by December 31. No entry fee. "All Louisiana-related books which committee members can locate are considered, whether submitted or not. Interested parties may correspond with the committee chair at the address above. All books considered *must* be on subject(s) related to Louisiana or be written by a Louisiana author. Each year, there may be a fiction *and/or* nonfiction award. Most often, however, there is only one award recipient, and he or she is the author of a work of nonfiction."

LYRA **SHORT FICTION CONTEST (I)**, *Lyra, Journal of Poetry and Fiction*, Box 3188, Guttenberg NJ 07093. (201)861-6097. Co-Editor: Lourdes Gil. To encourage emerging writers and to provide a vehicle for publication. Annual competition for short stories. Award: $150, publication in *Lyra*, and 5 copies. Competition receives approx. 80 submissions/year. "Judges alternate; they are also writers." Entry fee $6. Guidelines for SASE. Deadline September 30, 1989. Unpublished submissions. "There are no limits in length, style or topic. They can be written in English, French, Spanish or Italian."

MACDOWELL COLONY RESIDENCIES (I), The MacDowell Colony, 100 High St., Peterborough NH 03458. (603)924-3886 or (212)966-4860. Admissions Coordinator: Shirley Bewley. "Private studios plus board and room at the MacDowell Colony are provided to competitively selected writers, composers, visual artists and filmmakers, allowing up to 8 weeks of uninterrupted time for creative projects." Colony operates year-round for writers of short stories, novels and story collections, as well as poets and playwrights. Colony helps support costs of residencies for accepted applicants. Colony receives approx. 5-6 applicants for each residency. Judges: panels of professionals in each creative field. Entry fee: $10. Guidelines for SASE. Deadline April 15 for Sept.-Dec.; Sept. 15 for Jan.-April; Jan. 15 for May-August. Submissions may be either unpublished or previously published. "Open to all professionally qualified writers. See application instructions for length of work sample. Accepted applicants are asked to contribute as much as they are able toward residency costs, but no applicant is rejected for financial reasons. Residencies average 5-6 weeks. Applications from fiction writers are pooled for review with writers of poetry, plays and nonfiction. Over 200 artists are accepted each year, of whom approx. 90 are writers. The Colony has 31 studios open in summer, 24 in spring and fall, 19 in winter."

MADEMOISELLE **FICTION WRITERS CONTEST (I)**, *Mademoiselle Magazine*, 350 Madison Ave., New York NY 10017. Send entries to Fiction Writers Contest. Each entry must be accompanied by the entry coupon or a 3x5 card with name, age, home address. Award: 1st prize: $1,000 plus $1,500 for publication in *Mademoiselle*; 2nd prize: $500 cash. Open to all short story writers, male and female, age 18-30, who have not published fiction in a magazine with a circulation over 25,000. Entries will not be returned.

MARYLAND STATE ARTS COUNCIL FELLOWSHIP (I, IV), 15 West Mulberry St., Baltimore MD 21201. (301)685-6740. Fellowships given to reward artistic excellence and to promote career development. Annual grant for writers of stories, novels, novellas and story collections. Award: $6,000 fellowship or up to $3,000 work-in-progress grants. Competition receives 200 applications for fellowships; 120 for work-in-progress grants annually. Judge: out-of-state selection panel. Further information available for SASE. Applicants must be Maryland residents over 18. Students are not eligible. Writers are required to submit a body of work demonstrating artistic accomplishment and skill.

MASSACHUSETTS ARTISTS FELLOWSHIP (I, IV), Artists Foundation—Artists Fellowship Program, 8 Park Plaza, Boston MA 02116. (617)227-ARTS. Contact: Netta Davis. Annual award. "To encourage artists who live and work in Massachusetts." Categories include playwriting, fiction, nonfiction, poetry. Massachusetts residents 18 years of age or older are eligible to apply as long as resident is not enrolled as a student in a degree-granting program in their field. "Specific instructions are detailed in the entry form which is available upon request." Previous publication is not necessary, but any published work must be submitted in typewritten form. Entry forms available upon request. Award: $9,500 for winners; $500 for finalists. "Looking for artistic excellence. Work is judged anonymously by a panel of professional working writers and experts in the field who live outside Massachusetts."

‡MCDONALD'S LITERARY ACHIEVEMENT AWARDS FOR WRITING ON THE BLACK EXPERI-ENCE IN AMERICA (I, IV), The Negro Ensemble Company, Box 778, Times Square Station, New York NY 10108. (312)443-8739. Contact: Larry Calhoun (with any phone calls). To offer developing writers a chance to compete for literary awards for writing about the black experience in America. Annual competition for short stories and novels. Award: $2,000 and a trip to New York to participate in a celebrity reading of their work and a literary reception. Guidelines for SASE. Deadline June 1, 1989. Word length: up to 50 pages of a long work or two short works. "Include a biographical statement, including a list of publications, if any, in which your work has appeared."

THE JOHN H. MCGINNIS MEMORIAL AWARD (I), *Southwest Review*, 6410 Airline Road, Southern Methodist University, Dallas TX 75275. Contact: Betsey McDougall, managing editor. Biannual award. (One year for fiction and the next for nonfiction). Stories must have been published in the *Southwest Review* within a two-year period prior to the announcement of the award. Award: $1,000. Stories are not submitted directly for the award, but simply for publication in the magazine.

MCKENDREE WRITERS' ASSOCIATION WRITING CONTEST (I, IV), McKendree Writers' Association, Box 1522, Belleville IL 62222. Contact: Mary Ellen Bertram. Annual award. "To encourage literary excellence." Unpublished submissions. Award: First place, $25; second place, $15; third place, $10. Honorable mentions when appropriate. Deadline: March or early April. "The Association sponsors an annual writing conference each spring. The winners are announced at the conference." Entry fee: $3. In addition, contestant must be a member of the organization. Contest rules for SASE.

‡THE ENID MCLEOD LITERARY PRIZE (II, IV), Franco-British Society, Room 636, Linen Hall, 162-168 Regent St., London W1R 5TB England. Contact: Mrs. Marian Clarke, executive secretary. "To recognize the work of the author published in the UK which in the opinion of the judges has contributed most to Franco-British understanding." Annual competition for short stories, novels and story collections. Award: copy of Enid McLeod's memoirs. Competition receives approx. 6-12 submissions. Judges: Lord Lansdowne (FBS President); Martyn Goff and Terence Kilmartin. Guidelines for SASE. Deadline: December 31, 1989. Previously published submissions. "Writers, or their publishers, may submit 4 copies to the London Office. No nominations are necessary."

THE VICKY METCALF BODY OF WORK AWARD (II, IV), Canadian Authors Association, Suite 104, 121 Avenue Road, Toronto, Ontario M5R 2G3 Canada. (416)926-8084. Contact: Office Manager. Annual award. "The prize is given solely to stimulate writing for children, written by Canadians, for a *number* of strictly children's books—fiction, nonfiction or even picture books. No set formula." To be considered, a writer must have published at least 4 books. Award: $2,000 for a body of work inspirational to Canadian youth." Entry deadline: December 31. No entry fee. "Nominations may be made by any individual or association by letter *in triplicate* listing the published works of the nominee and providing biographical information. The books are usually considered in regard to their inspirational value for children. Entry forms or rules for SASE."

VICKY METCALF SHORT STORY AWARD (II, IV), Canadian Authors Association, Suite 104, 121 Avenue Road, Toronto, Ontario M5R 2G3 Canada. (416)926-8084. Contact: Executive Director. "To encourage Canadian writing for children (open only to Canadian citizens)." Submissions must have been published during previous calendar year in Canadian children's magazine or anthology. Award: $1,000 (Canadian). Matching award of $1,000 to editor of winning story if published in a Canadian journal or anthology. Entry deadline: December 31. No entry fee. Entry forms or rules for SASE. Looking for "stories with originality, literary quality for ages 7-17."

MIDLAND AUTHORS' AWARD (II, IV), Society of Midland Authors, 840 E. 87th Ave., Chicago IL 60601. (312)994-7200. Awards Coordinator or Editor: "changes annually." "To honor outstanding works published during the previous year by Midwestern authors." Annual award for previously published novels or story collections. Award: $300, and plaque and Society of Midland Authors' "Seal" for book jackets. Competition receives approximately 30-50 submissions. Judges are usually members of Society of Midland Authors. Entry forms or rules for SASE. Authors must be residents of IL, IN, IA, KS, MI, MN, MO, NE, ND, OH, SD or WI. Send for entry form.

‡MILKWEED EDITIONS NATIONAL FICTION PRIZE (I), Milkweed Editions, Box 3226, Minneapolis MN 55403. (612)332-3192. Managing Editor: Deborah Keenan. Annual award for three short stories, a short novel or a novella. Award: publication, $3,000 advance against royalties. Received 270 entries for first award; "we expect many more this year and next. Already past 300 for 1988." Judges: "2 editors at Milkweed narrow it to 10 mss. Then, a final judge—last year, Phillip Lopate. This year, Rosellen Brown." Entry fee $5. Guidelines for SASE. Deadline October 30, 1989. "Please look at *Ganado*

Red, by Susan Lowell, our first winning NFP book, or at *Backbone*, by Carol Bly, or *The Country I Come From*, by Maura Stanton—this is the caliber of fiction we are searching for. Catalog available for 2 first class stamps, if people need a sense of our list."

MILLAY COLONY FOR THE ARTS (I), Steepletop, Austerlitz, NY 12017. (518)392-3103. Executive Director: Ann-Ellen Lesser. "The Millay Colony gives residencies to writers, composers and visual artists. Residencies are for one month and usually cover a period from the first to the 28th of each month." Judges: professional artists on admissions committee. Deadline February 1 (for June-September residencies); May 1 (for October-January residencies); September 1 (for February-May residencies).

THE MILNER AWARD (III), Friends of the Atlanta Public Library, 1 Margaret Mitchell Square, Atlanta GA 30303. (404)688-4636. First Vice-President: Carol Phillips. Award to a living American author of children's books. Annual competition for novels and story collections. Award: $1,000 honorarium and specially commissioned glass sculpture by Hans Frabel. Judges: children of Atlanta vote during children's book week. Prior winners not eligible. For previously published books. Children vote at will—no list from which to select. Winner must be able to appear personally in Atlanta to receive the award at a formal program.

‡MIND BOOK OF THE YEAR—THE ALLEN LAND AWARD (II, IV), MIND, 22 Harley St., London W1N 2ED England. Contact: Ms. C.E. Shaw. "To award a prize to the work of fiction or nonfiction which outstandingly furthers public understanding of the causes, experience or treatment of mental illness." Annual competition for novels and works of nonfiction. Award: £1,000. Competition receives approx. 50-100 submissions. Judges: a panel of judges drawn from MIND's Council of Management. Deadline September, 1989. Previously published submissions. Author's nomination is accepted.

MINNESOTA STATE ARTS BOARD/ARTISTS ASSISTANCE FELLOWSHIP (I, IV), 432 Summit Avenue, St. Paul MN 55407. (612)297-2603. Artist Assistance Program Associate: Karen Mueller. "To provide support and recognition to Minnesota's outstanding literary artists." Annual award for fiction, creative nonfiction writers and poets. Award: $6,000. Competition receives approx. 150 submissions/year. Deadline: January. Previously published or unpublished submissions. Send request or call the above number for application guidelines. *Minnesota residents only*.

MISSISSIPPI ARTS COMMISSION INDIVIDUAL ARTIST GRANT (I, IV), Suite 207, 239 N. Lamar St., Jackson MS 39201. (601)359-6030. Contact: Individual Artist Program. "To encourage and support the creation of new artwork, and to recognize the contribution that artists of exceptional talent make to the vitality of our environment. Awards are based upon the quality of previously created work." Award granted every 3 years on a rotating basis. Award for writers of short stories, novels and story collections. Grant: up to $5,000. Competition receives 10 + submissions/year. Judging: peer panel. Guidelines for SASE. "The next available grants for creative writing, including fiction, nonfiction and poetry will be in fiscal year 1991. In fiscal year 1990 artists may apply for play and screenwriting." Applicants should send previously published submissions. Applicants must be Mississippi residents. "The Mississippi Arts Commission's Art in Education Program contains a creative writing component. Mississippi Artists have first priority. For more information, contact the AIE Coordinator. The Mississippi Traveling Arts program offers writers the opportunity to give readings and workshops and have the Arts Commission pay part of the fee." For more information, contact the M.T.A. Coordinator.

‡MISSOURI WRITERS' BIENNAL (I, IV), Suite 105, Missouri Arts Council, 111 N. 7th St., St. Louis MO 63101-2188. (314)444-6845. Award to support and promote Missouri writers. Every 2 years competition for short stories and poetry. Award: $5,000 each to 5 writers. Competition receives approx. 400 submissions. Judges: panel of national judges. Guidelines for SASE. Deadline "approx." September 1, 1989. Unpublished submissions. "Writers must have lived in Missouri for at least 2 years immediately preceding submission. Writers *must* request complete written guidelines."

MONTANA ARTS COUNCIL FIRST BOOK AWARD (IV), New York Block, 48 North Last Chance Gulch, Helena MT 59620. (406)443-4338. Director of Artists Services: Julie Cook. Biannual award for publication of a book of poetry or fiction—the best work in Montana. Submissions may be short stories, novellas, story collections or poetry. Award: publication. Competition receives about 35 submissions/year. Judges are professional writers. Entry forms or rules for SASE. Deadline May 1, 1990. Restricted to residents of Montana; not open to degree-seeking students.

MONTANA ARTS COUNCIL INDIVIDUAL ARTIST FELLOWSHIP (IV), New York Block, 48 North Last Chance Gulch, Helena MT 59620. (406)443-4338. Director of Artists Services: Julie Cook. Biannual award of $2,000. Competition receives about 35 submissions/year. 1989 panelists are professional writers. Contest requirements avialable for SASE. Deadline May 1, 1989. Restricted to residents of Montana; not open to degree-seeking students.

MYTHOPOEIC FANTASY AWARD (III), The Mythopoeic Society, Box 6707, Altadena CA 91001. Chair, awards committee: Christine Lowentrout. Annual award for novels. "A statue of a lion is given to the author; magazines and publishers are notified, plus we announce the award in our publications." Judges: members of the Mythopoeic Society who volunteer for the selection committee. Guidelines for SASE. Nominations for 1989 books must be sent in, by Society members, by February, 1990. Fantasy novels only. "Books are nominated by Society members. If an author has published his/her work during the previous year, and is a member of the Society, he/she can nominate his/her own work."

NATIONAL BOOK AWARDS, INC. (III), 155 Bank St., Studio 1002D, New York NY 10014. Annual award to honor distinguished literary achievement in two categories, including fiction. Books published Nov. 1 through Oct. 15 are eligible. Deadline is July 15. Awards judged by panels of critics and writers. November ceremony. Award: $10,000 award to each winner. $1,000 to four runners-up in each category. Selections are submitted by publishers only, or may be called in by judges. A $100 fee is required for entry. Read *Publishers Weekly* for additional information.

‡NATIONAL BOOK COUNCIL/BANJO AWARDS (III, IV), The Book Printer, National Book Council, 1st Floor, 302 Lygon St. Carlton, Victoria 3053 Australia. "For a book of highest literary merit which makes an outstanding contribution to Australian literature." Annual competition for creative writing. Award: 1st prize $10,000; 2nd prize $7,500 for a book in a different category from that winning 1st prize. Competition receives approx. 90-100 submissions. Judges: 3 judges chosen by the National Book Council. Entry fee $20. Guidelines for SASE. Deadline mid-December. Previously published submissions. For works "written by Australian citizens and published in Australia during the qualifying period." Books must be nominated by the publisher.

‡NATIONAL BOOK COUNCIL/QANTAS NEW WRITERS AWARD (III, IV), Qantas Airways Ltd., National Book Council, 1st Floor, 302 Lygon St., Carlton, Victoria 3053 Australia. "To encourage new writers. It is open to writers under 35 or to a writer of any age who has not had a book published previously." Annual competition for creative writing. Award: a plaque and trip to Frankfurt Book Fair. Competition received approx. 16 entries in 1988. Judges: 2 judges chosen by the National Book Council. Entry fee $20. Guidelines for SASE. Deadline mid-December. Previously published submissions. "The books shall have been written by Australian citizens and published in Australia during the qualifying period. Books must be nominated by the publisher."

NATIONAL ENDOWMENT FOR THE ARTS FELLOWSHIP (I), Nancy Hanks Center, 1100 Pennsylvania Ave. N.W., Washington DC 20506. (202)682-5732. Program Specialist, Literature Program: Christine Prickett. "The mission of the NEA is to foster the excellence, diversity and vitality of the arts in the United States, and to help broaden the availability and appreciation of such excellence, diversity and vitality." The purpose of the fellowship is to enable creative writers "to set aside time for writing, research or travel and generally to advance their careers." Annual award: $20,000. 1989 judges: panel of writers. All mss are judged anonymously. Entry forms and guidelines available upon request. Competition open to fiction writers who have published a novel or novella, a collection of stories or at least 5 stories in magazines since 1979. Deadline: March.

NATIONAL FOUNDATION FOR ADVANCEMENT IN THE ARTS, ARTS RECOGNITION AND TALENT SEARCH (ARTS) (I, IV), 3915 Biscayne Blvd., Miami FL 33137. (305)573-0490. President: Dr. Grant Beglarian. "To encourage 17- and 18-year-old writers and put them in touch with institutions which offer scholarships." Annual award for short stories, novels, "fiction, essay, poetry, scriptwriting." Award: $3,000, $1,500 and $500 awards. Judges: nationally selected panel. Entry fee $25 by May 15; $35 until October 1. Guidelines for SASE. 17- and 18-year-old writers only.

NATIONAL JEWISH BOOK AWARDS (II, IV), JWB Jewish Book Council, 15 E. 26th St., New York NY 10010. Contact: Paula Gottlieb, director. Annual award. "To promote greater awareness of Jewish-American literary creativity." Previously published submissions in English only by a US or Canadian author/translator. Award judged by authors/scholars. Award: $750 to the author/translator plus citation to publisher. Over 100 entries received for each award. Contest requirements available for SASE. Awards include National Jewish Book Award—Children's Literature, William (Zev) Frank Memorial Award (for the author of a children's book on a Jewish theme); National Jewish Book Award—Children's Picture Book, Marcia and Louis Posner Award (for the author and illustrator of a children's book on a Jewish theme in which the illustrations are an intrinsic part of the text); National Jewish Book Award—Fiction, William and Janice Epstein Award (for the author of a book of fiction of Jewish interest, either a novel or a collection of short stories); and National Jewish Book Award—Yiddish Literature, The Workmen's Circle Award (for the author of a book of literary merit in the Yiddish language in fiction, poetry, essays and memoirs).

NATIONAL NOVELLA AWARD (I), Arts and Humanities Council of Tulsa, 2210 S. Main St., Tulsa OK 74114. (918)584-3333. Literary Arts Program Coordinator: Elizabeth Thompson. "To provide fiction writers with an opportunity to be awarded for work in a somewhat unrecognized field and to provide a publishing opportunity for a genre that is becoming increasingly important to contemporary literature." Annual award for novellas. Award: $2,500, publiction in quality trade paperback and royalties. Judge: nationally recognized fiction writer. Entry fee $10. Guidelines for SASE. Deadline December 1. Previously unpublished submissions. Word length: 18,000 to 40,000 words.

NATIONAL WRITERS CLUB ANNUAL BOOK CONTEST (I), National Writers Club, 1450 S. Havana, Aurora CO 80012. (303)751-7844. Contact: James L. Young, director. Annual award to encourage and recognize writing by freelancers in the field of the novel. Unpublished submissions. Entry deadline: August 19. Award judged by successful writers. Contest/award rules and entry forms available with SASE. Charges $25 entry fee. Award: $1,000 in prizes; $500 first prize.

NATIONAL WRITERS CLUB ANNUAL SHORT STORY CONTEST (I), National Writers Club, 1450 S. Havana, Aurora CO 80012. (303)751-7844. Contact: James L. Young, director. Annual award. To encourage and recognize writing by freelancers in the short story field. Unpublished submissions. Award judged by professional writers. Write for entry form and rule sheet. Charges $10 entry fee.

‡THE NATIONAL WRITTEN & ILLUSTRATED BY . . . AWARDS CONTEST FOR STUDENTS (I, IV), Landmark Editions, Inc., Box 4469, Kansas City MO 64127. (816)241-4919. Contact: Nan Thatch. "Contest initiated to encourage students to write and illustrate original books and to publish exceptional works by students." Annual competition. "Each student whose book is selected for publication will be offered a complete publishing contract. To insure that students benefit from the proceeds, royalties from the sale of their books will be placed in an individual trust fund, set up for each student by his or her parents or legal guardians, at a bank of their choice. Funds may be withdrawn when a student becomes of age, or withdrawn earlier (either in whole or in part) for educational purposes or in case of proof of specific needs due to unusual hardship. Reports of book sales and royalties will be sent to the student and the parents or guardians annually." Winners also receive an all-expense-paid trip to Kansas City to oversee final reproduction phases of their books. Books by students may be entered in one of three age categories: A—6 to 9 years old; B—10 to 13 years old; C—14 to 19 years old. Each book submitted must be both written and illustrated by the same student. Any books that are written by one student and illustrated by another will be automatically disqualified." Book entries must be submitted by a teacher or librarian. Deadline: May 1 of each year. For a free copy of the rules and guidelines, send a #10 SASE to the above address.

NEBULA AWARDS (III, IV), Science Fiction Writers of America, Box H, Wharton NJ 07885. Contact: Peter D. Pautz, executive secretary. Annual awards for previously published short stories, novels, novellas, novellettes. SF/fantasy only. "No submissions; nominees upon recommendation of members only." Deadline: December 31. "Works are nominated throughout the year by active members of the SFWA."

‡NEGATIVE CAPABILITY SHORT FICTION COMPETITION (I), *Negative Capability*, 62 Ridgelawn Dr. E., Mobile AL 36608. (205)343-6163. Contact: Sue Walker. "To promote and publish excellent fiction and to promote the ideals of human rights and dignity." Annual award for short stories. Award: $1,000 best story award; $1,000 for the story which best exemplifies concern for human rights and dignity. Judge: Leon Driskell in 1988. Judge is a well-known author; changes each year. Entry fee $10, "includes copy of journal publishing the award." Guidelines for SASE. Deadline December 15, 1989. Length: 1,500-4,500 words. "At least one $1,000 award will be offered each year. Award honors an outstanding author each year, and the award is given his or her name."

THE NENE AWARD (II), School Library Services, Department of Education, 641 18th Ave., Honolulu HI 96816. Contact: Shirley Noito, chairperson (chairperson changes annually). Annual award. "To help the children of Hawaii become acquainted with the best contemporary writers of fiction for children; to become aware of the qualities that make a good book; to choose the best rather than the mediocre; and to honor an author whose book has been enjoyed by the children of Hawaii." Award: Koa plaque. Judged by the children of Hawaii. No entry fee.

NEUSTADT INTERNATIONAL PRIZE FOR LITERATURE (III), *World Literature Today*, 110 Monnet Hall, University of Oklahoma, Norman OK 73019. Contact: Dr. Ivar Ivask, director. Biennial award. To recognize distinguished and continuing achievement in fiction, poetry or drama. Awards: $25,000, an eagle feather cast in silver, an award certificate and a special issue of *WLT*. "We are looking for outstanding accomplishment in world literature. The Neustadt Prize is not open to application. Nominations are made only by members of the international jury, which changes for each award. Jury meetings are held in February of even-numbered years. Unsolicited manuscripts, whether published or unpublished, cannot be considered.

NEW HAMPSHIRE STATE COUNCIL ON THE ARTS INDIVIDUAL ARTIST FELLOWSHIP (I, IV), 40 N. Main St., Concord NH 03301-4974. (603)271-2789. Contact: assistant director, Rebecca Lawrence. Fellowship "for career professional to professional artists who are legal/permanent residents of the state of New Hampshire." Annual award: up to $2,000. Competition receives 150 entries for 7 awards in all disciplines. Judges: panels of in-state and out-of-state experts (music, theatre, dance, literature, film, etc.). Guidelines for SASE. Deadline March 24. Submissions may be either previously published or unpublished. Applicants must be over 18 years of age, not enrolled as full-time students, permanent, legal residents of New Hampshire. Application form required.

NEW JERSEY AUTHOR AWARDS (II, IV), NJIT Alumni Association, New Jersey Institute of Technology, 323 King Blvd., Newark NJ 07102. (201)889-7336. Contact: Dr. Herman A. Estrin, professor of English-Emeritus. Annual award. "To recognize New Jersey writers." Previously published submissions. Award: Citation inscribed with the author's name and the title of his work. Author is an invited guest at the author's luncheon, and a photograph of author receiving the citation is sent to the author's hometown newspaper. Entry deadline: February. No entry fee. Entry forms or rules for SASE.

NEW JERSEY STATE COUNCIL ON THE ARTS PROSE FELLOWSHIP (I, IV), 109 W. State St., CN 306, Trenton NJ 08625. (609)292-6130. Annual award for writers of short stories, novels, story collections. Award: maximum is $15,000; other awards are $8,000 and $5,000. Receives approx. 15 applications for each award. Judges: a peer panel. Guidelines for SASE. Deadline January. For either previously published or unpublished submissions. "Previously published work must be submitted as a manuscript." Applicants must be New Jersey residents. Applicants must not be matriculated students in an undergraduate program at the time of application. There is a maximum limit on total number of pages submitted.

NEW LETTERS LITERARY AWARD (I), *New Letters*, UMKC 5216 Rockhill, Kansas City MO 64110. (816)276-1168. Editorial Assistant: Glenda McCrary. Award to "discover and reward good writing." Annual competition for short stories. Award: $500. Competition receives 350 entries/year. Entry Fee $10. Guidelines for SASE. Deadline May 15. Submissions should be unpublished. Length requirement: 5,000 words or less.

‡**NEW YORK FOUNDATION FOR-THE-ARTS FELLOWSHIP (I, IV)**, New York Foundation for the Arts, #600, 5 Beekman St., New York NY 10038. (212)233-3400. Contact: R. Bruce. Annual competition for short stories and novels. Award: $6,000. Competition receives approx. 450 submissions. Judges: fiction writers. Call for guidelines (send SASE). Deadline September 5, 1989. Previously published or unpublished submissions. "Applicants must have lived in New York state at least 2 years immediately prior to application deadline."

‡**NEW YORK EDITH WHARTON CITATION OF MERIT (III,IV)**, NYS Writers Institute, Humanities 355, University at Albany/SUNY, Albany NY 12222. (518)442-5620. Contact: Thomas Smith, associate director. Award "to honor an outstanding writer of fiction, closely associated with New York state." Biannual competition. Award: $10,000 honorarium; title of "State Author." Judges: "distinguished panel which advises the governor and which is convened by the Institute. Nominees must be closely associated with New York State; residency preferable. Nominations of names to advisory panel only."

JOHN NEWBERY AWARD (III), American Library Association (ALA) Awards and Citations Program, Association for Library Service to Children, 50 E. Huron St., Chicago IL 60611. Annual award. Entry restricted to US citizens-residents. Only books for children published during the preceding year are eligible. Award: Medal.

‡**THE NOMA AWARD FOR PUBLISHING IN AFRICA (III, IV)**, Box 56, Oxford OX1 3EL England. Sponsored by Kodansha Ltd. Administered by Hans Zell Associates. Award "to encourage publications of works by African writers and scholars in Africa, instead of abroad as is still too often the case at present." Annual competition for scholarly or academic, books for children, literature and creative writ-

ing, including fiction, drama and poetry. Award: $3,000. Competition receives approx. 100 submissions. Judges: a committee of African scholars and book experts and representatives of the international book community. Chairman: Professor Eldred Jones. Guidelines for SASE. Previously published submissions. Submissions are through publishers only.

‡NORDMANN-FORBUNDET TRANSLATION GRANT (II, IV), Nordmann-Forbundet, Rädhusgt 23B, N-0158 OSL01 Norway. Contact: Dina Tolfsby, information officer. Annual award for translation of Norwegian poetry or fiction, preferably contemporary. Award: maximum NOK 15,000. Competition receives approx. 10 submissions. Judges: a committee of three members. Deadline March 1. Previously published submissions. "The grants awarded to foreign publishing houses that want to publish Norwegian literature in translation." Payment is made at the time of publication.

NORTH CAROLINA ARTS COUNCIL FELLOWSHIP (IV), 221 E. Lane St., Raleigh NC 27611. (919)733-2111. Contact: Don Linder, Literature Coordinator. Competition "to recognize and encourage North Carolina's finest creative writers." Annual award: $5,000. Competition receives approximately 200 submissions. Judges are a panel of professionals from outside the state. Writers must be over 18 years old, not currently enrolled in degree-granting program on undergraduate or graduate level, and must have been a resident of North Carolina for 1 full year prior to applying. Writers may apply in either poetry or fiction.

NORTHWOOD INSTITUTE ALDEN B. DOW CREATIVITY CENTER FELLOWSHIP (I), Midland MI 48640-2398. (517)832-4478. Carol B. Coppage, director. Annual fellowship: 10-week residency, including travel, housing and food, small stipend, and project costs. Competition receives approximately 80-100 submissions each year. Judges: board, staff and evaluators. Write or call for entry forms. Deadline December 31.

THE JULIAN OCEAN LITERATURE AWARD (I), Triple "P" Publications International, Box 1321, Kendall Square, Cambridge MA 02142. (617)437-1856. Contact: Eugene F.P.C. de Mesne, editorial manager. Annual award, named after Julian Ocean, publisher, author, poet, critic, book designer and artist. "To further new talent; to promote art and publishing; to give incentive to artists and writers who would like to compete for an award; to give fiction a broader scope and presentation." Unpublished submissions. Award: $20 prize money and a large certificate, plus recognition via Canadian Writers Ltd., International Writers Journal and the Kiosk Newsletter (winners announced in these publications). Entry deadline: December 31. Entry fee: $1. SASE is a *must* for entry forms; rules sent on request. "No taboos. Only requirement for entry is excellence and professionalism in presentation, development and theme. New writers are encouraged to submit."

THE FLANNERY O'CONNOR AWARD FOR SHORT FICTION (I), The University of Georgia Press, Terrell Hall, Athens GA 30602. (404)542-2830. Contact: award coordinator. Annual award, "to recognize outstanding collections of short fiction. Published and unpublished authors are welcome." Award: $500 and publication by the University of Georgia Press. Deadline: June 1-July 31. "Manuscripts cannot be accepted at any other time." Entry fee: $10. Contest rules for SASE.

FRANK O'CONNOR FICTION AWARD (I), *Descant*, Department of English, Texas Christian University, Fort Worth TX 76129. (817)921-7240. Contact: Betsy Colquitt, editor. Estab. 1979 with *Descant*; earlier awarded through *Quartet*. Annual award. To honor achievement in short fiction. Submissions must be published in the magazine during its current volume. Award: $300 prize. No entry fee. "About 12 to 15 stories are published annually in *Descant*. Winning story is selected from this group."

THE SCOTT O'DELL AWARD FOR HISTORICAL FICTION (II, IV), Scott O'Dell (personal donation), c/o Houghton Mifflin, 2 Park St., Boston MA 02108. (617)725-5000. Contact: Mrs. Zena Sutherland, professor, 1100 E. 57th St., Chicago IL 60637. Annual award. "To encourage the writing of good historical fiction about the New World (Canada, South and Central America, and the United States) for children and young people." For books published during the year preceding the year in which the award is given. To be written in English by a U.S. citizen and published in the U.S. Award: $5,000. Entry deadline: December 31. Entry forms or rules for SASE. Looking for "accuracy in historical details, and all the standard literary criteria for excellence: style, setting, characterization, etc."

OHIO ARTS COUNCIL AID TO INDIVIDUAL ARTISTS FELLOWSHIP (I, IV), 727 E. Main St., Columbus OH 43205-1796. (614)466-2613. Susan Dickson, coordinator. "To recognize and support Ohio's outstanding creative artists." Annual grant/fellowship. Award: cash awards of $5,000 or $10,000. Competition receives approximately 200-300 submissions/year. Judges: panel of experts. Entry guidelines for SASE. Writers must be residents of Ohio and must not be students.

OHIOANA BOOK AWARD (II, IV), Ohioana Library Association, 1105 Ohio Departments Bldg., 65 S. Front St., Columbus OH 43266-0334. Contact: Linda R. Hengst, director. Annual award (only if the judges believe a book of sufficiently high quality has been submitted). To bring recognition to outstanding books by Ohioans or about Ohio. "Books to be submitted on or before publication date, two copies. Each spring a jury considers all books received since the previous jury. Award judged by a jury, selected each year from librarians, book reviewers and other knowledgeable people. No entry forms are needed. We will be glad to answer letters asking specific questions." Award: Certificate and medal. "Books must be by an Ohioan (defined as a person born in Ohio or who has lived there for a total of at least 5 years), or about Ohio or the state's people. The submission must be of high quality."

OKTOBERFEST (I), Druid Press, 2724 Shades Crest Road, Birmingham AL 35216. Editor: Anne George. Competition "to encourage short fiction writers and to publish 10 stories a year." Annual award for short stories. Award: $150 (1st prize); $75 (2nd prize); $50 (3rd prize). The top 10 stories will be published in the Oktoberfest anthology. Competition receives approx. 300 entries/year. Final judging is done by members of the UAB English Department who are also writers. Entry fee $3. Guidelines for SASE. Deadline October 31, 1988. Submissions should be previously unpublished. "Sample copies of our first three anthologies are available at minimum cost so contestants can see what kind of stories we lean toward."

OREGON INDIVIDUAL ARTIST FELLOWSHIP (I,IV), Oregon Arts Commission, 835 Summer Street NE, Salem OR 97301. (503)387-3625. Artist Services Coordinator: Nancy Lindburg. "Award enables professional artists to undertake projects to assist their professional development." Annual competition for short stories, novels, poetry and story collections. Award: $3,000 and $10,000. (Please note: 8 $3,000 awards and 2 $10,000 Master Fellowship Awards are spread over 5 disciplines—literature, music/opera, media arts, dance and theatre awarded in even-numbered years.) Competition receives approx. 50 entries/year. Judges: professional advisors from outside the state. Guidelines and application available for SASE. Deadline September 1. Competition limited to Oregon residents.

***THE OTHER SIDE* SHORT FICTION AWARD (I)**, 1225 Dandridge St., Fredericksburg VA 22401. (703)371-7416. Barbara Moorman, fiction editor. "To recognize excellence in short fiction writing among people who have a commitment to Christian faith and an active concern for peace and justice." Annual award for short stories. Award: $250 plus a year's subscription to *The Other Side*. Winning story is published in *The Other Side*. Competition receives approximately 50 submissions/year. Judges are the magazine's editors. Entry forms for SASE. Deadline May 1, 1989.

PACIFIC NORTHWEST WRITERS CONFERENCE (I), 17345 Sylvester Road SW, Seattle WA 98166-3327. Contact: Executive Secretary. Annual award. "To encourage writers." Unpublished submissions. Entry deadline: early spring. Entry fee: $5 (plus $15 regular, or $5 senior citizen—62 or over, and students' membership dues). Entry forms and rules for 65¢ postage. Looking for adult short fiction; juvenile short story; novel (juvenile and adult); nonfiction book; poetry; articles; playwriting; screenplay/ scriptwriting. Awards in all categories. Grand prize for best manuscript selected from all contests: $400."

JUDITH SIEGEL PEARSON AWARD (I), Wayne State University, Detroit MI 48202. Contact: Chair, English Dept. Competition "to honor writing about women." Annual award. Short stories up to 20 pages considered every third year (poetry and drama/nonfiction in alternate years). Plays and nonfictional prose in 1989. Award: up to $400. Competition receives up to 200 submissions/year. Submissions are internally screened; then a noted writer does final reading. Entry forms for SASE.

WILLIAM PEDEN PRIZE IN FICTION (I), *The Missouri Review*, 107 Tate Hall, University of Missouri, Columbia MO 65211. (314)882-2339. Contact: Speer Morgan, editor. Annual award. "To honor the best short story published in *The Missouri Review* each year." Submissions are to be previously published in the volume year for which the prize is awarded. Award: $1,000 cash. No deadline entry or entry fee. No rules; all fiction published in *MR* is automatically entered.

PEGASUS PRIZE (III), Mobil, 150 E. 42nd St., New York NY 10017. (212)883-3896. Manager, Special Publications: G. Vitiello. To recognize distinguished works from literature not normally translated into English. Award for novels. "Prize is given on a country-by-country basis and does not involve submissions."

PEN/NELSON ALGREN FICTION AWARD, *Pen American Center*, 568 Broadway, New York NY 10012. (212)334-1660. Contact: Christine Friedlander. Annual award for short stories, novels and story collections. Award: $1,000 and one-month residence at Edward Albee Foundation. Competition receives approximately 300 submissions/year. 1989 judges: 3 writers. Deadline November 1.

THE PEN/FAULKNER AWARD (III), c/o The Folger Shakespeare Library, 201 E. Capitol St. SE, Washington DC 20003. Attention: Janice Delaney, PEN/Faulkner executive director. Annual award. "To award the most distinguished book-length work of fiction published by an American writer." Published submissions only. Publishers submit four copies of eligible titles published the current year. Deadline for submissions, December 31. No juvenile. Authors must be American citizens or permanent residents of the U.S. Book award judged by three writers chosen by the Trustees of the Award. Award: $7,500 for winner; $2,500 for nominees.

PENNSYLVANIA COUNCIL ON THE ARTS, FELLOWSHIP PROGRAM (I, IV), 216 Finance Bldg. Harrisburg PA 17120. (717)787-6883. Peter M. Carnahan, Literature Program director. Annual awards to provide fellowships for creative writers. Award: up to $6,000. Competition receives approximately 175 submissions for 12 to 15 awards/year. Six judges: three poetry, three fiction, different each year. Guidelines mailed upon request. Deadline October 1. Applicants must be Pennsylvania residents.

JAMES D. PHELAN AWARD (I,IV), The San Francisco Foundation, 685 Market St., Suite 910, San Francisco CA 94105. Contact: Adrienne Krug, assistant coordinator. Annual award "to author of an unpublished work-in-progress of fiction, (novel or short story), nonfictional prose, poetry or drama." Unpublished submissions. Applicant must have been born in the state of California and be 20-35 years old. Entry deadline: January 15. Rules and entry forms available after November 1 for SASE. Award: $2,000 and a certificate.

PHILOMATHEAN BOOK AWARD (II), Philomathean Society, Box H, College Hall, Philadelphia PA 19104. (215)898-8907. Senior Member: E.A. Bolt. Book award of the world's oldest collegiate literary and debate society. Annual award for novels. Award: monetary award, publication, presentation. Competition receives 130 submissions/year. Judges: Executive Board of Stewards. Guidelines for SASE. Deadline Decemer 31. For first novels by American authors.

PLAYBOY COLLEGE FICTION CONTEST (I), *Playboy* Magazine, 919 North Michigan Ave., Chicago IL 60611. (312)759-8000. Fiction Editor: Alice K. Turner. Award "to foster young writing talent." Annual competition for short stories. Award: $3,000 plus publication in the magazine. Judges: staff. Guidelines available for SASE. Deadline January 1. Submissions should be unpublished. No age limit; college affiliation required. Stories should be 25 pages or fewer. "Manuscripts are not returned. Results of the contest will be sent via SASE."

PLOUGHSHARES DENISE AND MEL COHEN AWARD (I), *Ploughshares*, Box 529, Cambridge MA 02139. (617)926-9875. DeWitt Henry, director. The purpose of competition/award is "to highlight outstanding work in each volume of *Ploughshares*." Annual award for short stories. Award: $300. Judges are coordinating editors. For *Ploughshares* writers from the preceding volume year only.

EDGAR ALLAN POE AWARDS (II), Mystery Writers of America, Inc., 236 West 27th St., New York NY 10001. Annual award. To enhance the prestige of the mystery. For manuscripts published during the calendar year. Entry deadline: December 1. Contact above address for specifics. Award: Ceramic bust of Poe. Awards for best mystery novel, best first novel by an American author, best softcover original novel, best short story, best critical/biographical work, best fact crime, best young adult, best juvenile novel, best screenplay, best television feature and best episode in a series.

KATHERINE ANNE PORTER PRIZE FOR FICTION (I), *Nimrod*, Arts and Humanities Council of Tulsa, 2210 S. Main St., Tulsa OK 74114. (918)584-3333. Editor: Francine Ringold. To award promising young writers and to increase the quality of manuscripts submitted to *Nimrod*. Annual award for short stories. Award: $1,000 first prize; $500 second prize. Receives approx. 650 entries/year. Judge varies each year. Past judges have been Rosellen Brown, Alison Lurie and Gordon Lish, George Garrett. Entry fee: $10. Guidelines for SASE. Deadline for submissions, April 1. Previously unpublished manuscripts. Word length: 7,500 words maximum.

PRAIRIE SCHOONER THE LAWRENCE FOUNDATION AWARD (I), University of Nebraska, Lincoln NE 68588. (402)472-1812. Contact: Hilda Raz, editor. Annually. "The award is given to the author of the best short story published in *Prairie Schooner* during the preceding year." Award $500. "Only short fiction published in *Prairie Schooner* is eligible for consideration."

THE *PRESENT TENSE*/JOEL H. CAVIOR LITERARY AWARD (III, IV), *Present Tense Magazine*, 165 E. 56th St., New York NY 10022. (212)751-4000. Senior Editor: Adam Simms. Award "to encourage the flourishing of Jewish literary and intellectual life by stimulating the writing of serious works with Jewish themes." Annual competition for novels. Award: $500 U.S. savings bond and a framed print.

Competition receives approx. 1,000 entries/year. Judges: independent panel of judges. Deadline November 15, 1989 for books published in 1989. "Books published in 1989 (official publication date) for the awards given in 1990 can *only* be nominated by book publishers, *not* by author.

PRISM INTERNATIONAL SHORT FICTION CONTEST (I), *Prism International*, Dept. of Creative Writing, University of British Columbia, E455-1866 Main Mall, Vancouver, British Columbia V6T 1W5 Canada. (604)228-2514. Contact: Publicity Manager. Annual award for unpublished short stories. Entry fee $12 plus $5 reading fee for each story. SASE for rules/entry forms.

‡LE PRIX MOLSON DE L'ACADÉMIE CANADIENNE-FRANÇAISE (II,IV), Union des écrivains québécois, 1030 rue Cherrier #510, Montréal, Québec H2L 1H9 Canada. (514)526-6653. Prize for a novel in French by a writer from Québec or another province in Canada. Annual award for novels. Award: $5,000 (Canadian). Judges: 7 persons chosen by the Académie canadienne française, the Molson brewery and the Union des écrivains québécois. Guidelines for SASE. Deadline June 10, 1989. Seven copies of the work must be submitted. Write for guidelines and entry forms (in French).

PULITZER PRIZE IN FICTION (III), Columbia University, Graduate School of Journalism, 702 Journalism Bldg., New York NY 10027. Contact: Robert C. Christopher. Annual award for distinguished fiction published in book form during the year by an American author, preferably dealing with American life. Submit 4 copies of the book, entry form, biography and photo of author and $20 handling fee. Open to American authors. Deadline: November 1. Award: $3,000.

PULP PRESS INTERNATIONAL, 3 DAY NOVEL-WRITING COMPETITION (I), Arsenal Pulp Press, 1150 Homer St., Vancouver, British Columbia V6B 2X6 Canada. (604)687-4233. Contact: Brian Lam, manager. Contest to write the best novel in 3 days, held every Labor Day weekend. Annually, for unpublished novels. "Prize is publication." Receives approximately 1,000 entrees for each award. Judged by Arsenal Pulp Press editorial board. Entry forms for SASE/IRC. Deadline: last week before Labor Day. "Entrants must register either with Pulp Press or with one of our sponsor bookstores throughout North America, a list of which is available with SASE. Winner is announced October 31."

PURE BRED DOGS/AMERICAN KENNEL GAZETTE (I), 51 Madison Ave., New York NY 10010. (212)696-8331. Executive Editor: Marion Lane. Annual contest for short stories under 2,000 words. Award: Prizes of $500, $350 and $150 for top three entries. Certificate and complimentary one-year subscription for nine honorable mention winners. Top 3 entries published in magazine. Judge: panel. Contest requirements available for SASE. "The *Gazette* sponsors an annual fiction contest for short short stories on some subject relating to pure-bred dogs. Winning entries are published one per month. Fiction for our magazine needs a slant toward the serious fancier with real insight into the human/dog bond and breed-specific pure-bred behavior."

PUSHCART PRESS EDITORS BOOK AWARD (III), Box 380, Wainscott NY 11975. (516)324-9300. Bill Henderson, president. "Award celebrates an important and unusual book ms that has been overlooked." Award: publication and $1,000. Competition receives approximately 80 submissions/year. Judged by B. Henderson. Entry forms for SASE. Deadline August 15, 1987. For book-length mss of literary distinction that have made the rounds of commercial publishers without acceptance. Mss may arrive from any source (agent, author, etc.), but must be nominated by an editor.

PUSHCART PRIZE (III), Pushcart Press, Box 380, Wainscott NY 11975. Contact: Bill Henderson, editor. Annual award. To publish and recognize the best of small press literary work. Previously published submissions; short stories, poetry or essays on any subject. Must have been published during the current calendar year. Deadline: Oct. 15. Nomination by small press publishers/editors only. Award: Publication in *Pushcart Prize: Best of the Small Presses*.

QUARTERLY WEST NOVELLA COMPETITION (I), University of Utah, 317 Olpin Union, Salt Lake City UT 84112. Biennial award for novellas. Award: 2 prizes of $300 + . Deadline postmarked by December 31. Send SASE for contest rules.

RAGDALE FOUNDATION RESIDENCIES FOR WRITERS AND VISUAL ARTISTS (I), 1260 N. Green Bay Rd., Lake Forest IL 60645. (312)234-1063. Director: Ron Wray. Award "to provide living and work space, as well as uninterrupted time to writers and visual artists for a modest weekly fee ($70/week). Financial assistance is available." The Foundation is open year-round, except for the last two weeks of June and December. Award: includes work and sleeping space, and food for all meals. Residencies for 12 artists and writers for periods of two weeks to two months. Applicants are reviewed by a selection committee composed of professionals in the arts. Guidelines available. Applications should be submitted at least several months in advance, if possible; however there is no application deadline. Submissions may either be previously published or unpublished.

SIR WALTER RALEIGH AWARD (II, IV), North Carolina Literary and Historical Association, 109 E. Jones St., Raleigh NC 27611. (919)733-7305. Secretary-Treasurer: Jeffrey J. Crow. Award "to promote among the people of North Carolina an interest in their own literature." Annual award for novels. Award: statue of Sir Walter Raleigh. Competition receives approx. 10 entries/year. Judges: University English and history professors. Guidelines for SASE. Book must be published between June 30, 1988 and June 30, 1989. Writer must be a legal or physical resident of North Carolina. Authors or publishers may submit 3 copies of their book to the above address. "(1)Must be an original work published during the twelve months ending June 30 of the year for which the award is given. (2)Its author or authors must have maintained either legal or physical residence, or a combination of both in North Carolina for the three years preceding the close of the contest period."

RAMBUNCTIOUS REVIEW, **ANNUAL FICTION CONTEST (I)**, 1221 W. Pratt, Chicago IL 60626. Contact: Nancy Lennon, co-editor. Annually. Short stories. Requirements: Typed, double-spaced, maximum 15 pages. SASE for deadline, rules/entry forms.

REDBOOK SHORT STORY CONTEST (I), *Redbook*, 224 W. 57th St., New York NY 10019. (212)262-5690. Contact: Deborah Purcell, fiction editor. Annual award. "The purpose of this contest is to recognize and reward the mastery of the short story form by writers whose fiction has never appeared in a major publication. There are no restrictions with regard to subject matter." Open to men and women 18 years and over. See March 1989 *Redbook* for complete rules. Award: 1st prize: $2,000, publication in *Redbook* Magazine; 2nd prize: $1,000; 3rd prize: $500. Competition receives 5,000-8,000 entries/year. Deadline: May 31, 1989. No entry fee.

REGINA MEDAL AWARD (III), Catholic Library Association, 461 W. Lancaster Ave., Haverford PA 19041. Contact: John T. Corrigan, executive director. Annual award. To honor a continued distinguished contribution to children's literature. Award: Silver medal. Award given during Easter week. Selection by a special committee; nominees are suggested by the Catholic Library Association Membership.

RHODE ISLAND STATE ARTS COUNCIL (I,IV), Individual Artist's Fellowship in Literature, 95 Cedar St., Suite 103, Providence RI 02903-1034. (401)277-3880. Contact fellowship program director, Edward Holgate. Annual fellowship. Award: $3,000. Competition receives approximately 50 submissions. In-state panel makes recommendations to an out-of-state judge, who makes the final award. Entry forms for SASE. Deadline March 15. Artists must be Rhode Island residents and not undergraduate or graduate students.

HAROLD U. RIBALOW PRIZE, (II, IV) *Hadassah Magazine*, 50 W. 58th St., New York NY 10019. (212)355-7900. Contact: Alan M. Tigay, Executive Editor. Estab. 1983. Annually. "For a book of fiction on a Jewish theme. Harold U. Ribalow was a noted writer and editor who devoted his time to the discovery and encouragement of young Jewish writers." Book should have been published the year preceding the award. Award: $500 and excerpt of book in *Hadassah Magazine*. Deadline: Dec. 31.

THE MARY ROBERTS RINEHART FUND (III), *George Mason University*, 4400 University Dr., Fairfax VA 22030. (703)323-2221. Roger Lathbury, director. Bienniel award for short stories, novels, novellas and story collections by unpublished writers (that is, writers ineligible to apply for NEA grants). Award: Two grants whose amount varies depending upon income the fund generates. 1989 awards will be around $950 each. Competition receives approximately 75-100 submissions annually. Entry forms or rules for SASE. Deadline November 30. Writers must be nominated by a sponsoring writer or editor.

‡ROBERTS WRITING AWARDS (I), H. G. Roberts Foundation, Box 1868, Pittsburg KS 66762. (316)231-2998. Awards Coordinator: Stephen E. Meats. "To reward and recognize exceptional fiction writers with money and publication." Annual competition for short stories. Award: $500 (first place); $200 (second place); $100 (third place); publication for prize winners and honorable mention receipts. Competition receives approx. 300 submissions. Judges: established fiction writer, different each year. Entry fee $5/story. Guidelines for SASE. Deadline: Sept. 1, 1989. Previously unpublished submissions. "Open to any type of fiction, up to 15 typed pages. Open to all persons with U.S. social security number."

ROCKLAND CENTER FOR THE ARTS WRITER-IN-RESIDENCE (II, IV), 5 Old Farm Ct., West Nyack NY 10994. (914)358-0877. Executive Director: Julianne Ramos. "Provides residencies to write and perform community service (e.g. workshops, readings, etc.)." Award: up to $3,750 for 4 month residency. Judges: literary committee. Guidelines for SASE. Deadline December 1. Applicants "must be previously published writers of fiction or poetry. Award does not include additional room and board. Therefore, we prefer applicants from New York, New Jersey and Connecticut in commuting distance."

ROMANCE WRITERS OF AMERICA GOLDEN HEART/GOLDEN MEDALLION AWARDS (I, II, IV), 5206 FM 1960, W#208, Houston TX 77069. (713)440-6885. "To recognize best work in romantic fiction in 7 categories by members of RWA, both published and not-published." Annual award for novels. Golden Heart Award: heart and certificate; Golden Medallion Award: etched placque. Golden Heart award receives 600+ submissions/year; Golden Medallion Award receives 250+ submissions/year. Judges: published writers, editors. Entry fee $15. Guidelines for SASE. Deadline November 30. Previously published submissions for Golden Medallion; unpublished for Golden Heart. Categories are "traditional, short and long sensuous, historical, single title, historical, regency, young adult."

‡SACRAMENTO PUBLIC LIBRARY FOCUS ON WRITERS CONTEST (I, IV), 1010 8th St., Sacramento CA 95814. (916)440-5926. Contact: Lois Jack. Award "to support and encourage aspiring writers." Annual competition for short stories and novels. Awards: $100 (first place); $50 (second place); $25 (third place). Competition receives approx. 147 short story entries; 78 novel chapters; 71 children's stories. Judges: local teachers of English, authors and librarians. Entry fee: $5/entry. Guidelines for SASE. Deadline February 1, 1989. Previously unpublished submissions. Length: 2,500-word short story; 1,000-word story for children. Open to all writers in northern California. Send for guidelines.

CARL SANDBURG AWARDS (I, IV), Friends of the Chicago Public Library, 78 E. Washington, Chicago IL 60602. (312)269-2922. Annually. To honor excellence in Chicago area authors (including 6 counties). For books published during the period of July 1 of preceding year and June 30 of current year. Cash honorarium for fiction, nonfiction, poetry and children's literature. Trophy awarded also. Deadline: September 1. Rules for SASE.

SCHOLASTIC WRITING AWARDS (I, IV), Scholastic Inc., 730 Broadway, New York NY 10003. (212)505-3440. Contact: Director of Awards Program, Margaret O'Keeffe. To provide opportunity for recognition of young writers. Annual award for short stories. Award: Cash awards, scholarships and grants. Competition receives 22,000 submissions/year. Judges vary each year. Deadline January 21. Previously unpublished submissions. Contest limited to junior high and senior high school students; grades 7-12. Entry blank must be signed by teacher. "Program is run through school and is only open to students in grades 7 through 12, regularly and currently enrolled in public and non-public schools in the United States and its territories, U.S.-sponsored schools abroad or any schools in Canada"

SCIENCE FICTION WRITERS OF EARTH (SFWoE) SHORT STORY CONTEST (IV), Science Fiction Writers of Earth, Box 121293 Fort Worth TX 76121. (817)451-8674. SFWoE Administrator: Gilbert Gordon Reis. Purpose "to promote the art of science fiction/fantasy short story writing." Annual award for short stories. Award: $100 (1st prize); $50 (2nd prize); $25 (3rd prize). Competition receives approximately 75 submissions/year. Judge: author Edward Bryant. Entry fee: $5 for 1st entry; $2 for additional entries. Guidelines for SASE. Deadline October 30. Submissions must be unpublished. Stories should be science fiction or fantasy, 2,000-7,500 words. "Although many of our past winners are now published authors, there is still room for improvement. The odds are good for a well-written story."

THE SEATON AWARDS (I,IV), *Kansas Quarterly*, 122 Denison Hall, Kansas State University, KS 66506. Annual awards. To reward and recognize the best fiction published in *KQ* during the year from authors native to or resident in Kansas. Submissions must be unpublished. Anyone who submits unpublished material which is then accepted for publication becomes eligible for the awards. No deadline. Material simply may be submitted for consideration at any time with SASE. Award: Recognition and monetary sums of $250, $200, $150, $100 and $50. "Ours are not contests. We give monetary awards and recognition to Kansas writers of national literary stature."

THE SEATTLE WEEKLY ANNUAL HOLIDAY SHORT STORY CONTEST (I,IV), 1931 Second Ave., Seattle WA 98101. (206)441-6239. Senior Editor: Rose Pike. Annual award to "find a short story, preferably set in the Northwest, for publication in our issue closest to Christmas." Award: $500 for first rights publication in *The Weekly*. Competition receives approx 50 entries. Judges: Editorial staff of the magazine. Guidelines for SASE. Deadline November 1. Submissions should be unpublished. Writers must reside in Washington. "Only those manuscripts with SASE or return postage will be returned. All writers will be notified by letter of the editors' decision."

WILLOUGHBY F. SENIOR MEMORIAL AWARD FOR DESERVING WRITERS (I), *Wyoming, the Hub of the Wheel . . . A Journal for Universal Spokesmen*, Box 9, Saratoga WY 82331. (307)326-5214. Lenore A. Senior, managing editor. To provide urgent financial assistance, without which the writer would be unable to continue to survive and create. Annual award for short stories, novellas, story collections. Award: $50, plus publication and two free copies of magazine in which work appears. Receives up to 100 entries for each award. Judges are editors. Deadline August 1. "Send 39¢ SASE for information about this award, plus other contests each year."

***SEVENTEEN* MAGAZINE/ SMITH CORONA FICTION CONTEST(I,IV)**, *Seventeen Magazine*, 850 3rd Ave., New York NY 10022. Contact: Sara London. To honor best short fiction by a young writer. Rules are found in the October issue. Contest for 13-20 year olds. Deadline: January 31. Submissions judged by a panel of *Seventeen*'s editors. Award: $2,000 plus a Smith Corona word processor (first prize); Smith Corona word processor (second prize); Smith Corona electronic typewriter with word processing capabilities (third prize); Smith Corona electronic typewriters for the ten honorable mention awards.

‡THE SIERRA CLUB AWARD FOR DISTINGUISHED NATURE WRITING, Sierra Club, 730 Polk St., San Francisco CA 94109. (415)776-2211. Contact: James Cohee. Award "to further the American tradition of nature writing and promote environmental consciousness. Award granted occasionally; (this is not an annual award) for fiction and nonfiction that explores the natural environment in human affairs. Award: $20,000 advance, guaranteed. Competition received approx. 100 submissions in the first year. Judges: a panel appointed by Sierra Club Books; first year: Wallace Stegner and Paul Brooks. SASE for guidelines. No deadline. Unpublished submissions. "Book-length ms, any region; works of literature—we do not consider pictorial books for the award."

CHARLIE MAY SIMON BOOK AWARD (III, IV), Arkansas Department of Education, Elementary School Council, State Education Building, Capitol Mall, Division of Instruction, Room 301B, Little Rock AR 72201. (501)682-4361. Contact: Larry Robertson, coordinator of elementary education. Annual award. "To encourage reading by children in quality children's literature." Previously published submissions. Award: Medallion. No entry fee. "The committee doesn't accept requests from authors. They will look at booklists of books produced during the previous year and check recommendations from the following sources: *Booklist, Bulletin of the Center for Children's Books, Children's Catalog, Elementary School Library Collection, Hornbook, Library of Congress Children's Books, School Library Journal*."

‡KAY SNOW CONTEST (I, IV), Willamette Writers, Box 2485, Portland OR 97208. (503)233-1877. Contact: Judith Renton. Award "to create a local showcase for writers of all fields of literature." Annual competition for short stories; also poetry, nonfiction, juvenile, script and student writers. Award: 1st prize $100 in each category except poetry $75; student $50. Competition receives approx. 300-500 submissions. Judges: local writers and teachers. Entry fee $10-nonmembers; $7-members. Deadline June 30. Previously unpublished submissions. Contest covers Oregon, Washington and Idaho. Maximum 1,500 words. "This contest is held in association with our annual conference. Prizes are awarded at the banquet held during the conference in early August."

‡SOCIETY OF CHILDREN'S BOOK WRITERS GOLDEN KITE AWARDS (II), Society of Children's Book Writers, Box 296, Mar Vista Station, Los Angeles CA 90066. Contact: Sue Alexander, chairperson. Annual award. "To recognize outstanding works of fiction, nonfiction and picture illustration for children by members of the Society of Children's Book Writers and published in the award year." Published submissions should be submitted from January to December of publication year. Deadline entry: December 15. Rules for SASE. Award: Statuette and plaque. Looking for quality material for children. Individual "must be member of the SCBW to submit books."

SOCIETY OF CHILDREN'S BOOK WRITERS WORK-IN-PROGRESS AWARDS (I,IV), Box 296, Mar Vista, Los Angeles Ca 90066. (818)347-2849. Contact: SCBW. Award to "aid childrens book writer complete a project." Annual competition for novels. Award: 1st-$1,000; 2nd-$500 (work-in-progress). 1st-$1,000; 2nd-$500 (Judy Blume/SCBW contemporary novel grant). Competition receives approx. 30 submissions. Judges: members of children book field—editors, authors, etc. Guidelines for SASE. Unpublished submissions. Applicants must be *SCBW* members.

***SONORA REVIEW* FICTION CONTEST (I)**, Dept. of English, University of Arizona, Tucson AZ 85721. (602)621-1836. Contact: fiction editor. Annual award. "To encourage and support quality short fiction." Unpublished submissions. Award: $100 first prize, plus publication in *Sonora*; $50 second prize, plus publication in *Sonora*. "We accept manuscripts all year, but manuscripts received during the summer (May-August) will not be read until fall." Contest rules for SASE.

SOUTH CAROLINA ARTS COMMISSION AND *THE STATE NEWSPAPER* **SOUTH CAROLINA FICTION PROJECT (I,IV)**, 1800 Gervais St., Columbia SC 29201. (803)734-8696. Steve Lewis, director, Literary Arts Program. The purpose of the award is "to get money to fiction writers and to get their work published and read." Annual award for short stories. Award: $500 cash and publication in *The State Newspaper*. Competition receives approximately 400 submissions for 12 awards (up to 12 stories chosen). Judges are a panel of professional writers and senior writer for *The State Newspaper*. Entry forms or rules for SASE. Deadline November 19. South Carolina residents only.

SOUTH CAROLINA ARTS COMMISSION LITERATURE FELLOWSHIP AND LITERATURE GRANTS (I, IV), 1800 Gervais St., Columbia SC 29201. (803)734-8696. Steve Lewis, director, Literary Arts Program. "The purpose of the fellowships is to give a cash award to two deserving writers (one in poetry, one in creative prose) whose works are of the highest caliber." Award: $5,000 fellowship. Matching grants up to $7,500. Competition receives approximately 40 submissions per fellowship. Judges are out-of-state panel of professional writers and editors for fellowships, and in-state panels and SCAC staff for grants. Entry forms or rules for SASE. Deadline September 15. South Carolina residents only.

‡SOUTH DAKOTA ARTS COUNCIL, ARTIST FELLOWSHIP (IV), 108 West 11th, Sioux Falls SD 57102. (605)339-6646. Award "to assist artists with career development. Grant can be used for supplies or to set aside time to work, but cannot be used for academic research or formal study toward a degree." Annual competition for writers. Award: $1,000 for emerging artists; $5,000 for established artists. Competition receives approx. 80 submissions. Judges: panels of in-state and out-of-state experts in each discipline. Guidelines for SASE. Deadline February 1, 1989. Previously published or unpublished submissions. Fellowships are open only to residents of South Dakota. "Writers with specific projects may apply for a Project Grant. They would not be eligible for fellowship grants in that case. Deadline is Feb. 1, 1989 and guidelines are available by writing SDAC."

‡SOUTHERN ARTS LITERATURE PRIZE (IV), 19 Southgate St., Winchester, Hampshire S023 9DQ England. Award "to recognize good works by authors (known or unknown) in the southern region (of the U.K.)." Annual competition for short stories, novels and poetry. Award £1,000. Competition receives approx. 20-30 submissions. Judges: 3 people (involved in literature or authors themselves), different each year. Guidelines for SASE. Southern arts region covers Hampshire, Berkshire, Wiltshire, Oxfordshire, West Sussex, Isle of Wight and East Dorset. 1989 award will be for nonfiction; 1990 for fiction.

SOUTHERN REVIEW/**LOUISIANA STATE UNIVERSITY ANNUAL SHORT FICTION AWARD (II)**, *Southern Review*, 43 Allen Hall, Louisiana State University, Baton Rouge LA 70803. (504)388-5108. Contact: Editors, *Southern Review*. Annual award. "To encourage publication of good fiction." For a first collection of short stories by an American writer appearing during calendar year. Award: $500 to author. Possible campus reading. Deadline a month after close of each calendar year. The book of short stories must be released by a U.S. publisher. Two copies to be submitted by publisher or author. Looking for "style, sense of craft, plot, in-depth characters."

SPUR AWARD CONTEST (II, IV), Western Writers of America, Fairgrounds 1753 Victoria, Sheridan WY 82801. Contact: Barb Ketcham, secretary-treasurer. Annual award. To encourage excellence in western writing. Entries are accepted only from the current calendar year for each year's award; that is, books can only be entered in the year they are published. Entry deadline: December 31. Award judged by a panel of experienced authors appointed by the current Spur Awards Chairman. Contest/award rules and entry forms available with SASE. Award: A wooden plaque shaped like a W with a bronze spur attached. "A special Medicine Pipe Bearer Award, is offered in the Best First Western Novel competition. First novels may be entered in both Spur and Medicine Pipe Bearer competition. Books must be of the traditional or historical western theme, set anywhere west of the Mississippi River before the 20th century, ideally from 1850 to 1900." A spur is awarded for Best Historical Fiction, Best Juvenile Fiction and Best Short Fiction works.

STAND MAGAZINE **SHORT STORY COMPETITION (I)**, *Stand Magazine*, 19 Haldane Terrace, Newcastle upon Tyne NE2 3AN England. Biennial award for short stories. Award: 1st prize $1,500; 2nd prize $750; 3rd prize $375; 4th prize $225; 5th prize $150. 1989 judges are Beryl Bainbridge, Malcolm Ross-MacDonald. Entry fee $5. Deadline: March 31, 1989. "For contest requirements *only*, send SASE to *Stand*, Jack Kingsbury, Stand US, Box 1161, Florence AL 35631-1161. All submissions must be sent directly to England at address above."

WALLACE E. STEGNER FELLOWSHIP (I, IV), Creative Writing Program, Stanford University, Stanford CA 94305-2087. (415)723-2637. Contact: Gay Pierce, program coordinator. Annually. 14 fellowships for unpublished or previously published fiction writers. Author must relocate to study at Stanford. Deadline: January 1. Entry fee $20.

STORY TIME **SHORT-STORY CONTEST (I)**, Hutton Publications, Box 1870, Hyden, Idaho 83835, (208) 772-6184. Contact: Linda Hutton, editor. Estab. 1982. Annual award. "To encourage short-story writers." For previously published submissions. Award: $15 first prize; $10 second prize; $7.50 third prize. Entry deadlines: March 1, June 1, August 1, December 1. Looking for "tightly written plot and well developed characters."

SUNTORY AWARDS FOR MYSTERY FICTION (I), c/o Dentsu Incorporated, 1-11 Tsukiji Chuo-Ku, Tokyo 104 Japan. Address work to Steering Committee. Contest for unpublished mystery, suspense, detective or espionage novels, 60,00-120,000 words. Grand prize: 5 million yen (approximately $25,000); Reader's Choice prize: 1 million yen (approximately $5,000). Judges are four Japanese writers and an American columnist. Entry forms or rules for SASE. No U.S. alcoholic beverage retailers or employees may submit work. Writers should include brief personal history along with manuscript. Manuscripts will not be returned.

TALES OF THE OLD WEST **"WESTERNER AWARDS," (I, IV)**, Bane K. Wilker's *Tales of the Old West*, Box 22866, Denver CO 80222. (302)722-9966. Publisher-Editor, Keith Olsen. Award to promote Western writing. Annual contest for previously published or unpublished stories and poetry. Award: $50, inscribed plaque and publication in *TOTOW*. Judged by magazine staff. Entry fee $5 (free to magazine subscribers, subscription costs $10). Entry forms or rules for SASE. Deadline December 1. "It is our hope that *TOTOW* 'Westerner Awards' stimulate an interest in fiction about the Old West. We know there are many good writers out there writing about the American frontier. We would like to help them."

TENNESSEE ARTS COMMISSION INDIVIDUAL ARTISTS FELLOWSHIP (I,IV), 320 6th Ave. N. Sta. 100, Nashville TN 37219. (615)741-1701. Contact: Alice Swanson, director of literary arts. Competition "recognizes outstanding writers in the state." Annual award for fiction in 1989-90; poetry in 1990-91. Award: up to $5,000 ($2,500 minimum). Competition receives approximately 40 submissions. Judges are 3 out-of-state jurors. Entry forms available. Writers must be residents of Tennessee.

THURBER HOUSE RESIDENCIES (II), The Thurber House, 77 Jefferson Ave., Columbus OH 43215. (614)464-1032. Literary Director: Michael J. Rosen. "Four writers/year are chosen as writers-in-residence, one for each quarter." Award for writers of novels and story collections. $5,000 stipend and housing for a quarter in the furnished third-floor apartment of James Thurber's boyhood home. Judges: advisory panel. Guidelines for SASE. Deadline: January 15, 1989. "The James Thurber Writer-in Residence will teach a class in the Creative Writing Program at The Ohio State University in either fiction or poetry, and will offer one public reading and a short workshop for writers in the community. Significant time outside of teaching is reserved for the writer's own work in progress. Candidates should have published at least one book with a major publisher, in any area of fiction, non-fiction or poetry, and should possess some experience in teaching."

TOWSON STATE UNIVERSITY PRIZE FOR LITERATURE (I, IV), Towson State University Foundation, Towson State University, Towson MD 21204. (301)321-2128. Contact: Annette Chappell, dean, College of Liberal Arts. Annually. Novels or short story collections, previously published. Requirements: writer must not be over 40; must be a Maryland resident. Deadline: May 1. SASE for rules/entry forms.

JOHN TRAIN HUMOR PRIZE (I), *The Paris Review*, 541 E. 72nd St., New York NY 10021. Fiction Editor: George Plimpton. Award for the best previously unpublished work of humorous fiction, nonfiction or poetry. Annual competition for short stories. Award: $1,500 and publication in *The Paris Review*. Guidelines for SASE. Deadline March 31. Submissions should be unpublished. Manuscripts must be less than 10,000 words. No formal application form is required; regular submissions guidelines apply.

TRANSLATION CENTER AWARDS (I, IV), The Translation Center, 307A Mathematics Bldg., Columbia University, New York NY 10027. Contact: Award Secretary. Annual awards. "For outstanding translation of a substantial part of a booklength *literary* work." Award: $1,000-$2,000. Entry deadline: January 15. No entry fee. Write for application form.

‡TRANSLATORS ASSOCIATION AWARDS (III, IV), 84 Drayton Gardens, London SW10 9SB England. Scott Moncrieff Prize for best translation into English of 20th century French work; Schlegel Tieck Prize for translations from German; John Florio Prize for translations from Italian into English. Annual competition for translations. Award: Scott Moncrieff Prize: £1,500; Schlegel-Tieck Prize: £2,000; John Florio Prize: £650. Judges: 3 translators. Deadline December 31, 1989. Previously published submissions. Awards for translations published in U.K. during year of award. U.K. publishers submit books for consideration.

‡UCROSS FOUNDATION/RESIDENCY (I), Residency Program/Ucross Foundation, 2836 U.S. Highway 14-16 East, Clearmont WY 82835. (307)737-2291. Award "to allow artists uninterrupted time to work in their field creatively." Biannual competition for short stories, novels, story collections and translations. Award: time to spend at Ucross to accomplish their works and ideas. Competition receives approx. 50 submissions. Judges: three-member selection committee. Guidelines for SASE. Deadline March 1, 1989. Previously published or unpublished submissions.

‡UNIVERSITY OF EAST ANGLIA WRITING FELLOWSHIP (II), University of East Anglia, Norwich, Norfolk NR4 7TJ UK. Contact: Mrs. B. Watson, assistant registrar. Award "to recognize a writer of established reputation." Annual competition for work from any genre. Award: a fee of £2,500 plus free accommodation and office. Competition receives approx. 30 submissions. Guidelines for SASE. Deadline November 3, 1989 for fellowship in summer term 1990. Previously published submissions. "Candidates are invited to submit a copy of at least one of their works. The fellowship is tenable for period of 14 weeks, made up of the summer term (10 weeks) and 4 weeks of vacation. It provides an opportunity for purusing one's own work. It also involves teaching an undergraduate creative writing course, informal consultations with student writers and making a contribution to the artistic activity of the region. The fellow is expected to reside in the university for the period stated."

UNIVERSITY OF MISSOURI BREAKTHROUGH SERIES (I), 200 Lewis Hall, Columbia MO 65211. Contact: Susan McGregor Denny, associate director or Janice Smiley, administrative assistant. Biennial competition for authors whose work has not appeared in book form or who are publishing in another media other than the original book publication. Entry fee is $10. Fiction and poetry mss are read only in odd-numbered years. Receives approximately 500 entrants for each award. Competition judged by professional writer or critic. Award: Publication in series. SASE for guidelines.

UTAH ORIGINAL WRITING COMPETITION (I,IV), Utah Arts Council. 617 East South Temple, Salt Lake City UT 84012. (801—)533-5895. Literary Arts Coordinator: G. Barnes. "An annual writing competition, now entering its 31st year." Annual competition for short stories, novels and story collections. Award: varies; last year between $200-$1,000. Competition receives 700 entries. Judges: "published and award-winning judges from across America." Guidelines available, no SASE necessary. Deadline mid-February, 1989. Submissions should be unpublished. *Limited to Utah·residents.* "Some limitation on word-length. See guidelines for details."

‡VICTORIAN FELLOWSHIP OF AUSTRALIAN WRITERS ANNUAL NATIONAL LITERARY AWARDS (I, II, IV), 1/317 Barkers Rd., Kew (Melbourne) Victoria 3101 Australia. Contact: J.S. Hamilton, president, Victorian FAW. Sponsors 20 awards for Australian writers, both published and unpublished. Annual competition for shorts stories, novels and story collections. Award varies: largest award is $1,000. Competition receives over 50 entries for books, at least 100 for manuscripts. Judges: writers and critics appointed by the organizer. Entry fee. Guidelines for SASE. Deadline: Dec. 31, 1989. Published or previously unpublished submissions. Awards offered to Australians (including those living overseas) or residents of Australia. Send for guidelines.

JAMES F. VICTORIN MEMORIAL AWARD (I,IV), Dialogue Publications, Inc., 3100 Oak Park Ave., Berwyn IL 60402. (312)749-1908. Contact: Bonnie Miller, editor. Annual award. "To recognize the best short story published in *Dialogue* during the previous year." Award: $100. No entry fee. Publication of any story constitutes entry. Only blind or visually handicapped entrants are eligible.

VIRGINIA CENTER FOR THE CREATIVE ARTS RESIDENCY FELLOWSHIP (I), Mt. San Angelo, Sweet Briar VA 24595. (804)946-7236. Director: William Smart. Award to "provide residencies to

✝ *The double dagger before a listing indicates that the listing is new in this edition. New markets are often the most receptive to freelance contributions.*

writers in order that they may work without interruption on their own projects. Approximately 250 fellowships awarded annually. Periodic deadlines. Award: 1 to 3 month residencies. Receives 1,000 applications/year. Judges: poets, playwrights, and fiction writers. Application fee $15. Write for application form.

THE VIRGINIA PRIZE FOR FICTION (I,IV), Virginia Commission for the Arts, 101 N. 14th St., 17th Floor, Richmond VA 23219. (804)225-3132. "The Commission has established these awards to support and encourage the work of Virginia's professional writers, and in recognition of exceptional talent. The prizes are intended to assist writers in the creation of new works, and to support writers' efforts to advance their careers. Annual competition for novels and story collections (150-page minimum submission). Award: 1st: $10,000; 2nd: $5,000; 3rd: $2,500. Competition receives approx. 115 submissions. Judges: a different out-of-state judge each year. Guidelines for SASE. Deadline February 1, 1989. Unpublished submissions (short stories may have been published individually, but the collection unpublished). Award available to writers who have resided in Virginia since January 1987. Program administered by Virginia Center for the Creative Arts, Sweet Briar, VA. Funded by Va. Commission for the Arts, a state agency.

HAROLD D. VURSELL MEMORIAL AWARD (III), American Academy and Institute of Arts and Letters, 633 W. 155th St., New York NY 10032. (212)368-5900. Annual award. "To single out recent writing in book form that merits recognition for the quality of its prose style. It may be given for a work of fiction, biography, history, criticism, belles lettres, memoir, journal or a work of translation." Award: $5,000. Judged by 7-member jury composed of members of the Department of Literature of the American Academy and Institute of Arts and Letters. *No applications accepted.*

EDWARD LEWIS WALLANT MEMORIAL BOOK AWARD (II, IV), 3 Brighton Rd., West Hartford CT 06117. Sponsored by Dr. and Mrs. Irving Waltman. Contact: Mrs. Irving Waltman. Annual award. Memorial to Edward Lewis Wallant, which offers incentive and encouragement to beginning writers, for books published the year before the award is conferred in the spring. Books may be submitted for consideration to Dr. Lothar Kahn, one of the permanent judges. Address: 41 Dayl Drive, Kensington CT 06037. Award: $250 plus award certificate. "Looking for creative work of fiction by an American which has significance for the American Jew. The novel (or collection of short stories) should preferably bear a kinship to the writing of Wallant. The award will seek out the writer who has not yet achieved literary prominence."

WASHINGTON STATE ARTS COMMISSION ARTIST FELLOWSHIP AWARD (I,IV), 110 9th and Columbia, Olympia WA 97504-4111, (206)753-3860. Arts Program Manager: Karen Gose. "Unrestricted award to a mid-career artist." Biannual award for writers of short stories, novels and literary criticism. Award: $5,000. Competition receives 50 entries. Judges: peer panel. Guidelines upon request. Deadline Spring/Summer of 1990—to be determined. Literary arts award made in even-numbered years. Submissions can be either previously published or unpublished. "Applicant must be 5 years out of school in field they're applying to. No emerging artists."

WEST VIRGINIA DEPARTMENT OF CULTURE AND HISTORY, ARTS AND HUMANITIES DIVISION, ARTIST-IN-RESIDENCE PROGRAM (I), The Cultural Center, Capitol Complex, Charleston WV 25305. (304)348-0240. Director: James Andrews. Awards to "assist with artist-in-residence programs in West Virginia." Three deadlines per year. Award: financial support for residencies. Judges: West Virginia Commission on the Arts. Write or call for guidelines. Deadlines February 1, April 1, and August 1 of each year. In-state and out-of-state writers are eligible.

WESTERN HERITAGE AWARDS (II, IV), National Cowboy Hall of Fame, 1700 NE 63rd St., Oklahoma City OK 73111. (405)478-2250. Contact: Marcia Preston, public relations director. Annual award. "To honor outstanding quality in fiction, nonfiction and art literature." Submissions are to have been published during the previous calendar year. Award: The Wrangler, a replica of a C.M. Russell Bronze. Entry deadline: January 1. No entry fee. Entry forms and rules available November 1 for SASE. Looking for "stories that best capture the spirit of the West."

WESTERN STATES BOOK AWARDS, Western States Arts Federation, 207 Shelby St., Santa Fe NM 87501. (505)988-1166. Contact: Gina Briefs-Elgin, Program Assistance. Estab. 1984. Biannual award. "Recognition for writers living in the West; encouragement of effective production and marketing of quality books published in the West; increase of sales and critical attention." For unpublished manuscripts submitted by publisher. Award: $2,500 for authors; $5,000 for publishers. Write for information on deadline. Contest rules for SASE.

WHITING WRITER'S AWARDS (III), Mrs. Giles Whiting Foundation, Rm 3500, 30 Rockefeller Pl., New York NY 10112. Director: Dr. Gerald Freund. To encourage the work of emergent writers and to recognize the work of older, proven writers. Annual award for writers of fiction, poetry, nonfiction and plays. Award: $25,000 (10 awards). Writers are submitted by appointed nominators and chosen for awards by an appointed selection committee. Direct applications and informal nominations nominations not accepted by the foundation.

LAURA INGALLS WILDER AWARD (III), American Library Association/Association for Library Service to Children, 50 E. Huron St., Chicago IL 60611. Award offered every 3 years; next year 1989. "To honor a significant body of work for children, for illustration, fiction or nonfiction." Award: bronze medal.

LAURENCE L. WINSHIP BOOK AWARD (III, IV), *The Boston Globe*, Boston MA 02107. (617)929-2649. Contact: Marianne Callahan, public affairs department. Annual award. "To honor *The Globe's* late editor who did much to encourage young talented New England authors." Previously published submissions from July 1 to July 1 each year. To be submitted by publishers. Award: $2,000. Deadline: June 30. Contest rules for SASE. Book must have some relation to New England—author, theme, plot or locale.

WISCONSIN ARTS BOARD LITERARY FELLOWSHIP (II,IV), 131 W. Wilson St., Suite 301, Madison WI 53702. (608)266-0190. Deputy Director:Paula McCarthy-Panczenko. Annual award for short stories, poetry, novels, novellas. Award: 3 awards of $5,000. Competition receives approximately 75 submissions. Judges are 3 out-of-state jurors. Entry forms or rules for SASE. Deadline September 15, 1989. Wisconsin residents only.

WORDS AT WORK WRITING CONTEST (I), Box 235, Sedona AZ 86336. Fiction and non-fiction (2,000 word limit) and poetry, unpublished. Open to everyone. Deadline: April 30, 1989. Winner announced June 15, 1989. Entry Fee $10. Prizes: $50 first place; $25-second; $15-third, with additional endowment awards for best of category. SASE for rules.

WORLD'S BEST SHORT SHORT STORY CONTEST (I), English Department Writing Program, Florida State University, Tallahassee FL 32306. (904)644-4230. Contact: Jerome Stern, director. Annual award for short-short stories, unpublished, under 250 words. Prize-winning story gets $100 and broadside publication; winner and finalists are published in *Sun Dog: The Southeast Review*. Open to all. Deadline: February 15. SASE for rules.

‡WRITERS AT WORK FELLOWSHIP COMPETITION (I), Writers At Work, Box 8857, Salt Lake City UT 84108. (801)355-0264. Contact: Steve Wanderli, director. "To award new talent—and in addition to the prizes listed below, winners are invited to attend the Writers at Work Conference (June 12-18) free of charge. Award: first: $500 and publication in *Quarterly West*; second: $200. Competition receives approx. 600 submissions. Judges: preliminary judges *Quarterly West* staff; final judges Francois Camoin, W. D. Wetherell and Peggy Schumaker. Entry fee $6. Guidelines for SASE. Unpublished submissions.

WRITER'S DIGEST ANNUAL WRITING COMPETITION (Short Story Division) (I,II), *Writer's Digest*, 1507 Dana Ave., Cincinnati OH 45207. (513)531-2222. Entry deadline: May 31. All entries must be original, unpublished and not previously submitted to a *Writer's Digest* contest. Length: 2,000 words maximum, one entry only. No acknowledgment will be made of receipt of mss nor will mss be returned. Grand Prize is a trip to New York City with arrangements to meet editors in writer's field. Other awards include electronic typewriters, reference books, plaques and certificates of recognition. Names of grand prize winner and top 100 winners are announced in the October issue of *Writer's Digest*. Top two entries published in booklet ($4.50). Send SASE to *WD* Writing Competition for rules or see January-May issues of *Writer's Digest*.

WRITERS' JOURNAL ANNUAL FICTION CONTEST (I), Box 9148, N. St. Paul MN 55109. (612)433-3626. Valerie Hockert, publisher/managing editor. Annual award for short stories. Award: 1st place: $200; 2nd place: $75; 3rd place: $25. Also give honorable mention awards. Competition receives approximately 100 submissions/year. Judges are Valerie Hockert, Marilyn Bailey, Betty Ulrich and others. Entry fee $5 each. Maximum of 2 entries/person. Entry forms or rules for SASE. Maximum length is 3,000 words. Two copies of each entry are required—one *without* name or address of writer.

‡WYOMING COUNCIL ON THE ARTS NELTJE BLANCHAN MEMORIAL AWARD (I, IV), 2320 Capitol Ave., Cheyenne WY 82002. (307)777-7742. Contact: Jean Hanson, literature consultant. To "honor best new writing inspired by nature. This does not mean the work need be traditional nature writing. Rather, the view presented should arise from a relationship with the natural world." Annual award, no genre restrictions. Award: $1,000 grant. Competition receives 30-40 entries. Judge: A well-known writer whose work is informed by nature (changes each year). Guidelines for SASE. Contact for 1989 deadline. Maximum length for fiction, nonfiction and drama 40 pages; poetry 14 pages. "Writers must have been Wyoming residents for one year prior to entry deadline; must not be a full-time student."

‡WYOMING COUNCIL ON THE ARTS FRANK NELSON DOUBLEDAY MEMORIAL AWARD (I,IV), 2320 Capitol Ave., Cheyenne WY 82002. (307)777-7742. Contact: Jean Hanson, literature consultant. To "honor the most promising work by a woman writer." Annual award; no genre restrictions. Award: $1,000 grant. Competition receives 30-40 entries. Judge: A well-known female author (changes each year). Guidelines for SASE. Contact for 1989 deadline. Maximum length for fiction, nonfiction and drama 40 pages; poetry 15 pages. "Writers must have been Wyoming residents for one year prior to entry deadline; must be a woman writer; must not be a full-time student."

‡WYOMING COUNCIL ON THE ARTS, LITERARY FELLOWSHIPS; (I, IV), Wyoming Council on the Arts, 2320 Capitol Ave., Cheyenne WY 82002. (307)777-7742. Contact: David Romtvedt. Award to "honor the most outstanding new work of Wyoming writers—fiction, nonfiction, drama, poetry." Annual competition for short stories, novels, awards, story collections, translations, poetry. Award: 4 awards of $2,500 each. Competition receives approx. 100 submissions. Judges: panel of writers selected each year from outside Wyoming. Deadline: Fall. Applicants "must be Wyoming resident for one year prior to application deadline. No genre exclusions. 40 pages doublespace maximum; 15 pages maximum for poetry. Guidelines for SASE. Winners may not apply for 4 years after receiving fellowships."

YADDO RESIDENCIES (I), Box 395, Saratoga Springs NY 12866-0395. President: Myra Sklarew. To provide undisturbed working time for writers and artists. Award for authors of short stories, novels, translations, story collections. Award: one to two month residency at Yaddo. Judges: advisory committee. Filing fee $10. Guidelines for SASE. Deadline January 15. "Those qualified for invitation to Yaddo are writers, visual artists and composers who have already published (or exhibited or had performed) work of high artistic merit. Sometimes, but not customarily, unpublished work may serve as the sole basis for admission, if the advisory committee feels that it shows unusual promise."

YOUNG ADULT CANADIAN BOOK AWARD (II, IV), Young Adult Services Interest Group, c/o Saskatoon Public Library, 311 23rd St., E, Saskatoon, Saskatchewan S7K OJ6 Canada. Contact: Nancy E. Black, convener of book award committee. Estab. 1980. Annual award given when merited. To recognize an outstanding Canadian work of fiction written for young adults. Submissions should have been published during the previous calendar year. Award: Recognition through media press releases; leatherbound copy of book; "usually an author tour." Judged by Young Adult Services Group of the Canadian Library Association.

MORTON DAUWEN ZABEL AWARD (III), American Academy and Institute of Arts and Letters, 633 W. 155th St., New York NY 10032. (212)368-5900. Awarded annually, in rotation, to a poet, writer of fiction or critic. "To honor writers of progressive, original and experimental tendencies." For previously published books. No applications accepted. Award: $2,500. Judged by 7-member jury composed of members of the Department of Literature of the American Academy and Institute of Arts and Letters.

Contests and awards/'88-'89 changes

The following contests, grants and awards appeared in the 1988 edition of *Fiction Writer's Market* but are not in the 1989 edition of *Novel and Short Story Writer's Market*. Those contest, grants and awards coordinators who did not respond to our request for an update of their listings may not have done so for a variety of reasons—the contest may not be an annual event, for example, or last year's listing might have resulted in their receiving too many unsuitable manuscripts.

Allegheny Review Awards (did not respond)

American Academy and Institute of Arts and Letters Literary Awards (did not respond)

Antietam Review Literary Award (did not respond)

Asted/Prix Alvine-Belisle (did not respond)

Black Ice Margaret Jones Fiction Award (asked to be deleted)

Brandeis University Creative Arts Awards (did not respond)

Bulwer-Lytton Fiction Contest (did not respond)

Caddo Writing Center Spring/Fall Literary Competition (did not respond)

Calliope Fiction Award (did not respond)

The Chattahoochee Prize (did not respond)

Miles Franklin Literary Award (did not respond)

Friends of American Writers Juvenile Book Award (did not respond)

The Journal President's Award (did not respond)

Lakes & Prairie Press Award (did not respond)

Irene Leache Memorial Literary Contest (did not respond)

Maine Novel Award (asked to be deleted)

The Marten Bequest Award (did not respond)

Minnesota Voices Project (did not respond)

MS Magazine Fiction Contest (no longer offered)

The Okanagan Short Fiction Award (did not respond)

Peak Output Writer's Grant (asked to be deleted)

PEN/Southwest Houston Discovery Awards (asked to be deleted)

Permafrost 'Three stories by Three Writers' Contest (no longer offered)

Shenandoah Jeanne Charpiot Goodheart Prize for Fiction (asked to be deleted)

Sun Dog Awards (asked to be deleted)

Sydney Taylor Manuscript Competition Award (did not respond)

Texas Institute of Letters Jesse H. Jones Award (did not respond)

Texas Institute of Letters Short Story Award (did not respond)

Mark Twain Award (did not respond)

Vogelstein Foundation Grants (did not respond)

William Allen White Children's Book Award (did not respond)

Word Beat Press Fiction Book Award Competition (asked to be deleted)

The Writers of the Future Contest (did not respond)

Yellow Silk Magazine Annual Erotic Fiction Contest (asked to be deleted)

Literary Agents

If you hope to sell your novel to a major commercial publisher, it's almost unquestionably in your best interest to find a literary agent. We've included over 50 literary agents more in this year's edition of *Novel and Short Story Writer's Market* than appeared in last year's book. The growing number of agents in the business is fortunate for writers, since it's a fact that an increasing number of publishers will not even consider unsolicited manuscripts or query letters sent by individual writers. In addition, today's publishing houses are in such flux, with the takeovers and the changes in editors, that writers are much more likely to achieve a stable relationship with an agent than with an individual editor. Just at the point when your manuscript could be on the verge of acceptance, for example, the editor with whom you had been working might be fired. Most literary agents, on the other hand, are self employed.

Writers of category fiction and books for children are less likely to find publishers' doors closed to them if they don't have agents than writers of mainstream and contemporary fiction. And if you haven't yet written a novel, you almost definitely do not need an agent. Many of the most respected and successful agents will represent only those writers of short stories who already have a substantial list of publication credits with literary or commercial magazines. Beginning story writers should submit their fiction on their own, as should writers who plan to submit only to literary magazines or very small presses that pay little or nothing: the 10%-20% commission an agent would earn on a story placed in most literary magazines would not come to very much. Writers whose manuscripts are likely to appeal to a limited audience might also find it difficult to find an agent. While many agents are personally interested in religious fiction, for example, most will not take it on if they doubt they will make money on it.

If you do manage to sell your manuscript on your own to a commercial publisher, it might still be to your advantage to find an agent to help you negotiate the contract. An agent will almost certainly help you earn more money from your book than you would be able to do otherwise, and will act as a welcome buffer between you and your publisher over money matters. Of course, some writers, having sold manuscripts on their own, are understandably unwilling to share their advances and royalties with an agent. If you've received an offer for your book and only need help going over the contract before signing it, remember there are agents who are also lawyers and will consult with writers on an hourly basis.

Agents' commissions

For years, the standard agent's commission was 10% of all advances and royalties earned by an author. In the last few years, many agencies have raised their fees to 12%, 15% or even 20%—usually a necessary response to general rising costs and overhead. Still, it makes sense for writers first to try agents charging lower commissions. Note that some agents also ask authors to pay for expenses such as photocopying, messenger services and long-distance phone calls.

Fee-charging agents

In order to provide readers with as much information as possible, we have included listings in *Novel and Short Story Writer's Market* for agents who charge fees to read manuscripts. Clearly, it is to a writer's advantage to submit manuscripts first to agents who do not charge fees. However, many agents with perfectly respectable records of placing manuscripts do charge reading fees. Some charge fees only to new writers; others give refunds if they decide to take on the writer's manuscript. In any case, keep in mind that there are some agents who make most or all of their living from reading fees and seldom actually sell a manuscript to a publisher. Even well-intentioned agents might feel a less-than-urgent need to place manuscripts with publishers if they earn a good income from reading fees.

Here are some things to watch out for if, after submitting your complete manuscript, you get a letter from an agent offering to represent you for a fee:

• Letters with grammatical or spelling errors. If you have trouble respecting your agent's use of language, an editor is also likely to be contemptuous.

• "Acceptance" letters personalized only with your name and the title of your manuscript. An agent who is really interested in your work will not correspond with you via a form letter.

• Fees that are higher than those stated in *Novel and Short Story Writer's Market*, or requests for money from agents who do not mention fees in their listings in *Novel and Short Story Writer's Market*.

Criticism services

Some agents offer criticism services as part of, or in addition to, their reading fee. Before you send an agent money to critique your manuscript, consider what evidence you have that the criticism you receive will actually be useful. Some agents are experts in particular genres of fiction (romance, westerns, etc.) and are likely to give you advice about your novel that is quite accurate as far as its marketability is concerned. Tastes in mainstream fiction are more subjective, however, and you probably have no proof that the agent who offers to critique your manuscript is someone whose judgment you should trust. Your payment of a criticism fee usually does not guarantee that the agent will represent your work, either. If you do want criticism on your work, it might well make more sense to join a writer's group or take a writing class from an instructor whose opinion you respect.

Some writers have complained of critiques from agents who had obviously read only the first chapters of their novels, or commented at length only on minor grammatical or spelling flaws. You might want to make a point of talking on the phone to the agent who will be reading your manuscript: It's often easier to get a sense of whether to trust a person's judgment through conversation than through written correspondence alone.

Submitting your manuscript

You might have to show your manuscript to a number of different agents before you find one to represent you. This is one reason why it is rarely advisable to send your complete manuscript to an agent without querying first. It's expensive! Many writers consider it standard procedure to begin by querying a number of agents simultaneously, and then sending the complete manuscript to agents who express an interest, one at a time. Your query letter should be written as carefully as the pages of your manuscript—an agent unimpressed with your writing style in a query letter is unlikely to ask to see your complete manuscript. If your manuscript falls into a particular genre such as romance or horror, a two-paragraph description of the plot is probably all that is necessary in your query letter; if it's a mainstream novel, it's more likely you'll want to enclose a detailed outline or a sample chapter or two with your letter. Check the individual agent listings for specific information on what to send first. In any case, you'll want to enclose a SASE; mail sent without return postage to literary agents does not usually receive a reply.

Check the Agents' Category Index on page 651 for a list of the types of manuscripts agents in the book are particularly interested in seeing. It's a waste of time to send your science-fiction novel to an agent who specializes in screenplays. Browse through the listings, too, to find agents who may not have specified a particular category interest but whose listings particularly appeal to you. Before submitting, read the listings *carefully* to learn each agent's preferred way of considering new material. Since most publishers are in New York City, many writers consider a New York location to be advantageous—but don't ignore agents in other locations: many have perfectly good records of placing manuscripts. Looking under the "recently published" heading in each listing is a good idea. Has the agent you're considering placed books with publishers with which you are familiar? If you have both the 1988 edition of *Fiction Writer's Market* and the 1989 *Novel and Short Story Writer's Market*, compare listings to see if the agent lists new books in the "recently published" category. Agents who sell new fiction titles every year to different publishers are obviously to be preferred.

Other sources of information

Literary Agents; How to Get and Work with the Right One for You, by Michael Larson (Writer's Digest Books) contains a great deal of helpful information on finding an agent and avoiding problems common to writers looking for representation. *Literary Agents of North America* (Author Aid/Research Associates International, 340 E. 52nd St., New York NY 10022) is a useful annual directory of agents indexed by agency name, geography, specialty and size. The newly updated *Literary Agents: A Writer's Guide*, by Debby Mayer (Poets & Writers, Inc., 201 W. 54th St., New York NY 10019) may be helpful, as might Poets & Writers' annual *Directory of Poets and Fiction Writers*. Many of the most well-known writers in the country are listed in this directory but can be written to only in care of their agents—and finding out the names of the agents of writers you admire is a good way to narrow down your own list of prospective agents.

Two professional organizations for agents, the Independent Literary Agents Association, Inc. (I.L.A.A.), and the Society of Author's Representatives (S.A.R.) offer brochures and membership lists for SASEs. Fewer than half of the agents we list here belong to these organizations, but an agent's membership in either can reassure a writer that the agency is thriving and reputable. Their addresses are: *I.L.A.A.*, Suite 1205, 432 Park Ave. So., New York NY 10016; and *S.A.R.*, 10 S. Portland Ave., Brooklyn NY 11217.

DOMINICK ABEL LITERARY AGENCY, INC., 498 West End Ave., #12C, New York NY 10024. (212)877-0710. Agency estab. 1975. Adult fiction and nonfiction only. Adult fiction specialty: mystery and suspense. Usually obtains new clients via recommendations. Currently represents 75 authors. Occasionally accepts new clients. Query with SASE. Responds to queries in 1 week; to mss in 3 weeks. New/unpublished writers: 10%. member of I.L.A.A.
Terms: Agent's commission: 10% on domestic sales; 20% on foreign sales. Charges for photocopying expenses, overseas mailing and authors' books.

EDWARD J. ACTON, INC., 928 Broadway, New York NY 10010. (212)473-1700. Agent contact: Ed Novak. Agency estab. 1975. Novels. Also reviews nonfiction (50%-50% fiction to nonfiction). Special interests: literary and commercial works. Usually obtains new clients via author references. Currently represents 100 authors. Presently accepting limited number of new clients. Query first. No unsolicited mss. Responds to queries in 2 weeks. New/unpublished writers: 10%. Member of I.L.A.A.
Recent Sales: *The Spitfire*, by Bertrice Small (Ballantine); *Seconds*, by Lois Wyse (Crown); and *The Year I Bought the Yankees*, by Sparky Lyle (Bantam).
Terms: Agent's commission: 15% on domestic sales; 19% on foreign sales.

‡LEE ALLAN AGENCY, Box 18617, Milwaukee WI 53218. (414)463-7441. Agent contact: Lee A. Matthias. Estab. 1983. Novels and feature film screenplays. Also reviews nonfiction (95%-5% fiction to nonfiction). Special interests: genre fiction, including mystery, thriller, horror, science fiction, western. Usually obtains new clients via "market directory listings, such as *L.M.P.*, *L.A.N.A.*, *Writer's Market*, Writer's Guild List, and various other directories and lists; also recommendations." Currently rep-

 The double dagger before a listing indicates that the listing is new in this edition. New markets are often the most receptive to freelance contributions.

resents 50 authors. Presently accepting new clients. Send query. Responds to queries in 3-4 weeks; to mss in 4-6 weeks. New/unpublished writers: 80%. Member of WGA; Horror Writers of America.

Recent Sales: *The Jihad Ultimatum*, by John Randall, (Saybrook Pub. Co.); *Fire Arrow and The Fire Dream*, by Franklin Allen Leib (Presidio Press); *Sea Lion*, by Franklin Allen Leib (New American Library).

Terms: Agent's commission: 10% on domestic sales; 20% on foreign sales. 100% of income derived from commission on ms sales. "From new, unpublished writers, we are most interested in material directed toward an established market. If a novel, we prefer fresh, innovative and strong mysteries, thrillers and horror stories. If a feature theatrical-release type screenplay, we prefer low-to medium-budgeted contemporary genre scripts of high quality—no exploitation or trend-followers—written with an immediately compelling, hook-type premise, engaging characters, and a strong point of view. Scripts need to be quite distinctive to get serious consideration. No television material, articles, poetry, or short stories considered. Proper length and format essential. Return postage and/or SASE must accompany all correspondence until we represent the prospective writer."

LINDA ALLEN AGENCY, 2881 Jackson St., San Francisco CA 94115. (415)921-6437. Reviews novels. Also reads nonfiction (40%-60% fiction to nonfiction). Usually obtains new clients through recommendations. Currently represents 50-60 writers. Presently accepting new clients. Query. Responds in 4-6 weeks.

Terms: Agent's commission: 15%.

MARCIA AMSTERDAM AGENCY, 41 W. 82nd St., New York NY 10024. (212)873-4945. Agency estab. 1969. Novels. Also reviews nonfiction (90%-10% fiction to nonfiction). Special interests: young adult, horror, humor, mainstream, science fiction, romance, men's adventure, mysteries. Usually obtains new clients via recommendations and query letters. Presently accepting new clients. Query with first three sample chapters and outline. Responds to queries in 2 weeks; to mss in 1 month. New/unpublished writers: 80-90%. Member of WGA.

Recent Sales: *The Midnight Hour*, by Donald Bacon (Pinnacle); *Silvercat*, by Kristopher Clark Franklin (Bantam); *Ash Ock*, by Christopher Hinz (St. Martin's).

Terms: Agent's commission: 15% on domestic and foreign sales. Charges for legal fees when agreed upon, occasional cable, telex, etc. 100% of income derived from commissions on sales. "If there is no SASE, we do not return queries or submissions."

AUTHORS' MARKETING SERVICES LTD., 217 Degrassi St., Toronto, Ontario M4M 2K8 Canada. (416)463-7200. Agency estab. 1978. Novels. Also reviews nonfiction (60%-40% fiction to nonfiction). Special interests: mainstream, male-adventure/thriller, horror, contemporary, regency. Usually obtains new clients via recommendations, word of mouth and advertising. Currently represents 25 authors. Presently accepting new clients. *Fiction:* We require a query letter first and then, from unpublished authors, the entire manuscript. *Nonfiction:* We require a query letter and then a proposal containing outline and two sample chapters. Responds to queries in 1 week; to mss in 6 weeks. New/unpublished writers: 35%.

Recent Sales: *Winter Place*, by Dennis Jones (Little, Brown); *Paxos Tiger*, by Ted Simon (Worldwide); *Anatomy of a Nightmare*, by Martyn Kendrick (Macmillan).

Terms: Agent's commission: 15% on Canadian/US sales; 20% on foreign sales. Charges $175 to review full mss by unpublished authors. "Fee includes a detailed critique and evaluation, which will indicate the weaknesses of the work, and offer specific suggestions as to how they can be eliminated." 95% of income derived from commission on ms sales; 5% from criticism service.

THE AXELROD AGENCY, INC., Room 5805, 350 Fifth Ave., New York NY 10118. (212)629-5620. Agency estab. 1983. Novels. Also reviews nonfiction (50%-50% fiction to nonfiction). Special interests: mainstream, mysteries. Usually obtains new clients via recommendations from others; at conferences. Currently represents 30 authors. Presently accepting new clients. Query. Responds to queries in 1 week; to mss in 1 month. New/unpublished writers: 20%.

Terms: Agent's commission: 10% on domestic sales; 20% on foreign sales. Charges extra for photocopying expenses. 100% of income derived from commission on ms sales.

Read the Manuscript Mechanics section to learn the correct way to prepare and submit a manuscript.

MAXIMILIAN BECKER, 115 E. 82nd St., New York NY 10028. (212)988-3887. Agent contact: Maximilian Becker. Agency estab. 1950. Novels. Also reviews nonfiction (75%-25% fiction to nonfiction). Special interests: adventure, mainstream, science fiction, suspense. Usually obtains new clients by recommendations from others. Currently represents 50 authors. Presently accepting new clients. Query. Responds to queries in 1 week; to mss in 2 weeks. 20% of clients are new/unpublished writers.
Recent Sales: *Goering*, by David Irving (William Morrow); *Time to Choose*, by Janine Boissard (Little, Brown); *The Enigma*, by David Kahn (Houghton Mifflin).
Terms: Agent's commission: 15% on domestic sales; 19% on foreign sales. 100% of income is derived from commission on ms sales and film rights.

BILL BERGER ASSOCIATES, 444 E. 58th St., New York NY 10022. (212)486-9588. Fiction and nonfiction. Query; send outline/proposal or outline plus sample chapters with SASE.
Terms: Agent's commission: 10%.

MEREDITH BERNSTEIN LITERARY AGENCY, 470 West End Ave., New York NY 10024. (212)799-1007. Agent Contact: Meredith Bernstein. Agency estab. 1981. Novels. Also reviews nonfiction (50%-50% fiction to nonfiction). Usually obtains new clients via recommendations from others, solicitation, at conferences. "Some, I go out and seek, if I have a prospect in mind." Currently represents 75-100 authors. Presently accepting new clients. Query first. Responds to mss within 2 weeks. Member of I.L.A.A.
Recent Sale: *The Visitors*, by Raymond Fowler (Bantam).
Terms: Agent's commission: 15% on domestic sales; 20% on foreign sales. Charges $45 reading fee to unpublished authors. Offers criticism service: "My assistant and I collaborate on our suggested ideas."

‡THE BLAKE GROUP LITERARY AGENCY, One Turtle Creek Village, Suite 600, Dallas TX 75219. Director/Agent: Ms. Lee B. Halff. Agency estab. 1979. Novels, novellas, story collections. Also reviews nonfiction (50%-50% fiction to nonfiction). Special interest: general. Usually obtains new clients via recommendations from others and publications. Currently represents 40 authors. Presently accepting new clients. Query first with sample chapters. Responds to queries within 1 month; to mss or chapters in 3 months, "depending on workload." New/unpublished writers: 50%.
Recent Titles: *Captured on Corregdor*, by John M. Wright, Jr. (McFarland & Co.); *Modern Languages for Musicians*, by Julie Yarbrough (Pendragon Press); *Linda Richards* article, by Katherine Kelly (*Cricket* magazine).
Terms: Agent's commission: 10% on domestic sales; 20% on foreign sales. Offers criticism service "if author wants a critique": $100 for book-length manuscript; $75 for less than 100 pages. "Written critique done by a qualified consulting editor." 95% of income derived from commission on ms sales; 5% from criticism service. "All submissions must be accompanied by a self-addressed, pre-stamped return mailer or envelope."

‡HARRY BLOOM AGENCY, Suite 404, 1520 S. Beverly Glen Blvd., Los Angeles CA 90024. (213)556-3461. Agent Contact: Patrice Dale. Estab. 1956. Novels. Also reviews nonfiction (80%-20% fiction to nonfiction). Special interest: mainstream. Usually obtains new clients via recommendations from others. Presently accepting new clients. Send in query. Responds to queries in 2 weeks; to mss in 3-4 weeks. New/unpublished writers: 10%.
Terms: Agent's commission: 10% on domestic sales; 10% on foreign sales. 100% of income derived from commission on ms sales.

REID BOATES LITERARY AGENCY, 44 Mt. Ridge Dr., Wayne NJ 07470. (201)628-7523. Agent nonfiction (25%-75% fiction to nonfiction). Special interests: mainstream, literary and popular. Usually obtains new clients via referral. Currently represents 40 authors. Presently accepting new clients. Query first. Responds to queries in 1 month. New/unpublished writers: 20%.
Recent Sales: *Survival*, nonfiction thriller by Ron Arias (New American Library); Untitled ms on collapse of E. F. Hutton (Doubleday).
Terms: Agent's commission: 15% on domestic and movie sales; 20% on foreign sales. Charges for photocopying complete ms. 100% of income derived from commission on ms sales.

❝ *Writing is making sense of life.* ❞

—Nadine Gordimer

BOOK PEDDLERS OF DEEPHAVEN, 18326A Minnetonka Blvd., Deephaven MN 55391. (612)475-3527. Agent contact: Vicki Lansky. Agency estab. 1983. Reviews mainly nonfiction (10%-90% fiction to nonfiction). Usually obtains new clients via recommendations, publicity. Currently represents 25 authors. Accepting few new clients. Query with outline/proposal or outline plus sample chapters and SASE. Responds to queries in 2 weeks. New/unpublished writers: 70%. Member of I.L.A.A.
Recent Sales: *The American-Jewish Baby Name Book*, by Smadar Sidi (Harper and Row); *What You Need to Know About Medicare*, by Mason and Noehgren (NAL).
Terms: Agent's commission: 15% on domestic sales; 20% on foreign sales. 100% of income derived from commission on ms sales.

GEORGES BORCHARDT INC., 136 E. 57th St., New York NY 10022. (212)753-5785. Agency estab. 1967. Novels, novellas, short stories, story collections. Also reviews nonfiction (35%-65% fiction to nonfiction). Special interest: literary. Usually obtains new clients via recommendations from others. Currently represents 200 authors. Presently accepting "very few" new clients. Query. No unsolicited mss.
Recent Sales: *World's End*, by T. Coraghessan Boyle (Viking); *Biography of Ronald Reagan*, by Edmond Morris (Random House); *Richard Burton*, by Melvyn Bragg (Little Brown).
Terms: Agent's commission: 10% on domestic sales; 20% on foreign sales. Charges for photocopying expenses. 100% of income derived from commission on ms sales.

‡THE BARBARA BOVA LITERARY AGENCY, 207 Sedgwick Rd., West Hartford CT 06107. (203)521-5915. Agent contact: Barbara Bova. Agency estab. 1978. Novels. Also review nonfiction (30%-70% fiction to nonfiction). Special interests: science, mysteries, science fiction. Usually obtains new clients via "recommendations from others, occasionally over-the-transom mss." Currently represents 20 authors. Presently accepting new clients. Send query. Responds to queries in 2 weeks; to mss in 2 months. New/unpublished writers: 18%.
Recent Sales: *Alvin Maker*, by Orson Scott Card (St. Martin's); *Peacekeepers*, by Ben Bova (Tor Books); *Stellar Shepherd*, by Kevin Egan (Crown).
Terms: Agent's commission: 10% on domestic sales; 10% on foreign sales. Charges reading fee to unpublished writers: $50 for 300-page novel, which includes an analysis of work, my recommendations and suggestions, opinion of marketability." 99.9% of income derived from commission on ms sales; .01% from criticism service. "I do not accept anything without a letter of inquiry first with a self-addressed return envelope included."

THE BRADLEY-GOLDSTEIN AGENCY, 7 Lexington Ave., New York NY 10010. (718)672-7924. Agency estab. 1985. Specializes in nonfiction (10%-90% fiction to nonfiction). Fiction *only* from agency clients. Usually obtains new clients via referrals. Currently represents 20 authors. Presently accepting new clients. Query by letter first. Include SASE, please! Responds to queries in 8 weeks. New/unpublished writers: 20%.
Recent Sales: *Oscar Wilde's Circle*, by Natasha Gray (Dutton); *Croquet: The Gentle but Wicket Game*, by Christopher Reaske (Dutton); *Women of the Third World*, by Maxine Fisher (Franklin Watts).
Terms: Agent's commission: 15% on domestic sales; 25% on foreign sales. Charges for expenses incurred in handling published work—for mail/phone, publicity, travel. 90% of income derived from commissions on ms sales; 10% from negotiating non-client contracts or consultations. "We mainly handle fiction for our nonfiction clients and through referrals. We *never* read unsolicited manuscripts."

BRANDT & BRANDT LITERARY AGENTS, INC., 1501 Broadway, New York NY 10036. (212)840-5760. Agency Contact: Carl Brandt. Agency estab. 1913. Novels, novellas, short stories, story collections, nonfiction. Usually obtains new clients via recommendations by editors and current clients. Currently represents 150 authors. Accepting new clients. Query first. Responds in 1 week. Member of S.A.R.
Terms: Agent's commission: 10% on domestic sales; 20% on foreign sales. 100% of income derived from commissions on ms sales.

RUTH HAGY BROD LITERARY AGENCY, 15 Park Ave., New York NY 10016. (212)683-3232. Agent contact: Wanda Hite or Michael Brad. Agency estab. 1977. Novels, story collections. Also reviews nonfiction (60%-40% fiction to nonfiction). Special interests: mainstream, mystery. Usually obtains new clients via solicitation. Presently accepting new clients. Query. Responds to queries in 1-2 weeks; to mss in 1-2 months.
Terms: Agent's commission: 15% on domestic sales. 100% of income derived from commissions on ms sales.

CURTIS BROWN, LTD., 10 Astor Pl., New York NY 10003. (212)473-5400. Contact: Perry Knowlton, Peter Ginsberg, Emilie Jacobson, Marilyn Marlowe, Henry Dunow, Irene Skolnick,Maureen Walters or Clyde Taylor. Fiction and nonfiction (50%-50% fiction to nonfiction). Presently accepting new clients. Query by letter with SASE. Responds to queries in 2 weeks; to mss in 1 month. Member of S.A.R. and I.L.A.A.
Terms: Charges for special postage (e.g., express mail), telexes, book purchases for subsidiary-rights sales. 100% of income derived from commissions on ms sales.

‡NED BROWN INC., Box 5020, Beverly Hills CA 90210. Full-length fiction and nonfiction. Send query with SASE. Presently accepting new clients "only if published commercially or recommended by another author, client or publisher."
Terms: Agent's commission: 10%.

PEMA BROWNE LTD., 185 E. 85th St., New York NY 10028. (212)369-1925. Agent contact: Pema Browne, Perry J. Browne. Novels. Also reviews nonfiction (60%-40% fiction to nonfiction). Special interests: mass-market romance, thrillers, horror, young adult, some mainstream. Usually obtains new clients via editors, listings, word-of-mouth. Currently represents 25 authors. Presently accepting new clients. Send outline plus sample chapters and SASE. Responds to queries in 1 week; to mss in 1 month. New/unpublished writers: 50%.
Recent Sales: *Death Merchant Series*, by J. Rosenberger (Dell); *Hills of Oil*, by Virginia Fox (Silhouette).
Terms: Agent's commission: 15% on domestic sales; 20% on foreign sales. 100% of income derived from commissions on ms sales. "We only review manuscripts not sent out to publishers or other agents."

JANE BUTLER, ART & LITERARY AGENCY, (ASSOCIATE, VIRGINIA KIDD LITERARY AGENTS), Box 278/538 East Harford St., Milford PA 18337. (717)296-7266. Agency estab. 1980 (Jane Butler); 1966 (Virginia Kidd). Novels. Also reviews nonfiction (75%-25% fiction to nonfiction). Special interests: science fiction, fantasy, horror, historicals, mystery and young adult novels. Usually obtains new clients by recommendations and unsolicited queries. Query with outline plus sample chapters. "NO SASE NO RESPONSE!" Responds to queries in 3 weeks.
Recent Sales: *Godslayer*, by Mickey Zucker Reichert (DAW); *A Time For Dragons*, by Gary Gentile (Berkley); *Earthwitch*, by Eileen Kernaghan (Berkley).
Terms: Agent's commission: 10% on domestic sales; 20% on foreign sales.

RUTH CANTOR, Rm. 1133, 156 5th Ave., New York NY 10010. (212)243-3246. Agency estab. 1952. Novels. Also reviews nonfiction. Special interests: mainstream, workmanlike novels, mysteries, psychological novels, anything that sells in the marketplace. Usually obtains new clients via recommendations from others. Currently represents 40-50 authors. Presently accepting new clients. Query with outline plus sample chapters.
Recent Sales: *Golf Humor*, by Blumenfield (Price/Stern/Sloan); *The Hurry Up Summer*, by Mary Mahoney (Putnam); *Mary*, by Mary Sherrod (Warner Paperback).
Terms: Agent's commission: 10% on domestic sales; 20% on foreign sales. 100% of income derived from commissions on ms sales.

MARIA CARVAINIS AGENCY, INC., 235 West End Ave., New York NY 10023. (212)580-1559. Contact: Maria Carvainis.Agency estab. 1977. Novels, story collections. Also reviews nonfiction (65%-35% fiction to nonfiction). Special interests: mainstream, historicals, regencies, suspense, mysteries, westerns, category romance and young adult novels. Obtains new clients through the recommendations of clients, editors, attendance of conferences and letters of query. Currently represents 80 clients. Presently accepting new clients on a selective basis. Query with SASE. Responds to queries in 2-3 weeks "if not earlier"; to mss in 4-12 weeks. New/unpublished writers: 15%. Member of Writers Guild of America, The Authors Guild, Romance Writers of America.
Recent Sales: *Slow Heat in Heaven*, by Sandra Brown; *Dance of the Gods*, by Norma Beishir; *Mask of Sapphire*, by Deana James.
Terms: Agent's commission: 15% on domestic sales; 20% on foreign sales. 100% of income derived from commissions on ms sales. "I view the project's editorial needs and the author's professional development as integral components of the literary agent's role, in addition to the negotiation of intricate contracts and the maintenance of close contact with the New York City publishing industry."

MARTHA CASSELMAN LITERARY AGENCY, 1263 12th Ave., San Francisco CA 94122. (415)665-3235. Agency estab. 1979. Novels. Also reviews nonfiction (20%-80% fiction to nonfiction). Special interests: mainstream; food-related books; biography; children's. Usually obtains new clients via referrals from clients and editors. Currently represents 25 authors. Query with outline/proposal. No multiple

submissions. No unsolicited mss. Responds to queries in 2-4 weeks. New/unpublished writers: 40-60%. Member of I.L.A.A.
Terms: Agent's commission: 15% on domestic sales; 10% for foreign agent and other sub agents. Charges for copying and overnight mail expenses.

‡THE LINDA CHESTER LITERARY AGENCY, 265 Coast, La Jolla CA 92037. (619)454-3966. Agent contact: Linda Chester. Estab. originally 1977-1984; reopened 1987. Novels, novellas, short stories and short collections. Also reviews nonfiction (40%-60% fiction to nonfiction). Special interest: mainstream. Usually obtains new clients via recommendations from others, solicitation, at conferences. Currently represents 50 authors. Presently accepting new clients. Send query and outline/proposal. Reports on queries in 1 week; on mss in 2-3 weeks. New/unpublished writers: 50%.
Recent Sales: "My agency has been closed for four years and was recently reopened in 1987. I am presently developing fictional writers, and several are on the verge of selling. The following authors, works and publishers are ones I worked with in the past: *The Singer and the Stone*, by John Willet (Houghton Mifflin); *Epidemic 9*, by Richard Lerner (William Morrow & Co.); and *Leaving the Enchanted Forest*, by Stephanie Covington and Linda Beckett (Harper & Row)."
Terms: Agent's commission: 15% on domestic sales; 20% on foreign sales. "I charge a nonrefundable deposit to cover ordinary expenses incurred (phone calls, clerical, etc.)." 99% of income derived from commission on sales; 1% reading fees. "When the agency was in operation between 1977-1984, I mostly handled nonfiction. But since I reopened in 1987, I am trying to develop a strong fiction side to my agency."

‡CINEMA TALENT INTERNATIONAL, 7906 Santa Monica Blvd., Suite #212, Los Angeles CA 90046. (213)656-1937. Agent contact: George Kriton. Agency estab. 1979. Motion picture and television scripts and stories. Also reviews nonfiction. Special interests: motion picture and television. Usually obtains new clients via solicitation and recommendations. Currently represents 19 authors. Presently accepting new clients. Send query. Responds to queries in 3 weeks. New/unpublished writers: 35%.
Recent Sales: Motion picture and TV scripts on assignment to my clients.
Terms: Agent's commission: 10% on domestic sales. 100% of income derived from commission on ms sales.

SJ CLARK LITERARY AGENCY, 101 Randall St., San Francisco CA 94131. (415)285-7401. Agent Contact: Sue Clark. Novels and story collections. Also reviews nonfiction (75%-25% fiction to nonfiction). Special interests: mystery, mainstream, psychic, children's. Usually obtains new clients by word of mouth. Represents 8 writers. Presently accepting new clients. Query or send outline plus sample chapters. New/unpublished writers: 90%.
Terms: Agent's commission 15%.

DIANE CLEAVER, INC., 55 Fifth Ave., New York NY 10003. (212)206-5600. Affiliated with Sanford Greenburger Assoc. Estab. 1979. Novels. Also reads nonfiction (40%-60% fiction to nonfiction). No science fiction or romances. "I do like mysteries, suspense mainstream." Usually obtains new clients via recommendations from others; listings in directories. Occasionally accepts new clients. Query. Responds to queries in 1 week. Member I.L.A.A.
Terms: Agent's commission: 15% on domestic sales; 10% on foreign sales and 10% sub agent's commission.

HY COHEN LITERARY AGENCY, 111 W. 57th St., New York NY 10019. (212)757-5237. Fiction and nonfiction. Send sample chapters with SASE "if ms is to be returned." Represents approximately 30 writers. Obtains writers via recommendation, conferences, unsolicited mss and queries. New/unpublished writers: 95%.
Terms: Agent's commission: 10%.

RUTH COHEN, INC., Box 7626, Menlo Park CA 94025. (415)854-2054. Novels. Also reviews nonfiction (60%-40% fiction to nonfiction). Special interests: detective mysteries, juvenile, young adult, quality fiction, historical romance. Usually obtains new clients via recommendations from others; at conferences. Currently represents 70 authors. Presently accepting new clients. Query. Responds to queries in 2-3 weeks; no unsolicited mss. Member of I.L.A.A.
Recent Sales: *No Way Out* (Harper and Row); *Dear Baby* (Macmillan); *Knaves and Hearts* (Avon).
Terms: Agent's commission: 15% on domestic sales; 20% on foreign sales. Charges for photocopying expenses. 100% of income derived from commissions on ms sales. Writers must include SASE.

JOYCE K. COLE LITERARY AGENCY, 797 San Diego Rd., Berkeley CA 94707. (415)526-5165. Contact: Joyce K. Cole. Novels. Special interests: mainstream and literary; all genre fiction. Query or send

outline plus sample chapters (up to 50 pages). Also reviews nonfiction (35%-65% fiction to nonfiction). Represents 25 writers. Obtains new clients via recommendations, conferences and queries. Not presently accepting new clients. New/unpublished writers: 30%.
Terms: Agent's commission: 15% on domestic sales; 25% on foreign sales.

SHIRLEY COLLIER AGENCY, 1127 Stradella Rd., Los Angeles CA 90077. (213)270-4500. Contact: Shirley Collier. Novels and biography. Prefers "good writing; no smut." Query first with SASE. Also reviews nonfiction (75%-25% fiction to nonfiction). Interested in new/beginning novelists when time permits. Writer must demonstrate a minimum of three sales to top magazines.
Terms: Agent's commission: 10%; foreign translations additional 10%.

COLLIER ASSOCIATES, 2000 Flat Run Rd., Seaman OH 45679. (513)764-1234. Agency estab. 1976. Novels. Also reviews nonfiction. Special interests (adult only): mainstream, historical, detective, s/f, fantasy, war. Usually obtains new clients via recommendations and queries. Currently represents 75 authors. Occasionally accepts new clients. Query with outline/proposal or outline plus sample chapters and SASE. Responds to queries in 3-4 weeks; to mss in 6-8 weeks. Member of S.A.R. and I.L.A.A.
Recent Sales: *Fair Weather Foul*, by Sean Freeman (William Morrow); *Matters of the Heart*, by Mayo Lucas (Avon).
Terms: Agent's commission: 15% on domestic sales; 20% on foreign sales. Charges for express mail and copies of books ordered from publisher if author approves. 100% of income derived from commissions on mss sales. "This is a small agency run by two people, and it handles authors and contracts dating back to the 1960s from predecessor agencies. So agency is extremely selective in accepting new authors of fiction—at most two or three new clients a year are tried out, including through referrals."

‡COLUMBIA LITERARY ASSOCS., INC., 7902 Nottingham Way, Ellicott City MD 21043. (301)465-1595. Contact: Linda Hayes. Novels (mass market). Special interest: mainstream and category, woman's fiction. Represents 40-50 writers. Query with synopsis plus first chapter and submission history (pubs/agents). Cannot respond without SASE. Also reviews commercial nonfiction (50%-50% fiction to nonfiction). Writer is billed for specific project expenses (shipping, long distance calls, photocopy). Obtains new clients via recommendations from others and queries. Presently accepting "a selected few" new clients. New/unpublished writers: 1/3.
Terms: Agent's commission: 12-15%.

BILL COOPER ASSOCIATES, INC., Suite 411, 224 West 49th St., New York NY 10019. (212)307-1100. Agency estab. 1964. Novels. Also reviews nonfiction. Special interest: mainstream. Usually obtains new clients via recommendations. Send outline/proposal. Responds to queries in 2 weeks.

‡ROBERT CORNFIELD LITERARY AGENCY, 145 W. 79th St., New York NY 10024. (212)874-2465. Agent Contact: Robert Cornfield or Jeffrey Essmann. Estab. 1979. Novels. Also reveiws nonfiction (30%-70% fiction to nonfiction). Special interests: adventure, mainstream. Usually obtains new clients via recommendations from others. Currently represents 60 authors. Presently accepting new clients. Send query. Responds to queries in 2 weeks; to mss in 1 month. New/unpublished writers: 20%. Member of I.L.A.A.
Recent Sales: *Muragan's Chariot*, by Indira Ganesan (Knopf); *The Hanged Man*, by Denis Johnson (Knopf); and untitled new novel, by Joyce Maynard (Knopf).
Terms: Agent's commission: 15% on domestic sales; 20% on foreign sales. 100% of income derived from ms sales.

BONNIE R. CROWN, 50 E. 10th St., New York NY 10003. (212)475-1999. Agency estab. 1976. Novels, novellas, story collections, including translations from Asian languages. Also reviews nonfiction (80%-20% fiction to nonfiction). Special interests: originality of style and tone, mainstream, and anything related to Asia. Usually obtains new clients via recommendation. Currently represents 12 authors. "I am a very small specialized agency." Presently accepting new clients. Send query with SASE for policy. Responds in 2 weeks. New/unpublished writers: 10%.
Recent Sales: *Wings of Stone*, by Linda Casper (Readers International); translation of the *I Ching*; *The Haiku Handbook*, by William Hisginson (Kodansha International).
Terms: Agent's commission: 15% on domestic sales; 20% on foreign sales. "I am particularly interested in any work which has been influenced by some Asian experience or is set in a foreign country."

RICHARD CURTIS ASSOCIATES, INC., 164 East 64th St., New York NY 10021. (212)371-9481. Agency estab. 1978. Novels, story collections. Also reviews nonfiction (75%-25% fiction to nonfiction). Special interests: genre fiction such as science fiction and fantasy, romance, westerns, male action-adventure, mystery and international thriller. Usually obtains new clients via referrals. Currently represents 75 authors. Presently accepting new clients. Query with outline/proposal. New/unpublished writers: 10%. Member of I.L.A.A.

Recent Sales: *Heiress*, by Janet Dailey (Little, Brown); five science fiction novel package by Gregory Benford (Bantam); *Indian Heritage* western series novels 4, 5, and 6, by Paul Lederer (New American Library).

Terms: Agent's commission: 10% on domestic sales; 20% on foreign sales. "Only occasionally do we charge fee, but we have no systematic program." Charges a $175 reading fee for a 300-page novel. 99% of income derived from commissions on ms sales; less than 1% derived from criticism services.

‡ELAINE DAVIE LITERARY AGENCY, Village Gate Square, 274 N. Goodman St., Rochester NY 14607. (716)442-0830. President: Elaine Davie. Agency estab. 1986. Novels. Also reviews nonfiction (60%-40% fiction to nonfiction). Special interests: "all types of adult, popular fiction. Both mainstream and category manuscripts are reviewed." No juvenile fiction. "I write several articles each year on 'agenting' for various trade journals. These articles generate a great response from writers." Currently represents 60 authors. Presently accepting new clients. Query or send outline plus sample chapters. Reports on queries in 2 weeks; on mss in 4 weeks. New/unpublished writers: 30.

Recent Titles: *Perfect Morning*, by Marcia Evanick (Bantam); *Night Dancer*, by Paul Bagdon (Dell); *John Wayne Trivia Book*, by Leonard Brideau (Crown).

Terms: Agent's commission: 15% on domestic sales; 20% on foreign sales. 100% of income derived from commission on ms sales. "Our agency specializes in adult fiction and nonfiction by and for women. We are particularly successful in placing genre fiction (romances, historicals, mysteries, suspense, westerns). We welcome queries from non-published writers as well as published authors, and we never charge a fee of any kind."

‡ATHOS DEMETRIOU, #6C, 211 West 10th St., New York NY 10014. (212)741-0035. Agent Contact: Athos Demetriou, Dale Reyer. Estab. 1986. Novels. Also reviews nonfiction (50%-50% fiction to nonfiction). Special interests: mainstream, mysteries, thrillers. Usually obtains new clients via recommendations. Currently represents 50 authors. Presently accepting new clients. Send query plus outline/proposal or outline plus 3 sample chapters. Responds to queries in 1 week; to mss in 4-6 weeks. New/unpublished writers: 50%.

Recent Sales: *Something to Live For*, by Christine Macarte (Dutton); *The Prospect of Detachment*, by Lindsley Cameron (St. Martin's); *Heritage*, by Heather Hay (Berkley).

Terms: Agent's commission: 15% on domestic sales; 20% on foreign sales. 100% of income derived from commission on mss.

ANITA DIAMANT: THE WRITERS' WORKSHOP, INC., 310 Madison Ave., New York NY 10017. (212)687-1122. Agency estab. 1917. Novels. Also reviews nonfiction (50%-50% fiction to nonfiction). Special interests: "any areas except children's and science fiction." Usually obtains new clients via recommendations and unsolicited queries. Currently represents 100 authors. Presently accepting new clients. Query. Responds to queries in 1 week; to mss in 4-6 weeks. New/unpublished writers: 25%.

Recent Sales: *Fallen Hearts*, by V.C. Andrews (Pocket Books); *Surrogate Child*, by Andrew Neiderman (Berkley Books); *Making Life Right*, by Herbert Fensterheim and Jean Baer, etc.

Terms: Agent's commission: 10-15% on domestic sales; 20% on foreign sales. 100% of income derived from commissions on ms sales. "Queries by mail preferred over telephone queries and unannounced visits."

‡SANDRA DIJKSTRA LITERARY AGENCY, 1237 Camino del Mar St. 515C, Del Mar CA 92014. (619)755-3115. Agent contact: Sandra Dijkstra. Associates: Laurie Fox, Kathy Goodwin. Agency estab. 1978. Novels and story collections. Also reviews nonfiction (20%-80% fiction to nonfiction). Special interests: mainstream, literary. Usually obtains new clients via "recommendations from authors, editors, reviewers, booksellers, etc.; conferences; 'over the transom.'" Currently represents 70 authors. Presently accepting new clients selectively. Send query, synopsis and sample chapters. Responds to queries in 3-4 weeks; to mss in 5-7 weeks. New/unpublished writers: 30%. Member of I.L.A.A.

Recent Sales: *The Joy Luck Club*, by Amy Tan (Putnam's); *Dessa Rose* by Sherley Anne Williams (Morrow/Berkley); *A Genuine Monster*, by David Zielinski (Atlantic Monthly Press)..

Terms: Agent's commission: 15% on domestic sales; 20% (British)-30% (translation) on foreign sales. Will critique 300-page novel for $300 "if we think the ms is ¾ of the way there, we ask the author to resubmit revised version within 6 months and we shall read it at no charge. Extensive assessment of the ms's potential—market, literary, etc. with suggestions for revision and enhancement so that maximum potential can be realized." Charges for postage, Xerox and phone expenses. "We ask an expense fee of $175/year which seems to be average expended." 90% of income derived from commission on ms sales; 10% from criticism service. Payment of fees does not ensure agency representation. "But we only ask to evaluate those mss which we feel have a true potential."

Close-up

Elaine Davie
Agent

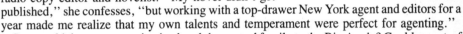

"An agent doesn't have to be based in Manhattan to be topnotch!"

So says Rochester, New York's Elaine Davie, who began to realize her dream of starting a local literary agency in 1986, after paying her dues as a high-school English teacher, daily columnist for the *Clearwater Sun* in Florida, radio copy editor and novelist. "My novel didn't get published," she confesses, "but working with a top-drawer New York agent and editors for a year made me realize that my own talents and temperament were perfect for agenting."

But would that mean moving husband, home and family to the Big Apple? Could an out-of-town agent be effective? Davie thought she'd see by starting small and keeping things simple.

"First *Fiction Writer's Magazine* did an article about me, in which I promised to give a personal and prompt response to anyone who consulted me." Davie says. "Then I sponsored a local writing competition which brought TV and print exposure. Then the IWWG (International Women's Writing Guild) listed me as an agent specializing in literature by and about women, and goodbye, small and simple!" Davie says this publicity helped her agency to take off, and forced her to move to a larger office during her first year in business.

Davie now travels to New York City at least twice a month to visit editors, and when she's not talking things over with them in person, she's on the phone. "It makes no difference to these editors whether I'm across town or across the country, as long as I have the goods to sell," she says. "And I think I do. My main criterion is that every manuscript I take on, no matter what its type, class or genre, must be the best of its kind." Quality manuscripts, Davie says, are what sales are made of, and an agent who can deliver them will build a reputation and a solid career.

Unlike many agents, who are leery of the unsolicited manuscripts that often come after public appearances, Davie enjoys making contact with writers through conferences and at other events. "I love to go to all the conventions, and I love public speaking," she says. "Give me a crowd and ask my advice, and I'm in heaven!"

Davie's advice to writers on working with a literary agent is simple: "Remember," she says, "that it's not always dollars and cents your agent is negotiating. Together, we're building a relationship with editors and publishers, a future for us all. And it doesn't matter where your agent is; each manuscript stands or falls on its own merit. Excellent writing is always hot."

Even if your agent sends it in from Iceland.

—Barbara Wernecke Durkin

CANDIDA DONADIO & ASSOCIATES, INC., 231 West 22nd St., New York NY 10011. (212)691-8077. Agency estab. 1973. Novels, novellas, short stories, story collections. Also reviews nonfiction (80%-20% fiction to nonfiction). Special interest: literary. Usually obtains new clients via recommendations. Currently represents 100 authors. Presently accepting new clients. Query with outline and sample chapters. Responds to queries in 1-4 weeks; to mss in 1-8 weeks. New/unpublished writers: 5%. Member of S.A.R.
Recent Sales: Untitled novel by Robert Stone (Weidenfeld & Nicolson); *And Venus is Blue*, by Mary Hood (Ticknor & Fields); *On the River Styx*, by Peter Matthiessen (Random House).
Terms: Agent's commission: 10% on domestic sales; 15%-30% on foreign sales. 100% of income derived from commissions on ms sales.

THE DORESE AGENCY, Suite 210, 1400 Ambassador St., Los Angeles CA 90035. (213)556-0710. Agent contact: Alyss Dorese. Estab. 1979. Novels, story collections. Also reviews nonfiction (50%-50% fiction to nonfiction). Special interest: mainstream. Usually obtains new clients via recommendations from others. Currently represents 35 authors. Presently accepting new clients. Query or send outline/proposal. Responds to queries in 3 weeks; to mss in 3 months. New/unpublished writers: 20%. Member of WGA.
Terms: Agent's commission: 15% on domestic sales; 20% on foreign sales. Charges $75 reading fee to unpublished authors. 95% of income derived from commissions on ms sales; 5% of income derived from criticism service.

‡DUPREE/MILLER AND ASSOC., INC., 5518 Dyer St., Ste. 3, Dallas TX 75206. (214)692-1388. Agent contact: Jan Miller. Agency estab. 1984. Novels. Also reviews nonfiction (60%-40% fiction to nonfiction). "No hard-core science fiction. Will review romance but very difficult to get published. Interested in everything else." Usually obtains new clients via recommendations. Currently represents 45-50 authors. Presently accepting new clients. Send sample chapters. Responds to queries in 6-8 weeks. New/unpublished writers: 60%.
Recent Sales: *The Great Depression of 1990*, by Ravi Batra (Bantam/Schwartz); *Star Mothers*, by Georgia Holt, Sally Quinn, Sue Russell (Simon and Schuster); *The Mansion Cookbook*, by Dean Fearing (Weidenfeld and Nicolson).
Terms: Agent's commission: 15% on domestic sales; 15% on foreign sales "plus 10% for foreign sub agent." "$150 handling fee due when contract to represent project is signed." 85% of income derived from commission on ms sales.

JOSEPH ELDER AGENCY, #6D, 150 W. 87th St., New York NY 10024. "Must query first, include SASE ('query' means query letter, not detailed outline, sample chapters)." Reviews book mss (75%-25% fiction to nonfiction). Represents 30 writers. Usually obtains clients via recommendations. Presently accepting new clients, but very selectively. Writer need not demonstrate a number of sales "but it's unusual to take on a new client with no track record." Member of I.L.A.A.
Terms: Agent's commission: 10%.

ETHAN ELLENBERG LITERARY AGENT/CONSULTANT, 548 Broadway, #5-C, New York NY 10012. (212)431-4554. Agency estab. 1983. Quality fiction and nonfiction. (75%-25% fiction to nonfiction.) Special interests: first novels, thriller, horror, spy, science fiction. Usually obtains new clients via referrals (75%) or solicitations (25%). Currently represents 25 clients. Query. Responds to queries in 30 days; to mss in 60 days. New/unpublished writers: 75%.
Recent Sales: *Jason Cosmo*, by Dan McGirt (NAL); *Springblade*, by Greg Walker (Berkley); *The Defenders*, by Jerry and Sharon Ahern (Dell).
Terms: Agent's commission: 15% on domestic sales. "75% of income derived from commission on ms sales; 25% of my business is derived from selling translations and performance rights. I only take clients I feel I can help, and I will not take a new client lightly. I usually give a quick response. I am actively seeking clients."

NICHOLAS ELLISON, INC., 55 Fifth Ave., New York NY 10003. (212)206-6050. Agency estab. 1984. Novels. Also reviews nonfiction (70%-30% fiction to nonfiction). Special interest: mainstream. Usually obtains new clients via recommendations. Currently represents 70 authors. Presently accepting new clients. Send entire ms. Responds to mss in 1-2 months. New/unpublished writers: 15%.
Recent Sales: *Word of Honor*, by Nelson DeMille; *To Kill the Potemkin*, by Mark Joseph; *The Secrets of Eva Hathaway*, by Janice Weber.
Terms: Agent's commission: 15% on domestic sales; 20% on foreign sales. Charges a portion of photocopying expense. 100% of income derived from commissions on ms sales.

‡ANN ELMO AGENCY INC., 60 East 42nd St., New York NY 10165. (212)661-2880. Agent contact: Ann Elmo or Lettie Lee. Agency estab. 1940s. Novels. Also reviews nonfiction. Special interests: mainstream, children's. No science fiction or fantasy. Usually obtains new clients via recommendations. Currently represents 50 authors. Not presently accepting new clients. Send query or entire ms. Responds to queries within a week; to mss "depending on length." Member of S.A.R.
Recent Sales: "Six romances. 2 western series going at one a month. 2 nonfiction (Harlequin, NAL and Berkley; Wm. Morrow for nonfiction.)"
Terms: Agent's commission: 15% on domestic sales; 20% on foreign sales.

‡ESTRADA LITERARY AGENCY, 8288 Gilman Dr., #47, La Jolla CA 92037. (619)457-3087. Agent contact: Patricia Estrada. Estab. 1985. Novels. Special interests: mysteries, horror, science fiction, suspense, romance, other genre fiction. Usually obtains new clients via referrals and recommendations; occasionally at conferences. Currently represents 20 authors. Presently accepting new clients. Query or send outline with sample chapters. Responds to queries in 1-2 weeks; to mss in 4-6 weeks. New/unpublished writers: 50%.
Recent Titles: *To Capture a Rake*, by Valerie Bosna (Berkley); *Man in a Wire Cage*, by Mark Perakh (Critic's Choice); and *Deadly Grounds*, by Patricia Wallace (Zebra).
Terms: Agent's commission: 15% on first novel for previously unpublished writers, reduced to 10% on subsequent books; 15% on foreign sales. Charges $35 one-time-only marketing fee for previously unpublished writers. 95% of income derived from commission on ms sales; .05% from marketing fees. "We are a small agency and offer highly personalized service to our clients, but we are *very* selective. Don't query us until your book is complete, and please submit your very best work in a professional manner. We will work with you to make a good book better, but haven't time for writing clinics."

‡FELICIA ETH LITERARY REPRESENTATION, Suite 62, 140 University Ave., Palo Alto CA 94301. (415)365-1276. Agent contact: Felicia Eth. Estab. 1988. "Though this is a brand new agency, I was an agent at Writers House Inc. in N.Y. from 1977 to 1985, handling some 65 clients." Novels, story collections, "also shorter material if book is in progress." Also reviews nonfiction (45%-55% fiction to nonfiction). Special interests: "accessible high-quality fiction. Not particularly interested in series romance, historicals, sf, men's action, ya novels or juveniles. Primarily developing a client list of Western based writers deserving strong representation to N.Y." Usually obtains new clients via "recommendations of editors, writing instructors, reviewers, as well as soliciting new writers whose short fiction I've read in literary magazines." Presently accepting new clients. Send 2-3 sample chapters (fiction). Reports to query letters in 10-14 days; to mss in 4 weeks. Member of I.L.A.A.
Recent Sales: "In light of my unique situation of just starting up in California (having been an West Coast editor for one of the N.Y. houses till I founded this agency) I'm just in the process of getting material to sell. Some sales from my days at Writers House: *Tales of the City*, by A. Maupin (Harper & Row); *Firelord*, by P. Godwin (Bantam); *Letters to Alice*, by Fay Weldon (HBJ reprint)."
Terms: All income derived from commission on sales of ms; no reading or consulting fees. "I believe I may be the only agent on the West Coast who's been an active agent in N.Y. for many years previously, which places me in a unique position to handle West Coast authors."

JOHN FARQUHARSON LTD., 250 W. 57th St., New York NY 10107. (212)245-1993. Agent contact: Deborah Schneider. Agency estab. 1919. Novels. Also reviews nonfiction (50%-50% fiction to nonfiction). Special interests: mainstream, literary, mysteries. Usually obtains new clients via recommendations. Currently represents 125 authors. Presently accepting new clients, but very few. Query. Responds to queries in 1-2 weeks; to mss in 4-6 weeks. Member of S.A.R. and I.L.A.A.
Terms: Agent's commission: 10% on domestic sales; 20% on foreign sales. 100% of income derived from commissions on ms sales.

FLORENCE FEILER LITERARY AGENCY, 1524 Sunset Plaza Dr., Los Angeles CA 90069. (213)652-6920. Agent Contact: Florence Feiler. Reviews novels. "No short stories." Special interest: mainstream, how-tos. Usually obtains new clients via recommendations from others. Query. Responds to queries in 6 weeks.
Recent Sales: *Out of Africa/Shadows of the Grass, Babette's Feast*, by Isak Dinesen (Random House); *Gay Priest*, by Malcolm Boyd (St. Martin's Press); *All that Sparkles*, by Stella Cameron (Harlequin Intrigue).
Terms: Agent's commission: 10% on domestic sales; 20% on foreign sales.

MARJE FIELDS—RITA SCOTT, Room 1205, 165 W. 46th St., New York NY 10036. (212)764-5740. Agent Contact: Ray Powers. Agency estab. 1961. Novels. Also reviews nonfiction. Special interests: "All kinds, but we do not represent children's books." Currently represents 40 authors. Presently ac-

cepting new clients. Query. Responds to queries in 1 day.
Recent Sales: *Manhattan is My Beat*, by Jeff Deaver (Bantam); *People Next Door*, by Caroline Crane (Dodd-Mead); *High Crimes*, by John Westermann (Soho Press).
Terms: Agent's commission: 15% on domestic sales; 20% on foreign sales.

FRIEDA FISHBEIN LTD., 2556 Hubbard St., Brooklyn NY 11235. (212)247-4398. Contact: Janice Fishbein. Agency estab. 1926. Novels. Also reviews nonfiction: (75%-25% fiction to nonfiction). Special interest: mainstream. Usually obtains new clients via recommendations and referral by staff readers. Currently represents 37 authors. Presently accepting new clients. "Responds to query letters in two weeks. Partial or complete manuscripts are not to be sent with query letter; sends criticism of manuscripts accepted for review in 4-6 weeks."
Recent Sales:*Dr. Death*, by Herb Fisher (Berkley); /*French Azilum*, by Jeanne Mackin (St. Martin's Press). .
Terms: Agent's commission: 10% on domestic sales; 15% on foreign sales. Charges reading fee for new, unpublished authors—$60 for first 50,000 words, pro-rated thereafter at $1 per thousand. Offers cricitism service. "Analysis (criticism) and summary done by staff reader. If ms found marketable, it is referred to myself or an associate." 75% of income derived from commission on ms sales; 25% from criticism service.

‡FLAMING STAR LITERARY, 320 Riverside Dr., New York NY 10025. Agent Contact: Joseph B. Vallely. Estab. 1985. Fiction and nonfiction (50%-50% fiction to nonfiction). Special interests: mainstream—adult, no children's. Usually obtains new clients via referrals. Presently accepting new clients. Send query with SASE. Reponds to queries "immediately"; to mss in 1 week. New/unpublished writers: 75%.
Recent Sales: "Confidential."
Terms: Agent's commission: 10% for published authors; 15% for unpublished. "No fees." 100% of income derived from commission on ms sales.

THE FOLEY AGENCY, 34 E. 38th St., New York NY 10016. (212)686-6930. Contact: Joan or Joe Foley. Novels and nonfiction (50%-50% fiction to nonfiction). Query first by letter with SASE. No manuscripts. Accepts very few new clients.
Terms: Agent's commission: 10%.

‡THE RICARDO HUNTER GARCIA AGENCY, 301 W. 45th St. New York NY 10026. (212)247-4320. Agent contact: Ricardo Hunter Garcia. Estab. 1988. Novels. Also reviews nonfiction (80%-20% fiction to nonfiction). Special interests: "mainstream popular fiction, romance, 'brat pack' fiction, gay novels, thrillers." Usually obtains new clients via recommendations and queries. Currently represents 15 authors. Presently accepting new authors. Send query and outline/proposal. Responds to queries in 3 weeks; to mss in 6-8 weeks. New/unpublished writers: 60%.
Terms: Agent's commission: 15% on domestic sales; 15% on foreign sales. 100% of income derived from commission on ms sales.

JAY GARON-BROOKE ASSOCIATES, INC., 415 Central Park West, New York NY 10025. (212)866-3654. Contact: Jay Garon. "Mainstream, male and female action, adventure, mainstream romance (contemporary), frontier novels with authentic research, non-category horror novels, generational suspense sagas." Area of specialization: "whatever is selling at a given time; fiction and nonfiction." Query first; no phone calls. No magazine shorts or articles. Represents approximately 110 writers. Presently accepting new clients with credits via queries and recommendations only. New/unpublished writers: queries only.
Terms: Agent's commission: 15% domestic; 30% foreign sales.

MAX GARTENBERG, LITERARY AGENT, 15 W. 44th St., New York NY 10036. (212)860-8451. Contact: Max Gartenberg. Novels. Special interests: mainstream, suspense and mystery novels. Represents 30 writers. Query. Also reviews nonfiction (50%-50% fiction to nonfiction). Obtains clients chiefly via queries and recommendations from others. Presently accepting few new clients. "Approximately 20% of my sales each year are for new clients, who are rarely, however, unpublished writers."
Terms: Agent's commission: 10%.

GELLES-COLE LITERARY ENTERPRISES, 320 E. 42d St., New York NY 10017. (212)573-9857. Agency estab. 1983. Novels. Also reviews nonfiction (75%-25% fiction to nonfiction). Special interests: mainstream and "relationship" novels. Usually obtains new clients via recommendations from others or at conferences. Currently represents 25 authors. Presently accepting new clients. Query. Responds to queries in 2 weeks; to mss in 3½-4 weeks. New/unpublished writers: 5%.

Recent Sales: *The Seduction*, by Art Bourgeau (Donald Fine Inc.); *Nothing More Than Love*, by De-wanna Pace (Crown/Pageant).
Terms: Agent's commission: 15% on domestic sales; 20% on foreign sales. Charges reading fee: $75-proposal; $100-novel under 250 pages; $150-over 250 pages. Offers criticism service: "This is very var-ied from project to project. We've charged between $500 and $10,000. The book is completely analyzed and then edited by me." Charges for overseas phone calls, photocopying for multiple submissions, overnight mail expenses. "These two areas of the agency (ms sales and editorial service) are separate—many writers in editorial service come to me from other agents or publishers. I frequently place writers in editorial service with other agents. Usually the literary agency clients are *not* out of the editorial serv-ice. In fact there are only two."

‡LUCIANNE S. GOLDBERG LITERARY AGENTS, INC., 255 W. 84th St., New York NY 10024. Es-tab. 1974. Novels. Also reviews nonfiction (25%-75% fiction to nonfiction). Special interest; main-stream. Usually obtains new clients via recommendations from others. Currently represents 68 writers. Presently accepting new clients. Send sample chapters. Responds to queries in 1 month. New/unpub-lished writer: 2%.
Recent Sales: *Lovers of the African Night* (Delacorte); *Time Capsule* (Morrow); *Fantasies* (Simon & Schuster).
Terms: Charges $150 reading fee for full manuscript. Will critique a 300-page novel for $150. Charges for "long distance, extensive Xerox, express mail." 98% of income derived from commission on ms sales; 2% on criticism service. Payment of fee does not ensure agency representation.

GOODMAN ASSOCIATES, 500 West End Ave., New York NY 10024. 1976. Contact: Elise S. Good-man. Agency estab. 1976. General adult fiction and nonfiction. Usually obtains new clients via letters of inquiry, recommendations. Currently represents approximately 100 authors. Presently accepting new clients on a very selective basis. Query with SASE. Responds to queries in 10 days; to mss in 4 weeks. Member of I.L.A.A. (Arnold Goodman is currently president of I.L.A.A.)
Terms: Agent's commission: 15% on domestic sales; 20% on foreign sales. Also bills for certain ex-penses: telexes, toll calls, overseas postage, photocopying of mss and proposals, book purchases. 100% of income derived from commissions on ms sales. Does not handle "poetry, sci fi and fantasy, articles, individual stories, or children's or YA material."

SANFORD J. GREENBURGER ASSOCIATES, 55 5th Ave., New York NY 10003. (212)206-5600. Adult novels only (no short fiction, poetry). Send query letter and detailed description or approximately 50-page sample with synopsis of balance. Also reviews nonfiction (50%-50% fiction to nonfiction). Presently accepting new clients. Interested in new/beginning novelists. Member of I.L.A.A.
Terms: Agent's commission: 15%.

MAIA GREGORY ASSOCIATES, 311 East 72nd St., New York NY 10021. Agent contact: Maia Gre-gory. Estab. 1976. Novels, novellas, story collections. Also reads nonfiction (25%-75% fiction to non-fiction). Special interests: literary fiction—no romance or popular fiction. Currently represents 10 cli-ents. Presently accepting very few new clients. Query or send outline/proposal. Responds to query in 2 weeks; to mss in 1 month. New/unpublished writers: 50%.
Terms: Agent's commission: 10 or 12% on domestic sales; 20% on foreign sales. Charges for Xeroxing and foreign calls and mailings. 100% of business is derived from commissions on ms sales.

REECE HALSEY AGENCY, 8733 Sunset Blvd., Los Angeles CA (213)652-2409. Query only with SASE. Also reviews nonfiction ("no set ratio"). Interested in new/beginning novelists, but not present-ly accepting new clients.
Terms: Agent's commission: 10%.

‡ALEXANDRIA HATCHER AGENCY, 150 W. 55th St., New York NY 10019. (212)757-8596. Agen-cy estab. 1976. Novels. Also reviews nonfiction (20%-80% fiction to nonfiction). Special interest: mainstream. Usually obtains new clients via recommendations. Currently represents 15-20 authors. No unsolicited mss. Not presently accepting new clients. Query by telephone. Responds to queries in 3 weeks; to mss in 8 weeks. New/unpublished writers: 75%. Member of I.L.A.A.
Terms: Agent's commission: 15% on domestic sales; 20% on foreign sales, including foreign agent's fee. Charges $50 handling fee with all new material submitted for the first time. Responds with com-ments on "why I think I can't sell it—what needs to be done to make it saleable, if possible." Charges for out-of-pocket expenses. 95% of income derived from commissions on ms sales; 5% from criticism services.

HEACOCK LITERARY AGENCY, INC., Suite 14, 1523 6th St., Santa Monica CA 90401. (213)393-6227. Contact: James B. Heacock, president; Rosalie Heacock, vice president. Agency estab. 1978. Also reviews nonfiction (10%-90% fiction to nonfiction). Usually obtains new clients via recommendations from others; solicitations; at conferences. Currently represents 50 authors. Presently accepting new clients. Query with sample chapters and SASE. Responds to queries in 3 weeks. New/unpublished nonfiction writers: 20%. Member of I.L.A.A. and Association of Talent Agents.
Recent Sales: *Moonflute*, by Don and Audrey Wood (Harcourt Brace Jovanovich); *Skin Secrets*, by Dr. Joseph Bark (McGraw Hill); *Country Bear's Good Neighbor*, by Larry Brimner (Franklin Watts).
Terms: Agent's commission: domestic is 15% of first $50,000 author earnings each calendar year and 10% for the balance of the year. Foreign 25% "only when a foreign agent is used. If sold directly to a foreign publisher it's 15%." 97% of income derived from commission on ms sales; 3% from "consulting to authors who are not represented providing advice on contract matters at $125/hour. Our agency presently represents only previously published novelists due to market conditions which favor nonfiction. We do not invite even queries from other novelists."

‡THE JEFF HERMAN AGENCY, INC., 166 Lexington Ave., New York NY 10016. (212)725-4660. Agent contact: Jeffrey H. Herman. Estab. 1985. Novels. Also reviews nonfiction (25%-75% fiction to nonfiction). Usually obtains new clients via referrals. Currently represents 50 authors. Presently accepting new clients. Send query. Responds to queries in 10 days; to mss in 4 weeks. New/unpublished writers: 25%. Member of I.L.A.A.
Recent Sales: 36 nonfiction titles sold; no fiction yet sold.
Terms: Agent's commission: 15% on domestic sales; 10% on foreign sales. Charges for manuscript/proposal Xeroxing costs, overseas electronic communications. 100% of income derived from commission on ms sales.

‡SUSAN HERNER RIGHTS AGENCY, 666 Third Ave. 10th Fl., New York NY 10017. (212)983-5230/1/2. Agent contact: Susan Herner, Sue Yuen. Agency estab. 1986. Novels. Also reviews nonfiction. Special interests: mainstream, romance, mystery, science fiction/fantasy, horror. Usually obtains new clients via referrals, conferences, unsolicited query letters. Currently represents 20 authors. Presently accepting new clients. Send 3-5 sample chapters. Responds to queries in 1-2 weeks; to mss in 4-6 weeks. New/unpublished writers: 75%.
Recent Sales: *Quest*, by Richard Ben Sapir (E. P. Dutton); *Bad Voltage*, by Jonathan Littell (New American Library); *Natural History*, by David Rosenthal (Alfred A. Knopf).
Terms: Agent's commission: 15% on domestic sales; 20% on foreign sales. 50% of income derived from commission on ms sales. "Our agency also handles subsidiary rights for middle and small publishing companies and other literary agents and packagers. That income is 50% of our business."

HHM LITERARY AGENCY, Box 106, Rahway NJ 07065. Agency estab. 1985. Agent Contact: Haes Hill Monroe. Novels and nonfiction. Obtains new clients through referrals only. Represents 20 writers. Query first with outline plus sample chapters. No response without SASE.
Terms: Agent's commission: 15% domestic; 20% foreign.

FREDERICK HILL ASSOCIATES, 2237 Union St., San Francisco, CA 94123. (415)921-2910. Agency estab. 1979. Novels. Also reviews nonfiction. Special interests: literary and mainstream fiction. Usually obtains new clients via recommendations from others; solicitation; at conferences. Currently represents 75 authors. Presently accepting new clients. Query.
Terms: Agent's commission: 15% on domestic sales; 20% on foreign sales. 100% of income derived from commissions on ms sales.

‡ALICE HILTON LITERARY AGENCY, (formerly Warren/Hilton Agency), 13131 Welby Way, Suite B, North Hollywood CA 91606. (818)982-2546. Agent contact: Alice Hilton. Agency estab. 1985. Novels, novellas, stories and story collections. "Preliminary query appreciated." Also reviews nonfiction (80%-20% fiction [and films] to nonfiction). "Approximately 60% of my work is cinematic." Special interests: mainstream, science fiction, romance, quality humor and wit, children's. Usually obtains new clients via *Writer's Market*, *LMP*, other trade publications, referrals. Currently represents 22 clients. Presently accepting new clients. Query or send entire ms. Responds to queries in 2 weeks; to mss in 6 weeks. New/unpublished writers: 60%.
Terms: Agent's commission: 10% on domestic sales; 20% on foreign sales. Charges reading fee: approx. $150 for 300-page ms. "Mostly, I do the evaluating myself. Sometimes I use outside readers, especially if special expertise is required." 80% of income derived from commission on sales; 20% derived from reading fees. Payment of fees does not ensure agency representation.

HINTZ & FITZGERALD, INC. LITERARY AGENCY, 207 E. Buffalo, Milwaukee WI 53202. (414)273-0300. Agent contact: Sandy Hintz. Agency estab. 1975. Novels. Also reviews nonfiction (75%-25% fiction to nonfiction). Usually obtains new clients via recommendations, listings and editors. Currently represents 25 authors. Query. Responds to queries in 1 month; to mss in 4-6 weeks. New/unpublished writers: 5%.
Recent Sales: *Bimbos of the Death Sun*, by Sharyn McCrumb; *Too, Too Solid Flesh*, by Nick O'Donohoe (TSR).
Terms: Agent's commission: 12% on domestic sales; 15% on foreign sales. 100% of income derived from commissions on ms sales.

JOHN L. HOCHMANN BOOKS, 320 E. 58th St., New York NY 10022. (212)319-0505. Agency estab. 1976. Novels. Also reviews nonfiction (50%-50% fiction to nonfiction). Special interests: mainstream, adventure, romance. Usually obtains new clients via recommendations. Currently represents 22 authors. Presently accepting new clients. Send detailed outline/proposal plus letter describing previously published work. New/unpublished writers: 0%. Responds to queries in 1 week; to outline plus sample chapters in 4 weeks. Member of I.L.A.A.
Terms: Agent's commission: 15% on domestic sales; 25% on foreign sales. "We charge only for photocopies of manuscripts; fees for extraordinary services are charged if clients agree in advance." 100% of income derived from commissions on ms sales. "Our agency also originates ideas for books and series, in which case we act as an agency with an interest."

YVONNE HUBBS LITERARY AGENCY, Box 342, San Juan Capistrano CA 92693-0342. (714)496-1970. Contact: Yvonne Hubbs. Estab. 1983. Reviews novels. Also reviews nonfiction (80%-20% fiction to nonfiction). Special interests: romance, mainstream, glitz, horror, suspense/intrigue. Usually obtains new clients through references from other writers and at conferences. Presently accepting new clients. Query. Responds to queries in 2 weeks.
Terms: Agent's commission: 15% on domestic sales; 20% on foreign sales. Charges fee to new writers for full critique of "basic plot problems, typos, suggestions to improve manuscript. I write the critiques." $45 for 250 pages; $65 for 300 pages. 70% of income derived from commission on ms sales; 30% from criticism service. Payment of fees ensures agency representation "if writer can rewrite for marketability. I operate my business as a doctor/patient or attorney/client set-up. My clients are my best references for new clients."

INTERNATIONAL CREATIVE MANAGEMENT, 40 W. 57th St., New York NY 10019. (212)556-5600. Contact: Suzanne Gluck. Novels. Query preferred; send outline plus sample chapters and biographical thumbnail. Also reviews nonfiction. Presently accepting new clients. Interested in new/beginning novelists. Member of S.A.R.
Terms: Agent's commission: 10%; 15% British; 20% foreign. Unsolicited mss will not be accepted.

‡SHARON JARVIS & CO., INC., 260 Willard Ave., Staten Island NY 10314. (718)273-1066. Agency estab. 1982. Novels. Also reviews nonfiction (80%-20% fiction to nonfiction). Special interests: "category/genre fiction, esp. science fiction, fantasy, horror; mainstream, nonfiction occult." Usually obtains new clients via conferences and references; mail queries. Currently represents 80 authors. Presently accepting new clients. Send query. Responds to queries immediately; to mss in 2-3 months. New/unpublished writers: 20%. Member of SFWA, WWA, MWA, RWA, I.L.A.A., INFO.
Recent Sales: *Vietnam: Gound Zero* series, by Eric Helm (Gold Eagle); *The Star Trek Interview Book*, by Allan Fasherman (Pocket Books); *Came a Spider*, by Michael Hammonds (Berkley).
Terms: Agent's commission: 15% on domestic sales; 10% on foreign sales; "split 15% for movie/TV." Charges $40 reading fee for first 3 chapters and outline; if we request balance of manuscrpt, there is no further fee; authors can choose to have their entire ms read for $60 instead of chapters." 100% of income derived from commission on ms sales. "Reading fee goes to outside reader." Payment of fees does not ensure agency representation. "Queries should include SASE; partials and manuscripts should include postage and mailing instructions."

ASHER D. JASON ENTERPRISES, INC., 111 Barrow St., New York NY 10014. (212)929-2179. Agency estab. 1983. Novels. Also reviews nonfiction (20%-80% fiction to nonfiction). Special interests: mainstream, suspense/espionage/mystery and romance. Usually obtains new clients via recommendations. Currently represents 30 authors. Presently accepting new clients. Query with outline plus sample chapters. Responds to queries immediately; to mss in 3 weeks. New/unpublished writers: 35%.
Terms: Agent's commission: 15% on domestic sales; 20% on foreign sales. Charges for photocopying expenses. 100% of income derived from commission on ms sales.

JCA LITERARY AGENCY, INC., 242 West 27th St., New York NY 10001. (212)807-0888. Agent Contact: Jane Cushman, Jeff Gerecke. Agency estab. 1978. Novels. Also reviews nonfiction (40%-60% fiction to nonfiction). Special interests: "literary fiction, thrillers/adventure and mysteries, commercial fiction." Currently represents 100 authors. Presently accepting new clients. Send query. Responds to queries in 2 weeks; to mss in 6 weeks. New/unpublished writers: 10%. Member of S.A.R.
Recent Sales: *Michigan Roll*, by Tom Kakonis (St. Martin's Press); *The Aviators*, by W. E. B. Griffin (Putnam); *Dead Run*, by Tony Gibbs (Random House).
Terms: Agent's commission: 10% on domestic sales; 15/20% on foreign sales. Charges for cost of bound galleys and copies of books to be submitted are deducted from author earnings. 100% of income derived from commission on ms sales.

JET LITERARY ASSOCIATES, INC., 124 E. 84th St., New York NY 10028. (212)879-2578. Agency estab. 1976. Novels. Also reviews nonfiction (40%-60% fiction to nonfiction). "Mainstream only. No children, sci fi or young adult." Usually obtains new clients via recommendation. Currently represents 80 authors. Not presently accepting new clients. Query. Responds to queries in 2 weeks; to mss in 1 month. New/unpublished writers: 5%.
Recent Sales: *In La La Land*, by Robert Campbell (Mysterious Press); *A Fragile Peace*, by Jonellen Heckler (Putnam's); *Summer Long A Coming*, by Barbara Finkelstein (Harper & Row).
Terms: Agent's commission: 15% on domestic sales; 25% on foreign sales. Charges for Xeroxing, long distance phone calls, postage expenses. 100% of income derived from commissions on ms sales.

LARRY KALTMAN LITERARY AGENCY, 1301 S. Scott St., Arlington VA 22204. (703)920-3771. Agent contact: Larry Kaltman. Agency estab. 1984. Novels, novellas. Also reviews nonfiction (75%-25% fiction to nonfiction). Special interest: mainstream. Usually obtains new clients via recommendations from others and solicitation. Currently represents 10 authors. Presently accepting new clients. Send entire ms. Responds to queries in 2 weeks; to mss in 2 weeks. New/unpublished writers: 75%.
Recent Sales: *RASTUS on Capitol Hill*, by Samuel Edison (Hunter House).
Terms: Agent's commission: 15% on domestic and foreign sales. Charges reading fee of $150 to 300 pages; $50 for each succeeding 100 pages for mss. "The author receives an approximately 1,000-word letter commenting on writing style, organization and marketability." 80% of income derived from commissions on ms sales; 20% from criticism service.

KIDDE, HOYT & PICARD, 335 E. 51st St., Apt. 1G, New York NY 10022. (212)755-9461. Novels and nonfiction (70%-30% fiction to nonfiction). Special interests: mainstream, literary and romatic fiction. Usually obtains new clients via recommendations from others, solicitations. Currently represents 50 authors. Presently accepting a few new clients. Query. Responds to queries in 1-2 weeks; to mss in 2-4 weeks. Associate member S.A.R.
Recent Sales: *Twilight of Innocence*, by Helene Lehr; *Silver Lining*, by Norma Seely; *Where has My Brother Gone*, by Lydia Long.
Terms: Agent's commission: 10% on domestic sales. Charges postage and phone call expenses. 100% of income derived from commissions on ms sales.

HARVEY KLINGER, INC., 301 W. 53rd St., New York NY 10019. (212)581-7068. Agency estab. 1977. Novels. Also reviews nonfiction (40%-60% fiction to nonfiction). Special interest: mainstream. Usually obtains new clients via referrals from publishers and existing clients. Currently represents 75 authors. Presently accepting new clients. Query with outline/proposal. Responds to queries in 2 weeks; to mss in 6-8 weeks. New/unpublished writers: 15-20%.
Recent Sales: *Green City in the Sun*, by Barbara Wood (Random House); *Butterfly*, by Kathryn Harvey (Villard); *The Final Opus of Leon Solomon*, by Jerome Badanes (Knopf).
Terms: Agent's commission: 15% on domestic sales; 25% on foreign sales.

BARBARA S. KOUTS, LITERARY AGENT, 788 Ninth Ave. 3A, New York NY 10019. (212)265-6003. Agency estab. 1980. Novels. Also reviews nonfiction (50%-50% fiction to nonfiction). Special interests: literary, mainstream, women's and children's novels. Usually obtains new clients via recommendations from others; at conferences; by queries. Currently represents 50 authors. Presently accepting new clients. Query with outline/proposal. Responds to queries in 3 weeks; to mss in 4-8 weeks. New/unpublished writers: 70%.
Recent Sales: *Short and Shivery*, by Robert San Souci (Doubleday); *Bed and Breakfast Across North America*, by Hal Gieseking (Simon & Schuster).
Terms: Agent's commission: 10% on domestic sales; 20% on foreign sales. 100% of income derived from commisssions on ms sales.

LUCY KROLL AGENCY, 390 West End Ave., New York NY 10024. Send mss to 2211 Broadway, New York NY 10024. (212)877-0556. Contact: Lucy Kroll or Barbara Hogenson. Novels. Special interest: contemporary. Represents 35 writers (including playwrights and screenwriters). Query. Also reviews nonfiction (50%-50% fiction to nonfiction). Obtains new clients via recommendations from others; queries occasionally. "Not actively seeking new clients, but we take them on occasionally."

PETER LAMPACK AGENCY, INC., Suite 2015, 551 5th Ave., New York NY 10017. (212)687-9106. Agent Contact: Peter Lampack. Agency estab. 1977. Novels, novellas. Also represents nonfiction (60%-40% fiction to nonfiction). Special interests: commercial fiction, especially contemporary relationships, out-of-category male-oriented action adventure, distinguished issue-oriented nonfiction and literary fiction. Usually obtains new clients via recommendations from others. Currently represents 60 authors. Presently accepting new clients. Query —no unsolicted mss. Responds to queries in 2 weeks. New/unpublished writers: 15%.
Recent Sales: *First Born*, by Doris Mortman (Bantam); *Treasure*, by Clive Cussler (Simon & Schuster); and *Stinger*, by Robert McCammon (Pocket Books).
Terms: Agent's commission: 15% on domestic sales; 20% on foreign sales. Author is responsible for supplying all submission copies. 100% of income derived from commissions on ms sales.

THE LANTZ OFFICE, 888 7th Ave., New York NY 10106. (212)586-0200. Contact: Joy Harris. Special interest: mainstream. Also reviews nonfiction (50%-50% fiction to nonfiction). Represents 60 writers. Usually obtains new writers via recommendations and writer's conferences. Presently accepting new clients on limited basis. New/unpublished writers: 10%. Member of S.A.R.

MICHAEL LARSEN/ELIZABETH POMADA LITERARY AGENTS, 1029 Jones St., San Francisco CA 94109. (415)673-0939. Agency estab. 1972. Novels. Also reviews nonfiction. Special interests: mainstream, historical, contemporary, literary, commercial, romance and mysteries. Usually obtains new clients via recommendations from others. Currently represents 100 authors. Presently accepting new clients. Send first 30 pages of completed manuscript and a synopsis with SASE. Responds to queries in 6-8 weeks. New/unpublished writers: 50%. Member of I.L.A.A.
Recent Sales: *Chantal*, by Yvone Lenard (Delacorte)' *Darkspell*, by Katharine Kerr (Foundation); *The Gathering of Winds*, by June Lund Shiplett (NAL)..
Terms: Agent's commission: 15% on domestic sales; 20% on foreign sales. As agents, we desperately seek new novelists, who are the lifeblood of the publishing world."

‡THE L. HARRY LEE LITERARY AGENCY, Box 203, Rocky Point NY 11778. (516)744-1188. Agent contact: Vito Brenna, Lisa Judd, Holli Rovitti, Dawn Dreyer. Agency estab. 1979. Novels. Does not review nonfiction. Special interests: mainstream, sf, historical, war, horror, occult, mystery, suspense, modern sexy romance, western, adventure, thrillers, spy and literary works. Usually obtains new clients via recommendations, solicitations, conferences, watering holes. Currently represents 155 authors, 94 of whom are screenwriters or playwrights. Presently accepting new clients. Query. Responds to queries in 3-4 weeks; to mss in 4-6 weeks. New/unpublished writers: 20%. Member of S.A.R., I.L.A.A., WGA, East, Inc.
Recent Sales: *Gatekeeper*; by Dana Reed (Dorchester); *The Hermit Kingdom*, by Don Kraus (Dell); *The Tel-Star Conspiracy*, by James G. Kingston (Warner Books).
Terms: Agents commission: 15% on domestic sales; 20% on foreign sales. Charges $50 reading fee "for 1st 50 pages; $100 for the rest of the novel regardless of length. That's with a critique." Offers criticism service by "competent associates who have years of experience. Critiques range from 3-6 pages. Plus a marked-up manuscript." Charges fee for "postage, handling (includes phone calls, letters, packaging), file set-up, responses to rejections etc. Copyright forms available, Associates available at all times." 90% of income derived from commissions on mss; 10% from criticism service. "Good story telling essential. Good writing essential. The market is getting tougher and tougher, so you got to be good to sell today."

ELLEN LEVINE LITERARY AGENCY INC., Suite 1205, 432 Park Ave. S, New York NY 10016. (212)889-0620. Agents: Ellen Levine, Diana Finch. Reviews novels and nonfiction (50%-50% fiction to nonfiction). Usually obtains new clients through recommendations from clients and editors. Presently accepting new clients. Query. Responds to queries in 1 week; to mss in 4-6 weeks. Member of S.A.R. and I.L.A.A.
Terms: Agent's commision: 10% on domestic sales; 20% on foreign sales.

THE NORMA-LEWIS AGENCY, 521 5th Ave., New York NY 10175. (212)751-4955. Agency estab. 1980. Novels, novellas. Also reviews nonfiction (50%-50% fiction to nonfiction). Special interests: children's, young adult and mainstream adult fiction. Usually obtains new clients via recommendations

and listings in directories. Presently accepting new clients. Query. Responds to queries in 2 weeks.
Terms: Agent's commission: 15% on domestic sales; 20% on foreign sales; 15% on Canadian sales.
100% of income derived from commissions on ms sales.

‡LIGHTHOUSE LITERARY AGENCY, 1112 Solana Ave., Box 2105, Winter Park FL 32790. Agent
contact: Sandra Kangas. Agency estab. 1988. Novel, novellas, story collections. Also reviews nonfiction (71%-29% fiction to nonfiction). Special interests: genre fiction, contemporary, literary, adventure, young adult. Usually obtains new clients via recommendations and professional organizations.
Currently represents 31 authors. Presently accepting new clients. Send entire ms if complete; otherwise,
send query or proposal package. Responds in 2 weeks. New/unpublished writers: 35%. Member of the
Authors Guild.
Terms: Agent's commission: 10% on domestic sales; 20% on foreign sales. No charge to review unsolicited mss for acceptance or rejection. Offers criticism service: will critique 300/page novel for $300;
write for fee schedule. "Within 2 months, author receives a written critique, one or more pages long.
Discussed are clarity, plot, characterization, viewpoint, style, credibility and market potential. Any critiques not done by me personally are done by published specialists in a particular field and overseen by
me." 93% of income derived from commissions on ms sales; 7% from criticism service. "The aim of
our analysis service is to turn an already good manuscript into a marketable one. After the rewrite, if we
feel the work is then salable, we will offer to represent the author. We promise prompt response to proposals, submissions and analysis requests, whether we offer to represent the author or not. We do not believe in holding up an author's work."

‡MAXWELL J. LILLIENSTEIN, 7 Rest Ave., Ardsley NY 10502. Agent Contact: Maxwell J. Lillienstein. Agency estab. 1979. Novels. Also reviews nonfiction (80%-20% fiction to nonfiction). Special
interests: mainstream, historical romances, fantasy, science fiction. Usually obtains new clients via recommendations from others. Currently represents 6 authors. Presently accepting new clients "only
published authors." Send 3 sample chapters. Responds to ms in 30 days.
Terms: Agent's commission: 10% on domestic sales; 10% on foreign sales.

RAY LINCOLN LITERARY AGENCY, 4 Surrey Road, Melrose Park PA 19126. (215)782-8882. Agency estab. 1974. Novels. Also reviews nonfiction (50%-50% fiction to nonfiction). "I particularly like
biographies and popular science." Special interests: "mainstream—contemporary, historical, science
fiction children's—only for ages 8 and upward; mostly young adult; no picture books; no plays; no poetry." Usually obtains new clients by recommendation. Presently accepting new clients "on recommendation." "I prefer a query letter first (with SASE); then if I'm interested I ask for two sample chapters
with overview, then on to full ms if promising." Responds to queries in 1-2 weeks; to mss in 3-4 weeks.
Recent Sales: *Silk Road*, by Jeanne Larsen (Henry Holt); *Dellas*, by Steven Lo (Algonquin Books);
Upchuck Summer's Revenge, by Joel Schwartz (Dell).
Terms: Agent's commission: 15% on domestic sales; 20% on foreign sales. "If I think a ms is very
promising and agree to handle it, then I'll make suggestions for changes in order to make it even better.
For this there is no fee."

LITERARY/BUSINESS ASSOCIATES, Box 2415, Hollywood CA 90078. (213)465-2630. Contact:
Shelley Gross. Agency estab. 1979. Novels, novellas. Also reviews nonfiction (40%-60% fiction to
nonfiction). Special interests: mystery, New Age, occult and contemporary, business. Usually obtains
new clients via recommendations; solicitations; at conferences. Currently represents 5 authors. Presently accepting new clients. Query with outline/proposal. Responds to queries in 1 month; to mss in 2
months. SASE. New/unpublished writers: 85-90%.
Terms: Agent's commission: 15% on domestic sales; 20% on foreign sales. Charges $65 evaluation fee
for up to 300-page ms. "Critique includes detailed written letter plus free literary nonfiction or fiction 1-
page guide sheet." Charges marketing fee of $50. 60% of income derived from commissions on ms
sales; 40% from criticism service. "Marketing fee is refundable after sale has been made."

PETER LIVINGSTON ASSOCIATES, INC., 143 Collier St., Toronto, Ontario M4W 1M2 Canada.
(416)928-1019 (queries) or 465 Park Ave., New York NY 10022. (212)755-5000 (sales). Contact: Peter
W. Livingston, president, David Johnston, agent. Janine Cheeseman, agent. Agency estab. 1981. Novels. Also reviews nonfiction (25%-75% fiction to nonfiction). Special interests: mainstream, commercial and literary. No children's, science fiction or westerns. Usually obtains clients via recommendations from editors and clients. Currently represents 80 clients. Presently accepting new clients. Query.
Responds to queries in 1 week; to mss in 6 weeks. New/unpublished writers: 50%. Member of I.L.A.A.
Recent Titles: *Gray Eagles*, by Duane Unkefer (Morrow, 1985); *The Cross Killer*, by Marcel Monte-
cino (Arbor House, 1988); and *Anna Delaney's Child*, by John Thorndike (MacMillan, 1986).
Terms: Agent's commission: 15% on domestic sales; 20% on foreign sales. "We only charge a reading

fee for previously unpublished book authors for works of fiction. For $75 we will review first two chapters of novel and outline, which we prefer to do to charging full ms fee. If authors want detailed criticism of their novel, they should go and pay elsewhere. Our fees are for screening purposes only. We sell 90% + of all fiction we represent and over 50% of our fiction writers are first-book authors." Does not offer criticism service "but we provide some criticism with our readings." 99% of business derived from commission on ms sales; 1% derived from reading fees and other services. "We refund reading fee if we take on and sell ms. We charge no reading fee under any circumstances for nonfiction. Queries should be sent to our Toronto office. The New York office is primarily a sales office. We are a US corporation. We have co-agents in all major foreign markets and in Hollywood."

LOS ANGELES LITERARY ASSOCIATES, 8955 Norma Place, Los Angeles CA 90069. (213)275-6330. Contact: Joel Gotler. Agency estab. 1987. Novels. Also reviews nonficiton (70%-30% fiction to nonfiction). Special interest: mainstream. Usually obtains new clients via recommendations from others. Query. Responds to queries in 2 weeks. New/unpublished writers: 10%.
Recent Titles: *Brain Building*, by Marilyn Vos Savant (Bantam); *Rockets Red Glare*, by Greg Dinallo (St. Martin's Press).
Terms: Commission: 10% on domestic sales; 20% on foreign sales.

‡LOWENSTEIN ASSOCIATES, 121 W. 27th St., New York NY 10001. (212)206-1630. Agent contact: Lori Perkins. Agency estab. 1978. Novels. Also reviews nonfiction (50%-50% fiction to nonfiction). Special interests: horror, thrlllers—Lori Perkins; romance—Eileen Fallon; women's fiction—Barbara Lowenstein. Usually obtains new clients via recommendations from clients and published authors, conferences. Currently represents 300 authors. Presently accepting new clients. Send query. Responds to queries in 4 weeks; to mss in 6-8 weeks. New/unpublished writers: 20%. Member of I.L.A.A.
Recent Sales: *The Night of the Weeping Women*, by Lawrence Naumoff (Atlantic Monthly Press); *Revelations*, by Peggy Payne (Simon & Schuster); *Beastmaker*, by James V-Smith, Jr. (Dell). "All first novels."
Terms: Agent's commission: 15% on domestic sales; 20% on foreign sales. 100% of income derived from commission on ms sales.

DONALD MacCAMPBELL INC., 12 E. 41st St., New York NY 10017. (212)683-5580. Agent Contact: Donald MacCampbell. Agency estab. 1940. Book-length fiction only. Special interests: adult fiction, specializing in the women's market. Usually obtains new clients via recommendations from others. Presently accepting new clients; no unpublished writers. Query with entire ms. Responds to queries in 2 weeks.
Recent Sales: *Kate*, by Joanna McGauran (Pocket Books); *Thunder*, by Lynne Scott-Drennan (Doubleday); *China Silk*, by Florence Hurd (Ballantine).
Terms: Agent's commission: 10% on domestic sales; 20% on foreign sales. 100% of income derived from commissions on ms sales. "This is a small, highly selective agency for professional writers who write full time in the commercial fiction markets."

GINA MACCOBY LITERARY AGENCY, 124 W. 24th St., Suite 3D, New York NY 10011. Agent contact: Gina Maccoby. Agency estab. 1986. Novels, short stories, story collections. Also reads nonfiction, (50%-50% fiction to nonfiction). Special interests: high quality fiction and nonfiction for adults and children. Usually obtains new clients through referrals from authors, editors, etc. Currently represents 45 clients. Presently accepting new clients. Query or submit outline/proposal plus 1-2 sample chapters and SASE. Responds to queries in 1-2 weeks; to mss in 2-6 weeks. 50% of clients are new/unpublished writers, "although almost all have published in magazines or quarterlies."
Recent Titles: Novel-in-progress by Anne Bernays (Weidenfeld & Nicolson); *Free For All* (first novel), by Jacoba Atlas (E.P. Dutton); and *The Woman Who Was Not All There* (first novel), by Paula Sharp (Harper & Row).
Terms: Agent's commission: 10% on domestic sales; 20% on foreign sales. 100% of income derived from commissions on ms sales. "If multiple copies of a manuscript are required for a multiple submission, I will charge the author for the cost of the copying. I would always tell the author in advance that this expense will be charged to them. Although I indicated above that I will review short stories, it is rare that I would offer representation to an author who is at the stage of circulating one or two stories to magazines. It is, however, one way of introducing me to the writer's work and perhaps establishing a connection that will lead to representation in the future."

JANET WILKENS MANUS LITERARY AGENCY INC., 370 Lexington Ave., New York NY 10017. (212)685-9558. Agency estab. 1981. Novels, novellas. Also reviews nonfiction (50%-50% fiction to nonfiction). Special interests: mainstream, psychology, thrillers, suspense, young adult fiction. Usually

obtains new clients via conferences, recommendations from others. Currently represents 35 authors. Presently accepting new clients. Query with sample chapters. Responds to queries in 2 weeks; to mss in 5-6 weeks. New/unpublished writers: 30%. Member of I.L.A.A.
Recent Sales: *Quarry's Contract*, by Robin Hunter; *Unorthodox Practices*, by Marissa Piesman; *Careless Whispers*, by Carlton Stowers.
Terms: Agent's commission: 15% on domestic sales; 20% on foreign sales. 100% of income derived from commissions on ms sales. "We do offer criticism service for those writers whom we take on to represent."

DENISE MARCIL LITERARY AGENCY, INC., 316 West 82nd St., Suite #5F, New York NY 10024. Agency estab. 1977. Novels. Also reviews nonfiction (65%-35% fiction to nonfiction). Special interests: women's fiction, commercial fiction, horror, psychological suspense. Usually obtains new clients via recommendations from others, conferences, and through query letters. Currently represents 100 authors. Presently accepting few new clients. Query. Responds to queries in 2 weeks; to mss in 3 months. New/unpublished writers: 80% "were unpublished at the time I began representing them." Member of I.L.A.A.
Recent Sales: *Good Bosses Do*, by Betsy Lazary (Amacon); *This Time Forever*, by Rosanne Bittner (Warner Books); *Corsican Woman*, by Madge Swindells (Warner Books).
Terms: Agent's commission: 15% on domestic sales; 20% on foreign sales. Charges $45 for first three chapters and outlines only if we request material. "If I sell the author's work, I charge for disbursements." 99.9% of income derived from commissions on ms sales; .1% from reading service.

ELAINE MARKSON LITERARY AGENCY, 44 Greenwich Ave., New York NY 10011. (212)243-8480. Query letter first. *Do not* send unsolicited mss. "Authors should write to us (*don't call*) and we will respond." Also reviews nonfiction (about 50%-50% fiction to nonfiction). Presently accepting new clients. ("Very rarely, but we do accept clients if we are very impressed with their potential.") Interested in new/beginning novelists. Member of I.L.A.A.
Terms: Agent's commission: 15%.

MARGARET McBRIDE LITERARY AGENCY, Box 8730, La Jolla CA 92038. (619)459-0559. Contact: Winifred Golden, associate. Fiction and nonfiction for adult mainstream market. Prefers query letter. No unsolicited mss. Member of I.L.A.A.
Terms: Agent's commission: 15%.

‡KIRBY McCAULEY LTD., #1509, 432 Park Ave. S., New York NY 10016. (212)683-7561. Agent Contact: Claire Morgan. Agency estab. 1971. Novels. Also reviews nonfiction (99%-1% fiction to nonfiction). Special interests: science fiction, fantasy, horror fiction. Usually obtains new clients via recommendations from others; reading through submissions. Currently represents 25 authors. Presently accepting new clients. Send query. Responds to queries in 1 week.
Recent Sales: *The Dark Tower II: The Drawing of the Three*, by Stephen King; *Communion*, by Whitley Strieber; *Red Dreams*, by Dennis Etchison (Berkley).
Terms: Agent's commission: 10% on domestic sales; 10% on foreign sales.

HELEN MERRILL, LTD., 435 W. 23rd St., New York NY 10011. Agent contact: Helen Merrill, Lourdes López. Estab. 1970. Novels, novellas, short stories and story collections. Also reviews nonfiction. Usually obtains new clients via recommendations from others. Presently accepting new clients. Query. Responds to queries immediately to three months. Member S.A.R.
Recent Sales: *Social Disease*, by Paul Rudnick (Knopf); *Prejudice and Passion*, by Sallie Bingham (Knopf); and *Exiled in Paradise*, by Anthony Heilbut (Viking).
Terms: Agent's commission: 10% on domestic sales; 15% on foreign sales.

ELINOR MIDLIK ASSOCIATES, 254 Willardshire Rd., East Aurora NY 14052. (716)652-9518. President: Elinor R. Midlik. Novels, novellas, short stories, story collections. Fiction and nonfiction. Spcecial interests: mainstream, children, historical, romances, detectives, espionage, adventure serials. Usually obtains new clients by queries from writers. Currently represents 30 clients. Presently accepting new clients. Submit outlne plus sample chapters. Responds to queries in 3 weeks; to mss in 4-5 weeks. New/unpublished writers: 40-50%.
Terms: Agent's commission: 15% on domestic and foreign sales. 100% of income derived from commissions on mss sales.

‡THE PETER MILLER AGENCY, INC., Box 760, Old Chelsea Sta., New York NY 10011. (212)929-1222. Agent contact: Peter Miller. Agency estab. 1976. Novels of all kinds. Also reviews nonfiction (40%-60% fiction to nonfiction). "Interested in category fiction, particularly fiction (or nonfiction)

WOULD YOU USE THE SAME CALENDAR YEAR AFTER YEAR?

Of course not! If you scheduled your appointments using last year's calendar, you'd risk missing important meetings and deadlines, so you keep up-to-date with a new calendar each year. Just like your calendar, *Novel & Short Story Writer's Market®* changes every year, too. Many of the editors move or get promoted, rates of pay increase, and even editorial needs change from the previous year. You can't afford to use an out-of-date book to plan your marketing efforts!

So save yourself the frustration of getting manuscripts returned in the mail, stamped MOVED: ADDRESS UNKNOWN. And of NOT submitting your work to new listings because you don't know they exist. **Make sure you have the most current writing and marketing information by ordering** *1990 Novel & Short Story Writer's Market* **today.** All you have to do is complete the attached post card and return it with your payment or charge card information. Order now, and there's one thing that won't change from your *1989 Novel & Short Story Writer's Market* — the price! That's right, we'll send you the 1990 edition for just $17.95. *1990 Novel & Short Story Writer's Market* will be published and ready for shipment in February 1990.

Let an old acquaintance be forgot, and toast the new edition of *Novel & Short Story Writer's Market.* Order today!

(See other side for more helpful writing books)

MORE BOOKS TO HELP YOU GET PUBLISHED!

NEW! 1989 Children's Writer's & Illustrator's Market®
edited by Connie Eidenier

This new annual brings together the two key aspects of children's publishing — the writing and the illustrating — in one handy volume of book publishers and magazine markets. You'll find over 300 detailed publisher listings, including such special markets as comic books, coloring books, and greeting cards. A helpful article on *how* to freelance in this lucrative market, plus a resource section with listings and information on agents, clubs, and workshops round out this definitive children's market guide.
300 pages/$14.95, paperback

Handbook of Short Story Writing: Volume II
edited by Jean M. Fredette

When you need expert help, go to the experts! Volume II brings fresh insight from a variety of established writers on everything from creating powerful plots to making trouble-free transitions. You'll find inspiration and advice on every aspect of short story writing from Lawrence Block, Gary Provost, Janet Burroway, John Updike, and more.
252 pages/$15.95

Writing the Novel: From Plot to Print
by Lawrence Block

Lawrence Block, author of more than 100 published novels, covers every step of the novel writing and selling process — from developing plot ideas to researching backgrounds — to help you deliver a salable manuscript to the right editor's desk!
197 pages/$8.95, paperback

Use coupon on other side to order your copies today!

which has television and motion picture potential." Usually obtains new clients via referral and reputation as established literary agent for over 12 years. Also writing conferences, and speaking engagements at colleges and universities. Currently represents 50 authors. Presently accepting new clients. Send query. Responds to query quickly; to mss in approximately 3-6 weeks. New/unpublished writers: 40%.
Recent Sales: *Lullaby and Good Night*, by Vincent Bugliosi (NAL); *Night of the Ranger*, by Mark D. Harrell (Lynx Communications, Inc.); *The Jersey Devil*, by Christopher Cook Gilmore (Lynx Communications, Inc.).
Terms: Charges fee (refundable out of first monies earned for author) for full-length novels. Will critique 300-page novel for $225 (nonrefundable out of first moneys earned for author). Critiques are 3-5 pages in length and written by the owner, Peter Miller, and a staff of highly qualified editorial consultants. Charges minimal marketing expenses, including photocopies, deliveries, Federal Express, long distance phone calls, and legal fees. 97% of income derived from commission on ms sales; 2-3% from criticism service. Payment of fees does not ensure agency representation. The agency specializes in representing "true-crime projects and all books that have significant television and motion picture potential and is particularly interested in developing agent/client relations. Agency has established relationships with co-agents throughout the world."

HOWARD MORHAIM LITERARY AGENCY, 175 5th Ave., Room #709, New York NY 10010. (212)529-4433. Novels principally. Query. Also reviews nonfiction (70%-30% fiction to nonfiction). Member of I.L.A.A.
Terms: Agent's commission: 15%.

WILLIAM MORRIS AGENCY, INC., 1350 Avenue of the Americas, New York NY 10019. (212)586-5100. Contact: Literary Department. Unsolicited authors should send letter of inquiry with description of material and author's background. Reviews fiction and nonfiction. Very occasionally accepts new clients. Member of S.A.R.
Terms: Agent's commission: 10%.

MULTIMEDIA PRODUCT DEVELOPMENT, INC., Suite 724, 410 S. Michigan Ave., Chicago IL 60605. (312)922-3063. Agent Contact: Jane Jordan Browne. Agency estab. 1971. Novels. Also reviews nonfiction (35%-65% fiction to nonfiction). Special interests: mainstream, historical, mystery, science fiction, fantasy and romance. Usually obtains new clients via recommendations, word-of-mouth, conferences. Currently represents 100 authors. Presently accepting new clients. Query. Responds to queries in 5 days; to mss in 3 weeks. New/unpublished writers: 5%. Member of I.L.A.A.
Recent Sales: *Swing Sisters*, by Jeane Westin (McGraw Hill); *The Dieter*, by Susan Sussman; *The Fifth Script*, by Ross H. Spencer (Donald I. Fine).
Terms: Agent's commission: 15% on domestic sales; 20% on foreign sales. Charges for photocopying expenses and overseas phone calls. 100% of income derived from commissions on ms sales. "We also review contracts or consult for an hourly fee if someone wants information."

JEAN V. NAGGAR LITERARY AGENCY, INC., 336 E. 73rd St., New York NY 10021. (212)794-1082. Agent contacts: Jean Naggar, Teresa Cavanaugh. Novels and nonfiction. Special interests: mainstream fiction (literary and commercial), suspense, science fiction and mystery; no category romances. Query with SASE. No unsolicited mss. Represents 80 writers. Obtains clients via recommendations, solicited mss, queries and writers' conferences. Presently accepting new clients only on a highly selective basis. Interested in some new/beginning novelists. Member of I.L.A.A. and S.A.R.
Terms: Agent's commission: 15% domestic; 20% foreign.

RUTH NATHAN, 242 W. 27th St., Suite 4A, New York NY 10001. (212)685-0808. Agency estab. 1980. Novels. Also reviews nonfiction (20%-80% ficton to nonfiction). Special interests: mainstream, biography, illustrated books on art and decorative arts and show biz. Usually obtains new clients through recommendations, solicitation or at conferences. Currently represents 12 authors. Presently accepting new clients. Send sample chapters. Responds to queries in 4 weeks; to mss in 6-8 weeks. New/unpublished writers: 20%.
Terms: Agent's commission: 15% on domestic sales; 10% on foreign sales.

CHARLES NEIGHBORS, INC., Suite 3607A, 7600 Blanco Rd., San Antonio TX 78216. (512)342-5324. Agent contact: Margaret Neighbors, vice president. Agency estab. 1966. Novels, story collections. Also reviews nonfiction (60%-40% fiction to nonfiction). Special interest: mainstream, male adventure, romance, mysteries, suspense, westerns and historical. No juveniles. Usually obtains new clients via 90% recommendations from clients and editors, 5% conferences, 5% inquiries. Currently represents 55 authors. Presently accepting new clients. Query with outline/proposal, ms samples and SASE. New/unpublished writers: 15%. Responds to queries in 1 week; to mss in 1 month.

Recent Sales: *War Horse*, by Wayne Barton and Stan Smith (Pocket Books); *Manual of the Mercenary Soldier*, by Paul Balor (Dell); *The Silent Sorority*, by Rhonda Aldrich and Lee Chichester (British American).
Terms: Agent's commission: 15% on domestic sales; 20% on foreign and co-agent motion picture sales. 100% of income derived from commissions on ms sales.

B.K. NELSON LITERARY AGENCY, 149 Madison Ave., Sute 806, New York NY 10016. (212)889-0637. Agency estab. 1979. Novels. Also reviews nonfiction (10%-90% fiction to nonfiction). Special interest: mainstream. Usually obtains new clients via recommendations by others. Currently represents 12 authors. Presently accepting new clients. Query. Responds to queries in "a few days"; to mss in 2 weeks. New/unpublished writers: 100%.
Recent Sales: *Brecher's Odyssey*, by Gerhard Brecher (Pueblo Press); *Cafe Pierre*, by W. Ware Lynch and Charles Romine (Random House).
Terms: Agent's commission: 15% on domestic sales; 10% on foreign sales. Charges a reading fee of $230 for a completed ms. 99% of income derived from commissions on ms; 1% on criticism service.

THE BETSY NOLAN LITERARY AGENCY, 50 West 29th St., 9W, New York NY 10001. (212)779-0700. Contact: Betsy Nolan, Michael Powers, Donald Lehr. Agency estab. 1982. Novels. Also reviews nonfiction (30%-70% fiction to nonfiction). Special interest: mainstream. Presently accepting new clients. Query with outline/proposal. Responds to queries in 2 weeks; to mss in 1 month. New/unpublished writers: 50%.
Terms: Agent's commission: 15% on domestic sales; 20% on foreign sales.

‡NUGENT & ASSOCIATES, INC., 170 10th St. N., Naples FL 33940. (813)262-7562. Agent contact: Ray E. Nugent. Agency estab. 1983. Novels. Also reviews nonfiction (60%-40% fiction to nonfiction). Special interests: "mainstream fiction, particularly historical novels, espionage and mystery/suspense fiction. We do also handle a fairly large amount of juvenile." Usually obtains new clients via publicity, other writers, writing conferences. Currently represents 40 authors. Presently accepting new clients. Send query and sample chapters and summary along with SASE. Responds to queries in 30 days; to mss in 90 days. New/unpublished writers: 60%.
Recent Sales: *Osteoporosis*, by MacIlwain, et al (John Wiley & Sons); *Disney's World*, by Mosley (Stein & Day); *Anti-Patriots*, by Mowl (Book Guild).
Terms: Agent's commission: 15% on domestic sales; 25% on foreign sales. "We charge for all clerical expenses directly associated with the preparation, mailing and materials required for the offering of a client's material. Long distance calls and wires are also billed to the clients." 100% of income derived from commission on ms sales. "On new writers, we request that they deposit in an account with us to offset the clerical expenses as they are incurred. A statement of this account is provided quarterly, and all unused funds in the account are reimbursed to the client in the event the contract is either terminated or the author's first book is sold for publication. The advance payment account is waived after the first book is sold. We only charge our clients for expenses that they would normally incur if they were to attempt to bring their material to market without an agent."

HAROLD OBER ASSOCIATES, INC., 40 E. 49th St., New York NY 10017. (212)759-8600. Novels and general nonfiction. Reads all kinds, category and mainstream. Query first. About 75%-25% fiction to nonfiction. Currently representing 400 writers. Presently accepting new clients but very limited numbers. Represents British agencies also. Member of S.A.R.
Terms: Agent's commission: 10% US; 15% British; 20% other foreign.

FIFI OSCARD ASSOCIATES, 19 W. 44th St., New York NY 10036. (212)764-1100. Novels. Also reviews nonfiction (50%-50% fiction to nonfiction). Special interests: literary, mainstream. Usually obtains new clients via recommendations. Currently represents over 100 authors. Presently accepting new clients. Query. Responds to queries in 2 weeks; to mss in 2-3 weeks. New/unpublished writers: 10%. Member of S.A.R.
Recent Sales: *The Man Who Met The Train*, by Harold Adams (Mysterious Press); *Cardinal Numbers*, by Hob Broun (Knopf); *Two Ways to Count to Ten*, by Ruby Dee (Henry Holt).
Terms: Agent's commission: 15% on domestic sales; 10% on foreign sales. 100% of income derived from commissions on mss.

PEEKNER LITERARY AGENCY, INC., 3418 Shelton Ave., Bethlehem PA 18017. Contact: Barbara Puechner, president. Novels only. Special interests: lead quality adult fiction, suspense. Query. Represents 50-60 writers. Not presently accepting new clients.
Terms: Agent's commission: 10%.

‡**RODNEY PELTER, LITERARY AGENT**, 129 E. 61st St., New York NY 10021. (212)838-3432. Contact: Rodney Pelter. Fiction and nonfiction. Query with SASE, résumé and first 50 pages. Represents 15-25 writers. Obtains clients via recommendations, unsolicited mss and queries. Presently accepting new clients. New/unpublished writers: "probably a majority."
Terms: Agent's commission: 15% on US book sales.

PICKERING ASSOCIATES, INC., 432 Hudson St., New York NY 10014. (212)627-5900. Contact: John Pickering or A. Elizabeth Davidson. Novels, nonfiction, and short story collections. Query. Also reviews nonfiction (50%-50% fiction to nonfiction). Represents 35 writers. Usually obtains clients via recommendations, "but I sometimes write to writers I admire, and am always glad for queries."
Terms: Agent's commission: 15%; standard split on foreign rights.

SIDNEY PORCELAIN AGENCY, Box 1229, Milford PA 18337. (717)296-6420. Agent contact: Sidney Porcelain. Agency estab. 1952. Novels, novellas, short stories. Fiction and nonfiction (75%-25%, fiction to nonfiction). Special interests: novels, mysteries, children's. Usually obtains clients through recommendations; market lists. Currently represents 20 clients. Presently accepting new clients. Query. Responds to queries in a few days; to mss in 2 weeks. New/unpublished writers: 60%. SASE.
Terms: Agent's commission: 10%. "If foreign agent, his fee is separate."

‡**JULIAN PORTMAN & ASSOCIATES**, 8033 Sunset Blvd., Suite 964, Los Angeles CA 90046. (213)281-7391. (CTV/motion picture scripts); Julian Portman and Associates, 7337 N. Lincoln Avenue, Suite 283, Chicago IL 60646. (312)509-6421. (book manuscripts). Agency estab. 1972. Novels. Also reviews nonfiction (45%-55% fiction to nonfiction). Special interests: mainstream, bios, adventure, historical. Usually obtains new clients via recommendations, conferences. Currently represents 17 authors. Presently accepting new clients. Query with outline/proposal. Include SASE. Responds to queries within 4 weeks. New/unpublished writers: 73%.
Recent Sales: *Shadow Over China*, by Julian Portman and Jean Kipfer (Paperjack Books); *The Senator Must Die: The Assassination of Robert Kennedy*, by Robert Morrow (Roundtable); *My Life With Errol Flynn*, by Bill DiNato (Roundtable).
Terms: Agent's commission: 15% on domestic and foreign sales. $150 reading fee for up to 275 pages; charges $200 reading fee for 300-page or more novel. Offers criticism service: "It is part of our reader's fee." "Readers used, but final approval by Julian John Portman." Payment of fees ensures agency representation if writers follow constructive critiques. Our agency is heavily involved in turning out mss that would be suitable for television."

THE AARON M. PRIEST LITERARY AGENCY INC., 122 East 42nd St., New York NY 10168. (212)818-0344. Contact: Aaron Priest, Robert Colgan or Molly Friedrich. Fiction and nonfiction. Presently accepting new clients. Send SASE with ms.
Terms: Agent's commission: 15% (foreign mailing and copying charged to author).

SUSAN ANN PROTTER, LITERARY AGENT, 110 West 40th St., New York NY 10018. (212)840-0480. Agent contact: Susan Ann Protter. Agency estab. 1971. Novels. Fiction and nonfiction (50%-50% fiction to nonfiction). Special interests: contemporary and medical novels, thrillers, mysteries, science fiction and fantasy. Currently represents 45 clients. Presently accepting some new clients. Query. Responds to queries in 2 weeks. New/unpublished writers: 20%. Member of I.L.A.A.
Recent Sales: *Sleeping Dogs Die*, by Frank King (E.P. Dutton); *No Special Hurry*, by James Colbert (Houghton-Mifflin); *Fire on the Mountain*, by Terry Bisson (Avon/Arbor House).
Terms: Agent's commission: 15% on domestic sales; 25% on foreign sales. Charges handling charge of $10 on ms submissions. 100% of income derived from commissions on ms sales.

‡**QUICKSILVER BOOKS, INC.**, 50 Wilson St., Hartsdale NY 10530. (914)946-8748. Agent contact: Bob Silverstein, president. Agency estab. 1973 (as packager); 1987 (as literary agency). Novels. Also reviews nonfiction (50%-50% fiction to nonfiction). Special interests: mainstream, science fiction, mystery/suspense. Usually obtains new clients via recommendations from others, listings in sourcebooks. Currently represents 25 authors. Presently accepting new clients. Send query with outline. Responds to queries in 1 week; to mss in 2-3 weeks. New/unpublished writers: 50%.
Recent Sales: *The Dogs*, by Jerrold Mundis (Berkley); *The Hypnotist*, by Brad Steiger (Berkley); *Coronation*, by W. J. Weatherby (Pocket Books).
Terms: Agent's commissions: 15% on domestic sales; 20% on foreign sales. 100% of income derived from commission on ms sales.

‡**HELEN REES LITERARY AGENCY**, 308 Commonwealth Ave., Boston MA 02116. (617)262-2401. Agent contact: Catherine Mahar. Agency estab. 1980. Novels, novellas, short stories, story collections. Also reviews nonfiction (15%-85% fiction to nonfiction). Special interests: mainstream, mystery, sus-

pense, gay, literary. Usually obtains new clients via solicitations, referrals, some through submissions. Currently represents 60 authors. Presently accepting new clients. Query. Responds to queries in 5-10 days; to mss in 2 weeks. Member of I.L.A.A.
Recent Sales: *Moscow Metal* (mystery), by Rick Boyer (Houghton Mifflin); *Love Letters*, by Alison Tyler (Harlequin, Temptation); *Silverglass* (3rd in Trilogy), by J.F. Rivkin (Ace Charter).
Terms: Agent's commission: 15% on domestic sales; 20% on foreign. Charges "reimbursement for expenses (mail, phone, copying)." 100% of income derived from commissions on ms sales.

‡SHERRY ROBB LITERARY PROPERTIES, Box 2787, Hollywood CA 90078. (213)653-7734. Contact: Sherry Robb, Rosemary Sneeringer. Agency estab. 1979. Novels, short story collections, "but mainly novels." Also reviews nonfiction (50%-50% fiction to nonfiction). Special interests: commercial mainstream, offbeat and literary, mysteries, thrillers and women's genre. Usually obtains new clients via client referrals, introductions via conferences and directories. Presently accepting new clients. Send entire ms (for literary, mystery, thrillers and offbeat novels); outline or proposal plus 3 sample chapters for mainstream or genre. Responds to queries in 2 weeks; to whole ms in 3 months; 2 months for outline/proposal. New/unpublished writers: 60%.
Recent Sales: *No Easy Place To Be* (literary), by Steven Corbin (Simon & Schuster); *Mistresses* (mainstream), by Trevor Meldal-Johnsen (Pinnacle); *Magnificent Passage* (historical romance) by Kat Martin (Crown).
Terms: "We do require authors—especially since we work with so many 'first-timers'—to pay for their own Xeroxing and postage charge. We don't charge, but we also will not refer any author to an editor or a critique service unless we plan to represent them (after re-doing their manuscript)."

THE ROBBINS OFFICE, INC., 12th Floor, 866 2nd Ave., New York NY 10017. (212)223-0720. Agency estab. 1978. Novels, story collections. Also reviews nonfiction (25%-75% fiction to nonfiction). Special interests: mainstream hardcover, literary. Usually obtains new clients via recommendations from others. Currently represents 150 authors. Presently accepting new clients. Query. Responds to queries in 2 weeks.
Recent Sales: *When We Get Home*, by Maud Carol Markson (Bantam New Fiction); *Yellow Dogs*, by Donald Zochert (Atlantic Monthly Press).
Terms: Agent's commission: 15%. "Specific expenses incurred in doing business for a client are billed back." 100% of income derived from commissions on ms sales.

MARIE RODELL-FRANCES COLLIN LITERARY AGENCY, 110 W. 40th St., New York NY 10018. (212)840-8664. Agent contact: Frances Collin. Also reviews nonfiction (50%-50% fiction to nonfiction). Special interests: general adult trade books. Query. Member of S.A.R.
Terms: Agent's commission: 15% on domestic sales; 25% on foreign sales.

‡THE MITCHELL ROSE LITERARY AGENCY, Suite 410, 799 Broadway, New York NY 10003. (212)418-0747. Agent contact: Mitchell Rose. Agency estab. 1986. Novels, story collections. Also reviews nonfiction (40%-60% fiction to nonfiction). Special interests: commercial fiction, mystery and literary fiction. Usually obtains new clients via recommendations. Currently represents 45 authors. Presently accepting new clients. Query or send outline plus sample chapters. Responds to queries in 3 weeks; to mss in 6 weeks. New/unpublished writers: 20%. Member of Authors Guild.
Recent Sales: *Victorian Tales*, by Michael Patrick Hearn (Pantheon/Random House); *To Laredo*, by Jim Shaffer (St. Martin's); *Chain Reaction*, by Josh Pachter (Alliance Entertainment).
Terms: Agent's commission: 15% on domestic sales; 20% on foreign sales involving a sub-agent. Charges fee for high-volume photocopying, telexes, overseas phone calls. 100% of income derived from commission on mss sales. "For talented writers with promising projects, we can offer extensive editorial guidance when required."

‡ROSENSTONE/WENDER, 3 E. 48th St., New York NY 10017. (212)832-8330. Novels, novelettes, short stories, short story collections, plays and screenplays. Query. Does not accept unsolicited mss. Also reviews nonfiction (50%-50% fiction to nonfiction).
Terms: Agent's commission: 10%. Member of S.A.R.

JANE ROTROSEN AGENCY, 318 E. 51st St., New York NY 10022. (212)593-4330. Agents: Jane Rotrosen Berkey, Donald Cleary, Andrea Cirillo, Margaret Ruley, Gretchen van Nuys, Stephanie Laidman, Andrea Barr. Agency estab. 1973. Reviews novels, novellas, story collections. Also reviews nonfiction (60%-40% fiction to nonfiction). Special interest: commercial fiction. Usually obtains new clients through referrals. Represents 140 + writers. Presently accepting new clients. Query. Responds to queries in 10 days if SASE included; to mss in 6-8 weeks. Member of I.L.A.A.
Terms: Agent's commission: 15% on domestic sales; 20% on foreign sales (10% to co-agent; 10% to JRA).

RUSSELL & VOLKENING, INC., 50 W. 29th St., Apt. 7E, New York NY 10001. (212)684-6050. Novels, nonfiction. Send query letter with SASE. Member of S.A.R. Agents in all countries.

‡SBC ENTERPRISES, INC., 11 Mabro Dr., Denville NJ 07834-9607, (201)366-3622. Agent contact: Alec Bernard. Agency estab 1979. Novels and story collections (where bulk are previously published). Also reviews nonfiction (75%-25% fiction to nonfiction). Special interest: mainstream, science projection, espionage. Usually obtains new clients via recommendations, conferences, advertising. Currently represents 25 authors. Presently accepting new clients. Query. Responds "immediately" to queries. New/unpublished writers: 90%.
Recent Sales: *Maximizing Cash Flow*, by Emery Toncré (Wiley); *Action-Step Plan to Owning & Operating Business*, by Toncré (Montclair Press reprint).
Terms: Agent's commission: 15% on domestic sales if advance under $10,000, 10% thereafter; 20% on foreign sales. Will critique 300-page novel for $2/page reading fee. 100% of income derived from commission on ms sales.

JACK SCAGNETTI, 5330 Lankershim Blvd. #210, N. Hollywood CA 91601. (818)762-3871. Agency estab. 1974. Novels. Also reviews nonfiction (40%-60% fiction to nonfiction). Special interest: mainstream. Usually obtains new clients by referrals from other clients or free listings. Currently represents 35 authors. Presently accepting new clients. Query with outline. Responds to queries in 2 weeks; to mss in 4-6 weeks. New/unpublished writers: 75%. Signatory to Writers Guild of America—West.
Recent Sales: *Superstition Gold*, by Melissa Bowesock (Dorchester Publishing). Script sales: *Highway to Heaven, Family Ties*.
Terms: Agent's commission: 10% on domestic sales; 15% on foreign sales. No reading fees for screenplays. No reading fees for books unless detailed critique is requested. Offers criticism service: $100 for 400 pages; $125 for 500 pages. Will detail critique 300-page novel for $75. "Experienced readers/analysts write critiques." Charges for one-way postage for multiple submissions. 100% of income derived from commission on ms sales. Payment of fees does not ensure agency representation. "Also handle screenwriters; spend more time reading/selling screenplays than books; represent more screenwriters than authors."

JOHN SCHAFFNER ASSOCIATES, INC., 264 5th Ave., New York NY 10001. (212)689-6888. Agency Contact: Timothy Schaffner or Patrick Delahunt. Agency estab: 1948. Novels and story collections. Also reviews nonfiction. Special interest: mainstream, science fiction, fantasy and literary fiction. Usually obtains new clients via referrals, conventions and by reading magazine fiction. Currently represents 75 authors. Presently accepting new clients. Query with outline. Responds to queries in 2 weeks; to mss in 4-6 weeks. Member of S.A.R. and I.L.A.A.
Recent Sales: *Life During Wartime*, by Lucius Shepard (Bantam Books); *Proud Monster*, by Ian Macmillan (North Point Press); *Man Ray*, by Neil Baldwin (biography).
Terms: Agent's commission: 10% on domestic sales; 20% on foreign sales. Charges for return postage or $5 if SASE not included. 100% of income derived from commission on ms sales.

‡SCHLESSINGER-VAN DYCK AGENCY, 2814 PSFS Bldg., 12 S. 12th St., Philadelphia PA 19107. (215)627-4665. Agent contact: Blanche Schlessinger or Barrie Van Dyck. Agency estab. 1987. Novels and story collections. Also reviews nonfiction (40%-60% fiction to nonfiction). Special interests: mainstream, children's, mysteries. Usually obtains new clients via recommendations from others. Currently represents 30 clients. Presently accepting new clients. Send query or outline plus sample chapters. Responds to queries in 2 weeks; to mss in 4 weeks. New/unpublished writers: 20%.
Recent Titles: *Indecent Proposal*, by Jack Engelhard (Donald I. Fine); *Maggie Among the Seneca* and *The Bread Sister of Sinking Creek*, by Robin Moore (Harper & Row).
Terms: Agent's commission: 15% on domestic sales; 20% on foreign sales. 100% of income derived from commission on sales.

HAROLD SCHMIDT LITERARY AGENCY, 67 Morton St., #3D, New York NY 10014. (212)989-0056. Contact: Harold Schmidt. Novels; short story collections if writer has prior publishing credits. "All polished, quality writing." Query with SASE. Also reviews nonfiction (60%-40% fiction to nonfiction). Represents 30 writers. Obtains new clients via recommendations from others and solicitations primarily. Interested in new/beginning clients. New/unpublished writers: 25%. "Agency founded in 1984 by Harold Schmidt, formerly affiliated with William Morris Agency and International Creative Management." Member of I.L.A.A.
Terms: Agent's commission: 15%. "Once a client is accepted for representation, client is responsible for paying any necessary long distance calls, copying charges, messenger fees, etc. incurred by us in handling his/her work."

SUSAN SCHULMAN LITERARY AGENCY, INC., 454 West 44th St., New York NY 10036. (212)713-1633. Agent contact: Susan Schulman. Estab. 1979. Novels and story collections. Also reviews nonfiction (50%-50% fiction to nonfiction). Special interests: mainstream, science fiction, romance. Usually obtains new clients via recommendations from current clients and colleagues in the trade. Presently accepting a few new clients, especially in nonfiction. Send complete proposal and/or sample chapters. Responds to queries in 2 weeks; to ms in 6 weeks. New/unpublished writers: 20%. Member of S.A.R., I.L.A.A., WGA, Dramatist Guild.
Recent Titles: *Queen's Gambit*, by Walter Lewis (film rights to Weintraub Entertainment Corp.); *Wife-in-Law*, by Ann Creptes (Simon & Schuster); *Overparenting*, by Ashner & Myerson (Wm. Morrow).
Terms: Agent's commission: 10% on domestic sales; 15% on English sales; 20% on foreign sales. "In response to an unsolicited query we submit a letter to the writer stating we will read any length ms for $50 within six weeks. I write these reports myself. They usually run about 4-6 single-spaced pages for a complete ms, and I am as detailed and specific as I think will be helpful." Agency clients are charged back only for expenses they ask me to incur such as travel, special messenger or quantity of copying charges. 99% of income is derived from commissions on ms sales; 1% from reading fees or criticism services. Payment of fee does not ensure representation.

‡ARTHUR P. SCHWARTZ, 435 Riverside Dr., New York NY 10025. Branch office: Box 9132, Christchurch 2 New Zealand. Novels only. Area of specialization: commercially oriented fiction (i.e., frank, realistic sex and themes), adult-oriented romantic fiction, mainstream, family sagas, women's historical, contemporary romantic fiction, and science fiction. No "Harlequin" type books. Represents approximately 70 writers. Query. "Do not register, certify or insure; retain original ms for your file. Enclose ms-size SASE." Also reviews nonfiction (33%-66% fiction to nonfiction). Presently accepting new clients. New/unpublished writers, 33%. Member of I.L.A.A.
Terms: Agent's commission: 12½%.

BOBBE SIEGEL AGENCY, 41 West 83rd St., New York NY 10024. (212)877-4985. Associate: Richard Siegel. Agency estab. 1975. Novels. Also reviews nonfiction (45%-55% fiction to nonfiction). Special interests: mainstream, literary, science fiction, mystery, historical, any fiction. "But I do not handle children's books or cookbooks." Usually obtains new clients via "referral from editors and authors I know or whom I represent." Currently represents 60 authors. Presently accepting new clients. Query with letter. Responds to queries in 2-3 weeks; to mss in 6-8 weeks. New/unpublished writers: 30%.
Recent Sales: *The Drowned and The Lost Souls*, by Anthony Schmitz (Ballantine); *Choke Hold*, by Lew Dykes (Berkley).
Terms: Agent's commission: 15% on domestic sales; 10% on foreign sales. Charges for airmail, overseas phone, photocopy etc. 100% of income derived from commission on ms sales. "I will not read any manuscript or proposal that is not preceded by a letter. Do not send unless I ask to see—and always send with return postage, otherwise material will not be returned."

EVELYN SINGER LITERARY AGENCY INC., Box 594, White Plains NY 10602. Contact: Evelyn Singer. Agency estab. 1951. Novels. Also reviews nonfiction (25%-75% fiction to nonfiction). Special interests: fiction and nonfiction adult and juvenile books. Interested in fiction for general trade departments and suspense or mystery. Usually obtains new clients via recommendations. Currently represents 50-75 writers. Not presently accepting new fiction writers. Query or send outline plus 2-3 sample chapters. New/unpublished writers: 15%. Responds to queries in 2-4 weeks; to mss in 2-6 weeks.
Recent Sales: *The Rebuilt Man*, by William Beechcroft (Dodd, Mead); *Macmillan Book Of The Human Body*, by Mary Elting (Macmillan); *Run Baby Run*, by Cruz with Buckingham (Bridge).
Terms: Agent's commission: 15% on domestic sales; 20% on foreign sales. Charges for: "Long distance calls; copyright; charges other than local postage, phone and overhead, that are special for a particular property." 100% of income derived from commission on ms sales. "Include bio pertinent to literary background; type double-space (or use letter-quality printer; I cannot read dot matrix) on 8½x11 paper. Do not bind ms. Paginate consecutively. Do not send sample material from a section of the ms; send first part and outline. Include SASE for reply and/or return of material. Write; do not phone."

‡SINGER MEDIA CORPORATION, 3164 Tyler Ave. Anaheim CA 92801. (714)527-5650. Agent contact: Natalie Carlton. Agency estab. 1945. Novels. Also reviews nonfiction (95%-5% fiction to nonfiction). Special interests: contemporary romance, adventure, suspense, mysteries. Usually obtains new clients via conferences, word of mouth. Presently accepting new clients. Query or send entire ms. Responds to queries by return mail; to mss in 6 weeks. New/unpublished writers: 80%.
Terms: Agent's commission: 15% on domestic sales; 20% on foreign sales. Charges reading fee for unpublished authors; $200 for 300-page novel. "Compilation of readers' reports." Payment of fees does not ensure agency representation.

‡**MICHAEL SNELL LITERARY AGENCY**, Box 655, Truro MA 02666. (508)349-3718. Contact: Patricia Smith. Estab. 1980. Reviews novels. Also reads nonfiction (20%-80% fiction to nonfiction). Special interests: mystery, suspense, thrillers. Usually obtains news clients through *LMP*, word of mouth, publishers. Currently represents 200 clients. Presently accepting new clients. Send outline/proposal and query. Reports on queries in 1 week; on mss in 2 weeks.
Recent Sales: *Blood Dawn, Blood Moon, Blood Tide*, by Kalish (3-book series) (Harvest/Avon); *The Brothers K*, by Duncan (Doubleday).
Terms: Agent's commission: 15% on domestic and foreign sales. 100% of business is derived from commission on mss sales.

‡**ELYSE SOMMER, INC.**, 110-34 73 Rd., Forest Hills NY 11375. (718)263-2668. Area of specialization: bestseller types: family sagas, some mysteries. No westerns, science fiction, futuristic books. Send outline plus 2 sample chapters with SASE. Entire manuscript should be available. "Send cover letter explaining status of ms—complete, partially finished, any previous marketing efforts." Also reviews nonfiction (1-4 fiction to nonfiction). Presently accepting new clients. Interested in new/beginning novelists and fiction only if "ms is unusual." Member of I.L.A.A.
Terms: Agent's commission: 15%.

SOUTHERN WRITERS, INC., Suite 1020, 635 Gravier St., New Orleans LA 70130. (504)525-6390. Agent contact: Pamela Ahearn. Agency estab: 1979. Novels and novellas. Also reviews nonfiction (65%-35% fiction to nonfiction). Special interest: fiction with a Southern flavor or background and romances—both contemporary and historical. Usually obtains new clients via recommendations from others, at conferences, and from listings. Currently represents 20-25 authors. Presently accepting new clients. Query. Responds to queries in 2 weeks; to mss in 4 weeks. New/unpublished writers: 35%.
Recent Sales: *An Age of Difference*, by Marie Goodwin (Macmillan); *My Wicked Enchantress*, by Meagan McKinney (Dell); *Second Son*, by Kate Moore (Pageant Books).
Terms: Agent's commission: 12-15% on domestic sales; 20% on foreign sales. Foreign Representatives: Abner Stein (UK); Uwe Luserke (Europe). Charges $150 reading fee to new writer on 300-page ms. "We charge a reading fee to unpublished authors and to those writing in areas other than that of previous publication." Offers criticism service for $250. Descripton of criticism service: "A letter (3-4 pp. single-spaced) evaluating work on the basis of style, content and marketability, offering constructive advice on this work and pointers for future writing." Charges for office expenses, which are deducted from royalties if book is sold. 65% of income derived from commission on ms sales; 35% from criticism service and reading fees.

‡**F. JOSEPH SPIELER LITERARY AGENCY**, 410 W. 24th Street., New York NY 10011. (212)242-7152 or (212)757-4439. Contact: Joseph Spieler. Estab. 1982. Reviews novels, novellas, short stories, story collections. Also reads nonfiction (40% to 50% fiction to nonfiction). Special interests: mainstream, children's, history, economics and contemporary issues, especially those dealing with the environment. Obtains clients through recommendations only. Currently represents 45 clients. Presently accepting new clients. Prefers query, outline/proposal or sample chapters. Reports in 1 week on queries; 3 weeks on mss. 20-30% of clients are new/unpublished writers.
Recent Sales: *Intimacy*, Susan Chace (Random House); *The Age of Miracles*, Catherine MacCoun (Atlantic/Little Brown); and *Service for the Dead*, by Robert A. Anderson (Arbor House/Avon).
Terms: Agent's commission: 15% on domestic sales; 20% on foreign. Sometimes charges criticism fee. "Exceptionally rare: done only at writer's request and then only if I feel it would be useful to the writer." Will critique 300-page, typed, double-spaced ms for $100. "Usable critiques. I write them." Charges for bulk Xerox, long-distance telephone, bulk mailing. 95 + % of business derived from commissions on mss sales; less than 5% derived from criticism services. Payment of fee does not guarantee representation.

PHILIP G. SPITZER LITERARY AGENCY, 788 9th Ave., New York NY 10019. (212)265-6003. Agency estab. 1969. Novels and nonfiction (50%-50% fiction to nonfiction). Special interest: quality fiction, suspense fiction. Obtains new clients primarily via recommendation. Currently represents 50 authors. Query. Also reviews nonfiction (50%-50% fiction to nonfiction). Accepting few new clients. Send outline/proposal. Responds to queries in 1 week; to mss in 6 weeks. New/unpublished writers: 25%.
Recent Sales: *King of the Hustlers*, by Eugene Izzi (Bantam); *I, J.F.K.*, by Robert Mayer (E.P. Dutton); *Hotel*, by Sonny Kleinfield (Simon & Schuster).
Terms: Agent's commission: 10% on domestic sales; 20% on foreign sales. 100% of income derived from commission on ms sales.

‡**LYLE STEELE & CO.**, 511 E. 73d St., Suite 7, New York NY 10021. (212)288-2981. Agent contact: Lyle Steele. Agency estab. 1984. Novels. Also reviews nonfiction (50%-50% fiction to nonfiction).

Special interests: mysteries, horror, particularly continuing series. Usually obtains new clients by recommendations from others. Currently represents 25 clients. Presently accepting new clients. Query. Responds to queries in 2 weeks; to mss in 6 weeks. New/unpublished writers: .05%.
Recent Sales: Eileen Fulton's eight book *Take One for Murder* series (Ballantine/Ivy).
Terms: Agent's commission: 10% on domestic sales; 10% on foreign sales (foreign agent also takes 10%). 100% of income derived from commission on mss sales.

STEPPING STONE, 59 West 71st St., New York NY 10023. (212)362-9277. Agent contact: Sarah Jane Freymann. Agency estab. 1974. Novels. Also reviews nonfiction (50%-50% fiction to nonfiction). Special interests: mainstream, self help, women's fiction, women's issues, spiritual themes, current events. Currently represents 60 clients. Presently accepting new clients. Query with outline/proposal. Responds to queries in 2 weeks; to mss in 1 month. New/unpublished writers: 10%. Member of I.L.A.A.
Terms: Agent's commission: 15%. 100% of income derived from commission on ms sales.

CHARLES M. STERN ASSOCIATES, Box 790742, San Antonio TX 78279-0742. (512)349-6141. Agency estab. 1977. Novels, nonfiction and how-to. Special interests: adventure, children's books, mainstream, women's, romance and mystery. Send query with SASE and/or send outline/proposal. Represents approximately 30 + writers. Obtains clients via recommendations and queries. Presently accepting new clients. Interested in new/unpublished novelists/writers.
Terms: Agent's commission: 15%. "Return postage must accompany every query or submission. Phone calls made to authors to discuss their work will be made collect."

GLORIA STERN AGENCY, 1230 Park Ave., New York NY 10028. (212)289-7698. Agent contact: Gloria Stern. Agency estab. 1976. Also reviews nonfiction (10%-90% fiction to nonfiction). Represents 35 writers. Not presently accepting new clients unless referred by established writer or editor. Query with outline plus 1 sample chapter. Member of I.L.A.A.
Terms: Agent's commission: 15% on domestic sales; 20% on foreign sales. "I am sorry that I cannot take any new fiction at the present time. This may change in the future."

JO STEWART AGENCY, 201 E. 66th St., New York NY 10021. (212)879-1301. Agent contact: Jo Stewart. Agency estab. 1976. Novels. Also reviews nonfiction. Special interest: "all kinds of fiction and nonfiction—young adult fiction." Usually obtains new clients via recommendations of other writers and editors. Presently accepting new clients. Query first or send synopsis plus 2-3 sample chapters. Responds to queries within 2 days, "depends on my schedule and length of manuscript." Member of I.L.A.A.
Terms: Agent's commission: 10% on domestic sales; 15% on unpublished authors; 20% on foreign sales.

GUNTHER STUHLMANN AUTHOR'S REPRESENTATIVE, Box 276, Becket MA 01223. (413)623-5170. Agent Contact: Barbara Ward. Agency estab. 1954. Fiction and nonfiction books; no sci-fi. Special interest: quality literary fiction. Usually obtains new clients via recommendations. Query with outline and SASE. Responds to queries in 2 weeks.
Recent Sales: *Prisoner's Dilemma*, by Richard Powers (Morrow).
Terms: Agent's commission: 10% on domestic sales; 20% on foreign sales; 15% Britain Commonwealth. 100% of income derived from commission on ms sales.

H.N. SWANSON, INC., 8523 Sunset Blvd., Los Angeles CA 90069. (213)652-5385. Agent Contact: B.F. Kamsler. Agency estab. 1932. Novels, novellas and story collections. Also reviews nonfiction (90%-10% fiction to nonfiction). Special interests: mainstream, adventure and thrillers. Usually obtains new clients via recommendations from others. Currently represents 125 authors. Presently accepting new clients. Query with outline plus sample chapters. Responds to queries in 1 week; to mss in 4 weeks.
Recent Sales: *Basil of Baker Street, (Great Moose Detective)*, (McGraw-Hill); *You Must Remember This*, by Joyce Carol Oates (E.P. Dutton); *Freaky Deaky*, by Elmore Leonard (Arbor House).
Terms: Agent's commission: 10% on domestic sales; 15% on foreign sales. 100% of income derived from commission on ms sales.

‡ROSLYN TARG LITERARY AGENCY, INC., 105 W. 13th St., New York NY 10011. (212)206-9390. Agent contact: Roslyn Targ. Estab. 1969. Novels. Also reads nonfiction. Special interest: mainstream. Usually obtains new clients via recommendations from others. Query. Responds to mss in 2-3 weeks. Member of S.A.R. and I.L.A.A.
Terms: Agent's commission: 15% on unpublished authors; 10% on published authors; 20% on foreign sales. 100% of income derived from commission on ms sales.

‡**PATRICIA TEAL LITERARY AGENCY**, 2036 Vista Del Rosa, Fullerton CA 92631. (714)738-8333. Contact: Patricia Teal. Agency estab. 1978. Novels. Also reviews nonfiction (75%-25% fiction to nonfiction). Special interest: category novels. Usually obtains new clients via recommendations from others, solicitation, at conferences. Currently represents 60 authors. Presently accepting "a few" new clients. Query. Responds to queries in 2 weeks; to mss in 1 month. New/unpublished writers: 50%. Member of I.L.A.A.
Recent Sales: *Polo's Ponies*, by Jerry Kennealy (St. Martin's Press); *Murder by Masquerade*, by D. R. Meredith (Ballantine); *Honorbound*, by Laura Taylor (Franklin-Watts).
Terms: Agent's commission: 10-15% on domestic sales; 20% on foreign sales. "We do not read entire manuscripts, only queries or partials. Would not charge a fee for a book we asked to see." Charges for postage and telephone calls. 100% of income derived from commission on mss sales. "We do not welcome mainstream fiction by unpublished writers except through professional writer referral or through contact at conferences."

‡**THOMPSON TALENT AGENCY**, Box 4272, Modesto CA 95352. (209)523-6035. Agent contact: Sharon Harris, director of literary talent. Agency estab. 1982. Novels, novellas, short stories, story collections. Also reviews nonfiction (60%-40% fiction to nonfiction). Special interests: screenplays, novels. Usually obtains new clients by recommendations from other writers, movie studios, etc. Presently accepting new clients. Query. Responds to queries in 1 month; to mss in 3 months. New/unpublished writers: 25%. Member of S.A.R., I.L.A.A.
Terms: Agents commission: 10% on domestic sales. Offers criticism service. "We request that the writer provide all postage expense to and from us and to the publishers we suggest if we accept."

‡**PHYLLIS R. TORNETTA LITERARY AGENCY**, 15 Laurel Hill Rd., Crugers NY 10520. (914)737-3464. Agent contact: Phyllis Tornetta. Agency estab. 1978. Novels. Special interests: romance, mainstream. Usually obtains new clients via recommendations from others, conferences. Currently represents 15 authors. Presently accepting new clients. Send outline/proposal. Responds to mss in 1 month. New/unpublished writers: 50%.
Recent Sales: *Cats and Kings*, by Beverly Simmons (Harlequin); *Intimate Strangers*, by Sally Hoover (Harlequin).
Terms: 15% on domestic sales. Charges $75 reading fee. "I will answer all inquiries at no charge."

RALPH M. VICINANZA LTD., 432 Park Ave. S., New York NY 10016. (212)725-5133. Agent contact: Chris Lotts. Estab. 1978. Novels, short stories. Also reviews nonfiction. Special interests: science fiction, fantasy, thrillers, mysteries. Usually obtains new clients via recommendations. Currently represents 50 clients. Presently accepting new clients. Query first. Responds to queries in 2 weeks. New/unpublished writers: 10%.
Terms: Agent's commission: 10% on domestic sales; 20% on foreign sales.

VICTORIA MANAGEMENT CO., 150 W. 82d St., #2F, New York NY 10024. (212)873-0972. Agent contact: Frank Weimann. Agency estab. 1984. Novels. Also reviews nonfiction (25%-75% fiction to nonfiction). Special interests: how-to, biography and mainstream. Obtains new clients primarily through referrals. Currently represents 25 clients. Presently accepting new clients. Submit sample chapters. Responds in 1 month. New/unpublished writers: 50%.
Recent Sales: *Stars & Bars*, by Robert Pack/Bob Hayes (Salem House); *The Monopoly Companion*, by Philip Orbanes (Bob Adams, Inc.); *Time-Based Competition*, by George Stalk, Jr. (The Free Press).
Terms: Agent's commission: 10% on domestic sales; 19% on foreign sales. 100% of income derived from commission on ms sales.

MARY JACK WALD ASSOCIATES, INC., Box 347, 70A Greenwich Ave., New York NY 10011. (212)254-7842. Contact: Mary Jack Wald. Agency estab. 1985 (1983-1985 was Wald-Hardy Associates, Inc.). Novels, "novellas if in or with a short story collection." Also reviews nonfiction (50%-50% fiction to nonfiction). Special interests: mainstream and literary fiction and nonfiction for the adult and juvenile audience. Usually obtains clients via recommendations from others. Currently represents 40 writers. Presently accepting new clients. Responds to queries in 3-4 weeks; to mss in 1-2 months. Member of The Authors Guild, The Society of Children's Book Writers and Authors League of America.
Recent Sales: *View from KWAJ*, by Patricia MacInnes (Beech Tree Books/Wm. Morrow); *The Battle of Gettysburg*, by author/photographer Neil Johnson (Four Winds Press/Macmillan); *Underwater Dog*, by Jan Wahl (Grosset & Dunlap/Putnam's).
Terms: Agent's commission: 15% on domestic sales; 15% on foreign sales.

THE GERRY B. WALLERSTEIN AGENCY, 2315 Powell Ave., Suite 12, Erie PA 16506. (814)833-5511. Contact: Ms. Gerry B. Wallerstein. Agency estab. 1984. Novels, novellas, short stories, story

collections. Also reads nonfiction (25%-75% fiction to nonfiction). Usually obtains new clients through (1) ongoing ad in *Writer's Digest*; (2) recommendations; (3) referrals from existing clients; (4) writers' groups. Currently represents 40 clients. Presently accepting new clients. Query. "Brochure is sent right away; responds to ms in approximately 4 weeks; no ms until writer sees brochure." New/unpublished writers: 25%. Member of Author's Guild and Society of Professional Journalists.
Terms: Agent's commission: 15% on domestic sales; 15% on dramatic sales; 20% on foreign sales. "I charge a reading/critique fee (waived for some published writers), which must accompany your material, on the following basis: $50 for each manuscript under 5,000 words; $100 for each manuscript of 5,000 to 20,000 words; $200 for each manuscript 20,000 to 65,000 words; $250 for each manuscript 65,000 to 85,000 words; $300 for each manuscript 85,000 to 105,000 words; $350 for each manuscript 105,000 to 125,000 words. A critique will be provided, including my assessment of the work's marketability. If the work requires revision or editing to make it saleable, it will be up to you to do it, if you so decide, based on the advice I give you, I will re-read the revised manuscript without additional charge. Charge for copyright applications, photocopying manuscripts, typing manuscripts, legal fees (if required and approved by author), my travel (if approved by author)." 50% of income derived from commissions on ms sales; 50% derived from reading fees and criticism services. "Only about 10-15% of the manuscripts I see have marketing potential, and of that percentage perhaps 5% are really likely to sell at all. Quality must be high for today's fiction marketplace."

JOHN A. WARE LITERARY AGENCY, 392 Central Park West, New York NY 10025. (212)866-4733. Agency estab. 1978. Novels and story collections "if individual stories have been placed." Also reviews nonfiction (40%-60% fiction to nonfiction). Special interests: literary, thrillers, mysteries, mainstream. "No romances, men's adventure or science fiction, please." Usually obtains new clients via referrals or at conferences. Currently represents 50 authors. Presently accepting new clients. Please query first. Responds to queries in 2 weeks; to mss in 1 month. New/unpublished writers: 25%.
Recent Sales: *Fool's Sanctuary*, by Jennifer Johnston (Viking); *We're Not Here*, by Tim Mahoney (Delacorte); *Terraplane*, by Jack Womack (Weidenfeld & Nicolson).
Terms: Agent's commission: 10% on domestic sales; 20% on foreign sales.

‡JAMES WARREN LITERARY AGENCY, (formerly Warren/Hilton Agency), 13131 Welby Way, Suite B, North Hollywood CA 91606. (818)982-5423. Agent contacts: James Warren, Romilde-Ann Dicke, Bob Carlson. Agency estab. 1969. Novels, novellas, stories and story collections, "but query first." Also reviews nonfiction (70%-30% fiction to nonfiction). Special interests: mainstream, adventure, gothic, history, historical romance, science fiction, mystery, horror, humor. Usually obtains new clients via *Writer's Market, LMP*, other trade publications, referrals. Currently represents 48 clients. Presently accepting new clients. Query or send entire ms. Responds to queries in 1 week to mss in 1 month. New/unpublished writers: 60%.
Terms: Agent's commission: 10% on domestic sales; 20% on foreign sales. Charges reading fee: $150 for 300-page ms typed with pica typeface; $225 or more for ms typed with elite typeface. "On rare occasions we may charge a submission fee if we think the material is excellent but has little chance of publication." 80% of income derived from commission on sales; 20% derived from reading fees. Payment of fees does not ensure agency representation.

WATERSIDE PRODUCTIONS, INC, 832 Camino Del Mar, Del Mar CA 92014. (619)481-8335. Contact: Julie Castiglia, agent, fiction. Novels. Also reviews nonfiction (12%-88% fiction to nonfiction). Special interest: mainstream novels. Usually obtains new clients through recommendations from others. Currently represents 150 authors. Presently accepting new clients. Query, then send outline/proposal. Responds to queries in 2 weeks. New/unpublished writers: 25%.
Recent Sales: *Good Friday*, by Bob Holt (Tab-hardcover, NAL-paperback); *Ashes to Empire (Paperjacks); Mission Bay Murder, Tartan Murders*, by Philip Wiliams (Paperjacks).
Terms: Agent's commission: 15% on domestic sales; 25% on foreign sales. No initial reading fee. Editorial services for pre-determined fee. Charges for postage and photocopies. 99% of income derived from commission on ms sales; 1% from criticism service. "We are only interested in writers with track records in national magazines, film experience, drama experience or superlative recommendations from known writers or writing teachers."

SANDRA WATT AND ASSOCIATES, 8033 Sunset Blvd., Suite 4053, Los Angeles CA 90046. (213)653-2339. Agent contact: Sandra Watt or Robert Drake. Agency estab. 1977. Novels and some short stories. Special interests: gay fiction, women's fiction, men's action/adventure, mystery, thrillers and YA. Usually obtains new clients via client referrals and conferences. Currently represents 100 + clients. Presently accepting new clients. Query first. Responds to queries in 1 week; to mss in 8 weeks. Always SASE. New/unpublished writers: 35%. Member I.L.A.A. and Writer's Guild West.
Recent Titles: *Lemons . . . & Lemonade*, by Portia Toples (NAL); *Hungry Women*, by B. Laramie

Dunaway (Warner); and *Stolen Houses*, by Wendy Hornsby (Crown/Pageant).
Terms: Agent's commission: 15% on domestic sales and 25% on foreign sales. "We charge an unpublished writer of fiction a $100 marketing fee." 100% of income derived from commission of ms sales.

CHERRY WEINER LITERARY AGENCY, 28 Kipling Way, Manalapan NJ 07726. (201)446-2096. Agency estab. 1977. Novels, novellas and short stories. Also reviews nonfiction (80%-20% fiction to nonfiction). Special interests: mainstream, science fiction, romance. Usually obtains new clients via recommendations from others. Currently represents 40 authors. Query or send outline plus sample chapters. Responds "immediately" to queries; to mss in 4-6 weeks. New/unpublished writers: 15%—not taking without recommendation.
Terms: Agent's commission: 15%. 100% of income derived from commission on ms sales. Sub agents: Germany, Scandinavia, Japan, England, France.

RHODA WEYR AGENCY, 216 Vance St., Chapel Hill NC 27514. (919)942-0770. Novels. Also reviews nonfiction. Query or send outline plus sample chapters. "The query letter should give any relevant information about the author and her/his work, publishing history, etc." Also represents nonfiction (about equal fiction to nonfiction). Presently accepting new clients. Interested in both fiction and nonfiction writers. Member of S.A.R and I.L.A.A. "Send letter/material, etc., with SASE to fit mss."
Terms: Agent's commission: 10% for domestic; 20% foreign.

WIESER & WIESER, 118 East 25th St., New York NY 10010. (212)260-0860. Agent contact: Olga Wieser. Agency estab. 1976. Novels. Also reviews nonfiction (40%-60% fiction to nonfiction). Special interests: mainstream, literary, historical and regency. Usually obtains new clients via recommendations from clients and other professionals. Currently represents 60 authors. Presently accepting new clients. Send outline plus sample chapters. Responds to queries in 1-2 weeks; to mss in 4 weeks.
Recent Sales: *Remember Santiago*, by Douglas C. Jones (Henry Holt); *Born of the Sun*, by Joan Wolf (NAL hardcover); *Silver Tower*, by Dale Brown (Donald I. Fine, Inc.).
Terms: Agent's commission: 15% on domestic sales; 20% on foreign sales; 15% motion picture rights sale. Offers criticism service. "No fees; if we decide to critique a work, we feel our input will improve the chances for publication." Charges for overseas cables and duplicating manuscript. 100% of income derived from commission on ms sales.

RUTH WRESCHNER, AUTHORS' REPRESENTATIVE, 10 W. 74th St., New York NY 10023. (212)877-2605. Contact: Ruth Wreschner. Agency estab. 1981. Novels. Also reviews nonfiction (15%-85% fiction to nonfiction). Special interests: mainstream, some romantic fiction, mysteries and science fiction. Usually obtains new clients via recommendations from others, solicitation, at conferences and listings. Represents about 40 writers. Send query and outline/proposal. Responds to queries in 2 days; to mss in 2-3 weeks. "Must enclose SASE."
Terms: Agent's commission: 15% on domestic sales; 20% on foreign sales. Charges for photocopy expenses "and when a book has been sold, I withhold certain funds for foreign mailings from the second advance." 100% of income derived from commission on ms sales. "While I avidly review fiction, I sell much more nonfiction. A first novel is very difficult to place, unless it really is superb."

ANN WRIGHT REPRESENTATIVES INC., 136 East 57th St., New York NY 10022. (212)832-0110. Agent contact: Dan Wright, head—literary department. Agency estab. 1962. Novels, novellas, short stories. Special needs: fiction that applies both to publishing and motion pictures/TV. Usually obtains clients via word of mouth, references from film industry. Currently represents 48 clients. Not presently accepting new clients. Query first. Responds to queries in 8 weeks; to mss in 3 + months. New/unpublished writers: 20%. Member of WGA.
Terms: Agent's commission: 10% on domestic sales; 20% on foreign sales.

WRITERS HOUSE, INC., 21 W. 26th St., New York NY 10010. President: Albert Zuckerman. Novels. Also reviews nonfiction (50%-50% fiction to nonfiction). Usually obtains clients via recommendations. Represents around 120 writers. Presently accepting new clients. Query. Responds to queries in 2 weeks; to mss in 8 weeks. New/unpublished writers: "about 75% when they started with us."
Recent Sales: *Lie Down With Lions*, by Ken Follett; *Sweet Valley High*, by Francine Pascal; *Robin Hood*, by Robin McKinley.
Terms: Agent's commission: 15% on domestic sales; 20% on foreign sales. 100% of income derived from commission on ms sales. "We are always on the lookout for skilled and talented writers."

WRITERS' PRODUCTIONS, Box 630, Westport CT 06881. Agent contact: David L. Meth. Agency estab. 1981. "Literary quality fiction; dramatic photo-essay books of exceptional quality on unique subjects; and works of nonfiction that are well researched, carefully planned and thought out, with a high degree of originality. We have a special interest in work by Asian Americans; work about Southeast Asia and the Far East." Usually obtains new clients by "word of mouth, though we read and respond to all work." Presently accepting new clients. Send one-page cover letter plus 30 pages and a SASE for return of ms. Responds to queries in 1 week; to mss in 1 month. New/unpublished writers: 50%.

Recent Sales: *White Badge*, by Ann Jung Hyo (Korea), (Soho Press); *Vessels of Sand*, by Matsumoto Seicho (Japan), (Soho Press); *Last Traces: The Lost Art of Auschwitz*, by Joseph Czarnecki (Poland), (Atheneum).

Terms: Agent's commission: 15% on domestic sales; 20% on foreign sales; 20% dramatic sales. SASE must accompany ms for its return and any correspondence. No phone calls please.

WRITERS WORLD FORUM, Box 20383, Midtown Station, New York NY 10129. (201)664-0263. President: William Parker. Agency estab: 1985. Novels, novellas and story collections. Also reviews nonfiction (70%-30% fiction to nonfiction). Special interest: "all except romances and westerns." Usually obtains new clients via recommendations, advertising. Currently represents 8-15 authors. Presently accepting new clients. Query with SASE. Responds to queries in 2 weeks; to mss in 3-5 weeks. New/unpublished writers: 80%.

Terms: Agent's commission: 10% on domestic sales; 10% on foreign sales. 100% of income derived from commission on ms sales. "We are seeking high-quality, book-length ficton and nonfiction on important topics, including women's, Third World, current issues, ethnic and other. Always looking for new writers."

MARY YOST ASSOCIATES, 59 E. 54th St., New York NY 10022. (212)980-4988. Contact: Mary Yost. Novels. Special interest: mainstream. Query or send outline plus 50 pages. Also reviews nonfiction (40%-60% fiction to nonfiction). Obtains new clients via recommendations from other clients, editors, a few unsolicited mss. Presently accepting new clients. Member of S.A.R.

Terms: Agent's commission: 10%.

SUSAN ZECKENDORF ASSOCIATES, 171 W. 57th St., New York NY 10019. (212)245-2928. Contact: Susan Zeckendorf. Agency estab. 1979. Novels. Also reviews nonfiction (60%-40% fiction to nonfiction). Special interests: mainstream, thrillers, mysteries, and literary, historical, and commercial women's fiction. Usually obtains new clients via recommendations and solicitation. Represents 45 writers. Presently accepting new clients. Query. Responds to queries in 2 weeks; to solicited mss in 3 weeks. New/unpublished writers: 25%. Member of I.L.A.A.

Recent Sales: *Temptations*, by Una Mary Parker (New American Library); *A Killing in Dreamland*, by James Frey (Bantam); *Headlong*, by James Underwood (Pageant/Crown).

Terms: Agent's commission: 15% on domestic sales; 20% on foreign sales. Charges for photocopying expenses. 100% of income derived from commission on ms sales.

Literary agents/'88-'89 changes

The following literary agents appeared in the 1988 edition of *Fiction Writer's Market* but are not in the 1989 edition of *Novel and Short Story Writer's Market*. Those agents who did not respond to our request for an update of their listings may not have done so for a variety of reasons—they may no longer be in business, for example, or last year's listing might have resulted in their receiving too many unsuitable manuscripts.

Glossary

The following words are used differently when applied to writing and publishing than they are when spoken or written in other situations. For more general definitions and terms, check a standard dictionary.

Advance. Payment by a publisher to an author prior to the publication of a book, to be deducted from the author's future royalties.

All rights. The rights contracted to a publisher permitting a manuscript's use anywhere and in any form, including movie and book-club sales, without additional payment to the writer.

Backlist. A publisher's list of its books that were not published during the current season but which are still in print.

Book auction. Sale of rights (e.g. paperback, movie) by a book publisher to the highest bidder.

Book producer/packager. An organization that plans all elements of a book, from its initial concept to writing and marketing strategies, and then sells the package to a book publisher and/or movie producer.

Category fiction. See Genre.

Chapbook. A booklet of 15-30 pages of fiction or poetry.

Clean copy. Manuscript free of errors, cross-outs and smudges, ready to be typeset for printing.

Cliffhanger. Fictional event in which the reader is left in suspense at the end of a chapter or episode, so that interest in the story's outcome will be sustained.

Clip. Sample, usually from newspaper or magazine, of a writer's published work.

Cloak-and-dagger. A melodramatic, romantic type of fiction dealing with espionage and intrigue.

Collective. A group of writers and editors who work together to publish books, usually collaborating on editing tasks and sharing financial risk.

Commercial. Publishers whose chief concern is with salability, profit and success with a large readership.

Confession. Genre of love story where a sympathetic narrator, usually a female from a blue-collar family, faces and eventually solves an emotional problem with a husband, lover or family members.

Contemporary. Material dealing with popular current trends, themes or topics.

Contributor's copy. Copy of an issue of a magazine or published book sent to an author whose work is included; often the only form of payment from little/literary magazines and small presses.

Co-publishing. An arrangement in which the author and publisher share publication costs and profits.

Copyediting. Editing a manuscript for writing style, grammar, punctuation and factual accuracy.

Copyright. The legal right to exclusive publication, sale or distribution of a literary work.

Cover letter. A brief descriptive letter sent along with a complete manuscript submitted to an editor.

Cyberpunk. Type of science fiction, usually concerned with computer networks and human-computer combinations, involving young, sophisticated protagonists.

Descenders. "Tails" of letters like "g" and "y," which sometimes do not extend below the line on inexpensive dot-matrix printers.

Division. An unincorporated branch of a company (e.g. Penguin Books, a division of Viking, Penguin, Inc.).

Dot-matrix printer. Computer printer on which the letters are formed with tiny dots rather than with a single key or other element.

Edition. All copies of a work printed from a single setting of type.

El-hi. Elementary to high school.

Escape literature. Writing, often genre fiction, that allows a reader to forget the realities of life and dwell in fantasies.

Experimental fiction. Fiction that is innovative in subject matter and style; avant-garde, non-formulaic, usually literary material.

Exposition. The portion of the storyline, usually the beginning, where background information about character and setting is related.

Faction. A combination of fact and fiction, depicting both real people under their own names and real people under fictitious names.

Fair use. A provision in the copyright law that says short passages from copyrighted material may be used without infringing on the owner's rights.

Fantasy. Literary work in which the action occurs in a non-existent and unreal world with incredible, imaginary characters.

Fanzine. A noncommercial, small-circulation magazine usually dealing with fantasy, horror or science-fiction literature and art.

First North American serial rights. The right to publish material in a periodical before it appears in book form, for the first time, in the United States or Canada.

Formula. A fixed and conventional method of plot development, which varies little from one book to another in a particular genre.

Galleys. The first typeset version of a manuscript that has not yet been divided into pages.

Genre. A formulaic type of fiction such as romance, western or horror.

Gothic. A genre in which the central character is usually a beautiful young woman and the setting an old mansion or castle, involving a handsome hero and real danger, either natural or supernatural.

Guidelines. A magazine or publishing house's rule sheet for potential contributors.

Honorarium. A small, token payment for published work.

Horror. A genre stressing fear, death and other aspects of the macabre.

Imprint. Name applied to a publisher's specific line of books (e.g. Aerie Books, an imprint of Tor Books).

Interactive fiction. Fiction in book or computer-software format where the reader determines the path the story will take by choosing from several alternatives at the end of each chapter or episode.

International Reply Coupon (IRC). A form purchased at a post office and enclosed with a letter or manuscript to a foreign publisher, to cover return postage costs.

Juvenile. Fiction intended for children 2-12.

Kill fee. A percentage of the agreed-upon purchase price paid to an author for a completed story or book that was assigned but subsequently canceled by the publisher.

Letter-quality printer. Computer printer with a typeface that is identical to that of a good-quality typewriter.

Libel. Written or printed words that defame, malign or damagingly misrepresent a living person.

Literary. The general category of serious, non-formulaic, intelligent fiction, sometimes experimental, that most frequently appears in little magazines.

Literary agent. A person who acts for an author in finding a publisher or arranging contract terms on a literary project.

Literary magazine. A special-interest publication of small circulation, often publishing literary, experimental fiction.

Little magazine. Publication of limited circulation, usually concerned with literary or political subjects.

Mainstream. Traditionally written fiction on subjects or trends that transcend experimental or genre fiction categories.

Manuscript. The author's unpublished copy of a work, usually typewritten, used as the basis for typesetting.

Mass market paperback. Softcover book on a popular subject, usually around 7" x 4," directed to a general audience and sold in drugstores and groceries as well as in bookstores.

Ms(s). Abbreviation for manuscript(s).

Multiple submission (also simultaneous submission). The practice of sending copies of the same manuscript to several editors or publishers at the same time.

Narration. The account of events in a story's plot as related by the speaker or the voice of the author.

Narrator. The person who tells the story, either someone involved in the action or the voice of the writer.

New age. A term including categories such as astrology, psychic phenomena, spiritual healing, UFOs, mysticism and other aspects of the occult.

Novella (also novelette). A short novel or long story, approximately 7,000-15,000 words.

#10 envelope. 9½"x4" envelope, used for queries and other business letters.

Offprint. Copy of a story taken from a magazine before it is bound.

One-time rights. Permission to publish a story in periodical or book form one time only.

Over the transom. Slang for the path of an unsolicited manuscript into the slush pile.

Page rate. A fixed rate paid to an author per published page of fiction.

Payment on acceptance. Payment from the magazine or publishing house as soon as the decision to print a manuscript is made.

Payment on publication. Payment from the publisher after a manuscript is printed.

Pen name. A pseudonym used to conceal a writer's real name.

Plot. The carefully devised series of events through which the characters progress in a work of fiction.

Proofreading. Close reading and correction of a manuscript's typographical errors.

Proofs. A typeset version of a manuscript used for correcting errors and making changes, often a photocopy of the galleys.

Proposal. An offer to an editor to write a specific work, usually consisting of an outline of the work and one or two completed chapters.

Prose poem. Short piece of prose with the language and expression of poetry.

Protagonist. The principal or leading character in a literary work.

Public domain. Material that either was never copyrighted or whose copyright term has expired.

Purple prose. Ornate writing using exaggerated and excessive literary devices.

Query. A letter written to an editor to elicit interest in a story the writer wants to submit.

Reader. A person hired by a publisher to read unsolicited manuscripts.

Reading fee. An arbitrary amount of money charged by some agents and publishers to read a submitted manuscript.

Regency romance. A genre romance, usually set in England between 1811-1820.

Remainders. Leftover copies of an out-of-print book, sold by the publisher at a reduced price.

Reporting time. The number of weeks or months it takes an editor to report back on an author's query or manuscript.

Reprint rights. Permission to print an already published work whose rights have been sold to another magazine or book publisher.

Roman à clef. French "novel with a key." A novel that represents actual living or historical characters and events in fictionalized form.

Romance. The genre relating accounts of passionate love and fictional heroic achievements.

Royalties. A percentage of the retail price paid to he author for each copy of the book that is sold.

SASE. Self-addressed stamped envelope.

Scene. Unit of dramatic action in which a single point is made or one specific effect is attained.

Science fiction. Genre in which scientific facts and hypotheses form the basis of actions and events.

Second serial rights. Permission for the reprinting of a work in another periodical after its first publication in book or magazine form.

Self publishing. An independent publishing effort where full financial and editorial responsibility for the printing and marketing of a work is taken by its author.

Sequel. A literary work that continues the narrative of a previous, related story or novel.

Serial rights. The rights given by an author to a publisher to print a piece in one or more periodicals.

Serialized novel. A book-length work of fiction published in sequential issues of a periodical.

Setting. The environment and time period during which the action of a story takes place.

Shelf life. Length of time that a book is sold in a bookstore or other retail outlet.

Short short story. A condensed piece of fiction, usually under 1,000 words.

Simultaneous submission. See Multiple submission.

Slant. A story's particular approach or style, designed to appeal to the readers of a specific magazine.

Slice of life. A presentation of characters in a seemingly mundane situation which offers the reader a flash of illumination about the characters or their situation.

Slick. Popular, commercial, usually non-literary publication. (Name derived from the coated or polished stock on which it is printed.)

Slush pile. A stack of unsolicited manuscripts in the editorial offices of a publisher.

Speculation (or Spec). An editor's agreement to look at an author's manuscript with no promise to purchase.

Subsidiary. An incorporated branch of a company or conglomerate (e.g. Alfred Knopf, Inc., a subsidiary of Random House, Inc.).

Subsidiary rights. All rights other than book publishing rights included in a book contract, such as paperback, book club and movie rights.

Subsidy publisher. A book publisher who charges the author for the cost of typesetting, printing and promoting a book. Also Vanity publisher.

Suspense. A genre of fiction where the plot's primary function is to build a feeling of anticipation and fear in the reader over its possible outcome.

Tearsheet. Page from a magazine containing a published story.

Trade paperback. A softbound volume, usually around 8" x 5," published and designed for the general public, available mainly in bookstores.

Unsolicited manuscript. A story or novel manuscript that an editor did not specifically ask to see.

Vanity publisher. See Subsidy publisher.

Viewpoint. The position or attitude of the first- or third-person narrator or multiple narrators, which determines how a story's action is seen and evaluated.

Western. Genre with a setting in the West, usually between 1860-1890, with a formula plot about cowboys or other aspects of frontier life.

Whodunit. Genre dealing with murder, suspense and the detection of criminals.

Young adult. The general classification of books written for readers 12-18.

Category Index

The category index is a good place to begin searching for a market for your fiction.

Below is an alphabetized list of subjects of particular interest to the editors and agents listed in *Novel and Short Story Writer's Market*. The category index is divided into five sections: little/literary magazines, commercial periodicals, small presses, commercial publishers and literary agents.

If you have prepared a manuscript for a children's novel, for example, check the small press, commercial publisher or agent sections under Juvenile. Then look up that publisher or agent you have selected in the general index (page 653) to find the correct page number. Read the listing *very* carefully.

The category index is a useful—but very general—guide to help you save time as you market your work. The categories are broad, and different editors—especially periodical editors—interpret them differently. For example, the romance fiction desired by *Cosmopolitan* is obviously different from that used by *Wyoming Rural Electric News*.

Remember too that some periodicals, presses and agents choose not to specify their needs for fiction too exactly, preferring not to be limited by categories. Their specifications may be *quality* fiction only—including literary or mainstream work in all categories. It would be a mistake to use this category index as your *only* guide for choosing markets for your work, especially in the little/literary magazine category. Browse through the book, and order sample copies of the magazines that interest you.

Little/literary magazines

Adventure. Abyss; Adara; Adroit Expression; Amelia; Amherst Review; Another Point of View; Apple Blossom Connection; Arnazella; Atalantik; Ball State University Forum; Belladonna; Black Jack; Blizzard Rambler; Breakfast Without Meat; Brilliant Star; Bugle; Il Caffè; Calli's Tales; A Carolina Literary Companion; Choplogic; Cochran's Corner; Cold-Drill; Common Lives/Lesbian Lives; Couch Potato Journal; Crazyquilt; Cross Timbers Review; Crystal Rainbow; Cube Literary; Dan River Anthology; Deviance; Door County Almanak; Dream International Quarterly; Edges; Evergreen Chronicles; Expressions; F.O.C. Review; Felicity; Fighting Woman News; Fright Depot; Galactic Discourse; Gas; El Gato Tuerto; Generation; Green Mountains Review; Harvest; Hawaii Pacific Review; Hibiscus; Hob-Nob; Hoofstrikes Newsletter; Icelandic Canadian; In Transit; Innisfree; Japanophile; Jeopardy; Journal of Regional Criticism; Kallisti; Kana; Kids Lib News; Lactuca; Pablo Lennis; Lighthouse; Little Balkans Review; Long Shot; MacGuffin; Magical Blend; Meal, Ready-to-Eat; Merlyn's Pen; Microcosm; Mind's Eye; Minnesota Ink; Mirror-Northern Report; Monocacy Valley Review; Muse's Mill; Negative Capability; New Press; Nimrod; Nocturnal Lyric; Northern Review; Open Wide; Ouroboros; P.I.; Pig Paper; Passages Travel; Perceptions; Portable Wall; Prisoners of the Night; Proof Rock; Pub; Pulpsmith; Queen's Quarterly; Rag Mag; RaJAH; Rambunctious Review; Read Me; Reflections; Riverwind; Samisdat; Scream; Scribbler; Serendipity; Shawnee Silhouette; Shoe Tree; Shooting Star Review; Slate and Style; Sneak Preview; Space and Time; Stamp Axe; Stories & Letters; Thema; Tucumcari Literary Review; Tyro; Uncommon Reader; Village Idiot; Vintage Northwest; Virginia Quarterly Review; Wide Open; Writers' Bar-B-Q; Writer's Bloc; Writers' Gazette; Writers' Haven Journal; Writers-in-Waiting Newsletter; Writers Newsletter; Written Word.

Condensed Novel. Alabama Literary Review; Art:Mag; Atalantik; Ball State University Forum; Blonde on Blonde; Breakfast Without Meat; Il Caffè; Choplogic; Connecticut Writer; Cube Literary; Deviance; Ellipsis; F.O.C. Review; Helicon Nine; Hob-Nob; Housewife-Writer's Forum; Jacaranda Review; K; Kenyon Review; Kiosk; Lactuca; Muse's Mill; Northland Quarterly; Perceptions; Pub; Quimby; Scribbler; Serendipity; Sneak Preview; Stamp Axe; Timbuktu; Tucumcari Literary Review; TV-TS Tapestry Journal; Tyro; Vintage Northwest; Willow Springs; V̶ d Row; Word & Image.

Confession. Allegheny Review; Amherst Review; Another Point of View; Art:Mag; Breakfast Without Meat; Burning Toddlers; Il Caffè; Columbus Single Scene; Creative Spirit; Cube Literary; Dream Interna-

Ethnic. ACM; ACTA Victoriana; Adrift; Aegean Review; Alabama Literary Review; Amelia; Amherst Review; Antietam Review; L'Apache; Apple Blossom Connection; Arba Sicula; Arnazella; Art:Mag; Atalantik; Aura; Azorean Express; Backbone; La Bella Figura; Bilingual Review; Black Dog; Black Jack; Black Writer; Boston Review; Breakfast Without Meat; Brilliant Star; Brontë Street; Broomstick; Il Caffè; Calapooya Collage; Callaloo; Carolina Literary Companion; Central Park; Chiricú; Chronoscope; Clifton; Cold-Drill; Collages and Bricolages; Conditions; Coydog Review; Crazyquilt; Cream City Review; Cross Timbers Review; Cube Literary; Dan River Anthology; Deviance; Dream International Quarterly; DV-8; Earth's Daughters; Edges; Elephant-Ear; Epoch; Evergreen Chronicles; Expressions; Feminist Studies; Festivals; Five Fingers Review; Footwork; El Gato Tuerto; Gay Chicago; Gingerbread Diary; Groundswell; Harvest; Hawaii Pacific Review; Hawaii Review; Helicon Nine; Hill and Holler; Hoofstrikes Newsletter; Icelandic Canadian; Innisfree; Jeopardy; Jewish Currents; Journal; Journal of Regional Criticism; Kana; Kenyon Review; Lake Street Review; Left Curve; Lilith; Lime; Little Balkans Review; Long Shot; Long Story; MacGuffin; Mark; Maryland Review; Midland Review; Mind's Eye; Miorita; Mirror-Northern Report; Muse's Mill; Musicworks; Negative Capability; New Letters; New Press; NeWest Review; Nimrod; Nocturnal Lyric; North Dakota Quarterly; Northern New England Review; Northward Journal; Notebook: A Little Magazine; Now & Then; Oak Square; Obsidian II; Open; Open Wide; Oxford; Painted Bride Quarterly; Pennsylvania Review; Permafrost; Pig Iron; Portable Wall; Pottersfield Portfolio; Puerto Del Sol; Quimby; Rag Mag; RaJAH; Rambunctious Review; Ransom; Read Me; Real Fiction; Reaper; Response; Riverwind; Rohwedder; Salt Lick Press; Samisdat; San Jose Studies; Scream; Seattle Review; Sequoia; Shattered Wig Review; Shmate; Sing Heavenly Muse! Skylark; Slipstream; Sonoma Mandala; Sore Dove; South Carolina Review; South Dakota Review; Southern California Anthology; Sou'Wester; Spindrift; Spirit That Moves Us; Spoofing!; Stamp Axe; Star-Web Paper; Stories; Streamlines; Struggle; Sub Rosa; Tampa Review; Tara's Literary Arts Journal; Third Woman; Timbuktu; Tucumcari Literary Review; Tyro; Valley Grapevine; Valley Women's Voice; Village Idiot; Virginia Quarterly Review; Wicazo Sa Review; Wide Open; Working Classics; Writers' Bar-B-Q; Writers' Forum; Writers-in-Waiting Newsletter; Wyoming, The Hub of the Wheel; Xavier Review; Yellow Silk; Z Miscellaneous; Zonë.

Experimental. ACM; ACTA Victoriana; Action Time; Adrift; Adroit Expression; Aerial; Alabama Literary Review; Alaska Quarterly; Albany Review; Allegheny Review; Alpha Beat Soup; Alternative Fiction & Poetry; Amelia; American Fiction; American Voice; Amherst Review; Another Point of View; Antietam Review; Antioch Review; Arnazella; Art Brigade; Art:Mag; Asymptotical World; Atalantik; Azorean Express; Baby Sue; Backbone; Bad Haircut Quarterly; Bad Newz; Ball State University Forum; Belladonna; Black Dog; Black River Review; Blonde on Blonde; Bogg; Book of Contemporary Myth; Boston Review; Boulevard; Breakfast Without Meat; Brontë Street; Bugle; Burning Toddlers; BVI; Cache Review; California Quarterly; Calliope; Capilano Review; Caribbean Writer; Cathedral of Insanity; Ceilidh; Central Park; Chattahoochee Review; Chicago Review; Chiricú; Choplogic; Chronoscope; Clockwatch Review; Cold-Drill; Collages and Bricolages; Columbus Single Scene; Comet Halley; Common Lives/Lesbian Lives; Conjunctions; Cotton Boll; Coydog Review; Cream City Review; Cube Literary; Dan River Anthology; Dark Starr; Death Realm; Denver Quarterly; Deviance; Dream International Quarterly; Dreamshore; DV-8; Earth's Daughters; Edges; Elephant-Ear; Ellipsis; emPo; Eotu; Evergreen Chronicles; Exquisite Corpse; F.O.C. Review; Fat Tuesday; Felicity; Fiction International; Fiction Review; Five Fingers Review; Flipside; Footwork; Gamut; Gargoyle; Gas; Generation; Georgia Review; Gettysburg Review; Gingerbread Diary; Grain; Green Mountains Review; Greensboro Review; Groundswell; Hawaii Pacific Review; Hawaii Review; Heaven Bone; Helicon Nine; Hobo Stew Review; Hoofstrikes Newsletter; Housewife-Writer's Forum; Hurricane Alice; Ice River; Impulse; In Transit; Inside Joke; Jabberwocky; Jacaranda Review; Jeopardy; Journal; Journal of Regional Criticism; K; Kairos; Kallisti; Kana; Kenyon Review; Kindred Spirit; Kingfisher; Kiosk; Lake Street Review; Left Curve; Pablo Lennis; Lime; Limestone; Linington Lineup; Little Balkans Review; Long Shot; Lost and Found Times; Louisville Review; Lyra; MacGuffin; Madison Review; Mage; Mark; Meal, Ready-to-Eat; Merlyn's Pen; Microcosm; Mid-American Review; Midland Review; Mill Hunk Herald; Mind in Motion; Mind's Eye; Minnesota Ink; Minnesota Review; Mississippi Review; Monocacy Valley Review; Monthly Independent Tribune Times Journal Post Gazette News Chronical Bulletin; Mount Thrushmore Monument; Muse's Mill; Musicworks; Naked Man; Nebo; Negative Capability; New Blood; New Delta Review; New Letters; New Moon; New Press; new renaissance; New Virginia Review; NeWest Review; Night Slivers; Nightmares of Reason; Nightsun; Nimrod; Nocturnal Lyric; North Dakota Quarterly; Northern New England Review; Northwest Review; NRG; Oak Square; Ogre; Ohio Review; Open; Open Wide; Other Voices; Ouija Madness; Ouroboros; Oxford; Painted Bride Quarterly; Pangloss Papers; Paper Radio; Partisan Review; Pennsylvania Review; Perceptions; Permafrost; Phoebe; Pig Paper; Portable Wall; Pottersfield Portfolio; Prairie Fire; Primordial Eye; Prisoners of the Night; Proof Rock; Puerto Del Sol; Quarry; Queen's Quarterly; Quimby; Raddle Moon; Rag Mag; RaJAH; Rambunctious Review; Ransom; Real Fiction; Reaper; Red Bass; Response; Rohwedder; Round Table; Salt Lick Press; Samisdat; Scream; Seattle Review; Sequoia; Serendipity; Shattered Wig Review; Shmate; Shooting Star Review; Sign of the Times; Skylark; Slipstream; Sneak Preview; Sonoma Mandala; Sore Dove; South Dakota Review; Southern California Anthology; Sou'Wester; Spindrift; Stamp Axe; Star-Web Paper; Stories & Letters; Streamlines; Struggle; Sub Rosa; Swift Kick; Sycamore Review; T.W.I.; Tampa Review; Thema; Thin Ice; Timbuktu; Touchstone; Turnstile; 2 AM; Tyro; Village Idiot; Virgin Meat Fanzine; Washington DC Periodical; West Coast Review; Whetstone; James White Review; White Walls; Wide Open; Widener Review; Wind Row; Wisconsin Academy Review; Wisconsin Review;

Cochran's Corner; Common Lives/Lesbian Lives; Connecticut Writer; Crazyquilt; Creative Spirit; Cross Timbers Review; Dan River Anthology; Deviance; Door County Almanak; Dream International Quarterly; Expressions; Felicity; Generation; Gettysburg Review; Gingerbread Diary; Harvest; Helicon Nine; Hoofstrikes Newsletter; Housewife-Writer's Forum; In-Between; Japanophile; Jefferson Review; Jewish Currents; Journal of Regional Criticism; Kana; Kenyon Review; Lake Effect; Left Curve; Lighthouse; Liningron Lineup; Little Balkans Review; MacGuffin; Meal, Ready-to-Eat; Merlyn's Pen; Mickle Street Review; Midland Review; Mill Hunk Herald; Mind's Eye; Minnesota Review; Miorita; Mirror-Northern Report; Monocacy Valley Review; Montana Senior Citizens News; Mountain Laurel; Negative Capability; NeWest Review; North Dakota Quarterly; Northern New England Review; Notebook: A Little Magazine; Ouroboros; Passages Travel; Pipe Smoker's Ephemeris; Pleiades; Portable Wall; Queen's Quarterly; RaJAH; Rambunctious Review; Read Me; Response; Riverwind; Samisdat; Scream; Seattle Review; Serendipity; Shawnee Silhouette; Shmate; Shoe Tree; Skylark; Sneak Preview; Southern California Anthology; Spindrift; Stamp Axe; Stories; Streamlines; Struggle; Sub Rosa; Sycamore Review; Tampa Review; Tucumcari Literary Review; TV-TS Tapestry Journal; Tyro; Uncommon Reader; Village Idiot; Vintage Northwest; Wide Open; Wisconsin Academy Review; Word & Image; Working Classics; Writers' Bar-B-Q; Writer's Bloc; Writers-in-Waiting Newsletter; Writers Newsletter; Xavier Review; Zonë.

Horror. Abyss; Action Time; Alpha Adventures SF&F; Amherst Review; Another Point of View; Apple Blossom Connection; Argonaut; Art Brigade; Art:Mag; Asymptotical World; Bad Haircut Quarterly; Bad Newz; Belladonna; Bellingham Review; Blizzard Rambler; BVI; Cache Review; Chronoscpe; Cochran's Corner; Cold-Drill; Cosmic Landscapes; Creative Spirit; Cube Literary; Dan River Anthology; Dark Starr; Death Realm; Dementia; Desert Sun; Deviance; Dream International Quarterly; Edges; Eldritch Tales; Fantasy & Terror; Felicity; Fright Depot; Gas; Generation; Grue; Haunts; Hawaii Review; Hoofstrikes Newsletter; Horror Show; Hor-tasy; Housewife-Writer's Forum; In Transit; Jabberwocky; Journal of Regional Criticism; Kana; Pablo Lennis; Lime; Little Balkans Review; Long Shot; Mage; Meal, Ready-to-Eat; Merlyn's Pen; Microcosm; Midland Review; Mind's Eye; Mount Thrushmore Monument; Muse's Mill; New Blood; Night Slivers; Nocturnal Lyric; Ogre; Open Wide; Ouija Madness; Ouroboros; Pleiades; Portents; Primordial Eye; Prisoners of the Night; Pub; Pulphouse; Pulpsmith; RaJAH; Read Me; Riverwind; Science Fiction Randomly; Scream; Scribbler; Seattle Review; Serendipity; Shoe Tree; Skylark; Space and Time; Stamp Axe; Starsong; Stories & Letters; Tapestry; Terror Time; Thin Ice; Trajectories; Twisted; 2 AM; Tyro; Var Tufa; Village Idiot; Virgin Meat Fanzine; Washington DC Periodical; Weirdbook; Wide Open; Witness to the Bizarre; Writers' Bar-B-Q; Writers' Gazette; Writers' Haven Journal; Written Word; Z Miscellaneous.

Humor/Satire. ACM; ACTA Victoriana; Action Time; Adara; Alabama Literary Review; Albany Review; Allegheny Review; Alpha Adventures SF&F; Amelia; American Atheist; American Screamer; American Voice; Amherst Review; Anglican; Another Point of View; Apple Blossom Connection; Arnazella; Art Brigade; Art:Mag; Atalantik; Axe Factory Review; Azorean Express; Baby Sue; Bad Haircut Quarterly; Bad Newz; Ball State University Forum; Bellingham Review; Big Two-Hearted; Black Jack; Black River Review; Blizzard Rambler; Blonde on Blonde; Blue Sky Journal; Boston Review; Breakfast Without Meat; Brilliant Star; Broomstick; Bugle; Burning Toddlers; BVI; Cache Review; Il Caffè; Callaloo; Canadian Author & Bookman; Caribbean Writer; Carolina Literary Companion; Cathedral of Insanity; Chattahoochee Review; Chiricú; Choplogic; Chronoscope; Clifton; Clockwatch Review; Cochran's Corner; Cold-Drill; Collages and Bricolages; Columbus Single Scene; Common Lives/Lesbian Lives; A Companion in Zeor; Connecticut Writer; Cotton Boll; Coydog Review; Crab Creek Review; Crazyquilt; Cream City Review; Creative Spirit; Creative Woman; Cross Timbers Review; Cube Literary; Dan River Anthology; Dekalb Literary Arts Journal; Desert Sun; Deviance; Door County Almanak; Dream International Quarterly; DV-8; Earth's Daughters; Edges; Elephant-Ear; Ellipsis; Evergreen Chronicles; Expressions; F.O.C. Review; Farmer's Market; Fat Tuesday; Felicity; Festivals; Five Fingers Review; Freelancer's Report; Freeway; Fright Depot; Galactic Discourse; Gamut; Gargoyle; Garland; Gas; Generation; Gettysburg Review; Gingerbread Diary; Goofus Office Gazette; Green Mountains Review; Groundswell; Harvest; Hawaii Pacific Review; Hawaii Review; Helicon Nine; Hibiscus; High Plains Literary Review; Hill and Holler; Hob-Nob; Hobo Stew Review; Hoofstrikes Newsletter; Housewife-Writer's Forum; Hurricane Alice; Icelandic Canadian; In Transit; In-Between; Inlet; Inside Joke; Jabberwocky; Japanophile; Jeopardy; Jewish Currents; Journal of Polymorphous Perversity; Journal of Quantum Pataphysics; Journal of Regional Criticism; K; Kaleidoscope; Kallisti; Kana; Kindred Spirit; Kiosk; Lake Effect; Lake Street Review; Pablo Lennis; Left Curve; Lighthouse; Lime; Limestone; Little Balkans Review; Live Letters; Lone Star; Long Shot; MacGuffin; Mark; Maryland Review; Meal, Ready-to-Eat; Merlyn's Pen; Mill Hunk Herald; Mind in Motion; Mind's Eye; Mirror-Northern Report; Mississippi Review; Minnesota Ink; Monocacy Valley Review; Monthly Independent Tribune Times Journal Post Gazette News Chronical Bulletin; Mount Thrushmore Monument; Mountain Laurel; Muse's Mill; Naked Man; Nebraska Review; New Crucible; New Delta Review; New Letters; New Press; new renaissance; NeWest Review; Nightmares of Reason; Nocturnal Lyric; North Dakota Quarterly; Northern New England Review; Notebook: A Little Magazine; Oak Square; On Our Backs; Open Wide; Oregon East; Other Voices; Ouija Madness; Ouroboros; Oxford; P.I.; P.U.N.; Pangloss Papers; Pegasus Review; Pennsylvania Review; Peregrine; Permafrost; Piedmont Literary Review; Pig in a Pamphlet; Pig Paper; Pipe Smoker's Ephemeris; Plough: North Coast Review; PM; Poetry Magic; Portable Wall; Pottersfield Portfolio; Poultry; Primavera; Proof Rock; Pulpsmith; Queen's Quarterly; Quimby; Quintessential Space Debris; RaJAH; Rambunctious Review; Ransom; Read Me; Reaper; Red Cedar Review; Response; Right Here; Riverwind; Rohwedder; Samisdat; San Jose Studies; Science Fiction

Randomly; Scream; Scribbler; Seattle Review; Sequoia; Serendipity; Shattered Wig Review; Shawnee Silhouette; Shmate; Shoe Tree; Shooting Star Review; Sing Heavenly Muse!; Skylark; Slate and Style; Slipstream; Sneak Preview; Sonoma Mandala; Sore Dove; South Carolina Review; Southern California Anthology; Southern Humanities Review; Space and Time; Spirit That Moves Us; Spoofing!; Stamp Axe; Starsong; Star-Web Paper; Stories; Stories & Letters; Streamlines; Struggle; Sub Rosa; Sycamore Review; T.W.I.; Tampa Review; Thema; Thin Ice; Touchstone; Trajectories; Tucumcari Literary Review; Turnstile; TV-TS Tapestry Journal; 2 AM; Tyro; Uncommon Reader; Var Tufa; Village Idiot; Vintage Northwest; Virgin Meat Fanzine; Virginia Quarterly Review; Voices in the Wilderness; Washington DC Periodical; James White Review; Wide Open; William and Mary Review; Wisconsin Academy Review; Wooster Review; Working Classics; World Humor and Irony Membership Serial Yearbook: Whimsy; Word & Image; Writers' Bar-B-Q; Writers' Gazette; Writers' Haven Journal; Writers-in-Waiting Newsletter; Writers Newsletter; Writers' Rendezvous; Writing Pursuits; Written Word; X-It; Yellow Silk; Z Miscellaneous; Zoiks!.

Juvenile. Apple Blossom Connection; Atalantik; Breakfast Without Meat; Brilliant Star; Calli's Tales; Cochran's Corner; Common Lives/Lesbian Lives; Creative Kids; Day Care and Early Education; Dream International Quarterly; Dreamshore; Felicity; Hobo Stew Review; Hoofstrikes Newsletter; Housewife-Writer's Forum; In-Between; Kids Lib News; Lighthouse; McGuffey Writer; Portable Wall; Reflections; Shattered Wig Review; Shoe Tree; Skylark; Sneak Preview; Spoofing!; Stone Soup; Tyro; Writer's Bloc; Writers Newsletter; Written Word.

Lesbian. ACM; Adrift; Alabama Literary Review; Amelia; American Voice; Amherst Review; Arnazella; Art Brigade; Art:Mag; La Bella Figura; Belladonna; Bellingham Review; Black Dog; Central Park; Chiricú; Chronoscope; Cold-Drill; Common Lives/Lesbian Lives; Conditions; Coydog Review; Deviance; Edges; Evergreen Chronicles; Feminist Studies; Five Fingers Review; Frontiers; Galactic Discourse; Gay Chicago; Gingerbread Diary; Groundswell; Heresies; Hurricane Alice; Kallisti; Kana; Kindred Spirit; Kiosk; Lilith; Lime; Live Letters; Long Shot; Mill Hunk Herald; Mind's Eye; Minnesota Review; Moving Out; On Our Backs; Open; Ouija Madness; Oxford; Painted Bride Quarterly; Pennsylvania Review; Permafrost; Pottersfield Portfolio; Primavera; Prisoners of the Night; RaJAH; Real Fiction; Reaper; Room of One's Own; Salt Lick Press; Samisdat; Scream; Seattle Review; Shattered Wig Review; Shmate; Sign of the Times; Slipstream; Sonoma Mandala; Sou'Wester; Spirit That Moves Us; Sub Rosa; Valley Women's Voice; Village Idiot; Visibilities; Washington DC Periodical; Wide Open; Working Classics; Writers' Bar-B-Q; Yellow Silk; Zonë.

Mainstream. ACTA Victoriana; Adroit Expression; Albany Review; Allegheny Review; Amelia; American Fiction; Amherst Review; Apple Blossom Connection; Arnazella; Art:Mag; Atalantik; Bad Haircut Quarterly; Ball State University Forum; Bellowing Ark; Beloit Fiction Journal; Black Warrior Review; Bloomsbury Review; Blue Sky Journal; Boston Review; Brontë Street; Cache Review; Caesura; Il Caffè; Calapooya Collage; Caribbean Writer; Carolina Literary Companion; Chattahoochee Review; Chiricú; Choplogic; Chronoscope; Clockwatch Review; Cold-Drill; Collages and Bricolages; Connecticut Writer; Columbus Single Scene; Coydog Review; Crazyquilt; Creative Spirit; Cube Literary; Dan River Anthology; Dream International Quarterly; Edges; Emrys Journal; Evergreen Chronicles; Fiction Review; Folio: A Literary Journal; Gamut; Gas; Generation; Gettysburg Review; Gingerbread Diary; Grain; Green Mountains Review; Groundswell; Handicap; Hawaii Pacific Review; Hibiscus; High Plains Literary Review; Hoofstrikes Newsletter; Housewife-Writer's Forum; In Transit; Inlet; Innisfree; Jacaranda Review; Japanophile; Jeopardy; Journal of Regional Criticism; K; Kana; Kenyon Review; Lactuca; Lake Effect; Lake Street Review; Lighthouse; Limestone; Little Balkans Review; Louisiana Literature; MacGuffin; Maryland Review; Meal, Ready-to-Eat; Merlyn's Pen; Mid-American Review; Mind's Eye; Minnesota Ink; Mirror-Northern Report; Monocacy Valley Review; Muse's Mill; Naked Man; Nebo; Nebraska Review; New Blood; New Delta Review; New Letters; New Press; New Virginia Review; NeWest Review; Nocturnal Lyric; Northern New England Review; Northland Quarterly; Oak Square; Open Wide; Ouroboros; Pasages North; Pembroke; Phoebe; Plough: North Coast Review; Portable Wall; Pottersfield Portfolio; Proof Rock; Puerto Del Sol; Pulpsmith; Quarry West; Queen's Quarterly; Quimby; Rag Mag; RaJAH; Rambunctious Review; Read Me; Right Here; Ripples; Riverwind; Round Table; Samisdat; Seattle Review; Serendipity; Shawnee Silhouette; Shoe Tree; Shooting Star Review; Skylark; Slipstream; Sneak Preview; Sonoma Mandala; Sore Dove; Southern California Anthology; Sou'Wester; Stories & Letters; Sun; Sycamore Review; Tampa Review; Thema; Threepenny Review; Touchstone; Tucumcari Literary Review; Tyro; Uncommon Reader; Village Idiot; Washington DC Periodical; Whetstone; Whiskey Island; Wide Open; Widener Review; Wisconsin Academy Review; Wooster Review; Writers' Bar-B-Q; Writer's Bloc; Writers' Forum; Writers' Gazette; Writers-in-Waiting Newsletter; Writers Newsletter; Writers' Rendezvous; X-It; Z Miscellaneous.

Preschool. Breakfast Without Meat; Brilliant Star; Calli's Tales; Cochran's Corner; Day Care and Early Education; Dreamshore; Housewife-Writer's Forum; Kids Lib News; Lighthouse; Shattered Wig Review; Spoofing!; Portable Wall; Tyro; Written Word.

Prose Poem. Abbey; ACM; ACTA Victoriana; Action Time; Adara; Adroit Expression; Agni Review; Alabama Literary Review; Alaska Quarterly Review; Albany Review; Antigonish Review; L'Apache; Argonaut; Arnazella; Art:Mag; Bad Haircut Quarterly; La Bella Figura; Belladonna; Bellingham Review; Beloit Fiction Journal; Big Two-Hearted; Black Dog; Black Warrior Review; Black Writer; Blizzard Rambler; Blonde on Blonde; Bogg; Book of Contemporary Myth; Boulevard; Brontë Street; Cache Review; Capilano Review; Caribbean Writer; Ceilidh; Chelsea; Chiricú; Chronoscope; Clifton; Cochran's Corner; Collages and Bricolages; Colorado-North Review; Columbia; Common Lives/Lesbian Lives; Companion in

Zeor; Cotton Boll; Couch Potato Journal; Cream City Review; Creative Spirit; Creative Woman; Cross-Canada Writers'; Crystal Rainbow; Cube Literary; Dan River Anthology; Deviance; Dream International Quarterly; Dreamshore; Earth's Daughters; Edges; Ellipsis; emPo; Eotu; F.O.C. Review; Fat Tuesday; Felicity; Fiction Review; Five Fingers Review; Folio: A Literary Journal; Fright Depot; Galactic Discourse; Gamut; Gargoyle; Gas; El Gato Tuerto; Gingerbread Diary; Goofus Office Gazette; Grain; Green Mountains Review; Harvest; Hawaii Review; Helicon Nine; Housewife-Writer's Forum; Ice River; In Transit; In-Between; Independent Review; Jacaranda Review; Journal of Regional Criticism; Kaleidoscope; Kenyon Review; Kids Lib News; Kiosk; Lake Street Review; Left Curve; Letters; Lighthouse; Lilith; Lime; Little Balkans Review; Long Shot; Loonfeather; Lost and Found Times; Louisville Review; Lyra; MacGuffin; Madison Review; Magic Changes; Meal, Ready-to-Eat; Midland Review; Mill Hunk Herald; Mind in Motion; Mind's Eye; Mirror-Northern Report; Monocacy Valley Review; Montana Review; Mount Thrushmore Monument; Muse's Mill; Mythic Circle; New Delta Review; New Moon; New Press; new renaissance; Nightsun; Nimrod; Now & Then; NRG; Oak Square; Oregon East; Pangloss Papers; Paper Radio; PM; Pegasus Review; Perceptions; Peregrine; Permafrost; Phoebe; Pig in a Pamphlet; Pig Paper; Plough: North Coast Review; Ploughshares; Poetry Magic; Portable Wall; Porfland Review; Pottersfield Portfolio; Prairie Fire; Prairie Journal of Canadian Literature; Prairie Schooner; Prism International; Prisoners of the Night; Puerto Del Sol; Pulpsmith; Quimby; Rambunctious Review; Ransom; Redneck Review of Literature; Reflections; Renaissance Fan; Response; Right Here; Ripples; Riverwind; Samisdat; Seattle Review; Seems; Serendipity; Shattered Wig Review; Sing Heavenly Muse!; Sinister Wisdom; Skylark; Slipstream; Sneak Preview; Sonoma Mandala; Sonora Review; Sore Dove; Soundings East; Southwest Review; Spindrift; Spirit That Moves Us; Starsong; Star-Web Paper; Struggle; Sub Rosa; T.W.I.; Tampa Review; Tara's Literary Arts Journal; Thema; Thin Ice; Trajectories; Twisted; 2 AM; Tyro; Unknowns; Unmuzzled Ox; Unspeakable Visions of the Individual; Village Idiot; Vintage Northwest; Virgin Meat Fanzine; Webster Review; West Branch; West Coast Review; What; Whiskey Island; James White Review; White Wall Review; Willow Springs; Wisconsin Academy Review; Wooster Review; Word & Image; Worcester Review; Writers Gazette; Writers-in-Waiting Newsletter; Writers Newsletter; Wyoming, The Hub of the Wheel; Xavier Review; Zoiks!; Zonë; Zyzzyva.

Psychic/Supernatural/Occult. Abyss; Alpha Adventures SF&F; Amherst Review; Art:Mag; Asymptotical World; Atalantik; Bad Haircut Quarterly; Bad Newz; Ball State University Forum; Belladonna; Bellingham Review; Blonde on Blonde; Book of Contemporary Myth; Breakfast Without Meat; BVI; Cathedral of Insanity; Chronoscope; Common Lives/Lesbian Lives; Cube Literary; Dan River Anthology; Death Realm; Deviance; Dream International Quarterly; Dreamshore; Edges; Eldritch Tales; Fat Tuesday; Felicity; Fright Depot; Galactic Discourse; Gas; Generation; Golden Isis; Green's; Grue; Haunts; Heaven Bone; Hob-Nob; Hoofstrikes Newsletter; Housewife-Writer's Forum; Ice River; In Transit; Inside Joke; Jabberwocky; Journal of Regional Criticism; Kallisti; Kana; Kids Lib News; Kindred Spirit; Pablo Lennis; Lilith; Lime; Little Balkans Review; Live Letters; Long Shot; MacGuffin; Magical Blend; Microcosm; Midland Review; Mind's Eye; Mirror-Northern Report; Mount Thrushmore Monument; Muse's Mill; Negative Capability; New Blood; New Frontier; Night Slivers; Nocturnal Lyric; Open Wide; Ouija Madness; Ouroboros; Perceptions; Piedmont Literary Review; Pig Paper; Prisoners of the Night; Proof Rock; Pub; Quimby; Scream; Seattle Review; Serendipity; Shattered Wig Review; Skylark; Space and Time; Stamp Axe; Starsong; Star-Web Paper; Tara's Literary Arts Journal; Thema; Thin Ice; Trajectories; Twisted; 2 AM; Tyro; Var Tufa; Virgin Meat Fanzine; Washington DC Periodical; Weirdbook; Wide Open; Witness to the Bizarre; Writers' Bar-B-Q; Writer's Bloc; Writers' Gazette; Writers' Haven Journal; Written Word; Zoiks!.

Regional. Abbey; Alabama Literary Review; Amelia; Amherst Review; Another Point of View; Antietam Review; Appalachian Heritage; Apple Blossom Connection; Arba Sicula; Arnazella; Art:Mag; Aura; Azorean Express; Bellingham Review; Big Two-Hearted; Blonde on Blonde; Boston Review; Cache Review; Callaloo; Carolina Literary Companion; Chattahoochee Review; Clifton; Clockwatch Review; Common Lives/Lesbian Lives; Confrontation; Coydog Review; Cream City Review; Creative Spirit; Cross Timbers Review; Cross-Canada Writers' Quarterly; Dan River Anthology; Descant (Texas); Door County Almanak; Edges; Elephant-Ear; Emrys Journal; Expressions; Farmer's Market; Five Fingers Review; Gamut; Gingerbread Diary; Glens Falls Review; Green Mountains Review; Groundswell; Hawaii Pacific Review; Hawaii Review; High Plains Literary Review; Hill and Holler; Hob-Nob; Hoofstrikes Newsletter; Icelandic Canadian; Innisfree; Jeopardy; Journal; Journal of Regional Criticism; Kana; Kenyon Review; Lactuca; Lake Effect; Left Curve; Lighthouse; Lime; Limestone; Little Balkans Review; Live Letters; Loonfeather; Louisiana Literature; Mark; Meal, Ready-to-Eat; Merlyn's Pen; Midland Review; Miorita; Minnesota Ink; Mount Thrushmore Monument; Mountain Laurel; Naked Man; Negative Capability; New Mexico Humanities Review; Northern New England Review; Northern Review; Northland Quarterly; Notebook: A Little Magazine; Now & Then; Oak Square; Oregon East; Partisan Review; Pennsylvania Review; Phoebe; Piedmont Literary Review; Plainswoman; Plough: North Coast Review; Portable Wall; Pottersfield Portfolio; Prairie Journal of Canadian Literature; Quimby; Rag Mag; RaJAH; Real Fiction; Red Cedar Review; Redneck Review of Literature; Response; Riverwind; Rohwedder; Samisdat; San Jose Studies; Scream; Seattle Review; Shattered Wig Review; Shawnee Silhouette; Shooting Star Review; Skylark; Sneak Preview; Sonoma Mandala; South Dakota Review; Southern California Anthology; Southern Humanities Review; Sou'Wester; Spindrift; Spoofing!; Streamlines; Struggle; Sycamore Review; Tara's Literary Arts Journal; Thema; Tucumcari Literary Review; Turnstile; Tyro; Widener Review; Wind; Wisconsin Academy Review; Word & Image; Working Classics; Writers' Bar-B-Q; Writers' Forum; Writers' Haven Journal; Writers Newsletter; Writing Pursuits; Wyoming, The Hub of the Wheel; Xavier Review.

Religious/Inspirational. Apple Blossom Connection; Arnazella; Ball State University Forum; Black Writer; Breakfast Without Meat; Brilliant Star; Cochran's Corner; Creative Spirit; Crystal Rainbow; Felicity; Freeway; Gettysburg Review; Handicap; Heaven Bone; Hob-Nob; Hoofstrikes Newsletter; Journal of Regional Criticism; Kana; Lilith; Meal, Ready-to-Eat; Modern Liturgy; Ouija Madness; Pegasus Review; Perceptions; Rampant Guinea Pig; Reflections; Reformed Journal; Response; Right Here; Shmate; Stories & Letters; Tyro; Vintage Northwest; Voices in the Wilderness; Word & Image; Writers' Gazette; Writers Newsletter; Xavier Review.

Romance. Adroit Expression; Amherst Review; Apple Blossom Connection; Arba Sicula; Aura; Atalantik; Belladonna; Il Caffè; Chronoscope; Cochran's Corner; Common Lives/Lesbian Lives; Couch Potato Journal; Creative Spirit; Dan River Anthology; Dream International Quarterly; Evergreen Chronicles; Felicity; Freelancer's Report; Fright Depot; Gay Chicago; Gingerbread Diary; Handicap; Hob-Nob; Hoofstrikes Newsletter; Housewife-Writer's Forum; Icelandic Canadian; Jeopardy; Journal of Regional Criticism; Lighthouse; Lime; Meal, Ready-to-Eat; Merlyn's Pen; Mind's Eye; Minnesota Ink; Mirror-Northern Report; Muse's Mill; Negative Capability; Nocturnal Lyric; Northern New England Review; Northland Quarterly; Open Wide; Proof Rock; PSI; Rambunctious Review; Read Me; Scribbler; Shawnee Silhouette; Shooting Star Review; Sneak Preview; Stories & Letters; Timbuktu; Tyro; Village Idiot; Virginia Quarterly Review; Word & Image; Writer's Bloc; Writers' Gazette; Writers' Haven Journal; Writers-in-Waiting Newsletter; Writers Newsletter; Writers' Rendezvous.

Science Fiction. Abbey; Abyss; Action Time; Adara; Alabama Literary Review; Alpha Adventures SF&F; Amelia; Amherst Review; Another Point of View; Apple Blossom Connection; Argonaut; Arnazella; Art Brigade; Art:Mag; Atalantik; Aura; Bad Haircut Quarterly; Ball State University Forum; Belladonna; Bellingham Review; Beyond . . . Science Fiction & Fantasy; Blonde on Blonde; Brilliant Star; Brontë Street; BVI; Cache Review; Callaloo; Ceilidh; Chiricú; Chronoscope; Cochran's Corner; Cold-Drill; Collages and Bricolages; Comet Halley; Common Lives/Lesbian Lives; A Companion in Zeor; Cosmic Landscapes; Couch Potato Journal; Coydog Review; Crazyquilt; Creative Spirit; Cube Literary; Dan River Anthology; Dark Starr; Death Realm; Desert Sun; Deviance; Dream International Quarterly; Edges; Elephant-Ear; Ellipsis; Exit; F.O.C. Review; Felicity; Fighting Woman News; Fright Depot; Galactic Discourse; Gas; El Gato Tuerto; Generation; Green's; Hawaii Pacific Review; Hibiscus; Hob-Nob; Hobo Stew Review; Hoofstrikes Newsletter; Housewife-Writer's Forum; Hurricane Alice; Ice River; In Transit; Innisfree; Inside Joke; Jabberwocky; Jam To-Day; Jeopardy; Journal of Regional Criticism; K; Kallisti; Kana; Kenyon Review; Kindred Spirit; Lake Street Review; Left Curve; Pablo Lennis; Letters; Little Balkans Review; Long Shot; Lyra; MacGuffin; Mage; Mad Engineer; Magic Changes; Mark; Merlyn's Pen; Microcosm; Midland Review; Mind in Motion; Mind's Eye; Minnesota Ink; Minnesota Review; Mirror-Northern Report; Muse's Mill; Negative Capability; New Blood; New Moon; NeWest Review; Night Slivers; Nightmares of Reason; Nimrod; Nocturnal Lyric; Northern New England Review; Ogre; Open Wide; Other Worlds; Ouija Madness; Ouroboros; Owlflight; Pandora; Paper Radio; Permafrost; Piedmont Literary Review; Pig Paper; PM; Portable Wall; Pottersfield Portfolio; Primavera; Primordial Eye; Prisoners of the Night; Pulphouse; Pulpsmith; Quarry; Queen's Quarterly; Quintessential Space Debris; Rampant Guinea Pig; Read Me; Reflections; Renaissance Fan; Samisdat; Science Fiction Randomly; Scream; Scribbler; Seattle Review; Serendipity; Shattered Wig Review; Shawnee Silhouette; Shmate; Shoe Tree; Shooting Star Review; Skylark; Slipstream; Sneak Preview; Space and Time; Spindrift; Stamp Axe; Starsong; Stories & Letters; Struggle; Thema; Trajectories; Twisted; 2 AM; Tyro; Village Idiot; Washington DC Periodical; Wide Open; Wind Row; Wisconsin Academy Review; Witness to the Bizarre; Wooster Review; Writers' Bar-B-Q; Writer's Bloc; Writers' Gazette; Writers' Haven Journal; Writers Newsletter; Yellow Silk; Z Miscellaneous; Zonë.

Senior Citizen/Retirement. Amelia; Apple Blossom Connection; Arba Sicula; Breakfast Without Meat; Broomstick; Carolina Literary Companion; Common Lives/Lesbian Lives; Dan River Anthology; Deviance; Dream International Quarterly; Edges; Felicity; Harvest; Hob-Nob; Hobo Stew Review; Icelandic Canadian; In-Between; Jewish Currents; Kana; Kenyon Review; Lighthouse; Lilith; Live Letters; Meal, Ready-to-Eat; Mill Hunk Herald; Minnesota Ink; Mirror-Northern Report; Montana Senior Citizens News; Negative Capability; Perceptions; Pleiades; Portable Wall; Reflections; Right Here; Shmate; Sneak Preview; Struggle; Tyro; Village Idiot; Vintage Northwest; Wide Open; Word & Image; Writers' Haven Journal.

Serialized/Excerpted Novel. Adara; Agni Review; Alabama Literary Review; American Voice; Another Point of View; Antaeus; Art Brigade; Ball State University Forum; Bellingham Review; Bellowing Ark; Black Jack; Boston Review; Burning Toddlers; Cache Review; Il Caffè; BVI; Callaloo; Cathedral of Insanity; Ceilidh; Central Park; Chiricú; Chronoscope; Cold-Drill; Columbia; Coydog Review; Crazyquilt; Deviance; Dream International Quarterly; DV-8; Elephant-Ear; Evergreen Chronicles; F.O.C. Review; Farmer's Market; Fat Tuesday; Fiction International; Fright Depot; Gettysburg Review; Green Mountains Review; Groundswell; Hob-Nob; Housewife-Writer's Forum; In-Between; Jabberwocky; K; Kaleidoscope; Kallisti; Kenyon Review; Kindred Spirit; Kingfisher; Madison Review; Mage; Montana Review; Muse's Mill; New Blood; New Press; New Virginia Review; Nightmares of Reason; Nocturnal Lyric; Northland Quarterly; Now & Then; Oak Square; Other Voices; Perceptions; Phoebe; Pikestaff Forum; Pleiades; PM; Prairie Journal of Canadian Literature; Pub; Puerto Del Sol; Quarry; RaJAH; Read Me; Real Fiction; Red Bass; Samisdat; Scream; Seattle Review; Serendipity; Shattered Wig Review; Skylark; South Dakota Review; Southern California Anthology; Spindrift; Star-Web Paper; Timbuktu; Trajectories; Tyro; Uncommon Reader; Unspeakable Visions of the Individual; Virginia Quarterly Review; Washington DC Periodical; Webster Review; West Coast Review; Widener Review; Willow Springs; Stephen Wright's Mystery

Notebook; Writ; Writers' Bar-B-Q; Writers' Rendezvous; Xavier Review.

Spiritual. Beloit Fiction Journal; Brilliant Star; Brontë Street; Clifton; Creative Woman; Deviance; Dream International Quarterly; Festivals; Freeway; Gingerbread Diary; Green Mountains Review; Heaven Bone; In Transit; Pablo Lennis; Lilith; Magical Blend; New Delta Review; New Frontier; New Press; Now & Then; Pig Paper; Prairie Schooner; Response; Right Here; Ripples; Riverwind; Samisdat; Skylark; Sub Rosa; Sun; Trajectories; Tyro; Writers Gazette; Writers Newsletter; Zonë.

Sports. Amelia; Beloit Fiction Journal; Cache Review; Creative Woman; Edges; F.O.C. Review; Folio: A Literary Journal; Gargoyle; Green Mountains Review; Lighthouse; Magic Changes; Meal, Ready-to-Eat; Mind's Eye; Mirror-Northern Report; Muse's Mill; New Delta Review; New Press; Now & Then; Ouija Madness; Portable Wall; Prairie Schooner; Ripples; Riverwind; Shmate; Sinister Wisdom; Skylark; Sneak Preview; Sub Rosa; Sun; Sycamore Review; Thema; Tyro.

Suspense/Mystery. Alabama Literary Review; Amelia; Amherst Review; Another Point of View; Apple Blossom Connection; Arnazella; Art:Mag; Atalantik; Ball State University Forum; Belladonna; Bellingham Review; Blizzard Rambler; Breakfast Without Meat; Brilliant Star; Brontë Street; BVI; Byline; Cache Review; Carolina Literary Companion; Chronoscope; Cochran's Corner; Cold-Drill; Columbus Single Scene; Common Lives/Lesbian Lives; Couch Potato Journal; Crazyquilt; Creative Spirit; Crystal Rainbow; Cube Literary; Dan River Anthology; Dark Starr; Detective Story; Deviance; Door County Almanak; Dream International Quarterly; Edges; Elephant-Ear; Evergreen Chronicles; Exit; F.O.C. Review; Felicity; Folio: A Literary Journal; Fright Depot; Galactic Discourse; Gas; El Gato Tuerto; Generation; Groundswell; Hawaii Pacific Review; Hibiscus; Hob-Nob; Hoofstrikes Newsletter; Housewife-Writer's Forum; In Transit; In-Between; Innisfree; Japanophile; Kana; Letters; Lighthouse; Linington Lineup; Little Balkans Review; Long Shot; Merlyn's Pen; Mind's Eye; Minnesota Ink; Mirror-Northern Report; Monthly Independent Tribune Times Journal Post Gazette News Chronical Bulletin; Muse's Mill; Mystery Time; Negative Capability; New Blood; Nocturnal Lyric; Open Wide; Ouroboros; P.I.; Perceptions; Pleiades; Prisoners of the Night; PSI; Pub; Pulpsmith; Quimby; Read Me; Reflections; Right Here; Samisdat; Scream; Seattle Review; Serendipity; Shawnee Silhouette; Shoe Tree; Shooting Star Review; Sing Heavenly Muse!; Skylark; Sneak Preview; Stories & Letters; Struggle; Thema; 2 AM; Tyro; Uncommon Reader; Village Idiot; Vintage Northwest; Wide Open; Wisconsin Academy Review; Witness to the Bizarre; Wooster Review; Stephen Wright's Mystery Notebook; Writers' Bar-B-Q; Writer's Bloc; Writers' Gazette; Writers' Haven Journal; Writers-in-Waiting Newsletter; Writers Newsletter; Writers' Rendezvous; Writing Pursuits; Written Word.

Translations. ACM; Adrift; Aerial; Agni Review; Alabama Literary Review; Alaska Quarterly; Albany Review; Alternative Fiction & Poetry; Amelia; American Voice; Amherst Review; Another Point of View; Antaeus; Antigonish Review; Antioch Review; L'Apache; Arba Sicula; Arnazella; Art Brigade; Artful Dodge; Art:Mag; Atalantik; Bad Haircut Quarterly; Ball State University Forum; La Bella Figura; Bellingham Review; Black Dog; Boston Review; Cache Review; Il Caffè; Callaloo; Ceilidh; Central Park; Chariton Review; Chattahoochee Review; Chiricú; Chronoscope; Cold-Drill; Columbia; Comet Halley; Conditions; Confrontation; Conjunctions; Crab Creek Review; Cream City Review; Cube Literary; Denver Quarterly; Descant (Canada); Deviance; Dream International Quarterly; Exit; Expressions; Fighting Woman News; Folio: A Literary Journal; Footwork; Gamut; Gargoyle; El Gato Tuerto; Green Mountains Review; Groundswell; Hawaii Pacific Review; Hawaii Review; Helicon Nine; Hobo Stew Review; Hurricane Alice; Icelandic Canadian; Jabberwocky; Jacaranda Review; Jefferson Review; Jeopardy; Jewish Currents; Kairos; Kana; Kenyon Review; Kingfisher; Kiosk; Left Curve; Pablo Lennis; Lilith; Lime; Little Balkans Review; Live Letters; Lyra; MacGuffin; Mark; Mid-American Review; Midland Review; Mind's Eye; Miorita; Mirror-Northern Report; Mississippi Review; Montana Review; Mount Thrushmore Monument; Negative Capability; New Blood; New Delta Review; New Laurel Review; New Letters; New Moon; New Orleans Review; New Press; new renaissance; Nimrod; Northern New England Review; Northwest Review; Oak Square; Oregon East; Oxford; Painted Bride Quarterly; Partisan Review; Pennsylvania Review; Phoebe; Portable Wall; Prism International; Proof Rock; Puerto Del Sol; Quarry; Quarterly West; Raddle Moon; RaJAH; Read Me; Real Fiction; Red Bass; Response; Riverwind; Rohwedder; Samisdat; Seattle Review; Sequoia; Shattered Wig Review; Shooting Star Review; Sonoma Mandala; Sore Dove; South Dakota Review; Sou'Wester; Spindrift; Spirit That Moves Us; Star-Web Paper; Streamlines; Struggle; Sub Rosa; Sycamore Review; Tampa Review; Third Woman; Touchstone; Translation; Triquarterly; Unmuzzled Ox; Village Idiot; Virginia Quarterly Review; Webster Review; West Branch; West Coast Review; James White Review; Willow Springs; Wind Row; Writ; Writers' Bar-B-Q; Writers' Rendezvous; Wyoming, The Hub of the Wheel; Xavier Review; Yellow Silk; Zoiks!; Zonë.

Western. Amelia; Amherst Review; Another Point of View; Apple Blossom Connection; Azorean Express; Ball State University Forum; Black Jack; Blizzard Rambler; Bugle; Chronoscope; Cold-Drill; Common Lives/Lesbian Lives; Cross Timbers Review; Dan River Anthology; Dream International Quarterly; Elephant-Ear; Felicity; Fright Depot; Generation; Hibiscus; Hoofstrikes Newsletter; Kana; Kenyon Review; Lighthouse; Little Balkans Review; Long Shot; Meal, Ready-to-Define; Merlyn's Pen; Minnesota Ink; Mirror-Northern Report; Montana Senior Citizens News; Muse's Mill; Oak Square; Pleiades; Prisoners of the Night; Pulpsmith; Read Me; Reflections; Riverwind; Samisdat; Seattle Review; Skylark; Sneak Preview; Sonoma Mandala; Stories & Letters; Tales of the Old West; Thema; Valley Grapevine; Village Idiot; Voyager; Wide Open; Writers' Forum; Writers' Gazette; Writers' Haven Journal; Writers-in-Waiting Newsletter; Writing Pursuits.

Young Adult/Teen. Apple Blossom Connection; Arba Sicula; Brilliant Star; Calli's Tales; Chronoscope;

Cochran's Corner; Common Lives/Lesbian Lives; Creative Kids; Dream International Quarterly; Dreamshore; Enfantaisie; Felicity; Fright Depot; Helicon Nine; Hob-Nob; Hobo Stew Review; Hoofstrikes Newsletter; Housewife-Writer's Forum; Kids Lib News; Lighthouse; Lilith; Little Balkans Review; McGuffey Writer; Merlyn's Pen; Minnesota Ink; Mount Thrushmore Monument; Muse's Mill; Mythic Circle; Open Wide; Riverwind; Serendipity; Shattered Wig Review; Shoe Tree; Sneak Preview; Spoofing!; Stone Soup; Struggle; Tyro; Village Idiot; Writer's Bloc; Writers Newsletter.

Canadian. Anglican; Antigonish Review; Canadian Fiction; Cross-Canada Writers' Quarterly; Descant (Canada); Grain; Icelandic Canadian; The New Quarterly; NeWest Review; Pottersfield Portfolio; Prairie Fire; Prairie Journal of Canadian Literature; Prism International; Quarry; Queen's Quarterly; Raddle Moon; Room of One's Own; Scrivener; University of Windsor Review; West Coast Review; Whetstone; White Wall Review; X-It.

Commercial periodicals

Adventure. American Accent Short Story; American Newspaper Carrier; American Squaredance; American Trucker; Arete; Art Times; Arthritis Today; Associate Reformed Presbyterian; Bay & Delta Yachtsman; Bike Report; Bowbender; Bowhunter; Boys' Life; Bread; Buffalo Spree; Canadian Forester; Cavalier; Chesapeake Bay; Children's Digest; Christian Life; Chrysalis; City Paper; Clubhouse; Cobblestone; Corvette Fever; Cosmopolitan; Crusader; Dialogue; Drummer; Easyriders; Equilibrium; Essence; Flyfisher; Flyfishing News, Views and Reviews; Friend; Gallery; Gem (Ohio); Gent; Guide; The Guide; Hang Gliding; Hi-Call; High Adventure; High Times; Horse Illustrated; Indian Life; Jack and Jill; Kid City; Lighted Pathways; Lighthouse; Llamas; Magazine for Christian Youth; M.A. Training; Messenger of the Sacred Heart; Michigan; Modern Short Stories; Modern Woodmen; Mountain; New Alaskan; New England Senior Citizen/Senior American News; New Methods; Northcoast View; Ocean Sports International; Oh! Idaho; On the Line; Outlaw Biker; Penthouse; Playboy; Pockets; Portland Monthly; Prime Times; R-A-D-A-R; Radiance; Ranger Rick; Road King; Rose Arts; San Gabriel Valley; Saturday Evening Post; Seacoast Life; Senior Life; Shofar; Skyline; Southern; Sports Afield; Straight; Student; Sunday Journal; 'Teen; Touch; TQ; Trailer Boats; Wave Press; Wee Wisdom; Western People; Wisconsin Restaurateur; Wyoming Rural Electric News; Young Judaean.

Condensed Novel. Arete; Bakersfield Lifestyle; Bay & Delta Yachtsman; Campus Life; Cape Cod Compass; Cornerstone; Equilibrium; Essence; Flyfishing News, Views and Reviews; Guide; Inside Texas Running; Michigan; New Methods; Northcoast View; Seacoast Life; Senior Life; Tikkun; Virtue.

Confession. City Paper; Conputor Edge; Crusader; Equilibrium; Flyfishing News, Views and Reviews; Hot Shots; Indian Life; Jive; Lady's Circle; Modern Short Stories; Screw; Student.

Contemporary. American Accent Short Story; American Trucker; Arete; Art Times; Associate Reformed Presbyterian; Atlanta Singles; Atlantic Monthly; B'nai B'rith International Jewish Monthly; Boys' Life; Buffalo Spree; Cape Cod Compass; Canadian Forester; Chrysalis; Clubhouse; Cornerstone; Cosmopolitan; Dialogue; Ensign; Equilibrium; Family; Gent; Good Housekeeping; Harper's; Home Life; Inside; Junior Trails; Kindergarten Listen; Lighted Pathway; Lighthouse; Lutheran Journal; Mademoiselle; Magazine for Christian Youth; Mature Living; McCalls; Michigan; Midstream; Military Lifestyle; Milwaukee; Modern Short Stories; Modern Woodmen; Moment; Mountain; Na'amat Woman; New England Senior Citizen/Senior American News; New Methods; Northcoast View; Northeast; Northwest; Omni; Other Side; Oui; Penthouse; Playboy; Pockets; Portland Monthly; Prime Times; Radiance; Redbook; Rose Arts; St. Anthony Messenger; St. Joseph's Mesenger and Advocate of the Blind; San Gabriel Valley; Seacoast Life; Shofar; Southern; Splash; Straight; Student; Tikkun; Trailer Boats; Virtue; Wave Press; Wee Wisdom; Western People; Wisconsin Restaurateur; With; Woman's Day.

Erotica. Cavalier; Chic; Drummer; Equilibrium; First Hand; Fling; Gallery; Gem (New York); Gent; Gentleman's Companion; The Guide; Guys; Harvey for Loving People; Hot Shots; Modern Short Stories; Hustler; Hustler Letters; In Touch For Men (California); In Touch Talks (California); Jock; Manscape; Manscape 2; Northcoast View; Nugget; Oui; Penthouse; Pillow Talk; Private Letters; Radiance; Rose Arts; Screw; Swank; Texas Connection; Torso.

Ethnic. Aloha; American Dane; Américas; Arete; Art Times; B'nai B'rith International Jewish Monthly; Buffalo Spree; Canadian Forester; Christmas; City Paper; Crusader; Equilibrium; Friend; Guide; The Guide; Hadassah; Indian Life; Inside; Inside Kung Fu; Jewish Monthly; Magazine for Christian Youth; Middle Eastern Dancer; Midstream; Moment; Na'amat Woman; New England Senior Citizen/Senior American News; Northcoast View; Other Side; Pockets; Prime Times; Radiance; Reconstructionist; Rose Arts; Screw; Shofar; Skyline; Student; Teens Today; Touch; Vision; With; Wyoming Rural Electric News; Young Judaean.

Experimental. Arete; Art Times; Chrysalis; City Paper; Cornerstone; Equilibrium; Essence; Guide; The Guide; Hang Gliding; High Times; Modern Short Stories; Mountain; New Methods; Northcoast View; Northwest; Other Side; Rose Arts; Screw; Splash; Wave Press.

Fantasy. Amazing Stories; American Accent Short Story; American Squaredance; Art Times; Isaac Asimov's Science Fiction; Bay & Delta Yachtsman; Bike Report; Campus Life; Cape Cod Compass; Chesapeake

Bay; Cornerstone; Dragon; Drummer; Equilibrium; Essence; Fling; Gentleman's Companion; The Guide; Hang Gliding; High Times; Kid City; Magazine for Christian Youth; Magazine of Fantasy & Science Fiction; Northcoast View; Northwest; Omni; Oui; Playboy; Pockets; Portland Monthly; Radiance; Ranger Rick; Relix; Road King; Rose Arts; Seacoast Life; Rod Serling's Twilight Zone; Shofar; Skyline; Splash; Starwind; TQ; Trailer Boats; Wave Press; Wee Wisdom; Weird Tales; Woman's Day; Young American; Young Judaean.

Feminist. Arete; Art Times; Buffalo Spree; Canadian Forester; Computor Edge; Daughters of Sarah; Equilibrium; Essence; Gem (Ohio); The Guide; Lighted Pathway; Lutheran Woman Today; Milwaukee; Mountain; Na'amat Woman; Other Side; Playgirl; Radiance; Rose Arts; Screw; Tikkun; Wisconsin Restaurateur.

Gay. Arete; Art Times; Drummer; First Hand; Guide; The Guide; Guys; Hot Shots; In Touch For Men (California); In Touch Talks (California); Jock; Manscape; Manscape 2; Pillow Talk; Rose Arts; Screw; Tikkun; Torso.

Historical. American Accent Short Story; American Squaredance; Arete; Art Times; Arthritis Today; Atlantic Advocate; Atlantic Salmon Journal; Bay & Delta Yachtsman; Bike Report; B'nai B'rith International Jewish Monthly; Cape Cod Compass; Chesapeake Bay; Christmas; Chrysalis; City Paper; Clubhouse; Cobblestone; Country Woman; Daughters of Sarah; Ensign; Equilibrium; Flyfishing News, Views and Reviews; Friend; Guide; The Guide; Hang Gliding; High Adventure; Indian Life; Inside Texas Running; Jack and Jill; Jewish Monthly; Juggler's World; Lady's Circle; Lighted Pathway; Llamas; Michigan; Midstream; Modern Short Stories; Modern Woodmen; Moment; Mountain; New Alaskan; New England Senior Citizen/Senior American News; New Methods; Northcoast View; Ocean Sports International; Pockets; Portland Monthly; Purpose; R-A-D-A-R; Radiance; Rose Arts; Senior Life; Skyline; Sunday Journal; Tikkun; Wyoming Rural Electric News; Young Judaean.

Horror. Amazing Stories; Arete; Cavalier; Drummer; Equilibrium; Gent; Guide; Hang Gliding; Michigan; Modern Short Stories; Northcoast View; Omni; Penthouse; Playboy; Rod Serling's Twilight Zone; Wave Press; Weird Tales.

Humor/Satire. American Accent Short Story; American Newspaper Carrier; American Squaredance; American Trucker; Arete; Art Times; Arthritis Today; Atlanta Singles; Atlantic Advocate; Atlantic Salmon Journal; Bay & Delta Yachtsman; Beckett Baseball Card Monthly; Bike Report; B'nai B'rith International Jewish Monthly; Boys' Life; Buffalo Spree; Campus Life; Cape Cod Compass; Canadian Forester; Chesapeake Bay; City Paper; Computor Edge; Cornerstone; Corvette Fever; Country Woman; Dialogue; Drummer; Ensign; Equilibrium; Essence; Flyfishing News, Views and Reviews; Friend; Gallery; Gem (New York); Gem (Ohio); Gent; Golf Journal; Guide; The Guide; Hang Gliding; Harper's; Hi-Call; Home Life; Ideals; In Touch (Indiana); Inside; Inside Texas Running; Jack and Jill; Jewish Monthly; Juggler's World; Lady's Circle; Latter-Day Woman; Lighted Pathway; Lighthouse; Llamas; Magazine for Christian Youth; Mature Living; McCalls; Meridian; Metro Singles Lifestyles; Michigan; Midstream; Modern Short Stories; Mountain; National Lampoon; New Alaskan; New England Senior Citizen/Senior American News; Northcoast View; Northwest; Ocean Sports International; Oh! Idaho; Other Side; Oui; Playboy; Portland Monthly; Prime Times; Radiance; Ranger Rick; Reform Judaism; Relix; Road King; Rose Arts; St. Joseph's Mesenger and Advocate of the Blind; San Gabriel Valley; Saturday Evening Post; Screw; Seacoast Life; Senior Life; Shofar; Singlelife; Skyline; Southern; Splash; Sports Afield; Starwind; Straight; Student; Sunday Journal; 'Teen; Teens Today; Tikkun; Trailer Boats; Virtue; Vista; Wag; Wave Press; Western People; Wisconsin Restaurateur; With; Woman's Day; Wyoming Rural Electric News; Young American; Young Judaean.

Juvenile. Action; Associate Reformed Presbyterian; Beckett Baseball Card Monthly; Boys' Life; Chickadee; Child Life; Children's Digest; Children's Playmate; Cobblestone; Cricket; Crusader; Equilibrium; Faces; Friend; Highlights for Children; Home Altar; Humpty Dumpty's; Ideals; Indian Life; Insights; Jack and Jill; Junior Trails; Kid City; Kindergarten Listen; Lady's Circle; Lefthander; Lighted Pathway; Lighthouse; Lollipops, Ladybugs and Lucky Stars; Modern Woodmen; My Friend; Noah's Ark; Pennywhistle Press; Pockets; R-A-D-A-R; Ranger Rick; Shofar; Single Parent; Story Friends; Sunday Journal; Teens Today; Touch; Wee Wisdom; Wisconsin Restaurateur; Woman's Day; Wonder Time; Young American; Young Crusader; Young Judaean.

Lesbian. Arete; Art Times; The Guide; Rose Arts; Tikkun.

Mainstream. American Accent Short Story; Arete; Art Times; Cape Cod Compass; Canadian Forester; Christmas; Chrysalis; City Paper; Cornerstone; Country Woman; Dialogue; Disciple; Ensign; Equilibrium; Explorer; Family; Friend; Gallery; Gem (Ohio); Guide; Lady's Circle; Latter-Day Woman; Lighthouse; Michigan; Midstream; Milwaukee; Modern Short Stories; Modern Woodmen; Mountain; New England Senior Citizen/Senior American News; New Methods; Northwest; Other Side; Portland Monthly; R-A-D-A-R; Radiance; St. Joseph's Mesenger and Advocate of the Blind; Seacoast Life; Southern; Tikkun; With.

Preschool. Equilibrium; Highlights for Children; Humpty Dumpty's; Lighthouse; Lollipops, Ladybugs and Lucky Stars; New Alaskan; Radiance; Sunday Journal; Turtle Magazine for Preschool Kids; Wee Wisdom.

Prose Poem. Arete; Christmas; Midstream; Mountain; Other Side; Skyline.

Psychic/Supernatural/Occult. Bay & Delta Yachtsman; Equilibrium; Gent; Modern Short Stories; Northcoast View; Penthouse; Rose Arts; San Gabriel Valley; Rod Serling's Twilight Zone; Wave Press; Weird Tales; With.

Regional. Arete; Atlantic Advocate; Bike Report; Cape Cod Compass; Canadian Forester; Chesapeake Bay; Cobblestone; Dialogue; Ensign; Equilibrium; Flyfishing News, Views and Reviews; The Guide; Maine Life; Michigan; Milwaukee; Modern Short Stories; Mountain; New Alaskan; New Methods; Northcoast

View; Northeast; Palouse Journal; Portland Monthly; Rose Arts; San Gabriel Valley; Seacoast Life; Southern; TQ; Tristate; Washingtonian; Wave Press; Wisconsin Restaurateur; Wyoming Rural Electric News; Yankee.

Religious/Inspirational. Alive now!; American Newspaper Carrier; Arete; Associate Reformed Presbyterian; Baltimore Jewish Times; B'nai B'rith; International Jewish Monthly; Bread; Canadian Messenger; Christian Life; Christmas; Church Herald; Church Musician; Clubhouse; Companion of St. Francis & St. Anthony; Cornerstone; Country Woman; Crusader; Daughters of Sarah; Disciple; Discoveries; Ensign; Equilibrium; Evangel; Explorer; Friend; Gem (Ohio); The Guide; Hi-Call; High Adventure; Home Altar; Home Life; In Touch (Indiana); Indian Life; Jewish Monthly; Junior Trails; Kindergarten Listen; Lady's Circle; Latter-Day Woman; Lighted Pathway; Lighthouse; Liguorian; Live; Living With Teenagers; Lookout; Lutheran Journal; Lutheran Woman Today; Magazine for Christian Youth; Mature Living; Mature Years; Messenger of the Sacred Heart; Metro Singles Lifestyles; Miraculous Medal; Modern Short Stories; Moment; My Friend; Noah's Ark; North American Voice of Fatima; On the Line; Our Family; Pockets; Purpose; R-A-D-A-R; Reform Judaism; Relix; St. Anthony Messenger; St. Joseph's Mesenger and Advocate of the Blind; San Gabriel Valley; Saturday Evening Post; Seek; Senior Life; Shofar; Standard; Story Friends; Straight; Student; Teens Today; Touch; TQ; Virtue; Vision; With; Woman's Day; Wonder Time; Young Judaean; Young Salvationist.

Romance. American Accent Short Story; American Squaredance; Bay & Delta Yachtsman; Cosmopolitan; Country Woman; Equilibrium; Essence; Explorer; Five Great Romances; Good Housekeeping; Guide; The Guide; Jive; Lady's Circle; Lighthouse; Lutheran Journal; McCalls; Metro Singles Lifestyles; Modern Short Stories; Northwest; Playgirl; Prime Times; Rose Arts; St. Anthony Messenger; St. Joseph's Mesenger and Advocate of the Blind; Straight; 'Teen; Teens Today; TQ; Virtue; Vista; Woman's World; Wyoming Rural Electric News.

Science Fiction. Aboriginal SF; Amazing Stories; American Accent Short Story; American Squaredance; Analog Science Fiction/Science Fact; Arete; Art Times; Isaac Asimov's Science Fiction; Bakersfield Lifestyle; Bay & Delta Yachtsman; Boys' Life; Campus Life; Chrysalis; Computor Edge; Cornerstone; Crusader; Dragon; Drummer; Equilibrium; Explorer; Gent; Guide; The Guide; Hang Gliding; High Times; Jack and Jill; Juggler's World; Kid City; Lighthouse; Magazine of Fantasy & Science Fiction; Michigan; Modern Short Stories; New Methods; Northcoast View; Northwest; Omni; Penthouse; Playboy; Radiance; Ranger Rick; Relix; Road King; Rose Arts; Seacoast Life; Senior Life; Rod Serling's Twilight Zone; Starwind; TQ; Trailer Boats; Vista; Wave Press; Wisconsin Restaurateur; Young Judaean.

Senior Citizen/Retirement. Arete; Arthritis Today; Bakersfield Lifestyle; Bay & Delta Yachtsman; Bike Report; Canadian Forester; Dialogue; Equilibrium; Gem (Ohio); The Guide; Lady's Circle; Lighthouse; Liguorian; Lutheran Journal; Mature Living; Mature Years; Meridian; Modern Woodmen; Mountain; New Alaskan; New England Senior Citizen/Senior American News; Our Family; Prime Times; St. Joseph's Mesenger and Advocate of the Blind; Seacoast Life; Sunday Journal; Vista; Wyoming Rural Electric News.

Serialized/Excerpted Novel. Analog Science Fiction/Science Fact; Campus Life; Cape Cod Compass; Equilibrium; Essence; Guide; High Times; Michigan; Moment; Mountain; Penthouse; Playgirl; Seacoast Life; Western People.

Spiritual. Junior Trails; Liguorian; Other Side; Southern; With.

Sports. Arete; Beckett Baseball Card Monthly; Black Belt; Junior Trails; Midstream; Modern Short Stories; Ocean Sports International; Prime Time Sports & Fitness; Senior Life; Volleyball Monthly; With.

Suspense/Mystery. American Accent Short Story; American Newspaper Carrier; Arete; Associate Reformed Presbyterian; Bakersfield Lifestyle; Bay & Delta Yachtsman; Boys' Life; Buffalo Spree; Canadian Forester; Chesapeake Bay; Children's Digest; Chrysalis; Cosmopolitan; Dialogue; Drummer; Equilibrium; Gallery; Gent; Guide; The Guide; Hang Gliding; Hi-Call; High Adventure; Alfred Hitchcock's Mystery Magazine; Horse Illustrated; Jack and Jill; Lighthouse; Magazine for Christian Youth; Michigan; Modern Short Stories; Mountain; New England Senior Citizen/Senior American News; Northcoast View; Other Side; Oui; Playboy; Pockets; Portland Monthly; Ellery Queen's Mystery Magazine; Radiance; Ranger Rick; Redbook; Road King; Rose Arts; Seacoast Life; Senior Life; Shofar; Southern; Straight; 'Teen; Trailer Boats; Wave Press; Wisconsin Restaurateur; Woman's World; Young American; Young Judaean.

Translations. Arete; Equilibrium; Inside; Magazine for Christian Youth; Midstream; Moment; Northcoast View; Rose Arts; Seacoast Life; Shofar; Tikkun; With; Young Judaean.

Western. American Squaredance; Bowbender; Boys' Life; Drummer; Equilibrium; Guide; Hi-Call; High Adventure; Horse Illustrated; Lighthouse; Modern Short Stories; New England Senior Citizen/Senior American News; New Methods; Penthouse; Playboy; Road King; San Gabriel Valley; Wisconsin Restaurateur; Wyoming Rural Electric News.

Young Adult/Teen. Alive now!; American Newspaper Carrier; Associate Reformed Presbyterian; Beckett Baseball Card Monthly; Boys' Life; Bread; Campus Life; Christian Living For Senior Highs; Clubhouse; Cobblestone; Equilibrium; Faces; Gem (Ohio); Hi-Call; High Adventure; Home Life; Horse Illustrated; In Touch (Indiana); Indian Life; Insights; Junior Trails; Lady's Circle; Lefthander; Lighted Pathway; Lighthouse; Liguorian; Lutheran Journal; Magazine for Christian Youth; Modern Woodmen; Noah's Ark; On the Line; Pennywhistle Press; Radiance; Scholastic Scope; Senior Life; Seventeen; Shofar; Straight; 'Teen; Teens Today; TQ; Vision; Vista; Wee Wisdom; Wisconsin Restaurateur; With; Young Salvationist.

Canadian. Atlantic Advocate; Atlantic Salmon Journal; Bowbender; Canadian Biker; Chickadee; Indian Life; Meridian; Messenger of the Sacred Heart; Our Family; St. Anthony Messenger; Score; Wag; Western People.

Small press

Adventure. Ariadne; Barlow; Black Heron; Bookmaker's Guild; Bryans & Bryans; Cave; Council for Indian Education; Creative Arts; Dan River; Fasa; Goose Lane; Liberty; Ltd. Edition; Lucky Heart; Mother Courage; New Victoria; Night Tree; Overlook; Pentagram; Ranger; Read 'N Run; S.O.C.O.; Scojtia; Soho; Triple 'P'; Unicorn; University Editions; Woodsong Graphics; Wyrick & Company; Yanaria.

Condensed Novel. Loft.

Contemporary. American Atheist; Androgyne; Applezaba; Ariadne; Arsenal Pulp; Arte Publico; Barlow; Barn Owl; BkMk; Black Hat; Black Heron; Bryans & Bryans; Carpenter; Catbird; Children's Center; Confluence; Coyote Love; Creative Arts; Crossing; Dan River; Dawnwood; Double M; Dragonsbreath; Esoterica; Exile; Feminist; Fiction Collective; Four Walls Eight Windows; Goose Lane; Green Street; Guernica; Lapis Educational Association; Liberty; Lincoln Springs; Loft; Lucky Heart; Mainspring; McDonald; Milkweed; Mother Courage; New Rivers; North Point; Overlook; Owl Creek; Padre; Papier-Mache; Paycock; Peachtree; Perivale; Pikestaff; Pineapple; Pocahontas; Porcepic; Porcupine's Quill; Press Gang; Primal; Pulp; Read 'N Run; Red Deer; Rowan Tree; Scojtia; Sea Fog; Second Chance; Seven Buffaloes; Station Hill; Studia Hispanica Editors; Sun & Moon; Talon; Teal; Tide; Times Eagle; Unicorn; University Editions; University of Illinois; Woelfinger; Women's; Woodsong Graphics; York; Zephyr.

Erotica. Banned; Black Heron; Caravan; Carlton; Creative Arts; Dancing Bear; Dragonsbreath; Gay Sunshine; Lucky Heart; New Victoria; Perivale; Press Gang; Primal; Red Alder; Slough.

Ethnic. Alaska Native Language; Arte Publico; Barn Owl; Bilingual Review; BkMk; Black Hat; Blind Beggar; Breakwater; Catbird; China; Clarity; Council for Indian Education; Creative Arts; Eighth Mt.; Esoterica; Feminist; Floricanto; Goose Lane; Guernica; Heritage; Kitchen Table: Women of Color; Lincoln Springs; Loft; Lucky Heart; Mina; New Seed; New Victoria; Overlook; Path; Perivale; Pocahontas; Press Gang; Read 'N Run; Scojtia; Sea Fog; Seal; Second Chance; Seven Buffaloes; Soho; Stormline; Studia Hispanica Editors; Third World; University Editions; Waterfront; Woelfinger; Wyrick & Company; Zephyr.

Experimental. Androgyne; Applezaba; Arsenal Pulp; Artifacts; BkMk; Black Heron; Blind Beggar; Carpenter; Catbird; Clothespin Fever; Coyote Love; Dancing Bear; Dragonsbreath; Exile; Feminist; Fiction Collective; Four Walls Eight Windows; Gay Sunshine; Goose Lane; Green Street; Laughing Bear; Lincoln Springs; Lintel; Loft; Lucky Heart; Milkweed; New Directions; New Rivers; North Point; Overlook; Papier-Mache; Paycock; Pentagram; Perivale; Pikestaff; Pineapple; Porcepic; Prairie Journal; Primal; Proper Tales; Quarry; Read 'N Run; Red Deer; Re/Search; Scojtia; Score; Second Chance; Station Hill; Sun & Moon; Thistledown; Turnstone; Ultramarine; University Editions; University of Illinois; Women's; Wyrick & Company; York; Zephyr.

Faction. Applezaba; Lucky Heart; Mainspring; Proper Tales; University Editions.

Fantasy. Ansuda; Applezaba; Ariadne; Balance Beam; Banned; Carpenter; Dan River; Dancing Bear; Double M; Dragon's Den; Dragonsbreath; Fasa; Kubicek & Associates; Liberty; Lucky Heart; New Victoria; Overlook; Porcepic; Porcupine's Quill; Press of MacDonald and Renecke; Read 'N Run; S.O.C.O.; Scojtia; Space and Time; Triple 'P'; Ultramarine; Unicorn; University Editions; W.W.; Yanaria; Yith.

Feminist. Applezaba; Ariadne; Arte Publico; Artifacts; Barn Owl; Cleis; Clothespin Fever; Creative Arts; Crossing; Double M; Eighth Mt.; Feminist; Firebrand; Kitchen Table: Women of Color; Lapis Educational Association; Lincoln Springs; Lintel; Loft; Lucky Heart; Metis; Mina; Mother Courage; Naiad; New Seed; Papier-Mache; Porcepic; Press Gang; Proper Tales; Pulp; Quarry; Read 'N Run; Samisdat; Sea Fog; Seal; Silverleaf; Spinsters Ink/Aunt Lute; Talon; Tide; Triple 'P'; University Editions; Vehicule; Woman Sleuth; Women's; Zephyr.

Gay. Alyson; Applezaba; Artifacts; Banned; Barn Owl; Black Heron; Crossing; Eighth Mt.; Feminist; Gay Sunshine; Jayell; Knights; Liberty; Lintel; Loft; Lucky Heart; Mina; Mogul Books & Filmworks; Primal; Proper Tales; Samisdat; Talon; Triple 'P'; Zephyr.

Historical. Acadia; And; Ariadne; Beil; Bilingual Review; Barlow; BkMk; Breakwater; Bryans & Bryans; Caravan; Children's Center; Confluence; Council for Indian Education; Creative Arts; Dan River; Dragon's Den; Esoterica; Feminist; Goose Lane; Heart of the Lakes; Homestead; Jayell; Kruza Kaleidoscopix; Kubicek & Associates; Liberty; Library Research; Lincoln Springs; Ltd. Edition; Lucky Heart; Mainspring; Melior; Micah; Misty Hill; Mosaic; New Victoria; Night Tree; Overlook; Path; Pineapple; Pocahontas; Porcupine's Quill; Press of MacDonald and Renecke; Quarry; Ranger; Read 'N Run; S.O.C.O.; Scojtia; Second Chance; Soho; Spiritual Fiction; Still Point; Third World; Tide; Triple 'P'; Unicorn; University Editions; Women's; Woodsong Graphics; Zephyr.

Horror. Ansuda; Bryans & Bryans; Dan River; Dragon's Den; Lucky Heart; Kubicek & Associates; McDonald; Proper Tales; Read 'N Run; Space and Time; Triple 'P'; University Editions; Yanaria; Yith.

Humor/Satire. American Atheist; Applezaba; Ariadne; Balance Beam; Banned; Barlow; Black Heron; Bryans & Bryans; Caravan; Catbird; Corkscrew; Creative With Words; Dancing Bear; Dragonsbreath; Eden; Exile; Liberty; Lucky Heart; Metamorphous; Mosaic; Mother Courage; New Victoria; Night Tree; Overlook; Paycock; Press Gang; Press of MacDonald and Renecke; Read 'N Run; S.O.C.O.; Scojtia; Silverleaf; Stormline; Tide; University Editions; Woodsong Graphics; Wyrick & Company; Zephyr.

Juvenile. Acadia; Advocacy; Annick; Artifacts; Blind Beggar; Bookmaker's Guild; Breakwater; Bright Ring; Canadian Stage & Arts; Carnival; Children's Center; Council for Indian Education; Creative Arts; Creative With Words; Dancing Bear; May Davenport; Double M; Esoterica; Floricanto; Green Tiger; Heart of the

Lakes; Homestead; Kar-Ben Copies; Kruza Kaleidoscopix; Kubicek & Associates; Lollipop Power; Lucky Heart; McDonald; Metamorphous; Mina; Misty Hill; Mosaic; New Seed; Overlook; Pippin; Prairie; Read 'N Run; Scojtia; Sea Fog; Aaron Smirnoff; Star; Third World; Unicorn; University Editions; Windriver; Women's; Woodsong Graphics.

Lesbian. Alyson; Applezaba; Artifacts; Banned; Barn Owl; Black Heron; Cleis; Clothespin Fever; Crossing; Eighth Mt.; Feminist; Firebrand; Kitchen Table: Women of Color; Liberty; Lintel; Lucky Heart; Metis; Mina; Mogul Books & Filmworks; Mother Courage; Naiad; New Victoria; Press Gang; Primal; Proper Tales; Samisdat; Seal; Silverleaf; Spinsters Ink/Aunt Lute; Talon; Triple 'P'; Woman Sleuth; Women's; Zephyr.

Mainstream. Ansuda; Ariadne; Barlow; Black Heron; Blood & Guts; Bottom Dog; Bryans & Bryans; Catbird; Confluence; Creative Arts; John Daniel; Four Walls Eight Windows; Kubicek & Associates; Liberty; Loft; Lucky Heart; McDonald; Peachtree; Perivale; Porcepic; Press of MacDonald and Renecke; Read 'N Run; S.O.C.O.; Scojtia; Second Chance; Soho; Stormline; Sun & Moon; Tide; Ultramarine; University Editions; University of Arkansas; Windriver; Woodsong Graphics; Wyrick & Company; Zephyr.

Military/War. Ariadne; Black Heron; Kubicek & Associates; Nautical & Aviation; Ranger; Read 'N Run; Sea Fog; Second Chance; University Editions; John Westburg.

Preschool. Advocacy; Annick; Artifacts; Blind Beggar; Bright Ring; Children's Center; Council for Indian Education; Dancing Bear; Double M; Green Tiger; Homestead; Lucky Heart; Read 'N Run; Scojtia; Star; Third World; Unicorn; Women's.

Psychic/Supernatural/Occult. Ansuda; Artifacts; Dan River; Dragon's Den; Hickman Systems; Knoll; Kubicek & Associates; Lapis Educational Association; Lintel; Lucky Heart; Overlook; Read 'N Run; Space and Time; Spiritual Fiction; Triple 'P'; Westgate; Woodsong Graphics.

Regional. And; Barlow; Barn Owl; Beil; Black Hat; Bryans & Bryans; Cinco Puntos; Coteau; Council for Indian Education; Creative Arts; Dan River; Feminist; Floricanto; Green Street; Heart of the Lakes; Kubicek & Associates; Laughing Bear; Lintel; Loft; Lucky Heart; Melior; Millers River; Mosaic; New Seed; Night Tree; Padre; Peachtree; Perivale; Pineapple; Pocahontas; Press Gang; Read 'N Run; Samisdat; Studia Hispanica Editors; Tide; Times Eagle; Triple 'P'; University Editions; Vehicule; Woelfinger; Zephyr.

Religious/Inspirational. Another Way; Double M; Garber; Hickman Systems; Kar-Ben Copies; Knoll; Kubicek & Associates; Lapis Educational Association; Liberty; Lucky Heart; Magnificat; Micah; Mosaic; Read 'N Run; St. John's; Sea Fog; Aaron Smirnoff; Spiritual Fiction; Star.

Romance. Bryans & Bryans; Liberty; Ltd. Edition; Lucky Heart; Mosaic; Mother Courage; New Victoria; Read 'N Run; S.O.C.O.; Scojtia; Star; Tide; Triple 'P'; University Editions; Woodsong Graphics.

Science Fiction. American Atheist; Balance Beam; Banned; Black Heron; Blood & Guts; Bryans & Bryans; Carpenter; Dan River; Dancing Bear; Dragon's Den; Dragonsbreath; Fasa; Feminist; Kubicek & Associates; Liberty; Lucky Heart; Mainespring; Mina; Mother Courage; New Victoria; Overlook; Porcepic; Press Gang; Primal; Proper Tales; Read 'N Run; Re/Search; S.O.C.O.; Sandpiper; Scojtia; Space and Time; Third World; Triple 'P'; Ultramarine; University Editions; W.W.; Woodsong Graphics; Yanaria; Zephyr.

Short Story Collections. Ansuda; Applezaba; Arsenal Pulp; Arte Publico; Artifacts; Banned; Barlow; Beil; Bilingual Review; Blind Beggar; Bookmaker's Guild; Bryans & Bryans; Caravan; Catbird; Clarity; Clothespin Fever; Confluence; Coyote Love; Creative Arts; Creative With Words; Dan River; Dancing Bear; John Daniel; Dragon's Den; Ecco; Eighth Mt.; Esoterica; Exile; Faber and Faber; Feminist; Four Walls Eight Windows; Gay Sunshine; Goose Lane; Graywolf; Green Street; Homestead; Kitchen Table: Women of Color; Kubicek & Associates; Lincoln Springs; Loft; Ltd. Edition; Lucky Heart; McDonald; Micah; Night Tree;20North Point; Owl Creek; Padre; Papier-Mache; Path; Peachtree; Porcepic; Press Gang; Press of MacDonald and Renecke; Proper Tales; Pulp; Quarry; Read 'N Run; Red Alder; Red Deer; Rowan Tree; St. John's; Sandpiper; Seal; Seven Buffaloes; Silverleaf; Slough; Station Hill; Still Point; Stormline; Studia Hispanica Editors; Sun & Moon; Third World; Thistledown; Triple 'P'; Ultramarine; University Editions; University of Arkansas; Vehicule; Westgate; Woman Sleuth; Women's; Yanaria; Zephyr.

Serialized/Excerpted Novel. Liberty.

Spiritual. Dragon's Den; Garber; Hickman Systems; Read 'N Run.

Suspense/Mystery. Ansuda; Ariadne; Black Heron; Blood & Guts; Bryans & Bryans; Carlton; Cliffhanger; Creative Arts; Dragon's Den; Eden; Kubicek & Associates; Loft; Ltd. Edition; Lucky Heart; Mother Courage; New Victoria; Perseverance; Press Gang; Proper Tales; Ranger; Read 'N Run; Rowan Tree; S.O.C.O.; St. John's; Scojtia; Second Chance; Soho; Triple 'P'; Unicorn; Windriver; Woman Sleuth; Women's; Woodsong Graphics.

Translations. Applezaba; Arsenal Pulp; Beil; Bilingual Review; BkMk; Blind Beggar; Catbird; Cleis; Confluence; Dancing Bear; Esoterica; Feminist; Floricanto; Four Walls Eight Windows; Gay Sunshine; Green Street; Lawrence Hill; Loft; Lucky Heart; Micah; New Rivers; North Point; Overlook; Owl Creek; Paycock; Perivale; Pocahontas; Porcepic; Read 'N Run; St. John's; Sea Fog; Seal; Station Hill; Studia Hispanica Editors; Sun & Moon; Threshold; Translation Center; University Editions; University of Arkansas; Vehicule; Waterfront; York.

Western. Bryans & Bryans; Council for Indian Education; Creative Arts; Homestead; Kubicek & Associates; Liberty; Ltd. Edition; Lucky Heart; New Victoria; Read 'N Run; Scojtia; Aaron Smirnoff; Sunstone; Woodsong Graphics.

Young Adult/Teen. Acadia; Blind Beggar; Bookmaker's Guild; Breakwater; Council for Indian Education; Dancing Bear; May Davenport; Double M; Dragon's Den; Esoterica; Homestead; Kubicek & Associates;

Lucky Heart; McDonald; Metamorphous; Mosaic; New Seed; Pocahontas; Porcupine's Quill; Read 'N Run; S.O.C.O.; Scojtia; Sea Fog; Aaron Smirnoff; Square One; Third World; W.W.; Women's; Woodsong Graphics.

Canadian. Annick; Breakwater; Canadian Stage & Arts; Coteau; Eden; Goose Lane; Guernica; Porcupine's Quill; Prairie; Press Gang; Red Deer; Talon; Thistledown; Turnstone; Vehicle; Women's; York.

Commercial publishers

Adventure. Avon; Bantam; Bart; Bethany House; Blackthorne; Bradbury; Branden; Broadman; Carroll & Graf; Critic's Choice; Crossway; Crown; Dell; Dodd, Mead; Fawcett; Fearon Education; Holloway House; Holt; Horizon; Joy Street; Morrow; Naval Institute; New American Library; New Readers; Pageant; Paperjacks; Pocket; Popular Library; Clarkson N. Potter; Random House; Richardson & Steirman; St. Martin's; Scribner's; Seal (McClelland/Bantam); Gibbs M. Smith; Stoddart; Lyle Stuart/Irma Heldman; Tor; Troll; TSR; Vesta; Villard; Walker; Warner; West End Games of Pennsylvania; Western; Worldwide Library; Zebra.

Contemporary. Bantam; Bart; Blair; Bookcraft; Bradbury; Branden; Carroll & Graf; Crossway; Crown; Delacorte; Dembner; Dodd, Mead; Doubleday Canada; Dutton; Fearon Education; Godine; Holloway House; Holt; Houghton Mifflin; Joy Street; Knopf; Little, Brown & Co.; Louisiana State University; Mercury House; Morrow; Newmarket; W.W. Norton; Paperjacks; Pocket; Poseidon; Clarkson N. Potter; Random House; St. Martin's; Scribner's; Seal (McClelland/Bantam); Sierra Club; Silver Arrow; Simon & Pierre; Simon & Schuster; Gibbs M. Smith; Stemmer House; Lyle Stuart/Irma Heldman; Summit; Texas Monthly; Ticknor & Fields; Vesta; Viking Penguin; Villard; Warner; Zebra.

Erotica. Carroll & Graf; Greenleaf Classics; Holt; Pocket; St. Martin's.

Ethnic. Bantam; Blair; Branden; Dodd, Mead; Fearon Education; Gemstone; Godine; Holloway House; Holt; Paperjacks; Pocket; Three Continents; Vesta.

Experimental. Carroll & Graf; Dutton; Holloway House; Mercury House; Morrow; Paperjacks; St. Martin's; Gibbs M. Smith; Vesta.

Faction. Leisure; Pocket; St. Martin's; Vesta.

Fantasy. Avon; Baen; Bantam; Berkley; Berkley/Ace; Blackthorne; Carroll & Graf; DAW; Delacorte/Dell Books for Young Readers; Del Rey; Dodd, Mead; Doubleday-Foundation; Holloway House; Holt; Iron Crown; Leisure; New American Library; Omeiga; Pageant; Popular Library; St. Martin's; Spectra; Starblaze; Summit; Tor; TSR; Vesta; Warner; West End Games of Pennsylvania.

Feminist. Bantam; Braziller; Holt; Morrow; Pocket; St. Martin's; Scribner's; Vesta.

Gay. Bantam; Holt; Morrow; New American Library; St. Martin's.

Historical. Avon; Ballantine; Bantam; Bart; Bookcraft; Branden; Broadman; Crown; Dembner; Dodd, Mead; Fawcett; Fearon Education; Godine; Harmony; Holloway House; Holt; Horizon; Leisure; Morrow; Naval Institute; New American Library; Paperjacks; Pocket; Clarkson N. Potter; Presidio; Random House; St. Martin's; Seal (McClelland/Bantam); Silver Arrow; Simon & Pierre; Stemmer House; Summit; Troll; Vesta; Villard; West End Games of Pennsylvania; Winston-Derek; Zebra.

Horror. Bantam; Bart; Berkley; Blackthorne; Critic's Choice; Crown; DAW; Dell; Dorchester; Doubleday-Foundation; Holloway House; Leisure; Morrow; Pageant; Pocket; Popular Library; St. Martin's; Scribner's; Seal (McClelland/Bantam); Starblaze; TAB; Tor; TSR; Villard; Walker; Warner; Wildstar/Empire; Zebra.

Humor/Satire. Bantam; Bart; Berkley; Blackthorne; Broadman; Crown; Dodd, Mead; Doubleday Canada; Dutton; Godine; Harvest House; Holloway House; Holt; Horizon; Leisure; Morrow;20New Readers; Paperjacks; Pocket; Clarkson N. Potter; Price Stern Sloan; St. Martin's; Scribner's; Simon & Pierre; Gibbs M. Smith; Summit; Vesta; Villard; West End Games of Pennsylvania; Western.

Juvenile. Antioch; Apple; Bethany House; Blackthorne; Bradbury; Branden; Broadman; Camelot; Carolrhoda; Childrens; Child's World; Clarion; David C. Cook; Crossway; Crown; Delacorte/Dell Books for Young Readers; Dell; Dial Books for Young Readers; Dodd, Mead; Doubleday Canada; Dutton; Eakin; Farrar, Straus & Giroux; Four Winds; Gemstone; Godine; Grosset & Dunlap; Harcourt Brace Jovanovich; Harper & Row Junior Books; Herald; Holiday House; Holt; Horizon; Joy Street; Knopf Books for Young Readers; Little, Brown & Co. (children's); Lodestar; Macmillan; Macmillan Children's; Margaret McElderry; Modern; Morrow Junior Books; Oddo; Orchard; Pelican; Philomel; Clarkson N. Potter; Prentice-Hall; Price Stern Sloan; Random House (juvenile div.); St. Paul Books & Media; Scholastic; Scribner's Books for Young Readers; Simon & Pierre; Tor; TSR; Vesta; West End Games of Pennsylvania; Western Producer Prairie; Western; Whitman; Winston-Derek; Yearling; Charlotte Zolotow.

Lesbian. Bantam; Morrow; St. Martin's.

Mainstream. Avon; Bart; Berkley; Blackthorne; Branden; Carroll & Graf; Crown; Doubleday Canada; Eriksson; Holloway House; Holt; Horizon; Houghton Mifflin; Little, Brown & Co.; Louisiana State University; Macmillan of Canada; New American Library; Newmarket; W.W. Norton; Paperjacks; Pocket; Popular Library; Poseidon; Random House; Seal (McClelland/Bantam); Silver Arrow; Lyle Stuart/Irma Heldman; Summit; Texas Monthly; Ticknor & Fields; Vesta; Viking Penguin; Villard; Warner.

Military/War. Avon; Bantam; Berkley; Branden; Carroll & Graf; Critic's Choice; Crown; Dell; Dodd, Mead; Dutton; Holloway House; Holt; Horizon; Morrow; Naval Institute; Paperjacks; Pocket; Popular Library; Presidio; St. Martin's; Vesta; Warner; West End Games of Pennsylvania; Worldwide Library; Zebra.

Preschool. Atheneum; Blackthorne; Childrens; Dial; Dutton; Farrar, Straus & Giroux; Four Winds; Grosset & Dunlap; Harcourt Brace Jovanovich; Harper & Row Junior Books; Harvest House; Holiday House; Joy Street; Knopf Books for Young Readers; Margaret McElderry; Modern; Morrow Junior Books; Orchard; Pelican; Philomel; Prentice-Hall; Random House (juvenile div.); St. Paul Books & Media; Scribner's Books for Young Readers; Troll; Vesta; Warner; West End Games of Pennsylvania; Western; Whitman.

Psychic/Supernatural/Occult. Avon; Bantam; Berkley; Dell; Fawcett; Holt; Paperjacks; Pocket; St. Martin's; Vesta; Wildstar/Empire; Winston-Derek.

Regional. Bethany House; Blair; Fearon Education; Paperjacks; Texas Monthly; Three Continents; Vesta.

Religious/Inspirational. Accent; Augsburg; Ballantine/Epiphany; Bantam; Berkley; Bethany House; Bookcraft; Branden; Bridge; Broadman; David C. Cook; Crossway; Gospel; Harvest House; Herald; Horizon; Pageant; Paperjacks; Resource; Standard; Tyndale House; Vesta; Winston-Derek.

Romance. Accent; Avalon; Avon; Bantam; Bart; Berkley; Bethany House; Bookcraft; Thomas Bouregy; Branden; Critic's Choice; Crown; Dell; Dodd, Mead; Dorchester; Doubleday; M. Evans; Fearon Education; Harlequin; Harvest House; Holloway House; Holt; Horizon; Keepsake; Leisure; Loveswept; Morrow; New Readers; Pageant; Paperjacks; Pocket; Popular Library; Second Chance at Love; Silhouette; Sweet Dreams; Vesta; Villard; Walker; Warner; Wildstar/Empire; Zebra.

Science Fiction. Avon; Baen; Bantam; Berkley; Berkley/Ace; Blackthorne; Bradbury; Carroll & Graf; Crossway; Crown; DAW; Del Rey; Dorchester; Doubleday; Doubleday Canada; Doubleday-Foundation; Fearon Education; Holloway House; Horizon; Iron Crown; Morrow; New American Library; New Readers; Omeiga; Pageant; Popular Library; Spectra; Starblaze; Tor; Vesta; Warner; West End Games of Pennsylvania; Worldwide Library.

Short Story Collections. Berkley; Blackthorne; Branden; Braziller; Crossway; Doubleday-Foundation; Fearon Education; Louisiana State University; Macmillan of Canada; New American Library; New Readers; Random House; Gibbs M. Smith; University of Georgia; Vesta.

Serialized/Excerpted Novel. Macmillan of Canada.

Spiritual. Horizon; New American Library; Paperjacks.

Sports. Contemporary; New Readers.

Suspense/Mystery. Avon; Bantam; Bart; Berkley; Bethany House; Blackthorne; Bogie's Mystery Books; Branden; Carroll & Graf; Dell; Dembner; Dodd, Mead; Doubleday; Doubleday Canada; Dutton; Fawcett; Fearon Education; Godine; Harvest House; Holloway House; Holt; Houghton Mifflin; Joy Street; Knopf; Macmillan of Canada; Morrow; Mysterious; New Readers; Pageant; Paperjacks; Pocket; Random House; Richardson & Steirman; St. Martin's; Scribner's; Seal (McClelland/Bantam); Silver Arrow; Simon & Pierre; Stoddart; Lyle Stuart/Irma Heldman; Summit; Tor; TSR; Vesta; Villard; Walker; Warner; West End Games of Pennsylvania; Western; Wildstar/Empire; Worldwide Library; Zebra.

Translations. Branden; Braziller; Dutton; Holt; Mercury House; Morrow; Simon & Pierre; Gibbs M. Smith; Vesta.

Western. Avalon; Avon; Bantam; Berkley; Bookcraft; Critic's Choice; M. Evans; Fearon Education; Holloway House; Holt; Jameson; Leisure; New American Library; Pageant; Paperjacks; Pocket; Popular Library; Summit; Walker; Warner; Wildstar/Empire.

Young Adult/Teen. Archway; Atheneum; Augsburg; Avon; Bantam; Berkley; Bradbury; Broadman; Carolrhoda; Clarion; David C. Cook; Crossway; Crosswinds; Crown; Delacorte/Dell Books for Young Readers; Dell; Dial Books for Young Readers; Dodd, Mead; Dutton; Eakin; M. Evans; Fearon Education; Flare; Four Winds; Harcourt Brace Jovanovich; Harper & Row Junior Books; Herald; Holiday House; Holt; Horizon; Keepsake; Knopf Books for Young Readers; Little, Brown & Co. (children's); Lodestar; Macmillan Children's; Margaret McElderry; Modern; Morrow Junior Books; New Readers; Orchard; Pelican; Philomel; Point; St. Paul Books & Media; Scholastic; Scribner's Books for Young Readers; Silhouette; Simon & Pierre; Stoddart; Sweet Dreams; Tab; Tor; Troll; TSR; Vesta; Walker; West End Games of Pennsylvania; Western Producer Prairie; Winston-Derek; Yearling.

Canadian. Doubleday Canada; Macmillan of Canada; Seal (McClelland/Bantam); Simon & Pierre; Vesta; Western Producer Prairie.

Literary agents

Adventure. Marcia Amsterdam; Authors' Marketing; Maximilian Becker; Richard Curtis; Estrada Literary Agency; Jay Garon-Brooke; John Hochmann; JCA; Peter Lampack; L. Harry Lee; Lighthouse; Elinor Midlik; Charles Neighbors; Julian Portman; Singer Media Corporation; Charles M. Stern; H. N. Swanson; James Warren; Sandra Watt.

Contemporary. Authors' Marketing; Anita Diamant; Dupree/Miller; Felicia Eth; Ricardo Hunter Garcia; Lucy Kroll; Peter Lampack; Michael Larsen/Elizabeth Pomada; Ray Lincoln; Lighthouse; Literary/Business Associates; Lowenstein Associates; Gina Maccoby; Mitchell Rose; Arthur P. Schwartz; Philip Spitzer; Writers World Forum.

Erotica. Arthur P. Schwartz.

Ethnic. Bonnie Crown; Writers' Productions; Writers World Forum.

Experimental. Andrews & Robb; Bonnie Crown; Sherry Robb.

Fantasy. James Allen; Jane Butler; Joyce Cole; Collier Associates; Richard Curtis; Estrada Literary Agency; Susan Herner Rights; Sharon Jarvis; Maxwell Lillienstein; Kirby McCauley; Multimedia Product Development; Susan Ann Protter; John Schaffner; Ralph Vicinanza.

Gay. Ricardo Hunter Garcia; Helen Rees; Sandra Watt.

Historical. James Allen; Andrews & Robb; Blake Group; Jane Butler; Maria Carvainis; Collier Associates; Elaine Davie; Jay Garon-Brooke; Michael Larsen/Elizabeth Pomada; L. Harry Lee; Ray Lincoln; Elinor Midlik; Multimedia Product Development; Charles Neighbors; Nugent & Associates; Julian Portman; Bobbe Siegel; F. Joseph Spieler; James Warren; Wieser & Wieser; Susan Zeckendorf.

Horror. Lee Allan; James Allen; Marcia Amsterdam; Authors' Marketing; Pema Browne; Jane Butler; Joyce Cole; Ethan Ellenberg; Estrada Literary Agency; Jay Garon-Brooke; Susan Herner Rights; Yvonne Hubbs; Sharon Jarvis; L. Harry Lee; Lowenstein Associates; Denise Marcil; Kirby McCauley; Lyle Steele; James Warren.

Humor/Satire. Marcia Amsterdam; Alice Hilton; James Warren.

Juvenile. Martha Casselman; SJ Clark; Ruth Cohen; Ann Elmo; Alice Hilton; Barbara Kouts; Norma-Lewis; Ray Lincoln; Gina Maccoby; Elinor Midlik; Nugent & Associates; Sidney Porcelain; Schlessinger-Van Dyck; Evelyn Singer; F. Joseph Spieler; Charles M. Stern; Mary Jack Wald.

Literary. Edward Acton; Andrews & Robb; Georges Borchardt; Ruth Cohen; Joyce Cole; Sandra Dijkstra; Candida Donadio; John Farquharson; Maia Gregory; Frederick Hill; JCA; Kidde, Hoyt & Picard; Barbara Kouts; Peter Lampack; Michael Larsen/Elizabeth Pomada; Lighthouse; Peter Livingston; Jean Naggar; Fi-fi Oscard; Sherry Robb; Robbins Office; Mitchell Rose; John Schaffner; Bobbe Siegel; Philip Spitzer; Gunther Stuhlman; Mary Jack Wald; John Ware; Writers' Productions; Susan Zeckendorf.

Mainstream. Edward Acton; James Allen; Marcia Amsterdam; Andrews & Robb; Authors' Marketing; Axelrod; Maximilian Becker; Blake Group; Harry Bloom; Reid Boates; Barbara Bova; Ruth Hagy Brod; Pema Browne; Ruth Cantor; Maria Carvainis; Martha Casselman; Linda Chester; SJ Clark; Diane Cleaver; Joyce Cole; Collier Associates; Columbia Literary Assocs.; Bill Cooper; Bonnie Crown; Athos Demetriou; Anita Diamant; Sandra Dijkstra; Dorese Agency; Dupree/Miller; Nicholas Ellison; Ann Elmo; Felicia Eth; John Farquharson; Florence Feiler; Frieda Fishbein; Flaming Star; Ricardo Hunter Garcia; Jay Garon-Brooke; Max Gartenberg; Gelles-Cole Literary Enterprises; Lucianne Goldberg; Goodman Associates; Alexandria Hatcher; Susan Herner Rights; Frederick Hill; Alice Hilton; John Hochmann; Yvonne Hubbs; Sharon Jarvis; Asher Jason; JCA; Jet; Larry Kaltman; Kidde, Hoyt & Picard; Harvey Klinger; Barbara Kouts; Peter Lampack; Lantz Office; Michael Larsen/Elizabeth Pomada; L. Harry Lee; Norma-Lewis; Maxwell Lillienstein; Ray Lincoln; Peter Livingston; Los Angeles Literary Associates; Donald MacCampbell; Gina Maccoby; Janet Wilkins Manus; Denise Marcil; Margaret McBride; Elinor Midlik; Peter Miller; Multimedia Product Development; Jean Naggar; Ruth Nathan; Charles Neighbors; B. K. Nelson; Betsy Nolan; Nugent & Associates; Harold Ober; Fifi Oscard; Peekner; Julian Portman; Quicksilver Books; Helen Rees; Sherry Robb; Robbins Office; Marie Rodell-Frances Collin; Irene Rogers; Jane Rotrosen; SBC Enterprises; Jack Scagnetti; Schlessinger-Van Dyck; John Schaffner; Susan Schulman; Arthur P. Schwartz; Bobbe Siegel; Evelyn Singer; Elyse Sommer; F. Joseph Spieler; Stepping Stone; Stern Associates; Charles M. Stern; Jo Stewart; H. N. Swanson; Roslyn Targ; Phyllis R. Tornetta; Victoria Management; Mary Jack Wald; John Ware; James Warren; Waterside Productions; Cherry Weiner; Wieser & Wieser; Ruth Wreschner; Ann Wright; Mary Yost; Susan Zeckendorf.

Military/War. L. Harry Lee; Sandra Watt.

Psychic/Supernatural/Occult. SJ Clark; L. Harry Lee; Literary/Business Associates.

Romance. Marcia Amsterdam; Authors' Marketing; Pema Browne; Maria Carvainis; Ruth Cohen; Joyce Cole; Richard Curtis; Estrada Literary Agency; Ricardo Hunter Garcia; Jay Garon-Brooke; Susan Herner Rights; Alice Hilton; John Hochmann; Yvonne Hubbs; Asher Jason; Kidde, Hoyt & Picard; Michael Larsen/Elizabeth Pomada; L. Harry Lee; Lighthouse; Maxwell Lillienstein; Lowenstein Associates; Elinor Midlik; Multimedia Product Development; Charles Neighbors; Sherry Robb; Susan Schulman; Arthur P. Schwartz; Singer Media Corporation; Southern Writers; Stern Associates; Charles M. Stern; Patricia Teal; Phyllis R. Tornetta; James Warren; Cherry Weiner; Wieser & Wieser; Ruth Wreschner.

Science Fiction. Lee Allan; James Allen; Marcia Amsterdam; Maximilian Becker; Barbara Bova; Jane Butler; Joyce Cole; Collier Associates; Richard Curtis; Ethan Ellenberg; Estrada Literary Agency; Susan Herner Rights; Alice Hilton; Sharon Jarvis; L. Harry Lee; Maxwell Lillienstein; Ray Lincoln; Gina Maccoby; Kirby McCauley; Multimedia Product Development; Jean Naggar; Susan Ann Protter; Quicksilver Books; SBC Enterprises; John Schaffner; Susan Schulman; Arthur P. Schwartz; Bobbe Siegel; Ralph Vicinanza; Victoria Management; James Warren; Cherry Weiner; Ruth Wreschner.

Short Story Collections. Georges Borchardt; Brandt & Brandt; Curtis Brown; Maria Carvainis; SJ Clark; Molly Malone Cook; Bonnie Crown; Richard Curtis; Candida Donadio; Dorese Agency; Maia Gregory; Gina Maccoby; Helin Merrill; Elinor Midlik; Charles Neighbors; Pickering Associates; Sherry Robb; Robbins Office; Rosenstone/Wender; Jane Rotrosen; SBC Enterprises; John Schaffner; Harold Schmidt; Susan Schulman; F. Joseph Spieler; H. N. Swanson; Thompson Talent; Mary Jack Wald; Gerry Wallerstein; John Ware; Ann Wright; Writers World Forum.

Spiritual. Stepping Stone.

Suspense/Mystery. Dominick Abel; Lee Allan; James Allen; Marcia Amsterdam; Axelrod; Maximilian Becker; Barbara Bova; Ruth Hagy Brod; Pema Browne; Jane Butler; Ruth Cantor; Maria Carvainis; SJ Clark; Diane Cleaver; Ruth Cohen; Joyce Cole; Collier Associates; Richard Curtis; Athos Demetriou; Ethan Ellenberg; Estrada Literary Agency; John Farquharson; Ricardo Hunter Garcia; Jay Garon-Brooke; Max Gartenberg; Susan Herner Rights; Yvonne Hubbs; Asher Jason; JCA; Michael Larsen/Elizabeth Pomada; L. Harry Lee; Literary/Business Associates; Lowenstein Associates; Janet Wilkins Manus; Denise Marcil; Elinor Midlik; Peter Miller; Multimedia Product Development; Jean Naggar; Charles Neighbors; Nugent & Associates; Peekner; Sidney Porcelain; Susan Ann Protter; Quicksilver Books; Helen Rees; Sherry Robb; Mitchell Rose; SBC Enterprises; Schlessinger-Van Dyck; Bobbe Siegel; Evelyn Singer; Singer Media Corporation; Michael Snell; Elyse Sommer; Philip Spitzer; Lyle Steele; Stern Associates; Charles M. Stern; H. N. Swanson; Patricia Teal; Ralph Vicinanza; John Ware; James Warren; Sandra Watt; Ruth Wreschner; Susan Zeckendorf.

Translations. Bonnie Crown.

Western. Lee Allan; Maria Carvainis; Joyce Cole; Richard Curtis; Jay Garon-Brooke; L. Harry Lee; Charles Neighbors.

Young Adult/Teen. Marcia Amsterdam; Pema Browne; Jane Butler; Maria Carvainis; Ruth Cohen; Norma-Lewis; Lighthouse; Ray Lincoln; Janet Wilkins Manus; Jo Stewart; Sandra Watt.

Markets Index

A

Other Books of Interest for Fiction Writers

Annual Directories
    Artist's Market, edited by Susan Conner $18.95
    Children's Writer's & Illustrator's Market, edited by Connie Eidenier (paper) $14.95
    Photographer's Market, edited by Connie Eidenier $19.95
    Poet's Market, by Judson Jerome $17.95
    Songwriter's Market, edited by Julie Whaley $17.95
    Writer's Market, edited by Glenda Tennant Neff $22.95
Fiction Writing Instruction
    The Elements of Fiction Writing Series:
        Characters & Viewpoint, by Orson Scott Card $12.95
        Dialogue, by Lewis Turco $12.95
        Plot, by Ansen Dibell $12.95
        Revision, by Kit Reed $13.95
    The Writer's Digest Genre Writing Series:
        How to Write Romances, by Phyllis Taylor Pianka $13.95
        How to Write Western Novels, by Matt Braun $13.95
    The Art & Craft of Novel Writing, by Oakley Hall $16.95
    Creating Short Fiction, by Damon Knight (paper) $8.95
    Dare to Be a Great Writer: 329 Keys to Powerful Fiction, by Leonard Bishop $15.95
    Fiction is Folks: How to Create Unforgettable Characters, by Robert Newton Peck (paper) $8.95
    Handbook of Short Story Writing, Vol. I, edited by Frank Dickson & Sandra Smythe (paper) $9.95
    Handbook of Short Story Writing, Vol. II, edited by Jean M. Fredette $15.95
    How to Write & Sell Your First Novel, by Oscar Collier, with Frances Spatz Leighton $15.95
    How to Write Tales of Horror, Fantasy & Science Fiction, edited by J.N. Williamson $15.95
    Mystery Writer's Handbook, by The Mystery Writers of America (paper) $10.95
    One Great Way to Write Short Stories, by Ben Nyberg $14.95
    Spider, Spin Me a Web: Lawrence Block on Writing Fiction, by Lawrence Block $16.95
    Storycrafting, by Paul Darcy Boles (paper) $10.95
    Writing Short Stories for Young People, by George Edward Stanley $15.95
    Writing the Modern Mystery, by Barbara Norville $15.95
    Writing the Novel: From Plot to Print, by Lawrence Block (paper) $9.95
    Writing Young Adult Novels, by Hadley Irwin & Jeannette Eyerly $14.95
Writing Reference
    Beginning Writer's Answer Book, edited by Kirk Polking (paper) $12.95
    How to Write a Book Proposal, by Michael Larsen $9.95
    Literary Agents: How to Get & Work with the Right One for You, by Michael Larsen $9.95
    Make Every Word Count, by Gary Provost (paper) $9.95
    12 Keys to Writing Books that Sell, by Kathleen Krull (paper) $12.95
    The 29 Most Common Writing Mistakes & How to Avoid Them, by Judy Delton $9.95
    The Writer's Digest Guide to Manuscript Formats, by Dian Dincin Buchman & Seli Groves $16.95

A complete catalog of Writer's Digest Books is available FREE by writing to the address shown below. To order books directly from the publisher, include $2.50 postage and handling for one book, 50¢ for each additional book. Allow 30 days for delivery.

WRITER'S DIGEST BOOKS
1507 Dana Avenue
Cincinnati, Ohio 45207

Prices subject to change without notice.